THE ORIGINS OF THE CULTURAL REVOLUTION

3 The Coming of the Cataclysm 1961–1966

Studies of the East Asian Institute, Columbia University

The East Asian Institute is Columbia University's center for research, publication, and teaching on modern East Asia. The Studies of the East Asian Institute were inaugurated in 1962 to bring to a wider public the results of significant new research on modern and contemporary East Asia.

THE ORIGINS OF
THE CULTURAL REVOLUTION

3 THE COMING OF THE CATACLYSM
1961–1966

RODERICK MACFARQUHAR

Published for
The Royal Institute of International Affairs
Studies of the East Asian Institute
by
Oxford University Press and Columbia University Press
1997

Oxford University Press, Great Clarendon Street, Oxford OX2 6DP
Columbia University Press, New York   Chichester, West Sussex

Oxford is a trade mark of Oxford University Press

First published in 1997

Published in the United States
by Columbia University Press, New York

British Library Cataloguing in Publication Data
Data available

ISBN: 0–19–2149970

1 3 5 7 9 10 8 6 4 2

Library of Congress Cataloging in Publication Data
MacFarquhar Roderick. The Origins of the Cultural Revolution
(Studies of the East Asian Institute)
Includes bibliographic references and index.
Contents: 1. Contradictions among the people, 1956–1957—
2. The great leap forward, 1958–1960—
3. The coming of the cataclysm, 1961–1966.
1. China—Politics and government—1949–1976.
2. China—History—Cultural Revolution, 1966–1969.
I. Royal Institute of International Affairs.   II. Columbia University.
East Asian Institute.   III. Columbia University. Research Institute on
Communist Affairs.   IV. Columbia University.
Research Institute on International Change.   V. Title.   VI. Series.
DS 777.75.M32   1974   951.05   73–15794

ISBN 0–231–03841–0 (v.1)
ISBN 0–231–08385–8 (v.1, pa.)
ISBN 0–231–05716–4 (v.2)
ISBN 0–231–05717–2 (v.2, pa.)
ISBN 0–231–11082–0 (v.3)

c 10 9 8 7 6 5 4 3 2 1

Typeset by Jayvee, Trivandrum, India
Printed in Great Britain
on acid-free paper by
Bookcraft Ltd., Midsomer-Norton
Nr. Bath, Somerset

For Benjamin Schwartz
The pioneer in the study of Chinese communism

So many deeds cry out to be done,
And always urgently;
The world rolls on,
Time presses.
Ten thousand years are too long,
Seize the day, seize the hour!
The Four Seas are rising, clouds and waters raging,
The Five Continents are rocking, wind and thunder roaring.
Away with all pests!
Our force is irresistible.

MAO ZEDONG, 9 Jan. 1963
(*Chinese Literature*, No. 5, 1966)

PREFACE

Scanning the shelves of the main Shanghai bookshop in the summer of 1990, I happily noted out of the corner of my eye that a new translation of the first two volumes of this work was prominently displayed on a table. A Chinese who was glancing through one of the volumes was approached by my escort from the Chinese Academy of Social Sciences (CASS) and told that if he bought the book he could get it signed by the author. The reader replied: 'I'm waiting for volume three.' I have often thought of that canny consumer since I slunk mortified out of the shop, and I hope he, and all my kind colleagues and friends in China and the West who have questioned me about the imminence of this final volume, will be satisfied that it is at least, and at last, out.

I have persisted in my original purpose, formulated over a quarter-century ago, to examine the impact of the main events of the decade prior to the Cultural Revolution on the thinking, actions, and interaction of the Chinese leaders in order to understand why Mao decided to tear down and rebuild a regime he had done so much to create. Readers of the earlier volumes may remember that I have been particularly interested in the human tragedy represented by Mao's purge of his longtime comrades of the Long March and the base areas, his dissolution of the Yan'an 'Round Table'.

As in the case of Volume Two, a bonus from, and an important cause of, the delay in the production of this book has been the vast increase in the availability of Chinese sources. What was a rushing mountain torrent a decade ago is now the broad Yangtze River, and I am acutely conscious that in attempting to cover so wide a canvas, I will inevitably have missed important materials, perhaps ones that would have cleared up questions which still puzzle me; some issues, however, will be resolved only when the party archives are eventually opened up.

How has the new material affected this study? The argument still proceeds along the original path, but more easily, thanks to the light shed by Chinese documents and secondary works. Masochistic readers who sat down to read all three volumes in a sitting might find two shifts of perception. My image of Mao is now less the stern but unifying sovereign of the Round Table, more a suspicious Olympian

Jove, ready to strike down with lightning bolts. To some extent, this reflects the changing environment in which Mao found himself (and which he helped to create) in the decade covered by this work, but I am more inclined now to believe in his original sin. Secondly, while the countryside has been evidently a critical factor in the Chinese political process in the earlier volumes, here it emerges as fundamental to an understanding of the origins of the Cultural Revolution.

Another cause of delay in completing this volume, ironically, was my move to Harvard's ivy tower in 1984. As a visiting professor two years earlier, spared of all duties but teaching, I could not understand why scholars were not more productive. Now I know. The pleasures of contributing in various small ways to the running of the institution, and in particular the challenge of following Philip Kuhn to direct the Fairbank Center for six years, have meant that my research and writing have been confined mainly to that bourn from which no academic returns happily, the summer recess.

One great compensation for my change of career has been moving on to a new learning curve as a result of regularly interacting with China scholars and political scientists. Editing the PRC volumes of the *Cambridge History of China* with John Fairbank enabled me to tap into the knowledge and wisdom of many distinguished specialists, as my endnotes indicate. Fairbank Center seminars—too many to keep up with—have been a constant stimulation. The regular canteen lunches with Center familiars and visitors have been peculiarly valuable, a time when longtime colleagues probe each other's views free of the constraints of the seminar room, or maybe just bemoan the state of the world. In the past, working mainly alone, it was relatively easy for me to acknowledge my debts; today, my mind boggles at the thought of listing *everyone* from whom I have gleaned an idea or a fact or a reference.

But at the Center, Merle Goldman's pathbreaking works on some of the wretched of the earth—the 'stinking ninth category' of Chinese intellectuals—have informed mine. Stuart Schram's monumental edition of the revolutionary writings of Mao is enriching my understanding of where the Chairman was coming from. Lucian Pye's ever-sceptical vision of Mao has worn the test of time better than most. The works of Jean Oi and David Zweig have helped me perceive the Chinese countryside in new ways. Michael Schoenhals stimulated and enlightened me when he spent a year with us under a generous Luce Foundation grant for the Center's Cultural Revolution project, run by Andrew Walder; Michael and I are collaborating on a book (one volume!) on the Cultural Revolution. Farther afield,

Frederick Teiwes has continued to produce great vintages from a vineyard close to my own. Jonathan Mirsky's essays in the *New York Review of Books* and frequent conversations have forced me to keep re-examining assumptions.

Another great boon at the Fairbank Center has been the Library, absolutely critical to my gaining access to the mass of new Chinese documentation. My heartfelt thanks go to Nancy Hearst, its devoted Librarian. Since expanding the scope of the collection to include Chinese materials in the mid-1980s, she has built up a network of contacts within China and the West which enables her to learn of and obtain the best new books almost immediately. As so many scholars from all over the world know well, if you tell her your interests, she will seek high and low, only too successfully, to satisfy your needs. Her late summer safaris to China result in Christmas cornucopias, as book packages arrive off slow boats from China.

Since I wrote the previous volumes, all China specialists have gained enormously from much freer access to Chinese citizens. In the summers of 1984 and 1986, I paid two research visits to Beijing under the auspices of the British Academy-CASS exchange scheme, and was attached to the Institute for Marxism-Leninism-Mao Zedong Thought, under the aegis of its kindly director, Su Shaozhi, and had access to the Library of the Chinese Academy of Sciences. Then and later, there and here, I have talked to and learned from a wide range of writers, scholars, and scholar/officials. For reasons best known in the higher reaches of CASS, my requests to interview even retired central committee cadres, prominent in the period I was studying, never bore fruit. (In 1980, I sat in on meetings between former Prime Minister James Callaghan and Deng Xiaoping and Hua Guofeng, but somehow the origins of the Cultural Revolution did not crop up.) Caution begets caution, and I have thought it prudent to allude to all interview data by an alphabetic identification, e.g. Informant A, etc. In place of all those Chinese who were so generous with their time and knowledge, let me mention others who have increased my understanding of their country, our graduate students—Ding Xueliang, Fu Jun, Gong Xiaoxia, Gu Weiqun, Huang Jing, Huang Yasheng, Jing Jun, Pei Minxin, Tian Dongdong, Xiao Yanming, Xu Guoqi, Yang Bingzhang, Yang Jianli, Yin Xiaohuang, Zhang Wei, Zheng Shiping—half of whom are now professors and some of whom have produced their first books. I also owe a large debt of gratitude (even if OUP does not) to the teams who have translated the earlier volumes of this study and the *Cambridge*

History of China; their toil has resulted in my hearing from people all over China, offering information and advice.

In the final stages of preparing the manuscript I accumulated fresh obligations. I owe Nancy Hearst another great debt for proof-reading the manuscript with typically meticulous care, a considerable labour which involved matching up the bibliography and the notes, supplying missing references, and putting it all into OUP style. On receiving his copy, Michael Schoenhals opened up a fusillade of e-mail messages from Stockholm, correcting and supplementing my findings, particularly on Part Four. Nicholas Lardy read the chapters on the economy to try to keep me from gross error; Timothy Cheek shared with me the final draft of his manuscript on Deng Tuo, and commented perceptively on Chapter 11; Fu Jun checked the translations of Chinese works in the Bibliography and proof-read the manuscript; Huang Jing, whose dissertation on party factionalism has taught me much, examined Anhui newspapers and the output of Liao Mosha. The revised text was submitted to the Royal Institute of International Affairs, at Chatham House, where it was received by Margaret May, Chief Editor of Publications, with gratifying warmth, doubtless tinged with surprised relief. At OUP, the MS was carefully prepared for publication by Anna Illingworth, Michael Belson, and Jeff New. Anne Holmes brought professional and China skills to preparing a complex index.

Emily MacFarquhar, to whom the first volume was dedicated and who has lived patiently through the production of the second and third, read the whole manuscript with her customary sharp editorial pencil, and asked probing questions based on a store of China lore stretching back over her years as a correspondent for *The Economist* and *US News & World Report*; as usual her input added weeks to the work, but with the replacement of typewriters by computers, I have found that I can bear such spousal abuse with equanimity, responding to rewrite orders with sweetness and light, even if I still have to take sole responsibility for the final product.

I dedicate this volume to Benjamin Schwartz, teacher, colleague, and friend, who did so much to bring me to Harvard, and whose sceptical intelligence, broad knowledge, deep wisdom, and wry wit shine through his writings and conversation and continue to inform my understanding of China.

RODERICK MACFARQUHAR

Cambridge, Mass.
October 1995

CONTENTS

LIST OF TABLES

LIST OF PLATES

ABBREVIATIONS*

ACFTU	All-China Federation of Trade Unions
APC	Agricultural Producers' Co-operative
CAS	Chinese Academy of Sciences
CASS	Chinese Academy of Social Sciences
CC	Central Committee
CCP	Chinese Communist Party
CONEFO	Conference of the New Emerging Forces
CPPCC	Chinese People's Political Consultative Conference
CPSU	Communist Party of the Soviet Union
CRG	Central Cultural Revolution Small Group
FYP	Five-Year Plan
GANEFO	Games of the New Emerging Forces
GLF	Great Leap Forward
GPD	General Political Department
GZAR	Guangxi Zhuang Autonomous Region
KMT	Guomindang
MAC	Military Affairs Commission
NEFA	North-East Frontier Agency
NPC	National People's Congress
PLA	People's Liberation Army
PRC	People's Republic of China
PSC	Politburo Standing Committee
SEM	Socialist Education Movement
SMC	Supply and Marketing Co-operative
SSC	Supreme State Conference
SSTC	State Science and Technology Commission
UFWD	United Front Work Department
YCL	Young Communist League

* For abbreviations used in notes, see pp. 474–8 below.

INTRODUCTION

Fengyang county's claim to fame is as the native place of the founder of the Ming dynasty, Zhu Yuanzhang. Situated in the northeast of the central China province of Anhui, the county's perennial poverty is underlined by an old saying that after Zhu's birth, nine years in every ten were hit by famine.[1] But even by Fengyang's grim standards, the famine brought about by the Great Leap Forward (GLF, 1958–60) was disastrous. In 1959 and 1960, 60,245 people died, 17.7 per cent of the county's population of 335,698. In the worst-hit communes, the percentages ranged as high as 26.9 per cent, 26.6 per cent, and 24.2 per cent. In one of these communes' component brigades, the percentage was 39.7 per cent; 1,627 people died out of a total population of 4,100. In one hamlet, the death toll was forty-eight out of seventy people. In the county as a whole, 8,404 complete households (including one of twelve) were wiped out, 3.4 per cent of the total; in one hamlet the figure was four households out of twenty. As a result of the death toll and the flight of survivors, twenty-seven of Fengyang's villages, twenty-one in one commune alone, became ghost communities.[2] Survival strategies in the worst period between winter 1959 and spring 1960 included wives migrating and taking up with other men; cases of bigamous marriage increased 27.5 times between 1960 and 1961 and the number of divorces 2.9 times.[3] In another Anhui county, a teacher 'sent down' to learn from the poor peasants during the Cultural Revolution found herself in a village where half the population had died in 1960. As late as 1969, boiled water was a luxury because fuel was scarce! Conditions were so primitive that a scholar of ancient Chinese history compared this village to a neolithic site uncovered near Xi'an.[4]

Fengyang's plight may have been exceptional, but the whole province suffered terribly. By the early 1960s, 'it was an open secret that millions . . . mostly peasants, had died of starvation' in Anhui.[5] Even in the provincial capital, Hefei, the grain ration had been cut to as little as 312 catties a year by the summer of 1959. 'The staples supplied were dried sweet potato strips, sweet potato flour, corn flour, and sorghum flour. Rice and wheat flour were supplied in small quantities on national holidays only'.[6] According to official statistics, the provincial output of grain declined precipitously in 1958 (13.9 per cent) and 1959 (a further 20.7 per cent) and continued to fall through 1961, causing the provincial population to drop from 34.2 m. at the end of 1959 to 29.8 m. at the end of 1961. In a normal year, 250,000 people died in Anhui; in 1954, when the province was devastated by floods, 515,000 people died. In 1960, 2,200,000 died—almost ten times the toll of a normal year and almost four times that of the worst previous year;[7] the province's population dropped by 11.2 per cent.[8] According to a former senior official, 8 million people died in the province as a result of the GLF.[9]

TABLE Intro. 1. *Anhui province: grain and population, 1957–1962*

	Grain (m. tons)	Population
1957	10.270	33,370,244
1958	8.845	33,941,565
1959	7.010	34,265,037
1960	6.746	30,425,058
1961	6.290	29,876,855
1962	6.707	31,335,852

Source: Anhui sheng tongjiju (ed.), *Anhui Sishi Nian* (40 years of Anhui), pp. 40, 102, 123.

The population data for Sichuan, where grain output fell from a 1958 peak of 22,455,000 tons to 13,395,000 tons in 1960, tell a similar story.[10] China's most populous province reached a post-revolution peak of 70,810,100 inhabitants at the end of the 1st FYP in 1957. Four years later, in 1961, the figure had dropped by over 6 million to 64,591,800. The 1957 high was not exceeded until 1965.[11] In 1957, the province's population increased by 100,217 people a month; by 1962, when the country would be beginning to recover from the post-GLF disaster, the monthly increase would be down to 72,219. In 1957, there were 170,744 births a month; in 1962, 151,097.[12]

In Shandong, China's most populous province after Sichuan, there were 650,000 extra deaths in the year following the relaunching of the GLF in September 1959, and 4.2 m. people were affected by diseases like oedema caused by malnutrition. With the average provincial per capita consumption of the staple food, grain, falling to 0.42 lb. a day, between a quarter and a third of the province's 54+ m. people were reckoned to be going hungry, and 1.1 m. fled their homes seeking food.[13] The Shandong provincial committee issued an emergency directive on 27 October 1960, a week before a national Twelve-Article Emergency Directive of 3 November. The province's plight was so grave that in the last two months of the year the central government shipped in half-a-million tons of grain and 2,000 tractors and donated 80 m. yuan to help the relief effort. Other East China provinces supplied 100,000 tons of grain, 125,000 tons of other foodstuffs, and 1,700,000 items of padded cotton clothing.[14]

We also have a glimpse of the grass-roots impact in Henan province, where GLF leftism had run riot under the leadership of then 1st secretary, Wu Zhipu.[15] In Xinyang, the death toll amounted to 1,136,000, 14.2 per cent of that district's 8 million population, and there was massive emigration. So notorious was this so-called Xinyang 'incident' that a task force of 4,633 officials, including 359 from the centre and 1,223 from provincial headquarters, was sent in to deal with the crisis and the 'counter-revolutionary' activities which it had provoked.[16]

The overall impact on Henan and other badly hit provinces is shown in Table 2.

TABLE Intro. 2. *Numbers of deaths for selected provinces, 1957 and 1960*

	Gansu	Guangxi	Henan	Hubei	Hunan	Jiangsu
1957	142,041	261,785	572,000	290,600	370,059	424,500
1960	538,479	644,770	1,908,000	670,300	1,068,118	785,900

Sources: *Zhongguo Renkou* (China's population), various provincial fascicles (*fence*); *Gansu Fence*, p. 121; *Guangxi Fence*, p. 113; *Henan Fence*, p. 106; *Hubei Fence*, p. 106; *Hunan Fence*, p. 138; *Jiangsu Fence*, p. 113.

Even in less-devastated provinces like Hebei, the sick, the elderly, and infants died. Wives were sold as 'cousins' for food and cash. Brigades issued certificates permitting peasants to go begging. Robber bands attacked grain stations and trains, and troops had to be deployed to defend them.[17] In Beijing, presumably a privileged environment, per capita annual pork consumption dropped from 13.3 catties in 1958 to 5.3 catties in 1960. It would fall to 2.1 catties in 1961.[18] The annual number of deaths in China's capital rose from 320,000 in 1957 to 790,000 in 1961.[19] In Shanghai, retail sales of pork dropped from 65,800 tons in 1958 to 17,600 tons in 1960, and then again to a post-GLF low of 7,500 tons in 1961.[20] These figures were hardly surprising, since state purchases of hogs fell from 46,337,000 head in 1958 to 19,913,000 in 1960 and would decline further to 8,071,000 in 1961.[21]

In the Chinese gulag, conditions were far worse. In one prison camp, working hours had to be reduced, and experiments were made with feeding the prisoners paper pulp and marsh water plankton. The former produced dire constipation, while the latter killed off the weaker prisoners. In the twelve months starting in the late summer of 1960, three-quarters of one brigade died or were sent off to a camp for the dying.[22] A prisoner there described how starvation killed:

I began to understand the process of starvation. When death strikes in the camps, malnutrition is rarely the direct cause. The heart does not stop beating from lack of nourishment. Depending on your overall health, you can survive for a week, even two, with no food or water at all. In such a depleted state, it is other things that kill you. Sometimes you catch cold, your lungs fill with fluid, and finally you stop breathing. Sometimes bacteria in the food cause continuous diarrhea that leads to death. Sometimes infection from a wound becomes fatal. The cause of death is always noted in your file as pleurisy or food poisoning or injury, never as starvation.[23]

In Qinghai, according to another prisoner:

We could not believe that death could come so easily. The dead bodies were like raindrops, and we stood in stormy purgatory for three years on end ... If you saw us, you would find each face starved into a pale mask, without flesh or life. Such faces were little different from those of the departed. No matter its shape, the face of a starvation victim is covered by only a fragile layer of skin. The eyes are hardly eyes but rather the pits of nuts fitted into sockets of bone. Such eyes shed no light. Yet, they bespeak the urgency of their owner's case ... they plead better than any words.

According to this prisoner's calculation, possibly 200,000 people died in the labour reform units in Qinghai.[24] It was much the same throughout China as birth rates dropped and death rates rose, as shown in Appendix 1. In some provinces, as in the country as a whole, the population actually *decreased* in at least one year.[25]

As the figures make grimly clear, at the start of the 1960s China was in the grip of the worst man-made famine in history. With the GLF (chronicled in Volume 2 of this work), CCP Chairman Mao Zedong had hoped with one supreme national effort to lift his nation and people out of poverty. Instead he had brought about a human catastrophe. The most recent Western demographic analysis indicates that there were 30 m. excess deaths between 1958 and 1961.[26]

TABLE Intro. 3. *Chinese provinces with negative population growth, 1959–1961* (per thousand)

	1959	1960	1961
China		−4.57	
Anhui		−57.20	
Gansu		−25.79	
Guangxi		−10.06	−1.77
Guizhou		−19.41	−0.21
Henan		−25.58	
Hubei		−5.00	
Hunan		−9.43	−4.97
Liaoning			−0.30
Qinghai		−27.66	−0.25
Shandong		−4.10	
Sichuan	−30.26	−42.24	−17.61
Yunnan		−2.07	

Source: Guojia Tongjiju Zonghesi (ed.), *Quanguo Gesheng, Zizhiqu, Zhixiashi Lishi Tongji Ziliao Huibian (1949–1989)*: Anhui, p. 405; Gansu, p. 829; Guangxi, p. 642; Guizhou, p. 721; Henan, p. 523; Hubei, p. 555; Hunan, p. 585; Liaoning, p. 213; Qinghai, p. 859; Shandong, p. 492; Sichuan, p. 690; Yunnan, p. 751.

As the death toll mounted, China's leaders reportedly rationed themselves, though they still ate relatively well.[27] Mao denied himself meat for seven months in 1960.[28] Premier Zhou Enlai, who used to calculate the population's grain needs on his desk abacus, reportedly confined himself to about 15 lb. of grain a month, saving the remainder of his ration for when he had to entertain, and, according to his bodyguard, never ate meat or eggs during this period. He upbraided his staff for accepting vegetables sent by provincial authorities to top leaders.[29]

But high-level guilt trips were no solution to the disaster which Mao and his colleagues had wrought in their hubris. Initial remedial measures taken in the first half of 1959 were largely aborted after Mao angrily rejected an attack on the GLF by then-Defence Minister Peng Dehuai at the Lushan conference that summer. Colossal human error was compounded by floods and droughts in 1959–60. Not till the autumn of the latter year, when China was experiencing the worst natural calamities in a century, did Mao allow the retreat to be sounded;[30] even so, 1961 would be a third 'bitter year'. It was indeed the worst of times.

But at least the Chairman called off—for ever, as it turned

out—what some colleagues had rightly called 'reckless advance'. This study began in 1956 partly because it was then, after collectivization, that Mao first entertained visions of leaping economic progress. Now, after five years of pressing, he reluctantly abandoned the delusion that China could become a superpower overnight.

The failure of the GLF changed the thinking of most CCP leaders about China's economic development—even those who, like head of state Liu Shaoqi, had enlisted enthusiastically under the 'three red banners' (of the 'general line', the GLF, and the communes) in pursuit of socialism with Chinese characteristics. Their agonizing reappraisals in the early 1960s made Mao inordinately suspicious of their private perceptions of him as a post-revolutionary leader. His paranoia blended with a genuine concern about China's political future in the context of both domestic demoralization and what he saw as the renunciation of Leninism in the Soviet Union.

The other reason why this study began in 1956 was because it was then that the Sino-Soviet dispute started festering. The anti-Stalin 'secret speech' of CPSU 1st secretary Nikita Khrushchev had embarrassed Mao, who, like the late Soviet dictator, luxuriated in a hyperbolic 'cult of personality'. The Hungarian revolt, which the speech triggered, prompted Mao to challenge Khrushchev's competence to set the ideological guidelines for the world communist movement. By 1960, Beijing and Moscow were engaged in bitter polemics over a range of national and international issues, and Khrushchev abruptly withdrew thousands of Soviet technical-assistance personnel. During the early 1960s, as relations worsened, Mao pondered how to avert a similar betrayal of the revolution in China.

The collapse of his hopes for a collectivist utopia at home and a fraternity of communist nations abroad had a profound impact on the Chairman's thinking. This volume chronicles how Mao, having failed in the material transformation of China, came to focus all his energies upon the nation's spiritual metamorphosis. It seeks to explain why, in the course of that endeavour, the Chairman decided to tear down and rebuild a regime he had done so much to create.

APPENDIX 1: BIRTH AND DEATH RATES

TABLE App. 1.1. *Provincial birth rates, 1957–1962* (per thousand)

	1957	1958	1959	1960	1961	1962
Anhui	29.75	23.83	19.89	11.35	12.34	53.26
Beijing	42.10	37.02	30.70	33.03	25.70	35.92
Fujian	37.88	29.12	27.56	25.11	17.42	40.16
Gansu	30.00	31.50	19.30	15.50	14.80	41.10
Guangdong	34.99	30.10	24.67	18.96	21.27	43.31
Guangxi	34.52	32.87	24.52	19.40	17.73	39.08
Guizhou	41.12	30.08	26.76	25.97	17.32	41.54
Hebei	29.62	24.45	23.09	20.51	15.13	28.68
Heilongjiang	36.58	32.98	30.38[a]	32.50	27.27	35.46
Henan	33.71	33.16	28.07	14.01	15.31	37.50
Hubei	34.36	30.49	26.42	16.41	27.34	42.51
Hunan	33.47	29.96	24.00	19.49	12.52	41.40
Jiangsu	34.48	24.83	20.91	18.56	18.83	33.30
Jiangxi	38.34	30.28	28.64	26.87	21.00	37.19
Jilin	35.46	33.31	28.04	32.51	26.45	40.70
Liaoning	41.90	38.70	28.00	31.80	17.20	34.10
Nei Menggu[b]	37.20	28.40	30.80	29.40	22.10	38.20
Ningxia	43.24	39.32	23.80	16.58	13.03	44.60
Qinghai	32.18	27.97	23.02	13.07	11.43	35.72
Shaanxi	32.20	26.70	26.60	27.70	21.10	34.60
Shandong	35.80	25.00	20.90	19.50	21.40	38.10
Shanghai	45.60	36.00	27.80	27.60	22.40	26.30
Shanxi	33.30	28.70	27.50	27.30	19.10	37.70
Sichuan	29.22	24.03	16.71	11.73	11.81	28.01
Tianjin	37.28	34.56	28.49	27.38	20.42	33.68
Xinjiang	31.48	31.03	29.87	28.13	25.16	32.02
Yunnan	36.27	23.61	20.93	24.19	19.40	39.71
Zhejiang	34.94	34.10	26.28	23.52	17.58	36.08[a]

Notes: [a] A figure after the decimal point is smudged in the source; [b] Inner Mongolia.

Sources: As for Table Intro.2: *Anhui Fence,* p. 100; *Beijing Fence,* p. 85; *Gansu Fence,* p. 94; *Guangdong Fence,* p. 93; *Guangxi Fence,* p. 82; *Hebei Fence,* p. 102; *Heilongjiang Fence,* p. 84; *Henan Fence,* p. 73; *Hubei Fence,* p. 83; *Hunan Fence,* p. 99; *Jiangsu Fence,* p. 89; *Jilin Fence,* p. 77; *Liaoning Fence,* p. 53; *Nei Menggu Fence.* p. 75; *Ningxia Fence,* p. 90; *Qinghai Fence,* p. 97; *Shaanxi Fence,* p. 89; *Shanghai Fence,* p. 72; *Shanxi Fence,* p. 64; *Sichuan Fence,* p. 87; *Tianjin Fence,* p. 75; *Xinjiang Fence,* p. 82; *Zhejiang Fence,* p. 88. Some figures have been culled from Guojia tongjiju zonghesi (ed.), *Quanguo Gesheng, Zizhiqu Zhixiashi Lishi Tongji Ziliao Huibian (1949–1989)* (Compendium of historical statistical materials for the nation's provinces, autonomous regions and cities directly under the central government [1949–1989]): Fujian, p. 433; Guizhou, p. 721; Jiangxi, p. 464; Shandong, p. 492; Yunnan, p. 751. No figures were collected for Xizang (Tibet) before 1965. Figures in this source often differ from those in the *fence,* but only slightly.

TABLE App. 1.2.   *Provincial death rates, 1957–1962* (per thousand)

	1957	1958	1959	1960	1961	1962
Anhui	9.10	16.72	n.a.	68.58[a]	n.a.	8.23
Beijing	8.19	8.08	9.66	9.14	10.80	8.77
Fujian	7.85	7.46	7.88	15.34	11.87	8.28
Gansu	11.32	21.11	17.47	41.46	11.47	8.24
Guangdong	8.43	9.13	11.74	15.12	10.67	9.32
Guangxi	12.35	11.74	17.49	29.46	19.50	10.25
Guizhou	8.77	13.69	16.18	45.38	17.73	10.41
Hebei	11.30	10.92	12.29	15.84	13.63	9.06
Heilongjiang	10.40	9.10	12.80	10.50	11.10	8.70
Henan	11.81	12.70	14.12	39.60	10.18	8.03
Hubei	9.64	9.64	14.50	21.19	9.19	8.76
Hunan	10.41	11.65	12.99	29.42	17.49	10.23
Jiangsu	10.26	9.40	14.55	18.41	13.35	10.36
Jiangxi	11.48	11.34	13.01	16.06	11.54	11.00
Jilin	9.10	9.10	13.40	10.10	12.00	10.00
Liaoning	9.40	8.80	11.80	11.50	17.50	8.50
Nei Menggu	10.50	7.90	11.00	9.40	8.80	9.00
Ningxia	11.06	14.98	15.82 .	13.90	10.71	8.49
Qinghai	10.40	12.99	16.58	40.73	11.68	5.35
Shaanxi	10.30	11.00	12.70	12.30	8.70	9.40
Shandong	12.10	12.80	18.20	23.60	18.40	12.40
Shanghai	6.00	5.90	6.90	6.80	7.70	7.30
Shanxi	12.70	11.70	12.80	14.20	12.20	11.30
Sichuan	12.07	25.17	46.97	53.97	29.42	14.62
Tianjin	9.35	8.66	9.88	10.34	9.89	7.36
Xinjiang	14.00	13.00	18.84	15.67	11.71	9.71
Yunnan	16.29	21.62	17.95	26.26	11.84	10.85
Zhejiang	9.32	9.15	10.81	11.88	9.84	8.61

Note: [a] The source gives this figure in two places, but 65.58 in a third.

Sources: As for Table Intro. 2: *Anhui Fence*, pp. 78–9, 91, 130–1; *Beijing Fence*, pp. 112–13; *Gansu Fence*, p. 121; *Guangdong Fence*, p. 121; *Guangxi Fence*, p. 113; *Hebei Fence*, p. 135; *Heilongjiang Fence*, p. 118; *Henan Fence*, p. 110; *Hubei Fence*, p. 106; *Hunan Fence*, p. 138; *Jiangsu Fence*, p. 113; *Jilin Fence*, p. 104; *Liaoning Fence*, p. 53; *Nei Menggu Fence*, p. 75; *Ningxia Fence*, p. 111; *Qinghai Fence*, p. 124; *Shaanxi Fence*, p. 124; *Shanghai Fence*, p. 72; *Shanxi Fence*, pp. 64, 97; *Sichuan Fence*, pp. 118–20; *Tianjin Fence*, p. 75; *Xinjiang Fence*, p. 109; *Zhejiang Fence*, p. 115. As in the previous table, some figures come from *Quanguo Gesheng, Zizhiqu, Zixiashi Lishi Tongji Ziliao Huibian (1949-1989)*: Beijing, p. 62; Fujian, p. 433; Guizhou, p. 721; Jiangxi, p. 464; Shandong, p. 492; Sichuan, p. 690; Yunnan, p. 751. No figures were collected for Tibet (Xizang) before 1965. As in the case of the birth rate data, figures in this source often differ from those in the *fence*, but only slightly.

PART ONE

THE THIRD BITTER YEAR

1 THE CENTRAL COMMITTEE'S NINTH PLENUM

Reason began to prevail in the summer of 1960 as a gloomily pensive Mao realized the enormity of what he had perpetrated.[1] At an expanded Politburo conference in Shanghai in June, Mao gave a series of speeches in which he talked of adjusting targets and emphasizing quality and variety instead of just quantity; a true leap forward, as he now characterized it, left room for manoeuvre. There was still a 'vast, uncomprehended kingdom of necessity' with respect to socialist economic development which demanded investigation.[2] At the customary summer central work conference, held at the northern seaside resort town of Beidaihe from 15 July to 10 August 1960, a directive was issued ordering the CCP to concentrate its efforts on agriculture in general and grain production in particular. But no action was taken on the proposal by Li Fuchun, the chairman of the State Planning Commission, that the CCP should adopt a policy of 'adjustment, consolidation, and improvement' (*tiaozheng, gonggu, tigao*); only after Premier Zhou Enlai had added the phrase 'filling out' (*chongshi*), did the lengthened slogan finally gain currency on 30 September in the State Planning Commission's report on the control figures for the 1961 plan.[3] But at the beginning of 1962 Liu Shaoqi was forced to admit that, regrettably, in practice this 'eight character' policy was not implemented in many ways.[4]

Unfortunately also, Mao was still in the grip of steel fever.[5] He told Li Fuchun and Bo Yibo, the chairman of the State Economic Commission, that 70 m. people should be thrown into another mass steel campaign that winter, apparently believing that a target of 22 m. tons, an increase of 9 m. tons over 1959, was attainable; he still hankered to reach what he evidently saw as the magic figure of 100 m. tons, though he was now prepared to wait until the end of the PRC's second decade in 1969.[6] The abrupt withdrawal of all Soviet technical advisers,[7] which was communicated to the Chinese as the Beidaihe conference was convening, put the Chairman on his mettle. Lagging output in the first half of 1960 had indicated that even the original 1960 steel target of 18 m. tons would be desperately hard to reach, but Mao evidently felt that the national honour was now at stake, and said so in an emergency directive issued on 3 December urging one final push. At great economic cost, 18,660,000 tons were produced.[8]

Fortunately, Mao was readier to listen to reason on the agricultural front. By October, Premier Zhou Enlai was suggesting more drastic measures than those agreed at Beidaihe, and on 3 November, the CC circulated a Twelve-Article Emergency Directive designed to restore incentives to the peasantry by encouraging private plots and reducing the power of the communes to enforce egalitarianism among their component production brigades. The brigade, called variously *dui*, *da dui*, and *guanliqu*, but corresponding to the former advanced or 'higher stage' (fully socialist) Agricultural Producers' Co-operative (APC), was again to be the basic level of ownership in the three-tier hierarchy—commune, brigade, team—and was supposed to remain so for at least seven years. All possessions taken over by the communes during the egalitarian upsurge of 1958 were to be replaced. In effect, this directive reaffirmed and developed those more moderate policies originally laid down by Mao from the first Zhengzhou conference in November 1958 until Lushan.[9]

On 15 November, the CC issued a further directive calling for the elimination of the 'five [work] styles' (*wu feng*) which derived from the euphoric 'high tide' of 1958: the communist wind (excessive collectivism/egalitarianism within the communes); boastfulness and exaggeration; commandism (relying simply on orders without employing persuasion and explanation); special privileges for cadres; the issuing of arbitrary and impracticable directives.[10] On 28 November, the CC circulated a report from Gansu province to which Mao appended a remarkable note, acknowledging a personal error made in 1958 when he had predicted an excessively rapid transition from socialist to communist forms of ownership in the countryside.[11] Doubtless he felt constrained to make this admission because, despite the CC directives, some provincial officials still felt leftism was safer than rightism, and were reluctant to reveal the extent of the disaster over which they had presided.[12]

On 24 December, leading officials met for a central work conference which would last until 13 January, the eve of the 9th plenum.[13] A number of important decisions were taken and formally ratified by the plenum. Agricultural procurement prices were to be raised in two stages: grain, edible oils, hogs, poultry and eggs in 1961, and cotton and other products in 1962. One billion yuan was allocated solely for raising the grain procurement price; at the subsequent CC plenum, it was laid down that the increase should start with the summer harvest and should average 20 per cent, though in practice it worked out at 25 per cent as a result of a retrospective bonus awarded to the main grain-producing areas for their efforts in 1960.[14]

A second set of decisions concerned paying compensation for the depredations wreaked on peasant lives as a result of GLF egalitarianism. The considerable sum of 2.5 billion yuan was allocated for this purpose. Of this, 1.5 billion yuan would be disbursed in cash during the following five months while the communes, 20 per cent of which were said to be in a bad way, were being rectified; the other 1 billion would be issued by banks in the form of IOUs. Other decisions taken to stimulate agriculture included raising the percentage of land assignable to peasants for private sideline occupations from 5 per cent (laid down as recently as November in the Twelve-Article Emergency Directive) to 7 per cent, and giving permission for rural markets to be encouraged.[15] In his speech, Mao admitted that socialist construction could not be hurried as it would take half-a-century.[16] Speaking on 13 January, he emphasized a theme that would become increasingly important, the need for leaders to undertake thorough grass-roots research to establish facts as bases for policy.[17]

The Leap is over; Long live the Three Red Banners!

The CCP's Central Committee met in Beijing for its 9th plenum from 14 to 18 January 1961. Its task was formally to endorse the measures already adopted to alleviate the economic crisis, and also to consider the diplomatic disasters suffered by China in the seventeen months since the previous plenum at Lushan. The most urgent item on the agenda was the catastrophic food situation which had already resulted in millions of deaths and a precipitous drop in the number of births from 21.2 million in 1957 to 12.5 million in 1960.[18]

In 1960, grain output had declined by 15.5 per cent (following a drop of similar proportions in 1959), falling to 143.5 m. tons, the lowest figure since 1950 when China was only just beginning to benefit from internal peace. On an assumed annual need of 250 kg. per capita, the shortfall was the equivalent of the rations for over 24 million people. Stocks in state granaries had dropped disastrously from almost 30 m. tons in 1957 to just over 18 m. tons in 1960. The stock figures seem to have weighed more heavily with the authorities than the output figures, for in 1960 the government had attempted to raise its compulsory procurements by 3 m. tons to over 51 m. tons, severely squeezing the amount of grain available in the countryside for human consumption, animal fodder, and seed. Consequently, the number of pigs, the major source of meat, had dropped by almost a third to the lowest figure since 1950. Even so, in December the State Statistical Bureau had to report that grain procurement was down 34 per cent through November.

Oil crops, essential for cooking, had plummeted 47.7 per cent, even more drastically than grain, to a figure lower than the output in 1949 when China was still engulfed in civil war, and procurement was down 42 per cent. In addition, the output of cotton, the basic material for the nation's clothing, had declined 37.8 per cent to the lowest figure since 1951 and procurement was down 23 per cent.[19]

The shortages were compounded by an increase in the amount of currency in circulation by over 80 per cent, from 5,280 m. yuan in 1957 to 9,592 m. yuan in 1960, due to the expansionary policies of the GLF, leading to sharp inflation in the open markets outside the state sector. Grain prices rose ten-to-twelve times to 1–2 yuan for 1.1 lb.; an egg cost half a yuan; 1.1 lb. of pork cost 5 yuan, and a chicken over 10 yuan.[20]

As a consequence of the rural crisis, the government was forced to reduce the agricultural tax for 1961 to 11,100,000 tonnes, a 42 per cent drop from 1960.[21] Its value, which had reached a post-1949 peak in 1959, fell to 2,804 m. yuan in 1960 and would plummet to 2,166 m. yuan in 1961, the lowest figure since 1950.[22]

The catastrophic drops in the outputs of major necessities had to be set beside a population rise of over 100 million since those early years of the regime.[23] The consequent decline in consumption standards, particularly in the countryside, is shown in Table 1.1.

TABLE 1.1. *Per capita consumption of major food items, 1957 and 1960* (in catties[a])

	1957	1960
Grain	406.0	327.0
urban	392.0	385.0
rural	409.0	312.0
Vegetable oil	4.8	3.7
urban	10.3	7.1
rural	3.7	2.9
Pork	10.2	3.1
urban	18.0	5.4
rural	8.7	2.4

Note: [a] A catty is about 1 lb. or 0.5 kg.
Source: DSYJ, No. 6, 1980, p. 24.

At the 9th plenum, Mao reiterated the need to extirpate the five styles, the keynote of his address on the final day being the importance of realism.[24] 'Seeking truth from facts' (*shishi qiushi*) had to be the watchword for 1961;[25] investigation and research were to be the means of attaining the goal.[26] The practice of having two targets— one public and certain of achievement, the other unpublished but to be striven for—would be dropped.[27] The 'four high' system—high targets, high estimates of production, large-scale government purchases of grain, and large-scale use of grain—adopted by Henan, the path-breaking province during the GLF, would also be abandoned.[28] Rigid bureaucrats (*si guanliao*) who could not reform their work style even after a considerable time—presumably by the end of the rectification campaign currently under way—would have to be dismissed.[29]

Mao gave little public evidence of contrition for his own role in helping to bring about the disasters of the GLF; indeed, in an interview with a leading French socialist, François Mitterand, a few weeks later, he would categorically deny that there was any famine in China. At the plenum, he alluded instead to the anti-leftist directives he had issued in the first half of 1959, effectively blaming provincial officials for not implementing them.[30] He recalled that at the Lushan conference people had said: 'You too have made mistakes.' He was untroubled; everyone made mistakes. The real question was the severity of the errors.[31] He admitted that the effect of the campaign against 'right opportunism' launched at Lushan (i.e. the counter-attack on Peng Dehuai and his sympathizers) had been to throw the correction of leftism into disarray, but reasserted that the campaign had been essential. Moreover, the relaunching of the GLF after Lushan had led to considerable achievements, especially in water conservancy.[32] It was probably on this occasion that Mao repeated his customary upbeat appraisal of the domestic situation: 'The situation is very good, there are numerous problems, but the prospects are bright.'[33]

As always, Mao's strongest card was an appeal for solidarity. 'The unity of the Central Committee is the core of the unity of the whole party', he said.[34] To emphasize his personal commitment to the concept, he added a conciliatory reference to his Lushan opponent: 'Peng Dehuai's letter to me reporting on his year of study is to be welcomed, regardless of whether or not he has made progress'.[35] In that single sentence, Mao managed to convey the impression that he himself was magnanimous, but Peng was incorrigible. Mao was prepared to accept the end of the Leap, but not the return of its chief critic.

But for the planners who had to effect China's economic recovery from the GLF, rehabilitation for Peng, who had had the courage to voice their doubts, was less important than Mao's re-endorsement of the main elements of the recovery programme: priority to agriculture over industry and to light industry over heavy industry;[36] a virtual moratorium on the expansion of heavy industry. Mao was prepared to accept that steel output could remain at 18 m. tons or rise not more than a further million tons, and to embrace the new slogan of 'adjustment, consolidation, filling out, and raising (standards)', thought of as 'emergency measures for an emergency period'.[37]

Moreover, provincial freedom of manoeuvre—a disastrous feature of the GLF which had led to competitive escalation of targets and claims—was to be curbed and central economic management reasserted.[38] Under the 1959 slogan of taking the whole country as a chessboard (*quanguo yipan qi*), recentralization of financial control was agreed, in large part to curb extra-budgetary expenditure which had grown from 4.7 billion yuan in 1957 before the GLF to 13 billion yuan in 1960.[39] The plenum approved the creation of six regional CC bureaux—North China, Northeast, Northwest, East China, Central-South, Southwest—designed to act for it 'in strengthening leadership over the Party committees in the various provinces, municipalities and autonomous regions'; evidently party leaders were no longer concerned that such organs would provide bases for ambitious officials to emulate Gao Gang's activities in the Northeast in the early 1950s and build 'independent kingdoms'.[40]

Yet Mao was still not prepared to abandon even parts of the main slogan of the GLF—'Go all out, aim high, and achieve greater, faster, better, and more economical results' (*guzu ganjin lizheng shangyou, duo, kuai, hao, sheng*)—and warned that he did not want to have to oppose rightism again at the central work conference scheduled for March.[41] Privately, he expressed the thought that the failure of the GLF should really be attributed to people not having been ideologically prepared for it.[42]

Mao's reiteration of the language of the GLF may or may not have been indicative of ambivalence towards the new economic policies, but unquestionably it was designed to exhibit his determination that they should not provide the justification for renewed political attacks on the GLF, and by implication on himself. Nevertheless, although the official communiqué of the 9th plenum made complimentary references to the role of the 'three red banners'—the general line, the GLF, and the people's communes—it did not spell out the GLF slogan. The 9th plenum marked the end of the GLF.[43]

The planners were evidently prepared to toe the Chairman's political line. The economics of the communiqué, which reaffirmed Mao's policy of 'taking agriculture as the foundation' adumbrated a year earlier by Li Fuchun,[44] were based on the latter's 'opinions' on the 1961 plan, given on the first day of the plenum.[45] Li's strikingly upbeat appraisal of the recent past seemed designed to set Mao at ease: 1960 was a year of victory for the continuing leap of the national economy; the GLF had achieved great and unprecedented successes. Li backed up such claims with copious comparisons with 1957, the year before the GLF, with 1952, the eve of the 1st FYP, and with the economy which the CCP inherited in 1949. In that perspective, one could face squarely current 'partial, temporary difficulties', and shortcomings in work which amounted, in a favourite phrase of Mao's, to 'one finger [in ten]', though Li was candid enough to mention that for certain areas and enterprises the shortcomings were a good deal more than a single finger.[46]

Li gave six reasons for the setbacks: natural calamities; imbalances, particularly between agriculture and industry; inexperience, leading to over-ambitious targets, though Li did not self-criticize on this account; excessive decentralization; the bureaucratic work style of a few leading officials: the infiltration of bad elements into positions of leadership.[47] Nowhere, of course, did Li hint at, let alone point even a single finger at, the man who was ultimately responsible for the GLF disaster. Instead, with a couple of judicious quotations from Mao, Li managed to imply that many of the problems would not have occurred had the Chairman's words been heeded![48]

Li's favourable assessment of 1960 was based on the industrial figures. When he came to agriculture he did not reveal outputs, even *in camera* to this high level audience, telling his colleagues only that the worst natural calamities in a century had affected some 60 m. hectares (over half the arable acreage as a result of the GLF policy of seeking higher yields from smaller areas) and seriously damaged perhaps up to 26.8 m. hectares, though there are indications that his figures may have involved a considerable amount of guesswork. Li attempted to bolster his colleagues' morale by pointing out that fluctuations in agricultural output were not peculiar to China, but had also happened in the Soviet Union in the late 1950s.[49]

Looking ahead, with mantra-like invocations of his own, now official, slogan 'adjustment, consolidation, improvement, and filling out', Li stated that getting the various sectors of the economy back in balance would take two to three years. The critical problems were the shortages of food and industrial raw materials, particularly coal and timber. In industry, production would have to take precedence over capital construction, extraction over processing, maintenance over manufacture, complete sets of equipment over main engines, and quality and variety over quantity.[50]

Despite his cautionary words, Li forecasted output figures for the major items in the Chinese economy which turned out to be absurdly optimistic (see Table 1.2).[51]

TABLE 1.2. *Major economic figures, 1960–1961* (million tons)

	1960 output	1961 target	1961 output
Grain	143.5	225.5	162.3
Oil crops	2.1	4.0	2.0
Cotton	1.3	1.8	.9
Pigs (m.)	82.3	150.0	75.5
Steel	18.7	19.0	8.7
Coal	397.0	436.0	278.0

Sources: Nongye Nianjian, 1980, pp. 34, 36, 38; *TJNJ, 1981*, p. 223; Guofang Daxue, *Cankao Ziliao* 23, pp. 439, 441. The figures have been rounded to one decimal place.

While Li clearly considered these projected 1961 increases to be appropriately modest, he was fully aware of the importance of swingeing cuts in the output of industrial goods. Only in the case of alternative power sources to coal and items critical to industrial production did he look for increases. In both sets of cases, his projections again turned out wildly far off the mark (see Table 1.3).

TABLE 1.3. *Plan and performance, 1961: major industrial goods* (% change)

	Planned	Actual
Electric power	+11	−19
Oil	+25	+2
Cement	0	−60
Sulphuric acid	+20–8	−32
Soda ash	+8	−40
Electricity-generating equipment	−44	−80
Machine tools	−53	−63
Cars	−23	−84

Sources: TJNJ, 1981, pp. 221–6; Guofang Daxue, *Cankao Ziliao* 23, p. 441.

These figures suggest that, despite the new tolerance of realism, the planners were labouring under two constraints: lingering political fears and sheer ignorance. Outside those areas of economic activity, like steel, over which they once again had some control, the planners were working in the dark, probably mainly because of the disruption of the statistical services during the GLF. Misreporting had continued through 1960. Indeed, a firm reassertion of the importance of accurate central statistics would not occur until April 1962.[52]

Li's figures for coal, much of which was produced by small local mines,[53] illustrate this point. He stated that the 1961 target of 436 m. tons would only represent an increase of 11 m. tons, which meant that he believed that the 1960 output was 425 m. tons, whereas we are now told that the actual figure was 397 m. tons.[54] In the light of his problems, Li was fortunate in not having to go public with his forecasts for 1961. China was entering a period when economic data would become state secrets; official figures for these years would not emerge for two decades.[55]

Thus the plenum formally endorsed the decisions taken earlier at the work conference to end the GLF and lay greater stress on agriculture, but was not the occasion for wide-ranging discussion on possible new economic initiatives. Characteristically, Mao reserved this for the more informal conditions of the March work conference. The Chairman seems never to have liked substantive debate within bodies formally authorized to take decisions, presumably in case the debate and the decision went against him.[56]

Verdict on the Moscow conference

In human terms, the state of the economy was the most urgent matter considered at the 9th plenum. Millions were still dying as a result of the ravages of the GLF. A third 'bitter year' of death and deprivation lay ahead. But in cold political terms, the state of the Sino-Soviet alliance was ultimately more serious. The Chinese economy would slowly recover; the rupture between Beijing and Moscow that occurred in 1960 would swiftly worsen, with disastrous results for the world communist movement and Chinese domestic politics.

At the plenum, CCP General Secretary Deng Xiaoping reported on the conference of eighty-one communist parties held the previous November in Moscow, at which he had spearheaded the Chinese attack on the policies of Nikita Khrushchev, the Soviet premier and CPSU 1st secretary. The plenum resolution on his report 'expressed satisfaction' with the work of the CCP delegation led by Liu Shaoqi and 'fully approved' the Statement adopted unanimously at the conference. But the resolution made it clear that the compromises agreed to by the Chinese in the Soviet capital in the interests of world communist solidarity had not altered Beijing's views on the correct global strategies to be pursued by the international communist movement in general and its strongest component, the CPSU, in particular.

Essentially the resolution emphasized the most militant and anti-Western passages of the Statement, while in Moscow, almost simultaneously, Khrushchev was toning it down. The resolution declared that the world was in a 'time of struggle between two opposing social systems, a time of socialist revolutions and national liberation revolutions, a time of the breakdown of imperialism, of the abolition of the colonial system . . .' The present situation 'imperatively demands that the peoples all over the world further unite and wage an unremitting struggle against the policies of aggression and war of imperialism headed by the United States . . . the chief imperialist country of our time, being the biggest international exploiter, the world gendarme, the chief bulwark of world reaction and modern colonialism and the main force of aggression and war of our time . . .' Strong words—which Khrushchev significantly failed to use—and hardly calculated to win friends within the incoming American administration of President John F. Kennedy.

The Statement contained a reference to a 'definite section of the bourgeoisie' in the West who feared war, which could have referred merely to Western peace campaigners. Khrushchev reaffirmed the existence of 'saner' representatives of the Western ruling classes with whom peaceful coexistence could be agreed, clearly leaving himself an opening to negotiate with the new American president. But the Chinese resolution made no specific mention of peace-lovers, either among the peoples or the rulers of the West.

The Chinese listed the 'national liberation movement' as one of the forces to prevent war; Khrushchev did not, and while the Soviet leader did evince support for liberation struggles as domestic insurrections, he was careful in his report on the Moscow conference to indicate that communist powers should seek to prevent them being internationalized, a process which of course carried with it the danger of confrontation between the Soviet Union and the United States.

By signing the Statement, the Chinese had subscribed to Khrushchev's view as elaborated in his speech to the CPSU's 21st Congress that the balance of forces was such that there was a real possibility of averting world war. But in their plenum resolution, the Chinese phrased this concept in a very different and far more negative manner, asserting that the 'danger is not yet over that imperialism will launch a new and unprecedentedly destructive world war'.[57]

However chastened the Chinese leaders may have felt as a result of their domestic problems, they were clearly in no mood for compromise on Marxist theory or in international affairs. Mao reportedly regarded the break with the Russians as a 'second liberation' of China, leaving the CCP free to chart its own ideological course, and he set up a brains trust to help him do it.[58] At the work conference prior to the plenum, Mao had denounced Khrushchev's theory of a state and a party of the whole people;[59] and though the Chinese had signed the Moscow Statement in the interest of unity and under pressure from other communist parties, they had no intention in practice of abandoning their militant foreign-policy posture.

Even before the CC met, Mao was planning the publication of a book designed to show by parable the mistakenness of Soviet foreign policy. The book was a compendium of old Chinese legends collected together under the title *Stories About Not Being Afraid of Ghosts*. Compilation of the book had been initiated in the spring of 1959 on Mao's instructions; at that time the principal objective appears to have been to revive national confidence at a time when the domestic problems brought on by the GLF were becoming acute. Natural calamities were still among the 'ghosts' to be confronted, but the principal ones listed in the preface were 'international imperialism and its henchmen in various countries' and 'modern revisionism represented by the Tito clique'.[60]

The compiler of the collection was the noted poet He Qifang, but as his own later account makes clear, Mao went over He's introduction with a fine-tooth comb, spending four hours on it at their first meeting on 4 January. The introduction stated that a 'big question' in China and throughout the world was how to assess the forces of revolution and the forces of reaction in the world. People still harboured superstitions, not understanding that the apparent power and strength of these forces were 'merely a transient phenomenon, a factor playing only a temporary role'.[61] The introduction summed up the correct attitude:

On the whole, strategically, we have every reason to despise, and we must despise, all of them. Those who dare not despise the enemy and all that obstructs our advance and are frightened out of their wits by imperialism and reaction, or who succumb before difficulties and setbacks, are ghost-fearing men of the 20th century.[62]

Mao personally inserted a passage clearly poking fun at Khrushchev's policy of peaceful coexistence: 'Is it possible that the more we fear "ghosts", the more they will love us? And that suddenly all will go swimmingly for our cause, and everything will be bright and rosy, like the flowers that bloom in the spring?'[63]

Conscious that in the selection of stories, stress had been put on men's fearlessness in standing up to and striking at ghosts—that is, on strategically despising the enemy—Mao and He Qifang felt constrained to draw attention in the introduction and with some stories to the other prong of the Chairman's military thinking: respecting the enemy tactically. It was necessary for men 'to be prudent and resourceful before they can win final victory'.[64]

At his second meeting with He Qifang on 23 January, after the CC had formulated its resolution on the Moscow conference, Mao added a final paragraph to the introduction in which he asserted that the ' "ghost-defying" [Moscow] Statement has greatly augmented the power and influence of the revolutionary people all over the world, plunged the devils and goblins into dejection and in the main broken up the anti-China chorus. But readers should understand that there are still plenty of devils, ghosts and goblins in the world, and it will take some time to wipe them out.'[65]

But though penning such phrases—and writing two (still unpublished) poems against revisionism[66]—probably gave Mao much satisfaction, he was aware that during 1960 the Chinese leadership had unwisely neglected domestic problems to engage in the polemics with the CPSU. Neither he nor his colleagues had any intention of making a similar error in 1961. After the passage of the plenum resolution on the Moscow conference, and the publication of *Stories About Not Being Afraid of Ghosts* shortly thereafter, the Chinese seemed content to let matters rest. It was not until Khrushchev provoked them by attacking their ally Albania at the CPSU's 22nd Congress in October that year, that they would return to the fray.

2 EMERGENCY MEASURES

The food crisis

The catastrophic decline in grain output and its impact on people's food consumption forced Beijing to take unprecedented remedial measures. Grain stocks declined sharply as a result of the GLF. In mid-1957, before it was launched, stocks stood at 18.2 m. tonnes (i.e. metric tons); by the winter of 1960–1 stocks were down to about 5.05 m. tonnes, or a little over a month's rations for the urban population.[1] Every five to ten days, reports on the grain situation were sent to Premier Zhou, who was in overall charge of grain work from 1959 to 1966. He kept a particularly close eye on the handling of the food situation from June 1960 to September 1962, adding numerous comments to the food balance sheets, engaging in long late-night discussions with Food Ministry officials several times a week, 115 times in all, and even personally devising a 'Central food allocations plan table' (*zhongyang liangshi diaobo jihua biao*) to enable him to monitor central and provincial grain flows.[2] By December 1960, Zhou would have been aware that food supplies for Beijing, Tianjin, Shanghai, Shenyang, and other major cities were down to only a few days' worth, in some cases just one day's, a grimly small margin for the government to operate with.[3] The monthly per capita cooking fat ration in the big cities was down to 3.5 oz.[4]

The desperate nature of the urban situation is underlined by the seat-of-the-pants decision-making forced upon the Chinese leadership. At some point in December, Zhou Enlai and Chen Yun, the only distinguished economic specialist in the Politburo Standing Committee,[5] persuaded their colleagues to agree to what some saw as the humiliating policy of purchasing grain from abroad.[6] At the end of the month, as Zhou prepared to board his plane at Beijing airport to leave on a goodwill mission to Burma,[7] he and Chen together with Ye Jizhuang, the Minister of Foreign Trade, agreed on 1.5 m. tonnes as the amount to be bought.[8] A few hours later, when Zhou's plane touched down in Kunming in Yunnan, there was a phone message stating that the figure had been increased to 2.5 m. tonnes. Zhou immediately called Chen Yun, who told him that the food situation was so critical that the higher figure was essential.[9]

The assessment of grain import needs became even more confused in the New Year. On 18 January, the State Council's General
Office on Finance and Trade[10] presented the central leadership with
its opinion that 4 m. tonnes of grain imports would be needed to alleviate the food crisis, stabilize the market, and provide support for
agriculture; this figure did not include 1 m. tonnes of grain destined
for re-export.[11] Yet in a speech the following day, Premier Zhou also
used a new figure, but his was only 3 m. tonnes.[12] It is unclear whether
this confusion masked a policy dispute; what is clear is that by
20 March the grimmer views of China's needs formulated in the
General Office on Finance and Trade had been accepted, for on that
day its director, Vice-Premier and Finance Minister Li Xiannian,
told the Canton work conference that 'it has already been decided'
to import 5 m. tonnes of grain in 1961 and between 3.5 m. and 4 m.
tonnes in 1962.[13] Even these figures turned out to be underestimates.[14]

In the meantime, organizational measures had been taken to
implement the decision on grain imports. On 29 December, the Ministry of Food summoned a conference to prepare to handle what the
central authorities were calling 'entrepot grain' (zhuankou liang).[15]
Why the imports should have been given that description is unclear:
perhaps the ministry was working on the basis of some earlier directive which talked only of the need to buy foreign grain and then re-
export it to fulfil China's export obligations; perhaps the term was
used for cosmetic purposes to prevent people from realizing that
China was about to become heavily dependent on foreign food.

Equally, it is unclear why this ministry took this initiative, since a
month later, on 30 January 1961, the centre issued an emergency
directive setting up a blue riband Central Grain Imports Reception
and Transportation Work Group (Zhongyang Jinkou Shiliang
Jieyun Gongzuozu) under the leadership of officials concerned with
commerce and transportation to handle the 'entrepot grain'.[16] Perhaps the explanation is simply more confusion, as the centre reacted
to ever-more pessimistic estimates of the grain situation.

However great the internal confusion surrounding Beijing's grain
import policy-making, in the outside world it had already become
clear by the end of 1960 that China had decided to seek assistance
from the granaries of Australia and Canada; direct trading with the
third great Western grain producer, the United States, was ruled out
for political reasons. In December 1960, the Australian Wheat
Board announced the sale of 240,000 tonnes of wheat and then a fur-

ther 60,000 tonnes, worth a total of £6 m.[17] In the same month, a tight-lipped, two-man Chinese trade delegation arrived in Montreal expecting to stay three-to-four months. By the beginning of February 1961, the Canadian Minister of Agriculture was able to announce that 750,000 tonnes of wheat and 260,000 tons of barley, worth about £20 m., would be shipped to China during the next few months.[18]

As it turned out, these initial purchases were in the nature of stopgap measures, with freighters being diverted by radio to Australian and Canadian ports,[19] designed in part to spare China's grain stocks without reneging on international obligations. Despite the growing agricultural crisis, grain exports had mounted in leaps and bounds since 1957, until the exigencies of 1960 forced a drastic reduction (see Table 2.1).

TABLE 2.1. *Chinese grain exports, 1958–1960*

Year	Amount (m. tonnes)	Increase (%)
1958	3.25	73.1
1959	4.74	45.9
1960	1.00	−78.9

Source: Dangdai Zhongguode Liangshi Gongzuo, pp. 122–3.

At Beijing's request, some 60,000 tonnes of wheat were shipped directly from Canada to Albania in the spring of 1961; 160,000 tonnes went directly to East Germany later in the year.[20] Similarly, China purchased 300,000 tonnes of rice from Burma in 1961, mainly to cover its agreements to exchange 160,000 tonnes for 17,000 tonnes of Ceylonese rubber, and another 100,000 tonnes for 350,000 tonnes of Cuban sugar.[21]

In China's emergency, even Khrushchev offered to help, despite the bitter Sino-Soviet polemics of 1960. In a letter to Mao on 27 February, he alluded to Soviet domestic food problems and obligations to Eastern Europe and North Korea, but offered to lend China 300,000 tonnes of wheat, 700,000 tonnes of rye, and 500,000 tonnes of Cuban sugar by August. Zhou Enlai replied orally on 8 March expressing China's wish to avoid adding to the Soviet Union's burden and indicating that Beijing hoped to obtain its needs on the international market. He asked that the Soviet grain be kept in reserve in case international purchases fell through, in which case

China would call for the loan. Zhou did, however, accept the sugar.[22] In due course, he arranged to borrow 200,000 tons of grain from the Soviet Far East to feed China's Northeast, repaying the loan with subsequent imports from the West.[23]

But China's leaders were increasingly conscious that the gravity of the domestic food crisis demanded more than short-term emergency measures. In a long letter to Mao on 17 May, Li Xiannian spelled out the hard facts and indicated that the estimate for 1962 grain imports would have to be raised from the 3.5 m. tonnes figure, which he had cited in Canton less than two months earlier, to 5 m. tonnes. At the Canton conference, it had been agreed to set the figure for the state's compulsory grain purchases during the 1961–2 crop year (July–June) at 44 m. tonnes, but the Food Ministry had since discovered that provinces had lowered their targets, and the total was now only 42 m. tonnes; almost half this grain, 20 m. tonnes, came from the surplus produced in only 250–300 of China's roughly 2,000 counties, and it was clearly felt that if they were squeezed further, production would suffer.

The revision of the overall figure for state grain purchases meant that the provinces would not be able to supply the centre with the 6 m.–6.5 m. tonnes agreed in Canton. The overall state grain deficit from domestic sources, estimated in Canton at 3.5 m. tonnes, now looked more like 7.5 m. tonnes, only 5 m. tonnes of which would be covered by imports. A larger import figure was not feasible because the external sources of supply were undependable, China lacked the requisite foreign exchange, and its shipping and port facilities could not cope. These calculations had dire implications for the 24 m. people in Beijing, Tianjin, Shanghai, and Shenyang dependent on central grain, not to mention the additional 110 m. urban residents dependent upon the provincial authorities. Li was concerned to prevent the average per capita grain consumption from dropping below the 1960–1 level of 140 kg., especially as he feared that the regime's enemies might take advantage of China's troubles to foment unrest.[24]

Li Xiannian's views were shared by Chen Yun. After a period of retirement attributable to both illness and discretion,[25] Chen Yun had returned to economic policy-making in the autumn of 1960 as Mao was abandoning the GLF. He had been put in charge of a Food Price Problem Small Group (*Liang Jia Wenti Xiaozu*) that had recommended raising procurement prices,[26] and he was the principal architect of the grain import policy.[27]

For Chen, as for Li, the overriding imperative was to increase supplies of food and clothing to the domestic market; food took precedence over clothing, and grain was the key foodstuff. It would be 'very perilous' if grain were not available, he said on 30 May 1961, and since agricultural production would take some years to recover, the main source had to be imports.[28]

Chen discarded Li's practice of making annual forecasts of grain import needs. As a result of his urging, the Chinese government decided to enter into long-term arrangements with Canada and Australia to ensure grain supplies until production recovered. Chen Yun even got Mao to agree to the import of American grain, laundered through France.[29] In the event, long-term dependence once begun did not readily cease. In the years ahead, imported grain accounted for a significant share of urban consumption; although net imports only equalled 2.7 per cent of national grain output in 1961–2, this was in fact the equivalent of 55 per cent of the average annual grain transfers from surplus provinces during the 1st FYP. Per capita grain supplies to cities could be raised from 235 kg. to 274 kg. in 1961 as a result of the imports, and from 258 kg. to 296 kg. in 1962.[30]

The first Sino-Canadian agreement was signed in May 1961 and allowed for a maximum purchase of 5,081,000 tonnes of wheat and 46.7 m. bushels (1,016,000 tonnes) of barley over the period June 1961 to December 1963; of these amounts, 762,000 tonnes of wheat and 17 m. bushels of barley were to be shipped by 30 November 1961.[31] This agreement was later followed by a second three-year agreement for 5,080,000 tonnes of wheat covering 1963–6, a third for 6.1 m. tonnes covering 1966–9, then a series of annual contracts (presumably due to the disruption of normal governmental activities during the Cultural Revolution), followed by yet another three-year agreement in 1973 for 6,096,000 tonnes.[32] Australian sales of grain to China totalled almost 11 m. tonnes between 1961 and 1966, with 1,965,000 exported in 1961–2.[33]

The first grain ships docked in Chinese ports in February 1961. In the first quarter of that year, 500,000 tonnes arrived, in the second, another 1.65 m. tonnes. Those first shipments were immediately despatched to the places where there was a danger of food running out: Beijing, Shanghai, Tianjin, Liaoning, and the worst-hit disaster areas.[34] Over the whole of 1961, grain imports amounted to 5,809,700 tonnes, well over six times the total imported in the 11 years since the founding of the People's Republic, and 800,000 tonnes more than Chen Yun thought China's foreign exchange and transporation resources would permit.[35] Wheat imports alone— 3,881,700 tonnes—represented 27 per cent of China's wheat crop, which had dropped to 14.25 m. tonnes in 1961 from 22.17 m. tonnes the year before; over the succeeding five years, imports amounted to around 25 per cent of production. As recently as 1959, China had exported 4,157,500 tonnes of grain; in 1961, the figure dropped to 1,335,000 tonnes, presumably to cover obligations that could not be escaped. The total burden on China during the years subsequent to the GLF can be seen from Table 2.2.

TABLE 2.2. *Grain output and trade figures, 1959–1966* (m. tonnes)

	All grains			Wheat	
	Output	Imports	Exports	Output	Imports
1959	170.0	0.002	4.15	22.18	0.00
1960	143.5	0.06	2.72	22.17	0.04
1961	147.5	5.80	1.35	14.25	3.88
1962	160.0	4.92	1.03	16.67	3.53
1963	170.0	5.95	1.49	18.48	5.58
1964	187.5	6.57	1.82	20.84	5.36
1965	194.5	6.40	2.41	25.22	6.07
1966	214.0	6.43	2.88	25.28	6.21

Source: *TJNJ, 1983*, pp. 158, 422, 438.[36]

The grain import policy had a considerable impact on the composition of China's trade. In the early years of the regime, agricultural products had accounted for over 50 per cent of the value of China's exports, and the figure was still over 40 per cent in 1957, the last year of the 1st FYP. During the GLF, 1958–60, the share of agricultural products fell further and fluctuated but remained above 30 per cent. But in 1961, it fell sharply to 20.7 per cent and the following year dropped to 19.4 per cent, the lowest level of the 1960s and 1970s. Food imports which had been less than 10 per cent of total imports since the start of the 1st FYP in 1953 and had only been 4.6 per cent in 1960, rose to 38.1 per cent in 1961 and were over 44 per cent in the three subsequent years.[37]

The foreign exchange cost of the food import policy was also enormous, even though credits provided some leeway. Speaking in January 1962, Liu Shaoqi estimated the total cost for 1961 and 1962 combined at $660 m., which he stated was the equivalent of forty Luoyang tractor plants or 17 m. tons of imported fertilizer.[38] China's trade with Canada, which had been roughly in balance until 1959, was heavily in deficit in 1960 and thereafter even more so. With Australia, China had always had a deficit, but again in 1961 the figure rose sharply. More importantly, imports from these two states alone, primarily grain, soared from 1.7 per cent of the total import bill in 1960 to 24.5 per cent in 1961, rose as high as 28 per cent in 1963, falling below 20 per cent in 1965 and 1966 only because of a jump of almost one third in the total import bill in the former year. Table 2.3 details the impact of the new food import policy.[39]

TABLE 2.3. *Value of Chinese imports and exports, 1958–1966* ($ m.)

	Canada		Australia		Global	
	Imports	Exports	Imports	Exports	Imports	Exports
1958	6.53	4.20	31.18	4.72	1,890	1,980
1959	2.37	4.23	31.27	5.28	2,120	2,260
1960	13.77	3.68	21.69	5.02	1,950	1,860
1961	167.88	2.29	187.75	3.88	1,450	1,490
1962	156.87	3.52	106.19	7.06	1,170	1,490
1963	111.10	4.83	245.60	10.81	1,270	1,650
1964	161.99	10.12	184.05	18.44	1,550	1,920
1965	125.77	15.63	214.97	20.88	2,020	2,230
1966	230.19	22.72	104.46	21.72	2,250	2,370

Source: *TJNJ*, *1981*, pp. 353 366, 367.

The Chinese were determined not to renege on their massive new financial obligations and thus damage their international credit; Premier Zhou told Foreign Trade Minister Ye Jizhuang: 'Pay close attention to contracts; safeguard our credit-worthiness' (*zhong hetong, shou xinyong*).[40] To ensure this, Zhou and his colleagues set out to keep China's trade in balance despite this major new ingredient in its imports. They appear to have employed two principal means. They cut imports from the Soviet Union sharply, from $845.16 m. in 1960 to $291.65 m. in 1961 and $210.92 m. in 1962. The figures declined further thereafter and did not rise again above $200 m. until 1976, though a short-lived rise of $52.19 m. in 1965 was an important component of the overall jump in imports that year. The 1961 cutback was doubtless dictated in part by the outbreak of the Sino-Soviet dispute in 1960 and the withdrawal of Soviet technical specialists in August of that year, but even without the Moscow–Beijing quarrel, China would have had to reduce industrial imports, of which the Soviet Union was the major supplier, partly because of the general need for economic retrenchment, partly because of the need to find foreign exchange to pay for the Australian and Canadian grain.[41]

The other means used to keep trade in balance was to increase exports. Indeed, import policy was tailored with the aim of purchasing precisely those raw materials that could be used in the production of exports.[42] In May 1961, explaining the new obligation to import grain, Chen Yun admonished foreign trade officials on the basic principles of international marketing and the importance of increasing high-quality traditional exports with cachet abroad:

We're not the only people doing business on the international markets and only those of our products which are better and cheaper will compete. To do business, one must be victorious in competition and not allow things to be decided subjectively by producers . . . In the past famous brand commodities . . . all had their own bases [and had] stable production, high output, good quality, and low cost . . . For example, there is a special kind of chicken that is worth $3 (US) with which we can buy 100 catties [50 kg.] of grain. That is economical. Many people like to eat this kind of chicken, so there is a good market. That is stability. To ensure exports we must work on commodity bases. We should spend one and a half years to establish bases for export commodities.[43]

The main export target was Hong Kong, an avid purchaser of traditional Chinese products and a major source of foreign exchange. Exports to Hong Kong and Macao almost doubled, though this took longer to achieve than import cutbacks, indeed roughly the one-and-a-half years envisioned by Chen Yun. During the 2nd FYP period (1958–62), Chinese exports to the two colonies averaged $200 m., rising to $227.87 m. in 1962. In 1963, they shot up to $300.64 m., and rose sharply again the following year to $404.31 m. By 1966, the figure had reached $580.57 m., from which it declined abruptly during the early years of the Cultural Revolution. Chinese imports from these sources, always low, dropped to $8.16 m. in 1963, hovering around $16 m. in the following three years.[44]

Rustication

In his letter to Mao on 17 May, Li Xiannian had cautiously suggested that perhaps the only additional way of tackling the grain problem was to reduce the number of urban residents. He professed himself concerned lest an exodus damage the industrial advances of the GLF, which he took care to praise.[45] But by the end of the month, presumably with Mao's encouragement, Chen Yun was more forthright.

Addressing the CC's work conference on 31 May, Chen Yun stated that the import of grain was one of four policies for tackling the food problem. The basic approach was to unleash peasant initiative by implementation of the Sixty Articles on Agriculture (discussed in the next chapter). Next, industrial support for agricultural development had to be stepped up. He pointed out, however, that just as there was a financial constraint in the case of food imports, so there was a time constraint in the case of industrial goods: the output of chemical fertilizer, tractors, and irrigation machinery could not be rapidly increased. He therefore concluded that the fourth policy was indispensable and had to be adopted immediately: the mobilization of urban residents to move to the countryside in order to reduce the amount of grain taken from the peasantry for sale in the cities. If excessive grain were procured, peasant enthusiasm would be extinguished and the Sixty Articles would be irrelevant.[46]

Chen reminded his audience that three out of the four grain crises since the creation of the PRC—in 1953, 1954, 1957, and since 1959—had been caused by excessive growth of the urban population. During the GLF, the urban population had increased from 99 m. to 130 m., including 24 m. extra workers, and grain stocks had dropped drastically in consequence. Chen estimated that at the conclusion of the crop year at the end of June, after the spring and early summer harvests, stocks would have risen only 7.4 m. tons.[47]

Chen acknowledged that to get people to abandon a 'much pleasanter' urban life to return to the countryside would be very hard. But not to do so would be worse. The cost of grain imports aside, it would mean severe pressure on the most productive areas; peasants might bear with only 150 kg. of grain per capita as their annual ration for a year, but after that their willingness to increase production for the sake of the cities would evaporate.[48] Chen perhaps did not need to remind his audience that 150 kg. was starvation rations for peasants engaged in heavy farm work.[49]

Hungry peasants would inevitably consume grain that should have been reserved for fodder. Draught animals would die, immobilizing an agriculture that depended on them more than on machines. Planters of cash crops would abandon them in favour of grain if food supplies were insufficient. In sum, agriculture, the foundation of the national economy would be crippled if forced to feed a swollen urban population.[50]

Obviously, if a rapid agricultural recovery could be expected, there would be no urgency about returning people to the countryside. But according to Chen, an analysis by Premier Zhou Enlai had indicated that rapid recovery was impossible. It would take three to four years with annual increases of 10–15 m. tonnes to reach 1958 levels, and the fertilizer and machinery to facilitate such a recovery was not available.[51]

Would industrial production be affected if workers were siphoned off to the countryside? No, because industry was in such a parlous condition that large numbers of workers had nothing to do; the industrial front would have to be shortened.[52] Some suggested that rusticated urbanites would have to eat the same amount wherever they were. But Chen calculated that on average each person sent back to the countryside would require 75 kg. less grain from the state. If 10 m. were rusticated that would amount to 750,000 tonnes; if 20 m., then 1.5 m. tonnes, and these figures would be for the first year alone. Thereafter, as the returnees started helping to produce in collective fields and on private plots, he reckoned the savings could be doubled.[53] In effect, the state would reduce friction with the peasantry over grain procurement, but until the returnees started pulling their weight, the friction would be transferred to the villages.

Chen's speech suggests that there was some resistance within the Central Committee to a policy which would impose a severe strain on the organizational skills both of the cadres responsible for mobilizing candidates for rustication and of those who would have to supervise their resettlement in the countryside. But with Liu Shaoqi warning that if such emergency measures were not carried out, the country might be plunged into a situation like the Soviet Union in 1921 during its civil war,[54] CCP officials realized that they had no option, and the massive operation was rapidly carried out.

A nine-point plan was issued on 16 June. The decision was to reduce urban population by 20 m. in three years: 10 m. in 1961, 8 m. in 1962, and the final 2 m. in 1963.[55] The evacuation of the first 10 m. was in fact accomplished between June and September 1961.[56] By mid-1963, the evacuees would total about 26 m.[57] By the time of the census of mid-1964, the urban population had been reduced to 97.91 m., which was below the 1957 level.[58]

The CCP accomplished this feat in part by rapid mobilization of senior officials. A three-man 'small group' consisting of Li Fuchun, the chairman of the State Planning Commission, Yang Shangkun, the head of the CC's General Office, and An Ziwen, director of its Organization Department, was entrusted with its implementation. Li called a series of separate meetings with top officials from the 1st Ministry of Machine Building (20 June), Light Industry (21 June), Railways (25 June), Culture and Education (28 June); in all, between 20 June and 5 July, the small group had nineteen meetings with various groups of officials, issuing instructions as to how the goal of urban population reduction could be achieved with the help of appropriate cutbacks in economic activity. In the case of light industry, for instance, Li ordered that decisions on combining plants and shutting down production should be made not on the basis of the needs of the population, but strictly on the basis of the amount of raw materials that agriculture could supply.[59]

The Tianjin experience

Tianjin data provide an example of how swiftly some local CCP committees reacted to the central directives.[60] The standing committee of the Tianjin city party was discussing the CC's 'Nine methods for reducing urban population and urban grain consumption' as early as 7 June, even before it had been formally issued.[61] A second standing committee conference on 16 June laid down a target of reducing the urban population by 300,000 within three years, 100,000 by the end of 1961. Then on 19 June, at a conference of party secretaries at the district level and below, arrangements for the implementation of this plan were made. On 21 July, a further work conference dealt with ideological and organizational problems resulting from the policy, while on 21 August, at a conference held by the city's party secretariat, a call was issued to fulfil the 1961 target as soon as possible, presumably in response to a decision in Beijing to fulfil the first annual target by September.[62]

The continuing importance of the policy was underlined by the personal supervision accorded it by the Tianjin 1st secretary Wan Xiaotang in assigning tasks in March 1962, and by the formation of a special 'leading small group' (*lingdao xiaozu*) to take charge by April. This activity may have been in response to continuing agitation in Beijing about the issue, for the small group formulated a plan in response to a central demand that Tianjin had to reduce its population by 390,000—not the originally planned 300,000—and its work-force by 260,000. On the basis of the statistics available on the reductions achieved in 1961, the small group concluded that Tianjin would have to shed 262,000 people in 1962. But by late May this latter figure had again been raised dramatically, this time to 400,000, a little under 7 per cent of the city population; between 14 April and 8 June, the target for the reduction in workers was raised in two steps from 180,000 to 220,000.[63]

It is difficult to assess the success of Tianjin's plans. Currently available statistics show that emigration from greater Tianjin in the years 1961–3 totalled 264,620, but the net reduction of population was only 136,448 when account is taken of the figures for immigration. The net decrease for the city proper (presumably including people migrating to Tianjin suburban villages) was 100,406 during those three years.[64]

Rusticating workers

As the Tianjin plans indicate, a second essential ingredient of the national plan issued in June was the mandated reduction of workers and staff, the national target being 9.6 m., almost 10 per cent of the 1960 figure.[65] Shanxi province had initiated its measures with a special work conference from 1 to 10 April, at which it was decided to reduce the work-force by 200,000 to 350,000 by the end of June. Then on 1 June, the provincial party committee agreed to the figure, now 300,000 non-agricultural population, suggested by the small group in charge of the weeding-out operation, only to raise it again two days later to 500,000–600,000.[66]

One factor in the success of the effort to reduce the non-agricultural work-force would seem to have been that the number of industrial workers had shrunk already in 1959, presumably as a result of Mao's first retreat from the excesses of the GLF at the end of 1958; many were doubtless employed in rural commune-run industry, but some were probably peasants leaving urban industrial establishments and returning to nearby villages. Although numbers expanded again after the GLF was revived at the Lushan plenum in August 1959, they did not reach the 1958 peak as Table 2.4 illustrates.

TABLE 2.4. *Employment figures, 1957–1966* (millions)

	Total[a]	Industrial workers	Farm labour
1957	237.71	14.01	193.10
1958	266.00	44.16	154.92
1959	261.73	28.81	162.73
1960	258.80	29.79	170.19
1961	255.90	22.24	197.49
1962	259.10	17.05	212.78
1963	236.00	16.32	219.68
1964	277.36	16.95	228.03
1965	286.70	18.28	233.98
1966	298.05	19.74	242.99

Note: [a]This column includes managerial and other non-manual workers.

Source: *TJNJ, 1983*, pp. 120, 122.

The 'extremely important and complex' task of rusticating workers was the subject of a CC circular issued on 28 June which dealt with the nuts and bolts of the logistical process.[67] The principal targets of rustication were all those temporary, contract, apprentice, and regular workers who had started work since January 1958. Except where they had become vital to their new units—a category clearly susceptible of abuse—they had to return home to work on the farms. Earlier urban immigrants could move back to the countryside on a voluntary basis. Workers who were genuine urban dwellers should generally not be moved.[68]

Those who left town before the middle of a month were to be given half-a-month's wages; those who left after it, a whole month's. There was also detailed provision for additional financial benefits to sweeten the pill (see Table 2.5).

TABLE 2.5. *Financial compensation for rusticated workers*

Employment period	Temporary/Contract	Regular/Apprentice
Less than $\frac{1}{2}$ year	None	
Less than 1 year		1 month's wages
$\frac{1}{2}$–2 years	$\frac{1}{2}$ month's wages	
1–2 years		$1\frac{1}{2}$ month's wages
2–3 years	1 month's wages	2 months' wages
3+ years	$1\frac{1}{2}$ month's wages	$2\frac{1}{2}$ months' wages

Source: Guofang Daxue, *Cankao Ziliao* 23, p. 490.

All such outlays, including travel expenses if necessary, had to be provided by the units where the workers were employed; the state would not provide any funding, though hard-pressed units might get bank loans. A time-consuming but vital part of the logistical operation was for the appropriate housing and grain bureaux to ensure that each departing worker had proof of legal change of residence.[69]

Cadres in charge of areas where the evacuees were to be decanted were told to deliver a somewhat contradictory message: on the one hand, they had to extol the glories of returning to the agricultural front line; but at the same time, they were permitted to dangle the consolation carrot of preferential status for returning to the cities when the economy picked up again.[70]

In the case of Tianjin, the reduction in the number of workers in state-owned enterprises in 1962 was only 59,061, but if figures for the collapse of commune industries were available, the total could be far larger.[71] In Guangdong province, the claimed figure was 2 m.[72]

On the staff side, the displaced personnel included central bureaucrats. By June 1961, Mao was able to commend Vice-Premier Xi Zhongxun, the Secretary-General of the State Council, on his report that there had been a cut of one-third in the central bureaucracy, which had been 240,000 strong. Mao, who was immensely pleased and impressed with the CCP's ability to handle the rustication operation,[73] urged a further reduction by 40,000 to make a total cut of one-half. He also recommended that the report be widely circulated so that provincial governments would be encouraged to do the same.[74]

A third element set out in the June plan, indeed the object of the whole massive exercise, was that the reduction in urban inhabitants would allow the regime to reduce the amount of grain it had to supply to the cities from the 1960 figure of 26 m. tonnes to between 24 m. and 24.5 m. tonnes by the end of 1962.[75]

Inflation

After food, prices were probably the most pressing of popular concerns. The shortages of light-industrial and agricultural products brought on by the concentration on heavy industry during the GLF resulted in an excess of purchasing power over commodities. State expenditure surpassed revenue and banknotes were issued on a massive scale. During the GLF the amount of currency in circulation increased 81.7 per cent; for the period 1957–61, the figure was 140 per cent.[76] One of the earliest and most notable successes of the new communist government had been to bring under control the catastrophic inflation of the civil war years. Now, only a decade later, mismanagement had resulted in a new inflation, not nearly as severe as that of the late 1940s, but nevertheless profoundly disturbing to China's leaders (see Table 2.6):

TABLE 2.6.   *Retail price indices*

1959	100.0
1960	103.1
1961	119.8
1962	124.4

Source: Luo Gengmo, 'Socialism and Inflation', *PR*, No. 44, 1982, p. 20.

The rise in the retail price index was mitigated by the government's decision to protect the urban consumer in the case of eighteen key household commodities—notably grain, cloth, and coal—while sharply raising the prices of special or luxury foodstuffs to help mop up spare cash. But in China's major city, Shanghai, free market prices were more than double the state prices.[77]

The marketing of expensive cakes and sweets began in forty large and medium-sized cities in January, and by March it was in place in towns of all sizes throughout the land. By the end of 1961, sales amounted to 3.3 billion yuan, 5.9 per cent of all consumer goods purchase.[78] In February 1962, Chen Yun would propose to expand the policy by allocating 40–50 m. yuan to the purchase of delicacies 'from the mountains and the seas' and elsewhere for sale in restaurants and to guesthouses. While the policy was targeted on the urban areas in 1961, for 1962 Chen advocated spreading sales to the rural areas where there was much excess cash.[79]

The success of the policy led to its extension: some bicycles, clocks, watches, liquors, teas, and knitwear were sold as luxury goods. The total figure for sales of all high-priced consumer goods in 1961 was 7.45 billion yuan, of which 3.85 billion yuan represented profit for the state.[80]

TABLE 2.7. *Retail prices of major consumer items, 1957–1962* (yuan)

	Grain (ton)	Vegetable oil (ton)	Sugar (ton)	Eggs (100 kg.)	Vegetables (ton)	Pork (100 kg.)	Cotton cloth (m.)	Coal (ton)
1957	220.0	1,131.2	1,138	105.0	108.8	118.0	1.10	19.2
1958	220.0	1,154.0	1,143	140.0	98.8[a]	118.0	1.11	19.2
1959	220.0	1,180.0	1,143	151.4	107.4	125.0	1.11	19.2
1960	227.2	1,210.0	1,273	159.4	120.0	134.0	1.20	20.0
1961	231.0	1,393.0	1,264	196.0	133.4	171.4	1.31	25.3
1962	229.4	1,471.0	1,279	201.8	135.0	171.4	1.54	25.3

Note: [a] This drop in price was due to the over-production of vegetables in 1958. This resulted in much being fed to animals or going to waste because of the shortage of storage facilities.
Source: *TJNJ, 1983*, pp. 470–2, 477.

Since the government could not afford to discriminate against the peasants, it was forced, as agreed at the work conference prior to the 9th plenum, to raise its purchase prices of farm products, at great budgetary cost, as tables 2.8 and 2.9 indicate:

TABLE 2.8. *Agricultural purchase prices, 1957–1962* (yuan)

	Grain (ton)	Edible oil (ton)	Pork (head)	Eggs (100 kg.)	Aquatic products (ton)	Tea (100 kg.)
1957	162	940	47.7	94.2	341	137.4
1958	168	940	45.0	98.6	383	145.6
1959	164	1000	42.4	115.0	383	146.2
1960	170	1100	34.0	123.8	363	146.2

TABLE 2.8. (*contd.*) *Agricultural purchase prices, 1957–1962* (yuan)

	Grain (ton)	Edible oil (ton)	Pork (head)	Eggs (100 kg.)	Aquatic products (ton)	Tea (100 kg.)
1961	213	1300	55.0	162.6	526	164.2
1962	214	1314	56.7	166.4	548	171.0

Source: *TJNJ, 1983*, pp. 478–9; the grain price is for traded grain (*maoyi liang*).

TABLE 2.9. *Agricultural purchase prices index numbers 1950 = 100*

1957	146.2
1958	149.4
1959	152.1
1960	157.4
1961	201.4
1962	200.1

Sources: *TJNJ, 1983*, p. 455, and Table 2.7.

At the 1960 work conference, it had been estimated that the additional cost to the state of the higher purchase price for grain would be 1 billion yuan, to which would have to be added the cost of higher prices for edible oil crops, pigs, poultry, and eggs.[81] In the event, the peasantry benefited to the tune of 3 billion yuan from higher crop prices, though their compensation for confiscated property was less than the government had set aside, 1.85 billion yuan as compared with 2.5 billion yuan.[82]

3 A NEW COURSE IN THE COUNTRYSIDE

Mao takes an initiative

The 9th plenum had drawn a line under the GLF. Emergency measures were being taken to relieve the famine. Now China's leaders had to devise detailed measures to flesh out the general precepts agreed by the CC to help reinvigorate agriculture over the long term. The principal task was to build incentives into the commune system. The CCP could do nothing about the weather, but it could encourage the peasants to produce more. Measures to accomplish this objective were taken at a central work conference in Canton in March 1961 which agreed on a draft Sixty Articles on Agriculture. Some mystery still surrounds the background to this meeting, at which, according to Cultural Revolution sources, Mao criticized CCP General Secretary Deng Xiaoping and his powerful deputy in the CC secretariat, Beijing 1st secretary Peng Zhen.

Immediately after the 9th plenum, on 20 January, Mao gave his political secretary Tian Jiaying extremely detailed instructions for the immediate organization and dispatch of three high-level seven-man teams to investigate communes for up to fifteen days in Guangdong, Hunan, and Zhejiang. Mao was apparently struck by the failure of the Twelve-Article Emergency Directive issued the previous November to solve the fundamental problems in the rural areas. The teams, which departed on 21 January,[1] were to report to Mao and then converge on Canton to investigate the industrial situation there for a further month.[2] In addition, Mao despatched six members of his household staff, including bodyguards, with instructions to investigate in Xinyang district in Henan and report back.[3] Mao himself set off by rail on the evening of 26 January to make what was little more than a whistle-stop tour, calling in on Tianjin, Ji'nan, and Nanjing in January, and continuing on through Shanghai, Hangzhou, Nanchang, and Changsha, before arriving in Canton on 24 February.[4]

The importance Mao placed upon this operation was underlined not only by the precision of his initial directive, but also by the level of leadership which he laid down: the Guangdong team was to be led by Chen Boda, an alternate member of the Politburo and a former political secretary to Mao, the Hunan team by Hu Qiaomu, another of Mao's secretaries and an alternate member of the CC's secretariat,[5] while Tian Jiaying would head the Zhejiang team. Members of the teams included: Deng Liqun, Liu Shaoqi's political secretary, later one of Chen Boda's assistants on the staff of *Red Flag*; Xu Liqun, director of the theoretical section of the CC's Propaganda Department, soon to become one of the department's deputy directors; Wang Li, another propaganda specialist, then working in the CC's International Liaison Department; Mei Xing, an economic specialist; Wang Lu, a section head in the CC's Rural Work Department; Yang Po, a statistician; Hu Jiwei, a deputy editor of the *People's Daily*; Pang Xianzhi, Mao's librarian; and Wu Jiamin, a *Red Flag* journalist.[6]

Mao stipulated that each seven-man team would split into two three-man sub-units, each with its own leader, with Chen Boda, Hu Qiaomu, and Tian Jiaying in overall charge. One sub-unit in each team would investigate a well-off brigade, the other a poor one; average brigades were to be ignored.[7]

Keeping to the time limits laid down by the Chairman, Tian reported to Mao on 6 February in Hangzhou and urged that regulations be drawn up for the communes. Mao later credited Tian with his decision to do just that.[8] Having heard Tian out, Mao summed up his preliminary thoughts on the rural situation under seven heads:

a. The five (communist or ultra-leftist work) styles had to be changed, particularly with respect to leaving some land to be farmed by teams;
b. peasants had to be compensated for confiscated property;
c. peasants should be allowed 'private' plots (*ziliudi*) for cultivation of vegetables and the rearing of small farm animals like ducks and pigs;
d. how the three levels of the communes should relate to each other needed to be laid down;
e. the scale of the commune units might be too large and perhaps the production team should be made the basic unit of accounting;
f. communal mess-halls should be run in accordance with the views of the peasants;
g. cadre corruption should be dealt with, again in accordance with peasant opinion.[9]

Mao was clearly already willing to contemplate drastic reform of the communes, though he still clung to some of the utopian vision he had laid out in 1958, notably on sprouts of collectivism like communal mess-halls. On the basis of the work of the three teams and his own inspections, Mao sent Tian Jiaying and his colleague Pang Xianzhi down to Canton on 21 February where, two days later, members of the three teams met to start drafting regulations for the communes. On the 25th, Mao held a meeting with Tao Zhu, the 1st secretary of the newly reinstated Central-South party bureau and concurrently the Guangdong provincial 1st secretary; Chen Boda; Hu Qiaomu; Liao Luyan, the Minister of Agriculture; Zhao Ziyang, Tao Zhu's principal deputy in the Guangdong party organization; and Tian Jiaying. It was decided to set up a drafting committee, headed by Tao Zhu, with Chen Boda as his deputy.[10] Years later, Chen Boda claimed to have been the chief drafter;[11] apparently Mao was impressed by the report of Chen's Guangdong investigation team.[12]

On the 26th, the larger drafting committee met. In addition to Tao and Chen, it consisted of: Hu Qiaomu; Liao Luyan; Zhao Ziyang; Deng Liqun; Xu Liqun; Wang Li; Wang Lu; as well as Tian Jiaying; and Pang Xianzhi. On the 27th, a sub-committee of the group, consisting of Liao Luyan, Tian Jiaying, Wang Lu, and Zhao Ziyang met for detailed drafting work;[13] Hu Qiaomu acted as rewrite man.[14] All these meetings apparently took place under Mao's direct supervision, but not with him in the chair.[15] A preliminary version consisting of sixty-seven articles (which Mao deemed to be too long) was ready on 6 March and was sent to members of the Politburo Standing Committee (PSC); after consultations with a variety of people, a final version of a first draft was completed on 10 March.[16]

Then from 10 to 13 March, Mao chaired a 'three southern regions' conference in Canton, comprising cadres from the CCP's Central-South, Southwest, and East China regions. Hu Qiaomu took notes of the comments on the draft and by 15 March had completed a second draft.[17] This meeting reissued Mao's 1930 article 'Investigation work'.[18] Simultaneously, Head of State Liu Shaoqi, Premier Zhou Enlai, Chen Yun, the CCP's senior economic planner, General Secretary Deng Xiaoping, and Peng Zhen, Deng's senior deputy in the CC secretariat, were running an equivalent meeting for the three northern regions (Northeast, North China, and Northwest) in Beijing.[19]

While the concept of holding two conferences might seem like a sensible division of labour, it seems unusual that the four politically active members of the Politburo Standing Committee besides

Mao—Liu, Zhou, Chen, and Deng—would be at the one, while the Chairman presided over the other by himself.[20] It seems more likely that the northern conference was an official one, summoned formally by the CC secretariat, and presided over by the men Mao himself had decreed should be in the 'first front' of the leadership while he retired to the 'second front'.[21]

Some proof of this proposition is offered by the behaviour of the provincial party committee in the northern province of Shanxi. From 17 to 22 March, its standing committee met to discuss and to implement the 'spirit' of the northern meeting. While this provincial meeting was still in progress, another had to be summoned to discuss and implement the results of the combined Canton conference, a duplication of effort unlikely to have been undertaken had the provincial party understood that the northern meeting was merely a preliminary one.[22]

Mao's meeting in the south, on the other hand, had an impromptu air, as if it were an outgrowth of his personal initiative in organizing his own post-plenum investigation teams. There was no hint of a conference or of drafting new regulations for the communes in Mao's original instructions to Tian Jiaying; instead he talked of the initial rural research being followed by investigations into industry in Canton,[23] though once Mao's men started drafting, the operation could no longer be seen as *ad hoc*.

Some confirmation of the impromptu genesis of the southern conference and of the more formal nature of the northern one is provided by the fact that at the end of the former, on the morning of 13 March, Mao wrote to his colleagues in the capital, summarizing some of the opinions raised in Canton, intending to send Tao Zhu with the letter to Beijing. In his letter, Mao encapsulated his findings of the past two months: the basic problem was egalitarianism, the levelling of richer and poorer production teams and of richer and poorer individuals. He called on first secretaries at all levels to investigate egalitarianism personally after returning to their units. Without such first-hand inquiries, they would not be able to grasp and solve the problem.

The letter was far more striking, however, for the contemptuous tone which Mao used to his senior colleagues: 'I think that, up till now, you really don't know much about this problem of the two egalitarianisms. Isn't that so? Am I wrong? Provincial, district, *xian*, and commune party 1st secretaries are the same; in brief, they don't know much or just have a vague idea.' Mao accused them all of being so busy with routine work that they had no time to carry out personal investigations, being satisfied instead to listen to reports.[24]

Possibly it was his sense that his colleagues needed a spur that led Mao to change his mind; or even more probably, it was simply that the Chairman found it very irksome to accept the discipline of staying back in the second front, especially on the issue of agricultural collectivization which he regarded as very much his own. At any rate, instead of sending Tao Zhu to Beijing, he summoned the northern group to Canton, and a combined central work conference was held there from 15 to 23 March.[25]

The Canton conference

Both the northern and southern meetings had discussed reforming the communes. The northern meeting probably did not discuss the southern draft since it was not completed in time.[26] Instead, it may have considered a detailed set of proposals for a commune constitution drawn up by the director of the CC's Rural Work Department, Deng Zihui.[27] At the request of Liu Shaoqi, Deng Zihui had investigated communes in Shanxi and Jiangsu provinces the previous summer and drawn up a forty-article proposal. Since Liu attended the northern conference along with Deng Xiaoping, it seems likely that Deng Zihui's proposals were fed into that meeting. Certainly, at the Canton conference, Mao acknowledged the positive contribution of Deng Zihui's forty articles, which had been sent to him at the end of 1960, and accompanying report.[28]

Either in the secretariat draft or in the discussions at the Canton conference, there was a proposal for dividing the country into two, putting the three northern areas—presumably those covered by the CC's North, Northeast, and Northwest bureaux—into one category and the three southern ones—East, Central-South, and Southwest—into another.[29] Perhaps this explained the logic of having a separate meeting for the northern bureaux. Possibly communes varied significantly enough between the mainly wheat-growing areas of the north and the mainly rice-growing areas of the south to justify this.

Why Mao should have found the proposal—no trace of which is to be found in the Sixty Articles—intrinsically unpalatable is unclear, but he apparently held Deng Xiaoping responsible.[30] Mao's reaction, reported during the Cultural Revolution, suggests that he objected to the manner rather than the matter of the proposal. He is quoted as saying: 'Which emperor made this decision?' This sounds as if—and various Chinese sources confirm this—he objected to Deng Xiaoping ordering the preparation of a new proposal without consulting him first.[31] Indeed, Deng Xiaoping was accused during the Cultural Revolution of not reporting to Mao from 1959 on, when the Chairman began to retire to the 'second front'. On this particular occasion, Mao may have been annoyed that his colleagues in the 'first front' had gone ahead and drawn up a plan, especially if it were superior to that drafted under his own supervision, or had tried to modify his own.

Mao is said to have upbraided Deng and Peng Zhen—whether in public or private is not clear—for making such a proposal without adequate prior investigation.[32] Again, the implication was that Mao had toured three regions before coming to conclusions, whereas his colleagues had simply been sitting at their desks in Beijing. The fact that the draft Sixty Articles were principally the work of Chen Boda and were finalized by a committee chaired by Tao Zhu rather than an appropriate central official suggests that Mao was insisting on the primacy of his preliminary southern conference and his own staff. According to one participant, Deng Zihui's forty articles, despite Mao's approving comment, were not used as a basis for the Sixty Articles.[33]

Indeed, one of the most striking aspects of the Canton conference, to judge by the most detailed account of its proceedings available, is how Mao discussed drafts of the Sixty Articles with members of successive drafting committees without his senior colleagues being present. Liu Shaoqi, Zhou Enlai, and Deng Xiaoping, as well as Zhu De and Lin Biao who both attended the Canton conference though not the preliminary northern or southern meetings,[34] presumably talked with Mao during the conference, but it seems strange that, although members of the PSC, they did not participate when the Chairman gave his instructions on the emerging document. All we know is that Liu and Zhou made speeches to a combined meeting of delegates from the Central-South and North China groups on 19 March.[35]

Certainly the choice of Tao Zhu to head the drafting committee, with Hubei 1st secretary Wang Renzhong as his deputy,[36] was a tribute to his ability and increasing prominence. Two of the other regional 1st secretaries—Li Jingquan (Southwest) and Ke Qingshi (East)—were members of the Politburo and thus outranked Tao within the party; Li had the additional political clout of leading Sichuan, one of China's major grain surplus provinces.[37] Yet neither Li nor Ke was called on to chair the committee. Tao had had his problems with Mao in the past,[38] but the Chairman evidently admired his practical abilities and had recently praised the quality of the Canton evening paper, *Yang Cheng Wan Bao*, which had been set up under Tao's aegis and was the only provincial evening paper rated good enough for national distribution.[39] More important, Tao Zhu had rendered Mao vital political service at the 1959 Lushan conference, where he was the official chosen to pressure General Huang Kecheng to admit his 'guilt' as a member of Peng Dehuai's alleged anti-party 'military club'.[40]

The Sixty Articles on Agriculture

The Twelve-Article Emergency Directive issued the previous November had been the skeleton of a plan for reviving agriculture. It was the basis for the much more comprehensive 'Work rules for the rural people's communes (Draft)' agreed at the Canton conference. Thereafter, the draft was promulgated for discussion, and then distributed in June in revised form after further top-level consultations.[41]

The Sixty Articles on Agriculture (as the 'Work rules' are usually known) were an attempt to put the clock back. Their inspiration was officially declared to be Mao's speeches at the second Zhengzhou conference in early 1959 together with the instructions he subsequently circulated to provincial party officials.[42]

Unfortunately, no full text of Mao's speech at the Canton conference has so far surfaced, but from the fragments of his remarks made in March that are available, the Chairman appears to have stressed yet again that the key problem was egalitarianism, a matter on which he had instructed the secretariat to take action the previous October. Mao referred to the issue with the GLF formula '*yi ping er diao*': one, egalitarianism; two, [indiscriminate] transfer [of resources].[43] He argued now that the Twelve-Article Emergency Directive had solved the problem of physical transfers of resources like farm tools and animals from rich brigades to poor ones, but had not dealt with the equalization of family incomes within communes which was greatly resented by members of richer brigades and teams. If those problems could not be solved then the initiative of the peasantry could not be encouraged.[44] These views were reflected in the document produced at Canton.

Like the earlier Twelve Articles, the Sixty Articles sought to limit the rights and functions of the commune in favour of the brigade (*da dui*),[45] the former advanced or 'higher stage' (fully socialist) APC.

The very first article affirmed that the commune was a 'union [*lianhe zuchengde*][46] based on the advanced APCs to meet the requirements of the development of *production*' (emphasis added). The implications of this description were twofold: the units were more important than the union; and production was more important than the socializing elements of commune life—crèches, mess-halls, and old peoples' 'happiness homes'.

The article emphasized three principles: 'From each according to his ability, to each according to his work', which had been formally acknowledged from the start of the commune movement; 'more pay for more work', which had been introduced after the second Zhengzhou conference in 1959 and reaffirmed at the 8th (Lushan) plenum in August that year; and 'he who does not work does not eat', which was apparently newly introduced in the Sixty Articles to emphasize the grimmer atmosphere of 1961.[47]

The brigade was to be the basic level of ownership and of accounting. This provision was designed to restore the *status quo ante* the GLF, when commune cadres transferred various forms of wealth from rich to poor brigades with an egalitarian enthusiasm which, as Mao had observed, aroused enormous resentment among those who lost out.[48] Moreover, the brigade in turn was enjoined to avoid enforcing egalitarianism between its component teams (*dui*), the sub-units which 'directly organise the production and livelihood of the commune members'. To this end, the scale of the commune at each level ought not to be excessively large. The commune itself should correspond to the *xiang* (township), rather than the *qu* (district) or *xian* (county); the brigade to the old higher-stage APCs. As a result of these provisions, the number of units at all levels increased during 1961.[49]

One particularly long article was designed to discourage commune cadres from interfering with or coercing brigade and team cadres. Where intra-brigade co-operation was necessary—e.g. for water conservancy projects—the commune management committee was supposed to secure agreement all round, issue contracts, and pay compensation. Communes were entitled to expropriate parts of their brigades' reserve funds, but were warned against doing so.[50]

In view of this emphasis, it was hardly surprising that almost three times as many of the Sixty Articles were devoted to the brigades and teams as to the commune level. The relationship between the brigade and the team was clearly fundamental to the success of the Sixty Articles. The brigade was 'the independently operated unit' responsible for its own accounting, profits, and losses, which, in a key phrase, 'carries out unified distribution within the entire scope of the production brigade but also respects the differences between various production teams'.[51]

The meaning of this phrase was spelled out in a later article which delineated the relationship between brigade and team. This was to be defined by the slogan 'three guarantees and one reward' (*san bao, yi jiang*). The team had to guarantee a certain quantity of production, labour, and costs; over-production would result in a reward for the team. To avoid egalitarianism even at this level, the article instructed brigades to compensate richer teams that had suffered as a result of unified distribution, by alloting them additional rewards and special guarantees.[52]

At the grass roots, the teams themselves had to avoid egalitarianism by strict adherence to the principle of 'to each according to his work', and ensuring that the cash component of wages should not be less than 70 per cent. The up-to-30 per cent paid in kind—the supply system—would include the food allotted to commune members at the public mess-halls. Nevertheless, teams were entitled to subsidize the old, the weak, orphans, widows, the disabled, and the sick, as well as commune members with large families but few wage-earners. Up to 5 per cent of the land could be allocated to families for subsidiary occupations, including growing vegetables and pig-rearing.[53]

The successful implementation of the Sixty Articles depended ultimately on cadres. Their numbers had to be kept down and, at brigade and team level, they had to pull their full weight in farmwork. They had to seek truth from facts and carry out investigation and research. 'They should speak honestly and should report the situation as it is; one is one and two is two. They should oppose faking and falsification'.[54]

An indication of how commune cadres had behaved at the height of the Leap was conveyed by an article insisting on a democratic work style. 'Beating, cursing, or any other forms of physical punishment are strictly forbidden. The use of "no meals" or "no food rations" and the arbitrary subtraction of work-points as methods of punishment are strictly forbidden'.[55]

But while the March version of the Sixty Articles aimed to reduce egalitarianism, the size of communes, and excessive control of lower-level units by higher-level units, it failed to tackle two crucial issues: the 'free supply' component of income was still set at 30 per cent, with wages according to work set at 70 per cent; and the viability and desirability of mess-halls were reaffirmed, except in teams where dwellings were scattered or fuel was short.[56]

'No investigation, no right to speak'

At the 9th plenum, and again at the Canton work conference, Mao strongly re-emphasized the importance of investigations.[57] He had needled Deng Xiaoping and Peng Zhen on this issue. Mao's slogan was: 'Energetically encourage the practice of conducting investigations and research' (*da xing diaocha yanjiu zhi feng*). This call had a galvanizing effect upon his senior colleagues, who agreed that a CC letter on the subject should be sent to the standing committees of provincial party committees, ordering first secretaries at the *xian* level and above to investigate at the grass roots. It was this letter which included the dictum: 'No investigation, no right to speak' (*bu diaocha meiyou fayan quan*).[58]

In their speeches at the Canton conference, both Liu Shaoqi and Zhou Enlai had addressed the same topic. As Liu put it: 'These past few years, investigation and research work has been weak'. Since 1958, despite the successes of the GLF, the party had committed several errors, big and small, some avoidable, some not. One had to believe reports from the grass roots, but some reports were not wholly credible and some were simply incredible. The CC had decided on policies without sufficient preliminary fact-finding, and newspapers had escalated the problem with unsubstantiated reports that contributed to the feverish atmosphere. Like Liu, Zhou praised Mao's article on investigation and the principle of seeking truth from facts. The party's current shortcoming was that 'we issue too many orders instead of practising the mass line'.[59] According to one Chinese analyst, the profusion of investigations at all levels which these speeches and documents produced was unprecedented in the history of the PRC.[60] Nobody pointed out at the time that Mao did not himself conform to his own strictures, but preferred simply to listen to reports from officials.[61]

Mao now resumed the pattern he had set after the adjournment of the 9th plenum, going himself to Wuhan, Changsha, and Shanghai. In July, he would hold a meeting with Hebei and Shandong cadres and commune members in Handan in Hebei. He sent his three investigation teams initially back to their original sites, and during the course of the following year he sent Tian Jiaying to Shanxi, Hunan, and Sichuan.[62] Mao spent twenty days supervising Hu Qiaomu's team investigating Hunan. Hu held a meeting in Mao's home village,

Shaoshan, to discuss the Sixty Articles in general and mess-halls in particular.[63]

Zhou Enlai visited a Hebei commune in Wuan *xian* immediately after the Canton conference, and then sent a work team to investigate Handan district for three weeks. Despite being busy with preparations for the Geneva conference on Laos, he went there himself from 28 April to 14 May,[64] and was also seen in Yunnan.[65] In Handan, the starkness of the situation was apparently brought home to the premier when a particularly blunt peasant told him: 'If things go on like this, even you may have nothing to eat'.[66] Zhou telephoned a preliminary report to Mao in Shanghai at 3 a.m. on 7 May, making then and later three main points: the mess-halls were universally disliked and where they had already been dissolved, the peasants had described the event as a 'second liberation'; the egalitarian free supply system was resented by those who worked hard, and anyway was unable to cater for the truly needy; peasants demanded a return to the pre-commune assessment of work points on the basis of work done and the principle of more work, more pay. Mao was impressed enough to order the report distributed down to district party committee level.[67] Zhou's findings may have been the reason Mao stopped off in Handan a few months later.

Deng Xiaoping collaborated with Peng Zhen who organized the five teams from the Beijing city party to conduct investigations in communes around the capital.[68] Deng Xiaoping went to Shunyi *xian*; his eight-person team included his wife, Zhuo Lin, and Liao Mosha, head of the city's United Front Work Department. Peng Zhen led twenty-three people in a forty-day survey of Huairou *xian* (and in December he would return to his home village in Shanxi for the first time in thirty years).[69] The Beijing party's 2nd secretary, Liu Ren, was in charge of a six-person team that went to a commune in Feng-tai district. The Beijing report of 10 May was prepared by Deng Tuo, who had lost his job as editor-in-chief of the official *People's Daily* during the Hundred Flowers period as a result of Mao's anger with him; he was now a senior member of the Beijing party secretariat.[70] Despite hostile commentary on the Beijing investigators during the Cultural Revolution, it was Mao who ordered that their report, as well as Zhou's, be circulated.[71] Like Zhou's, their report recommended urgent changes in the supply system, the mess-halls, and the work-point system, and also included suggestions on compulsory grain purchases.[72]

Vice-Premier Li Xiannian sent out teams from the ministries to Hebei, Henan, Shandong, Jiangsu, and Hubei, accompanying the Hebei group himself.[73] Zhu De went to Sichuan, Henan, and Shaanxi.[74] Tan Zhenlin, who had been in charge of the agricultural sector during the GLF, revisited one of the pathbreaking communes of 1958, Qiliying in Henan province, from April to July.[75] Similar activities took place in other provinces.[76] The disgraced former Defence Minister Peng Dehuai was allowed to return to his native village in Hunan to work and examine local conditions.[77] Even Peng's successor, the perennially ill Lin Biao, spent seven days investigating, causing Mao to send him a message stressing how important it was to guard his health.

Liu's rural rides

Probably the lengthiest investigation was carried out by Liu Shaoqi, who revisited his native Hunan. His tour of inspection—denounced during the Cultural Revolution as '44 days of counter-revolutionary restorationist activity'—was part of a learning process that would have profound long-term effects upon his relationship with the Chairman.[78]

Liu arrived in Hunan on 1 April and stayed until 15 May.[79] On arrival, he announced that he would conduct his investigation 'guerrilla-style', living and dressing simply, going where the spirit moved him, travelling in two jeeps, accompanied only by his wife, Wang Guangmei, who doubled as his secretary (*mishu*),[80] and a few relatively low-level provincial cadres, the most senior being the head of the provincial public security apparatus, Li Qiang.

All of this suggests that Liu deliberately excluded 1st secretary, Zhang Pinghua, and other top Hunan officials, and eschewed the large caravanserai that would have been his prerogative, in the belief that their presence would inhibit peasants from speaking to him freely. As he put it at the outset: 'If we don't turn up as workers, our investigations won't get very far.' He carried his own light luggage, including bowl and chopsticks, and determinedly roughed it and maintained a spartan regimen despite the protests of his escorts. He upbraided cadres who despatched sofas and bathtubs to villages he was scheduled to visit.[81]

Liu went first to the county of his birth, Ningxiang *xian*, to the west of the provincial capital, Changsha. There he spent five days with Wangjiawan production team which formed part of Donghutang commune. He had intended at this point to revisit his home village,

Tanzichong in Huaminglou commune, when he suddenly learned that Mao had arrived in Changsha. How normal it was for the Chairman to wander around the country without apprising his closest colleagues of his movements, we do not know.[82] But Liu's reaction to the news does seem to encapsulate the relationship between the two men.

He immediately rearranged his plans, hurried south to Xiangtan *xian*, passing through his own village with just a brief stop outside his old house—the first time he had seen it in forty years—to inspect Mao's home village Shaoshan on the morning of 9 April. His only reported action there was to change the Chinese character for 'old' in the sign 'Chairman Mao's Old Home', substituting *jiu* for *gu*, which he said conveyed the idea that Mao was dead. Leaving Shaoshan on 10 April, he proceeded to Changsha, touring Xiangtan, the county town, *en route*, and reported personally to Mao. The Chairman, we are told, was highly impressed with Liu's account, telling companions: 'I too can learn from Comrade Shaoqi.' He vowed to return to Shaoshan himself, but does not appear to have done so at this time.[83]

On 12 April, Liu left the provincial capital for Guangfu commune in Changsha *xian* for what is officially described as an eighteen-day investigation of its Tianhua brigade; however, from 15 to 17 April, he was back in Changsha for a major conference of provincial officials. While in Tianhua, Liu was apparently visited by three top officials of the region: Tao Zhu (Central-South Bureau 1st secretary), Wang Renzhong (Central-South Bureau 2nd secretary, Hubei province 1st secretary), and Zhang Pinghua (Hunan 1st secretary). From Tianhua, Liu returned to Huaminglou commune where he stayed eleven days. At the end of his forty-four-day inspection tour of Hunan, he quickly prepared a written report on his findings and despatched it by special messenger to Mao who was by then in Hangzhou, the Chinese beauty spot which the Chairman seems to have loved best.[84]

Liu spent about a month in the villages of Hunan. In three *xian*, he visited three communes and six of their component brigades. By any standards, it was an extraordinarily extended and intensive inspection tour for a head of state to pay to the grass roots. Liu stayed so long clearly because he was well aware of the difficulties involved in getting peasants to complain and cadres to confess. On arrival, he would say: 'We have done some things wrong during the past few years and this has been a consequence of not doing investigation and research. Only if you help us by exposing the true conditions can we help you. Only if you tell the truth can you help us to formulate correct policies'.

But the successive political campaigns of the previous years had made everyone wary of speaking up. The leaders of the Tianhua brigade, for instance, covered up faults to protect its 'Red Flag' status. Liu instructed investigating cadres confronted with silent peasants to study whether they had smiling or gloomy faces, whether their eyes were lively or narrowed, whether they held their heads high or lowered them. As he put it rather turgidly to a group of cadres on 30 April: 'It's not easy to do investigation and research well; to get man's subjective world to reflect the objective world is not simple . . .The object of investigation and research is to get to know the real world, and the object of doing that is to transform the world. While transforming the world we improve our understanding of it. Understanding the world and transforming it must be combined'.[85]

Liu was interested in every aspect of commune life where problems were to be found: grain supplies, mess-halls, the supply system, subsidiary occupations, private plots, housing, forestry, commerce, rural fairs.[86] To get at the truth about food supplies, he would launch 'surprise attacks', entering peasant homes without warning at mealtimes. On one occasion, he was so shocked to find a family eating 'substitute' foodstuffs (*dai shipin*) that he did not utter a word for several hours. Once he even wandered behind a peasant house and inspected the dried human faeces piled there to confirm his view that the peasants were not getting enough to eat. On a visit to a pig farm, he was put up in the forage store. To soften his bed board, his escorts scoured the place for some rice straw, normally common in paddy-growing areas like Hunan. Their failure to find any depressed Liu further.[87]

Before going to Tianhua brigade, Liu had read a report which stated that 90 per cent of all goods confiscated during the GLF had either been restored or paid for. During his eighteen-day investigation, during which he convened eleven meetings and visited numerous peasant households, he found out that virtually no restitution had been carried out. Restitution had to do with two major subjects of investigation: communal mess-halls and housing, subjects on which cadres and peasants disagreed totally.[88]

In the hamlet where Liu stayed, Wangjiatang, there was a mess-hall for seventy-two people. It employed a five-man team of 'specialists'—one each for cooking, cutting wood, looking after the rice, growing vegetables, and carrying water—who accounted for one-third of the total amount of work points awarded locally. Yet the mess-hall was still badly run, the cause of frequent wrangles and much apathy. Liu, who had hitherto cherished the notion that the advantage of mess-halls was that they economized on labour power and released women for production, was clearly flabbergasted.

Nearby was another hamlet, Shijiachong, consisting of eleven households divided in earlier years among nine houses. A mess-hall for so small a group was presumably not cost-effective, so the inhabitants of three other hamlets had been compelled to crowd into those nine houses to justify setting one up. As a result, land had gone to waste, there was insufficient water for lavatories and pig pens, household and natural fertilizer decreased, food production dropped, and household subsidiary occupations almost totally disappeared. In Tianhua brigade as a whole, there had been an average of 1+ rooms per capita prior to the formation of the communes. After the collectivization of living, accommodation had been reduced to only half a room per capita. The situation was serious enough for Liu to give a directive on housing to Hunan provincial 1st secretary, Zhang Pinghua.

At a mass meeting of brigade members, Liu found it impossible to get the wary peasants to commit themselves on the mess-halls. When he asked them whether there should be mess-halls or not, they replied that running mess-halls was fine, cooking individually was also fine! He tried reassuring them: communes could be run with or without mess-halls; one could not say that without the mess-halls one could have neither communes nor socialism. Still the peasants hesitated: they would not advocate having mess-halls, but nor would they press for their abolition. Doubtless they remembered the abrupt turn-around on the communes which the party had executed in the autumn of 1959 after the Lushan plenum, and they did not want to leave themselves open to criticism after any future U-turn.

The one concrete indication of their feelings that Liu noticed was their reminiscing about how good life had been in 1957, the year before the communes had been set up: there was plenty for the pigs and chickens to eat, the private plots produced a wide variety of products, everyone's stomach was full.

One afternoon, Liu invited eight of the original residents of Shijiachong for a chat over tea and cigarettes to discuss the mess-hall problem. Put at ease, they told him that the mess-hall did not provide enough to eat and that the supply system had made people lazy. Their 'small freedoms' had been done away with, and so household production of sweet potatoes, sesame, and beans had been cut back drastically; and there were cases of pigs not bearing young and hens not laying eggs.

To the peasants' delight, Liu agreed that the mess-hall should be closed. He ordered the provision of transportation to enable people to return home and a supply of cooking utensils to replace the ones that had been confiscated. Under his supervision, a ten-man team solved the resettlement problem in under two weeks. Commenting on what he had learned, he told local cadres that since the advent of the communes everyone up to the level of the CC had been asleep and not looking at the facts. Now they had awakened.[89] Shortly thereafter, the CC formally permitted the dissolution of mess-halls.[90]

In the course of Liu's investigation of the negative effects of the 'communist wind' of the GLF, he also came out against excessive egalitarianism in the distribution of rewards. Its principal manifestation had been a supply system, that is, 'free' food and other items, which accounted for 70 per cent of peasant income, payment on the basis of work done accounting for only 30 per cent. The proportions appear to have been reversed even before Liu came on the scene, and he ruled against this incentive-destroying system on the grounds that it overstepped the present socialist phase, advocating that free supply should be reduced to 20 per cent. During the Cultural Revolution, it was alleged that as a result of the move back towards a work-point system, a number of poor peasant families with many dependents but few workers had suffered great hardship.[91]

But the main attack on Liu's activities in Tianhua focused on his disciplining of the brigade party secretary, a long-time provincial 'labour model' of poor peasant stock named Peng Meixiu. Liu is said to have described her as a puppet of the class enemy, to wit, two other members of the Peng clan who held senior official posts within the brigade. Cultural Revolution sources acknowledged that these two Pengs hailed from landlord families and should not have been officials, but denied that they controlled the brigade.[92]

More importantly, Liu accused Peng and her colleagues of falsifying output figures in the interests of preserving the brigade's 'Red Flag' status, adding that her refusal to dissolve the mess-halls had been precisely for that reason. Most extraordinarily, Liu is quoted as saying later that Peng Meixiu had attempted to banish him from her brigade: 'After I had stayed there for ten days and more, she accused my presence of impeding production . . . I knew that she was trying to drive me out. I wouldn't let her do so and I refused to go. There she called me bearded Liu and lied that I had disrupted the order of the brigade. She wanted the brigade thrown into chaos . . . In retrospect, our anger has not entirely vanished.'[93]

Wang Guangmei later recalled that her husband had sought out cadres who had been dismissed for opposing the communist 'five styles' and encouraged them to return to work. Upon hearing of this, Peng apparently had taken up a position at a major crossroads and in a loud voice had shouted out: 'Bearded Liu, you have the audacity to use rightist elements.' When a public security official reported this to Liu, he only smiled. When Liu next ran across Peng, he made her blush by remarking: 'We CCP members work on behalf of everyone; one cannot only think of one's own fame and gain, wouldn't you say?'[94]

The Cultural Revolution accounts admitted that Peng did call the head of state 'Bearded Liu'—was he not shaving while in the countryside?—but suggested that this was legitimate retaliation for his description of her as a 'puppet' and a 'whore'. Nor does it seem unlikely that Peng could, with some justice, have spread it around that Liu's presence was extremely disruptive of the normal agricultural round. What seems unlikely is that she did it to Liu's face.

The confrontation had an unhappy ending. Post-Cultural Revolution accounts emphasize how Liu gave Peng credit for her good points, while Cultural Revolution accounts stressed a brusque leave-taking. In any case, Peng was dismissed at Liu's instance and transferred to another commune. She died a year later of cancer of the throat—for which the cultural revolutionaries also tried to blame Liu![95]

It is difficult not to feel some sympathy for the luckless Peng, a mere corporal in the party hierarchy whose command was suddenly exposed to inspection by a general. Doubtless thousands of other brigades up and down the country would have suffered at least as badly under Liu's relentless scrutiny. Perhaps it was the memory of the confrontation with Peng as well as the difficulty of getting peasants to speak up that would lead Liu to send his wife, incognito, on a village investigation in late 1963.

Liu goes home again

Liu seems to have had a less trying experience on his native heath to which he returned on 2 May for an eleven-day inspection. Quite possibly word of his activities in Tianhua had preceded him, because he persuaded the Tanzichong brigade secretary to think again about mess-halls after a single interview, during which he bolstered the latter's courage by informing him that both he (Liu) and Mao had worn rightist caps in their time. That evening a mass meeting was held and the mess-hall was dissolved, an example swiftly copied by all the other mess-halls in the *xian*. This was not the end of the problem, however. Several families no longer had cooking implements, many of which had doubtless been melted down during the backyard steel drive in 1958. Liu ordered them to be manufactured and forbade cadres to assign the first lot to their own families.[96] In the Chinese gulag, prisoners were put to turning out cheap aluminium pots and pans.[97]

In Liu's home village, as in Tianhua, housing was a problem, and was again aggravated by the winding up of the mess-halls. Some houses had been knocked down during the GLF, in one case to make way for a collective pig pen. Others had been taken over as part of an egalitarian redistribution of accommodations. One widow whom Liu met had moved house eight times in the previous two years. The order went out that owners should be allowed to move back to their houses, but in many cases the households they displaced had nowhere to go because their own houses had been knocked down or taken over. Liu reportedly laid down four principles which provided a basis for solving the *xian*'s housing problems.[98] As for his own family house, he refused permission for it to be made into any kind of museum like Mao's in Shaoshan, although Cultural Revolution sources alleged that it was refurbished at considerable cost. A poor peasant family was installed, which explains why the building was not demolished during the Cultural Revolution.[99]

The fundamental problem in Tanzichong was again food. Output was below the 1957 level. Liu had been told that production problems were primarily due to the weather, but during the previous two years, according to Wang Guangmei's retrospective account, there were no natural disasters which could be blamed for the shortfalls. Everywhere the peasants said: 'Three parts natural calamities, seven parts man-made disasters.' On investigation, Liu concluded that the peasants were right, and he blamed the 'five styles' in particular.[100]

Liu was fortunate in having siblings resident in the village who were not reticent in briefing him. He was reportedly struck dumb by the story of a woman forced to eat weeds, without cooking oil to prepare them, and was appalled at the number of cases of malnutrition in the local hospital. On 7 May, he apologized publicly for the food shortages:

I haven't returned home for nearly 40 years. I have disappointed you. I am guilty of bureaucratism. I heard only reports from below. The Central Committee had no knowledge of the 'five kinds of wind' [i.e. the five styles]. Some people below reported a per mou output of a thousand catties, one thousand five hundred catties, two thousand or five thousand catties. The Central Committee knew only how to procure more grain. The result was that people were starved and families torn apart.[101]

Liu also warned cadres against securing supplies for themselves by back-door methods. He later sent his 70-year-old sister $2\frac{1}{2}$ kg. of rice together with small quantities of other foodstuffs. Local opinion concluded that he could have afforded more, but did not want to place his sister in a privileged position. One may assume he also had his own admonition to cadres in mind. According to one of his daughters, Liu forswore meat and cut his own salary at this time.

Post-rehabilitation accounts, clearly designed to clear Liu of Cultural Revolution accusations that he favoured private enterprise, state that Liu opposed dividing up the collective fields *among households* (*fen tian dao hu*), but advocated a production responsibility system (*shengchan zerenzhi*), presumably a version of the one spread throughout China as a result of Deng Xiaoping's post-Mao reforms. Liu held that the strips of land separating fields and waste land in the hills could be assigned to households (*baochan daohu*), and he criticized cadres for confiscating private plots and forbidding household subsidiary occupations. His admonitions are said to have resulted in a dramatic improvement in output within a few months.[102]

While he was in Hunan, Liu evidently made some highly critical comments on CCP policies during the GLF, especially when talking to cadres. Isolated quotations in Cultural Revolution sources were clearly designed to prove Liu's apostasy; but post-Cultural Revolution versions of Liu's speeches may have been watered down to prove him studiously correct. There is certainly sufficient correspondence between the two versions, and little inherently implausible in the Cultural Revolution source, for the latter not to be taken seriously.

For instance, Wang Guangmei quotes Liu as rejecting the comforting excuse that mistakes were unavoidable due to inexperience: 'During the 1st FYP we had no experience, yet we did not make major mistakes. By the time we got to the 2nd FYP period, we had a bit of experience, but we have nevertheless made major mistakes.

Why is this? It's because not a few of us responsible comrades were insufficiently modest and prudent, were arrogant and self-satisfied, and neglected the spirit of seeking truth from facts.'[103]

A key issue in this context is his implicit reference to Mao. In the post-Cultural Revolution text of his speech to the peasants in his own village, he clearly indicated that the Chairman, too, must bear some of the blame: 'Coming back this time and seeing the way that work has been carried out, I must admit mistakes to you and the responsibility of the centre. There's no one who doesn't make a mistake; *in the whole world there is no man who doesn't make mistakes.* Making mistakes is unimportant; what's important is acknowledging and correcting them.'[104]

A Cultural Revolution quotation, starkly illustrating the change in the thinking of a strong advocate of the GLF as a result of his new comprehension of the catastrophe it had generated, seemed to target Mao by a reference to the great founding emperor Qin Shi Huang, to whom the Chairman was sometimes compared by his colleagues:

The Great Leap Forward has caused morale to drop in some places, many people have died . . . recovery will take some time. In these places, it should be said destruction has been caused . . . We must know that Emperor Ch'in [Qin] Shi[h] Huang and Emperor Sui Yang-ti[di] fell because of their building the Great Wall and the Grand Canal. Actually, more people have died now than in those times . . . Now is not a time of prosperity. The number of deaths exceeds that of births.[105]

But overtly, Liu was not out of line, since only two years earlier Mao himself had warned the CCP against repeating the mistakes of the Qin and Sui.[106]

In an earlier comment in his home village, Liu had linked the drop in morale to the excessive collectivism of the GLF period; there is considerable similarity between the Cultural Revolution version and the more recent one:

You have taken away the things of the commune members. You have taken over the private plots. Is there any system of ownership left? . . . Why do the commune members show no respect for the system of ownership . . . for anything that belongs to the public, to the collective? There are two reasons for this. First, they have less to eat, they do not have enough to eat. Secondly, as a result of readjustments over the past two years, things have been taken away from the commune members. So they also take things from the commune now. But in the first place, the commune and the brigades have taken away the things from the commune members and shown no respect for ownership by the commune members.[107]

Liu also strongly criticized 'commandism' or lack of democracy in the management of the GLF. Commune mess-halls had been 'simply set up by order on 1 October 1958' by the use of the CC's prestige. If harmful policies were promulgated by the CC in the future, they could be 'refuted, supplemented, or revised'. If individuals found it difficult to resist them, they should do so through the commune congress (formally, the organization's supreme decision-taking body), although Liu acknowledged that cadres could easily manipulate such bodies by frightening people into voting for their policies.[108] Again, startling though some of these views were made to seem during the Cultural Revolution, they were very similar to those of Mao when he took up the cudgels in the spring of 1959 on behalf of the peasants and the lower-level cadres.[109]

The need for honest journalism

A principal lesson derived by Liu from his experiences in Hunan, especially his sojourn in Tianhua brigade, was the critical importance of investigative journalism. Prior to his arrival in Tianhua, reporters had conducted a three-month-long investigation of the brigade and had triumphantly confirmed its claims of outstanding progress. After Liu had uncovered the truth, he delivered an important speech on the press and propaganda on 28 April.[110]

Liu defined three purposes of investigation: ascertaining whether or not CC policies were correct; checking on whether such policies were still adequate; and looking for previously unanticipated problems. But his experience of the deliberate cover-up in Tianhua had left him with no illusions as to the difficulty of the task. He concluded that the low-key investigative approach advocated by Mao in the past—'Be a willing pupil, with earnestness and sincerity' (chengxin chengyi, gan dangxiao xuesheng)—was no longer valid.[111]

Liu did not claim to have a sure-fire alternative. Indeed, the difficulty of getting people to speak the truth, particularly serious in Hunan, was not new and was in itself a problem worthy of investigation.[112] Talking to relatives was one possibility—Liu's daughter Aiqin told him of the hardness of life in Inner Mongolia during these years—and it seems as if the CC may have decided at this time of crisis to despatch senior officials to their native places to carry out investigations. Tao Zhu returned to his home in Hunan. Deng Zihui returned to his native district with a fellow Fujianese, Procurator General Zhang Dingcheng, and like Liu concluded that mess-halls should be immediately shut down. But Liu warned that one had to guard against relatives exaggerating for their own purposes. Another of Liu's suggestions was to talk to people away from their homes, presumably because they would then be uninhibited by the pressure of local cadres. The best method was to raise problems, or to advance opinions contrary to the current line and watch for reactions.[113]

At about this time Liu ordered a major investigation of journalistic coverage of the GLF—'habitual lying'—but whether this was a direct consequence of the failure of the press to uncover the truth about the Tianhua brigade is unclear.[114] Both he and Mao had earlier blamed journalists for helping to foment the wilder flights of fancy during 1958, and Liu had returned to the attack at the Canton conference. Zhou Enlai had expressed his concern about the precision of newspaper reporting even earlier.[115]

Now Lu Dingyi, the director of the CC's Propaganda Department, sent a work team to the Journalism Department of China People's University, which was apparently regarded as a hotbed of press leftism. Thirty teachers were sacked, clearly as a demonstration of the new approach required of reporters, for Lu Dingyi issued two circulars on the People's University case to the country's newspapers. The punitive work team was under the supervision of Deng Tuo, chosen doubtless because of his expertise as the former editor of the *People's Daily*.[116] Five years later it would be Deng Tuo whose journalistic activities would bring calamity down upon his head at the outset of the Cultural Revolution.

The problem of lawlessness

From Hunan, Liu went north to Henan, the pace-setting province during the GLF.[117] As on his previous visit a year earlier, Liu's main concern was the underestimation of problems by the provincial leadership.[118] But whereas in April 1960 he was unable or unwilling to curb the headstrong enthusiasm of Henan's 1st secretary, Wu Zhipu, in the crisis atmosphere of May 1961, Liu appears to have initiated his demotion. Indeed he had singled out Henan for critical mention at the Canton conference.[119] Henan had been one of the provinces worst hit by the famine, and a massive calamity in Xinyang district was attributed to local cadre error, for which Wu Zhipu assumed responsibility.[120] By July, Wu was revealed to have become 2nd secretary, ceding the top party post to Liu Jianxun, a troubleshooter with experience of taking over from a discredited provincial leader senior to himself.[121]

At the time of Liu Shaoqi's visit, Henan was in dire need of firm but sound leadership. It was in the grip of famine, and in some parts of the province there had been a breakdown of law and order during the latter part of the GLF. Rapes, muggings, armed highway robbery, and even killings took place in a number of *xian*, committed mainly by members of the militia who numbered nominally some 20 million as a result of the heady expansion of 1958. They were referred to by the peasantry as 'mad dogs', 'gangsters', 'bandit kings', 'beat up gangs', and 'tiger bands', and at the end of 1960 the CC's Military Affairs Commission had been obliged to despatch a forty-man work team under the command of a full general to clean up the militia. After a six-week investigation, all training was suspended until June to allow militiamen to work in the fields. Though Henan was the worst afflicted, there had been similar cases of lawlessness in other provinces, notably Shandong.[122]

The Beijing work conference

The combination of hunger, crime, and discontent which Liu and other leaders uncovered during their grass-roots investigations must have contributed to a sober mood when a new CC work conference met in Beijing from 21 May to 12 June.[123] Mao had underlined the gravity of the situation the previous month when he had given Deng Xiaoping a long list of problems which he wanted the conference to discuss, including: revision of the Sixty Articles; rectification of the 'communist' five styles of work; mess-halls; grain; the supply system; whether draught animals and farm tools should be owned by brigades (*da dui*) or teams (*dui*); restoration of or compensation for confiscated property. Urban problems could be postponed until the July work conference. Deng had circulated Mao's topics to provincial organizations the day he received them, 25 April. Until well into May, Mao was corresponding with provincial 1st secretaries, soliciting the results of their investigations into these issues.[124]

The work conference was held in three stages. During the first five days, there was a general discussion of four items raised by Mao: compensation for lost property; investigations; the mass line; and the rehabilitation of people wrongly punished during the campaign against right opportunism after the 1959 Lushan conference—the final figure was a staggering 6 million. During the ten-day second stage, participants discussed the CC drafts of the Sixty Articles and the accompanying directive, rulings on compensation, handicrafts, commerce, the problems of mountain areas, and a directive on the food problem. The final two-and-a-half days were devoted again to the food problem, with speeches by Zhou, Chen Yun, and Li Xiannian.[125]

During the proceedings, gloomy speeches were made by Liu and Deng. On 31 May, Liu spoke of acute contradictions, stating that neither peasants, workers, nor cadres had any ease of mind. He declared the food problem to be central: the shortages of grain, cooking oil, pork, fish, and other products were causing sharp tensions between town and countryside, threatening the survival of the regime.[126] Carefully quoting the Hunanese peasantry, and buttressing himself with support from the Shanxi 1st secretary, Tao Lujia, and unnamed comrades from Henan, Shandong, and Hebei, Liu repeated their attribution of the agricultural problems: 30 per cent to natural calamities, 70 per cent to man-made disasters.[127] The centre had to take responsibility for the many serious shortcomings and errors in CCP policy on the communes and in the GLF, which had resulted in deaths from hunger. Some mistakes were due to inexperience or were unavoidable, but great losses had resulted from the CCP's failure to discover and remedy them earlier.[128]

I believe the comrades present here ought to have gained experience! You ought to after two years without enough to eat. Do you still want to build tens of thousands of kilometres of railways? Do you still want to build many small modern enterprises? Do you still want to build many factories? Are you still reluctant to close some factories and let some workers go back to the countryside? Do you still want to build many guesthouses? I am afraid you should have learned from your experience. The peasants have suffered from hunger in the past two years; some have suffered from dropsy, some have died. City dwellers also didn't have enough to eat. Now the Party membership and people all over the country have had personal experience. In my view, it is high time we looked back and summed up our experience. We cannot go on like this.[129]

Liu stressed the overriding importance of a recovery of agriculture to turn the situation around. To accomplish this, people had to be moved from the urban areas to the countryside to engage in production and lessen the numbers whom the peasants had to feed in the cities. Light industry had to be geared to supplying the peasants with goods that would persuade them to sell their food products for the benefit of urban residents. Liu recalled that agriculture, light industry, heavy industry had been the order of priorities which Mao himself had proclaimed at the Lushan conference in 1959.[130]

Deng was equally gloomy. It would not be three-to-five years but more like seven or eight—Liu had said eight or ten—before agriculture recovered:

As things look at present, there is tension as regards production relations, between the party and the masses, among the cadres, and over the ownership system. In the past three years, the ownership system has been disrupted and enthusiasm has been undermined . . . Human error has been more serious than natural calamities . . . Henan's peasants attribute 30 per cent to natural calamities, 70 per cent to human failings. Shortcomings and errors are the prime cause; don't keep saying they're just one finger [out of ten].[131]

Liu had also dismissed the one-finger estimation. Neither he nor Deng needed to remind their audience that it was Mao himself who was fondest of glossing over errors and shortcomings in this way.

Mao later stated that he made a self-criticism in his speech on 12 June, the final day of the Beijing work conference, but that it was not distributed.[132] Certainly, in the apparently truncated version of that speech which is available, there is no hint of any personal apology. On the contrary, Mao described a process of correcting errors dating back to the first Zhengzhou conference in November 1958, and blamed the failure of these measures on the inability of cadres to understand their significance. He reinforced this impression of cadres' incompetence by calling for a campaign for their renewed education with rectification methods.[133]

Perhaps there was self-criticism in the remarks he made on the problems of the 1959 Lushan conference, and in his reported willingness to allow the rehabilitation of those mistakenly disciplined 'after' Lushan, that is, presumably not including Peng Dehuai and Zhang Wentian who were disciplined 'at' Lushan.[134] Certainly, there was an uncharacteristic humility in his praise for Liu Shaoqi's Hunan investigation and his avowed desire to learn from it, a tacit admission perhaps of the superficiality of his own recent investigations.[135] Notably absent from Mao's remarks, however, was the note of urgency, almost panic, that infused Liu's speech.

The 'revised draft' of the Sixty Articles

Nevertheless, Mao was sufficiently aware of the critical nature of the economic situation to back major amendments to the Sixty Articles, which were revised and reissued on 15 June on the basis of what had been found out. Only eight articles were left unchanged.[136] Permission to close down mess-halls was conceded, and the egalitarian supply system was wound up, except for specified cases of extreme penury or need.[137] The rights of the lower levels vis-à-vis the higher were affirmed in order to modify the extremes of collectivization.[138]

Communes, brigades, and teams still had to implement state policy, but with attention to local conditions and rationality. The various levels of representative and management bodies now had to be formally elected by secret ballot. They could not be run by a minority, and poorer peasants were no longer to be preferred members. Most importantly, the team was no longer to be in direct control of peasants' production and livelihood (*shenghuo*), only of production and collective subsidiary occupations.[139]

Communes had to supply seed, tools, fertilizers, and pesticides, but brigades and teams now had the right to pick and choose for quality. Communes could undertake water conservancy only with the agreement of affected brigades and teams. Even when undertaking a project to benefit a brigade, no more than 12 per cent of the brigade's accumulation fund could be used by the commune.[140]

The rights of teams as well as brigades to own animals and tools were buttressed. Team ownership rights were more clearly spelled out. In March, teams that over-fulfilled their grain targets had to be given a portion or a large portion of the surplus as a reward; in June, they could be given all of it.[141] On the other hand, brigade enterprises which in March could not utilize more than 3 per cent of team labour power now had the limit raised to 5 per cent. Two other contributions to brigade flexibility doubtless reflected economic reality: the ritual use of '90 per cent' to indicate how many commune members' incomes should be increased was abandoned, and the injunction that the cash value of work points should not be decreased was omitted.

But the brigade was now constrained by an upper limit of 3 per cent for the percentage of labour days which it could demand of peasants for basic construction work, and a crucial new article laid down a maximum of 5 per cent of public funds to be used for welfare; in the March version, teams were still permitted to use up to 30 per cent of their funds for the supply system, covering both mess-halls and the indigent.[142] The mess-halls were not publicly discarded in the June text; they simply disappeared from the relevant articles.[143]

Within the teams, the portion of land that could be allocated for peasants' private plots was raised from 5 per cent to 7 per cent.[144] In a further reflection of what China's leaders had heard on their tours, another important new article affirmed that peasants owned their houses in perpetuity (*yongyuan*), and had the right to buy, sell, or rent them. Organizations could not force a peasant to move house, nor commandeer his home, except with suitable compensation if construction needs demanded it.[145]

In the final tenth section, on the role of the CCP in the commune, a couple of surprising omissions in the March version were remedied in June: party members were enjoined to propagate not merely the general line of socialist construction but also Marxism-Leninism and Mao Zedong Thought; and party organs were instructed strictly to respect not the 'centralist' system but the 'democratic centralist' one![146]

In discussions of the revisions, the existence of a time-bomb was briefly hinted at from a surprising direction. Zhu De asked: 'Has anyone investigated how much individual farming is going on nationwide? Should one insert an article about it? That would make it legitimate. There will still be families farming individually in eight or ten years time. Even if you don't write it in, it'll still exist.'[147] For the moment, Zhu's forthright query could be ignored as the rumbling, perhaps even the rambling, of an elder statesman with little political clout, but in 1962 the issue emerged as a major dispute.

Mao's leadership style

While rewriting the Sixty Articles was a vital step towards setting China's countryside on a new course, the most salient political aspect of the Beijing work conference was that Mao effectively pre-empted its conclusions. In fact, the Chairman had characteristically short-circuited any real debate on the mess-halls at the conference, by authorizing on 26 April the circulation of a report to him by Hu Qiaomu on conditions in Sichuan, an illustration of the major role played in Mao's policy-making of the reports of trusted personal aides.

In late March, as already noted, Hu had held discussions on mess-halls in Mao's home village in Hunan province, and on 16 April (in response to an order from the Chairman), the provincial party committee issued a report on the Shaoshan discussions, which was later said to have solved the mess-hall problem, and sent Liu Shaoqi a copy of Hu's report.[148] Presumably Hu's conclusions in Hunan were similar to those he reached thereafter in Sichuan, from where he wrote that mess-halls were 'an impediment to developing production and a cancer in relations between party and masses . . . the sooner this problem is solved the better'.[149] Perhaps out of caution, probably out of reluctance to retreat from GLF leftism, and certainly to Mao's irritation, the Sichuan (and Southwest Bureau) 1st secretary, Politburo member Li Jingquan, did not write to him with his own findings and suggestions until 8 and 11 May, after being prompted by the Chairman. At this point, he reasserted the viability of the majority of mess-halls.[150] However, after seeing Hu's report, Marshal Zhu De felt able to confirm its correctness with his own findings, writing to Mao with a long list of complaints about the mess-halls which he had heard on tour in the same province, as well as in Shaanxi and Henan.[151]

It is a significant indicator of the crucial role of Mao in the CC's decision-making process, that until he had ordered Hu's report to be disseminated on 26 April, even the CCP committee in Sichuan province which had provided the data for it apparently did not have a 'deep understanding' of the mess-hall issue! Indeed the record suggests that even China's senior leaders rarely dared to make on-the-spot pronouncements on this or any other issue until Mao's own thinking was indicated by the documents he authorized for circulation, despite the fact that in some cases they found that desperate local cadres or peasants had already taken the law into their own hands.

Zhou Enlai wrote to Mao on 19 April about some early findings in various parts of the country in post-Canton discussions, but he did not address the issue of the supply system head on and did not mention mess-halls at all;[152] his own report did not reach Mao till 7 May—in fact the premier did not start his investigation until two days after Hu's report had been ordered circulated—Zhu De's not till 9 May, Deng Xiaoping and Peng Zhen's not till 10 May, Deng Zihui's not till 13 May.[153] It is notable, too, that Liu Shaoqi gave permission for mess-halls to close in the Hunanese villages which he visited only after he had a chance to gauge the Chairman's thinking at their meeting in Changsha, and after the report of Hu Qiaomu's March meeting in Shaoshan had been circulated by the provincial party.

Mao's final concession

With the decisions agreed at the May–June work conference, the CC had effectively restored to the countryside, in practice if not in nomenclature, the organizational *status quo ante* 1958. Even though the commune level still retained certain functions, the brigade, equivalent to the pre-GLF higher-stage APC, was the principal unit of decision-making. Some of Mao's colleagues had realized that even these measures were not radical enough to solve rural production problems, but again, nobody would anticipate him. It was three months before the Chairman moved again.

Why Mao changed his views on brigade accounting is unclear. On 23 August, the first day of the CC's customary summer work conference, the Chairman warned his colleagues not to overestimate what they had achieved by hammering out the Sixty Articles in Canton and Beijing. More work remained to be done. Yet he was sufficiently buoyed to believe that the economic crisis had bottomed out, and even Tian Jiaying, who was still desperately worried by the industrial situation, was inclined to agree that things were looking up in the countryside. No one wanted to dwell on the fact that the conference venue was again the mountain resort of Lushan where Mao had had his epic confrontation over the economic crisis with Defence Minister Peng Dehuai in 1959. Better to let bygones be bygones.[154]

One reason for general optimism was an upbeat report prepared by the CC's Rural Work Department which Mao read after his cautionary opening remarks. The report put great stress on the considerable changes brought about by the Sixty Articles, and Mao described it as very good and ordered it distributed at the conference.[155]

The report balanced ten improvements with ten problems. The major improvement was the extraordinarily rapid reduction in the size of rural work units, and thus the increase in their numbers, decreed as early as Canton. By the end of the year, the figures were as shown in Table 3.1.[156]

TABLE 3.1. *Numbers of communes and their sub-units,*
1959–1961

	1959	1960	1961
Communes	25,450	24,317	57,855
Brigades	518,000	464,000	734,000
Teams	3,299,000	2,892,000	4,089,000

Source: *Nongye Nianjian, 1980*, p. 5. The drop in the number of units in 1960 presumably reflects the post-Lushan leftist resurgence.

Most of the other improvements also represented restoration: 25 billion yuan distributed in compensation for lost property; the primacy of the brigade; private plots; a return to home cooking, with only 20 per cent of farm families still eating in mess-halls; concentration on production, and the provision of appropriate rewards for work.[157]

This assessment bore the hallmark of hope rather than the resonance of reality, especially in the light of the reported ten problems, which Mao urged cadres to solve in the six months between the autumn harvest and spring sowing. There was not enough grain to satisfy both peasants and compulsory state purchase targets, to feed both town and country. Where the harvest was better, hard-pressed peasants wanted to enjoy the surplus, but their less fortunate brethren were starving. Despite the payment of compensation, only about 20 per cent had so far found its way into the hands of peasant families, and very little of it consisted of commodities. In some places, wheat produced on private plots was being confiscated; in others, private plots had not been returned because the cadres clung to egalitarianism and regarded them as capitalist.

At the opposite end of the spectrum, in every province there were peasants and cadres who wanted effectively to dismantle collective agriculture with slogans like 'distribute land according to labour [power]' (*anlao fentian*) and 'fix output quotas by household' (*baochan daohu*). A *laissez-faire* attitude in some areas had led to a reduction of the size of the brigades and teams beyond the point at which collectivism had any meaning; in effect they had become family units known as 'father-son teams' (*fuzidui*) or 'brothers' teams' (*xiongdidui*). Not surprisingly, some saw all this as retrogression, and peasants and cadres on both sides of the argument, observing that the Sixty Articles were a 'draft' programme, anticipated the possibility of a policy reversal like that in the autumn of 1959 after the first Lushan conference.[158]

It was in this confused situation that Mao cut the Gordian knot. Shortly after the Lushan meeting, from 22 to 24 September, Mao hosted Field-Marshal Viscount Montgomery in Wuhan, revealing to a Westerner for the first time almost the full extent of the crop shortfall.[159] Three days later, on 27 September, Mao held a small meeting in Handan district in southern Hebei where Zhou Enlai had been earlier in the year. This seems not to have been a grass-roots survey, because the nine people listed in Mao's notes as attending were senior officials of Hebei and neighbouring Shandong. It seems likely that he stopped his special train as he journeyed north and summoned the officials to his carriage. This was indeed the 'viewing flowers from horseback' (*zou ma kan hua*), which Mao had accused his colleagues of practising in lieu of real investigation in his March letter from Canton.[160]

The point is worth stressing because it again illustrates Mao's decision-making procedure. He had raised the issue of making the team the accounting unit at Canton, but it was controversial and he did not push it.[161] During the three weeks he had just spent closeted with his colleagues, the 1st and 2nd secretaries of the Central-South region, Tao Zhu and Wang Renzhong, one of Mao's favourite provincial leaders, had again raised the matter, talking of the contradiction between the ownership rights of the team and the accounting rights of the brigade. Subsequent accounts give no indication, however, that Mao reopened the matter in a major way or that he indicated any inclination to carry out another fundamental revision of the Sixty Articles. Yet two days after his Handan meeting, he wrote to his most senior colleagues saying that he now believed that the accounting unit should be the team not the brigade.[162] Why?

His interlocutors, how emboldened we are not told, apparently informed him bluntly that one of the laboriously devised flagship slogans of the Sixty Articles, 'three guarantees and one reward', was far too complex to operate. It involved observing thirty-seven work procedures, calculating forty-nine percentages, keeping 1,128 accounts, and abiding by over 400 quotas. In place of this unworkable system, people were using one in which tasks were assigned (*baoganzhi*). In the case of a particular commune in Hebei, nominally the eleven brigades operated the prescribed system, but that was only to placate the *xian*; in practice they operated *baoganzhi*. The cadres ignored criticism of being rightist, and the peasants supported them. Their grain output went up each year, and in other respects they had managed at least to maintain 1957 levels while elsewhere figures were plummeting. Even the state was able to increase its compulsory grain purchases.

The counter-arguments which Mao heard were that this represented a return to primary-stage APCs; was not helpful for capital construction; made state purchasing more problematic; left disaster victims helpless; was harmful to mechanization; and would be difficult to reverse. He commented tersely and uncharacteristically: 'These six contrary opinions can all be answered.'[163]

In his letter to his colleagues, Mao stressed that only by team accounting could the problem of egalitarianism, which he had been battling since 1959, be overcome. He quoted peasants who said that the Sixty Articles lacked this one article on team accounting.[164]

Mao may have been motivated by two factors. It was reported to him that the peasants who had abandoned 'the three guarantees and the one reward' system hated people who engaged in commerce and neglected collective production and public works.[165] Perhaps he calculated that the peasants were opposed to genuine capitalism and only wanted to make the collective system work better.

More profoundly, he may have been desperately anxious to save the collective system, however nominally. Since his victorious leadership of the revolution and the takeover of power, he had taken four major personal initiatives. He had overridden his colleagues and taken China into the Korean War;[166] he had launched the 1955 collectivization drive against the advice of the director of the CC's Rural Work Department and many of his senior colleagues; he had launched the 1957 rectification campaign in a form which displeased many of his colleagues and subordinates; and he had launched the GLF, in the face of the opposition of the economic planners and their Soviet advisers, and had endorsed the communes.[167]

Participation in the Korean War had been costly, but it had won China international prestige for being able to defeat the world's leading superpower in campaigns and secure a draw in the final outcome; but that glory had faded and was irrelevant to the tasks which the CCP currently faced.[168] The rectification campaign had been a severe setback for the CCP, as it was forced to come to terms with nationwide criticism of its rule, and had to retaliate with an Anti-Rightist Campaign which had undermined its hopes of harnessing the intellectual community to economic development. The GLF had been a national disaster as a result of which millions were still dying.

The one hitherto seemingly unblemished triumph was a swift collectivization campaign which had confounded the experts and had exposed Stalin as a deadly bungler in this area. Now in 1961, even this remaining triumph was at risk, eroded by the desperate efforts of peasants to stay alive and of cadres trying to repair the damage wreaked by their earlier actions.

Thus Mao's second reason may have been a feeling that one last concession of permitting team accounting was needed as a safety valve if collectivization was not to collapse under the impact of famine and demoralization. He would go this far and no further; it was his 'final frontier'.[169] On 7 October, a week after Mao signed his letter, the CC issued a directive authorizing experimentation with team accounting.[170] Formal approval of the system would not come until 1962, when Mao carefully went over the relevant directive to ensure it did not go too far;[171] it was later incorporated into a further revision of the Sixty Articles that was approved at the 10th plenum. But it can be assumed that, if there had been widespread abandonment of brigade accounting even when it was mandatory, team accounting now spread rapidly.

Mao, it turned out, had only bought time. He had restored the *status quo ante* 1956, before the wholesale changeover from primary to advanced APCs.[172] As he wrote to his colleagues: 'We've been running around in confusion for six years; shouldn't we wake up in this seventh year?'[173] Profit and loss, sufficiency and need, were now to be more closely related to effort and the luck of location. But Mao had still not solved the problem of how best to combine prosperity and collectivism in rural China. He would soon face a new challenge on that issue.

4 A PLETHORA OF PLANS

The prospect of persisting mass starvation in the countryside and its spread to the cities brought out the best and the worst of the CCP's traditional approaches to crises. With Mao ready to acknowledge, if not to accept blame for, the economic disaster, a leadership consensus finally emerged on such key measures as the establishment of a less egalitarian accounting system, the dissolution of the mess-halls, the restoration of or compensation for confiscated private property, the renewed acceptance of 'private plots', the importation of Western grain, and the transfer of millions of urban residents back to the countryside. Each of these policies posed grave issues of ideology, organization, or national self-reliance, but after two years of fatal dithering, nothing was now allowed to delay rapid implementation. Having acknowledged the dire emergency, a party trained to cope with the sudden exigencies of guerrilla warfare responded rapidly and effectively.

It was in its longer-term policies that the regime fell back on more formalistic methods. The critical issue was to restore sanity and stability to the running of the economy after the chaotic, helter-skelter development of the GLF, and the central leadership sought to do this by lengthy statements of principle and prescription, all criticized later during the Cultural Revolution as 'revisionist'. The main ones were mini-charters for commerce (the 'Forty Articles'), handicrafts (the 'Thirty-five Articles'), industry (the 'Seventy Articles'), and forestry (the 'Eighteen Articles'), and in intellectual arenas—science (the 'Fourteen Articles'), higher education (the 'Sixty Articles'), and literature and the arts (the 'Eight Articles').[1] While programmes like the Forty Articles on Commerce and the Seventy Articles on Industry may have provided hard-pressed managers and officials with authorization for reasserting control and common sense, they simultaneously reimposed a conformity inimical to dynamic growth.

The Forty Articles on Commerce

Reorganization of the industrial sector of the economy was crucial for the long-term development programme, but in the short term, stabilizing the commercial sector was even more important because it affected the lives of all China's hard-pressed citizens. During the turbulent years of the GLF and its disastrous aftermath, senior officials paid a great deal of attention to commerce until the situation eased;[2] the mini-charter for this sector, the Forty Articles on Commerce, was put on the agenda of the Beijing work conference by Mao and circulated on 19 June 1961, three months before the Seventy Articles on Industry.[3]

The main aim of the Forty Articles was to provide a framework for repairing the damage done to China's domestic commercial activity by the more utopian concepts of the GLF.[4] While commerce was already state-controlled and organized on complex collectivist lines by the mid-1950s,[5] during the GLF radicals rejected the production of goods for sale and the law of value as the basis of exchange. In practice, this meant radically reshaping existing commercial networks, mainly by decentralization, discarding tried management practices, amalgamating trading enterprises, closing down rural markets, and laying off pedlars. A preliminary effort at repairing some of the damage took place in early 1959, but in the nature of the times, it did not get far.[6] In the more propitious political atmosphere after the 9th plenum, the Forty Articles could be drawn up, even if still only as an 'experimental draft'.

The Forty Articles reflected the urgency imbuing the post-plenum approach to the economy: production had rapidly to be increased; living standards had to be restored; a proper balance between the interests of peasants and urbanites had to be drawn; and trade had to be restored.[7] Key to these issues was how to persuade the peasants to produce and sell more in exchange for consumer goods and agricultural inputs. This meant setting fair prices and speeding up commodity flows, ironing out difficulties between the state commercial sector and village commerce, and improving the management of commercial enterprises.[8]

A major step in this direction had been taken with the raising of procurement prices at the end of 1960.[9] The Forty Articles embraced the possibility of further price rises as appropriate, and advocated that the state sign contracts with the peasants to guarantee deliveries.[10] The further raising of procurement prices would necessarily remain a high-level political decision. The Forty Articles was, understandably, principally concerned with re-establishing the mechanisms by which to maintain an adequate flow of goods, should the prices be appropriate to bring them to market. State commercial enterprises, supply and marketing co-operatives (SMCs), and rural fairs were reaffirmed as the three major channels for those flows.[11] State enterprises had to be separated from bureaucratic administration of the ministry, and specialized state trading companies had to be restored.[12] SMCs had to be revived, small shops and pedlars, whose disappearance had caused enormous inconvenience during the GLF, should be brought back, and rural fairs had to be reopened. All goods except for grain and cotton could be sold at the fairs once contracts with the state had been honoured.[13] Improved economic management was a familiar cry in 1961, but the Forty Articles also suggested what appear to have been interesting innovations: the right of trading enterprises to select what they distributed, a policy which would have excused them from the duty of simply buying all they were offered, no matter what the quantity or quality; and the creation of consumer councils to act as price watchdogs.[14]

The term 'experimental draft' was no misnomer. The Forty Articles appears to have created an atmosphere in which experiments could be initiated, but neither it nor the 'experimental draft' Hundred Articles which the Commerce Ministry issued on 25 December 1961—which never even achieved the status of a formal document[15]—had the effect of decisions. The caution probably reflected an ongoing ambivalence towards private commerce, an attitude which was reflected by Commerce Minister Yao Yilin when he spoke in support of the Forty Articles in June. He called for opening up (*kaifang*) moribund commercial channels, but was careful to argue, albeit somewhat casuistically, that the revival of small trading groups could not be defined as the revival of private trading. Some comrades, he revealed, were saying the party should 'open the cage to release the bird' (*kai long fang niao*), but his preference was to 'open the cage to release the chicken' (*kai long fang ji*). Yao's meaning seems to have been that private commerce was a bird which could not be controlled, whereas a chicken was confined to the ground and could be easily retrapped and caged. By referring to chickens he may also have wanted to stress that the Forty Articles was designed as a down-to-earth policy calculated to improve access to commodities important to daily living, and did not represent an ideological turnabout.[16]

In this atmosphere, even the restoration of co-operative shops could be resisted by radicals as a retrograde step in terms of ownership, precisely because the CC had made no formal determination of the issue.[17] In Shenyang in 1957, there were 15,312 retail outlets, of which 1,100 were state-run, 624 were joint state-private, and 13,588 were co-operative shops and pedlars. By 1960, the overall figure had been reduced to 2,683, of which 1,507 were state-run and 1,080 were nominally co-operatives; there were virtually no pedlars left. Of Shenyang's pre-GLF 2,892 catering outlets, only 432 were left in mid-1961.[18] In some smaller towns, even orders by officials to increase the frequency of markets could not bring back discouraged traders.[19] Nationwide, the convenience of customers continued to be neglected despite the new thinking of the early 1960s: for all cities above the county level, the number of catering-industry retail outlets shrank, as in Shenyang, as a result of amalgamation or closure, from a million in 1957 to 400,000 in 1962, and by 1978 there were only 190,000.[20]

Nevertheless, there was progress in 1961. By the end of the year, 31,000 SMCs had been restored at the grass roots, along with 13,000 at the county level and eighteen at the provincial level.[21] In addition, about 99 per cent of the rural markets existing prior to the GLF— some 41,000—reopened.[22] Perhaps these moves were widely acceptable because they were clearly vital for ensuring supplies of grain and other rural products for the cities and within the countryside itself; in Shanghai, for instance, between 1957 and 1962, the flow of agricultural sideline products declined by 50 per cent.[23] More contentious ideas in the commercial and other fields had to await the further improvement in the political atmosphere that would be heralded by the Seven Thousand Cadres Conference at the beginning of 1962. Thereafter, 'hesitation, wait-and-see attitude and refusal to implement the Party's policies, which were prevalent among some cadres, decreased considerably'.[24] Even so, although Liu Shaoqi stated in January 1962, that the Forty Articles were currently under revision in the light of comments and would be reissued for implementation, for unexplained reasons the document never emerged.[25] Moreover, the director of the CC's Rural Work Department, Deng Zihui, revealed in May 1962 that outside Guangdong and Guangxi, where trading at country fairs was lively, in most areas too many restrictions applied.[26]

The Thirty-five Articles on the Handicraft Industry

When the CCP took over China, the handicraft industry accounted for 23.1 per cent of the value of all industrial output.[27] By 1954 when a survey was carried out, handicraft production was valued at 10.46 billion yuan, still equal to over 20 per cent of total industrial production and over 10 per cent of the total value of industry and agriculture. If one included craftsmen working either on their own or in co-operatives, peasants who engaged in part-time handicraft production, and workers in tiny enterprises of between four and ten employees, total employment in this sector amounted to 20 m. people, 57.7 per cent of them working in the rural areas, 54 per cent in inland China, the vast majority producing consumer goods without the benefit of machinery. This meant, adding in their families, that the livelihood of something like 100 m. people was totally or partially dependent upon handicraft production. By 1957, the relative importance of handicrafts had declined slightly, but the gross value of their output had risen by almost a third in three years to 13.36 billion yuan. It was thus a sector which the CCP did not take lightly, economically or politically.[28]

By the end of the 1st FYP in 1957, over 90 per cent of the full-time handicraft workers had been organized into co-operatives,[29] but with the advent of the GLF this no longer seemed ideologically advanced enough. By the end of 1958, 85 per cent of the over 5 m. members of the 100,000 co-ops existing a year earlier were now working in 'factories', of which almost 80 per cent were run either by the state or by communes.[30] Responsibility for the livelihood of these handicraftsmen, which had hitherto rested upon their own collaborative efforts, now devolved upon the 'owners' of the new factories.

This transformation of ownership and responsibility turned out to be a massive disincentive to effort, and very harmful to the interests of consumers. As employees rather than collective owners, handicraftsmen could now expect to eat from the same 'big pot' (daguofan) as the envied workers in state factories, and be assured of the 'iron rice bowl' (tiefanwan) of lifetime employment. Moreover, the new masters of the handicraft industry developed grandiose plans for their factories and discarded the production of consumer staples which they felt were 'low, crude, or small' (di, cu, xiao). As a result, supplies of wooden basins, vegetable baskets, bamboo beds, iron cooking pots, scissors, and small and medium agricultural implements were drastically reduced, and repair services were sharply cut back.[31] As one commentator put it, urbanites found it 'difficult to get clothing made, have their hair cut or styled, eat out in restaurants, buy nonstaple foodstuffs, buy furniture, or get repairs done'.[32]

A well-known Beijing knife factory diverted most of its 300 workers into making expensive equipment for China's disastrous backyard steel campaign. By this method, the factory was able to over-fulfil its target for value of output, but the twenty workers left making knives were able to produce only 3,000 knives monthly as compared with the previous 35,000 and they had to reduce the number of types from 200 to eleven. In Shanghai, street industries were developed, employing 116,000 people by the end of 1962, almost as many as were in handicraft trades there before the GLF. But though their output was valued at over 95 m. yuan, most of it was for use in factories and not to replace the consumer goods produced by handicraftsmen.[33]

In Chengdu, between 1951 and 1957, the value of the output of collectivized handicraft production rose massively from 60,000 yuan to 79,900,000 yuan. But after the more than 400 collective workshops producing over thirty types of goods were transformed into state ownership in 1958—a transition from 'china rice bowl' (*cifanwan*) to 'iron rice bowl' was the local description—value of output dropped 20 per cent, by implication largely due to decreased incentives. A remarkably successful musical instruments factory, with a strongly motivated work-force turning out products that sold throughout southwest and northwest China, resulting in an annual profit of 100,000 yuan, was losing 50,000 yuan on greatly reduced output by the end of the second year of the GLF, and its workers, assured that their wages were guaranteed, had lost their hitherto keen interest in company performance.[34]

The 'CC's [experimental draft] stipulations on certain problems in the urban and rural handicraft industry'—the Thirty-five Articles—were on the agenda of the Beijing work conference and were issued on 19 June 1961 in an attempt to alleviate the problems of consumers, but even more importantly, to judge by the relative attention accorded the topic in the document, to relieve the state and communes of the financial burden of paying wages to (and presumably of being responsible for the welfare benefits of) handicraftsmen.[35]

Ten articles, the first and easily the largest section, were devoted to the question of ownership. It was emphatically laid down that of three permissible forms—state, collective, and individual—collective ownership should be the main one. But whatever the form, neglect of economic accounting in favour of 'eating from the same big pot', and the idea of relying on the state's 'iron rice bowl' had to be opposed.[36] In order speedily to restore and develop output, there had to be a rational adjustment in the current handicrafts ownership pattern, with the criteria being: raising workers' motivation and efficiency, increasing the quantity, quality, and variety of goods, economizing on raw materials and lowering costs, benefiting agricultural production and people's needs, and adhering to the principle of 'from each according to his ability, to each according to his work'.[37]

Self-sufficient individual handicraftsmen (*geti shougongyezhe*) were also sanctioned, though expected to pay a fee to the collective under whose umbrella they operated. Private family handicrafts (*jiating shougongye*) were encouraged for urban areas.[38] The losses of re-established handicraft collectives had to be borne by the state enterprise responsible for them during the GLF, and prior capital, equipment, and premises had to be restored or replaced.[39] Succeeding sections dealt with the scale of operation, material benefits—'the more you work the more you get' was the watchword, and egalitarianism was to be eschewed—supplies, prices, management, and overall leadership, but the main thrust remained the restoration of the *status quo ante* the GLF.[40]

The Thirty-five Articles are credited with having had a considerable and speedy impact, and this may have been partly because the need to implement them was reinforced by mention in the CC directive on industry in September.[41] Yet even in this sector, insiders say that it was not till 1962 that a breakthrough came.[42] Statistics from sixteen cities in the provinces of Hubei, Zhejiang, Hebei, and Yunnan, indicate that within a few months in 1961, the prescribed readjustments had been carried out in 72,000 enterprises employing 2,240,000 people. Of the organizations emerging from the process, almost 85 per cent were handicraft or some other form of co-operative, almost 10 per cent were co-operative factories, and only 4.5 per cent were state- or commune-run.[43] The value of handicraft production, which had dipped drastically in 1958, but then started rising again, reached the 1957 level again in 1964:[44]

TABLE 4.1. *Handicraft industry: value of output, 1957–1966* (100 million yuan)

1957	1958	1959	1960	1961*	1962	1963	1964	1965	1966
83.12	47.00	62.00	71.40	52.40	68.50	70.40	83.10	96.10	110.00

Note: *The sharp dip in the 1961 figure was presumably due partly to reorganization and partly to a return to less-profitable consumer products.

Source: Ma Hong and Sun Shangqing, *Jingji Jiegou Wenti Yanjiu*, pp. 177, 178.

Shortening the front

An illustration of the lopsided manner in which the CCP leaders approached their task of readjusting their economic programme is provided by their handling of industry. The drafting of what eventually emerged as the Seventy Articles, a long-term overall programme for the management of the industrial sector, began before they had taken adequate measures to deal with short-term problems which needed urgent attention. At the 9th plenum, Li Fuchun, the chairman of the State Planning Commission, had underlined the need to curtail the scale of industrial production and the meeting had formally agreed to the need to 'readjust the tempo of development'. But food shortages were more compelling and comprehensible than budget deficits; starving millions were more obviously a potential threat to the regime than an overheated economy. Thus disagreement persisted about the extent to which industrial production needed to be cut back, and in this atmosphere targets remained high and 'no substantial results were achieved' in the readjustment of the non-agricultural sector.[45] Liu Shaoqi and Zhou Enlai were said to be on opposite sides of the argument at first, with Liu wanting to cut back drastically, and Zhou insisting on preserving at least some of the small and medium-sized iron and steel works set up during the GLF, as advocated also by the Ministry of the Metallurgical Industry.[46] Gradually during 1961, the realities of the situation forced the CCP leadership to overrule dissenters and take drastic action.

As mentioned in Chapter 2, a sharp reduction of the urban population was in part a function of the inevitable cutback in construction and output imposed by the need to restore a desperately overstretched economy to balance. During the three years of the GLF, investment in capital construction had totalled 99,600 m. yuan, a staggering 80 per cent more than during the whole of the 1st FYP. That construction leap had been based on the enormously exaggerated agricultural output figures for 1958, leading to a belief that the agricultural problem had been solved (*guo guan*), and a demand for a 1962 steel output of 50–60 m. tons. In the cold light of the actual 1960 figures it was seen that this massive investment in construction had placed considerable strain on all sectors of the economy and could not be maintained. The nation's financial, material, and human resources were totally out of balance.

During the three years of the GLF, national income had increased by 31,200 m. yuan. During the same period, investment in capital construction increased by 24,600 m. yuan, absorbing almost 80 per cent of the increase in national income. Indeed, in 1960, when national income had actually fallen by 200 m. yuan, capital construction had still increased by 3,900 m. yuan.

Nor could the output of the basic materials for building-work keep pace with the 40.7 per cent average annual increase in capital construction: during the three years, the output of steel products had gone up on average only 38.8 per cent, timber 14.8 per cent, and cement 31.7 per cent.[47] When the planners had sat down to draft the 1959 annual plan they had not been able to make the figures add up even on paper and were forced to leave a shortfall of materials worth 5,000 m. yuan! As a result, it had been impossible to complete some projects, due to either a shortage of materials or money; and even though the number of workers on construction work increased by 4,210,000, on all sides there were complaints of shortages of personnel.

The demands placed on heavy industry had led to damage to equipment, with many enterprises being unable to continue manufacturing. The dislocation had been particularly serious in the extractive and processing industries. By 1960, the amount of coal mined had reached 390 m. tons, an increase of 200 per cent over the 1957 pre-GLF figure, but even this massive rise fell short of demand by 3.5 per cent. Moreover, in order to satisfy the needs of the steel and electrical power industries, the use of coal for domestic purposes was curtailed and many plants had to close. In Shandong province in 1960, three-quarters of the spinning, chemical, and machinery plants had shut down.

In addition, three years of obeying blind directives from on high had completely demoralized management. Product quality and labour efficiency had both declined. Waste was widespread and heavy losses were incurred. In 1957, 99.4 per cent of pig iron output had been up to standard; in 1960, only 74.9 per cent. During the 1st FYP, the ash content of the coal produced at the most important mines had averaged 21 per cent; by 1960, it was up to 24 per cent. In industry, the overall efficiency of labour declined 12 per cent between 1957 and 1960. Economic losses rose sharply and by 1961 reached 10,500 m. yuan, of which industry accounted for 4,650 m. yuan. By 1960, the value of construction projects abandoned and subsequently written off totalled 15,000 m. yuan.[48]

These disastrous trends continued into the first post-GLF year. 'In the first quarter of 1961, the production level of 25 important industrial goods ... dropped by 30 to 40% as compared with the level in the fourth quarter of 1960, and only 10 to 20% of the annual planned production quotas were fulfilled, the lowest since 1949.' The trend continued through the second and into the third quarters.[49] A major factor was the shortage of energy, discussed in Chapter 2. 'Faced with these harsh facts',[50] China's leaders finally acted.

Lushan revisited

At Lushan in 1959, at the annual CC summer work conference, Mao had anathematized Marshal Peng Dehuai's criticisms of the GLF, and had relaunched the movement to prove himself right.[51] At Lushan in the summer of 1961, Mao was relaxed enough to write a brief paean to nature, which he inscribed upon a photograph of himself on Lushan taken by his wife, Jiang Qing, during the 1959 conference:[52]

> Amid the growing shades of dusk stand sturdy pines,
> Riotous clouds drift past, swift and tranquil.
> Nature has excelled herself in the Fairy Cave,
> On perilous peaks dwells beauty in her infinite variety.

Under Mao's aegis, the CC work conference began to take decisive action to repair the GLF industrial disaster which his headstrong action two years earlier had so gravely compounded. The recently appointed executive vice-chairman of the State Planning Commission, Cheng Zihua, had a simple *reculer-pour-mieux-sauter* rationale for the needed cutbacks, drawn from Maoist guerrilla tactics: when one met a stronger enemy, one retreated to seek a position of greater advantage from which to liquidate one's opponent. This attitude was reflected in the deliberations at Lushan.[53]

The 1961 Lushan conference produced two major documents on industrial policy: a directive on current industrial problems and the Seventy Articles, issued on 15 and 16 September respectively. The Seventy Articles, as we shall see, was another programmatic document. The directive was designed to have more immediate impact. It began with a paragraph of obligatory praise of the GLF, but then went on to admit 'many shortcomings and errors', and 'several difficulties', principally high targets, excessively fast pace of development, uneven growth, waste, bad management, lower efficiency, worse quality. Though these difficulties were transient, they were nevertheless serious.[54] The eight sections of this long directive laid down how they were to be overcome.

The slogan 'adjustment, consolidation, filling out, and raising (standards)', first articulated a year earlier,[55] but evidently not taken seriously enough for 'we have already lost over a year of opportunities',[56] had now to be resolutely implemented for seven years;[57] during the next three years the most important of these guidelines should be 'adjustment', evidently the rubric under which closures and cutbacks could be implemented. Industrial output targets and plant construction had to be reduced to dependable levels, and had to allow room for manoeuvre.

The CC's seriousness contrasted strongly with attitudes at the 9th plenum in January. At that time, Mao's willingness to accept for 1961 the same steel output as in 1960—18 m. tons, or a modest rise to 19 m. tons[58]—indicated an agreement at best to mark time rather than cut back. In the case of coal, Li Fuchun had forecast an output of the order of 436 m. tons. But now, only nine months later, hopes and expectations for these bellwether industries had been drastically revised: *for 1961 and 1962 together*, coal output was to be only about 500+ m. tons, steel only about 15+ m. tons. As a result of this new realism, steel output dropped over 50 per cent to 8.7 m. tons in 1961 and a further 23 per cent to 6.67 m. tons in 1962, for a total of 15.37 m. tons, very much in line with the directive.[59] Coal production dropped almost 30 per cent to 278 m. tons in 1961 and a further 20 per cent to 220 m. tons in 1962, for a total again very much in line with the directive.[60]

With the planning system still in disarray, managers abruptly being told to reverse direction, and much of 1961 already elapsed, such precision targeting is surprising. There is no information on other targets that may have been agreed on at Lushan, and it is difficult to gauge from the figures whether or not Chen Yun or Li Fuchun suggested some rough rule of thumb which the CC accepted. Possibly in the case of major items critical to industrial construction, targets were set for the two-year period 1961–2, as in the case of steel, to be roughly 75–85 per cent of the figures for just 1960, but if so there was slippage (see Table 4.2).

TABLE 4.2. *Selected industrial output figures, 1960–1962*

	1960	1961	1962	1961–2 as % 1960
Pig iron (m. tons)	27.16	12.81	8.05	76.76
Steel (m. tons)	18.66	8.70	6.67	82.36
Steel products (m. tons)	11.11	6.13	4.55	96.12
Cement (m. tons)	15.65	6.21	6.00	78.01
Plate glass (m. units)	6.70	3.32	3.99	109.10
Timber (m. cu. metres)	41.29	21.94	23.75	110.65

Source: *TJNJ, 1983*, pp. 244–5.

Whatever the overall plan, if any, the CC hoped that this drastic readjustment would produce big results by the end of 1963.[61] None of this could be accomplished, however, without a reassertion of central economic control at the national or at least the regional level, and so this was the theme of the directive's second section. The GLF devolution to the provincial level and below was reversed; investment, materials, labour, wages, cash reserves would follow central guidelines.[62] Central control was particularly urgent for major items like raw materials, building materials, and energy which were in critically short supply. Among these, energy was the most crucial, and within the energy sector, coal was king.

The energy gap

In 1961, China's oil industry had not yet begun the spectacular spurt which was to take it to an output of 100 m. tons in 1978. Output in 1960 had only been 5.2 m. tons.[63] Coal was, and indeed remains, the prime source of energy, but the massive increase in output during the GLF had imposed severe strains on the industry. In the second half of 1960, daily production had averaged 630,000 tons. In the first half of 1961, that figure dropped to 520,000 tons, and by the third quarter of the year it had dropped again to 440,000 tons, a decrease of 30 per cent in less than a year.[64] In 1961, total output would decline 30 per cent to 278 m. tons.[65]

In 1961, as during the GLF, Chen Yun devoted special attention to the energy problem, but again only when he was certain that Mao was ready to swallow unpleasant medicine. In a speech to a forum on coal work after the Lushan meeting, he pinpointed the reasons for the industry's parlous condition:[66]

The basic cause of the decrease in coal production is that the production target is set too high and the scale of capital construction is too large. As a result mining is uncontrolled, equipment is unrepaired, part of the equipment is barely working, and the supply of materials and equipment is insufficient. Meanwhile, the living standard of workers has declined and this affects their health and production initiative and causes an increase in the mobility of production workers. Chaotic management, poor ideological work, bad [work] styles of cadres and other factors also directly cause coal production to decrease.

Chen called for targets to be set in line with capacity. Capacity had to be determined in terms of the availability of machinery and materials. If targets were discovered to be still too high, they should be reduced. With China now dependent on itself for whole sets of equipment—a function of the Sino-Soviet dispute and shortage of foreign exchange—calculations would have to be made with particular care.

Equipment standards should not be set too high, but it would be even worse to set them too low. Construction timetables should not be made too tight while China was feeling its way forward.[67]

The figures make clear how disastrous the situation was with respect to mining equipment. There had been an enormous increase in output during the GLF, presumably much of the machinery being sub-standard. Output then dipped precipitously in 1961 and thereafter kept declining until 1964. But as a result of another dip after the start of the Cultural Revolution, the pre-GLF high was not surpassed until 1969 (see Table 4.3).

TABLE 4.3. *Mining equipment*

1957	52.9
1958	95.6
1959	229.8
1960	251.9
1961	90.3
1962	34.5
1963	22.0
1964	28.2
1965	40.0
1966	51.9
1967	37.7
1968	29.3
1969	61.6

Source: *TJNJ, 1983*, p. 248.

There had been arguments about the siting of new mines. Most mines were in the north, and some people felt it was absurd to be continually transporting coal from north to south; southern resources should be developed. But while Chen conceded the rationality of this position, he pointed out that the development of production would suffer if the north (the location of the bulk of the reserves)[68] were not given priority development.

To keep miners down in the pits, Chen advocated greater incentives in the form of bonus food and firewood, higher wages, and greater safety. Technical personnel should be given positions and authority, and their 'class' problems should be tackled in a sympathetic manner. Managers should be given more responsibility and party committees should refrain from mass movements and excessive interference.[69]

All these were sensible prescriptions for setting the industry on an even keel—reducing production to a level appropriate for the reduction in the rate of investment—and top leaders attempted to see that they were followed; at one point in 1961, Premier Zhou Enlai went personally to the Northeast to investigate the coal supply problem.[70] But the sharp decline in coal production already noted for 1961 and 1962 continued thereafter, and output only began to rise again on the eve of the Cultural Revolution (see Table 4.4).[71]

TABLE 4.4. *Coal output (m. tons)*

1957	131
1958	270
1959	369
1960	397
1961	278
1962	220
1963	217
1964	215
1965	232
1966	252

Source: *TJNJ, 1983*, p. 244.

Key links

In addition to coal, the Lushan industrial directive singled out steel products as a cause for particular concern. They were lacking in variety and quality. If the coal and steel problems could not be solved soon, there would be no way to assist the factories that had shut down or were working on a part-time basis. In addition, there had to be strict economy in the use of other essential materials like pig iron, timber, cotton, and tobacco. Industrial plants that had insufficient supplies of raw materials and other supplies, or used them in an inefficient or costly fashion, had to halt production, shut down, or partially shut down. The centre would also take a firm grip of various types of construction: new, expansion, refurbishment. All this in the interests of 'overall balance' (*zonghe pingheng*), long the watchword of the planners, though normally disturbing to Mao.[72]

In the overall economic picture, grain and cotton were also key links, especially in the light of the dire shortages of food and clothing anticipated over the next two or three years, and the directive reiterated the importance of heavy industry supporting agriculture—notably by the provision of tools, machinery, and chemical fertilizer—as well as the consumer goods industries.[73] The directive went on to order the restoration of ruptured pre-GLF economic linkages; to underline the importance of the 'five fixes', a key element of the Seventy Articles, discussed below; to stress the importance of paying attention to living standards, and, probably most importantly, to threaten serious punishment for those who flouted discipline by disobeying central economic plans and directives such as this one.[74]

The Seventy Articles on Industry

The Seventy Articles on Industry, which was the other major document on this subject to emerge from the Lushan conference, had originated in investigations initiated in early January 1961 by Li Fuchun. Li led a team drawn from the State Economic Commission, the First Ministry of Machine Building, the Central Party School, the Economic Research Centre of the Academy of Sciences, along with cadres from Beijing municipality, to examine ten factories and other units in the capital. The major investigation, at the Beijing No. 1 Machine Tool Factory, lasted five to six months.[75]

In June, Bo Yibo, Chairman of the State Economic Commission, replaced Li Fuchun as team leader,[76] and was told to lead a specially set up '10-man small group', originally proposed by Zhou Enlai in January, to consider the results of all these investigations and to transform them into a concrete set of proposals. This the group carried out in the industrialized Northeast, basing themselves in Shenyang, where they organized a 350-man investigation task force,[77] and visiting Harbin and Changchun to hold consultations. In July, Deng Xiaoping presided over a series of secretariat discussions which hammered the draft document into seventy articles. The final draft was considered at Lushan. On 16 September, it was ordered to be distributed for further discussion.[78]

Despite attacks on the Seventy Articles during the Cultural Revolution, the document was promulgated with Mao's consent.[79] Perhaps Mao and his more radical supporters were propitiated by language deferential to the GLF and the Chairman's thought in the Seventy Articles.[80] In Article 6, under the overall rubric of 'General Principles', the draft surprisingly reaffirmed the slogan of the GLF, asserting that it was the duty of the enterprise party committee to lead workers and staff to implement the general line of constructing socialism by 'going all out, aiming high, and achieving greater, faster, better, and more economical results'. This article also called on the party committee to promote the study of Mao's works and Marxism-Leninism, though significantly with the provisos that the personnel had to be capable of studying, and that it should be on a voluntary basis.[81] Elsewhere the draft declared that politics took command and was the soul of all work.[82]

Despite such phraseology redolent of the GLF, later proponents and critics of the Seventy Articles on Industry agreed that major features of the document were the 'five fixes' (*wu ding*) and the 'five guarantees' (*wu baozheng*), laid down in the first section on the management of the plan, clearly designed to restore central control and predictability after the uncertainties of the GLF.[83] The state imposed 'five' fixed items on the enterprise: product plan and production scale; personnel and organizational structure; consumption quotas and sources of supply of major raw materials, processed materials, fuel, power, and tools; fixed capital and liquid capital; and co-operative relationships. The enterprise had to guarantee 'five' items to the state: product variety, quality and quantity; not to exceed the wage bill; to fulfill its cost target and struggle to reduce costs; to turn over profits to its superior unit; the allotted utilization period of the principal equipment.[84]

Once the content of these ten items were laid down for an enterprise, they 'basically' (*jiben*) could not be changed for three years, but there was provision for annual adjustment based on the exigencies of the state plan.[85] And in an effort to restore horizontal as well as vertical predictability, the crucial nature of binding inter-enterprise relationships was stressed.[86]

While the overall leadership of the enterprise party committee was reaffirmed and the significance of the enterprise workers' congress was acknowledged, a key objective of the Seventy Articles was to restore the authority of factory managers and their subordinate production, financial, and technical officials, so that they could in turn reinstate regularized operations after the heady days of the GLF mass movement.[87] This had already been indicated in a spate of press articles prior to the formulation of the Seventy Articles. As early as February 1961, the *People's Daily* had stated editorially: 'The collective leadership of the CCP Committee cannot replace the day-to-day administrative management of an enterprise. Nor is it necessary for the Party Committee to manage the daily routine affairs of the enterprise . . .'[88] In June, a Shanghai periodical had argued: 'Without a perfect system of responsibility of the factory director, or a system of command over day-to-day administration, the Party Committee will trap itself in daily routine, and be unable to concentrate force for solving important matters of policy or to step up the day-to-day ideological and political work of the Party.'[89]

Managerial authority was ideologically grounded in the notion that the essence of modern industry everywhere was the material and technical conditions of production, not the social relationships in which they were placed. An article in the specialist journal *Jingji Yanjiu* (Economic Research) said baldly: 'The conditions under which a machine is used, operated, and maintained is the same in both a socialist enterprise and a capitalist enterprise.'[90]

The practical implication of this ideological position was the partial shielding of the factory manager from the party committee. He presided over the factory administrative and executive meetings where he had the final say, and these were clearly differentiated from party committee meetings at which majority rule applied. Whereas the party committee met only once a month, the manager's committees met weekly. The party committee acted as a final court of appeal only if 'important matters' could not be resolved at administrative or executive meetings.[91]

During the GLF, much power over production, personnel, and finance was devolved from the manager to the workshop level. This process was now reversed. Emphasis on 'scientific' management also resulted in the reversal of many GLF organizational changes, notably by the greater articulation of functional departments. In the Shenyang steel plant, thirty-two such departments had been reduced to six during the GLF; now the number was increased to twenty-three.[92]

Technical management under the leadership of the chief engineer was accorded a long section to itself in the Seventy Articles.[93] Simultaneously, engineers and other technical personnel were publicly lauded in a series of articles in the CC's theoretical journal *Red Flag*, which in 1962 stated unequivocally that problems occurring in the execution of technological policies 'should be solved by the responsible technological personnel concerned in accordance with the assigned duties. *No one else should interfere.*'[94] This concern for technical specialists was underlined in 1963 when systems of financial rewards for scientific discoveries (ranging from 500 to 10,000 yuan) and technological innovations (ranging up to 1,000 yuan) were laid down by the State Council.[95]

Financial discipline and control of wages and bonuses were also accorded their own sections in the Seventy Articles, and egalitarianism was firmly rejected in favour of payment according to work:

The wage and bonus system of state enterprises must embody the principle of payment according to work and set aside egalitarianism. The amount of compensation for work of workers, technical personnel, and staff members must be fixed according to the degree of skill in the individual's technical specialisation or the amount and quality of his work, and not in accordance with any other standard.[96]

Among the 'other standards' were presumably political activism and reliability which figured importantly during the GLF.[97] This official respect for expertise over 'redness' or political merit appears to have persisted within Chinese industry into 1966, though changes were appearing as the Cultural Revolution got under way. According to a first-hand report on that period by a foreign specialist on business management:

At all of the [thirty-eight] enterprises surveyed I was told that enterprise management was under the leadership of the party committee. However, it did appear that at a majority of the enterprises the management still had considerable leeway and authority in running the firm . . . There seemed to be a fairly reasonable balance between Reds and Experts, with the Experts generally making the types of managerial and technical decisions that they were best suited to make at the majority of firms. In most instances, managers seemed to be treated with respect and often with considerable spontaneous warmth and friendliness by other enterprise personnel, including workers. I got the general feeling during my visits to Chinese enterprises that higher-level managers and key experts still had quite a bit of status and prestige.[98]

Behind the scenes the reality seems to have been more ambiguously complex. Party officials moved with understandable caution.[99] Elements of GLF management practices appear to have persisted in some factories even after the promulgation of the Seventy Articles.[100] According to one analysis of fifty-three factories, 'strong' continuity of various such practices ranged from 5 per cent to 53.6 per cent, while 'some' continuity ranged from 35.9 per cent to 67.5 per cent.[101] The Seventy Articles thus turned out to be a benchmark, not tablets of stone, and even as such its full implementation had to await the convening of the Seven Thousand Cadres Conference in January 1962.[102] By the end of 1962, with renewed advocacy of class struggle, the balance of advantage would shift again, and from 1964 on, debate was joined on which management pattern to follow.[103]

5 REDS AND EXPERTS

As the debates generated by the Seventy Articles on Industry illustrated, the struggle between 'redness' and expertise, between virtue
(*de*) and ability (*cai*),[1] over the relative importance of politics versus
knowledge, was one of the perennial dialectics of the CCP. Mao's
preferred position was to have his cake and eat it, to proclaim the
primacy of redness and the importance of expertise.[2] During the
GLF, however, the Chairman, angered at what he felt was a lack of
appropriate co-operation on the part of the bourgeois intellectuals
during the Hundred Flowers period, led the way in sweeping aside
expertise, both domestic and Soviet, and putting politics totally in
command.[3]

A significant element in recovering from the GLF was to re-enlist
the intellectuals in China's economic enterprises, and to recast the
education system so that it could once more produce well-trained
young men and women. More broadly, the whole cultural sphere
had to be involved. Writers and artists—novelists and painters,
actors and musicians, dramatists and film-makers—were the 'engineers of the human soul'[4] whose inspirational talents were critical to
reviving battered morale and flagging energies in town and country.

Moreover, there was no possibility of engendering new attitudes
within the CCP or the population at large if the intellectuals were
still labouring under leftist restraints. There was obviously a wide
gulf between the worlds of an urban intellectual and a barely literate
peasant, but one spin-off of 'politics taking command' was that all
spheres of activity were interrelated. No Chinese was an island. If
the intellectuals were under leftist attack, rural cadres could assume,
correctly, that they should gear up for a leftist assault in the countryside.[5] Equally, if egalitarianism and the 'communist five styles' were
criticized in the rural areas, officials in charge of culture would know
that new measures were also called for in the intellectual sphere.

Thus on 24 November 1960, three weeks after the Twelve-Article
Emergency Directive for Agriculture was issued, the CC's Culture
and Education 'Small Group' (*wenjiao xiaozu*), whose head was Lu
Dingyi, the director of the CC's Propaganda Department, held a

work conference with central and provincial officials to discuss the relationships between politics and professional activities, quality and quantity, and how cultural enterprises could help serve agriculture.[6] This meeting spawned a series of investigations, meetings, and, finally, a number of programmatic documents on the lines of those for the economy, sanctioned by a directive from Mao and the CC.[7] They included the Fourteen Articles on Science, issued on 19 July 1961,[8] the Sixty Articles on Higher Education, issued on 15 September 1961,[9] the Eight Articles on Literature and Art, issued on 30 April 1962,[10] and the more focused Ten Articles on Theatres and Troupes and Thirty-two Articles on Films.[11] Again, the order in which these successive programmes emerged indicated both the priorities of China's leaders and current political problems, for work on all of them began about the same time.

The Fourteen Articles on Science

Mao had developed little taste for the natural sciences during his youth, though his catholic reading habits did imbue him with an abiding interest in the theories of Charles Darwin. He was of course aware of the importance of science and technology to China's development programme, but he tended to stress them more during those relatively brief periods—for instance, in the first half of 1956—when he was not obsessed with politics and class struggle.[12] The immediate aftermath of the GLF was one such time, and if Mao's participation in the discussions leading up to the drafting of the Fourteen Articles on Science seems to have been negligible, his imprimatur at the end of the process was nevertheless vital.[13] It was doubtless the absence of Maoist utterances that later enabled Cultural Revolution radicals to denounce the Fourteen Articles.[14]

During the GLF, scientific organizations were not immune from disruption by the campaign mania;[15] some scientists were criticized as 'white and expert' (*bai zhuan*), and all were spending 50 per cent of their time on political study or manual labour.[16] At the end of 1960, the Shanghai branch of the Chinese Academy of Sciences (CAS), a body which embraced the social sciences,[17] held a 'meeting of immortals' (*shenxian hui*) at which all could air their views freely in order to resolve problems. There were complaints that the GLF had resulted in research projects being wiped out; science, it was argued, had no class character.[18] Outsiders could not lead experts, and novices should not outrank established scholars, familiar cries from the Hundred Flowers period.[19]

The Shanghai forum seems to have been of great importance in alerting Beijing officials charged with handling the intellectuals to the need to take new initiatives if scientists and others were to be energized for a helpful role in the nation's crisis. On 3 January, Zhou Yang, a deputy director of the CC's Propaganda Department, telephoned Zhang Jingfu, a vice-president of the CAS, secretary of its leading party members group, and a deputy director of the State Science and Technology Commission (SSTC), and asked: 'Could CAS come up with some proposals to reassure people [*anmin gaoshi*] which we could distribute nationwide?'[20]

Two days later, Zhang mobilized Du Runsheng, who would become secretary-general of CAS in May, and Wu Mingyu, a young academy official, who drafted a science programme for the CAS embodied in fifteen articles. This February draft, along with the complaints raised at the Shanghai forum, were discussed from 22 February to 6 March 1961, at an expanded meeting of the CAS party members leading group. Interestingly, Zhang felt it necessary to preface this new effort to provide scientists with greater leeway by differentiating them from the 'bourgeois rightists' who had attacked the CCP four years earlier: 'Today's intellectuals are different from 1957; the great majority of them listen to the party.' But this did not short-circuit controversy at the Beijing meeting over what some academicians apparently felt was a retrograde policy being peddled in Shanghai.[21]

After the Beijing conference, Zhang Jingfu set in train a series of intensive consultations on the draft with various scientific establishments. It seems to have been at this point that the nation's most senior science policy official, Marshal Nie Rongzhen, took a hand, transforming what was up till that time a CAS project into a national programme.[22]

Marshal Nie, one of only ten generals promoted to that rank in 1955, had been deputy and then acting chief-of-staff of the People's Liberation Army (PLA) in the aftermath of the communist takeover. In 1956, after a three-year hiatus due to ill health, the marshal began a decade-long career in charge of the nation's science and technology.[23] In the CCP scheme of things, his power lay not so much in his directorships of the SSTC and the Defence Science and Technology Commission,[24] but rather in his behind-the-scenes leadership of the important 'central science small group' (*zhongyang kexue xiaozu*) and probably, too, his long friendship with Deng Xiaoping.[25]

The members of the science small group were: Song Renqiong, until recently minister of the Second Ministry of Machine Building, in charge of China's nuclear programme, now 1st secretary of the CC's new Northeast regional bureau;[26] Wang Heshou, minister of the Ministry of the Metallurgical Industry; Zhang Jingfu; Han Guang, like Zhang a deputy director of the SSTC; and Yu Guangyuan, a future SSTC deputy director, currently head of the science section of the CC's Propaganda Department.[27] Throughout most of the Cultural Revolution, Marshal Nie was in good standing and fairly immune to criticism, and so Zhang Jingfu and Han Guang, along with leaders of the CC's Propaganda Department, bore the brunt of criticism as the most influential figures in the preparation of the Fourteen Articles, though in his memoirs the marshal assumed final responsibility.[28]

In March 1961, Marshal Nie was resting in Hangzhou, perhaps convalescing (*tiyang*) after a renewal of his earlier health problems. He summoned there both the CAS drafters and a team from the Shanghai branch of the academy that had drawn up its own programme, and told them to hammer out a compromise draft programme. A combined team consisted of Han Guang, Zhang Jingfu, Du Runsheng, with Liu Shuzhou, a municipal party secretary who doubled as president of the Shanghai academy, and Shu Wen, also representing Shanghai, set to work in Hangzhou and Shanghai, with Wu Mingyu again acting as drafter under Du's supervision. A fourteen-article programme was presented to Marshal Nie in Hangzhou and after further revision it became the April draft.[29]

This second version of a science programme, along with a draft report on it to the CC, was then discussed and further revised in Beijing in May at yet another expanded conference of the CAS leading party members group, most of the conferees coming from north and east China. Zhang Jingfu and others criticized themselves for excessive harshness during the Anti-Rightist Campaign in 1957 and the struggle against right-opportunism after the purge of Marshal Peng Dehuai in 1959, and they called for 'reversals of verdicts' (*pingfan*) and the opportunity for scholars to bloom and contend (*ming fang*) as during the Hundred Flowers. An important focus of discussion was an experiment carried out in the Chemistry Institute to have less politics in its activities (*zhengzhi tuipei*).

Finally, after the conclusion of the conference, Zhang Jingfu, Du Runsheng, Gong Yuzhi, a chemistry graduate from Qinghua University working for the CC's Propaganda Department, and Wu Mingyu prepared a final (June) draft of the Fourteen Articles and the report that would accompany it to the Politburo. It was this version that earned the vigorous criticism of Cultural Revolution radicals. The burden of that criticism was the omission of key political phrases mandated by Nie Rongzhen.[30]

The February, April, and June drafts

An examination of the February, April, and June drafts does reveal small but significant changes, with the April version being arguably the most politically correct: it was more strident in its affirmation of past successes than the February version and contained key phrases omitted in the June version, though the June preamble in most respects simply repeated April phraseology.[31] The first sentence of the April preamble read: 'In the past three years, under the guidance of the Thought of Mao Zedong and the party's general line, scientific enterprises have advanced along a broad highway of high speed development'. There was no reference to Mao's Thought in the February version and it was excised in the June version.[32] This was in line with the dropping of the reference to Mao's Thought from the CCP constitution at the 8th Congress in 1956,[33] and the decision, confirmed by Mao himself as early as 1953, that the correct phrase to be used was 'the works of Chairman Mao' (*Mao Zhuxi zhuzuo*), which would have sounded bizarre in the quoted passage.[34] The force of this Cultural Revolution complaint is further diminished by the fact that in two more appropriate places elsewhere in the June version, the importance of studying Mao's works is stressed; in one case, the equivalent article in the April version has no reference to Mao's works.[35]

Yet it seems unlikely that this was a bogus issue dreamed up by Cultural Revolution polemicists. The 'Thought of Mao Zedong' was used again during the GLF, notably by Defence Minister Lin Biao and Kang Sheng, an alternate member of the Politburo, both of whom emerged as key allies of Mao at the outset of the Cultural Revolution. During the GLF, another alternate member of the Politburo, the director of the Propaganda Department, Lu Dingyi, had attempted to moderate the extravagant claims made for Mao Thought.[36] In early 1961, the radical style of the GLF still lingered, and in April Lu Dingyi remarked sarcastically: 'At present there is still another new label, namely the "Thought of Mao Zedong," which one sees stuck on everywhere as if just sticking it on is itself the Thought of Mao Zedong . . . Sticking on labels is simplistic and crude, better left than right; in my view this is not struggle . . . Doing it is not just worthless, it is positively harmful.'[37]

Other differences in the preambles include descriptions of achievements during the GLF: 'significant' (*you yiyi*) in February, but 'great' (*weida*) in April, and 'tremendous' (*juda*) in June. The February version talked hopefully of the emergence of a corps of red and expert scientists, but the April version expressed no such explicit confidence in the political reliability of the scientific community. Whereas the February version talked of the mistakes made by CAS 'party organizations' in running science, the April version avoided criticizing the party by referring more neutrally to 'units' and by inserting a phrase about the novelty of the problems arising during the GLF to excuse errors. This latter phrase was omitted from the June version, along with the reaffirmation in the April version of the GLF slogan 'Go all out, aim high' (*guzu ganjing, lizheng shangyou*).[38] Summing up the lessons of success, the April preamble stated: 'All these fully prove that the party's various general and specific policies towards scientific enterprises are correct, and that the road on which we are travelling is correct.' The June version omitted the assertion of the correctness of the party's policies, just referring to the correctness of the national road.[39]

There was a fair degree of correspondence between the topics of the articles in the three versions, but with some differences in their titles, ordering, content, and phraseology.[40] All three versions put at or near the top the importance of research work being carried on in conditions of 'relative stability' (*xiangdui jiding*) after the (unmentioned) upheaval of the GLF, and the April and June versions laid down a 'five fixed' formula to ensure it: fixed direction, duties, personnel, equipment, system. The April and June versions also placed high value upon taking practicality and the special features of science into account when making plans, again a backward glance at the GLF. Professionals who were understandably wary after the scorn poured upon expertise by Mao during the GLF, were encouraged in another article to do what he had told the masses to do then: dare to think, speak, and act.[41]

All three versions sought to guarantee research time, five days out of six; all advocated the systematic rearing of new cadres, and the strengthening of scientific collaboration between units;[42] all reaffirmed Mao's 'Let a hundred flowers bloom, let a hundred schools contend' policy aborted four years earlier by the Anti-Rightist Campaign; all echoed Mao's recent re-emphasis on investigation and research.[43]

One way to see if there were justification for the complaints made during the Cultural Revolution is by comparing what the acceptable April draft had to say about politics with how the other two versions handled this topic. The February version had no equivalent of Article 11 in the April version entitled 'Strengthen political and ideological work', which became Article 12, 'Strengthen ideological and political work', in the June version. The preamble of the April Article 11 led off with the ringing declaration that 'scientific work must be on behalf of proletarian politics'—a phrase missing from the June version—but the force of this assertion was diminished by the explanation that it simply meant raising the scientific basis for the modernization of agriculture, industry, and defence, which was by implication the criteria for calling a scientist red and expert.[44] The preamble of the June Article 12 omitted all but the final sentence of the April preamble, but this was firmly politically correct: 'Ideological and political work is the lifeblood of scientific research work; at no time ought it to be weakened, rather it must be continually strengthened.'[45]

The sub-clauses of the two articles did not correspond precisely, but there was a fair degree of overlap. A striking feature of both was the emphasis on a Hundred Flowers-style 'gentle breeze, mild rain' (*he feng xi yu*) approach to political problems, and on self-study methods.[46] The April version dealt with how party groups in scientific units should respond to major national political campaigns, whereas by June the drafters apparently felt that this was a remote enough issue to be omitted. Instead, party organs were instructed how to look after the living conditions of scientific personnel.

An examination of these specifically political articles, along with references to politics in other articles, does not suggest that the June version significantly watered down a radical April version as alleged during the Cultural Revolution. Indeed, in some places the June version sounds more orthodox by radical standards. For instance, in the April version of an article on promoting investigation and research, this work method is depicted as one which enables leading cadres to direct scientific work. In the identically entitled June version, investigation is enlarged to include the study of Marxism-Leninism and Mao's works, as well as CCP's policies, and is seen as a means by which outsiders, that is, party non-scientists, can lead science.[47]

Again, in another two identically entitled and largely similar articles (14) on leadership systems, the April version warned against substituting party leadership for administrative leadership, whereas the longer June version seemed to lay more stress on party supervision of administrative leadership.[48]

Analysis of the differences in content and terminology between the three versions suggests that in February the focus was on preparing an internal document to revive a demoralized CAS, and political considerations were assumed rather than stated; but by April the object had become to prepare a document for national application, and political concerns had to be addressed four-square, perhaps at the instigation of Marshal Nie. In the process of injecting greater political content, opinions on precise formulations may have fluctuated between April and June, but it does not seem that there was an underhand attempt by the drafters to undercut any April guidelines that the Marshal may have issued.

Nie Rongzhen's summary

According to the memoirs of Marshal Nie, who summarized the main purposes of the final version of the Fourteen Articles in some detail,[49] there were three articles that were key to the whole document's purpose and that aroused the particular ire of the cultural revolutionaries.

First was the assertion in Article 1 that the fundamental tasks of research organizations were to produce results and train competent personnel. This responded to a sense that research institutions worked in haphazard manner. The June provisions were also in the April version, though in the document's preamble.

The second was the definition of 'red' intellectuals and the relationship between redness and expertise, which Nie discussed at some length at the top of his written report to Mao and the Politburo.[50] Article 11 of the Fourteen Articles laid down that to be a red scientist, one had to support CCP leadership and socialism, and use one's specialized knowledge on behalf of socialism, criteria adopted from Mao's 1957 speech on contradictions among the people. To be red and expert meant just that: one without the other was no use. Scientists had gradually to develop a proletarian world view, but in most cases, keenness in research was the concrete manifestation of a socialist consciousness. According to Nie, these criteria aroused 'enthusiasm' among intellectuals.[51]

In his written report, Nie advocated dropping the use of the term 'white expert' (*bai zhuan*). One could criticize the politics of someone who was against the party and socialism, but using this epithet tended to make people feel that expertise was always associated with whiteness.[52]

In the April version, there was no specific article on red and expert, but it was mentioned in the preamble to Article 11 and, as indicated above, the definition was implicitly similar. Presumably consultations on the basis of the April version caused the drafters to realize that to reassure scientists fully, the concept of red and expert would have to be much more explicit. Thus most of the brief preamble to Article 11 on strengthening political leadership in the April version became an expanded new Article 11 on uniting with, educating, and remoulding the intellectuals in the June version, in which the definition of red and expert was spelled out. The rest of the April Article 11 resurfaced as Article 12 in the June version, as already pointed out.

The third article pinpointed by Marshal Nie was the final one adjuring the party not to interfere in academic leadership of science. This was designed to prevent arrogant party commandism which led to 'empty political talk, formalism, and issuing arbitrary directives'. Hence there were stipulations that grass-roots party committees could not supervise research, and that the views of individual party members were just that and no more. Again, as indicated above, the two versions were similar, and if anything, the June one appeared more politically correct by Cultural Revolution standards.[53]

Politburo discussion of the Fourteen Articles

Whatever Marshal Nie's precise role in the drafting process, he led the team which presented the final version to the Politburo on 6 July, and both he and Zhang Jingfu made presentations. Mao was not there, but Liu Shaoqi, Zhou Enlai, Deng Xiaoping, Peng Zhen, and Li Fuchun are quoted by Nie as making approving statements.[54] In a Cultural Revolution denunciation of this session, there is no mention of Nie Rongzhen being there—because that would have made a nonsense of the attack on the June draft—only of Zhang Jingfu making the report. But the quotations in it, though only from Liu and Deng among those mentioned by the Marshal, correspond so precisely to parts of the longer quotations in Nie's memoirs,[55] that it seems reasonable to suppose that other quotations in the Cultural Revolution version may be accurate even though not confirmed by Nie.

Both versions quote Liu Shaoqi as saying that the 'current problem was there were deviations and we should admit this. Whatever deviations there were must be rectified. The Party had been in power these years. That's a good thing, an achievement. We were obeyed even if our directives were arbitrary. But we could not go on like that, or we would trip and fall.'[56] Marshal Nie does not mention Liu as also saying: 'Are our achievements [*chengji*] in fact great [*weida*], is there no boastfulness in saying that! . . . False claims must be denied by oneself and a self-criticism must be quickly made.'[57] This seems and may indeed have been harmless enough, but presumably it was quoted in this hostile source because it could be implicitly seen as a criticism of Mao's well-known optimistic summary of the state of the GLF on the eve of the 1959 Lushan conference: 'In general, achievements are great [*chengji weida*], the problems are numerous, [but] the future is bright.'[58]

Deng is quoted by both Marshal Nie and by the Cultural Revolution source as saying: 'Leading Party cadres should befriend scientists . . . What was needed was to work conscientiously as the orderlies of the scientists . . .'[59] Harmless enough in ordinary times, but in the fevered anti-intellectual atmosphere of the Cultural Revolution enough to damn a leader who had already been targeted.

The Cultural Revolution source does not quote Zhou Enlai's approval of the Fourteen Articles presumably because that would have tarred him as another anti-party person, but he apparently gave it, and asked that the document be distributed additionally through the finance/trade and culture/education systems, to both of which it would be beneficial.[60] The source does quote, however, from Kang Sheng, who emerged as one of Mao's leading collaborators during the Cultural Revolution:

The crucial problem is how Marxism-Leninism should lead science. There should be a few more sentences [on this]. Marxism-Leninism has a function in leading science . . .. As for 'natural science has no class character': do we want this formulation which has never before been used in a party document. Science becomes a system, and so there is the problem of its philosophy and its world outlook. At that point can we say it has no class character? Lenin and Engels said: 'Many natural scientists have special skills in science, but are fools when it comes to philosophy'.[61]

According to cultural revolutionaries, there were further revisions in the document after the meeting. But Kang Sheng's intervention had no effect, because Article 10 continued to maintain that science had no class character, and to assert the need to learn from Western achievements. This had been the line laid down in April by propaganda director, Lu Dingyi, when he had criticized labelling at an education conference: 'It is not only in the natural sciences that one shouldn't stick on labels at will, saying this is socialist, that's capitalist, this is capitalist, that's proletarian; in my view, one cannot stick on labels at will in the social sciences either.'[62]

Marshal Nie's memoirs make clear his satisfaction at the passage of the Fourteen Articles, and subsequently Mao gave his approval. Even if China's crisis made it inevitable, this was clearly a major achievement. But though the memoirs talk of momentum being generated by the Fourteen Articles, it is significant that in this case too, a further meeting had to be held in the more hopeful atmosphere generated by the Seven Thousand Cadres Conference at the start of 1962, to produce a new science programme;[63] and even so, in the same year, probably after he had swung the CCP leftwards again, Mao talked of the need for considerable modification of some of the articles.[64]

Chen Yi on red and expert

A month after the Fourteen Articles had been discussed by the Politburo, one of its members, Nie Rongzhen's fellow marshal, Foreign Minister Chen Yi, conveyed the ruling consensus on red and expert to the graduating seniors of Beijing's institutions of higher learning.[65] Perhaps because of his customary downright manner, of which more below, or because he was speaking to young people whom he considered politically unsophisticated or teachers whom he considered excessively doctrinaire, Chen Yi made his points bluntly.

The effort to build socialism in China demanded various types of talents, among them specialists in politics who graduated from the party, Young Communist League (YCL), and similar schools. But politics and professional skills should not be seen as in opposition to each other. Marx and Mao had both acquired considerable specialist knowledge on the way to becoming politicians. All Chinese leaders combined professional and political skills. In case these polymaths might overawe his audience, Chen Yi cited the case of China's most famous Peking Opera star, Mei Lanfang; there was no need and no point for him to become familiar with political texts. But to attain Mei Lanfang's level of fame in order to be excused politics would also have seemed a remote possibility, so Chen Yi then cited the case of trainee diplomats who had to learn foreign languages and about foreign affairs, and by implication had no time to study Marxist tomes. So long as such people followed the lead of the party, that was sufficient.[66]

In the early years of the regime, it had been right to stress politics, Chen argued, but the young people of today had been nurtured for some years by the party and steeled by successive political movements. China had now to strengthen professional studies, to foster a large corps of specialists for economic development. 'What one calls modern industry, agriculture, science, and culture are the manifestation of socialist politics. This is our most important political duty', Chen stated. Citing a favourite analogy of his, he said that a pilot deficient in political training might flee to the enemy, but a badly trained pilot would simply be shot down by the enemy and what use would he be?[67]

The principal time and the bulk of the effort of students in specialist schools should be directed towards acquiring professional knowledge; one cannot demand that they emulate students at party schools and devote their principal time to studying politics and high-level Marxist-Leninist theory. Nor can one expect them to do deep research into political theory and various concrete policies (like the various policies on the communes).[68]

Chen Yi quoted admonitions to work hard from Confucius and his Han dynasty disciple Dong Zhongshu to strengthen the resolve of his audience, but even more striking was his criticism of a current conventional wisdom among students conveyed by the phrase 'thoroughly red and specialized' (*hongtou zhuanshen*). He expressed his disbelief that an individual would have the time truly to become both a politician and a specialist. Like Nie Rongzhen, Chen also rejected the epithet 'white specialist'. So long as people contributed to socialist construction, taking less part in political movements was not blameworthy. Chen Yi's only concern was that neglect of politics should not mean coming into conflict with the party leadership.[69]

Drafting an educational programme

That Chen Yi's speech to the graduating seniors came under fire during the Cultural Revolution was hardly surprising since a main focus of that movement was rearing new generations of radical successors.[70] For the same reason, while all the programmatic documents prepared during 1961 were later denounced, the Sixty Articles on Higher Education came in for particularly sharp attack as representing a retreat from Maoist ideals laid out during the GLF: stronger CCP leadership, greater concentration on politics, the integration of mental and manual labour, and the encouragement of schools run by the people (*min ban*).[71]

In fact, the GLF programme for education, like other GLF innovations, was supported in 1958 by Liu Shaoqi and other leaders responsible for this area, like propaganda chief Lu Dingyi.[72] With massive devolution of control to provinces and lower-level administrations—responsibility for 187 out of 229 institutions of higher learning was transferred downwards[73]—the State Council lost contact with reality, plans were abandoned, unbridled expansion took place, and quality plummeted. In the first eight months of 1958, the following claims were reported: 90 m. people had attained literacy, with 67 per cent of all counties reporting the elimination of illiteracy; 93.9 per cent of all school-age children were in school, 87 per cent of counties having universalized primary education; there were 26,000 new middle schools, and the total number of students had increased 47 per cent; there were 800 new institutions of higher education, and many provinces vowed to universalize higher education within fifteen years.[74]

As in other areas, a retreat began in 1959. Claims and plans for educational expansion were scaled down, greater emphasis was placed on quality, unviable schools were closed down, and the amount of manual labour in the curriculum was more precisely delineated.[75] Even so, as in other spheres, the reining in of the GLF in the first half of 1959 was aborted after the Lushan conference, and educational expansion spurted again in 1960.[76] Realism and retrenchment began only in 1961, though the educational ideals of the GLF had been put on the back burner by Chinese leaders even earlier.[77]

TABLE 5.1. *Expansion and contraction in higher education, 1957–1963* (numbers of institutions)

Year	Comprehensive universities	Industrial colleges	Agricultural colleges	Teachers colleges	Medical colleges
1957	17	44	28	58	37
1958	27	251	096	171	134
1959	29	274	99	175	142
1960	37	472	180	227	204
1961	32	269	106	163	158
1962	31	206	69	110	118
1963	29	120	44	61	85

Source: *Jiaoyu Nianjian*, p. 965.

In October 1960, Lu Dingyi had sent his deputy Zhou Yang to make some preliminary enquiries into the state of education at

Peking University, the China People's University, and Beijing Teachers College, from which he apparently concluded that there was too much manual labour and that the curriculum had been altered too much.[78] The formal turning point, as in other intellectual spheres, seems to have been the national work conference summoned by the CC's Culture and Education Small Group (*wenjiao xiaozu*) from 24 November to 12 December 1960. Members of the small group almost certainly included: Lu Dingyi (chair); Kang Sheng (deputy chair); Lin Feng, a senior official who had filled a number of leading posts in the educational field; Zhang Jichun, director of the State Council office on culture and education, a job which Lin Feng had done earlier; possibly Zhou Yang, a deputy director of propaganda in charge of culture; and Yang Xiufeng, Minister of Education.[79]

Members of the small group reported to the conference, and, presumably basing themselves in part on the ensuing criticism of 'communist style', extravagance, and commandism, finalized a statement on cultural and educational work for 1961 and the succeeding period. The report, which was approved by the CC secretariat in February 1961, made three sets of points: if labour power was to be freed up to help agriculture, then students over 16 in rural schools ought to amount to no more than about 2 per cent of the rural labour force; attempts to universalize primary education should take account of differences between town and country, middle-school education should be spread in different forms, and control should be kept on the growth of spare-time education; in higher education, the raising of quality should be the number-one task.[80]

When the CC secretariat met to discuss educational and cultural work in the first half of 1961, Deng Xiaoping's comments indicated the main worries of Chinese leaders. He affirmed that in science and education, standards should be set not by quantity but by quality. Universalization had to do with ordinary education; higher education demanded the raising of quality. Deng gave his blessing to running fewer schools but running them well, and to running keypoint (*zhongdian*) or high-quality schools. Schools needed order, and he looked to the production of the Sixty Articles to provide them with rules and regulations.[81] After the central work conference in Beijing in May–June, the Ministry of Education called its own meeting to discuss how to 'shorten the front' in education too. Decisions were taken to reduce the number of students in higher institutions by 22 per cent during 1961–3, upper middle-school students by

16 per cent, and lower middle-school students by 18 per cent.[82] The actual reduction in college students was by almost 21 per cent.

TABLE 5.2. *Numbers of students in higher education*

1957	441,181
1958	659,627
1959	811,947
1960	961,623
1961	947,166
1962	829,699
1963	750,118

Source: Jiaoyu Nianjian, p. 966.

Detailed investigations on which the Sixty Articles were based had begun in early 1961. In February, Lin Feng led a team that included Jiang Nanxiang, one of the deputy ministers of education, to Peking University.[83] On Lu Dingyi's orders, investigations were carried out at Qinghua University by Zhang Jichun, at Tianjin University by Yang Xiufeng, and at Wuhan University by Zhang Ziyi, a deputy director of the CC's Propaganda Department. Yang's inspection lasted over two months and led to his drafting some provisions on how the system of university presidents taking responsibility under party committees might work. In March, a CC directive authorized the preparation of what turned out to be the Sixty Articles and in April, Jiang Nanxiang began to draft them.[84] It turned out to be a controversial process, involving successive revisions, the final document being the seventeenth. The whole process apparently evolved as follows:[85]

Drafting of the Sixty Articles

1960
Oct.   Zhou Yang investigates three Beijing universities.
Nov.–Dec.   *Wenjiao xiaozu* conference on education.
1961
Jan.–Feb.   Ministry of Education conference on keypoint colleges.
Jan.–Mar.   Education officials investigate Peking, Qinghua, Tianjin, Wuhan universities.
Mar.   Ministry of Education gives *Wenjiao xiaozu* a report on keypoint colleges.
Mar.   CC issues directive ordering a plan for higher education to be drafted.

Mar.–Apr?	Lin Feng and party secretaries of some Beijing universities discuss drafting work.
Apr.	Jiang Nanxiang starts drafting Sixty Articles, focusing only on keypoint schools.
Apr.	Propaganda Department/Ministry of Education/Ministry of Culture conference on college teaching materials.
May	Conference of university party secretaries from various regions.
June	Jiang Nanxiang convenes 'three thirds' conference: university party secretaries, veteran specialists newly admitted to the party, and non-party specialists.
July	*Wenjiao xiaozu* discusses Sixty Articles; after meeting, new draft prepared but rejected in favour of further revisions of original draft; Ministry of Education conference on Sixty Articles.
July–Aug.	CC secretariat discusses and agrees on Sixty Articles at Beidaihe; Deng co-signs letter to PSC explaining document and directive, authorizing experimental implementation.
Aug.	Opinions of party secretaries at major universities and at provincial level sought. Chen Yi addresses graduating college seniors on red and expert.
Sept.	Lu Dingyi explains Sixty Articles at CC Lushan work conference; seventeenth revision approved.
Sept.–Oct.	Ministry of Education conference on Sixty Articles.

Trouble with the drafting process appears to have started at the May conference of university party secretaries summoned to discuss Jiang Nanxiang's first version. While the party secretaries of Peking and Tianjin universities were supportive, others argued that the 1958 educational revolution ought to be fully affirmed and that the new elements in education ought to be protected. When Jiang reported all this to Lu Dingyi, the latter waxed sarcastic, allegedly accusing the defenders of GLF educational ideas of fearing criticism. Lu told Jiang to call the 'three thirds' conference, at which party secretaries would be outnumbered two to one by experts. This occasion proved to be more in tune with Lu's current thinking. Complaints were aired about the disruptiveness of GLF educational policies; about the tension between teachers and students, between the party and non-party people, and between old and young; about excessive extramural activities and manual labour, which had disrupted the normal teaching schedules; about how, compared to 1957, students were required to attend too few classes, read too few books, and acquire too little knowledge. Everything had been a mess since 1958 and the quality of teaching had declined. With Lu Dingyi's approval, Jiang prepared his fourth draft on the basis of the opinions expressed at the conference.[86]

The July meeting of the Culture and Education Small Group under Lu Dingyi's leadership was held to discuss the new version. According to Cultural Revolution sources, at this meeting Lu and others expressed opposition to the inappropriately constraining use of Mao Zedong Thought in all academic matters, which Lu compared to the Buddha's palm (*rulaifo zhangxin*), from which not even the legendary Monkey King could escape.[87] In place of Mao's educational aim of rearing 'cultured workers with a socialist consciousness', the small group preferred the formulation 'various specialist talents for the needs of socialist construction'; it downplayed class struggle, emphasizing uniting with the bourgeois intellectuals and not stressing educating and remoulding them; and it restricted the role of the departmental-level party committees.

Lu decided that Jiang Nanxiang's draft concentrated too much on nuts-and-bolts academic and administrative affairs, and spent too little space on ideology, policy, and principles, so another group of propaganda officials, led by Tong Dalin, was entrusted with revising the fourth draft.[88] The forty-eight-article new version which they produced was allegedly 'even more reactionary' than the draft they were revising. It stressed collaboration with bourgeois intellectuals even more strongly; further diminished the role of the party; preferred professorial to collective academic leadership; abolished university-run factories; and opposed the trinity of teaching, scientific research, and manual labour. The 'revisionism' in this fifth draft was too 'barefaced' to be seen outside the small group; it was suppressed and the long-suffering Jiang Nanxiang was ordered to prepare a sixth draft. Regrettably, from the radicals' point of view, Kang Sheng, although a deputy head of the small group, rarely attended its meetings to fight their corner, apparently because of his involvement in the propaganda struggle with the CPSU.[89]

There followed another conference, called by Yang Xiufeng, the Minister of Education, and the party group of the ministry, which passed the document, only to have matters reopened by Lu Dingyi. Under the propaganda director's supervision, five major changes were agreed:

1. Running colleges should be the responsibility of the 'college administration committee, with the college principal at its head, under the leadership of the college party committee'.
2. Scientific research institutions should not be committed to the three unities of teaching, research, and productive labour.
3. Teaching and research sections, as well as teachers, had a responsibility for nurturing new talent.
4. The amount of time that students had to spend in physical labour should be reduced and teachers and students in particular specialities need not participate in productive labour.
5. Militia training should not consume excessive time.[90]

An agreed draft was then taken to a series of meetings of the secretariat, presided over by Deng Xiaoping, in Beidaihe in late July through 5 August, to discuss the Sixty Articles as well as the Seventy Articles on Industry.[91] Deng seems to have done little to the draft except drop the phrase 'foster proletarian ideology, eliminate bourgeois ideology' (*xing wu mie zi*), and limit the political demands upon students to patriotism, a socialist spirit, communist morality, and supporting CCP leadership and socialism, and being willing to serve socialist enterprises and the people. He explained that it was demanding too much to write in that students had to establish a proletarian communist world outlook. Rightist professors also had their uses. Comparing the Sixty Articles with equivalent documents from Sweden, the Soviet Union, and the KMT period, Deng observed: 'Ours is best. This is a good document which has something of the past, something of the modern, something Chinese, something foreign; it solves the big problems.'[92]

Kang Sheng, it was later claimed, made a strong and principled, but ultimately unsuccessful struggle to insert demands for strengthening basic-level party leadership, the Hundred Flowers policy, and colleges running production units, and tried vainly to have more emphasis put on GLF success than failure in the directive that was drawn up to accompany the Sixty Articles.[93]

On 5 August, the secretariat agreed that Lu Dingyi would present the final draft to the forthcoming work conference and that three work teams would be sent to Peking University, Tianjin University, and Fudan University in Shanghai to solicit further opinions. Thereafter, Deng co-signed a letter to Mao and the rest of the PSC, explaining both the draft of the Sixty Articles and a CC directive authorizing their experimental use.[94]

The seventeenth draft of the Sixty Articles was examined at the Lushan work conference in September, which was presided over by Mao, a fact not acknowledged by hostile accounts during the Cultural Revolution. The PSC formally approved it for experimental use on 15 September.[95] Then Lu Dingyi held another conference of education officials in Beijing, at which he said that the programme would be tried out till 1963 at half the nation's higher institutions.[96]

The Sixty Articles on Higher Education[97]

The general principles of the Sixty Articles began with a series of politically correct references, ignored by Cultural Revolution critics, to the need for education to serve proletarian politics and to be integrated with productive labour, along with a quote from Mao laying down that 'Our educational guiding principles ought to bring about the moral, intellectual and physical education of those receiving education in order to turn them into cultured workers with a socialist consciousness'. Deng's phrasing about the demands on students was there, immediately followed by requirements to study Marxism-Leninism and Mao's works and to be steeled through productive labour and practical work, in order to establish gradually the viewpoints of the proletarian class, of manual labour, of the masses, and of dialectical materialism.

Higher institutions had to take teaching as their main focus; had to strengthen party leadership and co-operation with non-party people; implement the Hundred Flowers policy within the compass of the six political criteria laid down in Mao's 1957 contradictions speech;[98] encourage free discussion in the natural sciences; critically inherit the Chinese tradition in philosophy and the social sciences in order to develop Marxist-Leninist theory; help in the ideological remoulding of the intellectuals while taking care to draw lines between their political problems, problems of world view, and academic problems; and had to distinguish between contradictions among the people and contradictions between the people and the enemy.[99]

A clear attempt was made to draw a line between the present and the frenetic days of the high tide of the GLF, when students and teachers spent long hours smelting 'steel' and performing other manual-labour jobs.[100] Theoretical analysis—'book larnin'—was not to be slighted in favour of practical work (art. 11). Political courses (art. 10) were limited to about 10 per cent of the mandatory eight months of teaching (art. 8) in science and engineering faculties and up to about 20 per cent in liberal arts faculties. Students still had to spend between a month and a month-and-a-half doing manual labour (art. 8), but there was a proviso for dropping this requirement in special cases (art. 16). Militia activities were not to be excessive and party and youth league activities were to occupy not more than six hours a week (art. 33). Two to two-and-a-half months were set aside for vacation, when teachers were supposed to be allowed to pursue their own researches, unbothered by demands from the school or outside units (art. 8). Faculty members were also supposed to be guaranteed five-sixths of their working time for professional activities (art. 30).[101]

Political messages remained in place. Since teaching was the basic mission of the college or university, teachers had to prepare themselves for their mission by the diligent study of Marxism-Leninism and Mao's works and self-conscious reform of their world view (art. 29). The party organization had the responsibility for propagating these doctrines among faculty and students (art. 44). However, the document cited some of Mao's more moderate approaches from 1957, instructing the party that all ideological work was designed to bring about a 'political climate in which there is both centralism and democracy, discipline and freedom, unity of purpose and personal ease of mind and liveliness'. Problems among the people had to be handled on the basis of 'unity-criticism-unity', using the methods of democracy, self-education, and 'gentle breeze and mild rain' (art. 45).[102]

Superficially the Sixty Articles was a politically acceptable document. Since it was prepared by the chief propagandists of the regime and passed by Mao, this is hardly surprising. The question arises: why did it arouse so much sound and fury during the Cultural Revolution? Probably for two reasons. First, it signified a return to order after the heady days of continuous revolution during the GLF, the golden era which the cultural revolutionaries looked back to and intended to restore. It was also a reaffirmation of conventional educational principles and thus implicitly a denial of the GLF experiments encouraging the fusing of work and education. Mao's continuing preference for the latter was underlined by his ringing letter of endorsement to the Jiangxi Labour University on its third anniversary on 1 August 1961.[103]

Secondly, and this applies to all the documents produced in 1961, the key did not really lie in the clauses or their language, but in how they were implemented. In a carefully balanced document like the

Sixty Articles, the general political atmosphere and the guidance of the appropriate leadership body, in this case the Propaganda Department, would determine whether officials emphasized moderation or political correctness. Clearly the guidance of the propagandists in 1961 was in the direction of moderation. But like the other programmatic documents of that year, the Sixty Articles was not implemented with full enthusiasm until the political atmosphere changed.

Chen Yi revives the Hundred Flowers

The Sixty Articles dealt with the intellectual élite. The propagandists had also to be concerned about the spiritual health of the 'broad masses', without whose toil the graduates of China's key-point universities would be able to achieve nothing. This meant reviving art forms beloved of the people, particularly the various types of Chinese opera.

The theatre had always been seen by the regime as a powerful vehicle with which to mobilize the masses. During the Anti-Japanese and civil wars, the CCP had organized thousands of village drama groups and sent its own teams to stage appropriate propaganda messages. After the CCP victory, the Ministry of Culture took over the task: in 1953, there were 41,000 performances by state and semi-private troupes before audiences totalling over 45 m.; in 1954, the figures rose to 57,000 performances and audiences of over 62 m.[104] In 1959, it was reported that there were amateur drama groups in all reasonably sized state factories, colleges, and middle schools, and an average of seven performing groups in each of the then 24,000 communes. Beijing had half-a-dozen opera houses and each province maintained at least one company to stage the local operatic form in the regional dialect.[105]

By the mid-1960s, according to Mao's ex-actress wife Jiang Qing, there were about 3,000 theatrical companies nationwide, excluding amateur and unlicensed groups. Of this figure, about 170 were either cultural troupes or professional companies performing modern drama. The remaining 2,800 were opera companies of various types performing traditional plays with their panoply of 'feudal' VIPs centre stage.[106] These were the dramas beloved of the masses which had to be protected and promoted by the party propagandists as part of the CCP's effort to raise national morale.

But the propagandists lacked credibility with the intellectuals who would have to nourish and perform traditional drama. As Zhou Enlai implied in a speech around this time, it was the CC's United

Front Work Department (UFWD) whose job it was to cosset non-party people, while the Propaganda Department was charged with remoulding them.[107] Lu Dingyi had been chosen to explain Mao's Hundred Flowers policy to the intellectuals in 1956, but had shown himself reluctant to support the Chairman's later invitation to outsiders to criticize the CCP.[108] Lu's deputy for literary affairs, Zhou Yang, had been a strong supporter of the Hundred Flowers, but the criticisms of the CCP raised at that time had revealed that he was widely distrusted within the intellectual community.[109] So the propagandists needed high-level backing if their message was to have any impact. The first spokesman to emerge was Marshal Chen Yi. Why? Probably *faute de mieux*.

Mao himself could not again come before the intellectuals with any credibility. They had trusted him in the spring of 1957, accepted his invitation to proffer criticisms of the CCP, only to have the Anti-Rightist Campaign unleashed against them that summer. Either he had been unable to protect them against his colleagues, or he had, as he later claimed, been trying to trap them all along.[110] Subsequently, he had derided their value during the GLF.[111] Liu Shaoqi, who had objected to Mao's invitation to non-party intellectuals to 'contend' with the CCP in 1957, was an equally unlikely advocate of a revival of the Hundred Flowers.[112] Of the other members of the PSC, Zhu De and Lin Biao had never been prominent in dealings with the intellectuals. Chen Yun liked to talk about the Suzhou ballad form Pingtan, but was an unlikely spokesman on culture in general.[113] Deng Xiaoping had supported Mao in early 1957, but as party General Secretary he had subsequently supervised the Anti-Rightist Campaign. Of China's top seven leaders, only Zhou Enlai still combined the credentials and the track-record to revive the Hundred Flowers, but he allowed Chen Yi to make the first major speech on this issue in 1961.

Kang Sheng was a credible spokesman on intellectual matters, and had a great taste for the theatre. According to hostile post-Cultural Revolution biographies, Kang spent the early months of 1961 seeing plays in Yunnan and Sichuan, rather than inspecting the economy, and took a somewhat unradical view of what could be staged.[114] However, his status as an alternate member of the Politburo was no higher than that of Lu Dingyi, and he was probably not prepared publicly to acknowledge his 'bourgeois' tastes. There is no indication that he took part in the conference on traditional opera held in the Zhongnanhai in March 1961 at the instance of Chen Yi.[115]

Of the full members of the Politburo under the PSC, Chen Yi was the most likely candidate to support the propagandists. He had had a better education than most high-ranking PLA leaders. Like Zhou Enlai, Deng Xiaoping, Li Fuchun, and Nie Rongzhen, he had been a worker-student in France for a couple of years after World War I.[116] Later he had a spell at the Université Franco-Chinoise in Beijing.[117] Marshal Chen was a reputable poet, worthy of mention alongside Mao, and, despite his military background and diplomatic portfolio, a credible spokesman on intellectual affairs, and accepted as such by his less well-read Politburo colleagues. Indeed, as a young man, he had at first resisted accepting the discipline of party membership, preferring the freedom of a literary career. When he was transferred from Shanghai to Beijing in 1954, this background was doubtless the reason why he was made the vice-premier in charge of culture.[118]

The speeches which Chen made in 1961–2, possibly encouraged by his predecessor as Foreign Minister, Zhou Enlai, were an important part of the regime's efforts to revive the spirit of the Hundred Flowers in the inauspicious aftermath of the Anti-Rightist Campaign and the GLF during which intellectuals and their pursuits had come under ferocious fire.[119] The activities which he encouraged would be a major target of the Cultural Revolution. Bolder and more headstrong than the ever-politic Zhou, the other senior spokesman for intellectual liberalization during this period, Chen Yi did his best to inspire his audiences with some of his own spirit.[120] The previous year he had written a poem which his comrades later convincingly suggested could stand for himself:

> Heavy snow weighs down the pine,
> But straight and proud stands the tree.
> When the snow melts you will see
> Its unbowed integrity.[121]

Chen's declared motive for speaking at the March conference was his horror at hearing Sichuan opera troupes talk about the need for root-and-branch transformation of traditional dramas in the interests of political correctness.[122] Coupling his remarks with a sideswipe at the excessive iconoclasm of the May Fourth Movement, Chen asserted: 'If this kind of opinion became current, our ancient drama would be done for [wandanle]. Over a thousand years of traditional opera, created in suffering from the Tang dynasty on, including Yuan qu and right up to the Beijing and local opera of today, would be ruined [zaotadiaole] in just our single generation.'[123] Chen's primary argument had to do with 'constraints' (*juxianxing*). Though one could dream dreams, in practice one was limited by the possibilities of one's era. He asserted that if Mao attempted to surpass current constraints to solve problems, even he would inevitably commit mistakes, a somewhat daring assertion in the light of Mao's hubris and failure during the GLF. Indeed, Chen went on to add that one might be able to bring about a leap forward (*gao yige yuejin*), but then new constraints emerged.

That being the case, historical personages like Cao Cao, the Empress Wu, and Zeng Guofan, who had been constrained by the possibilities of their times but had nevertheless made some contribution, should still be studied, even if they had no affinity with the people (*renminxing*). After all, Mao had once said that the CCP should study landlords and capitalists. Of course, such people had their shortcomings, but so did everyone; Mao himself had never claimed to be error-free. Mao should not be deified; anyone who tried to do so had ulterior motives, as the Stalin case proved.[124]

Chen derided those who anachronistically sought not just Marxism but even Mao Zedong Thought in old plays: 'Plays should give us pleasure and artistic satisfaction, not a political lesson. After eight hours of work, if we can derive a bit of "relaxation" [*yi*] from a play, enabling us to combine labour and leisure, it fills us with joy. Even if it's a tragedy, it can still give one artistic satisfaction.'[125] If a play were totally out of tune with the times then one should forget about it; otherwise, one should basically not change it except for some appropriate editing. He rejected the editing of *Xi xiang ji* (The West Chamber) by the noted playwright Tian Han and poked fun at the 'leftist' practice of the historian Wu Han (whose play about an upright Ming dynasty official *Hai Rui ba guan* [The Dismissal of Hai Rui] had recently been performed) who gave strange names to emperors as if to protect his audiences from thinking they were their rulers.[126]

In his role as Foreign Minister, Chen thanked members of his audience for reviving old plays and operas which had had a tremendously beneficial effect on China's image abroad. They had been performed all over South-East Asia, Europe, Latin America, and in Canada, where they had been seen even by Americans. China had a rich cultural heritage, a priceless treasure, which on no account should be ruined. 'It's nothing less than criminal for a Chinese to adopt a nihilistic attitude towards that heritage.'[127]

Having delivered himself of these evidently deeply felt views, Chen concluded by trying to bolster the courage of his listeners.

Critics, editors, and writers had too many inhibitions, he said. China had the system of democratic centralism which meant democracy as well as centralism, and officials with power should ensure that they did not criticize people to death. But artists should not fear a little criticism; after all Mao himself had borne it throughout the CCP's early years. 'We still want a hundred flowers to bloom, so cast aside your inhibitions, and speak up with your opinions.'[128]

As in his speech to graduating college seniors later in the year, Chen Yi said he was speaking off his own bat and not for the 'organization', and doubtless his vehemence was characteristically his own.[129] But no Politburo member spoke only for himself, and this speech must have been designed to cheer the cultural community in general, even though every intellectual would have been conscious of lacking Marshal Chen's political status, revolutionary record, and personal connections to fall back on in time of trouble.

Zhou Enlai intervenes

Three months after Chen Yi's speech, Zhou Enlai finally added his even more considerable voice to the promotion of a livelier artistic scene. His failure to lead the campaign as he had the similar one in January 1956 may have been due to the pressure of economic and diplomatic work; Zhou described his speech of 19 June 1961, as 'impromptu remarks, not a formal commentary', and confessed that he had spent 'only' two days preparing it.[130]

Or the delay may have been the product of discretion. Certainly by the time Zhou spoke, the political atmosphere had lightened as a result of Mao's acceptance at the Beijing work conference of the dispensability of commune mess-halls and the supply system. But Mao was not at his side as he had been in 1956, and Zhou's remarks, laced with many references to the Chairman, were far more carefully balanced than Chen Yi's. Though he did describe the banning of one particular opera as 'absolute nonsense', he tended to make this kind of point most strongly by reference to colleagues. He mentioned Chen Yun's comment that people went to the theatre to relax, not to attend a political class, and he quoted Marshal Zhu De as saying: 'I've been fighting all my life. I want to see some films that are not about fighting.'[131]

Zhou, who was addressing a joint meeting of participants attending forums on literature, art, and film scenarios, started by deploring the undemocratic work styles which prevented people from responding to Mao's call to dare to think, speak, and act. 'Of course, they still think, but they do not dare to speak or act.' Zhou told his audience that anything he said that day could be criticized or negated. Like Chen Yi, he pointed out that '[n]o one under the sun says the right thing 100 per cent of the time'; but unlike Chen, he did not specifically name Mao in this context.[132]

People lacked courage, Zhou indicated, because '[w]hatever a person says is judged by prescribed patterns, and if it doesn't fit them, it is held against him, his past is dug up, he is labelled and attacked'.[133] But though Zhou evidently disapproved of this practice, the creak of the fence as he sat firmly upon it was unlikely to persuade his audience to throw caution to the winds:

So I'm not advocating that the proletariat should abandon all formulas, pay no attention to a person's conduct, give no consideration to his past record and family background, attach no labels whatsoever to him and never punish him even if he really deserves it. No, that's not my view. I mean to call your attention to certain wrong, unreasonable practices that are quite common nowadays, primarily the five following: 1) judging a person according to a fixed criterion, 2) finding fault with him, 3) digging up his past record and family background, 4) attaching political labels to him, and 5) attacking him. It's time to put a stop to these practices. But that doesn't mean we should throw away our formulas altogether and pay no attention to serious mistakes. Everyone should let the proper authorities know his record and family background, so that they can help him remedy his mistakes . . . So we should adhere to our major principles and try to get rid of the bad practices. That is the only way to develop healthy practices and bring about a favourable atmosphere and a political environment in which there will be both centralism and democracy, both freedom and discipline, both unity of will and personal ease of mind and liveliness.[134]

Or, as he put it more succinctly later on: 'On the one hand we must wage class struggle; on the other we must consolidate the united front.'[135] Easier said by China's premier than done by the CCP's cadres.

Zhou made many of the right gestures, stressing quality over quantity, pillorying simplistic sloganeering, advocating official apologies to wronged artists, opposing illegal levies on writers' earnings, supporting popularly organized theatre troupes, upholding free choice of subject-matter, and, at the request of Marshal Nie Rongzhen, deploring attacks on professionals as 'white experts'.[136] But he recognized that there remained a credibility gap: 'Recently some people have begun wondering whether we have abandoned the policies adopted in 1956 with regard to intellectuals. No! Those policies remain valid. Being preoccupied with other matters in the past three years, we have not given them enough publicity.' Zhou's audience surely welcomed this forthright reaffirmation of the Hundred Flowers period—though Zhou never actually mentioned the Hundred Flowers policy by name—and may have been prepared to gloss over his feeble excuse about the GLF era, but they could hardly ignore his immediate return to the fence: '[W]e must heighten our political vigilance against class enemies at home and abroad and at the same time expand and strengthen internal unity.'[137]

One has to assume that Zhou's speech was not counter-productive, and that his remarks strengthened the hands of his less-senior colleagues in the CC's Propaganda Department who had the task of encouraging renewed cultural vitality in those grim days. But after Chen Yi's robustness, Zhou's nuances, not to mention his approving reference to the Anti-Rightist Campaign, gave writers and artists grounds for wondering whether the political weather might be too variable for the blooming of new flowers.[138]

The Eight Articles on Literature and Art

The propagandist assigned to the job of stimulating a new Hundred Flowers was Lin Mohan, head of the Literature Section of the Propaganda Department and Vice-Minister of Culture.[139] With Zhou Yang as his supervisor, Lin called six meetings to discuss problems in various artistic realms. To reassure his audiences, he guaranteed that in the event of any future rectification campaign his department would not give out the records of their remarks, especially not to their units, nor doctor (*zhengli*) them![140] Despite their previous buffetings, conferees aired familiar complaints: excessive politicization of the arts, insufficient creative freedom, even deficient cultural leadership as compared with the Soviet Union.[141]

By May 1961, Lin and a group of colleagues had started drafting ten articles on literature and art, which were discussed at a national conference in June–July, when Zhou Yang made the formulaic party self-criticism of excessive control and discrimination against non-party intellectuals familiar from the Hundred Flowers period and even earlier.[142] The draft was circulated to the provinces, revised, and recirculated. Then further revisions were begun in October under the leadership of Lu Dingyi himself. His principal collaborators were Zhou Yang and two literary figures, He Qifang and Zhang Guangnian.[143] On Lu's instructions, the ten articles were revised into the Eight Articles. According to a hostile Cultural

Revolution account, the main purpose was to excise many hard-core revisionist viewpoints on the relationship between politics and culture in order better to conceal their intentions.[144] Even if the motivation was other than that alleged during the Cultural Revolution, a comparison of the ten articles and the final version of the Eight Articles issued in April 1962 does suggest a far more circumspect approach to the problem of loosening up in the cultural sphere.[145] According to an authoritative source, this was because leftists fought a strong rearguard action over the course of a year.[146]

Indications of the debate emerge first from examination of the introductions to the two documents, normally the section in which the tone is set. Both documents contained an almost identically phrased encapsulation of the objectives of cultural policy as laid down at the Third National Congress of Literary and Art Workers held in 1960:[147]

Under the overall direction of serving the workers, peasants and soldiers and serving socialism, implementing the policies of Let a hundred flowers bloom, let a hundred schools contend [*Bai hua qi fang, bai jia zheng ming*], and Weed through the old to bring forth the new [*Tui chen chu xin*], is the most correct and the broadest road for developing our country's socialist literature and art.[148]

But the introduction to the Eight Articles took greater pains over political correctness by giving in far more detail an approving account of the party's earlier cultural policies, including under the 'three red banners' of the GLF when populism seemed likely to overwhelm conventional writers and artists.[149] Not only was there no mention of the GLF in the introduction to the ten articles; that earlier document, unlike the Eight Articles, also referred neither to Mao's Yan'an talks on literature and art, the *locus classicus* for CCP policy in this area, nor to the Anti-Rightist Campaign which had cut so wide a swathe through the cultural sphere.[150]

Both documents discussed the deleterious effects of incorrect implementation of past policies in similar terms, but the Eight Articles excised the ominous warning in the ten articles of what would happen if the mistakes were not corrected. The aim of issuing the ten articles was said to be 'to create even more good works, to reflect the people's life and struggle through lively artistic images and beautiful artistic forms, to educate the people in the vigour of socialism and communism, to encourage the people's enthusiasm for labour and revolution, to enrich the people's cultural life, and to satisfy the many and various needs of the people.' This was apparently not militant enough for leftists and the goal of the Eight Articles was proclaimed to be 'to enable our country's socialist literature and art to be even more useful for combat, even more effectively to "unite the people, educate the people, strike the enemy, wipe out the enemy".'[151] Finally, presumably in response to the wave of high level self-criticism at the Seven Thousand Cadres Conference (including by Mao) which took place between the gestation of the two documents, the Eight Articles placed the blame for mistakes not just on 'some comrades' but squarely on the cultural leadership, particularly the party group in the Ministry of Culture.[152]

The greater circumspection of the Eight Articles was also shown in its omission of a full-frontal discussion of how art should serve politics, broadly interpreted, which formed the first of the ten articles. Works had to have politically correct content, but also correct artistic forms. Instead, the Eight Articles made similar points by indirection, enumerating in the first article how to implement the Hundred Flowers policy: the party advocated the themes of revolutionary struggle and socialist construction and would help writers and artists become more familiar with them.[153] But[154] they were also allowed to base themselves on their personal experience and write comedies or tragedies, about the present or the past, about sharp political struggle or about ordinary everyday life, about positive or negative characters, about contradictions with the enemy or among the people. Any subject-matter was permissible to serve the people's needs, with two caveats: a correct attitude and good writing. Equally, though the CCP advocated a combination of revolutionary realism and revolutionary romanticism, any style was permissible.[155]

The different tones of the two documents were also evident in their respective discussions of the importance of promoting creativity and avoiding over-enthusiastic criticism. The drafters of the Eight Articles (arts. 2 and 4) took care to quote from Mao to the effect that artistic works, however worthy politically, had no force without artistic quality; and they advocated the voluntary study of Marxism-Leninism, Mao's works, and CCP policy as part of the process of improving creativity. Only then did they expatiate on the need for greater tolerance of the creative patterns of the individual artist, a theme plunged into far more precipitately by the drafters of the ten articles (arts. 3 & 6). The Eight Articles also omitted the emphasis placed in the ten articles on distinguishing between political problems on the one hand and ideological and artistic ones on the other.[156]

Both documents referred to the six criteria in the published version of Mao's contradictions speech as the benchmark for critics attempting to assess a work's political correctness.[157] But while the ten articles baldly stated that works and criticisms departing from the criteria were anti-people and anti-socialist, the Eight Articles described them only as 'weeds', and asserted (as Mao had done in 1956–7) that flowers and weeds were not always easily distinguishable, and that flowers were strengthened by struggle.[158] While the ten articles talked of the need 'to strengthen unity and mobilize all positive forces', the Eight Articles wanted to 'strengthen unity and continue [ideological] reform'.[159]

There is significant evidence of greater political subtlety at work in the drafting of the Eight Articles, but the ten articles was not just a crass effort at cultural liberalization; it also contained its caveats and quotes from Mao. Both documents were in broad agreement, sometimes with identical wording, on such issues as drawing critically upon traditional art forms[160] and foreign culture; creative time and leisure had to be safeguarded;[161] criticism should not be simplistic and politically motivated; talent should be encouraged and material rewards should be offered; party leadership should be exercised in a generally united-front atmosphere.[162]

In fact, both the ten articles and the Eight Articles were but a shop-worn recycling of the major speeches by Mao Zedong, Zhou Enlai, Lu Dingyi, and Zhou Yang and other spokesmen for the Hundred Flowers in their earlier blossoming during 1956–7, except that now the cautionary codicils were far more explicit and the trumpeting of freedom was more muted, hardly surprising in the light of what had happened in the intervening four years.[163] Cultural Revolution objections to the ten articles may have had some justification in the behind-the-scenes drafting process, but the contents of both documents were far less permissive than Mao himself in 1956–7. There was nothing in either document that was likely to encourage anyone who had lived through the Anti-Rightist Movement and the GLF to allow their creative juices to flow freely, which was of course why the encouragement of men like Zhou Enlai and Chen Yi—and in the provinces, prominent leaders like Tao Zhu[164]—was so vital.[165]

Consideration of the two sets of articles on literature and the arts indicates unsurprisingly that political considerations were involved in their compilation, probably more so than in the case of the Fourteen Articles on Science. Detailed comparison in both instances does not, however, support Cultural Revolution allegations of malevolent anti-Maoism at work. Rather, leading cadres in the various fields, who themselves had much to lose from conceding too much, were trying to steer a course between excessive liberalization and over-zealous political control.

The implication of the Cultural Revolution criticisms was that Lu Dingyi agreed with the 'revisionism' of the drafters of the ten articles, but took over control of the drafting process which transformed them into the Eight Articles because he thought his colleagues had been too blatant and unsubtle. In fact, it is more likely that Lu instituted the changes because on policies towards the literary intellectuals he was more 'Maoist' than cultural revolutionaries were prepared to concede. Lu reportedly disagreed strongly with the line taken by Zhou Enlai and Chen Yi in Canton.[166]

As in the case of the Sixty Articles on higher education, the real grievance of the cultural revolutionaries about all these documents was that they symbolized the retreat from the anti-intellectual cultural line of the GLF years. Even so, the weight of recent history prevented any of these documents from having real impact until there was a decisive change in the political atmosphere. The intellectuals were far too cautious, fearing yet another reversal of policy.[167] Despite later fulminations against the machinations of capitalist-roaders within the leadership of the CCP during 1961, that change did not take place until after the Seven Thousand Cadres Conference which convened in January 1962.[168]

For a brief few months, that meeting would seem to have ushered in a new era in Chinese domestic politics, and perhaps even a way out of the international isolation in which China found itself at the end of its 'third bitter year'.

6 CHINA'S ISOLATION

Even when swamped by domestic problems, Mao and his colleagues always placed such concerns within the overall context of world affairs, which, as Marxist-Leninists, they were convinced were of great relevance; in major addresses, they usually included sketches of the international background even if the principal focus was domestic. The Seven Thousand Cadres Conference would be no exception, but the problem for China's leaders as they prepared their speeches for that meeting was that the foreign scene looked almost as grim as the domestic one.

At the end of 1961, the principal international worry of the Chinese leadership was the worsening dispute with Nikita Khrushchev, the Soviet premier and CPSU 1st secretary, and his colleagues. Despite the document signed in Moscow at the eighty-one-party meeting in November 1960, subsequently endorsed at the CC's 9th plenum,[1] the easing of tension between the two communist superpowers was brief[2] and the conflict 'continued to smolder'[3] throughout 1961. This dispute was a major factor behind China's rejection of tentative olive branches offered by the new Kennedy administration, which took office in January 1961, and this hostility in turn served to increase Beijing's isolation.

Yet the continuation of the Sino-Soviet dispute into 1961 was surprising, for the Russians had made some conciliatory gestures. Early that year, Khrushchev had written to Zhou Enlai offering to share data on the Mig 21 and the Chinese premier had replied indicating Beijing's keen interest in producing this combat aircraft.[4] In February, Khrushchev had made a significant offer of food aid,[5] and in April the Russians had agreed to a five-year interest-free repayment of China's 1960 trade debts, both moves prompted by China's economic crisis.[6] In July 1961, when Foreign Minister Chen Yi was returning home through Moscow from Geneva, Khrushchev went out of his way to show courtesy towards the man who had railed at him in Beijing two years earlier.[7]

The Berlin crisis

More importantly in the context of the earlier arguments, one of China's principal complaints against Khrushchev—his softness on the United States—seemed to be less valid. The Soviet leader was taking an increasingly tough attitude towards the United States, apparently convinced that the new young American president, John F. Kennedy, shaken by the Bay of Pigs fiasco, could be bullied.[8] The Kennedy–Khrushchev summit meeting in Vienna in June 1961, later described by the president in his radio and TV address to the American people as 'somber',[9] ended with a clash over the issue of Berlin and the two Germanys. Khrushchev spelled out his terms: peace treaties with East and West Germany, the eventual withdrawal of West Germany from NATO and of East Germany from the Warsaw Pact, the demilitarization of Berlin and its transformation into a free city, thus ending its joint occupation by the four victors of World War II, the United States, the USSR, Britain, and France. The proposal was also designed to end the rights of the Western allies to access to West Berlin across the territory of East Germany.[10] At the end of the discussion, Khrushchev banged the table and said: 'I want peace. But if you want war, that is your problem', to which Kennedy replied, 'It is you, and not I, who wants to force a change.' As they parted, Khrushchev reaffirmed his intention of signing a peace treaty with East Germany in December, prompting Kennedy to comment: 'If this is true, it's going to be a cold winter.'[11]

Instead it turned out to be a hot summer. On the night of 12–13 August, the East German regime started building the Berlin Wall—which Khrushchev referred to euphemistically in his memoirs as the 'establishment of border control'[12]—causing a sharp deterioration of East–West relations, even after the immediate danger of a superpower clash faded. Recalling the Berlin crisis over a decade later, the Soviet leader wrote: 'To put it crudely, the American foot in Europe had a sore blister on it. That was West Berlin. Anytime we wanted to step on the Americans' foot and make them feel the pain, all we had to do was obstruct Western communications across the territory of the German Democratic Republic.'[13] Shortly thereafter, the Russians stepped on the other American foot by announcing on 30 August their intention of resuming nuclear testing.[14]

Beijing naturally welcomed these developments. By mid-1961, the editorial writers of the *People's Daily* were writing almost exclusively on foreign affairs, presumably constrained by the CC's inability to provide them with good domestic news and clear policy directives on which to comment.[15] On the eve of the Soviet–American summit, in an editorial entitled 'John Kennedy is facing a severe test', the paper cited the meeting as proof of the 'sincere desire of the Soviet Union for peace'. The editorial criticized Kennedy's 'aggressive policy' with respect to Cuba and Laos and his emphasis on closing the supposed missile gap between the United States and the Soviet Union. Kennedy's decision to meet Khrushchev was held to be a *volte face* and thus a defeat for the American president, but 'the people the world over are watching closely to see what attitude Kennedy will take towards the Vienna meeting'.[16]

Doubtless the Chinese leaders were also watching closely to see what attitude Khrushchev would take. While they may have been buoyed up by Kennedy's statement that the meeting had been sombre, indicating that Khrushchev had given nothing away, they did not sanction another editorial on the subject, perhaps because the Russians did not brief them on what happened behind the scenes. On 10 August the paper strongly supported the demand for a German peace treaty, though it did not comment editorially when the Berlin Wall was begun a few days later; and on 1 September it also backed the Soviet decision to resume nuclear testing.

A likely reason for the tepid support of China's leaders for Khrushchev's diplomatic moves against the West was that they did not trust his sincerity or his resolution or both. Their criticisms of the Kennedy administration in mid-June after the summit were far stronger than the Russians', and they consistently warned against American duplicity.[17]

The Laos conference

More concretely, Beijing was particularly concerned with American actions in Indo-China and disagreed with Moscow's tactical handling of the crisis in Laos,[18] where there was a struggle between right-wing forces supported by the United States and left-wing forces armed by the Communist bloc, mainly the Soviet Union,[19] with the perennial premier, the neutralist Prince Souvanna Phouma, vainly attempting to make the centre hold.[20] This was an issue of far more immediate significance for China's national security than Berlin,[21] especially since there were several thousand remnant KMT troops in Laos.[22] In April 1961, Foreign Minister Chen Yi warned that if SEATO intervened in the Laotian struggle, China would send troops if requested by Prince Souvanna Phouma, though otherwise the Chinese remained silent about committing themselves to military action there.[23] When the prince visited Beijing that month, the Chinese did agree, however, to build a road to connect the kingdom with Yunnan province.[24] In fact, China's aims in Laos were in harmony with those of the Soviet Union—removing US influence without provoking US intervention—and there was some diplomatic co-ordination at the Geneva conference on Laos which began in May 1961.[25] But throughout the period of the conference, which did not end until July 1962 and was punctuated by successive military incidents on the ground, the Chinese took a far harder line publicly than the Russians, and their combination of tough rhetoric and covert support for the pro-communist forces, laced with a willingness to compromise when necessary, would in the end suggest that Beijing's way of dealing with the Americans was more effective than Moscow's.[26] Thus when the Geneva conference was getting under way in mid-1961, China's leaders doubtless awaited an assessment of Soviet performance from Chen Yi, who led the Chinese delegation.

Khrushchev's attack on the Albanian communists

But as the Geneva negotiations dragged on into the autumn, the Chinese were faced with the more immediate prospect of renewed struggle over Soviet ideological leadership and political control of the Communist bloc. The issue was first posed by the publication of the new programme of the CPSU in late July 1961: the Russians again reiterated positions on a number of points on which the Chinese had expressed disagreement at the 1960 Moscow conference.[27] The *People's Daily* published the programme in its entirety in early August, but significantly without comment. It was left to Deng Xiaoping to indicate a month later that the Chinese leadership considered this a document relevant only to the Soviet Union. But probably ideological differences over issues like the possibility of peaceful transition to socialism in non-communist countries, the progressiveness of 'national democracies' in the Third World and whether or not East–West war was inevitable could have been papered over had the issue of Soviet hegemony in East Europe not been posed.[28]

The boil on the Russians' foot in Europe was Albania. At the Romanian party congress in Bucharest in June 1960, which had been the scene of a stormy confrontation between Khrushchev and the head of the Chinese fraternal delegation, Peng Zhen,[29] the Albanians had refused to join the CPSU and the other East European Communist parties in condemning the CCP. Immediately thereafter Moscow cut off all aid to and trade with Tirana, and similar measures were taken by its East European satellites, greatly aggravating an already severe economic situation caused by drought and grain shortages.[30] At the eighty-one-party conference in November 1960, the Albanian party leader, Enver Hoxha, violently denounced Khrushchev, particularly for courting Tito whom the Albanians feared wanted to annex their country, and he supported all the Chinese positions on bloc policy. Hoxha accused Khrushchev of attempting to split the Albanian party and army and of holding up grain shipments at a time of bitter hardship: 'The Soviet rats were able to eat whilst the Albanian people were dying of hunger; we were asked to produce gold'.[31] Immediately thereafter Hoxha began taking precautions against a Soviet assassination attempt, and when he left Moscow for home ten days later, he travelled by train because he feared that it was too easy for an 'an accident' to befall him and his colleagues on a Soviet plane.[32]

During 1961, China emerged as a strong backer of Enver Hoxha. In a fraternal speech to the Albanian Communist party's 4th Congress in February, Li Xiannian repeatedly and emphatically praised the 'correct leadership' of the Albanian party,[33] though behind the scenes he advocated caution and counselled against a rupture with the Russians, reflecting Beijing's own posture. Hoxha recorded in his diary that Li 'sat in stony silence through the sessions when he saw the enthusiasm of the delegates',[34] and it is possible that the Chinese vice-premier's personal demeanour was influenced by the friendly reception he had been given in Moscow *en route* to Tirana.

On that occasion, Li had heard a frank account of Soviet–Albanian differences by Frol Kozlov, Khrushchev's senior colleague and likely successor.[35] In reply, Li had to admit that he had not been authorized to speak on this subject and was moreover uninformed about the issues which Kozlov had laid out. He therefore offered his 'personal opinion' that one had to take the large view: geography had placed the Albanians in the most strategically exposed position in the Communist bloc, but they nevertheless fought hard against imperialism and for socialism. It was the earnest hope of the CCP and Mao that Soviet–Albanian relations would improve as Sino-Soviet relations had done after the Moscow conference. Perhaps fearing that the Russians were planning a sudden verbal assault on the Albanians in Tirana of the kind which they had launched against the Chinese in Bucharest in 1960, Li pointed out that the Chinese and Soviet delegations at the Albanian congress would both be guests and should behave as such. He received an appropriate reassurance from Kozlov.[36] In the event, it turned out to be the hosts who 'got' the (Russian) guests, and the Soviet delegation formally protested.[37]

There is no indication that Li Xiannian discussed with his Albanian hosts the substitution of Chinese economic support for Soviet aid. Yet already China had granted Albania a loan of 500 m. roubles,[38] and one reason why Beijing chose its Finance Minister to lead the Chinese delegation to Tirana may have been that he would be the appropriate official to enter into further discussions with the Albanians on this issue. At any rate, in what could well have seemed like calculated snubs in Moscow, just after the signature of a new Soviet–Chinese trade agreement in April, the Chinese pledged credits of $123 m. to Albania and paid for the shipment of 60,000 tons of Canadian wheat there.[39]

Further violent disagreements between Moscow and Tirana erupted over control of the Soviet submarine base in Vlorë, resulting in the withdrawal of the Soviet boats, and thus the abandonment of the Soviet navy's only Mediterranean base, at the end of May.[40] But the final break between the Soviet Union and Albania was initiated by Khrushchev on 17 October 1961, in his first speech to the CPSU's 22nd Congress. He accused the Albanians of flouting decisions agreed by the world Communist movement at their Moscow meetings in 1957 and 1960,[41] and denounced them for their purges of pro-Soviet Albanian party members, including the execution of a pregnant woman. He used these actions and Hoxha's alleged unwillingness to discuss them, to justify his own flouting of agreed bloc policy not to interfere in other parties' internal affairs nor to publicize inter-party disputes.[42]

In his memoirs, Khrushchev wrote surprisingly little about Albania, and then only in the context of his discussion of Sino-Soviet relations. This suggests that, although he may have wanted to demonstrate to other East European communist leaders that they should not think of emulating Hoxha and step out of line, his real reason for publicizing the quarrel with the Albanians was publicly to humiliate the Chinese at a time of national weakness by forcing them to swallow this denunciation of their new protégé.[43] Knowledgeable Chinese officials had no doubt that the real target was the CCP.[44]

The Chinese response

The CCP fraternal delegation was led by Zhou Enlai who had not been personally involved in any of the confrontations during 1960. This suggested a willingness on Beijing's part not to rock the boat.[45] Zhou had also led the delegation to the previous CPSU congress in early 1959, a time of modest reconciliation and the allocation of more Soviet aid, after the claims for the communes had been moderated and the Taiwan Straits crisis was over.[46] But in case the Russians should read excessive symbolism into his leadership of the delegation, Zhou was flanked by the doughty Peng Zhen, who had stood up to Khrushchev in the 1960 Bucharest clash, and by the crafty, Moscow-trained Kang Sheng, who had given the first formal exposition of the Chinese alternative to Soviet foreign policy at the Warsaw Pact meeting in February 1960.[47]

There is, anyway, no evidence that Zhou Enlai's views on the conduct of Sino-Soviet relations were markedly different from those of his colleagues. Certainly, his more rational approach to running the economy cannot be called in aid. It seems likely that, whatever their differences on domestic affairs, most Chinese leaders were united in their indignation at the way the Soviet Union and Khrushchev in particular had treated China in the past few years. For instance, Deng Zihui, who had been and would again be punished for his rightist views on collective agriculture, referred critically to Soviet revisionism and Khrushchev in a speech to the central party school some months later.[48] Tao Zhu, another member of the Chinese delegation to the 22nd Congress, seen by some as a moderate in support of Zhou,[49] was later described by his daughter as a Chinese first and a Marxist second.[50] Chinese patriotism had to include resentment at Soviet behaviour towards China.

But had Zhou believed that China should be less provocative and more circumspect in its dealings with the Soviet Union, party discipline and political discretion would have dictated that he not stray out of line. Moreover, those who had been prominent in the angry Sino-Soviet debates in 1960 realized that now was not the time to provoke the Soviet Union. Peng Zhen told Ambassador Liu Xiao in Moscow that even if the quarrel between the two *parties* became very fierce, friendly relations between the two *countries* should be preserved.[51] Peng's instruction, however unrealistic, clearly reflected a decision taken in Beijing, presumably ultimately by Mao, and it helps to explain the CCP delegation's behavior during the CPSU's 22nd Congress.

When the Russians learned that Zhou would be leading the Chinese delegation, they offered to send a plane to Beijing to bring him and his team to Moscow. The Chinese informed the Russians that the delegation would be accompanied by the Albanian first vice-premier, Manush Myftiu, returning home after a tour of China, but

Moscow balked, saying that the aircraft was for the exclusive use of the Chinese delegation—whereupon Zhou decided to refuse the Soviet offer and hired a special plane![52]

On arrival in Moscow, the Chinese delegation demonstrated that, however much they felt it in their interest to maintain Sino-Soviet cordiality, this did not reflect an abandonment of principles. At the obligatory wreath-laying at the Lenin–Stalin mausoleum in Red Square, Zhou and his colleagues placed a separate one, 'Dedicated to the great Marxist, Comrade Stalin', to indicate that they still regarded Khrushchev's denunciation of him in his 'secret' speech to the CPSU's 20th Congress in 1956 as intemperate and unbalanced. But once the 22nd Congress began, they had to sit through ferocious attacks on the late dictator, which were capped at the end of the congress by a resolution to remove his corpse from the mausoleum.[53]

The Chinese delegates could hold their peace on the Stalin issue without loss of face because, by this time and in this context, like the renewed attacks on the Soviet 'anti-party' group, it was an internal matter for the CPSU; and in so far as Stalin was the common property of the world communist movement, their opinion was already on the record.[54] But they could not swallow the sudden and unprecedented public attack on a fraternal party which had backed them under similar circumstances in the past, especially since the Albanians were not there to defend themselves.[55] Zhou's response to Khrushchev was designed to demonstrate China's outrage while maintaining the niceties of protocol. Instead of taking sides in the dispute, he focused on the Soviet leader's violation of communist internationalism. Speaking on 19 October, two days after Khrushchev, Zhou reaffirmed Albania's status as a member of the Communist bloc, and added that '[a]ny public, one-sided censure of any fraternal party does not help unity and is not helpful to resolving problems. To lay bare a dispute between fraternal parties or fraternal countries openly in the face of the enemy cannot be regarded as a serious Marxist-Leninist attitude.'[56]

Having made his *démarche*, Zhou seems to have been prepared to sit grimly through the rest of the congress, but finally decided to leave it early, on 23 October, after his remarks were attacked by subsequent speakers. Even so, in an effort to minimize the damage to Sino-Soviet relations and to demonstrate how inter-party disputes ought to be handled, Zhou tried to avoid the appearance of a walk-out by giving as his excuse the need to prepare for the imminent meeting of the National People's Congress (NPC) in Beijing, and by appointing Peng Zhen to lead the delegation in his absence. But if anyone was deceived, Zhou's real message was underlined by the public demonstration of support which Mao gave by turning up at Beijing airport to greet him on his return.[57] In Zhou's absence, Khrushchev referred ironically to the Chinese intervention in his second speech to the congress on 27 October:

Comrade Chou En-lai, the leader of the delegation of the Communist Party of China, expressed in his speech concern over the open discussion at this congress of the issue of Albanian–Soviet relations. The main point in his statement, as we see it, was anxiety lest the present state of our relations with the Albanian Party of Labour might affect the unity of the whole socialist camp. We share the anxiety expressed by our Chinese friends, and appreciate their concern for greater unity. If the Chinese comrades wish to make efforts towards normalising the relations between the Albanian Party of Labour and the fraternal parties, *there is hardly anyone who could contribute more to the solution of this problem than the Communist Party of China.* (Emphasis added)[58]

Khrushchev's speeches provoked a series of diatribes from Tirana, combining 'traditional Balkan fury and left-wing Marxist-Leninist fanaticism . . . as violent as, and certainly more colorful than, anything in the "high Stalinist" period in the Soviet Union'.[59] The Russians responded and ensured that they were backed up by their East European satellites and other friendly parties.[60] By mid-December, Soviet–Albanian diplomatic relations had been broken and embassy staffs withdrawn.[61]

Despite what had almost certainly been a genuine desire to minimize intra-bloc conflict at this time, the Chinese were trapped by the intransigence of the two sides. Solidarity demanded that they reprint these Albanian polemics in the *People's Daily*, which they did through January 1962, along with the attacks on the CCP by 'fraternal' parties, and this policy doubtless helped to worsen Sino-Soviet relations.[62] Solidarity also required the Chinese to reaffirm their support for the Albanian party and its leadership, which they did strongly.[63] In December, in international fora dominated by communists and their fellow-travellers, like the World Peace Council and the World Federation of Trade Unions, Chinese delegates repeated their tactics of 1960 and disputed forcefully the Soviet positions on international affairs.[64] But discretion and discipline prevailed over solidarity when it came to overt attacks on the CPSU or Khrushchev personally; the Yugoslavs and Tito were used as surrogates.[65]

The Beijing view of the Kennedy administration

As in 1960, the principal concern of the Chinese in their dispute with the Russians was what they saw as Moscow's appeasement of Washington, which they considered bad for China and worse for world revolution. Despite his table-thumping in Vienna, the building of the Berlin Wall, and a confrontation between American and Soviet tanks at Checkpoint Charlie in October, well before the end of 1961 Khrushchev was making secret overtures to Kennedy, trying to get himself off the hook on which he had impaled himself. At the end of September, he secretly sent a twenty-six-page letter to the president, bypassing Soviet foreign ministry channels. At the party congress, he was almost the only Russian speaker to mention the Berlin crisis, and in early November, he told reporters that 'for the time being it is not good for Russia and the United States to push each other'. While it is unlikely that the Chinese knew of Khrushchev's secret correspondence with Kennedy, the nuances of his behaviour suggested a diminished will on Moscow's part to test the president. They would have been deeply suspicious that in late November the Soviet leader's son-in-law and confidant, Alexei Adzhubei, the editor of the Soviet government organ *Izvestia*, interviewed Kennedy and took the unprecedented step of publishing the full text of an American president's remarks on the Cold War in his newspaper.[66] The Chinese public reaction, however, was to criticize what Kennedy said in the interview.[67]

At the end of the year, Beijing was arguing that there had been nothing in the 'criminal record' of the eleven months of his administration or 'President Kennedy's personal criminal record' to justify any illusions about the unchanged nature of 'US imperialism'.[68] The Chinese representative at the regular Sino-American ambassadorial talks in Warsaw, Ambassador Wang Bingnan, repeated in his memoirs almost a quarter-of-a-century later the 1961 Beijing line that '[a]fter Kennedy took office, the United States launched an overbearing offensive all over the world ... After a few rounds of talks, Kennedy showed that he was no different from his predecessors.'[69]

In fact, these were not new assessments, but mainly restatements of what the Chinese had said about Kennedy even *before* he took office. This attitude puzzled the new president, who was appalled that Beijing had 'spewed unremitting vituperation upon him' since his inauguration.[70] Given all its domestic problems in 1961, it is curious that China would be prepared to risk provoking a confrontation with the United States. Two explanations seem likely.

During his campaign for the presidency, Kennedy had reaffirmed his long-standing position that the Nationalist regime should be persuaded to abandon the offshore islands of Quemoy and Matsu, because they represented a threat to peace in the region, and the United States might well be dragged into any conflict, as seemed dangerously likely during the 1958 Taiwan Straits crisis. From Mao's point of view, this apparently more rational American attitude was actually more dangerous, because at least from 1958 he seems to have seen the offshore islands as umbilical cords ensuring that Taiwan's links with the mainland were never severed. Even worse from the Chinese perspective, Kennedy and his advisers seemed to be moving towards a so-called 'two Chinas' policy of recognizing that there were now two successor states as a result of the Chinese civil war and subsequent developments.[71]

By themselves, these perceptions of the new administration's China policy might account for Beijing's constant fault-finding with respect to Kennedy. To this has to be added Mao's need to maintain towards the United States the same degree of hostility which he was urging Khrushchev to adopt. In the aftermath of the polemics of 1960, and with Khrushchev now blowing cold on Berlin, he could not afford to give the Soviet leader any justification for 'going soft' on America. This meant, among other things, withdrawing an offer to exchange journalists, originally proposed by Beijing in 1956, and now revived by the Americans at the Warsaw talks. In addition to their concern about how such an agreement would look to Moscow, the Chinese must have been unwilling to allow inquisitive foreigners to wander around China at a time of economic crisis.[72]

In short, by the end of 1961, a set of external exigencies had again led China into a state of simultaneous confrontation with both superpowers. In the face of this potentially dangerous situation, the Chinese leaders revealed themselves united on external policy.

Chinese leaders' assessments of the international situation in early 1962

The first and most formal survey of the international situation presented by the Chinese leadership to the Seven Thousand Cadres Conference was contained in Liu Shaoqi's written report.[73] This assessment, which has never been published, may be assumed to represent as frank a briefing as senior leaders were prepared to offer their subordinates at that time. It would have been passed out in written form to 7,000 officials, and presumably to many others after it had been approved. So the Chinese leaders had to be wary about a copy falling into the hands of a Soviet or East European diplomat, courtesy of one of the many contacts they had made in China over the previous twelve years. In fact the report was standard fare; at no point, even though it was confidential, did it attack the Soviet Union or Khrushchev by name. Yet his audience would have known from reading the *People's Daily* whom Liu meant by the 'modern revisionists'. His reference to railroading other communist parties could only have meant the Soviet Union; this time he did not bother to use the Yugoslavs as surrogates.[74]

Liu's basic message was plain: the world-wide revolutionary forces were gaining strength; the imperialist camp had never been so weak; the revisionists assessed this situation wrongly, and the resulting split in the socialist camp might cause problems for true Marxist-Leninists like the CCP. He started off with a reassuring show of confidence by stating that Mao's famous maxim, 'the enemy rots with every passing day, while for us things are getting better and better', was the basic direction of the current international situation.[75] Neither imperialists nor revisionists could hold back the tide of revolution in Asia, Africa, and Latin America, where the peoples had been immensely encouraged by the victory of the Chinese revolution. In Cuba, Algeria, the Congo, Angola, Japan, Laos, South Korea, and elsewhere, the revolutionary struggle was surging forward. Even in Western Europe, North America, and Australasia, the workers' movements were developing, as was the world peace movement.[76]

Liu explained that the split between the CCP and the modern revisionists was over fundamentally differing views on the fate of imperialism and on the desirability of supporting revolution. China's general line in foreign policy was to strengthen co-operation within the Communist bloc, pursue a policy based on the five principles of peaceful coexistence towards non-communist countries, to oppose the imperialists' policies of aggression and war, and to support the revolutionary struggle of all oppressed peoples and nations.

The modern revisionists, however, cherished the un-Marxist belief that if you wanted peace you could not have revolution, and vice versa. Adopting an attitude of superiority, they demanded that ruling and non-ruling communist parties obey them. Those who would not, they attacked and expelled, vainly trying to reverse the truth. Albania was a small country, but a socialist one led by a Marxist-Leninist political party. In an unmistakable reference to Khrushchev's handling of Albania, Liu added: 'Even if there are people who want to kick it down, history will prove that it cannot be kicked down.'[77]

The modern revisionists were serving the interests of imperialism and of reactionaries like Nehru, the Indian prime minister, and they were all joining together in an anti-China chorus, which would prove to be in vain. But like everything else, the international communist movement would pursue a tortuous path, and one had to calculate that the activities of modern revisionism could deal a severe blow to its development. All this could lead to new difficulties for the CCP and a few fraternal parties. Indeed, revisionist activities had already led to a new split in the movement.[78]

Liu drew comfort from the historical precedent of Lenin's break with the revisionists of the socialist 2nd International. Though in the minority at the time, Lenin defeated his opponents after a long struggle and went on to lead the October revolution. The current situation was similar, and in many countries there were very few true Marxist-Leninists, and there would have to be a protracted and arduous struggle against the revisionists and opportunists. But so long as the revolutionaries stuck to their principles, they would eventually triumph. The anti-revisionist forces were now far stronger than they had been in Lenin's day, and there were numerous helpful contradictions in the international arena, which could only be solved by the popular revolutionary struggle. Liu listed first the contradiction between the socialist and imperialist camps, 'including the contradiction between imperialist America and the *socialist* Soviet Union' (emphasis added).[79] Perhaps that passage was for Soviet consumption in case there was a leak, but it contrasted oddly with the unusually brief remarks Mao devoted to this topic in his speech to the Seven Thousand Cadres Conference a few days after the distribution of Liu's report.

Mao was as upbeat as Liu, but he was characteristically blunter:

The Soviet Union was the first socialist country, and the Soviet Communist Party was the party created by Lenin. Although the Party and the state leadership of the Soviet Union *have now been usurped by the revisionists*, I advise our comrades to believe firmly that the broad masses, the numerous Party members and cadres of the Soviet Union are good; that they want revolution, and that the rule of the revisionists won't last long. (Emphasis added)[80]

While Mao advocated continued learning about the good people and things of the Soviet Union, it was left to his audience to puzzle out how a country whose leadership had been usurped by revisionists could still be 'socialist'. Certainly, when the Chinese polemics against the Soviet Union started the following year, Mao would readily subscribe to the idea of a capitalist restoration in the homeland of Lenin.

In the final speech of a major leader to the Seven Thousand Cadres Conference, Zhou Enlai warned of the danger of the United States instituting an even more thorough economic blockade or partial war, and spelled out the heavy economic impact of the Sino-Soviet dispute: the repayment of all remaining debts to the Soviet Union and its East European allies by 1967 and the maintenance of a generous aid programme to sympathetic countries like North Korea, North Vietnam, Mongolia, and Albania. China had to honour its international duties, despite its internal problems.[81]

Mao had blithely rejected the idea that China was isolated, even though it was 'being cursed' by revisionists, imperialists, and reactionary nationalists: 'I myself don't feel isolated. In this room alone there are already over 7,000 people; how can we be isolated with over 7,000 people? The popular masses of all countries of the world are already standing, or are going to stand, together with us. Can we be isolated?'[82] But of course by posing the question, Mao answered it. China was isolated. North Korea and North Vietnam were keen to remain friendly with the richer and more powerful Soviet Union, and the prickly loyalty of little Albania hardly made up for the loss of the security blanket of the Soviet bloc. Inevitably, this isolation increased the tension under which the Chinese leaders worked as they strove to deal with their grave internal problems. Because of the hostility of the 'imperialists' and the 'modern revisionists', they knew that they could rely only upon themselves (zili gengsheng).[83] Yet, they could face this situation with confidence if they were agreed on what measures they had to take. The Seven Thousand Cadres Conference was supposed to bring about the requisite meeting of minds and the establishment of a consensus. In that, it would be only partially and temporarily successful.

PART TWO

FALSE DAWN

7 THE SEVEN THOUSAND CADRES CONFERENCE

Origins

When, why, and how a meeting is called in China—and how it is run and by whom—is sometimes as illuminating as the documents produced at it. The Canton conference in March 1961 was a case in point.[1] But none is more intriguing than the central work conference held at the start of 1962, dubbed the Seven Thousand Cadres Conference because of the unprecedented number of attendees; even the 8th Congress had had only 1,026 delegates.[2] Held from 11 January to 7 February 1962, the conference's origins are particularly important because it was a watershed in the post-GLF reform process. All members of the PSC, with one important exception, made speeches, and the result was a change in the political atmosphere which enabled the policy proposals laboriously drawn up during 1961 to be seriously implemented.[3]

Summer work conferences were by now a regular form of CCP leadership interaction, consultation, and decision-making, and indeed remain so as of this writing. But year-end midwinter meetings were also not unusual for the CC. They provided an opportunity to assess the successes and failures of the annual plan and to reshape the plan appropriately for the coming year. The work conference of December 1960, and the subsequent 9th plenum in January 1961, were major meetings to initiate post-GLF policies in the light of the catastrophes of 1960. That policy process had been continued at the Canton conference in the spring and the Beijing conference in the summer, and was seemingly completed at the second Lushan conference in the autumn. Key policy proposals on agriculture, commerce, industry, higher education, importing grain, and population relocation had gradually been evolved and agreed to. The CCP's job now was surely to get on with implementing them. Instead, its leadership decided at a brief central work conference held on 21 December 1961 to convene a bigger meeting than ever held before.[4]

A gathering of seven thousand officials meant that attendees included not merely the usual suspects from the centre, regional bureaux, and the provincial and major city *apparats*, but also considerable numbers from districts, counties, industrial enterprises, and relatively small PLA units. Of course, quite humble officials might attend a meeting like the 8th Congress as delegates, but a congress was a highly structured occasion when leaders gave the word and the role of the rank-and-file participants was largely to absorb and later transmit their message. Work conferences normally had agendas, but the possibility of postponing formal decisions to a subsequent plenum meant that the proceedings could be, and indeed were designed to be, more freefloating. To allow so many junior officials to witness and participate in such discussions among the CCP's top leaders at a time of severe national crisis was a risky enterprise according to the standard operating procedure of democratic centralism. Why was it undertaken?

Clearly one factor necessitating the summoning of another midwinter conference was that the measures initiated at the 9th plenum and thereafter had failed to transform the economic situation.[5] A Planning Commission briefing for Zhou Enlai, Chen Yun, Deng Xiaoping, and Li Fuchun in the second week of December 1961 revealed an economy still in the throes of a deep depression. Government measures to breathe life into agriculture had had some effect, but food was still the main problem, and industrial adjustment had been postponed till the following year.[6] Agriculture's contribution to national income had been restored almost to its pre-GLF level (Table 7.1). The agricultural labour force had

TABLE 7.1. *Changing proportions of economic sectors in national income, 1957–1961* (%)

Year	Agriculture	Industry	Construction	Transportation	Commerce
1957	46.8	28.3	5.0	4.3	15.6
1960	27.2	46.3	6.5	6.9	13.1
1961	43.4	34.6	2.5	4.8	14.7

Source: TJNJ, 1983, p. 24.

been dramatically increased, while the number of industrial workers had been slashed (Table 7.2). But the 1961 grain output of 147.5 m. tons was a marginal 2.8 per cent increase on the 1960 low, and still represented only 75 per cent of the 1957 pre-GLF high. Moreover, due to the widespread starvation in the countryside, six provinces still registered a negative population growth rate; in China's most populous province, Sichuan, it was 17.61 per thousand.[7] Consequently, the procurement of grain and of other major

TABLE 7.2. *Changing numbers of agricultural and industrial workers, 1957–1961*

Year	Agricultural	%	Industrial	%
1957	193,100,000	93.2	14,010,000	6.8
1960	170,190,000	85.1	29,970,000	14.9
1961	197,490,000	89.9	22,240,000	10.1

Source: *TJNJ, 1983*, p. 122.

agricultural products had had to be reduced well below the 1957 and 1960 levels (Tables 7.3, 7.4), causing widespread distress in the cities, where the cost of most foodstuffs had gone up dramatically (Table 7.5).[8] The Planning Commission bureaucrats had come up

TABLE 7.3. *Grain output and procurement, 1957–1961* (tons)

Year	Output	Procurement	% procured
1957	195,045,000	48,040,000	24.6
1960	143,500,000	51,050,000	35.6
1961	147,500,000	40,470,000	27.4

Source: *TJNJ, 1983*, p. 393.

TABLE 7.4. *State procurement of other major agricultural products, 1957–1961*

Year	Vegetable oil (ton)	Pigs (head)	Fresh eggs (ton)	Aquatic products (ton)	Cotton (ton)
1957	1,338,000	40,500,000	390,000	17,170,000	1,412,000
1960	830,000	19,913,000	142,000	19,030,000	1,005,000
1961	571,000	8,701,000	130,000	13,910,000	660,000

Source: *TJNJ, 1983*, pp. 389–90.

TABLE 7.5. *Changing retail prices of consumer goods, 1957–1961* (yuan)

Year	Grain (ton)	Vegetable oil (ton)	Pork (100 jin)	Fresh eggs (100 jin)	Aquatic products (ton)	Fresh vegetables (ton)
1957	220.0	1,131.2	118.0	105.0	628	108.8
1960	227.2	1,210.0	134.0	159.4	617	120.0
1961	231.0	1,393.0	171.4	196.0	873	133.4

Source: *TJNJ, 1983*, p. 470.

with a solution: soybeans (*douzi*). With an additional output of about 1.2 billion catties (about 600,000 tons), each urban resident could be supplied with 3 jin (3.3 lb.) of beans per month for the next eight months.[9]

In the industrial sector, the collapse which Tian Jiaying had correctly foreseen in early 1961 had taken place, and Li Fuchun's forecasts for 1961 industrial output had turned out to be totally unrealistic. Value of output had in fact fallen by over 40 per cent, and many enterprises had shut down either wholly or partially due to shortages of raw materials and fuel.[10] In the prison system, 'reform through labour' often became a mockery as the public security authorities had to close down mines and factories.[11] The resulting drastic reduction in state revenue from the industrial sector combined with a reduction in the agricultural tax burden (Table 7.6), and the raising of agricultural procurement prices agreed at the beginning of 1961 (Table 7.7) meant that state finances were still in a parlous condition. An excessive amount of currency was in circulation.[12] The slashing of government expenditure (Table 7 8) had reduced the 1960 deficit of 8.18 billion yuan sharply, but it still stood at 1.09 billion yuan (Table 7.9).

TABLE 7.6. *State revenue by major source, 1957–1961* (100 m. yuan)

Year	Enterprises: total	Enterprises: industrial	Taxes: total	Agricultural tax	Industrial and commercial taxes
1957	144.2	59.3	154.9	29.7	113.1
1960	365.8	215.8	203.7	28.0	160.6
1961	191.3	80.4	158.8	21.7	120.5

Source: TJNJ, 1983, p. 446.

TABLE 7.7. *State procurement prices for major agricultural products, 1957–1961* (yuan)

Year	Grain (ton)	Vegetable oil (ton)	Pigs (head)	Fresh eggs (100 jin)	Aquatic products (ton)
1957	162	940	47.7	94.2	341
1960	170	1,100	63.8	123.8	363
1961	213	1,300	70.0	162.6	526

Source: TJNJ, 1983, pp. 478–9.

The reform measures devised to deal with these problems were unlikely to be implemented with enthusiasm, if at all, while party officials feared that yet another shift in the wind would expose them to criticism like the 'right opportunists' faced in 1959 for opposing the 'three red banners' that had defined the policy environment of the 1958–60 period. Large numbers of cadres who had been totally committed to the GLF were waiting to pounce on deviationists.[13] Hence the need for a conclave at which officials could be reassured that the leaders were committed to the new course.

TABLE 7.8.   *Major items of state expenditure, 1957–1961* (100 m. yuan)

Year	Construction	Enterprises' revolving funds	Education, culture, and health	Defence	Administration
1957	123.7	20.8	27.8	55.1	21.7
1960	354.5	67.5	50.5	58.0	28.0
1961	110.2	29.4	41.2	50.0	26.8

Source: TJNJ, *1983*, p. 448.

TABLE 7.9.   *State revenue and expenditure, 1957–1961* (100 m. yuan)

Year	Income	Expenditure	Surplus/Deficit
1957	310.2	304.2	+6.0
1960	572.3	654.1	-81.8
1961	356.1	367.0	-10.9

Source: TJNJ, *1983*, p. 445.

But if the economic and political situation demanded yet another meeting, whose idea was it to expand so substantially the central work conference already in progress? Some authoritative accounts state unequivocally that it was Mao; another equally authoritative account asserts that Liu Shaoqi, Zhou Enlai, Deng Xiaoping, and others wanted a bigger meeting than usual to analyse the experience of the past twelve years, and that Mao went along with the suggestion.[14]

It can be taken as axiomatic that so unusual a procedure could not have been adopted if Mao had rejected it; we have no evidence that his closest colleagues forced him to take this step. The idea fitted so well with his practice when his back was against the wall, that he may have welcomed it, even if he did not suggest it. In 1955, the Chairman had appealed over the heads of his central colleagues to provincial officials for a rapid collectivization drive; in 1957, he had done the same with the bourgeoisie to mobilize them to take part in the rectification campaign. Those were aggressive steps, and Mao succeeded in getting his way. He may have seen the Seven Thousand Cadres Conference, wherever the idea came from, as a means of rallying a broader community behind him, though for more defensive purposes than on those earlier occasions.

We do not know whether Mao's personal position was threatened at the end of 1961. We do know that at the Seven Thousand Cadres Conference he would feel obliged to assume greater responsibility for the GLF catastrophe than ever before. But the leaders of the State Council whose policies had been thrust aside at the outset of the GLF, Zhou Enlai and Chen Yun, never showed any disposition to use the disastrous consequences of Mao's actions against him. Liu Shaoqi and other senior party officials were themselves deeply mired in the GLF débâcle, even if the main responsibility lay with Mao. Marshal Peng Dehuai, who had the temerity at Lushan in 1959 to underline the problems caused by the GLF, had been disgraced, and Mao showed no sign of allowing him to be rehabilitated.[15]

Even if unthreatened by any cabal, the economic crisis constrained Mao's options. He had led a forced retreat on the communes, and allowed his colleagues to devise a series of plans for the industrial front, the common characteristic of which was the restoration of the *status quo ante* the GLF. By the end of 1961, the economic situation had not yet bottomed out and Mao may have sensed further retreats in the air, particularly on agriculture, even though he proclaimed the situation to be not too bad.[16] He may have been prepared to try to convince cadres to implement the new measures agreed with his colleagues by holding a very large meeting at which comparatively junior officials could hear him and his colleagues tell them what to do. But under these circumstances, it also seems likely that he would have felt that lower-level party leaders, the shock troops of the GLF who had invested much political capital in carrying out Mao's disastrous policies, would be likely to rally to his banner and eschew further retreats, partly out of loyalty, partly out of a sense of self-preservation.

One piece of evidence which lends credence to this hypothesis is the unusual procedure which Mao proposed at the outset of the Seven Thousand Cadres Conference:

At the start of the conference Comrade Liu Shao[qi] and several other comrades prepared a draft report. Before this draft had been discussed by the Political Bureau, I suggested to them that instead of first holding a meeting of the Political Bureau to discuss it, we should rather immediately issue it to the comrades who are participating in this conference so that everyone could comment on it and put forward ideas.[17]

Mao justified his proposal, which was of course accepted, by invoking participants' deep understanding of the grass roots, as compared with that of the top leadership. In fact most of his colleagues had spent a good deal of time at the basic levels in 1961 at Mao's insistence, and the policies subsequently adopted reflected their findings. Mao's real reason may have been that he did not want junior officials to be inhibited from expressing their views at the conference.

For there was a key difference between the people interviewed by Liu Shaoqi and others in their rural safaris and those represented at this conference. Peasants had been deeply unhappy with the GLF and the havoc it had wreaked upon their lives; the changes agreed in Beijing and Lushan reflected their concerns. The grass-roots representatives at the conference, on the other hand, were local officials who had forced the peasants to accept those policies in 1958. A high proportion were hardened veterans who had joined the CCP before 1949.[18] Many of them were doubtless as unhappy as Peng Meixiu, the woman party secretary with whom Liu Shaoqi had his confrontation during his Hunan investigation, feeling that they were being blamed simply for loyally carrying out the policies of the leadership. They had lost face and authority, and the policies now being introduced gave them less power over the peasantry. Mao may well have calculated that if they were encouraged to speak up at the Seven Thousand Cadres Conference, there would be a groundswell of support for holding the line on any further retreats from the GLF, at least in the countryside. If that was his calculation, it was wrong. Far from being a last-ditch stand for the supporters of the GLF, the conference turned into a launching pad for new radical measures to deal with the economic crisis.

Liu Shaoqi's written report

Chinese party historians divide the Seven Thousand Cadres Conference into two stages: from 11 January until the morning of the 29th, which Zhou Enlai called the 'first high tide' (*di yige gao chao*); and the second high tide, from the afternoon of the 29th, when Mao prolonged the conference, calling on the conferees to let off steam (*kai chuqi*), till the afternoon of 7 February.[19] The timetable was as follows:

Seven Thousand Cadres Conference: Timetable[a]

16 Dec.		Deng Xiaoping gives Mao secretariat report on GLF decision-making.
21 Dec.		Central work conference decides to hold much larger meeting.
21 Dec.–11 Jan.		Liu Shaoqi's 'written report' drafted under supervision of Deng, then Liu.
11 Jan.	a.m.	*Seven Thousand Cadres Conference convenes*; Regional groups hear reports on how leaders want conference to go.
	p.m.	1st draft of Liu's 'written report' presented to conferees.
12 Jan.–25 Jan.		Provincial groups discuss Liu's report.
17 Jan.		Redrafting committee begins eight days of meetings to prepare 2nd draft.
24 Jan.		Mao accepts 2nd draft.
25 Jan.		Politburo meeting.
26 Jan.		2nd draft of Liu's report, reflecting criticisms, presented to conferees.
27 Jan.	p.m.	Liu addresses plenary session on 2nd draft.
28 Jan.–29 Jan.	a.m.	Provincial groups discuss Liu's 2nd draft and speech.
29 Jan.	p.m.	Lin Biao addresses plenary session. Mao initiates second stage of conference with call for frankness.
30 Jan.	a.m.	Provincial groups caucus.
	p.m.	Mao addresses plenary session on democratic centralism.
31 Jan.–6 Feb.	a.m.	Provincial groups criticize provincial committees, regional bureaux, and central organs.
3 Feb.		Zhu De addresses Shandong provincial group.
6 Feb.	p.m.	Deng Xiaoping addresses plenary session on party's work.
7 Feb.	a.m.	Small groups discuss Deng's speech.
	p.m.	Zhou Enlai addresses plenary session on State Council's mistakes; *Seven Thousand Cadres Conference closes.*

8[/9?] Feb.   Chen Yun addresses Shaanxi provin-
                              cial group.
                              New work conference discusses 3rd
                              draft of Liu's report.
17 Feb.   3rd draft finalized.
23 Feb.   Mao approves 3rd draft.
26 Feb.   3rd draft circulated within CCP.

([a]*Sources*: Zhang Tianrong, 'Guanyu yijiuliuer nian qiqian ren dahuide jige wenti', pp. 6–10; Cong Jin, *Quzhe Fazhande Suiyue*, pp. 399–413; Teng Wenzao, 'Guanyu qiqian ren dahuide pingjia wenti', p. 4; Li Xiangqian, 'Qiqian ren dahui shimo', p. 28; Bo Yibo, *Ruogan Zhongda Juece*, op. cit., 2, pp. 1017, 1019–20.)

Liu Shaoqi's written report was prepared under the supervision first of Deng Xiaoping, who as General Secretary was responsible for organizing the conference, and then of Liu himself.[20] It was drawn up between 21 December, when the decision to hold the Seven Thousand Cadres Conference was taken, and 11 January when the report was presented.[21] This suggests a very hurried process, in the light of the immense length and considerable importance of a document supposed to sum up twelve years of experience.[22] On the other hand, since much of the report consisted of lists of problems and duties, most of which had been spelled out many times, it should not have been difficult for senior Beijing officials to string them together for the report. Furthermore, Liu revealed in his written report that the party secretariat had very recently drawn up its own report on policy-making, based on a study of central documents issued in the past few years, which had been submitted to Mao and the PSC on 16 December.[23] This document, which Mao seems to have approved, with reservations about its failure to castigate the media,[24] may have been distributed at the conference.[25] Thus some of the groundwork on which Liu's report was based may have been largely done before the December work conference, possibly by the Beijing party committee.[26]

The only available text of the written report is the revised version presented to the conference on 26 January; but Liu's speech on the 27th explaining the changes gives a fairly clear idea of the problems which the conferees found with the original draft.[27] The report embodied the rule of thumb of any government in trouble: put the best face on it.[28] It consisted of three major sections—the present situation and tasks, strengthening democratic centralism and unity, and party problems—with many subsections. After a laudatory but cursory review of the CCP's record from 1949 to 1958, the report listed twelve achievements of the GLF, covering all branches of economic and social activity, the first few focusing on industrial expansion.[29] By contrast, current problems were subsumed under only four heads, albeit at slightly great length: the distortions and setbacks produced in the economy by over-ambitious targets, in turn due to inexperience and lack of prudence; excessive collectivism in the commune movement; the dislocation caused by attempts to set up comprehensive industrial systems all over the country after the decentralization of much economic decision-making; and the massive growth of industry and people in the cities. The drastic reductions of agricultural output in 1959–60 and the industrial collapse in 1961, along with the numerous current difficulties, could be attributed in part to natural calamities, but also 'to a very great degree' (*hen da chengdu*) to human error.[30] Where did responsibility lie?

At this point, Liu's report went into a lengthy defence of the GLF, Mao's role in it, and, in passing, his own, all of which was excluded from Liu's posthumous selected works, doubtless in order to protect his reputation.[31] The report admitted that people were asking if the three red banners of the general line, the GLF, and the communes were correct. Were successes or failures the main characteristic of CCP work since 1958? Clearly, many party members would have given negative answers to these and other questions, for the report affirmed the right of CCP members to debate them and hold contrary positions.[32]

The report reminded readers that the general line had been formally passed at the second session of the CCP's 8th Congress in May 1958. Its basic ideas were attributed to Mao, but the report added that the central committee had affirmed that congress's political report which, as his audience would have known well, Liu himself had presented. Thereafter, under the aegis of the general line, there had been successes on many fronts. The report described the formation of the communes in a disingenuous manner which could have deceived nobody: 'In some places, APCs united and organized people's communes. The centre affirmed this creation of the masses and issued a decision on their measured expansion.'[33]

The report argued that the centre had always laid down the correct policy parameters, insisting, for instance, on the equal importance of all four elements in the GLF slogan 'more, faster, better, and more economically', and distinguishing between the socialist and communist stages in the development of the communes. Now, it added, 'all can see clearly that the fixing of these policy limits truly had the significance of important principles'. Doubtless, all could see clearly, too, the patent effort to shift blame from the centre to its subordinates: 'The very great successes in our work in these past few years prove that the basic direction and important principles of the three red banners of the general line, the GLF, and the people's communes are correct. The shortcomings and errors in our work are not errors of line but problems of concrete implementation.'[34] It was insufficient to judge the three red banners from a partial or a short-term perspective; they should be seen in the context of the whole historical period of the construction of socialism. Clearly the three red banners would have to be re-examined hereafter in the light of concrete work, but 'the experience of the past few years causes us to affirm even more firmly: these three red banners are correct . . . the successes have been very great and the shortcomings and errors have been secondary.'[35]

The report returned to this theme later in a brief bravura passage:

Ahead of us we say are the problems of adjustment work in agriculture, industry, commerce, and other fields. What is this adjustment work for? It is simply to enable us to implement even better the general line of constructing socialism by going all out, aiming high, and achieving greater, faster, better, and more economical results, to bring about even more successfully the leap forward in our national economy, and to develop the superior nature of the people's communes even better.[36]

The one concession to reality in this passage was, of course, the omission of 'great' in front of 'leap forward'.

The exoneration of the three red banners was accompanied by a eulogy of their progenitor:

Comrade Mao Zedong penetrates very deeply and is very far-sighted with respect to problems of construction just as he was with the problems of revolution. He is very good at analysing and summing up the experiences of the masses and carefully separating out mistaken things while supporting and promoting correct things. He has always reminded us that in the life of the party and of the state we must support the principle of democratic centralism. In these past few years, he has always been the earliest to discover our shortcomings and errors.[37]

After giving examples of Mao's prescience from the GLF, the report went on:

If all of us many comrades had grasped the Thought of Mao Zedong better, and were good at utilizing the methods of seeking truth from facts and investigation and research which he has consistently advocated, if we had sincerely implemented the guiding opinions which Comrade Mao Zedong has put forward at every critical moment, if we had truly and not just formally spread popular and party democracy, if we had correctly implemented the system of democratic centralism, then the various errors in our work in the past few years could have been avoided or greatly mitigated, or could have been corrected more swiftly after they had occurred.[38]

The report then turned to the question of Peng Dehuai, repeating the allegation that the former defence minister and his 'right opportunist anti-party clique' had plotted to utilize the few errors associated with the GLF to achieve his long-cherished goal of 'usurping the party'. Unfortunately the struggle against the Peng clique had resulted in the resuscitation of leftist errors and an excessive expansion of the struggle against right opportunism.[39]

After this ringing defence of the centre in general and Chairman Mao in particular, the subsequent portion of the report read extremely strangely, for it spelled out what must have been obvious to every reader at the conference: 'The centre considers that there is a necessity at this expanded work conference to point out that the primary responsibility for the shortcomings and errors in our work in these past few years lies with the centre.'[40]

The 'centre', in which the report specifically included the Politburo as well as CC departments and State Council ministries, had often been deficient not merely in experience, but also in ability. It had lacked the capacity to set appropriate and timely concrete policies, and to monitor correct policies when they had been decreed; instead, it had been too ready to believe, without investigation, reports which had little or no basis in reality.[41]

Among the central officials and departments criticized in various parts of the report were various 'comrades responsible for central work', which might conceivably have referred to the CC secretariat; the *People's Daily* and *Red Flag*, for publishing opinions not in accord with central policy and material not in accord with reality;[42] parts of the State Council for going their own way and ignoring central policies; the Ministry of the Coal Industry, for issuing instructions on introducing new technology without consulting the party centre or the appropriate State Council supervisory office, with serious damage to the industry as a result; and the Ministry of the Metallurgical Industry for bartering steel products for other products and then trying to conceal its activities from the State Council.[43]

The report's criticisms of the State Planning and Economic Commissions for habitually failing to supply the PSC with accurate and analytical economic materials provided an interesting insight into how policy was made at the highest levels of Chinese government. When plans were being finalized, these commissions did not put forward alternate versions for the PSC to compare and choose from, and often they did not supply materials in advance to enable the PSC to examine and discuss the plan at leisure, but pressured the centre to make hasty decisions. This revealing criticism, which echoed Mao's attack on the Ministry of Finance and its chief, Li Xiannian, four years earlier,[44] clearly pointed the finger at the commissions' directors, Li Fuchun and Bo Yibo, respectively member and alternate member of the Politburo.[45]

There was no overt criticism of Mao, but the report's attack on the Anshan Iron and Steel Company, where units had changed old systems of operation, reflected on the Chairman, for he had praised the striking down of superstitions there as a result of its new 'charter'.[46] Below the centre, provincial organs bore a share of responsibility because of the devolution of tasks to them.[47] Here again, Politburo members were being implicitly criticized, for Peng Zhen's Beijing, Ke Qingshi's Shanghai, and Li Jingquan's Sichuan, along with Anhui, Hebei, Heilongjiang, Henan, and Liaoning came under fire.[48] This allocation of responsibility, the report stated, was designed to show that the CCP was fully conscious of its responsibilities to the people and was determined to overcome current difficulties; as proof, it proceeded to list a series of measures adopted since late 1958.[49]

One possible conclusion to be drawn from this strange juxtaposition of self-criticism by the centre following on its stout self-defence earlier is that the drafters proved inept at reconciling diametrically opposed positions within the Chinese leadership. The debate within the committee preparing the second draft indicates that the centre's self-criticism was in the first draft, which would suggest that the self-defence was added to appease disgruntled leftists in the leadership who, as we shall see, made their views plain in the committee's discussions.[50]

The report then went on to list sixteen lessons to be derived from the development experience of the PRC, particularly since 1958. All were familiar to the audience: for instance, that quality and economy were as important as quantity and speed; that agriculture was the basis of the economy; that commerce was crucial; that socialism was not egalitarianism.[51] The issue was of course not education, but implementation.

The duties for 1962 were, again, a familiar laundry list of ten items, repeatedly adumbrated during 1961, including strengthening agriculture, increasing the output of light industry and handicrafts, reducing staff sizes, cutting back on basic construction, implementing the various sets of articles drawn up for each sector.[52] More interesting was Liu's revelation that the centre had decided on the need for a ten-year 'plan', and the few sets of figures he gave for it. The grain targets proved in the end to be over-cautious, the cotton targets were of varying reliability as predictors, while the steel and coal targets turned out to be hopelessly over-optimistic. Both Liu and Mao understood the dubious validity of such figures,[53] and the exercise served only to show yet again that the CCP could neither control the weather nor run industry, especially during a Cultural Revolution which erupted half-way through the ten-year period, and that after a decade of experience, 'planning' was still hit-or-miss (see Table 7.10).

TABLE 7.10.   *1962 ten-year plan targets* (tons)

Product	1961: actual	1967: plan	1967: actual	1972: plan	1972: actual
Grain	147,500,000	190,000,000	217,820,000	215,000,000	240,480,000
Cotton	800,000	1,600,000	2,354,000	2,100,000	1,958,000
Steel	8,700,000	18,000,000	10,290,000	28,000,000	23,380,000
Coal	278,000,000	350,000,000	206,000,000	450,000,000	410,000,000

Sources: Liu Shaoqi, Xuanji, xia, p. 369; *TJNJ, 1983*, pp. 158, 159, 244, 245.

The second section of Liu's written report on strengthening the democratic centralist system as well as centralism and unity was contradictory. In the context of the Seven Thousand Cadres Conference, as Mao's speech a few days later would show, democratic centralism meant more democracy rather than more centralism: it was vital to exhibit more tolerance towards citizens and cadres who wished to warn against foolhardy policies. But this section of the report also opposed 'dispersionism' and laid down ten rules for re-establishing the grip of the central government on the economy.[54] The perennial dilemma in implementation would be, how were cadres to allow their flocks more leeway and at the same time rigidly adhere to the plans sent down from the centre? This was illustrated in examples given by Liu.[55]

The contradictions persisted in the third section on CCP problems. Liu's written report repeated the demand, so common in speeches over the previous year, that cadres should establish a style of work that sought truth from facts (*shi shi qiu shide zuofeng*), as well as adhere to the mass line.[56] If these strictures meant anything, they had to entail a sceptical view of unrealistic central orders and a greater willingness to listen to popular opinion about their local applicability. What was a loyal cadre, the rustless screw in the well-oiled CCP machine, to do when he knew that a policy was wrong and unpopular? This was the question posed, more diplomatically, by a local party committee to the centre. The written report gave an unequivocal answer: 'How to resolve this contradiction? There is only one road, that is, the whole party must obey the centre.'[57] The organizational implication was inescapable. The written report inveighed against party organs which would not permit members to express different opinions or discuss problems, which used tough methods against erring colleagues, and which ignored the party constitution in expelling members, often confusing internal contradictions and those between the people and the enemy. But if the centre insisted on obedience, then lower-level officials would almost certainly invoke the centre in insisting on obedience to their own commands. The time-honoured antidote for such misbehaviour was criticism and self-criticism, and especially bottom-up criticism. Now Liu's written report also demanded adherence to a relatively new set of precepts, the 'three main rules for discipline and the eight points for attention for party and government cadres' (*dang zheng ganbu san da jilu, ba xiang zhuyi*).[58]

The original 3/8 formulation, dating back to the late 1920s, had provided the guidelines for Mao's revolutionary soldiers' behaviour towards civilians. During the course of 1961, an equally simplistic but different 3/8 formulation had been devised for political use. First hints of it were visible in the March draft of the Sixty Articles on Agriculture and then it had appeared fully formed in Article 47 of the June version of that document. Simultaneously, in a parallel attempt to devise a code of conduct for commercial workers, eight rules (*guiju*) embracing some of the same sentiments were inserted as Article 40 of the Forty Articles on Commerce. In September, the version in the June draft of the Sixty Articles reappeared as Article 68 of the Seventy Articles on Industry.[59] Now it was repeated here for a broader and more politically oriented audience.

The three rules were: (1) Tell it like it is (*ru shi fanying qingkuang*); (2) Carry out party policy correctly; (3) Implement the democratic centralist system. The eight points were: (1) Participate in manual labour; (2) Treat others as equals; (3) Be fair; (4) Don't assume airs and privileges; (5) Work must be discussed with the masses; (6) No investigation, no right to speak; (7) Do things in keeping with the real world; (8) Raise your political level.[60]

In truth, there was nothing novel about these eleven injunctions except their incorporation into a single formulation. CCP cadres were regularly enjoined to adhere to conduct along these lines. The constant repetition of such slogans was possibly thought necessary for the motivation of a relatively uneducated cadre base, but it also underlined the regularity with which rules of conduct were flouted. This may have been one reason why the following year, the PLA and soon thereafter the whole political system came up with the alternative approach of providing real-life examples of model conduct like Lei Feng.[61]

Group discussions of Liu Shaoqi's written report

Bearing in mind that it was circulated *in camera* to a supposedly united and supportive party, not a howling opposition in open parliamentary assembly, Liu's written report was a curiously anodyne document. Despite its acknowledgement of crisis and the errors which had brought it on, and its acceptance of the centre's prime responsibility, even the revised version, with its familiar if contradictory formulae and its long lists of desiderata, seemed designed to cover over the fundamental political issues posed by the GLF disaster. These issues were raised, at least by implication, in the group discussions which occupied the conferees from the start of the meeting until the day before the circulation of the revised version of Liu's report on 26 January.[62] Chinese commentators tend to agree that these were lively meetings, but Mao himself later referred to a session which fell silent when the provincial secretary entered, and this was probably not an isolated phenomenon.[63]

According to one Chinese scholar, there were disagreements (*fenqi*) over two major issues at the conference. Firstly, the assignment of blame for the GLF catastrophe as between natural and human causes. While there was some evidence for those who claimed that natural disasters were the principal cause, this seems not to have been persuasive for the majority. How to explain that the catastrophe was nationwide while natural calamities had hit only parts of the country? Moreover, natural calamities mainly affected agriculture, whereas industry, transportation, the national finances, indeed the whole national economy, was in dire straits. Liu Shaoqi had acknowledged the primacy of human agency in May 1961, and his analysis was backed up in the discussions within the Southwest and North China groups at this conference. Indeed, the more effective the economic readjustment measures, the more compelling the argument that this disaster had been 70 per cent man-made (*ren huo*).[64]

But this consensus raised an even more important and politically far more sensitive issue. If human agency was the main factor, who should be held to blame? On this issue, the majority accepted the familiar and comforting charge of implementation failures, along with subjectivist ideological methods and bureaucratic work style of (lower-level) cadres.[65] But there were apparently some braver souls who dissented sharply from this view. One asked:

If the shortcomings and errors are not mistakes of line but problems of implementation, why has the whole country produced mistakes? The losses suffered during the past few years are no less than those produced by the third left line. After all, the country has lost so many people and so much livestock from abnormal deaths, there has to be a clear reckoning of the account. One can't just generalise by saying that the three red banners are correct and that shortcomings and errors are problems of implementation.[66]

A more cautious and therefore commoner complaint against the three red banners went like this: 'It's easy enough to say that in principle the three red banners are correct, but difficult in practice; speaking abstractly, they're fine, speaking concretely, it's not easy to say.'[67] Even a cadre who claimed not to doubt the three red banners echoed the uneasiness about their widespread impact by asking 'why have there been so many problems, and why have the difficulties produced been so serious and so universal?' The impact of the 1959 Lushan conference in reinvigorating GLF leftism and attacking 'right opportunism' was also queried by a number of conferees who felt that the real danger at that time had been leftism. One cadre in the Northwest group stated that the principal error over the past few years had been 'blind leftist empiricism',[68] which sounded like an oxymoron.

A group consisting of government cadres, dissatisfied with Liu Shaoqi's list of four major problems and needing clear guidelines, compiled its own list of twelve problems in neutral, theoretical language which concealed a number of sharp points. Citing the relationship between production relations and the productive forces or between the superstructure and the economic base was another way of asking whether the basic philosophy of the GLF—where there's a will there's a way—should be carried to the extremes of 1958. They queried the operational effectiveness of simultaneous adoption of the slogans, taking agriculture as the base and promoting both industry and agriculture, which taken together were clearly meaningless. They asked what should be the speed of construction and the relationship of accumulation and consumption. And they questioned the policy of walking on two legs (i.e. making use of both foreign and native technology), presumably in an attempt to probe whether the leadership was prepared to forgo costly experiments such as the backyard steel furnaces of 1958. What about balanced growth, the law of value, payment according to work, and the relationships between quality and quantity, between politics taking command and material interests, between technical change and the speed of construction, between the centre and the localities? What was the validity of using mass movement methods (as in the GLF) for economic development? And, finally, they wanted to discuss party leadership and its ideological work style, clearly the most fundamental question of all.[69]

The drive for rapid economic growth during the GLF was the focus of a number of interventions. For one conferee, the high targets were a function of the one-sided stress on speed as the very soul (*linghun*) of the general line. Another cadre criticized Liu's written report for weakly saying that speed had resulted in lack of co-ordination; the right word was 'dislocation' (*shitiao*).

Another set of attacks was levelled against using lack of experience as an excuse for error: why had there not been even greater errors during the 1st FYP when there had been even less experience?[70] This was of course precisely the point made by Liu during his Hunan sojourn in spring 1961,[71] but in front of this larger audience and having to offer some defence of the centre, Liu would reply cleverly: during the 1st FYP period, the CCP had focused on socialist transformation rather than development, taking its cues on economic construction from the Soviet model; it was only when China struck out on its own, choosing self-reliance (*zili gengsheng*) during the GLF that their lack of experience became a negative factor.[72]

Other attacks raised the issue of subjectivism (*zhuguanzhuyi*), the blind application of Marxist theory, as the source of high targets, commandism, dispersionism, and 'punishmentism' (*zhengbanzhuyi*);[73] one critic boldly said that only if the major theoretical construct to emerge from the GLF, the three red banners, were thoroughly aired would the conference be a success. That the theoretical underpinnings of the GLF were the brainchild of Mao, and that accusations of subjectivist theorizing without reference to lower-level cadres could apply only to him, was of course left unstated.

Although only a minority dared voice these views, the points were often expressed sharply and uncompromisingly.[74] Such comments, and the general rumbling among the seven thousand participants, had an impact upon the twenty-one members of the committee which Liu Shaoqi put together from senior central leaders—Zhou Enlai, Chen Yun, Deng Xiaoping, Peng Zhen, Li Xiannian, Bo Yibo[75]—and top regional officials to help him prepare the second draft of his written report.[76] On this occasion, unlike in Canton in March 1961 when he had masterminded the drafting of the Sixty Articles on Agriculture, Mao chose to remain aloof, allowing his cronies to defend his corner. In his absence, splits emerged and statements were made which unquestionably reflected and exacerbated the tensions within the Chinese élite.

Redrafting Liu Shaoqi's written report

The very first speaker when the eight days[77] of redrafting sessions began on 17 January was the Shanghai and East China regional 1st secretary, Ke Qingshi, who had enjoyed a long relationship with Mao and been a leading proponent of the GLF. He posed a set of innocent-sounding but provocative questions:[78] Was the Twelve-Year Agricultural Programme (1956–67)—one of the flagship schemes in Mao's attempts to achieve leaping progress in 1956 and 1958—still in place?[79] Ke asserted that the programme was still viable except in a few areas; a total grain output of 300 m. tons was not possible, but 250 m. tons was attainable; his own region alone could be producing 200 m. tons of grain by 1967! How many years before problems of food, clothing, and everyday necessities were solved? Was China still going to overtake Britain in fifteen years? Should one continue to 'go all out' (*[guzu] ganjin*), a reference to the general line of the GLF?[80] If not, there would be less and less vigour.[81]

Had Mao himself been at the meeting, he could not have framed the questions and comments more pointedly. Evidently they highlighted lacunae in the first draft of Liu's written report. But Ke was jumped on. Liu, Zhou Enlai, and others said that the Twelve-Year Programme had not been properly researched or tested. The targets for grain yields were not very scientific (*bu da kexue*).[82] Deng Xiaoping said that the higher the figures went, the more difficult it was to achieve them. Peng Zhen, who spoke on the 18th, appears to have given the strongest rebuttal. His view was that the general line was easy to explain, but not the GLF. In 1960, the extent of the agricultural disaster and the impact of the increase of the urban population had been underestimated. The 'eight character programme'—

adjustment, consolidation, improvement, and filling out—had been merely empty talk because there had been no directive; targets had not been lowered, and there had been no adjustment until it had been made a central issue at the 1961 Lushan conference, so a year had been wasted. Peng's remarks, intentionally or not, underlined the relative powerlessness of Zhou Enlai in late 1960; the premier had improved and embraced the slogan,[83] but lacked the authority to get it translated into a directive.

Bo Yibo agreed with Peng that it was easier to defend the general line than the GLF, saying that it was not a good idea to invoke the name of the GLF because under some conditions a leap was not possible. Liu closed this discussion by saying that one could still use the term GLF, because it would not be a good idea to drop one of the three red banners, but that one should look at the GLF in a new, more historical perspective.[84]

Among the other major points of dispute in the redrafting committee's meetings, the most sensitive was the question of whom to blame for the three bitter years. The assignment of prime responsibility to the centre was apparently already included in the first version of Liu's written report, and in an intervention in the committee proceedings on 18 January,[85] Peng Zhen stated that, at the centre, the CC secretariat had to shoulder the responsibility. As the second-ranking leader of the secretariat under General Secretary Deng Xiaoping, Peng seemed to be making a self-criticism, but he then moved on to more dangerous ground.

Should the blame assigned to the centre include the Chairman, Liu Shaoqi, and other members of the Politburo Standing Committee? If they deserved it, his answer was 'yes'. Could Peng's question and answer have been an expression of a generalized personal resentment at the fact that he was not a member of the Politburo Standing Committee? Allegations of this resentment were made by Cultural Revolution sources, and while all such politically motivated accusations must be treated with care, in the light of Peng's distinguished career they are quite credible. Indeed, he could have been excused for believing in the early 1950s that he, not Deng Xiaoping, would become General Secretary.[86] One has to ask why, on the occasion under consideration here, Peng Zhen referred to the PSC. In its acceptance of central responsibility, Liu's written report referred to the Politburo but not to the PSC, probably because narrowing it down to a seven-man body which Mao normally summoned would definitely have been seen as pointing the finger at the Chairman. But in this intervention, Peng Zhen referred to Mao by name, and thus his reference to the PSC could not have been a face-saving circumlocution. It did serve, however, to draw a line between Peng himself and Deng Xiaoping, who was a member of the PSC, as well as Peng's boss in the secretariat. Peng could have been hinting that although the CC secretariat had an institutional obligation to accept responsibility, it was in fact the members of the PSC who really deserved the blame; Deng's guilt was a function of his PSC membership, not his secretariat membership. Thus he, Peng, was making only a pro-forma self-criticism. From Deng's perspective, it might seem irrelevant whether it was the PSC or the secretariat which was assigned the principal responsibility since he was a member of both; however, since Deng was the leader of the secretariat but not the PSC, his acceptance of secretariat responsibility, again presumably to shield Mao, was the greater sacrifice.

But obviously the politically sensitive issue was Peng Zhen's reference to Mao. Mao was not without mistakes. It was the Chairman who had suggested that China could make a transition to communism in three to five years.[87] This was possibly the most direct attribution to Mao of this particular piece of GLF utopianism; even in his excited speeches at the 1958 Beidaihe conference, the Chairman had indulged in his habitual practice of putting forward extravagant visions of the future hedged around with cautionary remarks, in the full knowledge that his supporters would ignore the warnings as they enthusiastically attempted to fulfil his aims.[88] Since Mao had not included this mistake among those he admitted to at the 1959 Lushan conference, and indeed specifically indicated that he had suggested that the transition would take perhaps ten or even twenty-five years, he could not have liked Peng Zhen pointing the finger at him in this way.[89]

Peng also stated that it was the Chairman who had advocated universalizing mess-halls, humiliatingly abandoned at the Beijing central work conference the previous June. In quoting Peng, one Chinese scholar stated that this was probably the first time since the founding of the PRC that Mao had been so directly criticized from within the core of the CCP leadership.[90]

At this point, Deng Xiaoping interrupted to support his deputy by citing Mao himself. When the Chairman had been handed the secretariat's report on policy-making on 16 December, he had commented, almost certainly disingenuously: 'You have made me into a sage [*shengren*]. [But] there are no sages. Everyone has shortcomings and makes mistakes, the only question is how many. Don't fear to talk about my shortcomings . . .' [91] Despite this reminder of Mao's apparent equanimity about being accused of error, and perhaps conscious of the dubious sincerity of this remark, Peng Zhen hedged his temerity with expressions of respect for the Chairman which probably made matters worse: 'If Chairman Mao's prestige isn't Mt Everest, it is certainly a high mountain, so much so that even if you take a few tons of earth away, it is still very high. But, if Chairman Mao has committed a 1 per cent error or even a one in a thousand error, it would be odious [elie] to us if he did not self-criticize.' [92]

The following day, Mao's trusty Chen Boda counter-attacked fiercely:[93] 'Comrade Peng Zhen's remarks about Chairman Mao yesterday are worth thinking about. We've messed up [luanqibazao] so many things—does Chairman Mao have to take responsibility for them all? Should we investigate Chairman Mao's work?' [94] Not content with exonerating Mao from any responsibility for the errors of the centre during the GLF, Chen glossed over Mao's 'arbitrary' work style by claiming that the basic current problem was insufficient centralization. Peng Zhen immediately retorted: 'Let's get the problem of Chairman Mao quite clear. It seems that Peng Zhen saying he can be criticized isn't popular. My idea was to counter the impression that anyone could be criticized except Mao. That would be bad.' [95] Bad it might be, but Chen Boda, who had presumably reported to the Chairman before he intervened, knew that the only kind of criticism which Mao was prepared to tolerate was self-criticism. After all their years of working with him, Deng and Peng must have understood that too. The question remains: Did Peng Zhen want the second draft to include an attribution of error to Mao, and was that idea abandoned in the light of Chen Boda's response? Or did Mao indicate that he would self-criticize, thus inducing his colleagues to decide that pointing formally at him in the second draft would be unnecessary and excessively humiliating? Either way, the Chairman accepted the second draft on 24 January.

Liu Shaoqi's speech to the conference[96]

Liu Shaoqi's speech of 27 January explaining the revised version of his written report to the Seven Thousand Cadres Conference was arguably the most important one he made after the founding of the PRC.[97] Another 'bitter year' of economic collapse and widespread famine could only have undermined the faith of the Chinese leaders in the effectiveness of the successive readjustment measures on which they had agreed since the previous January. Liu must have realized that to instil sufficient confidence in CCP cadres for them to implement those measures wholeheartedly, there had to be a radical change in the political atmosphere. This meant that he had to disavow many GLF policies; but he had to accomplish that task in such a way as not to offend the Chairman.

Liu started carefully by invoking the Chairman: for China to be able to fulfil its international duties, domestic work had to be done well. That meant, Liu pointed out, tackling the serious difficulties which the country faced: the shortages of grain, pork, cooking oil, clothing, everyday goods. Why were there shortages? Because agricultural production had dropped massively in the three years 1959–61, and in 1961 industrial output had dropped by 40 per cent or more, and it would continue to do so in 1962. Instead of a leap forward, the country had gone backwards. What was the principal cause, natural calamities or human error?

While there had been strong support for human agency as the principal culprit in the group discussions, this issue, too, had been a cause of controversy in the redrafting committee sessions.[98] Liu trod carefully, perhaps made even more cautious by a disgruntled interruption from Mao.[99] In the second version of his written report, which he quoted in his speech, the crisis was attributed on the one hand to natural calamities, and on the other, and to a very great degree, to human error and shortcomings, that is, natural calamities were put in first place, but human agency was weighted more heavily.[100] This placatory, semi-even-handed approach was repeated in Liu's use of examples. On the one hand, two districts in Shandong—Huimin and Dezhou—were examples of the primacy of natural calamities.[101] On the other hand, there were areas—and here Liu cited what he had been told in Hunan the previous spring—where human error was the key. When he reached the bottom line, he defused the issue by postponing it: 'As for investigating how it was in such and such a province, or district, or county, looking at the conditions there, you can discuss it and make a judgement on the basis of seeking truth from facts.'[102]

Liu then invited those who had thought the first draft too upbeat to send in lists of additional errors committed, but held the line on the main issue: 'Speaking generally, since 1958 our successes have been primary; they occupy the first position. Shortcomings and errors are secondary, occupy the second position.'[103] At this point Liu strayed on to dangerous ground again. What, he asked, was the ratio of achievements to setbacks: seven to three? It was not possible today to apply everywhere the standard CCP analogy of nine fingers to one, a favourite phrase of Mao's.[104] Liu singled out Henan's Xinyang district and Gansu's Tianshui district as being places where nobody would believe that achievements amounted to as many as seven fingers.[105] It was of course still true of some areas, he went on, at which point Mao interrupted to say that there were 'not a few' (*bushao*) such areas.[106] Despite this defensive but implicitly threatening remark, Liu boldly went on to state that from the perspective of the whole country, it would be more accurate to assess achievements and setbacks as seven fingers to three, and in some areas it was even worse than that, with setbacks outweighing achievements.

Again, Liu clothed himself in the protective garb of popular opinion, quoting the same Hunanese peasants whom he had visited the previous spring: 'If you don't acknowledge this, they won't be convinced.'[107] Again, he attempted to dampen controversy, first by postponing the issue, adjuring each province, district, and county to investigate and make their judgements, and discuss the matter again in a few years, and secondly by pointing out that the errors were no longer being committed: the supply system and mess-halls had been abandoned, ambitious targets were not being set, basic construction and water conservancy works had been cut back.

Liu was clearly in a dilemma. The delicacy of his task was underlined by a cautionary rule of thumb that was in vogue during the GLF: 'Don't part from the three [red banners], six [hundred million Chinese people], or nine [fingers/one finger].'[108] Liu had to maintain the centre's position that achievements were primary, partly because Mao would not have tolerated anything else, and partly because he and his colleagues were probably agreed that to admit otherwise would be too demoralizing.[109] Mao believed that unless the CCP was making a mistake of *line*—which Liu stoutly denied in his speech[110]—the nine-to-one ratio should not be tampered with. Even if many mistakes were made, they were all to be subsumed under the one finger. It was only when assessing the seriousness of an *individual* error that it was permissible to juggle the one-finger/nine-fingers formula and estimate the negatives as higher than one. For Mao, the plethora of plans produced during 1961 were all efforts to mitigate the ill effects of such individual errors, not an admission of a more general failure of leadership.

But Liu had to make a reasonably realistic assessment of the current crisis, otherwise the seven thousand cadres would be frustrated because their leaders would seem out of touch with the real world. He attempted to finesse this problem by disaggregating the crisis into a set of regional problems of varying severity and by conceding three fingers rather than just one as the extent of the setbacks. He seems to have relied on casuistry to placate the Chairman while simultaneously hinting that he no longer believed in Mao's one-finger/nine-fingers metaphor.

The 'three red banners'

Liu also had to defend the 'three red banners' in the face of the criticisms made at the conference.[111] The general line was still completely correct, but in implementing it, the CCP had one-sidedly emphasized quantity and speed at the expense of quality and economy; a small number of cadres had failed to involve the masses in a realistic manner, but instead had ordered them to implement the general line in a formalistic manner.[112] The GLF had also been misunderstood as meaning annual increases in production of 90 to 100 per cent, whereas the correct approach—and here Liu quoted Mao at length—was to view China's progress in long-term comparison with what the Soviet Union had achieved from 1920 to 1941. The CCP's ability to lead a GLF should be judged by whether or not over the course of twenty-one years, China could surpass the 14 m. ton increase in Soviet steel production during that period.[113] Again, Liu finessed the issue by postponing the verdict.

Liu used the same device with the third red banner. The communes had also been a matter of controversy in the redrafting committee, with Ke Qingshi complaining that the first draft had not praised their achievements enough. Liu had refused to accept this criticism,[114] but a paean to them, with a catechismal style worthy of Stalin in his heyday, was included in the second draft of his report, and its odd placing in the text suggests that it may have been grafted on to appease the critics:

In the history of mankind, advanced individuals early on raised the question of the commune. Can one or can one not now put it this way: the very great experience of the people of our nation has already indicated that the development of people's communes is a practical road, and so in our villages we have already begun to take the concept of the commune and transform it into reality? We consider that one can put it this way.[115]

In his speech, Liu felt obliged to defend this encomium against critics from the opposite quarter who queried the timing and even the *raison d'être* of the communes. The communes had been trumpeted as being 'large and public' (*yi da er gong*), and though Liu admitted that these characteristics were no longer so obvious, he insisted that the slogan should not be dropped, only reconsidered in the future. Liu admitted that the peasants had been much happier about being members of the primary stage semi-socialist APCs than the higher stage, fully collective ones;[116] for political reasons, he could not admit that the peasants had been even less happy about being hustled into the communes, so he evaded the issue by arguing that as a result of the changes agreed over the past year, the communes embraced the best features of both levels of APC! Should the team, the former primary stage APC, have been the basic accounting unit from the start? Yes, but though the CCP's leadership was guided by Marxism-Leninism, it had not recognized the problem at the time.

He even extolled largely abandoned features of the 1958 communes: a limited form of supply system was still in place for indigent families; temporary mess-halls could still be useful at busy agricultural seasons, even if the attempt to make them a universal system had been wrong.[117] Were the communes set up too early as some comrades had suggested? Perhaps it would have been better not to have set them up in 1958, but now that they were there—the masses had 'already stood up' (*yijing qilaile*), as Liu put it, tongue presumably in cheek—should one abandon them or endorse them and gradually improve them? Liu obviously came down in favour of preservation.[118]

But if Liu had to defend the sacred cows of the GLF, he was able to shelve its more precise aims: the fifteen-year goal of overtaking Britain and the Twelve-Year Agricultural Programme. Responding to Ke Qingshi's questions in the redrafting sessions, Liu stated that the fifteen-year target had not been included in the written report because the new projections for 1972 indicated that it might not be attainable. Taking refuge in the original formulation having been fifteen years 'or a little bit more', a customary cautionary codicil in CCP documents and one regularly employed by Mao, Liu asserted that the goal's omission did not mean it had been cancelled. The Twelve-Year Programme was also still extant if also excluded from the report. The original targets were based upon incomplete investigation and further study suggested that twice as long would be needed. But what if it did take twenty-four years? The heavens would not collapse, Liu argued.[119] Possibly not, but Mao who had personally generated both proposals could not have been happy.[120]

Liu on Peng Dehuai

Liu replied either directly or indirectly to most of the points raised by critics and proponents of the GLF. Chinese party historians do not tell us if Liu's defence of what his report (but not his speech) described as the 'glorious illumination' (*guanghui zhaoyao*) of the three red banners won grudging acceptance from his audience,[121] or whether his shelving of the GLF's extravagant goals engendered more relief than anger. But it is unlikely that his recycled explanation of the purge of the only leader to have had the courage to pose questions to Mao about such matters proved convincing.[122] After all, like Marshal Peng Dehuai, others had now criticized the backyard furnaces, the mess-halls, the supply system, and the wisdom of setting up the communes.[123]

Liu's response was that the campaign against right opportunism (launched at the 1959 Lushan conference), reaffirmed in Liu's written report, had not been initiated just because of Peng Dehuai's letter to Mao criticizing aspects of the GLF.[124] Many of Peng's concrete points had been accurate, and a Politburo member did not commit an error by writing to the Chairman, even if his letter did contain some mistakes.

The reason for the struggle against Peng was his incorrigible antiparty behaviour. In addition to participating in the Lushan 'antiparty group' (*fandang jituan*), he was the left-over evil (*yunie*) of the Gao Gang–Rao Shushi anti-party group in 1953–4.[125] At this point both Mao and Zhou Enlai interrupted to say that Peng was the principal member, and Liu agreed.[126] This was why at Lushan, Mao had asked: 'In the last analysis, was it a Gao–Rao alliance or a Gao–Peng alliance? Perhaps one should say it was a Peng–Gao alliance [because] the most important factor was not that Gao Gang used Peng Dehuai but that Peng Dehuai used Gao Gang.'[127] Mao interrupted again to reiterate that as between Peng and Gao, Peng had been the leader.[128] Liu went on to allege that both men had an 'international background' (*guoji beijing*) and their anti-party activities were related to the 'subversive' (*dianfu*) activities of foreigners— Liu presumably meant Russians[129]—in China. Peng had engaged in factional activities and had plotted to usurp the party (*cuan dang*).[130] So the struggle against Peng Dehuai at Lushan had been completely necessary and correct.[131]

Liu also recapitulated other points made in 1959: the CC was already engaged in eradicating problems raised by Peng; he had failed to voice any criticisms at several earlier meetings; he spoke at

Lushan only because he thought it would be his last opportunity to exploit the difficulties and usurp the party. The issue of usurpation was fundamental to the struggle against Peng Dehuai; others who had criticized the GLF had not committed that sin and so had not been criticized. Peng had come back from leading a military delegation to the Soviet Union and Eastern Europe and had hastily written his letter. That was proof of his plot. Liu concluded with the last defence of government officials anywhere when arguing a weak case: 'Obviously those comrades who do not understand the conditions, don't see matters clearly.'[132]

Liu's remarks clearly showed that there must have been considerable sentiment among the conferees for the rehabilitation of Peng Dehuai. His refusal to envisage such a move should not be seen simply as a loyal defence of the Chairman. Though Mao had chosen at the 1959 Lushan conference to treat Peng's letter as a personal challenge, Liu had been far more vulnerable. Mao's resignation, let alone dismissal, as the outcome of Lushan showed, was inconceivable to CCP leaders at that time, whatever their views on the rights and wrongs of the Mao–Peng quarrel. But Liu, as an equally ardent supporter of the GLF, could conceivably have been made a scapegoat had Mao chosen to accept Peng's letter rather than denounce it.

A key issue in Liu's justification of the case against Peng was the Gao Gang–Rao Shushi episode. While Mao went along with the condemnation of Gao Gang, there is no doubt that Gao's aim was not to attack the Chairman, but to replace Liu Shaoqi as his successor. Gao's contention, as he tried to muster support for his scheme, was that in the post-1949 division of spoils, the heroes of the 'red' base areas had lost out to the party officials like Liu Shaoqi who had worked a great deal in the 'white' areas behind Japanese or Nationalist Chinese lines. If Peng Dehuai had been seduced by this argument before, Liu had to regard the former Defence Minister as a long-term threat, the potential leader of military opposition to his succeeding Mao. Thus the last thing Liu needed was for the outspoken Peng Dehuai to return, vindicated, to the Politburo.[133]

Entrepreneurship

In his discussion of Peng Dehuai and the three red banners, Liu was essentially letting the seven thousand cadres in on the consensus within the PSC. But one of the most fascinating passages in his speech dealt with a matter probably more familiar to his audience than to himself: the immense trading network that had sprung up all over the country as a result of decentralization and necessity. It was a foretaste of what was to happen in China in the 1980s with official encouragement. Liu revealed that Fujian's Lianjiang county bartered its kelp for other goods in over ten provinces. Then he spoke of the representative of a brigade in Henan's Linying county who had travelled well over a thousand miles to buy 200 carts in Canton. When the railways would not transport the carts, he was at his wits' end until he found an air-force officer who was prepared to put them on a plane to Wuhan, from where he managed to get them home. According to Liu, every district, *xian*, city, enterprise, commune, and brigade had many people involved in commerce, including purchasing agents who were flying all over the country to get things the state could not supply. He estimated that there were at least a million people, perhaps a few million, involved in such activities; there were over 50,000 in Beijing alone.

What kind of commerce was this? Socialist or non-socialist, nationally owned, collectively owned, or capitalist? Clearly troubled, but unwilling to clamp down on such activities for fear of precipitating shortages, Liu prescribed investigation, cessation of unreasonable activity, and rectification of the rest, with tough treatment for corrupt groups who had embezzled thousands, perhaps tens of thousands, of yuan. Lianjiang county's activities, for instance, should be taken over by the state trading network.[134] Liu's concern over these unorthodox activities may be part of the explanation for his extreme leftism during the Socialist Education Movement two years later.

Liu Shaoqi's accomplishment

Had the second draft of his written report been the only message which Liu Shaoqi sent to the Seven Thousand Cadres Conference on behalf of the central leadership, it is doubtful if his audience would have been encouraged enough to go forth and rectify the manner in which they ran the country. To be sure, the centre accepted the principal blame, but discredited slogans were reaffirmed and there was scant probing of the causes of the catastrophe. Any experienced CCP cadre could see how the phrasing could serve equally to justify a new course or a U-turn, depending on the balance of forces in the Politburo and the overall state of the economy. Liu's written report was an uncertain trumpet at best. It had to be elaborated.

Liu's speech, for all its compromises and obfuscations, gave the report the appropriate spin. He did not contradict his report, but in replying to the conference debate, he probed more deeply into the issues troubling his auditors, utilizing linguistic nuances so that they could grasp the political realities, but understand that these were not going to be allowed to stand in the way of the restoration of sane operating procedures. In particular, his discussion of the nine/one fingers issue may have been calculated to suggest that he was even prepared to stand up against the cherished shibboleths of the Chairman in the national interest. Liu had assumed the mantle of head of state and heir-presumptive to the party chairmanship in April 1959; in January 1962 he may have convinced the junior officials of the CCP that he had the mettle to succeed in those roles. Reportedly there was general satisfaction that he had said many things that had needed saying for years.[135] If the seven thousand cadres had any doubt after Liu's speech about the distinction between respecting the *amour propre* of the Chairman and kowtowing to him, their uncertainties should have been cleared up when Defence Minister Marshal Lin Biao spoke on the afternoon of 29 January.

Lin Biao supports Mao[136]

Apart from Liu Shaoqi, Lin Biao was the PSC member most threatened by a root-and-branch reappraisal of the GLF. True, he could not be held guilty of stoking up ideological fervour and mishandling economic affairs. Pleading illness, Lin had maintained a low political profile during most of the 1950s, even after his elevation to the Politburo in 1955 and to the PSC in 1958;[137] he appears to have made only one major speech during the decade between the establishment of the PRC and the Lushan conference in 1959. Though it was given in 1958, it was on military affairs.[138] But when summoned to Lushan by Mao to denounce and replace Peng Dehuai, he readily complied, and any rehabilitation of his predecessor as Defence Minister, which would probably have been an inevitable consequence of a 'reversal of verdicts' on the GLF, would have made his position untenable.[139] Thus on this one issue, his interests coincided with those of Liu Shaoqi,[140] and in his speech he briefly indicated his continuing antipathy to Peng's crimes.[141]

Lin Biao's main concern, however, was not to bury Peng but to praise Mao:

In times of troubles, we must rely even more on the leadership of the centre, on the leadership of Chairman Mao, and trust Chairman Mao's leadership even more. If we just do that it will be even easier to overcome our troubles. The facts prove that these troubles spring precisely from our failure in many instances to act according to Chairman Mao's directives. If we proceed according to Chairman Mao's directives, if we listen to what Chairman Mao says, then our troubles will be very much smaller, and there will be fewer curves in the road. I have not been in the centre long, but from what I have seen and heard, there are three types of thinking among the comrades: one is the thought of Chairman Mao; the second is 'leftist' thought; and the third is rightist thought . . .

Whenever in the past our work was done well, it was precisely when Chairman Mao's thought received no interference. Every time that Chairman Mao's thought was not respected or suffered interference, there has been trouble. That is essentially the history of the last few decades. Therefore, in times of difficulty, the party must unite even more and must follow Chairman Mao even more closely. Only in this way can the party go from victory to victory and the country improve further.[142]

Lin was equally unquestioning in his support of the GLF and its symbols. The party's successes were very great and its shortcomings were minute and secondary compared to them. The three red banners were 'correct, a reflection of real life, a creation springing from the development of the Chinese revolution, a creation of the people, a creation of the party'. Facts proved that one could and ought to leap forward. Although the output figures for the previous year and the current year were not very large, and would not be next year either, compared with other periods in the nation's history, it was still a GLF. Only if measured against excessively large targets and attempts at excessively rapid completion, the product of subjectivism, did it fail to qualify as a GLF.[143]

There had been difficulties over the past few years, and the supply of food, clothing, and necessities was rather tight everywhere, but, Lin asserted, these were temporary problems which could be overcome, and already there was a turn for the better. And the causes? Lin cited first natural calamities, which had virtually wiped out (*huimie*) some areas. Of course, there were always mistakes in the implementation of directives, not deliberate and often due to inexperience, but no error of line had been committed. Only a very few cadres had assumed special privileges.

Lin made a point of tackling the issue on which Mao had attacked Peng Dehuai at Lushan: did gains outweigh losses or vice versa? Agriculture and industry had suffered, he admitted, but on the construction front there had been a great increase of income. Incautiously, he appears to have repeated Peng Dehuai's Lushan error of saying there had been losses and gains, *in that order*. Even if the losses were more obvious now, the gains would become more obvious in the future. It was like paying for an education: for seventeen years a pupil was fed and clothed and produced nothing, but thereafter the training brought dividends. Superficially the losses were larger; but in reality and over the long haul, gains greatly exceeded losses.[144]

In his peroration on this subject, Lin pulled out all the stops in his effort to enthuse his audience and rally it behind Mao. The party had the very heavy responsibility of combating both imperialism and what Mao had called its running dog, revisionism, that is, the Americans and the Russians, though Lin did not specify. At home the tasks were especially heavy, to make the nation glorious, rich, and powerful. Unquestionably, China had all the attributes to enable her to move out of backwardness to become an advanced nation. Economic advance demanded productive forces, the key productive force was man, and China had the largest population in the world. China could overtake not just Britain but also America. Lin cited America as one of a number of encouraging examples of speedy economic growth. A century earlier, America had been nothing more than a wasteland inhabited by a few Indians, yet today it was a most advanced country—materially only, spiritually it was corrupt (*fushi*). To achieve greatness, countries needed unity and leadership. In a passage reminiscent of the appeals of other leaders in other countries at other times, Lin Biao asserted that the Chinese people could without doubt establish their country as a major force in the world if they would just unite and 'trust the party, trust Chairman Mao, trust Marxism-Leninism, have faith in China and in reality'.[145]

Mao's 'self-criticism'

Lin Biao's speech was allegedly out of harmony with the mood of the conference,[146] but Lin's praise of the Chairman almost certainly did not seem as egregious to the rank and file then as is now made out. Indeed Zhou Enlai, in his self-criticism at the second session of the party's 8th Congress in 1958, had expressed similar views on the importance of sticking closely to Mao's precepts and the defeats that ensued when the CCP did not. Faith in the god-like leader was built into the Leninist system, encouraging followers to suspend doubts and trust that everything would turn out well in the end even if his current activities clearly defied common sense.[147] At any rate, Mao was extremely appreciative;[148] he presumably felt the gratitude pithily expressed by another dominating twentieth-century leader: 'He supported me steadfastly when I was right and, more important, when I wasn't.'[149] After listening to Lin, Mao reportedly asked PLA Chief-of-Staff Luo Ruiqing if he could make that kind of speech. Luo, honestly perhaps, foolishly certainly, replied that he could not.[150] Nor is it surprising that Mao chose Luo as the man he would put on the spot. He must have been told that Luo had argued violently with Lin's wife, Ye Qun, against including excessive praise for Mao when they were drafting the written version of Lin's speech, and had been accused of revisionism by Lin Biao for his pains.[151] Mao would not forget. As for his critics, Mao commented privately: 'They complain all day long and get to watch plays at night. They eat three full meals a day—and fart. That's what Marxism-Leninism means to them.'[152]

But in public, on 30 January, and for now, the Chairman was at his most avuncular,[153] a gentle giant spouting Chinese history, citing classical fiction, an Olympian deity ready to admit that he, too, could err:

On 12 June last year, during the last day of the [Beijing] Conference called by the Central Committee, I talked about my own shortcomings and mistakes. I said I wanted the comrades to convey what I said to their various provinces and districts. I found out later that many districts did not get my message, as if my mistakes could be hidden and ought to be hidden. Comrades, they mustn't be hidden. Any mistakes that the Centre has made ought to be my direct responsibility, and I also have an indirect share in the blame because I am the Chairman of the Central Committee. I don't want other people to shirk their responsibility. There are some other comrades who also bear responsibility, but the person primarily responsible should be me.[154]

This 'self-criticism' was part of a long disquisition on democratic centralism in which Mao urged his colleagues not to be afraid of criticism from the masses or their subordinates. In his customary earthy style, Mao told those who thought of themselves as tigers, shirking responsibility and repressing criticism, that they would all fall: 'You think that nobody will really dare to touch the arse of tigers like you? They damn well will!'[155]

But Mao knew there was one exception, a tiger that nobody would confront directly: himself. Liu's report did not do it, nor did his speech. Even Peng Zhen made his remarks in Mao's absence. There was a revealing moment towards the end of the Chairman's speech when he said: 'As for me, I will not go out during the day; I will not go to the theatre at night. Please come and criticize me day and night [*laughter*]. Then I will sit down and think about it carefully, not sleep for two or three nights, think about it until I understand it, and then write a sincere self-examination.'[156] The laughter was the give-away. Nobody could conceive of Mao being criticized. Nor did Mao give any indication of changing his ways. He told the conference that in the PSC he would always give way if everyone (*daj.a*) disagreed with him! Even if Mao had been in the habit of holding regular meetings of the PSC to discuss policies before announcing them instead of running China guerrilla-style, this would not have been much of a concession. There was always at least one member of the PSC who would go along with the Chairman.

More importantly, Mao's self-criticism amounted to little more than acknowledging the truth of the legendary motto found on President Truman's desk: 'The buck stops here';[157] and he may have have been prepared to acknowledge that much, only in order to remind everyone that, though retired to the second front, he, not Liu, was still the ruler of China.[158]

Much of Mao's speech was a justification of the mistakes of the past four years on the grounds of inexperience, his, yes, but everyone else's too. He rehearsed the history of the communist revolution to show how long it took, and with how many setbacks, to work out a winning strategy, and to remind his audience that it was he who had led them to victory (making no concession, incidentally, to the proposition of post-Mao historians that the 'Thought of Mao Zedong' was the collective product of many minds). He recited a long list of admiring foreigners to whom he had protested the CCP's inexperience in economic development, and he freely admitted his personal ignorance, particularly of industry and commerce. '[U]nderstanding the laws of socialist construction , Mao said, 'must pass through a process.'[159] For the Chairman, as for Lin Biao the day before, the greatest man-made human catastrophe perpetrated in the peace-time history of the world's longest continuous civilization with the world's largest population was simply part of the learning curve.

As in 1959 when he had last had to acknowledge *force majeure*, Mao trotted out a line from Engels, 'Freedom is the recognition of necessity', an acceptance that man alone, however well led and motivated, could not achieve everything.[160] But there was no self-criticism for his personal role in framing the general line that demanded leaping progress; no acknowledgement that he had godfathered the communes and promoted their mess-halls and supply system that had now been abandoned. There was certainly no expression of regret for the millions of deaths resulting from his Promethean urges. Significantly, Mao referred a few times to Liu Shaoqi's report which had reaffirmed that there had been no mistakes in line, but never to Liu's speech in which the latter had hinted at line error by indicating that the Chairman's customary upbeat nine-fingers/one-finger appraisal of any crisis no longer had any validity.

Under the circumstances, it is difficult to see why Mao's speech had so ameliorating an impact on the political situation. True, he specifically re-endorsed the plethora of plans that the CCP had laboriously generated the previous year, and this accolade would give saner policies a boost:

It is not enough to have the General Line; it is also necessary that, under the leadership of the General Line, in the domains of industry, agriculture, commerce, education, army, government and Party, there should be a complete set of concrete general and specific policies and methods which are suited to our conditions. Only then is it possible to persuade the masses and the cadres.[161]

True, he also endorsed working with even unrevolutionary intellectuals so long as they were patriotic. He reaffirmed that 95 per cent of the population could be classified as 'the people' with whom the CCP should unite, though there was just a hint of future turmoil:

The reactionary classes are now no longer as ferocious as hitherto ... But we may on no account underestimate these remnants. We must continue to struggle against them ... The reactionary classes which have been overthrown are still planning a come-back. In a socialist society, new bourgeois elements may still be produced. During the whole socialist stage there still exist classes and class struggle, and this class struggle is a protracted, complex, sometimes even violent affair.[162]

Perhaps in the context of Mao's self-criticism and the general atmosphere of the conference these words seemed only the harmless rumblings of an extinct volcano.

Indeed, one cannot read the later party histories or talk with older Chinese scholars and officials without concluding that the Chairman's 'self-criticism' had a profound effect upon the political atmosphere. Even a minimal apology was so unusual as to be electrifying.[163] The headline told the story; the message was the message. Mao himself was pleased enough with the speech to decide immediately to review the text, presumably for publication.[164] Nevertheless, those who knew Mao best should perhaps have reflected on how the Chairman must have felt about paying even this slight obeisance to the party norms which governed the behaviour of every other CCP member.

Despite his 'self-criticism', Mao did not hint publicly at formally handing over power to his more sober colleagues. Could he have done so in private? The timing would have been right. Depending on whether one reckoned from its first session in September 1956, or its second in May 1958 (presumably the former), the constitutional five-year term of the CCP's 8th Congress was either already or almost over. Mao could have resigned at the 9th Congress with honour simply by exchanging his party chairmanship for the honorary chairmanship tailor-made for him in the constitution adopted at the CCP's 8th Congress, thus completing his retirement to the 'second front' of the leadership.[165] The behaviour of Mao's colleagues after the Seven Thousand Cadres Conference certainly suggests that they considered a new era had begun even if a formal rite of passage had not yet been celebrated.[166] But however they interpreted Mao, they would find that he had only beat a temporary retreat after the conference was over.

A chorus of criticism

Even if Mao's own behaviour was unlikely to change, his stress on the democratic element in democratic centralism unleashed a spate of criticism of lesser men if not of himself. Responsible officials from the centre, the regional bureaux, and the provinces made self-criticisms, as their work over the past few years came under the severe scrutiny of their subordinates.[167] Among those forced to self-criticize was Ke Qingshi. On 6 February, he admitted to having been over-excited after the bumper 1958 summer harvest, to have believed in the extravagant claims for unit output, and to have become convinced as a result that China's grain problem was finally solved. Tan Zhenlin, the agricultural overlord during the GLF had been criticizing himself frequently for some time.[168] The Liaoning 1st secretary, Huang Huoqing, said that the worst leftism had occurred after the Lushan conference of 1959, and he detailed the errors over which he had presided: speeding up the transition to communism, preventing private pig-rearing, high production estimates, excessive levels of grain procurement, massive promotion of mess-halls, abolishing peasants' private plots. In Guizhou, according to 1st secretary Zhou Lin, peasants had not only been subjected to excessive procurement, but had been persecuted on the assumption that they must be hiding and distributing among themselves the surplus grain they supposedly had.[169] Zhao Ziyang, who ran Guangdong province under Tao Zhu,[170] probably spoke for all provincial leaders when he said that in his area they had neglected two fundamental party traditions: treating the illness to save the patient when conducting internal party struggles; and seeking truth from facts, making investigations and following the mass line. The Shanxi 1st secretary, Tao Lujia, took a similar line. As a result of such self-criticism, senior provincial officials who had suffered in those struggles had their cases re-examined and overturned: Pan Fusheng, the Henan 1st secretary who had been displaced by the disastrous Wu Zhipu; Jiang Yizhen and Wei Jinshui, both Fujian officials; and Li Zhongyun from the northeast, whose letter detailing the problems of the GLF had been blasted by Mao at the 1959 Lushan conference.[171]

PSC speakers

Finally it was time for the other PSC members to speak. Chen Yun, who had been briefly recalled by Mao in 1959 to institute more rational economic policies,[172] was invited by the Chairman to address the conference but cautiously declined.[173] The remaining three members of the PSC, Zhou Enlai, Zhu De, and Deng Xiaoping did speak, however, adding their voices to the chorus of self-criticism. Zhu De, who addressed the Shandong provincial group on 3 February, made an interesting revelation and startling recommendation:

In the last few years, the wealth of peasant families, accumulated over a long time, has all been spent. They should be allowed to accumulate their family wealth again. This doesn't mean turning back the clock because, after all, production teams remain the foundation of our agricultural economy. When they are in good shape and the peasants have once again built up their family wealth, everything else will be easy to do.[174]

What Zhu De meant by family wealth, other than surplus grain, is unclear, but this brief passage was a vivid reminder of how close to the margin of subsistence Chinese peasants lived and how the GLF and the three bitter years had wiped out that margin. Theoretically, they were cocooned in the collective security of the production team, but the straightforward Zhu De realized they needed the protection of their own parsimony as well, building up savings by selling the produce of their private plots. Perhaps, too, Zhu wished to return circumspectly to the issue of family farming which he had raised at the Beijing work conference in mid-1961.[175]

Deng Xiaoping addressed the conference on 6 February on party matters.[176] Like Liu Shaoqi at the start of the conference, Deng at its end felt obliged to accentuate the positive by listing five special aspects of the CCP, five 'goods' (*wu hao*): its guiding ideology; its central leadership; a large contingent of tried cadres; its traditions and its work style; and the people of China. Under the headings of ideology, leadership, and traditions, Deng naturally referred approvingly to Mao, but when congratulating himself and his colleagues in the central leadership for being willing to make self-criticism, he cited Liu's report but not Mao's speech. Was the Chairman's self-criticism too sensitive a topic for Deng to risk touching the 'tiger's arse?'[177] Nor did Deng refer to Liu's speech at all, even though it was the state chairman's more individual and important contribution to the conference. Formally, perhaps he did not need to, but politically it would have been a powerful gesture of solidarity.[178] Was Deng trying to avoid straining his relations with Mao by openly aligning himself with Liu's daring modification of the Chairman's nine/one formula?

Deng went on to explain how this 'five good' party had gone off the rails by failing to live up to its traditions. Since the conquest of power, some party officials had forgotten that they were the servants not the masters of the people.[179] As officials, they neglected to investigate, lost contact with reality, did not speak the truth. Struggle became too fierce. The restoration of democratic centralism would be an important means of correcting these problems. For Deng, as a general secretary wishing to restore control over the party's 17 million members,[180] insufficient centralism in the form of dispersionism seemed to be the principal problem. Dispersionism, he argued, led to commandism and a weakening of democracy, implying that when the centre's grip slackened, local party leaders turned into petty tyrants. The ultimate objective for the party, as for the country, was the one expressed by Mao at Qingdao in the summer of 1957: to create 'a political climate in which there is both centralism and democracy, discipline and freedom, unity of purpose and personal ease of mind and liveliness'.[181]

Deng stressed two essentials for restoring the CCP's traditions: it was impermissible not to carry out party decisions; and it was impermissible to form factions (though Mao interrupted to say that only secret factions were unacceptable).[182] But turning to the democratic element in democratic centralism, Deng re-emphasized the warning issued by both Mao and Liu against arbitrarily labelling opponents, a practice which had led to party members writing anonymous letters instead of standing up openly to make their criticisms.[183] At every level, cadres working together should supervise each other.[184] Deng suggested on behalf of the centre, with Mao interrupting to reinforce the message, that after the conference was over, units at every level should have a letting-off-steam (*chuqi*) session, and that within the leadership cores there should be frank exchanges and self-examinations.[185]

Deng had three further proposals for averting future disasters: the regularization of daily work so often disrupted by mass movements; the careful selection and nurture of cadres; and the careful study of Marxist-Leninist theory and Mao's works. But his extended discussion of democratic centralism had exposed the heart of the problem without pointing the way to a solution. It was all very well for the leadership cores of provinces, districts, and *xian* to have heart-to-heart chats about where they had gone wrong, and for local tigers to have their 'arses touched', but if the centre had to bear the principal blame for the GLF disaster, then this process had also to take place at the centre. The missed opportunity of the Seven Thousand Cadres Conference was that all but one of Mao's colleagues seemed unprepared to face up to that challenge in the manner that they had urged upon their subordinates. In the available texts of top leaders' speeches to the conference, only Zhou Enlai's, delivered on the final day of the conference when it was useless as a spur to his colleagues, contains genuine *self*-criticism, and its sincerity is questionable.

Zhou Enlai's self-criticism

Zhou took responsibility for both institutional and individual mistakes. He summarized the institutional ones under the rubric of the State Council's 'five highs': excessively high production figures, excessive procurement of grain, excessive consumption, excessive transfers of grain from the provinces to the centre, and excessive exports.[186] The current economic figures which Zhou gave, and their policy implications, will be discussed in the next chapter; here we are concerned with their political aspect of the premier's self-criticism.

Looking back over the GLF, Zhou mused about how one could have thought that a 1957 grain output of 180–5 m. tons could overnight become 325 m. tons, the median 1958 target, which was translated at the end of the year into a claimed output of 350 m. tons. Even 250 m. tons, the revised output claim issued after the Lushan conference in 1959 was impossible. The steel target had been forced up 18 m. tons in 1960, affecting the production of other departments and forcing many enterprises to cease operations. Forcing the coal target up to 400 m. tons in the same year had resulted in damage to equipment and a precipitous drop in output in 1961.[187]

Planning in the GLF had been a total muddle, Zhou's account made clear. Plans had to be changed often because figures did not accord with reality. The pattern was of high figures at the start of the year, followed by a mid-year downward adjustment; by the end of the year, the government was clearly ready to accept whatever figures could actually be achieved. In 1960, the centre was given first one and then a second draft of the plan, and later a third when some ministries had revised their figures. Since there may have been fourth and fifth drafts at the local levels, everything was done wrong.[188] The planners had not done well at seeking truth from facts or in achieving any kind of an overall balance in the economy. The premier went on to explain this planning wonderland:

We were not in accord with Chairman Mao's directives to start from reality, to take agriculture as the basis, to arrange appropriately the proportions between agriculture, light industry, and heavy industry, to put emphasis on having a variety of goods and on their quality to achieve an overall balance, to leave room for manoeuvre. Instead, we disobeyed Chairman Mao's directives and objective laws, worked from a subjectivist viewpoint, stressed quantity and speed, did not leave room for manoeuvre, allowed the gaps [in the plans] to expand, neglected variety and quality, and solely and one-sidedly sought figures and high targets. In organizing production and work, we messed things up, blindly issuing directives, held telephone and on-the-spot conferences; documents and commendations cascaded downwards, and in the end a large quantity of duties descended upon the *xian*, communes, and factories. The upper levels wanted various figures and statistical tables, and raised various strange problems, to which the lower levels had no means of responding; all the communes could do was to telephone in replies, and the only thing for some telephonists to do was embrace their machines like crying infants.[189]

Zhou had earlier cited in passing such personal lapses as his suggestions that universities should hold winter vacation entrance exams and that factories and mines should run institutions of higher learning, the result being that there was an excessive enrolment of students. Now he expatiated on two concrete examples of his own errors. The first had occurred on 26 August 1959, when he reported to the NPC's standing committee on the key figures for the 1959 plan. Zhou confessed that he had 'mistakenly and one-sidedly laid down that industry and agriculture should increase production at leap forward pace each year'. He had suggested that a 10 per cent +

increase in agricultural output should be regarded as a leap forward, a 15 per cent + increase as a great leap forward, and a 20 per cent + increase as a specially great leap forward. In the light of the earlier demands for doubling output in 1958 and a further 40 per cent increase in 1959, Zhou said, these percentages looked comparatively realistic, but in fact they were neither practical nor scientific, and one had only to investigate the development of agriculture world-wide to see this. Setting the speed of the leap forward not in accord with reality was 'to disobey Chairman Mao's repeated demands that plans should be settled on the basis of seeking truth from facts and overall balance, leaving room for manoeuvre, and the result was more haste less speed' (yu su ze bu da).[190]

Zhou's second example was the devolution of economic powers in the drive to create regions with relatively complete industrial systems. To achieve this goal, control over 98.5 per cent of light industry and 76 per cent of heavy industry was handed down to lower levels of government, along with appropriate financial, commercial, cultural, and technological powers.[191]

Zhou's self-criticisms were unusual enough coming from a member of the PSC that a later Chinese historian drew attention to them.[192] Two caveats are in order. Firstly, Zhou gave two very broad hints that the State Council was not totally to blame. He imputed responsibility to various organs under his leadership because 'we did the concrete work under the leadership of the CC secretariat', clearly a dig at Deng Xiaoping. When he had prepared the document introducing excessive devolution of powers, it was 'passed by the centre'. This could have meant Mao, though the Chairman was unlikely to have pored over a detailed planning document, or, more likely, Liu and Deng.[193] These comments served to underline the degree to which control of economic policy had passed from the government's State Council to the party's secretariat since the second session of the CCP's 8th Congress at the outset of the GLF. It was convenient to remind officials of this fact in order to diffuse blame. Conceivably, too, Zhou was angry that in his speech the previous day, Deng Xiaoping had not accepted responsibility for any of these matters. Zhou may have decided not to let him get away with it.[194]

The more important point is that Zhou's self-criticism was meaningless. While various vice-premiers of the State Council and senior officials of its subordinate ministries—Zhou Enlai singled out the Ministry of Agriculture and financial and trade departments—had doubtless made many errors of judgement in the previous few years, they had devised the 'five highs' policies in response to the overarching demand of Mao, supported by Liu Shaoqi, for leaping progress. Zhou's redefinition of leaping progress had been a loyal attempt to lower expectations and yet justify what had been achieved; in his decentralization document, he had simply been following Mao's orders. Zhou Enlai and his State Council colleagues had been criticized by Mao and Liu for opposing 'blind advance' at the beginning of the GLF, and had no recourse but to swim with the tide thereafter.[195] Zhou's assertion now that they had disobeyed the sage council of a cautious Mao who had consistently warned against flights of fancy, and his warm endorsements of the three red banners, represented a degree of kowtowing to the Chairman at the Seven Thousand Cadres Conference which Chinese historians have so far pinned only on Lin Biao.[196] No wonder the editors of the *Selected Works of Zhou Enlai*, doubtless solicitous of the premier's so-far untarnished reputation in the PRC, decided not to include this important speech.

A ludicrous self-criticism of this type was hardly likely to encourage the rank and file. Perhaps the junior officials at the Seven Thousand Cadres Conference were not *au fait* with the intimate details of policy disputes in the capital, but everyone in Zhou's audience knew that Mao had been the driving force behind all the most extravagant GLF policies, even if he had not micro-managed the details. The example Zhou was setting was that everyone who had been proved right about the GLF should make a confession in order to allow those who had been wrong to get off scot free!

But Zhou's action did underline the coyness of his colleagues. The admissions by Mao, Liu, and others of the culpability of the centre were all very well—the speeches of PSC members were circulated to the party[197]—but a blanket confession implicated all while pinpointing none. Liu Shaoqi, unlike Zhou, did not specify how and when he personally had gone over the top in 1958, in the manner clearly expected of lower-level leaders in their heart-to-heart sessions.[198] Had he done so, conceivably Mao, too, would have had to beat his own breast more convincingly.

At the 1959 Lushan conference, there was some excuse for members of the PSC and the Politburo not to confront Mao. Despite difficulties, the GLF seemed to have registered some spectacular successes. The problems were being tackled before Peng Dehuai intervened and Mao was leading that process. A public admission of massive statistical exaggeration was about to be made. Liu, Zhou Enlai, and their colleagues may not have expected that, despite this admission, a counter-attack against Peng would result in the GLF being relaunched; and they could not have known that they were in the middle of the first of three bitter years which would cost millions of lives. Above all, Mao had confronted them with choosing between Peng and himself, and in those circumstances, they had to back their Chairman.[199]

The situation in January 1962 was completely different. The human disaster of the GLF was plain, even though the available texts indicate that no leader was prepared to spell it out by alluding to the massive death toll. The economy was in ruins. Apart from the communes, where Mao had played an important role, Liu, Zhou, and Deng were spearheading its rehabilitation. The Chairman was on the defensive. The only choice to be made was between realism and megalomania in the governance of the country. Now, if ever, was the moment for his PSC colleagues to attempt to ensure that Mao could never again perpetrate a similar disaster. Instead, they allowed him to save face, presumably partly because they believed that they had the reins of power securely in their hands, and partly because Khrushchev's secret speech had warned all communist élites of the dangers of tampering with the cult of a leader. If the repercussions had been so immense in the case of a dead dictator, how much more potentially catastrophic might they be with a live leader, especially one who, as Lushan had shown, would use all his considerable resources to resist his dethronement.

The Peng Dehuai issue

Behind these calculations, at the heart of the matter, was the case of the wronged Peng Dehuai. Mao and Liu seem to have had an agreement, probably tacit, certainly unprincipled, that Peng could not be rehabilitated as part of the massive campaign to 'reverse verdicts' on cadres and others innocently washed away in the tide of anti-right opportunism in the wake of the marshal's disgrace. Overseen by Deng Xiaoping, the extent of the amnesty programme revealed the widespread impact of the 1959–60 purges and underlined why in 1961 it was difficult to persuade officials to move forward on what at some future date might be described as right opportunist policies. Seventy per cent of the 3,650,000 cadres and CCP members and all of the over 3,700,000 ordinary citizens whose cases were investigated were adjudged to have been wronged.[200]

The justification for not including Peng in this amnesty was given by Liu in his speech to the Seven Thousand Cadres Conference.

Peng did not participate in the meeting, but the previous November he had been allowed to return to his native village for a fifty-day visit. It had been his findings there in December 1958 that had helped to increase his awareness of the damage being done by the GLF.[201] On his visit in 1961, the last time he would be allowed to leave his place of confinement on the outskirts of Beijing for another four years, the responses of local officials to his questions led him to exclaim: 'Ai! I was afraid of hunger in the old society, and so I joined the revolution. I never thought that twelve years after the victory of the revolution our people would still not be able to fill their stomachs. What a profound lesson!'[202] With this visit fresh in his mind, no wonder the former defence minister was infuriated when he read Liu's attack on him. He sat down and wrote an 80,000-word autobiographical apologia rejecting the charges of participating in anti-party groups. He sent this document to Mao and his colleagues on 16 June 1962, calling for a comprehensive investigation, and reiterated this appeal in a further letter on 22 August.

In his apologia, Peng rejected the allegation that he had been party to the Gao–Rao conspiracy. He admitted to have been hoodwinked by Gao for a time, but after Deng Xiaoping had talked to him, he had seen the light and told Deng whatever he knew. Peng seemed even more incensed by the imputation of treacherous relations with foreign countries. He admitted only that he had not talked enough about the three red banners (i.e. had not praised them) while touring the Soviet Union and Eastern Europe prior to the Lushan conference, but said that this was because he had focused on the 1959 Tibetan rebellion and the 1958 bombardment of Quemoy. Since he knew no foreign languages, a Chinese interpreter was present at every meeting and he suggested that the CC should examine the interpreters' records to see if he had said anything wrong.[203]

Peng's rebuttal was an explosive document which still has not been published in full.[204] At the time, even a PSC member like Chen Yun was not shown it, and when the existence of the missive was revealed at the CC's 10th plenum in August–September 1962, only extracts were distributed. At the plenum, a special investigation committee was set up under one of Peng Dehuai's old adversaries, Marshal He Long, which ultimately proved unable to pin any crimes on Peng.[205]

But Peng's anger had confirmed that his return was too threatening a prospect for too many people at the top of the Chinese leadership. Perhaps the spate of attempted and successful military coups in

Asia in 1958—in Burma, Indonesia, Iraq, Pakistan, and Thailand—had been one reason why, in 1959, Mao had talked of Peng's 'military club' and the PSC had united against the marshal; and there may well have been fears, even in 1962, (after two more coups, in Laos and South Korea, the previous year) of the power implications of the return of a vindicated military hero.

What Liu and his colleagues could not or would not understand or face up to—not even Zhou Enlai, who had got very drunk in Lushan in 1959 when Peng Dehuai was disgraced[206]—was that only by rehabilitating Peng Dehuai could Mao be visibly and therefore effectively tamed, and that only by so taming Mao would his leftist demons be exorcised. It would be a costly mistake, for them personally and for China.

APPENDIX 2: THE CHANGGUANLOU INCIDENT

During the Cultural Revolution, much vitriol was poured upon the perpetrators of the so-called Changguanlou incident, a meeting of senior Beijing city officials in December 1961 under the leadership of Deng Tuo, the former editor of the *People's Daily*, which produced a critical review of central policy documents from the GLF. The meeting, named for a building near the Beijing Zoo where it took place, was the culmination of an investigation process originally sparked by Mao's demand for grass-roots surveys. Deng Tuo and his colleagues were later accused of having prepared a ringing indictment of the 'three red banners' for Peng Zhen to use against Mao. Western scholars, who have had to contend with a curious silence on this episode in post-Mao historiography, have tended to assume that the meeting did take place and did indeed produce a document highly critical of the GLF, but that Peng Zhen, either out of discretion or because it was unnecessary, decided not to report on the Beijing party's findings at the Seven Thousand Cadres Conference.[1]

Recent Chinese revelations suggest that the explanation of the Changguanlou affair may be less dramatic than alleged in Cultural Revolution accounts. In his written report to the Seven Thousand Cadres Conference in January 1962, Liu Shaoqi stated that the CC secretariat had very recently submitted a report on policy-making to Mao and the Politburo Standing Committee.[2] It was based on a study of central documents issued in the past few years. The authoritative account of the Seven Thousand Cadres Conference given by Zhang Tianrong states that Deng Xiaoping oversaw an investigation into central documents in order to assess the work of the secretariat.[3] Another Chinese account reports that the report was handed to Mao by Deng and possibly Peng Zhen on 16 December 1961. It also indicates that it carefully insulated Mao from criticism.[4]

In early December, Peng Zhen told a subordinate about the central secretariat's investigation and ordered that a Beijing task force be set up under Deng Tuo to replicate it. At this time, the Beijing party committee was completing a report summing up its investigations earlier in the year in the city's Huairou county, where Peng had spent considerable time. Having examined the grass roots, the Beijing cadres were being told to see how the problems which they had found had come about. In a sense, they would be complementing the central secretariat's bird's-eye view with their own worm's-eye view. According to a hostile but detailed Cultural Revolution account, the Beijing investigation lasted from 9 to 20 December. The work was divided up under nine heads to allow appropriate officials to investigate their areas of responsibility; the final product was a 20,000 word 'Extracts from central documents' prefaced only by a brief note periodizing when central directives caused problems, a periodization which jibed with the two upsurges of the GLF.[5]

By this time the central secretariat report had been handed to Mao. As Deng's second-in-command in the secretariat, Peng Zhen would have been aware of the contents of that document. Inevitably, the two reports would have included many of the same materials. Even if Peng had originally contemplated submitting the Beijing materials to the forthcoming Seven Thousand Cadres Conference, he would now have known that they would simply be repetitious.

Indeed, since Deng himself had to supervise the first stage of the writing of Liu's report—a more important document than the secretariat report since it would have to be circulated among so many party officials—and the conference arrangements,[6] Peng Zhen may anyway have played a central role in overseeing the secretariat report to the PSC.

If so, the likelihood of an overlap with the Changguanlou document would have been even greater. This would explain why Peng did not speak to the Beijing document at the Seven Thousand Cadres Conference. It would also explain why cultural revolutionaries, who were presumably angered by implicit if not explicit criticism of Mao's GLF policies, attacked the Changguanlou document but not, to my knowledge, Deng's report.[7] The Changguanlou collection of materials may have been damningly factual without the verbal window-dressing which made the final secretariat report acceptable to Mao.[8] Or it may simply have been the highly critical oral comments made by the Beijing team as they sifted through the documents which constituted the 'Changguanlou incident'.[9]

8 ECONOMIC CRUNCH

Economic burdens

It is not clear why Zhou Enlai's exposition of the economic burdens under which China was labouring was given only on the last day of the Seven Thousand Cadres Conference. Perhaps the figures were not available before,[1] but clearly knowledge of the extent of China's predicament at the beginning of the conference would have concentrated minds even more. Zhou sought to illustrate three major problems: China's parlous grain supply situation; the relationship of that problem to the urban population; and China's external liabilities. The figures he revealed are set out in the four tables below.

As Zhou was at pains to emphasize, the peasants were under great pressure. The state had procured excessive amounts of grain from the countryside, partly because it initially assumed that the harvest was much larger than later acknowledged, and partly because of the need to feed the greatly expanded number of urban residents. In the 1st FYP, the state had left about 125 m. tons of unprocessed grain in the countryside each year after procurement; in 1962 it would be down to 100 m. tons. In consequence, the amount available for seed and fodder was down, and the average rural ration had dropped from 200 kg. per capita a year to 150 kg. (Table 8.1).

The centre's policies had squeezed the grain surplus provinces, principally Sichuan, Heilongjiang, and Jilin (Table 8.2). They had responded loyally, particularly Sichuan, to calls for the transfer of supplies to the centre for emergency use, but now the granaries in the surplus provinces were almost bare. In the 1st FYP period, these three provinces had supplied a total of about 4 m. tons a year to the centre, but this was no longer possible and other provinces could not make up the deficit. Indeed, a central report a few weeks later revealed that Sichuan and Heilongjiang were now deficit areas. Yet the centre was still responsible for vastly increased shipments of grain to the cities (Table 8.3). The government had already moved to ameliorate the urban problem with large shipments of grain from Canada and Australia to make up the urban deficit, but China's foreign exchange had to be stretched also to cover the repayment of debts, mainly to the Soviet Union (Table 8.4).[2]

TABLE 8.1. *Zhou Enlai's summary of grain figures* (m. tons)[a]

	Output[b] (Calendar)	Procurement[b] (June–June)	(2) as % of (1)	Grain returned to countryside	Rural ration (kg. per yr)
1st FYP	180	43.5	28.4	18.5	200
1958	250?				
1958–9		55.0	[26.4] [33][c]	25.0	
1959					
1959–60		60.0		25.0	
1960					
1960–1		41.8		20.0	
1961	140				
1961–2		34.0	29.1	13.4	
1962 plan	150				
1962–3 plan		39.0	32.1	13.4	150

Notes: [a]Zhou gave the figures in *yi jin*, i.e. 100 m. jin; I have converted at 2,000 jin to the ton. [b] Production figures are for unhusked grain; procurement figures are for processed grain. Using Zhou's percentages, it is possible to calculate that the ratio of a unit of processed grain to a unit of unhusked grain was 1:1.2. However, using this multiplier means that the percentage of grain procured in the 1st FYP plan period should average 29 per cent of output not 28.4 per cent as given by Zhou. [c]This is calculated from Zhou's figures; clearly the doubts he expressed about the size of the 1958 harvest reflected his knowledge of food shortages in early 1959 (*Origins* II, p. 144) which that level of procurement should not have produced. If one accepts the second officially revised estimate of 1958 output of 200 m. tons, then procurement stood at 33 per cent, well above the 1st FYP average.

Source: Zhou Enlai, *Qi Qian Ren Dahui Ziliao*, pp. 88–9.

TABLE 8.2. *Supplies of grain to centre from main surplus provinces* (m. tons)

	1st FYP average	1958	1959	1960	1961
Sichuan	1.7	2.10	2.1	1.25	0?
Jilin and Heilongjiang	2.1	2.15	2.7	1.50	0.75[a]

Note: [a]Heilongjiang alone; some residents of Jilin's capital Changchun told me in 1991 that they had not suffered the hardships felt elsewhere in China in the early 1960s.

Source: Zhou Enlai, *Qi Qian Ren Dahui Ziliao*, p. 80.

TABLE 8.3. *Zhou Enlai's depiction of the urban problem*

	Population (m.)	Grain supply (m. tons)	Workers (m.)	Wage bill (billion yuan)
1957	99.49	21.10	24.50	15.6
1960	130.00	26.25	50.44	26.3
1961	120.00	24.00	41.70	24.8

Source: Zhou Enlai, *Qi Qian Ren Dahui Ziliao*, p. 89.

TABLE 8.4. *Zhou Enlai's summary of China's international liabilities* (billion yuan)

Borrowings	Repayments	Debts	Aid pledged	Aid given	Aid due	Obligations debts + aid
7.75	4.7	3+	6.9	3.7	3.1[a]	6.2

Note: [a]It is not clear why Zhou did not give this figure as 3.2 billion yuan, i.e. 6.9 minus 3.7.
Source: Zhou Enlai, *Qi Qian Ren Dahui Ziliao*, p. 100.

The Xilou conference

Zhou's gloomy outline ensured that the most important immediate result of the Seven Thousand Cadres Conference was to unleash a flurry of activity among senior economic officials. In particular, Chen Yun clearly decided that the Chairman's 'self-criticism' and post-conference retreat meant that he would go along with radical measures to turn the economic situation around. Chen had discreetly declined Mao's invitation to address a plenary session of the Seven Thousand Cadres Conference, but now for a few months he became very active, taking the lead in devising recovery measures.

Lower down the CCP hierarchy, however, the impact of the conference was more ambiguous. Fear of retribution persisted. The failure of his colleagues openly to criticize Mao, and the Chairman's failure to perform a true self-criticism, meant that the waters still seemed muddy. Equally, Liu Shaoqi's preference for indulging in semantic sparring with the Chairman over how many fingers one should assign respectively to success and failure, instead of presenting in detail the terrible human toll of the GLF, may have angered Mao, but it meant that the vast majority of CCP cadres were ignorant of the extent of the disaster nationwide. There was a tendency to drag feet on radical recovery measures in the hope that the situation would turn around. In so far as this sentiment was widespread, the Seven Thousand Cadres Conference had failed in its primary mission of developing a unified perception of the extent of the crisis and the appropriate measures for its alleviation.

There was no top-level split, however, over the first major decision taken after the Seven Thousand Cadres Conference, which was further to reduce the urban population and the industrial work-force. By the end of 1961, the urban population had been decreased by 13 m. people and this had meant a cut of 9.5 m. workers. Most of these people had left the cities as a result of the central committee decision of June 1961.[3] On 14 February 1962, the centre decided to press on with the policy and ordered the evacuation of a further 7 m. people from the cities in the first half of the year; of these, over 5 m. would be workers. The vast majority of these workers had come into the cities after the start of 1958; those who had come before the cut-off date at the end of 1957 and were therefore not part of the GLF influx, were to be reassigned to other urban units or given financial inducements to go home. Workers who had managed to settle with their families in the cities were entitled to decide for themselves whether or not it would be a good idea for them to return to their villages.[4] It turned out to be only a preliminary decision.

Disputes did arise, however, when the first line of the leadership followed up the Seven Thousand Cadres Conference with gloomier reassessments of the economic situation and radical measures to deal with them. This process started at a PSC work conference convened by Liu Shaoqi in the Xilou, a building in the Zhongnanhai where the principal party and state offices are housed, from 21 to 23 February.[5]

The agenda of the Xilou conference included finance, banking, markets, and the overall economic situation. The principal policy paper presented for discussion was the report of the Finance and Trade Office of the State Council, which laid out national performance on the 1961 budget and credit projections and budget proposals for 1962. Supposedly revenue and expenditure in 1962 would balance out at 30 billion yuan each.

On examination, Liu Shaoqi and his colleagues were horrified to discover that these figures bore no relation to reality. Some income items in the report were bogus and some expenditures had not been counted in. The real bottom line was a 1962 budget deficit of between 5 and 6 billion yuan. This meant that the financial situation was far more precarious than the Seven Thousand Cadres Conference had been told. This was political dynamite.[6]

Behind this fiasco lay miscalculations—or a cover-up—of the financial situation during the previous four years. The original estimates had envisaged a surplus of 3.9 billion yuan. In fact, there had been massive deficits every year from 1958 on (see Table 8.5).

TABLE 8.5. *Chinese financial deficits resulting from the GLF* (billion yuan)

1958	2.18
1959	6.58
1960	8.18
1961	1.09
1958–61	18.03

Source: Cong Jin, *Quzhe Fazhande Suiyue*, p. 414; Zhong Pengrong, *Zhongguo Zhangjia Fengbo* (China's inflationary storm), p. 17.

The vice-premier responsible for the Finance and Trade Office, Li Xiannian, who estimated that the 1962 deficit would be 6 billion yuan if measures were not taken, does not appear to have taken responsibility for his officials' revelation of this colossal discrepancy.[7]

The cause of the crisis was a combination of the over-extension of credit during the GLF, and highly dubious public accounting. During the GLF, bank loans to industry had increased 12 times and to commerce 2.3 times. But as Li Xiannian admitted privately at the time and Chinese economists explained publicly twenty years later, the financial outlays and bank loans were 'to a large extent, sham in character'. Much of the capital investment was paid for out of funds earmarked for maintenance, and other aspects of daily operation, and from bank credits. The nation's bookkeeping was kept in notional balance only by counting some of the enterprises' circulating capital as taxes and interest, whereas in fact they represented loans from the state banks. During the GLF, 1958–60, the amount of currency in circulation had increased by 81.7 per cent, the fastest rise since 1950, just after the CCP takeover. By the end of 1961, currency in circulation totalled 12.53 billion yuan, a further increase of almost 7 per cent since February that year. By early February 1962, on the eve of the Xilou conference, the figure had risen to 13.7 billion yuan, representing a further rise of 11 per cent in a little over a month.[8] China's finances were out of control.

Liu Shaoqi and others berated the luckless officials and ordered them to go back and produce another report explaining what had gone wrong, a task which took them another month.[9] It was under these inauspicious circumstances that Chen Yun once more came back into his own with a speech analysing the financial and economic crisis and proposing ways to tackle it.[10]

Chen Yun's prescriptions

Chen first discussed the five major areas of crisis in the economy: agricultural output; capital investment; inflation; excessive currency in the countryside; and declining urban living standards. The first two were basic, the other three derived from them. Chen put the key problem starkly: 'There is not enough grain to eat. We imported more than 10 billion jin [5 m. tons] of grain last year, and we still need to import 8 billion jin [4 m. tons] this year. We lack oil in our stomachs and we lack clothes to wear. This result is caused directly by the decline in agricultural production.'[11] Chen acknowledged arguments among Chinese leaders over the extent of the problem; some comrades claimed that in some villages the peasants ate well and had chickens and ducks. Chen characterized that kind of village as a 'tiny minority'; in most of the country, he asserted, peasants 'do not have enough to eat'.[12] He professed himself unable to predict whether recovery would be fast or slow, pending a major investigation under way by the State Council's Agriculture and Forestry Office. But he pointed out that grain output had increased on average by only a little over 6 m. tons a year in the 1st FYP (1953–7), and since then output had declined by 40 m. tons.[13] While Chinese peasants now had more machinery and better water conservancy systems at their disposal, they were much worse off in terms of land, animals, fertilizer, tools, and seed. Over the past four years, for instance, 6.25 per cent of the country's 266 m. acres sown to crops, including some of the best land, had been lost to industry and other uses.[14]

Chen rejected the argument, however, that agriculture was holding back industry; current capital investment in the industrial sector was at too high a level even for a normal harvest year. There had been grain shortages four times since the revolution and on three of those occasions the cause had been excessive growth of the urban population due to over-investment in industry. Moreover, the number of workers was increasing much faster than industrial output, so industry was unable to meet demand in terms of volume, quality, or variety, and semi-finished goods were being stockpiled in large amounts. The whole GLF industrial drive had been premised on the false assumptions that grain output in 1958 was 350 m. tons and cotton output was 3.5 m. tons and that the country would soon be producing 50–60 m. tons of steel. Thus the level of capital investment was way out of line with the industrial base.[15] In fact, in 1961 capital investment had already been reduced by two-thirds of the 1960 level, and in 1962 it would go down to 17.6 per cent of the 1960 figure.[16]

The drastic shortfall in agricultural and industrial commodities combined with a 6–7 billion yuan increase in the money supply to cover the financial deficit were prime causes of the current inflation. Most of the extra cash had flowed to the countryside where, because of the market shortages, peasants had been able to sell goods worth a billion yuan for three times that amount over the past year. The state had insufficient goods in stock to be able to reverse this flow and prevent speculation, and was not producing enough to mop up the spare cash in the countryside. For every 100 yuan of agricultural products which peasants sold to the state, the government could furnish only perhaps 60 yuan of goods and perhaps 10–20 yuan of services in return, leaving a shortfall of the order of 20–30 yuan. Unless this situation could be stabilized there was a danger that peasants would stop selling their output.[17] On most of these issues, Chen revealed, there was disagreement over the facts and the remedies, but on one issue all were agreed: in urban areas, prices had risen and real wages had decreased sharply.[18]

Listing the conditions favourable to overcoming these problems, Chen Yun must have been conscious of the weakness of what was presumably an obligatory portion of his speech, dictated by Mao's relentless insistence on overall optimism: the general line had achieved 'a certain success', said Chen, but whereas for most people this referred to the three red banners, he defined it by output; the harvest was up; poultry and pig production were recovering; industrial capacity and infrastructure were greater than before. The people would be understanding and fair if problems were explained; and leading cadres had gained both negative and positive experience. But he warned that if officials failed to speak honestly, then the revolution could go down to defeat.[19]

Finally, Chen Yun listed six essential elements of a recovery plan. The ten-year plan should be divided into two stages, recovery and development, so that there would be no confusion about the need to continue cutting back in the first phase, which he suggested should last another three years. To prevent provincial foot-dragging in the first phase, he called for greater central control.

Secondly, Chen re-emphasized the importance of continuing to move people out of cities. While persuading people to return to the countryside was difficult, the alternative was worse. If the 1961 transfer had not taken place, the state would have needed to procure an additional 2 m. tons of grain from the peasants for the cities and that simply could not have been done.

Thirdly, inflation had to be checked by strict control of cash flows, the increased production of daily necessities, if necessary by importing raw materials or transferring them from heavy to light industry, the manufacture of a few high-priced luxury items to help mop up purchasing power, and strict controls on speculative activities by better market management.[20]

For his fourth set of prescriptions, Chen Yun turned to what he clearly considered the critical importance of ensuring at least subsistence standards in the urban areas. Here he produced three suggestions, exhibiting that penchant for detailed analysis of nuts-

and-bolts issues which had stood the CCP in good stead in 1959 when Mao had commissioned him to get the steel industry back on track.[21] Chen posited that everyone needed at least 70 grams of protein a day and pointed to soybeans as the ideal way of delivering that dosage to the urban resident. He informed his audience that each jin (0.5 kg.) of grain contained 45 grams of protein, each jin of vegetables contained 5 grams, while each liang (50 g.) of soybeans contained 20 grams. Chen's figures meant that soybeans were about 4.5 times as efficient as grain and 40 times as efficient as vegetables as a source of protein. He concluded that the objective should be to supply three jin of soybeans per month to each urban resident. This works out at one liang (a tenth of a jin) or 20 grams of protein a day, leaving a gap of 50 needed grams, presumably to come from grain and vegetables since meat and eggs were in short supply.

Basing himself on an urban population figure of 100 m., Chen called for the delivery of 3 billion jin of soybeans to the cities every year to achieve this aim (a sizeable increase on the 1.2 billion jin for eight months which the Planning Commission had called for as recently as December).[22] He stated that this should be possible within the next two years; production had been 19 billion jin before the GLF and had been 12 billion in the past two years. A quick calculation shows that even using Chen's estimate of an urban population of 100 m., this plan still left a gap of 600 m. jin.[23] In fact, the urban population at the end of 1961 was later estimated at over 127 m. This meant that 4.5 billion jin was actually needed to fulfil Chen's plan, leaving a shortfall of 1.5 billion jin.[24] Two weeks later, as we shall see, Chen began talking about supplying not all urban residents but only the 60 m. residents of big and medium-sized cities. That group alone could certainly have been catered for under his policy.[25]

Chen Yun's second suggestion for improving the lives of urban residents was to supply tens of millions of pairs of nylon socks every year!

For families with many children it is a real headache to darn socks. If we spend US $4 m. to import 1 thousand tons of nylon, we can make 40 m. pairs of nylon socks. If we make socks with nylon bottoms, we can double the output. One pair of socks can be sold for several yuan and buyers are happy, and the state can also withdraw several hundred million yuan of currency every year.[26]

Chen's third proposal might have been subtitled 'Let them eat bears' paws', for though logical, it was strangely reminiscent of

Marie Antoinette. At a time of shortages of basic necessities, Chen re-emphasized the sale of luxury foods. He suggested expanding high-priced restaurants, stocking them with 40–50 m. yuan of culinary delicacies from all over the country, thus improving the city-dwellers' life-style and mopping up spare cash.

The fifth plank of Chen's recovery programme was the fundamental importance of increasing agricultural output. He pinpointed three aspects of the problem. The output of cash crops had to grow to ensure urban commodity supplies. For every yuan the state spent purchasing cotton, it could earn 4 yuan from cotton cloth and even more if the yarn were processed into knitted goods. But producers of cash crops also had to eat. Under the present arrangement peasants got 35 jin of grain for every 100 jin of ginned cotton. This was insufficient for their needs so they converted cotton fields to grain. Chen advocated raising the rate nearly six times to 200 jin of grain for every 100 jin of ginned cotton; he also urged similar increases for the producers of other cash crops.[27]

Chen's second suggestion for improving agricultural production was revolutionary only in the sense that it went against the uniformity encouraged by the simplistic GLF preference for selecting national models and urging everyone to copy them: since the provinces producing marketable grain surpluses were very different, the government should devise appropriately different methods for each to increase their output. The one common factor should be chemical fertilizer, because it was a more cost-effective import than grain. Chen's third point was the need to allocate steel, iron, and wood for producing medium and small farm tools which were far more critical than tractors.[28]

Chen Yun's final major recommendation was that the nation's planners should shift their attention from industry to agriculture, a suggestion more easily made than implemented because planners, reared on Soviet practice, were industry-oriented.[29]

When Chen Yun repeated his Xilou remarks to a meeting of State Council officials on 26 February, his audience burst spontaneously into enthusiastic and prolonged applause.[30] Over thirty years on, it is difficult fully to grasp why. Chen was humming his favourite tune—planned and proportionate development—and repeating lessons his audience had been taught before. Possibly it was the contrast between his careful, dry-as-dust analysis and down-to-earth prescriptions on the one hand and the heady rhetoric of the GLF and the insouciant optimism of Chairman Mao on the other that was appealing. Possibly, too, the audience derived confidence from Chen Yun's belief that sensible policies could see China through the current crisis. They may also have been cheering because they had heard that Chen Yun would be in charge of the recovery effort. On 24 February, immediately after the Xilou conference, Liu Shaoqi, Zhou Enlai, and Deng Xiaoping had gone to Wuhan to see Mao. Liu had outlined the assessments and decisions made and indicated that if the Chairman did not agree with them, they would have to go back to the drawing-board and hold another conference. However, Mao gave his consent, and also agreed to the revival of the Finance and Economics Small Group under the leadership of Chen Yun.

Chen had been reluctant to accept the post, pleading ill health, perhaps reluctant to assume what would inevitably be a high-risk political role. At first it was agreed that he and Zhou Enlai would simply be members of the group under Li Fuchun's chairmanship. But at the Xilou meeting, while Chen was absent, Liu Shaoqi announced that it had been put to him by various people that Chen Yun should be chair and Li his deputy. Li indicated his willingness to serve under Chen and it was so agreed. When Chen learned what had transpired, he tried to resign—and later he strongly opposed the reprinting and distribution of any of his speeches—but Liu Shaoqi told him he would have to serve and promised him his total personal support.[31]

Perhaps the audience on 26 February would have cheered less heartily, and Chen Yun would have been less persuadable, had they all known that Mao was in fact deeply unhappy about the assessments of the Xilou meeting and had agreed to Chen's reinstatement and the distribution of his speech to cadres throughout the country only because he felt he had no other option at this point. Liu Shaoqi himself did not realize that Mao was opposed to the measures agreed; and for the moment, most officials knew only that with Chen Yun in charge, they could be at ease.[32]

On 1 July, the forty-first anniversary of the founding of the CCP, the *Guangming Ribao*, the newspaper broadly oriented towards intellectuals and professionals, printed a picture on its front page to pass on the comforting message that Mao and Chen were again working together, and that the camaraderie of the Yan'an 'round table' had been re-established. Taken at the Seven Thousand Cadres Conference, it showed a smiling Mao chatting with Chen Yun, the two men surrounded by all the other members of the PSC, also all smiling: Liu Shaoqi, Zhou Enlai, Zhu De, Lin Biao, and

Deng Xiaoping.[33] Regrettably for the readers of this enterprising paper, the message was by then almost out of date. Perhaps that was why no such picture appeared in the *People's Daily*.

The implications of Chen Yun's strategy

Planning Commission Chairman Li Fuchun also addressed the State Council meeting on 26 February, but it was left to Finance Minister Li Xiannian to spell out the harsh implications of Chen Yun's strategy.[34] He ticked off the measures needed to fulfil the centre's goal of balancing the accounts and reducing currency in circulation.[35]

1. *Increase production*: The recent PSC conference had decided that the unfeasible 900 m. yuan worth of light industrial goods written into the plan had to be made feasible and that billions of yuan worth of additional goods had to be produced. These should include grain, cotton, tobacco, alcohol, and pigs. Following Chen Yun's lead, Li said that industry needed to produce more sneakers, chemical fertilizers, chemical industry products, hardware, nylon socks, and small and medium farm tools. The aim was to produce an additional 2 billion yuan of such goods.

2. *Economize*: The overall wage bill had to be kept within the limit of 22.4 billion yuan fixed by the Planning Commission and the Ministry of Labour. The Ministry of Commerce would have to cut back 900 million yuan on its declared goal of having 23.3 billion yuan of goods available in order to meet that target. Administrative, cultural, and educational expenses would have to be cut by several hundred million yuan; to set an example, four days earlier the central committee had concurred with a proposal to reduce the strength of state organs and mass organizations by two-thirds, from 2.68 m. to 940,000.[36] Payment of 700 m. yuan of promissory notes, issued to peasants the previous year to compensate for lost property and due for payment this year, would be deferred three years. Bonus prices for grain procured by the state would be eliminated, and localities that had themselves raised procurement prices would have to lower them in order to save several hundreds of millions of yuan. The purchasing power of various mass organizations would have to be reduced by several hundred million yuan. Investigations would be initiated to see if it were possible to reduce capital investment further.

3. *High-priced goods*: The policy of producing expensive candies and foods had paid off the previous year, helping to mop up over 2 billion yuan net from circulation. This policy would be extended to a number of other goods to help cope with the deficit: alcohol

(except for 100,000 tons earmarked for those working underground or at high altitudes); knitwear purchasable without clothing coupons; rare seafood delicacies and mountain produce, hitherto reserved for use at state guest-houses, would now be available at high-priced food stores; expensive watches and bicycles.

Selling expensive consumer goods was a temporary and subsidiary measure, but there was a lot of cash in the hands of rural speculators, and if it were not mopped up the peasants might withhold their goods, putting further strain on the cities. Three principles governed the policy: it had to be concentrated on a few goods and it had to be swift to be effective; it should focus on the rural areas rather than the cities as in 1961; it should be directed only to villages where there was surplus cash.

Li proclaimed himself a sceptic on the fourth policy, encouraging increased savings. He was prepared grudgingly to support the three-pronged policy of voluntary savings, freedom to withdraw savings, and the confidentiality of savings accounts, but he doubted that this would result in increased savings. While the market was tense, withdrawals from savings would increase; when the market was settled deposits would increase.

For Li, the critical issue was increasing rural production of the key consumer goods. In 1957, sales of seven principal items—grain, cotton cloth, knitwear, cooking oil, pork, tobacco, and alcohol—had totalled 20.3 billion yuan and accounted for 46 per cent of sales of consumer products. In 1961, sales of these items had dropped by 29 per cent to 14.6 billion yuan.

The second part of Li Xiannian's address was focused on the overriding importance of rigorous financial discipline, which meant reinstituting greater central control, particularly over the banking system. Li's warnings against certain bank activities indicated how provincial and lower-level local governments had misused their new financial powers during the GLF: bank funds were not to be used to generate profits, pay wages, to finance investment in basic construction projects, or to cover expenses.[37]

Li's speech leaves a curious impression. On the one hand he seemed to have a distaste for the methods prescribed by Chen Yun to coax money out of the countryside. On the other hand he clearly relished the opportunity to consolidate his own power. Despite the mistakes made by his subordinates in estimating the size of the deficit, Li's bureaucratic position was strengthened by the nation's dire financial straits and the agreed need for greater central control.

Two days after the meeting with the State Council cadres, the centre issued an emergency notification recalling banking, financial, and commercial cadres who had been seconded to local units during the GLF. Local branches of the central bank and the Commerce Ministry had to be crack units, and their links with local administrative and financial departments, which had presumably milked them during the GLF, had to be severed. During 1962, the Finance Ministry would increase its staff by 40,000 bureaucrats, the banking system by 60,000, and the Commerce Ministry by 500,000.[38] Four years after the Finance Ministry was excoriated by Mao Zedong at the Nanning conference on the eve of the GLF,[39] it bid fair to regain its central position in economic policy-making. By July 1963, it would be able to claim that the financial situation was again under control.[40]

A stream of central directives laid down the rules by which Li's policies were to be implemented. On 10 March, the CC and the State Council issued six rules on tightening banking controls; the following month, they issued six articles on banking, equivalent to those on industry, commerce, and other fields of economic activity. On 20 March, the centre banned extra-plan construction by local governments, which had got into the habit of flouting central guidelines during the GLF, and ordered the immediate cessation of work under way. On 25 March, the Finance and Trade Office presented its revised report, making three recommendations: 2 billion yuan worth of extra goods for daily use should be produced to increase revenue by 400 m. yuan; state spending should be reduced by 3.1 billion yuan, including defence as well as development; seven new types of high-priced goods should be marketed to mop up another 2 billion yuan worth of currency and increase state revenues by about 1 billion yuan. In addition, tough credit restrictions could reduce the state's exposure by 500 m. yuan. The total financial effect on the budget would be a reduction of 5 billion yuan.

On 26 March, the Finance Ministry took steps to prevent further erosion of its tax base. As a result of adjustments forced upon the ministry by the previous two years of natural calamities, the agricultural tax had shrunk from 38.8 billion yuan in 1958 to a budgeted 21.5 billion yuan in 1962, roughly the 1949 level. The ministry ordered provinces to increase their reserve stocks by 7 per cent, to be earmarked for the central government as compensation for drops in agricultural tax receipts in disaster-struck areas.[41]

All these measures underlined the grim news given to the State Council cadres on 26 February. None the less, Li Xiannian was mindful enough of Mao to make his final words on that occasion an uplifting declaration that the current crisis was secondary compared with CCP successes and the valuable experience gained![42]

Chen Yun's last word

Chen Yun's swan-song was on 7 March 1962, when he addressed the Finance and Economics Small Group.[43] With two important exceptions, he spoke less about details and more about approaches to running the economy based on his own experience. He argued against haste in drawing up the 3rd FYP which was supposed to start in 1963 and was due to be discussed at the central work conference scheduled for July. He pointed out that it had taken three years to devise the 1st FYP and that it had not been published until two-and-a-half years after it had started. He reiterated that the proposed ten-year plan period should be divided into two phases with the first one focusing on recovery. 'We can only talk about development after we have recovered completely', he insisted. It was the 1962 annual plan that demanded immediate attention, and once settled, it should not be continually readjusted as in the past, a process which was the bane of planning officials. Nor should there be any hesitation over sharply reducing the targets.[44]

Chen Yun seems to have wanted above all to impress upon his colleagues the importance of his favourite theme, comprehensive balance. He had long believed in the key importance of three balances: of government expenditure and revenue, of bank loans and deposits, and of supply and demand for commodities.[45] This time he took on an old GLF antagonist, the Minister of the Metallurgical Industry, Wang Heshou, and again got the better of him.[46] Wang apparently favoured setting a long-range target—such as 25–30 m. tons of steel in seven years—allowing the implications of that target for other targets to be worked out over time; in short, muddling through. Chen Yun's experience was that if short-term balances were not calculated in advance, there would be no long-term balances; as a result, large quantities of materials and semi-finished goods remained in storage and went to waste.

In his argument with Wang, Chen had asked if the seven-year target would result in a full range of steel products, and was told it would not. Taking up the issue of balance, Wang posited that if a 25 m. ton steel target demanded more non-ferrous metals than available, then they could be imported. Chen replied with the kind of calculations that must have infuriated those colleagues who preferred management methods of the seat-of-the-pants, back-of-the-envelope variety. An increase of 3 m. tons of steel, he estimated, would require 150,000 tons of non-ferrous metals. Since 1949, the largest amount of non-ferrous metals imported in any one year had been 130,000 tons. If, nevertheless, 150,000 tons were imported and the 3 m. tons of steel produced, then even more non-ferrous metals would have to be imported the following year in order to permit a further increase in steel production. Even if China had the foreign exchange, such purchases would be difficult to make. Hence the need for calculating balances on a short-term basis.[47]

Chen also tried to persuade his colleagues that fixating on steel was wrong. Such leading industrial powers as the United States, Britain, Germany, Japan, and the Soviet Union had put in place balanced industrial structures before expanding their steel industries in a big way. Chen indicated that he did not trust Wang Heshou to abide by his demand for balance. He insisted on central control of the management of materials by the State Planning Commission; otherwise, '[w]e let the Ministry of [the Metallurgical Industry] take care of steel products, but they "steal what is entrusted to their care" . . .' Nor was the Planning Commission blameless. It traditionally gave its primary attention to industrial development; now it had to refocus and put agriculture first.[48]

The other important matter of detail with which Chen dealt reflected his understandable obsession with urban diets. Chen supplemented his proposals for a tofu diet, perhaps in response to criticisms reflected in Zhou Enlai's wry interruption of this speech:

[Comrade] Chen Yun's earlier proposal that we supply one liang daily of soybeans to each person is very good. However, human nutrition requires more than plant protein; animal protein is also needed. Perhaps Buddhist monks and nuns who sit in meditation every day only need plant protein. That will not suffice for people like us, and certainly not for people who do more labour than we do. We should have plant protein as well as animal protein.[49]

Chen's solutions were fish and pork. Ever inventive, he suggested allocating more steel to the manufacture of motorized sailboats and additional fishing equipment, asking the appropriate ministry to increase the supply of fish by 150,000 tons a year. This would enable each of the 60 m. people living in big and medium-sized cities to have half a jin (i.e. a little over 1/2 lb.) a month. In addition, some of the catch could be allocated to restaurants. Chen argued curiously but revealingly that if more people could afford to dine out this would reduce resentment of preferential treatment for cadres. Chen also advocated allocating what would amount to half the planned state pork purchases in 1962 for urban residents, to enable them to have half a jin of pork per month along with their fish. By Chen's reckoning, an urban family of five would thus be able to share five jin of animal protein a month composed of equal parts of fish and pork. Chen grimly emphasized the political importance of solving this problem:

If 600 million people do not have good health and we do not find ways to solve their problems, people will have objections. People want to know whether the Communist Party is really concerned about them and can solve living problems. This is a political issue . . . Comrades, we spent dozens of years to achieve a successful revolution, and we must not let our revolutionary achievements slip from our hands.[50]

Chen concluded with a moment of nostalgia, recalling his methods of controlling the economy during his glory days in the early years of the regime.[51] It was an appropriate coda, a reminder to his colleagues of what they lost when he slipped off-stage. This he would shortly do again. Chen Yun would not make another major speech for almost exactly fifteen years.[52]

The May central work conference

Immediately after making this speech, Chen Yun repaired to Shanghai pleading ill health. The chairmanship of the meeting was taken over by Zhou Enlai, even though he was supposedly only a member and not one of the two vice-chairmen of the Finance and Economics Small Group, and the premier made a very long speech, expanding on Chen Yun's points.[53] In early April, the small group convened a meeting of State Council personnel dealing with finance to discuss, as Chen Yun had wanted, the immediate and not the distant future. At about the same time, Zhou forwarded the revised report of the State Council's Finance and Trade Office on the deficit to Mao. The Chairman returned it on 12 April, commenting that it was very good and giving permission for it to be distributed; it was duly sent out with a covering note explaining that this was a slight upward (*gengda yixie*) revision of the deficit figures produced at the Seven Thousand Cadres Conference.[54] On the basis of the small group discussions and Mao's apparent approval, Zhou Enlai and Li Xiannian submitted a draft report to the centre on the 1962 plan. This report provided the basis for another major work conference summoned by Liu Shaoqi and organized by Zhou Enlai in Beijing from 7 to 11 May.[55]

The importance of the new meeting was attested to by the attendance: four of the seven members of the PSC (all of whom spoke in plenary session),[56] six of the remaining ten full members and four of the five alternate members of the Politburo still in good standing, along with all the full members of the CC secretariat. Significant absentees were the two provincial members of the Politburo who had keenly supported Mao during the GLF, Ke Qingshi of Shanghai and Li Jingquan of Sichuan. For the first two days, the 105 officials attending pored over the small group's report and other documents before splitting into five discussion groups. The four PSC members spoke on the final day.[57]

The report of the Finance and Economics Small Group

The small group's report was clearly an attempt to provide as comprehensive and as honest an appraisal of the economic crisis as possible and to propose measures to combat it.[58] It is not clear whether it exposed the human dimensions of the famine, but it did lay out the details of the country's economic predicament. The economy was in serious imbalance: the relationships between industry and agriculture, between various branches of industry and between the cities and the countryside were inappropriate; expenditure on culture, education, and administration was inappropriate for the current economic situation; and the relationship between accumulation and consumption was very much out of joint.

To illustrate these problems, the report pointed out that whereas in 1961 the value of industrial output increased by 45 per cent over 1957, agriculture had not only failed to improve on the backwardness of 1957, but the value of production had actually fallen 26 per cent. While heavy industrial output had increased 79 per cent since 1957, light industry had gone up only 16 per cent. Even though 10 m. people had returned to the countryside in 1961, there were still 20 m. more people in the urban areas than in 1957. The number of urban workers had been cut by 8.7 m. in 1961, but there were still almost 17.24 m. more workers than in 1957. Despite the 1961 measures, 1962 targets for most agricultural produce were below 1952 levels, and the overall value of agricultural output was expected to be 22 per cent less than in 1957. The value of light industrial output would increase by 9.6 per cent, but six types of foodstuffs would go down by 37 per cent, and fourteen types of clothing would go down by 39 per cent. Yet at the same time heavy industry would still manage to increase by 42 per cent.

Eight critical areas

The report analysed eight critical nodes in the economy.

1. *Agriculture*: Output had seriously declined since 1957. The total 1961 grain output including soybeans amounted to 142.5 m. tons, a drop of 42.5 m. tons since 1957.[59] As a consequence, in 1961 per capita grain availability in the rural areas had declined by well over a third from 215 kg. to 150 kg. The report predicted that it would take three-to-five years for grain production to regain 1957 levels and for agriculture as a whole it would be even longer.[60]

A critical aspect of the problem was that during those three-to-five years, the state could not expect to get much more grain for the cities from its traditional sources. As Zhou Enlai had indicated earlier, two key grain surplus provinces, Sichuan and Heilongjiang, which had together supplied the state with 3.1 m. tons a year on average during the 1st FYP, were now deficit areas.[61] Provincial statistics later revealed that in Sichuan's 1st FYP peak year for grain sales to the state, 1954, the net amount supplied had been 6.48 m. tons, just over a third of total output; in 1962, it would be 2.705 m. tons, just under 19 per cent of output.[62] In Heilongjiang, output tended to fluctuate wildly and it had plummeted as a result of the GLF (see Table 8.6).

TABLE 8.6. *Key agricultural outputs for a grain surplus province, Heilongjiang, 1953–1961* (tons)

Year/Crop	Grain	Soybeans
1953	7,140,000	1,735,000
1954	7,035,000	1,370,000
1955	8,205,000	1,415,000
1956	7,925,000	1,660,000
1957	6,650,000	1,500,000
1958	8,780,000	1,650,000
1959	8,510,000	1,795,000
1960	5,340,000	1,180,000
1961	4,250,000	1,020,000

Source: Zhang Xiangling (ed.), *Heilongjiang Sishi Nian* (Forty years of Heilongjiang), p. 466.

The report, basing itself on current computations of urban and other needs, estimated that the state would have to supply at least 7 m. tons of grain between mid-1962 and mid-1963, which meant that the short-fall which had to be made up with imports stood at 4 m. tons. But if the urban population and workers could be further reduced and if grain production gradually picked up, the availability of surplus grain could increase each year by a million tons, and then imports could be cut. But even if supply and demand for grain came into balance, the report recommended that the nation should continue to import 1–1.5 m. tons of grain a year to restock its granaries for emergencies.[63]

2. *Industry*: The report stated bluntly that without agricultural recovery and without large-scale industrial restructuring, industrial output could not rise.[64]

3. *Basic construction*: After cutbacks, it would take two or three years before investment could pick up again. Between 1958 and 1961, total investment of this type totalled 111.2 billion yuan, of which 24.5 billion had been outside the plan. This was not only way above the nation's capacity; the results had not in any way justified the expenditure. And in order to finance it in various unorthodox ways, popular living standards had been depressed. This was really a case of 'undermining the east wall to shore up the west wall'. Any project which could not fulfil the aims of the investment had to be halted.

4. *Transportation*: The rail crisis had temporarily eased, but there was a grave shortage of short-distance transport capacity.[65]

5. *Excessive numbers of workers*: At the end of 1961, there were still 41,700,000 urban workers, an increase of 17,200,000 over 1957. China's agriculture was not capable of feeding that many workers. In the past four years, grain production had gone down 23 per cent, while the number of workers had risen 17 per cent. Even if the number of workers was reduced this year by another 9 m., agriculture still could not cope, and unless there was a massive reduction there would be no way to improve workers' living standards.

6. *Market conditions*: There would be no improvement in the supply problem, especially of foodstuffs and clothing, for three to five years.

7. *Foreign exchange*: The amount could not be increased; about half of China's earnings was being spent on grain imports.

8. *Finance*: The nation was in deep deficit, too much currency had been issued, and while the nation's warehouses had been cleaned out of commodities, capital goods were greatly overstocked. The combination of these factors together with the expenditure of foreign exchange, excessive lending, and the losses incurred by numerous state firms, meant that a total deficit of over 25 billion yuan had been incurred during the last four years. In 1961 alone, national receipts were down to 79 billion yuan, 14.2 billion less than the 1957 figure of 93.2 billion yuan. If this situation were not turned around, investment would dry up and consumption standards could not be improved.[66]

Three policy proposals

In its third section, the report offered three broad policy prescriptions to allow the nation to deal with the crisis it had described:

- Restore overall balance (*zonghe pingheng*) between various sectors of the economy, the overriding concern of Chen Yun, Li Fuchun, and other planners for many years;[67]
- strive for speed in financial work, but prepare for slowness because accidents happened;
- cut back on industry in order to help agriculture.

Chen Yun's style was to make precise, concrete analyses as the basis for policy prescription, as we have seen. This report was no exception. He was well aware that general admonitions would have no effect on provincial leaders or industrial managers. So he had commissioned a special investigation of the current industrial situation to illustrate what had to be done.

At the end of 1961, there were 41,700,000 workers in 61,800 industrial firms and 849 construction companies. Such a vast industrial establishment was unsuitable not merely for the current level of agriculture but also for the adjusted 1962 plan. Despite the considerable reduced amount of agricultural products available for processing, there were still over 21,000 light industrial firms. As a result, utilization of capacity in the sugar, cigarette, and canning plants was between 20 and 25 per cent. This year's target for cotton yarn output was only 2,600,000 pieces, and, even allowing for increased output next year and thereafter, this required only 5–6 m. spindles and fewer than a hundred cotton mills; but the cotton spinning industry had 10 m. spindles and 236 mills in operation.

The report did not spare heavy industry either. The revised 1962 plan called for the output of 12,000 machine tools; 50–60 machine-tool plants could do the job, but at the moment there were over 110 plants. The productive capacity of other parts of the machinery industry was also greatly in excess of what was needed; in some lines, the situation was worse than in the case of machine tools. The capacity of the steel industry was 12 m. tons (a figure which China did not produce again until 1965), compared with the target for 1962, when China produced 6.67 m. tons.[68]

The small group's conclusion was inevitably that many state plants did not have sufficient or indeed any duties to perform, but they were still consuming fuel, electricity, and raw materials and other inputs, as well as paying wages. Hence the need for down-sizing, amalgamating, and even closing plants, or at least changing their functions. There would be difficulties, but they would be worse if this course was not followed. To ensure that orders to close or reduce production would be obeyed, and that materials would not be disposed of illegally, the report indicated that controls on finance and materials, already outlined in directives issued, would be strictly enforced.[69]

The revised 1962 plan

The small group's report laid down four principles for the revised 1962 plan:

1. Priority for agriculture. The allocation of steel products would be increased by almost 13 per cent to 750,000 tons; the timber allocation would be raised 16 per cent.
2. Increased production of goods for daily use by 1.9 billion yuan.
3. Reduced targets for heavy industries by amounts ranging from 5 to 20 per cent.
4. Reduction in capital construction by almost a quarter to a value of 4.6 billion yuan.

The Planning Commission was told to ensure that these principles were enforced. Liu Shaoqi pointed out that, with one exception, every year since the start of the GLF had witnessed the lowering of targets towards the end of the year. 'We've been "leftist" these many years, let us be "rightist" for a bit', he said.[70]

Rustication revisited

If factories were to be closed down without provoking serious urban unrest, the process of decanting large numbers of workers and other urban residents into the countryside would have to continue. Premier Zhou Enlai took the lead on this topic, quoting from a participant: 'Yesterday a comrade said: Last year we sent down 10 m. workers; this year and next year, we are going to send down in excess of another 20 m., making 30 m. in all—this is like moving a medium-sized country. It's unprecedented historically and globally, and perhaps it's also unique.'[71] Zhou explained that the decision on population transfer had been brewing gradually; it would not have been possible earlier. The aim was to reorder the economy in order to have a new basis for development. No other Chinese government could have done this, only 'our proletarian dictatorship'.[72] The main outlines of the plan Zhou presented to the conference was for a reduction of 10 m. workers, 20 m. urban residents in all, over the course of two years, and he reportedly indicated in detail how the operation should be carried out.[73]

In supporting Zhou, Liu Shaoqi revealed why both men talked of the need for strong determination in the execution of the rustication policy, with Liu describing it as more difficult to implement than the GLF. Among the urbanites to be rusticated would be students, and Liu spent some time talking about the possibility of student riots. He expressed particular concern about avoiding disturbances in cities like Beijing, Shanghai, Tianjin, Wuhan, Shenyang, Harbin, and Canton. If disturbances could not be prevented, then efforts must be made to ensure that they were few in number and small in size. And if all measures failed and disturbances broke out, then martial law should be introduced and transport links with other cities should be cut until order was restored. But, he added, 'Opening fire and killing people is impermissible'.[74]

The Guangdong exodus

Events in Guangdong exemplified the turbulence which Liu feared. As early as July 1961, the provincial authorities had decided to ease their economic problems by allowing easier access to Hong Kong. A conference of public security officials agreed to increase by seven the number of exit points on the border with the British crown colony so as to circumvent its border controls. Even production teams were permitted to issue exit permits. To justify relaxing China's own movement restrictions, presumably in presenting the case in Beijing, the provincial 2nd secretary Zhao Ziyang argued that, since the southern Guangdong countryside was effectively a suburb of Hong Kong, it was entirely natural for Chinese citizens to go there. Guangdong hoped that Chinese citizens would bring back food, fertilizer, and other goods.[75]

Faced with the order to engineer further population flows in 1962, 1st secretary Tao Zhu and his colleagues eventually decided on an even more radical measure: allowing mass emigration. At a frontier defence conference in March, the seven additional exit points were increased to ninety. At another conference in the same month, plans were worked out for profiting from the imminent emigration by charging for arranging illegal entry into the colony; an undisclosed sum, but over a million Hong Kong dollars, was earned by the end of the episode. During April the situation appears to have been confused, with pressure increasing at exit points, and 'bloody incidents' occurring as frontier guards fired on determined émigrés and even at each other. The minister of public security, Xie Fuzhi, cabled Tao Zhu, apparently trying to take the pressure off his forces by getting the provincial authorities to use political measures to stem the exodus. Instead, Tao Zhu allegedly visited the border and ordered the number of guards reduced.[76] At the end of April, the Guangdong border guards stopped preventing emigration.[77] Once it became generally known that the provincial authorities were prepared to connive at flight from China, the exodus became a 'tidal wave'.[78] The worst earthquake in almost half a century had hit Canton on 19 March and was probably seen by many as a bad omen, hastening people on their way.[79]

Within a few days, 30,000–40,000 peasants had entered the colony. They were quickly followed by urban residents, many doubtless wanting to avoid rustication by emigrating to the one city where they could avoid it,[80] and during the three weeks of uncontrolled emigration in May, almost 100,000 people crossed the border. Hong Kong fever reached Fujian, Hunan, Zhejiang, and Jiangsu. The Hong Kong authorities, who did not welcome the prospect of a massive population increase, arrested as many as possible and shipped them back across the border. Some tried again and again to get back in,[81] but by 12 May it was virtually impossible for border-crossers to escape arrest. Guangdong was now able to deflect dissatisfaction from the provincial government, against whose policies people were voting with their feet, to the British colonial government which was refusing them refuge.[82]

Some time after the middle of May, probably around the 20th, Premier Zhou Enlai cabled Tao Zhu and ordered him to stop the exodus by 25 May.[83] On 22 May, the Guangdong authorities closed the border, but the popular pressure continued. On 5–6 June, there was a demonstration by several thousand people at the Canton–Kowloon railway station and elsewhere demanding to be allowed on the train to Hong Kong. According to Mayor Zeng Sheng's later memoir about this 'East Station Incident', among the 'reactionary' leaflets they handed out were demands to be allowed to go to celebrate the Queen's official birthday in the colony! The protest was successfully contained and damped down, but the alarmed mayor appealed to Premier Zhou and managed to get the local public security forces increased from about 5,000 to 7,000.[84]

Rehabilitation of cadres

It was not only public security cadres who faced dilemmas engendered by the economic crisis. If planning and financial officials were blithely to adopt 'rightist' attitudes, they clearly had to be reassured that it would be safe to do so. The previous month the centre had issued a notification indicating that the work of rehabilitating cadres, party members, and ordinary citizens caught in the backlash against 'right opportunism' in 1959–60, as well as earlier campaigns, had proceeded too slowly since its initiation in June 1961, because officials were giving it low priority or using inappropriate methods.[85] As CCP General Secretary, Deng Xiaoping was in charge of this work, and at the May work conference, he re-emphasized the importance of the operation and the simplified procedures to be adopted in order to hasten the rehabilitation process.

The root of the problem was in the countryside, where most of the people affected were working below the *xian* level in teams and brigades. Since the CCP was pinning its hopes of an agricultural upturn on the new deal for the teams—Deng rated this as important for recovery as reducing the urban population[86]—it was critical that the peasants should not feel unhappy or resentful. The numbers involved were very large. Deng estimated perhaps 10 m. people nationwide needed their cases re-examined; assuming three adults per family plus a circle of acquaintances, the total affected could be several tens of millions. In Henan province, which had been 'leftist' during the GLF, and where Deng felt the work could have been done better, there were 400,000 cases so far. To improve the process, Deng advocated the Sichuan method of rehabilitating completely and *en masse*, and not leaving stains on people's records.[87]

The mood of the May work conference

The accounts and speeches of the May central work conference induce a sense of *déjà vu*. As with the Canton, Beijing, and Lushan work conferences in 1961, and especially with the Seven Thousand Cadres Conference, they give an impression of a fresh beginning. New measures are adopted, and even greater resolve is proclaimed to fulfil them. Officials leave with renewed enthusiasm.

On this occasion, participants welcomed the frankness of the report, and comments from the discussion groups underlined the failure of the Seven Thousand Cadres Conference to give a true picture of the nation's dire straits. The comparatively universal condition was said to be blind optimism and an inclination to trust to luck, as if a good harvest this year would make everything fine next year. Bureaucrats and factory managers watched and waited, clinging on to manpower; in this way, half-a-year had been lost. One participant implied that the reason for the minimal impact of the Seven Thousand Cadres Conference was the failure of CCP leaders to lay all the facts on the table: 'Say clearly why there has to be retrenchment, why there has to be reduction [of the urban population], don't hide things.'[88]

The senior leaders attempted to respond appropriately. Liu Shaoqi described the situation as 'very difficult' (*hen kunnan*); one could no longer use the term 'very good' as everyone (and of course particularly Mao) had done in the past: 'If we here don't open our mouths, the people won't be able to talk about it.' Liu added that the principal danger was underestimating the peril the nation was in: better to overestimate than to underestimate. He effectively admitted that he had been foolish to tell the Seven Thousand Cadres Conference that the 'most difficult period had already passed'. Everyone had seized hold of that phrase, but was it correct? 'I'm afraid what one has to say is that there are a few areas where the most difficult period is already past, but in the cities and in industry, the most difficult period has not yet passed.'[89] Zhou Enlai had delivered the same message.[90] Deng Xiaoping added a twist by suggesting that those who feared being accused of rightism if they acknowledged problems were in fact rightist.[91]

But how deep and how wide was the consensus even now? And how likely were the new measures to be implemented? The CCP would prove equal to moving the equivalent of a medium-sized nation from town to country, but how could its fundamentally revolutionary or 'leftist' ethos be transformed unless its soberer leaders confronted Mao and the CCP membership with the human balance sheet of the GLF famine? And if Mao were allowed to save face, either for his own sake or the CCP's prestige, could more rational policies be long maintained even if he formally consented to them?[92] That issue was already joined and would soon be decided in that decisive battlefield of CCP politics, the countryside.

9 THE DISPUTE OVER COLLECTIVIZATION

Among the many contentious issues discussed at the May work conference, none was potentially more divisive than whether or not to bring in further drastic modifications of the structures of rural collectivization in order to stimulate agriculture. No conclusion was reached on this problem and no decisions were taken.[1] Everyone from Liu Shaoqi on down knew that for Mao this was a, probably *the* central issue of Chinese politics. It had been simmering in a few provinces; it had already come to the boil in the East China province of Anhui.[2]

The Anhui responsibility system

The Anhui 1st secretary, Zeng Xisheng, was a party veteran who had been on the Long March and had risen by 1949 to be a senior political commissar in the PLA.[3] He had become the ranking Anhui party official in the early 1950s, and been elected to the CC at the CCP's 8th Congress in 1956. In 1961, he became 2nd secretary of the CCP's East China region as well.[4] He was probably one of the most widely known provincial leaders, because he wrote often for official publications.[5] Zeng was trusted by Mao,[6] presumably because he had what appears to have been a justifiable reputation for leftism,[7] as a result of which the province had suffered probably more than any other during the GLF. Some 2,200,000 people died in Anhui in 1960. One estimate places the total number of abnormal deaths as a result of the GLF as 8 million. In 1962, grain production was 35 per cent below the 1957 level, oil crops 20 per cent, and cotton 15 per cent.[8] Under the circumstances, even a leftist might be tempted to experiment with 'rightist' measures to restore the province's agricultural situation. Zeng initiated a major investigation of the whole collectivization process.[9]

In fact, Anhui had made two earlier experiments with varying collective production methods. In 1957, as a result of serious problems stemming from the hasty creation of higher-stage APCs in 1955–6, some areas had practised a household contracting system (*chengbao daohu*) while nominally operating under the guise of collective management. Again in 1959, as a result of the problems stemming from the amalgamation of the higher-stage APCs into communes the previous year and the egalitarianism which it unleashed, some areas devolved responsibility for land (*tudi xiafang*) and assigned fields to peasant households (*dingtian daohu*), which meant that virtually all agricultural activity was performed by households (*baogong daohu*).[10] It is unclear if Mao was aware of these experiments, but he certainly knew that parts of Anhui were badly hit by famine as early as 1958, for late that year he received a letter from one county where 500 people had died of starvation and ordered an investigation by Zeng and his colleagues.[11]

In 1960, Zeng's high standing in Beijing had led to him being appointed 1st secretary in Shandong, where the problems were thought to be even worse than in Anhui, while retaining his leadership of the latter province. In December 1960, a group of senior Anhui party officials reported to him in Shandong, and he ordered them to experiment with assigning responsibility for production to households (*baochan daohu*) in mountain areas, a system which Mao seemed to have endorsed. He repeated this injunction the following month when other Anhui officials reported that the situation in the province was worsening. Blaming himself for committing a crime against the people of Anhui, he immediately sought and obtained permission from Mao and the East China Bureau to give up his Shandong post, and returned to Anhui on 6 February 1961. The following day he called a meeting in Fengzhui to hear local reports and discuss the crisis. It was now that he formally raised the issue of a responsibility system, which, whatever its name, was essentially *baochan daohu*. He compared it to the 'responsibility system' in factories, where responsibility was assigned to the shop and from the shop to the individual machine, with workers rewarded by the piece, with bonuses for over-production. Zeng compared the team to the shop and the field to the machine, and said that peasants like workers should be held responsible for their machines: 'Isn't this simply transplanting the responsibility system of industrial production to agricultural production? Since working this way in industry is not individual operation [*dan'gan*] or restoration or retreat, so if we use it in agriculture, the caps of individual operation, restoration, and retreat can't be stuffed on our heads.'[12]

It was at this meeting that a responsibility system success story with the flavour of legend helped convince Zeng and his colleagues that they were on the right track. In 1960, a 73-year-old peasant in

Suxian district, whose neighbours thought he ought to go to an old people's home, got permission to take his sick son to a mountain area to convalesce, undertaking to provide for the two of them unaided, which he did with spectacularly successful results. Zeng Xisheng commented that this was an example of socialism not individual operation because the old man had supplied the collective with more than half of his output. In the spring of 1961, Quanjiao *xian* in Chuxian district demanded to be allowed to emulate the old man.[13]

On returning to the provincial capital, Hefei, on 14 February, Zeng summoned the provincial party secretariat and ordered immediate research into responsibility systems, which he characterized as the way to safeguard socialism. The principle was to transplant the industrial responsibility system; the methods, which had to be discussed with the peasants, could include fixing production per field, responsibility to the individual, bonuses for over-production, and penalties for under-fulfilment. Within a couple of days he had deputed four senior colleagues to supervise a responsibility system experiment in Dushan commune near Hefei. When they drew his attention to all the articles and editorials that had been published after the 1959 Lushan conference inveighing against *baochan daohu*, Zeng shrugged them off, saying that this should serve only to make them examine problems more carefully. He alone would bear responsibility for the experiment. The umbrella title for the new method was the 'field management responsibility system plus rewards' (*tianjian guanli zerenzhi jia jiangli*), usually shortened to 'responsibility fields' (*zeren tian*). The system turned out to be so effective in encouraging the recovery of output that it became popularly widely known as the 'life-saving fields' (*jiuming tian*).[14]

On 7 March 1961, after two inspections of Dushan, Zeng took what would turn out to be for him the fateful step of ordering the experiment to be popularized, and described it as 'guaranteeing production according to teams, fixing production according to the field, assigning responsibility to the individual' (*baochan daodui, dingchan daotian, zeren daoren*). It was regarded as a form of the suspect 'guarantee work and production responsibility system' (*baogong baochan zerenzhi*).The same day, he went to Canton to attend the central work conference.[15]

In Canton, Zeng reported at length on his experiment to colleagues from the East China region. He seems to have come under attack from the region's leftist 1st secretary, Ke Qingshi, and Zeng telephoned his provincial colleagues and ordered them temporarily to halt the spread of the reform.[16] On 15 and 16 March, Zeng reported to Mao on what he was trying to do, and the Chairman said: 'All right, you people can experiment, but if it goes wrong, you'll just have to make a self-criticism.' Zeng immediately telephoned this go-ahead to his colleagues.[17] But Zeng was getting contradictory signals in Canton. Ke Qingshi relayed to Zeng a message from Mao stating that the responsibility system should only be a small-scale experiment.[18] Since this was at variance with what Zeng had heard personally from the Chairman—perhaps it was a caveat which Ke had persuaded Mao to add—the Anhui 1st secretary gave a written explanation of what his province was doing in a letter on 20 March to Mao and other senior leaders in Canton.[19]

To follow Zeng's argument, one needs to understand the system which the Anhui party was in the process of modifying. After the introduction of the higher-stage APCs, and equally under the communes, the basic income of the peasant came from labour, under the socialist principle of 'From each according to his ability, to each according to his work'. This principle was usually implemented through a system of work points. In Yangyi commune in southern Hebei province, as observed by two Western scholars resident in China, the day's work of an average man was rated at ten work points. An exceptionally strong peasant or a very experienced older man might have a higher rating, say twelve points, a teenager starting out would probably rate seven points, while the standard woman's rate was eight points.[20] The value of the work points was not known in advance, being dependent on the size of the harvest, though estimates were made, on the basis of which cash was advanced. When the harvest was known, the total income of the brigade (until Mao decreed it should be the team) was divided by the total number of work points earned by members of the brigade to establish the value of the work point. Individual peasants would then be paid according to the number of points they had earned.[21]

Even under the production-oriented Sixty Articles, this system was of enormous complexity, as Mao was informed at his Handan meeting in September 1961, requiring the keeping of accurate records and accounts by peasants who might be barely literate. A key issue was assessment: had a peasant on a given day in fact worked as hard as his 10-point norm demanded or had he been a free-rider, a question which often could not be settled without recrimination. But if, in the interests of maintaining neighbourly solidarity, no such assessment were made, then there was the risk that a lazy peasant would encourage others to be lazy too since it entailed no forfeit.[22] A former peasant described how this applied to 'odd jobs':

For this type, you received the same amount of work points no matter how much you produced. You had to stay for a fixed period of time, but people laughed and played while working. One morning, for instance, the leader might say, 'See that pile of firewood? Just move it over there. It's an odd job.' Many people worked slowly and carried a light load. Some honest people carried a heavy load, but their work points were just the same as the others—ten points for the day.[23]

It was only if the number of work points depended on the amount of firewood carried that peasants had an incentive to work hard.[24]

Of course, there was a collective penalty for slacking off since the income of the brigade would go down and the value of the work point would be diminished. But a key problem was that the links between hard work, harvest size, and peasant reward were not sufficiently direct and personal to provide adequate incentives. The devolution of accounting from brigade to team in September 1961 brought a closer connection between a village's ecology and the work effort of its inhabitants on the one hand and average village incomes on the other, but the link between household effort and household income was still too distant to provide real motivation, and plenty of reasons remained for disputation among commune members.

According to a middle-ranking official from northwestern Hebei province, peasants had four 'resentments': other work groups came to work late, theirs came early; other groups had long rests, theirs had short ones; other groups stopped work early, their's stopped late; and other groups had high work points, but their's had low ones. As a result, peasants worked without enthusiasm; it was still necessary for team leaders to go from door to door calling them out.[25]

The modification of the system in Anhui and elsewhere was designed to remedy these defects. The political conundrum was how to do so without being accused of restoring family farming or even capitalist agriculture as Anhui had been charged with doing at the Canton conference.

Zeng Xisheng's defence

In his letter of 20 March 1961, Zeng Xisheng offered two defences: the provincial party had resisted the masses' desire for 'fixing output quotas by households' (*baochan daohu*), which would represent a complete return to family farming; and collective agriculture was still dominant. According to Zeng, the peasants had wanted output and work fixed field by field (*zhuqiu dingchan, zhuqiu dinggong*). Households, depending on the extent of their labour power, would contract for a certain amount of land. Output would be divided by labour to obtain the output per labour day, and this would be used to fix the work point. In fact, as Zeng hinted, this final step was unnecessary, since the output would simply be divided up within the contracting household. Indeed, Zeng said that one of the advantages of the system favoured by the masses was that work points would not have to be calculated, only the total amount of labour, thus relieving incompetent officials of impossible tasks. Even more importantly, under this system the quality of work—energetic or half-speed—did not have to be measured; and whereas previously only cadres were concerned about output, now every household had an incentive to be so.

Zeng acknowledged that there were dangers: selfishness, competition for preferential treatment for one's fields, and difficulties for labour-poor and other weaker households. The province's response was the 'five unities', of which the two most important were unified distribution of grain by the team and the performance of big farm jobs by collective groups. Individual or household activity was confined to managing fields and various odd jobs. The incentive was that if a field produced more than its output norm, the family responsible for its well-being—for instance, by ensuring it was properly fertilized—divided a bonus with the members of the collective group which had worked on it. The essence of the system was to split up farm tasks into big and small; it was not what was generally understood by household responsibility for production (*baochan daohu*) and certainly not 'independent operation' (*dan'gan*).

Finally, Zeng listed the advantages: the outputs guaranteed by households were realistic; the output targets were increasing; turnout for work had dramatically improved; the number of people engaged in agricultural production had increased; care of the fields had improved; everyone now collected manure for fertilizer; peasants were keen to repair tools; people no longer paid close attention only to their private plots, but were keen on collective projects as well.[26]

Zeng's letter was a holding operation, an instant response to a difficult political situation, like his telephone call to Anhui. He did not convince Mao's secretary Tian Jiaying, who forwarded the Anhui materials to the Chairman with a passionate covering letter, dilating upon the deleterious impact of *baochan daohu* upon widows and other disadvantaged members of rural society; Mao was sufficiently impressed to circulate it among members of the PSC and the regional 1st secretaries,[27] but he vouchsafed no opinion of his own.[28] Zeng now had the duty of making a more formal case, and this followed in a report by the Anhui party to Mao and others on 27 April. The difference in terminology between this report and Zeng's letter is indicative of the experimental nature of what was being attempted in Anhui, the political exigencies of the moment, and possibly Zeng's inability to lay down a considered formulation on the spur of the moment.[29]

The Anhui formula was no longer called 'fixing production according to the field and responsibility to the individual', which perhaps smacked too much of family farming, but rather the 'guarantee labour and production responsibility system' (*baogong baochan zerenzhi*), though an attempt was made to finesse the change by suggesting that this particular experiment was initiated only on 6 March.[30] Guaranteeing labour (*baogong*) was done by calculating the ease or difficulty of a task for a certain piece of land, dividing the task up between big jobs, assigned to a collective work group (*zuoye zu*), and small jobs, assigned to a household which would regard the land as its responsibility (*zeren tian*); labour contracts were agreed by both. Then likely output for the same piece of land would be calculated in order to arrive at a guaranteed figure (*baochan*), again agreed to by both the work group and the household. Compensation for major and minor duties would then be calculated. The brief report finished by listing advantages and disadvantages, much as Zeng had done in his letter, but inserting a new disadvantage designed to pre-empt political criticism: some peasants were mistakenly calling the new system *baochan daohu* or claiming it was dividing the fields (*fentian*), that is, for cultivation by individual households. The Anhui report claimed that the system was in fact neither of these things, but was precisely in line with the 'field management responsibility system' (*tianjian guanli zerenzhi*) advocated in the Sixty Articles.[31]

The fall of Zeng Xisheng

However persuasive Zeng may have considered these explanations to be, he could not ignore the Chairman's second thoughts, relayed by Ke Qingshi, that the Anhui experiment had to be kept small. Between the formal decision to popularize the experiment on 15 March and the 1st secretary's return to Hefei from Canton on 28 March, 39.2 per cent of Anhui's production teams had begun to engage in some form of the new incentive system. Zeng seems to have frozen the experiment till the end of April, for the figure of 39.2 per cent is given for both periods.[32] But on 12 July, Mao stopped in Bengbu on his way back to Beijing from the south, and Zeng, bolstered by his own month-long on-the-spot investigation, again explained the Anhui experiment to the Chairman in minute detail for over an hour. Finally Mao reluctantly said: 'If you think that there are no faults [in the system] you can universalize it.' The Anhui leader telephoned his colleagues, with jubilant instructions to press on. By the time the provincial party presented a really substantive discussion of what it was doing in a written report on 24 July, the percentage of teams taking the initiative (*zidong*) to use the new methods had risen to 66.5 per cent; by mid-August it would be 70.8 per cent, by mid-October, 84.4 per cent, and by the end of the year, 90.1 per cent.[33]

Clearly seeking to align itself as closely as possible with central policy, the report once more renamed the policy 'field management responsibility system with bonuses' (*tianjian guanli zerenzhi jia jiangli*). It emphasized the collective and downplayed the household's role: production was guaranteed by the team; production was fixed by fields; big agricultural duties were guaranteed by the work group (*baogong daozu*); only small agricultural duties like field management were guaranteed by the household; a substantial role for the brigade, conspicuous by its absence from the two earlier reports, was written in.[34] Finally, Zeng again drew parallels with operations in state-owned factories to obtain additional legitimation.[35] In essence, however, it was recognizably the same system described in the two earlier Anhui communications. An experienced party veteran, Zeng Xisheng, was clearly trying desperately to pursue what in the end turned out to be mutually contradictory objectives: rescuing his province and saving his career.

One Chinese historian has argued that Mao agreed to the experiment only because in the summer of 1961, he saw that even the revised Sixty Articles was failing to solve the problem of egalitarianism in the brigade accounting system. He was prepared to authorize any experiment that might offer a way out, but this did not constitute approval of its methods.[36]

It was in this context that Mao made the crucial decision to permit team accounting, spelled out in his letter to his colleagues on 29 September. This was, it turned out, his final concession, and once it had been made, any experiments that went beyond it were to be ruled unacceptable.[37] On 13 November, the CC issued a directive on rural socialist education which was clearly aimed at halting what was being done in Anhui and elsewhere. It called for solidifying and developing the collective economy, and, while admitting that the five communist styles of the GLF had been harmful to the peasantry and the collective economy, it warned against mistakenly confusing the five styles with the collective economy or the basic system of the communes:

The household responsibility system [*baochan daohu*] and some covert independent operation [*bianxiang dan'gan*] methods that are currently appearing in various places are all inconsistent with the principles of the socialist collective economy and are therefore incorrect. In those places, work to amend the situation must be initiated, the collective economy must be run well and careful education must be carried out so as gradually to get the peasants to change these methods.[38]

The deliberation process that took place after the decision on team accounting and before the publication of the directive on socialist education is unclear. Nor do we know on whose initiative the directive was issued. In the light of what ensued, however, we can only assume that Mao played a significant role in any discussions and that his position was endorsed by the PSC. By December, the Chairman was quizzing Zeng Xisheng in Wuxi as to whether the responsibility system should now be abandoned as production had recovered.[39] Perhaps Mao was giving Zeng a broad hint, but Zeng asked for permission to continue the experiment since it had only just started. Mao gave no formal prohibition, and Anhui persisted,[40] but in February 1962, at the Seven Thousand Cadres Conference, Zeng Xisheng was criticized on all sides and was dismissed as Anhui 1st secretary.[41] Liu Shaoqi was the designated hitter.

During the conference, Liu spent several long days with the Anhui delegation.[42] Finally, after listening to Zeng's self-criticism, he pronounced his verdict. Anhui's problems stemmed in the last analysis from its 1st secretary, a committed veteran with many achievements, but cursed, it would seem, with a hot temper and a dictatorial work style. Liu said that he and senior colleagues had been long aware of Zeng's personal shortcomings, but not until now had he appreciated their impact upon the Anhui party organization

and Anhui society because Zeng had run it as an independent kingdom, refusing to allow error to be admitted and resisting central
inspection.[43]

Liu emphasized that Zeng was not being dismissed because
Anhui was in such bad straits; the centre bore responsibility for the
policies of the GLF. But whereas other provinces might be in worse
shape, they had been open and above board.[44] Despite this disclaimer, Zeng was a convenient scapegoat. His dismissal might
appease Anhui cadres and citizens who had suffered from his leftist
stewardship of the province during the GLF and the subsequent
famine. 'Responsible people' of the Anhui provincial committee
were among those accused of causing considerable destruction and
waste due to undemocratic work styles in Liu Shaoqi's written
report to the Seven Thousand Cadres Conference.[45] Simultaneously, sacking Zeng rid Mao of a senior official whom he felt was
flouting him on rural policy. The one concrete policy error for which
Liu blamed Zeng was parlaying the centre's permission to experiment with the responsibility field system (*zerentian*) in one district
into a province-wide phenomenon.[46] It is highly unlikely that an
experienced veteran like Zeng would have taken such liberties with
a Mao directive, but Zeng was even more unlikely to dare openly to
deny that the Chairman had issued so precise a directive.

The Anhui party fell into line. It held a major cadre conference
and on 20 March issued an abject self-criticism, accepting that the
responsibility field system was in fact a household responsibility
(*baochan daohu*) system heading in the direction of independent
operation, and blaming the error on Zeng Xisheng's leadership. The
Anhui document stated that, with the directive on team accounting
added to the Twelve Articles and the Sixty Articles, it was now possible to solve the problems of lack of correspondence between work
and reward and of intra-team egalitarianism. The document laid
down methods by which the responsibility field system would be
amended in 1962–3.[47] Zeng was replaced by Li Baohua (the son of
one of the two founding fathers of the CCP, Li Dazhao), whom Liu
had endorsed in less than ringing terms.[48]

Appeals from the grass roots

Zeng's disgrace was not the end of the Anhui affair. In late spring
1962, a local propaganda official, Qian Rangneng, in poverty-
stricken Taihu *xian* in southwest Anhui, sent an extraordinary
appeal to Mao himself.[49] Qian argued that the responsibility field

system (*zerentian*) was a peasant creation and an important out-growth of the Sixty Articles and team accounting. For agricultural production, it was the equivalent of water for a fish, or adding flowers to brocade.[50] He described the parlous condition of production during the GLF, when some areas were annihilated (*huimie*). The CC's attack on the five communist styles in winter 1960 had had little impact because the masses were at their last gasp; when the field responsibility system was instituted a few months later in March 1961, there was a burst of peasant energy (*gu jintou*) greater than anything Qian had seen since land reform. Disaster areas became productive, emigration became immigration, hunger turned into sufficiency, illness gave way to health, and death to life as women became pregnant again.

Citing the poorest area of the *xian*, Qian listed the production increases from 1960 to 1961: grain—81 per cent (exclusive of private plots which would normally do even better); oil crops—750 per cent; cotton—1,100 per cent; pigs and poultry—several hundred per cent.[51] The current year was even better. This could not be attributed simply to the responsibility field system, but was also a natural product of CC policies, and he reminded Mao: 'The Chairman has said that any idea that does not fit with objective reality, whose objective existence is not needed, and which is not seized by the masses, cannot be used, even if it is a good thing, even if it is Marxist-Leninist.'[52] Qian clearly felt that it had been downhill since 1955 and the rapid spread of higher-stage APCs (at Mao's signal, though he did not mention that). That had been Taihu *xian*'s best year, and as a result of the GLF it would be years before the 1955 production figures would be surpassed, though Qian expressed the obligatory confidence in the therapeutic effects of the Sixty Articles, team accounting, plus the field responsibility system.[53]

Qian's argument for this system was based on his belief that it solved the critical problem for peasants under collective ownership, how to safeguard their individual interests. To raise efficiency, peasants had to be motivated, they had to be made to care about production and to be clear about their responsibilities. Qian quoted Stalin on the importance of individual responsibility in industry, and commented that it must be even more true for agriculture, which was so much more complicated. One could not get that sense of responsibility with the time-consuming and complicated work point system.[54]

Qian insisted that the field responsibility system was simply a management method of the socialist collective economy: it did not transform the ownership of the means of production. Land was still collectively owned, incomes were based on payment according to labour, and collective labour was still practised except for complicated and minor tasks more appropriate to individual labour. Collective production and individual labour coexisted in any socialist production unit, he asserted.[55] Finally, Qian derided the claim in the Anhui decision to amend the field responsibility system that 70 per cent of the peasants were neutral about the system. He asserted that 80–90 per cent supported it, and he invited the Chairman to send someone to Anhui to get at the truth.[56] It seems that his appeal fell on deaf ears,[57] but his analysis was corroborated two months later by another grass-roots communication from the north of the province.[58]

Every member of the Fuli district committee in Su *xian*, party members all, agreed that the field responsibility system had resulted in very great successes on the production front since being proclaimed in March 1961, so that after the committee members heard of the provincial decision to change the system earlier in 1962, they became very anxious, as if there were 'an ideological millstone on our backs'. Despite reading and discussing the decision several times, they still could not fathom it,[59] and they proceeded to explain, in terms similar to Qian Rangneng, why they liked the system and did not think it was anti-socialist. What is not clear is whether these officials were encouraged to write, either directly or indirectly, by the work team of the CC's Rural Work Department, which was conducting an investigation in Su *xian*. While the work team's report, issued in the same month as the Fuli one, was overtly a neutral presentation of facts, it clearly leaned in favour of the local methods.[60]

Nor were Anhui cadres the only ones to try to protect the new agricultural production systems. Hu Kaiming, a prefectural 1st secretary in northwest Hebei, also wrote to the Chairman.[61] Hu cited three main reasons for the lack of peasant enthusiasm for production: state procurement policies, state pricing policies, and the lack of production responsibility systems. Since the economic situation precluded much being done about the first two, he argued that it was crucial to fix the third. Hu repeated the two familiar handicaps of the current work point system: it was too complicated—200–300 norms—and involved too much hassle and provoked resentment if evaluation were done properly. Hu reported that at two conferences which he had summoned, cadres were unanimous that the system of 'evaluating work and allotting work points' (*pinggong jifen*) had never been done well, from primary-stage APCs to the present. They found it easier to eschew evaluation and substitute a simple egalitarian work point system, which meant that hard-working groups were penalized and lazy ones rewarded.[62]

Hu maintained that to separate work from output was fruitless, and he dismissed various labour guarantee (*baogong*) systems as empty.[63] His preferred solution was the ' "three guarantees" production responsibility system' (*'sanbao' shengchan zerenzhi*), whose essential ingredients were the formation of very small work groups on a voluntary basis, the assignment of land, animals, and tools to the groups on a long-term basis, and the evaluation of land according to likely output, labour needs, and investment requirements. Those evaluations would be the three guarantees made by the work group to the team. After the harvest, excess output went to the group for distribution according to labour.

Because the production unit was small, the connection between collective and individual interests was more direct than under the current system and mutual supervision was easier. Another advantage was that work did not have to be evaluated.[64] Hu was careful to indicate his disapproval of household, as opposed to group, guarantee of production (*baochan daohu*)—though he was prepared to accept it if the peasants were adamant—arguing that it precluded the advantages of mutual aid.[65] Even more carefully, however, he gave no indication that when a group allocated its surplus it might well do so on the basis of individual or household responsibility for certain tasks, like field management or care of animals.

The Guangxi experience

The punishment of Zeng Xisheng and the Anhui reversal of policy should have been a salutory lesson, ending further experimentation in responsibility systems. But these systems responded so closely to the need to resuscitate rural production that they had sprung up in a number of provinces. Even before the Anhui decision reversing the province's rural policy, the centre had received an alarming report from Guangxi province about independent operation: a quarter of cadres coming to rural conferences were in favor of independent operation (*dan'gan*); in well-off areas, independent operation was only 15 per cent, but it was as high as 60 per cent in badly hit areas or where the five communist styles had been rampant during the GLF. In Liucheng *xian*, 65 per cent of cadres advocated independent operation, of whom four were commune committee secretaries and another fourteen were commune committee members; in the case of Longsheng *xian*, 42 per cent of the teams were implementing house-hold responsibility (*baochan daohu*) systems. Among the arguments advanced by those cadres who described *dan'gan* as their 'general line' to persuade others to copy them were that the system resolved the problem of egalitarianism, improved production, and prevented oppression. They contrasted the collective period negatively with the pre-collective period and with the private plot system.[66]

The resolution of the Guangxi situation was striking in the light of what had happened in Anhui. In early June 1962, the two leaders of the CC's Central-South region, Tao Zhu and Wang Renzhong, made a two-day inspection of the situation in Longsheng *xian* and declared that the problem of independent operation, which they strongly condemned in principle, had been exaggerated due to incorrect local understanding of that term. Tao and Wang divided the forms of team operation which they observed into five types, only one of which was clearly independent operation, though one other could degenerate into it in the absence of firm leadership. Their conclusion was that collective economy could take many forms, provided certain principles were adhered to.[67]

Tao and Wang laid down four criteria by which collective agriculture could be distinguished from independent operation: collective ownership of the principal means of production; a unified arrangement of production; collective labour; and unified distribution of income from production. Three of these four were easy to understand; only collective labour puzzled people. So Tao and Wang explained that the principal content of collective labour was that the team ought to allocate labour in a unified manner, though this did not mean that all agricultural work had to be done collectively. Manpower and tasks ought to be fitted to each other, both in collective and individual work. The rational division of labour was an advanced feature of socialist development which individual operation could not match. Thus one could not deduce whether production was collective or not simply from the amount of work that was collectively done. In order to ensure that the four principles were being applied, teams should grasp six points: collective ownership of the major means of production; a unified production plan and assignment of production duties for both agriculture and sideline activities; unified distribution of labour; unified settlement of the amount of fertilizer to be handed over by the family to the team (which presumably meant that families could retain some) and unified control of team fertilizer supplies; unified harvest and income distribution; appropriate care of distressed households.[68]

The analysis and dicta of Tao, who had expressed his opposition to *baochan daohu* at the 1961 Canton conference,[69] and Wang are strikingly similar to the successive communications from Anhui to the centre. Zeng had early on grasped the importance of stressing that the province's teams practised unified distribution of income, unified management and allocation of labour, and that collective ownership and labour remained the principal characteristics of the rural scene in Anhui. Although Zeng did not think to talk artfully about the superiority of the collective residing in its ability to assign labour to appropriate labour forces, collective or individual, the Anhui line that their arrangements did not differ from those within state-owned factories was equivalent.

Lending land

The willingness of Tao Zhu and Wang Renzhong to find a way around ideological considerations was exhibited even more strikingly in other parts of the Central-South region. In Hunan and Henan, they were prepared to tolerate the lending of land to peasants to farm privately. In August 1961, the Hunan party leadership pointed out to its officials that up to 6 m. mou (about a million acres) of land was lying idle in the winter. Along with another 1 m. mou of calamity-struck land, it could be used for planting winter vegetables and crops that could be harvested in the spring. If the collectives could not make use of all this land, portions could be lent to the peasants, up to three strips per head in ordinary areas, and up to five strips in famine areas. All the produce of peasant strips belonged to those who cultivated them, and should not be used to fulfil the state procurement quotas or to lower the grain ration except in desperate circumstances. The Hunan circular underlined that this was a policy of allowing people to rescue themselves by producing (*shengchan zijiu*), and that cadres and peasants had to be told that it was 'absolutely not dividing the fields among the households' (*fentian daohu*). The fields had to be returned to the collective for the 1962 spring sowing.[70]

This stern admonition was probably unrealistic, to judge by the experience of the even worse-hit province of Henan. In July 1962, Henan 1st secretary Liu Jianxun, who had been brought in to clear up the mess resulting from the ultra-leftism of his predecessor, sent a report on lending land to his regional bosses, Tao Zhu and Wang

Renzhong, and requested that it be transmitted to Mao. Liu reported that as a result of successive bad harvests and serious salinity, peasants in north and east Henan were deserting their villages, taking their clothes and furniture to neighbouring provinces to exchange for grain. The provincial party considered providing emergency shipments of state grain, but concluded that this would not serve to jump-start the collective economy. Henan may also have been informed by the centre that extra grain was simply not available; this would certainly explain why the centre decided to tolerate Henan's land-lending policies. With the agreement of Tao Zhu, Liu Jianxun and his colleagues decided to lend land and donate seed to the peasants where there had been serious salinity, considerable migration, or massive deaths among the farm animal population; a million iron spades were supplied courtesy of State Planning Commission chief, Li Fuchun, to substitute for the dead animals. The disaster areas were centred in four special districts comprising 22 *xian* with a population of about 4 m. The amount of land lent was between six and eight pieces per household, which, with a private plot, might amount to about a mou (a sixth of an acre) per head. As Hunan had done, Henan described the policy as allowing the peasants to rescue themselves by producing (*shengchan zijiu*); this phrase may have become a term of art in the Central-South region to justify emergency measures that would otherwise be unthinkable for ideological reasons.

Once adopted, the policy seems to have taken root. In May, there were serious food shortages in Henan and early wheat was growing badly. Everyone became nervous, and lower-level cadres suggested lending a small quantity of early autumn harvest land to be planted with sweet potatoes for a one-off harvest in August. The land would be returned in time for collective wheat planting. Again the provincial committee got the agreement of the Central-South Bureau, only to find that the policy was too popular. Now all areas wanted to adopt it. Party officials realized that lending land for just one crop could affect soil fertility; peasants would try to extract maximum output, knowing that they would soon have to relinquish the land. The provincial committee therefore made a formal ruling that land lent should not, when taken together with private plots, amount to more than 15–20 per cent of arable land, and the loan period should be from three to five years. Almost immediately, every area implemented the higher time limit, and the policy was modified to a flat five years. All the produce of the land was exempt from state procurement, but the provincial committee laid down that there would no longer be an automatic grain ration in addition to payment for collective labour, except for families in distress. Yet 1st secretary Liu estimated that a household might raise only about 150 catties of grain from their lent land, less than the previous ration. Thus it only made economic sense for the peasants to put in the extra labour if they could add the product to the ration.

From the statistics available to Liu Jianxun for his mid-July report, it is clear that the lower-level cadres and peasants had exploited the new policy to the hilt. Only a minute fraction of the province's teams had lent no land. In the worst-hit saline areas, the total amount of land lent and assigned to private plots was as much as 28.6 per cent of the arable area; in the less badly hit areas with a population of about 40 m., the proportion was just over the upper limit at 16.5 per cent; even in five presumably better-off districts near such major cities as Kaifeng and Luoyang, 11 per cent of the teams had reported 20 per cent or over, and 83 per cent of the teams had reported the maximum 15 per cent.

Liu effectively acknowledged that the policy had got out of control, but justified it by claiming that it was paying dividends. Emigration had been halted and many peasants were returning home. Peasant enthusiasm had risen and production was taking a turn for the better. In short, though Liu of course could not say so, collectives had collapsed as their starving members had wandered off in search of food, and only the prospect of farming privately had attracted them back.[71] As it turned out, 1962 was indeed a better year for Henan, with the value of agricultural production rising to 115.4 per cent of the 1961 figure. This was the first year since 1957 that production had not fallen.[72] Yet in mid-1962, Liu clearly still felt his position to be politically vulnerable enough to admit problems—the collective was in competition with private farming for labour and fertilizer, and nobody needed to be told which normally won. He also announced measures to take back lent land where it exceeded the 15 per cent limit or where it was not really needed.[73] Even so, for most of the province for three to five years, some 15 per cent of the arable land would have been lost to collective farming, and reclaiming it would require a massive political effort.

Regional variations

The Anhui reform seems to have been much less radical. It is not easy to understand, therefore, why the permissiveness towards

Henan and Hunan could not have been applied to Anhui, where the economic situation was at least as desperate. The Tao Zhu/Wang Renzhong analysis of what was at stake in Guangxi, which Mao described as Marxist and at one point wanted to see used as the basis for a CC decision,[74] would surely have exonerated Zeng Xisheng if it had been applied to the earlier case. The different handling of the southern provinces may have reflected confusion over criteria or an evolution of views of what was acceptable. More likely, they underline the conflict within the CCP CC over the right methods for solving the post-GLF rural crisis, and the importance of the post-GLF CCP power structure in the promotion of rival solutions.

While Tao and Wang cannot be exonerated for their roles in the GLF, the evidence of their report on Guangxi and their behaviour towards Henan and Hunan suggests that they now put recovery as a top priority. They apparently had the ideological skills and the standing with Mao to be able to define rural collectivism in the Central-South region in such a way as to include certain types of responsibility system.[75] There seems to have been similar realism and tolerance in the North China region. Hu Kaiming's analysis, first presented in a speech to a regional agricultural conference, must have been well received or he would not have had the temerity to forward it to the Chairman. This contrasts sharply with the harsh judgement on Anhui's reforms.

Unhappily for Zeng Xisheng, his superior as East China regional leader was an unreconstructed leftist as well as another Mao favourite, Ke Qingshi, whose reputation was bound up with GLF collectivism, and who led the criticism of his subordinate;[76] from the very beginning, he had been prepared to sanction only experimentation, not popularization of the responsibility system.[77] The aim of the reintroduction of CC bureaux in 1961 had been to increase central control of the provinces after the decentralization of the GLF. But the issue of rural responsibility systems suggests that an unintended consequence may well have been to confer upon the new regional overlords, rather than the centre, the power to dictate what happened in the provinces under their jurisdiction.

Deng Zihui's last hurrah

The realism if not the persuasiveness of Tao Zhu and Wang Renzhong was matched higher up in the party hierarchy. The director of the CC's Rural Work Department, Deng Zihui, thought the rural situation so parlous that it was wrong simply to condemn out of hand the experimental systems that were being tried in various parts of the country. That he was prepared to put forward controversial views despite the rough treatment he had received from Mao in the mid-1950s is a testament to Deng Zihui's courage and sense of responsibility, if not to his discretion. Perhaps he believed that Mao had finally ceded power to Liu Shaoqi, Zhou Enlai, and Deng Xiaoping.[78] In two major reports in May and July 1962, he exposed the problems that persisted in the countryside despite successive concessions to the peasantry embodied in the Twelve Articles of 1960, the Sixty Articles of 1961, and the adoption of team accounting.[79] In espousing the cause of *baochan daohu*, he was reasserting views he had maintained from April 1954 when the collectivization process had begun to speed up.[80]

The symptoms of the rural problem were low attendance rates, low efficiency, with three peasants often doing what one could have done before, carelessness, and malingering. Deng attributed these widespread phenomena to continuing egalitarianism and the attendant lack of incentives plus cadre privileges and poor management. All were compounded by the continuing economic depression in the countryside. As a result, individual operation in different forms was now being practised by 20 per cent of peasant households nationwide, rising to 60 per cent in some *xian*. Deng predicted this would spread further if appropriate measures were not taken to deal with the problems.[81]

Egalitarianism was most evident in land ownership. Villages resented the fact that, since 1958, significant portions of agricultural land had been taken over by construction and other enterprises, official organs, schools, and even military units, and had still not been returned. But the basic problem was deeper, and could be traced, said Deng, to hurried collectivization in the wake of Mao's clarion call of 31 July 1955.

Deng's argument was that the land distributed during land reform in the early 1950s was legally assigned to peasant households and thus to the villages in which they lived. The formation thereafter of primary-stage APCs, usually comprising single villages, did not affect this basic situation because the peasants retained ownership of their land and principal assets, such as farm tools and animals, though in many cases land owned by peasants in one village was enclosed by the landholdings of another village.

Mao's rejection of Deng Zihui's caution in mid-1955 effectively meant that for most of China, primary-stage APCs were a brief way-station, and often not even that, as the cadres proved their redness by bundling the peasants into the fully socialist higher-stage APCs, and land recently acquired under land reform became the property of the APC. These higher-stage APCs embraced several primary-stage ones. The new rural leadership imposed neatness, order, and equality by redistributing land among component villages. While the division of property at the time of land reform had been based on village population, now it was based on labour power in a group of villages. The result was often that good land was exchanged for bad. This process continued three years later when the communes were set up with even greater haste and land was reallocated again in the interests of equality. These changes in village land ownership were resented, but nevertheless had little impact since all peasants within the confines of a commune were notionally treated the same.

The devolution of management and, most recently, accounting to the team level revived the issue. The teams were in most cases the old primary-stage APCs, or what would have been primary-stage APCs if the area had gone through that phase in a serious manner. Team members all over China suddenly found that the village units of the early 1950s no longer existed, and that in many cases the new landholding patterns made some villages much worse off and others much better off than they had been a decade earlier. This mattered greatly now that the teams/villages were responsible for their own profits and losses.

Deng Zihui pointed out that, while the post-GLF policies involved the handing back of property, both public and private, to its former owners, the base line for adjudication was 1957, by which time the damage had already been done. He advocated that the land reform land settlement should be the baseline, and he called for a law enshrining the CCP's promise that the new deal in the country-side would remain untouched for thirty years. In that way, cadres would be forced to acknowledge and peasants would come to believe that the new land settlement was not simply a cynical, temporary expedient, and could begin to build on it.[82]

A second aspect of egalitarianism which dismayed peasants and sapped their enthusiasm for production had to do with food. Three of the five grain-allocation systems which Deng found to be wide-spread in his year-long investigations in a number of provinces were flawed, in his opinion, because they offered little or no incentive. In the worst, the basic ration was set according to age only; no matter how hard a peasant worked, or indeed whether he worked at all, he would still receive the same amount of grain as everyone else in his category. Deng preferred the system which combined three types of grain distribution: a basic ration (*jiben kouliang*), labour grain (*laodong liang*), and 'consideration' grain (*zhaogu liang*). About one-third of the grain available to the team was given in the form of a basic ration of anywhere between 20 to 30 lb a month to those who were genuinely unable to work; another two-thirds of the available grain would be distributed to working peasants (who would not get the basic ration) on the basis of work points; and about 5 per cent (the 'consideration' grain) would be set aside for such groups as the needy, the long-term sick, women in pregnancy, and the families of revolutionary martyrs.[83]

Egalitarianism was also prevalent in the assessment of work because it was simpler and involved less hassle. Tasks might not be assessed for their difficulty or laboriousness. The quality of work might not be inspected, or if so, only cursorily, partly in order to avoid controversy, partly because the young team leader was not qualified to make an assessment. There was no proper system of checking and accepting (*yanshou zhi*) and no system of rewards and punishments regularly or widely used. Thus someone who worked slowly but carefully and well would end up with fewer work points than someone who worked faster but carelessly. By the time crop yields demonstrated who had worked to better effect, the work points would have been awarded long since.[84]

The nub of the efficiency issue for Deng Zihui as for so many other officials concerned with rural China in the early 1960s was how to instil a sense of responsibility in the peasants as they went about their daily tasks. The answer was to provide incentives, which were of course the bases of the various responsibility systems being debated in 1961 and 1962. Deng cited a 1957 decision that, within the new higher-stage APCs, output should be guaranteed by the team (*baochan daodui*), that tasks would be contracted down to work groups within the team (*baogong daozu*), while responsibility for the management of individual fields could be assigned to households (*tianjian guanli bao daohu*). Field management included hoeing up weeds, putting on fertilizer, and making sure there was a sufficient supply of water. This system, which Deng may have devised, had been swept away in the fervour of the GLF, but there were signs of its revival in various parts of the country.[85]

For the collective economy to be successful, Deng argued, the peasants had to be motivated, and the only way to achieve that was through a responsibility system under which work was shared and people co-operated (*fengong hezuo*).[86] Like others, he used the industrial analogy: industry could not function without a responsibility system; agriculture was no different. Distribution had to be according to labour, with clear and reasonable rewards; work must be assessed and work points recorded; responsibilities must be strictly adhered to; and there had to be political work.[87]

Deng Zihui offered concrete examples from his various inspection tours. A striking one concerned a brigade in a mountainous area of Guangdong. When the current brigade leader became a team leader in 1955, he would sound a bell when the sun came up. But peasants got up at about 8 or 9 a.m. to go to the fields and returned about 11, and he soon realized that this method was no good. So he ruled that every person had to work for eight hours or be docked work points: people then stayed the full time, but loafed on the job, and eight hours only amounted to about three hours of hard work. The leader's third scheme was to fix duties, but make the time flexible; people could come and go as they pleased without benefit of bells or gongs. This worked better but quality suffered and the peasants' attention was focused solely on increasing their work points. Currently he was working successfully with a fourth system: eight points were awarded for completion of the agreed quantity of work and another two points were awarded on the basis of the quality of the work.[88]

From this and other examples Deng Zihui gave, it is clear that household responsibility for production (*baochan daohu*), especially when all the land was so assigned, was his ideal, so long as there was a reward for over-production; at the very least, 80 per cent of the excess should go to the household. Under those circumstances, all family members got up early, groping in the dark as they went off to the fields, and collective land was treated with loving care and lavished with fertilizer as if it were a private plot. This was not equivalent to individual operation (*dan'gan*), said Deng, because the soil and the means of production were collectively owned; but there had to be strong political leadership for there was a danger, he admitted, of descent into the individualized economy (*geti jingji*).[89]

Another important incentive was ensuring the peasants' 'small freedoms' (*xiao ziyou*). As a result of the reaffirmation of private plots in the Twelve Articles and the Sixty Articles, peasants had become very enthusiastic about rearing poultry and other domestic animals, and sideline occupations had been revived. At a time when the principal means of production were human and animal power rather than machines, the small freedoms stimulated a sense of responsibility, and so long as the social system took the collective and state-owned economy as its main element and political power was in the hands of the CCP, there was no danger of a revival of capitalism. Deng saw no problem in expanding the amount of land allocated to households for private plots from the 5–7 per cent in the Sixty Articles to 10 per cent (which was already the practice in some areas), and advocated allocating additional land for growing fodder. He even endorsed the lending of land to households for up to five years, especially in disaster areas. The total amount of land assigned to households under the various rubrics ought not to exceed 20 per cent of the total arable land, and thus could present no possible capitalist menace. To those who argued that the existence of private plots discouraged attention to the collective fields, he pointed out that during the GLF all private activities had been eliminated but peasant turn-out for collective work had been very unsatisfactory.[90]

In addition to increasing incentives, Deng Zihui was keen to remove disincentives, notably the excessive procurement burden. He argued that since the value of the currency was unstable (*bu wending*), current grain procurement resembled the forced collection of surplus grain during the civil war period in the Soviet Union. Moreover, the peasants were not fairly rewarded for their produce with equivalent quantities of consumer goods. Deng had two suggestions. In May, he proposed fixing the national grain procurement target at 35 m. tons and to keep it at that level for three to five years, or even ten to twelve years for poorer areas; by July he had reduced the figure to 32.5 m. tons, divided into about 12.5 m. tons of tax grain and 20 m. tons of procurement grain. At the very least, quotas should be fixed for the hard-pressed 400 *xian* which produced a substantial amount of grain and cotton for the market. Deng's second suggestion was to issue industrial certificates, exchangeable eventually for consumer and other manufactured goods, since the state was currently able to produce only up to 30 per cent of the goods the peasants could rightly expect in return for the procured grain. Alternatively, there could be barter of, say, grain for cotton. To get the best out of the peasants, it was best to fix the obligations low and maintain them at that level for a period (*ding qing, ding si*).[91]

In addition, exchanges between the state and the peasantry should be supplemented by country fairs. According to Deng, only in Guangdong and Guangxi were there lively country fairs, because in those provinces, grains, other than rice or wheat, and prepared foods were freely traded, whereas elsewhere there were strict controls. The only result of the controls in the rest of the country, however, was that there was a flourishing black market.[92]

Finally Deng dealt with the problems associated with the rural cadres: special treatment and poor management. Deng had found that brigade and team cadres often earned about 14 per cent more than a peasant turning up for a full day's work; some cadres earned 600 labour days a year for their official duties. If they went to an evening meeting or made an inspection tour, they would add on an extra ten points. The peasants said that the CCP had nurtured a group of idlers and their enthusiasm for work was correspondingly affected. Deng advocated limiting the number of cadres whose living was subsidized, and limiting the amount of subsidy to up to 150 labour days for a brigade cadre and up to thirty for a team cadre. If such reforms were not carried out, those cadres would form the basis of revisionism, and China would go revisionist in twenty years.[93] As it would turn out, Deng Zihui was right in his timing, but wrong in his implicit assumption that, in two decades, the existence of a privileged cadre class fostering peasant capitalism would still be regarded as a defeat for socialism. By the early 1980s, with Deng Xiaoping's regime proclaiming that 'to get rich is glorious' in the search for 'socialism with Chinese characteristics', rural cadres were maintaining their special position on top of the peasantry with new strategies, while overseeing the abandonment of collective agriculture.[94]

Back in 1962, however, cadres did not have to justify themselves by displaying entrepreneurial skills but rather by ensuring compliance with directives from on high. Deng Zihui revealed that such, presumably politically loyal, team and group leaders had far less experience than the managers of the fields of landlords and rich peasants in the past. The old system was worth copying, albeit with experienced older peasants rather than hired foremen in leading roles.[95]

Deng Zihui's assessment clearly overlapped considerably with those of lower-level officials, which was not surprising since he and officials of his department had been soliciting the views of team leaders and others. His intervention had even greater potential impact than the activities of Tao Zhu and Wang Renzhong. As director of the CC's Rural Work Department, however diminished his role had been in recent years, Deng's authority and experience were being exerted at the national rather than the regional level in favour of far-reaching rural reforms in the face of the famine.

More important still, and perhaps accounting for a courage which might otherwise be deemed reckless, Deng Zihui had backers in high places. At a meeting of the CC secretariat at the end of June to hear agricultural officials from the East China region justifying their suppression of the Anhui experiment,[96] he heard Chen Yun and Deng Xiaoping express themselves in favour of household guarantees of production (*baochan daohu*), though there was disagreement on the issue. It was on this occasion that Deng Xiaoping endorsed a saying of the peasants of Anhui, later inextricably linked with his own name: 'It doesn't matter if a cat is black or white, so long as it catches the mouse it's a good cat.' Chen Yun, in early July, advocated *baochan daohu* to Mao and other senior colleagues.[97] Even the politically cautious chairman of the State Planning Commission, Li Fuchun, endorsed the system of responsibility fields after a visit to Anhui.[98]

This was formidable support for the kind of reforms advocated by Deng Zihui. The implementation of some of them would constitute an admission that the whole hectic process of collectivization and commune-ization from 1955 to 1960—Mao's greatest post-1949 successes—had been disastrously bungled, and that the whole rationale of the key slogan defining the communes—large (of size) and public (in ownership)—was fatally flawed.[99] Mao perhaps felt he had no option but to sanction drastic but temporary reforms of the commune system on a local, case-by-case basis. The political fallout could be minimized. But to endorse Deng Zihui's programme would have been a major defeat on a nationwide basis and was not tolerable. Fortunately for Mao, circumstances conspired to provide him with the basis for rejecting Deng's ideas.

10 RESUSCITATING THE UNITED FRONT

Deng Zihui's outspokenness on collectivization reflected not just his own courage, but also the general amelioration of the political atmosphere that had taken place since the end of the GLF, and in particular after the Seven Thousand Cadres Conference. The combination of political change and economic necessity had led Chinese leaders to revalidate expertise and try to coax a hundred new flowers to bloom. Since the majority of China's intellectuals, professionals, and managers were non-party, that is, not CCP members,[1] and often had 'complicated' political pasts, this meant a revival of 'united front' policies. These had been severely damaged by the 1957 Anti-Rightist Campaign when so many leaders of China's eight non-communist or 'democratic' parties, the CCP's united front partners, and others— some 500,000 people in all—had been denounced.[2] Thereafter, most non-party people feared to say anything, although during the relaxation in the middle of the GLF, leading rightists had been able and willing to offer criticisms of the CCP's actions in 1958.[3]

Further anxiety had been caused by the 1959 struggle against 'right opportunism'. While this was intended to be a purely intra-CCP campaign, many leftists used it as an opportunity to attack non-party people too.[4] The watchword for cautious members of the bourgeoisie was 'The three looks and the three don't speaks': look for the direction of the wind—if you're unclear about the direction of the wind in the upper levels, don't speak; look at the colour of the eyes—if the colour of a leader's eyes is wrong, don't speak; look for the intent—if a leader's intent is unclear, don't speak.[5]

Such fears complicated the work of Li Weihan, the director of the CC's UFWD, who, with Liu Shaoqi's backing, began to cultivate bourgeois industrialists and merchants as early as December 1959, to get their help in China's increasingly difficult economic situation.[6] According to the statistics Li compiled, the key target constituency was made up as follows: 710,000 businessmen, of whom 550,000, almost 78 per cent, had less than 2,000 yuan of capital invested in the joint state–private commercial and industrial sector; over 10,000 engineers; and about 150,000 medium and big capitalists, of whom

70,000 had employed over ten workers in the old days. Many of the more prosperous national capitalists were members, along with intellectuals, of the democratic parties. Below the level of their leadership, who rubbed shoulders with the CCP élite, these parties had over 5,700 grass-roots branches, of whom Li estimated 80 per cent were politically 'good' or 'comparatively good'.[7]

In 1961, Li made a series of investigations of these groups, which led to the circulation of a set of guidelines designed to diminish leftism among local authorities, keen to 'haul down white flags' (*ba bai qi*).[8] (It is illustrative of the sometimes divided and confused nature of policy-making at the higher levels of the CCP, that both Zhou Enlai and Chen Yi, frequent spokesmen on united front issues, were unaware that hauling down white flags was not, as they thought, dreamt up at the grass roots, but had appeared in a CC document.[9])

That summer, after Mao had expressed the view that the campaign against right opportunism had spread too widely and proposed reversals of verdicts where mistakes had been made,[10] Li Weihan was informed by Deng Xiaoping that the centre had decided that anyone criticized during the campaign against right opportunism at the *xian* level and below would simply have his case dismissed; above the *xian* level, cases would be re-examined one by one.[11] Li accordingly set up a small task force in the UFWD to draft a document laying out what was necessary for the improvement of relations between the CCP and outsiders. He himself helped the Shanghai party UFWD draft a similar document which was rejected by the leftist city 1st secretary and Politburo member, Ke Qingshi. The UFWD draft eventually disappeared in the revived leftism of late 1962.[12]

Information gap

A significant problem in attempting to revive the united front was that non-party people had been left out of the loop as the GLF crisis worsened. In the 1950s, they had been able to hear or read speeches by leaders; Zhou Enlai's annual report on government work to the NPC, in particular, had always been published, and at the very least it amounted to a sanitized state-of-the-nation address. But at the beginning of the 1960s, CCP leaders apparently decided not to share bad news with non-party people,[13] let alone the Chinese people in general, perhaps out of embarrassment, perhaps because they feared it would leak overseas. Even when the leadership began to speak again to trusted 'democratic personnages' in 1962, the speeches were not published.[14]

The editorial policy of the CCP's major propaganda organ, the *People's Daily,* suggests a failure of nerve and loss of direction in the immediate aftermath of the GLF. At a time when Chinese propagandists might have coined the slogan 'The economy, stupid!',[15] the *People's Daily* cut the number of editorials and shifted the focus of its columns to foreign affairs.[16]

Since *People's Daily* editorials were the principal means by which the CCP informed the great mass of the people, including most non-party people, of its thinking on the whole gamut of policy issues, this self-censorship meant that there was widespread ignorance, outside the magic circle of bureaucratic power, about how Mao and his colleagues thought the nation's woes should be alleviated. If thoughtful Chinese citizens wondered if CCP silence reflected unsureness at the top, this conclusion would have been reinforced by the CCP newspaper.

In 1958, when Mao was greatly exercised by the Middle East crisis and initiated a major confrontation with the United States in the Taiwan Straits, just over 31 per cent of the *People's Daily*'s editorials were on international affairs. In 1960, when by Mao's own account the leadership spent an inordinate amount of time on the Sino-Soviet dispute,[17] just over 28 per cent of the paper's editorials were on international affairs. These proportions suggest an underlying assumption that the proper business of Chinese is China. But in 1961, when Chinese citizens desperately needed guidance on domestic affairs, the proportion of editorials on international affairs rose to 46.9 per cent, and rose again in 1962 to 59 per cent. At a time when the Chinese leadership had rightly decided that everything must take second place to the recovery of agricultural production, the average number of editorials dedicated to rural-related concerns shrank from 13.66 a month in 1960 to 5.5 in 1961, to 3 in 1962, rising barely perceptibly to 3.3 in 1963. In place of many of the predictable seasonal exhortations on sowing, collecting fertilizer, water conservancy, hog-rearing, and harvesting, *People's Daily* readers were informed in 1961 about British 'armed intervention' in Kuwait, delays in signing a German peace treaty, and a successful Tokyo conference against nuclear weapons; they were reminded of the anniversaries of the Mongolian and Cuban revolutions and the patriotic Laotian *coup d'état*, and told to welcome distinguished guests from Brazil, Cuba, Ghana, Nepal, and North Korea. Even allowing for the leaders' sense that China had to play a more prominent international role as the last major bastion of world revolution, this was an extraordinarily lopsided use of their 'bully pulpit' at a time of domestic crisis.[18]

Zhou Enlai's efforts

But if the leadership felt that guidance of the 'broad masses' could be left to party cadres, who in turn were informed through internal channels, they could not hope to enlist the active co-operation of top-flight non-party professionals without giving them some general picture of the country's condition. Consequently, national institutions in which non-communists participated were reconvened. The Supreme State Conference (SSC)—an *ad hoc* body summoned by the head of state whenever he saw fit, with members he chose[19]—was convened by Liu Shaoqi on 21 March 1962, for the first time in over two-and-a-half years. Mao had held fifteen meetings of the SSC in his four-and-a-half year tenure as head of state, and had often used it as a major policy platform, from which to reach out to the non-party élite.[20] Liu had been head of state for three years, but had summoned it only once before, in the late summer of 1959.

This time Liu made a frank speech, recounting the conclusions of the Seven Thousand Cadres Conference and the Xilou meeting and detailing the nation's economic problems and the CCP's solutions. The audience was said to be deeply moved by the tenor of Liu's speech, and doubtless relieved that he had excused all non-party people from any serious responsibility for the crisis.[21]

But the principal responsibility for reviving the united front fell to Zhou Enlai, who dealt with it in four speeches in the spring of 1962, first in Beijing, then in Canton, and thereafter at the NPC and the Chinese People's Political Consultative Conference (CPPCC),[22] neither of which had met for two years. Mao commented favourably on the way Liu and Zhou had handled these meetings, feeling that they had adequately compensated for the CCP's neglect of the non-communists in recent years.[23]

On 2 March, Zhou gave the keynote address to the joint opening session of the National Conferences on Science and of Playwrights which were being held in Canton.[24] He started on a flattering and fraternal note:

It is a great pleasure for me to have this chance today to meet and talk with you—the senior and most accomplished scientists and playwrights of our country. Since time is limited, I shall only discuss one question: intellectuals.

This is a question that involves me personally, because I too come from an intellectual background. And talking about it, I shall feel closer to you.[25]

After a brief disquisition on the intellectuals as a social stratum of mental workers, Zhou gave a thumbnail sketch of his social origins and intellectual development to illustrate that he, like his audience, had his roots in China's 'feudal' past. Born into a mandarin family, he had worshipped Buddha as a child and later believed in anarchism and flirted with Fabian socialism.[26] 'In short, there is a fact we must admit, namely, that all of us come from the old society and that no matter who we are now, we were all bourgeois intellectuals in the past.'[27] Zhou took this occasion to acknowledge his debt to Zhang Shenfu, who had saved him from that bourgeois background by introducing him to the CCP. Zhang had helped Li Dazhao found a Marxist cell in Beijing, but had soon quit the CCP, became a nonperson for decades, and then, in 1957, was condemned as a rightist. Older members of the audience, familiar with the details of the party's early history, would have realized that this mention of Zhang was a breakthrough, signifying a new honesty.[28]

Zhou went on to claim, less honestly, that the CCP had always stressed allying with the intellectuals because—and here he buttressed himself by quoting Mao and Liu from the Hundred Flowers period, 1956–7—the great majority of them were patriotic and had made progress towards socialism. Despite the Anti-Rightist Campaign, that fundamental assessment had not changed, though some CCP members did not understand this; but the intellectuals had to remould themselves in order gradually to eradicate the bourgeois thinking attributable to their origins.[29]

Zhou then turned to the vexed question of how the CCP should lead the intellectuals, a subject much discussed in 1957.[30] It had to be responsible for overall principles and policies and could provide political, ideological, and organizational guidance, but should not interfere with detailed or professional work. The CCP had to trust and help the intellectuals, improve its relations with them, solve their problems, admit errors and correct them. For their part, the intellectuals had to continue to remould themselves.[31] This speech was a vintage Zhou performance for an intellectual audience, reasoned rather than strident, stressing persisting commonalities, glossing over past differences, appealing to patriotism, minimizing class struggle.

At some point in the next four weeks, it seems to have been agreed that Zhou could be even more forthcoming. Addressing the NPC on

28 March, the premier said that the great majority of intellectuals who served socialism and obeyed the party were 'without doubt intellectuals who belonged to the working people' (*shuyu laodong renminde zhishifenzi*), a comforting assurance if hardly a guarantee, since Zhou did not go so far as to call them intellectuals of the proletarian *class*. Reaching back again to the more moderate Mao of 1957, Zhou quoted the Chairman berating CCP members for not treating intellectuals correctly, and added that letting a hundred flowers bloom and a hundred schools contend was a major CCP goal.[32]

On this occasion, the premier dealt with all the various constituencies within the united front. Turning to the national minorities, Zhou expressed satisfaction with 'democratic reform' in Tibet, where socialist transformation had been halted in April 1961,[33] but admitted that in some minority areas, cadres had disobeyed the party policy of treating all peoples equally and had caused unnecessary damage. Indeed, there were shortly to be major incidents among the nationalities in Xinjiang which probably confirmed Zhou's analysis, even though they could conveniently be blamed on provocations by Soviet consular authorities in the autonomous region. On 16 April, 60,000 Kazakhs living in three counties along the Soviet border—Tacheng, Yumin, and Huocheng—started moving into the Soviet Union, doubtless attracted by the hopes of a better standard of living among their ethnic brothers there. The following month, on 25 May, there was a rebellious incident in Ili, again blamed on the Soviets, again probably reflecting also Han mishandling of the Xinjiang minorities.[34]

Zhou also made cursory mention in his speech of the overseas Chinese and religious believers, asserting the CCP's determination to carry out its policies well.[35] Later in the year, the CC approved more detailed reports on how to improve relations with the overseas Chinese, national minorities, and united front work in general.[36]

But at the NPC, the only group that received a promise of a tangible benefit from Zhou was the 'national bourgeoisie' or businessmen. When their firms had been transformed into joint state–private enterprises in early 1956, they had been promised interest for seven years, to represent 35 per cent of the capital they had contributed. During the blooming of the Hundred Flowers in 1957, some capitalists had argued for a longer buying-out period, perhaps twelve or even twenty years, so that the government could compensate them 100 per cent. In the Anti-Rightist Campaign, this plea was denounced.[37] When Liu Shaoqi had courted the capitalists in early 1960, he had been very cautious on this subject, promising nothing.[38] Now, however, Zhou was able to tell them that the government had 'already decided' to extend the buying-out period for an additional three years, and then would look again at the matter.[39]

Zhou gave his most extensive discussion of united front policy to the 897 delegates at the CPPCC meeting on 18 April.[40] The CPPCC was the institutional embodiment or 'organizational form of the people's democratic united front', dating back to the pre-PRC period,[41] so it was appropriate that Zhou Enlai should try to persuade its members of a 'new development' in this policy arena.[42] The shift which he laid out was from emphasizing socialist transformation to emphasizing socialist construction; in other words, the CCP was prepared to relax ideological remoulding in return for the active co-operation of non-communists in combating the current economic crisis. In line with Mao's speech to the Seven Thousand Cadres Conference, Zhou also dangled the prospect of a 'broadening of democratic life', provided people did not violate the six criteria laid down in the official version of Mao's contradictions speech in 1957.[43]

Concretely, Zhou asked the members of the CPPCC to engage in more investigation, study, and academic discussions, an indication of the CCP's renewed awareness of its need for independent feedback on policy performance. Zhou revived the policy of 'long-term coexistence and mutual supervision' which Mao had devised in 1956 precisely for that end, despite grumbling among his followers.[44] But though he talked longer on this subject than at the NPC, Zhou had no additional concessions to offer. Effectively, all he could do was ask his audience to trust him that the old line meant something in the new political atmosphere. But would the bourgeoisie buy a second-hand policy from the premier after their long years of harsh ideological remoulding? Li Weihan attempted to ensure a positive answer by summoning a national united front work conference in May.[45]

Flowers and schools

As in 1961, so in 1962, a significant part of the effort in the united front field was the continuing attempt by bourgeois-friendly CCP leaders like Zhou and Chen Yi to revive the Hundred Flowers policy.[46] Two of Zhou's three major speeches on this subject, as published or cited by PRC authors and editors, were the ones he made in these two years, the third having been in 1959.[47] On 17 February

1962, the premier addressed a meeting of over a hundred play-wrights in Beijing.[48]

Zhou started with an admission which could not have been very reassuring to his audience. Some provincial and city leaders had refused to distribute his 1959 speech.[49] What he said next, however, was in contrast with his remarks about that same speech only eight months earlier. In June 1961, Zhou had disclosed unease, though without revealing the resistance of provincial officials:

In 1959 I gave a talk on the need to pursue 'a policy of walking on two legs' in the sphere of literature and art. As I now see it, not everything I said then was necessarily right. Perhaps I went a bit too far on one point, or failed to make myself clear on another. After that talk I felt rather uneasy, because there was no response. It seemed that it was soon consigned to limbo. I could not but be disturbed about that. Now you have invited me to come to this meeting and give a talk. And I do have some ideas that I shall be very glad to share with you. But I hope you won't expect me to be correct on every point ... [50]

Now, in February 1962, in a far more confident comment, Zhou stated simply that he had reviewed the 1959 speech that very day and found the content to be 'basically correct'.[51]

The premier's revelations underlined the constraints on even a very senior leader in the leftist atmosphere unleashed by the GLF. Zhou had made his speech in 1959 at a time when his authority had been diminished by criticism by Mao and by the transfer of control over the economy either to the CC secretariat or the provinces.[52] Although he was speaking during the brief rational interlude in the GLF, leftism had not been quelled, and presumably a GLF enthusiast like Shanghai 1st secretary Ke Qingshi felt sufficiently in tune with the times and the Chairman to refuse to distribute among the numerous intellectuals in his bailiwick what to him must have seemed like a subversive document.[53] Zhou's reaction to that 1959 boycott and his disclaimers in his 1961 speech indicate that, even after the formal end of the GLF, he was not totally certain that the political atmosphere had radically changed. Thus his confident reaffirmation now, in 1962, of his 1959 remarks, and his willingness to shrug off their fate at the time, must be seen as a reflection of a new confidence, signalled also by fewer references to Mao.[54] This could only have sprung from the Seven Thousand Cadres Conference which had ended ten days earlier.

Yet for Zhou's audience in February 1962, some of whom had probably heard both the earlier speeches, it was a cautionary tale.

A major speech on policy towards the intellectuals by the third-ranking member of the CCP élite, a man of enormous national and international prestige, had been ignored or set aside as if it had been made by a *xian* secretary. If even Zhou could be rendered powerless by the tide of events, how advisable was it for intellectuals to respond boldly to his proposals to shatter superstition and liberate their thinking?

Zhou attempted to reinforce his message by indicating that a new stage had begun in the field of literature and the arts. Charting a fuzzy chronology with overlapping dates,[55] Zhou said that from 1949 to the GLF had been the first stage, characterized at first by unfamiliarity with the problems and uncertainty as to what to preserve from the old society. Then, as a result of the Hundred Flowers policy, creativity had been unleashed, consciousness had been raised, and people had been inspired to dare to think, speak, and act, and to throw out the old and bring in the new—until the 1957 Anti-Rightist Campaign.

Zhou's second stage seemed to start with the campaign against right opportunism in the autumn of 1959, or what he described as 'deviations in the implementation of the general line in concrete work', which inevitably affected all fields of activity. Zhou put the principal blame, however, on developments in the arts themselves. New superstitions had replaced the old. It had been right to reject the myths that anything old was better than anything new or that anything foreign was better than anything Chinese. But now anything new was said to be good and everything old was bad, anything Chinese was good, everything foreign bad. This was contrary to Mao Zedong Thought, and the latter idea was a deviation redolent of the ideas of the Boxers at the beginning of the century; and whereas the Boxers were responding to imperialist oppression, the current revival of anti-foreignism smacked of 'big nation chauvinism' (*da guo shawenzhuyi*).[56]

Zhou also objected to the new constraints embodied in rigid model characters, which meant that party secretaries or reactionaries could be described only in certain formulaic, politically correct terms, greatly easing the tasks of critics and of party cadres in charge of culture. To illustrate what he meant, Zhou criticized his 'old friend' the distinguished playwright Cao Yu, who had been bold in Chongqing during the anti-Japanese war and in the PRC's early years. Cao had since joined the CCP (in 1956) and should have got bolder, but, comparing his earlier work with his latest, he was acting as if he were hedged in by even more restrictions.[57]

Zhou proclaimed that literature and the arts were now entering a third stage which involved the 'negation of the negation' (*fouding zhi fouding*), a highly uncharacteristic and even risky reference to one of Engels's contributions to Marxist theory. Zhou was using this theoretical window-dressing for purely practical purposes, however: he wanted writers to revert to his rose-tinted image of the earlier period and to rediscover their boldness.[58]

How could party leadership facilitate this? Citing Mao's Sixty Articles on Work Methods issued in January 1958, Zhou argued that party committees should leave specialized matters to the experts. Overall party leadership was successful, but at the grass roots the achievements/errors ratio was not always nine fingers to one. Was there not this kind of phenomenon in the field of literature and the arts? Zhou asked rhetorically. Mistakes should be corrected by self-criticism, and party committees should be readier to listen to others; here Zhou repeated Mao's assertion two weeks earlier at the Seven Thousand Cadres Conference that the secret of the success of the founder of the Han dynasty, Liu Bang, had been his willingness to listen. Trust in the party was high but this did not amount to trust in every party member nor to an endorsement of the correctness of the work of every party committee; non-party people should speak up to help correct mistakes.[59]

Zhou blamed the new political straitjacket upon party committee leaders who could not write, but simply assigned labels like 'conservative' or 'right opportunist'. This in turn led to the formulization and vulgarization of artistic works. The centre had to take principal responsibility and the provinces secondary responsibility, but unit party committees could not be excused from blame and some had to be reformed. With the exercise of democracy, correct opinions would emerge and it would be possible to achieve the aim which Mao had articulated in 1957, the creation of a 'political climate in which there is both centralism and democracy, discipline and freedom, unity of purpose and personal ease of mind and liveliness'. To get there one needed the negation of the negation.[60]

Zhou then turned to particular problems of writers. They had to express the 'spirit of the times' (*shidai jingshen*), but this did not mean that CCP policies and decisions had to be enacted on stage. As Mao had said, if plays were like conferences, what would be the point of having plays? Nor did all the characters have to be heroes; everyone had shortcomings and limitations. In a phrase which could have been grounds for condemnation by Red Guards during the

Cultural Revolution had Mao wished it, Zhou added: 'There is no absolutely correct person.'[61]

Zhou acknowledged that it was more difficult to write about contradictions among the people than about contradictions with the enemy, for the latter lent themselves to easy formulaic treatment. But daily life was principally about internal contradictions and they had to be described. Zhou of course knew, though he did not articulate it, that writers had to worry about official displeasure at 'incorrect' analysis of such internal contradictions, for many of the latter resulted from the shortcomings and limitations of cadres. Nor would his audience have been reassured by the advice Zhou gave on how to deal with the shortcomings of the proletariat in his discussion of artistic and historical truth. He counselled against emulating people like the purged writer Hu Feng,[62] who went to cities like Tianjin in search of proletarian faults. Rather one should copy Gorky, who had written about the faults of workers, but had attributed them to the old system.

In fact, despite his encouraging talk of democracy and the negation of the mistaken approaches in the new era he proclaimed was starting, Zhou was actually offering cold comfort: 'Even if all windows are thrown wide open and the two stages of superstitions are dispelled, writers themselves will still need self-cultivation—ideological self-cultivation and artistic self-cultivation.'[63] In short, leaders like Zhou and Chen Yi might be sympathetic and helpful, but in the final analysis it was the writer's responsibility to make the necessary compromises between artistic honesty and political survival.

Chen Yi takes courage

With Zhou Enlai, one has to deduce that the bolder and more optimistic tenor of his speech to playwrights in Beijing had its roots in what happened at the Seven Thousand Cadres Conference. In Chen Yi's marathon speech[64] to the national playwrights conference in Canton, he admitted as much: 'I attended the seven thousand man conference, and I then plucked up the courage to speak . . . Today, the centre has decided to take the initiative to improve relations with writers and scientists.'[65] Chen's semi-official biography confirms that this was not just a rhetorical flourish. It notes that there were those who believed that Chen's boldness in making this speech was a result of Mao's self-criticism at the Seven Thousand Cadres Conference, and it comments that there were grounds for thinking that.[66] It appears that Chen did not seek advice from senior colleagues in preparing his speech, merely ticking off the main points two days before delivery to Zhou Enlai when the premier was leaving Canton for Beijing. While Zhou approved the outline,[67] he could not have fully anticipated what appears to have been a bravura performance, interrupted over sixty times by laughter or applause and remembered by intellectuals as the crowning moment in Chen's dealings with cultural affairs.[68]

Chen began with a long discussion of the general state of the party's relations with the intellectuals. His verdict: 'very abnormal' (*hen bu zhengchang*). The scientists had kept quiet about absurd claims and campaigns during the GLF for fear of being labelled conservative; writers had kept their own counsel when people vowed to write sixty plays in a night. Had the party been prepared to listen, perhaps the country would have gone down a less tortuous path:

Yesterday I said at the scientists' conference: the important thing today is that we ought to foster scientists. They are the people's intellectuals, socialist scientists, workers for the people, workers with their brains who serve the proletariat. The workers, peasants, and intellectuals are the three component elements of our nation's working people, they [too] are masters [in our society]. After twelve years of remoulding and testing, we cannot continue to put the cap of bourgeois intellectual on all the existing intellectuals, because that would not be in accord with actual conditions.[69]

Ideological remoulding was a long-term process, Chen maintained, and should be done voluntarily and not through campaigns. He advised all comrades involved in party and administrative work to indulge in introspection and self-criticism. In the past, the intellectuals were not united with or listened to and things went wrong as a result; like Zhou, Chen reminded cadres that Mao attributed Liu Bang's success in founding the Han dynasty to his willingness to listen. Chen derided wholesale attacks on the intellectuals, and again taking advantage of Mao's admission of CCP crassness at the Seven Thousand Cadres Conference, he shouted: 'What you [i.e. leftists] are doing is very stupid.'[70]

Turning to specific issues which he had been asked to address, Chen revealed that Mao, Zhou, and other central comrades—interestingly, Chen referred several times to Mao and Zhou, but not once to Liu Shaoqi[71]—had never had a special discussion about modern drama. Chen deduced that Mao had no objection to it because in all fields he believed in utilizing things ancient and modern, Chinese and foreign, and he explained the Chairman's indifference with a quotation: 'I don't go to plays because I'm "acting out a drama" every day, and to go and see one in addition would be tedious. But I don't oppose plays. I hear that the mass of young people and people in general are very fond of them, so we ought to promote these things.'[72] Zhou, on the other hand, was very keen on plays of all kinds and had discussed relevant issues many times with Chen. The premier strongly deplored the prevailing lack of respect for playwrights and actors and the attempts to hedge their artistic freedom with political slogans and duties. As for himself, Chen said he had nothing new to add to the views he had often expressed. He rejected the notion that peasants did not like plays that had been written in a capitalist society; this had been disproved during the anti-Japanese war. He also refused to acknowledge that films were an adequate substitute for plays. People liked all sorts of different artistic forms, and laws could not be based on personal preferences.[73]

Chen Yi expressed his personal belief in the 'democratic rights of the writer' (*zuojiade minzhu quanli*); no party secretary, or even a vice-premier, should be able to compel him to revise his work. Only one thing was forbidden, propagating reactionary propaganda, but Chen did not believe that there was a single writer who wished to write that way.[74]

Even more importantly, Chen insisted upon the primacy and the inviolability of the individual writer as the principal element in artistic creation. Talented individuals were essential for such specialized work as writing. The writer alone was responsible for his spiritual product. Collective creation—much trumpeted during the GLF[75]— was only a style: 'The poems I have published are simply mine alone. If you want to work with me, I won't do it (*Laughter*).'[76]

The individual writer's responsibility extended to subject-matter, and he could legitimately choose to describe internal contradictions. Chen was still wrestling with this issue but he boldly modified the view put forward by Mao in his talks on literature in Yan'an that such works could be used by the imperialists against China. Rather they should be seen as examples of self-criticism, Chen felt, though he was realistic enough to add later that current rural conditions were too serious to be described publicly yet; they indeed could give imperialism cause for rejoicing. Apparently at Zhou Enlai's suggestion, Chen took as his text the film *Dong xiao heng chui* (The panpipe is played horizontally), referring to it several times in his speech. Its author Hai Mo had been purged during the Anti-Rightist Campaign for his critical depiction of two venal local party officials, but had now been rehabilitated. Chen pointed out that the film proved that an appeal to Beijing and Chairman Mao could produce results and so encouraged people to oppose error.[77]

Chen took a similar line on the 'internal contradictions' of characters in dramas, asserting that tragedy was a permissible art form, and again attempting to amend Mao's view, following Engels, that writers should stress only the heroic aspects of characters. Their shortcomings could also be described, Chen argued, because this highlighted their virtues.[78]

And what should one do about the Hai Mos who were wronged? The audience was composed entirely of supporters of the revolution, mainly party members, and they should understand that the course of a revolution was turbulent. The general situation was bright, but from time to time there could be dark spells. In a passage that was all too soon to be borne out in practice, Chen said that although the weather was currently sunny in Canton, one could not predict that it would always be so, and the political weather was similarly uncertain. One could not say that there were no 'black spots in the sun'.[79] From time to time there would be oppression under the party, but in the end the CCP would rectify such problems. Taking examples of such victimization from his own career and that of Mao, Chen told his audience that under such circumstances they should stand firm, accept discipline, and exhibit patience.[80]

For all his brave and encouraging words, Chen was honest enough to acknowledge that whatever a leader like himself said, and whatever undertakings might be given at meetings like this, neither was any protection against retribution back at one's unit. He knew he was preaching to the converted, that those in the CCP who oppressed intellectuals were not present, and so Chen called for a debate on the basis of the record of the conference.[81]

It was not to be. Chen's insight was correct. Though the ripples of the Canton conference did benefit intellectuals in various parts of the country, including former rightists[82]—'How the temperature warmed up in 1962', one remembers[83]—they only lapped the walls of leftist bastions. Two conferees from Shanghai—which had been captured by Chen Yi's 3rd Field Army in 1949, and where he had presided as mayor for five years before being transferred to Beijing—returned home enthusiastically to advocate distribution of his speech, but 1st secretary Ke Qingshi absolutely forbade it. Local party members of similar leftist persuasion who were permitted to read it remarked that if Chen Yi's name had not been clearly written on it, they would have thought it the speech of a 'rightist element'.[84]

Perhaps Ke knew that when Zhou Enlai had requested Mao's guidance on policy towards the intellectuals, the Chairman had refused to comment.[85]

Even if they could not control Shanghai, the national literary bureaucrats were able to use Chen Yi's speech to some effect. In August, the Chinese Writers' Union held a small seminar in Dalian in northeast China, at which sixteen leading authors, including Mao Dun, Zhao Shuli, and Zhou Libo, discussed subjects for short stories on rural themes. The meeting was presided over by the Writers' Union's party secretary, Shao Quanlin, and addressed by the propaganda official in charge of the literary world, Zhou Yang, both of whom had earlier been merciless critics of writers who deviated from the narrow path of orthodoxy. Now, in a meeting to explore the complexities of portraying the real world, with its 'internal contradictions', rather than the idealized world of the Stakhanovite peasant, both men reversed themselves by advocating the honest portrayal of 'middle characters' (*zhongjian zhuangtaide renwu*), the great majority of the population, with all their faults and prejudices. Their words would be held against them during the Cultural Revolution.[86]

11 THE CURIOUS CASE OF THE 'THREE-FAMILY VILLAGE'

The words and actions of responsible senior party leaders and bureaucrats like Chen Yi at Canton and Zhou Yang at Dalian confirmed an important aspect of the post-GLF recovery period: officials were prepared to think the unthinkable. Radical measures could be proposed for any field. Orthodox cadres condoned what they had condemned. For some, doubtless, it was simply a case of 'orders are orders'. For others, it may have been a heaven-sent opportunity to express long-suppressed thoughts.

That, at least, was the implicit allegation later made by Cultural Revolution polemicists against a trio of senior party propagandists, Deng Tuo, Wu Han, and Liao Mosha, who were accused of unleashing a series of bitter if veiled attacks on Mao and his policies in their newspaper columns at this time.[1] Some outside observers believed these charges, often sympathizing with the disgraced writers and admiring their courage.[2] Yet to this day, the truth of the charges is unclear; and although the denunciations of the three men's articles are historically important because they were the first salvoes of the Cultural Revolution, it is not certain that their writings had any political impact when originally published in the early 1960s.

Despite the continuing obscurity of the case of the so-called 'Three-Family Village', a judgement must be made about it. If the writings were totally innocent, then the subsequent attacks on the authors reflected either paranoia or a cynical manipulation of evidence as a pretext for the assault on leading party officials at the outset of the Cultural Revolution. If, on the other hand, the articles were intended to criticize Mao, as later alleged, then the collapse of morale and discipline in the Communist party in the early 1960s must have been considerable, and the concern of the Chairman to revive its revolutionary vigour is more comprehensible.

Fortunately for historians, one member of the 'Three-Family Village' survived the Cultural Revolution to give his version of events. Liao Mosha, a former journalist and historical novelist, was in 1961 a 54-year-old senior official of the Beijing municipal party organization with experience in propaganda and educational work. In September that year he became director of the local United Front Work Department which exercised control over non-party intellectuals.[3] In the middle of the month, Deng Tuo and his fellow editors of the municipal party's theoretical journal *Qianxian* (Front Line) invited him to a lunch at the Sichuan restaurant, where he found that the company included another leading figure in the intellectual life of the capital, Wu Han.[4]

Deng Tuo and 'Evening Chats at Yanshan'

Deng Tuo was a distinguished party journalist, who had won his spurs during the revolution as editor of the main newspaper in the Jin-Cha-Ji base area, where his civilian boss was Peng Zhen.[5] In Jin-Cha-Ji, on the instructions of the military commander, Nie Rongzhen, Deng Tuo had also edited the very first official edition of Mao's selected works.[6] After the communist capture of Beijing in January 1949, Deng Tuo became propaganda director for the municipal committee, but that autumn, as the communist forces completed their victory nationwide, he was appointed editor-in-chief of the *People's Daily*, established as the CCP's principal national newspaper the previous year.[7]

It is unclear why the occupant of so responsible a post should not have been made at least an alternate member of the CC at the first post-Liberation CCP congress in 1956.[8] What is clear is that during the Hundred Flowers period, 1956–7, Deng Tuo incurred Mao's increasing wrath and finally lost his editorial chair at the *People's Daily* in 1958 at the Chairman's insistence.[9] Since Deng had not actually committed any errors of line or indiscipline, he was transferred to the Beijing municipal party secretariat to be the secretary in charge of culture and education and editor-in-chief of *Qianxian*, from its inception in November 1958,[10] working once again under Peng Zhen. During the early period of the GLF, he trumpeted its virtues.[11] In 1960, Deng Tuo became in addition an alternate secretary of the newly formed North China Bureau of the CCP.[12] In 1961, Deng started writing a column for the *Beijing Wanbao* (Beijing Evening News), which, despite its local origins, distributed half its 300,000 print run outside the capital.[13]

Impressed by his wide-ranging knowledge of both history and the arts, the editors of *Beijing Wanbao* had cultivated Deng Tuo for a couple of years, coaxing occasional pieces out of him, before finally pinning him down to a regular column. In the darkness of the three bitter years, they felt their readers needed articles that could 'expand their horizons, enrich their knowledge, and raise their spirits'. In March 1961, Deng Tuo agreed.

When the delighted editors called at his house to cement the arrangements, Deng presented them with two pieces of paper. One carried the title he had chosen for the column: *Yanshan yehua* (Evening Chats at Yanshan); Yanshan was an important range of hills in the Beijing area, while *yehua* was designed to convey the idea of the kind of heart-to-heart talks that can only take place after dark. On the other piece of paper he had inscribed his chosen pseudonym, Ma Nancun, a variation on the name of the fondly remembered hamlet of Malancun in north China where he had edited the *Jin-Cha-Ji Ribao* (Jin-Cha-Ji Daily) during the anti-Japanese war. He indicated that his busy schedule would permit him to write only twice a week, and that his preference was for the column to be printed on the top right-hand corner of the page so that it could be easily cut out by those wanting to preserve it![14] He would be paid 15 yuan per article, above the going rate.[15]

What seems to have struck Deng Tuo at first as an extra chore he could well do without had clearly now become an exciting new venture which would give him a free hand to write on any subject under the sun. Three years after his humiliating departure from the editorship of the *People's Daily* at Mao's insistence, this was doubtless a welcome boost to his ego. His first column appeared on 9 March 1961, and the series continued until September 1962, by which time he had written 152 'Evening Chats'.[16]

This term, as it turned out, implied more than just intimacy. In his first piece, 'One third of life', Deng Tuo cited an ancient Chinese practice of reckoning the evening hours as equivalent to half a day, because a conscientious person could pack so much study or work into it, including, presumably, reading Deng's column.[17] He himself set an example by dashing off his columns in the evenings in less than hour.[18]

The subject-matter of 'Evening Chats at Yanshan' was wide-ranging, cultural in the most general sense: philosophy, science, history, geography, literature, the arts, as well as policy, current events, study, work, and work style. Deng brought in the Confucian classics, the dynastic histories, novels, and much else. Liao Mosha described the column as 'an all-embracing feast for the eyes, much like a small encyclopaedia'.[19] Deng Tuo seemed obsessed with 'knowledge'.[20] Perhaps the main appeal of the column was that the vast majority of the articles, even those with a subliminal political message, could be enjoyed by all and sundry for what they purported to say. After long humourless years of movement politics, simply to relax briefly over Ma Nancun's latest literary excursion must have been an enormous relief. Ironically, this may have been a more subtly subversive aspect of the column than any political innuendoes later 'uncovered' by Yao Wenyuan, for it legitimized a private space in which politics did not take command.

The column was enormously popular. In its first year, Deng Tuo received some 400 letters from readers, from as far away as Yunnan, Guizhou, Xinjiang, and Tibet, and from workers, teachers, students, scientists, and leaders.[21] Marshal He Long was alleged during the Cultural Revolution not to have missed an instalment.[22] Even Yao Wenyuan, who would claim that Deng Tuo slandered Chairman Mao and all his works, held the column in high esteem at the time.[23] Ironically, the column does not appear to have been read by the men who would later be held accountable for it, Deng's immediate superiors, Peng Zhen and Beijing 2nd secretary, Liu Ren—Peng Zhen because his cultural interests were limited and Liu because, as he later claimed, he was too busy coping with the capital's cabbage problem![24] Since Deng Tuo was the colleague whom they had deputed to oversee *Beijing Wanbao*, he did not need to consult them, let alone submit his articles to them for approval prior to publication.[25]

Wu Han and *The Dismissal of Hai Rui*

Those within the Chinese leadership who were aware of Deng Tuo's stormy relationship with Mao might have found Yao's later accusations against him credible. Yet Yao's first target on the eve of the Cultural Revolution would be someone whom Mao admired, Wu Han,[26] the third major figure at the Sichuan restaurant lunch.[27] Deng Tuo and Liao Mosha had both joined the CCP in 1930.[28] Wu Han, in contrast, was a long-time fellow-traveller, active in the China Democratic League. His value to the CCP as a non-communist sympathizer was such that, although he applied for party membership in 1948, he was permitted to join only in 1957 at the age of 47.[29] Wu Han's political activism had earned him early on a supporting role in public life as a deputy mayor of Beijing,[30] but by profession he was an academic, a distinguished historian of the Ming dynasty and the author of a widely acclaimed life of its founder.[31]

In 1959, complaining privately that even long-time comrades-in-arms like Liu Shaoqi did not dare to speak up in front of him,[32] Mao had called on party members to emulate a courageous and outspoken Ming dynasty official called Hai Rui.[33] Hu Qiaomu, one of Mao's earliest secretaries and a deputy director of the CC's Propaganda Department, had thereupon pressed Wu Han into deploying his expertise to describe for more ignorant party officials how Hai Rui had confronted local tyrants and even defied the emperor. Wu Han wrote a series of articles on Hai Rui, culminating in the publication of a collection of Hai Rui's works in 1962.[34]

Wu was also prevailed upon by leaders of a Peking Opera company to branch out into what was for him a new genre by writing a historical drama about Hai Rui for them to perform. After repeated criticisms and rewriting, the play was completed on 13 November 1960. Wu Han had titled it simply 'Hai Rui', but this was considered inappropriate by his theatrical collaborators since it was not a complete life; for five drafts it was called 'Hai Rui Returns the Land' (*Hai Rui Tui Tian*), but at the suggestion of a friend, the last two drafts bore the final title *The Dismissal of Hai Rui* (*Hai Rui Ba Guan*).[35] The play was staged early in 1961,[36] and immediately sparked an interchange in the *Beijing Wanbao* between Liao Mosha and Wu Han, in which Liao asked Wu whether there was any difference between historical and dramatic truth.[37]

Shortly after the play had been staged and its text published, and Mao had had a chance to appraise it, the Chairman invited the actor who played Hai Rui, Ma Lianliang, to dinner at his residence, prevailed upon him to recite lines from his part, and voiced the opinion: 'The play is good, and Hai Rui was a good man! *Hai Rui Ba Guan* is written pretty well [too].'[38] Later in the year, Mao presented Wu Han with a personally inscribed copy of the fourth volume of his *Selected Works*.[39] Evidently at this time, Mao was not angry in any way about *The Dismissal of Hai Rui*, and bore no grudge against its author. As late as 1963, Mao sought out Wu Han at a reception for philosophers and social scientists and asked him how the revision of his biography of the Ming founder was going.[40] Whether he changed his mind about Wu Han will be discussed in a later chapter. But Yao Wenyuan was to charge that Wu Han, in partnership with Liao Mosha and Deng Tuo, had already 'formed a deliberate, planned and organized major attack on the Party and socialism, masterminded in detail by Three-Family Village'.[41]

The 'Three-Family Village'

At the fateful lunch in mid-September 1961, Deng Tuo informed Wu Han and Liao Mosha that his journal *Qianxian* wanted to emulate the practice started by other papers of having a column co-authored by a number of writers.[42] His proposition was that the three of them should collaborate on a column to be called *Sanjia Cun Zhaji* (Notes from a Three-Family Village). As they ate, the conversation rambled over many topics, and it was only at the end of the meal that they settled the details of an enterprise which seems to have been readily agreed to.

They would write under a single pseudonym: Wu Nanxing, derived from *Wu* Han, Ma *Nan*cun (Deng Tuo's other pseudonym), and Fan *Xing* (a pseudonym of Liao's), though the Beijing intellectual *cognoscenti* soon penetrated their disguise.[43] They would publish one column in each issue of *Qianxian*, and on the rare occasions—it turned out to be five—when all of them were too busy to write, some outsider would be invited to fill in. According to Liao Mosha's later account, the editors made no attempt to suggest topics, let alone impose them; they were more interested in ensuring that the columns should be no longer than 1,000 characters.[44] As Liao himself indicates, the members of the trio were by background and talent a natural combination. They belonged to the same generation, and knew each other well.[45] Each had a long history of writing for the communist cause and they were all deeply engaged in the intellectual life of the capital. Between them they spanned the fields of literature, drama, academia, journalism, and propaganda.[46] Is it conceivable that jointly they conspired to attack the party and Chairman Mao?

Liao Mosha later insisted that no agreements were reached at the lunch except those concerned with technicalities. He recalled choosing all his own topics and never having any of his articles altered. Deng Tuo exercised no editorial prerogative in an effort to mould the column to a fell design. He 'pointed to the heavens and swore by the sun' (*zhitian shiri*) that 'Notes from a Three-Family Village' was unorganized and unplanned, and its authors operated as three individual writers without leadership and without direction.[47] Yao Wenyuan argued otherwise.

The case against the 'Three-Family Village'[48]

There was nothing inherently absurd about Yao's contention that the targets of his polemics had made political points by the use of Aesopian language. Deng Tuo's work in the 'red' base areas in the 1930s and 1940s, had provided less opportunity for this, but Wu Han and Liao Mosha had both used the technique against the KMT prior to the CCP conquest of power.[49] In his polemic against the three men, however, Yao directed his main fire at Deng Tuo, linking 'Notes from a Three-Family Village' with Deng's 'Evening Chats at Yanshan', fingering him as the prime mover, the 'black hand', in the alleged conspiracy.[50] Yao made his case by analysing a number of the essays.

In 'Welcome "the Miscellaneous Scholars" ', Deng had classified such people as 'those with a wide range of knowledge' knowing 'an assortment of bits of everything', much like the leading scholars of the past, and said: 'It will be a great loss to us if we now fail to acknowledge the great significance of the wide range of knowledge of the "miscellaneous scholars" for work.'[51] From these brief quotes, Yao deduced that 'miscellaneous scholars' were none other than the 'unregenerate elements and intellectuals of the bourgeois and land-lord classes, a handful of characters of dubious political background, as well as such reactionaries as the "scholars" of the landlord and bourgeois classes . . . Using their "knowledge" as their capital, such characters are trying desperately to intrigue themselves or climb into leading positions at different levels and change the nature of the dictatorship of the proletariat.' Deng Tuo was 'in effect, demanding that the Party open the door to those "miscellaneous scholars" who had taken the capitalist road . . . so as to prepare public opinion for the restoration of capitalism'.[52]

In an article on agricultural policy, 'Guide Rather than Block', Deng Tuo allegedly 'demanded' that 'everything' should be 'actively guided to facilitate its smooth development'. On the basis of these few words, Yao Wenyuan was able to execute one of those extraordinary leaps of imagination that are permissible only to a polemicist who fulminates without fear of correction. He wrote: ' "Everything", please note, including those dark things that are anti-Party and anti-socialist' such as 'bourgeois liberalization' and 'surrender to the ill winds which were blowing at the time, the winds of "going it alone" [i.e., the restoration of individual economy] and of the extension of plots for private use and of free markets, the increase of small enterprises with sole responsibility for their own profits or losses, and the fixing of output quotas based on the house-hold'.[53]

In another flight of fancy, Yao attacked Deng Tuo for writing in an article on 'This Year's Spring Festival': 'The bitter cold of the north wind will soon come to an end. In its stead a warm east wind will blow and a thaw will soon set in on this earth.' Yao asked rhetorically if it were not significant Deng used the word 'thaw', 'one of the terms in the out-and-out counter-revolutionary vocabulary used by the Khrushchov [sic] revisionist clique against Stalin?' According to Yao, Deng was predicting the demise of 'socialist New China' by the end of the year. Perhaps some of Yao's readers wondered contrarily whether by north wind Deng meant the Soviet Union, which lay in that direction from China, so that he was in fact describing how Mao, customarily associated with any manifestation of the east, would overcome Khrushchev.[54]

Yao Wenyuan's more preposterous accusations should not lead one to conclude that Deng Tuo never used his scholarly tales and historical analogies to make pointed observations about the current scene. One article strongly criticized by Yao was 'On Treasuring Labour Power', in which Deng cited examples from Chinese history to warn against the excessive use of corvée workers. Yao's claim that this was an oblique critique of the methods of the Great Leap Forward may well be justified, but if so, it was mild, non-recriminatory, and in line with current official sentiment.[55] Deng Tuo's Western biographer argues that 'The Kingly Way and the Tyrannical Way' and 'Three Kinds of Zhuge Liang', both published after the Seven Thousand Cadres Conference, were clearly attacks on Mao.[56]

Yao Wenyuan probably directed most of his fire at Deng Tuo, not just because he saw him as the kingpin of the Three-Family Village, but precisely because his writings were easier to attack. Wu Han's esssays were 'by and large not blatantly satirical, but rather quite straightforward . . . He identified problems openly and proposed solutions that often combined traditional wisdom and socialist consciousness'. Understandably, he tended to argue from historical analogy.[57] Liao Mosha's contributions to the column were allusive, and 'neither as cuttingly sarcastic as Deng Tuo's, nor as doggedly committed to preserving certain elements of the Chinese cultural heritage as those of Wu Han'. Nevertheless, his early columns contained more references to the Chinese heritage than to Marx, Lenin, and Mao, and he evidently valued the traditional student–teacher relationship, seeing the party as the teacher and the broad masses' as the pupil.[58] Had Wu Han and Liao Mosha allowed themselves to get tied up with a man seeking to wound Mao in return for the humiliations which he had suffered at the Chairman's hands? Was Yao, despite his india-rubber logic, correct in asserting that there had been something afoot? Or was there less in the columns than met the eye?

Trimming the sails

One way of getting at this problem is to examine the chronology of the two columns and see how they correspond to the fluctuations in the political atmosphere. Taking Deng Tuo, for instance, it is clear that only a few of his essays in either column, possibly a little over a quarter, might have carried a political *double entendre*; the rest were either purely cultural or simply echoed the current line.[59] How did they reflect what was happening in high politics?

One analysis suggests that Deng was a 'politically astute creature who chose his time carefully'. According to this view, Deng's writings display five high tides of critical commentary on Maoist leftism and on Mao himself: in March–April 1961, sparked presumably by the Canton conference; in June 1961 at the time of Mao's 'self-criticism' at the May–June work conference; in August, around the time of the second Lushan conference; in November, when Deng Tuo was playing a leading role in compiling the Beijing party dossiers on the GLF at the Changguanlou meeting;[60] and in February 1962, just after Mao's second self-criticism at the Seven Thousand Cadres Conference.[61] More importantly, it is clear that after the CC's 10th plenum in September 1962, when Mao proclaimed the primacy of class struggle, the 'Three-Family Village' column became more cultural, more orthodox, and more anodyne.[62] Indeed, Deng Tuo closed down 'Evening Chats at Yanshan' in early September, by which time Mao's rumblings on the class struggle issue at the summer work conference must have been common knowledge among senior Beijing bureaucrats. Presumably Deng Tuo felt more exposed in a single-author vehicle.

Tacking with the wind does not, however, amount to guilt.[63] As we have seen, that hammer of the bourgeois intellectuals, Zhou Yang, had changed course in line with new policy directions after the 9th plenum. About-turns, whether in response to orders or as an adjustment to new realities, have always been key to survival in communist states. Yao was, of course, correct in suggesting in the very different atmosphere four years later that some essays in the two columns had been critical of GLF practices. But Mao himself was guilty on that score with his attacks on the five 'communist styles'. The only difference was that the critiques in the 'Three-Family Village' and 'Evening Chats' were undoubtedly a good deal less turgid, not to say shorter, than the cascade of official speeches and directives.

Since the evidence clearly shows that Wu Han's play about Hai Rui pleased rather than offended Mao when it appeared in January 1961, the only interesting question to be settled about the members of the Three-Family Village is whether or not Deng Tuo committed *lèse-majesté* by sniping at Mao in his essays. His widow, his collaborator Liao Mosha, and his friends all claim he did not, but Deng Tuo took that secret to the grave when he committed suicide at the beginning of the Cultural Revolution. Suicide could have been a confession of guilt; more likely it was a protest, a decision not to endure any more suffering in a revolution which was now devouring its own children.

What seems highly unlikely is that an experienced cadre like Deng Tuo would deliberately set out to avenge the humiliations he had suffered at the Chairman's hands. It was far too dangerous. As the behaviour of men considerably more senior than Deng Tuo at the Seven Thousand Cadres Conference demonstrated, even at a time when Mao felt compelled to apologize, it was foolhardy to rub it in. Deng Tuo would undoubtedly have learned of the reaction to the modest suggestion from his chief, Peng Zhen, about ascribing some blame to the Chairman.

Deng Tuo clearly took advantage of the general attack on the communist styles to vent his own exasperation at the leftism of which Mao was the source. In a few cases he chose analogies and illustrations which he probably realized were susceptible of the kind of interpretation which Yao Wenyuan and others later put upon them. But he may have done so less with deliberate intent to denigrate Mao—as other scholars have indicated, virtually all his barbs applied to cadres at all levels—than with the thought 'If the cap fits . . .' Had Deng Tuo been as clearly attacking Mao as Yao later alleged, it would surely have been a scandal among Beijing bureaucrats at the time, but in fact readers of the column appear to have missed such innuendoes completely.[64]

It was rather the anti-GLF aspect of Deng Tuo's essays which Mao's supporters disliked, for it induced an atmosphere antipathetic to the leftism revived at the 10th plenum, which developed into the Socialist Education Movement (SEM) and finally burst forth into the Cultural Revolution. But that was insufficient reason for retrospectively making the 'Three-Family Village'—just one column among many—a *cause célèbre* at the outset of the Cultural Revolution; in 1965–6, Deng Tuo, Wu Han, and Liao Mosha became catspaws in a larger political intrigue. And back in the summer of 1962, Mao had more pressing matters on his mind than putative, obscure *ad hominem* jibes by pseudonymous columnists.

PART THREE

CLASS STRUGGLE

12 MAO CHANGES THE SIGNALS[1]

On 11 July 1962, the CC secretariat circulated a document seeking answers to forty-one specific problems. The questions on agriculture were political dynamite:

What do you consider to be the problems in rural production relations and agricultural production after the implementation of the Sixty Articles and the transfer of basic accounting to the team? What methods do you consider should be selected to consolidate the collective economy and to encourage peasant production to recover and develop a bit faster? Do you consider that selecting the methods of *baochan daohu* or *fentian daohu* [dividing the fields down to the household] could restore and develop agricultural production more quickly? If we selected these kinds of methods, what economic and political outcomes would they produce? What policies do you consider we should adopt towards those areas which are already practising *baochan daohu* or individual operation [*dan'gan*]? What kind of policies do you think we should adopt towards those teams which, because of massive disruption, bad cadre work styles, and a badly run collective economy, demand *baochan daohu*?[2]

This document was presumably a product of the pro-*baochan daohu* meeting of the secretariat in late June. In the light of the dismissal of Zeng Xisheng and the abject 180-degree turn subsequently executed by the Anhui provincial party, such questions should not have been necessary. Every street-wise party official could have been expected to give a thumbs down to *baochan daohu* to avoid a similar fate. But simply by posing the questions, the secretariat was reopening the issue, implying that a reversal of verdicts on the Anhui experiment was under consideration; and indeed, despite its superficial neutrality, the questionnaire was effectively soliciting the kind of answers to make it possible. Deng Xiaoping seemed to be copying the tactics adopted by Liu Shaoqi over the previous year: when advocating a controversial policy, cling firmly to the coat-tails of the broad masses, however defined.

Since this secretariat document merely requested information and did not issue any orders, strictly speaking it probably did not require Mao's prior approval. But even if he had not seen it in advance, the Chairman would soon have been informed about it by Maoist recipients like Ke Qingshi, the 1st secretary of the East China region. However he got hold of it, Mao would have realized instantly upon reading the questionnaire that he could no longer rely upon the man whom he had placed in the post of General Secretary in order to ensure the loyalty of the party to himself [3]

Liu Shaoqi takes the helm

After the Seven Thousand Cadres Conference, the Chairman had gone to Shanghai for almost two weeks and then on to Hangzhou,[4] and had conspicuously and almost unprecedentedly absented himself from such major party meetings as the Xilou conference and the May work conference.[5] This was a period when the central leadership clearly had to make hard policy choices on the basis of the apparent consensus reached at the Seven Thousand Cadres Conference. The previous year, after the 9th plenum, Mao had played the leading role in the search for new policies, particularly in the countryside. His abdication in favour of Liu Shaoqi during the first half of 1962,[6] attested to by the Chairman's order to his secretary Tian Jiaying to report to Liu on his rural investigation and request instructions,[7] was thus particularly startling, bearing in mind the sense of crisis gripping the leadership.

The most significant public manifestation of Liu's enhanced stature was the publication on the occasion of the forty-first anniversary of the founding of the CCP of a revised version of his famous 1939 tract 'How to be a Good Communist'. It occupied most of that day's edition of the *People's Daily*. During the next four years, over 18 million copies of a pamphlet version were printed.[8] Liu took the opportunity to draw a lesson from CCP history by inserting a long new section about the 1930s, describing how the party changed its strategy, tactics, and allies in response to changes in the objective situation. An official close to Liu explained twenty-five years later that this was designed to justify more moderate class policies, including presumably stressing the united front.[9]

The publication was as significant a tribute as the placing of Liu's picture in the *People's Daily* side-by-side with and equal in size to Mao's after he had taken over Mao's title as head of state in 1959.[10] Even though the revised version included substantial quotes from Mao which were not in the original—some quotes from Soviet sources were dropped—it still represented an official acknowledgement of Liu's status as a theoretician, a role reserved since the founding of the PRC exclusively for the Chairman. Behind the scenes, a first volume of Liu Shaoqi's selected works was being prepared at Mao's suggestion,[11] by a small group under the leadership of Kang Sheng,[12] though in the event it would be published posthumously twenty years later.[13]

Additional indicators of Liu's new role in the first half of 1962 were provided by the speeches of other leaders. Zhou's new-found confidence and freedom has been mentioned above as suggesting less concern about leftism. This had to mean that the chief sponsor and inciter of the leftists, Mao himself, was, in some sense, out of the picture.

Equally barometric in a different way were the speeches of Li Xiannian. A canny political operator who survived the Cultural Revolution virtually unscathed, Li had a well-developed sense of power relationships. His pre-Cultural Revolution speeches were on the whole very businesslike, full of figures, problems, and policies. They were not replete with fawning references to the Chairman, though there was normally a deferential quotation or an allusion or two. By contrast, two important speeches he made after the Seven Thousand Cadres Conference had references to Liu Shaoqi instead. One, on 6 June, was particularly indicative as to who was in charge: 'Comrade Shaoqi puts very great stress on the unified management of goods and materials.' Three months later at the 10th plenum, on 25 September, by which point Mao's resumption of leadership was more than apparent, Li noted that: 'Chairman Mao personally grasps commerce...' In fact as early as 12 July, when senior officials may have had an inkling that Mao would be resuming control at the forthcoming Beidaihe conference, Li was already referring again to Mao and his thought.[14]

Mao's behaviour in early 1962 suggests that he was reluctant to put his imprimatur upon any of the unpalatable alternatives now facing the country, even though he had to agree to them when his senior colleagues sought his approval. But although the draconian policies advocated by Chen Yun for the industrial sector underlined the disastrous legacy of the GLF, they did not seek to dismantle the state or collective sectors of the economy. A reversal of verdicts on *baochan daohu*, however, would threaten Mao's whole vision of a collectivist rural China and had to be resisted. On this issue, the Chairman found that he had been deserted even by his secretary, Tian Jiaying.

Tian Jiaying's 1962 rural investigation

Shortly after the Seven Thousand Cadres Conference, Mao decided to repeat the rural investigation he had mounted in 1961.

Summoning Tian, he again gave him detailed instructions. He had to take four teams down to Hunan province: one was to investigate Mao's home village, Shaoshan; another was to go to the village of Mao's grandparents; a third was to go to Liu Shaoqi's home village; and the fourth was to visit Tianhua brigade where Liu had carried out part of his 1961 investigation. In the event, Tian's seventeen-person team investigated only the first three.

On 22 March, before departing for Hunan, the team's members were received by Mao in the guest-house on the East Lake at Wuchang in Hubei. The Chairman put everyone at ease by carefully asking each one's name and telling a few political jokes. Then he explained what he expected them to do: collaborate closely with local cadres at all levels; not to issue instructions off the top of the head; to carry no preconceptions except Marxism; to pay attention to the historical context; to draw attention only to good people and good things, not bad ones; and to perform some light manual labour.[15]

Tian's own hope was that out of the exercise would come a ten-point program for reviving the rural economy. He did, however, have a preconception. He was still opposed to *baochan daohu*. He was thus totally unprepared to find the peasants of Shaoshan, a village which had escaped some of the worst ravages of the GLF, besieging him and his colleagues with demands for the institution of that system, or even the division of fields among households (*fentian daohu*). Production had fallen continuously since the collectivist high tide of 1955. Ironically, while Mao's one-time neighbours had deserted his cause, the team found that in Liu's home village the peasants were more prepared to live with the modified collectivist system sanctioned in 1961, largely because of the groundwork done by the head of state during his visit then.[16]

Tian, however, was won over by the Shaoshan peasants. After listening to their arguments, he became convinced that his aim of increasing production could best be achieved by adopting *baochan daohu* and even *fentian daohu*; in the present crisis, the collective economy was 'difficult to preserve' (*nan yi weichi*). Though Tian vouchsafed his conclusions only to one trusted colleague, he organized what were often heated debates within his team on the issue. Tian's view turned out to be in the minority, but he encouraged like-minded team members to continue their research into the question. Later he sent two team members to examine the Anhui experience.

Tian was in a quandary. All the locals knew that he was Mao's secretary and had been sent by the Chairman personally. For him to advocate *baochan daohu* in Mao's home village would thus be a major political *démarche* resonating immediately throughout Hunan, and thereafter the rest of the country. The provincial party was lending land, but it had not endorsed *baochan daohu*, even though in practice some localities had instituted the system surreptitiously as early as March 1961. So in Hunan, Tian held his peace.[17]

But he now had the unenviable task of reporting his findings to the Chairman. First he went to Beijing and told Liu Shaoqi about the situation in *his* home village. Liu received the report with equanimity. Then Tian went to Shanghai to talk to the Chairman. Before doing so he showed his report to Chen Yun who was also there. Chen, who had disagreed with Tian's earlier views at the Canton conference, was very supportive.

Unlike Chen, the Chairman appeared not to have read Tian's report, contenting himself with listening coolly to his oral summary. Finally, in a revealing comment, he indicated his total rejection of peasant sentiment and, incidentally, of the tactic of sheltering behind grass-roots opinion employed by Liu and Deng: 'We want to follow the mass line, but there are times when we cannot completely heed the masses. For example, if they want to institute *baochan daohu*, we cannot listen to them.'[18]

Tian's subsequent conduct is probably the clearest indication that in some sense the Chairman had ceded power at this time. While he was in Shanghai, Tian was called by Yang Shangkun, the head of the CC's General Office, and told that the premier wanted to know if it was all right to enlarge somewhat the portion of private land in the countryside. Without hesitating, or consulting Mao, Tian gave his agreement.[19]

The next pointer is that when Tian returned to Shaoshan, where his team was winding up its investigation, he did not pass on Mao's views. Possibly this was formally correct, since Mao had given an opinion rather than issued a directive. But as Deng Tuo had found out to his cost when editing the *People's Daily*, following formal procedures and failing to pass on the views of the Chairman was dangerous. Moreover, it was at this time that Tian sent two team members off to investigate the Anhui experience. Tian would have been well aware of the risks involved in this behaviour, and would surely have taken them only if he believed that Mao was no longer in operational control.[20]

This seems confirmed by events in Beijing where Tian returned at the end of June. In the capital, he found that there was as much talk about *baochan daohu* as down in rural Hunan, the main difference being that here it was dressed up in theoretical garb. A model worker who was a member of the NPC advocated keeping the Anhui system for six years. Li Fuchun reported to Liu Shaoqi and Deng Xiaoping that the Anhui masses still wanted the system.[21] When Tian reported to Liu, the latter cut him short, saying he was well aware of the situation and revealing his own support for *baochan daohu*, and for its legalization. It may well have been on this occasion that he stated: 'In industry, we must retreat adequately, and in agriculture, too, we must retreat adequately, including *baochan daohu* and individual operation [*dan'gan*].'[22] He asked Tian to sound out policy experts[23] on the issue, without revealing that the second-ranking member of the party had such views. Tian asked if he could pass on Liu's opinion to Mao and Liu readily agreed.

Tian then told Deng Xiaoping about his idea of preparing a ten-item policy document on reviving the rural economy. Tian intended to advocate many types of ownership: collective, semi-collective, *baochan daohu*, and even division of the fields and individual operation (*fentian dan'gan*). In his typically businesslike way, Deng simply said, 'Approved'. Tian, who took part in Zhongnanhai meetings on the issue at this time,[24] got equally supportive reactions from other leaders to whom he confided his views. Almost all the PSC members other than Mao favoured *baochan daohu* or at least some form of responsibility system.[25]

In the meantime, however, Tian Jiaying had the difficult task of acquainting Mao with his final analysis. Whatever leadership arrangements were in place at the time, Tian was well aware that *baochan daohu* needed to get the Chairman's approval. He telephoned Hebei where Mao was again touching base in Handan, the site of his decision nine months earlier to give the green light for team accounting. When he was informed that the Chairman had passed a message saying not to hurry, Tian knew that it indicated Mao's impatience. Two days later, after returning to Beijing, the Chairman summoned his secretary.

Tian expounded his views. About 30 per cent of China's peasants were farming either under *baochan daohu* or *fentian daohu*, and the number was growing.[26] Tian estimated that the proportion could reach 40 per cent, leaving the rest of the peasantry farming collectively or semi-collectively. These methods were the best for reviving production and once that had been achieved, the peasants could be led back to collectivism.

One does not know if Tian actually believed his final sweetener. Almost certainly Mao knew better, but the Chairman heard Tian out in silence. Unlike Liu, Mao neither interrupted nor offered his own opinion. But when Tian had finished, the Chairman skewered him with a devastatingly unexpected question for which he had no prepared reply: 'Which are you advocating as the main form of agriculture, collective or private?' Mao immediately followed up by asking if Tian were expressing his own opinion or other people's. Tian apparently took full responsibility upon himself and did not mention Liu's position, despite the latter's permission to do so. The Chairman expressed no opinion, but his aides knew him well enough to realize that this signified a negative reaction.[27]

From 9 to 11 July, Mao consulted with provincial leaders from Henan, Shandong, and Jiangxi.[28] Shortly thereafter, Mao called a staff meeting to which Chen Boda was summoned. The Chairman criticized Tian for having advocated *baochan daohu* instead of working on a revision of the Sixty Articles on Agriculture. Without consulting his PSC colleagues, he entrusted Chen with drafting a central decision to consolidate the collective economy and develop agricultural production.[29] As in 1955, Mao had lost faith in his chief aide's opinions on rural affairs, and turned to a leftist ideologue upon whom he could rely to devise a preferred solution.[30] But when Tian requested a transfer to the countryside, Mao refused permission, presumably because he needed his considerable talents for the intensive political activity he anticipated.[31]

Embarrassment in the PSC

Tian was not the only official to brave Mao's wrath on this issue. After a summer tour, Chen Yun wrote to Mao in early July asking for an hour of his time to explain a few ideas he had for agricultural recovery. Chen had his interview on the night that Mao returned to the capital, and expressed a conviction that the collective and individual economies would have to coexist in the countryside for a lengthy period, and that in order to combat the current crisis, the individual economy should be stressed.[32] Mao did not comment, but the following day Chen Yun learned that the Chairman had angrily stated that dividing the fields for individual operation was revisionism that would unravel the collective system. Chen thereupon wrote to Deng Xiaoping, as CCP General Secretary, with a copy to the

Chairman, requesting leave on the grounds of ill health, and expressing support for the CC resolution on strengthening the collective economy which Chen Boda had drafted for Mao.[33] Three years later, he would write to Mao from hibernation criticizing himself for his 1962 positions.[34]

The General Secretary also had to cope with his own embarrassment as a result of Mao's return. In a speech to the YCL CC on the morning of 7 July, Deng had advocated letting a hundred schools contend to discover the best form of rural organization, allowing everyone to express his opinion. He made his own view clear by repeating his black cat/white cat aphorism, advocating that the peasants be allowed to adopt whatever system they wanted; if it were not legal, it should be made legal![35] That same afternoon, Deng telephoned the YCL's 1st secretary, Hu Yaobang, to tell him that Mao had just returned and indicated his distaste for *baochan daohu*. Deng, according to Hu, who passed the news on to the YCL CC, ordered that the passage about the colour of cats be deleted from his speech.[36] The following morning he called again and ordered Hu to strengthen the paragraph on the collective economy.

On 18 July, addressing central officials on their way to the countryside to strengthen leadership there, Liu Shaoqi attempted to square the circle. Liu told his audience that the CC would soon be deciding on *baochan daohu* and individual operation,[37] and indicated his preference for a Henan responsibility system 'where major farm work is done collectively and odd jobs are done separately by individuals. Every production team is responsible for a stretch of land and every household for a plot, and those who overfulfill the quotas are rewarded.'[38] But in the light of the attitude Mao was now known to hold, he also defended the collective system, attributing its current problems to mistakes of implementation, and calling on his audience to struggle against incorrect views and attitudes in an effort to consolidate it, admitting, as he well knew, that doubts about the collective system were shared from the highest to the lowest in the land. Liu was left in no doubt that his hope of retaining some form of responsibility system was a forlorn one, for the Chairman summoned him to his swimming-pool and upbraided him for not halting *baochan daohu*.[39]

Mao was ready to resume control. He was probably spurred by a challenge to his thinking in another arena which he regarded as his particular preserve: foreign affairs in general and relations with the Soviet Union in particular. The challenge came from a once-prominent CCP leader, whom Mao had transformed, like several others, into one of yesterday's men.

'The three reconciliations and the one reduction'

Wang Jiaxiang, like Zhang Wentian who had challenged the GLF at Lushan in 1959, had been one of the '28 Bolsheviks', the derisive nickname conferred by less privileged China-bound colleagues upon the group of young men trained in Moscow in the 1920s as future CCP leaders. Despite his support for Mao in Jiangxi[40] and, even more importantly, at the Zunyi conference in January 1935, when Mao emerged as the CCP's *de facto* leader,[41] ten years later, in 1945, Wang lost his Politburo seat and CC membership at the party's 7th Congress. Mao made an appeal to the congress delegates to ensure that Wang, despite his 'line errors', was elected second among the CC alternates.[42] Wang continued to be of service to Mao, and his wife to Jiang Qing.[43] From October 1949 to April 1951, he was ambassador to the Soviet Union, at which point he returned home to become director of the CC's International Liaison Department which dealt with foreign communist parties.[44] It was in that capacity that his counsel had again been sought by Mao at the 1959 Lushan conference on the latest phase of the Sino-Soviet dispute.[45] But during Mao's absence from the helm in early 1962, Wang had offered what the Chairman would later deem less palatable advice on this and other foreign policy issues.

Wang's ideas had been gestating for a year. As a result of one of his bouts of recurrent illness,[46] Wang had happened to be convalescing in Canton during the conference there in March 1961 which was deliberating on the Sixty Articles on Agriculture. He was visited by one of the drafters of that document, Wang Li, who was currently on his department staff.[47] Wang Li reported to him about deaths from starvation in Hunan province which he had learned about during a recent inspection tour. Wang Jiaxiang became emotional and wept. He said that the CCP needed to concentrate all its attention on such dire domestic problems, and therefore should adopt more conciliatory external policies in order to avoid crises with the United States, the Soviet Union, and India. He also wanted to see less money spent on various types of foreign aid; it would do great harm to the international communist movement if China became unstable because it invested blood and treasure in foreign entanglements. One of Wang's notions was that the PRC should issue a general statement of foreign policy principles in which it would stress its basically peaceful posture.

Later Wang Jiaxiang explained his ideas, derided subsequently by his critics as the 'three reconciliations and the one reduction' (*san he yi shao*), in a long conversation with Liu Shaoqi, who agreed with him.[48] Wang was encouraged by this and other discussions to write, on 27 February 1962, to the three men running foreign affairs: Zhou Enlai, Deng Xiaoping, and Chen Yi.[49] That he did not see or write to Mao is further evidence of the Chairman's withdrawal from affairs after the Seven Thousand Cadres Conference. The deputy directors of the International Liaison Department, Liu Ningyi and Wu Xiuquan, also signed the letter.[50]

To borrow the language of the Cultural Revolution, Wang Jiaxiang's proposals 'raised the red flag in order to knock down the red flag'. Wang quoted liberally from Mao's earlier writings and statements to buttress positions to which the Chairman no longer adhered, whether on strategic grounds or out of the tactical imperatives of the struggle with Khrushchev. Wang's device was to attack the CPSU's line, but then to reject the more extreme versions of the CCP's line. Since Wang considered the preservation of a peaceful international environment essential to allow China to focus on domestic recovery, he harked back to the polemics about war in 1960, and asserted, for instance: 'We do not support one-sidedly stressing that it is already settled that world war can be avoided or saying that there no longer exists a danger of world war . . . But we also do not consider that world war absolutely cannot be avoided.'[51]

To reduce the cost of foreign policy entanglements to the Chinese exchequer, Wang Jiaxiang advocated a 'seeking truth from facts' approach to expenditure on aid to revolutionary and nationalist movements. There was a range of possible policies, from the moral support of speech-making and declarations, through material assistance, right up to sending volunteers.[52] But socialist countries could not be expected under all conditions and at all times to provide aid. At times like the present economic crisis, China had to consider very carefully what it spent overseas and not go overboard,[53] whether to thwart imperialism or to deflect allegiance from the CPSU to the CCP. Wang's views were in striking contrast to those expressed by Zhou Enlai at the Seven Thousand Cadres Conference, when, perhaps because of Mao's presence, the premier had stressed China's international obligations.[54]

In referring to volunteers, Wang cited the 1930s Spanish Civil War, when there were many genuine volunteers on the 'progressive' side, and not the closer-to-home example of the Korean War, when the 'Chinese People's Volunteers' was simply a PRC expeditionary force and an instrument of Beijing's national security policy. As Wang saw it, the last thing China needed in the early 1960s was another commitment on the scale of the Korean War.

Wang Jiaxiang's final plea for a more restrained posture in foreign affairs was dated 29 June 1962; until then, it seems, his ideas had not met with significant criticism. Deng Xiaoping, like Liu Shaoqi, supported him totally.[55] Moreover, the elaboration of Wang's ideas coincided with a period of relative quiescence in the Sino-Soviet dispute. During most of 1961, internal crises had been too severe for even Mao to pay too much attention to the CPSU. He seemed content to rest with the resolution on the Moscow conference passed at the 9th plenum. After the flare-up at the CPSU's 22nd Congress, when Khrushchev openly attacked the Albanian communist leadership for diverging from Soviet views on bloc foreign policy and de-Stalinization,[56] Sino-Soviet polemics resumed via the familiar attacks on surrogates: the Chinese targeted the Yugosolavs and the Soviets maintained their barrage against the Albanians. The veneer of civility wore thin as the Moscow and Beijing media increasingly reprinted open attacks by third parties upon the other.[57]

In early 1962, a group of five 'neutral' communist parties, led by Ho Chi Minh and his Vietnamese party, had proposed that a new international conference be held to iron out intra-party differences, and that until then there should be a suspension of propaganda hostilities.[58] This proposal was accepted by the CCP, and on 7 April, the CC addressed a letter to the CPSU indicating a readiness for bilateral talks.[59] Both sides noticeably toned down their public comments, despite the ethnic problems which China was experiencing in Xinjiang, later blamed upon the Russians.[60] In consequence, the Albanian leader, Enver Hoxha, began to get perturbed about possible opportunism on the part of his Chinese ally. In his diary notes for April through July 1962, he described Chinese policy variously as vacillating, centrist, conciliatory, with tendencies to softening, fear, and passivity. His concern was exacerbated because Beijing was extremely reticent about revealing its dealings with Moscow to Tirana.[61]

The new Chinese line was publicly in evidence for the first time at the World Peace Congress held in Moscow from 9 to 14 July, when both sides acted with restraint. Beijing's delegation was officially headed by the famous writer Mao Dun, but Deng Xiaoping and Wang Jiaxiang had sent Wang Li as a member, and he had conversations with Yuri Andropov. Though both sides maintained their positions, some agreements were reached. On Wang Li's return to Beijing, his handling of the contacts, as well as Wang Jiaxiang's general formulation, were apparently endorsed by Deng and Peng Zhen.[62]

The United States also helped to engender a less fraught relationship at this time, by seeking to restrain the KMT on Taiwan. Nationalist agents were being infiltrated into the mainland on sabotage missions, and the American commander-in-chief in the Pacific and the CIA's station chief in Taipei urged US support.[63] On 1 May, the KMT imposed 'return to the mainland' consumer taxes amid reports of military preparations on the island. Taiwanese newspapers trumpeted calls for action at a time of weakness on the mainland; the mass exodus from Guangdong to Hong Kong in May was seen as proof that the communist regime was on its last legs. Behind the scenes, 'Taipei's long-standing invasion plan was revised with instructions to make it operational in the shortest possible time', and purchases of additional naval vessels and amphibious craft were negotiated.[64] All this Nationalist excitement reportedly caused a certain amount of panic among Chinese leaders,[65] and it resulted in a massive reinforcement of the PLA positions in Fujian province opposite Quemoy, perhaps by as many as half-a-million troops, in case a full-scale assault should take place.[66] General Luo Ruiqing, the PLA Chief-of-Staff believed that it was not a question of whether there would be a war, but how the PRC should fight the war: repel the enemy before he reached the coast or lure him deep into the hinterland.[67] The Chinese ambassador to the Warsaw talks, Wang Bingnan, was ordered by Zhou Enlai to cut short his home leave and return to his post to ascertain the American position, which was regarded as the crucial determinant of whether the Nationalists would attack. On 23 June 1962, a session of the Sino-American ambassadorial talks in Warsaw was held at Chinese request at twenty-four hours notice, and over tea at his residence, Ambassador Wang Bingnan warned his American interlocutor, John Moors Cabot, against supporting a KMT invasion.[68] Cabot assured Wang that Washington would not support any attempt by the Taiwan regime to attack the mainland, a position which President Kennedy publicly confirmed a few days later,[69] while simultaneously renewing the US commitment to defend Taiwan in case the Fujian buildup was not defensive but the prelude to an attack on the offshore islands.[70] The PLA airforce shot down a Nationalist U-2 spy plane for the first time, on 9 September over east China, and between

1 October and 6 December, nine groups of armed Nationalist agents, 217 men in all, either seaborne or parachuted in, were reportedly liquidated in Guangdong.[71] But war fever in the Taiwan Straits diminished considerably after the end of June. In his memoirs, Ambassador Wang confirmed that the statement of American policy 'had a great impact on policy decisions at home'.[72]

In the case of India, Wang Jiaxiang seemed to be seeking at least a partial revival of the 'Bandung line' of the mid-1950s, according to which non-communist independent nations of the Third World were regarded as allies in the overarching struggle against imperialism. The line had effectively been discarded in the aftermath of the 1959 Sino-Indian border clash, and as a result of the Sino-Soviet dispute. In his argument with Khrushchev, Mao had rejected the possibility of 'peaceful transition' from bourgeois regimes like Nehru's India to proletarian dictatorship and insisted that they would have to be overthrown by revolution.[73] Wang's effort to improve Sino-Indian relations may have sparked a remarkably optimistic, even nostalgic, *People's Daily* editorial on Sino-Indian relations on 3 June,[74] though it would be given particularly short shrift later in the year after Mao's return to active duty. Pro-Indian sentiment was probably not very widespread in Beijing and Mao had not abandoned his views on peaceful transition.

The Geneva conference on Laos concluded on 23 July with agreements signed by both the Chinese Foreign Minister and the American Secretary of State, after fourteen months of negotiation during which the American and Chinese delegates had often exercised restraint in their interventions. Chen Yi described the agreement on the peaceful settlement of the Laos question as 'a major contribution to the cause of world peace. The Chinese delegation hails it.'[75] Indeed, the Geneva conference, at which Beijing had deployed a sizeable delegation, had been a chance for the PRC to come in from the cold, mitigating the isolation and hostility resulting from the offshore islands crisis of 1958, the Sino-Indian border clashes of 1959, and the Sino-Soviet dispute of 1960.

Thus in mid-1962, Mao's colleagues were moving towards a number of policies not favoured by the Chairman: they had accepted the arguments for a household responsibility system in the countryside; they were offering new freedoms and status to intellectuals; and they were moderating China's approaches towards its principal antagonists, the United States, the Soviet Union, and India, and discovering the potentialities of successfully negotiating differences with them. Mao was in danger of being marginalized; his policy preferences were being implicitly questioned as irrelevant at best and harmful at worst.

Mao's Beidaihe speeches

The decision to hold a summer work conference on agriculture had been taken in May. While the work conference held then was considered a success, it had dealt primarily with industry and construction; there was still no agreement on what needed to be done about agriculture. When circulating the report of the Finance and Economics Small Group on 26 May, the centre ordered the regions systematically to investigate production relations and productive forces in the countryside so that adequate preparations could be made for taking steps at the next work conference to solve the problems of agricultural production.[76] The conference met in Beidaihe.

As he had so often before, Mao seized the initiative. He discarded the agenda and substituted his own: class, contradictions, and the current situation.[77] He focused his attack on the three winds: the wind of excessive pessimism (*heian feng*), the wind of going it alone (*dan'gan feng*) in the countryside, and the wind of reversing correct verdicts (*fan'an feng*).[78]

Opening the work conference on 6 August,[79] Mao gave his immediate agreement to a proposal by Liu Shaoqi to set up a core group of twenty-two senior leaders to discuss six (unspecified) issues too sensitive to be shared with everyone attending the meeting.[80] The proposal evidently represented an attempt by Liu to put together a collective directorate within which the elusive consensus on the changes demanded by the economic situation could be brokered. The group was small and secret enough to enable Mao's colleagues to feel less inhibited about forcing the Chairman to face facts than they had at plenary sessions of the Seven Thousand Cadres Conference, and equally to allow him the leeway to retreat on policy issues without again suffering the humiliating embarrassment of public self-criticism. This kind of structured bureaucratic exercise was alien to Mao's preferred personal work style; besides, he would almost certainly have seen it as a trap. In fact, the group contained several men, not all of whom were ultra-leftists of the Cultural Revolution variety, who would support him as a result of their dissatisfaction with some aspect or another of current policies: for instance, Ke Qingshi, Li Jingquan, Tan Zhenlin,[81] Chen Boda, Lu Dingyi, Tao Zhu, and Liu Lantao.[82] Others, he could expect, would swim with the tide.

But the role of the new group was anyway rendered moot by what Mao said next:

Do classes actually exist in a socialist state? There are people in other countries who hold that classes no longer exist and the Party is thus the Party of the whole people, and not a class instrument, not the instrument of the proletariat ... Does this apply to a country like ours? Let us discuss this question. I have spoken to several comrades from the large regions about this, and understand that there are some people who are very surprised when they hear that classes still exist in China.[83]

As Mao rambled on, he interwove classes, and the contradictions between them, with current policy issues, clearly warning his colleagues that he considered the rural issue a matter of principle. Mao did not talk yet about class *struggle*, but he insisted that conflict was basic to Marxism; he talked mainly about contradictions among the people, but the solution to such problems in 1957 had turned out to be the Anti-Rightist Campaign, with its disastrous impact upon the united front and the CCP's ability to use non-party professionals.

If we recognize the existence of classes in our country, we should also recognize the existence of a contradiction between socialism and capitalism. The vestiges of classes are long-lasting, as are contradictions ... If there were no classes there would be no Marxism, and it would turn into a theory of no contradictions, a theory of no conflict. There are at the moment some peasants who are kicking up a fuss and wanting to go it alone [*dan'gan*], but just what is the percentage? Some say 20 or 30 per cent, and more than that in Anhui ... In the final analysis, are we going to take the socialist road or the capitalist road? Do we want rural co-operativization or don't we? Should we have 'fixing of farm output quotas for each household' [*baochan daohu*] or collectivization?[84]

Mao was adamant that none of the responsibility systems adopted in Anhui or elsewhere could legitimately be categorized as merely a form of division of labour within the collectivist system. Those wanting to go it alone were the well-to-do, the middle peasants, and even remnants of the landlords and the rich peasants. If the poor peasants were not persuaded by the CCP to reject this option, they might well engage in capitalism.

Mao thus clearly established his defensive perimeter around the current collective system, and sought to safeguard it by sallying forth on the attack, excoriating Deng Zihui's career from 1950 on in the process.[85] Mao's first tactic was to decry pessimism. Those people who felt there was no future or who had lost confidence were ideologically confused and wrong. He repeated his notorious pronouncement from the 1959 Lushan conference—'Our achievements are great. There are quite a lot of problems. The future is bright'[86]—and added: 'I tend to be not particularly pessimistic with regard to the problem of the current situation. All is not gloom.'[87] In a series of revealing remarks in Beidaihe on 9, 15, and 20 August, Mao made plain his resentment at having felt constrained since 1960 from inveighing against pessimism. He berated colleagues who had failed to emulate his penchant to look on the bright side: 'What is one to do about those people who haven't gone all out? They energetically trumpet individual operation [dan'gan] and darkness, and eagerly discuss shortcomings and errors, but they have no energy for discussing brightness or the collective economy. What is one to do?' On a later occasion he fumed, 'We have been discussing difficulties and darkness for two years now; it's become illegal to discuss brightness.'[88] His targets here were Liu Shaoqi, Zhou Enlai, and Chen Yun, whose handling of the economy since the spring had been predicated on a worst-case analysis of the economic situation.[89] Mao's estimate of the proportion of peasants wanting to try a responsibility system, evidently a deliberate reduction of Tian's figures, was designed to reinforce his qualified optimism by suggesting that the rural problem was less deep than, for instance, Deng Zihui had indicated.

Mao's second tactic was to impugn the competence of his colleagues. 'We' (meaning himself) had been talking about making agriculture the foundation, but this had not actually been practised (by his colleagues in charge of implementing the Chairman's goals) in the four years from 1959 to 1962. By including the six months of 1962 during which he had abdicated in favour of Liu, the Chairman was again making clear whom he blamed. In case there was any doubt, he added that since the Seven Thousand Cadres Conference, 'I consider that no solution has been reached' on the contradiction between centralization and dispersionism.[90] In other words, Liu, Zhou, Chen Yun, Deng, et al. had failed to get a grip on the situation in the country in his absence.

Mao's underlying strategy was to change the grounds of debate.[91] Once it was accepted that class, that is, politics not economics, was the real issue in the countryside, then Mao had the legitimacy to resume control. In addition, he unsettled his colleagues. The last time a dispute over economic policy had been transmuted into political struggle was at the 1959 Lushan plenum, as Mao's reference reminded them, and then it had resulted in the purge of four senior officials.

Three days later, Mao pressed home his advantage by raising the stakes in the first of six speeches to the new central small group (*zhongxin xiaozu*).[92] 'Today I will only talk about whether or not the the CCP could fall . . . The KMT lasted twenty-three years; we still have a few years.'[93] Political leaders in all systems occasionally dangle the prospect of losing power in front of their senior followers to concentrate their thinking and rekindle their loyalty. Mao was certainly not above such devices.[94] On this occasion, too, he was attempting to link regime survival with his own policy preferences. But more importantly, behind Mao's tactical devices in this relatively brief speech on 9 August 1962, one can detect elements of the thinking which would lead eventually to his decision to launch the Cultural Revolution: the degeneration of the Soviet revolution, the danger of China becoming infected, the need for class struggle to prevent that, the shortcomings of Chinese senior cadres, their failure to deliver the goods.

Mao's characterization of the Soviet Union was particularly harsh at a time of relative *détente* between the two communist giants, indicating that it was no accident that this thaw had coincided with his absence from policy-making. But it was the juxtaposition of the degeneration of the Soviet revolution and the failure to eliminate the capitalist class in China that revealed the way his mind would increasingly be working in the coming years:

The Soviet Union has been in existence for several decades, but it's still revisionist and serving international capitalism. In reality, it's counter-revolutionary. In the book *Socialist Upsurge in [China's] Countryside* there was a sentence which said that the capitalist class had been eliminated, and all that remained were the remnants of capitalist thinking. That was wrong and must be changed . . . The capitalist class can be reborn; that's how it is in the Soviet Union.[95]

Mao saw the danger of a slide towards the Yugoslav model, while someone in the audience compared current phenomena to land reform on Taiwan.[96] The Chairman repeatedly attributed the failure to eliminate rural capitalism to a relatively mild land reform movement in the later liberated areas—in contrast to the more thorough process in the early liberated areas of north and northwest China, which the CCP had controlled, in some cases for well over a decade before coming to power, and where they had experimented with many of the rural policies and processes which they later used in the rest of China.[97]

But Mao was not content to blame only past mistakes for current ideological backsliding in the countryside, the demands for the *baochan daohu* system, which he now admitted was practised by 40 per cent of peasant households. Part of the problem, he argued, was failing to give a clear direction to cadres sent down to the rural areas, with the result that they went with all sorts of different notions. Perhaps he was blaming himself for assuming his preferences would be known to and accepted by Tian Jiaying; more likely, he was sniping at Liu Shaoqi for failing to give the right lead in his speech of 18 July. Li Jingquan, the leftist 1st secretary of the Southwest Bureau and of Sichuan, interrupted to blame the speeches of Deng Zihui, and Mao took the opportunity to query why Deng had not been invited to join the central small group. He ordered Deng Zihui, Wang Jiaxiang, Kang Sheng, Wu Lengxi (the director of the NCNA and editor-in-chief of the *People's Daily*), and the historian Hu Sheng (Chen Boda's deputy on *Red Flag*) to be co-opted into the group.[98] While the addition of Deng and Wang may have seemed like a gesture of fairness on the Chairman's part, enabling them to present their viewpoints at the highest level, Mao was also admitting additional sympathizers, Kang Sheng and Hu Sheng, upon whom he could rely for trenchant criticism of 'revisionist' viewpoints. Moreover, by enlarging the group, Mao was adulterating its original purpose; it was becoming less of a directorate and more of an ordinary work conference, thus inhibiting potential opponents and enabling him to play off one group against another.

With some justice, the Chairman depicted the current rural scene as pitting families with labour power against those without. He argued that the Soviet Union had tried individual farming for almost a decade without achieving an agricultural breakthrough before Stalin collectivized; Kang Sheng, he revealed, was preparing materials on this point. It is less clear on what he based his claim that an American farm averaged sixteen families, which was not much less than the Chinese team with its twenty families. More threatening was his suggestion that senior provincial officials like Zeng Xisheng had been suborned by rich peasant aspirations. Nor was the luckless Hebei cadre, Hu Kaiming, who had written to Mao advocating *sanbao daozu*, too insignificant to escape the Chairman's derision.[99]

Mao declared that the mistake of taking the capitalist road in the countryside was far worse, indeed of a different order, than excessive leftism. Revisionism had its roots in the capitalist class, and if China did not practise class struggle for 10,000 years, the CCP would become like the KMT and the revisionists. Again he criticized undue pessimism and poked fun at cadres who, like petty-bourgeois peasants, lost their bearings at the first sign of troubles, like grass trembling in a gust of wind.[100]

Typically, Mao proceeded to take the credit for more sensible policies, even when as in the commercial realm they might be described as 'rightist';[101] he suggested that the Ministry of Commerce might be renamed the ministry of disruption for failing to carry out his instructions after the first Zhengzhou conference in November 1958.[102]

More importantly, as at Canton in March 1961, he severely criticized departments run by some of his most senior lieutenants, implicitly laying the basis for his own return to the first line. Having stated that military affairs and foreign affairs had been well run, both sectors where Mao normally had the last word on major matters, he proceeded to attack the Planning Commission, the Economic Commission, and the offices (in the State Council) for finance and trade and agriculture for seeming never to be able to solve their problems. As in Nanning in 1958, Mao took particular exception to organs in the finance and economic realm:

They never report; before taking action they don't ask permission; after taking it, they don't report. They are independent kingdoms. Whenever it may be, they force one to give approval; the upper levels don't liaise with the centre; the lower levels don't liaise with the masses . . . Everyone knows about foreign affairs, even about what Kennedy wants to do, but who knows what the ministries in Beijing are doing? I don't know what's happening in the various economic ministries, and if I don't know, how can I propose principles.[103] I understand that the provinces have the same problem[104]

Mao was of course being totally disingenuous. In so far as there had been less reporting to him in recent months, his voluntary absenteeism was doubtless to blame. But in fact, Liu Shaoqi, Zhou Enlai, Chen Yun, and Deng Xiaoping were still far too cautious to go it alone. They had taken care to solicit Mao's approval for Chen Yun's drastic economic prescriptions. Totally unfairly, the Chairman was blaming the current economic crisis on officials who were attempting to remedy it, rather than the architect of the policies which had caused it, himself. He was implying too that, if consulted, he would have had better ideas about how to proceed.

Mao was adopting a characteristic tactic to divide any potential coalition against him: without mentioning names, he was obviously exonerating a few, at least for their work in some areas—Lin Biao and Luo Ruiqing (military), and Zhou Enlai and Chen Yi (foreign affairs)—while criticizing most others—Li Fuchun (planning), Bo Yibo (economic commission), Li Xiannian (finance and trade), and Deng Zihui (agriculture). Zhou Enlai of course shared with Liu Shaoqi and Chen Yun the blame for poor oversight of the economy, while Chen Yun shared the blame with Deng Zihui for advocating *baochan daohu*.[105]

Zhou, along with Chen Yi, also came under fire when Mao queried the notion that the bourgeois intellectuals had really been transformed, indicating his disapproval of the extent of his colleagues' courtship of them, and warning Chen Yi not to spout his views all over the place.[106] Neither Zhou nor Chen Yi made another major speech on the subject. Later in the year, those who had earlier disagreed with Zhou and Chen on the class status of the intellectuals were encouraged to speak up at a propaganda conference. Lu Dingyi reported Mao's views, seemingly approvingly, to a meeting of the secretariat, of which he became a member at the 10th plenum; Lu himself had made no secret within the Propaganda Department of his disagreement with Zhou's speeches at the time they were made, commenting that he had heard of proletarian intellectuals and bourgeois intellectuals, but never of intellectuals belonging to the working people.[107] On this occasion at which Zhou was present, the premier defended himself by saying that he had been propounding party policy. Deng Xiaoping supported him, telling Lu to get things straight. Deng, who had also backed Chen earlier when he was on the defensive, told Lu that he had got Mao's agreement that the proceedings of the propaganda conference would not be distributed.[108]

In this new leftist atmosphere, united front policy, of which the Hundred Flowers was a component and which Zhou had backed, also came under fire. Mao particularly objected to what he apparently considered to be excessively hasty rehabilitation of intellectuals who had been denounced as bourgeois rightists in 1957.[109] After the 10th plenum, the head of the CC's United Front Work Department, Li Weihan, had to self-criticize for allegedly wanting to transform the democratic parties into socialist parties and part of the core of socialist leadership.[110]

Mao took care to enlist provincial leaders on his side, not for the first time,[111] tapping their resentment of the stern measures they were being ordered to carry out, at the loss of powers that recentralization meant, and, above all, of the blame assigned them for faulty implementation of correct policies—the very device used by Mao's colleagues to insulate the Chairman from responsibility.

In the tense atmosphere generated by Mao, in which most senior politicians must have felt threatened, it is not surprising that nobody was prepared to stand up for the luckless Peng Dehuai. Peng was so angered by the attacks on him at the Seven Thousand Cadres Conference that he had written an immensely long apologia which reached the CC on 16 June. Mao simply dismissed it out of hand as an unjustified attempt to reverse the verdict passed on Peng at the 1959 Lushan conference. Nobody attempted to gainsay him.[112]

It is not difficult to understand why Mao launched this sudden counter-attack. He was faced with what he saw as fundamental and unacceptable changes in key areas of policy: a rolling back of collectivization in the countryside which would have undermined his whole vision for a socially transformed China; and a *détente* with the Soviet Union, which could have undermined his search for a distinctive Chinese road.[113] In his eyes, this was 'peaceful evolution' towards capitalism.[114] Moreover, the changes were reversals of his own past policies: rapid collectivization followed by rapid commune-ization, and the frontal attack on Soviet revisionism. At the outset of the Cultural Revolution, in his famous polemic 'Bombard the Headquarters', he would describe what happened in 1962 as a 'rightist deviation'.[115] The rehabilitation of Peng Dehuai would have been the final straw, constituting a devastating admission of error during the GLF far greater than Mao's acceptance of responsibility at the Seven Thousand Cadres Conference. It could not be tolerated.

The timing of Mao's counter-attack

Mao had ample motives for confronting his colleagues and reasserting his dominance, but there remains the question of timing. How was it that at the end of January he felt obliged to make what his colleagues clearly felt was an extraordinary self-criticism, freeing them to explore radical policy options, whereas by early August he could launch an unapologetic counter-attack that had them scurrying for cover? What had happened to give Mao this surge of confidence?

The decisive factor was probably the size of the summer harvest, which tended to be a reliable indicator of the size of the larger autumn harvest and thus of annual output.[116] When touring the country after the Seven Thousand Cadres Conference, Mao was apparently being told on all sides that 1961 had been better than

1960 and that 1962 was better than 1961.[117] On 11 May, Zhou Enlai informed his colleagues that '[e]xcept for a few regions, agricultural production in most parts of the country has stopped declining and taken an upward turn'.[118] In Ji'nan in June, Mao was given this appraisal by Shandong officials on the basis of the recent wheat harvest.[119] By the time he got to Beidaihe, he should have been able to buttress this anecdotal evidence with statistical data. Though no announcement was made about the summer harvest in 1962, we know that the data for computing its size should have been available at least by the end of the third week in July, for in 1958 the Ministry of Agriculture issued the summer harvest figures on 22 July, and they had been made available to Chinese leaders by mid-June.[120] In his first Beidaihe speech on 6 August 1962, Mao revealed that he had seen an assessment of the industrial achievements for the first half of the year, and it seems likely that this was part of an overall statistical brief.[121] Since the first estimates of the autumn harvest were normally made in August, Mao may have seen them too.[122]

Though we do not know the size of the 1962 summer harvest, we do know the total output for the year. Grain production went up from 147.5 m. tons in 1961 to 160 m. tons in 1962, an increase of almost 8 per cent, a higher increase than in any year but one during the 1st FYP, even if from a lower base. Assuming that the summer harvest figures provided a harbinger of this encouraging trend, Mao must have been convinced that Chinese agriculture had turned the corner, without the wholesale dismantling of the collective system. Indeed, this was generally recognized before the autumn harvest.[123] On 11 August, a defensive Liu Shaoqi admitted that one of his two errors at the May work conference had been to state as a foregone conclusion that the 1962 summer harvest would be smaller than the previous year's.[124]

Mao's previous two major rural initiatives—collectivization in 1955 and the commune movement in 1958—were launched at the end of July or in August, presumably after he had indications of bumper harvests to come; in 1955, as in 1962, the first signs of a turnaround after two difficult years were visible as early as May.[125] In 1962, since he was planning only to stem a retreat, Mao did not need a bumper harvest, just an assurance that output would be healthy enough so that no blame could be attached to his ban on *baochan daohu*. That he had received.[126]

In addition, though probably less importantly, by the time of the Beidaihe meeting, Mao knew that the United States would restrain the KMT from launching an invasion of the mainland. He therefore had no need to worry about preserving leadership unity because of an impending international crisis.

The 10th plenum

The Beidaihe conference lasted well into the second half of August, whereupon the great majority of the participants repaired to Beijing where a preparatory meeting for the CC's 10th plenum began on the 26th. Discussions on the various matters raised by Mao, as well as on agriculture, commerce, industry, and planning,[127] continued until 23 September. At 10 a.m. the following morning, Mao opened the plenum in the Huairentang in the Zhongnanhai and made the first speech.[128]

Mao's primary focus was again on issues which would permeate the ideology of the Cultural Revolution: class struggle, especially in the socialist world, and the danger that, without it, communist regimes would be overthrown. His aim was to oppose revisionism abroad and prevent it at home (*fan xiu fang xiu*).[129]

Now then, do classes exist in socialist countries? Does class struggle exist? We can now affirm that classes do exist in socialist countries and that class struggle undoubtedly exists ... We must acknowledge that classes will continue to exist for a long time. We must also acknowledge the existence of a struggle of class against class, and admit the possibility of the restoration of reactionary classes. We must raise our vigilance and properly educate our youth as well as the cadres, the masses and the middle- and basic-level cadres. Old cadres must also study these problems and be educated. *Otherwise a country like ours can still move towards its opposite* ... Therefore, from now on we must *talk about this* every year, every month, every day [*niannian jiang, yueyue jiang, tiantian jiang*]. We will talk about it at congresses, at Party delegate conferences, at plenums, at every meeting we hold, so that we have a more enlightened Marxist-Leninist line on the problem. (Emphasis added)[130]

We do not know if Mao had followed his own injunction and discussed classes and class struggle every day since his opening remarks to the Beidaihe conference seven weeks earlier, but once he gave the lead, his cronies would take up the refrain. None of Mao's senior colleagues, who had been trying in his absence to chart pragmatic new courses, attempted to stem his ideological revivalism. Chen Yun appears to have absented himself from the meetings.[131] Deng Xiaoping and Peng Zhen significantly chose not to display to posterity any contributions they made to the discussions at Beidaihe or at the

10th plenum. Similarly, the editors of the posthumous volumes of speeches and articles of Liu Shaoqi and Zhou Enlai preferred to draw a veil over their subjects' contributions or these occasions. Mao's colleagues seem simply to have collapsed in the face of his implacable determination and overpowering personality.

Mao had begun to soften up Liu immediately upon his return to the conduct of affairs. In a brilliant tactical stroke, the Chairman asked why Liu had not prevented Chen Yun's advocacy of *baochan daohu*.[132] Liu was not being accused of supporting *baochan daohu* himself, even though Mao may well have suspected him of it, but instead was offered the chance of redeeming himself by disavowing Chen Yun, Deng Zihui, and *baochan daohu* from now on, and, by implication, any other leaders and policies opposed by Mao. Liu capitulated.

At Beidaihe, he had self-criticized for making two errors at the May work conference: underestimating the summer harvest and putting private farming at 20 per cent of the total.[133] In his address to the plenum on its final day, 26 September, which was frequently interrupted by Mao,[134] Liu's first concern was to range himself alongside the Chairman. Under Mao's leadership, development had been relatively smooth up till 1959, when a combination of natural calamities and some errors in work had led to a few quite big difficulties. The real question, however, was what attitude one took towards these problems. Most comrades had confronted the difficulties, supported the socialist road and Chairman Mao and the centre's revolutionary road; this had been the line taken at the Xilou and May work conferences. But some people had been intimidated into abandoning the socialist path and adopting individual operation in the countryside. This was Deng Zihui's attitude. At this point, Mao interrupted to say that nominally such people had not abandoned the socialist path, claiming that they were only seeking managerial changes, but in fact it was individual operation. Liu added that many had written to the CC supporting individual operation, and Deng Zihui, whose advocacy he went on to describe as a 'poisonous weed', was representative of them. Not surprisingly, Deng, who unflinchingly maintained his support for the responsibility system despite the criticism he sustained, was deprived of his roles in agricultural affairs after the plenum.[135]

Finally, there were those who, like Peng Dehuai, sought to make use of China's difficulties to attack the CCP, plotting to overthrow the Marxist-Leninist leadership of the CC and Chairman Mao. Of these three attitudes, the first was correct, the second indicated wavering, the third was antagonistic. Mao interrupted again to say that the second group did not understand Marxism, and had not realized that after the communist victory there was still the question of whether to practice socialism or capitalism. Liu added that if the leaders advocated individual operation, the CCP would change its nature. He adopted Mao's Beidaihe line of minimizing the problem of reining in individual operation by suggesting that it was largely confined to Anhui and Gansu.[136]

Liu's next concern was to clear himself of any imputation of having exaggerated the blackness of China's situation. The worst difficulties, he stated unequivocally, had now passed, but propaganda should continue to emphasize them. At the May work conference, the estimate of the difficulties had been a little excessive (*duole yi xie*); that approach was not a problem. But if one's estimate of the difficulties was too great (*tai duo*), it indicated a wavering of faith in socialism. Presumably Liu had got Mao's agreement to a compromise on private optimism and public pessimism, and at least his tacit consent, on that basis, to define Liu's earlier estimates as being within the bounds of the acceptable. In return, Liu endorsed Mao's view that even after a communist seizure of power, a two-line struggle between socialism and capitalism would inevitably last several decades, perhaps centuries, or, Mao interjected, five to ten generations. Liu would eventually be the principal victim of this theory. But at this moment he took the opportunity to offer a little gratuitous flattery to the Chairman: Stalin had got this wrong, Mao had got it right—to which Mao modestly responded that he was only following Lenin.[137]

Insulating the economy

Possibly as a result of this total support for Mao, Liu won his agreement not to let ideological issues interfere with the economy.[138] The Chairman was anyway understandably cautious. He was well aware that if he launched a nationwide struggle against revisionism—his new term for Peng Dehuai's 'right opportunism'—the painful economic recovery process might be aborted as disastrously as in 1959–60, and then his colleagues might finally unite against him.[139] If some notion of a 'cultural revolution' of the kind he eventually launched four years later was already in his mind, he knew that the time was not yet ripe. Instead, he warned the plenum to

please take care that the class struggle does not interfere with work. The first Lushan Conference of 1959 was originally concerned with work. Then up jumped P'eng Te-huai [Peng Dehuai] and said: 'You fucked my mother for forty days, can't I fuck your mother for twenty days?' All this fucking messed up the conference and the work was affected . . . Work and the class struggle should proceed simultaneously. The class struggle must not be placed in a very prominent position . . . We have to engage in the class struggle, but there are special people to take care of this kind of work. The security departments are specially charged with carrying on the class struggle.[140]

Liu followed up on this. There were not many unmasked inner-party revisionists, and there was no need for the whole party to be involved and have its work disturbed. Cadres should continue as normal while special task forces took care of domestic and international revisionism. All that was necessary was a bit of education. Mao added that only the 100,000 cadres at the level of section chief and above should discuss it.[141]

This dispensation placed the 10th plenum in odd contrast to the two GLF conferences—in 1958 at Beidaihe and in 1959 at Lushan— when great stress was placed on both production and ideological correctness. Whereas during the GLF it was assumed that the two were interrelated and mutually reinforcing, in 1962 it was tacitly acknowledged that they were potentially contradictory. The result was that, although the 10th plenum is rightly seen as marking a decisive turn to the left that would lead eventually to the Cultural Revolution, it also produced a series of economic decisions in line with the adjustment process already under way.[142] Nevertheless there is evidence to show that, however sincere Mao's strictures, the leftist shift at the 10th plenum did in fact affect economic work.[143]

The Sixty Articles on Agriculture in final form

Since the revival of agriculture was the CCP's prime task, probably the most important document to emerge from the 10th plenum was the final version of the Sixty Articles on Agriculture. The September 1962 version differed considerably from the one circulated in June 1961, reflecting the discoveries, debates, and decisions since the earlier document was drawn up.

The main changes reflected the diminution of the role of the brigade, confined now to leading, supervising, and helping (*lingdao, ducu, bangzhu*) the team, and the expansion of the role of the team to take over as the basic unit of accounting, which Mao had accepted a year earlier, and now also of ownership.[144] The impracticality of separating ownership from financial responsibility, which had been argued after Mao's concession on team accounting, had been conceded. The unworkable *sanbao yijiang* system of brigade control over the team naturally disappeared in the drastic diminution of brigade functions; brigades (and communes) were in general not to seek to accumulate capital out of team resources; brigade cadres' work points for official duties were to be limited to 1 per cent of team work points. Indeed, with the commune now seen as conforming to the old rural administrative unit, the *xiang*, the CCP was prepared to see the brigade level disappear if appropriate, presumably where the *xiang* was quite small.[145] As a result of the earlier post-GLF downsizing there had been a considerable growth in the numbers of units at all three levels in the communes;[146] now there was further growth in the numbers of communes and teams, but a reduction in the number of brigades as some were phased out (see Table 12.1).

TABLE 12.1. *Numbers of communes and their sub-units, 1961–1964*

	1961	1962	1963	1964
Communes	57,855	74,771	80,956	79,559
Brigades	734,000	703,000	652,000	644,000
Teams	4,089,000	5,530,000	5,643,000	5,590,000

Source: Nongye Nianjian, 1980, p. 5.

Despite the attacks on Deng Zihui during the summer of 1962, the final form of the Sixty Articles bore his imprint. The peasants were given the closest thing to a legal guarantee—enshrinement in an official CC programme—that the new accounting arrangements would remain unchanged for 'at least' the thirty-year period which Deng had espoused.[147] Team ownership was not guaranteed for thirty years, but for a 'long period' (*chang qi*), but this, too, may have represented an acknowledgement of the validity of Deng's analysis. He had pointed out that there was considerable dissatisfaction in many teams about their landholdings, because they had been radically altered as a result of collectivization, leaving many villages worse off now that they had to resume responsibility for their own profit and loss.[148] A thirty-year guarantee of current land-ownership patterns would have perpetuated those injustices and the attendant resentments. On the other hand, the last thing the CCP needed in the countryside at this point was a massive redistribution of village landholdings with all the anger and disputation it would have generated. By guaranteeing current land-ownership for a substantial but indeterminate period, the CCP bought time while retaining the option of redressing grievances under more prosperous circumstances.

Other changes reflected the odd juxtaposition of production imperatives and ideological compulsions. Under the old rules, brigades could accumulate up to 5 per cent of distributable income as capital, but the figure was reduced to 3–5 per cent for the teams; the brigade welfare fund could be up to 3–5 per cent of the same income figure, but for the team it would be 2–3 per cent, both changes clearly designed to leave more funds for distribution as family income.[149] Peasants had the right to purchase medium-sized farm tools, not just 'little' ones.[150] In stressing the importance of establishing norms, the previous ranking of quantity before quality was reversed to reflect the widely observed negative effect on peasant performance of a one-sided emphasis on gross figures.[151] Private plots adjacent to dwellings were still limited to 5–7 per cent of the land, but in view of the special attention lavished on such land by peasants, the total amount of privately run land was expanded to up to 15 per cent, to include forests, barren hillsides, and wasteland; peasants could also plant trees in designated areas outside their own backyards.[152] Later in the year, the authorities amplified these measures with a directive designed to encourage the peasants in their traditional sideline activities and to prevent cadres from designating these as capitalist.[153]

The combination of aims enshrined in the 1962 draft of the Sixty Articles was clearly exemplified in the articles on membership of the commune congress and management committee. To the categories of desirable delegates to congresses previously listed—such as experienced old peasants, youth, women, ethnic minorities, and returned overseas Chinese—were added specialized workers (i.e. handicraftsmen) to increase the amount of technical know-how available to the bodies, and demobilized servicemen and members of the families of revolutionary martyrs to guard against ideological backsliding.[154] When congresses selected members of management committees, they had hitherto been adjured to ensure a preponderance of poor and lower middle peasants; this requirement was maintained in 1962, but in the search for valuable experience, the adjective 'old' was inserted to qualify those categories.[155]

A similar mixture of aims was visible in a revised version of the three/eight work style for cadres, hammered out the previous year and reaffirmed in Liu Shaoqi's written report to the Seven Thousand Cadres Conference.[156] The three main rules for discipline were reordered and altered: implementing party policy, hitherto number two, became number one. Obeying government directives and actively participating in socialist construction were added, underlining the greater emphasis on production. Simultaneously, hard-pressed cadres were given more leeway to implement directives 'sincerely' rather than 'correctly'. Implementing democratic centralism was elevated from number three to number two, presumably a reflection of Mao's speech on the subject at the end of January; and the relegation of telling the truth from number one to number three may have meant that the CC felt its access to accurate information was now more secure.

The first of the eight points for attention was entirely new—'Pay attention to the masses' livelihood'—and changes in other points also expressed a heightened realization of the gap that had opened up between cadres and peasants. Cadres had to participate not just in labour, which could mean working on their private plots, but in 'collective' labour, side by side with the peasants; they had not merely to eschew special privileges, but also to bond (*dacheng yi pian*) with the masses.

Ideological requirements were not forgotten in the changes, however: cadres had not only to raise their political level, but also their proletarian consciousness;[157] peasants had not only to do their duty and respect state policy, but also to raise their socialist consciousness;[158] party branches had to reaffirm in their propaganda not just the general line, but also the other two red banners, the GLF and the communes.[159]

The sage of the eastern sea

Mao's colleagues charged with running the economy were doubtless relieved at the balance achieved in the Sixty Articles. It seemed concrete proof of Mao's agreement that the readjustment programme should not be halted and his undertaking that class struggle would be handled by specialists and not be prominent. But however limited, class struggle boded ill for individuals who fell foul of the Chairman. At the 10th plenum, Mao revealed that Peng Dehuai and the three men denounced with him at the Lushan conference were to be subjected to further investigation, by a 'special case review commission' (*zhuan'an shencha weiyuanhui*). Deng Xiaoping announced that, as suggested by Kang Sheng,[160] they would no longer be entitled to attend meetings of the party bodies of which they were still members, though this was almost certainly only a formal confirmation of the current situation.[161] Mao was indicating to all and sundry that Peng could write as many letters at whatever length he pleased, but he would be rehabilitated only over his dead body—which is what eventually happened. All and sundry suited their words to the Chairman's mood, and Peng was roundly denounced at the plenum for his latest missives which, among other things, were said to be in concert with China's enemies, labelled for convenient memorization as the 'three *ni*'s and the one *tie*' that is, Kennedy (*Ken-ni-di*), Nikita Khrushchev (*Ni-ji-ta He-lu-xiao-fu*), Nehru (*Ni-he-lu*), and Tito (*Tie-tuo*).[162]

Whether Mao's colleagues had any compunctions about colluding in his further act of vengeance against the already disgraced marshal is unknown. But they should have been more alarmed at the Chairman's announcement of the creation of a second special case review commission to investigate a totally new victim, for it exhibited Mao's readiness to believe in plots against him. The new 'anti-party' figure was a key vice-premier in Zhou Enlai's State Council, Xi Zhongxun, who sometimes acted as premier when both Zhou and Deng Xiaoping were absent from Beijing.[163] The identity of his chief persecutor, Kang Sheng, and the grounds for and manner of Xi's disgrace provided a foretaste of the early months of the Cultural Revolution.

Kang Sheng was a sinister and shadowy figure even to his colleagues, sinister because of his activities in the Soviet Union and Yan'an prior to 1949, shadowy because for the first six years after the CCP's conquest of power he had been almost invisible, apparently ill.[164] Nevertheless, he was evidently a man of considerable ability; Tian Jiaying regarded him with great respect, and referred to him as 'the sage of the eastern sea' (*donghai shengren*).[165] Born in 1898 (like Liu Shaoqi and Zhou Enlai) to a rich Shandong landowning family, Kang[166] was first tutored at home with his siblings in the Chinese classics, and later sent to a German missionary school in Qingdao where he was exposed to modern Western knowledge in addition to Confucian texts.[167] Though his nationalism was aroused by the anti-foreign May Fourth incident in 1919,[168] Kang stayed home for five years, teaching at a local primary school, before moving to Shanghai in 1924, leaving behind his wife and two children. Kang enrolled in the social sciences department at Shanghai University, run by CCP supporters. The following year he met a student Cao Yiou, whom he later married, and both joined the CCP.[169]

In March 1927, already a senior local official, Kang took part in the successful Shanghai workers uprising, and managed to escape the subsequent massacre of communists ordered by Chiang Kaishek. He had already displayed a talent for organizing, and by 1930, he was general secretary of the CCP's Organization Department.[170] In 1931, Zhou Enlai appointed him to head the CCP's security and spying operations throughout KMT-run China, thus initiating Kang's subsequent lifelong *métier*.[171]

During this period, as a result of the convulsions in the communist movement after the split with the KMT, the baton of CCP leadership was passed from one pair of clumsy hands to the next. Kang's biographers allege that he managed to keep rising within the party as a result of his nimble opportunism, adroitly changing allegiances as the political winds shifted.[172] Western commentators have made similar comments about Zhou Enlai. At any rate, by the early 1930s, Kang had attached himself to Wang Ming, the leader of the '28 Bolsheviks', the group of Chinese communists who had been trained in the Soviet Union and brought back to China by their patron, Pavel Mif, to run the CCP. Under Wang's aegis, Kang Sheng became a member of the CC and director of its Organization Department in 1931, and a member of the Politburo in 1934. From 1933 to 1937, Kang served in Moscow as Wang Ming's deputy in the leadership of the Chinese delegation to the Comintern, able to observe Stalin's great purge at close quarters, and, allegedly, to try out some of its techniques among the Chinese *émigré* community there.[173]

In late November 1937, Kang Sheng returned to China, arriving in Yan'an in Wang Ming's entourage, and the following month was appointed a secretary of the CC secretariat. But Kang quickly discerned that power relations on Chinese soil were far different from those he might have envisaged from Moscow, and he now transferred his allegiance to Mao.[174]

Kang Sheng was a valuable catch for Mao as he strove to consolidate the power he had won at the Zunyi conference in January 1935. Kang could betray all the secrets of Wang Ming and his supporters. He was *au fait* with Moscow politics and police methods, and sufficiently fluent in Russian to act as a major contact with Soviet visitors. He had absorbed sufficient Marxism-Leninism and Stalinist polemicizing to affect the patina of a theorist, and he was a fluent writer.[175] Perhaps most importantly at that time, Kang was able to introduce Mao to a young Shanghai actress whom he had known back in Shandong, and to certify to those of Mao's colleagues who resisted his marriage to Jiang Qing that she had impeccable political credentials.[176] His talents and new-found loyalty were rewarded with two critical posts: the directorship of the Central Party School, with a key role in imparting Maoist ideology; and the directorship of the CC's

Social Affairs Department, the innocuously named CCP security organ.[177]

In the early 1940s, after the defection of Zhang Guotao and the humiliation of Wang Ming, Mao's principal rivals, the victorious party leader initiated a rectification campaign to instil his principles among his followers.[178] While this began as a campaign of ideological education, wartime exigencies and the danger of infiltration by KMT agents allegedly enabled Kang Sheng to launch a widespread search for spies and fifth columnists, fabricating cases against loyal party members. At one point Kang is quoted as stating that 70–80 per cent of the youth and cadres who had flocked to Yan'an were politically undependable. The relentless criticism and self-criticism sessions were terrifying enough. Besides, there were widespread arrests on trumped-up charges. Senior party officials became alarmed and many such cases were re-examined and verdicts adjusted. The most notorious incident was the execution in 1947 of the writer Wang Shiwei along with a hundred other suspects before their cases were processed.[179] But Kang Sheng had been relieved of his security portfolios before that because of rumbling at the CCP's 7th Congress in 1945 about his activities during the rectification campaign. Yet Mao saved him his position on the Politburo.[180]

By 1962, the reason for Kang Sheng's seat on the Politburo may have been a mystery to the 80 per cent of the CCP's 17 million plus members who joined after 1949.[181] Kang had been almost invisible during the early years of the PRC. Apparently angered at being assigned the leadership only of the Shandong region rather than the whole of East China under the new regime, he took to his bed pleading illness, spending years in hospital, baffling doctors who found themselves unable to offer a diagnosis. He surfaced in public only in the mid-1950s after the man who had been assigned the East China Bureau, Rao Shushi, was disgraced along with Gao Gang.[182] Such malingering would be punishable by dismissal in many political cultures, but though Kang's ranking fluctuated oddly in the run-up to the 8th Congress in 1956, he survived in the Politburo, albeit reduced from full to alternate membership.[183] He was the beneficiary of Mao's practice of preserving and protecting those whom he trusted and relied upon, and for whom he foresaw a future use.[184] Kang Sheng immediately confirmed his value to Mao by using his ideological expertise to boost the Chairman's ideas and cult, and by indiscriminately backing both his 'rightist' policies in 1957 and his leftist policies during the GLF.[185] He was given a number of appointments which he exploited to the full: deputy head of the CC's Cultural and Education Small Group in March 1957; deputy head of the editorial committee for Mao's *Selected Works* in March 1959; and later in 1959, he reassumed responsibility for the Central Party School.[186] The collapse of the GLF temporarily beached him; he spent some time touring the country and reviving his youthful interest in the traditional theatre, occasionally in the company of Jiang Qing, now recovered from her more genuine ailments.[187] But when Mao sounded the leftist tocsin at Beidaihe, Kang Sheng responded with alacrity, making an 180-degree turn.[188] His stratagem was to attack the manuscript of a novel about a revolutionary martyr, Liu Zhidan.

The *Liu Zhidan* affair

Liu Zhidan was born in 1903 in the northwestern province of Shaanxi. In 1926, already a CCP member, he entered the fourth class (along with Lin Biao) at the Whampoa Military Academy, directed by Chiang Kai-shek with Soviet military advisers.[189] After the CCP–KMT split in 1927, he had returned to his native province and set up a guerrilla group. For a time he was under attack by 'leftists' in the CCP leadership, but after Mao and the Long Marchers reached Shaanxi in 1935, he was rehabilitated. He died in battle against the KMT in 1936, still in his early thirties.[190]

The origins of the novel about his life resembled that of the play about Hai Rui. Wu Han had no intention of writing a play about the Ming official, but did so after being importuned by a theatrical company. His reluctance stemmed from his not being a playwright. Li Jiantong, the author of *Liu Zhidan*, also had grave doubts about accepting the commission when approached in the mid-1950s. She thought she did not have the appropriate artistic or ideological talents. The matter was complicated because she was married to Liu Zhidan's younger brother, Liu Jingfan, a vice-minister of geology, and had had a complicated 'struggle relationship' with Liu Zhidan. Li's husband was against her accepting the commission. But the Workers' Publishing House had decided that Liu would make a good subject for a planned series of uplifting and edifying revolutionary sagas. By sponsoring fictionalized accounts, the publishers could hope to invoke artistic licence as an excuse for either mistakes or gaps, and perhaps this was what persuaded Li Jiantong. Liu Zhidan's most senior surviving comrade-in-arms, Vice-Premier Xi Zhongxun, warned her, when he learned of the project, that it would bring her grief because of all the intra-party disputes in which Liu had been involved, but she eventually decided to ignore his advice and, like Wu Han, took on an assignment for which she had little experience. After two years of collecting materials and interviewing many of Liu's one-time comrades-in-arms, she began to write in 1958 and submitted her third draft to the publishing house in 1959. The editors found it acceptable, but Li asked them to submit it to Xi Zhongxun for his approval.[191]

Like Liu Zhidan, Xi hailed from Shaanxi. Born in 1913, he had joined the YCL in 1926 and the CCP in 1928. By 1932, still in his teens, he had set up a guerrilla force in the Shaanxi–Gansu border region.[192] It was there that he became associated with Liu and Gao Gang, who were the two leading communists in the northwest prior to the arrival of Mao and the Long Marchers. During the civil war, as the PLA moved south, Xi remained in the northwest as the leading party official in the region, a role he maintained into the early 1950s, until he moved to the capital. After a brief spell as director of the CC's Propaganda Department, Xi took on a pivotal bureaucratic role as secretary-general of the State Council in 1954, a post which he still occupied in 1962.[193]

Xi was unhappy with the manuscript, and it went through three more drafts, at which point he appears to been worn down by the persistent author, and he gave the project his blessing without reading any of the later drafts thoroughly.[194] But Li Jiantong took the additional precaution of submitting the fifth draft to her old teacher Zhou Yang in the spring of 1962, and harried him into reading it. Zhou, whose position as the CC Propaganda Department's deputy director in charge of literature gave him the authority to issue an imprimatur, raised some issues, but did not forbid publication. At least one senior cadre, originally from Shaanxi, did take exception to the book. In a letter to the author in the summer of 1962, Yan Hongyan, an alternate CC member, a three-star general, the 1st secretary of Yunnan province, and a one-time companion-in-arms of Liu Zhidan, expressed the view that no writer could assume the responsibility for making historical judgements; that was up to the CC. In view of Yan's objections, it was decided to publish a few chapters from the sixth draft in the *Gongren Ribao* (Workers' daily) and *Zhongguo Qingnian* (China youth) in order to gauge public reactions. At Beidaihe, Yan immediately lobbied the All-China Federation of Trade Unions (ACFTU) and YCL leadership—Liu Ningyi and Hu Yaobang then headed those organizations—to have publication stopped. Yan also raised the matter in writing with the head of the CC's General Office, Yang Shangkun, and again on 8 September at a preparatory meeting for the 10th plenum.[195] Unfortunately for Li Jiantong, Xi Zhongxun, and a number of senior CCP officials, Yan Hongyan took the further step of mentioning the matter to Kang Sheng, claiming that the aim of the novel was to reverse the verdict on Gao Gang.[196]

Unlike Liu Zhidan, Gao Gang survived the warfare in the northwest, rising high in Mao's favour. But he overreached himself in 1953, when he attempted to supplant Liu Shaoqi as Mao's eventual successor and allegedly plotted with the head of the CC's Organization Department, Rao Shushi, to bring about a major reshuffle of the CCP's top leadership.[197] Both men were purged; Gao was put under house arrest and later shot himself.[198]

The day of the jackal

The Gao Gang affair was still a live issue in 1962. As we have seen, by the time of the Seven Thousand Cadres Conference, it was Peng Dehuai's alleged involvement in it that had to be used as the major justification for Mao's refusal to rehabilitate the marshal, since his trenchant criticisms of the GLF had been proved correct. Thus it was no wonder that Kang Sheng should prick up his ears at the mention of a new Gao Gang angle. In the tense atmosphere of intra-party struggle revived at Beidaihe by Mao, here was a heaven-sent opportunity for Kang to prove again to the Chairman his indispensability in ferreting out traitors.

Among Kang's current positions was vice-head of the CC's Culture and Education Small Group and head of its theory section, and on that authority he ordered the Propaganda Department to stop any further publication of chapters from *Liu Zhidan*, even though at this point he had not even seen the manuscript. He ordered 300 copies of the third draft and 600 copies of the fifth draft to be printed and distributed for examination by the Beidaihe conferees. On 24 August, he wrote to the CC's General Office to say that this was not simply a literary issue but had political implications. He coined the phrase 'using novels to promote anti-party activities is a great invention', which Mao embraced with enthusiasm, and which indeed was subsequently attributed to the Chairman.[199] But author Li Jiantong was small fry, and so Kang Sheng concocted the idea of a high-level plot masterminded by Xi Zhongxun.

Why did Mao seize on the *Liu Zhidan* affair and give Kang Sheng his head without really looking into the matter, or indeed believing the charges?[200] Did he not have enough to do discouraging his colleagues from pursuing revisionist policies in the countryside and abroad? One reason was probably that he welcomed a fresh case seemingly tailor-made to justify his warnings on the need for class struggle and eternal vigilance. Secondly, ever since the Hungarian revolt and the Hundred Flowers in China, he had been extremely wary of the ability of intellectuals to use their professional skills for nefarious political purposes, what might be called the Petöfi Circle syndrome.[201] Kang's new concept resonated with him, and as the 1960s progressed, Mao would increase the pressure on the intellectuals. Finally, as Kang Sheng doubtless intuited, attacking *Liu Zhidan* was an excellent way to demonstrate the continuing relevance of the Gao Gang affair, and thus provide additional justification for the refusal to rehabilitate Peng Dehuai.

For his own reasons, Liu Shaoqi had to fall in with this strategy *vis-à-vis* Peng Dehuai, but at the 10th plenum he also condemned Xi Zhongxun and *Liu Zhidan* in the same terms.[202] There is no record of Zhou Enlai attempting to save a man he evidently regarded as a key member of his State Council team; with Mao's permission and Chen Yi in attendance, the premier tried only to comfort Xi Zhongxun with an assurance that if the *Liu Zhidan* accusation was a mistake, it would be corrected.[203] At the 10th plenum, Kang Sheng was thus free to lead the attack on Xi, and thereafter to lead the second special case review commission in its investigation of the supposed 'anti-party group' led by Xi; Jia Tuofu, a one-time associate of Liu Zhidan and currently a CC member and a vice-chairman of the State Planning Commission;[204] and the author's husband, Liu Zhidan's brother, Liu Jingfan. Kang Sheng alleged that a character in the novel named Luo Yan represented Gao Gang, just as three years later he would claim that Hai Rui was Peng Dehuai. Officials at the publishing house and throughout the northwest were investigated, and the case had still not been concluded when the Cultural Revolution broke out and it became public knowledge.[205] Kang Sheng's reward was promotion to the CC's secretariat at the 10th plenum. Two months later, he moved to the Diaoyutai guest complex in the capital to mastermind a team of ideologues for the campaign against Soviet revisionism.[206] The most cynical hit-man of Mao's Cultural Revolution swat team was now an agent in place helping to initiate the domestic and foreign policies that were the prelude to that cataclysm.

WAR IN THE HIMALAYAS, CRISIS IN THE CARIBBEAN

The dual role of Kang Sheng in Mao's campaign against revisionism at home and abroad symbolized the close relationship between Chinese domestic and foreign policy. Mao opened many of his major speeches with *tours d'horizon* which clearly showed that he considered the Chinese revolution to be part of a world-wide series of events, with interaction both ways. This was particularly true of events within the Communist bloc. Khrushchev's attack on Stalin had implications for Mao personally. The Hungarian revolt helped precipitate a new kind of rectification campaign in China.[1] Mao admitted that Soviet anger over the communes led him to modify the ideological claims made for them.[2] By the early 1960s, Mao was beginning to speculate about the implications of Soviet revisionism for Chinese domestic politics.[3]

The connection between Chinese military actions and domestic politics is more obscure. China's involvement in the Korean War enabled the CCP's leaders to launch a patriotic campaign to solidify the people behind them, but that was a windfall benefit. The despatch of the Chinese expeditionary force to defend the crumbling Kim Il Sung regime was clearly a response to the threat of a united, anti-Communist Korea, allied to the United States, on China's borders.[4]

In the case of the Taiwan Straits crisis of 1958, again the Chinese were responding to external events: the Middle East crisis and the Soviet failure to take strong action.[5] There was no direct threat to the PRC, as there arguably was in the case of Korea. Honour might have been satisfied had the Chinese government merely repeated its behaviour at the time of the 1956 Suez Canal crisis, staging large-scale protest rallies and threatening to send volunteers. But by bombarding Quemoy (Jinmen) from 23 August 1958, Mao was better able to whip up fervour for the commune movement as well as to teach Khrushchev a lesson in how to confront imperialism.[6]

China's renewed militancy in foreign affairs in the autumn of 1962 similarly helped to create an appropriate atmosphere for the domestic class struggle which Mao had demanded at Beidaihe and at the 10th plenum. But China was perforce responding to decisions taken in foreign capitals, New Delhi and Moscow. Mao did not like Wang Jiaxiang's *san he yi shao* policy, and events conspired to enable him to destroy it.

India's forward policy

It is clear, for instance, that the Sino-Indian border war of October 1962 was, at least in part, China's reaction to what came to be known in New Delhi as India's 'forward policy'.[7] This policy was conceived in 1960, after the April summit in the Indian capital between premiers Jawaharlal Nehru and Zhou Enlai failed to resolve the border dispute that had led to clashes and casualties the previous year.[8] The forward policy envisaged Indian troops patrolling as far forward as possible into the disputed Aksai Chin area on the Tibet–Kashmir border, up to what India considered to be the frontier. It was not implemented, however, due to the army's reluctance to push forward with inferior military resources and very poor resupply facilities.

In September 1961, however, a major appraisal made by New Delhi's Intelligence Bureau concluded that the Chinese did not challenge Indian outposts once they had been established, and on 2 November Nehru held a meeting with his Defence Minister and close confidant, Krishna Menon, and senior military officers, at which a firm decision was taken to advance and establish new posts in Ladakh. Orders were issued that gave the cautious commander of the western region no further grounds for delay. Even in the eastern sector, along the border between Tibet and India's North-East Frontier Agency (NEFA), which was quiescent at the time, the existing prohibition on operations within 3 km. of the frontier was lifted, and the local commander was ordered to 'plug the gaps' with a 'systematic advance' towards the Indian-claimed McMahon Line.

Nehru was apparently unaware of the parlous condition of India's forces on the border, and certainly unwilling to contemplate emergency purchases of arms from abroad, but his policy was anyway posited on the belief that war between India and China was unthinkable, which was in turn based on the assumption that the Chinese would not launch a major attack.[9] This latter misapprehension would be bolstered as late as September 1962 by Soviet advice to the same effect.[10] Indian misperceptions were compounded by the lack of any systematic attempt by the New Delhi intelligence community to analyse Chinese domestic and diplomatic developments. Instead, reliance was placed on CIA briefings, newspaper accounts, and, presumably, despatches from the Indian embassy in Beijing about China's economic crisis, its split with the Soviet Union, and the threat of invasion from Taiwan. India concluded that the Chinese were too hard pressed to contemplate any major hostilities.[11] Moreover, the swift victory of the Indian forces in the takeover of the Portuguese colony of Goa in December 1961 produced a false euphoria in which it was easy to gloss over the 'military inadequacies' exposed by that relatively simple operation.[12]

In the first half of 1962, the Indian forces in Ladakh were gradually reinforced, attaining a strength of four battalions, broken down into sixty posts and patrols, but were still outnumbered five to one and greatly outgunned. In NEFA, new posts were established, higher up the mountain slopes, closer to the Tibetan border. In both sectors, these moves were made despite a continuing lack of adequate logistical support, at the insistence of the Chief of General Staff, B. M. Kaul.

After a lull lasting from the beginning of December 1961 through February 1962, the Chinese foreign ministry renewed its protests against these Indian movements on 1 March. In its seventh note of the year on 30 April, Beijing issued a threat. After listing fifteen alleged new intrusions made by Indian troops between 15 and 27 April, the Chinese note stated that the PLA would resume patrolling in the disputed area, from the Karakoram Pass to the Kongka Pass, suspended since the hostilities of 1959, and that if the Indian forward movement continued, PLA patrols would take place all along the frontier. Nehru was undeterred, still convinced that Beijing would not engage in a major war. His judgement seemed to be confirmed in May: a superior PLA force advanced on a new Indian post, apparently intending to liquidate it, but then did nothing.[13]

The Chinese rules of engagement, which began to be laid down by the Military Affairs Commission on 1 February, were quite strict. Within the band of territory 30 km. inside their line of control, Chinese units were not permitted to fire weapons, patrol, go hunting, or even put down rebellious Tibetans; within the 20 km. band inside their line of control, there were additional restrictions: no target shooting, manoeuvres, or demolition. If Indian troops penetrated its lines, a Chinese unit had first to issue a warning and try to push them into retreating; if this did not work, it had then to confiscate their weapons according to international custom, and after an explanation, return their weapons and allow them to leave.[14] All easier said than done, was probably the comment of the average PLA platoon commander, but there was a reason for Chinese caution.

In May–June 1962, the main concern in Beijing was over the threat of an invasion from Taiwan. While India's actions may have been seen as part of a strategy, backed by both the United States and the Soviet Union, to encircle China, Chinese leaders would have been reluctant to provoke hostilities in the Himalayas, which might have meant diverting military resources from the main danger point along the Fujian coast. A two-front war was certainly undesirable, and the Chinese press played down events on the Indian border.[15] The *People's Daily* editorial of 3 June, possibly a reflection of the *san he yi shao* policy favoured by Beijing leaders at the time,[16] expressed regret at India's refusal to renew the 1954 trade treaty, and affirmed that 'the Chinese government and people will never change their stand of safeguarding Sino-Indian amity.'[17] It was only from July on, after American assurances had lifted the threat of a KMT invasion,[18] that the Chinese could focus on the Indian border as a discrete foreign policy issue.

The first clash

At first there appeared to be no change in PLA behaviour. A risky advance by an Indian platoon to a position behind a Chinese outpost provoked a confrontation in the first half of July, but though the Chinese forces had been built up to battalion strength from late May, they did not attack, thus providing further encouragement to the Indian side.[19] On 21 July Chinese troops fired on an Indian patrol for the first time since 1959, causing two Indian casualties.[20]

Despite brave words in the Indian parliament, and Indian purchases of Soviet aircraft,[21] no knowledgeable Indian officials could have had any doubts about China's military superiority on the ground if this small clash escalated into full-scale hostilities. A major paper on defence policy prepared by the Indian Chiefs of Staff in January 1961 stated: 'Should the nature of the war go beyond that of a limited war . . . and develop into a full-scale conflagration amounting to an invasion of our territory, then it would be beyond the capacity of our forces to prosecute war . . . beyond a short period . . .'[22] In July 1962, a respected former Indian Chief of Army Staff, Gen. K. S. Thimayya, under whom this appraisal had been drafted, wrote: 'I cannot even as a soldier envisage India taking on China in an open conflict on its own. China's present strength in man-power, equipment and aircraft exceeds our resources a hundredfold with the full support of the U.S.S.R. and we could never hope to match China in the foreseeable future. It must be left to the politicians and diplomats to ensure our security.'[23] Extraordinarily, the Chiefs of Staff paper had not even attempted to demand from the Indian government the level of forces that might have stood a better chance of withstanding a full-scale Chinese invasion, but limited itself to indicating the forces needed better to cope with continuing border clashes. On reading the paper in early 1961, the incoming Director of Military Operations at HQ in New Delhi, Brigadier D. K. Palit, concluded that its proposals for counter-measures to the Chinese threat were 'perfunctory to the point of being simplistic . . . It seemed incredible that so grave a matter could have been despatched so heedlessly . . .'[24]

It was perhaps consciousness of this fundamental weakness that led the Indian government to adopt a relatively conciliatory tone in its note about the clash. On 21 July, a Chinese note had included the statement: 'The Chinese Government has repeatedly stated that China is not willing to fight with India and the Sino-Indian boundary question can be settled only through routine negotiations.'[25] The Indian reply on 26 July said, 'the Government of India fully reciprocate this desire for settlement by peaceful negotiations'.[26]

Even before the clash, Prime Minister Nehru had seemingly made a major concession at a lunch which he hosted for the departing Chinese ambassador, Pan Zili, by indicating that India would be prepared to hold discussions without demanding withdrawal from disputed areas as a pre-condition.[27] The 26 July note reiterated this position by indicating a willingness to talk 'as soon as the current tensions have eased and the appropriate climate is created'.[28] Almost simultaneously, at the Laos conference in Geneva, Foreign Minister Chen Yi was seeking out Defence Minister Menon, the chief Indian delegate for informal discussions on the border,[29] 'and only a failure in communication with New Delhi prevented the issuance of a joint communiqué proposing further talks'.[30] Another factor encouraging a more receptive Indian attitude to talks at this time may have been the visit to New Delhi of the Soviet first deputy premier, Anastas Mikoyan. The Indians were keen to have Soviet support, while the Russians were almost certainly anxious to avoid disrupting their truce with the Chinese by having to take a position if the Sino-Indian border dispute escalated as in 1959.[31]

Unfortunately for Mr Nehru, the pressure of parliamentary and public opinion gave him no room for manoeuvre at any time during the growing crisis. The publication of the Indian note of 26 July occasioned widespread accusations of a sell-out. The Chinese also embarrassed Mr Nehru in their reply by agreeing that there should be no pre-conditions for talks but suggesting that an Indian withdrawal would smooth away all difficulties. The Indian premier had to explain to parliament that the removal of tension referred to in the Indian note meant that previous alterations of the boundary by force had first to be rectified. This nullified the earlier concession.[32]

China changes tack

Despite the less flexible position which Mr Nehru, willingly or not, was now adopting, from 5 to 26 August Chinese diplomatic *démarches* and open propaganda diminished considerably, perhaps with the intention of reducing tension while chances of negotiation might still exist.[33] Another explanation, in the light of what is now known of Mao's political activities in 1962, is that this diminution of activity had to do with the summoning of the Beidaihe conference on 6 August. Officials running the Chinese foreign ministry in Beijing would have been reluctant to take major steps in the absence of Zhou Enlai and Chen Yi.[34] More importantly, Zhou and his colleagues would immediately have appreciated that Mao's new leftist line would have implications for the conduct of foreign affairs, and that further initiatives could not be taken until these had been fully understood. At the very least it meant the end of *san he yi shao*.

According to one analysis, a 'critical change occurred in Chinese behavior following the collapse of negotiatory prospects in late August . . . manifested in fresh diplomatic protests to New Delhi after a hiatus of several weeks, sharpened warnings over the consequences of Indian activity, and actual military clashes on the border'. In place of the mixture of carrot and stick employed in July and most of August, the Chinese now employed only the stick.[35] This new pattern emerged on 27 August, after the conclusion of the Beidaihe conference, and the day after preparatory meetings for the 10th plenum began in Beijing.[36] Confirmation that the end of the Beidaihe conference was a watershed in Chinese attitudes on the border crisis is provided by an Indian reconstruction of the events leading up to the Sino-Indian war, which dated the major buildup of war *matériel* and an increase in the number of Chinese posts as starting on 29 August.[37]

China's Changing Attitude towards India

27 Feb.	Wang Jiaxiang formally writes to Zhou, Deng, Chen Yi on *san he yi shao*, having got Liu Shaoqi's earlier endorsement.
3 June	Nostalgic *People's Daily* editorial on Sino-Indian relations.
16 June	Peng Dehuai letter reaches CC.
29 June	Wang's final programmatic statement on *san he yi shao*.
Late June	United States tells PRC it won't support KMT attack on mainland.
1st half July	Indian advance; confrontation but no clash.
7 July (*c.*)	Mao reasserts himself on collectivization.
9–14 July	Peace conference in Moscow.
21 July	PRC troops fire on Indians for first time since 1959.
23 July	Laos conference agreement.
26 July	Indian moderate note (Chen Yi seeks out Menon for informal talks in Geneva).
5–26 Aug.	PRC diplomatic activity *vis-à-vis* India diminishes.
6 Aug.	Mao opens Beidaihe conference.
	Peng Dehuai's letter rejected as being in line with three 'Ni's and one 'Tie'.
29 Aug.	Buildup of PRC forces on border starts.

Mao takes charge

It seems unlikely that contingency plans for military action would have been discussed at Beidaihe, except in very general terms.[38] This was too sensitive a topic for wide dissemination.[39] According to one official account, Zhou took personal charge of all arrangements, including notes, letters, news releases, and negotiations, and every move went to Mao for his approval. According to another, Liu Shaoqi also played a role, presumably presiding over a CC secretariat conference on 14 July, at which he and Zhou both reported on the border and the general staff issued appropriate orders thereafter. Mao is said to have approved and given two linked reasons why, despite ample justification, China should not yet hit back: Nehru had to be allowed to expose himself and the international community had to be convinced of India's aggression. On 16 July,

Chief-of-Staff Luo Ruiqing relayed the Chairman's eight-character comment on the situation: *wuzhuang gongchu, quanya jiaocuo* (armed coexistence, jigsaw pattern); presumably Mao was contemplating the long-term persistence of the situation that had begun to develop already, whereby Indian and Chinese posts were on the 'wrong' side of each other.[40] Chinese accounts stress that because of the diplomatic implications of a border clash, all decisions were taken at the highest level: 'No matter to do with border defence is small; every matter must be checked with Beijing.'[41]

Chinese defensive measures translated into dividing the Chinese units into three commands. In the disputed Aksai Chin area, the commander of the southern Xinjiang military district, He Jiachan, headed the western sector headquarters. Along the frontier roughly defined by the McMahon Line, separating Tibet from India's NEFA, an eastern sector headquarters was set up under the commander of the Tibet Military Region, Lt.-Gen. Zhang Guohua, who had commanded a corps of three divisions in the 2nd Field Army led by Liu Bocheng and Deng Xiaoping in the final period of the civil war.[42] Zhang was backed by two of his deputies Deng Shaodong, Zhao Wenjin, and a deputy political commissar, Lü Yishan. According to Indian estimates made after the border war, these men had three divisions at their disposal, a slightly larger force than that eventually assembled by the Indians before the final confrontation.[43] Left in charge in Lhasa were the region's political commissar, Tan Guansan, a deputy commander, Chen Mingyi, an assistant political commissar, Zhan Huayu, and the Chief-of-Staff, Wang Kang.[44]

These allocations of top brass suggested that the Chinese both anticipated more serious fighting in the east than in the west and were sufficiently concerned about their grip on Tibet, only three years after the flight of the Dalai Lama, to retain a strong reserve to keep the region under control. The Chinese dispositions also reflected their continuing overwhelming superiority over any Indian probing from Ladakh into the disputed Aksai Chin area, despite the desperate plea of the local Indian commander for reinforcements and his warning that India's diplomatic posture should be consonant with its military capabilities.[45] But even with their superiority, the Chinese left nothing to chance. As early as May 1962, Zhang Guohua's old chief, Marshal Liu Bocheng, one of the PLA's most brilliant commanders and head of the Military Affairs Commission's (MAC) strategy small group, had predicted an Indian attack, and was deputed to oversee the planning of a Chinese counter-attack.[46]

Neither Mao's comments nor the Chinese command structures along the Indian border shed much new light upon the reasons for Chinese behaviour in the weeks after the Beidaihe conference.[47] On the one hand, Chinese words and deeds unquestionably became more and more forceful. On the other hand, Indian words and deeds, including the establishment of forty-five new forward posts on the NEFA front, thirty-five of them on the McMahon Line, were also more and more forceful, and could have been construed in Beijing as legitimate grounds for Chinese reaction. Indeed, the Chinese appraisal was that having been checked in Aksai Chin, the Indian government decided in September to push forward north of the McMahon Line; the general staff decided to match the Indians man for man.[48]

Moves and missives

On 8 September, a Chinese force crossed the Thag La ridge. This topographical feature was regarded by the Indians as part of the eastern frontier, though it was north of the McMahon Line, the Indian standard for defining the frontier elsewhere in this sector. The Chinese troops moved into positions enabling them to threaten a small Indian unit at Dhola post, though they did not attack. But the Dhola post had been set up only in June 1962, the first contravention of the implicit agreement between the two sides dating from 1959 that no new forward movement should take place in the area, pending a comprehensive settlement. The Dhola post was within the territory claimed by India, but again, it was on the Tibet side of the McMahon Line. In New Delhi, the area was seen as indisputably Indian; in Beijing, it was claimed as Chinese, but recognized as disputed territory and thus subject to negotiation as part of a formal boundary delimitation.[49]

On 13 September, the Chinese delivered two notes which took strong lines. One protested recent incidents in the western sector, warning that 'he who plays with fire will eventually be consumed by fire'.[50] The other, part of the ongoing correspondence about the border situation in general, accused India of 'persisting in advancing into Chinese territory, changing the *status quo* by force and aggravating the border tension', and of using negotiation as a cover for 'nibbling Chinese territory', but proposed that there should be talks, starting on 15 October.[51] On 16 September, a Chinese note protested the establishment of the Indian post at Dhola, again describing this as part of India's 'systematic nibbling activities' which 'fully reveal how ambitious the Indian side's aggressive designs are'.[52] An Indian note of 19 September noted Beijing's 'undiplomatic language' and 'threats of force', countered that it was the Chinese who were attempting to alter the *status quo* by 'unilateral action and aggressive activities', but accepted the idea of talks starting on 15 October 'to define measures to restore the *status quo* in the Western Sector which has been altered by force in the last few years and to remove the current tensions in that area'.[53]

Although both sides professed a willingness to talk, they differed considerably on the topics they were willing to discuss. More crucially, while the Indian government had seemed ready to live with what Mao had called a jigsaw situation in the western sector, it was not prepared to accept what appeared to it an encroachment on a well-defined frontier in the eastern sector. Indian official thinking was bolstered by the belief that, however outclassed their troops might be in the western sector, in the eastern sector India possessed the power to drive the Chinese out, despite reports to the contrary by local commanders who appreciated only too well the PLA's local superiority in manpower, weapons, logistics, and position. Overriding the warnings of junior commanders, on 9 September, immediately after the Chinese crossed the Thag La ridge, Defence Minister Menon ordered the army to evict them.[54]

Increasing troop movements and escalating intransigence on both sides inevitably led to bloodshed. A clash took place at Dhola on 20 September. One Chinese was killed, one seriously wounded; five Indians were wounded.[55] By this time both the Indian Prime Minister and the Defence Minister were abroad, Nehru at the Commonwealth Prime Ministers' conference in London, Menon at the UN in New York, and in the light of the increasingly evident strength of the PLA, the chief of army staff requested written confirmation from his minister of the order to evict the Chinese from the eastern sector. It was promptly cabled back from New York.[56] On 24 September, there was a further clash and three more Chinese soldiers were killed.[57] Further notes were exchanged; again, both sides offered to talk, but neither was yet prepared to accept the other's conditions. Both Beijing and New Delhi were quite conscious of the importance of influencing opinion throughout Asia, and so their notes combined truculence directed at each other and reasonableness addressed to the outside world.[58]

On 4 October, due to disagreements between senior officers on the NEFA front, the Indian government appointed the Chief of General Staff, General Kaul, to take charge of the effort to throw the Chinese out, and despite Kaul's minimal combat experience, the Indian press immediately reported that his mission presaged an all-out effort. At this stage, desultory fire was regularly exchanged between the two sides. Unbeknownst to Kaul, however, the PLA general staff had just transmitted a critical directive from the centre and the Chairman.

Sometime earlier, Mao had complained that the Indians had been pressing the Chinese along the border for three years, 1959–61; if they tried it a fourth year then China would strike back. The Dhola clash apparently decided the Chinese leaders that a military engagement was inevitable. On 6 October, the order was sent to the border forces: 'If the Indian army attacks, hit back ruthlessly . . . If they attack, don't just repulse them, hit back ruthlessly so that it hurts.' During fateful discussions held by the Chinese leadership in October, Mao and Zhou were in charge, but Liu Shaoqi and Deng Xiaoping also participated, along with Marshals Liu Bocheng, He Long, and Xu Xiangqian, and General Luo Ruiqing as chief-of-staff. In the light of subsequent events, Marshal Liu's recommendations were clearly taken very seriously. He rejected the idea of simply dealing with border troops by removing them, forcing them back, breaking up their attack, and surrounding them. Rather, he advocated taking on India's best troops and swiftly beating them. Only that could be called a decisive victory.[59]

General Kaul had fixed on 10 October for starting his assault, but the Chinese attacked first and a major clash took place. Analysis of Chinese behaviour and orders suggests, however, that they intended the attack to serve as a deterrent and not as the beginning of an all-out offensive. General Kaul, whose reports to Army HQ in New Delhi had combined stark realism regarding the weakness of the Indian position with unrealistic optimism about his mission, was sufficiently alarmed to fly back to New Delhi to consult with Prime Minister Nehru on whether it should be aborted.[60]

As a result of the meeting on the evening of 11 October, it was agreed neither to build up Indian strength in order to attack the Chinese—a decision made for military reasons—nor to retreat to less exposed positions, but simply to hold the line—a decision made for political reasons. But the next day, at the airport *en route* to Sri Lanka, in off-the-cuff exchanges with Indian journalists about what orders had been given to troops in the eastern sector, Nehru did not reveal this fact. Instead he said, 'Our instructions are to free our territory', hedging only on when this might be accomplished. In addition, he effectively ruled out talks while the Chinese remained on the southern slope of the Thag La ridge.[61]

Mao's India war

The Chinese seized on Nehru's unguarded remark, and indeed to this day it figures in Chinese accounts of the border war as the essential proof that India was the aggressor.[62] In an editorial two days later, the *People's Daily*, declaring that a 'massive invasion of Chinese territory by Indian troops in the eastern sector . . . seems imminent', went on to issue an implicit warning:

How could the Chinese possibly be so weak-kneed and faint-hearted as to tolerate this? It is high time to show to Mr Nehru that the heroic Chinese troops with the glorious tradition of resisting foreign aggression, can never be cleared by anyone from their own territory . . . All comrade commanders and fighters of the People's Liberation Army guarding the Sino-Indian border, redouble your vigilance! Indian troops may at any time attempt to carry out Nehru's instructions to get rid of you. Be well prepared! Your sacred task now is to defend our territory and be ever-ready to deal resolute counterblows at any invaders.[63]

Some credence was given to the Chinese charges by the Indian decision, apparently taken for domestic publicity purposes and against the advice of the local commander, to reinforce the line their troops were holding,[64] which could have been seen in Beijing as preparations for attack rather than for defence. Defence Minister Menon's public statements would have confirmed that impression.[65]

On 16 October, four days after Nehru's fateful remark, the MAC decided to annihilate Indian troops north of the McMahon Line; the following day the operational order was given 'liquidate the invading Indian army'. During the days that followed, the Indian forces observed helplessly as the PLA prepared methodically for battle. In the east, the Chinese mustered a force of 10,300 men to attack the Indian 7th Brigade, whose strength they estimated at 6,000.[66] In the west, their front-line troops were two battalions, the Chinese having increased their strength by 4,000 men, including an extra infantry battalion.[67] The eastern sector was chosen for the main assault, both because it was militarily more advantageous and because the Chinese wished to demonstrate once and for all that they did not accept the McMahon Line.[68] Finally, shortly after dawn on 20 October, the PLA attacked in overwhelming strength, both in the west and across the McMahon Line in the east, and within four days had captured virtually all the posts established so laboriously by the Indian army in both sectors over the previous several months.[69] After a week, the Chinese halted their advance in NEFA and hostilities ceased there, though Indian posts in the western sector continued to be picked off.[70] In the immediate aftermath of the Chinese victory, Nehru formally took over the defence portfolio, but kept Menon in the cabinet; on 8 November, however, the Prime Minister was forced by his parliamentary party to discard his long-time political ally. General Kaul was flown back to New Delhi with pulmonary problems, acquired during his visits to NEFA units stationed at high altitudes.[71]

Had Nehru at this stage agreed to talks after the two sides had returned to their positions prior to the start of India's forward policy as the Chinese demanded, presumably Mao and Zhou would have considered that their punitive expedition had achieved its purpose and no further use of force was needed. But what might have made military and diplomatic sense given the balance of forces on the ground was political nonsense in New Delhi. Far from cowing the Indians, the Chinese attack had induced a national mood of unity, defiance, and determination. Had Nehru decided that discretion was the better part of valour and agreed to sit down with the Chinese prior to their evacuating all the military gains they had just made and India returning to its posts in the disputed territory, even he might not have survived in office.[72] As it was, he was roundly criticized for the relatively mild tone of his first letter rejecting Zhou Enlai's offer of talks, and his subsequent correspondence was markedly more hostile in tone. Nevertheless, he refused to break off diplomatic relations with Beijing or to take the matter to the UN.[73]

Though the position on the ground in both sectors was still unfavourable to the Indian forces, and made worse by inappropriate tactical dispostions in the eastern sector, New Delhi, fortified by the conviction that Beijing would not order another major assault, prepared confidently to drive the Chinese out of NEFA. In contrast to China, where the official media played down the military aspects of the dispute at this time, Indian newspapers reported every indication of Indian troops preparing for an offensive. Nehru was quoted as saying that though India was not 'technically' at war, 'the fact is that we are at war, though we have not made any declaration to that effect—it is not necessary at the present moment to do so, I do not know about the future.'[74]

The Chinese pursued a two-pronged diplomatic policy after

halting their initial assault. On the one hand, Zhou Enlai pressed Nehru to come to the conference table in measured language—indeed, in his first letter he did not sign his name to the Chinese propaganda allegation that it had been India which had attacked first. Simultaneously, he wooed leaders of the Afro-Asian non-aligned movement.[75]

But after Nehru had rejected Zhou's initial proposal for talks, an all-out denunciation of the Indian Prime Minister was made in a 15,000-word *People's Daily* article on 27 October, entitled 'More on Nehru's philosophy in the light of the Sino-Indian boundary question'. This was a sequel to the paper's article on Nehru's 'philosophy' and the Tibetan revolt, published three years earlier when the Dalai Lama had fled to India, but it was a still more virulent and personal attack on the Indian Prime Minister, and Mao contributed significantly to it. Its major contention was that Nehru was a 'lackey' of US imperialism and had become a pawn 'in the international anti-China campaign', an allegation that may have gained a spurious credibility from Nehru's appeal for American military aid in the aftermath of the Chinese attack.[76]

The tone and content of the article were consonant with that of Beijing's anti-Soviet polemics of 1960 and prefigured its anti-Soviet polemics of 1963–4, thus marking it as a weapon in the ideological struggle with Moscow rather than in the military struggle with India. Mao was again condemning Khrushchev's theoretical position that there could be peaceful transitions to communism in developing countries in general, and the consequent Soviet policy position of making friends with countries like India in particular. It was an 'I-told-you-so' riposte for Khrushchev's neutrality in the 1959 Sino-Indian border clashes which had so angered the Chinese leadership.[77]

The second Chinese attack

Nehru might have shrugged off Chinese abuse and could have lived with the personal enmity of China's leaders.[78] Far more serious for him was the evidence of continuing Chinese military preparations in the eastern sector. Even before the first Chinese attack, the staff of the Sichuan-based 54th Corps, which had fought in the Korean War, including the commander, Ding Sheng, and deputy commander, Wei Tongtai, were formed into a separate command to take charge of the 'defence' of the eastern section of the eastern sector, bringing their 130th division with them; a regiment was despatched from Qinghai.[79]

Yet the inexperienced General Kaul, now recovered and back in command in NEFA,[80] was as ebullient as ever, and decided to attack the Chinese on 14 November, in one area only and not as part of a general offensive, for no better reason than that it was Nehru's birthday. He happened to choose the eastern section of the eastern sector, where arrayed against him were Ding Sheng's Korean War veterans. Indian HQ staff appraisals of superior Chinese strength were ignored, and the result was a shattering defeat for brave but outmatched Indian units, prompting Kaul finally to acknowledge that he had insufficient forces for his assignment and to urge New Delhi to recruit foreign forces to come to India's aid![81] As one Indian historian later put it, 'It was clear that the Indian army command was in desperate confusion. Grip, insight and poise were wholly lacking.'[82]

This was even more the case when the Chinese followed up with what was clearly their pre-planned attack in both east and west on 18 November, deploying eight infantry regiments and three artillery regiments on the NEFA front.[83] Insufficient attention to military considerations and excessive concern for political ones had placed the main Indian forces in the eastern sector in highly vulnerable positions,[84] and they were decisively routed as the Chinese pushed forward. Rumors spread that the Chinese would soon arrive on the plains of Assam, perhaps parachute troops into New Delhi itself, and morale in the capital collapsed. Nehru appealed privately to President Kennedy for American warplanes.[85] A US carrier force steamed towards the Bay of Bengal, and a squadron of transport planes arrived. But on 21 November, Beijing unilaterally proclaimed a cease-fire and announced that its forces would soon start withdrawing from NEFA.[86]

This time there was no question of India preparing for a counter-offensive. The Chinese had convincingly taught their lesson. China had no intention of giving up Aksai Chin and it had the means with which to defend that disputed territory. Moreover, a renewal of India's forward policy could once again result in a massive threat along the whole frontier.[87]

But the protection of Chinese security interests and the concomitant humiliation of China's Asian 'rival' were not the only benefits achieved by this successful punitive expedition.[88] Nehru's appeal for Western aid in his hour of need dented, if it did not destroy, India's image as a non-aligned nation, thus diminishing its status both in the Communist bloc and the Third World. China, on the other hand, had dispelled its most recent image as a country crippled by economic disasters, ripe perhaps for revolt and invasion. Beijing had also demonstrated to a deaf Moscow the unwisdom of choosing India over China as an ally. Most importantly, it had signalled to its erstwhile communist partner that the banner of militant Marxism-Leninism had once more been unfurled over Beijing. The question that remains unanswerable is: if Mac had still been in retirement, would Liu Shaoqi and Zhou Enlai have chosen to teach Mr Nehru a lesson in quite so brutal a fashion? Probably not, in the light of their support for *san he yi shao*.

Khrushchev's position on the border war

In fact, Moscow had tilted more towards Beijing in the border dispute this time than in 1959, though the Chinese were still aggrieved about Soviet weapons sales to India. On 8 October, a

Chinese leader[89] told the Soviet Ambassador that China had information that India was about to launch a massive attack along the Sino-Indian border and that should India attack we would resolutely defend ourselves. He also pointed out that the fact that Soviet-made helicopters and transport planes were being used by India for airdropping and transporting military supplies in the Sino-Indian border areas was making a bad impression on our frontier guards . . .'[90]

In the week following this conversation, Khrushchev demonstrated how eager he was to propitiate the Chinese at this juncture by his unusually cordial handling of Ambassador Liu Xiao as he prepared to return home after eight years in his post.[91] When Liu paid his formal parting call, Khrushchev gave him a two-hour *tour d'horizon* of his views on world affairs, and on 14 October the Soviet 1st secretary summoned the whole of the CPSU Presidium (Politburo) to a farewell dinner, seating the ambassador's wife between himself and his senior colleague, Frol Kozlov. Rising to his feet, Khrushchev recalled with nostalgia the strength of the Sino-Soviet relationship prior to 1958, and expressed the hope that the two countries would cease dwelling on past quarrels, and instead could turn a fresh page in their relationship. Socialist countries should respect each other's domestic policies, and if there were differences between Moscow and Beijing on the issue of transition to socialism, life itself would instruct them who was right.

On the question of the Sino-Indian border dispute, the Soviet Union was on China's side, Khrushchev said. This was the unanimous position of the CPSU Presidium. Nehru's comments as he left

New Delhi airport for Sri Lanka showed that he was propitiating domestic reaction. If unhappily there were an attack on China, 'we stand together with China'. If the Chinese wished, the Soviet Union would proclaim this the following day; it had not done so previously to avoid driving the Indians into the arms of the Americans, who were trying to sell them arms. Turning to the aircraft issue, Khrushchev apparently did not refer to past Soviet sales to India, though in a subsequent memorandum the Soviet government claimed that the planes which the Chinese had complained about had no military significance and did not affect the balance of power on the border. At the dinner, Khrushchev refrained from so impolitic a claim. Instead he expressed as his personal view, but with Kozlov and others indicating assent, that the Soviet Union should postpone selling Mig-21s to India until after the border dispute was settled, not because a few aircraft would make India stronger than China but to prevent 'our enemies' from sowing discord. Of course, after his experience in Beijing in 1959, Khrushchev was well aware that it would not be enemies but his 'friends' in China who would take him to task,[92] and indeed the announcement of the Mig deal by the Indians in mid-August had been given prominent play in the Beijing media.[93]

Liu Xiao informed Khrushchev that Indian troops were massing on the eastern sector of the frontier, and that if they attacked, China would resist them. Khrushchev said that this information coincided with the Soviet Union's, and, again mindful of 1959, added: 'If the Soviet Union were placed in China's position it would select the same measures.' A neutral attitude on the border issue was impossible; if China were attacked, it would be an act of betrayal to declare neutrality.[94]

How sincere Liu Xiao thought Khrushchev was is unclear. But his wife, Zhang Yi, reminded Liu that in pursuit of its strategic aims, the Soviet leadership had treated Indians with special courtesies since the 1950s. As a result of her own round of farewell visits, she was able to inform her husband that this policy was still in place. The wife of the Indian ambassador to Moscow had informed Zhang Yi that she and her husband, also about to relinquish his post, had been invited to spend a month in the Crimea prior to returning home. This was contrary to diplomatic practice, and all that Liu Xiao and Zhang Yi rated was a more customary invitation from Mikoyan to return at some future time.[95]

Zhou Enlai would have been sensitive to such diplomatic niceties;

he never forgot Dulles's refusal to shake his hand at the 1954 Geneva conference.[96] For Mao, they were doubtless bourgeois irrelevancies; he had hated having to receive ambassadorial credentials when he was head of state. Neither man trusted Khrushchev, however, and by the time Liu Xiao returned home and reported in minute detail to the centre about the Khrushchev dinner, they decided that the Soviet leader's expressions of support did not warrant a response.[97]

Nevertheless, shortly after the Chinese attack began on 20 October, Nehru received a letter from Khrushchev in which the Soviet leader alluded to earlier reports of India's intention to initiate hostilities and urged him to agree to Zhou's offer of talks. Soviet officials followed through on Khrushchev's undertaking to Liu Xiao on Mig-21s, telling the Indian embassy in Moscow that the Soviet commitment to sell these to New Delhi would not be fulfilled. The closest that Khrushchev came to a public commitment to the Chinese was a *Pravda* editorial on 25 October, which said only that the McMahon Line had been imposed on both Indians and Chinese, that the Chinese had never recognized it, and that Beijing's statement of the previous day constituted a satisfactory basis for opening negotiations.[98] Slim pickings, from the Chinese point of view. Whereas a speech of support by the North Vietnamese Foreign Minister was accorded front-page treatment by the *People's Daily*, the *Pravda* editorial was reported on the back page, after stories of similar press support in North Korea and North Vietnam.[99]

The Cuban missile crisis

Khrushchev's restraint in the Sino-Soviet dispute in the summer and early autumn of 1962, his modest tilt to Beijing and away from New Delhi, and his cordial treatment of Ambassador Liu Xiao, probably had less to do with a change of heart on the Sino-Indian border issue and more to do with his anticipated confrontation with the United States. Khrushchev needed to face Kennedy with a united Communist bloc behind him. The Chinese had not wanted a two-front war in the summer of 1962; Khrushchev did not want to have to confront both America and China in the autumn.

Khrushchev anticipated provoking this confrontation in early November, after America's mid-term congressional elections. At that point, he would reveal to Kennedy that the Russians had placed nuclear missiles in Cuba. If Chinese 'militancy' in its relations with India could in part be attributed to Nehru's forward policy in the Himalayas, equally Beijing's renewal of the Sino-Soviet polemics in the autumn of 1962 could in part be attributed to Khrushchev's 'forward' policy in the Caribbean, which led to the Cuban missile crisis.[100]

According to his own account, the Soviet leader had long worried that the Americans, unreconciled to the existence of a communist state on their doorstep, would again attempt to overthrow his ally Castro, and that next time they would be more successful than during the Bay of Pigs fiasco of April 1961. If the Soviet Union 'lost' Cuba, it would be 'a terrible blow to Marxism-Leninism. It would gravely diminish our stature throughout the world, but especially in Latin America.'[101] Finally, in April–May 1962,[102] Khrushchev came up with the idea of secretly emplacing Soviet missiles in Cuba to deter an American attack. This policy would have the additional advantage of exposing the United States to a threat equivalent to that experienced by the Soviet Union from American missiles in Turkey. Indeed, though Khrushchev did not admit this in his memoirs, the missiles he planned to send to Cuba could have 'quadrupled the number of nuclear warheads that Soviet missiles could drop on the United States'.[103] Conceivably, this, and not Cuban security, was the real reason for Khrushchev's gamble.

The Soviet leader managed to persuade his colleagues and, with much greater difficulty, Castro to agree to the policy.[104] His assumption was that if Kennedy were presented with a *fait accompli*, he would accept it. He failed to appreciate that an operation of this magnitude could not be kept secret from the myriad American instruments of surveillance on Cuba, and he totally miscalculated Kennedy's reaction. Khrushchev planned to reveal what he had done after the November elections to prevent embarrassing Kennedy into a heated response. But on 14 October, the same day as the Soviet leader entertained Liu Xiao to dinner, the CIA concluded that film taken over Cuba that morning by a U-2 aircraft showed that missile silos were being constructed on the island.[105]

Thereafter, the crisis developed rapidly. On 22 October, Kennedy revealed America's discovery, demanded that the missiles be removed, and announced a naval quarantine of Cuba to prevent further shipments of Soviet weapons. No arms-carrying vessels tested the blockade, and after a tense week, and exchanges of notes between Kennedy and Khrushchev, the latter agreed on 28 October to remove the Soviet missiles and dismantle the installations for them. Despite Khrushchev's claim then and in his memoirs that his policy had been worthwhile, for it had forced the Americans to pledge not to invade Cuba, this *dénouement* was a humiliation, and the whole episode cost the Soviet Union a billion dollars.[106]

The chronology of this period illustrates the overlapping development of the crises in the Caribbean and on the Himalayas:

Crises Timetables

October	Himalayas	Caribbean
14	Khrushchev pledges support for China	United States discovers missile silos on Cuba
20	First Chinese attack Khrushchev letter to Nehru	
22		Kennedy reveals Soviet missiles, demands removal, imposes naval quarantine
24	China proposes talks	Soviet ships halt *en route* Cuba
25	*Pravda* editorial tilts to China	
26		First ship stopped by US Navy
27	First Chinese offensive ends	
28		Khrushchev agrees to remove missiles
November		
Early	Moscow resumes neutrality	
5–14	[Chinese criticized at Bulgarian party congress]	
14	Indian attack; Soviet ambassador conveys good wishes to Nehru (Before 21st: Mig-21 sales confirmed)	
16	Second Chinese attack	

| 20–4 | [Sino-Soviet clashes at Hungarian party congress] |
| 21 | Chinese cease-fire |

December

| 1 | Chinese withdrawal commences |
| 4–8 | [Sino-Soviet clashes at Czech party congress] |

Ambassador Liu Xiao reportedly informed Beijing in advance about Khrushchev's missile plan,[107] though the Chinese probably knew about it anyway, for they had excellent sources of information in Cuba. But while Khrushchev undoubtedly handled the Himalayan crisis with the Caribbean in mind, it is highly unlikely that the Chinese did the same. The Himalayan crisis was clearly looming long before the first Chinese attack, with Chinese communications to Moscow as well as their propaganda giving Khrushchev ample warning of what might happen. But the Caribbean crisis did not erupt until after the first Chinese attack, and the Chinese had no means of foreseeing American reactions, which, if Khrushchev's calculations had been correct, would not have resulted in a potential Armageddon.[108] Moreover, if the Chinese had any inkling of Soviet plans, they would have known that any Soviet–American confrontation was unlikely to be precipitated by Khrushchev before the second week of November.[109] By that time, had Nehru agreed to negotiate after their first attack, the Himalayan crisis would have been over.[110]

The conjunction of the crises was crucially important for Mao, enabling him forcefully to remind his colleagues of what he clearly saw as Khrushchev's perfidy and cowardice: perfidy in the Himalayas, as he had displayed under similar circumstances in 1959, and cowardice in the Caribbean, as he had displayed in the Middle East in 1958.[111] A year later, when open polemics had begun between Beijing and Moscow, the Chinese revealed how they had felt about Soviet behaviour during the Himalayan crisis: 'During the Caribbean crisis, they spoke a few seemingly fair words out of considerations of expediency. But when the crisis was over, they went back on their words. They have sided with the Indian reactionaries against China all the time . . . a complete betrayal of proletarian internationalism . . .'[112] After the end of the missile crisis but before the Chinese cease-fire, the Soviet ambassador in New Delhi had conveyed his country's good wishes to Nehru, indicating that Moscow was tilting back into neutrality, though the sales of Mig-21s proceeded only after the Chinese cease-fire.[113] In that respect,

Khrushchev kept his word.

Unlike the Russians on the border war, the Chinese were anything but lukewarm on the missile crisis. Massive rallies—which had not been mounted in connection with the border war—were held and Chinese leaders spoke in support of the Russians and Cubans. This was a strong testimonial to CCP belief in the importance of bloc solidarity in East–West crises, for Beijing's leaders actually disapproved of Khrushchev's policy of placing missiles in Cuba, regarding it, as they later revealed, as unnecessary and 'adventurist'. Far worse, however, was Khrushchev's agreement to pull the missiles out, which they characterized as 'capitulationist'.[114] In the light of these events, very few of Mao's colleagues would have been prepared to stand up for the policy of *san he yi shao*, and it was inevitable that Mao would eventually call an end to the uneasy Sino-Soviet truce that had prevailed since the beginning of 1962.

Polemics resume

Again, however, it appears to have been the Russians who struck first. The arenas were four East European communist party congresses, held successively from early November 1962 through mid-January 1963. Almost thirty years later, the leader of the Chinese fraternal delegations to all four meetings, Wu Xiuquan, gave the CCP's version of how the Moscow–Beijing split grew wider as congress followed congress.

At the first congress, that of the Bulgarian party in Sofia, there were many open attacks on the Albanian communist party along with veiled ones on the CCP, with a few delegations naming it too.[115] Clearly, critics were taking their lead from the CPSU; the Bulgarian leader, Todor Zhivkov, had been in Moscow only a couple of days before the congress opened. Wu did not attempt to debate the allegations. Instead, to indicate his disapproval of a critical passage, which he immediately picked up on from the simultaneous translation in Russian, Wu would neither rise to his feet nor applaud along with everyone else, and since he was on the platform, his behaviour was widely noted. Wu's own speech was composed only of the customary greetings and brief report on domestic developments, with a comment that the CCP thought that the criticisms of the Albanians served only the imperialists. The audience stood and applauded at its start and end, perhaps, Wu felt, because he had been polite. At the banquet thrown by the Bulgarian party for its guests, however, he was less polite. Protocol meant that Wu had to sit next to the chief

CPSU delegate, Suslov, whom he studiously ignored throughout the meal because of the criticisms the Soviet ideologist had voiced in his speech.

At the customary formal call on Zhivkov after the close of the congress, Wu's main concern was to explain the Chinese position on the border war in order, he later wrote, to combat any wrong impressions the Bulgarian leader might have got from the Western media—an interesting acknowledgement of communist leaders' willingness to believe Western reports on a fraternal country rather than the latter's own information, presumably because they were only too well aware of the mendaciousness of their own propaganda.[116] Zhivkov, like János Kádár at the subsequent Hungarian congress, had in fact followed the resumed Soviet line of urging peace in the Himalayas while remaining neutral on the issues.[117]

The widespread official antagonism to the CCP in Eastern Europe was further illustrated when the Chinese delegation went from Sofia to Bucharest for a few days' rest. When they went to buy their airline tickets in the Romanian capital to go to Budapest to attend the Hungarian party congress, the Chinese were told that none were available, and they got tickets only by appealing to the Hungarian embassy. The plane of course turned out to be far from full.[118]

The Hungarians took precautions to avoid embarrassment from a repeat of Wu's tactics in Sofia by issuing an instruction that there was to be no standing up to indicate approval of speeches at their communist party congress. But of course, as Wu commented, they could not forbid applause and he would still be able to sit on his hands if he had cause to object to a speech. In fact, the CCP fared even worse under the auspices of the Hungarians than under those of the Bulgarians. The Chinese delegation calculated that twenty of the sixty-four parties attending the Sofia meeting attacked them, but in Budapest it rose to thirty out of sixty. Only the North Vietnamese delegation openly expressed friendship for the CCP. Wu reported all this to Beijing and requested instructions.

On the morning of the final day of the Hungarian congress, 24 November, an official asked the CCP delegation if there would be a Chinese speech at the closing reception that night. Since no directive had yet arrived from Beijing, the delegation had to temporize, promising a reply in the afternoon. Fortunately a telegram arrived in the lunch interval with instructions to use the reception to rebut critics, making three major points: the worsening of relations between the CPSU on the one hand and the CCP and the Albanians on the other was attributable to Moscow; the current anti-China chorus was being directed by the CPSU; party congresses should be the occasion for promoting unity not fomenting splits. The telegram included an official Chinese statement which had to be read out.

Wu's heart sank, presumably because he knew the furore this would cause. Nevertheless, he quickly had the statement translated into Russian and Hungarian and devised a plan to prevent his being stopped in mid-protest. If he followed the normal practice of paragraph by paragraph translation, he anticipated being interrupted as soon as the audience got the drift, so on the pretext of saving time, he got his hosts to agree to his interpreter simply reading the speech in Hungarian. The trick worked, but after the strong Chinese protest had been read, a Latin American communist was put up by the Russians to counter-attack. Kádár personally came up to Wu Xiuquan and said: 'I did not think that your delegation could make a speech like this, and we can only express our regret at your conduct.' Wu replied that he understood what Kádár was saying and that his delegation could stay no longer at the reception.[119]

Wu and the delegation then went to Poland to spend time with his colleague Ambassador Wang Bingnan before the Czech congress opened on 4 December. He found the Poles much more hospitable than the Romanians, and he accepted an invitation to go boar hunting, a pastime he had learned while ambassador to Yugoslavia. But after a pleasant week he had to face the music in Prague.[120]

Clearly stung by Wu's seizure of the initiative at the Hungarian congress, the CPSU delegation, which included a hefty contingent of specialists from its international department, came well prepared for the Czech one. A few days earlier, at the Italian party congress, attacks on the Chinese had increased, and the member of Wu's delegation who had represented the CCP was heard in silence.[121] The *People's Daily* replied with a criticism of the Italian party leader, Palmiro Togliatti.[122]

On the eve of the Hungarian congress, the *People's Daily* and *Red Flag* had published indirect criticism of Khrushchev's behaviour in the missile crisis though without naming him, and the CPSU had by now had a chance to assess these attacks and to co-ordinate counter-measures with its satellites.[123] The Czech 1st secretary, Antonin Novotný, accused the Albanians—read the Chinese—of egging the Cubans on to a nuclear war,[124] and attacked unnamed 'dogmatists, sectarians, and nationalists' who supported them.[125] The leader of the Soviet delegation, Leonid Brezhnev, expressed concern that people who called themselves Marxists could regret that the Cuban revolution had been saved without war.[126] From then on, there was an unremitting drumbeat of criticism of the Albanians and their Chinese allies from Czech and foreign speakers. The Chinese delegation again made a little list: of over sixty fraternal delegations, fifty attacked the Albanians by name, and of these, twenty attacked the CCP by name. Even the North Koreans were attacked for disagreeing with this procedure and strongly supporting the Chinese. The odds against Beijing were increasing.

Wu, cautioned by Beijing not to retreat, once again protested the use of a party congress to attack a fraternal party, and once again, with a clever manoeuvre, he outwitted his host, Novotný, and won the right to hand out a copy of a new official Chinese statement to that effect to every foreign delegation.[127] Almost certainly, these petty Chinese tactical successes in manipulating local procedural conventions infuriated the leaden-footed leaders of the East European satellites far beyond their intrinsic importance and increased the venom with which they imitated their master's voice.[128] Equally, the East Europeans, doubtless guided by Moscow, got some revenge with protocol victories, though Wu Xiuquan did not record this in his memoirs: in his speech, Novotný listed the CCP in eighth place, below all the East European parties, instead of second, after the CPSU, as had been customary; at the East German congress, Walter Ulbricht would list them ninth, below Mongolia as well.[129]

These events, big and small, were viewed with intense interest back in Beijing. On 14 December, the day that Wu and his colleagues returned there for a brief vacation before the East German congress, the *People's Daily* published a selection of Novotný's anti-Chinese remarks, and followed it up the next day with an editorial calling on proletarians of the world to unite against their common imperialist enemy. More significantly, Mao summoned Wu to Hangzhou and had him give a blow-by-blow description of his experiences. The Chairman pronounced himself satisfied, and commended Wu for his conduct.[130]

Wu returned to East Berlin for his final bout in mid-January 1963 to find that Khrushchev was leading the Soviet delegation, and that the East Germans had devised even tougher measures to prevent dissident foreign voices being heard. Only delegations led by the first secretary had the right to deliver their fraternal greetings orally; others would have to be content with presenting them in writing and having them published in the local press. Realizing that this would provoke an enormous row if followed rigidly, the East Germans excused China and Czechoslovakia—Novotný had not come—from the rule. Other parties had to be content with regional spokesmen: the Cubans spoke for Latin America, the Japanese for Asia. This meant that pro-Chinese parties like the North Koreans and the Indonesians could not speak, and their messages were in fact not published in the East German press.[131] Worse still, in his opening report the East German party leader, Walter Ulbricht, blamed the Chinese for abandoning peaceful coexistence on the Sino-Indian border.

In what seems to have been a variation of the old 'bad cop/good cop' routine, Khrushchev followed up Ulbricht's hatchet job with a partially conciliatory speech, perhaps another attempt to corral the Chinese delegation and to avert a Prague-type fiasco. He spent considerable time justifying Soviet behaviour in the missile crisis on the lines he later adopted in his memoirs, and went on to deride the Chinese, though without naming them, for the polemics they had issued on this subject:

Some people who consider themselves Marxists opine that the way to combat imperialism is not, above all, by building up the socialist countries' economic strength—that tangible factor with which our enemies reckon; no, they have invented a new method of doing it, probably the cheapest ever known. This method, you see, does not depend on a country's economic level, it does not depend on the quality and quantity of armaments; it consists in nothing but abuse. These people imagine that to engage in endless swearing and cursing at imperialism is to do what will best help the socialist countries. This is a sort of voodoo belief in the power of curses and incantations.[132]

Khrushchev proposed that, from now on, public intra-party debates should cease, that within their own ranks parties should desist from criticizing fraternal parties, and that the Albanians should abandon their mistaken viewpoints and return to the large and fraternal socialist family. The East Germans immediately supported this 'correct advice', and demanded to know the Chinese delegation's response.

Wu and his colleagues reasoned that, despite the heated atmosphere, Khrushchev had not yet decided on precipitating a split and anyway did not want to assume the responsibility for one—which probably mirrored Mao's position, though Wu did not comment on that—and so had put up a smoke-screen to deceive middle-of-the-road foreign communists. This placed the Chinese in a dilemma: if they did not fall in with Khrushchev's suggestion, they would be seen as the splitters, but if they agreed to it, they would lose the opportunity of making their case. New instructions arrived from Beijing along with the text of the CCP's official greeting. The latter was translated and printed, and all available Chinese officials were impressed into distributing copies in an effort to evade the anticipated East German refusal to publish it. On 18 January, with Khrushchev pointedly absent, Wu Xiuquan went to the podium to read it out. The Chinese line was that everyone should pay more attention to deeds than to words, in order to be able to distinguish between false unification and actual splitting. Wu also expressed 'extreme regret' that the host party had chosen to use their congress as the occasion for attacking a fraternal party.

Provoked by Wu's criticisms of Yugoslavia, whose representatives were at the congress, the East German chairman repeatedly tried to cut Wu's speech short by ringing his bell, but Wu read on. The East German delegates, led by their senior cadres, tried to drown him out with shouts and whistles, stamping their feet and beating on their desks. When they finally subsided, Wu started up again, briefly departing from his text to say: 'You German comrades have done well for you've let us see your "civilization".' When the German interpreter failed to translate this unscripted comment, a German-speaking Chinese jumped into the breach, provoking another noisy outburst of barracking. In protest at this rudeness, the Chinese delegation took no further part in the proceedings except to attend the final session. When Khrushchev and Ulbricht entered, Wu and his colleagues refused to stand or applaud and at the end of the meeting they did not even wait to sing the *Internationale*. Wu's coolness under fire earned him good coverage in the foreign press and hearty appreciation from his Chairman.[133]

But despite this unprecedented public confrontation, on the key issue, Wu indicated the CCP willingness to talk to the CPSU after a suitable preparatory period. The running battle of the congresses later in 1963 notwithstanding, the CCP and the CPSU would sit down together in one last, futile effort to resolve their differences.

14 MAO IN CHARGE

As Mao reasserted control over the main lines of foreign and domestic policy in the second half of 1962, he began to assemble an informal *cabinet* to assist him, an *ad hoc* coalition of trusted supporters like Kang Sheng which would become a truly 'anti-party group' when the Cultural Revolution was launched. One reason given by Maoists for this extra-bureaucratic approach to that struggle, and accepted for the most part by contemporary foreign observers, was that the party machine was disloyal to the Chairman. It was no longer responsive to his commands; it no longer shared his vision.

Liu Shaoqi's quick surrender at the 10th plenum, in contrast to his modestly forthright performance at the Seven Thousand Cadres Conference, suggests that this explanation is simply incorrect. Nobody listening to Liu's performance at the plenum could have had any doubt that, despite his title as one of China's two Chairmen, despite the equal status accorded his photograph with Mao's on National Day, he was still the loyal lieutenant, coming quickly to heel when Mao cracked the whip. Zhou Enlai was even more deferential, allegedly servile.[1]

The role of CC plenums

Moreover, Mao was able not only to dominate his most senior subordinates, but also to ignore party procedures. The 10th plenum was the first formal meeting of the CCP's constitutionally supreme body which Mao had called in over eighteen months. It would be the last for four years. This pattern was quite different from the early years of the 8th CC.[2] In the three-year period from September 1956 to August 1959, the CC had met eight times, an average of almost three times a year. If one includes the 9th plenum in January 1961, the average was still two a year, in conformity with the CCP constitution.[3] During the next five-and-a-half years till the 11th plenum in August 1966, there would be only one.

While the lengthy gap between the 8th and 9th plenums might be explained by a combination of a focus on urgent economic problems and the Sino-Soviet dispute, the post-10th plenum was a period of

economic recovery during which the centre systematically and successfully set about restoring administrative order and resuming economic advance. Nor did the centre stop holding work conferences of
the type that normally preceded plenums. What accounts for this
change in the pattern of élite rule?

The answer must start with Mao. As Chairman of the CC, it was
his prerogative to summon that body. During his leadership of the
PRC, nobody else ever presided over a CC plenum. To judge by the
pattern that prevailed for most of the period from 1956 to 1961, Mao
saw the prime function of the CC as formalizing a consensus, arrived
at in the more free-and-easy, and perhaps rough-and-tumble,
atmosphere of the preceding work conference. Thereafter, everyone would notionally understand the centre's aims and policies, and
act in unison to fulfil them.

The 2nd plenum in November 1956 was held only six weeks after
the post-8th Congress 1st plenum, probably in order to allow the
CC to respond to rapidly moving events in Eastern Europe, most
importantly to agree the CCP's attitude towards the Hungarian
revolt and the subsequent disarray in the world communist movement.[4] Between the 2nd and 3rd plenums, there was the longest
inter-plenary gap of the first three years of the 8th CC, ten months,
almost certainly explicable by the difficulty in resolving the top-level
controversy over the rectification campaign and its subsequent
reversal.[5] With one unimportant exception, the average period
between plenums from the 3rd through the 8th was five months, very
close to the constitutional ideal.[6] The second session of the 8th Congress, preceded by the 4th and succeeded by the 5th plenums, articulated the consensus on launching the GLF hammered out at work
conferences in the first four months of 1958;[7] the 6th agreed the modifications to the GLF, again negotiated at earlier work conferences;[8]
the 7th formalized the nomination of Liu Shaoqi as head of state;[9]
and the 8th, after a particularly stormy work conference, ratified the
purge of Peng Dehuai, though that could not have been the original
aim.[10]

But though there is a sharp contrast between the constitutional
regularity of the first nine plenums, and the unconscionable delays in
summoning the 10th and 11th plenums, by dividing these meetings
in a different way, one can perhaps get a better insight into Mao's
behaviour. The 1st through the 7th plenums were consensus
plenums, as just discussed. But from the 8th through the 11th,
plenums were struggle sessions at which the CC was divided among

itself, and senior leaders got purged.[11] In this grouping, the 9th plenum was exceptional in harking back to earlier practices. Looked at through this prism, from the 8th plenum through the onset of the Cultural Revolution, formally launched at the 11th plenum, Mao summoned such meetings only when he felt able successfully to impose a settlement which he foresaw would cause considerable unhappiness. This in turn stemmed from the growing cleavage between Mao's vision and what he suspected his colleagues thought vital for the good of the country.

Mao's work practices

There is another way of looking at the way Mao ran the top institutions of the CCP in the early 1960s. In the mid-1950s, after the consolidation of the regime, the PRC had embraced Soviet-style systems and procedures; after all, the Soviet today was to be China's tomorrow. The Soviet constitution was examined and copied when the PRC's was being written.[12] A vast central economic and planning apparatus was created on the Soviet model.[13] The educational system aped the Soviet one.[14] Simple PLA uniforms were redesigned to give Chinese marshals and generals something of the heavy gilt appearance of their Soviet counterparts.[15] Even Soviet dietary strictures were faithfully adhered to. How much the Chairman chafed under this system he revealed during the GLF, when he revelled in what has been called a guerrilla style of running the country.[16]

In fact, an examination of Mao's private office indicates that even at the height of China's 'Soviet period', Mao personally maintained a system of rule that seemed better suited to Yan'an than to Beijing. Mao did not 'go to the office', but operated from his home, often from his bedroom, whether in the Zhongnanhai, in Hangzhou, or some other favoured provincial city, or on his special train. In Beijing in the mid-1950s, he resided in the Feng Zi Yuan complex in the Zhongnanhai, in which the main buildings were the Yi Nian Tang, which comprised a conference hall and smaller meeting rooms, and the Ju Xiang Shu Shi, which held his living quarters.[17] The mountain of officialdom came to Mahomet—except when he had a toothache.[18]

Mao had four political secretaries, though only Tian Jiaying was full-time and officially assigned to and paid for the job. Chen Boda and Hu Qiaomu had their other official responsibilities, but, as we have seen, were often called on by Mao to conduct investigations or to draft documents. Jiang Qing was the fourth secretary, also unofficial, and only employed by Mao to read material.[19] From time to time, Mao might take on a part-time 'secretary' on an *ad hoc* basis, like Li Rui during the first half of the GLF.[20]

Mao's access to information seems to have been equally haphazard. The first thing he always did on waking was to have one of his secretaries bring in the latest documents and materials which had arrived for him. These would normally have been pre-selected; sometimes the secretary would report on them orally or in writing.[21] Mao would normally read the *People's Daily* and the NCNA bulletins—though he often expressed dissatisfaction with the CCP's official organs[22]—and the local press when on tour; Jiang Qing culled the press for items to draw to his attention. There was no routine of daily formal presentations by Tian Jiaying or anyone else on national or international developments over the previous twenty-four hours, a strong contrast with the American system of a daily briefing of the president by the national security adviser, on the basis of a paper summarizing the findings of the various branches of the intelligence community.[23] The nearest equivalents were the various 'internal' reference materials, nominally a journalistic product of the NCNA,[24] much of which, however, consisted simply of reprints from the foreign press.[25] Mao told the Soviet ambassador in 1960 that he was brought two large volumes of 'routine information' on international affairs twice a day.[26]

The flow of official documents to Mao and other top leaders was controlled by the CC's General Office, directed by Yang Shangkun, an alternate member of the secretariat. Yang and his subordinates would decide to whom any particular document should go, depending on the responsibilities and interests of individual leaders. It was then up to Tian Jiaying and other political secretaries to decide which documents to put before their masters. In Mao's case, there was not a big flow of documents.[27]

Mao's guerrilla style

How then did Mao rule? First and foremost, by placing men he felt he could trust in charge of the major engines of bureaucratic power, the CCP, the PLA, and the government: Deng Xiaoping at the CC secretariat, Lin Biao over the PLA, and Zhou Enlai at the State Council. While Lin Biao's health, and probably his natural disposition, prevented him from exercising detailed daily supervision over the PLA, both Zhou and Deng had the talents and energy to run their operations efficiently, and Mao seems to have assumed that they and their subordinates would loyally report on problems to him as they arose.[28] The Chairman's perennial dilemma, however, was that, since he had no personal staff of experts to monitor the various departments, he often found himself at a disadvantage when presented with technical, especially financial, measures for approval, as he complained at Nanning in 1958 and at Beidaihe in 1962. It was an irritation he shared with at least some Chinese emperors.[29]

But Mao was far from being a remote imperial figure, passively awaiting bureaucratic input. The Chairman was passionately concerned with the problems of governing China. He personally sought information on his visits outside the capital, though the value of some of it may be doubted,[30] or, more effectively, through investigations by staff members, initiated by himself. When a major policy was in the making, as in the case of the Twelve-Year Agricultural Programme and the ten great relationships in 1956, the GLF and the communes in 1958, his investigations and interviews would become intensive.[31] His findings and the reports of his staffers would then provide the basis for a speech and/or a programme, as at Canton in 1961. Looked at through the prism of imperial Chinese practices, it was a use of 'inner court' officials to outflank procrastination or resistance on the part of the 'outer court' of the regular bureaucracy.[32] Looked at in terms of the Chinese revolution, it reflected a preference for guerrilla government over standard operating procedures.

Mao's communications[33]

When he was not presiding over a work conference, the Chairman's principal routine method of informing his colleagues of his views was by way of comments, *piyu*, on all kinds of documents sent to him. This imperial-style means of communication was used by him far more often, almost eleven times a month from 1949 through 1957, than speeches or articles.[34] He wrote most often about mass movements, the military, and provincial affairs, surprisingly seldom about agriculture, even when land reform and collectivization are included. His most productive periods were around the turn of the year, and his fallow ones were in the summer when he was normally at the annual work conference. While Mao's comment was often one indicating approval or disapproval, the problem which must sometimes have arisen for receiving officials was how to treat a document with a laconic message which might not fully indicate the Chairman's own opinion of the matter.

The CC secretariat

Mao's work style might have induced bureaucratic confusion had he not valued organization, at least for others.[35] In his absence, and with his authorization, his deputy Liu Shaoqi had the right to convene meetings of the PSC, Politburo, and all meetings centring on those bodies. Small Groups could be set up to tackle special tasks requiring supra-bureaucratic authority. The locus of authority was clear. Under Mao and Liu, and responsive to them, the CC secretariat had played the central role in the Chinese political process since the start of the GLF.[36] The 10th plenum confirmed that position.[37] Zhou Enlai may not have liked it but he never challenged it. Deng Xiaoping, though he appears less prominent than Zhou or Liu in the currently available Chinese sources, effectively ran China on a day-to-day basis.[38]

At the 10th plenum, in addition to Kang Sheng, Lu Dingyi, director of the CC's Propaganda Department, was made a secretariat member, clear evidence of the prospective importance of ideological issues, and PLA Chief-of-Staff Luo Ruiqing formally replaced his predecessor Huang Kecheng on that body.[39] Thus the secretariat was led by a member of the PSC, Deng Xiaoping, included four other Politburo members—Peng Zhen, Li Fuchun, Li Xiannian, and Tan Zhenlin—and now in addition, two Politburo alternates, Lu Dingyi and Kang Sheng. Military affairs clearly came under its aegis, since Deng Xiaoping was the only civilian member of the MAC other than Mao himself, and Luo Ruiqing was in executive charge of that body as its secretary-general.[40] With Chen Yun again voluntarily *hors de combat*, Li Fuchun and particularly Li Xiannian were the nation's chief economic officials. While the re-centralization of economic control in the aftermath of the GLF must have meant renewed importance for their concurrent roles as vice-premiers of the State Council, at least for policy *implementation*, the State Council does not seem to have recovered the centrality it had in the mid-1950s, and policy *formulation* was finalized in the secretariat.[41] Even Zhou Enlai felt obliged to sit in on meetings.[42]

Thus the issue for Mao in the early 1960s was the responsiveness of Liu and the secretariat to his wishes. There was no point in him issuing *piyu* if they were ignored. He had successfully cracked the whip over the State Council in 1958 and the PLA in 1959. Would he have to pursue similar tactics with the secretariat? He had rewritten the national agenda in the summer of 1962 and his colleagues had fallen into line, but would they follow through loyally? As the poem at the front of this volume indicates, in early 1963 Mao felt a surge of confidence and a sense of urgency about the need and possibility of ridding himself of his enemies. He knew that they existed in Moscow. The emerging question was: did they exist in Beijing? The first test was his latest campaign, the Socialist Education Movement.

APPENDIX 3: COMPARATIVE DICTATORIAL ROLES AND STYLES

Looked at from Moscow, Mao's work style represented a sharp departure from the practices of Lenin and Stalin. Both Soviet leaders had operated through bureaucracies, Lenin through the Sovnarkom or Council of Ministers, Stalin through the CPSU secretariat. Lenin, in sharp contrast to Mao, 'distrusted "spontaneity" ' and believed that 'every situation had to be approached with a preconceived plan and an organizational chart'.[1] Within three years of Stalin's appointment as General Secretary in 1922, he had built the CPSU secretariat into an organization of 767 full-time employees which became and remained the real centre of authority in the party.[2] While Mao accorded the much smaller CC secretariat the key role in the Chinese bureaucratic structure, it remained an instrument of his power rather than its locus.

Mao did not deign to be a mere general secretary, with the myriad bureaucratic routines the post demanded. He had a predilection for delving into Chinese history and literature or anything else that took his fancy and discussing them with intellectuals.[3] Knowing that he also spent long hours in dalliance,[4] Mao's colleagues might sometimes have wondered, as did Adolf Hitler's, when their leader actually worked. Hitler was more gregarious within a less intellectual circle, and on most days spent long hours at table in general conversation. But as their colleagues knew, for both Hitler and Mao such activities were periods of gestation not indications of sloth.[5]

Stalin, on the other hand, 'lived in only one dimension, and that was in his work. He was a slave to it',[6] and he ran the Soviet Union from his office in the secretariat.[7] Yet Stalin, like Mao and Hitler, left the capital for long periods, taking annual vacations in the south, two to three months in the 1930s, as much as four-and-a-half months in his later years.[8] Though he kept in touch with Moscow, this meant that Stalin, like the two other leaders, had to depend on trusted subordinates such as Molotov.[9]

Mao, unlike Stalin, disliked regular work routines and was indifferent to bureaucratic norms. While the CC never fulfilled its supposedly supreme role in either Stalin's CPSU or Mao's CCP, it is instructive that Mao summoned plenums far less frequently than Stalin—twenty-one in the twenty-seven years he ruled China compared with twenty-two during the nineteen years between Stalin's 'Congress of Victors' in 1934 and his death in 1953.[10] Mao was even less concerned with constitutional niceties than the Soviet dictator.

Mao had a greater scorn for planners and experts than Stalin, and felt a compulsion to reduce complex problems to elemental contradictions. His work style thus differed markedly from his Soviet precursors' and recalled, rather, the behaviour and attitudes of Adolf Hitler. The Nazi leader also distrusted experts, refused to entertain complexities, disliked regular work routines, and insisted that all problems could be solved if there were a will to do so. Indeed, Mao's work style might have induced the same bureaucratic confusion as existed in Nazi Germany as a result of the Führer's,[11] had the Chairman, too, believed that most problems took care of themselves as long as one did not stir them up.[12]

But unlike Hitler, until the Cultural Revolution Mao worked with, even if he railed at, an articulated bureaucratic structure. In China all leaders came together in the CC and Politburo, whereas in Nazi Germany, there was a debilitating institutional struggle between the principal organs of the party and government for hegemony or spheres of influence. This gave Hitler the decided advantage of being omnipotent. He was not just the head of both party and state, but was indeed the only clear link between the two machines and the arbiter between them.[13]

In some of their core beliefs, Hitler and Mao were similar. Unlike Stalin—who seems to have used struggle primarily as a means of subduing his opponents—but very much like Mao, Hitler believed in struggle as the essence of existence: 'Man has become great through struggle . . .' Struggle was 'the father of all things'. 'He who wants to live must fight and he who does not want to fight in this world where eternal struggle is the law of life has no right to exist.'[14] As is well known, Mao considered that 'a revolution is not a dinner party, or writing an essay, or painting a picture, or doing embroidery; it cannot be so refined, so leisurely and gentle, so temperate, kind, courteous, restrained and magnanimous. A revolution is an insurrection, an act of violence by which one class overthrows another.'[15] While Mao did not embrace Hitler's racist theories, and normally talked of struggle in class terms, his theory of uninterrupted revolution resembled Hitler's,[16] and his philosophical justification of class struggle indicates that he, like the Nazi leader, considered struggle to be fun-

damental to life: 'One divides into two. This is a universal phenomenon, and this is dialectics.'[17] Or as he put it more personally to his
doctor during the Cultural Revolution: 'I love great upheavals.'[18]

As striking is the shared belief of Mao and Hitler in the primacy of
will. Hitler of course derived his ideas on the subject from Schopen-
hauer and Nietzsche.[19] We now know that in his twenties, Mao also
absorbed the ideas of those Western philosophers, as well as others,
from a translation of Paulsen's *System of Ethics*.[20] As he put it in an
annotation to that volume:

> Everything that comes from outside [the truly great person's] original
> nature, such as restraints and restrictions, is cast aside by the great motive
> power that is contained within his original nature . . . The great actions of the
> hero are his own, are the expression of his motive power, lofty and cleans-
> ing, relying on no precedent. His force is like that of a powerful wind arising
> from a deep gorge, like the irrestible sexual desire for one's lover, a force
> that will not stop, that cannot be stopped. All obstacles dissolve before
> him.[21]

Even prior to that arresting statement, as his 1917 essay on physical
education shows, he had taken to heart the Confucian aphorism: 'If
one has an unbreakable will, there is nothing that cannot be accomplished.'[22] As the GLF and the Cultural Revolution demonstrated,
he never lost that faith in the power of 'the foolish old man who
removed the mountains'.[23]

Where Mao seems to have resembled Stalin more than Hitler was
in his growing paranoia over the years.[24] Hitler, by contrast, was the
unquestioned leader of the Nazi movement from its inception, no
one ever disputed his position, and he never felt any need to purge
the Nazi party because he feared a palace coup. Nor at any stage did
he face an ideological challenge; to the party rank-and-file, 'Adolf
Hitler is our ideology'.[25] Hitler *was* the Nazi revolution; it began and
ended with him, and it is impossible to conceive of it without him.
Despite Mao's dominance and the importance of his Thought, it was
not until the Cultural Revolution that the Chairman seemed about
to assume a comparable role.

15 THE SOCIALIST EDUCATION MOVEMENT

The militant policies which Mao revived at the 10th plenum were neatly summarized in the phrase: 'Oppose revisionism, prevent revisionism' (*fan xiu, fang xiu*).[1] The CCP stepped up its campaign to oppose revisionism abroad after the 10th plenum in its polemics in the *People's Daily* and through the activities of Wu Xiuquan on his East European odyssey. Khrushchev's ability to swing the majority of the world communist movement against China undoubtedly rankled with Mao, and embittered the relationship between the two men.

More importantly, in contemplating Khrushchev's Soviet Union, Mao had seen the future and found it worked in a manner totally unpalatable to himself; no longer would he want to hold up the 'Soviet Union today' as 'China's tomorrow'. Mao would seek a different destiny for China. So while the CCP struggled with the CPSU in the international communist movement, simultaneously Mao limbered up for an even more serious task: to prevent revisionism at home. His first effort was the Socialist Education Movement, which was still in progress in some areas when its far more ambitious successor, the Cultural Revolution, got under way three years later. The SEM would be the setting for his decisive break with Liu Shaoqi.

The four clean-ups and the five-antis

There had been no mention of plans for an SEM in the communiqué of the 10th plenum, only a stress on the long and tortuous class struggle which lay ahead as a result of attempts to abandon the socialist road. But the communiqué did recognize that the behaviour of lower-level leading cadres had alienated the masses and added that the CCP 'should endeavour to change this state of affairs and improve the work of those units without delay'.[2] In January, the *People's Daily* complained that

a number of production teams are not well run . . . The work styles of the cadres in these teams are not pure . . . The cadres themselves lack socialist consciousness, and they even manifest spontaneous capitalist tendencies . . .

Such cadres lack all awareness of serving the people . . . They do not actively participate in labour, and they are always thinking about eating more and owning more. They not only fail to listen to the opinions of the masses, but they also force their demands upon the masses . . .[3]

Documents from Lianjiang, a rural county near Fuzhou on the Fujian coast, gave concrete examples of such phenomena.[4] Cadres used their authority to get peasants to build them houses, purloining collectively owned bricks and wood. They gave parties at the drop of a hat, and expected monetary gifts from guests for weddings and birthdays. Collective funds were wasted on feasts, staging plays and operas, and pointless construction. A minority of cadres was financially very corrupt. 'Superstition'—religion—was embraced or at least tolerated.[5]

The Lianjiang documents indicate that in Fujian, measures were being taken before the end of 1962 to remedy such misbehaviour and to re-indoctrinate the peasants with socialist ideals in line with the decisions of the 10th plenum. Similar action was taken in Heilongjiang, Shandong, and Sichuan.[6] Mao visited eleven provinces in the aftermath of the plenum, but found only two officials who talked 'fluently and unceasingly' about socialist education: Wang Yanchun in Hunan and Liu Zihou in Hebei, both senior secretaries in their provincial party *apparats*.[7]

On 21 October, the Hunan provincial committee reported that three gusts of the 'wind' of individual operation (*dan'gan feng*)—in the spring and autumn of 1961 and the spring of 1962—meant that there were now over 25,200 teams, 5.5 per cent of the total, which had divided up their fields for individual operation; more were preparing to go down that road, though some were turning back. Apparently, in the new political atmosphere, 'individual operation' included the whole range of responsibility systems, including *baochan daohu*, and did not simply mean the division of fields among families. The standard for pinning this label was the key role of the household in production planning and agricultural tasks, and in labour and income distribution, and not simply the abandonment of collective ownership of the principal means of production, which in fact still prevailed in most of these teams. Nor was it just 'landlords and rich peasants' who had been keen on individual operations; poor peasants and cadres had also supported it, their faith in socialism shaken by the famine. The motive force was clearly the desperate need to restore production and get food to eat, and a belief that individual operation was the best way to achieve that goal.[8]

Hunan's solution was to attempt to reinstil faith in socialism among cadres and former poor peasants, and to use them as the spearhead to halt and roll back the advance of individual operation. Peasants were reminded of their grim pre-communist past and were implicitly threatened that unless they farmed collectively, they would get no government help in mechanizing.[9] The Hunan report predictably claimed successes.[10]

In Hebei province, in the winter of 1962, the Baoding district experimented with a rural 'four cleans' (si qing) campaign, the 'four small cleans' as it was later known, to try to lessen peasant anger at cadre behaviour.[11] An investigation group ordered the 'cleaning up' of team management of accounts, granaries, property, and work points, all areas in which cadre malfeasance or incompetence generated peasant dissatisfaction, and to do a better job of income distribution.[12] Elsewhere, there were experiments with 'three cleans', 'five cleans', and 'six cleans'.[13]

At a central work conference held from 11 to 28 February 1963, Mao pressed the Hunan and Hebei models upon other provinces, asserting that 'once class struggle is grasped, everything will be solved'.[14] He interrupted a speech by Liu Shaoqi to say that the key to preventing revisionism lay in the countryside,[15] and that since cadres could be bribed for three catties of pork or a few packs of cigarettes, only class struggle could prevent revisionism.[16] The conference authorized a four clean-ups campaign in the villages and a five-antis campaign (wufan yundong) in the cities. The targets of the latter were graft and embezzlement, speculative activities, extravagance, dispersionism, and bureaucratism.[17] As a quid pro quo for this intensification of class struggle, Mao agreed that the economic adjustment period should extend from 1963 through 1965.[18]

The meeting galvanized some laggard provincial committees.[19] By April, the four clean-ups campaign had got down to the county level in Henan.[20] The provincial committee had devised a three-stage process: three-level cadres' conferences at the county level, three-level cadres' conferences at the commune level, these two stages being designed to energize the educators for the third stage, mass education. The first stage lasted about twenty days and involved 150,000 cadres above the brigade level and was basically wound up in mid-April.

As befitted a province where leftism had been rampant during the GLF, the statistics sent to the centre by the provincial party gave evidence of the need for the ferocious class struggle desired by Mao:

over 100,000 cases of speculation and profiteering; over 1,300 counter-revolutionary group activities; over 26,000 instances of landlords and rich peasants opposing the government; 8,000 secret societies and religious groups; over 50,000 witches, sorcerers, and geomancers; over 10,000 cases of maintaining family rites; and over 50,000 cases of marriages involving financial transactions.

Most serious of all, many cadres participated and even took the lead in these activities. Between 50 and 60 per cent of all basic-level cadres were youngsters who had not been tempered in the class struggle of land reform, and so were unlikely to crack down on illegitimate behaviour. One example was a team in which, in 1960, nobody had been engaged in commerce; by 1962, there were eight people, and by April 1963 there were over eighty people doing business. The attendance rate for agricultural tasks had fallen to 10 per cent and the collective enterprise had almost collapsed.[21]

In Jiangsu, the provincial party proceeded at a more leisurely pace. It began discussing the implications of the February conference even before it had ended, but launched a five-antis campaign only after a further meeting in the second half of March. Its four clean-ups campaign began on 30 April.[22] In Heilongjiang, the provincial committee seems to have been even slower off the mark, launching a five-antis campaign only on 23 April.[23] The first phase involved the cleansing of party, governmental, and other units of Harbin and seven other major cities and lasted till August. Presumably corrupt cadres were dismissed or disciplined, though the difficulty the CCP had in bringing prominent offenders to book during anti-corruption campaigns in the 1980s and 1990s make one retrospectively wary of SEM statistics. The second phase, which lasted till the end of the year, spread the movement to the county level. Each phase of the campaign involved three stages: increasing production and being more economical; blending those tasks with opposition to waste and extravagance, and reforming systems; and finally, merging the first two stages into a mass struggle against corruption and speculation. In the course of the campaign, fifty-five enterprises in four cities, including Harbin, uncovered waste amounting to almost 103,000,000 yuan.[24]

The unplanned nature of the rolling process by which the SEM unfolded is illustrated by the behaviour of the Inner Mongolian party, under the leadership of Ulanfu, an alternate Politburo member. In response to the successive central initiatives, the local party held a series of meetings, a long one from 8 October to 3 November, another on 27 December, a third lasting ten days in March, and a fourth on 1 April, at each of which a new decision was taken.[25]

'Learn from comrade Lei Feng'

After goading the provinces into action at the February conference, Mao unsheathed a new weapon for the struggle against domestic revisionism. That same month, the editors of *Zhongguo Qingnian* (China youth), wrote informing the Chairman that they were about to publish an article extolling a selfless young PLA officer called Lei Feng and invited Mao to brush an appropriate slogan in his own calligraphy exhorting people to study Lei's example.[26] The request was passed to Mao by one of his secretaries, Lin Ke, amidst the daily pile of documents. Over the course of the next few days, the editors telephoned twice to find out the Chairman's decision. On the second occasion, Lin told them that Mao would do it; the Chairman had been impressed by the magazine's account of Lei Feng's actions and told Chief-of-Staff Luo Ruiqing that the young man was really worthy of study. The editors asked if Mao's slogan could be ready by 25 February for the magazine's 1 March issue. Mao asked Lin Ke to devise a number of possible slogans; on 22 February, he called him in to say that he had rejected Lin's ideas in favour of his own: 'Learn from comrade Lei Feng.'

The slogan duly appeared on 2 March in *Zhongguo Qingnian*, and on 5 March, it was republished in the *People's Daily*, *Jiefang Jun Bao* (the Liberation Army News), and the *Guangming Daily*. The following day, *Jiefang Jun Bao* published similar slogans written by Liu Shaoqi, Zhou Enlai, Zhu De, and Deng Xiaoping. Subsequently Chen Yun followed suit. On 13 March, *Jiefang Jun Bao* published a major editorial on how to be a good warrior for Chairman Mao by studying Lei Feng.[27] In this somewhat haphazard manner, the nationwide 'study Lei Feng' campaign was launched.[28]

Lei Feng turned out to be the first of a series of heroic figures, most of whom had perished in the service of their fellow citizens. Their diaries, mostly banal and naïve, expressed a new communist morality. Two of Lei Feng's entries capture their flavour

I felt particularly happy this morning when I got up, because last night I had dreamt of our great leader Chairman Mao. And it so happens that today is the Party's 40th Anniversary. Today I have so much to tell the Party, so much gratitude to the Party, so much determination to fight for the Party . . . I am like a toddler and the Party is like my mother who helps me, leads me, and teaches me to walk . . . my beloved Party, my loving mother, I am always your loyal son . . .

Sunday today. I didn't go out; instead, I washed 5 mattresses for the comrades in my squad, repaired Kao K'uei-yun's bedcover, assisted the cooks to wash more than 600 catties of cabbage, swept inside and outside the room, and other things . . . In all, I've done what I should have done. I'm tired but happy . . . It's glorious to be a nameless hero.[29]

The essence of the Lei Feng campaign was to encourage total loyalty, devotion, and obedience to Mao and the party at a time of crisis. Liu Shaoqi and the Chairman's other senior colleagues who wrote in honour of Lei Feng could not have realized that there would come a time when Mao would exploit that kind of subservience to destroy them.[30]

The Former Ten Points

Although Lei Feng was held up as a model during the SEM,[31] class struggle demanded sterner measures of cadres than washing cabbages, to wit, 'washing hands and feet' (*xi shou xi jiao*) and even 'taking a bath' (*xizao*), in short, ridding themselves of corrupt practices.[32] Mao followed up the February work conference by summoning another at Hangzhou from 2 to 12 May. As in the case of the 1961 Canton conference, it seems to have started as a brainstorming session between Mao and some regional leaders, but it swiftly escalated into a more significant meeting which included most of the top leadership.[33] Liu Shaoqi, however, was abroad during this meeting, paying state visits to Indonesia, Burma, Cambodia, and Vietnam.[34] For Liu, the trip was an opportunity to achieve the higher media profile hitherto reserved for Zhou Enlai and Mao himself. For the Chairman, Liu's absence was a chance to define the SEM without interference from the man whom he had placed in charge of the first front within the PSC. Not that Liu would have opposed Mao, but in his absence the Chairman could give the SEM his own spin without interference. Liu was so supportive of the document produced at the meeting that there was no hint that he and Mao would eventually differ over where the post-GLF problems lay, at the grass roots as Liu saw it, or at the top, as Mao did.[35]

The Hangzhou document, the 'Draft resolution of the CCP CC on some problems in current rural work', which became known as the Former Ten Points, was drafted and revised by Peng Zhen and finalized by Chen Boda, with Mao closely supervising and correcting at all stages,[36] on the basis of the twenty reports that had come in from Hunan, Hebei, Henan, Hubei, Shanxi, Zhejiang, and the northeast. Point 1 was an upbeat appraisal of the current agricultural situation to demonstrate the illegitimacy of past pessimism and the correctness of the three red banners. Point 2 recalled the conclusions of the 10th plenum and reaffirmed the correctness of Mao's call for class struggle. The sharpness of this conflict was due to continuing attempts by exploiters to make a comeback, as evidenced by sabotage, speculation, profiteering, the hiring of labour, the sale of land, and the re-emergence of religious, clan, and secret societies (Point 3). The gravity of the situation was increased by the failure of some cadres to appreciate it (Point 4). In undertaking class struggle in the rural areas, the CCP had to rely on the poor and the lower-middle peasants (Point 5)—thus resolving a question which had been on the agenda for millennia, according to Mao[37]—and such peasants should be organized into associations at the commune, brigade, and team levels (Point 7). Socialist education meant teaching the revolutionary history of individual communes and brigades, the history of agrarian reform and collectivization, as reminders of past oppression. There should be a three-stage process: training of cadres; training more cadres and village activists; and finally mass education (Point 6). Basing itself on the Baoding model, the Former Ten Points called for a rural 'four clean-ups' campaign, with the masses mobilized to check accounts, warehouses, properties, and work points. Education rather than punishment was the objective, physical punishment 'of any sort' being strictly prohibited, so that cadres especially could be made 'clean of hand and foot'; unity with 95 per cent of the cadres and the masses against the enemy was sought.[38] In his speech at Hangzhou, Mao asserted that this year the prohibition on executions would not be lifted, though this could be reviewed in 1964.[39] Cases of serious corruption, however, could be settled by legal means (Point 8), though Mao professed a desire for leniency where restitution was made.[40] Point 9 was a reaffirmation of the perennial call by the centre for all cadres to engage in manual labour; the seven Zhejiang documents distributed with the Former Ten Points, all pronounced very good by Mao, dealt with this issue. Without this therapeutic process, the Chairman asserted, revisionism would appear.[41] Point 10 was another reaffirmation, this time of investigation through 'squatting' (*dun*) in specific localities.[42] Many of these points were emphasized in the four speeches and the written comments Mao made at the Hangzhou meeting.[43]

Embedded in the Former Ten Points was a basic problem which haunted the SEM till it petered out: were the 'teachers' (the cadres) and the 'classroom' (the Chinese countryside) appropriate for the task of educating the peasants in socialism? Clearly, cadres had to be clean if they were to carry conviction, which is why the campaign was soon nicknamed the 'four clean-ups' and retained that sobriquet even after the content of the 'clean-ups' had changed. Prior to collectivization, cadres reminded peasants of the brutalities and financial extortions of the landlords and their KMT patrons; since collectivization, many cadres had become corrupt, and used their positions to dominate and sometimes beat the peasants, much as landlords had done. Mao mused openly in Hangzhou about whether some cadres were indistinguishable from those of the KMT.[44] Indeed, cadre cleansing proved eventually to be so massive and intractable an endeavour that it swamped the ultimate objective of peasant education.

But even if the 'teachers' had been clean, the educational environment was poor. Prior to the GLF, collectivization had been accepted in the countryside, willingly or grudgingly, as the wave of the future. Now clearly many peasants and even cadres had grave doubts about that vision, and responsibility systems had provided a glimpse of an attractive alternative. Prior to the famine, cadres could remind the peasants with conviction about the bad living conditions of the pre-communist period when individual farming was practised; but few of even the oldest peasants alive in 1963 could have experienced privation as terrible as the post-GLF famine. More fundamentally, the Henan data, however exaggerated, revealed that traditional social and economic practices were deeply embedded and quickly re-emerged when the socialist veneer cracked.

Rural socialist education campaigns had been Mao's customary remedy at times of political crisis—in the summer of 1957, after the Lushan conference in 1959, at the beginning of the second bitter year in 1960, and at the end of the third bitter year in 1961.[45] Song Renqiong, the 1st secretary of the Northeast region, assured Mao and the centre that the historical reminiscences of poor peasants were very effective in redirecting peasants to the socialist path,[46] and a great many 'recitals of bitterness' did take place,[47] though even Song acknowledged the difficulty of convincing younger peasants that the past was worse than the present.[48] In fact 'education' probably had little to do with the abandonment of responsibility systems throughout China. What mattered was that the centre had recovered its nerve and issued a clear directive, and that CCP cadres, from the regional level down to the teams, understood that unless they followed through on it, they would suffer. So long as cadres were again united and determined, peasant resistance was unavailing. But in the vast spaces of rural China, there doubtless remained significant pockets of some form of 'responsibility system'.

In a coda, the Former Ten Points quoted from Mao's recent directive 'of extraordinary importance':

Class struggle, production struggle, and scientific experiment are the three great revolutionary movements that build up a powerful socialist nation. They are a guarantee for the Communists to do away with bureaucratism, to avoid revisionism and dogmatism, to stand eternally invincible . . . Otherwise, the landlords, the rich peasants, the counter-revolutionaries, the bad elements and the evils would all come out; our comrades would do nothing about it, and many people would even resort to collusion without distinguishing friend from foe, and thereby allow the enemy to erode and invade, to divide and dissolve, to abduct and penetrate . . . If things were allowed to go on this way, the day would not be too far off—few years, over ten years, or few decades at the most—when the resurgence of a nation-wide counter-revolution becomes inevitable. It would then become a certainty that the Party of Marxism and Leninism would turn into a party of revisionism, of Fascism. The whole of China would then change color. Let all fellow comrades give it a thought. Isn't that a most dangerous situation!

. . . This Socialist Education Movement is a great revolutionary movement . . . This is a struggle that calls for the re-education of man. This is a struggle for reorganizing the revolutionary class armies for a confrontation with the forces of feudalism and capitalism which are now feverishly attacking us. We must nip their counter-revolution in the bud.[9]

Here, prefigured, was the apocalyptic vision which would inform the Cultural Revolution: the Manichaean opposition of the forces of light (socialism) and darkness (revisionism); the need for eternal vigilance, and the prospect of China going capitalist if the CCP and the masses dropped their guard; and, finally, the fundamentalist demand for the 're-education of man'.

There was, however, a crucial difference between what Mao was ordering at this point and what he attempted in the final phase of the SEM and in the Cultural Revolution. In the spring of 1963, the Chairman was still acting on the assumption, which he had held for most of the lifetime of the PRC, that China's future would be determined in the countryside. In 1956–7, mistakenly concluding that the rural problem had been solved by collectivization, he had transferred his emphasis to intellectuals as the engineers of the Soviet-style modernization programme which he had embraced. In 1958, let down by the intellectuals and placing his hopes for rapid development in the GLF on brawn rather than brains, he had returned to his more typical emphasis on the peasantry.[50] That emphasis suffused the Former Ten Points. But by January 1965, Mao would espouse an alternative view: the key to China 'changing colour' was whether or not there were 'capitalist-roaders' in the CC.

The Latter Ten Points

After the Hangzhou meeting, the five-antis movement proceeded in the cities, and by September had been completed in central party and government units.[51] In the countryside, provinces established rural socialist education experimental sites. Despite Mao's instructions to provincial leaders to take things easy, and the injunctions in the Former Ten Points to educate rather than punish and the strictures against struggle meetings, the SEM apparently became as harsh as previous rural campaigns. The data is limited, but by the end of February, even before the campaign was officially started, between seventy-six and ninety-seven people had died in Hunan, apparently mostly suicides, and there were many cases of beatings and other strong-arm struggle methods there and in Hubei. Between mid-May and mid-June, Peng Zhen toured Hebei, Jiangxi, Hunan, Guangxi, Yunnan, Guizhou, Sichuan, and Shaanxi and discovered similar problems there. In his report to Mao on 4 July, Peng said that apart from a few cases where landlord or corrupt elements had seized power and outside work teams were needed, local cadres could be trusted to run the movement. He warned against repeating the leftist mistakes committed in the old liberated areas of north China during land reform. The centre decided it had to take steps to prevent the situation from getting out of hand.[52]

Mao did not dispute that problems had arisen as a result of his clarion call,[53] but seems to have retired to the second front again, while his colleagues discussed how to fine-tune the SEM. Peng's report was discussed at a central work conference in September; under the supervision of Deng Xiaoping and Tan Zhenlin, Tian Jia-ying drafted 'Some concrete policy formulations of the CCP CC in the rural socialist education movement', which became known as the Latter Ten Points. On 5 October, after repeated revisions, Deng pronounced the draft satisfactory (*keyile*) and sent it to Mao. The Chairman seems to have discussed the draft in those regions with whose leading cadres he felt most comfortable—East China (Ke Qingshi) and Central-South (Tao Zhu and Wang Renzhong)—and returned it with comments to the Politburo.

Liu Shaoqi's role in this process seems to have been marginal and formal. In a confession at the outset of the Cultural Revolution, he disclaimed knowledge of the origins of the document:

How did this 'second 10-point decision' come into being? I did not know. *Only recently* have I learned that after the 'first 10-point decision' was made, Peng Zhen toured seven provinces. After his return he submitted a report to Chairman Mao, which provided the basic ideas for the 'second 10-point decision.' (Emphasis added)[54]

In the serious political situation in which he found himself in October 1966, Liu would hardly have made a statement revealing a haphazard PSC decision-making process if it were unfounded. His confession reveals how Mao-centred the party was. The Chairman had reasserted his role in the summer of 1962, and had made the SEM a personal initiative. Under these circumstances, it appears that the CC secretariat under Deng and Peng Zhen did not feel it necessary to channel all SEM documents through Liu. Their actions could not have been justified by Liu's absence on a state visit to North Korea which occupied less than two weeks in the second half of September.[55]

At any rate, on 31 October, Liu Shaoqi summoned a meeting of the Politburo and it approved a sixth draft which was submitted by Deng to Mao in Shanghai the next day. A subsequent draft was given to the Chairman on 4 November by Tian Jiaying. Finally on 14 November, a Politburo conference meeting under Liu gave its formal blessing to the document, which was then issued with Mao's permission; though he would later reveal resentment that his colleagues thought it necessary to amend his original document so soon after its promulgation, he had participated in drafting the new document.[56]

The Latter Ten Points was effusive in its praise for Mao, the SEM, and the Former Ten Points, which it described as

a great document with guiding authority . . . on the basic reconstruction of our Party in the ideological, political, organizational and economic aspects . . . Experiences gained in . . . spot-testings have amply proved that Comrade Mao Tse-tung's analyses and instructions on such problems as classes, class contradictions and class struggle in a socialist society, have great revolutionary and historic significance. They have also proved that this Socialist Education Movement, launched in accordance with Comrade Mao's instructions, has long-range and far-reaching significance in repulsing the frantic offensive of the once loudly aggressive imperialist and feudalist forces, in consolidating the position of rural socialist and proletarian dictatorship, in destroying the social basis from which revisionism stems, in consolidating collective economy, and in developing agricultural production.[57]

Conscious that the Latter Ten Points would shape the future course of the SEM, the drafters clearly were at pains to indicate to the Chairman that their intention was to adhere strictly to his guidelines.[58] Did they? Yes and no, because they were trying to fulfil conflicting guidelines.[59]

On the one hand, Mao envisaged the SEM as the first thoroughgoing class struggle in the rural areas since land reform.[60] Indeed, in so far as he blamed the relative smoothness of land reform in many areas for the ill winds blowing through the countryside,[61] the SEM would be the *first* such struggle to be truly nationwide. Both the Former and the Latter Ten Points acknowledged the unprecedented nature of the SEM.[62] And if a thorough land reform were the minimum standard, then the SEM would involve considerable upheaval.[63]

On the other hand, in the Former Ten Points Mao had adhered to his undertaking given at the 10th plenum not to launch a movement deleterious to production. When listing the SEM's aims, that earlier document had stated that they were 'all for the development of agricultural production'; and later it stipulated that the SEM process must be broken down into phases and sectors '[u]nder the condition that production not be deferred and that all undertakings be closely coordinated with production'.[64] The Latter Ten Points re-emphasized this position: 'At no stage of the Movement should production be affected.'[65] How these two fundamentally contradictory aims were to be reconciled was not Mao's department; he left tricky, nuts-and-bolts issues like that to his colleagues, reserving for himself the right of final approval. In this case, they handled it by spelling out with considerable care and at great length in the Latter Ten Points— it was over one-and-a-half times as long as the Former Ten Points[66]—the methods and approaches which cadres should employ in the SEM. It laid down twelve items of work, seven methods of leadership (with six subheads), four ways of distinguishing between class enemies, minor peculators, and peasants engaged in legitimate sideline occupations, five principles for organizing associations of poor and lower-middle peasants, five ways (with four subheads) for handling errant cadres, and eight standards to which post-SEM party branches should be held.[67]

In this thicket of clauses and sub-clauses, the drafters had to find a way of reconciling the anti-capitalist fervour which the SEM was supposed to unleash with the encouragement to private plots and free markets given by the Sixty Articles on Agriculture which had finally and formally been ratified at the 10th plenum. In laborious prose, the drafters ordered local cadres to distinguish between 'speculators and those peasants who show a more serious spontaneous capitalist tendency', between 'speculative activities and proper activities of marketing and trading, vending of a temporary nature, and small scale peddling', and between 'spontaneous capitalism and proper family sideline occupations'.[68] But as experienced party officials, they must have known that, in the last analysis, at the local level, judgements would be shaped by local power structures, family and other personal relationships or *guanxi*, and existing class status.[69]

In an attempt to limit the scope of local infighting, of which there were already signs, the Latter Ten Points emphasized the need to unite with over 95 per cent of the peasants and cadres, and indicated that only a tiny percentage of either group would be found to be counter-revolutionaries or serious criminals. One of the ten points was devoted to the handling of former landlords, rich peasants, counter-revolutionaries, and undesirable elements, and another to their children.[70] The key group was the rich peasants, from which both Mao and Liu had sprung, and which probably included the most dynamic elements in the countryside, vital for the revival of agricultural production. A separate point was devoted to the middle peasants, also entrepreneurial, whose definition was a thorny issue, dating back to 1933.[71]

But the Latter Ten Points was more successful in stirring up class struggle than in subduing local prejudice. Some 2,000 people died in the first group of Hubei experimental sites; within twenty-five days after the initiation of the province's second group, seventy-four people had died in Xiangyang district alone. In Guangdong, 602 people tried to commit suicide and 503 succeeded.[72]

Doubtless such figures would have been higher had the Latter Ten Points not enjoined cadres to exercise caution and prevent the SEM from getting out of hand. This was no longer the KMT countryside of the late 1940s and early 1950s, virgin soil to be upturned by the CCP because the class struggle of land reform was a crucial stage in the destruction of existing power structures. This was a CCP countryside, already devastated by famine, for which the CCP would continue to have responsibility after the SEM was over. That was why the SEM was 'even more complicated' than land reform and why the

Latter Ten Points said there would be no wholesale reclassification of peasant status, except under extraordinary circumstances.[73]

The most fundamental difference between the two sets of Ten Points was on the issue of leadership in the SEM. The Former Ten Points stressed, as Mao had done, that cadres at all levels had to take the issue of class struggle seriously and get involved in the SEM through which it would be conducted. But in that earlier document, the cadres actually appeared more as investigators, teachers, and facilitators than as leaders. For instance, in giving directions on how the four clean-ups should be conducted, point 8 stated that: 'Now the first thing to be done is to set the masses in motion.'[74] The projected poor and lower- middle peasant associations were put on a par with the SEM itself.[75] In the Latter Ten Points, on the other hand, '[t]he key to the questions of whether the Socialist Education Movement can be carried out smoothly, and whether the Party's policies can be carried out correctly in the Movement, *lies in the leadership*'[76] (emphasis added). The formation of peasant associations was put on the back-burner.[77]

If the masses were to play the leading role in the four clean-ups as the Former Ten Points decreed, this had to mean a process of 'open-door' rectification, with the masses participating in the criticism and self-criticism sessions at which 'four unclean' cadres were exposed. The Latter Ten Points had work teams of higher-level cadres providing leadership and conducting 'closed-door' rectification of erring CCP cadres, along with a few representatives of the poorer peasantry.[78]

The contradictions between the documents reflected differences between Mao and Liu which had surfaced in the 1957 rectification campaign in arguments over allowing outsiders to criticize members of the party.[79] Most CCP members abhorred the idea of being criticized by outsiders, be they bourgeois intellectuals or poor peasants. They knew only too well what might come up. This conflict was in turn rooted in the contrasting approaches to the conduct of revolution of Mao on the one hand and Liu and most of their colleagues on the other. Even at the outset of the GLF, at a time when Mao and Liu were on the same side, the Chairman preferred to unleash the energy of the masses, while his chief lieutenant opted for organized mobilization.[80] Mao believed in learning to make revolution by making revolution; in this case, the medium was the message. For his first-front colleagues, concerned to nurse the countryside back to health, careful CCP control of the SEM was vital to prevent it from getting out of hand. This difference of approach w3s later to provide the grounds for Mao's attacks on Liu and Deng at the outset of the Cultural Revolution.[81]

Later denunciations of the Latter Ten Points,[82] however, did not acknowledge that Mao had approved the document or that he could have rejected it at the time. His launching of the SEM and his swift reversal of a later SEM document of which he disapproved were proof that he had the power to override his colleagues. Probably, he was biding his time, waiting to see how the SEM would develop, beginning to assess his colleagues' fitness for the rew revolutionary upsurge he felt necessary. Perhaps more importantly, he was distracted by the split with the CPSU which had now come into the open and seemed irrevocable.

16 THE SINO-SOVIET RUPTURE AND THE VIETNAM WAR

The East German party congress in January 1963 had been followed by series of polemics, emanating mainly from Moscow, Beijing, and Tirana. During a three-month period from the end of 1962, Beijing alone issued eight major broadsides.[1] About the only point of agreement between the CPSU and the CCP in these exchanges was that the situation was critical. The Russians referred to serious differences on 'cardinal issues of policy,' while the Chinese declared that the world communist movement was 'in more and more serious danger of a split'. Both sides maintained the façade of discretion by not attacking each other directly, but there was no doubt about their targets, especially since the *People's Daily* reprinted Albanian articles which excoriated Khrushchev by name. To justify their refusal to accept the Soviet leader's suggestion to suspend polemics, Beijing characterized it as a device to muzzle the CCP while allowing the CPSU free rein.[2]

A major focus of the rival polemics was Yugoslavia. Tito's visit to Moscow and the invitations to the Yugoslavs to send delegations to the East German and Italian party congresses were clearly in violation of the agreement hammered out at the 1960 communist summit in Moscow, in which the 'Communist Parties have unanimously condemned the Yugoslav variety of international opportunism, a variety of modern revisionist "theories" in concentrated form'. The 1960 Moscow statement stigmatized the 'Yugoslav revisionists' as carrying on 'subversive work against the socialist camp and the world Communist movement'. Further exposure of the 'leaders' (i.e. Tito) of the Yugoslav revisionists, the document stated, was to 'remain an essential task of the Marxist-Leninist parties'.[3]

The Chinese now argued that a party's attitude towards the Yugoslav question represented a choice: 'whether to adhere to Marxism-Leninism or to wallow in the mire with the Yugoslav revisionists . . . whether genuinely to strengthen unity or merely to pay lip-service to unity while in fact creating a split.'[4] The Soviet reply amounted to a plea for treating Tito as a prodigal son, asserting that the world communist movement had set itself the goal of helping the Yugoslav communists to correct their errors. For good measure, *Pravda* quoted earlier pro-Yugoslav Chinese utterances.[5]

Apart from reiterating some long-held positions in the dispute,[6] Beijing furiously attacked the CPSU for exercising hegemony over fraternal parties. By stressing the importance of revolution in the Third World, the CCP implicitly staked out its own claims for leadership of the world communist movement. In response to Khrushchev's provocative remarks the previous December about China's failure to recover Hong Kong and Macao, the *People's Daily* listed all Chinese territories lost as a result of 'unequal treaties' imposed by imperialist nations during the nineteenth century, including those parts of Soviet Central Asia and the Soviet Far East which had been acquired by the tsars. The paper hinted that any more sarcastic jibes on the part of Khrushchev would result in the Chinese demanding a renegotiation of the Sino-Soviet border.[7]

Sino-Soviet negotiations

The resumption of Sino-Soviet polemics perturbed many fraternal parties, who viewed a prospective split between Moscow and Beijing as extremely damaging to the world communist movement and to themselves. They lobbied for a meeting at which the CPSU and the CCP could try to reconcile their differences. Both parties eventually acceded to these pleas, if only to gain support by showing willing.[8]

The CPSU made the first gesture with an invitation to the CCP to hold bilateral talks, preparatory to another world communist conference. When the Soviet ambassador handed the letter to Mao on 23 February, the Chairman suggested that Khrushchev come to Beijing for an exchange of views.[9] The official CCP reply, which Deng Xiaoping handed to the ambassador on 9 March, welcomed the proposal for talks and repeated Mao's invitation.[10] On 30 March, the CPSU diplomatically contrasted Khrushchev's three visits to China with Mao's two visits to the Soviet Union, and made a countersuggestion: Mao should make the tour of the Soviet Union for which he had long expressed a desire. But whoever led the CCP delegation, the talks could take place around 15 May in Moscow.[11]

This Sino-Soviet correspondence was not simply concerned with debating points about who should lead the other's delegation. Only the first Soviet letter made even a pretence of attempting to reduce tension; the other letters were further polemics, restating hardened positions, the Chinese with particular sharpness.[12] The CCP reply to the CPSU letter of 30 March, drafted by a team led by Chen Boda, was entitled 'A Proposal Concerning the General Line of the International Communist Movement',[13] and represented the Chinese negotiating position, which Beijing had taken the precaution of discussing with the leaders of sympathetic fraternal parties, such as Kim Il Sung and Ho Chi Minh, prior to finalization.[14] The Russians refused to publish it, claiming it was too inflammatory, though one Soviet official later opined that Khrushchev's real concern was fear of being accused of departing from Marxism-Leninism.[15] When Chinese diplomats and students tried to distribute the 'Proposal', they were expelled from the Soviet Union and the display cabinets in front of the Chinese embassy were smashed by Russian youths.[16] But after further exchanges on dates, it was agreed that Deng Xiaoping, Peng Zhen, Kang Sheng, Yang Shangkun, Liu Ningyi, and the inevitable Wu Xiuquan would go to Moscow to hold talks with a Soviet delegation led by Suslov and including Andropov.[17]

The Moscow talks

When the Chinese delegation left for Moscow at 7.30 a.m. on 5 July 1963, every major Chinese leader except Mao was there to see them off.[18] A disgruntled ally, Enver Hoxha, confided to his diary: 'The delegation . . . was given a pompous farewell in Peking as if it were going to a wedding, while in Moscow it had an icy reception like a funeral. We shall see what this worthless, formal meeting will yield . . . What result can be achieved in talks with the Khrushchevite traitors . . .'[19] A few days later, Hoxha recorded that Foreign Minister Chen Yi had told the Albanian ambassador that the Moscow talks might be broken off but continued later. While Chen evidently made critical comments about Khrushchev, the Marshal affirmed that it was important to prevent him from 'going over to the imperialists', an argument which, as Hoxha disgustedly noted, replicated the Soviet justification for their courtship of Tito. Hoxha criticized the Chinese for vacillating, being unclear on their tactics, and often intimidated by pressure from the Soviets, suggesting that, despite Albania's 'lips and teeth' alliance with China, he was out of the loop of fraternal communists whose advice was heeded in advance of the meeting.[20] While the Chinese may have welcomed the unrestrained diatribes which Tirana fired at Moscow, they probably treated Hoxha like a loose cannon who might easily damage China's interests in his search for greater security for his isolated Balkan fastness.

Nevertheless, Hoxha's intuitions cannot be ignored. Despite the CCP's unyielding public statements, a split with the CPSU was a massive step for Beijing to contemplate, with a potential for highly damaging repercussions: the breakup of the world communist movement, in which Mao and his colleagues had enlisted so hopefully forty years earlier, and the loss of the Soviet nuclear shield against the United States. Even after the bitter hostilities of 1960, there must have been some other CCP leaders who, like Wang Jiaxiang felt that China's aim should be to improve relations with the CPSU, not to break with it. It would hardly have been surprising if even the Chairman had wanted to keep his options open until he judged that the point of no return had been reached. The Chinese negotiating team was instructed to give appropriate ripostes to Soviet attacks, but to work with the 'utmost patience and effort' to achieve unity with the CPSU on the basis of Marxism-Leninism and internationalism.[21]

Compromise would have been hard to reach under the best of circumstances, but it was well-nigh impossible with the unremitting exchange of diplomatic grapeshot outside the conference room.[22] Inside, there was a 'dialogue of the deaf'.[23] From the first meeting on 6 July, each side simply reaffirmed its own position and denounced the other's. Each attack was followed by a counter-attack. There was no common ground from which to set forth on a search for solutions. The choreography of the sessions fell quickly into a pattern: one side would bring in a prepared statement; this would be read out by a senior member of the delegation; with translation, two or three hours would elapse.[24]

Right from the outset, the talks assumed their own unique rhythm and form. They consisted of endless unilateral declarations intended, first, to rip the other side to shreds and, second, to defend one's own case and Marxist orthodoxy. The Soviet representative would get up and read his statement, and other members of the delegation would add their own statements, which had been orchestrated beforehand.[25]

The session would then be closed, and the other side would plunge into a bout of feverish activity, analysing what it had heard and constructing a reply. This would be read out at the next session and the cycle began again.[26] The speakers at the substantive sessions were: 6 July, Suslov; 8 July, Deng; 10 July, Suslov; 12 July, Deng, and, at the fifth session later the same day, Ponomarev; 15 July, Peng Zhen; 17 July, Andropov; 19 July, Kang Sheng.[27] The only benefit of this process, according to Wu Xiuquan, was that each side had the opportunity to explain its position in full.[28]

Grounds for divorce

As the meetings droned on, staff members of the Soviet delegation were suddenly called on to draft speedily a reply to the twenty-five-point CCP 'Proposal concerning the general line of the international communist movement'. 'This lengthy document was written in record time. We worked in the Central Committee building for about thirty hours straight and handed in the draft, page by page, to the secretaries of the Central Committee for editing.'[29] On 14 July, the CPSU published its response, and comparison of the two documents made it possible even for those outside the conference room to see how far apart Moscow and Beijing still were. As ever, the issues were framed in the language of Marxism-Leninism and were supported, at least on the Chinese side, with numerous quotations from the classics, but the substance concerned issues of foreign policy and intra-bloc politics.

The twenty-five-point Chinese 'proposal' was a catalogue of the issues in dispute that had emerged over the previous seven years, laid out as a series of propositions:

- There had to be a general line for the international communist movement, based on the use of Marxist-Leninist theory to analyse the fundamental contradictions in the world, as in the joint Moscow statements of 1957 and 1960.[30] This implied that there had to be an agreed bloc foreign policy, which meant that the Chinese would have a veto on Soviet attempts to improve relations with the United States.
- While the balance of forces between socialism and capitalism had altered in favour of the former since World War II, American imperialism was pursuing aggression and war world-wide;[31] in other words, the increased size of the bloc did not ensure victory, which still had to be struggled for.
- Various types of contemporary contradictions were concentrated in Asia, Africa, and Latin America, and were displayed, for instance, in liberation struggles: 'In a sense, therefore, the whole cause of the international proletarian revolution hinges on the outcome of the revolutionary struggles of the people of these areas, who constitute the overwhelming majority of the world's population.'[32] This was evidently part of the CCP's continuing effort to refocus Moscow's attention away from the bilateral struggle with the United States towards an area in which the CCP could claim far more expertise.

- If communist party leaders adopted a non-revolutionary line, they would be deposed by true Marxist-Leninists;[33] it was of course to see if this was what had happened in Moscow that the CCP would send Zhou Enlai there in the wake of the ouster of Khrushchev eighteen months later.
- The way to secure world peace was through struggle, not appeasement or naïve calls for universal disarmament.[34]
- The emergence of nuclear weapons did not alter the necessity for social and national revolutions, nor the relevant principles of Marxism-Leninism;[35] peaceful coexistence between states with different social systems did not mean an end to struggles for national liberation or the transition from capitalism to socialism and it was the duty of communist countries to support and assist the struggles of oppressed peoples and nations;[36] in other words, the Russians should not use the threat of a nuclear holocaust to soft-peddle revolutionary struggles in the Third World.
- Class struggle and the dictatorship of the proletariat persisted long after the creation of a communist state, and 'states of the whole people' and 'parties of the whole people' (as mentioned in the latest CPSU programme) were bourgeois concepts.[37]
- Attacks on the personality cult (i.e. de-Stalinization) had been transformed into a device to force fraternal parties to change their leaders.[38]
- Differences between fraternal parties, as in the Soviet–Albanian case, should be settled through intra-party consultation, not through public attacks at party congresses;[39] revisionism or right opportunism (i.e. Yugoslav ideas), not dogmatism (as the Russians characterized Chinese ideas), was the main danger to the international communist movement.[40]
- And finally, in the intra-bloc debate, the CPSU should publish Chinese polemics just as the CCP published Soviet ones.[41]

The Soviet reply of 14 July, couched in the form of an open letter from the CPSU CC to all Soviet communists, accused the CCP of 'arbitrary' interpretations of the 1957 and 1960 Moscow statements, and rejected 'groundless and slanderous' CCP attacks on the decisions of the CPSU's 20th, 21st, and 22nd congresses.[42] The open letter reminded readers of Soviet assistance to the Chinese revolution and economic development, and then proceeded to detail Chinese anti-Soviet and splittist activities in the international communist movement.[43] The CCP's 'Proposal' was an example, and the CPSU had refused to publish it because that would have necessitated a reply, which in turn would have exacerbated relations![44]

The letter then turned to the substance of the differences between the two parties. Perhaps to account for the sparseness of theoretical justifications in Soviet polemics, the letter derided the CCP's resort to what it called verbal 'camouflage', through which 'it might appear to the outsider that the controversy has acquired a scholastic nature, that it concerns individual formulas, far removed from vital issues. In point of fact, however, the controversy centres on issues affecting the vital interests of the peoples.'[45] These vital issues were:

• war and peace;
• the role and development of the world socialist system;
• the struggle against the personality cult;
• the strategy and tactics of the world labour movement; and
• the national liberation struggle.[46]

On a number of these issues, the open letter reaffirmed the Soviet position and hinted at ulterior motives for the Chinese theoretical assertions. On the personality cult, for instance, the open letter asserted that it was hard to ascertain why the CCP supported it: 'In effect, this is the first time in the history of the international communist movement that we meet with open extollation of the personality cult. It should be observed that even at the height of the personality cult in our country, Stalin himself was forced, at least in words, to reject this petty-bourgeois theory . . .'[47] The reader was obviously meant to draw the conclusion that the CCP position arose out of a need to protect the Mao cult in China. Elsewhere, the CCP's emphasis on armed struggle as the only route to revolution and its focus on Asia, Africa, and Latin America was alleged to be designed to win easy popularity in the Third World and to isolate national liberation movements from the international working class and the socialist world system, that is, the Soviet Union.[48]

But in fact the heart of the dispute was still the issue of war and peace. The open letter reaffirmed the line which Khrushchev had taken since the CPSU's 20th Congress in February 1956, which the Chinese had endorsed at the time.[49] The advent of nuclear weapons had led to a 'radical, qualitative change of the means of waging war': 'These weapons possess unprecedented destructive power. Suffice it to say that the explosion of only one powerful thermonuclear bomb surpasses the explosive force of all the ammunition used during all previous wars, including the first and the second world wars. And many thousands of such bombs have been accumulated.'[50] The Russians and their East European allies had been appalled at Mao's speech in Moscow in 1957[51] (from which they quoted in their 'Open Letter' without attribution), and Khrushchev had been extremely worried that the Chinese bombardment of offshore islands in the 1958 Taiwan Strait crisis could escalate into a Soviet–American confrontation. China's behaviour on the Indian border, and Beijing's propaganda about the Caribbean crisis,[52] had confirmed him in the view that Mao was a dangerously ignorant warmonger, who had no time for peaceful coexistence,[53] and would like nothing better than to involve the Soviet Union in a nuclear exchange with the United States, from which only the Chinese with their vast population would benefit. That had been why, in 1959, Khrushchev had cancelled his defence agreement with the Chinese and reneged on his undertaking to supply the Chinese with a sample atomic bomb.[54] These fears surfaced again in the open letter:

The Chinese comrades . . . frankly say: 'On the ruins of destroyed imperialism,' in other words, as a result of the unleashing of war, 'a beautiful future will be built'. . . . Apparently those who describe the thermonuclear weapon as a 'paper tiger' are not fully aware of its destructive power . . . The atomic bomb does not distinguish between imperialists and working people, it strikes at areas, so that millions of workers would be killed for every monopolist destroyed . . .

The way the Chinese comrades present the question can arouse legitimate suspicion that this is no longer a class approach to the struggle for the abolition of capitalism, but that there are entirely different aims. If both the exploiters and the exploited are buried under the ruins of the old world, who will build the 'beautiful future'? The fact cannot pass unnoticed in this connection, that instead of the class, internationalist approach expressed in the slogan 'Workers of all countries, unite!' the Chinese comrades stubbornly propagate a slogan deprived of all class meaning: 'The wind from the East prevails over the wind from the West.'[55]

When Mao used the terms East Wind and West Wind, he had of course included the whole of the Communist bloc within the East Wind, but here the Russians were deliberately misinterpreting his words to hint that he lumped the Russians within the West Wind and that the East Wind consisted only of China.

Despite this robust rejection of Chinese views, the CPSU's own position contained contradictions stemming from ambivalences and differences of opinion within the Soviet political and ideological establishments. These meant, according to one Soviet official who helped draft the Soviet reply, 'it was not all that difficult for Maoist propaganda to intimidate us and force us onto the defensive, causing us to adopt inconsistent or simply erroneous stands'.[56] On the one hand, the CPSU reply boldly stated for the first time that 'the atomic bomb does not draw class distinctions', but a few paragraphs further on proclaimed in almost CCP language that '[i]t stands to reason, of course, that if the imperialist madmen unleash a war, the peoples will sweep away capitalism and bury it'.[57]

The test-ban treaty

The strong CPSU reaffirmation of the dangers of nuclear war and the necessity of peaceful coexistence with the United States may have been permitted by a dramatic recent change in the Soviet leadership. On 11 April, Frol Kozlov had been removed from the political scene by a severe stroke or heart attack, twenty-four hours after he had summoned a meeting of the CPSU Presidium in Khrushchev's absence amidst rumours that the latter's resignation was being plotted.[58] Kozlov's support for Khrushchev against the Chinese on earlier occasions had been critical in demonstrating to them that the Soviet leadership was united against them,[59] but he was more hawkish on Soviet–American issues than the Soviet 1st secretary, and had he prevailed in the spring of 1963, Beijing might have benefited from a deterioration of relations between Moscow and Washington. Certainly Kozlov's absence made an immediate difference to Khrushchev's dealings with President Kennedy. Soviet policy softened considerably.[60]

Coincidentally, four days after Kozlov was struck down, Kennedy and British Prime Minister Harold Macmillan had addressed a joint letter to Khrushchev in an effort to revive the stalled negotiations on a nuclear test-ban treaty.[61] A principal concern of the Western allies was to try to prevent the Chinese acquiring nuclear weapons. In January 1963, Kennedy had told André Malraux, President de Gaulle's Minister of Culture, that a nuclear China would be the 'great menace in the future to humanity, the free world, and freedom on earth'; the Chinese 'would be perfectly prepared to sacrifice hundreds of millions of their own lives' for the sake of their 'aggressive and militant policies', for they attached a 'lower value' to human life.[62] The American administration hoped that a test-ban would strengthen Moscow's own efforts to head off China's nuclear programme.[63] Despite some harsh language, possibly designed to shore up his domestic position, Khrushchev's reply to the Western initiative on

8 May was positive.[64] There was a further exchange of letters, sufficiently encouraging for Kennedy to make a major 'peace speech' at
American University on 10 June, announcing that new high-level
test-ban talks would begin soon in Moscow. Khrushchev described it
as 'the best speech by any President since Roosevelt'; an American
historian has described it as the best of Kennedy's life.[65] In this suddenly mellower atmosphere, it was perhaps less of a coincidence that
the CPSU engaged in feverish activity in order to be able to publish
its open letter attacking the Chinese one day before Averell Harriman, a diplomat with long experience of dealing with the Russians,
and Lord Hailsham, a British cabinet minister, arrived in Moscow on
15 July for the test-ban negotiations.[66] On 20 July, the CPSU and
CCP delegations reached their one agreement: to adjourn their talks
sine die. The Chinese delegation left Moscow the same day, arriving
in Beijing on the 21st. This time even Mao turned up with all his
senior colleagues to demonstrate Chinese unity in the face of Soviet
revisionism. From the airport, the delegation was whisked immediately to the Zhongnanhai to give Mao and Zhou (but apparently not
Liu Shaoqi) a detailed briefing.[67]

The partial test-ban treaty was initialled by Gromyko, Harriman,
and Hailsham in Moscow on 25 July.[68] Immediately afterwards,
Harriman raised the question of Chinese nuclear weapons privately
with Khrushchev, but the Soviet leader could not afford to be forthcoming, especially without the French acceding to the treaty.[69] The
Chinese, however, were well aware that the treaty was designed to
freeze them out of the nuclear club.[70] It was the last straw. From now
on they would exert all their efforts in the international communist
movement and its front organizations against the CPSU and direct
the full force of their propaganda machine into open denunciations
of Khrushchev and his allies. The Sino-Soviet alliance had collapsed.[71]

The struggle in the world communist movement

The protagonists in the Sino-Soviet dispute now sought to rally supporters and neutrals to their side. The CPSU, long accustomed to
leading the world communist movement, had a natural advantage.
In Europe, apart from Albania, where Zhou Enlai paid a morale-
boosting visit in January 1964,[72] only in the Belgian party did a significant section of the leadership break away to form a pro-Chinese
faction. But the very existence of the dispute meant that parties, particularly outside the East European bloc, had greater freedom of

manoeuvre than before, particularly those which normally supported the CPSU but did not share its determination to declare the
CCP beyond the pale. Even within Eastern Europe there were more
options, which Romania at least began to exploit.[73]

In Asia, the CPSU could rely on the Mongolian and Indian parties, but the North Korean, North Vietnamese, Indonesian, and
Japanese parties, because of their own circumstances, preferred the
CCP's position on bloc policy towards America. The CCP's advantages over the CPSU in the Third World were particularly notice-
able in international front organizations, particularly when centred
on Asia and Africa; many bitter battles for influence were fought, to
the growing irritation of non-communist participants who objected
to becoming pawns in the Sino-Soviet dispute. Castro attempted to
maintain neutrality, but Cuba's economic dependence on the Soviet
Union made that an increasingly untenable position.

A key issue in the movement became whether or not to hold a new
international communist conference. In the Soviet view, this would
be the culmination of its campaign formally to declare the CCP
heretical and cast it out of the movement. The CCP leaders, who had
campaigned for such a conference as an opportunity to spread their
views within the movement before the dispute became public, now
opposed the idea, realizing that the inevitable Soviet success would
result in their marginalization as everyone realized how narrow was
their base of support. They were helped by some pro-Soviet parties
even after the polemics had become public, which used their new-
found influence to drag their feet on the conference proposal, precisely because it would bring the curtain down on the era of the
single world movement.[74]

The Sino-Soviet struggle was not confined to the communist movement and its fronts, as both sides attempted to build broader support
among sympathetic Third World nations. China's major effort was to
send Premier Zhou and Foreign Minister Chen Yi and several dozen
aides on a ten-nation tour of Africa,[75] which lasted seven weeks from
mid-December 1963 to early February 1964. While Zhou Enlai
impressed many of his hosts personally, some of whom had never
entertained so distinguished a visitor, he signally failed to convert any
of them to China's position on the test-ban treaty or the Sino-Indian
border dispute. The premier sought allies against both the West and
the Soviet Union, but while attacks on imperialism were well-
received in some quarters, the promotion of self-reliance was hardly
likely to appeal to countries heavily dependent on Western or Soviet

aid, and the concept of Africa as a storm centre, 'ripe for revolution', which he articulated at the end of his tour, may have been taken as threatening by uneasy rulers who had already made as much revolution as they thought necessary.[76]

The Chinese propaganda war

While Zhou was thus somewhat inhibited in what he could say, the mouthpieces of the CCP were not. As early as 1960, the CC had set up a five-man team at the VIP Diaoyutai guest-house complex to work on the anti-Soviet polemics published that year; it included Kang Sheng as leader; Wu Lengxi, the chief editor of the New China News Agency (NCNA) and the *People's Daily*; Wang Li, of the CC's International Liaison Department; Yao Qin, a deputy director of the CC's Propaganda Department; and Fan Ruoyu, a deputy chief editor of *Red Flag*, the party's main theoretical journal.[77] Building on this precedent, the CCP had been preparing for a renewed anti-Soviet propaganda campaign since just after Chinese New Year, 1963.[78] The best ideologists from all over China, about 120 in all, were brought to Beijing, where they were housed in the Eighteen Buildings Compound, another guest-house complex built in the western suburbs in the 1950s.[79] They were given special treatment, and, most importantly in those Spartan times, were served very good food. Some were allowed to bring their families. One winter's evening, some 400–500 people connected with the operation were treated to an entertainment at Diaoyutai where Kang Sheng, again in charge, was in residence. Even their regular manual labour assignment was a sort of a privilege, for their chore was merely to clear the grounds of the Liu Suo, a nearby six-building complex for members of the PSC.[80]

Eight groups were formed, each under the leadership of a different unit; the *People's Daily* was in charge of one, *Red Flag* of another, and so on. The responsible unit chose the group members, though not necessarily from among their own cadres. The *People's Daily* group had members from the PLA, a provincial party school in one province, and a propaganda bureau in another, as well as from the paper itself. The eight group leaders formed a leadership committee, responsible to Kang Sheng, who had effectively replaced Wang Jiaxiang as the head of the CC's International Liaison Department.[81]

Each group was assigned the preparation of a polemic on a specific topic: 'The origin and development of the differences between the leadership of the CPSU and ourselves'; 'On the question of Stalin'; 'Is Yugoslavia a socialist country?'; 'Apologists of neo-colonialism'; 'Two different lines on the question of war and peace' (assigned to the *People's Daily* group); 'Peaceful coexistence—two diametrically opposed policies'; 'The leaders of the CPSU are the greatest splitters of our times'; 'The proletarian revolution and Khrushchev's revisionism'. Later, the ninth and most important polemic was added: 'On Khrushchev's phoney communism and its historical lessons for the world'. At one point a tenth was planned.[82]

To prepare the polemics, each group was divided into teams. Four teams were charged with compiling books of relevant citations—from Mao, from Marxism-Leninism, from the imperialists, and from old and new revisionists—on the group's topic; in all over three-dozen books were prepared. A fifth team drawn from these four was then formed to check all the quotations. Altogether, about forty books were produced. Those on the old and new revisionists—Kautsky, Bernstein, Gramsci, Trotsky, Bukharin, and the theoreticians of contemporary Soviet Union, Eastern Europe, and Yugoslavia—were published internally and were known as the 'grey paperbacks' (*hui pi shu*).

This raw material was woven by the writing teams, composed of the more senior cadres in the groups, into their assigned polemics. Each polemic was vetted by the group leader, Kang Sheng, CC propaganda director Lu Dingyi, Deng Xiaoping, and finally by Mao himself. The nine polemics were published between 6 September 1963 and 14 July 1964, and the groups were finally disbanded in the autumn of the latter year.[83]

The whole operation was an immense labour of orthodox piety for which the Russians no longer had the manpower, the talent, or the inclination. The nine polemics, plus the CPSU letter of 30 March 1963, the CC's reply of 14 June (the 'proposal'), the CPSU's 'open letter' of 14 July, and a CCP comment on Khrushchev's fall in October 1964, filled a 585-page English-language book, *The Polemic on the General Line of the International Communist Movement.*

Even at the time, this was a largely pointless exercise, an intra-movement ideological GLF doomed to failure from the start. Few CCP theoreticians, let alone the Chairman himself, could have supposed that the dextrous juxtaposition of some well-chosen quotes from the classics would convince the targets of the polemics to change their policies. The issue of national survival in the nuclear age was too important for that. Rather, Mao was raising a banner of revolutionary Marxism-Leninism to replace Moscow with Beijing as the new Rome of the wretched of the earth, and to make himself the latest in the line of apostolic succession from Marx through Stalin. He hoped initially to rally to his side the communists and some nationalists of the Third World, and later Russians and East Europeans, once they had dispensed with their revisionist leaderships. Little did he realize that when the disgruntled peoples of the Soviet bloc took that course a quarter-century later they would prefer to abandon Marxism-Leninism totally—or that by then, China itself would be embracing far more radical versions of the revisionist policies which he halted in 1962.

But though much of the material in the nine polemics has, therefore, a somewhat antique air, the Sino-Soviet rift which those articles catalogued was critically important in bringing about the more recent developments.[84] The break between Moscow and Beijing shattered the myth of a remorseless tide of history, sweeping a global and united Marxist-Leninist movement towards inevitable victory. It was the most important reminder since the CCP conquest of power in 1949 that nationalism was a force even more potent than international proletarian solidarity.[85]

The nine polemics are also of immense significance for understanding the origins of the Cultural Revolution. The process of disenchantment with the Soviet elder brother, which started with the CPSU 20th Congress in 1956,[86] had reached its fruition. The CCP was now isolated from virtually all the major communist parties in the world movement, and could derive only cold comfort from the formation of Maoist *groupuscules* in parties outside the bloc.[87] The result was to turn China in upon itself. As Mao pondered why the Soviet leadership had gone astray, he determined to make China a laboratory in which revolution would be kept alive and revisionism would be snuffed out. His key ideas which began germinating in the summer of 1962 were finally laid out in the ninth polemic two years later.[88]

The ninth polemic

'On Khrushchev's phoney communism and its historical lessons for the world' started with a long section defining socialist society and the dictatorship of the proletariat on conventional Marxist-Leninist lines. Having established benchmarks, the polemic proceeded to argue that the contemporary Soviet Union did not measure up to these standards. A catalogue of 'the activities of the various bourgeois elements in the Soviet enterprises owned by the whole people' was intended to show how leading functionaries and their 'gangs' abused their positions and amassed fortunes.[89] Data culled from the Soviet press was used to prove that the Soviet Union was the scene of widespread attacks by the bourgeoisie on the proletariat. This would not have been surprising or worrying if the leadership of the country had been Marxist-Leninist,[90] but the next section of the polemic set out to prove that this was far from the case. The 'revisionist Khrushchev clique' was depicted as exalting material incentives at the expense of the socialist principle 'from each according to his ability, to each according to his work', widening income differentials by promoting high salaries, defaming the dictatorship of the proletariat by its attack on the personality cult, and substituting capitalist management for socialist planning.[91] The conclusion drawn was that the 'revisionist Khrushchev clique are the political representatives of the Soviet bourgeoisie, and particularly of its privileged stratum' which had taken control of the party and the government by a series of purges of genuine communists.[92] While the terminology differed, effectively the Chinese were denouncing the Soviet élite as a 'new class', similar to that described by the dissident Yugoslav communist theoretician Milovan Djilas.[93] The Chinese bottom line was that as a result of Khrushchev's revisionism, 'the first socialist country in the world built by the great Soviet people with their blood and sweat is now facing an unprecedented danger of *capitalist restoration*'[94] (emphasis added). Khrushchev's 'communism' took the United States as its model, and catered to the American policy of 'peaceful evolution' of the Soviet Union and other socialist countries.[95]

The polemic then stated that this danger of capitalist restoration should sound the alarm for all socialist countries and communist parties, including China and the CCP, who had to struggle to prevent 'peaceful evolution' that would mean the restoration of capitalism in their own societies. Fifteen principles were outlined to indicate how this struggle might be carried on.[96] But these familiar and largely conventional Marxist-Leninist or Maoist nostrums were insufficient. There was an additional task of supreme importance: rearing revolutionary successors:[97]

In the final analysis, the question of training successors for the revolutionary cause of the proletariat is one of whether or not there will be people who can carry on the Marxist-Leninist revolutionary cause started by the older generation of proletarian revolutionaries, whether or not the leadership of our

Party and state will remain in the hands of proletarian revolutionaries, whether or not our descendants will continue to march along the correct road laid down by Marxism-Leninism, or, in other words, *whether or not we can successfully prevent the emergence of Khrushchov's* [sic] *revisionism in China.* In short, it is an extremely important question, *a matter of life and death for our Party and our country.* It is a question of fundamental importance to the proletarian revolutionary cause for a hundred, a thousand, nay ten thousand years.[98] (Emphasis added)

Here, unveiled, was the apocalyptic vision of a dark future which would eventually convince Mao of the need for the Cultural Revolution. Only dimly glimpsed at this stage was the method by which succeeding generations would be educated in Maoist principles, but it, too, was there: 'Successors to the revolutionary cause of the proletariat come forward in mass struggles and are tempered in *the great storms of revolution.* It is essential to test and know cadres and choose and train successors in the long course of mass struggle'[99] (emphasis added). Possibly those of Mao's colleagues who actually read to the end of the ninth polemic dismissed this as revolutionary hyperbole, used by Kang Sheng to please Mao, convince allies. and combat revisionists. Surely none could have seen it as a storm-warning of the political typhoon which would engulf China and themselves.

The fall of Khrushchev

The CCP polemicists had expended so much vitriol on Khrushchev[100] that it was perhaps not surprising that his fall in mid-October 1964 should prompt the Chinese to make one last effort to come to terms with his successors, even though they too had been excoriated as members of the deposed leader's revisionist clique.[101] There was a quick exchange of reasonably cordial telegrams between Beijing and Moscow. Chinese polemics ceased and a conciliatory editorial was published in the *People's Daily*, which Hoxha considered scandalous, undignified, false, and hypocritical.[102] Zhou Enlai sounded out the ambassadors from communist countries and found them all, except for the Albanian,[103] enthusiastic about a tentative plan to send a high-level delegation to Moscow on the occasion of the annual November celebrations of the Bolshevik revolution in order to make contact with the new Soviet leaders. The Russians issued a formal invitation, and the Chinese decided not to send any of the leaders who had played prominent roles in the dispute. Instead, Zhou and Marshal He Long, accompanied by Wu Xiuquan, headed a delegation padded to 50–60 members to indicate how important Beijing considered the mission. The Chinese delegation was met at Moscow airport by the new Soviet premier, Alexei Kosygin, second only to Leonid Brezhnev, the new CPSU 1st secretary, in the post-Khrushchev leadership.[104]

In addition to assessing the intentions of the new men in Moscow and perhaps laying the foundations of a better relationship, Zhou and his colleagues had an immediate objective: the cancellation of the international communist conference at which Khrushchev had intended to anathematize the CCP and cast it out of the movement. Originally scheduled for the end of 1964, the new leaders had postponed it till March 1965. At the formal discussions between the two parties on 13 November, Zhou argued that it should be cancelled, or at least postponed until after the CPSU and the CCP had reached agreement. He found Brezhnev and his colleagues unyielding, reaffirming the political line of the CPSU's 20th, 21st, and 22nd congresses which Chinese polemicists had spent so much time denouncing. Even without Khrushchev, his China policy would be maintained.[105]

For the CCP delegation, the moment of truth had in fact occurred earlier. On 7 November at one of the Kremlin receptions, the Soviet Defence Minister, Marshal Malinovsky, had said to He Long: 'We've already got rid of Khrushchev; you ought to follow our example and get rid of Mao Zedong. That way we'll get on better.' After making an indignant response, He marched off to inform Zhou who immediately protested to Brezhnev. The Soviet 1st secretary tried to brush the matter aside by saying that Malinovsky was in his cups and had misspoken, an excuse which Zhou rejected with the equivalent of *in vino, veritas* (*jiu hou tu zhen yan*).

The CCP delegation arrived back in Beijing on 14 November, and once again Mao and all his colleagues turned up at the airport to signal to the Russians that the Chinese leadership was united against them.[106] Hoxha reflected mordantly that the Chinese premier 'went to Moscow like Napoleon and returned like Napoleon. He suffered an ignominious defeat.'[107] The Albanian leader was better pleased, however, when on 21 November, *Red Flag* published an editorial entitled 'Why Khrushchev fell'. It concluded, unsurprisingly, that the latter's revisionist line had been discredited. His supporters would not resign themselves to this failure, but hoped for 'Khrushchevism without Khrushchev'. This, however, was a blind alley.[108] Though Khrushchev's successors were clearly included among the supporters of his line, the magazine conspicuously did not subject Brezhnev or any other Soviet leaders to the kind of personal abuse which it had in the past heaped upon Khrushchev. Possibly Mao did not want to rule out an eventual change of heart in Moscow. If so, he would be disappointed.

China goes it alone

Despite their setback in Moscow, the Chinese still had some cards in their hand. Their willingness and their nation's capacity to go it alone on the world stage was symbolized by the explosion of the PRC's first nuclear device on the same day as Khrushchev fell.[109] Three years earlier, in the aftermath of the withdrawal of Soviet technical assistance and in the midst of the post-GLF famine, there had been a heated argument over the wisdom of continuing China's nuclear weapons programme. Mao, however, had long seen nuclear weapons as vital to the nation's standing in world affairs.[110] During the 1961 debate, this view was strongly defended by vice-premier Marshal Nie Rongzhen, the chairman of the National Science and Technology Commission, and his report, which was accepted by the CCP leadership, stated that, even going it alone, China could bring its nuclear and missile programmes to successful conclusions.[111]

China's achievement of nuclear status was part and parcel of the modernization of its armed forces and strategic planning under Lin Biao during the early 1960s. Coming two years after the PLA's defeat of the Indian army on the Tibetan border, China's nuclear breakthrough reinforced the image of an increasingly formidable military power, determined not to be browbeaten, even though now at loggerheads with both superpowers.

Nor was China totally bereft of diplomatic resources, despite being sidelined within the Soviet bloc. The international conference convened by Moscow to denounce the Chinese had turned into a fiasco.[112] Outside the bloc, the Chinese registered a major success when President de Gaulle defied his American ally and recognized the People's Republic in January 1964. Both France and China disputed the leadership of the hegemon in their respective blocs; neither was prepared to sign the partial test-ban treaty, being equally convinced that a nuclear armoury was a necessary buttress to an independent role in world affairs. De Gaulle was also delighted that the Sino-Soviet rift confirmed all that he believed about national interests prevailing over ideology.[113]

In Asia, President Sukarno was a firm friend whose emissaries could be relied upon to back Beijing's policies, including its opposition to the partial test-ban treaty, in the Afro-Asian People's Solidarity Organization and similar 'progressive' international bodies. Following on Liu Shaoqi's successful visit to Jakarta in April 1963, China shared the expenses and sponsorship of the Games of the New Emerging Forces (GANEFO), held in Jakarta in November 1963 in defiance of the International Olympic Committee. In return for Chinese support for his desire to 'crush' Malaysia, Sukarno increasingly parroted Beijing's line, meeting regularly with Chinese leaders. When Indonesia walked out of the UN and its agencies in January 1965 in protest at Malaysia's election to the Security Council, the Chinese backed Sukarno's proposal to convene a Conference of the New Emerging Forces (CONEFO) as a rival UN, and in May, Peng Zhen delivered a strongly anti-imperialist speech in Jakarta. Though even Sukarno was dismayed enough by the Sino-Soviet split to express his concerns in a letter to Mao, he was fortified in his pro-China stance by the backing of Aidit, the leader of the powerful Indonesian communist party.[114]

With Asian communist leaders of ruling parties, however, China's relationship was more ambiguous. North Korea, which had almost consistently taken the Chinese side on international and intra-bloc affairs since 1962, ceased anti-Moscow polemics immediately after Khrushchev fell. In return for economic and military assistance from Khrushchev's successors, Kim Il Sung now placed renewed stress on the need for bloc unity, thus combining 'organizational neutrality' with an ideological tilt to Beijing, a position which represented a gain for Moscow and was correspondingly resented by the Chinese.[115] With North Vietnam, the Chinese had an even more complex relationship as a result of the increasing seriousness and international implications of Hanoi's struggle to conquer the south.

The Vietnam War

In the cases of France, Indonesia, and North Korea, Chinese profits and losses were to be measured principally in terms of prestige. China's relationship with North Vietnam involved far more serious issues of national security, and these would also affect Mao's decisions on domestic economic and possibly political policies. Beijing was disturbed by the first major public decision of the Kennedy administration on helping South Vietnam survive the guerrilla insurgency directed from Hanoi.[116] During the first year of his presidency, Kennedy sent a series of emissaries to Saigon and solicited opinions from senior advisers in order to understand his policy options. In a decision taken on 13 November and publicized in mid-December, the President considerably increased the American commitment to the government of Ngo Dinh Diem, despite misgivings as to its stability, by undertaking to send in several thousand ground troops along with air combat and helicopter teams. There were 700 US military advisers in Vietnam when Kennedy came to office in January 1961; that figure had risen to 3,200 a year later.[117] In February 1962, the Military Assistance Advisory Group was turned into a 'full military field command', entitled the Military Assistance Command, Vietnam, with a four-star general replacing a three-star general in charge.[118]

The creation of this new command structure aroused particular concern in Beijing, leading to consultations in the Chinese capital between the PRC and North Vietnamese governments in the summer of 1962 on the possibility that the American buildup was in preparation for an attack on North Vietnam. The upshot was a decision by Beijing immediately to send Hanoi, free of charge, sufficient arms for 230 infantry battalions.[119]

The American commitment to South Vietnam continued to rise through the Kennedy years, reaching 16,732 men a few weeks before the President's assassination on 22 November 1963.[120] The Chinese continued to consult with North Vietnam. The PLA chief-of-staff, General Luo Ruiqing, led a military delegation to Hanoi in March 1963, to discuss again the possibility of an American attack on the north, and he was followed in May by Liu Shaoqi on a state visit.[121] It was doubtless this Chinese aid and solicitude, coupled with Hanoi's anger at Khrushchev's commitment to seeking peaceful coexistence with an American president engaged in arming their enemy in Saigon, that led the North Vietnamese, from March 1963 on, to veer from their preferred neutrality in the Sino-Soviet dispute and to adopt positions more in line with Beijing's, though always without severing their links to Moscow.[122]

Under Kennedy, American involvement in what came to be called the quagmire of Vietnam grew unceasingly, but he never made an unqualified commitment to saving the south from communism.[123] He also shied away from sending a full-fledged American expeditionary force to fight on the Asian mainland.[124] Under his successor, Lyndon Johnson, these hesitations were eventually swept aside.[125] Gripped by presumed analogies with the Korean War and Munich, the new President and the advisers whom he inherited came to see the struggle in Vietnam as one which the West had to win;[126]

otherwise the 'dominoes' of South-East Asia would fall to communism with catastrophic geopolitical results.[127]

Two major developments marked the escalation of the American commitment. In early August 1964, North Vietnamese torpedo boats purportedly attacked American naval vessels in international waters in the Gulf of Tonkin, and President Johnson ordered swift retaliation with air strikes against North Vietnam. What actually happened in the Tonkin Gulf later became the subject of controversy, but the incident enabled the President to persuade Congress to pass a resolution giving him virtual *carte blanche* to defend South Vietnam as he saw fit, including resort to war.[128] The reprisal was accomplished 'with virtually no domestic criticism, indeed, with an evident increase in public support for the Administration'. A threshold had been crossed; psychologically, the bombing of North Vietnam had been legitimized.[129] Limited air strikes against North Vietnam and unlimited air action over South Vietnam were sanctioned in February 1965, after a communist attack on American barracks at Pleiku.[130] That same month, President Johnson initiated the second major escalation of the American commitment when he approved the deployment of two battalions of marines in Danang. By May, he had agreed to increase American forces to 82,000, including thirteen combat battalions. In July, he ordered a further increase to 125,000 men.[131] American escalation had considerable implications for the Sino–North Vietnamese relationship.

China and Vietnam

Even before these Johnson watersheds had been crossed, the Chinese had been watching the American buildup in South Vietnam resulting from earlier Kennedy decisions with increasing concern. At a central work conference in May–June 1964, Mao proposed that the country should be put on a war footing by dividing it into three 'fronts',[132] and a decision to do so was taken in August.[133] The first front was to consist of the vulnerable coastal provinces; the second front was the inland provinces that would also become vulnerable in an all-out war.[134] The third front was the deep interior of the country, including the southwestern provinces of Sichuan, Guizhou, Yunnan, and the northwestern provinces of Gansu, Ningxia, and Qinghai, along with parts of Shaanxi, Henan, Hubei, and Hunan, roughly the area south of the Great Wall and west of a line drawn between Beijing and Canton, though its precise definition changed.[135]

From 1965 to 1971, the third front and China's non-oil development programme were virtually synonymous,[136] absorbing 50 per cent of basic construction expenditures at a cost of over 80 billion yuan.[137] To oversee the effort, Mao created a 'National Economic Supreme Command', responsible to himself and Liu Shaoqi, under the successful Petroleum Minister, Yu Qiuli, designed to bypass the State Planning Commission with which he was dissatisfied.[138] As Chinese sources have confirmed, the new economic programme was a reversal of the pro-coastal policy enunciated in Mao's 'Ten great relationships' speech in April 1956 and a reversion to the previous 1st FYP strategy, which had been based in part on defence considerations.[139] It was also brought about by a reordering of the development priorities adopted after the GLF: Mao ordered them to be changed from 'agriculture, light industry, heavy industry' to 'heavy industry, light industry, agriculture'.[140] This third front would be built up as an industrial war base, a replication of Chiang Kai-shek's strategy against the Japanese. But unlike Chiang, who had no option but to adopt such a policy in the face of a Japanese foe who had already occupied large areas of coastal and central China, Mao was apparently sufficiently alarmed just by the prospect of invasion to plunge the economy into costly confusion over the next seven years.

Because the Japanese invasion came from the northeast and the east, Chiang was forced to take refuge in southwest China. Mao put the lion's share of investment in the southwest,[141] even though in the event of American attacks from their bases in South Vietnam, that region would be particularly vulnerable.[142] This suggests that Mao's fear was that if the war widened, the danger to China would again be along its eastern coast: American strategy would be to 'unleash' the South Vietnamese to cross the 17th parallel into the north—General Nguyen Khanh, who took charge of the South Vietnamese government after the assassination of Ngo Dinh Diem in November 1963, was urging his American allies in early 1964 to allow him to do just that[143]—while Chiang Kai-shek would invade the Chinese mainland from the southeast.[144] No wonder that in June 1964, Mao told the North Vietnamese chief-of-staff, General Van Tien Dung: 'Our two parties must collaborate and work together against the enemy. Your affairs are our affairs, and ours are yours. That's to say, our two nations are unconditionally and jointly opposed to the enemy.'[145]

The three-fronts plan was a nightmare for the technocrats who by mid-1964 were beginning to see light at the end of the tunnel created by Mao's GLF; now the Chairman was proposing that the economy should be put through new contortions.[146] But the Tonkin Gulf incident seemed to demonstrate that the Chairman had been right to anticipate American escalation in Vietnam, with profound implications for China. Publicly, the Chinese mobilized 20 million people in nationwide protest rallies; privately, the visiting Vietnamese communist party 1st secretary, Le Duan, told Mao: 'The morale of our people and our army is so high and they fight so bravely because they are constantly aware that behind them is the support of China.'[147] In autumn 1964, Foreign Minister Chen Yi assured foreign experts that the Chinese were prepared for attack by the United States from the south, the Russians from the north, and the Japanese from the east, adding a typical rhetorical flourish: 'Let them all come. If necessary, we will give up some of our cities, retreat to the hills, and fight for a hundred years.'[148]

With the start of American air attacks on North Vietnam in February 1965, and the arrival of American marines in South Vietnam in March, Mao's prescience was confirmed and Beijing's concerns increased.[149] In interviews with foreigners, Zhou Enlai and Chen Yi expressed anger at American actions,[150] though Mao himself had earlier indicated that he believed Secretary of State Rusk when the latter said that the United States would not invade North Vietnam; Mao even implied that the Americans might withdraw from South Vietnam within a few years.[151] For public consumption, a government proclamation warned Washington that China was ready and unafraid; Mao and his senior colleagues attended an anti-American rally of 1.5 million people in Beijing on 10 February. Privately, on 12 April, the CC circulated a directive on preparing for war (*bei zhan*) which speculated that the Americans might attack Chinese military installations, industrial centres, communications routes, and large cities, and might even invade. Presumably to prevent panic, only people in frontier regions were to be mobilized to prepare for war at this point.[152]

In the early spring, the North Vietnamese leader Ho Chi Minh had come secretly to Changsha to talk to Mao, apparently just in search of assistance with road building north of Hanoi.[153] But after the American escalation, there was a second secret North Vietnamese mission in April 1965, when Le Duan came to Beijing with Defence Minister Vo Nguyen Giap. In a meeting with Liu Shaoqi on the 8th, Le Duan requested an expansion of Chinese aid, including volunteer pilots and soldiers (*zhiyuande feixingyuan, zhiyuande zhanshi*) and PLA support units.[154] He told Liu that he and his colleagues considered that only China, not the Soviet Union, could provide the emergency help needed at this moment of crisis.[155]

Despite these honeyed words, American escalation had changed the nature of the military equation for the North Vietnamese. Previously, the kind of assistance China could render was ideally suited to the type of warfare Hanoi was waging in the south. But faced with American troops armed with the latest weapons, the North Vietnamese needed equally advanced equipment of the kind that only Moscow could supply. With the dismissal of Khrushchev, who had effectively opted out of the communist struggle to unite Vietnam, the Russians once more indicated a willingness to help Hanoi. A visit by Premier Kosygin to the North Vietnamese capital in February 1965 resulted in new supplies of Soviet military aid, and this encouraged Vietnamese tendencies to neutralism in the Sino-Soviet dispute.[156]

The Chinese were in a dilemma. Failure to respond to North Vietnamese requests would deprive them of any influence in Hanoi. On the other hand, the changing nature of the war in Vietnam made increased Soviet influence inevitable. Furthermore, North Vietnamese determination to fight the Americans on the latter's terms rather than just continue to pursue protracted guerrilla warfare increased the risk of further escalation and spillover into China. Faced with diminishing choices, and probably in the hopes of retaining influence in Hanoi after a putative reunification of Vietnam under its leadership, the Chinese made the best of a bad job.[157]

For his meeting with Le Duan, Liu Shaoqi received instructions from Mao to 'satisfy Vietnam's demands unconditionally', so he told the North Vietnamese party leader that anything that he wanted which the Chinese had would be made available. If Hanoi did not issue an invitation, the Chinese would not come, but if they were invited, the Chinese would go wherever the North Vietnamese needed them. After these exchanges, Liu and Le Duan ordered their respective military aides to flesh their agreement out for signature.[158] On 10 April, at the request of the North Vietnamese, a group of Chinese officers and railway officials left for Vietnam to see how China could help with railway construction and anti-aircraft defences.[159] Between 12 and 21 April, the CC and the standing committee of the NPC formally backed the policy of supporting North Vietnam.[160] At that point, General Giap was able to discuss practicalities with the PLA chief-of-staff Luo Ruiqing (on the 21st) and with deputy chief-of-staff Yang Chengwu the following day.[161] On 25 May, Zhou Enlai, Luo Ruiqing, and Yang Chengwu fulfilled Mao's undertaking to Ho by holding talks with a Vietnamese delegation on road, rail, and other forms of transportation.[162] A highways repair agreement was signed on 30 May.[163]

At the suggestion of Luo Ruiqing, Zhou also set up two bodies to oversee the aid effort. Yang Chengwu and another deputy chief-of-staff, Li Tianyou,[164] were to be the principals in the CC and State Council Aid Vietnam Small Group. Both men were also appointed to a more senior small group charged with oversight of the aid group's activities on behalf of the CC. The latter's five other members were Li Xiannian, Bo Yibo, Luo Ruiqing, Liu Xiao (the former ambassador to the Soviet Union), and Li Qiang (a deputy minister of foreign trade specializing in intra-bloc exchanges).[165]

Under the Sino–North Vietnamese agreement, PLA SAM and anti-aircraft units, as well as engineering and railway construction battalions, logistics forces, and minesweepers were deployed in North Vietnam, starting from 9 June 1965.[166] While the Americans were certainly aware of the presence of PLA troops and the nature of their activities, they were apparently unaware of the size of the Chinese commitment. At the time of maximum strength, there were 170,000 Chinese troops playing various roles on behalf of Hanoi; in the almost three years from June 1965 to March 1968, a total of 320,000 Chinese were at some time assigned to the Vietnam War. In addition, 6,000 political and technical personnel were seconded to the Vietnamese forces for training purposes. After that time, the Chinese forces were gradually run down, as originally agreed, until by 1971 all ground units had been withdrawn. The minesweepers stayed until August 1973.[167]

According to possibly understated official figures, the PLA suffered 5,270 casualties of whom 1,070 were killed. The anti-aircraft batteries, the units which directly engaged American forces from August 1965 till 14 March 1969 when the last battery was withdrawn, claimed to have participated in 558 battles, shot down 597 aircraft, and damaged 479 others with its out-of-date equipment, for the loss of 280 killed and 1,166 wounded. China supplied North Vietnam with over 170 aircraft, 140 warships, 500 tanks, 16,000 motor vehicles, 37,000 artillery pieces, 2,160,000 rifles and machine guns, and 1,280 m. rounds of ammunition. The total cost of the Chinese aid-Vietnam war effort was $20 billion.[168]

Beijing signals to Washington

Despite this evidence of China's seriousness about its 'lips and teeth' relationship with North Vietnam,[169] Beijing also signalled to

Washington its desire to avoid becoming a full-fledged participant in the war across its southern frontier. At some time between 9 March and 2 April 1965, probably between 9 and 23 March, the Chinese agreed to a set of principles on which their policy on Vietnam would be based.[170] On 2 April, *a week before* Liu Shaoqi and Le Duan began discussing what military assistance Chinese could offer North Vietnam, Zhou Enlai stopped over in Karachi and privately asked President Ayub Khan of Pakistan, whom the Chinese premier had been encouraging to act as a bridge between Beijing and Washington,[171] to pass on four points to President Johnson during his visit to Washington later that month:[172]

1. China would not take the initiative to provoke a Sino-American war;
2. China, however, meant what it said: and would assist any country which was attacked by imperialists headed by the United States, and that if this led to the United States attacking China, it would fight to the end;
3. China was prepared: if America attacked China it would never be able to extricate itself;
4. Once war came, there would be no boundaries (presumably a threat that Chinese troops would flood into South Vietnam as they had into South Korea).[173]

The Pakistani president was an obvious candidate to bear a message of this type; Pakistan had been an ally of the United States long before it became a friend of China. Unfortunately for the Chinese, President Johnson abruptly postponed the Ayub visit at unprecedentedly short notice. Planned for 25 April, the visit's deferral was announced by the American President's press spokesman on April 16.[174] Ironically, the American action resulted precisely from the growing ties between Pakistan and China, and, more specifically, the remarks President Ayub had made about Vietnam in Beijing during his visit from 2 to 9 March.[175] Nevertheless, Zhou Enlai's message seems to have got through, though not apparently via the Pakistanis.[176]

To drive this message home, the PLA reinforced its air capabilities in South China, constructed an airfield specially for North Vietnamese aircraft, and engaged in joint exercises with the North Vietnamese aircraft, in the knowledge that the Americans would soon become aware of these efforts. The Chinese must have hoped that they would act as a deterrent to 'hot pursuit' over their airspace—the PLA shot down the first of nine or possibly more American planes in September 1965[177]—and that China would be able to remain a safe haven, as in the Korean War.[178] More publicly, an authoritative Chinese commentator justified Chinese aid to the north as a justifiable *quid pro quo* for American aid to the south. But the *People's Daily* reinforced the cautious private message sent via the Pakistani president: 'We will not attack unless we are attacked; if we are attacked, we will certainly counter-attack.'[179] In sum, the Chinese would send support troops to their ally, but no massive fighting force like the Chinese People's Volunteers in Korea to fight side by side with the North Vietnamese. Presumably that is why, despite Mao's blanket approval of all North Vietnamese requests, the Chinese did not send volunteer pilots or infantry units. Beijing adhered to the letter if not the spirit of its four-point policy.[180]

The international environment and the Cultural Revolution

The Sino-Soviet rupture confirmed Mao in his growing conviction that revolutions might be won by red armies, but could be lost by communist parties. Without the gradual emergence of strains, then tensions, disagreements, and finally an open rift between Moscow and Beijing, it would have been far less likely, if not inconceivable, that Mao would have developed the theories that underlay the Cultural Revolution. Indeed, China's increasing isolation within the Communist bloc may have contributed psychologically to his willingness to use his country as a massive revolutionary laboratory. Nor, one may assume, was it accidental that this emplacement of Chinese domestic affairs within the larger context of international communism ensured that Mao, who had always dominated foreign affairs, thus reinforced his overall policy-making role. A sulky retreat by China into an isolationist policy of 'socialism in one country' devoted to economic renewal could have diminished Mao's ability to override planners and pragmatists.

The desirability of co-operation with Moscow to help North Vietnam did not result in any revival of cordiality, despite some overtures by Kosygin during his visit to Beijing in February 1965.[181] On the other hand, the eruption of a major war on China's southern frontier should have given Mao pause, even if the actions of the United States in Vietnam showed him to be right and the Soviets wrong about imperialism. Could he afford to throw his country into political and social turmoil and thus make it more vulnerable to American attack and Nationalist invasion; might not policy-makers in Washington see that as an opportunity to nip Chinese nuclear developments in the bud?[182] Or, to turn the question around, was it not vital for Mao to ensure that there would be no Korea-type confrontation between China and the United States so that he would have the domestic room for manoeuvre necessary for launching the Cultural Revolution? It seems that Mao decided to get rid of Liu Shaoqi and perhaps to launch the Cultural Revolution at least as early as January 1965.[183] The attempt by Zhou to despatch China's four points to Johnson in April may have been designed to free Mao of the risk of a major foreign war which would force him to abort his plans. While the Chinese seem not to have received any private reassurance from President Johnson himself,[184] the American emissary at the Warsaw talks made it quite clear in sessions held in February and April 1965, that the United States had no intention of invading or bombing China or crushing the North Vietnamese regime.[185] That this was American policy was understood in Beijing.[186] In effect, Washington unwittingly gave Mao the green light for launching the Cultural Revolution.

A further question is whether or not the Vietnam War had a disruptive effect on the Chinese leadership. China was alienated from its erstwhile Soviet ally, and thus deprived of its notional nuclear shield. Simultaneously, it faced a growing threat from the other superpower on its southern border. Crises divide counsels in all political systems. The Chinese political system would have been unusual, indeed, if the international crisis of 1963–5 had not produced divergent opinions in Beijing, especially as in the first half of 1962, virtually all China's top leaders had been persuaded by Wang Jiaxiang that a more moderate policy in foreign affairs would serve the nation better in its current difficulties.

By the mid-1960s, however, the situation had evolved considerably since Wang had made his proposal, and reasonable men could have changed their minds, even without Mao glowering at them. Quite apart from the Chairman's resumption of control over foreign affairs, others things were not equal. Most importantly, China was no longer in the throes of economic depression, and the nation's leaders had much less reason to feel desperate. Khrushchev had undoubtedly behaved provocatively in lining up his East European cohorts against the Chinese, and he had tried to freeze China out of the nuclear club with the partial test-ban treaty. So Wang's advocacy of better relations with the Soviets probably ceased being a tenable position within the Chinese leadership until Khrushchev fell; thereafter Brezhnev and his colleagues clearly indicated that Beijing could expect no change of line from the new leadership in Moscow. While Liu Shaoqi's personal position on the Sino-Soviet dispute at this time is uncertain, two early senior victims of the Cultural Revolution, Deng Xiaoping and Peng Zhen, had performed well as Mao's hatchet-men against the Russians, and could not have been faulted for lack of fervour on this issue.

As for the United States, American willingness to restrain Chiang Kai-shek in mid-1962 had been swiftly succeeded by total sympathy for India in the Sino-Indian border war. As Chinese anger at the Russians for their neutrality in the earlier Sino-Indian crisis of 1959 had demonstrated, a third party's stance on this issue was in some ways a litmus test for Beijing. Washington, like Moscow, had failed it.

But the key issue was of course the increased US commitment to the struggle in South Vietnam. Could the Chinese leadership have differed over the correct line to be pursued towards the Vietnam War which carried the seeds of Chinese involvement? Could some leaders have believed it safer to shelve differences with the Soviet Union in the interests of a North Vietnamese victory and Chinese national security? Or wanted to do more for the north, possibly by sending in Korean War-style 'volunteers'? Or to do less, in order to avert American attacks? Possibly. But there is no sign that Mao's grip on foreign policy was challenged; and even if such differences did exist, there is no evidence that *views on Vietnam policy* played a significant or indeed any role in the purge of any of those involved in such a debate.[187]

Pending further evidence, one must conclude that the impact on China of its international environment in the mid-1960s was to confirm Mao in a view of the world that seemed to him to demand radical domestic surgery. His differences with his colleagues were less over the nature of the world than over the type of surgery. Those differences were focused by the dispute between Mao and Liu Shaoqi at the end of 1964 on the correct way to proceed with the Socialist Education Movement.

PART FOUR

THE END OF THE YAN'AN ROUND TABLE

17 WOMAN WARRIOR

The transformation of the Sino-Soviet dispute after mid-1963 from bitter attacks on or by surrogates into a no-holds-barred, open quarrel between Beijing and Moscow inevitably intensified the leftist climate of domestic policy-making within China. The publication of the first of the CCP's nine polemics against the CPSU on 6 September 1963, coincided with the opening of the CC's work conference to discuss the formulation of the Latter Ten Points. While the final version of the latter document attempted to set certain parameters for the conduct of the SEM, the movement was still about class struggle. Moreover, as the Latter Ten Points was being modified through successive drafts until its eventual passage in November, Mao and Liu Shaoqi were both moving leftward, developing even more sombre views of the extent of the task which faced the CCP. Unfortunately for Liu, he discovered a year later that the Chairman's leftism had diverged from his own.

Mao's view of the superstructure

As always, when resolved upon class struggle, Mao cast a baleful eye upon intellectuals. Mao, like Stalin and Hitler, 'was scornful of intellectuals, yet at the same time eager to establish his own intellectual authority'.[1] Moreover, ever since he had observed the seminal role of the Petöfi Circle in the Hungarian revolt of 1956, Mao had been obsessed with the key role which intellectuals could play in mobilizing the masses in critical political situations.[2] Thus, when sounding the trumpet for the fight against revisionism, the Chairman wanted to ensure that intellectuals were drummed into service on his side.[3] He began to indicate his dissatisfaction with their current orientation. At the 10th plenum he had eagerly adopted Kang Sheng's tag, 'using novels to promote anti-party activities is a great invention'. On 21 December 1962, Mao told his leftist acolytes in the East China regional leadership that there were few good plays and few bad ones and a lot in between, including many with emperors and generals in them. In some, the west wind overcame the east wind. There were too many drama troupes for old-style plays, including Peking Opera troupes in Beijing.[4]

To the East China and Shanghai 1st secretary, Ke Qingshi, a nod was as good as a wink where the Chairman was concerned. On 1 January 1963, at a forum of Shanghai cultural workers, he advocated 'writing about the thirteen years',[5] that is, the period of the PRC's existence, and senior Shanghai propagandists like Zhang Chunqiao and Yao Wenyuan began to promote the slogan. They argued that the subject-matter of literature and the arts determined its nature, and thus the only way to have socialist culture in China was for it to be about contemporary themes.[6] This meant the negation not merely of classical literature, but also of the works of communist and leftist intellectuals written from the 1920s through the 1940s, many of whom were grandees of the current cultural establishment. The Shanghai leftists were opposed by central literary bureaucrats like Zhou Yang, Lin Mohan, and Shao Quanlin, who regarded Yao as 'oversimple' and 'rude',[7] and prayed in aid of a 'directive' by Zhou Enlai that one should 'write about the thirteen years, and also about the 108 years'.[8] But at a work conference called by the CCs Propaganda Department in April, Zhang, undaunted by that kind of opposition, claimed that there were ten great advantages of portraying the thirteen years.[9] And even Zhou Yang, as he acknowledged after the Cultural Revolution, had to bend with the wind—when the Chairman pontificated, no official could afford to ignore him—and made speeches emphasizing the need to oppose Soviet-style revisionism in the cultural realm.[10]

This debate between Shanghai and Beijing, between provincial leftists and the central party establishment, prefigured what would happen two-and-a-half years later, on the eve of the Cultural Revolution. And in 1963, and even more so in 1965, Mao's wife, Jiang Qing, played a critical behind-the-scenes role.

Waiting in the wings

Jiang Qing's marriage to Mao in Yan'an in 1938 had caused considerable consternation among the colleagues of the future CCP Chairman. They had admired his previous wife He Zizhen who had accompanied him on the Long March, but who had become estranged as a result of his earlier affair with a previous Shanghai actress. They were critical of the 'colourful past' and sexual mores of this newly arrived actress Lan Ping (as Jiang Qing was then called),[11] and suspicious of her KMT connections back in Shanghai. The CCP's central organization took formal cognisance of the liaison, and there was clearly opposition to it, though accounts differ as to how much, and on whose part. The Organization Department made enquiries about her political past, without uncovering anything negative. Some accounts indicate that the discussions resulted in a three-point verbal CC admonition to Jiang Qing—not to take part in party political work; not to show her face in public; and to look after Mao well—each one of which she eventually flouted, and certainly there were persistent rumours to that effect.[12] Whatever prohibitions were placed on her, in the early years of her marriage Jiang Qing revealed herself as lively, strong-willed, and assertive, but seemingly relatively content with her status as the consort of the CCP's leader.[13]

After the founding of the PRC through the 1950s, Jiang Qing was little in evidence. She was afflicted with a variety of complaints, some serious, some trivial, some imaginary. Beginning in 1949, she had spells in the Soviet Union under the care of Russian doctors, one lasting almost a year. Back home, she soon began to live a courtyard apart from Mao, citing differences in life-styles—taste in food, sleeping patterns, timings of activities. She made a few forays into the countryside, but her most significant political activity in this period was in the sphere in which she felt most comfortable, the performing arts.[14]

Despite any constraints on her activities that may have been agreed in Yan'an, during the early 1950s, Jiang Qing briefly held a number of posts. Averse to high-pressure office work which aggravated her health problems, she did not last long in her most important job as chief of the secretariat of the CC's General Office.[15] More congenial was her role as head of the cinema section and deputy head of literature and arts in the CC's Propaganda Department, obtained for her by Zhou Enlai. Though she never turned up at the office,[16] this position legitimized her attacks on films which she considered capitalist. She campaigned against a Hong Kong import *The Inside Story of the Qing Court*, and while it was not condemned, she made sufficient waves behind the scenes for it effectively to be withdrawn. She had greater success with a film called *The Story of Wu Xun*, which had been approved by Zhou Yang, for she managed to persuade Mao to write an editorial in the *People's Daily* denouncing it.[17] Jiang Qing had found her *métier*, but this was only a flash in the pan. Poor health, lack of opportunity, and the unco-operative attitude of cultural officials kept her largely inactive throughout the decade. By the early 1960s, however, Mao was sending Jiang Qing documents for her to study.[18]

During this period she revived her friendship with Kang Sheng, with their mutual love of traditional drama as common ground.[19] Kang had been an *aficionado* since his youth, and had considerable knowledge of the theatre. During the 'three bitter years', he indulged his passion, and was instrumental in the performance of old and even erotic plays. He encouraged a very old friend, the dramatist Meng Chao, in adapting a Ming play under the title *Li Huiniang*, in which the eponymous heroine was a ghost, and took a close interest in it as it went through rehearsal. The play was blessed by Zhou Enlai and was performed to appreciative audiences in Beijing and round the country,[20] leading to a spurt of interest in ghost plays.[21] Mao himself ordered a special performance of *Li Huiniang* to be put on in the Zhongnanhai.[22] In the spring of 1962, after the Seven Thousand Cadres Conference, Kang and Jiang spent two months in Hangzhou, demanding performances by the local drama troupe.[23]

Their self-indulgence ended with the Beidaihe work conference and the 10th plenum. Both Kang and Jiang grasped that there were political opportunities presented by Mao's revival of class struggle, but that to seize them meant abandoning their bourgeois, even 'feudal', tastes in drama. Kang sent warnings to Meng Chao that he should write different kinds of plays and get his theatrical colleagues to stop performing plays about ghosts. It was the last favour he did him.[24] After the 10th plenum, as Kang got busy with the case against Xi Zhongxun and the nine polemics, Jiang Qing turned back to the arena in which she had briefly been an assistant stage manager in the early 1950s.

The leftist literary offensive

In March 1963, the party committee of the Ministry of Culture issued a report bewailing the prevalence of ghost plays, the support they received from critics, and the fact that contemporary playwrights were writing such plays; as an example of the latter, the report cited *Li Huiniang*.[25] In April 1963, Jiang Qing seized upon ghost plays in general and *Li Huiniang* in particular as her first targets;[26] the latter was additionally reprehensible because it could be construed as being opposed to the GLF.[27] With the co-operation of Ke Qingshi, she arranged for a critical article to be published in the Shanghai *Wenhui Bao* on 6 May, an event which she referred to during the Cultural Revolution as the first real assault on ghost drama.[28]

But, as in the case of *The Story of Wu Xun*, Jiang Qing had no real impact until her husband joined the fray. In May 1963, Mao had

PLATE 1. Liu Shaoqi quizzing peasants in Hunan, 1961

PLATE 2. Liu resting with Wang Guangmei in Heilongjiang, 1961

PLATE 3. Seven Thousand Cadres Conference: The PSC in harmony? Left to right: Zhu De, Zhou Enlai, Chen Yun, Liu Shaoqi, Mao, Deng Xiaoping, Lin Biao

PLATE 4. China's active leaders in discussion at the conference. Left to right: Zhou Enlai, Chen Yun, Liu Shaoqi, Mao, Deng Xiaoping, Peng Zhen

PLATE 5. Mao's leftist guerrillas: Jiang Qing emerges from seclusion to help Mao greet Mme Sukarno, Beijing, September, 1962

PLATE 6. Kang Sheng

PLATE 7. The MAC standing committee in Canton. Front row left to right: Marshals Chen Yi, Liu Bocheng, Lin Biao, He Long, Luo Ronghuan. Back row left to right: Chief of Staff General Luo Ruiqing, Marshals Nie Rongzhen, Xu Xiangqian, Tao Zhu (1st secretary, Central-South Region), Marshal Ye Jianying

PLATE 8. Deng Zihui addresses cadres in Fujian

stated that the theory that there was 'no harm in ghosts', whose main exponent was Liao Mosha, was a reflection of the rural and urban class struggle.[29] In September 1963, Mao warned dramatists who had been writing historical plays that they should weed through the old in order to bring forth the new—a familiar instruction—not more of the old by portraying the emperors, generals, and beauties of yesteryear.[30] He returned to this theme in November, when he criticized *Xiju Bao* (Drama News) and the Ministry of Culture: the paper was only propagandizing ghosts; the ministry was not doing its job, ignoring the prevalence of feudal things. If the ministry did not shape up, its name should be changed to the 'Ministry of Emperors, Princes, Generals, and Ministers' or the 'Ministry of Gifted Scholars and Beautiful Ladies', or even the 'Ministry of Foreign Dead People'.[31]

After these rumblings came what an authoritative account describes as Mao's first significant intervention in the emerging struggle in the cultural sphere. It was sparked by a report about Shanghai carried in the CC Propaganda Department's serial publication *Wenyi Qingkuang Huibao* (Report on the situation in literature and art) in the issue of 9 December 1963. Entitled, 'Comrade Ke Qingshi grasps folk art work', the article enthused the Chairman sufficiently for him to send a copy to the Beijing city party leaders, Peng Zhen and Liu Ren, presumably with the implication that they should set their own house in order. His appended comments were later cobbled together and circulated as Chairman Mao's directive on literature and the arts of 12 December:[32]

This document may be read. Problems abound in all forms of art such as the drama, ballads, music, the fine arts, the dance, the cinema, poetry and literature, and the people involved are numerous; in many departments very little has been achieved so far in socialist transformation. The 'dead' still dominate in many departments. What has been achieved in the cinema, new poetry, folk songs, the fine arts and the novel should not be underestimated, but there, too, there are quite a few problems. As for such departments as the drama, the problems are even more serious. The social and economic base has changed, but the arts as part of the superstructure, which serve this base, still remain[s] a serious problem. Hence we should proceed with investigation and study and attend to this matter in earnest.

Isn't it absurd that many communists are enthusiastic about promoting feudal and capitalist art, but not socialist art?[33]

This thunderbolt precipitated a flurry of activity among the propagandists who were formally responsible for the sorry state of affairs alleged by Mao. On 3 January 1964, Liu Shaoqi chaired a forum of thirty members of the CC's Propaganda Department and luminaries from the cultural field, at which Zhou Yang propounded Mao's directive, reaffirmed the successes of the past, but acknowledged the problems of the present. In his speech, Peng Zhen assumed that Mao had sent his directive to the Beijing party because its cultural work was pretty backward and he accepted that verdict.[34] Like Mao, Peng believed that intellectuals could wield enormous political influence. He pointed out that many Chinese intellectuals had joined the revolution because they had been inspired by novels and other cultural products, and he cited the role of Mao's *bête noire*, the Petöfi Circle, in the Hungarian revolt as an example of what could happen if bourgeois and feudal tendencies in the cultural realm were not curbed.[35]

It need not be assumed that this was simply a placatory gesture to deflect the Chairman. Peng Zhen was a genuine leftist in the cultural realm, who did not believe in conceding too much freedom to intellectuals. Precisely that viewpoint had brought him into conflict with Mao in 1957. At that time, Peng believed that the lesson which the CCP should learn from the Hungarian revolt was the need to tighten up on potential dissenters rather than open up to potential critics, and he dragged his feet on endorsing open-door rectification.[36] The example of Peng Zhen, like that of Lu Dingyi, demonstrates that, the simplistic criticisms of the cultural revolutionaries notwithstanding, victimization during the Cultural Revolution did not necessarily mean that a party leader had earlier or consistently been a rightist or opposed to Mao.

Spurred on by some 'vulgar' episode at a soirée given by the Dramatists' Union on 3 February 1964 to welcome Chinese New Year,[37] party officials[38] investigated the past few years' work, and decided towards the end of March to initiate a rectification campaign in the ranks of the cadres of the All-China Federation of Literary and Art Circles and various specialized bodies like the Writers' Union. On 8 May, the CC's Propaganda Department prepared a draft report on the progress of this rectification campaign.[39] It concluded that there were some serious problems in the cultural world:

(a) CCP cultural policy was not being implemented, and until the 10th plenum, the various cultural organizations were muddled in their aims and failed to understand class struggle;
(b) Literary criticism was weak;
(c) Ideological remoulding was being neglected.[40]

Before this report could be finalized, Jiang Qing forwarded a copy to Mao, and on 27 June, the Chairman appended another ferocious comment:[41]

In the last fifteen years these associations, most of their publications (it is said that a few are good), and by and large the people in them (that is not everybody) have *basically* not carried out the policies of the Party. They have acted as high and mighty bureaucrats, have not gone to the workers, peasants, and soldiers and have not reflected the socialist revolution and socialist construction. *In recent years* they have slid right down to the brink of revisionism. Unless they remold themselves in real earnest, at some future date they are bound to become groups like the Hungarian Petöfi Club.[42]

Again the propaganda officials swung hastily into action, summoning another meeting of cultural cadres on 2 July and ordering a second rectification campaign under the leadership of a special *ad hoc* group. This campaign would last ten months, until April 1965.[43]

The Peking Opera festival

Since Mao's critiques had revealed a particular concern about opera, the art form most likely to influence the masses, it was decided to hold a national meeting on the subject. Again, Ke Qingshi had led the way. At the time of the East China Drama Festival in December and January 1963–4, he had lauded new model revolutionary operas as ideological weapons to rally the people.[44]

This was followed from 5 June to 31 July 1964 by the festival of Peking Opera on contemporary themes held in the capital, a grand affair under the auspices of Zhou Enlai and Peng Zhen (but not Chen Yi, whose efforts on behalf of traditional opera seemed doomed). When Mao Dun, the Minister of Culture and one of the great writers of the pre-1949 period, opened the event, Lu Dingyi, Kang Sheng, Guo Moruo, and all the luminaries of the Peking Opera world were arrayed on the dais; in front of them sat 5,000 artistes and officials from all over the country. During the festival, over 2,000 actors drawn from nineteen provinces and twenty-eight troupes put on thirty-seven modern operas, some of which were seen by Mao.[45]

Both Zhou and Peng Zhen spoke, and the latter's remarks could hardly have been bettered by the Chairman himself; indeed Mao described them retrospectively as 'very good':

Our Peking Opera art form has already entered a new stage. In our country, the root contradiction today is between the socialist and capitalist roads, between communism and capitalism, and is also manifested in the contradiction between Marxism-Leninism and revisionism. Therefore, the basic problem we have to solve is: does our Peking Opera serve socialism or capitalism; does it serve the workers, peasants, and soldiers or oppose them; does it serve the general line or oppose it; does it support party leadership or not; does it take the road of Marxism-Leninism or the road of revisionism? This is also the prime standard for deciding whether Peking Opera is good or bad and is the critical problem for the art form which will settle whether it lives or dies, persists or disappears. Ours is a socialist society and each element of the superstructure must serve the socialist economic base.[46]

At the beginning of July, when Mao suggested that a small group should be formed to take charge of revolutionizing culture, Peng Zhen was the obvious choice to lead the five-man group, with Lu Dingyi as his deputy, and Kang Sheng, Zhou Yang, and Wu Lengxi, head of the NCNA and chief editor of the *People's Daily*, as members. These men were responsible for the tough rectification campaign in cultural units that ensued, yet, ironically, all but Kang Sheng were early victims of the Cultural Revolution.

Enter Jiang Qing, stage left

In this favourable climate, Jiang Qing came out of the political closet. Even before the Peking Opera festival, she had embarked on her self-appointed task of revolutionizing the Chinese stage. In May 1964, after watching the dress rehearsal of *Hong Deng Ji* (The Red Lantern), a Peking Opera drama of communist resistance to Japanese imperialism, she gave the first of five detailed commentaries on how it should be presented.[47] On 23 June, at a forum of performers arranged by Zhou Enlai, Jiang Qing made her first public speech, and gave a slightly longer version of it to another forum the following month, with the latter version later selected as the preferred text.[48] The only significant difference between the two versions with political implications was that in the earlier one, she clearly indicated her political allies, with respectful mentions of Lin Biao and Kang Sheng, who was simultaneously pursuing an equally aggressive leftist line.[49] Ke Qingshi was mentioned in both speeches, but on the earlier occasion his hands-on approach to the drama in Shanghai was implicitly contrasted favourably with that of an unnamed Peng Zhen. Privately, Jiang Qing liked to accuse Peng of 'Beijing chauvinism' (*da Beijingzhuyi*) because of his dismissive attitudes towards Shanghai's drama experiments.[50] Privately, Beijing party intellectuals would have agreed that neither Peng Zhen nor his deputy Liu Ren were normally interested in or competent to dabble in cultural matters.[51]

In her speech, Jiang Qing started with two sets of 'shocking' figures, contrasting the high proportion of drama troupes staging traditional, historical, or foreign plays with the small portion of the
national population—5 per cent or 30 million landlords, rich peasants, counter-revolutionaries, bad elements, rightists, and bourgeois
elements—who would welcome such performances.[52] Echoing the
earlier call of the Shanghai leftists, Jiang Qing stressed that 'our
foremost task' was performing operas 'on revolutionary contemporary themes which reflect real life in the fifteen years since the
founding' of the PRC. Historical operas 'portraying the life and
struggles of the people before our Party came into being' were also
needed. Good traditional operas, '[e]xcept for those about ghosts
and extolling capitulation and betrayal', could be staged, but would
require careful revision if they were to command an audience.
Remembering her husband's admonition that without investigation,
one had no right to speak, she put an acceptable political spin on her
1962 theatre spree with Kang Sheng, by adding: 'I have made systematic visits to theatres for more than two years and my observation of both actors and audiences led me to this conclusion.'[53]

Where should one start to transform Peking Opera? With good
new plays, too few of which had been written recently. Jiang Qing
commended Ke Qingshi who personally came to grips with the problem of creative writing, forming a three-way combination of leaders,
playwrights, and the masses. The alternative was adaptation of politically acceptable existing plays. Interestingly, Jiang Qing acknowledged that in Peking Opera, with its tendency to artistic
exaggeration, there were problems in depicting negative characters,
but the real difficulty lay in making heroes convincing.[54]

Mao soon indicated approval of Jiang Qing's June speech.[55]
Indeed, he continued to complain to all and sundry—foreign visitors,
economic officials, relatives—about the condition of PRC culture
and the officials who ran it.[56] Encouraged, Jiang Qing continued her
guerrilla activities. In July, she selected official materials depicting
the sorry state of contemporary Chinese culture and sent them on to
him to maintain his interest and his anger.[57] Building on her earlier
work on *Hong Deng Ji*, over the course of the following twelve
months she began to issue 'instructions' on other dramas and even
interfered in the musical realm.[58] At the end of 1964, she met with
five deputy directors of the Propaganda Department in an effort to
persuade them to criticize ten films. Spurned, she got the Shanghai
party to do it instead, and when this initiative was taken up

elsewhere, the Propaganda Department felt it had no option but to have two of them criticized for appearances' sake in the *People's Daily*.[59]

These activities infuriated cultural officials in general and Peng Zhen in particular, mainly because she was trespassing on their turf, but also because they felt she was draining the works of any artistic content.[60] According to one Western scholar,

the heroes and heroines of Jiang Qing's operas and ballets suffered no doubts, weaknesses, sorrows, or disorders, were thoroughly infused with ideological goals, and carried out superhuman feats for the revolution. Her effort to reform China's traditional opera dispensed with its content but retained its formulas, techniques, and styles. She repudiated Western culture, but injected the most banal and conventional Soviet dance, music, and song. These devices, along with the content of class struggle, military conflict, and heroic models, presaged the official culture that would emerge in the Cultural Revolution.[61]

Yet there is an alternative Western view: 'Despite the simplistic renderings of the good-and-evil struggles and the objections of the purists to Tchaikovskian orchestration and elaborate sets and lighting effects, the model plays offered splendid dramatic moments and were genuinely popular before reiterated performances dulled their impact.'[62]

The rectification of communist intellectuals

However jaundiced Peng Zhen's views of the merits of Jiang Qing's activities, the declared objectives of his five-man small group were identical to hers: the revolutionization of Chinese culture. While it was in the interests of the cultural revolutionaries to assign the credit—and of the post-Cultural Revolution historians to assign the blame[63]—to Jiang Qing and Kang Sheng, there is nothing in their previous records to suggest that Peng Zhen, Lu Dingyi, and Zhou Yang would have shirked the task of bringing intellectuals to heel. Under them, in every department, there were doubtless loyal cadres, be they time-servers or conviction politicians, who would crack the whip as readily as they had spared the rod only two years before.[64] The result was that a long list of plays, novels, short stories, and films, and their creators, came under fire. During the Cultural Revolution, a list of sixty-three reprehensible novels and the fifty-five writers responsible was published; many were first attacked before the Cultural Revolution began.[65]

As a result of the attacks on the depiction of contemporary reality during the Anti-Rightist Campaign in the 1950s, in the early 1960s many writers had sought refuge by setting their novels in the past rather than the present. Now, forced to depict reality and alarmed by the attacks on Shao Quanlin, the party secretary of the Writers' Union who had used the 1962 Dalian conference to promote the depiction of 'middle characters'—neither heroes nor villains, but vacillating between the old society and the new, like peasants unhappy with collectivization—writers found their subject-matter greatly restricted and their palettes for characterizations reduced to black and white. Lei Feng was the kind of model on which characters now had to be based.[66]

The rectification campaign under the aegis of the Ministry of Culture and the Federation of Literary and Art Circles was brought formally to a close in April 1965. After the discovery of so much revisionism in such high positions, official heads had to roll. The Minister of Culture was the famous playwright Mao Dun (Shen Yanbing), not a party member and therefore only in nominal charge of the ministry.[67] He could have been made a scapegoat, but was probably considered too important an international asset to be disgraced.[68] On the other hand, a non-party figurehead was clearly an inappropriate leader of the ministry in the new leftist era, so he was replaced by Lu Dingyi in January 1965 even before the campaign ended. Lu then presided over the dismissal on 7 April of the two senior CCP members at the ministry with responsibility for its day-to-day running, Qi Yanming and Xia Yan, the latter once a major figure in the 1930s Shanghai film world, and apparently another focus of Jiang Qing's resentments.[69] How much latitude Lu had in choosing their successors is uncertain, for, in a reflection of the shape of things to come, the new day-to-day party leadership in the ministry was brought in from the outside, and consisted of two generals and a Shanghai bureaucrat: Lt.-Gen. Xiao Wangdong, the PLA deputy political commissar in the Nanjing Military Region, Shi Ximin, a secretary of the Shanghai municipal party committee, and Maj.-Gen. Yan Jinsheng, a Korean War veteran, at this time deputy director of the political department of the Wuhan Military Region.[70]

One divides into two

During the 1964–5 rectification, culture was not narrowly construed to mean the theatre, films, fiction, and the fine arts. Once the leftist tide was in motion, it swept through all areas of intellectual activity.

On a number of occasions, Mao indicated his concern for simplifying the educational process and combining it with work, much as he had done during the GLF; he clearly felt that a lengthy period of book-learning was not the best way to rear new revolutionary successors.[71] Many prominent figures came under attack. The head of the Economics Institute, Sun Yefang, was tricked by Chen Boda into writing an article in 1962 and then attacked two years later for the views in it, and more generally for his advocacy of more rational economic policies than those adopted in the GLF.[72] Probably the country's leading Marxist historian, head of his department at Peking University, Jian Bozan, came under fire for advocating an equal reliance upon facts and theory and opposing the notion that history should be the handmaid of politics. He also questioned whether it had only been through revolution that the lot of China's peasantry had been bettered.[73] Another leading Marxist academic, the Peking University philosopher Feng Ding, was attacked for his earlier assertion that happiness could be private and nothing to do with class struggle. With Mao's concern for rearing the younger generation to emulate Lei Feng and think only of self-sacrifice, Feng Ding became an obvious target, especially since he had once seen fit to indicate distaste for the cult of personality.[74]

But undoubtedly the most significant political figure to be attacked at this time was another leading Marxist philosopher, Yang Xianzhen.[75] Elected an alternate CC member in 1956 and a full member in 1958, Yang had been assigned to the education of CCP cadres since Yan'an days. In 1949, he was a deputy director at the Academy of Marxism-Leninism and the head of teaching and research on philosophy. When the academy was transformed into the Central Party School in 1955, Yang became its director.[76] In this role, he was in a strategic position from which to influence the thinking of thousands of upwardly mobile central and provincial cadres who came as students.

Unfortunately for Yang, the importance of his post made it a focus of political ambition and struggle. One of his subordinates was another leading dialectician, Ai Siqi, who had been his rival even in Yan'an and on whose work Mao had relied at that time.[77] In 1955, Ai and Yang were on opposite sides of the debate on collectivization, with Ai as the protagonist of more rapid change, the position which Mao adopted shortly thereafter. Ai was a long-time protégé of Kang Sheng's. After the latter's appointment as the Politburo's supervisor of the school in 1956, and the infiltration of his wife Cao Yiou as an administrator there, a struggle ensued between him and Liu Shaoqi (who generally supported Yang) as to the school's programme and direction.[78]

During the three bitter years, Yang Xianzhen had been shocked at what he found on an inspection of the countryside in the path-breaking province of Henan, and later incautiously made criticial comments about the GLF. Since Yang had been closely associated with Peng Dehuai in the Yan'an period, and the latter was assigned to do remedial theoretical study under him after his disgrace at Lushan, Yang's enemies were able to add to their dossier on him.[79]

Among those enemies was Chen Boda, who treated Yang as he had treated Sun Yefang: asked him to write an article which was later used against him. In 1958, Chen commissioned Yang to draft a refutation of an entry in a Soviet encyclopaedia which had 'slan-dered' one of Mao's concepts. Yang did so, using orthodox Marxist-Leninist ideas, but his article was not published; only when he raised the matter directly with Chen four years later did he realize that the latter supported differing views espoused by Ai Siqi. The dispute was over the seemingly esoteric Hegelian assertion of the 'identity of thought and existence' which materialists had always rejected. Ai, and more importantly Mao, believed, however, that materialists could also accept this concept. For Mao, it was the philosophic basis of the GLF, the possibility of transforming ideas into actuality, and his contention that properly motivated human beings could achieve miracles. Kang Sheng used Yang's more conventional Marxist views against him.[80]

After the Seven Thousand Cadres Conference, Yang, like many others who had been subsidiary victims in the campaign against Peng Dehuai's 'right opportunism', was rehabilitated and able to make a comeback. Unfortunately for him, just as he was managing to wrest the school back from Kang Sheng's influence, the political wind shifted again.[81] Once more, Yang fell foul of Mao for his orthodox ideological views, this time as a result of an article written by two of his followers on another seemingly esoteric question: 'combining two into one'.

As early as 1957, speaking in Moscow, Mao had asserted that 'one divides into two' (*yi fen wei er*) was a universal phenomenon. At the time, he seemed concerned to play down divisions within the Soviet bloc, notably between the Russians and the Poles, by arguing that contradictions leading to disagreements were the natural order of things and nothing to be alarmed at. By the early 1960s, however, the bitterness of the Sino-Soviet dispute and its open acknowledgement in July 1963 provided a very different context in which to tease out the implications of this concept. In October that year, Zhou Yang used it to explain why the world communist movement had split, and implicitly to justify Mao's role in bringing about the rupture. The publication of the speech on Mao's birthday, 26 December, though it was made two months earlier, was clearly meant to suggest that Zhou was retailing the Chairman's ideas, and thereafter 'one divides into two' became the justification for the domestic class struggle Mao had launched with the SEM.[82]

On 11 November 1963, Yang Xianzhen, demoted by now to deputy director of the Central Party School, gave his first lecture since his rehabilitation, using it as an opportunity to attack the philosophic idealism behind the mistakes of the GLF. Because Kang Sheng did not monitor this address, it passed without any repercussions. Yang was less fortunate with his lecture on 3 April 1964, to the Xinjiang contingent at the school, in which he expounded his views on the law of the unity of opposites in doing work or 'combining two into one' (*he er er yi*). The lecture excited a young lecturer in the audience, Ai Hengwu, who persuaded a friend and colleague, Lin Qingshan, that they should write an article expounding Yang's ideas. As Ai explained the lecture to Lin, Yang gave examples to prove that everything represented the unification of two opposite things, which was why 'one divides into two' was an appropriate tool for analysis, that is, of secondary methodological importance.[83]

In fact, Yang later denied that this ordering of the two concepts represented his position.[84] According to his brief lecture notes:

To study dialectics is to gain the understanding of how to bring two opposite thoughts together, that is, one should learn to use the law of unity of opposites in one's practical work, and to learn to walk on two legs. The so-called unity of opposites is to walk on two legs. The meaning of the unity of opposites should be made clear: One divides into two; two combines into one. One dividing into two is the law of the unity of opposites, the doctrine that everything has two aspects, dichotomy . . .[85]

Yang went on to reject the 'revisionist' idea that the unity of opposites meant their 'conciliation'. Rather, it embraced the meaning of the 'struggle of contradictions because the characters of contradictions are different . . . Moreover, for the two opposite aspects, the unity is relative and the *struggle is absolute*. This is also the law of the unity of opposites.'[86] In sum, Yang seemed to be arguing that the two concepts were on a par; he certainly does not seem to have claimed that 'combining two into one' negated 'one divides into two', nor to have favoured class conciliation over class struggle.[87]

But Yang's true philosophical position was irrelevant in the political context of 1964. When Ai and Lin's article, entitled ' "One divides into two" and "Two combine into one" ' was published in *Guangming Ribao*, the paper read by intellectuals, on 29 May 1964, Kang Sheng seized upon it as his opportunity finally to encompass Yang's downfall. Believing, incorrectly, that the article had been published at Yang's suggestion or at least with his permission, Kang mobilized a young philosopher, Guan Feng. The latter, who headed the philosophy section of *Red Flag*, quickly organized the writing of a counterblast, which was published in *Guangming Ribao* on 5 June. Thereafter, Kang orchestrated a debate, encouraging the publication of other articles supporting Ai and Lin, which enabled him to demonstrate that this was a serious and widespread heresy which had to be dealt with summarily.[88]

The key to Kang's ability to deliver a *coup de grâce* to Yang was the angering of Mao. Kang got Jiang Qing to show the Chairman the 5 June rebuttal on the day of publication. Mao's reaction was that ' "two combine into one" is a theory of reconciling contradictions'. Three days later, he commented again: ' "One divides into two" is dialectics, "two combine into one" I'm afraid is revisionism and class reconciliation.'[89] In a long, rambling discussion of philosophy on 18 August, by which time the *People's Daily* had long since pinpointed Yang Xianzhen as the chief protagonist of 'two combine into one', Mao cited the example of the struggle between the CCP and the KMT to denounce Yang by name to Kang Sheng, Chen Boda, and others:

What is synthesis? You have all witnessed how the two opposites, the Kuomintang and the Communist Party, were synthesised on the mainland. The synthesis took place like this: their armies came, and we devoured them, we ate them bite by bite. It was not a case of two combining into one as expounded by Yang Hsien-chen [Xianzhen], it was not the synthesis of two peacefully coexisting opposites.[90]

Mao seems to have misinterpreted Yang's position, deliberately or as a result of Kang Sheng's priming. Yang, at any rate, was finished. At the Central Party School, he had already been condemned at a mass meeting. On 1 March 1965, the school sent the CC a report describing him as a 'representative of the bourgeoisie inside the party, a tool of Peng Dehuai, and a mini-Khrushchev'; the latter as it turned out was a particularly explosive epithet, for during the

Cultural Revolution Liu Shaoqi was regularly referred to as 'China's Khrushchev'.[91] On 9 June the school suggested that Yang be dismissed as deputy director and a member of the school management committee. On 24 September, the CC approved the report and concurred with the suggestion.[92]

Yang Xianzhen did not suffer alone. Lin Qingshan and Ai Hengwu were consigned to the countryside in the northeast. Another deputy director of the school was attacked and later arrested. Another colleague committed suicide rather than betray Yang. Altogether, 154 cadres underwent punishments ranging from imprisonment, forced labour, and expulsion from the party to various degrees of mass criticism.[93]

The struggle to be on the left

As the case of Yang Xianzhen brought home, for the first time since the Yan'an rectification campaign, senior communist intellectuals as a group were tasting the persecution which they had hitherto meted out to their 'bourgeois' colleagues. In Mao's eyes, these CCP intellectuals had failed to set revolutionary examples, whether out of negligence or with malice aforethought, and the members of Peng Zhen's group had to ensure that they took the consequences. Otherwise the next in line for blame would be themselves. Thus Zhou Yang personally conducted the campaign against Shao Quanlin whom he had supported at the Dalian conference two years earlier.[94] In the light of his speech of October 1963, he might also have attacked Yang Xianzhen had Kang Sheng not anticipated him.

At this stage, the major issues dividing the insider five-man group from Jiang Qing's guerrillas were not so much politics as turf and ties. Peng Zhen and his colleagues had been formally appointed by the CC and as such considered they were in charge, and Peng in particular had a low tolerance for independent entrepreneurship. But often there was nothing they could do about it, and Peng's troops were often forced to fan a blaze after Jiang's irregulars had lit the fire.

A case in point was Kang Sheng's criticism of two films, *Zao chun er yue* (Early Spring in February) and *Bei guo jiang nan* (North and South of the Country), in July 1964 during the Peking Opera festival. By the end of the month, the CC's Propaganda Department, the two key members of which—Lu Dingyi and Zhou Yang—were members of Peng's five-man group, felt obliged to issue a report requesting instructions on whether the two films should be publicly shown and openly criticized.[95] With his penchant for education by negative example, Mao ordered the films to be shown not just in the big cities but in 100 medium-sized towns up and down the land so that the masses could be exposed to this revisionist material. He asserted that there were many more films than just these two that ought to be criticized. A massive denunciation campaign ensued.[96]

In addition, there were personal considerations that differentiated the two groups vying for control of the campaign. Peng Zhen and Zhou Yang, it emerged, would try to protect at least some of the more famous party intellectuals and cultural officials with whom they had close links. As an outsider, Jiang Qing, abetted by Kang Sheng and Ke Qingshi, had no such *guanxi* ties. Moreover, she seems to have harboured resentments against many establishment figures, either for real or imagined slights when she had been a minor member of leftist artistic circles in the old days in Shanghai, or for being fobbed off with bit parts in the 1950s and 1960s when she auditioned unsuccessfully for the role of a cultural commissar.

A prominent example was the playwright Tian Han, chair and party secretary of the Dramatists' Association, who was one of Jiang Qing's *bêtes noires* from her actress past. As early as December 1963, Tian was cold-shouldered and humiliated at the East China opera festival.[97] At the Peking Opera festival, when Kang Sheng turned on his friend Meng Chao and publicly denounced his play *Li Huiniang* as reactionary, he coupled with it Tian Han's *Xie Yaohuan*.[98] This was a historical drama, admired by Chen Yi,[99] written, like Wu Han's *Hai Rui Ba Guan* (which will be considered in a later chapter) about an eponymous, virtuous—in this case, female—official who attempted to protect the people from corrupt colleagues. Within the play are layers of meaning and, written in 1961, it certainly refers by analogy to the sufferings caused by the GLF. Yet the imperial figure—in this case, also female, the famous Empress Wu, putatively Mao—enters the play at the end in a positive light, spurred to rectify abuses by her new-found knowledge of popular suffering. Whatever the justice of Tian Han's later critics, these attacks should have felled him forthwith, but his prestige, position, and perhaps the protection, in this case of Zhou Enlai, saved him from final disgrace until early 1966.[100]

Whereas Tian Han had offended Jiang Qing in the 1930s and erred ideologically in the 1960s, Zhou Yang's problem was that, possibly uniquely, he had personally offended Jiang Qing during both periods, and despite his senior bureaucratic position and his attempts always to fall into line with the Chairman's position, he too would disappear early on in the Cultural Revolution.[101] Because Mao supported Jiang Qing, in the end the five-man group was able only to procrastinate on behalf of favoured colleagues. Its members could not save even themselves.

18 FROM GREY EMINENCE TO RED LEADER

Wang Guangmei's Taoyuan experience

While Mao was encouraging Jiang Qing to investigate revisionism in the cultural arena, Liu Shaoqi was encouraging his wife, Wang Guangmei, to play a similar role in the countryside. The complementary roles played by the two wives should have made for harmony. But Jiang Qing resented the increasing public exposure which accrued to Wang Guangmei as the wife of the head of state. One hint of this occurred during the visit to China of the wife of Indonesia's President Sukarno in September 1962. After a number of pictures of Wang Guangmei in the company of Mme Sukarno had appeared in the *People's Daily*, the official party paper printed a picture of Mao and Jiang Qing with the Indonesian visitor on the front page, while printing a much smaller picture of Liu, Wang, and Mme Sukarno on page two. It was the first time Jiang Qing's picture had appeared in the paper and the first time that a photograph of her and Mao together had ever been released since the founding of the PRC.[1] From then on, occasional pictures of Mao and Jiang Qing, the latter unidentified, appeared in the official press.[2]

Wang, it will be remembered, had accompanied Liu on his inspection trip in Hunan in 1961, and so had experience of rural investigations. During that period, Liu had come to distrust the data provided by CCP officials and journalists, but simultaneously had had to confront the problems any well-known leader faced in seeking to gather information: peasants were reluctant to criticize CCP policy to august personages, especially if local officials were in the vicinity. Thus Liu decided to send his wife incognito to the countryside to ascertain the facts about cadre corruption in the wake of the GLF and the three bitter years.[3]

Using their wives as trouble-shooters was a high-risk strategy for both men. Initiatives by high-ranking spouses with no independent legitimacy arouses hostility and resentment in most political cultures,[4] and when their husbands disappeared both Wang and Jiang suffered. Liu at least tried to mitigate the risk, in vain as it later turned out, by obtaining Mao's approval for Wang's mission; according to Wang, every time she returned from the field, Mao would inquire about conditions at the grass roots.[5]

That Mao and Liu were prepared to adopt this controversial procedure of using their wives reflected their more general dissatisfaction with different parts of the system they had both done so much to create. Mao's increasing obsession with the cultural realm, and the failure of the relevant branches of the central CCP *apparat* to control it, led him to encourage his wife to make up for his subordinates' failures. Mao seems to have distrusted central officials because they did not always do exactly what he wanted them to do; he trusted provincial officials, perhaps because they tended to tell him what he wanted to hear.

Liu, on the other hand, trusted central officials because he worked with them and believed that their goals and methods were similar to his own; indeed, many key central officials had been members of the pre-1949 North China Bureau which he had headed. He was more concerned about the state of the CCP in the countryside where so much damage had been done during the GLF and the famine. His experience with Wu Zhipu in Henan in 1960 meant that he could never be sure that provincial officials would tell him the truth; his experience in Hunan in 1961 had given him an abiding impression of the difficulty of worming the truth out of peasants.[6] Hence in 1963, he sent his wife to find out for him. His instructions to her were: 'Don't have any preconceptions; always start out from the actual situation; and solve whatever problems there are. You must have a Marxist-Leninist standpoint, viewpoint, and method, and you must understand the basic policies of the party, but apart from that don't have any preconceptions, and always start out from the actual situation.'[7]

At the end of November 1963, Wang Guangmei joined an SEM work team in Hebei which was assigned the task of investigating Taoyuan (Peach Orchard) brigade in Tangshan district.[8] It was an area which she and Liu had visited in 1958, but this time she used the name Dong Pu, and wore a gauze mask and wrapped a large scarf round her head to disguise herself.[9] According to Mme Wang's own report, the team's original intention was to spend three months in Taoyuan, but the complexity of its mission kept it there for five. The crops were doing fine, but class struggle was a different matter.[10] The problem, it emerged, was the brigade party secretary, Wu Chen. As in the case of the clash between Liu Shaoqi and Peng Meixiu in

Hunan 1961,[11] this principal culprit was to be transformed during the Cultural Revolution into an almost blameless victim.

Wu Chen had some trumps in his hand. The commune authorities had commended him to the work team. The work team leader was a county cadre who was very familiar with the brigade cadres.[12] And, as Mme Wang found out, Wu was prepared to use all the resources of five years of incumbency. Her ace, like Jiang Qing's, was her husband, with whom she maintained contact while in the field.[13]

The work team launched three 'high tides' to try to induce cadres to 'take a bath' by confessing their faults, and to encourage the peasants to speak up against them. The first high tide consisted of summoning the three levels of local cadres—commune, brigade, and team—to a conference at which the commune party secretary was supposed to give a lead by publicly unburdening himself of his sins. This he failed to do, and so the Taoyuan cadres were also coy. After some prevarication, Wu Chen confessed only to beating a few commune members.

After a North China regional si qing conference in which the work team participated, a second high tide, characterized by more widespread investigations and careful ideological work, was launched. Wang's description gives the impression that this represented a breakthrough, as a result of which the cohesion of the brigade power structure began to fracture, and the balance of forces between the entrenched local cadres and the outsiders on the team began to change. The third high tide was launched by another three-level cadres conference, this one addressed by the Hebei provincial 1st secretary, Lin Tie, who called on cadres to engineer their personal revolutions and on the masses to help them, with a promise of mercy for reformed prodigals.[14]

Gradually the masses did speak up, but only after the team, at their suggestion, had set up a complaints box, and, again at their suggestion, had moved it from in front of the team's HQ to a public lavatory, so that a peasant could drop in a 'speak bitterness' note without fear of discovery by the cadres he sought to discredit.[15] Slowly, the team built up a dossier of charges of embezzlement, capitalist activities, and thirty-one beatings against Wu Chen. He was accused also of falsifying his class background; in fact, he started out as a pedlar, not a poor peasant, and was given to feasting, whoring, and gambling. This was not a party branch which had changed colour, the team concluded; it had always been a KMT-type organization.[16] Wu's backstage boss was a landlord who had cunningly avoided that classification at the time of land reform by selling off most of his holdings in advance.[17] Wu was expelled from the CCP, and the local militia chief, Guan Jingdong, replaced him as party secretary.[18]

In September 1967, the *People's Daily* published a major attack on Wang's activities in the Hebei countryside. A comparison of Wang Guangmei's account with the Cultural Revolution version reveals similarities and differences. Wang admitted that the new party secretary, chosen under the aegis of the work team, had a record of embezzling money and grain. She justified his appointment on the grounds of his ability to raise production.[19] The *People's Daily* admitted that Wu Chen had beaten peasants and had once been a pedlar.[20] It defended him on the grounds of his long-term commitment to socialist agriculture.[21]

It was hardly surprising that in the post-famine period, Wang and her work team would be particularly keen that their investigations and changes should result in a boost in agricultural output,[22] nor that at the height of the Cultural Revolution, the party paper would focus on ideology; both positions could be supported with quotations from Mao. But what the two accounts confirm is how widespread corruption was throughout the rural power structure. This meant that incoming work teams were presented with unpalatable alternatives: either to confirm the current cadres in power with admonitions to do better from now on, or to replace them with perhaps equally dubious cadres who had the good fortune not to be in the front line at that moment. Wang Guangmei stressed the importance and the difficulty of finding local stalwarts or 'roots' (*genzi*).[23] Almost certainly, all viable leadership material had been tapped at some time already, so that virtually every cadre or potential cadre might be tainted.[24]

It was politically inconceivable that a class struggle launched with so much fanfare should end up preserving the *status quo ante*. So work teams had little option but to replace one set of flawed cadres with another. For the peasants, it was doubtless a case of *plus ça change, plus c'est la même chose*—unless they happened to have a relative or friend in the new leadership line-up. The impact on the CCP was far more serious. By reshaping the rural institutional infrastructure that had been in place since land reform a decade-and-a-half earlier, the work teams precipitated a wholesale disruption of the bureaucratic ecology of the countryside. Since, as Wang Guangmei's report revealed, the current cadre leadership had close links with the power-holders immediately above, this in turn meant that the SEM could be carried out only by outsider work teams whose political clout exceeded that of county and district authorities. This was the revolution which Liu Shaoqi sought to unleash in the aftermath of his wife's return to Beijing. He had good reason to anticipate Mao's support.

The Revised Latter Ten Points

From the end of March to the end of April 1964, just as Wang Guangmei was winding up her spell in Taoyuan brigade, Mao did his usual whistle-stop tour *en route* to Hangzhou, and also heard reports from officials from eight provinces. He told everyone that the two sets of ten points had to be jointly propagandized, and he reprimanded one of his favourite 1st secretaries, Wang Renzhong of Hubei, for not having gone to the grass roots to investigate.[25]

When Mao and Liu met at the central work conference held from 15 May to 17 June, they seemed to be on the same wavelength. One major issue was the extent of the problem which the centre faced. The gloomy appraisal of rural cadres which Liu had gleaned from his wife and imparted to his colleagues was in line with what Mao had been saying since late 1960. In November that year, the Chairman had blamed bad elements for the poor economic conditions in one-third of all rural areas. Again in December and in January 1961, Mao blamed 'feudal forces' and the restoration of earlier power structures for the disasters that had been largely caused by his own utopian visions.[26] Mao returned to this theme on 14 June 1963, as the SEM got under way. A year later, on 4 June 1964, he told a North Korean visitor that almost a third of the teams in the countryside were controlled by the CCP's enemies and their allies; on the 8th, he told the central work conference that about one-third of national power structures were not in the hands of the CCP.[27] Even when engaged in a rambling discourse on philosophy on 18 August, he dragged in the problem of corrupt rural cadres, striking proof of how obsessed he was with the issue.[28] This was the line which Liu later echoed. At the work conference, Liu also accused basic-level cadres of attempting to subvert and derail the SEM by describing the 'four clean-ups' as 'anti-party'. He proposed that any such disruption should be characterized as counter-revolutionary and should result in expulsion from the party.[29] Liu also anticipated Mao on the question of where true responsibility for current problems lay: not at the grass roots where the 'four unclean' cadres were to be found, but higher up in the hierarchy, where he detected 'peaceful evolution' (*heping yanbian*) towards capitalism. He advocated uncovering such roots of corruption even if they were in the CC [30]

After many fire-eating speeches, with calls for the removal of stumbling-blocks (*ban shitou*) in the countryside and a reclassification of classes in the cities,[31] at the end of the conference the CC secretariat formally decided to revise the Latter Ten Points. The senior secretariat member concerned with agriculture, Tan Zhenlin, was put in charge of this task and of drafting regulations for poor and lower-middle peasant associations; and the senior secretariat member concerned with urban affairs, Peng Zhen, was assigned to draft a new directive for the urban five-antis campaign. The peasant association regulations were quickly drawn up and circulated on 25 June, with an accompanying directive which raised the spectre of reclassifying those who had illegitimately acquired the status of poor or lower-middle peasants.[32]

Liu Shaoqi spent much of July and August on tour, making speeches in many parts of the country: Tianjin, Jinan, Hefei, Nanjing, Shanghai, Zhengzhou, Wuhan, Changsha, Canton, and Nanning. He later explained that he became concerned that some articles in the Latter Ten Points 'would interfere with the free mobilization of the masses'.[33] He stressed Mao's line on the CCP losing political control over one-third of the country, and the need to seek out the upper-level bosses of bad basic-level cadres. Equally threateningly, he indicated that one could not depend on basic-level cadres, and that the 95 per cent figure for those who could be united with might have to be revised downward. He urged expanding the concept of the four cleans, suggesting that the four current ones could be subsumed under one—clean economics—and that clean politics, ideology, and organization should be added. Finally, he advocated concentrating one's forces and fighting battles of annihilation (*da jianmie zhan*), by which he meant sending in massive work teams which would swamp the local power structures in order to reform them.[34]

Liu's itinerary indicated both the crucial importance of the Central-South and East China regions and their leaders, Tao Zhu and Ke Qingshi, and their unequivocal endorsement of the SEM. More importantly, his innovative proposals were clear evidence of self-confidence, and an assumption that he was in charge of the SEM. Additional proof of this was provided by the behaviour of Mao's political trusty, Chen Boda. Ever one to hitch his wagon to the next star,[35] Chen suggested to Liu that the report on her Taoyuan experience which Wang Guangmei, at Peng Zhen's suggestion, had given to the Hebei provincial committee on 5 July, should be distributed more widely. Mao allegedly expressed disgust at this performance in an earthy peasant phrase,[36] but presumably in ignorance of this, Liu readily assented to Chen Boda's proposal and wrote an introduction. On 5 August, Deng and the secretariat formally transferred the revision of the Latter Ten Points from Tan Zhenlin to Liu (with Bo Yibo taking over the five antis from Peng Zhen),[37] and, on Chen Boda's suggestion, put Liu in charge of a new directorate in overall charge of the SEM and the five antis.[38]

It was presumably in this capacity that Liu wrote to Mao and the CC on 16 August, informing them that he had advised provinces in the Central-South region to alter their tactics for the SEM. Instead of forming *xian* work teams to attend to their sub-districts, he had suggested that Hubei and Hunan organize provincial and prefecture level teams to deal with the *xian* under them. This would create a force of several thousand, or perhaps ten thousand, for a battle of annihilation. He further proposed that central organs should send a third of their cadres in units of 10,000 or several tens of thousands down to the countryside.

Mao wrote back on 18 August expressing complete support, saying that he thought that these ideas were 'very good'. The Chairman may have been excited by the grandiosity of Liu's approach, a sort of GLF technique for ideological cleansing. He may also have considered it an appropriate response to the call, in the CCP's recently published ninth polemic, for the rearing of revolutionary successors. Mao told Liu that he had discussed his proposals with other central comrades, presumably including Deng as head of the secretariat who would have to organize implementation, and ordered the party to proceed swiftly on these lines; party thinking could be united around this approach at the October work conference. In the meanwhile, the centre, provinces, and lower levels should spend the next two months training work teams, to be ready for a flying start in the autumn. As a result of Mao's instruction, the various ministries and departments in the industrial and transportation sector organized 25 per cent of their cadre force into a team of 3,901 which included a third of the deputy ministers. Nationwide, 1,560,000 cadres were mobilized for the SEM and the urban five antis.[39]

On 19 August, Liu pressed on with a further letter to Mao and the CC, enclosing his suggested revisions to the Latter Ten Points. Tian Jiaying took the document from Canton to Beidaihe. A week later,

Mao passed on the revised draft to Deng Xiaoping with the instruction that it should be circulated as quickly as possible to members of the regional secretariats and others who had attended the work conference for their opinions so that the draft could be further revised.

Mao's support was surprising. When his secretary Tian Jiaying was leaving to accompany Liu on his tour at Liu's request, he had asked the Chairman for instructions and been given two points to bear in mind: (a) not to paint the lower-level cadres in pitch-black colours; (b) not to concentrate large work teams at a single spot. Tian duly passed these views on to Liu, but they seem to have had little effect on him. At this point, Mao apparently accepted Liu's position.[40]

Perhaps Mao was influenced by Wang Guangmei's report to him on her Taoyuan experience. He advised her to hold big meetings of 10,000 people and mobilize the masses on a grand scale.[41] Certainly Mao's most significant endorsement of Liu's activities took place on 27 August, when he supported Chen Boda's suggestion that Wang's report should be circulated. Among the report's recommendations which were seen as significant within the CCP were: first strike roots and establish ties (*zhagen chuanlian*), and then carry out the four clean-ups and struggle against the enemy; depend, but not totally, upon the basic-level cadres; the four cleans were not just work points, accounts, finances, and granaries, but were politics, economics, ideology, and organization. On 1 September, the CC circulated Wang's report with the comment, written by Liu, that it had general significance.[42] On 18 September, after consideration by a work conference chaired by Liu in late August, and after Mao, Zhou, Deng Xiaoping, and Peng Zhen had checked and approved it, the CC issued the Revised Latter Ten Points.[43] This was Liu Shaoqi's most notable achievement in the eyes of his colleagues since the Seven Thousand Cadres Conference, and it marked the transition from the 'little four clean-ups' to the 'big four clean-ups'.[44]

There were seven key changes and additions in the new document according to Bo Yibo, who was an alternate member of the Politburo at the time and had taken over supervision of the five antis in August:

- Mao's six criteria for judging whether the SEM was being conducted well. [These were: the degree of mobilization of the poor and lower-middle peasants; the elimination of the four uncleans among cadres; the participation of cadres in manual labour; the creation of a good leading nucleus; the conduct of struggle against undesirable elements of various types at the basic level; increase of production.];[45]

- leaders had to participate at the brigade level from beginning to end of the process and they should do it twice;
- the criterion for judging the thoroughness of SEM work was whether or not the masses in general and the poor and lower-middle peasants in particular were unleashed;
- one could only solve the problems of the masses on the basis of solving the problems of the cadres; the movement had to be led by the work teams;
- in areas where the democratic revolution [i.e. land reform] had not been thorough, it was necessary to undertake additional work [which included reclassification of former landlords or rich peasants who had managed to sneak their way into the ranks of the poor peasants];
- the movement should be divided into two stages, the first being to carry out the four clean-ups and struggle against the enemy, and the second being organizational reconstruction.

Of these seven points, the most significant was the stress on work team leadership.[46]

The new document exhibited the ruthless thoroughness which Liu Shaoqi felt crucial for the success of the SEM. It was estimated that the campaign would take five to six years in contrast to the earlier two to three. The minimum period for a work team's operations was extended from three to six months. Excessive concern for the 'face' of basic-level cadres was decried; in contrast to the original Latter Ten Points, the revised version warned that rightism in this regard was more serious than leftism. Not just serious offenders, but even cadres who had committed only minor sins now had to be confronted by the masses; peasant fears of being left to the mercy of local officials after the departure of work teams were addressed by an assurance of regular check-ups by work teams to ensure that their achievements had not been undermined. All cases of corruption had to be dealt with by the work teams, and not handed over to more senior local officials who had, under the earlier dispensation, tended to act leniently towards people with whom they had long working relationships. Persuasive education to reform working people who had become speculators or profiteers was dropped in favour of struggle. Liu had the bit between his teeth.[47]

The conduct of the SEM: the worm's-eye view

During the Cultural Revolution, it was possible to glean information about the conduct of the SEM from basic-level cadres and peasants who had fled to Hong Kong, mainly from south China. After the Cultural Revolution, accounts could also be had from work team members. From this worm's-eye viewpoint, the SEM was a terrible experience. Each *xian* selected for SEM treatment received a work team of over 10,000 people. Local cadres were completely bypassed, and in many cases had power 'seized' from them. In one commune in Qinghai province, perhaps cited as an example of leftism run rampant because it was one of the worst in the country, the work team decided that 47 per cent of the cadres required dismissal and disciplinary action.[48] In many places and at many times, cadres were beaten or trussed up, and there were cases of flight and suicide. In Tong *xian* on the outskirts of Beijing, to which a team of journalists, including forty from the *People's Daily*, was sent for a year,[49] there were well over a hundred cases of beatings; seventy people attempted suicide and fifty succeeded. In the Shanxi *xian* of Hongdong, forty-five people died. In Sichuan, more people were arrested in November and December than in the previous ten months of 1964.[50]

In one Guangdong county, all rural cadres were brought together in compounds in the county seat where for several weeks they were subjected to political study sessions; in time-honoured CCP fashion, a quota of fines for corruption was assigned to each commune's set of cadres. According to a cadre who weathered this struggle:

For the best part of a month we were made to study party documents and write confessions. I even had to confess how many free movies I had attended, and how many pieces of sugarcane I ate while working in the collective fields. I was fined 46 yuan but refused to pay. Many cadres were scared stiff . . . Some cadres felt so humiliated that they refused to resume their posts afterward.

According to another cadre, the ordeal did not end when the cadres returned to their communes from the compounds: 'When we returned home, the work teams mobilized the masses to criticize us. It was vicious. In previous rectification campaigns, the matter was largely confined within the party. This time, all hell broke loose.'[51]

There seems to have been a policy of targeting outstanding units, perhaps to demonstrate that the SEM would be conducted without fear or favour from now on, and that no cadres, however apparently worthy, would be excused investigation. In fact, the available accounts make it clear that there were serious problems everywhere. In Shandong, the whole family of the leader of the Dongguo brigade in Qufu *xian*, a famous provincial labour model who had greatly raised local living standards, was denounced and his eldest son was dismissed as head of the local militia.[52] The model Shengshi brigade in Guangdong's Pearl River delta, which had earlier been given a clean bill of health by the provincial 1st secretary, Zhao Ziyang, was revisited by a new work team, this time under the leadership of Wang Guangmei, again incognito, backed by members of the provincial and Beijing public security bureaux. The local party boss, another labour model, but guilty of rape and corruption, attempted unsuccessfully to flee by boat to Hong Kong. Even the famous Dazhai brigade in Shanxi province was reclassified by a work team from 'advanced unit' to a unit 'with serious problems'.[53] In the words of one Western scholar, it was 'in all probability the most intensive purge of rural Party members and cadres in the history of the Chinese People's Republic'.[54]

Urban radicalism

As the Beijing suburban suicides indicated, the radical thrust was not confined to the deepest countryside. Xiaozhan district in the suburbs of Tianjin, also in Hebei province, produced an even more threatening model than Wang Guangmei's Taoyuan. The SEM had started there in January 1964, but in March the city party decided to reinforce the work team considerably, perhaps because it had got wind of what was happening in Taoyuan. The new recruits included Zhou Yang, and ten staff members from *Red Flag*, including its chief editor Chen Boda, probably at his own suggestion.[55] On 4 August, pre-empting the Tianjin party's own report, Chen wrote to tell the CC that three counter-revolutionary cliques had been uncovered there. One was led by a rice specialist, one by a female labour model, and the third by a township party secretary. Chen's letter was circulated along with its supporting material; six weeks later, the Tianjin party's own report confirming Chen's findings was distributed with the comment that wherever leadership had been usurped by counter-revolutionaries there had to be a struggle to seize power.[56] According to one account, 250 cadres were purged as a result of Chen's activities.[57]

In many cases, such as the industrial and transport ministries, the urban five-antis campaign had been considered completed in 1963, but was revived in response to the new leftism in 1964. In that year the various ministries of the industrial and transportation system organized 130,000 cadres, including forty-five deputy ministers, into work teams, sending them into 1,800 state enterprises and 730 collective enterprises.[58] Though the movement was not as severe as some previous campaigns,[59] it produced the other notorious urban model, the case of the Gansu Silver and Non-Ferrous Metals Company, known as the Silver Plant. This large-scale enterprise, which had come on stream in 1962, employed 11,000 workers, producing copper and sulphur in addition to silver. A five-anti work team, sent by the province and the Ministry of the Metallurgical Industry had arrived as early as March 1963, but spurred on by the rising leftist tide, it depicted the company's problems as the transformation of a state enterprise into a 'landlord-capitalist' one. A struggle to recover power took place and several senior party officials at the plant were disciplined, some receiving criminal sentences.[60]

Liu ascendant

With the help of alarmist reports like these, Liu stoked the fires of class struggle. He fired off a series of instructions.[61] No central or provincial cadre who was a member of a work team wanted to be accused of failing to recover power from landlord-type elements or corrupted former poor peasants (who might be revealed to be landlords who had escaped proper classification). Since all reports, contemporary and subsequent, indicated that corruption was widespread, any accusation from a disgruntled peasant or worker had to be treated as a smoke signal indicating fire.

The most fervent support for Liu seems to have come from the Central-South region. In Liu's year-end dispute with Mao, discussed below, it would be Tao Zhu who shared Liu's opinions. Tao's principal aide, the Hubei 1st secretary Wang Renzhong, having heeded Mao's criticism and gone down to the grass roots, soon made a speech which Liu ordered circulated in early December.[62] Wang referred often to 'Comrade Shaoqi's' utterances, a striking indication of Liu's current role coming from a Mao crony. Wang also endorsed Liu's analysis that the previous year's SEM work had only scratched the surface; that there were workers who had become exploiters, CCP members who had changed into the KMT; and that the real problem lay not at the grass roots but higher up, even at the provincial level. This was, of course, Mao's position as well, but Wang referred only to Liu.[63] Could the Chairman have been irked by this shift of loyalty?

The Hubei 1st secretary gave three sets of reasons for 'peaceful evolution' and counter-revolutionary seizures of power, social, historical, and party work. He pointed out that the secretary of Anquan brigade in Hongan *xian* had been installed by the 'enemy' as long ago as 1947 when the area was liberated by the forces led by Liu

Bocheng and Deng Xiaoping, and thus had had seventeen years to disguise himself. State and collective enterprises had been taken over as counter-revolutionaries installed themselves from top to bottom in the brigade. Land reform had been thorough, but not thorough enough, and so the bad elements were not uncovered. Not every activist cadre who had emerged during land reform was bad, but 'these men are all peasants and peasants have a dual nature, a revolutionary activist nature, alongside a spontaneous tendency to be selfish and think only of enriching their own families'. The CCP's failure, Wang said, was to have talked perennially to these cadres about production, accounts, and distribution to the neglect of ideology, politics, and class struggle. If peasants were not educated to take the communist road, they would inevitably regress towards capitalism.[64] The economic depression of 1961 and 1962, and the emergence of two types of market and prices, had encouraged speculation, even within the CCP, as cadres struggled for more than their fair shares and became corrupt. Cadres and their families had become a privileged stratum, for whom money came with power; in 1961–2, some had even wanted to give up being cadres in order to go into business.[65] Inevitably, unclean economics corrupted politics and organization. Thus opposing the four uncleans meant a sharp, complicated two-class, two-line struggle, encompassing both contradictions among the people and with the enemy, with the one type mutating into the other.[66]

Wang Renzhong endorsed the proposition that the focus of the current struggle had to be the principal contradiction, which was that between the masses and the four unclean cadres—a Liu formulation, which Mao would later reject. Wang also undercut Mao's original assumption, embedded in the Former Ten Points launching the SEM,[67] that 'education' by means of comparison between now and then could be an effective means of convincing peasants of the virtues of socialism, for some peasants' lives were as miserable as before and most were oppressed by four unclean cadres. In another break with the Former Ten Points, Wang set aside the notion that unleashing the masses against the four unclean cadres could be like 'taking a warm bath' or a 'gentle breeze and mild rain'; on the contrary, it would be a 'violent revolutionary storm'.[68] Thus rural cadres were to be subjected to a far sterner rectification campaign than that to which senior cadres had been briefly exposed in 1957;[69] the wind would not be tempered to the shorn lamb, indeed, just the opposite. Moreover, oppressed peasants could be expected to be much blunter in their criticisms than cautious bourgeois intellectuals.

The Hubei 1st secretary was well aware that the kind of movement he was describing could wreak organizational havoc within the provincial party. Wang contemplated that during the SEM, brigade party branches would generally collapse and the work teams would have to assume control, handing over power to the poor peasant associations once they had been formed. After the completion of the movement, cleaned-up, healthier party branches could be established and once more become the core of brigade leadership. To encourage Hubei party members who must have been appalled at what was in store for them, Wang held out the optimistic prospect that if the SEM were conducted correctly, the victory of Marxism-Leninism over feudalism, capitalism, and revisionism would be assured. By implication, then, the SEM would be the last major revolutionary movement.[70] This concept of a *terminus ad quem* for revolutionary movements would be rejected by Mao during the Cultural Revolution in favor of regular upheavals to keep everyone's revolutionary *élan* ever on the boil.

Wang's apocalyptic vision of the wholesale collapse of party branches was not a figment of a fervid imagination. He must have heard that this had already begun to happen in neighbouring Hunan, also in the Central-South region. On 1 November, the governor, Cheng Qian, and the party 1st secretary, Zhang Pinghua, the latter as head of the preparatory committee of the provincial poor peasant association, signed a formal order licensing work teams to transfer the reins of power to local poor peasant associations where party branches had collapsed or were in the hands of the enemy. Liu had approved this move on 12 November, three days before Wang Renzhong gave his speech, though the speech was not distributed until 3 December.[71]

Resistance to Liu

But if the Central-South region were hell-bent on carrying out Liu Shaoqi's version of the SEM, elsewhere there was resistance. Sherlock Holmes would have noticed many dogs that did not bark, or at least not very loudly.[72] The 1st secretary of the Southwest region, Politburo member Li Jingquan, does not figure in any accounts, and Liu Shaoqi did not visit the region during the summer of 1964 although it included China's most populous province, Sichuan. Liu may have assumed, however, that, with a proven record of leftism, Li could be trusted to carry out his orders.[73] The Northeast region was so silent that on 6 December, Liu had to write plaintively to 1st secretary Song Renqiong, requesting at least a brief communication to bring him up to date on the SEM there.[74]

The North China region, the location of the Taoyuan brigade, was definitely unhappy. First secretary Li Xuefeng complained to Mao on 20 August, expressing his opposition to Liu's proposal to take the SEM out of the hands of *xian* committees; he also vouchsafed that there were those who had reservations about the Taoyuan model. Mao, however, had just approved Liu's plans and Li was not given any encouragement.[75] This may explain why Li wrote to Liu on 11 October, supporting Liu's approach, but justifying his own earlier position by spelling out the significant opposition he had faced at the *xian* level in trying to push through CC directives. At the outset, only 60–70 per cent of the *xian* had accepted that they should be sidelined in the SEM. Many *xian* officials, and also provincial and even regional officials, basically did not understand the seriousness of the class struggle problem. Effectively, Li Xuefeng conceded Liu's case by estimating that in the case of the ninety-six *xian* in Shanxi province, 44 or 45 per cent had serious problems: two committees were totally rotten, seventeen were seriously rightist, five were seriously factionalized, and another twenty were pretty rightist. Of the ninety-six *xian* secretaries, nineteen opposed or did not support the SEM and nineteen were compromisers, totalling 40 per cent.[76]

The North China region came reluctantly to heel, but not apparently East China, controlled by Mao's principal crony in the regions, Politburo member Ke Qingshi. While Liu visited four of the region's seven provincial-level units during his summer tour, including Shanghai, there is no indication of Ke giving him overt support. Moreover, Liu's only disclosed confrontation with a senior official over the SEM other than Mao was with an East China regional secretary, Jiang Weiqing, who had worked as Ke's deputy in Jiangsu province before succeeding him as provincial 1st secretary in 1955. Liu used this extraordinary episode to indicate to provincial leaders that he would not brook opposition.

Jiang Weiqing was a native of Jiangsu and had worked there since 1949. At the first session of the CCP's 8th Congress in 1956, he had been made an alternate member of the CC.[77] Jiang's speeches and reports had from time to time been praised by the centre and distributed for the edification of his colleagues, which was not unusual for a cadre of his rank and role.[78] The quarrel between him and Liu on this occasion arose because a speech Jiang had made on the SEM had been distributed for study within Jiangsu province. Liu had visited Jiangsu during the summer, but the confrontation between the two men took place in Beijing at some point before 8 September. At that meeting, Liu raised the issue of the speech's distribution, whereupon Jiang heatedly asserted that it had been done by the provincial general office without his knowledge, and insisted that Liu had no right to disbelieve the word of a party man. Liu dropped the matter, but Jiang was apparently so agitated that the rest of the meeting was unproductive.[79] The implication of Liu's account is that he had read Jiang's speech during his visit to Jiangsu, considered it inadequate and said so, and was affronted that the speech had been disseminated anyway. Jiang's defence was that he may not have exercised sufficient control over his subordinates, but that he had not defied Liu and so committed the far greater sin of flouting party discipline.

On 8 September, Jiang wrote Liu what Liu considered an unsatisfactory letter, indicating that Jiang had not understood Liu's concerns. On 30 September, Liu replied, pointing this out, and this reply prompted the Jiangsu provincial committee to send him a telegram on 15 October, containing an abject self-criticism by Jiang. Having asserted his authority, and fortified by Mao's approval, Liu distributed both his letter and the telegram down to the county level, as an object lesson to thousands of party officials nationwide, some of whom were allegedly worse than Jiang.[80]

Why was Jiang's report not worth distributing? Because, Liu wrote, it was just 'pages and pages of empty verbiage' (*konghua lianpian*), an uncreative exercise in dogmatism, which in this case meant simply repeating existing documents. The first section had been a rehash of the Former Ten Points and Mao's speech on the subject; the second section had referred to Liu's speech in the Jiangsu capital, Nanjing, without quotation, only because Liu had not spoken from a written text. The third and fourth sections had been purely administrative instructions on the conduct of the SEM.[81]

Jiang Weiqing was not the first and surely would not be the last Chinese official to avoid committing himself by the well-worn device of repeating what his superiors had said, and, when two superiors took different lines, repeating them both. Thus Liu was disingenuous when he charged Jiang with sitting on the fence. Moreover, had Jiang's boiler-plate been more to Liu's liking, he would likely not have incurred Liu's wrath. But Liu felt that it indicated reservations about his own Nanjing speech. Liu spelled out his objections, confident that he was fully in charge.

Liu proclaimed himself supportive of the current movement to study Mao's works and the slogan 'Study and apply Chairman Mao's works in a lively fashion'. He did not oppose calls to study the Former Ten Points and Mao's speech, but he felt that all this could have been covered in a few sentences; to make it the centre-piece of Jiang's speech was simply to dogmatize Mao's works.[82] Indeed, Liu's analysis of the SEM conference which Jiangsu had held was that at all levels of the provincial party, including the top, cadres were out of touch with reality and the masses. The Jiangsu *apparat* fell into the category of cadres characterized by Mao as arrogant, complacent, and conservative. During their meeting in Beijing, Liu had pressed Jiang into admitting that, despite over a decade in the province, he knew less about the situation there today than before, especially when it came to class struggle. Jiang, Liu now wrote, was unable to enforce party directives, for local committees did as they pleased; they led him rather than vice versa.[83]

Liu accused Jiang and many of his colleagues of failing to go among the masses and so passing on the opinions only of the basic level cadres. It was the misinformation disseminated by cadres that had resulted in the mistakes in the Latter Ten Points, with the result that the masses had been constrained. Hence the need to revise that document.

Liu ended his letter with an expression of confidence that Jiang was a good cadre, and of joy that he had finally gone down to the grass roots. But these pats on the head only underlined the devastating nature of the humiliation to which Liu had subjected Jiang, a lesson which other provincial secretaries doubtless took to heart.[84] Without minimizing his anger at Jiang's earlier defiance, which crackles off the page, Liu's real target may have been Jiang's immediate superior, Ke Qingshi, whose dumb insolence could have given the Jiangsu 1st secretary the courage to dig in his heels.[85] Certainly, by dressing down Jiang Weiqing in public, Liu served notice upon Ke and other regional bosses that if they did not enforce his directives, then he would interfere directly in their bailiwicks. This constituted the most powerful assertion of personal authority over the party machine that Mao's deputy had ever attempted to make. Mao may have chafed at the brusque treatment accorded his words and the Former Ten Points, but in its wake, Mao seemed ready to cede Liu formal authority as well.

'You be Qin Shi Huang'!

There is only one source providing testimony to the Chairman's innermost feelings about his principal deputy: the memoirs of Dr Li Zhisui. According to Dr Li, the Chairman's personal physician from 1954 to 1976, Mao had long been deeply suspicious of Liu, and his enmity was vividly shown when he learned, in early 1964, that Liu had contracted tuberculosis. Mao apparently displayed satisfaction rather than concern. More importantly, Dr Li believed that Mao's subsequent steps to limit the special care available to China's leaders by ordering the abolition of the Central Bureau of Health were aimed against Liu.[86] Whatever the accuracy of this intuition, the relationship between Mao and Liu entered a climactic phase in the last few months of 1964. As so often in the past, events in the Soviet Union probably had a critical impact upon Mao's thinking.[87]

The decisive period was between mid-October, when Khrushchev fell, and mid-November, when Zhou Enlai's delegation returned from Moscow empty-handed. Had Brezhnev and his colleagues been even partially accommodating, Mao could legitimately have claimed a victory. Instead, they indicated their intention, in the words of the *People's Daily*, of practising 'Khrushchevism without Khrushchev'. If Mao were afflicted by even a fraction of the paranoia attributed to him by Dr Li, these developments should have been profoundly disturbing.[88] Why not 'Maoism without Mao?' For the Chairman, Malinovsky's drunken suggestion that he should be removed was too close to the bone to be dismissed as simply bad manners.

The Soviets had purged Khrushchev not because they disagreed with all his policies, but because they considered his attempts to revamp the party and other 'hare-brained schemes' to be too damaging to the country and to their institutional interests.[89] As Brezhnev put it, Khrushchev 'swears at us, says we don't do a damn thing. . . he's impossible to work with . . . We just don't know what to do with him'.[90] Mao's penchant for sarcasm and bullying at the expense of his colleagues was at least on a par with Khrushchev's, and with a record which in the previous decade included the abortive Hundred Flowers, the GLF and the subsequent famine, the purge of a national military hero, the rejection of a sensible agricultural policy, the launching of the disruptive SEM, the adoption of a costly 'third front' policy in preference to a more moderate international stance, and now an attempt to revamp the party, Mao had espoused even

more 'hare-brained schemes' with far more disastrous consequences. During the Cultural Revolution, the Maoists would condemn Liu Shaoqi as 'China's Khrushchev', but after the fall of the
CPSU 1st secretary, Mao could have been forgiven for fearing that
he might end up with that soubriquet.[91]

Zhang Wentian, when under attack at Lushan in 1959 as a member of an anti-Mao clique, exclaimed: 'Who wants to topple Chairman Mao? And even if someone really wanted to topple him, they
wouldn't be able to do it.'[92] Probably virtually all of Mao's senior colleagues would have echoed that sentiment in 1964, but the Chairman could never be sure. He would have noted that the plot against
Khrushchev could be carried out only when he was out of the capital, because that was the only time when he was not in day-to-day
control of affairs; since the Chairman was out of the capital far more
often and never in charge of affairs on a daily basis, he was in principle far more at risk. When, in 1961, he discovered that his private
train and all his residences had been bugged, his immediate suspicion was that his colleagues intended to use the tapes in order to
compile a 'black report' against him as Khrushchev had against
Stalin.[93] After Khrushchev's 'secret speech' denouncing the late dictator, Mao had worried that he, too, might be denounced by colleagues after his death;[94] after the purge of Khrushchev, he had to
contemplate the far more alarming possibility of being toppled while
still alive. For Mao, from this point on, loyalty to his *person* had to be
more important than loyalty to his *policies*—which would be one
reason why a 'rightist' like Zhou Enlai would survive the Cultural
Revolution, while a 'leftist' like Liu would not. And loyalty included
promoting the Mao cult because, the Chairman concluded at that
time, '[p]robably Mr Khrushchev fell because he had no cult of personality at all . . .'[95]

Interestingly, Mao's reaction to potential danger resembled that
of Khrushchev when the Soviet leader had been under threat in
1963: he hinted at a willingness to step down.[96] On 26 November
1964, in the course of a meeting to discuss the 'third front', Mao said:

Shaoqi's still in command. The 'four clean-ups', the 'five antis', economic
work should all be run by you [i.e. Liu]. I'm Chairman, you're first deputy
chairman, but something unexpected could happen any time. Otherwise,
once I die you may not succeed. So let's change over now. You be Chairman;
you be Qin Shi Huang. I have my weak points. When I tell people off it has
no effect. You're vigorous. You should take over the role of telling people
off. You take control of Xiaoping and the premier.[97]

From the point of view of Mao's audience, the Chairman's initial remark may have seemed designed to emphasize that Liu was still in day-to-day charge despite the considerably augmented interest Mao had been displaying in economic affairs in general and the third front in particular during 1964.[98] Yet the passage is shot through with implicit reminders of Liu's secondary status: It is Mao who decides who's in command. Liu is referred to as first deputy chairman of the party under Mao, as if his other ranking as a fully fledged 'chairman' in his own right, albeit of the state, was of no consequence. There is a hint that without Mao's backing, Liu could not succeed him as party chairman. Even designating Liu as the new 'first emperor', to whom Mao was regularly compared, only served to underline how, by contrast, Liu was quite inappropriate for so imperial a role.[99] The great Chinese historian Sima Qian wrote: 'The king of Qin . . . is merciless with the heart of a tiger or a wolf. When he is in trouble, he finds it easy to humble himself, but when he is enjoying success, he finds it just as easy to devour human beings.'[100] That does not sound like Liu; it could be Mao.

Nevertheless, for Liu this was a tantalizing moment. Mao was apparently indicating a willingness finally to cede his party chairmanship to Liu and retire to the honorary chairmanship created for him and this eventuality at the CCP's 8th Congress.[101] Liu need no longer be a grey eminence; indeed, he was already proving that he could be as red as Mao in leading the party. But Liu's reaction suggests circumspection based on experience. Was this a poisoned chalice, he had to ask himself. Self-deprecatingly, he said he could not preside over so many matters: he could run the four clean-ups, but Peng Zhen[102] and Xie Fuzhi, the Minister for Public Security, were running the five antis, and the economy was being run by Deng Xiaoping and the premier. Mao was insistent: Deng and the others were very busy and if Liu did not take charge there would be no unity.[103]

But despite his disclaimers, the Chairman continued active. On 5 and 12 December, he commented in writing on reports on the five-antis campaign respectively from Xie Fuzhi and Chen Zhengren, one of his former secretaries. Similarly, on the 13th, he commented at length, again in writing, on the draft of Zhou Enlai's government report due to be submitted to the forthcoming NPC session. On the 14th, he wrote to Vice-Premier Bo Yibo agreeing with his suggestions about a proposed rail line needed for the third front.[104] Evidently, no attempt had been made to take Mao at his word and cut him out of the loop, and his subordinates' caution was justified by this continuing stream of comments from the Chairman.

The December work conference

At some point in December, Mao became unwell, sufficiently so for Deng Xiaoping to suggest that he not bother to attend what the General Secretary assumed would be a routine Politburo work conference on the SEM under the chairmanship of Liu Shaoqi. It was to be held simultaneously with the convocation of the new NPC. The agenda was to discuss Liu's appraisal of problems in the SEM and then to draft an appropriate document to deal with them.[105] Conceivably, Deng was also testing Mao's professed willingness to hand over affairs to Liu Shaoqi. If so, Mao's extraordinary behaviour quickly disabused his colleagues of any illusion that he would actually follow through on that commitment.

The conference opened with Liu's report on 15 December, and then split into small groups for discussion as was normal. Mao appears not to have attended until the 20th,[106] perhaps in the setting of a PSC meeting.[107] That day, Liu arrived after Mao and was told by him: 'You speak up first, and be the commander. If you don't speak up, we will adjourn the meeting.'[108] Again, Mao asserted leadership by demonstrating that it was his to cede. His displeasure with Liu emerged in the disagreements between them during the discussions on the SEM that day.[109]

According to one senior participant at the conference, the substance of the disagreement between the two men was (a) the basic issue or underlying contradiction at stake in the SEM, and (b) how to conduct the SEM.[110] The first issue was debated from the 20th through the 28th; the second issue did not surface seriously until January.[111]

Liu Shaoqi, supported by Tao Zhu, maintained the position he had taken as a result of Wang Guangmei's report and injected into the Revised Latter Ten Points three months earlier; Mao, it will be remembered, had endorsed the report and supported the policy. In that document, the original four clean-ups, drawn up under Mao's aegis and concerned purely with economic crimes, had been modified and expanded to embrace politics, economics, ideology, and organization. For Liu, the struggle was between the four cleans and the four uncleans. The uncleans which were to be uprooted consisted of three groups: former landlords and rich peasants; landlords and rich peasants who had escaped that fatal categorization at the time of land reform; and former poor and middle peasants who had degenerated into the equivalent of landlords and rich peasants as a result of their oppressive and exploitative behaviour after they became cadres in the wake of land reform and collectivization. Liu felt it was essential that this last category in particular be made to disgorge their ill-gotten gains if the peasants were to be appeased.[112]

One reason Mao favoured narrowing the number of people to be attacked was the sheer immensity of the task. It might amount, he suggested, to taking on 20 per cent of the population, about 140 m. people. As a result, he declared himself 'rightist' on this issue, and laid down that the percentage of families labelled as bad elements after struggle should not exceed 10 per cent, itself a concession since the normal campaign quota was 5 per cent. Mao's position in December 1964 closely resembled the line he had taken for similar reasons in early 1959 when he had called himself a rightist on the issue of extracting the peasantry's supposed hidden grain reserves.[113] The Chairman was always sensitive to the dangers of antagonizing too large a segment of the population, particularly in the countryside.

In opposition to Liu's Robespierre-like rectitude Mao even advocated going easy on those who had embezzled funds, rejecting the need for strictness and thoroughness in demanding repayment, and arguing for their quick admission into the revolutionary ranks. He was backed by the North China regional 1st secretary, Li Xuefeng, who had protested unsuccessfully to Mao about Liu's policies earlier in the year. Li now contended that Liu's tough line would diminish drastically the number of poorer peasants, which of course amounted to an admission that Liu's analysis of the rural scene was correct.

Liu countered by pointing out that the sums involved in many cases were not a few tens of yuan, as Mao had asserted, but rather hundreds or even thousands of yuan, to which the Chairman riposted that one could not squeeze all the toothpaste out of the tube, an oddly chosen analogy for a man whose concept of oral hygiene was the homely peasant procedure of rinsing with tea![114] Liu attempted vainly to pin the Chairman down to a percentage of embezzled funds which offenders would have to repay; Mao even suggested using state funds to reimburse those who had been exploited so that the offenders could be excused.[115]

Mao may have sincerely flinched at the enormity of the struggle that was being unleashed, but he also had a deeper motivation. By now he had decided that if revisionism were to be prevented from infecting China, it was the CCP that had to be purified, not pilfering peasants. Earlier in the month, he had talked darkly about the formation of a bureaucratic class who were or were becoming 'capitalist class elements drinking the blood of the workers';[116] in that same comment on 12 December for the first time, he apparently spoke of 'leaders taking the capitalist road'.[117] Now, at three points, he stressed the importance of focusing on the party members among the unclean cadres.[118] The problem about the rural SEM from this perspective was that there were relatively few party members among the cadres who were the campaign's targets. At the end of 1964, there were 18,011,000 CCP members, about 2.55 per cent of the population, but only 10,563,000, or 1.74 per cent of the rural population, were stationed in the countryside. After a massive intake—6,420,000 new members—during the GLF, there had been a virtual freeze from 1961 as the authorities attempted to absorb these often low-quality recruits. This meant, as Mao angrily pointed out, that there were relatively few party members at the brigade and team levels: 25 per cent of teams had no party member; two-thirds of all team leaders were not party members.[119] This in turn meant that the SEM, which Mao had launched, was a very blunt instrument for use in the countryside against what he now considered the prime target.

At this point in the discussion, Mao received support from Bo Yibo, Chairman of the State Economic Commission, who was supervising the urban five-anti campaign. Bo could readily target party members, for this directed the spotlight away from 'bourgeois' engineers, a result that accorded well with the pro-expert line of the Seventy Articles on Industry which Bo had been heavily involved in drafting three years earlier.[120] The following exchange took place:

Bo Yibo: Consequently, the first target should be clear, and we must concentrate our strength, to rectify the department, the factory and the party. For instance, in a department, members of the party group should be rectified first; in a factory, the secretary of the party committee and the factory director should be rectified first. It is necessary to make this stipulation clearly, for otherwise the cadres in power would slip away.

Chairman: By catching wolves first and foxes later, we have thus found the problem. It'd be impossible if we don't start with the power holders.

[Finance Minister] Li Xiannian: If we don't rectify the power holders, we will eventually rectify poor and lower-middle peasants.

Chairman: The basic problem lies here.

Bo Yibo: Strike at the wolf first and catch the fox later.[121]

Bo and Li seem to have had no hesitation in throwing the wolves to the wolves; indeed the Minister of the Metallurgical Industry, Wang Heshou, had already been dismissed, held responsible for the problems at the Gansu Silver Plant.[122] The proportion of party members in the arenas supervised by Bo and Li was far higher than in the countryside: 15.3 per cent in the industrial and communications system, 17.3 per cent in the financial and transportation system.[123] Perhaps they felt they could afford to cut out some fat.

Liu Shaoqi, too, seemed to feel obliged to appease the Chairman. He suggested letting off all guilty peasants, and that where cadres and peasants had collaborated in filching state moneys, only the cadres should pay compensation. In cultivating new cadres one might utilize 'brave elements' (*yonggan fenzi*), by whom Liu seemed to mean energetic people of dubious character, for Mao welcomed the idea, recalling that vagrants had been a mainstay of his early guerrilla force. In a revealing comment, the Chairman warned Liu that if he were obsessed with finding honest men he would accomplish nothing (*ni zhuan gao laoshi ren, bu hui ban shi*). Corrupt elements could also serve as prime ministers.[124]

But despite a few tactical retreats, Liu conceded little of substance. Perhaps he was emboldened by Mao's support in recent months. There was a genuine discussion, with Liu more than holding his own, speaking up and not allowing the Chairman to dominate the proceedings. The Chairman had indicated his desire that the SEM focus on the party, but that was no problem for Liu; it would not seriously affect the SEM in the countryside since party members would certainly be included among the targets. Mao had not managed to develop a coherent theoretical position on the fundamental contradiction underlying the SEM to which his colleagues had to respond. Towards the end of the session, the two men were agreeing that there should be no mass executions during the SEM, and Mao reaffirmed Liu's role as Qin Shi Huang, and his own as Liu's aide.[125]

On 23 December, the conferees met again to finalize a draft sixteen-point document. The document represented a partial concession to Mao with a compromise on semantics: As for the various verbal formulations regarding the nature of the movement, namely, a contradiction between the four cleans and the four uncleans, an overlapping of contradictions within and without the party and an overlapping of contradictions among the people and between the people and the enemy (these being Liu's alternate ways of characterizing the movement), and a contradiction between socialism and capitalism (Mao's), the 'last one is more appropriate in encompassing the nature of the problem'. 'The key issue is to rectify those power holders taking the capitalist road (including the corrupt and the speculators).' Mao accepted the document and agreed to its publication.[126] But he had actually gained little. Alternate formulations about the nature of the SEM were clearly seen to be acceptable, even if Mao's was *primus inter pares*; and attacks on capitalist roaders were to include attacks on corruption, which had been Liu's concern all along. If Mao's purpose was to establish the overriding importance of combating revisionism by attacking party power holders, then he should have focused the spotlight exclusively upon the contradiction between capitalism and socialism. Thus Mao's subsequent behaviour can be explained on the grounds that he realized, or was advised, that his victory had been Pyrrhic, and that Liu could still run the SEM the way he wanted. This seems to have enraged him. His anger erupted on 26 December, his 71st birthday.

Mao and his colleagues had always eschewed the kind of extravagant public celebrations held in the Soviet Union in honor of Stalin's birthdays. Stalin's seventieth birthday in 1949 had been a major international event, which Mao and other foreign communist leaders had attended,[127] whereas the Chairman had celebrated his own the previous year with four old Hunanese friends now resident in Beijing and a few of their offspring.[128] Close comrades might mark the occasion by sending him a poem.[129] Thus Mao's decision to summon a group of central and regional party leaders, a few ministers, some scientists, and some labour models to a banquet at the Great Hall of the People for a relatively unimportant seventy-first birthday in 1964 clearly had political significance.[130]

Mao seated the scientists and the labour models, including Chen Yonggui, the leader of the Dazhai brigade, at his own table and consigned PSC and other close colleagues to a separate table. During the dinner, he groused about incorrect formulations regarding the SEM (Liu's), describing them as being non-Marxist; attacked 'independent kingdoms' at the centre, apparently meaning the secretariat under Deng and the Planning Commission under Li Fuchun; and asserted that the party was in danger of producing revisionism. There was dead silence in the room.[131]

Mao's courtesy to Chen Yonggui was significantly more than just a snub to his colleagues. The Chairman was doubtless aware of the trouble which the Dazhai brigade was having validating its claimed achievements to its SEM work team.[132] While Mao had not yet issued his call for all agriculture to study Dazhai, he had invested some of his prestige in boosting this brigade's spirit of self-help (*zili gengsheng*). If Dazhai's claims proved to be bogus, he and other leaders would end up with egg on their faces. More importantly, the model system, of which Dazhai was a shining example, was vital to the way Mao and the CCP had traditionally run the country. It permitted the setting of high standards with proof that they could be met, and provided blueprints to simplify the tasks of lower-level officials struggling to reconcile party dictates with local conditions. Above all, models encouraged the centrally led campaign pattern of development, and the speed it engendered. If the national model system were now to be demolished by unsympathetic work teams, the alternative would be painstaking, unheroic, and, to judge by the development of the responsibility system at the beginning of the decade, unrevolutionary development, locality by locality. It was not a prospect which could have pleased Mao, and he demonstrated his rejection of it by his special treatment of Chen Yonggui—which effectively aborted the SEM in Dazhai—at that birthday dinner.[133]

The following day at the work conference he returned to the attack, allowing Chen Boda to make the running by deriding Liu's formulations for the SEM, though without mentioning their author. The concept of a contradiction between the four cleans and the four uncleans was inappropriate; after all, the problem of corruption had existed in imperial times too. The overlap of contradictions inside and outside the party could have been applied to the KMT. What is the principal contradiction, asked Chen: 'The Chairman has summed up *everyone's* view. The principal contradiction is the contradiction between socialism and capitalism' (emphasis added). Mao spelled out the implications: 'There are at least two factions in our party: one is the socialist faction, and the other the capitalist faction.'[134] According to one account, Liu accepted that there were capitalist roaders, but felt that to classify them as a faction implied larger numbers than was the case. He argued that practice would decide which were the fundamental contradictions, and they should not all be described as between the enemy and the people that is, between capitalism and socialism. The same day, perhaps as a result of the argument, Mao was again presented with the conference document, this time with an insignificant seventeenth clause added on for purposes of bureaucratic precision. Again, Mao approved the document.[135]

But Liu's continuing refusal to be walked over provoked the Chairman's most extraordinary action to date. On 28 December, at the end of a long monologue reasserting his view of the nature of the SEM, justifying it with a reprise of the line he had pursued since 1962, he brandished copies of the national and CCP constitutions, asserting that as a citizen and party member he had a right to speak out at party meetings. He accused one unnamed colleague (clearly Deng) of trying to set aside his right to attend the meeting, and another (clearly Liu) of wanting to suppress his right to express an opinion![136] The extravagance of his remarks recalls his threat at the 1959 Lushan conference to recruit a new army if the PLA would not support him in his struggle against Marshal Peng Dehuai.[137] On both occasions, Mao was emphasizing the importance of the issue to him and simultaneously threatening, in 1964 implicitly, drastic action if he were not obeyed. As it turned out, he was also laying the basis for the accusations which he made at the outset of the Cultural Revolution of being ignored by his colleagues, particularly Deng Xiaoping.[138]

Yet unlike in 1959, Mao's explosion on this occasion seems to have been either pointless or ineffectual, for on the same day, the 28th, Peng Zhen formally authorized the printing and distribution of the seventeen articles as agreed by Mao on the 27th as central document No. 811 of 1964, and the work conference prepared to adjourn, or perhaps formally did so.[139] Either Mao had already got the document that he wanted or his fulminations were ignored.[140]

Then on the 30th, at a 'small-scale conference',[141] Mao suddenly produced modifications to the seventeen articles suggested by Chen Boda, designed to strengthen the passage about power holders. The new formulation elaborated on the passage about some power holders being in front of the curtain, others behind; of those behind the curtain, some were at the lower levels, others at the higher levels. If 'Comrade Shaoqi' and the secretariat accepted them, Mao indicated, the new formulations should be issued.

At first glance, this *démarche* seems proof that Mao's fulminations on the 28th had indeed been ignored, that the conference had endorsed a document over his objections. But Liu's response showed how impossible it was to ignore the Chairman, even if he wished to violate the CC's standard operating procedures. The following day, 31 December, with Liu's agreement, the General Office circulated central directive No. 814, cancelling the distribution of No. 811 and ordering its destruction on the grounds that the centre was still in the process of revising it.[142] The ease with which Mao got his way suggests that he *had* been happy with the document issued on the 28th, but had been persuaded by Chen Boda that it should be made more explicit. As we shall see in the case of Yao Wenyuan's polemic against Wu Han in November 1965, Mao was far from infallible in the preparation of documents, even those designed to further his own cause.[143] An additional motivation could have been a simple desire to display raw power in order to intimidate his colleagues. If so, he succeeded.

From this point on, Mao appears to have taken over control of the proceedings from Liu,[144] who may have made a self criticism.[145] What followed may have been a series of *ad hoc* meetings summoned by the Chairman, guerrilla style, rather than the formal continuation of the work conference.[146] Having established to his own satisfaction the primacy of his version of the principal contradiction, Mao's second concern was to transform the conduct of the SEM by ending the human wave tactics which he had endorsed only a few months earlier. At a meeting on 3 January, the very day that the NPC was formally approving Liu's re-election as state chairman, Mao derided the idea of sending work teams totalling 18,000 people to a county with a population of 280,000, and that this horde would then take six weeks to study the relevant documents before making a move. He even chided Chen Boda for employing similar tactics in Tianjin; Chen refocused his loyalties back to Mao just in time. The streamlined SEM which Mao now propagated would focus exclusively on the party, and 'petty thieves and pickpockets' would be exempted. Indeed, the four clean-ups could be postponed to a later stage, and would be undertaken only if the masses wanted it.[147] On the 14th, as he prepared to issue the final document of the SEM, the Twenty-three Articles, he showed his resentment of an earlier document. What had been the need for the Latter Ten Points to be issued in September 1963 only three months after the Former Ten Points had been issued? How much experience could the party have accumulated in so short a time to justify such instant revision? This led him into a criticism of the 'independent kingdoms' of Beijing, the party secretariat under Deng Xiaoping (responsible for the Latter Ten Points), and the Planning Commission under Li Fuchun (responsible for drafting the 3rd FYP due to start in 1966).[148] At this point, Mao decided that the officials of the 'National Economic Supreme Command', set up to handle the third front, should take over the role of the Planning Commission—it became known in official circles as the 'small planning commission' (*xiao jiwei*)—responsible directly to Premier Zhou rather than to any of the vice-premiers in charge of economic policy, like Li Fuchun, Li Xiannian, and Bo Yibo.[149] Since the two Li's were members of the CC secretariat, this meant that Deng had lost effective control over economic policy.

The Twenty-three Articles

In keeping with Mao's predilection for simplicity and brevity, and despite the number of points it contained, the Twenty-three Articles, drawn up by Peng Zhen, was considerably shorter than the three previous programmatic documents of the SEM.[150] But its precedence over those documents was asserted in the covering note sent out by the CC: if there were any contradictions between the Twenty-three Articles and any previous document on the SEM, 'then this document shall uniformly be taken as the standard'.[151]

Yet for lower-level cadres unfamiliar with the 'legislative history',[152] that is to say the minutes of the work conference discussions, much of the document would have seemed repetitive. Class struggle was still acute. Class enemies were attempting by 'peaceful, evolution' to restore capitalism. Leadership of certain communes, brigades, and enterprises had either been 'corrupted or usurped' (art. 1). The six standards set by Mao in June 1964 for evaluating the SEM had been listed in full in the Revised Latter Ten Points and were repeated in the Twenty-three Articles (art. 4, a new article). The percentage of cadres and people with whom to unite remained at 95 per cent (art. 1). Criticism of the erring few with a view to reuniting with them after they had 'washed their hands and bodies' continued to be prescribed; but where local leadership had been seized by alien class elements whose errors were gross, then authority had to be seized from them as before (art. 9, a new article). The broad masses had still to be boldly mobilized (art. 5). Spot-testing or 'squatting at points' was still the recommended way for cadres to familiarize themselves with the problems of a new area (art. 7).

Even the key differences in the documents could have been seen, by those not privy to the party's inner councils, as adjustments based on experience gained since the last document. The nature of the movement was described, in the terms upon which Mao had insisted at the work conference, as a contradiction between socialism and capitalism rather than one between the four cleans and the four uncleans (art. 2). Yet the movement was now officially to be known as the four clean-ups (*siqing*), not as the SEM (*shejiao*); the urban movement's separate designation as the five antis was abolished in favour of the single all-embracing title of four clean-ups;

and the reinterpretation of the four cleans as comprising politics, economics, ideology, and organization and not just financial probity in various spheres was lifted from Wang Guangmei's Taoyuan report (art. 3).

For the average work team leader, there were probably only three changes that should have altered his practices. The first was the prohibition of 'human sea tactics'. Yet this article also stated that '[w]e must suitably concentrate our forces to fight a war of annihilation' (art. 6, a new article). How was the team leader to distinguish between the two? The second change was the insistence that the work teams should be open and above board, not work secretively— 'We must not be quiet; we must not be mysterious . . .' (art. 5)— clearly a criticism of Wang Guangmei's preference for working incognito.[153] Thirdly, an attempt was made to moderate and even excuse financial penalties that might be imposed on free-loading cadres (art. 9).

In post-Cultural Revolution analyses, these efforts to restrain the excessive leftism of Liu's Revised Latter Ten Points were commended as justified; at the time, Peng Zhen took advantage of the Twenty-three Articles to relieve leftist pressure on the president of Peking University.[154] But one passage in the Twenty-three Articles has attracted trenchant official criticism in the post-Mao era, because it became the scriptural authority for the high-level purge of the party during the Cultural Revolution, to which rampaging Red Guards could turn for justification:

The key point of this movement is to rectify those people in positions of authority within the Party who take the capitalist road, and to progressively consolidate and develop the socialist battlefront in the urban and rural areas. Of those people in positions of authority who take the capitalist road, some are out in the open and some are concealed. Of the people who support them, some are at lower levels and some are at higher levels . . . Among those at higher levels, there are some people in the communes, districts, *hsien [xian]*, special districts, and even in the work of provincial and *Central Committee departments*, who oppose socialism. (Emphasis added)[155]

Originally the offending passages, which appear to have been added to one of the earlier articles, referred simply to the CC, but Zhou Enlai managed to add the word 'departments' which mitigated its force.[156]

The impact of the Twenty-three Articles

The implications of this fateful passage probably escaped grass-roots SEM work team leaders. They already knew that if party members were unclean they had to be dealt with like any other cadre. Moreover, initially the Twenty-three Articles does not seem to have had much impact. It was issued on 14 January 1965. It was probably distributed by provincial committees within a few days.[157] Yet two or three weeks later, new work teams which should have been briefed on the revised procedures continued to practise the stealthy approach pioneered by Wang Guangmei at Taoyuan in violation of the new rule:

In the winter cold of early February 1965, a contingent of thirteen cadres entered Chen Village. They announced that they were a Four Cleanups workteam that had come to 'squat' at the brigade. For the first time since land reform, outside cadres had come in to take over control of the entire village's affairs.

The peasants were soon aware that this cadre workteam was only a branch of a larger team that had set up headquarters in the commune seat ... But no one in the village knew who any of the thirteen cadres were, where they were from, or what posts they had held before. No, the villagers were not supposed to know, they were told: 'Things that should not be asked, you shouldn't ask; things that should not be seen, you shouldn't see; things that should not be heard, you shouldn't hear.'[158]

Anonymity was supposed to convey an image of a work team 'composed not of fallible individuals but of sacrosanct representatives of the Communist party'. Anonymity was also thought to be an advantage in enabling work team members to present a united front to their charges; and it protected the members, who often hailed from neighbouring units, from rumour-mongering.[159]

Detailed accounts of work team behaviour nationwide that would permit a comprehensive assessment of the impact of the Twenty-three Articles on the SEM have either not been compiled or not been released. Probably reactions varied across and even within work teams. Some officials might have breathed sighs of relief at no longer having to enforce so brutal a policy; others may have relished their powers under the SEM and continued to oppress. In one Shandong brigade, where Beijing intellectuals were revelling in their power over the local cadres, hitherto their 'teachers', the SEM team leader refused to retool his procedures according to the Twenty-three Articles; but the cadres, aware that the wind had changed, began to stand up to the team, and it was eventually withdrawn.[160] This source concurred with the sentiments of Mao's doctor, Li Zhisui, who was appalled at the poverty of the peasantry which he found in rural Jiangxi in mid-1965, and at the stupidity of wasting so much money on sending hundreds of thousands of reluctant urbanites to 'clean up' the cadres under such conditions:

There was corruption. That was undeniable. But to focus on corruption at the level of poor teams like this one was absurd. Our socialist education work team had no way of inspecting account books. There were no account books to inspect. The peasant responsible for bookkeeping was barely literate and would not know how to keep books. And there were really no accounts to keep. The team was so poor, and the villagers lived and worked together so closely, that everyone knew everything about everyone else.[161]

Absurd or not, the SEM continued. By the time it was overtaken and subsumed by the Cultural Revolution on 15 December 1966, the movement had been completed in a third of the nation's counties. Among urban areas, Beijing and Shanghai had 'basically' completed the SEM. Fortunately for Bo Yibo, under 4 per cent of the units in the industrial and transportation system under his supervision had begun the disruptive process.[162] Close to 2 million cadres had taken part in the SEM nationwide.[163] But already, a year earlier, Mao had lost interest in it, convinced that it would not achieve his basic purpose of reforming the party.[164]

19 MAO STOOPS TO CONQUER

'When did you finally decide that Liu had to go?' I asked him
during our conversation in December of 1970. He replied that
the moment of decision came in January, 1965 ... The first point
of the [Twenty-three Articles] had specifically denounced and
demanded the removal of 'those in the Party in authority who
are taking the capitalist road'. Now it was to be the first point of
the new drive, the cultural revolution. Liu had strenuously
opposed that first point right at the meeting, said Mao. 'Was it
then in January, 1965 ... that the decision was made to launch
the cultural revolution?' The Chairman said that after October,
1965, when the criticism and repudiation of *Hai Jui Dismissed
from Office* was made, things had unfolded rapidly.[1]

Edgar Snow's report of the Chairman's brief explanation of his decision to purge Liu Shaoqi has become the *locus classicus* for Chinese
historians seeking to date the split between these two leaders.[2] Some
biographers of Liu have corroborated Mao's assertion that his deputy
opposed the 'capitalist-roader' formulation.[3] Mao's one-time secretary and party historian, Hu Qiaomu, stated however that Liu did not
directly oppose it, but only talked of the overlapping of contradictions
among the people and those between the people and the enemy.[4]

Whether Liu directly opposed Mao or not is less important than
the Chairman's version of what occurred, and the fact that *he had
taken steps in January 1965 to make his version of events credible*, and
to imprint it upon the minds of his colleagues at the time.

As we have seen, Mao was out to generate *Sturm und Drang* at the
year-end work conference. He made it vividly clear through his theatrical display of anger that he was accusing Liu and Deng Xiaoping
of trying to prevent him from combating revisionism in the CC by
excluding him from the meeting. His performance was so effective
that Bo Yibo recalled it with palpably bated breath almost twenty
years later. Doubtless everyone in attendance was equally
impressed. Certainly, no one present could have been in any doubt
about 'what' had happened—some kind of Rubicon had been
crossed—though the 'why' may have been puzzling.

If, as argued in the last chapter, the fall of Khrushchev was the precipitating event that had rung alarm bells in Mac's mind, then the Chairman was deceiving Snow. He had decided to rid himself of Liu some months before January 1965, but he gave that date because it provided credibility for his claim that he was *reacting* to Liu's unacceptable conduct of the SEM rather than *provoking* a clash out of fear for his own future. At the year-end work conference, he was justifying to his colleagues his abrupt change of attitude, from strong approval of Liu's conduct of the SEM to sharp hostility. He was beginning to build up a case against Liu. Fortunately for Mao, many of Liu's natural allies were dubious about the extremism of the Revised Latter Ten Points and welcomed the Chairman's intention of moderating it.[5]

This was not the first time that Mao had criticized Liu or been at odds with him. He had attacked him for 'leftism' in land reform in 1947–8 and 'rightism' for coddling capitalists in 1949 and on collectivization in 1951.[6] They had been at loggerheads over the conduct of the rectification campaign in 1957.[7] It was arguably not even the first time he had hoped to get rid of him.[8] But it was the first time that the Chairman personally played an active ongoing role in a plot to purge a senior colleague. He evidently felt that the combination of the ideological threat to China and the political threat to himself now demanded decisive action.[9]

Mao's caution

Even if one assumed that the Chairman was roughly accurate in the dating of his determination to get rid of Liu Shaoqi, one is faced with a puzzle: Why did it take Mao at least twenty months—from January 1965 to the 11th plenum in August 1966—to demote him, the first step in encompassing his total disgrace? By January 1965, Mao knew that his capacity to intervene decisively in party policy-making was undiminished. By May 1965, when the Chairman recharged his revolutionary batteries with a nostalgic and perhaps symbolic visit to his earliest military base in Jinggangshan,[10] he knew that the United States had no intention of extending the Vietnam War to China;[11] he could bring about domestic turmoil without fear of opening the country to attack. And as the *Götterdämmerung* of 1966–7 demonstrated, he could topple the giants of the CCP like ninepins. Why did he wait? And why did he proceed hugger-mugger, instead of confronting Liu Shaoqi directly?

Four overlapping hypotheses can be suggested First, Mao could not be sure of easily translating Liu's defeat into his demotion. Men like Liu, Zhou Enlai, Chen Yun, Peng Zhen, and some of the marshals had established independent reputations and followings long before Mao became Chairman and indisputable leader in 1943, a fact which his godlike dominance of the CCP during the Cultural Revolution obscured. Liu, as we have seen, normally deferred to Mao, but he was not his creature to be disposed of at will. Liu's status as a Marxist theoretician, party organizer, and labour expert predated Mao's chairmanship, and indeed had made him a crucial ally in Mao's consolidation of his leadership in the early 1940s.[12] From the CCP's 7th Congress in 1945, Liu always ranked second in the party hierarchy; the Gao Gang episode in 1953 had shown how difficult it would be to supplant him; the humiliation of Zhou Enlai in 1958 meant that Liu had no pre-eminent rival for the succession, which could only have increased Mao's worries about him;[13] and in 1961, as all senior party officials would have known, Mao had told Field-Marshal Montgomery that Liu was his designated successor.[14] From 1959, on May Day and National Day, the official newspapers had printed equal-sized pictures of the two chairmen side by side on the front page.[15] When study materials were prepared for cadres in 1961, they included extracts from Liu in addition to Marx, Engels, Lenin, Stalin, and Mao. In the 2nd polemic against the Soviet Union ('On the problem of Stalin') issued in September 1963, Mao personally added Liu Shaoqi's name in the phrase 'Chinese Marxist-Leninists as represented by Comrade Mao Zedong and Comrade Liu Shaoqi'; and in the 9th polemic in July 1964, overseen by Kang Sheng, a similar reference may have been made in an early draft.[16] By 1965, 'Chairman' Liu had been running the country on a daily basis for several years, and senior colleagues had become accustomed to his leadership. He was left in charge even after the year-end work conference.[17] In September 1965, Zhu De suggested that if war broke out again, it would be Liu not Mao who would be commander-in-chief.[18]

Secondly, Liu oversaw the party machine, whose upper ranks were salted with his supporters. A cautious guerrilla fighter, the Chairman could not ignore the possibility that a frontal assault on Liu on flimsy charges would finally unite the party against him, especially if he were correct in his suspicions that he could no longer command the allegiance of General Secretary Deng Xiaoping.[19] To understand why, a reminder of how Mao established his dominance over the government and army bureaucracies is necessary.

Mao's subjection of the State Council

None of Mao's colleagues lightly thwarted or opposed him, and in the post-1949 period, the Chairman had cracked the whip over the leaders of two of the three key bureaucratic establishments, and brought them to heel. In January 1958, he made a frontal assault on the leaders of the State Council for their earlier opposition to what they called 'blind advance' and he called leaping progress,[20] and from that time on, the State Council became less an initiator and more an executor of policy under the leadership of the CC secretariat.[21]

As premier of the State Council, Zhou Enlai seems always to have taken the line of least resistance, bending with whatever Maoist wind was blowing, be it leftist gale or rightist zephyr.[22] He had two instructions for his secretaries: if there were an international or domestic crisis, he had to be informed immediately, even if he were asleep; equally, if the Chairman wanted him, he was to be summoned whatever the hour.[23] Always at Mao's beck and call, Zhou responded immediately to any hint of Maoist displeasure, especially after the 1958 assault. That year, Zhou spent ten days preparing the abject self-criticism he made at the second session of the CCP's 8th Congress for his opposition to 'blind advance'.[24] At the Lushan conference in 1959, he had shrugged off Peng Dehuai's 'Letter of opinion' until Mao denounced it, whereupon he, too, decided it constituted a political problem.[25] In 1965, after a complaint from the Chairman, he acted with an alacrity hardly necessitated by the seriousness of the matter. At the year-end work conference, Mao had declared that Zhou's private office was too large, perhaps annoyed that the premier had many more secretaries than himself. Zhou virtually dissolved it immediately.[26] Independent personae do not necessarily entail independent attitudes.[27]

This was true also of Chen Yun, a man of considerable standing in the pre-Maoist leadership, who was a significant figure in Yan'an, and who, as the senior vice-premier in the State Council, played the major role in its economic policy-making in the first half of the 1950s. But his behaviour, too, was drastically affected by Mao's attack on the State Council planners in 1958. Thereafter, whenever Chen saw that Mao had got the leftist bit between his teeth, he chose discretion as the better part of valour, and simply retired, as during the GLF in 1958 and after the Lushan conference in 1959.[28] He cautiously refused Mao's invitation to present his views at the Seven Thousand Cadres Conference, and after the 10th plenum later that year, he went into hibernation till after Mao's death fourteen years later.[29]

His only political action in the interim was to make an unsolicited additional self-criticism on 18 June 1965. In the light of Mao's behaviour, and in particular his comments on the struggle against revisionism to foreign communist leaders, Chen wrote to the Chairman to blame himself for totally underestimating the speed with which the Chinese economy could recover from the post-GLF depression, and also for mistakenly advocating the responsibility system in the countryside.[30] Chen's prudence almost certainly helped him to escape becoming a prime target during the Cultural Revolution.[31]

Other senior economic ministers in the State Council also self-criticized in 1958 and were certainly no more willing than Zhou and Chen to challenge the Chairman thereafter. The other prestigious vice-premier was Foreign Minister Marshal Chen Yi. Courageous and often outspoken, he publicly admitted his inhibitions about airing his views on policy towards the intellectuals until after the Seven Thousand Cadres Conference.[32]

The success of Mao's intimidation of the State Council was facilitated by the tacit backing of the PLA marshals and the active support of the party bureaucrats. Indeed, the evidence suggests that Mao had to restrain Liu Shaoqi from further humiliating Zhou and his ministerial colleagues at the second session of the 8th Congress.[33] Liu's report on that occasion, coupled with the ministers' self-criticisms, provided all the justification needed to accept Zhou's offer to resign and perhaps sack others.

The loyalty of the PLA

The PLA, too, had been brought to heel in the late 1950s, with the assertion of party leadership in 1958,[34] and the replacement of Peng Dehuai by Mao's trusty Lin Biao as the marshal in day-to-day charge of the CC's MAC after the 1959 Lushan conference. Mao's success at Lushan is attributable to a number of factors: factionalism in the military;[35] the concern of party officials like Liu Shaoqi that a marshal should not upstage them; and the basic loyalty of the top brass to their victorious commander-in-chief when he made the issue a choice between Peng and himself.[36]

Thereafter, Lin Biao ensured that the image of the PLA should be precisely what Mao wanted: a totally loyal 'red' institution, bent upon maintaining the guerrilla traditions beloved of the Chairman, in particular the doctrine that man was more important than weapons, and committed to the view, as the new Defence Minister put it in 1960, that 'politics is the lifeline of the Liberation Army as well as the fundamental guarantee of all kinds of work'.[37] In 1962, Chief-of-Staff Luo Ruiqing and the head of the PLA's General Political Department Xiao Hua led senior officers in the study of Marxist-Leninist classics at the behest of Mao.[38]

But Lin Biao had what the Chairman, at least, must have considered an even better idea. At a conference of senior military officers in 1960, he referred to his theory of the 'apex' (*dingfeng lun*): 'What is Marxism-Leninism at this time? It is the Thought of our Chairman Mao. It is the highest peak in today's world; it is the apex of contemporary thought.'[39] Building on this concept, Lin subsequently advocated learning aphorisms from the Chairman's work so as to be able to recite them by heart.[40] But how could private soldiers or even officers know what aphorisms to be able to recite? The answer was the publication in May 1964 of the so-called 'Little Red Book' of brief quotations from the Chairman, a project first broached by Lin Biao with Mao in August 1961, destined to become the bible of the Red Guards during the Cultural Revolution.[41] At this time, however, when Mao was looking to his cult as a weapon of political struggle,[42] this distillation of his writings served to emphasize single authorship of his *Selected Works* and to undercut the more accurate notion that the Thought of Mao Zedong incorporated the collective wisdom of the top leaders of the CCP.[43]

Mao quotations were drummed into the soldiery, who were encouraged to become 'five good' elements like Lei Feng: good in politics, military training, style of work, fulfilment of tasks, and physical education. Recruits were instilled with Lin Biao's 'four firsts' which Mao called a 'great creation':[44] put the human factor first, political work first, ideological work first, and living ideas first. Lin presided over a swift increase in the number of company party committees and political instructors. The status of political commissars was considerably enhanced by a decision in 1963 to extend their responsibilities to purely military functions, hitherto the sole prerogative of the unit commander. Two years later, PLA ranks, awards, and insignia were abolished; officers and men were simply to be known as 'commanders' and fighters, and the PLA's elaborate Soviet-style uniforms were abandoned in favour of red stars on all hats and red badges on all collars.[45] The PLA was overtly returning to the simpler Yan'an way cherished by Mao.

Lin Biao's success in projecting an image for the PLA of selfless egalitarianism resulted in the extraordinary decision to make the PLA a model for the nation, extraordinary because in a communist country the model institution should of course be the communist party. But it was the party paper, the *People's Daily*, which called on the nation to 'Learn from the PLA' in February 1964, on the grounds that: 'The PLA ardently loves the country, the people, and socialism and is boundlessly loyal to the cause of the proletariat. The combatants . . . are impartial and selfless. They always render service to others without considering their own interests. They even sacrifice their valuable time and life for the sake of socialism.'[46]

The first unit to model itself on the PLA was the Daqing oilfield, which claimed to have overcome immense problems after it had studied the political work experience of the PLA. This in turn had excited the interest of other industrial enterprises, notably the ministries of water conservancy and electric power, the metallurgical industry, and the chemical industry. Bo Yibo, who was in charge of the industrial and communications system,[47] reported this to Mao. The Chairman sent a note to Lin Biao and other senior military figures on 16 December 1963, urging them to expand this effort.[48]

Learning from the PLA went beyond studying documents, though that was the conventional starting-point. In industrial and communications establishments, as a result of the Chairman's intervention, more party branches were created and political departments were set up. PLA officials were seconded as consultants, while civilian cadres took political courses in PLA units. The system held its first political work conference in March 1964, at which Bo reported on the historic significance of Mao's directive and presented a draft programme for implementing it. After dissemination by the CC secretariat as a draft for discussion, a final document was issued in May 1965.[49] Thus civilian leaders helped to increase the prominence of the PLA's political role in the mid-1960s, a prominence which prefigured its enhanced status during the Cultural Revolution, when Lin Biao would replace Liu Shaoqi as Mao's heir apparent.

The position of the party

The loyalty of Lin Biao and the subservience of Zhou Enlai meant that Mao could assume that neither the MAC nor the State Council would act contrary to his wishes, if they understood what his wishes were. Lin and Zhou were likely to consult the Chairman or ascertain his views before taking any major decision. Mao could not make the same assumptions about Liu Shaoqi, Deng Xiaoping, or Peng Zhen, though in practice they, too, took care to brief the Chairman and give him the chance to advise and consent. But Mao had not cowed the top ranks of the party bureaucracy as he had intimidated the government in 1958 and the PLA in 1959; indeed, party support had been critical to his campaigns against the leaders of those two institutions. On the one occasion when Mao had tried to expose party cadres to criticism, during the rectification campaign of 1957, the Chairman had been compelled to beat a hasty retreat, in large part because of their bitter resentment and opposition.[50] He could not lightly attempt a new rectification campaign involving the purge of senior party colleagues.

A third reason why Mao had to proceed against Liu in a circuitous manner was that certain proprieties had to be observed. Even Stalin felt obliged to justify his purges by holding show trials. The CCP had always been far more insistent than the CPSU, at least formally, upon the observance of the correct norms for intra-party struggle.[51] Mao could not simply say 'Off with their heads' and hope to preserve his own image as a just and righteous leader, intervening only when his colleagues in the first front went astray. There had to be cause and due process if the heir-apparent were to be removed.

Fourthly, as the Cultural Revolution would illustrate, Mao was groping towards a form of leadership renewal which would encompass revolutionary steeling of the successor generation. A simple purge, even assuming he could carry it off, would not achieve that purpose. Mao's dilemma in early 1965 was that he could not unleash the unprecedented campaign for revolutionary renewal, assuming that he already had a clear idea of what that might mean, without first removing obstacles by the very familiar means of intra-party struggle. Had his colleagues any inkling of what the Chairman intended to do, they might finally have banded together against him.

Mao could not rely on playing his seniormost colleagues off against each other. As the Gao Gang episode had demonstrated a decade earlier, if a Politburo member were to lobby his colleagues against Liu, it was very likely that one or more would report the matter to the Chairman, so forcing him to reveal his hand.[52] Equally, Mao could not use party organs for his purposes, since his intentions would immediately become plain to an even wider group.[53] Indeed, the bulwarks of the party machine which Liu oversaw had to be sapped before any assault on him could begin with an assurance of success.

Under these circumstances, Mao had to abandon the moral high ground that should have pertained to the office of party chairman and stoop to the secret scheming he was wont to warn his colleagues against. He turned to leftists who had demonstrated that their first loyalty was to him personally. Whether they occupied positions within the party hierarchy or were 'irregulars' operating from without,[54] their fealty to his designs would be ensured by the knowledge that by implementing them they could hope to attain the political preferment they sought. Even so, Mao could not convene them as a group;[55] his secretary Tian Jiaying, whom he no longer trusted after the events of 1962, would quickly realize that something was up.[56] For the most part, he would have to give general indications of his views, and hope that his trusties—Lin Biao, Chen Boda, Kang Sheng—would divine his intent, stirring the pot, though more circumspectly than Gao Gang.[57] But, as in the case of Gao Gang, Mao had to light the fire. As his agent, he chose the person closest to and most dependent upon himself: Jiang Qing.

The secret agent

During the prologue to her political career, Jiang Qing was in the habit of describing herself as 'just a plain soldier, a sentry of the Chairman patrolling on the ideological battle front. I am keeping watch and will report what I find to the Chairman.'[58] Mao's 'sentry' did well to be modest. As we have seen, she had been able to harass Peng Zhen's five-man small group in charge of revolutionizing culture, but though she now had talking roles, they were still bit parts. Even in the home, she was increasingly cast as a supporting character to the series of young *ingénues* who flitted through Mao's bedroom, and her consciousness of this probably intensified her hypochondria. Indeed, Mao's doctor has speculated that the Chairman may have encouraged Jiang's forays into the reform of Peking Opera in the mid-1960s to divert her attention from his growing passion for his latest paramour, Zhang Yufeng.[59] Be that as it may, by early 1965, Mao had a new production in mind in which Jiang Qing was at last to play the starring role she had so long coveted.

Her covert mission was to organize an assault on a prominent party intellectual, a task calculated to set her adrenalin going. Moreover, this was no ordinary intellectual, but someone of whom she had long been suspicious, a senior functionary of the Beijing city party *apparat*: Deputy Mayor Wu Han, the author of the Peking Opera *The Dismissal of Hai Rui*. According to one account, Jiang Qing had seen the play in July 1962 and had unsuccessfully lobbied the CC's Propaganda Department and the Ministry of Culture to have it criticized.[60] Mao, too, had not reacted to her indignation;

according to some accounts, it was Kang Sheng who eventually ignited his interest in the play as a possible object of criticism and led him to unleash Jiang Qing.[61]

In the second half of 1964, Jiang Qing tried to get the Beijing literary critic Li Xifan, the notorious ideological 'golden sweeper' (*jin saozhao*) of the north, to attack it, but he declined.[62] Li, who had earned his leftist nickname as a result of dragon-slaying activities a decade earlier,[63] was perhaps worried by the political problems he might face if he criticized a deputy mayor in good standing with the local party boss, Peng Zhen. This was a reason why Mao later remarked that Beijing under Peng was a place into which no needle could penetrate, no drop of water could enter.[64]

So in February 1965, Jiang Qing visited her leftist friends in Shanghai. She arranged with Zhang Chunqiao, whom she had first met through Ke Qingshi in Shanghai two years earlier,[65] to enlist the services of the 'golden sweeper' of the south, Yao Wenyuan, to write the polemic. Zhang, who became Jiang Qing's key ally in Shanghai after the death of Ke Qingshi in April 1965,[66] ensured that Yao's work over the next eight months, during which his article went through countless drafts, was done under conditions of maximum secrecy.[67]

A plot unfolds

From their respective later accounts, it is clear that while Jiang Qing had long sought to attack *The Dismissal of Hai Rui*, it was only when Mao gave her permission, or, as he put it, suggested it, that the enterprise got under way in a serious manner.[68] Mao's green light is critical in analysing the motivation for the project. Mao, as we have seen, had praised the play when it first appeared four years earlier, and had subsequently presented Wu Han with a mark of his esteem. Wu's play was evidently regarded by the Chairman as a legitimate response to his request for publicity for Hai Rui. Why did he change course in 1965?

It was not because he had suddenly seen that the play was a disguised defence of Peng Dehuai. Kang Sheng had made this suggestion as early as 1964, but Mao had either disagreed or taken no notice of it.[69] It was not until December 1965, that Mao told Chen Boda and other ideological acolytes that the essence of the play was that the emperor dismissed Hai Rui and that this was supposed to parallel the dismissal of Peng: 'Peng Dehuai is Hai Rui.' He did this in the course of an explanation of why Yao's polemic, good though it was in many respects, had not hit the nail on the head.[70] It will be remembered that Wu Han had originally intended to entitle his play 'Hai Rui returns the land' (*Hai Rui Tui Tian*), and indeed expropriation of peasants was its primary focus and therefore what Yao concentrated on. It was only at a late stage, in response to a suggestion from a friend, that Wu Han had adopted the title which Mao now found so provocative. What the Chairman did not reveal to his followers was that the failure to fasten on to the title was as much his fault as Yao's, for he had read the polemic three times prior to publication and obviously failed to make this point via Jiang Qing to the author.

Why did Mao stay quiet on this point during the writing of Yao's article? If the sole objective of Mao's campaign had been to target Wu Han and the main reason for this had been Wu's supposed support for Peng Dehuai, then that issue would surely have been made the centre-piece of Yao's article. On the other hand, if the objective was to get at Peng Zhen through Wu Han, then perhaps Mao allowed Yao to initiate the campaign on a less important issue, reserving the more serious one for a later assault. Or could Mao simply have forgotten about the alleged Hai Rui connection, only to be reminded about it *after the publication of Yao's article* by Kang Sheng, who had been kept in the dark about the preparations for the polemic?[71] Whatever the explanation, the Peng Dehuai issue was clearly a device in a larger scheme of things rather than the grounds for anger against Wu Han.

Peng Dehuai on probation

During the long gestation of Yao's polemic, Mao took a step which implied that he considered the Peng Dehuai affair over. On 11 September, Peng was summoned from the outskirts of Beijing, where he was under house arrest,[72] to the Great Hall of the People. There he was told by Peng Zhen that Mao Zedong and the centre wanted to send him to the 'third front' as a deputy commander under Li Jingquan. In the course of discussion, Peng Dehuai raised a number of objections while proclaiming his willingness to do whatever the party decided.[73] On 24 September, Peng Dehuai wrote to Mao indicating his preference for working at the grass roots, but agreeing to go to the southwest; he asked for an interview with Mao, Liu, Zhou, and Deng. The following day Mao, joined later by Liu, Deng, and Peng Zhen,[74] received Peng Dehuai at the Yi Nian Tang in the Zhongnanhai with great *bonhomie*: 'I've been waiting for you a long time and have not gone to bed. I received your letter yesterday afternoon, and I was too excited to fall asleep. You are a bull-headed person. You haven't written me for several years; but once you take up your pen, you write me a letter of 80,000 words.'[75] For five hours, including a meal, Mao reminisced with Peng Dehuai about all the political and military battles they had waged together, and regaled him with the importance of his new assignment. He even said that time would tell who had been right at Lushan in 1959.[76] In the end, Peng was won over and accepted the assignment. He arrived at the HQ of the 'third front' in Chengdu on 30 November.[77]

The dispatch of Peng Dehuai to the south-west may have had a political significance quite other than a desire to forgive an old warhorse and find him a useful job to do. Intentionally or not, Mao's radically revised attitude towards Peng Dehuai was likely to induce his colleagues to lower their guard. This Chairman was no longer the vengeful politician of 1959 and 1962, but rather the stern but ultimately benevolent patriarch of the Yan'an round table, seeking unity by acknowledging the contribution to the revolution of one of his oldest comrades-in-arms. Perhaps his outburst against Liu and Deng at the end of 1964 could be written off as a freak storm rather than a harbinger of a hurricane to come.

Moreover, on the eve of a wide-ranging assault on the party, it would have been prudent for Mao to ensure that Peng was far removed from the scene of action. Peng, after all, was the only senior Politburo member to stand up to him in recent memory, and a military hero whose dismissal and continuing disgrace had aroused considerable disquiet within the party. If Mao's plans went awry or provoked unexpected resistance, Peng Dehuai was a conceivable rallying point for opposition. Indeed, Mao himself had indicated his awareness of Peng's popular standing and potential power when, at the 1959 Lushan conference, he had stated that many party members feared that if he pre-deceased the marshal, the latter would be uncontrollable.[78] The hypothesis that Mao wished to guard against any possible danger from Peng Dehuai at a time of domestic political crisis is lent credence by the Chairman's ordering the simultaneous and hurried exiling from Beijing of General Huang Kecheng, the PLA Chief-of-Staff at the time of Lushan, who had been disgraced along with Peng Dehuai.[79]

But outwardly, the marshal and the general were now being pardoned, or at least put on probation, and Mao was prepared to talk of history being the judge of the rights and wrongs of their disagreements. Under those circumstances, it did not make logical sense to construct an elaborate plot against a mere intellectual who was alleged, contrary to the Chairman's assessment at the time, to have taken Peng's side four years earlier.

Since Mao kept a careful eye on the writing process, the plot against Wu Han cannot be seen as mere indulgence of Jiang Qing's whims. As his later comments about the tight cohesion of the Beijing party machine confirmed, the Chairman was well aware that an attack on Wu Han would necessarily be construed as an attack on the Beijing *apparat* of which he was part, and therefore on its 1st secretary, Peng Zhen. Mao could not lightly have sanctioned a plot to use Yao Wenyuan as an *agent provocateur* against the No. 2 man in the CC secretariat, one of the Politburo's most powerful and senior members, certainly not just to divert Jiang Qing's attention from his sexual dalliance. Why then?

Mau-Mauing the Flak Catchers

The most plausible explanation is that in Mao's eyes, getting rid of Peng Zhen was an essential prerequisite for getting rid of Liu Shaoqi and conducting a revolutionary regeneration of the whole top leadership. First, Mao had to have a firm base in Beijing; he could not run what turned into the Cultural Revolution from Shanghai, especially not after the death of his loyal ally Ke Qingshi in April 1965. The Chairman knew that Peng Zhen was the critical linchpin for the men he had privately designated as his opponents. While Liu and Deng were formally more senior and powerful, it was Peng Zhen as executive secretary who implemented their decisions via the secretariat; making the first approach to Peng Dehuai exemplified his trouble-shooting role in tricky situations.[80] The removal of this long-time friend and associate of Liu's[81] would simultaneously undermine the operations of the secretariat and shake the confidence and prestige of the head of state. Indeed, Mao's tactic was similar to that of Gao Gang in 1953, when Gao attempted to get at Liu by attacking Bo Yibo.[82]

Despite his key role in the party machine, Peng was to some extent an isolated and therefore vulnerable figure. During the communist conquest of Manchuria, he had started as regional 1st secretary, but was recalled by Mao after he quarrelled with Gao Gang, Lin Biao, and Chen Yun; those differences had not been forgotten.[83] Though Peng filled important posts in Yan'an in the early 1940s, he was seen primarily as a 'white area' cadre, that is, someone who worked behind Japanese or Nationalist lines and had no real experience of conducting revolutionary war. His only significant military connection was Nie Rongzhen, with whom he had served in the Shanxi–Chahar–Hebei Border Region, but Nie was an unpolitical marshal, one of only three who was not a member of the Politburo. Peng had no links to the State Council élite, except possibly of a competitive nature.[84] He had no provincial base, since Shanxi was poorly represented in the CC;[85] indeed, he was reputedly on bad terms with the only other Shanxi member of the Politburo, Bo Yibo.[86] Ability aside, Peng's strength lay in Liu's patronage and in the loyalty of other 'white area' cadres in the top ranks of the party bureaucracy. His strengths and his weaknesses made Peng an obvious target for anyone wishing to undermine the party machine.

If there were to be a true 'cultural' revolution, Mao had to gain control of the propaganda organs; he needed to have them as obedient as soldiers to his command.[87] Jiang Qing was a fierce woman warrior, but Mao needed a national network. That meant breaking the power of Peng Zhen's five-man small group, which included the director of the CC's Propaganda Department, Lu Dingyi; his deputy on the literary front, Zhou Yang; another deputy director, Wu Lengxi, the head of both the NCNA and the *People's Daily*.[88] Among these establishment figures, the group's fifth member, Mao's Trojan horse Kang Sheng, was effectively corralled.

An example of how these two motivations dovetailed occurred on 2 March 1965, when the secretariat under Liu Shaoqi's aegis had a meeting about the present state of literature and the arts. Deng stated that as a result of mistaken leftist criticisms, nobody dared write articles, the NCNA was receiving very few manuscripts, only fighting was depicted on the stage, and films were no good. While Deng's forthright remarks were later said to have had little effect in the face of the leftist tide,[89] the meeting illustrated once again to Mao the importance of seizing power over the cultural realm in which Peng Zhen played such a key role.

A possible third reason for Mao's decision to attack Peng Zhen was personal animosity. There is no post-1949 record of the Chairman rebuking Peng Zhen over major policy issues as he did Liu Shaoqi or Zhou Enlai; ironically, as the position of his long-time patron eroded early in 1965, and Deng Xiaoping, too, came under fire, Peng might have thought that *he* had a chance of succeeding Mao. Indeed, an underlying rivalry among Mao's potential successors was surely an important reason why he was able to divide and

conquer them in 1966. But the Chairman would neither have forgotten nor forgiven Peng's resistance to rectification in 1957 (when
Wu Han had been his collaborator),[90] nor his readiness to pin the
blame for the GLF disaster on Mao at the Seven Thousand Cadres
Conference.[91]

Mao's device for getting at Peng was to impale him on the horns of
an impossible dilemma.[92] By arranging for Wu Han to be publicly
attacked, Mao presented Peng Zhen with two unpalatable choices:
either he had to try to protect Wu and thus expose himself to charges
of colluding or sympathizing with an anti-party element; or he had to
disavow him and thus convict himself of incompetence in harbouring an anti-party element for so long.

The seige of Beijing

Yao Wenyuan's polemic against Wu Han, 'On the new historical
opera *Hai Rui Dismissed from Office*', appeared in the Shanghai
Wenhui Bao, a paper mainly for intellectuals, on 10 November.[93]
Jiang Qing's *groupuscule* had kept its secret well and there had been
virtually no advance warning for the Beijing party. At a work conference in October, Mao had asked regional leaders what they
would do if 'revisionism emerges in the central committee?' and
had answered the question himself: 'In that event, you must rebel.'
Peng Zhen apparently did not grasp what Mao was getting at. The
only inkling Peng received at the conference of what was to come
was when Mao asked him personally if Wu Han could be criticized,
to which Peng answered: 'If he has problems they can be criticized.'
But Peng took this to mean criticism from an artistic rather than a
political point of view. Earlier in the year his five-man small group
had forbidden the use of political labels in the course of the ideological struggle which it was conducting in literary and artistic
circles;[94] again on 23 September, he had ordered a conference of
senior cultural officials to distinguish between political and artistic
problems, and had boldly proclaimed, in a phrase that would later
bring down the wrath of cultural revolutionaries: 'Everyone is equal
before the truth.'[95] He could not have been more wrong.

Peng Zhen and Wu Han were both away from Beijing when Yao's
article was published.[96] In Peng's absence, consternation reigned in
the party *apparat* of the capital. Peng's five-man small group had also
forbidden any targeting of individuals without permission from the
CC's Propaganda Department and ordered that official party papers
had to set the standards for criticism. What had happened to party

discipline in Shanghai if Yao could criticize a vice-mayor of Beijing who was a party member, a leading member of the Democratic League, and a prominent scholar? On 13 November, Deng Tuo, as the Beijing party secretary overseeing propaganda and the press, conferred with the head of the city's propaganda department, Li Qi, and the editor of the municipal party paper, *Beijing Ribao*, Fan Jin, on whether or not they should reprint the article. They decided to seek an explanation from the *Wenhui Bao* to find out if Mao had sanctioned Yao's polemic—a decision that reflected Deng Tuo's considerable personal experience of the devious ways of the Chairman—and if the latter *were* involved then they would reprint. But under Zhang Chunqiao's orders, the *Wenhui Bao* would give nothing away, and so Deng Tuo contacted Peng Zhen for instructions. The 1st secretary said to do nothing till he returned.

Zhang and Yao eagerly awaited Beijing's reaction, and were baffled when nothing happened. Jiang Qing relayed Beijing's inaction to Mao who was on a whistle-stop tour of East China from the 13th to the 19th.[97] CCP discipline was so effective, in fact, that even the East China party paper did not republish till the end of November. On the 20th, Mao suggested bringing out the article as a small monograph, but when on 24 November the Shanghai Xinhua Bookshop solicited orders for the publication, the Beijing Xinhua Bookshop, instructed by the municipal party committee, replied that it would not take a single copy. This defiance did not last.

Peng Zhen returned to Beijing in late November. He decided to reconsider whether national organs like *Red Flag* should reprint Yao's article and ordered the municipal party secretariat to discuss the question of reprinting locally. But he laid down that any problems Wu Han might have had were not in the category of enemy versus people and insisted that incorrect aspects of Yao's article would have to be criticized.[98] The Beijing secretariat told Peng that it disagreed with the politically based criticisms in the fourth part of Yao's article,[99] and that if it were reprinted it would have to be accompanied by an editorial note making clear the Beijing party's position. Nudged by Zhou Enlai, and by now aware of Mao's interest, Peng Zhen finally took a decision. On 29 November, almost three weeks after Yao's article had been published, *Beijing Ribao* reprinted it with a note saying that differing opinions should be aired. The following day, the *People's Daily* followed suit, this time with an editorial note jointly revised by Zhou and Peng emphasizing the importance of free criticism in the search for truth through facts.[100] The paper's editors demonstrated their disapproval of the political dimensions of Yao's polemic by printing it on the fifth page in the section on academic discussion.

But if Peng Zhen thought he had stabilized the Wu Han controversy and protected his Beijing bailiwick, he must have been concerned at simultaneous political developments in different spheres which threatened his other power base, the CC secretariat.

The fall of Yang Shangkun

On the same day as the publication of Yao Wenyuan's attack on Wu Han, Mao abruptly dismissed Yang Shangkun, an alternate secretary in the CC secretariat, whose most important function was to head the CC's General Office which controlled the paper flow at the top of the CCP.[101] In his place, he installed Wang Dongxing, who, as head of the central guards (known as the 8341 unit), normally accompanied Mao everywhere.[102]

The ostensible reason for Yang's dismissal was that in 1959 he had arranged for the sleeping quarters and reception area in the railway carriage of Mao's special train to be bugged. Listening devices were also installed in provincial guest-houses which he habitually visited. According to the account of Mao's physician, who was privy to this operation, the objective was benign: to ensure that the many *obiter dicta* which Mao tossed off during his provincial tours should not be lost to his colleagues in the CC. More to the point, it would mean that the CC would be instantly aware of any change in the Chairman's thinking and be able to anticipate his commands. The matter was kept secret from Mao because he had once objected to the suggestion that a stenographer accompany him for the same purpose; he did not want to feel he had to watch his words in case some casual remark launched a movement.[103]

The sleeping car was presumably bugged because it was Mao's custom to conduct much of his business from his bed. One result was that Mao's many liaisons were also recorded. Indeed, the bugging was discovered early in 1961; the technician in charge teased one of Mao's young women about a conversation she had had with the Chairman which he had overheard. Mao was incandescent with anger when she revealed the bugging to him, believing that his colleagues were compiling a dossier to be used against him, and a number of his junior staff were dismissed. Though Yang's role was covered up, Mao apparently always suspected him of masterminding the operation.[104] If that is so, the most plausible reason for the

Chairman to stay Yang's execution for almost five years, in a matter which he regarded with the utmost seriousness, was that it was not until November 1965 that it became crucial for him to take control of Yang's office. Almost simultaneously, moves were being taken against the PLA chief-of-staff, General Luo Ruiqing, another member of the CC secretariat.

Lin Biao takes control of the MAC

In the early 1960s, Lin Biao maintained a low profile, perhaps because of illness, making only occasional forays either to defend Mao, as at the Seven Thousand Cadres Conference, or to set new standards for the study of the Chairman's thought. For the most part, Lin left the MAC and the daily conduct of military affairs in the hands of his chief-of-staff, Luo Ruiqing. Like Lin Biao, Luo had been appointed as a result of the purge of Defence Minister Peng Dehuai and *his* chief-of-staff, Huang Kecheng, in 1959, and he played a leading role in the subsequent purge of Peng's putative 'right opportunist' supporters in the PLA.[105] Luo's background was as a political commissar specializing in security matters. He had fought alongside Lin Biao during the 1930s and 1940s.[106] Luo appears to have been in charge of Mao's security on the Long March, and regularly accompanied the Chairman after 1949 when he rose to be Minister of Public Security and, in 1959, a vice-premier. During those years, Mao's complaint about Luo, according to his doctor, was that he tried to restrict his freedom of action too much for security reasons.

At the MAC, Luo seconded Lin Biao's efforts on the ideological front, but he also took his military duties seriously, and while the PLA was held up to the nation as the model of political correctness in the mid-1960s, it also managed to maintain and improve its professional standards. The apogee of its efforts was a two-day display of military training in June 1964, held at the Ming Tombs outside Beijing in front of Mao, Liu, Zhou, Zhu De, Deng Xiaoping, and other leaders. Post-Cultural Revolution accounts state that Mao indicated approval of what he saw, with the result that similar manoeuvres were conducted in various parts of China through August. But the Chairman's physician remembers Mao as being best pleased at those exercises which demonstrated the irrelevance of modern weapons, and as making a caustic comment at Luo's expense.[107]

Lin Biao did not attend the display, apparently stating that he did not believe in military exercises;[108] instead, he sent some trusties, headed by his wife Ye Qun, an army officer who doubled as the head of his private office, to see whether or not military training was diverting the PLA from political work at the grass roots.[109] On 30 November 1964, Lin told the PLA organizational work conference to give prominence to politics (*tuchu zhengzhi*); politics had to take precedence. A month later he criticized the PLA's General Political Department for failing to implement the 'four firsts'; training was too dominant and was leaving too little time for political work. In 1965, the PLA had to grasp politics, and it was in May that year that the abolition of military ranks was announced.[110]

Luo Ruiqing became extremely disgruntled with Lin, arguing that politics had not been neglected and that it could not be allowed to mess up everything else. If the PLA were untrained, in the event of war the party and nation would be finished.[111] Since many of Luo's remarks were made in the presence of colleagues, they naturally reached Lin's ears and angered him further. The last straw came when Luo Ruiqing, in the furtherance of Mao's policy of rearing revolutionary successors, urged Lin to allow certain older colleagues to retire. He got the head of the air force to tell Ye Qun that Lin Biao should look after his health and allow Luo to run the PLA. On 30 November 1965, Lin wrote to Mao, recounting all this, accusing Luo of trying to get rid of him. He sent Ye Qun to Hangzhou to convey the allegations in person. The air force chief, Liu Yalou, had died in May and so was unable to corroborate Ye's testimony, but Lin arranged for the new chief, Wu Faxian, and the navy commissar, Li Zuopeng, to write in support.[112]

Whatever he may have thought about the validity of Lin Biao's accusations, there was good reason for Mao to act against Luo Ruiqing. When Luo had been Minister of Public Security, Mao had resented his reporting to Liu Shaoqi and other party officials about his safety.[113] As a member of the CC secretariat since 1962, Luo was responsible to Deng Xiaoping and Peng Zhen. Though Luo was doubtless as loyal to Mao as any senior member of the CCP, his comment on Lin Biao's speech at the Seven Thousand Cadres Conference had indicated to the Chairman that he was not a mindless devotee.[114] If Luo was now at odds with Lin Biao, upon whose total loyalty Mao *could* count, then Luo had to go. In the turmoil that Mao was about to unleash against the party, he had to be totally certain of the firm backing of the military, the other major national institution. With Lin in perennial poor health, Mao could not afford to have in day-to-day control of the PLA a general who might conceivably feel a higher loyalty to the party than to its Chairman.

On 8 December, Mao summoned an expanded PSC conference in Shanghai at which Ye Qun was the principal prosecution witness against the absent Luo, speaking for ten hours, supported by Lin Biao, Wu Faxian, and Li Zuopeng. Liu Shaoqi, Zhou Enlai, and Deng Xiaoping were reportedly all taken aback by this sneak attack and at a loss as to what to make of it. After the session ended on the 15th, Mao ordered Zhou and Deng to conduct an investigation, another instance of Mao bringing in the premier to adulterate the power of the General Secretary and the CC secretariat; on a later occasion, he would describe this device as 'mixing in sand'.[115] Luo was summoned from Kunming to answer the charges, but instead of admitting his errors, he argued his case. This led to the establishment of a 'small group' to take charge of the Luo case. In Beijing from 4 to 16 March and from 22 March to 8 April, the small group conducted struggle sessions against the luckless general, with forty-two participants in the first session and ninety-five in the second. Between the sessions, on 18 March, Luo tried to commit suicide by jumping from a building, but succeeded only in breaking his leg. He was dismissed as chief-of-staff and replaced by a deputy, Yang Chengwu, on an acting basis.[116] Luo Ruiqing's successor in the CC secretariat would be a marshal, Ye Jianying, with close ties to Zhou Enlai;[117] Ye and two other marshals, Chen Yi and Xu Xiangqian, were made deputy chairmen of the MAC, perhaps as an inducement not to question the sudden purge of the chief-of-staff.[118] Having transferred control over the economy from the CC secretariat to Zhou Enlai and the 'small planning commission' at the beginning of 1965, Mao now seemed bent on ensuring that the PLA, too, would be more responsive to the premier than to the CC secretariat. The PLA was now Mao and Lin Biao's to command.

A marriage of convenience

The attack on Luo Ruiqing gave Jiang Qing an opening to develop a stronger base than the Shanghai propaganda department. When she had asked Luo Ruiqing in Shanghai towards the end of November 1965 why the PLA paper, *Jiefang Jun Bao* (Liberation Army News), had not reprinted the Yao Wenyuan article, he had telephoned a deputy head of the PLA's General Political Department, Liu Zhijian, and notified him that it should be reproduced. But the article was not published until the 29th, the same day that it appeared in the *Beijing Ribao*, though an editorial note did describe Wu Han's play as a 'big poisonous weed'. The PLA was clearly under the sway of the CC's secretariat and its propaganda department; perhaps Luo, as a member of the secretariat, had advised Liu Zhijian not to move faster than Peng Zhen.[119]

Lin Biao's attack on Luo and Luo's removal from office gave Jiang Qing her chance. Lin had again demonstrated his loyalty to Mao's ideas and the extent to which he was prepared to go to enforce them in the PLA. Accordingly, on 21 January 1966, Jiang Qing went from Shanghai to Suzhou to suggest to Lin that she might hold a cultural forum in the PLA. Lin readily agreed, doubtless seeing this as a way of further ingratiating himself with Mao. He issued an instruction that all PLA literary documents should henceforth be shown to Jiang Qing. A phone call from Ye Qun resulted in Liu Zhijian flying to Shanghai with three colleagues and two aides on 2 February, to be regaled with Jiang Qing's views on films, Peking Opera, and the cultural life of the 1930s.[120] Jiang Qing had eight conversations with Liu, presided over four group discussions, took the PLA team thirteen times to the movies and three times to Peking Operas, talking all the while, and sending them separately to twenty-one other films![121]

At the end of this intensive cultural course, on 20 February, Liu Zhijian produced a report to the GPD, but although it included 'many extremely important opinions' of Jiang Qing, she denounced it as an unacceptable distortion, and referred it to Mao, who in turn ordered it revised by Chen Boda, Zhang Chunqiao, and Yao Wenyuan.[122] Out of this exhaustive collective endeavour came the 'Summary of the army forum on literature and art work called by Jiang Qing at the behest of Lin Biao'.[123]

The most important point in the summary was that there was a sharp struggle in the literary and art field. Mao's instructions had not been carried out since the CCP came to power; his policies had been thwarted by the dictatorship of an anti-party, anti-socialist black line. This attack on the CCP cultural establishment in general and the CC's Propaganda Department in particular was only slightly modified by the comment that the socialist cultural revolution had begun to bear fruit in the past three years. This was meant not as a tribute to Peng Zhen and his five-man group but rather as a claim that Jiang Qing had managed to stir things up, for the summary asserted that the struggle between the two lines continued, including in the PLA. Most works of art were neutral or anti-party. The influence of the Chinese classics, European and Russian classics, and American movies was too strong. In a clear attack on one member of the five-man group, the literary tsar Zhou Yang, the summary denounced anti-Marxists who had espoused the slogan 'Literature of national defence'.[124] The summary concluded with a ten-point programme for the PLA's GPD to adopt to improve political work in the military.[125]

The summary did more than lay out a new cultural policy emanating from Jiang Qing with Mao's backing and careful supervision; it established a cultural HQ to rival Peng Zhen's. The Beijing 1st secretary understandably took alarm when he learned of Jiang Qing's activities and took steps to counter them.

Date Summary 1

November

10	Yao Wenyuan article; Wang Dongxing replaces Yang Shangkun.
29	Yao article reprinted by *Beijing Ribao* and *Jiefang Jun Bao* with disclaimers.
30	Yao article reprinted by *Renmin Ribao*.
	Lin Biao writes to Mao about Luo Ruiqing.

December

Start	Ye Qun describes Luo's misdeeds to Mao.
8–15	Mao presides over PSC conference in Shanghai to criticize Luo; Zhou Enlai, Deng Xiaoping summon Luo for interrogation.

January

21	Jiang Qing visits Lin Biao, suggests a PLA cultural forum.
Last ten days	Ye Qun tells Liu Zhijian to attend forum.

February

2–10, 16–20	Jiang Qing's PLA cultural forum.
3	Peng Zhen's five-man group meets; 'February Outline' drawn up.
5	February Outline approved by PSC.
8	Peng Zhen presents February Outline to Mao in Hangzhou.
Last ten days	Mao inspects PLA cultural forum document.

Peng Zhen's last stand

In December, the *People's Daily* and the *Beijing Ribao*, obedient to the five-man group, had published articles designed to redirect the Wu Han debate into purely literary channels. Deng Tuo defended his former literary collaborator with a pseudonymous article in the

Beijing local paper.[126] Comments in defence of Wu Han were published even in the *Wenhui Bao* where Yao Wenyuan's broadside had
appeared.[127] On 30 December, a long self-criticism by Wu Han,
replete with historical data, was published in the *People's Daily*; in it,
he rejected any connection between his play and the surge in favour
of individual farming and reversal of verdicts in the early 1960s.[128]

But Wu Han's self-criticism was already out of date. By now
Mao had the bit between his teeth, and during conversations with
Chen Boda, Tian Jiaying, Hu Sheng, Guan Feng, and Ai Siqi on
21–2 December in Hangzhou,[129] he had committed himself to the
view suggested by Kang Sheng: 'The damaging issue in *Hai Rui
Dismissed from Office* is "dismissal from office". The Jiaqing
emperor dismissed Hai Rui from office; in 1959, we dismissed Peng
Dehuai from office. Peng Dehuai is indeed "Hai Rui" '.[130] Even
though intellectuals around the country, presumably ignorant of
this Hangzhou dictum, continued to defend Wu Han into the new
year,[131] Mao's pronouncement transformed the Wu Han issue into
a political one. In Shanghai towards the end of January, Jiang Qing,
while discussing Mao's point with Guan Feng, one of the band of
leftist polemicists working with Chen Boda and Zhang Chunqiao,
gave a clear indication of the campaign's real aim by adding that
Beijing's initial failure to republish the article was 'an example of
the dictatorship of the black line'.[132] Articles attacking Wu Han
became more frequent.[133] To give the beleagured historian some
respite, a Beijing party secretary, Wan Li, sent Wu Han incognito to
participate in the four clean-ups in the suburbs, but there he soon
found himself being pressed to participate in local manifestations of
the anti-Wu Han campaign![134]

Peng Zhen persisted with such routine defensive efforts throughout December and January; in the Propaganda Department, earlier
articles of Guan Feng were examined to show that his viewpoint had
been similar to Wu Han's.[135] But on 3 February, having allowed two
months to go by without a major response to the campaign, Peng
summoned an enlarged meeting of the five-man small group in order
to discuss the Wu Han issue and its implications. The timing of this
meeting, and the speed with which its decisions were implemented,
suggests that Peng had learned from the PLA's GPD of the departure on 2 February of the Liu Zhijian group to meet Jiang Qing in
Shanghai. He would not have needed to know many details to realize the potential threat which the link between Jiang Qing and his
old nemesis, Lin Biao, represented.

At the meeting, Peng announced that background checks of Wu Han had failed to find organizational ties between him and Peng Dehuai. He also emphasized Mao's approval of *The Dismissal of Hai Rui* when it had first been performed, indicating that Mao had seen a performance as well as read the play. Perhaps intuiting that the whole Beijing *apparat* would soon be under fire, or possibly simply anticipating that the campaign against Wu Han could spread to his writings for the 'Three-Family Village' and thus to his collaborators in that enterprise, Peng Zhen called on his deputy, Liu Ren, and another municipal secretary to testify that Deng Tuo had always upheld the 'three red banners'. Peng reaffirmed his belief that *The Dismissal of Hai Rui* should not be discussed as a political issue, and that even academic criticism should be restrained and not exceed certain bounds. Kang Sheng, who was present as a member of the five-man group, apparently did not express any disagreement, despite his earlier allegations to Mao about Wu Han and Peng Dehuai.[136]

On the basis of these remarks and apparently supportive comments at the meeting, two of Peng Zhen's suborcinates, Xu Liqun and Yao Zhen, immediately drafted the 'Outline of a report of the five-man small group to the CC', later stigmatized by cultural revolutionaries as the 'February Outline'. Moving fast, doubtless keen to pre-empt whatever Jiang Qing had in mind as well as to stem or at least channel the tide of criticism before it got out of hand, Peng sent this to all members of the PSC and formally presented it at a meeting of all PSC members currently in the capital on 5 February.[137] Since Mao was in Wuhan,[138] Zhu De in Jiangxi,[139] and Lin Biao probably in Suzhou,[140] this meant Liu Shaoqi, Zhou Enlai,[141] and Deng Xiaoping.[142] Liu asked if there were any organizational links between Wu Han and Peng Dehuai, and Peng Zhen reaffirmed that there were none. Again, Kang Sheng remained silent and Peng Zhen obtained the PSC's formal approval.[143] On 8 February, Peng and colleagues flew down to Wuhan to get Mao's approval for the outline.[144] According to Wu Lengxi who was present, the Chairman agreed to the circulation of the outline in the name of the centre;[145] according to other accounts, the Chairman at least expressed no contrary opinions.[146] According to differing accounts, Mao then asked either if Wu Han was anti-party and anti-socialist or if he was tied up with Peng Dehuai, or perhaps both. Peng Zhen again explained that there were no organizational links. Mao seemed satisfied for he responded that, after criticism, Wu Han could stay on as a deputy mayor. He added that the link between Lushan and *The Dismissal of Hai Rui* was Kang Sheng's discovery.[147]

What was Peng Zhen to make of this encounter? The Chairman had vouchsafed no objection to the February Outline, and seemed to accept Wu Han staying on. He had brought up the issue of the Wu Han–Peng Dehuai link, but had indicated no dissatisfaction with Peng Zhen's explanation. He had even disclaimed responsibility for the suggestion, saying it was Kang Sheng's discovery. Kang Sheng, who seems to have been present in his unofficial capacity as adviser to the Chairman rather than as a member of the five-man group, was embarrassed by this accolade, and tried to disclaim it. He had been exposed as going behind the back of Peng Zhen and his other colleagues on the five-man group. Kang may have wondered if he had misunderstood Mao's intentions, and he was about to be thrown to the wolves in some devious manoeuvre of the Chairman's. Only as the Cultural Revolution got under way would Kang Sheng acknowledge authorship and claim credit.[148] At this moment, however, it seemed as if Peng Zhen had regained the initiative and could press ahead with damage limitation with the Chairman's consent.

The February Outline

The February Outline was a brief document which bore evidence of hasty preparation; one of the six sections was simply a heading with content to follow.[149] The Outline paid obeisance to the leftism of the moment by declaring that the current ideological struggle was between the socialist and capitalist roads. But the first section emphasized that it was a struggle within the field of scholarship rather than a political one, which in turn meant that it was complex and not always easy to distinguish right and wrong in the short run. Thus it was essential to seek truth from facts and, repeating Peng Zhen's formulation of the previous September, to abide by 'the principle that everyone is equal before the truth' (*zai zhenli mianqian renren pingdeng de yuanze*).[150] The self-reform of scholars whose viewpoints were reactionary or who had committed errors was to be welcomed. On Wu Han, the outline was somewhat contradictory, admitting that he had 'adopted the bourgeois world view towards history and committed political errors', but ordering that published criticisms should not stray into the political realm. In the vain hope of reining in ideological cowboys like Yao Wenyuan, the outline appealed to all leftist scholars to work together in 'mutual aid teams' or 'APCs', and announced the creation of the five-man group's own 'scholarly criticism general office', presumably to promote and enforce such co-ordination.[151] But even as Peng Zhen and his colleagues were putting these defences in place, Mao was only biding his time for a final assault on the capital.

The fall of Peng Zhen

Mao's opportunity came with the departure of Liu Shaoqi, Peng's long-time patron and friend, on a trip round South Asia on 26 March. Even though he stopped over twice for a few days in Xinjiang in between his visits to Pakistan, Afghanistan, and Burma, he did not return to Beijing.[152] By the time he did get back on 19 April, Peng's fate was sealed.

Date Summary 2

March

Uncertain	Peng Zhen inspects third front in Sichuan.
4–8 Apr.	Small group examines Luo case;(4–16) struggle sessions; (22–8 Apr.) larger sessions.
11	Angry exchange between Peng Zhen and Shanghai party.
Mid ten days	Jiang Qing, Chen Boda, Zhang Chunqiao discuss PLA cultural forum document.
Mid ten days	Mao complains to Zhou and Deng about Peng Zhen's independent kingdom.
14	Forum document sent to Mao.
17	Mao approves forum document.
18–20	Mao holds PSC expanded conference in Hangzhou; Liu Shaoqi, Zhou Enlai, Peng Zhen, Kang Sheng, Chen Boda present, Deng Xiaoping absent in SW; Mao criticizes *People's Daily* as semi-Marxist on 18th.
c.18	Luo Ruiqing attempts suicide.
19	Jiang Qing sends forum document to Lin Biao.
22	Lin Biao sends document to other marshals.
26	Liu Shaoqi and Wang Guangmei leave for Pakistan.
28, 30	Mao condemns Peng Zhen, wants five-man group disbanded.
30	MAC sends PLA cultural forum document and Lin Biao's letter to CC.
31–4 Apr.	Liu Shaoqi in Xinjiang.

April

1	Zhang Chunqiao prepares a document criticizing the February Outline.
2	*RMRB* publishes Qi Benyu/Guan Feng article.
4	Liu Shaoqi flies to Afghanistan.
8–15	Liu returns to Xinjiang.
9–12	Kang Sheng, Chen Boda criticize Peng Zhen at secretariat meeting; decision to draft document criticizing February Outline (May 16th directive); establish CRG.
10	CC passes PLA cultural forum document for distribution.
14	Mao begins redrafting the May 16th directive.
15	Liu flies to East Pakistan and thereafter goes to Burma.
16	*Beijing Ribao* publishes material against the 'Three-Family Village'.
19	Liu Shaoqi returns to Beijing from Rangoon.
22	Mao presides over Politburo conference.

May

4–26	Expanded Politburo conference in Beijing. Peng Zhen, Luo Ruiqing, Lu Dingyi, Yang Shangkun condemned. Beijing party and CC's Propaganda Department reorganized. CRG replaces five-man group. Lin Biao talks about Mao's concern about coups.

In early March, Zhang Chunqiao, in what was probably a deliberate provocation, tested the limits of the policy laid down in the February Outline by sending the head of the Shanghai propaganda bureau for discussions in Beijing about guidelines for criticizing offending scholars and writers. Peng Zhen's curt brush-off of this emissary prompted Zhang to label the Beijing party and the Propaganda Department as anti-Yao Wenyuan and even anti-Mao. The renewed hostilities between Beijing and Shanghai were brought to Mao's attention by Jiang Qing. He reacted in anger, simulated or otherwise. At some point in the middle of the month—which may well have been when Peng Zhen left Beijing to inspect the third front in Sichuan—the Chairman held an expanded PSC conference in Hangzhou at which he complained to Zhou Enlai and Deng Xiaoping that Peng Zhen ran an independent kingdom in Beijing; the ostensible grounds for this accusation was the treatment accorded the first of Jiang Qing's model operas, *Shajiabang*, in Beijing. When asked for their reactions, both Zhou and Deng said they had none.[153] But even if they had not realized it before, they must now have understood the intention behind the assault on Wu Han and foreseen the impending denouement.

On 28 and 30 March, just after Liu had left China, Mao summoned Kang Sheng, Jiang Qing, and Zhang Chunqiao for talks. He condemned the February Outline as failing to distinguish between right and wrong, and alleged that the Propaganda Department, Peng Zhen, and the Beijing party committee were protecting bad people. The department, the committee, and the five-man group should all be dissolved.

Within a few days, the Propaganda Department had been swept aside and an article by the leftist intellectuals Qi Benyu and Guan Feng which it had banned was published in the *People's Daily*. At a meeting of the secretariat from 9 to 12 April, Kang Sheng and Chen Boda attacked Peng Zhen. Deng Xiaoping's role at the meeting has not been disclosed, but presumably he assented to the decision to issue a condemnation of the February Outline. Mao revised this condemnatory document seven times before allowing it to go out as the 'May 16 notification', the first official document of the Cultural Revolution. The secretariat also decided to set up a 'cultural revolution document-drafting small group' which eventually became the Central Cultural Revolution Small Group (CRG).[154] On 22 April, Mao summoned a meeting of the PSC in Hangzhou to lay down the guidelines for the *coup de grâce*.[155] We do not know if Liu, hot off the plane, or any other member of the PSC objected to what Mao had in mind. Liu had been very circumspect in his dealings with Peng Zhen when the Yao Wenyuan article was published, apparently aware that Mao was behind it.[156] We do know that, in a gesture of cruel irony, Mao opted to stay in Hangzhou and allow Liu to preside over Peng's political demise.

The Politburo met in expanded session—eighty people were present—from 4 to 26 May in Beijing. Unusually, participation was confined to people working in the capital; no representatives of the CCP's regional bureaux or provincial-level committees were present. During the first three days, in a carefully co-ordinated series of speeches, the scene was set by Mao's surrogates, Kang Sheng, Zhang Chunqiao, and Chen Boda.[157]

Kang, who spoke for eight hours on 5 and 6 May, relayed Mao's unhappiness with Peng Zhen and Lu Dingyi from the 10th plenum on, but particularly since November 1965, and called for their dismissal and the reorganization of the Beijing party committee and the CC's Propaganda Department. Kang gave his own view of what Mao wanted: first, Peng and Lu were to be criticized for protecting the right and oppressing the left and refusing to permit revolution; second, everyone had a duty to support the left and create a new corps of revolutionary cultural cadres to promote a great cultural revolution. Already the CC had given birth to revisionism: Luo Ruiqing, Peng Zhen, Yang Xianzhen, Yang Shangkun, Tian Jiaying, and Liao Mosha were all examples.

On the afternoon of 6 May, Zhang Chunqiao took over the baton, attacking the cultural establishment—Lu Dingyi, Zhou Yang, Lin Mohan, Shao Quanlin—but again directing his principal fire against Peng Zhen and the Beijing party committee for their handling of the Yao article. The following morning, it was Chen Boda's turn. His job was to criticize the whole of Peng Zhen's long revolutionary career.[158]

But the bombshell was thrown by Lin Biao, who in a speech before a plenary session on 18 May, accused Peng, Luo, Lu, and Yang of plotting a *coup d'état*. The following day, in a five-minute rebuttal which hardly amounted to a self-criticism, Peng Zhen said that he had not even dreamed of a coup let alone plotted one; he challenged the CC to discover any improper links between him, Luo, and Lu.[159] Mao later expressed reservations about Lin's talk of coups, but he ordered Zhou to increase Beijing security, particularly in the Zhongnanhai.[160] Lin had hit a nerve.

Lu Dingyi's self-criticism on 20 May took place under bizarre circumstances. On each participant's seat was a document which stated baldly: 'Ye Qun was a virgin. Lin Biao.'[161] This was in response to a letter written by Lu Dingyi's apparently deranged wife alleging loose behaviour by Lin's wife Ye Qun. In a heated exchange, Lin Biao refused to accept Lu's insistence that he knew nothing about his wife's letter.[162]

The rest of the meeting followed the course laid down by Mao. No one defended any of the targets publicly. On 21 May, Zhou Enlai stated that Peng, Lu, Luo, and Yang 'had taken the "capitalist road"', and their recent exposure and the 'retaking of the positions they had usurped' was a 'victory for Mao Zedong Thought and a cause for celebration'.[163] The four men were dismissed from the CC secretariat; Peng was dismissed as Beijing 1st secretary and Lu as director of propaganda. Tao Zhu was helicoptered from the Central-South region to take over Peng's role as the executive secretary of the CC secretariat and Lu's job as head of propaganda,[164] and Marshal Ye Jianying, a long-time associate of Zhou Enlai's, took over Luo Ruiqing's role supervising the military in the secretariat.[165] On 24 May, the PSC set up a Case Examination Committee (later Group) to 'further examine the anti-party activities and irregular relationships of the four comrades [sic] Peng, Lu, Luo, and Yang'.[166] Before the session ended on 26 May, two officials had committed suicide: Deng Tuo, one-time chief editor of the *People's Daily* on 18 May; Tian Jiaying, secretary to Mao for ten years, on 23 May.[167]

Mao had removed powerful opponents from the CC secretariat, replaced them with new officials intended to be more responsive to himself, and put the cast of his leftist Cultural Revolution coalition on stage: Lin Biao to oversee the PLA; ideologues like Chen Boda, Kang Sheng, and the CRG to control propaganda, with the help of intellectuals like Qi Benyu and Guan Feng; Zhang Chunqiao and Yao Wenyuan and the propaganda wing of the Shanghai party; and, of course, his personal trouble-maker, Jiang Qing. All of them, apart from Lin Biao, who was represented by his wife, Ye Qun, and perhaps Yao Wenyuan, were made members of the new Case Examination Group, destined to emerge as the principal bureaucratic organ for hounding old comrades during the Cultural Revolution.[168] The prologue to the Cultural Revolution was over. The Chairman was ready for Act I.

Act 1, Scene 1 of the Cultural Revolution was played out in Beijing, with Mao directing from off-stage. Kang Sheng's wife, Cao Yiou, persuaded a group of Peking University teachers to put up a poster denouncing the university administrators in late May.[1] Predictably, the administration and its trusties unleashed a powerful counter-attack, but the ground was cut from under them when the *People's Daily*, now in the charge of Chen Boda, editorialized in support of the leftist dissidents on 2 June.[2] Soon all the Beijing campuses were in an uproar as teachers and students realized that it was now open season on the university party *apparats*.

Liu Shaoqi, Zhou Enlai, and Deng Xiaoping pondered a re-sponse. They telephoned Mao in Hangzhou to urge him to return to the capital, but he refused. They asked him if sending in work teams, standard operating procedure for the CCP, would be accept-able. Getting no clear response, Liu and Deng flew down to Hangzhou to pose the question in person. Mao still temporized, indicating that he was happy to leave them in charge.[3] They sent in work teams. The work teams attempted to bring the campuses under control.

Scene 2 took place in Wuhan on 16 July 1966. Chairman Mao took to the waves, floating down the Yangtze for two hours. Ten days later, this feat was trumpeted throughout China by films and news-papers. It was a dramatic return to public view. Despite his intensive backstage plotting over previous months, his only previous appear-ance since November had been a photo-opportunity with a visiting Albanian leader in May. The Chairman's absence from the capital in the first half of 1966 contributed significantly, and doubtless designedly, to political tension and bewilderment as pyres were lit under senior cadres by his adherents. Now Mao was demonstrating that, although 72, he was still fighting fit and ready to take charge of the unfolding Cultural Revolution.[4]

Back in Beijing by 18 July for Scene 3, Mao spent the night listen-ing to reports from Kang Sheng and Chen Boda and other leftists, and then on 19 July roundly castigated Liu and Deng Xiaoping for suppressing revolutionary students and teachers, the kind of behaviour, as he put it, that had been adopted by the Qing dynasty, the northern warlords, and the KMT.[5] As in the case of Peng Zhen, Mao's allies had stirred the pot to provoke a response, Mao's senior colleagues had asked for guidance which he had refused to provide, seeming to indicate acceptance of their conduct of affairs. Then, in an about-face, he turned on them. He ordered the work teams withdrawn. Zhou Enlai professed himself unable to understand what was happening.[6] The CC secretariat had been deprived of effective responsibility for a major campaign.

Act 1, Scene 4 was the 11th plenum of the CC, the first in four years, a measure of the extent to which Mao had preferred to rule without institutional restraint. But now he wanted formal ratification of the creation of a new power structure and a launch pad for Act 2. At the end of the plenum, held from 1 to 12 August, the final communiqué revealed how the comity of the Yan'an Round Table was shattering at the outset of the Cultural Revolution:

	Politburo	
	*8th Congress**	*11th Plenum*
PSC	Mao Zedong	Mao Zedong†
	Liu Shaoqi	Lin Biao
	Zhou Enlai	Zhou Enlai
	Zhu De	Tao Zhu
	Chen Yun	Chen Boda
	Lin Biao	Deng Xiaoping
	Deng Xiaoping	Kang Sheng
		Liu Shaoqi
		Zhu De
		Li Fuchun
		Chen Yun
Members	[Lin Boqu]	Dong Biwu
	Dong Biwu	Chen Yi
	Peng Zhen	Liu Bocheng
	[Luo Ronghuan]	He Long
	Chen Yi	Li Xiannian
	Li Fuchun	Li Jingquan
	{Peng Dehuai}	Tan Zhenlin
	Liu Bocheng	Xu Xiangqian
	He Long	Nie Rongzhen
	Li Xiannian	Ye Jianying

                    [Ke Qingshi]
                    Li Jingquan
                    Tan Zhenlin

Alternates   Ulanfu   Ulanfu
                    {Zhang Wentian}   Bo Yibo
                    Lu Dingyi   Li Xuefeng
                    Chen Boda   Song Renqiong
                    Kang Sheng   Xie Fuzhi
                    Bo Yibo

(*After the first and second sessions of the 8th Congress.† For an account of how Jiang Qing helped draw up this ranking, see Ye Yonglie, *Chen Boda Qiren*, pp. 263–4. '[   ]' = Died before the 11th plenum. '{   }' = Not a functioning member of the Politburo since the Lushan plenum in 1959.)

This drastically altered line-up exhibited Mao's deviousness. Since there were twenty-six members and alternates in the new Politburo, the same as in the old, the operation could at one level be passed off as a topping-up made necessary by deaths and by the disgrace of Peng Zhen and Lu Dingyi, the only two to lose their posts.[7] The appointment of the remaining three marshals who had not attained the Politburo at the 8th Congress sessions was doubtless calculated to solidify the most reliable and important constituency behind Mao and Lin Biao. The enlargement of the PSC was a familiar Stalinist device designed to minimize the danger of a small cabal uniting against him; and the promotion of Mao supporters like Chen Boda and Kang Sheng, and even the humiliated planner, Li Fuchun, ensured Mao an easy majority.

The most spectacular strategic change in the 11th plenum reshuffle was of course the substitution of Lin Biao for Liu Shaoq as heir-apparent. The man about whom Mao had grumbled indiscreetly to Gao Gang fourteen years earlier had finally been struck down.[8] Any threat which he might have constituted had been neutralized.

But the crucial tactical element in Mao's game plan was the differential treatment of Liu Shaoqi and Deng Xiaoping. Liu had clearly fallen from grace, demoted to eighth place in the PSC. But Deng Xiaoping, whose secretariat had been effectively stripped of all its major responsibilities and purged of some of its key personnel, who had been held equally responsible for sending in the work teams, and who in a few months time would be demonized just below Liu as the 'No. 2 power holder taking the capitalist road', was attacked only once in a small group, and actually came out of the session one place higher than before in the PSC rankings. But for Jiang Qing's protests, he might have ranked even higher, for he got the maximum possible number of votes.[9] He seemed not to have been punished. Yet had Mao given the signal to his ideological Rottweilers, Deng's reputation could have been torn to shreds, as was to be amply proven in succeeding months.

One explanation may be that at this key moment in the development of the Cultural Revolution, when there was considerable unhappiness, bewilderment, and even opposition in the CC,[10] Mao was seeking to prevent Liu and Deng joining forces to rally the CC against him. As an old guerrilla fighter, he knew better than to tackle all his foes simultaneously.[11] By maintaining Deng in a high position, Mao was perhaps lulling the General Secretary into a sense of false security: Liu would suffer, for the Chairman had never really got on with him, but he, Deng, would survive because of his long and loyal association with Mao. After all, Mao had told Khrushchev in 1957 of his high appraisal of Deng.[12] But as the Cultural Revolution moved into high gear thereafter, Deng, like Liu Shaoqi, Peng Zhen, and most other comrades of the Yan'an Round Table, would be purged in a hail of abuse.[13]

If the aim of the Cultural Revolution had been only to safeguard Mao's position and remove potential threats in the form of Liu and Deng, the movement would have run its course in the few months after the 11th plenum. But though Mao bore grudges and suspected plots, he also dreamed dreams and envisioned a brave new world. This was to be 'a great revolution that touches people to their very souls',[14] designed to revitalize China by training revolutionary successors to dare to think, speak, and act. The plenum's sixteen-point decision concerning the 'Great Proletarian Cultural Revolution' emphasized the need to 'boldly arouse the masses' and 'let the masses educate themselves in the movement'.[15]

So Act 2 of the Cultural Revolution began with a Nuremberg-style rally of hundreds of thousands of students chanting *Mao zhuxi wan sui*—Long Live Chairman Mao—in Tiananmen Square on 18 August, shortly after the 11th plenum had concluded. Mao was to present himself at seven more rallies in the following three months, a demigod enthusing hysterical disciples—the Red Guards—to obey his instructions to 'bombard the headquarters' of the CCP. While Red Guard organizations appear to have sprung up spontaneously at élite middle schools in the capital, Mao's decision to wear military uniform and accept a Red Guard arm-band at the first rally was an endorsement which ensured the formation of Red Guard units nationwide. Indeed, had the Red Guards not existed, Mao would have had to invent them. From long experience, from the May 4th Movement to the Hundred Flowers, the Chairman knew that students would always be the most fiery opponents of oppression and the *status quo*. Sure enough, the Red Guards 'tried' party cadres at mass rallies, beating many of them, in some cases to death. Never before had a dictator unleashed the forces of society against the state which he himself had created. This was indeed the mother of all mass movements.

CONCLUSIONS

The first volume of this work started with a mass movement. Another mass movement was the theme of the second volume. It was the ultimate failure of both collectivization and the Great Leap Forward that was one key element in the political process that led eventually, though not inevitably, to Mao's third major mass movement, the Cultural Revolution, the cataclysm whose coming completes this third volume.

The rapid and relatively peaceful completion of collectivization, in town as well as country, had been a stunning success for Mao, won in the face of his colleagues' doubts. The social fabric of the nation had apparently been transformed without the massive upheaval that had occurred in the Soviet Union. Within a few years, the Chairman had left his mark upon his nation's history. In war, he had bested Chiang Kai-shek; in peace, he had surpassed Stalin. The victor of the revolution had become the architect of national renewal, and would go on to pioneer new structures like the communes. Yet a decade later, Mao emerged at the head of a wrecker's crew, preaching 'destruction before construction'. That Jekyll-to-Hyde metamorphosis can be partly traced to collectivization.

Mao envisaged his collectivist triumph as the launch pad for his next labour: to transform China economically. He intended to make his nation rich and powerful. He also knew that economic success had to be the surest advertisement for and guarantor of the new social order. To get rich would be glorious for collectivism. Unfortunately for Mao, his hopes collided with reality. The economic 'little leap' of 1956 was aborted by the guardians of the Soviet model.[1] At this point, the Chairman had no alternative to offer, and anyway had more pressing concerns: the beginnings of the Sino-Soviet dispute, the other key element in the origins of the Cultural Revolution.

The confusion and heart-searching in the world communist movement precipitated by Khrushchev's attack on Stalin in his 'secret speech' at the CPSU's 20th Congress in February 1956, reaching its peak with the Hungarian revolt, caused Mao to distrust the CPSU 1st secretary and to ponder how to avoid a similar crisis within

China. Mao understood that the 'errors' of Stalin and his Hungarian satraps stemmed from their insistence upon ruthless class struggle.[2] Mao, too, believed implicitly in class struggle, but he felt it expedient to rectify the methods by which the CCP exercised its overweening power. He decided to expand the scope of the new united front, recently inaugurated in the interests of development. He called on non-party intellectuals and bureaucrats to help remould the CCP. But his unprecedented invitation to outsiders to participate in the previously intra-party process of rectification backfired. Criticisms mounted, campus agitation spread, cadre morale sagged. So Mao reneged, abandoning his first grand design, a great harmony.[3] Punishing the educated élite for answering his call, he sought new ways to transform China. He turned back to development, and to the peasants who had provided him with his greatest triumphs in war and peace.

Liberating China from Soviet formulae, Mao launched the GLF and the commune movement in a utopian effort to create a new form of socialism with Chinese characteristics. The peasants were to be the engine of development. Supposedly poor and blank, they could be transformed into renaissance men, equally proficient in agriculture, industry, commerce, education, or the military as occasion demanded. But his second grand design, a collectivist cornucopia, collapsed in the nationwide famine which the GLF precipitated. A majority of Mao's senior colleagues now realized that the peasants were not egalitarian pawns to be moved at will on the chessboard of Mao's imagination. Only with the traditional incentives associated with family farming would agriculture flourish. Collectivization may have been a victory for Mao, but it had been a defeat for China. The rapid spread of the responsibility system in the early 1960s demonstrated that the vaunted 'transformation' had been only superficial. The CCP should have left well alone after land reform.

But though Mao was prepared to lead a partial retreat, he could not sanction surrender without another humiliating loss of face and the sacrifice of his vision for the new China. Fortunately for him, as in the case of the GLF, only one old comrade was bold enough and responsible enough to challenge Mao. As at Lushan in 1959, so in Beidaihe in 1962, none of the whistle-blower's colleagues was prepared to stand by him, although they shared his views. At high noon, the party's rural chief Deng Zihui stood alone. Since he was not a general with potential for making mischief, his disgrace was less demeaning than Peng Dehuai's. The CCP and the peasants were compelled to muddle through with scaled-down communes. But at least Mao quit the economic arena, having been forced to accept that development was a marathon, not a sprint.

The Chairman had again bullied his colleagues into compliance. But his perception of their lack of ideological steel reinforced other concerns arising from the CPSU's 20th Congress. Khrushchev had declared, contrary to Lenin's dictum, that world war between capitalism and imperialism was *not* fatally inevitable; he had suggested that communist parties in Third World nations could come to power *without* armed revolution. Mao felt that the Soviet leader had gone soft on the international bourgeoisie. From Khrushchev's visit to Camp David in 1959 through his withdrawal of missiles from Cuba in 1962, to his signing of the partial nuclear test-ban treaty in 1963, the Soviet 1st secretary's behaviour was seen by Mao as appeasing the imperialist superpower. Khrushchev's withdrawal of Soviet experts in 1960, his attack on the Albanian communists in 1961, and his neutrality in the two Sino-Indian border clashes in 1959 and 1962 were even worse, a betrayal of proletarian solidarity. Gradually, as we have seen, Mao became convinced that the origins of Soviet treachery lay in the abandonment of Marxism-Leninism by CPSU leaders in the interests of a capitalist restoration.

As in the mid-1950s, so in the mid-1960s, the Chairman pondered the meaning of developments in the Soviet bloc for China, again asking the question: How can we avoid this fate? On both occasions, interwoven with the overall political issue was the personal one: in the 1950s, what the denunciation of Stalin might mean for himself; in the 1960s, the lesson of the fall of Khrushchev for Mao. The Chairman could have been forgiven for seeing Peng Dehuai's challenge at Lushan in 1959 as being encouraged by Khrushchev's assault on the 'cult of personality'. But if divinity no longer hedged the Chairman, he would ensure that fear did. In the mid-1960s, he pre-empted what he saw as an even more serious challenge with the Cultural Revolution.

But Mao's paranoia and the assertions of cultural revolutionaries are insufficient proof that in 1966 a beleaguered Chairman finally lashed out in desperate defence of himself and his 'Thought'. From the mid-1950s to the mid-1960s, the record shows that Mao was always in overall charge if not always in day-to-day command. He controlled the agenda. The force of his personality and prestige coupled with the institutional weight of the party chairmanship within the leader-friendly Leninist system ensured that. Mao bowed to *force majeure*, but not to his colleagues. When the economy over-heated, he allowed the 'little leap' to be halted. When students and intellectuals conjured up a hurricane instead of the 'gentle breeze and mild rain' he had forecast, he reversed course. When the Americans stood by the KMT in the Taiwan Straits, he held back. When the Soviets objected to the ideological aura imparted to the communes, he dispelled it. When the GLF produced a famine, he retreated. On such occasions, he might hibernate in his notional 'second front', a convenient device for saving face and eschewing responsibility. But his next spring was never far behind.

When Mao chose discretion, his lieutenants might feel obliged by circumstances to alter course, but they checked with him on every important issue. They assumed or hoped that silence or a mumble indicated consent. The brief interlude of 'rightist' policies in the early 1960s—in the countryside and in the cities, in agriculture, industry, and commerce, in education and in science, towards the intellectuals and the united front, and in the international arena—were rational responses by committed communists to domestic and international crises. Leftists grumbled, but through January 1962, Mao gave the policies his imprimatur. When the great helmsman returned to the bridge in mid-1962 and reversed course, his lieutenants aye-aye'd, and the pen-pricks of a Deng Tuo ceased. Prometheus bided his time; he was never bound. And he always made the difference.[4]

If this account of the decade leading up to the Cultural Revolution is correct—albeit at variance with earlier conventional wisdom—the question arises: why was the Cultural Revolution necessary at all? If Mao could call the shots, why shoot the piano-players?

It is not possible totally to disentangle Mao's motives, but the evidence suggests that 'Mao's ultimate dread—the image of extinction that stalk[ed] him—[was] the death of the revolution'.[5] He had to devise some new recipe for reinvigorating it. He had experienced the morning-after epiphany common to all revolutionaries: in victory, the revolution dies. Shades of the prison house begin to close upon the post-revolutionary state; after the initial transformative spasm, exhaustion replaces exhilaration, routine replaces voluntarism, responsibility clogs idealism.[6] Many revolutionary victors are happy to settle for power and stability. Mao was not.[7] The revolution was dead; long live the revolution!

But by the mid-1960s, the Chairman was running out of options as to how to achieve that rebirth.[8] His efforts to galvanize the country over the previous decade had all boomeranged. Two brave new worlds had proved chimeras. The intellectuals were silent. In place of GLF decentralization, China had a Soviet-style command economy again. The 'Anshan charter' system of industrial management had given way to the Seventy Articles on Industry, which embodied, in fact if not in name, the 'Magnitogorsk constitution', derided during the GLF.[9] People's communes had effectively reverted to Soviet-style collective farms. This was not socialism with Chinese characteristics; it was simply the Soviet model modified. Humiliatingly, for all its drawbacks, it worked better than Mao's hare-brained schemes.

The most serious setback for Mao was the failure of rural collectivism. The intellectuals he could shrug off; he often did. His persona was not invested in industry, though in fact workers in state factories were probably more satisfied with his revolution than any other segment of the population. But it was in the countryside that his first attempt at a revolution within the revolution had foundered. Mao built a field of dreams but the peasants would not come. It was not possible to bring about dynamic agricultural development through the collective system. Ironically, Mao who believed in unleashing people, shrank from freeing the peasantry. By 1965, he realized how right he had been a decade earlier to worry about the 'spontaneous and constant growth of capitalist elements in the countryside',[10] and how wrong to think he could snuff out that tendency by collectivization; he could barely contain it. And by early 1965, Mao felt also that the radicalized Socialist Education Movement which he had earlier supported could not be pressed forward on the lines envisaged by Liu Shaoqi.[11] The political costs were unacceptable.

At this point, having made good-faith efforts to keep the revolutionary fires burning by institutional and educational means, again most other leaders would have settled for second-best. Not Mao. Ruthlessly Machiavellian in the acquisition and retention of power, Mao remained recklessly utopian in the uses to which he put it. With the disintegration of the Sino-Soviet bloc, China was the last bastion of world revolution, and the Chairman had to find a way to implant his people with an ideological inner compass, ever pointing to magnetic Mao. If revolution from above was now impossible, it would have to be revolution from below. If the party could not change society, then Mao would unleash society to change the party.[12]

But the Cultural Revolution was rooted in personal as well as principled disputes.[13] The first necessity for any leader is to stay in power.[14] Mao's supremacy as Chairman of the CCP was unassailable so long as he could maintain a revolutionary agenda, on which no colleague would challenge him. From his experience in the mid-1950s and in early 1962, he knew that if he were to allow a Liu or a Deng or a Zhou to set the agenda, his 'hare-brained' utopian schemes would be set aside. Perhaps he himself would have to step aside. Khrushchev's dismissal increased his sense of threat from Liu and Deng. Mao, as both the Lenin and Stalin of the Chinese revolution, seemed in a uniquely unassailable position, but '[u]neasy lies the head that wears a crown', and from the CPSU's 20th Congress on, his paranoia grew.[15] Since Mao proved quite prepared to dump Liu Shaoqi, his close comrade-in-arms and heir-apparent of twenty years standing—transforming the next 'Qin Shi Huangdi' into 'China's Khrushchev'—why should he not have considered the earnest, uncharismatic but doggedly assertive Liu capable of equal treachery towards himself?

While Liu almost certainly never considered any kind of *coup d'état*, it does seem extraordinary that he put up no resistance. Instead, he dutifully presided over the demise of his principal political ally in May 1966. Did he think that this was the price for remaining Mao's heir? Or was this simply the disciplined behaviour of the ultimate Leninist *apparatchik*? Did he experience no 'conflict of loyalty' between the claims of the leader and the claims of the party, even the country?[16] Or did his behaviour represent, as with some of Stalin's victims, a refusal or an inability to comprehend the enormity of the anti-party actions which the leader had begun to commit?[17] Was there no 'higher kind of loyalty'?[18] Or was Liu simply transfixed, like a rabbit before a boa constrictor? Stalin's administrative system, according to his interpreter, depended for its effectiveness (in addition to faith and enthusiasm) upon discipline, fear, and reward.[19] Possibly all these influenced Liu's behaviour at this time.

Whatever the explanation, the restraint displayed by Liu, and by Deng, Peng Zhen, Lu Dingyi, Luo Ruiqing, Yang Shangkun, and many others subsequently, in the face of Mao's assault on the party was enormously helpful to the Chairman. He was able to safeguard his own position by getting rid of colleagues, suspect because of their independent stature and authority, and surround himself with toadies whose loyalty was to himself rather than to the party, Marxism-Leninism, or their peers. Mao thus stripped China of a priceless asset, a united and capable leadership, the Yan'an Round Table, that 'elect group' which had conquered China and guided it through the early travails of nation-building.[20]

To give Mao the benefit of the doubt, there were legitimate reasons, unconnected with the Chairman's personal security of tenure, why he might have wanted to prevent Liu succeeding him. Apart from differences between Mao and Liu on specific issues discussed in this and earlier volumes, there was a more fundamental divergence between the two men on how to run China. In the blooming of the Hundred Flowers, the GLF, the SEM, and at the beginning of the Cultural Revolution, Mao was for 'opening wide' and 'unleashing' mass movements, while Liu always opted to exercise tighter control through hands-on party leadership. Mao was an *à la carte* leader, choosing freely whatever policy seemed good at the time, content to take his chances with whatever came next; Liu was a *table d'hôte* man, preferring to stick with the prescribed menu of political techniques that had served him well in the past. Not surprisingly, like leaders elsewhere, Mao preferred a successor whom he considered 'one of us'.[21]

Mao could also legitimately have worried about Liu's lack of ballast, his tendency to yaw violently from one extreme to another. Mao beat tactical retreats from time to time, but without striking his colours. Liu, on the other hand, moved from ultra-leftism during the GLF to ultra-rightism during the post-GLF famine, and then back to ultra-leftism in the second half of the SEM.[22] While country and party undoubtedly faced severe difficulties during those years, Liu tended to over-react and say too much, perhaps even to panic, bad traits in a leader at any time, but particularly in crises. Even when Liu was keenly following the Chairman's lead, as in the SEM, it could be argued that he transgressed political limits which Mao himself instinctively perceived; indeed, Liu's anti-cadre policy at that time undermined his personal standing within his only constituency, the CCP, at what turned out to be the critical moment of his career. Perhaps most important of all, could Liu command the loyalty of the PLA?[23]

The degree to which such concerns about Liu as a leader played a significant role in Mao's discarding him must remain conjectural. What is less conjectural is that if Mao wished to revolutionize the CCP, he had to remove Liu Shaoqi and those who emulated his style of leadership;[24] and to do that Mao had first to capture the commanding heights of party control. This was clearly an important determinant of the manner in which the Cultural Revolution was launched. Why were Peng Zhen, Lu Dingyi, Luo Ruiqing, and Yang Shangkun all charged in quick succession, albeit apparently under differing indictments? Was it pure coincidence that in May 1966, in one fell swoop, Mao removed the man in charge of the capital, the man in charge of propaganda, the man in daily control of the PLA, and the man in charge of the CC's paper flow? Or had the Chairman decided in advance that controlling these four positions was crucial to his plans, and connived to unseat incumbents whom he or his allies did not trust? Whatever genuine if misbegotten idealism inspired Mao, his first resort was to sordid political intrigue. The Cultural Revolution bore the mark of Cain from birth.

If so, why did Mao not order show trials and executions like Stalin? Leaving aside Mao's undoubted contempt for spurious 'bourgeois' legalism, he may have intuited that even the most supine of his old comrades might have recoiled and perhaps even rebelled at bare-faced brutality.[25] The CCP of 1966 was not yet the CPSU of 1936. More importantly, Mao genuinely believed in spiritual rebirth. Uncertain, now, where the revolutionary Grail was to be found, Mao pinned all his hopes on the quest for it. Travelling hopefully would have to replace arriving, the means would become the end, making revolution would *be* the revolution.[26] He sent the comrades of the Yan'an Round Table out to face one ultimate test in the hope that, purified in the flames of class struggle, in *luan*,[27] at least some— a former favourite like Deng Xiaoping, for instance—might return, born again in Mao Thought, perhaps even bearing the Grail. If they perished, *tant pis*. He would assemble a new Round Table from the ashes of the old. The revolutionaries are dead; long live the revolutionaries! And if all else failed, the revolution was incarnate in its leader and the prime directive was: Long live Chairman Mao!

ABBREVIATIONS USED IN THE NOTES

Anhui Sheng Qing	Anhui Sheng Renmin Zhengfu Bangongting (ed.), *Anhui Sheng Qing*
Baochan Daohu Ziliao Xuan	Zhongguo Nongcun Fazhan Wenti Yanjiuzu (ed.), *Baochan Daohu Ziliao Xuan*
Biji Taozhu	'Tao Zhu Wenji' Bianjizu (ed.), *Biji Tao Zhu*
Caizheng Dashiji	Chen Rulong (ed.), *Zhonghua Renmin Gongheguo Caizheng Dashiji (1949–1985)*
CB	US Consulate General (Hong Kong), *Current Background*
Chen Yi Zhuan	'Dangdai Zhongguo Renwu Zhuanji' Congshu Bianjibu (ed.), *Chen Yi Zhuan*
Chen Yun's Strategy	Lardy and Lieberthal, *Chen Yun's Strategy for China's Development*
CHOC	*Cambridge History of China*
CQ	*China Quarterly*
CYWG	*Chen Yun Tongzhi Wengao Xuanbian*
CYWX	*Chen Yun Wenxuan*
Dangdai Zhongguo Jingji	'Dangdai Zhongguo' Congshu Bianjibu (ed.), *Dangdai . . .*
Dangdai Zhongguo Junduide Junshi Gongzuo	
Dangdai Zhongguo Kong Jun	
Dangdai Zhongguo Wai Jiao	
Dangdai Zhongguode Beijing	
Dangdai Zhongguode Henan	
Dangdai Zhongguode Hunan	
Dangdai Zhongguode Liangshi Gongzuo	
Dangdai Zhongguode Shandong	

Dangdai Zhong-guode Sichuan	
Dangdai Zhong-guode Zhejiang	
DSNB	Zhonggong Zhongyang Dangshi Yanjiushi (ed.), *Zhonggong Dangshi Dashi Nianbiao*
DSYJ	*Dangshi Yanjiu*
Eight Articles, source	pp. 260–73 of unnamed source
FBIS	Foreign Broadcast Information Service
Gongheguo Zhuxi Liu Shaoqi	Zhonggong Zhongyang Wenxian Yanjiushi and Xinhua Tongxunshe (eds.), *Gongheguo Zhuxi Liu Shaoqi*
Gongye Qiye Fagui	Guojia Jingji Weiyuanhui Jingji Faguiju and Beijing Zhengfa Xueyuan Jingjifa Minfa Jiaoyanshi (eds.), *Zhonghua Renmin Gongheguo Gongye Qiye Fagui Xuanbian*
Guangdong Teaching Materials	Guangdong Sheng Gaodeng Yuanxiao 'Zhongguo Gongchan Dang Jian Shi Jiangyi' Bianjizu (ed.), *Zhongguo Gongchan Dang Jian Shi Jiangyi*
Guofang Daxue, *Cankao Ziliao*	Zhongguo Renmin Jiefang Jun Guofang Daxue Dangshi Dangjian Zhenggong Jiaoyanshi (ed.), *Zhonggong Dangshi Jiaoxue Cankao Ziliao*
HQ	*Hong Qi*
HQPP	*Hong Qi Piaopiao*
Huainian Tao Zhu	Zhonggong Qiyangxian Weiyuanhui (ed.), *Huainian Tao Zhu Tongzhi*
Huainian Zhou Enlai	'Huainian Zhou Enlai' Bianji Xiaozu, *Huainian Zhou Enlai*
Jiangsu Sheng Dashiji	'Dangdai Zhongguode Jiangsu' Weiyuanhui and Jiangsu Sheng Dang' anju (eds.), *Jiangsu Sheng Dashiji, 1949–1985*
Jiaoyu Dashiji	Zhongyang Jiaoyu Kexue Yanjiusuo (ed.), *Zhonghua Renmin Gongheguo Jiaoyu Dashiji, 1949–82*
Jiaoyu Nianjian	'Zhongguo Jiaoyu Nianjian' Bianjibu (ed.), *Zhongguo Jiaoyu Nianjian, 1949–1981*
Jiefang Jun Jiangling Zhuan	Xinghuo Liao Yuan Bianjibu (ed.), *Jiefang Jun Jiangling Zhuan*
Jiefang Jun Liushi Nian Dashi	Junshi Kexue Yuan Junshi Lishi Yanjiubu (ed.), *Zhongguo Renmin Jiefang Jun Liushi Nian Dashiji, 1927–1987*
Jingji Dashiji	Fang Weizhong (ed.), *Zhonghua Renmin Gongheguo Jingji Dashiji*
JPRS	Joint Publications Research Service

Jueyi Zhushiben Xiuding	Zhonggong Zhongyang Wenxian Yanjiushi, *Guanyu Jianguo Yilai Dangde Ruogan Lishi Wentide Jueyi Zhushiben (Xiuding)*
Liu 27/1/62 mimeo version	'*Liu Shaoqi yu 1962 1 yue 27 ri zai guangdade zhongyang gongzuo huiyishangde jianghua*'
Liu Shaoqi Lun Dangde Jianshe	Zhonggong Zhongyang Wenxian Yanjiushi and Zhonggong Zhongyang Dangxiao (eds.), *Liu Shaoqi Lun Dangde Jianshe*
Liushi Nian Dashi Jianjie	Zhengzhi Xueyuan Zhonggong Dangshi Jiaoyanshi (ed.), *Zhongguo Gongchan Dang Liushi Nian Dashi Jianjie*
Lun Shangpin Liutong	Zhongguo Shehui Kexue Yuan Caimao Wuzi Jingji Yanjiusuo and Shangyebu Jiaoyuju (eds.), *Lun Shangpin Liutong: Shangpin Liutong Jingji lilun Taolunhui Wenji*
Mao, *Miscellany*	Mao Tse-tung, *Miscellany of Mao Tse-tung Thought (1949–1968)*
Mao, *Shuxin*	*Mao Zedong Shuxin Xuanji*
Mao Zedong he tade Mishu Tian Jiaying	Dong Bian, Tan Deshan, and Zeng Zi (eds.), *Mao Zedong he tade Mishu Tian Jiaying*
NCNA	New China News Agency
Nongye Jitihua	Zhonghua Renmin Gongheguo Guojia Nongye Weiyuanhui Bangongting, *Nongye Jitihua Zhongyao Wenjian Huibian*
NYT	*New York Times*
Origins	MacFarquhar, *The Origins of the Cultural Revolution*
PR	*Peking Review*
Qishi Nian Jianjie	Guofang Daxue Dangshi Dangjian Zhengzhi Gongzuo Jiaoyanshi, *Zhongguo Gongchan Dang Qishi Nian Dashi Jianjie*
RMRB	*Renmin Ribao*
SCMM	US Consulate General (Hong Kong), *Selections from China Mainland Magazines*
SCMP	US Consulate General (Hong Kong), *Survey of China Mainland Press*
SCMP (S)	US Consulate General (Hong Kong), *Survey of China Mainland Press (Supplement)*
Shangye Dashiji	'Dangdai Zhongguo Shangye' Bianjibu (ed.), *Zhonghua Renmin Gongheguo Shangye Dashiji, 1958–1978*
Shangye Shigao	Shangyebu Shangye Jingji Yanjiusuo (ed.), *Xin Zhongguo Shangye Shigao*
Shanxi Sishi Nian 1949–1989	Shanxi Sishi Nian Bianji Weiyuanhui (ed.), *Shanxi Sishi Nian, 1949–1989*

Sichuan Sheng Qing	Zhonggong Sichuan Shengwei Yanjiushi (ed.), *Sichuan Sheng Qing*
The Polemic	*The Polemic on the General Line of the International Communist Movement*
Tianjin Jingji Jianshe Dashiji	Tianjin Shehui Kexue Yuan Jingji Yanjiusuo (ed.), *Tianjin Jingji Jianshe Dashiji, 1949–1987*
TJNJ	Zhonghua Renmin Gongheguo Guojia Tongjiju (ed.), *Zhongguo Tongji Nianjian*
Wang Jiaxiang Xuanji	'Wang Jiaxiang Xuanji' Bianjizu (ed.), *Wang Jiaxiang Xuanji*
Who's Who in China	*Who's Who in China* Editorial Board, *Who's Who in China: Current Leaders*
Womende Zhou Zongli	'Womende Zhou Zongli' Bianjizu (ed.), *Womende Zhou Zongli*
Xinwenjie Renwu (5): Deng Tuo	'Xinwenjie Renwu' Bianji Weiyuanhui (ed.), *Xinwenjie Renwu (5): Deng Tuo*
Yongheng zhi Ri	Xinhua Tongxunshe Sheyingbu and Jilin Jiaoyu Chubanshe (eds.), *Yongheng zhi Ri*
Zhonggong Dangshi Renwuzhuan	Zhonggong Dangshi Renwu Yanjiuhui (ed.), *Zhonggong Dangshi Renwuzhuan*
Zhonggong Dangshi Zhongda Shijian Shushi	Zhonggong Zhongyang Wenxian Yanjiushi and Zhongyang Dang'an Guan, 'Dangde Wenxian' Bianjibu (eds.), *Zhonggong Dangshi Zhongda Shijian Shushi*
Zhonggong Dangshi Zhuan Ti Jiangyi	Zhonggong Zhongyang Dangxiao Zhonggong Dangshi Jiaoyanshi (ed.), *Zhonggong Dangshi Zhuan Ti Jiangyi: Kaishi Quanmian Jianshe Shehuizhuyi Shiqi*
Zhonggong Dangshi Ziliao	Zhonggong Zhongyang Dangshi Yanjiushi (ed.), *Zhonggong Dangshi Ziliao*
Zhonggong Renming Lu	'Zhonggong Renming Lu' Bianxiu Weiyuanhui, *Zhonggong Renming Lu*
Zhongguo Caizheng Wenti	Zhonghua Renmin Gongheguo Caizhengbu *et al.* (eds.), *Zhongguo Caizheng Wenti*
Zhongguo Gongye Guanli Bufen Tiaoli Huibian	Zhongguo Shehui Kexue Yuan Gongye Jingji Yanjiusuo Qiye Guanli Yanjiushi (ed.), *Zhongguo Gongye Guanli Bufen Tiaoli Huibian*
Zhongguo Gongye Jingji Fagui Huibian	Zhongguo Shehui Kexue Yuan Gongye Jingji Yanjiusuo Qingbao Ziliaoshi (ed.), *Zhongguo Gongye Jingji Fagui Huibian, 1949–1981*
Zhongguo Wenxue Yanjiu Nianjian	Zhongguo Shehui Kexue Yuan Wenxue Yanjiusuo and 'Zhongguo Wenxue Yanjiu Nianjian' Bianji Weiyuanhui (eds.), *Zhongguo Wenxue Yanjiu Nianjian, 1981*

Zhongyao Huiyiji, xia	Zhonggong Zhongyang Dangxiao Dangshi Jiao-yanshi Ziliaozu (ed.), *Zhongguo Gongchan Dang Lici Zhongyao Huiyiji, xia*
Zhou Enlai Tongyi Zhanxian Wenx-uan	Zhonggong Zhongyang Tongyi Zhanxian Gongzuobu and Zhonggong Zhongyang Wenxian Yanjiushi (eds.), *Zhou Enlai Tongyi Zhanxian Wenxuan*
Zhou Enlai yu Wenyi	Zhongguo Shehui Kexue Yuan Wenxue Yan-jiusuo Tushu Ziliaoshi (ed.), *Zhou Enlai yu Wenyi*

NOTES

INTRODUCTION

[1] Wang Jingjin *et al.*, *Xiangcun Sanshinian* (30 years of the countryside), editors' introduction, p. 1.

[2] Ibid., p. 194. For a description of the 'communist wind' that contributed so largely to this county's disaster, see ibid., pp. 177–86. For another description of the disasters that befell this county, see Wu Ren (ed.), *Gongheguo Zhongda Shijian Jishi* (A record of the republic's major incidents) 3, pp. 61–5. Fengyang *xian* is part of an ecologically unstable region which was the focus of Elizabeth Perry's study, *Rebels and Revolutionary in North China, 1845–1945*; for Fengyang's happier fate after the Cultural Revolution, see Perry, 'Implications of Household Contracting in China: The Case of Fengyang County', in Rhee, *China's Reform Politics*, pp. 195–217.

[3] Li Mo (ed.), *Xin Zhongguo Dabolan* (New China review), p. 365.

[4] Wu & Li, *A Single Tear*. pp. 266, 268.

[5] Ibid., p. 191. The authors were residents of Hefei, Anhui's capital.

[6] Ibid., p. 121.

[7] *Zhongguo Renkou: Anhui Fence* (China's population: Anhui fascicle), pp. 130–1.

[8] Anhui Sheng Renmin Zhengfu Bangongting (ed.), *Anhui Sheng Qing* (Information on Anhui province; hereafter, *Anhui Sheng Qing*), p. 124.

[9] This source is a senior Chinese cadre who, in the post-Mao era, was charged with investigating the impact of the GLF famine. According to an Anhui source, a provincial official gave a figure of 7 m. deaths at the Seven Thousand Cadres Conference in January 1962, but there is no written record of this oral report. This source calculates from the official figures in Anhui Sheng Tongjiju (ed.), *Anhui Sishi Nian* (40 years of Anhui) that Anhui lost 5 m. people as a result of the three bitter years. For a description of the parlous state of Chinese agriculture in the late 1970s as compared with the 1950s and even the 1930s, see Chen Yizi, *Zhongguo: Shinian gaige yu bajiu min yun* (China: The reform decade and the '89 democratic movement), pp. 17–25.

[10] The grain figures are in Sichuan Sheng Tongjiju (ed.), *SichuanTongji Nianjian, 1990* (Sichuan statistical yearbook, 1990), p. 135. Output fell further to 11,550,000 tons in 1961, and the 1958 figure would not be surpassed until 1970; ibid.

[11] Sichuan sheng tongjiju, *Sichuan Shehui Tongji Ziliao* (Statistical material on Sichuan society), p. 23.

[12] Ibid., pp. 56–7. According to the senior Chinese cadre quoted above, the death toll in Sichuan was 9 million. In relative terms the Anhui disaster was very much greater. In 1953, at the time of the first Chinese national census, the populations of the two provinces were: Anhui, 30.7 m.; Sichuan, 65.7 m. (Shabad, *China's Changing Map*, p. 34); in 1957, just before the GLF, the populations were estimated by the State Statistical Bureau at: Anhui, 33.56 m.; Sichuan, 72.16 m. (*Ten Great Years*, p. 11).

13 'Dangdai Zhongguo' Congshu Bianjibu (ed.), *Dangdai Zhongguode Shandong* (Contemporary China's Shandong; hereafter, *Dangdai Zhongguode Shandong*) 1, p. 193. The grain-short figure was 15,960,000 people; the per capita daily figure is calculated from the per capita annual figure given here of 142.7 catties. The drop in grain production is attributed to four factors: a 20% drop in the rural labour force and the reduced energy levels of those remaining in agriculture; massive drops in the livestock population, which meant fewer and weaker draught animals and less pig manure for fertilizer; reduced sown area due to GLF policies; and poor husbandry resulting from the previous factors (ibid., pp. 193-4). The population figure is for 1957; see State Statistical Bureau, *Ten Great Years*, p. 11. In Dingzhou, the rate of population increase dropped from 2.4% to just over 1%; 'Dingzhou Juan' Bianji Weiyuanhui (ed.), *Zhongguo Guoqing Congshu—Bai Xianshi Jingji Shehui Diaocha: Dingzhou Juan* (China national conditions series—investigation of the economy and society of 100 *xian* cities: Dingzhou volume), p. 17.

14 *Dangdai Zhongguode Shandong* 1, pp. 196-7.

15 See MacFarquhar, *The Origins of the Cultural Revolution* (hereafter, *Origins*) II, pp. 42-3, 302-3.

16 *Zhumadian Shi Zhi* (Annals of Zhumadian city), p. 101. I am grateful to Michael Schoenhals for bringing this source to my attention.

17 See Friedman, Pickowicz, & Selden, *Chinese Village, Socialist State*, pp. 240-5. Yet as late as Apr. 1960, ordinary residents of Beijing could be totally unaware of the starvation in the province surrounding the capital; Wu & Wakeman, *Bitter Winds*, p. 55.

18 Shangyebu Shangye Jingji Yanjiusuo (ed.), *Xin Zhongguo Shangye Shigao* (Draft history of commerce in new China; hereafter, *Shangye Shigao*), p. 193.

19 *Zhongguo Renkou: Beijing Fence*, p. 112.

20 Shanghaishi Tongjiju (ed.), *Shanghai Tongji Nianjian, 1983* (Shanghai statistical yearbook, 1983), p. 240.

21 Guojia Tongjiju Maoyi Wujia Tongjisi (ed.), *Zhongguo Maoyi Wujia Tongji Ziliao (1952-1983)* (Statistical material on China's commercial commodity prices, 1952-1983), p. 198.

22 See Bao & Chelminski, *Prisoner of Mao*, pp. 210, 213-15, 248. In addition to Bao's account, there are at least two other first-hand descriptions of the grim conditions of prison life at Qinghe State Farm near Beijing; see, Wu & Wakeman, *Bitter Winds*, pp. 99-153; Wu & Li, *A Single Tear*, pp. 127-37. For an account of Chinese prison camps, see Barmé & Minford, *Seeds of Fire*, pp. 454-62; Qinghe is discussed on pp. 460-1.

23 Wu & Wakeman, *Bitter Winds*, pp. 95-6.

24 Pu Ning, *Red in Tooth and Claw*, pp. 181-2; see also Zhang Xianliang, *Grass Soup*.

25 In a book of photographs published for the 40th anniversary of the PRC in 1989, there is a picture with the caption: 'Three Jiangsu peasant orphans living under broken thatched roof [literally true; the thatch is supported by bamboo poles not walls]. Their parents and another sister died of starvation which resulted mainly from 1958's Great Leap Forward'. What the picture underlines is that the tragedy hit even relatively better-off provinces of China; see Xinhua Tongxunshe Sheyingbu & Jilin Jiaoyu Chubanshe (eds.), *Yongheng zhi Ri* (The unforgettable days; hereafter *Yongheng zhi Ri*), p. 103.

²⁶ See Banister, *China's Changing Population*, p. 85. In *Origins* II, p. 330, I used the earlier estimates of another distinguished demographer, John Aird, who estimated the figure at anywhere between 16.4 and 29.5 m. The senior cadre referred to in n. 9 above estimated the total as 43 m. For a recent book-length study of the famine, see Becker, *Hungry Ghosts*.

²⁷ Officials often took advantage of the presence of leaders to indulge themselves and their underlings; Li, *The Private Life of Chairman Mao*, pp. 330, 344–5. In addition, cadres on special duties, such as the élite translation team working on the English version of Mao's selected works, continued to be fed special meals cooked by special chefs; see Rittenberg & Bennett, *The Man Who Stayed Behind*, pp. 257–8. 'Foreign experts' were also entitled to better rations; ibid., p. 259.

²⁸ Li, *The Private Life of Chairman Mao*, p. 340; Gao Jingzheng (ed.), *Pingfan yu Weida* (The greatness out of the ordinary: Photographic album of Mao Tse-tung's Zhongnanhai memorabilia), p. 117.

²⁹ For Zhou's grain consumption and use of an abacus, see *Renminde Hao Zongli* (The people's good premier) 3, p. 135. For his anger at gifts of vegetables, see ibid., p. 132. For his bodyguard's assertion that he ate no meat or eggs at this time, see *Jing'aide Zhou Zongli Women Yongyuan Huainian Ni* (Beloved Premier Zhou, we will always remember you) 3, p. 83; in *Renminde Hao Zongli* 2, p. 526, the claim is only that he seldom ate meat during the three bitter years. Zhou instructed Xi Zhongxun, the secretary-general of the State Council, to tell the unit's mess-hall staff to plant their own vegetables and raise pigs because the food for his officials was so poor; see ibid., 3, pp. 20–1. For accounts of Zhou's parsimonious eating habits at this time by a Vice-Minister of Food, see *Bujinde Sinian* (Inexhaustible memories), p. 236, and by staff aides, see Cheng Hua, *Zhou Enlai he tade Mishumen* (Zhou Enlai and his secretaries), pp. 81, 289, 463.

³⁰ See *Origins* II, *passim*.

PART ONE: THE THIRD BITTER YEAR

CHAPTER 1

[1] For Mao's mood in the second half of 1960, see Dong Bian, Tan Deshan, & Zeng Zi (eds.), *Mao Zedong he tade Mishu Tian Jiaying* (MaoZedong and his secretary Tian Jiaying; hereafter, *Mao Zedong he tade Mishu Tian Jiaying*), pp. 56–7.

[2] '*Yige hendade weibei renshide biran wangguo*'. See Zhonggong Zhongyang Dangshi Yanjiushi (ed.), *Zhonggong Dangshi Dashi Nianbiao* (A chronological table of major events in the history of the CCP; hereafter, *DSNB*), p. 306; Zeng Bijun & Lin Muxi, *Xin Zhongguo Jingj Shi* (An economic history of new China), p. 171. This phrase of Mao's obviously represented renewed acceptance of Engels's dictum on recognizing the dictates of necessity, evinced earlier during his more realistic period in 1959 before the revival of the GLF; see *Origins* II, p. 164.

[3] See *Origins* II, p. 323; for the indication that 30 Sept. was the date of the first official use of this slogan, see CCP CC Party History Research Centre (ed.), *History of the Chinese Communist Party—A Chronology of Events (1919–1990)*, p. 286.

[4] *Liu Shaoqi Xuanji* (Selected works of Liu Shaoqi), *xia*, p. 357.

[5] See *Origins* II, pp. 88–90.

[6] At Beidaihe two years earlier, Mao had hoped to achieve this figure by 1962; ibid., p. 90.

[7] Ibid., pp. 278–83.

[8] Mao's words and behaviour on the steel issue in the second half of 1960 are detailed in Liao Gailong *et al.* (eds.), *Xin Zhongguo Biannianshi* (The annals of new China), p. 181. For the economic dislocation caused in the non-rural sector of the economy by the GLF, see *Origins* II, pp. 326–30, and below, Ch. 4. For the text of the 3 Dec. directive, see Zhongguo Renmin Jiefang Jun Guofang Daxue Dangshi Dangjian Zhenggong Jiaoyanshi (ed.), *Zhonggong Dangshi Jiaoxue Cankao Ziliao* (Reference materials for teaching and studying CCP history; hereafter, Guofang Daxue, *Cankao Ziliao*) 23, pp. 411–13. For the impact of central demands on the key industrial area of the northeast, see *Song Renqiong Huiyilu* (The memoirs of Song Renqiong), pp. 376–8.

[9] Ibid., pp. 136–72; *Zhongguo Baike Nianjian, 1981* (China Encyclopaedic Yearbook, 1981), p. 563; Guangdong Sheng Gaodeng Yuanxiao 'Zhongguo Gongchan Dang Jian Shi Jiangyi' Bianjizu (ed.), *Zhongguo Gongchan Dang Jianshi Jiangyi* (Teaching Materials for a Short History of the CCP; hereafter, Guangdong Teaching Materials), pp. 357-8; Xu Dixin, *Wo Guo Shehuizhuyi Jingji Wenti Yanjiu* (Researches into the problems of our nation's socialist economy), p. 153. The latter source incorrectly gives Dec. as the date of this directive.

[10] *Zhongguo Baike Nianjian, 1981*, p. 563.

[11] Zhonghua Renmin Gongheguo Guojia Nongye Weiyuanhui Bangongting,

Nongye Jitihua Zhongyao Wenjian Huibian (1958–1981) (A collection of important documents on agricultural collectivization, 1958–1981; hereafter, *Nongye Jitihua, xia*, p. 407.

12 In fact, Gansu seems to have been a case in point. One of the provinces worst hit by famine, it was the target of a special investigation in Dec. 1960 by the former Minister of Internal Affairs, Mme Qian Ying, and a former Vice-Minister of Finance, Rong Zihe. They soon concluded that the claimed grain output of 7 billion catties (3.5 m. tons) was in reality only 4 billion (2 m. tons)—as compared with a pre-GLF high of 3.8 m. tons—but the *xian* secretaries were too frightened to speak up, and the official of the Northwest regional bureau of the CCP to whom they telephoned their findings—was it 3rd secretary Hu Yaobang?—tried to persuade them to accept the 1st secretary's figure; see Rong Zihe's account in 'Womende Zhou Zongli' Bianjizu (ed.), *Womende Zhou Zongli* (Our Premier Zhou; hereafter, *Womende Zhou Zongli*), p. 304. The Gansu grain figures can be found in Gansu Sheng Tongjiju (ed.), *Gansu Sishi Nian* (40 years of Gansu), p. 306. In 1961, grain output dropped below 2 m. tons and the pre-GLF high was not exceeded until 1967. There appears to have been something mysterious about the sequel to this investigation. Zhang Zhongliang, the Gansu 1st secretary, lost his job and disappeared into obscurity. But Qian Ying and Rong Zihe also dropped out of sight, Rong being reassigned to a provincial post. See their three biographies in Klein & Clark, *Biographic Dictionary of Chinese Communism*.

13 See *DSNB*, p. 310; *Huainian Mao Zedong Tongzhi* (Remember Comrade Mao Zedong), p. 216; Fang Weizhong (ed.), *Zhonghua Renmin Gongheguo Jingji Dashiji* (A record of the major economic events of the PRC; hereafter, *Jingji Dashiji*), pp. 287–9.

14 *Jingji Dashiji*, pp. 288–9, 296; 'Dangdai Zhongguode Jihua Gongzuo' Bangongshi (ed.), *Zhonghua Renmin Gongheguo Guomin Jingji he Shehui Fazhan Jihua Dashi Jiyao, 1949–1985* (A summary chronology of the national economic and social development plans of the PRC, 1949–1985; hereafter, *Jingji he Shehui Fazhan Jihua Dashi Jiyao*), p. 161; 'Dangdai Zhongguo Shangye' Bianjibu (ed.), *Zhonghua Renmin Gongheguo Shangye Dashiji (1958–1978)* (A chronology of commerce in the PRC, 1958–1978; hereafter, *Shangye Dashiji*), p. 210.

15 *Jingji Dashiji*, pp. 288–9, 296; *Jingji he Shehui Fazhan Jihua Dashi Jiyao*, p. 161; *Shangye Dashiji*, p. 210. In Guangdong province alone, the cost of compensating peasants for egalitarian policies was over 100 m. yuan; see 'Tao Zhu Wenji' Bianjizu (ed.), *Biji Tao Zhu* (Written memorials to Tao Zhu; hereafter, *Biji Tao Zhu*), p. 354. For examples of the impact of egalitarianism in the rural areas, see Ch. 2.

16 Liao Gailong *et al.*, *Xin Zhongguo Biannianshi*, p. 182.

17 Brief excerpts from Mao's speech are reprinted in a number of unofficial collections of the Chairman's speeches which surfaced as a result of the Cultural Revolution. I have used *Mao Zedong sixiang wan sui* (Long live Mao Zedong Thought) *(June 1967)*, *xia*, pp. 323–4.

18 The mortality rate more than doubled between 1957 and 1960, and in the latter year the population actually declined by 0.45%. See World Bank, *China: Socialist Economic Development*. Annex B: Population, Health and Nutrition, p. 71; *Origins* II, p. 330.

19 The percentages are calculated from the output figures published in detail for the first time in *Zhongguo Nongye Nianjian, 1980* (China agricultural

yearbook, 1980), pp. 34, 36, 38. For the grain procurement, stock, and shortfall figures, see Liu Suinian, ' "Tiaozheng, gonggu, chongshi, tigao" ba zi fangzhende tichu ji zhixing qingkuang' (How the eight character policy 'adjustment, consolidation, filling out, and raising standards' was put forward and implemented), *Dangshi Yanjiu* (Research into party history; hereafter, *DSYJ*), No. 6, 1980, p. 23. For the population figures, see Zhonghua Renmin Gongheguo Guojia Tongjiju (ed.), *Zhongguo Tongji Nianjian, 1983* (China statistical yearbook, 1983; hereafter, *TJNJ*), p. 103.

20 Xue Muqiao, *Wo Guo Wujia he Huobi Wenti Yanjiu* (An investigation into the problems of commodity prices and currency in our nation), pp. 44–5.

21 *Caizheng Gongzuo Sanshiwu Nian* (Thirty-five years of financial work), p. 137. According to this source, the total burden of the agricultural tax from 1950 through 1960 was 200,512,000 tonnes, which averaged out at 10.2% of output per annum.

22 See Zhonghua Renmin Gongheguo Nongyebu Jihuasi (ed.), *Zhongguo Nongcun Jingji Tongji Daquan (1949–1986)* (A compilation of statistics on China's rural economy, 1949–1986), pp. 96, 362. The drop in value was only 22.7%, presumably a reflection of the increase in the procurement prices.

23 For China's leaders responsible for national development, an equally stark contrast may have been between 1960 and 1957, the last year of a 1st FYP that had been a hopeful beginning to that effort: grain output down 26.4%; cotton output down one-third; oil crops down 54%; draught animals down 12.5%; see Ma Yuping & Huang Yuchong (eds.), *Zhongguo Zuotian yu Jintian: 1840–1987 Guoqing Shouce* (China yesterday and today: A handbook of national conditions, 1840–1987), p. 620.

24 *Miscellany of Mao Tse-tung Thought (1949–1968)* (hereafter, Mao, *Miscellany*) 2, p. 239.

25 Ibid., p. 242; *Mao Zedong sixiang wan sui (1967)*, p. 263. This favourite motto of Mao's dates back to the Han dynasty; see Zhonggong Zhongyang Dangxiao Keyan Bangongshi, 'Mao Zedong Sixiang Yuanli Jianghua' Bianxiezu (eds.), *Mao Zedong Sixiang Yuanli Jianghua* (Talks on the principles of Mao Zedong Thought), p. 338. According to a paper presented by Michael Schoenhals to the annual meeting of the Association for Asian Studies in 1991, the *locus classicus* of the phrase for the CCP is Mao's 1941 report 'Reform our study'.

26 Mao, *Miscellany* 2, pp. 237, 238, 241, 242.

27 Ibid., p. 239; for a discussion of this practice during the GLF, see *Origins* II, pp. 31–2.

28 Mao, *Miscellany* 2, pp. 237, 238.

29 Ibid., p. 240; *Mao Zedong sixiang wan sui (1967)*, pp. 261–2. The rectification campaign is mentioned in the plenum communiqué, *Peking Review* (hereafter, *PR*), No. 4, 1961, p. 6. For other mentions of it, see *Huainian Mao Zedong Tongzhi*, p. 221; *Selections from China Mainland Magazines* (hereafter, SCMM) 604, p. 27; *Survey of China Mainland Press (Supplement)* (hereafter, SCMP[S]) 221, p. 31. For a discussion of the campaign, see Teiwes, *Politics and Purges in China*, pp. 448–71.

30 Mao, *Miscellany* 2, p. 242. For Mao's interview with the future French President (on 8 Feb.; *Survey of China Mainland Press* [hereafter, SCMP] 2439, p. 21), see *L'Express*, 23 Feb. 1961, pp. 13–14; a shorter version appeared in *New Republic*, 23 Oct. 1961, pp. 17–21.

31 Mao, *Miscellany* 2, pp. 240, 244; *Mao Zedong sixiang wan sui (1967)*, pp. 261, 265.

32 Mao, *Miscellany* 2, pp. 238, 243–4.

33 *Liu Shaoqi fan-dang fan-shehuizhuyi fan-Mao Zedong sixiang yanlun yi bai li* (One hundred examples of Liu Shaoqi's anti-party, anti-socialist, anti-Mao Zedong Thought utterances) (Office for the study of Chairman Mao's works, Revolutionary Committee of Canton city's Military Control Committee, May 1967), p. 20. Mao's words (dated only 1961) were: '*Xingshi ta hao, wenti bushao, qiantu guangming*'. Cf. his words on the eve of the 1959 Lushan conference: '*Chengji weida, wenti bushao, qiantu guangming*'; see *Mao Zedong sixiang wan sui (1967)*, p. 63.

34 Ibid., pp. 261, 265. The two passages on CC unity are virtually identical, suggestive of an error by the compilers of this unofficial collection. But Mao's speeches are often repetitive, probably because they seem to have been virtually impromptu, unstructured, and therefore somewhat rambling. For Mao's appeal for unity at Lushan, see *Origins* II, p. 220. Mao's tactics on this difficult occasion were not unique; cf. this observation by former British Prime Minister Margaret Thatcher: 'So in an unvarnished speech I told them that they had had to take a lot of difficulties on the chin in the last year, but those difficulties had nothing to do with our fundamental approach, which was correct. They had resulted from throwing away the precious virtue of unity and also because . . . we had had to do genuinely difficult things which were right.' Thatcher, *The Downing Street Years*, p. 564.

35 *Mao Zedong sixiang wan sui (1967)*, p. 261.

36 Ibid., pp. 258–9, 265–6; again these passages are repetitive. Mao had articulated this policy earlier at the Lushan plenum in 1959; see Zhonggong Dangshi Yanjiuhui (ed.), *Xuexi Lishi Jueyi Zhuanji* (A special collection of articles for the study of the Resolution on CCP history), p. 121.

37 *Mao Zedong sixiang wan sui (1967)*, pp. 260, 265–6; SCMM 633, p. 18. For the genesis of this slogan, see *Origins* II, p. 323, and Liu Suinian, ' "Tiaozheng, gonggu, chongshi, tigao" ', pp. 21–33. For the role of the senior economic official Xue Muqiao in drafting this formula, see 'Huainian Zhou Enlai' Bianji Xiaozu, *Huainian Zhou Enlai* (Remember Zhou Enlai; hereafter, *Huainian Zhou Enlai*). p. 38; for a good summary of the whole series of economic measures taken by the CC from June 1960 through 1962, see 'Dangdai Zhongguo' Congshu Bianjibu (ed.), *Dangdai Zhongguo Jingji* (Contempor-ary China's economy; hereafter, *Dangdai Zhongguo Jingji*), pp. 353–61.

38 The provisions were issued on 20 Jan.: *Jingji he Shehui Fazhan Jihua Dashi Jiyao*, pp. 165–6; *Shangye Dashiji*, p. 212; 'Dangdai Zhongguode Jingji Guanli' Bianjibu (ed.), *Zhonghua Renmin Gongheguo Jingji Guanli Dashiji* (A chronology of economic management in the PRC; hereafter, *Jingji Guanli Dashiji*), p. 154.

39 The decision was issued on 15 Jan. in the form of CC approval of a report by the party group in the Finance Ministry; ibid., p. 154; *Shangye Dashiji*, p. 210; *Jingji he Shehui Fazhan Jihua Dashi Jiyao*, p. 165; cf. *Origins* II, pp. 142–4.

40 *PR*, No. 4, 1961, p. 7. The decision to set up the bureaux had been formally taken in Sept. 1960 (CCP CC Party History Research Centre, *History of the Chinese Communist Party*, p. 286); 1st secretaries of the new bureaux, apparently chosen by Mao personally, were notified during the July–Aug. Beidaihe work conference; *Song Renqiong Huiyilu*, pp. 361–2. For a discussion of the relationship of these bureaux to their predecessors, see Schurmann, *Ideology*

and Organization in Communist China, pp. 147–9; for an account of Gao Gang's 'independent kingdom', see Teiwes, *Politics at Mao's Court, passim*.

41 *Mao Zedong sixiang wan sui (1967)*, p. 261.

42 *Huainian Mao Zedong Tongzhi*, p. 261.

43 For the communiqué, see *PR*, No. 4, 1961, pp. 5, 6. For confirmation that the 9th plenum 'decided to end' the GLF, see *DSYJ*, No. 6, 1985, p. 39.

44 For Li Fuchun's 1960 article, see *Origins* II, pp. 300–1.

45 The text of Li Fuchun's speech is in Guofang Daxue, *Cankao Ziliao* 23, pp. 434–45.

46 Ibid., pp. 435–6.

47 Ibid., pp. 436–7.

48 Ibid., p. 438.

49 Ibid., pp. 435, 438. For the reduction in arable acreage during the GLF, see *Origins* II, p. 126. The sown acreage for grains and the most important economic crops in 1960 was almost 135 m. ha., according to *Zhongguo Nongye Nianjian, 1980*, pp. 34–5, but there is a problem with these figures. The sown grain acreage for 1960 is given in this latter source as 1,836,440,000 mou (123,041,480 ha.); whereas Li (Guofang Daxue, *Cankao Ziliao* 23, p. 439) talks of expanding the sown grain acreage in 1961 to 1,800,000,000 mou (120,600,000 ha.). Either Li was working in the dark, or the post-Cultural Revolution statisticians were making approximations in their attempts to present accurate figures. (The Chinese figures are given in mou; I am using a conversion rate of 1 mou = .067 ha.)

50 Ibid., pp. 438–9.

51 This is widely admitted in post-Mao China, even if in more restrained language; see, for instance, Jin Chunming, *Jianguohou Sanshisan Nian* (The thirty-three years after the founding of the state), p. 15c.

52 See Li, *The Statistical System of Communist China, passim*; Wang Yifu, *Xin Zhongguo Tongji Shigao* (A draft history of statistics in new China), pp. 120–5, 134; also Zhang Sai (ed.), *Zhonghua Renmin Gongheguo Tongji Dashiji, 1949–1991* (A chronicle of statistics in the PRC, 1949–1991).

53 According to Chen Yun, in 1960 only 200 m. tons of coal were produced in mines under the direct control of the Ministry of the Coal Industry; see Lardy & Lieberthal, *Chen Yun's Strategy for China's Development* (hereafter, *Chen Yun's Strategy*), p. 174.

54 Guofang Daxue, *Cankao Ziliao* 23, p. 441.

55 Li Fuchun's speech was not published.

56 An interesting example of Mao's wariness of allowing the CC as an institution to engage in major discussions occurred in the early 1940s in the handling of the CCP's 'Resolution on Certain Questions in the History of our Party' which was put before the 7th Congress.

57 For the 9th plenum resolution on the Moscow conference, see *PR*, No. 4, 1961, pp. 7–9. For Khrushchev's report on it, see Hudson, Lowenthal, & MacFarquhar, *The Sino-Soviet Dispute*, pp. 207–21. For comments on the Chinese and Soviet positions, see ibid., pp. 33–4, 206–7; Zagoria, *The Sino-Soviet Conflict*, pp. 367–9; Gittings, *Survey of the Sino-Soviet Dispute*, pp. 144–53.

58 Informant T. The brains trust was initially led by Chen Boda, later by Kang Sheng. There were no limits on the subjects which it could investigate and it had the right of access to archives and agencies.

59 Lieberthal, *A Research Guide to Central Party and Government Meetings in China, 1949–1975*, p. 165.

⁶⁰ *PR*, No. 10, 1961, p. 7.
⁶¹ Ibid., p. 6; *Huainian Mao Zedong Tongzhi*, pp. 214–17. He Qifang had come under fire during the GLF for being critical of poetry composed by the 'masses', and Mao asked him about his present position; see ibid., p. 215, and Goldman, *Literary Dissent in Communist China*, pp. 261–71. Mao respected He for his Marxist approach to the great 18th-century novel *Hong Lou Meng* (usually translated as *The Dream of the Red Chamber*, but more recently as *The Story of the Stone*), a literary work of which the Chairman was extremely fond; see Gong Yuzhi, Pang Xianzhi, & Shi Zhongquan, *Mao Zedongde Dushu Shenghuo* (Mao Zedong's life of learning), pp. 220–37, and Goldman, *Literary Dissent in Communist China*, pp. 119, 248. For another account of Mao and He's collaboration, see Zhonggong Zhongyang Wenxian Yanjiushi & Zhongyang Dang'an Guan, 'Dangde Wenxian' Bianjibu (eds.), *Zhonggong Dangshi Zhongda Shijian Shushi* (An account of major events in CCP history; hereafter, *Zhonggong Dangshi Zhongda Shijian Shushi*), pp. 138–43. For precise indications of Mao's editing of He's work, see *Jianguo Yilai Mao Zedong Wengao* (Manuscripts of Mao Zedong since the founding of the state) 9, pp. 425–9.
⁶² *PR*, No. 10, 1961, p. 7.
⁶³ Ibid.; *Huainian Mao Zedong Tongzhi*, p. 218.
⁶⁴ *PR*, No. 10, 1961, p. 9.
⁶⁵ Ibid.; *Huainian Mao Zedong Tongzhi*, p. 218.
⁶⁶ Ibid., p. 217.

CHAPTER TWO

¹ *Chen Yun Tongzhi Wengao Xuanbian (1956–1962)* (Selections from Comrade Chen Yun's manuscripts; hereafter, *CYWG*), p. 120; *Chen Yun's Strategy*, pp. xxix–xxx, 147. Grain stocks had been 21.35 m. tonnes in mid-1956. The calculation of the relationship of stocks to urban rations is by the editors of the latter volume, Nicholas Lardy and Kenneth Lieberthal.
² *Bujinde Sinian*, p. 233; Ji Xin'ge et al., *Wo Yanzhongde Zhou Enlai* (The Zhou Enlai I saw), p. 225; 'Dangdai Zhongguo' Congshu Bianjibu (ed.), *Dangdai Zhongguode Liangshi Gongzuo* (Contemporary China's grain work; hereafter, *Dangdai Zhongguode Liangshi Gongzuo*), pp. 112–13, 121. In the latter work, there are somewhat illegible photocopied reproductions of Zhou Enlai's annotations on a Food Ministry document (p. 112) and his food allocation table (p. 121). For the statement that Zhou was in overall charge of grain work from after the 1959 Lushan conference until the Cultural Revolution, see *Huainian Zhou Enlai*, pp. 78–9.
³ Ibid., p. 253. According to an earlier State Council emergency directive, dated 6 Apr. 1960, at that point Beijing had seven days of stocks, Tianjin ten days, the industrial cities of Liaoning between eight and nine, while Shanghai had no reserves of rice and was coping on a day-to-day basis; see the life of Li Fuchun in Zhonggong Dangshi Renwu Yanjiuhui (ed.), *Zhonggong Dangshi Renwuzhuan* (Biographies of personalities in CCP history; hereafter, *Zhonggong Dangshi Renwuzhuan*) 44, p. 93.
⁴ For a discussion of this dimension of the food crisis and its eventual solution, see *Dangdai Zhongguode Liangshi Gongzuo*, pp. 224–8.
⁵ For a discussion of Chen Yun's role in trying to bring order to the chaos of the GLF, see *Origins* II, pp. 163–70.

6 See for instance Tao Zhu's comments on importing grain in *Xinhua Yuebao* (New China monthly), No. 11, 1989, p. 50.

7 Zhou visited Burma from 2 to 9 Jan. 1961 to attend Burma's independence day celebrations, to exchange the instruments of ratification of the Sino-Burmese Boundary Treaty, and to sign an agreement extending an interest-free loan of £30 m. to the Rangoon government; Home News Library, Xinhua News Agency, *China's Foreign Relations: A Chronology of Events (1949–1988)* (hereafter, *China's Foreign Relations Chronology*), p. 209.

8 To judge by one authoritative biographical sketch, Ye Jizhuang was an executor rather than a formulator of policy; see *Zhonggong Dangshi Renwuzhuan* 45, pp. 273–6.

9 *Bujinde Sinian*, pp. 253–4. Accompanying Zhou to Rangoon was one of Ye Jizhuang's deputy ministers, Lei Renmin, who was sent to Hong Kong by the premier on the conclusion of their Burma visit to check up on grain availability on the world market, on shipping, and on foreign exchange; Li Ping, *Kaiguo Zongli Zhou Enlai* (The PRC's founding premier, Zhou Enlai), pp. 376–7.

10 This was one of five general offices under the State Council in existence at this time. It supervised the ministries of Finance, Food, Commerce, Foreign Trade, and the People's Bank of China. See Donnithorne, *China's Economic System*, p. 517.

11 *Jingji Dashiji*, p. 296.

12 *Womende Zhou Zongli*, p. 11. According to this account by Gu Mu, then a Vice-Chairman of the State Economic Commission, Zhou stated that the first estimate of import needs was 500,000 tonnes. Gu Mu dates Zhou's speech as being made on 19 Jan., the day after the plerum ended; presumably it was at the work conference which appears to have met that day, an indication that the plenum was only the launch-pad for further discussion and policy-making; see *Shangye Dashiji*, p. 211.

13 *Dangdai Zhongguode Liangshi Gongzuo*, p. 123.

14 See below Table 2.2.

15 *Shangye Dashiji*, p. 206.

16 Ibid. The group was chaired by Li Xiannian in his capacity as the head of the State Council's Finance and Trade General Office, and had the minister of Communications (which means transportation), Wang Shoudao, and the minister of Commerce, Yao Yilin, as vice-chairmen. Members of the group included a vice-chairman of the State Economic Commission (Zhang Guojian), a vice-minister of Communications (Yu Mei), a vice-minister of Railways (Liu Jianzhang), two deputy directors of the Finance and Trade General Office (Niu Peizong, Ma Dingbang), two vice-ministers of Food (Chen Guodong, Yang Shaoqiao), a vice-minister of Commerce (Liang Yao), a vice-minister of Finance (Li Shude), an assistant to the minister of Foreign Trade (Jia Shi), and Jiang Dongping, a CC official, at that time probably working on finance and banking. Yao Yilin presided over the group's executive office.

17 *Manchester Guardian*, 22 and 30 Dec. 1960; 11 Jan. 1961; *The Times*, 26 Jan. 1961.

18 *New York Times* (hereafter, *NYT*), 30 Dec. 1960; *The Times*, 3 Feb. 1961. The Chairman of the Canadian Wheat Board reportedly paid an exploratory visit to China in October 1960; *NYT*, 15 Oct. 1960.

19 *Manchester Guardian*, 27 Jan. 1961.

20 Barry, 'The Chinese Food Purchases', *The China Quarterly* (hereafter, *CQ*), No. 8, 1961, p. 24.

[21] Ibid., pp. 21, 24; *Daily Telegraph*, 27 Jan. 1961. These figures add up to 780,000 tonnes, somewhat short of the 1 m. tonnes that the Finance and Trade Office estimated would be needed for re-exports.

[22] Liu Xiao, *Chu Shi Sulian Ba Nian* (Eight years as ambassador to the Soviet Union), pp. 105–6.

[23] *Bujinde Sinian*, p. 232. For an account of the previous year's Sino-Soviet polemics, leading to the withdrawal of Soviet technical advisers, see *Origins* II, ch. 11.

[24] Li's letter is in *Li Xiannian Wenxuan, 1935–1988* (Selected works of Li Xiannian, 1935–1988), pp. 257–64.

[25] At the end of December 1959, Mao wrote to Chen Yun, acknowledging a letter from him reporting on his illness, and expressing satisfaction on his convalescence; *Mao Zedong Shuxin Xuanji* (Selected letters of Mao Zedong; hereafter, Mao. *Shuxin*), p. 568. A reference to Chen in another of Mao's letters dated 25 Aug. 1961 (ibid., p. 585) suggests that he had still not fully recovered. But it surely cannot be without political significance that the official compilation of Chen's speeches record none for the period from just before the 1959 Lushan conference, at which the then Defence Minister Peng Dehuai was disgraced, until May 1961, the month in which the Sixty Articles on Agriculture were adopted; see *CYWG*. Lardy & Lieberthal come to the same conclusion; see *Chen Yun's Strategy*, p. xxvi.

[26] *Shangye Dashiji*, p. 210.

[27] See *Origins* II, p. 323, for Chen Yun's role at the end of the GLF; see Deng Liqun, *Xiang Chen Yun Tongzhi Xuexi Zuo Jingji Gongzuo* (Study Comrade Chen Yun on how to do economic work), pp. 45–6, for his role in promoting grain imports.

[28] *CYWG*, pp. 117–18; *Chen Yun Wenxuan, 1956–1985* (Selected works of Chen Yun, 1956–1985; hereafter, *CYWX*), pp. 147–8; *Chen Yun's Strategy*, pp. 140–1.

[29] *CYWX*, p. 212. Chen consulted Mao during the Lushan conference in Aug.–Sept. 1961.

[30] See Walker, *Food Grain Procurement and Consumption in China*, p. 161, where it is estimated that net grain imports amounted to about 14% of urban requirements in 1961–2. Wang Gengjin, however, claimed that grain imports accounted for 40% of urban consumption in subsequent years; see 'Shehuizhuyi jianshe bixu zunzhong nongye shi jichude guilu' (Socialist construction must respect the law that agriculture is the basis), *Jingji Yanjiu* (Economic research), No. 12, 1979, pp. 36–8.

[31] International Wheat Council, 'Trade Arrangements Involving Wheat', Secretariat Paper, No. 2, Dec. 1961, p. 58; I am grateful to Mr S. J. Tjaardstra of the Council for supplying me with this and other papers published by its Secretariat. See also Barry, 'The Chinese Food Purchases', p. 26.

[32] Wilson, 'Grain Marketing in Canada', Canadian International Grains Institute, 1979, pp. 345–8. This source contains an interesting description of the negotiation of the 1973 contract, but its figures for the 1961–3 agreement seem to be wrong.

[33] International Wheat Council, 'Trade Arrangements Involving Wheat: 1962/63–1965/66', Secretariat Paper, No. 7, Mar. 1967, p. 15. Barry, ('The Chinese Food Purchases', p. 21) gives a figure of 2,789,000 tonnes for 1961 purchases, but this was probably a maximum figure and includes options which may not have been taken up.

³⁴ This was reported to Mao by Li Xiannian on 30 July; see *Dangdai Zhong-guode Liangshi Gongzuo*, p. 123.

³⁵ For Chen Yun's estimate of a 5 m. tonne limit on China's ability to import grain, see *CYWG*, p. 121.

³⁶ According to this source, the total amount imported from 1961 through 1965 was 29.64 m. tonnes. Another source puts the figure at 54,700 m. jin or 27.35 m. tonnes; see *Dangdai Zhongguode Liangshi Gongzuo*, p. 124. In January 1962, Liu Shaoqi gave a figure of 5.2 m. tons for 1961 grain imports and estimated the country needed 4 m. tons in 1962, underestimating in both cases; *Liu Shaoqi Xuanji, xia*, p. 358.

³⁷ *TJNJ, 1983*, pp. 420–1.

³⁸ *Liu Shaoqi Xuanji, xia*, pp. 358–9. Liu, who made this estimate at the Seven Thousand Cadres Conference, appears to have overestimated the foreign exchange cost (see Table 2.3).

³⁹ For credit terms, see International Wheat Council, Secretariat Papers Nos. 2 (p. 58) and 7 (p. 15). For Chen Yun's confirmation of the critical effect of grain imports on China's ability to pay for imports of industrial equipment and raw materials, see *CYWG*, p. 124.

⁴⁰ *Zhonggong Dangshi Renwuzhuan* 45, p. 275.

⁴¹ *TJNJ, 1981*, p. 359. For a discussion of the Sino-Soviet dispute in 1960, see *Origins* II, ch. 11.

⁴² *Jingji Dashiji*, p. 296. The slogan was '*Yi jin yang chu*'.

⁴³ *CYWG*, pp. 118–19; *Chen Yun's Strategy*, pp. 141–2.

⁴⁴ *TJNJ, 1981*, p. 356. It was of course Hong Kong that absorbed the great bulk of China's exports to the two colonies.

⁴⁵ *Li Xiannian Wenxuan*, pp. 261–2.

⁴⁶ *CYWG*, pp. 120–1.

⁴⁷ Ibid., pp. 122–3, 128.

⁴⁸ Ibid.

⁴⁹ See *Origins* II, p. 329, for ration figures at the end of the GLF.

⁵⁰ *CYWG*, pp. 123–4.

⁵¹ Ibid., pp. 124–5.

⁵² Ibid., pp. 125–8. For details of the conditions of industry, see Ch. 4, 'Shortening the front'.

⁵³ Ibid., p. 128.

⁵⁴ Quoted in Cong Jin, *1949–1989 Niande Zhongguo 2: Quzhe Fazhande Suiyue* (China 1949–1989, 2: Years of tortuous development), p. 382.

⁵⁵ Chen Rulong, (ed.), *Zhonghua Renmin Gongheguo Caizheng Dashiji (1949–1985 nian)* (Financial chronology for the PRC, 1949–1985; hereafter, *Caizheng Dashiji*), p. 212. In Li Fuchun's speech to the CC's 9th plenum, he referred to the release of 20 m. people from all walks of life to strengthen the agricultural front line in the fourth quarter of 1960, but this was presumably a short-term expedient at a time when the autumn harvest was threatened by bad weather; see Guofang Daxue, *Cankao Ziliao* 23 p. 438. However, as early as 12 Nov. 1960, the CC evidently saw the advantages of trying to transform temporary rustication into a permanent status; ibid., p. 403. The reference to 10 m. persons sent down in the whole of 1960 in Cheng, *The Politics of the Red Army*, p. 459 (quoted in the Conclusions to *Origins* II, p. 330) is presumably also to the same temporary draftees.

⁵⁶ Cong Jin, *Quzhe Fazhande Suiyue*, pp. 381–2.

⁵⁷ *Dangdai Zhongguo Jingji*, p. 360. According to this source, the work was

harder after 1961. For the 1962 decision to reduce the population further, see below Ch. 7.

58 *TJNJ, 1981*, p. 93. For Mao's delight with the CCP's ability to carry out this task without major popular resistance, see *Origins* II, p. 335.

59 See the biography of Li Fuchun in *Zhonggong Dangshi Renwuzhuan* 44, pp. 93–6.

60 The Zhejiang party discussed the matter between 27 June and 24 July at a large meeting held to communicate the decisions of the Beijing work conference; 'Dangdai Zhongguo' Congshu Bianjibu (ed.), *Dangdai Zhongguode Zhejiang* (Contemporary China's Zhejiang; hereafter, *Dangdai Zhongguode Zhejiang*) 2, p. 516. The Sichuan party issued a directive on the subject on 8 July; 'Dangdai Zhongguo' Congshu Bianjibu (ed.), *Dangdai Zhongguode Sichuan* (Contemporary China's Sichuan; hereafter, *Dangdai Zhongguode Sichuan*) 2, p. 713. The Hunan party issued 'opinions on certain problems' in the rustication process on 5 Dec., which presumably means that there was an original directive months earlier; 'Dangdai Zhongguo' Congshu Bianjibu (ed.), *Dangdai Zhongguode Hunan* (Contemporary China's Hunan; hereafter, *Dangdai Zhongguode Hunan*) 2, p. 632.

61 The party committee of the northern province of Shanxi held a telephone conference on 8 June to discuss the reduction of the urban population among other matters; Shanxi Sishi Nian Bianji Weiyuanhui (ed.), *Shanxi Sishi Nian, 1949–1989* (Forty years of Shanxi, 1949–1989; hereafter, *Shanxi Sishi Nian, 1949–1989*) p. III-80.

62 Tianjin Shehui Kexue Yuan Jingji Yanjiusuo (ed.), *Tianjin Jingji Jianshe Dashiji (1949–1987)* (A chronology of Tianjin's economic construction, 1949–1987; hereafter, *Tianjin Jingji Jianshe Dashiji*) pp. 164–5, 168.

63 Ibid., pp. 179–81.

64 *Zhongguo Renkou: Tianjin Fence*, pp. 85, 89. As compared with Tianjin's pre-GLF population of 3.2 m., Canton had a population of 1.8 m. (Shabad, *China's Changing Map*, pp. 113, 187); Canton moved out 130,000 people under this policy (*Zeng Sheng Huiyi Lu* [The memoirs of Zeng Sheng], p. 646).

65 *Caizheng Dashiji*, p. 212. The 1960 figure given here was 50,440,000; to judge by the statistical Table 2.4, this could not have included rural 'staff'. According to one source, the number of workers and staff actually released totalled 19,400,000 (1,940 *wan ren*); it is possible that this is a misprint for 9,400,000, but if not then presumably large numbers of workers were being hired while others were being dismissed. See *Dangdai Zhongguo Jingji*, p. 360.

66 *Shanxi Sishi Nian, 1949–1989*, p. III-80. The Tianjin and Shanxi data suggest two successive directives were sent from the centre in early June. An indication that the reduction of the non-agricultural work-force and the reduction of the urban population were treated as separate operations is provided by the fact that the Shanxi party held a telephone conference on the urban population question on 8 June and another on non-agricultural personnel on 11 June; ibid., pp. III-79, 80.

67 The text is in Guofang Daxue, *Cankao Ziliao* 23, pp. 489–91.

68 Ibid., pp. 489–90.

69 Ibid., p. 490.

70 Ibid., p. 491.

71 *Zhongguo Renkou: Tianjin Fence*, p. 88.

72 *Biji Tao Zhu*, p. 354. From the dating indicated by this source, it would seem that the major transfer of Guangdong workers back to agriculture occurred during 1960.

[73] See his remark quoted in *Origins* II, p. 335.
[74] Mao, *Shuxin*, pp. 583-4.
[75] *Caizheng Dashiji*, p. 212.
[76] For the 1958-60 figure, see Liu & Wu, *China's Socialist Economy*, p. 270; for the 1957-61 figure, see Xue Muqiao, *Dangqian Woguo Jingji Ruogan Wenti* (Certain problems in our country's economy at present), p. 170.
[77] Shanghai Shehui Kexue Yuan 'Shanghai Jingji' Bianjibu (ed.), *Shanghai Jingji, 1949-1982* (Shanghai's economy, 1949-1982; hereafter, *Shanghai Jingji*), p. 82.
[78] Liu & Wu, *China's Socialist Economy*, p. 278; Zhang Zerong (ed.), *Zhongguo Jingji Tizhi Gaige Jishi* (A chronology of China's economic system reform), p. 88; *Shangye Dashiji*, p. 211.
[79] *Chen Yun's Strategy*, pp. 196, 198.
[80] Liu & Wu, *China's Socialist Economy*, pp. 278-9.
[81] See above, Ch. 1.
[82] *Jingji he Shehui Fazhan Jihua Dashi Jiyao*, p.177. The actual gain to the peasants would have been less than the figures indicate since higher procurement prices would have been offset by rises in the prices of consumer goods and agricultural inputs; for this point, I am grateful to Nicholas Lardy, whose *Agriculture in China's Modern Economic Development* focuses on how rural–urban terms of trade were stacked against the peasants.

CHAPTER 3

[1] Bo Yibo, *Ruogan Zhongda Juece yu Shijiande Huigu* (A review of certain major decisions and incidents) 2, p. 902.
[2] Mao's letter of instruction to Tian is reproduced in *Jianguo Yilai Mao Zedong Wengao* 9, p. 421, and three times in *Mao Zedong he tade Mishu Tian Jiaying*, pp. 41-2, 107, 177; it is considered important enough to be reprinted in full in Mao, *Shuxin*, pp. 574-5. See also Zhengzhi Xueyuan Zhonggong Dangshi Jiaoyanshi (ed.), *Zhongguo Gongchan Dang Liushi Nian Dashi Jianjie* (A summary of the principal events in the 60 years of the CCP; hereafter, *Liushi Nian Dashi Jianjie*), p. 483. Hong Chenghua & Guo Xiuzhi (eds.), *Zhonghua Renmin Gongheguo Zhengzhi Tizhi Yange Dashiji, 1949-78* (A record of the major events in the evolution of the political system of the PRC, 1949-78), p. 219, talks of Mao's investigations in these provinces being 'personally organized and led'.
[3] Li Yinqiao, *Zai Mao Zedong Shenbian Shiwu Nian* (Fifteen years at Mao Zedong's side), pp. 268-71. In fact, the Henan provincial party committee sent the team to Xuchang district instead, where it spent six months. According to another member of the team, Lin Ke, this was because commune rectification had almost been completed there; see Lin Ke, Xu Tao, & Wu Xujun, *Lishide Zhenshi—Mao Zedong Shenbian Gongzuo Renyuande Zhengyan* (The historical truth—The testimony of personnel who worked at Mao's side), p. 242. Possibly the real reason was that the provincial authorities did not want so well-connected a work team visiting an area where there had been considerable trouble; see Introduction above. After reporting back to Mao, the team spent another six months doing manual labour in Guizhou province. This was not the first time that Mao had sent out his guards to do on-the-spot investigations; he employed them in this role also during the summer of 1955 during the collectivization drive; see

Jianguo Yilai Mao Zedong Wengao 5, pp. 208–11. Perhaps it was the earlier precedent that deceived Li Yinqiao into thinking that this was a genuine investigation, but Mao's doctor has revealed that the mission was in fact an elaborate hoax by which Mao, with the connivance of Wang Dongxing, was able to get rid of corrupt members of his household, including Li, without admitting that he had tolerated their behaviour within his entourage. On 25 Dec. 1960, to celebrate his 67th birthday the following day, Mao held a dinner at which only members of his family and staff were present, and used the occasion to hoodwink the men who were being sent away with an elaborate historical analogy. When they tried to postpone their departure until after Chinese New Year, he insisted that they leave immediately. For the real purpose of this 'investigation', see Li, *The Private Life of Chairman Mao*, pp. 337–45; for the text of Mao's speech, see *Yan Huang Chun Qiu*, No. 7, 1993, pp. 2–4.

⁴ *Zhonggong Dangshi Renwuzhuan* 50, p. 166; Bo Yibo, *Ruogan Zhongda Juece* 2, p. 902.

⁵ Hu became one of Mao's secretaries and concurrently secretary to the Politburo in February 1941 at the age of 28; although by 1961, Mao's main day-to-day secretary was Tian Jiaying, Hu formally retained those positions, despite illness, until June 1966; see the official obituary reprinted in *Xinhua Yuebao*, No. 10, 1992, pp. 77–9. Hu was probably the most important word-smith in the CCP's propaganda apparatus. During the 1950s he had written some of the key editorials in the *People's Daily*; see ibid., and *Hu Qiaomu Wenji* (Collected writings of Hu Qiaomu); he is also credited with helping draft the major documents for the CCP's 8th Congress in 1956; *Xinhua Yuebao*, No. 10, 1992, pp. 77–9; and Zhang Rong, *Fengyun Renwu Jianwen Lu* (A record of interviews with famous persons), p. 69. Mao and Hu also exchanged views on poetry; Xu Jizhi, 'Mao Zedong yu Hu Qiaomude shici jiaowang' (Exchanges on poetry between Mao Zedong and Hu Qiaomu), *Dangde Wenxian* (Party documents), No. 6, 1993, pp. 81–6; *Jianguo Yilai Mao Zedong Wengao* 11, pp. 231–6, 450–4.

⁶ Bo Yibo, *Ruogan Zhongda Juece* 2, p. 902; some local officials also joined the teams (ibid.). For Deng Liqun, see 'Zhonggong Renming Lu' Bianxiu Weiyuanhui, *Zhonggong Reming Lu* (A record of CCP personnel; hereafter, *Zhonggong Renming Lu*), p. 850; for Xu Liqun, URI, *Who's Who in Communist China* (2nd edn.), pp. 271–2; for Pang Xianzhi, see *Who's Who in China* Editorial Board, *Who's Who in China: Current Leaders* (hereafter, *Who's Who in China*), pp. 526–7.

⁷ *Mao Zedong he tade Mishu Tian Jiaying*, p. 107. For an account of the investigation process and the problems attending it by one of Tian's team, Pang Xianzhi, see ibid., pp. 42–5; for another account, see ibid., pp. 176–87. For the findings of the Guangdong team, preserved by Deng Liqun, see '1961 nian Guangdong nongcun diaochade yizu cailiao' (Materials from the 1961 investigation into Guangdong villages), *Dangdai Zhongguo Shi Yanjiu* (Research on Contemporary Chinese History), No. 1, 1994, pp. 62–70.

⁸ *Mao Zedong he tade Mishu Tian Jiaying*, p. 45. Mao also cited conversations in Hangzhou with Jiang Hua, the Zhejiang party 1st secretary, and Lin Hujia, a member of the provincial party secretariat; ibid. According to Bo Yibo, *Ruogan Zhongda Juece* 2, pp. 913–14, Mao had hitherto felt that the rapid pace of change militated against trying to lay down regulations for the communes.

⁹ *Mao Zedong he tade Mishu Tian Jiaying*, pp. 45–6.

10 Bo Yibo, *Ruogan Zhongda Juece* 2, pp. 915–16.
11 Ye Yonglie, *Chen Boda Qiren* (That man Chen Boda), p. 201; confirmed by Informant C.
12 Bo Yibo, *Ruogan Zhongda Juece* 2, p. 903. For an episode from 1958 indicating that Chen Boda, the head of the Guangdong team, could be easily fooled by rural cadres due to his ignorance of agriculture, see Zhang Xixian, *Chen Bulei yu Chen Boda* (Chen Bulei and Chen Boda), p. 326.
13 *Mao Zedong he tade Mishu Tian Jiaying*, p. 47.
14 Bo Yibo, *Ruogan Zhongda Juece* 2, p. 916.
15 *Mao Zedong he tade Mishu Tian Jiaying*, p. 47. See also, Zhonggong Zhongyang Dangxiao Dangshi Jiaoyanshi Ziliaozu (ed.), *Zhongguo Gongchan Dang Lici Zhongyao Huiyiji, xia* (Collection of various important conferences of the CCP, 2; hereafter, *Zhongyao Huiyiji, xia*), p. 148; Hao Mengbi & Duan Haoran (eds.), *Zhongguo Gongchan Dang Liushi Nian* (Sixty years of the CCP), p. 526.
16 Bo Yibo, *Ruogan Zhongda Juece* 2, pp. 915–16.
17 Ibid., pp. 916–17. For a summary of some of the discussions, see *Jianguo Yilai Mao Zedong Wengao* 9, pp. 446–50.
18 Hong Chenghua & Guo Xiuzhi, *Zhonghua Renmin Gongheguo Zhengzhi Tizhi Yange Dashiji*, p. 221. This article had been unearthed only two months previously by the Museum of the Chinese Revolution; see *Mao Zedong Nongcun Diaocha Wenji* (A collection of Mao Zedong's writings on rural investigation), p. 355, n. 1. One of the major items in this collection has been translated: Thompson, *Mao Zedong: Report from Xunwu*. While Mao perennially laid stress on investigation, it is conceivable that his renewed insistence on it at this time was sparked by this rediscovery. When the article was openly republished in 1964, it was retitled 'Oppose bookishness' (*Fandui benbenzhuyi*); see *Mao Zedong Zhuzuo Xuandu: jia zhongben* (Selected readings from the works of Mao Zedong: collection A), pp. 20–8.
19 *Liushi Nian Dashi Jianjie*, pp. 483–4. For the cautiously orthodox views expressed at this conference by the 1st secretary of the Northeast region, Song Renqiong, welcomed by Mao when he learned of them, see *Jianguo Yilai Mao Zedong Wengao* 9, pp. 454–5.
20 There were two other members of the Politburo Standing Committee, making a total of seven. Marshal Zhu De attended meetings and made occasional reports but probably his only significant act as a member of the Politburo Standing Committee in recent years had been his abortive attempt to protect Marshal Peng Dehuai at the 1959 Lushan conference; see *Origins* II, p. 229, and Cong Jin, *Quzhe Fazhande Suiyue*, p. 218. Marshal Lin Biao, who had taken Peng Dehuai's place as Defence Minister after Lushan, was politically significant, but only periodically active, and then mainly on military matters.
21 For a discussion of Mao's division of the CCP leadership into first and second fronts, see *Origins* I, pp. 152–6, and II, pp. 172–80. For an earlier example of senior leaders holding a regional meeting without Mao, see *Jianguo Yilai Mao Zedong Wengao* 4, p. 605, n. 1.
22 *Shanxi Sishi Nian, 1949–1989*, p. III–79 (under 17–22 and 20 Mar.). An interesting comparison can be made with the eve of the 1957 Rectification Campaign when two directives followed each other in quick succession with consequent confusion at the provincial level; see *Origins* I, pp. 207–10. For confirmation of the hypothesis elaborated there that there had to have been

an earlier directive preceding the rectification directive proper, see *Jianguo Yilai Mao Zedong Wengao* 6, pp. 432–3.

23 See above p. 39.

24 *Jianguo Yilai Mao Zedong Wengao*, 9, pp. 440–1. In Guofang Daxue, *Cankao Ziliao* 23, p. 448, the letter is not given in its entirety, nor is there any indication of the addressees. Cong Jin quotes from the letter, and names the addressees; see his *Quzhe Fazhande Suiyue*, p. 376. The letter was written at 8 a.m., but according to Bo Yibo, the Chairman later changed his mind about sending it; *Ruogan Zhongda Juece* 2, pp. 904–5.

25 Some sources say that the conference began on 14 March: *Liushi Nian Dashi Jianjie*, pp. 483–4; Liao Gailong *et al.*, *Xin Zhongguo Biannianshi*, p. 185; *Zhongyao Huiyiji, xia*, p. 148; and *Mao Zedong he tade Mishu Tian Jiaying*, p. 48. But equally authoritative sources say the Canton conference began on 15 March; see Bo Yibo, *Ruogan Zhongda Juece* 2, p. 905; Cong Jin, *Quzhe Fazhande Suiyue*, p. 376; Zhonggong Zhongyang Dangshi Yanjiushi (ed.), *Zhongguo Gongchan Dang Lishi Dashiji (1919.5–1987.12)* (A chronology of the history of the Chinese Communist party, May 1919–Dec. 1987), p. 253; *DSNB*, p. 312; *Jingji Dashiji*, p. 300; Zhonggong Zhongyang Wenxian Yanjiushi & Zhonggong Zhongyang Dangxiao (eds.), *Liu Shaoqi Lun Dangde Jianshe* (Liu Shaoqi on party building; hereafter, *Liu Shaoqi Lun Dangde Jianshe*), p. 685. One source opts for both dates: Jiang Huaxuan, Zhang Weiping, & Xiao Sheng (eds.), *Zhongguo Gongchan Dang Huiyi Gaiyao* (Essentials of CCP meetings), pp. 455, 457! This uncertainty may simply reflect legitimate vagueness about the 'formal' beginning of a hastily summoned work conference which was by its nature semi-formal, though normally the Chinese do not permit themselves such fuzziness. According to Informant S, there was a preparatory meeting after the arrival of the northern group at 9 p.m. on the 14th, which some writers have clearly not considered part of the conference proper. Anyway, it seems unlikely that any major business was conducted before the 15th, since on the 14th and 15th Mao's investigative team, together with the Guangdong provincial committee, was discussing rural problems with cadres of a brigade located some 75 miles west of Canton, presumably *in situ*; *Jianguo Yilai Mao Zedong Wengao* 9, p. 443. The issue may well turn out to be trivial, but awaits definitive official clarification.

26 Private communication from a participant in the Canton conference.

27 *Mao Zhuxide geming luxian shengli wan sui—Dangnei liang luxian douzheng dashiji* (Long live the revolutionary line of Chairman Mao: Major events in the two-line struggle inside the party), p. 595. In this source, Chen Boda is cited as the drafter of the Sixty Articles; Cultural Revolution radicals would not have wanted to give credit to Deng Zihui and especially not to Tao Zhu. Equally, post-Cultural Revolution historians would not want to give credit to Chen Boda, who was earlier cited by some sources as the chief drafter; Pang Xianzhi's account in *Mao Zedong he tade Mishu Tian Jiaying* stresses the key role of Tian Jiaying, though Chen's part in the process is also mentioned. These nuances make the job of the outside analyst more difficult. For particularly strong attacks on Chen's counter-productive role in economic affairs, see Zhongguo Shehui Kexue Yuan *et al.* (eds.), *Shehuizhuyi Jingjizhong Jihua yu Shichangde Guanxi, shang* (The relations between plans and markets in socialist economies, vol. 1), pp. 98, 253.

28 For Deng Zihui's contribution to the draft proposals agreed at the Canton conference, see *Zhonggong Dangshi Renwuzhuan* 7, pp. 372–3. Bo Yibo,

who refers to Deng's 66 articles rather than 40, points out that Wang Lu, who was one of Mao's investigators and an assistant draftsman in Canton, had helped Deng Zihui to draft his set of recommendations for the communes; *Ruogan Zhongda Juece* 2, pp. 912–13. Mao's tribute to Deng was remarkable, for although the latter had been close to the Chairman during the revolution, he had never really recovered from the political setback he had sustained in 1955. At that time, he had failed to follow Mao when the Chairman changed course and advocated faster collectivization. Deng Zihui's directorship of the CC's Rural Work Department was not purely nominal, but its political significance had diminished considerably by 1961. When Liu's summons to him to investigate the rural situation came in the summer of 1960, Deng was staying at home in enforced idleness because of the political cloud over him. For a discussion of Deng's setback, see *Origins* I, p. 19; for one of Deng's speeches which contributed to that setback, see *DSYJ*, No. 1, 1981, pp. 2–9; for a commentary on the debate within the party over collectivization at that time, see ibid., pp. 10–17; for Mao's change of line on the pace of collectivization in 1955, see *Zhonggong Dangshi Renwuzhuan* 7, pp. 366–72, especially p. 371; for Deng's enforced idleness, see ibid., p. 372. For post-Cultural Revolution analyses of Deng's views and contributions, see Zhongguo Nongye Jingji Xuehui & Zhongguo Shehui Kexue Yuan Nongcun Fazhan Yanjiusuo (eds.), *Deng Zihui Nongye Hezuo Sixiang Xueshu Taolunhui Lunwenji* (A collection of papers from the symposium on Deng Zihui's thinking on agricultural co-operation).

29 In the Twelve-Year Programme for Agriculture, produced under Mao's leadership, the country was divided into three areas when increases in yields were laid down; see Chao, *Agrarian Policy of the Chinese Communist Party*, p. 331.

30 SCMP(S) 167, p. 2; SCMM 574, p. 15; SCMP 3903, p 2; SCMP 3908, p. 2; *Deng Xiaoping Zibai Shu* (Deng Xiaoping's confession), p. 6.

31 'Shi neige huangdi juedingde?' See *Dongfang Hong* (East is red), No. 20, 18 Feb. 1967, p. 6 (translated in SCMP 3903, p. 2); see also *Deng Xiaoping fan-dang, fan-shehuizhuyi, fan-Mao Zedong sixiangde yanlun zhaibian* (Selection of Deng Xiaoping's anti-party, anti-socialist, anti-Mao Zedong Thought utterances), p. 4. These Cultural Revolution attacks have not been confirmed since, and the conventional wisdom among PRC historians is that at this time, in the face of the manifest national emergency, Mao was collaborative rather than confrontational with his colleagues. Yet this assessment underestimates the Chairman's swift swings of mood; and the issue seems too minor for cultural revolutionaries to have considered manufacturing the episode out of whole cloth.

32 'Meiyou diaocha jiu meiyou fayan quan'; see *Dongfang Hong*, No. 20, 18 Feb. 1967, p. 6, and SCMP(S) 187, p. 25. For a slightly different version of the injunction as purveyed after the Canton conference, see below, n. 58.

33 A private communication from a conference participant provided the information about the neglect of the forty articles. For Tao Zhu's role, see Zhonggong Qiyangxian Weiyuanhui (ed.), *Huainian Tao Zhu Tongzhi* (Remember Comrade Tao Zhu; hereafter, *Huainian Tao Zhu Tongzhi*), p. 80. It is possible that this source is referring only to the preliminary southern conference and not to the subsequent combined work conference. The obscurity surrounding Tao Zhu's exact role is increased by the revelation that what appears to have been a final drafting team was set up on

19 March—a final, third draft was completed on the 21st—with membership drawn from each regional bureau, with the Central-South being represented by Wang Yanchun and Zhao Ziyang but not Tao Zhu; *Mao Zedong he tade Mishu Tian Jiaying*, p. 48; Bo Yibo, *Ruogan Zhongda Juece* 2, p. 917. Yet Tao is reported in another source to have been doing rural investigations as late as May in pursuance of his role as chairman of the drafting committee; see *Xinhua Yuebao*, No. 11, 1989, p. 50. But when another source reports that he made a contribution to the drafting of the final document, it suggests his role was more to ensure that the committee functioned well than to be concerned with the draft's content in detail; see *Biji Tao Zhu*, p. 406. Whatever Tao's precise input into the drafting process, his leadership role is striking since, as claimed during the Cultural Revolution and corroborated by post-Cultural Revolution accounts and a private communication from a participant, Chen Boda played an important role in the southern conference. In addition to his Politburo position and closeness to Mao, Chen Boda was editor of the party's theoretical journal *Red Flag*, and head of the CC's Political Research Office (*Zhongyang Zhengzhi Yanjiushi*). Chen may have wanted to play a back-room role because he parented the original form of the commune now being altered. (For Chen's role in the genesis of the communes, see *Origins* II, pp. 78–82, and Bo Yibo, *Ruogan Zhongda Juece* 2, pp. 738–9; his position at the head of the CC's Political Research Office is mentioned in Mao, *Shuxin*, pp. 511, 575. Mao's current secretary, Tian Jiaying, became a/the deputy head of this office some time between Oct. 1958 and Jan. 1961.) Similarly, it was possibly felt that Tan Zhenlin—a member of the Politburo and the CC secretariat—the agricultural supremo during the GLF, ought also to maintain a low profile at this time of retreat. (For Tan's role in the GLF, see *Origins* II, pp. 60–1, 82–3, 122–4, 127, 221, 299.) But other appropriate central officials, notably Agriculture Minister Liao Luyan, could have done the job without any loss of face because of their role in the GLF.

34   Zhu De and Lin Biao are clearly visible in a picture of a session at the Canton conference reproduced at the front of *Mao Zedong he tade Mishu Tian Jiaying*.

35   Pang Xianzhi says Liu spoke on 15 March, while 19 March is given in a collection of Liu speeches which includes this one; see below, n. 59. Cf. *Mao Zedong he tade Mishu Tian Jiaying*, p. 48, and *Liu Shaoqi Lun Dangde Jianshe*, p. 685.

36   *Xinhua Yuebao*, No. 11, 1989, p. 50.

37   Tao Zhu was quoted during the Cultural Revolution as having once said, 'At a central work conference, whoever holds the largest of the food crop can out-talk anybody else'; SCMP 4018, p. 3. For a brief discussion of Sichuan's grain situation at this time, see below, Ch. 7.

38   At the time of the first Zhengzhou conference in Nov. 1958, when Mao was beginning his first retreat from the excessive leftism of the GLF, he criticized Chen Boda for suggesting the abolition of currency; *Origins* II, pp. 131–2. At that time, he said to Chen: 'You haven't studied Marxism-Leninism well; go to Guangdong and study Comrade Tao Zhu'; Ye Yonglie, *Chen Boda Qiren*, p. 191. However, in a strikingly sudden withdrawal of his favour a few months later, Mao criticized Tao and his deputy Zhao Ziyang for their excessive zeal in trying to uncover hidden stocks of grain, expressing his belief that there was not much Marxism along the banks of (Guangdong's) Pearl River! See *Origins* II, pp. 156–9.

³⁹ *Huainian Tao Zhu Tongzhi*, p. 104.
⁴⁰ *Huang Kecheng Zishu* (Huang Kecheng's autobiography), pp. 260–1.
⁴¹ The text of the March draft is contained in Guofang Daxue, *Cankao Ziliao* 23, pp. 452–61, and in *Nongye Jitihua, xia*, pp. 455–69 The text of the June draft is available in the latter source, pp. 474–91. For reports on discussions of the Sixty Articles on Agriculture in PLA units, see Cheng, *The Politics of the Chinese Red Army*, pp. 465–70, 491–8, 515–26, 58z. One report (p. 465) stated that 'a small number of people show that under the temporary difficult circumstances their beliefs are being shaken, and passing from uncertainty to doubt they are beginning to ask if the policies of the Party and the superiority of the system of people's communes are real or only imaginary. Some individuals even went so far as to violate the laws and ordinances and to damage the interests of the Party and the nation'. Soldiers were clearly well aware that the 'Sixty Articles were not a development but a retreat' (pp. 493, 515). They asked why markets were tight and prices were high (pp. 467, 515). In one unit, 30% of the cadres and 50% of the rank and file were conspicuously 'confused' about the rural situation (p. 466); in another, some commented that 'the standard of food ration in rural areas is so low that it does not provide enough for us to eat' and that 'the food ration in Army units is also not enough' (p. 495). Among the causes of their concern were frequent letters—in some units soldiers were receiving five or six a month—and increased numbers of visits from their peasant relatives living in hard-hit areas (p. 580).
⁴² Ibid., pp. 406, 456.
⁴³ Mao, *Shuxin*, pp. 570–1; *Mao Zedong he tade Mishu Tian Jiaying*, p. 49; Bo Yibo, *Ruogan Zhongda Juece* 2, p. 905. The October 1960 letter was addressed to Li Fuchun, presumably because his seniors in the secretariat, Deng Xiaoping and Peng Zhen, were in Moscow for the preparatory meetings for the 81-party Communist summit in November; see *Origins* II, p. 284. For Mao's attack on egalitarianism and transfer of resources in early 1959, see ibid., pp. 146 ff. Mao's criticism of *yi ping, er diao* was echoed by Peng Zhen at a Beijing party meeting in June, but this was one of the many things held against him during the Cultural Revolution see *Peng Zhen fangeming xiuzhengzhuyi yanlun zhaibian* (Extracts from Peng Zhen's counter-revolutionary revisionist speeches), p. 34.
⁴⁴ *Mao Zedong sixiang wan sui (June 1967), xia*, pp. 331–2; *Mao Zedong he tade Mishu Tian Jiaying*, pp. 48–9; Liao Gailong *et al.*, *Xin Zhongguo Biannianshi*, p. 185.
⁴⁵ It was at the Canton work conference that commune nomenclature was altered again, for the last time. Since the second Zhengzhou conference in early 1959, the principal subdivision of the commune, officially translated as the 'brigade', had been known as *shengchan dui* (production group), and its sub-unit, the 'team', had been known as the *shengchan xiao* (small) *dui*. Now, in a reflection of its increasing relative importance, the team became the *shengchan dui* and the brigade became the *shengchan da* (large) *dui*. An instance of the prevailing confusion is Shanxi province, where as recently as 30 Jan. the provincial party committee had decided to change the title for the administrative level below the commune from *guani qu* (administrative district) to *shengchan dui* (brigade) and of the lowest administrative level from *shengchan dui* (team) to *shengchan xiaodui* (team); there was a further change to the new national nomenclature after the Canton conference; see

Shanxi Sishi Nian, 1949–1989, p. III-79 (under 30 Jan. and 20 Mar.). For a discussion of this terminological turbulence in the communes, see *Origins* II, pp. 181–4.

46 Mao had said that the commune was a union (*lianhe zuzhi*) of brigades; ibid.
47 Guofang Daxue, *Cankao Ziliao* 23, p. 452.
48 Art. 2, ibid. For Mao's attacks on commune egalitarianism at the second Zhengzhou conference, see *Origins* II, pp. 146–55.
49 Arts. 2 and 5, Guofang Daxue, *Cankao Ziliao* 23, p. 452. For more details about the desired scale of the various levels of commune organization and a post-Cultural Revolution assessment that the reductions in their sizes was a key element in the Sixty Articles, see Zhonggong Dangshi Yanjiuhui, *Xuexi Lishi Jueyi Zhuanji*, pp. 121–2. For a discussion of the expansion of numbers, see Domes, *Socialism in the Chinese Countryside*, p. 48. In Ding *xian* (renamed Dingzhou *shi* in 1986), 120 miles south of Beijing, the number of communes grew almost five times, from nine to fifty-three, well over the national rate of expansion, each new commune averaging 12,000 people; see 'Dingzhou Juan' Bianji Weiyuanhui (ed.), *Zhongguo Guoqing Congshu— Bai Xianshi Jingji Shehui Diaocha: Dingzhou Juan*, p. 36. Ding *xian* was the site of a major economic and social survey from 1926 to 1933 which provides a bench-mark for assessing the changes described in the above volume; see Gamble, *Ting Hsien: A North China Rural Community*.
50 Arts. 10, 11, 14; Guofang Daxue, *Cankao Ziliao* 23, pp. 453–4.
51 Art. 16; ibid., p. 454.
52 Art. 20; ibid., p. 455.
53 Arts. 33, 37; ibid., p. 457.
54 Arts. 43–5; ibid., p. 459.
55 Art. 47; ibid.
56 Cong Jin, *Quzhe Fazhande Suiyue*, p. 377.
57 *Mao Zedong sixiang wan sui (June 1967), xia*, pp. 331–2.
58 Guofang Daxue, *Cankao Ziliao* 23, p. 462; Hong Chenghua & Guo Xiuzhi, *Zhonghua Renmin Gongheguo Zhengzhi Tizhi Yange Dashiji*, p. 222. The letter, which was drafted by Hu Qiaomu and revised by Mao and Tian Jiaying (Bo Yibo, *Ruogan Zhongda Juece* 2, pp. 905–6), was dispatched on 23 March. On 26 Dec. 1961 (his 68th birthday), Mao had written to the editor of *Poetry (Shikan)* explaining that until he did further research on the problems of poetry, he had no right to speak about it; Mao, *Shuxin*, p. 589.
59 *Liu Shaoqi Lun Dangde Jianshe*, pp. 685–8; *Selected Works of Zhou Enlai* 2, pp. 320–1. According to a private communication from a participant, in addition to his formal speech on 19 Mar., Liu also made remarks at a small group meeting on the 15th, during the course of which he described household sideline production as 'economic democracy' (*jingji minzhu*).
60 Zhang Tianrong, 'Guanyu yijiuliuer nian qiqian ren dahuide jige wenti' (Some problems relating to the 1962 Seven Thousand Cadres Conference), 12 May 1981, p. 2.
61 Few have remarked upon this even after his death; but see Shi Zhongquan, *Zhou Enlaide Zhuoyue Fengxian* (Zhou Enlai's outstanding contributions), pp. 341–2. A scathing analysis of investigation methods was prepared in May 1961 by Qi Benyu, a staff member of the CC's General Office, which Mao considered important enough to put on the agenda of the Beijing work conference; see *Jianguo Yilai Mao Zedong Wengao* 9, pp. 504–6, 512.
62 For Mao's own visits see *Renmin Ribao (People's daily*; hereafter, *RMRB*),

2 May 1961; *Zhonggong Dangshi Renwuzhuan* 50, p. 163. Mao's Hunan visit disturbed him sufficiently for him to order the Hubei 1st secretary, Wang Renzhong, to go to Changsha to help out; *Jianguo Yilai Mao Zedong Wengao* 9, pp. 465–7, 482–3, 494–5, 499–500, 510–12. See also Gong Guzhong, Tang Zhennan, & Xia Yuansheng, *Mao Zedong Hui Hunan Jishi, 1953–1975* (A record of Mao Zedong's returns to Hunan, 1953–1975), pp. 104–22. For Mao's teams, see Bo Yibo, *Ruogan Zhongda Juece* 2, p. 907. For Tian Jiaying, who was accompanied on some of his other trips by Yang Shangkun, director of the CC's General Office, and Wu Lengxi, editor-in-chief of *RMRB*, see *Renwu* (Personalities), No. 5, 1981, p. 82, and *Current Background* (hereafter, CB) 874, p. 53.

63 *Dangdai Zhongguode Hunan* 2, p. 631; Gong Guzhong, Tang Zhennan, & Xia Yuansheng, *Mao Zedong Hui Hunan Jishi, 1953–1975*, pp. 113, 116.

64 Bo Yibo, *Ruogan Zhongda Juece* 2, p. 907; *Zhongyao Huiyiji, xia*, p. 153; Zou Aiguo & Xue Jianhua, *Zhongguo Da Guang Jiao (1)* (A panoramic view of China, 1), pp. 9, 11. The latter source (p. 11) gives Zhou Enlai's work log for 7 May to demonstrate the premier's punishing schedule: the day started at 2 a.m. with a telephone conversation about the Laos conference with Zhang Hanfu, a deputy foreign minister, and finally ended at 7.50 p.m. There is a picture of Zhou talking with a group of peasants in Zhongguo Geming Bowuguan (ed.), *Jinian Zhou Enlai* (Remember Zhou Enlai), plate 367. For a full schedule of Zhou's period in Handan, see *Wenxian he Yanjiu 1983* (Documents and research, 1983), pp. 88–92; this is an extract from the detailed log of the premier's activities, kept by him and his secretary from Jan. 1950, which was presented to General Secretary Hu Yaobang by Zhou's widow, Deng Yingchao, in Jan. 1981. Zhou's Handan team may have been led by Xie Fuzhi, the Minister of Public Security, who is reported by Bo Yibo also to have investigated in that *xian*; *Ruogan Zhongda Juece* 2, p. 907. If so, the failure to indicate a direct link between Zhou and Xie (who is not referred to in the other sources) might be due to the unsavoury reputation which the latter gained during the Cultural Revolution.

65 Zhou's principal reason for going to Yunnan was to have further talks with Premier U Nu of Burma; see Huai En, *Zhou Zongli Shengping Dashiji* (A chronology of Premier Zhou's life), p. 421. According to one source, Zhou had had surgery for an unspecified reason shortly before this trip, but disregarded his doctor's advice to cancel it; see *Womende Zhou Zongli*, pp. 111, 471. Zhou's wife, Deng Yingchao, also had a spell in hospital in 1961; ibid., p. 468.

66 Zhang Quanzhen, Hou Guangwen, & Wang Yongsheng (eds.), *Zhou Enlaide Ganqing Shijie* (The emotional world of Zhou Enlai), pp. 107–8. Zhou restrained embarrassed local officials from punishing the peasant and quoted him at the subsequent Beijing work conference.

67 *Jingji Dashiji*, p. 302; Zou Aiguo & Xue Jianhua, *Zhongguo Da Guang Jiao (1)*, pp. 10–11. The latter source gives the purported record of the telephone report.

68 'Dangdai Zhongguo' Congshu Bianjibu (ed.), *Dangdai Zhongguode Beijing* (Contemporary China's Beijing; hereafter, *Dangdai Zhongguode Beijing*) 1, p. 155; *Xin Beida* (New Peking University), 12 June 1967, p. 4; SCMM 640, pp. 19–21; SCMP 4014, p. 2; Bo Yibo, *Ruogan Zhongda Juece* 2, p. 907. In his speech to the Canton conference, perhaps in response to Mao's criticism, Deng also emphasized the importance of investigation and sug-

gested that lack of it had resulted in the communes being set up too quickly: 'In these past few years we have abandoned the methods of investigation and research . . . Everyone has talked a bit wildly. We have substituted our personal feelings for policies . . . In the process of collectivization, from Mutual Aid Teams to lower-stage APCs, and from the latter to higher-stage APCs, there were laws. Even though the transformation of [private] industry and commerce was carried out with fanfare, it had been preceded by investigation and discussion, and the work was measured and steady. But in setting up the communes, we moved too quickly.' (See *Jin Jun Bao* [Advancing army news], 26 Mar. 1967, p. 4, col. 2 [here the remarks are dated Apr. 1961]; ibid., 14 June 1967, p. 2, col. 3; *Chedi qingsuan Deng Xiaoping fan-dang, fan-shehuizhuyi, fan-Mao Zedong sixiangde taotian zuixing* [Thoroughly settle accounts for Deng Xiaoping's monstrous anti-party, anti-socialist, anti-Mao Zedong Thought crimes], p. 4; SCMP[S] 208, p. 10.)

69 Shi Dongbing, *Zuichude Kangzheng: Peng Zhen zai 'Wenhua Da Geming' Qianxi* (The earliest resistance: Peng Zhen on the eve of the 'Great Cultural Revolution'), p. 18.
70 For Deng Tuo's problems with Mao during the Hundred Flowers period, see *Origins* I, pp. 193–4, 201, 282, 312.
71 *Jingji Dashiji*, p. 302; *Liushi Nian Dashi Jianjie*, p. 484. For hostile comments, see *Peng zei 'Huairou diaocha' shi Liu, Deng hei silingbu yinmo fanpi zibenzhuyide yanzhong buji* (Traitor Peng's 'Huairou investigation' is a serious step in Liu [Shaoqi] and Deng [Xiaoping's] black headquarters' secret plot to restore capitalism), *passim*. The membership of the investigation teams and the description of Deng Tuo's role is on pp. 25–6.
72 *Liushi Nian Dashi Jianjie*, p. 484; *Jianguo Yilai Mao Zedong Wengao* 9, pp. 492–3.
73 *Li Xiannian Wenxuan*, p. 257.
74 *Zhongyao Huiyiji, xia*, p. 153. Earlier in the year, Zhu De had visited Jiangxi; Guo Simin & Tian Yu (eds.), *Wo Yanzhongde Zhu De* (Zhu De as I saw him), p. 332. For a fuller record of Zhu's many tours in the early 1960s, suggestive of a search for a role on the part of this ageing (late seventies), sidelined, but still vigorous member of the PSC, see Qing Mu, *Zhongguo Yuanshuai Zhu De* (Chinese marshal Zhu De), p. 508. For a glimpse of the extraordinary precautions that could surround the visit of a leader as eminent as Zhu De, see the account of his return to his home province in March 1960 in *Zhu De fan-dang fan-shehuizhuyi fan-Mao Zedong sixiangde zuixing* (Zhu De's anti-party, anti-socialist, anti-Mao Zedong Thought crimes), p. 30.
75 *Zhonggong Dangshi Renwuzhuan* 31, pp. 94–5; Jin Ye (ed.), *Huiyi Tan Zhenlin* (Remember Tan Zhenlin), p. 395; Dong Baocun, *Tan Zhenlin Wai Zhuan* (An unofficial biography of Tan Zhenlin), pp. 72–4.
76 For Tao Zhu and others in the Central-South region, see for instance *Huainian Tao Zhu Tongzhi*, pp. 94, 96, and *Xinhua Yuebao*, No. 11, 1989, p. 50; for the Northeast region, see Liaoning Wuchanjieji Gemingpai Lianluozhan 'Fa Song Bingtuan', *Jianjue dadao dongbei diqu dangnei touhao zou zibenzhuyi daolude dangquanpai—Song Renqiong* (Resolutely topple the leading capitalist roader power-holding clique within the party in the Northeast region—Song Renqiong), p. 2. Other peregrinating central leaders included Xi Zhongxun, secretary-general of the State Council, who went

to Henan; YCL 1st secretary Hu Yaobang, who went to Liaoning; Chen Zhengren, who went to Sichuan; and Liao Luyan, who went to Shanxi; Bo Yibo, *Ruogan Zhongda Juece* 2, p. 907.

77 For Peng Dehuai, see the account by his widow, Pu Anxiu, in *Xinhua Wenzhai* (New China digest), No. 5, 1981, p. 174; see also the discussion in Ch. 7 below. For Lin Biao, see *Jianguo Yilai Mao Zedong Wengao* 9, p. 487.

78 *Huainian Liu Shaoqi Tongzhi* (Remember Comrade Liu Shaoqi), pp. 60, 335. In August, Liu went to Heilongjiang to inspect the Daqing oilfield; Kang Shi'en, 'Ji Shaoqi tongzhi guancha Daqing youtian' (Remembering comrade Shaoqi inspecting the Daqing oilfield), *Dangde Wenxian*, No. 5, 1993, pp. 24–6.

79 *Huainian Liu Shaoqi Tongzhi*, p. 60. Liu's visit received considerable attention in anti-Liu Cultural Revolution polemics and, as a consequence, in post-rehabilitation tributes to him. In the following account, I have utilized both types of sources. Cultural Revolution reports give the dates of the visit as 2 Apr.–16 May—see SCMM(S) 26, p. 1; *Dongfang Hong Bao* (East is red news), 9 Mar. 1967, p. 5; *Liu Shaoqi fan-geming zui'e shi* (The history of the counter-revolutionary crimes of Liu Shaoqi), p. 37.

80 Zou Aiguo & Xue Jianhua, *Zhongguo Daguang Jiao* (2), p. 19. *Mishu* is a term which can cover a number of different roles, but almost certainly Wang Guangmei was Liu's administrative secretary (*bangong mishu*) not his political secretary. For a discussion of the CCP staff system, see Li Wei, *The Chinese Staff System: A Mechanism for Bureaucratic Control and Integration.*

81 SCMM(S) 26, p. 6; *Huainian Liu Shaoqi Tongzhi*, pp. 68, 335, 342–3; Lü Xingdou, *Liu Shaoqi he tade Shiye* (Liu Shaoqi and his enterprises), p. 500. The escorting officials doubtless considered themselves privileged at the time, but during the Cultural Revolution they were all denounced as Liu's 'running dogs' at meetings, in print, and even in plays.

82 According to Li Wei, 'The Security Service for Chinese Central Leaders', only Zhou Enlai was kept informed about Mao's movements, and he only partially.

83 Mao had last been in Shaoshan in 1959, immediately prior to the Lushan conference; *Origins* II, pp. 187–90.

84 *Huainian Liu Shaoqi Tongzhi*, pp. 60, 65, 327, 331, 342–4, 346–62; *Hong Qi Piaopiao* (Red flags fluttering; hereafter, *HQPP*), No. 20, 1980, p. 242; SCMM(S) 26, pp. 16–17. For Mao's fondness for Hangzhou, see *Origins* I, p. 370(27).

85 *Huainian Liu Shaoqi Tongzhi*, pp. 60, 323, 325, 336; SCMM(S) 26, p. 16.

86 *Huainian Liu Shaoqi Tongzhi*, p. 66.

87 *HQPP*, No. 20, 1980, p. 187.

88 *Huainian Liu Shaoqi Tongzhi*, pp. 60, 323; Yang Shangkun, 'Huainian Liu Shaoqi Tongzhi' (In memory of Comrade Liu Shaoqi), *Hongqi* (Red flag; hereafter, *HQ*), No. 8, 1980, translated in JPRS 75921, pp. 13–14. According to a hostile Cultural Revolution account, Liu not only spent two days back in Changsha attending meetings, but also spent a third day visiting Mt Tianhua. Allegedly, his investigation consisted for the most part of sitting in his quarters receiving reports; see SCMM(S) 26, pp. 4, 17.

89 *Huainian Liu Shaoqi Tongzhi*, pp. 61, 324–5, 329, 346–8. In March 1962, Liu wrote to the brigade to make sure that progress had been maintained; ibid., p. 326. Other Chinese leaders were allegedly even blunter at this time. The Young Communist League 1st secretary, Hu Yaobang, told some of his

members: 'On the question of canteens, Hunan had the Chairman fooled. One can be fooled for lack of close investigation and study. As a result, when one gets fooled, one may fool others in return.' See SCMP(S) 194, p. 30.

90 *Huainian Liu Shaoqi Tongzhi*, pp. 324–5.

91 Ibid., p. 325; SCMM(S) 26, pp. 10–11.

92 SCMM(S) 26, pp. 3–6.

93 Ibid., p. 6. In this source, the passage 'In retrospect . . . vanished' is not included within the quotation marks, but the context suggests that it should have been.

94 Lü Xingdou, *Liu Shaoqi he tade Shiye*, pp. 516–17. The actual words used by Peng (to whom Wang refers only by her office not her name) were: '*Liu huzi, ni jinggan yong youqing fenzi.*' 'Youqing' was the epithet applied to Peng Dehuai and his notional supporters who were attacked after the Lushan plenum in 1959 for criticizing the GLF. Another account quotes Peng as saying: 'Bearded Liu, you haven't come here to get a grip on production, but to look for trouble' (*Liu huzi, bushi lai zhua shengchande, shi lai zhao chazide*); see 'Liu Shaoqi Yanjiu Lunwenji' Bianjizu (ed.), *Liu Shaoqi Yanjiu Lunwenji* (A collection of research papers on Liu Shaoqi), p. 377.

95 Ibid.; *Huainian Liu Shaoqi Tongzhi*, pp. 350–1.

96 Ibid., pp. 328–30; *HQPP*, No. 20, 1980, pp. 192–3; *Liu Shaoqi Xuanji, xia*, pp. 329–30.

97 Bao & Chelminski, *Prisoner of Mao*, p. 265.

98 *Huainian Liu Shaoqi Tongzhi*, pp. 328–9, 356–8.

99 Ibid., pp. 329–30, 358; *HQPP*, No. 20, 1980, pp. 207–8; *Liu Xuanji, xia*, pp. 330–1; SCMM 602, p. 10. After Liu's posthumous rehabilitation in 1980, the house his family had owned for 200 years was made into a place of pilgrimage. Only a 45-minute drive from Mao's family home in Shaoshan, it is considerably larger than the latter, comprising 23 rooms as compared with 13. Liu's three elder brothers lived in it till the last one died in 1970. A son of the last of the Liu brothers still farmed and lived in the neighbourhood as of 1986 when the present author visited the Liu ancestral home.

100 Lü Xingdou, *Liu Shaoqi he tade Shiye*; *Huainian Liu Shaoqi Tongzhi*, pp. 329–30.

101 SCMM(S) 26, p. 13; see also the briefer quotations in Wang Guangmei's account in Lü Xingdon, *Liu Shaoqi he tade Shiye*, p. 516.

102 *Liu Shaoqi Xuanji, xia*, p. 330; *Huainian Liu Shaoqi Tongzhi*, pp. 327–32, 354, 356, 359–60, 362; *HQPP*, No. 20, 1980, pp. 191–2, 193–4; Liu Zhanming, 'Liu bobo jiao wo bu pa "gui" ' (Uncle Liu taught me not to fear 'ghosts'), *RMRB*, 15 May 1980, p. 2; Chen Dianguo, 'Qunzhongde tie xin ren' (A close friend of the masses), ibid., 22 May 1980, p. 8; SCMM(S) 26, p. 9. Liu Aiqin, *Nüerde Huainian* (A daughter's memories), pp. 61–2; Aiqin was a daughter by an earlier marriage.

103 Lü Xingdou, *Liu Shaoqi he tade Shiye*, p. 504. Wang Guangmei quotes Liu in the context of her description of their Hunan trip, but does not specify when and where he made this remark. He would make a different, more nuanced, less self-critical assessment when addressing his senior colleagues at the central work conference in May 1961; see *Liu Shaoqi Xuanji, xia*, p. 338. In his speech to the Seven Thousand Cadres Conference in January 1962, Liu would use the exact words quoted by Wang Guangmei, but present them less baldly, introducing the point about the two FYPs with the

phrase 'Some people say', and prefacing the self-critical assessment precisely with the excuse 'On the one hand, our experience is still insufficient'; ibid., pp. 423–4.

[104] *Liu Shaoqi Xuanji, xia*, p. 329; emphasis added.

[105] SCMM(S) 26, p. 2; I have not found a post-Cultural Revolution equivalent. Liu was historically slightly inaccurate. Though both the Qin and Sui, the two great unifying dynasties in Chinese history, quickly collapsed as a result of their excessive oppressiveness, it was Qin Shi Huangdi's son who was overthrown. For a brief account of the cruelties perpetrated by Qin Shi Huangdi and Sui Yangdi, see Hucker, *China's Imperial Past*, pp. 42–7, 138–9. For a Cultural Revolution account alleging that Liu actually said that Mao had made mistakes, and, less convincingly, that he had called on Mao to retire, see *Mao Zedong-zhuyi Zhan Bao* (Mao Zedongism combat news), 1st ten days, Apr. 1967, p. 3, col. 2. For a comparison between Mao and Qin Shi Huang, see *Origins* II, p. 206. The grim picture that Liu saw during his Hunan visit may have accounted for his anger when he learned about the imprisonment of a young Hunanese girl who had put up wall posters at the offices of the State Council the previous year denouncing the communes in a protest at her family's plight; see *HQPP*, No. 20, 1980, pp. 188–90, and *Huainian Liu Shaoqi Tongzhi*, pp. 339–41.

[106] See *Origins* II, p. 153.

[107] SCMM(S) 26, p. 9; cf. *Liu Shaoqi Xuanji, xia*, pp. 331–2.

[108] SCMM(S) 26, p. 2; *Liu Shaoqi Xuanji, xia*, pp. 332–3.

[109] See *Origins* II, pp. 146–53.

[110] Xing Zhen, 'Everything should start from reality', *Xinwen Yanjiu Ziliao* (Material for research on the press), No. 3, 1980, p. 4; Geng Sheng, 'We must definitely seek truth from facts', ibid., p. 6. (The speech is not included in *Liu Shaoqi Xuanji, xia*.)

[111] *Xinwen Yanjiu Ziliao*, No. 3, 1980, p. 5; Lü Xingdou, *Liu Shaoqi he tade Shiye*, p. 501.

[112] For Wang Guangmei's account of Liu's difficulties in establishing the facts during his Hunan tour, see ibid., pp. 501–3. The problem for senior leaders of differentiating truth from lies, reality from exaggeration, is discussed by Bo Yibo in his explanation of Mao's decision to launch the 'high tide' of collectivization in 1955; see Bo Yibo, *Ruogan Zhongda Juece* 1, pp. 374–5. As a senior economic official in the period up to the Cultural Revolution, who was made an alternate member of the Politburo at the CCP's 8th Congress in 1956, Bo was in an excellent position to understand the problems faced by Liu and other top-level investigators when they got to the grass roots.

[113] *Xinwen Yanjiu Ziliao*, No. 3, 1980, p. 5. See also Liu Aiqin, *Nüerde Huainian*, pp. 59–62. For Tao Zhu's return to Qiyangxian, see *Xinhua Yuebao*, No. 11, 1989, p. 50. For Deng Zihui's 20-day investigation in Fujian, see *Zhonggong Dangshi Renwuzhuan* 7, pp. 373–4. During the Long March, Deng Zihui and Zhang Dingcheng, along with Tan Zhenlin (a Hunanese), were left behind to preserve the Soviet areas in Fujian; see ibid., pp. 329–40, and the biographies of the three men in Klein & Clark, *Biographic Dictionary of Chinese Communism.*

[114] SCMP(S) 201, p. 29. Shortly after the 9th plenum, Liu had allegedly told *RMRB* editors not to link news coverage too closely with what was going on if they wished to avoid mistakes! (See SCMP 4253, pp. 23, 24.)

[115] For Mao and Liu during the GLF, see *Origins* II, pp. 81, 220, 230. For Liu at

the Canton conference, see *Liu Shaoqi Lun Dangde Jianshe*, pp. 686–7. For Zhou's directive of 25 June 1957, see Xu Xiang, 'Premier Zhou's Chat with Reporters', *Xinwen Yanjiu Ziliao*, No. 3, 1980, pp. 24–8.

[116] SCMP(S) 201, p. 30.

[117] *Origins* II, pp. 42–3, 302–4, 363(5), 376(9). Liu later went also to Heilongjiang, spending 20 days there from 18 Jul. to 10 Aug. 1961, visiting the Daxingan, Xiaoxingan, and Zhangguangcai mountain ranges, inspecting the timber industry, which had been ravaged by excessive felling during the GLF; Zhonggong Zhongyang Dangshi Yanjiushi (ed.), *Zhonggong Dangshi Ziliao* (Materials on CCP history; hereafter *Zhonggong Dangshi Ziliao*), No. 30, pp. 71–83, 230–2. He found some forestry enterprises in a state of total anarchy; *Zhonggong Dangshi Yanjiu* (Research on CCP history), No. 5, 1988, p. 12. In the course of his trip, which would attract less attention during the Cultural Revolution than his Hunan visit, he relaxed with his wife for a couple of days beside the waters of Lake Jingpo; see Zhonggong Zhongyang Wenxian Yanjiushi & Xinhua Tongxunshe (eds.), *Gongheguo Zhuxi Liu Shaoqi* (State Chairman Liu Shaoqi; hereafter, *Gongheguo Zhuxi Liu Shaoqi*), p. 31. According to this source, p. 284, Liu was in Heilongjiang from 16 July to 11 August. The extent of the problem Liu was investigating is indicated by the contraction in the area covered by timber forests from 2,513,000 ha. in 1958 to 717,000 ha. in 1961; see *TJNJ, 1981*, p. 161.

[118] For Liu's 1960 visit, see *Origins* II, pp. 303–4; for his 1961 visit, see Duan Junyi *et al.*, 'Shaoqi tongzhi, Henan renmin huainian ni' (Comrade Shaoqi, the people of Henan remember you), *RMRB*, 21 May 1980, p. 2, col. 2.

[119] Liu stated that during the GLF the proportion of success to shortcomings nationally was 8 to 2, but in Henan it was 7 to 3; *Liu Shaoqi Lun Dangde Jianshe*, p. 687.

[120] At the end of 1960, Zhang Guohua, the ranking party and military official in Tibet, investigated the Xinyang tragedy and reported on it to Zhou Enlai, who promptly sent a State Council work team to the province; see Cheng Hua, *Zhou Enlai he tade Mishumen*, p. 286, and Quan Yanchi, *Tao Zhu zai 'Wenhua Da Geming' zhong* (Tao Zhu in the 'Great Cultural Revolution'), pp. 211–12; I am grateful to Michael Schoenhals for directing my attention to these sources. For the overall impact of the GLF on Henan, see above, Intro.

[121] See the biographies of Liu Jianxun and Wu Zhipu in Klein & Clark, *Biographic Dictionary*. Liu came to Henan from Guangxi where in 1957 he had replaced 1st secretary Chen Manyuan who had been disciplined along with ten other officials for failing to prevent deaths from starvation; see reports in *RMRB*, 18 June 1957, trans. in SCMP 1562, pp. 13–20.

[122] Cheng, *The Politics of the Chinese Red Army*, pp. 119, 120, 122, 138, 140, 142; John Wilson Lewis, 'China's Secret Military Papers: "Continuities" and "Revelations"', *CQ*, No. 18, 1964, pp. 68–78; John Gittings, 'China's Militia', ibid., pp. 113–17. See also SCMM(S) 32, p. 22.

[123] The conference had originally been scheduled for 15 May but on 5 May it was postponed until the 20th to give more time for investigations; see Mao, *Shuxin*, pp. 578, 580; *Jianguo Yilai Mao Zedong Wengao* 9, pp. 475–6. In fact, it opened on 21 May and lasted till 12 June; see *Zhongyao Huiyiji, xia*, p. 148.

[124] Mao, *Shuxin*, pp. 578–82; *Jianguo Yilai Mao Zedong Wengao* 9, pp. 465–72,

482–5, 488, 494–503, 507–11. Mao's decision to tell Deng to summon a new CC work conference was apparently sparked by the sombre report he had heard on 23 Apr. from Tian Jiaying, who had returned to Zhejiang on Mao's instructions for further investigations immediately after the Canton conference; see *Mao Zedong he tade Mishu Tian Jiaying*, pp. 50–3.

125 Guofang Daxue Dangshi Dangjian Zhengzhi Gongzuo Jiaoyanshi, *Zhongguo Gongchan Dang Qishi Nian Jianjie* (A summary of the principal events in the 70 years of the CCP; hereafter, Guofang Daxue *Qishi Nian Jianjie*), p. 487; Gong Yuzhi & Shi Zhongquan, *Deng Xiaoping Jianshe You Zhongguo Tese Shehuizhuyi Lilun Xinlun Dagang* (A new outline of Deng Xiao-ping's theory of constructing socialism with Chinese characteristics), p. 33.

126 *Liu Shaoqi Xuanji, xia*, pp. 335–6.

127 Ibid., p. 337. According to one Chinese scholar, quoting from a different source and perhaps a different text of Liu Shaoqi's speech, Liu indicated that this was his personal view, too; Informant S. Cultural revolutionaries naturally made much of Liu's gloomy views; see for instance 'Along the socialist or the capitalist road', *China Reconstructs*, Nov. 1967, Supplement, pp. 8, 11.

128 *Liu Shaoqi Xuanji, xia*, pp. 337–8.

129 Ibid., p. 338, translated in *Selected Works of Liu Shaoqi* 2, p. 316.

130 *Liu Shaoqi Xuanji, xia*, pp. 338–40.

131 See *Chedi qingsuan Deng Xiaoping fan-dang, fan-shehuizhuyi, fan-Mao Zedong sixiangde taotian zuixing*, p. 4; *Deng Xiaoping fan-dang, fan-shehuizhuyi, fan-Mao Zedong sixiangde yanlun zhaibian*, p. 25; SCMP(S) 208, p. 9. No text of this speech is included in *Deng Xiaoping Wenxuan, 1938–1965* (Selections from Deng Xiaoping, 1938–1965).

132 *Mao Zedong sixiang wan sui (1969)*, p. 406; Liao Gailong, Zhao Baoxu, & Du Qinglin (eds.), *Dangdai Zhongguo Zhengzhi Deshidian, 1949–1990* (A dictionary of contemporary Chinese politics, 1949–1990), p. 631. There is no record of Mao's 12th June speech in *Jianguo Yilai Mao Zedong Wengao 9*. See also Lieberthal & Dickson, *A Research Guide to Central Party and Government Meetings in China, 1949–1986*, p. 118.

133 *Mao Zedong sixiang wan sui (June 1967), xia*, pp. 332–4

134 Hong Chenghua & Guo Xiuzhi, *Zhengzhi Tizhi Yange Dashiji*, p. 223. As we shall see, Mao never permitted Peng to be rehabilitated.

135 Bo Yibo, *Ruogan Zhongda Juece* 2, p. 908.

136 Ibid., p. 925. A team began working on a revised draft in early May with Hu Qiaomu again in the role of wordsmith, but Hu dropped out ill before the draft was completed on the 22nd. A second revised version was circulated on 8 June and, after some verbal corrections, it was eventually agreed upon; ibid., p. 924. Mao urged Hu Qiaomu to take an extended rest; *Jianguo Yilai Mao Zedong Wengao 9*, p. 542.

137 Zhonggong Dangshi Yanjiuhui, *Xuexi Lishi Jueyi Zhuanji*, p. 122; Guangdong Teaching Materials 2, p. 360; *Jingji Dashiji*, pp. 306–7. Even in the revised version, the articles dealing with these topics, 33 and 34, were phrased so as to disguise the full extent of the retreat acknowledged by the above post-Cultural Revolution sources. One source underlines the extent to which the revised Sixty Articles exposed the shortcomings of the Twelve-Article Emergency Directive issued the previous November; Zhao Desheng (ed.), *Zhonghua Renmin Gongheguo Jingji Zhuanti Dashiji*,

1949–1966 (PRC chronology on specialized economic topics), p. 514. See also Bo Yibo, *Ruogan Zhongda Juece* 2, pp. 925–33.

138   I have compared the text of the March version of the Sixty Articles in Guofang Daxue, *Cankao Ziliao* 23, pp. 452–61, with the text of the June version in *Nongye Jitihua, xia*, pp. 474–91.

139   Arts. 1–6.

140   Arts. 10–15.

141   Arts. 17, 18, 20, 26 of the March version which correspond to arts. 17, 20, 28 of the June version.

142   Arts. 23, 24, 33 (Mar.), 24, 25, 26 (June).

143   In both versions, these are 52, 53, and 54.

144   Art. 37 (Mar.) and 39 (June).

145   Art. 43. Due to new articles like this being inserted in the June version, a number of articles from the March version disappeared, including one on the treatment of rich peasants and landlords (42) and four on cadre behaviour (45, 46, 48, 49).

146   Arts. 57 and 60 in both versions.

147   Informant S.

148   *Dangdai Zhongguode Hunan* 2, p. 631; *Jianguo Yilai Mao Zedong Wengao* 9, p. 467.

149   See ibid., pp. 467–70, for a summary of Hu Qiaomu's Shaoshan report; see also ibid., pp. 489–91. *Zhu De Xuanji* (Selected works of Zhu De), p. 440, n. 318.

150   *Dangdai Zhongguode Sichuan* 1, pp. 108–9. For Mao's unmistakable rebuke to Li Jingquan, see Mao, *Shuxin*, pp. 580–1; see also *Jianguo Yilai Mao Zedong Wengao* 9, pp. 484–5, 488, 496–8. Mao had, however, received a formal report about discussions in the Southwest region of the Sixty Articles; see *Zhou Enlai Shuxin Xuanji* (A selection of Zhou Enlai's letters), pp. 571–3. Li's failure to write personally may have reflected annoyance that Mao should have circulated a report by an outsider (Hu Qiaomu), junior to himself, about his bailiwick. For Li Jingquan's resentment of Tian Jiaying's efforts in 1958 to persuade the Sichuan provincial party not to push excessively close planting, see Li Rui, *Lushan Huiyi Shilu* (A true record of the Lushan conference), pp. 89–90. Despite a circular issued by Mao on the basis of Tian's findings, Li Jingquan maintained the close-planting policy in Sichuan. For Li Jingquan's attack on Tian at the Lushan conference, see Li, *The Private Life of Chairman Mao*, p. 319. At about the same time that Li was reaffirming his faith in mess-halls, the Zhejiang party 1st secretary, Jiang Hua, was reporting to Mao that the masses wanted their dissolution; *Dangdai Zhongguode Zhejiang* 1, p. 80.

151   Ibid.; *Zhu De Xuanji*, pp. 374–5.

152   *Zhou Enlai Shuxin Xuanji*, p. 571.

153   Cong Jin, *Quzhe Fazhande Suiyue*, p. 378; *Zhu De Xuanji*, p. 375; Jiang Boying, *Deng Zihui Zhuan* (A biography of Deng Zihui), p. 344. The premier may have been delayed by having to prepare Foreign Minister Chen Yi for the Geneva conference on Laos; Zou Aiguo & Xue Jianhua, *Zhongguo Da Guang Jiao (1)*, pp. 9–11. It seems unlikely that Liu Shaoqi was ready to tell Mao when they met in Changsha only ten days after his Hunan investigation had begun that mess-halls should be eliminated. According to a Cultural Revolution source, the Beijing municipal party report on the ownership of tools and draught animals was submitted to the CC on 17 May and its report

on mess-halls on 18 May; see *Peng zei 'Huairou diaocha' shi Liu, Deng hei silingbu yinmo fanpi zibenzhuyide yanzhong buji*, pp. 15, 21.

154 *Mao Zedong he tade Mishu Tian Jiaying*, pp. 57–8. Mao's caution on the Sixty Articles was belied shortly thereafter by the upbeat report which reached him from the CC's Rural Work Dept.; *Jianguo Yilai Mao Zedong Wengao* 9, pp. 548–9. For an insider's account of the Lushan clash, see Li Rui, *Lushan Huiyi Shilu*; for the present author's analysis, see *Origins* II, pp. 188–251.

155 *Nongye Jitihua, xia*, pp. 492–7.

156 The figures given in the Rural Work Department report were somewhat different from these year-end figures and may not be exactly comparable: 25,204 communes before the first draft of the Sixty Articles was issued in late Mar., 55,682 in late Aug.; 483,814 brigades then, 703,912 now; 2,988,168 teams then, 4,549,474 now. See ibid., pp. 492–3. I have used the later figures on the grounds that a report hurriedly prepared in the few weeks between the Beijing and Lushan conferences, doubtless in the hopes of pleasing leaders, would be more likely to contain errors than statistics re-calculated under less pressure afterwards. An indication of the slender basis and hurried nature of the report was that in discussing problems it cited only one province, Jiangsu. According to one report, teams were further divided into smaller units a year later; Chan, Madsen, & Unger, *Chen Village*, pp. 31–5. This account also indicates how cadres used their powers to gerrymander the reapportionment of land in favour of family and friends.

157 *Nongye Jitihua, xia*, pp. 492–3.

158 Ibid., pp. 494–6.

159 In the course of nine hours of conversation, Mao told Montgomery (who later described the Chairman as 'a very great man, a most uncommon man in an age of common men') that the 1960 harvest had only been 150 m. tons, but said that the 1961 one was expected to be 160 m. tons; the actual figures for those years were 143 m. and 147 m. tons respectively. After travelling widely throughout the country, Montgomery's unequivocal conclusion was: 'Talk of large-scale famine, of grim want, of apathy, of a restless nation, is nonsense, maybe even dangerous . . . The bad harvests of 1959 and 1960 did indeed create a food problem and necessitated the introduction of rationing; but there is enough for all though some may not now get as much as formerly. China has had to tighten its belts in parts, but there has been no large-scale famine'; *Sunday Times* (London), 15 Oct. 1961, Magazine Section, p. 25. Possibly Mao did not inform Montgomery as he did another foreign visitor: 'Don't listen to all those people. They just trot out the good figures to impress you. When they ask you to go with them to visit someplace, believe me, they're putting their best foot forward. The achievement is not as great as you think. *It's all been arranged beforehand for your benefit.* Don't believe it for a minute'; Phathanothai, *The Dragon's Pearl*, p. 194 (emphasis added).

160 *Nongye Jitihua, xia*, pp. 519–20; Guofang Daxue, *Cankao Ziliao* 23, p. 448; *Mao Zedong he tade Mishu Tian Jiaying*, pp. 59–60; *Jianguo Yilai Mao Zedong Wengao* 9, pp. 562–4. Mao also records details about a commune in Tang *xian* in Baoding district, west of the rail line to Beijing, over 200 miles further north. He did not, it seems, have time for a personal visit there on the same day, but got his information from the Baoding district secretary, Li Yuenong, who attended the Handan meeting; Zhonggong Hebei Shengwei Dangshi Yanjiushi (ed.), *Lingxiu zai Hebei* (Leaders in Hebei), p. 363.

¹⁶¹ Mao is said to have given a friendly reception to a report by Tao Zhu and Wang Renzhong concerning a radical departure from the collective system in Guangxi province, where a seven-family production group (*shengchanzu*) farmed as households with individuals taking responsibility for their work (*tudi daohu, zeren daoren*). On the basis of the success this system displayed in raising output, Tao and Wang suggested more widespread establishment of *shengchanzu*, implementing linked production (*lianxi chanliang*), individual responsibility, and bonuses for exceeding targets. Mao apparently commended the report, describing its content and suggestions as Marxist, and delegating Tao, Wang, and another Central-South official, Hunan 1st secretary Zhang Pinghua, to draft a decision for the CC based on this experience. In the end, the experience was not spread around, because there were 'comrades who disagreed with it'. The curious aspects of this account are (a) Mao's welcome for a proposal that could have undermined collectivism; (b) the ability of other officials to have dissemination of the experience aborted even if Mao were in favour of that course. Perhaps Mao was persuaded that a tiny experiment in a remote mountain area inhabited by ethnic minorities was inapplicable to the Han heartland. See *Xinhua Yuebao*, No. 11, 1989, p. 50.

¹⁶² *Jianguo Yilai Mao Zedong Wengao* 9, pp. 565–73, 580–3; *Mao Zedong he tade Mishu Tian Jiaying*, pp. 59–60. (According to one source, Mao was already persuaded of the preferability of team accounting as early as Apr. 1961 as a result of a meeting with Wang Renzhong and other Hubei officials; Zhonggong Hubei Shengwei Dangshi Ziliao Zhengbian Weiyuanhui [ed.], *Mao Zedong zai Hubei* [Mao Zedong in Hubei], p. 335.) Either even Mao had not yet got the nomenclature straight or he was determined that he should not be misunderstood as to what he meant by *dui* as he seems to have been in 1959, because he referred to the team by its old title *xiaodui* not by its current one, *dui*! For the 1959 problem, see *Origins* II, p. 161. For discussions of confusion over nomenclature see ibid., pp. 181–4, and the research note by Gao Yi in *DSYJ*, No. 1, 1982, p. 36, in which he points out that the official designation of the lowest level of rural collective organization (team) as *dui* was ordained in a central document issued on 22 Mar. 1961, though the old term *xiaodui* persisted even in the reports of Liu Shaoqi and old hands responsible for rural affairs like Deng Zihui, as well as Mao. See, for instance, 'Liu Shaoqi yu 1962 nian 1 yue 27 ri zai guangdade zhongyang gongzuo huiyishangde jianghua' (Liu Shaoqi's speech of 27 Jan. 1962 to the enlarged [Seven Thousand Cadres] central work conference; hereafter, Liu 27/1/62 mimeo. version), the unexpurgated version of Liu's speech on that occasion, p. 9.

¹⁶³ Guofang Daxue, *Cankao Ziliao* 23, pp. 519–20.

¹⁶⁴ *Mao Zedong he tade Mishu Tian Jiaying*, p. 60; see also Bo Yibo, *Ruogan Zhongda Juece* 2, pp. 938–42.

¹⁶⁵ Guofang Daxue, *Cankao Ziliao* 23, p. 520.

¹⁶⁶ *Peng Dehuai Zishu* (Peng Dehuai's autobiography), pp. 257–8.

¹⁶⁷ In *Origins* II, pp. 77–82, it was argued that Chen Boda elaborated the concept of the communes and that Mao endorsed and refined it. Years later, Chen Boda confirmed this; see Ye Yonglie, *Chen Boda Qiren*, pp. 181–3. According to Informant S, however, the commune concept was already in use in leadership circles, and Chen merely publicized it.

¹⁶⁸ As Winston Churchill discovered in 1945 and George Bush in 1992, the

political kudos from victory in war are a highly perishable political commodity.

169 The quotation is from a member of his staff, Pang Xianzhi; see *Mao Zedong he Tade Mishu Tian Jiaying*, pp. 68–9. For a confirmation of this judgement, see 'Deng Zihui Zhuan' Bianji Weiyuanhui, *Deng Zihui Zhuan* (A life of Deng Zihui), p. 566.

170 *Nongye Jitihua, xia,* p. 518.

171 *Mao Zedong he Tade Mishu Tian Jiaying,* p. 60; *Jianguo Yilai Mao Zedong Wengao* 10, pp. 48–50.

172 The internal version of the commentary on the 1981 resolution on party history confirms that ever since the formation of higher APCs in 1956, there had been a basic contradiction over the fact that the unit of management was the team or its equivalent, while the unit of accounting was the brigade or its equivalent. This contradiction was resolved by this decision of Mao's. See Zhonggong Dangshi Yanjiuhui, *Xuexi Lishi Jueyi Zhuanji,* pp. 122, 139. See also *Mao Zedong he Tade Mishu Tian Jiaying,* p. 60.

173 Hu Sheng & Zhonggong Zhongyang Dangshi Yanjiushi (eds.), *Zhongguo Gongchan Dangde Qishi Nian* (The seventy years of the CCP), p. 385.

CHAPTER 4

1 Liao Gailong *et al., Xin Zhongguo Biannianshi,* pp. 188–9. There were also 'Six Articles' on banking issued in March 1962 (see *Shanghai Jingji, 1949–1982,* p. 817), 'Six Articles' on finance (*Li Xiannian Lun Caizheng, Jinrong, Maoyi* [Li Xiannian on finance, banking, trade], *xia,* p. 86); 'Thirty-two Articles' on films (*Zhou Yang, Xia Yan, Chen Huangmei zai dianying fangmian fan-dang fan-shehuizhuyi fan-Mao Zedong sixiang zuixing lu* [A record of the anti-party, anti-socialist, anti-Mao Zedong Thought crimes of Zhou Yang, Xia Yan and Chen Huangmei in the film sector], pp. 42–8); 'Ten Articles' on public security (Zhou & Shao [eds.], *Xin Zhongguo Fazhi Jianshe Sishi Nian Yaolan*). (In 1968, a further 'Six Articles' on public security were issued: Chan, Madsen, & Unger, *Chen Village,* p. 143. For a village leader who used this later document to threaten peasants, see Wu & Li, *A Single Tear,* pp. 263, 279, 294, 305.)

2 According to a Chinese tabulation, the following were the numbers of directives and decisions on commerce laid down by the CC and/or the State Council during these years: 1958: 25; 1959: 12; 1960: 22, 1961: 13; 1962: 21; 1963: 18; 1964: 7; 1965: 9; 1966: 8. Mao made four major pronouncements on commerce in 1958, six in 1959, two in 1960, five in 1961, but only one each in 1962 and 1963, none in 1964, two in 1965, and one in 1966. The most influential figure in the making of commercial policy in the early 1960s, Chen Yun, is credited with three utterances in 1961 and two in 1962 before he fell silent again. Whenever Chen Yun was out of the picture, Li Xiannian seems to have emerged as the main spokesman on commerce: 1959: 7; 1960: 6; 1961: 1; 1962: 1; 1963: 4; 1965: 4. See *Shangye Dashiji,* pp. 872–4. During the 1961 spate of high-level investigations, Hu Yaobang, 1st secretary of the YCL, examined rural commerce in Liaoning and wrote a report which Mao pronounced very good; *Jianguo Yilai Mao Zedong Wengao* 9, pp. 507–9.

3 Ibid., p. 512. The formal title of the Forty Articles was 'Certain stipulations on the reform of commercial work (experimental draft)'; the text is contained in Guofang Daxue, *Cankao Ziliao* 23, pp. 484–9.

[4] The utopian views of GLF radicals are contrasted with those of bureaucrats in charge of the commercial sector in Solinger, *Chinese Business under Socialism*, p. 71.

[5] The socialization of commerce was basically started and completed in a few weeks in late 1955 and early 1956, a process so rapid that it brought about chaos similar to that experienced during the GLF; see *Origins* I, pp. 19–25. For an explication of the complexity of the commercial network, see Solinger, *Chinese Business under Socialism*, pp. 33–47; for a post-Mao orthodox description of commerce under the CCP, see Liu Fuyuan, Tang Gonglie, & Luo Lixing (eds.), *Zhongguo Shehuizhuyi Shangye Jingji* (The economy of socialist commerce in China).

[6] Zhonggong Zhongyang Wenxian Yanjiushi, *Guanyu Jianguo Yilai Dangde Ruogan Lishi Wentide Jueyi Zhushiben (Xiuding)* (Revised annotated edition of the Resolution on the History of our Party since the Founding of the State; hereafter, *Jueyi Zhushiben Xiuding*), p. 304. For a concise account of these changes, see 'Dangdai Zhongguo' Congshu Bianjibu (ed.), *Dangdai Zhongguo Shangye* (Contemporary China's commerce) 1, pp. 79–83. Without throwing doubt on the latter work's account of successive structural changes in the commercial sector, it is worth observing that it seems to have been written from the viewpoint of central planners who disliked loss of control almost as much as the chaos which was certainly precipitated by the GLF innovations.

[7] The Chinese phrase was *fazhan shengchan, fanrong jingji, chengxiang huzu, neiwai jiaoliu*. It appeared in art. 2; see Guofang Daxue, *Cankao Ziliao* 23, p. 484.

[8] Art. 4, ibid., pp. 484–5.

[9] See above, Ch. 1.

[10] Arts. 8 and 11, ibid., p. 485.

[11] Art. 13, ibid., p. 486.

[12] Art. 15, ibid.

[13] Sections 4–6, ibid., pp. 487–8.

[14] Arts. 16 and 17, ibid., p. 486.

[15] *Shangye Dashiji*, p. 266; perhaps its informal status explains why little appears to have been published about the Hundred Articles.

[16] *Jiti he Geti Shangye Wenjian Xuanbian* (Selected documents on collective and individual commerce), pp. 195–6. To judge by his conduct in the 1980s reform period, Yao Yilin's remarks in 1961 were dictated by conviction rather than expediency. He subscribed to Chen Yun's simile of the planned economy as the necessary cage within which the bird of free marketing and individual enterprise had to be confined.

[17] *Shangye Shigao*, pp. 206–7. The importance of a formal CC decision is illustrated by retrospective accounts of commercial activities in Sichuan and Liaoning provinces during these years; they refer neither to the Forty Articles nor to the Hundred Articles, but rather to the CC 'decision' on commercial work in 1962. See Zhonggong Sichuan Shengwei Yanjiushi (ed.), *Sichuan Sheng Qing* (Information on Sichuan province; hereafter, *Sichuan Sheng Qing*), p. 577; Zhongguo Shehui Kexue Yuan Caimao Wuzi Jingji Yanjiusuo & Shangyebu Jiaoyuju (eds.), *Lun Shangpin Liutong: Shangpin Liutong Jingji Lilun Taolunhui Wenji* (On the circulation of commodities: papers from the symposium on the economic theory of the circulation of commodities; hereafter, *Lun Shangpin Liutong*), p. 75.

18   Ibid., p. 74.
19   See Gu Hua's novel *A Small Town Called Hibiscus*, pp. 16–17, which closely reflects his observations in the Hunan countryside.
20   The implication of the 1978 nationwide figure was one retail outlet for every 1,000 people, an 80% reduction in the 1957 proportions; the drop in the number of shops was accompanied by a drop in the number of shop personnel just as the population of the cities was doubling. *Lun Shangpin Liutong*, pp. 30, 51–3. This source (p. 53) also comments on the high-and-mighty attitudes that could be adopted by shop assistants in their commanding positions.
21   The restoration of the SMCs had also been suggested at the Canton work conference in March; *Shangye Shigao*, p. 203.
22   Ibid., p. 210.
23   *Lun Shangpin Liutong*, p. 107.
24   Liu & Wu, *China's Socialist Economy*, p. 285. For other indications that it was not until 1962 that errors in the commercial sector began to be corrected, see *Lun Shangpin Liutong*, pp. 93, 190, 242; see also, *Dangdai Zhongguode Liangshi Gongzuo*, p. 135.
25   *Liu Shaoqi Xuanji, xia*, pp. 358, 500, n. 160.
26   *Nongye Jitihua, xia*, p. 575. Deng contrasted these two provinces where trade in grains other than rice and wheat was permitted with the rest of the country where it was mostly strictly forbidden.
27   Ma Hong & Sun Shangqing (eds.), *Zhongguo Jingji Jiegou Wenti Yanjiu* (Research into problems of China's economic structures), p. 172. This was considerably down from the 1936 figure of 65%; see Riskin, *China's Political Economy*, p. 20. For a succinct description of the handicraft industry, see Donnithorne, *China's Economic System*, pp. 220–4. For a description of CCP policy towards handicrafts in the first half of the 1950s by one of the leaders of the sector, see *Cheng Zihua Huiyilu* (Memoirs of Cheng Zihua), pp. 337–66.
28   Ma Hong & Sun Shangqing, *Jingji Jiegou Wenti Yanjiu*, pp. 172–3, 175. By 1957 the proportions of handicraft workers in town and country had changed dramatically, with only 35.9% placed in the rural areas.
29   Peasant part-timers were of course members of APCs.
30   The precise percentages were: locally managed factories, 48%; co-operative factories, 22%; commune factories, 30%; see Ma Hong & Sun Shangqing, *Jingji Jiegou Wenti Yanjiu*, p. 176. These percentages differ from those given at the time of the GLF, as quoted in Donnithorne, *China's Economic System*, p. 224. For uncertainty as to the exact number of full-time handicraftsmen, see ibid., p. 221.
31   Ma Hong & Sun Shangqing, *Jingji Jiegou Wenti Yanjiu*, pp. 175–7.
32   Quoted in Riskin, *China's Political Economy*, p. 275.
33   Ma Hong & Sun Shangqing, *Jingji Jiegou Wenti Yanjiu*, pp. 176–7.
34   'Zhongguo Shehui Kexue' Jingji Bianjishi (ed.), *Jingjixue Wenji, 1980* (Collection of articles on economics, 1980), pp. 514–15. For further instances of the impact of the GLF on handicraft production and on consumers, see Donnithorne, *China's Economic System*, p. 225.
35   *Jianguo Yilai Mao Zedong Wengao* 9, p. 512. The Thirty-five Articles are reprinted in Zhongguo Shehui Kexue Yuan Gongye Jingji Yanjiusuo Qingbao Ziliaoshi (ed.), *Zhongguo Gongye Jingji Fagui Huibian, 1949–1981* (A collection of laws and regulations on China's industrial economy,

1949–1981; hereafter, *Zhongguo Gongye Jingji Fagui Huibian*), pp. 18–23. Virtually all sources agree that the Thirty-five Articles were issued on the same day as the Forty Articles on Commerce, but one source says 22 June; see Hong Chenghua & Guo Xiuzhi, *Zhengzhi Tizhi Yange Dashiji*, p. 225.

36 Art. 1, *Zhongguo Gongye Jingji Fagui Huibian*, p. 18.

37 Arts. 2 and 3, ibid.

38 Arts. 7 and 8, ibid., p. 19.

39 Arts. 9 and 10, ibid.

40 Ibid., pp. 19–23.

41 Zhongguo Shehui Kexue Yuan Gongye Jingji Yanjiusuo Qiye Guanli Yanjiushi (ed.), *Zhongguo Gongye Guanli Bufen Tiaoli Huibian* (A collection of some regulations on China's industrial management; hereafter, *Zhongguo Gongye Guanli Bufen Tiaoli Huibian*), p. 208. The directive on industry is discussed in the next section.

42 *Cheng Zihua Huiyilu*, p. 402. The same source (p. 404) indicates that this hesitancy applied across the board.

43 Ma Hong & Sun Shangqing, *Jingji Jiegou Wenti Yanjiu*, p. 177.

44 Ibid., pp. 177, 178.

45 Liu & Wu, *China's Socialist Economy*, pp. 272–3, 279; *Cheng Zihua Huiyilu*, p. 404.

46 *Renminde Hao Zongli* 2, p. 288. This is a post-Cultural Revolution account, but one written several months before the restoration of the CCP old guard to power at the famous 3rd plenum of December 1978 which led, 18 months later, to Liu Shaoqi's rehabilitation. Thus it refers to the late state chairman as seizing the opportunity of the three years of 'temporary' economic difficulties to restore capitalism and cut back the iron and steel industry. This article was authored by the Theory Group of the Ministry of the Metallurgical Industry, the very ministry which, in 1959, led by its minister, Wang Heshou, had fought fiercely if unsuccessfully against the cutbacks in the steel target advocated at that time by Chen Yun; see *Origins* II, pp. 165–70. In 1978, Chen Yun was a CC member in good standing and re-emerging as a major political figure behind the scenes, as political insiders like this theory group might have known; he, therefore, could not be attacked with impunity, but with the CCP Chairman, Hua Guofeng, still proclaiming the correctness of the Cultural Revolution, Liu Shaoqi must have seemed like fair game. Since Zhou Enlai, like Chen Yun, had been criticized by Mao at the beginning of the GLF for opposing reckless advance (ibid., p. 25), he might seem like an unlikely hero in this context; but this theory group would have remembered that it was also Zhou who fulfilled the face-saving task assigned him by Mao of ensuring that the 1958 steel campaign should at least nominally reach its target (ibid., p. 113; *Renminde Hao Zongli* 2, pp. 293–4). Whether Liu and Zhou were as sharply opposed in 1961 as suggested awaits further documentation, but the brief reference cited here from *Renminde Hao Zongli*, clearly indicates that the Ministry of the Metallurgical Industry was defending its turf as fiercely in 1961 as two years earlier.

47 *DSYJ*, No. 6, 1980, p. 24. It is not clear how the percentages given in this authoritative article were arrived at since they do not seem to fit with those obtainable from the absolute figures given in *TJNJ, 1983*, pp. 245, 323. But the overall picture of construction outstripping raw-material supplies is confirmed in the latter source.

48 *DSYJ*, No. 6, 1980, pp. 24–5.

⁴⁹ Liu & Wu, *China's Socialist Economy*, pp. 279–80.
⁵⁰ Ibid., p. 280.
⁵¹ See *Origins* II, part 3. For an account of the worries and warnings of Zhuo Lin, Deng Xiaoping's wife, about her husband suffering Peng Dehuai's fate at Lushan if he did not restrain his speeches, see Liu Jintian (ed.), *Deng Xiaopingde Licheng: Yige Wei Ren he Tade Yige Shiji* (Deng Xiaoping's course: A great man and his century) 2, p. 5.
⁵² Translated in *Chinese Literature*, No. 5, 1966, p. 9. Mao refers to Jiang Qing as 'Comrade Li Jin'; Li was her family name, Li Jin an occasional pen name. One biographer reports that Chinese believed the poem was less about nature than about Mao's revived sexual interest in his wife; see Terrill, *The White-Boned Demon*, p. 238.
⁵³ *Cheng Zihua Huiyilu*, p. 403. For the same argument in a document produced at the Lushan meeting, see *Zhongguo Gongye Guanli Bufen Tiaoli Huibian*, p. 202. Cheng Zihua, who took up his post as executive vice-chairman of the State Planning Commission on 28 Jan. 1961, talks of Mao and Liu Shaoqi suggesting capital construction be cut back at the Shanghai conference as if it took place in 1961; but this conference, and the subsequent Beidaihe meeting to which Cheng also refers, both took place in 1960 before he took office, and there is no other evidence of Mao sanctioning industrial cutbacks that early. See *Cheng Zihua Huiyilu*, p. 403; for the date of his appointment, see p. 684. There is no obvious reason for Cheng's elevation to the key position on the State Planning Commission under Li Fuchun. Perhaps his role was to stiffen Li's resolve in the face of the resistance he would undoubtedly meet when trying to get GLF radicals to accept the cutbacks. As it was, Li went sick in early 1962 and Zhou Enlai took over supervision of the planning commission; *Cheng Zihua Huiyilu*, p. 404. For a brief discussion of Li Fuchun's possible inability to stand up to pressure, see below, n. 78. Interestingly, a long-serving senior member of the planning commission (Wang Guangwei) has revealed that even in the drafting of the 1st FYP, it was Zhou Enlai and Chen Yun rather than Li who took charge, and that in the case of the 2nd FYP, it was also Zhou. In the latter instance, Li was apparently in Moscow on a trip not recorded in the standard biographical dictionaries. See *Huainian Zhou Enlai*, pp. 42–3. For Mao's high appraisal of Zhou's work on the 2nd plan—totally undermined 18 months later by the GLF—see ibid., p. 44.
⁵⁴ *Zhongguo Gongye Guanli Bufen Tiaoli Huibian*, pp. 199–200.
⁵⁵ To judge by the way targets were set (see below), 1961 was taken as the first year of the periods laid down by the CC at Lushan, even though the language (*jinhou qiniannei*) suggests otherwise.
⁵⁶ *Tiaozheng, gonggu, chongshi, tigao*; see above, Introduction and *Origins* II, p. 323.
⁵⁷ *Zhongguo Gongye Guanli Bufen Tiaoli Huibian*, p. 202; Guofang Daxue, *Cankao Ziliao* 23, p. 532.
⁵⁸ See above, Ch. 1.
⁵⁹ *TJNJ, 1983*, p. 245.
⁶⁰ Ibid., p. 244. The drop in coal output, while precipitous, may have been less significant than the figures indicate, since the quality of much of the coal produced during the GLF was inferior; I am grateful to Nicholas Lardy for this point; see also *Origins* II, pp. 166–70.
⁶¹ *Zhongguo Gongye Guanli Bufen Tiaoli Huibian*, p. 202.

[62] Ibid., pp. 203–5.
[63] *TJNJ, 1983*, p. 244.
[64] *CYWG*, p. 127; *Chen Yun's Strategy*, p. 174.
[65] *TJNJ, 1983*, p. 244.
[66] *Chen Yun's Strategy*, p. 174. For Chen Yun's 1959 investigation into the coal industry, see ibid., pp. 120–1, and *Origins* II, p. 168.
[67] *CYWG*, pp. 148–9; *Chen Yun's Strategy*, pp. 175–6. This speech is not included in *CYWX*.
[68] See the estimates of the distribution of reserves in Wu, *Economic Development and the Use of Energy Resources in Communist China*, p. 36; according to Vaclav Smil, 'China's Energetics: A System Analysis', in Joint Economic Committee, *Chinese Economy Post-Mao*, p. 339, 60% of output came from the north and northeast and only 17% from the south.
[69] *CYWG*, pp. 147–52; *Chen Yun's Strategy*, pp. 174–80.
[70] Jilin Radio, 28 Aug. 1967.
[71] The serious implications of the parlous condition of the coal industry is underlined by comparison with the electrical power industry. While the output of electrical generating equipment declined even more precipately than that of mining equipment, the output of electric power only dipped to 77% of the GLF high, and by 1963 was rising again, whereas coal output had dropped by almost 50% before it started rising again in 1965; *TJNJ, 1983*, pp. 244, 248. This confirms that supplies of fuel to coal-fired power stations were maintained, while other customers were rationed. According to one almost contemporary Western analysis, in 1960 power plants accounted for 13.17% of coal consumption; calculated from Wu, *Economic Development and the Use of Energy Resources in Communist China*, p. 119. Though this analysis also estimated there to be a coal surplus of up to 73.18 m. tons in 1960, which would not seem to accord with the worries of China's leaders, the percentage seems to be about right to judge by later official figures. In 1976, the power industry was responsible for 16.6% of coal consumption, a figure which had risen to 20.1% by 1978; see World Bank, *China: Socialist Economic Development*, Annex E: Energy, p. 30.
[72] *Zhongguo Gongye Guanli Bufen Tiaoli Huibian*, pp. 205–6. For a discussion of Chen Yun's commitment to the concept of overall or comprehensive balance, see *Chen Yun's Strategy*, pp. xv–xviii. For Mao's attitude, see *Origins* II, p. 296.
[73] *Zhongguo Gongye Guanli Bufen Tiaoli Huibian*, pp. 207–8.
[74] Ibid., pp. 208–15.
[75] For a discussion of the investigation, see Li Guang'an, Wang Guizhen, & Qin Ming (eds.), *Jinian Li Fuchun* (Remembering Li Fuchun), pp. 120–6.
[76] 'Deng Xiaoping Da Cidian' Bianji Weiyuanhui, *Deng Xiaoping Da Cidian* (A compendium on Deng Xiaoping), p. 460.
[77] The size of the local task force is reported in a hostile Cultural Revolution account of Bo Yibo's activities; see *Liaolian Zhan Bao* (Liaoning Alliance Combat News), 21 July 1967, p. 4, cols. 1–2.
[78] *Jingji Dashiji*, pp. 292–3, 316–18. The fullest (and first-hand) account of the investigation and drafting process is contained in Bo Yibo, *Ruogan Zhongda Juece* 2, pp. 952–60. Even in this latter source, it is not clear why Li Fuchun, having led the investigation, was not charged with summarizing its findings and drafting a programme; nor why the ten-man group was set up in January at the suggestion of the premier, but not activated until June.

No mention of any connection between Li Fuchun and the Seventy Articles is given in his biography in *Zhonggong Dangshi Renwuzhuan* 44, pp. 1–112. There is evidence suggesting that Li was a weak leader, unable to unite the Planning Commission behind him during the GLF, and therefore dependent on support from elsewhere, notably Wang Heshou, Minister of the Metallurgical Industry; see Li Rui, *Lushan Huiyi Shilu*, pp. 88, 91. In one of his speeches at the 1959 Lushan conference, Mao referred to criticisms of Li as 'going to make a step forward but hesitates, and about to speak but stammers'; see *The Case of Peng Teh-huai, 1959–1968*, p. 26. Be that as it may, the members of the ten-man small group were Bo Yibo; Gu Mu, a vice-chairman of the State Economic Commission and Bo's deputy in running this team; Wang Heshou; Zhang Linzhi, Minister of the Coal Industry; Lü Zhengcao, acting Minister of Railways; Zhao Erlu, until recently Minister of the 1st Ministry of Machine Building (covering most civilian machinery), but at this time a vice-chairman of the State Economic Commission; Liu Lanbo, a vice-minister of the Ministry of Water Conservancy and Electric Power; Peng Tao, a vice-chairman of the State Planning Commission, who died in Nov. 1961; Chen Zhengren, a one-time secretary to Mao, now the Minister of Agricultural Machinery; and Sun Zhiyuan, Minister of the 3rd Ministry of Machine Building (conventional weapons). For the list of names, see *Womende Zhou Zongli*, p. 11. Despite Zhou's role in its formation, and although its members were recruited on the basis of their government portfolios, this small group was formally set up by Deng Xiaoping and was answerable to the CC secretariat; see ibid., and *Liushi Nian Dashi Jianjie*, p. 491; Zhonggong Zhongyang Dangshi Yanjiushi Keyanju (ed.), *Mao Zedongde Zuji* (The footprints of Mao Zedong), pp. 513–15; *Deng Xiaoping Wenxuan (1938–1965)*, p. 259; *Selected Works of Deng Xiaoping (1938–1965)*, p. 280. The preparation of the Seventy Articles differed from that of the Sixty Articles on Agriculture, in that economic specialists were consulted for the Seventy Articles; see Halpern, 'Economic Specialists and the Making of Chinese Economic Policy, 1955–1983', ch. 4. For the duties of the Ministries of Machine Building, see Donnithorne *China's Economic System*, pp. 150, 520. Zhao Erlu had been the founding minister of the 2nd Ministry of Machine Building in 1952 when it was in charge of aircraft, tanks, and munitions (*Jianguo Yilai Mao Zedong Wengao* 3, p. 529).

79 Zhonggong Zhongyang Dangshi Yanjiushi Keyanju, *Mao Zedongde Zuji*, pp. 513–15; *Selected Works of Deng Xiaoping (1938–1965)*, p. 280; *Deng Xiaoping Wenxuan (1938–1965)*, p. 259. Mao seems to have made only one modification of the directive promulgating the Seventy Articles, excising the phrase 'using Mao Zedong Thought'; *Jianguo Yilai Mao Zedong Wengao* 9, pp. 560–1.

80 For a full text of the Seventy Articles, see Guojia Jingji Weiyuanhui Jingji Faguiju & Beijing Zhengfa Xueyuan Jingjifa Minfa Jiaoyanshi (eds.), *Zhonghua Renmin Gongheguo Gongye Qiye Fagui Xuanbian* (A selection of the PRC's laws and regulations on industrial enterprises; hereafter, *Gongye Qiye Fagui*), pp. 45–73; substantial extracts are included in Zhonghua Quanguo Zonggonghui Zhengce Yanjiushi (ed.), *Zhongguo Qiye Lingdao Zhidude Lishi Wenxian* (Historical documents on the leadership system of Chinese enterprises), pp. 244–58. To the best of the present author's knowledge, no full text of the Seventy Articles, or of any of the other programmatic documents drawn up at this time, was openly published

contemporaneously. Prior to the early 1980s, foreign scholars' knowledge of the Seventy Articles was derived either from hostile accounts and short quotations in Cultural Revolution sources or from terse and not totally accurate summaries made available in Taiwan and Hong Kong.

81 *Gongye Qiye Fagui*, p. 48. For the evolution of the slogan of the GLF in 1958, see *Origins* II, pp. 42, 351, n. 54. For Cultural Revolution criticism of the Seventy Articles, see for instance 'Smash "70 Articles for Industry", a Revisionist Black Program', *Yu-tien Chan-pao* (Post and Tele-Communication combat bulletin), 28 June 1967, translated in SCMP(S) 210, pp. 27–31; for a sympathetic summary of attacks on the Seventy Articles, see Andors, *China's Industrial Revolution*, pp. 129–34, 187–91. One allegation made by Cultural Revolution sources was that the Seventy Articles 'mentions *nothing* about the invincible thought of Mao Tse-tung' (SCMP(S) 210, p. 28; emphasis added), whereas in addition to the admittedly nuanced advocacy of studying Mao's works in art. 6, art. 70 adjured enterprise party committees to lead cadres in the study of how 'Comrade Mao Zedong clarified the theoretical and practical problems of our national socialist construction'; *Gongye Qiye Fagui*, p. 73. Another allegation made by Cultural Revolution sources (SCMP[S] 210, p. 27) was that the Seventy Articles were in opposition to the 'Charter' of the Anshan Iron and Steel Company, praised by Mao in March 1960 for its emphasis, among other things, on the mass movement in industry; but cultural revolutionaries failed to cite any evidence of Mao fighting for the retention of the principles of the Anshan charter during the economic crisis of 1961. For a longer discussion of the Anshan charter, see *Origins* II, pp. 306–9; for a report on how, in the mid-1960s, Liaoning officials compared the Anshan charter unfavourably with the Seventy Articles, see *Liaolian Zhan Bao*, 21 July 1967, p. 3, col. 2.

82 In art. 64; *Gongye Qiye Fagui*, p. 70.

83 See Bo Yibo, *Ruogan Zhongda Juece* 2, pp. 960–2; *Jingji Dashiji*, pp. 316–17; Cong Jin, *Quzhe Fazhande Suiyue*, p. 390; *Liushi Nian Dashi Jianjie*, p. 492; SCMP(S) 210, p. 30.

84 These provisions are included in the document's lengthy art. 8; see *Gongye Qiye Fagui*, pp. 48–9.

85 Ibid., p. 49. This provision may have been designed to enable the state to tighten the screws annually, but it was doubtless also used by inefficient managers to justify a bail-out by their superior unit, as envisioned in Kornai's theory of the 'soft budget constraint'; see Kornai, *The Road to a Free Economy*, p. 62 and *passim*.

86 *Gongye Qiye Fagui*, pp. 62–4.

87 Ibid., pp. 64–6, 68–9; Bo Yibo, *Ruogan Zhongda Juece* 2, pp. 962–7. For a discussion of this issue, see Chung, *Maoism and Development*, pp. 163–8.

88 Quoted in Andors, *China's Industrial Revolution*, p. 69.

89 Ibid., p. 100.

90 *Jingji Yanjiu*, No. 15, 1962, quoted in Chung, *Maoism and Development*, p. 163.

91 Ibid., pp. 163–5.

92 Ibid., pp. 165–8. For another discussion of the new-found range of discretion of the factory manager at this time, see Schurmann, 'China's "New Economic Policy"—Transition or Beginning', in Li (ed.), *Industrial Development in Communist China*, pp. 76–80.

93 *Gongye Qiye Fagui*, pp. 51–4.

[94] Quoted in Cheng, *Scientific and Engineering Manpower in Communist China, 1949–1963*, p. 182; emphasis added here.

[95] *Gongye Qiye Fagui*, pp. 682–91.

[96] Ibid., pp. 56–62. The quotation is on pp. 56–7.

[97] Andrew Walder has pinpointed the 'vague' term *biaoxian* (manifestation) as a result of his interviews with Chinese workers as one which encompasses overlapping aspects of a 'good work attitude' which became an important element in the determination of wages, bonuses, and other compensations during the GLF; see Walder, *Communist Neo-Traditionalism*, pp. 132–43.

[98] See the report of Richman, *Industrial Society in Communist China*, pp. 234–42; the quotation appears on pp. 236–7. Richman, who did his factory survey in April–June 1966, appears not to have been informed about the Seventy Articles by his Chinese hosts.

[99] In Wuxi, Jiangsu, on 14 December, Mao scolded the municipal party 1st secretary for still experimenting with the Seventy Articles some two months after the document had been promulgated; Zhonggong Jiangsu Shengwei Dangshi Gongzuo Weiyuanhui & Jiangsu Sheng Dang'anju (eds.), *Mao Zedong zai Jiangsu*, p. 79.

[100] From the beginning there were party secretaries who resisted the Seventy Articles; see *Qi Qian Ren Dahui Ziliao* (Materials from the seven thousand man conference), p. 39.

[101] Andors, *China's Industrial Revolution*, pp. 104–32; the percentages are on p. 119. Chung also emphasizes the wide variety of management practices from industry to industry and factory to factory; see *Maoism and Development*, pp. 163, 167.

[102] *Dangdai Zhongguo Jingji*, pp. 357–8.

[103] Andors, *China's Industrial Revolution*, pp. 132–42.

CHAPTER 5

[1] As for instance in an article by An Ziwen, deputy director of the CC's Organization Department, discussed in *Origins* I, p. 306.

[2] In his speeches during the Hundred Flowers period (1956–7), Mao strove valiantly to persuade suspicious subordinates of the crucial importance of the talents of bourgeois professors to the CCP's economic enterprises; see for instance, MacFarquhar, Cheek, & Wu (eds.), *The Secret Speeches of Chairman Mao*, pp. 331–6.

[3] See *Origins* I, p. 314; II, pp. 40–2.

[4] This is Stalin's oft-quoted description of writers; see for instance, Conquest, *Stalin: Breaker of Nations*, p. 209.

[5] For the impact of the 1983–4 'spiritual pollution' campaign directed against the intellectuals upon rural attitudes and economic reform, see Schram, ' "Economics in Command?" Ideology and Policy Since the Third Plenum, 1978–84', *CQ*, No. 99, 1984, pp. 417–61.

[6] Zhongyang Jiaoyu Kexue Yanjiusuo (ed.), *Zhonghua Renmin Gongheguo Jiaoyu Dashiji, 1949–1982* (A chronicle of education in the PRC, 1949–1982; hereafter, *Jiaoyu Dashiji*), pp. 282, 285.

[7] Bo Yibo, *Ruogan Zhongda Juece* 2, p. 985.

[8] 'Fourteen opinions on the current work of natural science research institutes (draft)'; see the pamphlet published during the Cultural Revolution,

Zhanduan Liu, Deng shenxiang keji jiede hei shou (ziliao huibian 7): Keyan 'Shisi tiao' zhuanji (4) (Cut off the black hand of Liu [Shaoqi, and] Deng [Xiaoping] stretched out towards the scientific and technical circles (7th collection of material): Special edition on the 'Fourteen Articles' on science research [4]), pp. 23–33. Earlier drafts (Feb., fifteen articles; Apr., fourteen articles) are also printed in ibid., pp. 6–22. Although the science programme is normally referred to as the 'Fourteen Articles' to conform with the other programmatic documents produced in 1961, its authors actually advanced fourteen 'opinions', perhaps reflecting a caution born of experience.

⁹ The text of the 'Provisional articles on the work of institutions of higher learning directly under the PRC Ministry of Education (draft)' is published in 'Zhongguo Jiaoyu Nianjian' Bianjibu (ed.), *Zhongguo Jiaoyu Nianjian, 1949–1981* (China education yearbook, 1949–81; hereafter, *Jiaoyu Nianjian*), pp. 693–9. The CCP also started to draw up the Forty Articles on Primary Education and the Fifty Articles on Middle School Education (texts in ibid., pp. 699–705) in July 1961, but they were not distributed until March 1963; see *Jueyi Zhushiben Xiuding*, pp. 308–9.

¹⁰ 'Opinions on certain current problems in literature and art work (draft)'; see ibid., pp. 313–17.

¹¹ 'Articles on the work of theatres (and troupes) [revised draft]', and 'Opinions on strengthening the creation and management of fiction films (draft)'. These latter two documents were never formally approved by the CC, but the drafts were circulated for discussion and trial application. See *Zhou Enlai Xuanji, xia*, pp. 524–5, n. 288, and *Selected Works of Zhou Enlai 2*, p. 546, n. 262.

¹² Gong Yuzhi, Pang Xianzhi, & Shi Zhongquan, *Mao Zedongde Dushu Shenghuo*, pp. 83–97; *Origins* I, pp. 33–5.

¹³ There is no mention of his participation in the chapter on 'Mao Zedong and the natural sciences', in Gong Yuzhi, Pang Xianzhi, & Shi Zhongquan, *Mao Zedongde Dushu Shenghuo*, pp. 83–114, nor in the section on the Fourteen Articles in Nie Rongzhen, *Inside the Red Star*, pp. 713–27 (*Nie Rongzhen Huiyilu* [The memoirs of Nie Rongzhen], *xia*, pp. 822–38).

¹⁴ In addition to the source mentioned in n. 8 above, other collections of materials (*ziliao huibian*) in that series have items relevant to this topic: Nos. 2, 3, and 5. See also *Keji Geming* (Science and technology revolution), No. 1, 1967; *Keyan Pipan* (Scientific research criticism), No. 2, 1968, where there is a reference (p. 37) to 'Seventy-two Articles' on scientific research prepared under the auspices of Zhang Jingfu (see below) of the Chinese Academy of Sciences; *Keda Hongweibing: 1, Kexue geming zhuanji* (Science and Technology University Red Guard: 1, Special issue on science revolution), No. 2, 1968; *Da pipan beijing cailiao* (Background material on the great criticism), July 1967; *Chedi qingsuan jiu zhong xuanbu yanwangdian shenxiang kexue jishu gongzuozhongde hei xian* (Thoroughly settle accounts with the black line of the old CC Propaganda Department, Palace of Hell, towards science and technology work), July 1967. The following attempt to disentangle the way in which the Fourteen Articles emerged perforce relies partly on these sources, which, despite their obvious biases, are often quite precise. Marshal Nie Rongzhen's memoirs (*Inside the Red Star; Nie Rongzhen Huiyilu*) written after the Cultural Revolution, are another major source, for he played a crucial role in science policy-making. But though full they are less detailed, say nothing about changes in the successive drafts, and give the impression of

his being in hands-on charge throughout, whereas it does seem as if he were out of the loop in the early stages of the process. My analysis benefits from the spadework done on the Cultural Revolution materials by my research assistants at the Wilson Center, Bonnie Glaser and Jeffrey Wang.

15 See Klochko, *Soviet Scientist in Red China*, pp. 66–78.

16 Nie, *Inside the Red Star*, p. 714; *Nie Rongzhen Huiyilu, xia*, pp. 823–4. In the early 1960s, there were some 1,300 scientific research institutes and over 94,000 research personnel; Li Ping, *Kaiguo Zongli Zhou Enlai*, p. 406.

17 A separate Chinese Academy of Social Sciences (CASS) was set up after the Cultural Revolution.

18 *Da pipan beijing cailiao*, pp. 1–2; for a collection of what Cultural Revolution radicals termed reactionary utterances made at this meeting, see *Zhanduan Liu, Deng shenxiang keji jiede hei shou (ziliao huibian 5)*, passim.

19 See for instance, MacFarquhar, *The Hundred Flowers Campaign and the Chinese Intellectuals*, pp. 85–6.

20 *Zhanduan Liu, Deng shenxiang keji jiede hei shou (ziliao huibian 7)*, p. 1.

21 Ibid., pp. 1–2; *Chedi qingsuan jiu zhong xuanbu yanwangdian shenxiang kexue jishu gongzuozhongde hei xian*, p. 8; *Da pipan beijing cailiao*, p. 5.

22 The preamble and art. 1 of the February draft clearly indicate that the document was intended for in-house use.

23 Nie, *Inside the Red Star*, pp. 659–60.

24 Lewis & Xue, *China Builds the Bomb*, pp. 53–4.

25 *Nie Rongzhen Huiyilu, xia*, p. 825. For Nie's friendship with Deng Xiaoping, dating back to their worker/student days in France, see [Deng] Maomao, *Deng Xiaoping: Wode Fuqin* (Deng Xiaoping: My father), p. 80.

26 Lewis & Xue, *China Builds the Bomb*, pp. 48–59.

27 For the membership of the small group, see Nie, *Inside the Red Star*, p. 784, n. 120.

28 For attacks on Zhang Jingfu and Han Guang, see for instance, *Keyan Pipan*, No. 2, 1968, pp. 1–13; *Zhanduan Liu, Deng shenxiang keji jiede hei shou (ziliao huibian 7)*, pp. 1–2; *Keji Zhan Bao* (Science and technology combat news), 22 May 1967, pp. 3–7. Despite the attacks, Zhang Jingfu surfaced again towards the end of the Cultural Revolution as Minister of Finance 1975–9, and held a number of important posts thereafter; see his biographical entry in *Who's Who in China*, pp. 930–1. In his memoirs, Marshal Nie constantly uses the pronoun 'we' when describing the various actions taken in the formulation of the Fourteen Articles, but then says, 'I signed the document and submitted it to the Central Committee'; see Nie, *Inside the Red Star*, p. 715.

29 *Da pipan beijing cailiao*, p. 6.

30 Ibid., pp. 6–7.

31 The three texts are in *Zhanduan Liu, Deng shenxiang keji jiede hei shou (ziliao huibian 7)*, pp. 6–33.

32 Cf. ibid., pp. 6, 13, 23.

33 See *Origins* I, pp. 105–8, 149–50.

34 See Mao's letter to General Xiao Ke, 24 May 1953, in *Jianguo Yilai Mao Zedong Wengao* 4, p. 238; in another context, he had earlier sanctioned the excision of the 'Thought of Mao Zedong', ibid., p. 192. For a later allegation that this decision was a result of the machinations of Liu Shaoqi and Deng Xiaoping, see *Da pipan beijing cailiao*, p. 7.

35 In arts. 7 and 13; *Zhanduan Liu, Deng shenxiang keji jiede hei shou (ziliao*

huibian 7), pp. 27, 31; it is in art. 13 (p. 21) that the April version has no reference to Mao's works.

36 See *Origins* II, pp. 318–22.

37 *Jiaoyu Dashiji*, p. 291. The phrase 'better left than right' appears to have been used by Lu as an example of another simplistic utterance.

38 For the origins of this slogan, see *Origins* II, pp. 42, 351, n. 54.

39 *Zhanduan Liu, Deng shenxiang keji jiede hei shou (ziliao huibian 7)*, pp. 6, 13–14, 23.

40 The additional article—it was the first—in the February version concerned the duties of the CAS; ibid., pp. 6–7.

41 Ibid., pp. 7, 14–15, 16, 23–4, 25–6. According to *Nie Rongzhen Huiyilu, xia*, p. 828, the encouragement to scientists to be bold was known as *san gan*, the 'three dares'; for one of Mao's speeches on this theme, see *Origins* II, pp. 40–1.

42 One of the criticisms levelled by the Stalin Prize-winning Soviet chemist at Chinese science was the intense secrecy which cut scientific institutions off from each other; quoted in Pepper, 'New Directions in Education', *Cambridge History of China* (hereafter, *CHOC*) 14, p. 415.

43 *Zhanduan Liu, Deng shenxiang keji jiede hei shou (ziliao huibian 7)*, pp. 9–12, 13, 16–20, 21, 26–8, 29–30, 31–2.

44 Ibid., p. 20.

45 Ibid., pp. 20, 31.

46 Ibid., pp. 21, 31. For the use of the phrase during the Hundred Flowers, see *Origins* II, p. 212.

47 *Zhanduan Liu, Deng shenxiang keji jiede hei shou (ziliao huibian 7)*, pp. 21, 31.

48 Ibid., pp. 22, 32.

49 Nie, *Inside the Red Star*, pp. 717–19.

50 Marshal Nie's report, dated 20 June 1961, together with the leadership's favourable comment on it, is in Guofang Daxue, *Cankao Ziliao* 23, pp. 499–512.

51 Nie, *Inside the Red Star*, p. 719.

52 Guofang Daxue, *Cankao Ziliao* 23, p. 502.

53 Ibid., pp. 509–11; Nie, *Inside the Red Star*, pp. 720–1; *Zhanduan Liu, Deng shenxiang keji jiede hei shou (ziliao huibian 7)*, pp. 13–14, 20–1, 22, 23, 30–1, 32–3.

54 Nie, *Inside the Red Star*, pp. 715–17.

55 Cf. *Nie Rongzhen Huiyilu, xia*, pp. 826–7, and *Da pipan beijing cailiao*, pp. 7–8.

56 Nie, *Inside the Red Star*, p. 716; *Nie Rongzhen Huiyilu, xia*, pp. 826–7; *Da pipan beijing cailiao*, p. 7; see also, *Zhanduan Liu, Deng shenxiang keji jiede hei shou (ziliao huibian 2)*, p. 5.

57 *Da pipan beijing cailiao*, p. 7.

58 The whole phrase is: 'Zongde lai shuo, chengji weida, wenti bushao, qiantu guangming'; see *Mao Zedong sixiang wan sui (1967)*, p. 63.

59 Marshal Nie's quote is in fact longer: Nie, *Inside the Red Star*, p. 716; *Nie Rongzhen Huiyilu, xia*, p. 826; *Da pipan beijing cailiao*, p. 8.

60 Bo Yibo, *Ruogan Zhongda Juece* 2, p. 986.

61 *Da pipan beijing cailiao*, p. 8.

62 *Jiaoyu Dashiji*, p. 291.

63 Nie, *Inside the Red Star*, pp. 717, 721–2.

64 *[Mao Zedong] Xuexi Wenxuan* (Selected documents of Mao Zedong] for study) 3, p. 319.

65 The speech was on 10 Aug.; *Chen Yi Tan Hong yu Zhuan* (Chen Yi discusses red and expert), pp. 13–24.

66 Ibid., pp. 13–15.

67 *Na you shemme yong ne?*; ibid., pp. 15–18.

68 Ibid., p. 17. Probably the bulk of the students in Chen Yi's audience were from the numerous Beijing professional schools (which resembled the French *grandes écoles*), set up under various industrial ministries, rather than from the Chinese equivalent of a liberal arts college like Peking University.

69 Ibid., pp. 18–19.

70 See for instance *Wenge Fengyun* (Cultural Revolution storm), No. 5, 1967, pp. 12–13. While this source gives both 10 Aug. and 20 Sept. for the quotes here, nearly all appear to come from the 10 Aug. speech, unless he made a virtually identical one a month later.

71 For a description of educational radicalism in 1958, see *Jiaoyu Nianjian*, pp. 91–2; Pepper, 'New Directions in Education', pp. 400–11; *Origins* II, pp. 108–13. For major Cultural Revolution critiques, see *Dou Pi Gai Tongxun* (Struggle, criticism, transformation newsletter), No. 16, 29 June 1967, pp. 3–16.

72 Pepper, 'New Directions in Education'; *Origins* II, pp. 108–13.

73 *Jiaoyu Nianjian*, p. 236.

74 Ibid., p. 92.

75 Ibid., where it seems that the CC secretariat not the ministry of education was in charge; Pepper, 'New Directions in Education', pp. 411–14.

76 *Jiaoyu Nianjian*, p. 93; *Origins* II, pp. 315–18.

77 This point is illustrated by the decline in the number of major statements or decisions on education: *1958*: Mao—4; Liu—2; Zhou—1; Deng—0; Lu Dingyi—1; Lin Feng—1; CC/SC (State Council) directives—4; *1959*: Mao—0; Liu—0; Zhou—2; Deng—0; Lu—2; Lin Feng—0; CC/SC—7; *1960*: Mao—0; Liu—0; Zhou—0; Deng—0; Lu—1; Lin Feng—1; CC/SC—5; *1961*: Mao—1; Liu—0; Zhou—0; Deng—1; Lu—1; Lin Feng—0; CC/SC—2; *1962*: Mao—0; Liu—0: Zhou—2; Deng—0; Lu—0; Lin Feng—0. Source: *Jiaoyu Dashiji*, p. 683.

78 *Dou Pi Gai Tongxun*, No. 16, 29 June 1967, p. 12. Curiously, Zhou Yang is also quoted as complaining that another problem was excessive scientific research.

79 Lin Feng is identified as a member of the small group in *Jiaoyu Dashiji*, p. 290; Zhang Jichun, Zhou Yang, and Yang Xiufeng are identified as speakers at this conference which, in addition to their posts, suggests their membership; see ibid., p. 285. However, while Zhang and Yang attended the small group meeting summoned to discuss the Sixty Articles in July, Zhou did not; see *Dou Pi Gai Tongxun*, 29 June 1967, p. 14. This source indicates that Lu Dingyi chaired the small group and states that Kang Sheng was deputy chair. Attendees at this meeting also included Zhang Ziyi, a deputy director of the Propaganda Department, Jiang Nanxiang, the drafter of the Sixty Articles, and Liu Zizai, like Jiang a deputy minister of education. Since the CCP practice was to keep a 'small' group small, these three men were probably attending as expert advisers, but it is possible that they too were members.

80 *Jiaoyu Dashiji*, pp. 285, 288–9; *Jiaoyu Nianjian*, p. 93.
81 *Jiaoyu Dashiji*, pp. 294–5.
82 *Jiaoyu Nianjian*, p. 93.
83 *Dou Pi Gai Tongxun*, No. 16, 29 June 1967, p. 13.
84 Ibid.; *Jiaoyu Dashiji*, p. 298; 'A record of the great events in the struggle between the two lines in the field of higher education', *Jiaoxue Pipan* (Pedagogical critique), 20 Aug. 1967, translated in *Chinese Sociology and Anthropology*, Fall–Winter 1969–70, p. 55. In 'Chronology of the two-road struggle on the educational front in the past 17 years', *Jiaoyu Geming* (Educational revolution), 6 May 1967, translated in JPRS 41,932 (21 July 1967), p. 36, the drafters of the Sixty Articles are listed as Lin Feng, Zhang Jichun, and Jiang Nanxiang. Jiang was to become minister of higher education in Jan. 1965.
85 *Jiaoyu Dashiji*, p. 298; *Jiaoyu Nianjian*, pp. 93, 254, 511, 692–3, 942–3; *Chen Yi Tan Hong yu Zhuan*, pp. 12–24; *Dou Pi Gai Tongxun*, No. 16, 29 June 1967, pp. 13–16.
86 Ibid., No. 16, pp. 13–14. Among the colleagues Jiang asked to help him in this task was He Dongchang, the deputy party secretary at Qinghua, who in 1985 would become vice-minister in charge of the State Education Commission.
87 Ibid., pp. 14–15. For the origins of this phrase, see the description of the confrontation between Monkey and the Buddha in Yu, *The Journey to the West* 1, pp. 171–4.
88 *Dou Pi Gai Tongxun*, No. 16, 29 June 1967, p. 15. The other members of this group were Cheng Jinyu, a Propaganda Department official; Lin Jianqing, deputy chief of the science division of the Propaganda Department, who re-emerged in various party posts after the Cultural Revolution and became an alternate member of the CC at the CCP's 12th Congress in 1982; and Gong Yuzhi, a long-time researcher in the department, whose first post-Cultural Revolution job was as a senior official of the committee for publishing Mao's works, and who went back to the Propaganda Department as deputy head in 1988.
89 Ibid., pp. 14–15. This was not the only group of which Kang Sheng was a member which produced a 'revisionist' programme in the first half of the 1960s. He was the only member of Peng Zhen's five-man small group on cultural revolution not to be purged at the outset of the Cultural Revolution. Conceivably, as the radicals later claimed, Kang was for one reason or another not responsible for the supposedly sinister activities of these groups—it is certainly true that he played a key role in the drafting of anti-Soviet polemics—but it is also possible that Kang, while retaining radical views, thought discretion the best course in the post-GLF crisis. There is no record of him attending the small group meeting in July in the chronologies included in the education volumes.
90 Ibid., p. 15.
91 The participants on the educational side included Lu Dingyi, Kang Sheng, Lin Feng, Zhang Jichun, Tong Dalin, Cheng Jinyu, Jiang Nanxiang, and Li Shouci of Qinghua University; ibid. See also Bo Yibo, *Ruogan Zhongda Juece* 2, p. 987.
92 *Dou Pi Gai Tongxun*, No. 16, 29 June 1967, pp. 15–16. Unfortunately, there is no record of Deng's remarks at this meeting in *Deng Xiaoping Wenxuan (1938–1965)*, published after the Cultural Revolution.
93 *Dou Pi Gai Tongxun*, No. 16, 29 June 1967, p. 16.

94 Bo Yibo, *Ruogan Zhongda Juece* 2, pp. 987–8.

95 *Jiaoyu Nianjian*, p. 237.

96 *Dou Pi Gai Tongxun*, No. 16, 29 June 1967, p. 16.

97 The formal title was Provisional Work Articles for Institutions of Higher Education directly under the PRC Ministry of Education (Draft). The text is in *Jiaoyu Nianjian*, pp. 693–9. There were ten sections: general principles, teaching, productive labour, training graduate students, scientific research, teachers and students, facilities and living conditions, ideology and politics, leadership system and administrative organization, CCP organization and work.

98 These were the criteria introduced into the original speech when it was published after the period of free criticism was brought to a halt on 8 June 1957; see *Origins* I, pp. 262–9, and MacFarquhar, Cheek, & Wu, *The Secret Speeches of Chairman Mao*, pp. 131–89.

99 *Jiaoyu Nianjian*, p. 694. The two types of contradiction are again drawn from Mao's 1957 contradictions speech; see *Origins* I, pp. 184–6.

100 See *Origins* II, pp. 108–13.

101 *Jiaoyu Nianjian*, pp. 694–6.

102 See *Origins* II, pp. 225–7, 287.

103 See *Jianguo Yilai Mao Zedong Wengao* 9, pp. 535–6, and *Mao Zedong sixiang wan sui (1967)*, pp. 267–8; CB 891, p. 36. For a discussion of Jiangxi Gongda, see Pepper, 'New Directions in Education', pp. 406–8.

104 Tung & MacKerras (eds.), *Drama in the People's Republic of China*, pp. 2–5. The figures given here indicate that about one-third of the performances each year were staged specially in factories, mines, villages, and military bases, where the audiences of workers, peasants, and soldiers made up between 45% and 48% of the total.

105 Snow, *The Other Side of the River*, p. 257.

106 Chiang Ching (Jiang Qing), *On the Revolution of Peking Opera*, p. 2.

107 *Mao Zedong, Zhou Enlai, Liu Shaoqi, Zhu De, Deng Xiaoping, Chen Yun Lun Dangde Qunzhong Gongzuo* ([These leaders] discuss the party's work among the masses), p. 139. Only an extract from this speech, which was made on 19 June at a conference on artistic creation, is included in this source, and it appears to be one of the few the premier made on culture in 1961. It has not been widely publicized, so it presumably did not play a defining role at this time. The main function of the United Front Work Department was to deal with ethnic minorities and to work with the organizations of private businessmen and the minor ('democratic') parties, some of which included intellectuals among their number. But the UFWD was probably also discredited with the intellectuals. In May 1957, the UFWD had invited non-party people to air their criticisms of the CCP at a series of forums, but later some had their remarks there used against them; MacFarquhar, *The Hundred Flowers Campaign and the Chinese Intellectuals*, pp. 38–58. Certainly Li Weihan, the director of the UFWD, seems to have been more active with ethnic minorities and businessmen in 1961, and in late 1962 he would be criticized as a revisionist. See Li Weihan, *Huiyi yu Yanjiu* (Memories and researches) 2, pp. 859–78; *Li Weihan Xuanji* (Selected works of Li Weihan), pp. 362–431.

108 *Origins* I, pp. 53–6, 92–6, 190–1, 247.

109 Ibid., pp. 52, 201; MacFarquhar, *The Hundred Flowers Campaign and the Chinese Intellectuals*, pp. 175, 177–8.

110 See *Origins* I, parts 3 and 4.

111 See ibid. II, pp. 40–2.
112 This is a major part of the argument of *Origins* I, parts 3 and 4. According to the official line in post-Mao historiography as enshrined in the 1981 *Resolution on CPC History (1949–1981)*, there were no serious differences between Mao and Liu before the 1960s. This line was reaffirmed in the summer of 1984, when the present author expounded the arguments of *Origins* I and II in two lectures in Beijing at the CASS Institute of Marxism-Leninism–Mao Zedong Thought before an audience drawn from various CCP think-tanks in Beijing. During the question period after the second lecture, a senior party historian commented on the argument of the first lecture, stating flatly that 'we' do not believe that there were any differences between Mao and Liu over the Rectification and Anti-Rightist Campaigns. Acknowledging that the commentator clearly knew more about the inner history of the CCP than himself, the author repeated the main pieces of evidence that had led him to his conclusions and asked for further comment or rebuttal. Neither was forthcoming. One issue was whether or not Liu Shaoqi attended Mao's speech on contradictions on 27 Feb. 1957 (see *Origins* I, appendix 7). In an interview with a different party historian in 1984, the author was informed that Liu had been present on that occasion; but the historian was unable to explain why he had not been shown in the *RMRB* photograph taken of that historic occasion. In a subsequent interview some years later, the same party historian expressed forgetfulness as to whether Liu had indeed attended that occasion.
113 Chen Yun spoke and wrote a fair amount on Pingtan in the 1959–62 period; see 'Chen Yun Tongzhi guanyu Pingtande Tanhua he Tongxin' Bianji Xiaozu (ed.), *Chen Yun Tongzhi guanyu Pingtande Tanhua he Tongxin* (Comrade Chen Yun's talks and correspondence on Pingtan).
114 Zhong Kan, *Kang Sheng Pingzhuan* (A critical biography of Kang Sheng), pp. 144–5; and Lin Qingshan, *Kang Sheng Waizhuan* (An unofficial biography of Kang Sheng), pp. 181–4.
115 Zhongguo Shehui Kexue Yuan Wenxue Yanjiusuo & 'Zhongguo Wenxue Yanjiu Nianjian' Bianji Weiyuanhui (eds.), *Zhongguo Wenxue Yanjiu Nianjian, 1981* (Chinese literary research yearbook, 1981; hereafter, *Zhongguo Wenxue Yanjiu Nianjian*), pp. 483–4; 'Dangdai Zhongguo Renwu Zhuanji' Congshu Bianjibu (ed.), *Chen Yi Zhuan* (A biography of Chen Yi; hereafter, *Chen Yi Zhuan*), p. 530.
116 For accounts of his period in France, see *Renminde Zhongcheng Zhanshi: Mianhuai Chen Yi Tongzhi* (The people's loyal warrior: Remembering Comrade Chen Yi), pp. 14–62; *Chen Yi Zhuan*, pp. 8–19.
117 *Fifty Years of the Chinese People's Liberation Army*, p. 121. Chen had earlier been denied entry into the French branch of this university, the Institut Franco-Chinois in Lyons, and had been arrested and deported from France along with other Chinese worker/students for occupying the institute building in protest; Klein & Clark, *Biographic Dictionary of Chinese Communism* I, p. 105; *Chen Yi Zhuan*, pp. 16–19.
118 For his poetry, see *Chen Yi Shici Xuanji* (Selected poetry of Chen Yi). For a bracketing of his poetry with Mao's, see *Selected Works of Zhou Enlai* 2, p. 338; in *Zhongguo Dangdai Wenxue Shi Chugao* (A preliminary draft history of contemporary Chinese literature), *xia*, pp. 444–89, Mao's poetry rates a chapter, Chen Yi's rates a section, while Zhou Enlai, Dong Biwu, and Zhu De have to share a section. For a Chinese justification of Chen Yi's

right to speak on intellectual matters, see *Chen Yi Zhuan*, pp. 525–6. In June 1958, Chen Yi presided over the 750th anniversary celebration of the Yuan dynasty playwright Guan Hanqing; Wagner, *The Contemporary Chinese Historical Drama*, p. 25. For Li Xiannian's opinion of Chen Yi as a 'man of culture' whose opinion on a controversial film would be sounder than his own, see Zhongguo Shehui Kexue Yuan Wenxue Yanjiusuo Tushu Ziliaoshi (ed.), *Zhou Enlai yu Wenyi* (Zhou Enlai and literature and the arts; hereafter, *Zhou Enlai yu Wenyi*), *shang*, p. 67; for Chen Yi's admission that at one time he had intended to pursue a literary career, see ibid., p. 69; for his knowledge of Soviet novels, English and French poetry, and the plays of Shaw, Ibsen, and French authors, see ibid., p. 70; for Chen Yi's cultural responsibilities in 1954, see ibid., p. 72.

[119] See *Origins* I, part 4; II, pp. 40–2.
[120] For a brief discussion of Chen Yi's character, see *Origins* II, pp. 74–5.
[121] Translated in *Fifty Years of the Chinese People's Liberation Army*, p. 140; for an alternative translation, see Hsu, *Literature of the People's Republic of China*, p. 525; the original is in *Chen Yi Shici Xuanji*, p. 254.
[122] For a brief description of Sichuan opera in the early 1960s and a comparison with Peking opera, see Han, *My House Has Two Doors*, pp. 353–4.
[123] *Zhongguo Wenxue Yanjiu Nianjian*, pp. 483–4.
[124] Ibid., pp. 477–8, 479–80. Cao Cao was a wily statesman at the end of the Eastern Han dynasty in the early 3rd century AD; *CHOC* I, pp. 350–5. The Empress Wu ruled for fifteen years during the Tang dynasty and was excoriated ever after by Chinese historians who disapproved of her usurpation of the male line; *CHOC* 3, Pt. 1, pp. 306–21. The PRC's pre-eminent intellectual, Guo Moruo, the president of the Chinese Academy of Sciences, had recently written plays to rehabilitate Cao Cao (*Cai Wenji*, 1959) and the Empress Wu (*Wu Zetian*, 1960); Guo Moruo, *Five Historical Plays*, pp. vii–ix, 317–521. The leading playwright Tian Han would publish a Peking opera on Wu Zetian (*Xie Yaohuan*) later in 1961; see the discussion in Wagner, *The Contemporary Chinese Historical Drama*, pp. 80–138. Zeng Guofan was a mid-19th-century defender of the crumbling Qing dynasty, much admired by his fellow Hunanese Mao Zedong in his youth; see Kuhn, *Rebellion and its Enemies in Late Imperial China*, pp. 135–52, and Schram, *Mao Tse-tung*, p. 51. Among the other ambiguous historical characters alluded to by Chen Yi was Li Zicheng (*Zhongguo Wenxue Yanjiu Nianjian*, p. 479), who was responsible for bringing down the Ming dynasty in 1644, but was quickly overthrown by the invading Manchus. Chen pointed out that Li was obviously worthy since he had led a popular uprising against a dynasty, but that he also had shortcomings or he would not have been defeated. Two years later, conceivably encouraged by Chen Yi's speech, the writer Yao Xueyin published the first volume of a long-planned, multi-volume novel about this complex character, and was enabled by Mao's protection to continue working on his saga throughout the Cultural Revolution. See Yao Xueyin, *Li Zicheng* I, preface; and FBIS-CHI-91-076, p. 25.
[125] *Zhongguo Wenxue Yanjiu Nianjian*, p. 479.
[126] Ibid., pp. 479–80, 482. This play is discussed below in Ch. 18.
[127] Ibid., p. 481.
[128] Ibid., p. 486.
[129] Ibid., p. 477.
[130] See *Selected Works of Zhou Enlai* 2, pp. 333, 353. For Zhou's speech on the intellectuals in Jan. 1956, see *Origins* I, pp. 33–5.

131 *Selected Works of Zhou Enlai* 2, pp. 344, 348, 349. Chen Yun's comments were made on 14 Feb. 1961 to leading members of the literature and arts section of the CC's Propaganda Department, and are to be found in 'Chen Yun Tongzhi guanyu Pingtande Tanhua he Tongxin' Bianji Xiaozu (ed.), *Chen Yun Tongzhi guanyu Pingtande Tanhua he Tongxin*, p. 51.

132 *Selected Works of Zhou Enlai* 2, p. 331.

133 Ibid., p. 334.

134 Ibid., pp. 336-7. The description in the final sentence of the ideal political environment comes from remarks made by Mao at the Qingdao conference of July 1957, when the Chairman was trying to find a compromise formula that would enable him to salvage some of the aims of the Rectification Campaign amidst the hurly-burly of the Anti-Rightist Campaign. See *Origins* I, pp. 286-7.

135 *Selected Works of Zhou Enlai* 2, p. 345.

136 Ibid., pp. 337-40, 348, 353-4.

137 Ibid., p. 346. Zhou did refer to one of the major speeches during the course of which Mao had laid out the Hundred Flowers policy; ibid., p. 341.

138 For favourable post-Cultural Revolution recollections of Zhou's performance and its impact at the time, see *Zhou Enlai yu Wenyi, shang*, pp. 106-24, 129-41.

139 URI, *Who's Who in Communist China* I, p. 427. Lin was promoted to deputy directorship of the Propaganda Department in Aug. 1961. Little has been publicized about his behaviour during the Hundred Flowers period, but he did support the controversial author Wang Meng; see *Origins* I, p. 373, n. 37.

140 *Wenyi Zhan Bao* (Literature and arts combat news), 30 June 1967, p. 3. This hostile Cultural Revolution source was clearly condemning Lin Mohan's guarantee, not the practice of doctoring people's remarks so as to use them as evidence in struggle sessions.

141 Ibid.

142 His colleagues were Yuan Shuipai, Cai Ruohong (a painter), and Yi Bing; ibid.

143 Ibid., p. 4. For He Qifang, see Ch. 1 above. Zhang Guangnian was a literary critic, a secretary of the Union of Chinese Writers, and editor-in-chief of *Wenyi Bao* (Journal of literature and the arts). Ironically, He and Zhang had recently been at loggerheads as a result of Zhang's criticisms of He; see Goldman, *Literary Dissent in Communist China*, p. 268.

144 *Wenyi Zhan Bao*, 30 June 1967, p. 4.

145 The ten articles are reproduced in ibid., 30 June 1967, pp. 5-6, 8. The copy of the Eight Articles made available to the present author was xeroxed from pp. 260-73 of an unnamed text; despite the lack of provenance, the authenticity of the document seems strong. Referred to hereafter as Eight Articles, source.

146 Bo Yibo, *Ruogan Zhongda Juece* 2, p. 1004.

147 For a discussion of the congress, see Jerome Ch'en, 'Writers and Artists Confer', *CQ*, No. 4, 1960, pp. 76-81.

148 This is the version in the Eight Articles, source, p. 261. For earlier uses of these slogans, see *Origins* I, pp. 52-3.

149 One aspect of this populism, the 'million poem' movement, is discussed in S. H. Chen, 'Multiplicity in Uniformity: Poetry and the Great Leap Forward', *CQ*, No. 3, 1960, pp. 1-15.

150 For a translation of the earlier version of Mao's talks, see McDougall, *Mao Zedong's 'Talks at the Yan'an Conference on Literature and Art': A Translation of the 1943 Text with Commentary*; for a discussion of their political significance, see Goldman, *Literary Dissent in Communist China*, ch. 2; for accounts of the Anti-Rightist Campaign, see ibid., ch. 9, and *Origins* I, part 4.

151 This particular change was pinpointed by Bo Yibo, *Ruogan Zhongda Juece* 2, p. 1004.

152 The introductions to the two documents are in *Wenyi Zhan Bao*, 30 June 1967, p. 5, for the ten articles, and pp. 260–2 of the Eight Articles, source. Zhou Yang had been secretary of the party group in the ministry from perhaps 1951 to 1954; see his biography in Klein & Clark, *Biographic Dictionary of Chinese Communism*. Lin Mohan had probably been the secretary since becoming a vice-minister of culture in 1959.

153 Bo Yibo, *Ruogan Zhongda Juece* 2, pp. 1004–5, confirms that this omission of the distinction between the political and the artistic spheres was no accident.

154 In Chinese editorials, directives, programmes, and other documents giving guidance to cadres, the customary format was to reaffirm current policies in the first section, and then, after a 'but' (*danshi*), to lay out the real message, the innovations that were desired. In both the ten articles and the Eight Articles, the cautionary codicils came before the 'but', the new 'licence' after it.

155 Eight Articles, source, pp. 262–4. This topic is discussed in section 2 of the second of the ten articles; *Wenyi Zhan Bao*, 30 June 1967, p. 5. During the Cultural Revolution, much indignation was expressed against an article masterminded by Zhou Yang and Lin Mohan and published in *Wenyi Bao* in Mar. 1961, which advocated a broad approach to the question of subject-matter; see for instance SCMP 3860, pp. 10–16. For a Cultural Revolution attack on Zhou Yang's pre-PRC activities, coupled with his autobiographical account of the 1930s compiled under pressure, see *Jinggangshan Zhan Bao* (Jinggangshan combat news), 11 Aug. 1967.

156 Bo Yibo, *Ruogan Zhongda Juece* 2, p. 1005.

157 For a discussion of the introduction of these criteria into the published version of this speech, see *Origins* I, pp. 262–6; for the official version of this process, see *Jianguo Yilai Mao Zedong Wengao* 6, pp. 358–60; for the original text of the speech, minus the criteria, see MacFarquhar, Cheek, & Wu, *The Secret Speeches of Chairman Mao*, pp. 131–89.

158 Ten articles, art. 6, *Wenyi Zhan Bao*, 30 June 1967, p. 6; Eight Articles, source, art. 4, pp. 267–8.

159 Bo Yibo, *Ruogan Zhongda Juece* 2, p. 1005.

160 Whereas in this connection the Eight Articles cited the traditional operas validated by Chen Yi, the ten articles specifically referred to the heritage of the past 40 years, a provision presumably designed to legitimate acceptable works written since the May Fourth Movement of 1919, when the grandees of the communist literary establishment, and their fellow-travellers, began their careers.

161 Here the Eight Articles was more specific, calling for full-time writers to be guaranteed ten months for their calling, for those writers who had administrative, teaching, or editorial duties to be guaranteed one to three months time for creative work, and for manual labour to be restricted to a month or even half a month; art. 5, Eight Articles, source, p. 268. Presumably this

greater precision was motivated by a realization that the generalized strictures of the ten articles on this subject would be too easy for cultural cadres to circumvent.

[162] On the issue of CCP leadership of the arts, the ten articles was typically blunter: it was wrong to feel the party could not perform in this sphere (a rebuttal of a recurring criticism during the earlier Hundred Flowers), but in that leadership, the CCP had been guilty of subjectivism (the blind application of Marxist theory), commandism (the issuing of orders without checking on their feasibility), and sectarianism (discrimination against non-party people), precisely the sins which Mao had hoped to correct with the aborted Rectification Campaign of 1957; see *Origins* I, p. 111, where the term 'bureaucratism' rather than 'commandism' is used. The Eight Articles was vaguer and less accusatory; cf. its art. 8 with art. 10 in the earlier document, *Wenyi Zhan Bao*, 30 June 1967, pp. 8, 10, and Eight Articles, source, pp. 272–3.

[163] For the earlier speeches by these men, see *Origins* I, pp. 33–5, 51–6, 92–6, 184–9, 201, 204.

[164] Tao Zhu made a series of speeches in the second half of 1961 advocating a more conciliatory policy towards intellectuals and non-party people; see 'Tao Zhu Wenji' Bianji Weiyuanhui (ed.), *Tao Zhu Wenji* (Collected works of Tao Zhu), pp. 251–66.

[165] Bo Yibo, *Ruogan Zhongda Juece* 2, pp. 1005–6, admits that taken by themselves the changes embodied in the Eight Articles were not incorrect, but that at the time they represented an attempt to circumscribe correct policies with political criteria.

[166] Informant B. In his extended account of the emergence of the more constrictive Eight Articles, Bo Yibo significantly did not blame the ideological 'heavies' of the Cultural Revolution like Kang Sheng or Chen Boda. Bo could not directly point the figure at Lu Dingyi if he were the promoter of the changes, for he was a fellow victim of the Cultural Revolution, and because he was alive and in good political standing at the time when Bo's book was published. However, Bo was able to quote Deng Xiaoping to hint at Lu's leftism on a later occasion (Bo Yibo, *Ruogan Zhongda Juece* 2, p. 1007).

[167] Ibid., pp. 1008–9.

[168] For one of the many assertions that none of the 1961 policies was seriously implemented until after the Seven Thousand Cadres Conference, see Zhang Suhua, Bian Yanjun, & Wu Xiaomei, *Shuo bujinde Mao Zedong* (An endless story of Mao Zedong), p. 216.

CHAPTER 6

[1] See *Origins* II, pp. 283–92 and Ch. 1 above.

[2] This is the appraisal of the then-Chinese ambassador to Moscow; see Liu Xiao, *Chu Shi Sulian*, p. 105.

[3] Zagoria, *The Sino-Soviet Conflict*, p. 372.

[4] Liu Xiao, *Chu Shi Sulian*, p. 107.

[5] See above, Ch. 2, pp. 25–6.

[6] *CQ*, No. 6, 1961, 'Quarterly Chronicle and Documentation', p. 194.

[7] Liu Xiao, *Chu Shi Sulian*, p. 106; for Chen Yi's attack on Khrushchev over Soviet neutrality in the Sino-Indian border conflict, see *Origins* II, pp. 260–2.

[8] This was Kennedy's own reading of Khrushchev; see Beschloss, *The Crisis*

Years, Kennedy and Khrushchev, 1960–1963, p. 225. In his memoirs, Khrushchev naturally stressed his reasonableness and stated that he formed a high estimate of his American opposite number, especially in contrast to Eisenhower; *Khrushchev Remembers: The Last Testament*, pp. 560–75. But according to the account of the Soviet scientist Andrei Sakharov, in July 1961 Khrushchev commented witheringly on his encounter with the American president: 'Quite a guy! He comes to a meeting but can't perform. What the hell do we need a guy like that for? Why waste time talking to him?' (Quoted in Beschloss, *The Crisis Years*, p. 294.) Beschloss suggests that Khrushchev's toughness may have been partly in response to Chinese pressures; ibid., p. 217. If so, this may have been as a result of his failure to demonstrate to the Chinese that he could move the Americans by the softer approach which they had criticized. Soviet officials had tried to persuade their American counterparts of the importance of a success to Khrushchev and the danger that in its absence he might be succeeded by someone less flexible; see Watt, *Survey of International Affairs, 1961*, p. 212.

9   Watt (ed.), *Documents on International Affairs, 1961*, p. 282.
10 The *aide-mémoire* presented by Khrushchev to Kennedy in Vienna is in ibid., pp. 277–80.
11 Quoted in Beschloss, *The Crisis Years*, pp. 223–4.
12 *Khrushchev Remembers*, p. 455.
13 *Khrushchev Remembers: The Last Testament*, p. 572.
14 Ibid., pp. 271–96; Watt, *Documents on International Affairs, 1961*, pp. 339–74, 455–65; Watt, *Survey of International Affairs, 1961*, pp. 246–63.
15 See the titles listed in Oksenberg & Henderson, *Research Guide to* People's Daily *Editorials, 1949–1975*, pp. 57–9; for a further discussion of this point, see below, Ch. 10.
16 Translated in SCMP 2511, pp. 46–8.
17 Zagoria, *The Sino-Soviet Conflict*, pp. 372, 449, n. 13; SCMP 2511, pp. 46–8.
18 Zagoria, *The Sino-Soviet Conflict*, pp. 372, 448, n. 10.
19 The prevalence of a 'vast quantity' of Soviet arms among the Communist-backed Pathet Lao forces is attested to by one of only two Western correspondents allowed to visit their headquarters in the Plaine de Jarres in February 1961; see Field, *The Prevailing Wind*, pp. 115–22.
20 See Dommen, *Conflict in Laos*, pp. 117–70.
21 Garver, *Foreign Relations of the People's Republic of China*, pp. 292–4; Young, *Negotiating with the Chinese Communists*, pp. 248–50.
22 Dommen, *Conflict in Laos*, p. 193.
23 Ibid., pp. 193–4. Dommen comments that this was a riskless pledge since neither pre-condition was likely to be satisfied.
24 The Zhou Enlai–Souvanna Phouma statement is in SCMP 2486, pp. 24–6. For some details about the construction of the 81.5 km. road, see Li Cheng, Xiao Ji, & Wang Libing, *Jianguo Yilai Jun Shi Bai Zhuang Dashi*, p. 189.
25 Taylor, *China and Southeast Asia*, p. 21.
26 Whiting, 'The Sino-Soviet Split', *CHOC* 14, p. 525.
27 *Origins* II, pp. 283–92.
28 Zagoria, *The Sino-Soviet Conflict*, pp. 372–3; for the Soviet position on these issues, see *Programme of the Communist Party of the Soviet Union*, pp. 38–9, 47, 54–6.
29 *Origins* II, pp. 276–8.
30 Biberaj, *Albania and China*, p. 28.

31 Griffith, *Albania and the Sino-Soviet Rift*, pp. 54–6. It is a measure of the importance that China was now placing upon its diminutive ally within the context of the Sino-Soviet dispute, that Li Xiannian, who could doubtless have spent his time more profitably helping to sort out China's domestic economic problems, was sent to Tirana.

32 Halliday (ed.), *The Artful Albanian: The Memoirs of Enver Hoxha*, pp. 238–9.

33 Griffith, *Albania and the Sino-Soviet Rift*, p. 73.

34 Halliday, *The Artful Albanian*, p. 244.

35 Beschloss, *The Crisis Years*, p. 584.

36 Liu Xiao, *Chu Shi Sulian*, pp. 106–9. In addition to Kozlov, Li Xiannian's Soviet hosts included the Soviet ideologue Mikhail Suslov, and the senior members of the Soviet delegation to the Albanian party congress, P. N. Pospelov and Yuri Andropov. For the clash in Bucharest, see *Origins* II, pp. 276–8.

37 Griffith, *Albania and the Sino-Soviet Rift*, pp. 76–7. Hoxha's account of the petty-sounding exchanges between the Soviet delegates and their Albanian hosts is in Halliday, *The Artful Albanian*, pp. 244–6.

38 Floyd, *Mao against Khrushchev*, p. 311.

39 Griffith, *Albania and the Sino-Soviet Rift*, pp. 78–9.

40 Ibid., p. 81; Floyd, *Mao against Khrushchev*, p. 312. Hoxha's own account of this particular dispute is in Halliday, *The Artful Albanian*, pp. 240–4.

41 The texts of the declarations in question are in Hudson, Lowenthal, & MacFarquhar (eds.), *The Sino-Soviet Dispute*, pp. 46–56, 177–205.

42 Griffith, *Albania and the Sino-Soviet Rift*, pp. 89–93. Two leading Albanian women communists, one-time guerrillas, were executed by Hoxha: Liri Gega was pregnant when shot in 1956, apparently for conspiring to overthrow Hoxha; and Liri Belishova was allegedly strangled in 1960, perhaps for briefing Russian diplomats in Beijing on the anti-Soviet line taken by the Chinese in talks with her delegation. See also *Khrushchev Remembers*, p. 476; *Khrushchev Remembers: The Last Testament*, pp. 303–4; Halliday, *The Artful Albanian*, pp. 10, 223–4.

43 This is Zagoria's conclusion; *The Sino-Soviet Conflict*, pp. 374–5.

44 See Wu Xiuquan, *Huiyi yu Huainian* (Memoirs and reminiscences), p. 345. Wu was one of China's leading Soviet specialists. He had studied in the Soviet Union in 1926–31, and during his subsequent political and military career back in China was called upon from time to time to act as a Russian interpreter. After spending eight years in the foreign ministry, finishing with a three-year spell (1955–8) as the PRC's first ambassador to Yugoslavia, Wu had become a deputy director of the CCP's International Liaison Department which dealt with foreign communist parties (ibid., p. 321).

45 Zagoria, *The Sino-Soviet Conflict*, p. 371.

46 *Origins* II, pp. 92–100, 132–5. Zhou had also visited Moscow, Budapest, and Warsaw in early 1957 in an effort to shore up the Soviet position in Eastern Europe in the wake of the Hungarian rebellion; ibid., I, pp. 175–6. For an inside account of Zhou's activities on these two occasions, see Liu Xiao, *Chu Shi Sulian*, pp. 31–9, 78–82.

47 Kang Sheng's speech on that occasion is in Hudson, Lowenthal, & MacFarquhar, *The Sino-Soviet Dispute*, pp. 72–7; its negative impact on the Russians is discussed in Liu Xiao, *Chu Shi Sulian*, pp. 84–5, 88.

48 *Nongye Jitihua, xia*, p. 584.

[49] Zagoria, *The Sino-Soviet Conflict*, p. 371.
[50] Quan Yanchi, *Tao Zhu he tade Qinren: Nüer Yanzhangde Fuqin* (Tao Zhu and his family: A father in the eyes of his daughter), p. 113.
[51] Liu Xiao, *Chu Shi Sulian*, p. 114.
[52] Ibid., p. 112. The NCNA reported the departures of Myftiu and the Chinese delegation in separate reports on 15 Oct., but coyly neglected to intimate that they were travelling on the same 'special' plane; SCMP 2603, pp. 23, 45-6.
[53] Liu Xiao, *Chu Shi Sulian*, pp. 110-11. For a discussion of the immediate Chinese reaction to Khrushchev's 'secret' speech, see *Origins* I, pp. 39-41, 43-8.
[54] See 'On the historical experience of the proletarian dictatorship', and 'More on the historical experience of the proletarian dictatorship', both translated in *Communist China, 1955-1959: Policy Documents with Analysis*, pp. 144-51, 257-72.
[55] Even Enver Hoxha in his speech to the Albanian 4th Congress in February had not attacked the CPSU, but had adopted the Chinese custom of using the Yugoslavs as surrogates; see Griffith, *Albania and the Sino-Soviet Rift*, pp. 197-222.
[56] Floyd, *Mao against Khrushchev*, pp. 316-17; Liu Xiao, *Chu Shi Sulian*, p. 113. Griffith points out that within 24 hours of the Khrushchev attack, even before Zhou had had a chance to reply, Beijing had published a speech made several days earlier by the Chinese delegate to a women's congress in Tirana in which she had said: 'The friendship between the Chinese and Albanian peoples, based on the principles of Marxism-Leninism and proletarian internationalism, is unbreakable and no force can destroy it'; *Albania and the Sino-Soviet Rift*, p. 93.
[57] Liu Xiao, *Chu Shi Sulian*, p. 113. Liu says, '*Fortunately* our NPC was about to meet' (emphasis added) to show that Zhou used a legitimate excuse, but in fact the NPC was never convened in 1961 and the next meeting was not held until March 1962; *Renmin Shouce, 1962*, p. 3. Perhaps a meeting was scheduled for the autumn of 1961, but when writing his memoirs Liu Xiao forgot it had been cancelled.
[58] Floyd, *Mao against Khrushchev*, p. 319; Griffith, *Albania and the Sino-Soviet Rift*, p. 98.
[59] The comment is Griffith's; ibid., pp. 99-100; as an illustration, see Hoxha's speech of 8 Nov. 1961, in ibid., pp. 242-70.
[60] A list of the supportive statements is contained in Dallin, *Diversity in International Communism*, pp. 141-5; for the line-up of foreign parties at the 22nd Congress on Albania and other issues in dispute between Beijing and Moscow, see Griffith, *Albania and the Sino-Soviet Rift*, pp. 102-5.
[61] Floyd, *Mao against Khrushchev*, p. 321; for the diplomatic exchanges accompanying the rupture, see Dallin, *Diversity in International Communism*, pp. 145-56.
[62] Griffith, *Albania and the Sino-Soviet Rift*, p. 100; Dallin, *Diversity in International Communism*, pp. 220-1. The Russians also reprinted attacks on the CCP; Griffith, *Albania and the Sino-Soviet Rift*, p. 115.
[63] Dallin, *Diversity in International Communism*, pp. 208-11.
[64] Ibid., pp. 222-34; Griffith, *Albania and the Sino-Soviet Rift*, pp. 122-9. For the 1960 episodes, see *Origins* II, pp. 274-6.
[65] See for instance the *People's Daily* editorial on the first anniversary of the

1960 Moscow statement in Dallin, *Diversity in International Communism*, pp. 213–20.

66 Beschloss, *The Crisis Years*, pp. 317–19, 335–6, 342–6.

67 See the article 'Kennedy's Wishful Thinking', *RMRB*, 8 Dec. 1961, translated in SCMP 2639, pp. 38–42.

68 Dallin, *Diversity in International Communism*, p. 235.

69 Wang Bingnan, 'Nine Years of Sino-U.S. Talks in Retrospect', translated in JPRS-CPS-85-079, p. 46. The talks had started in Geneva in 1955 and were moved to Warsaw in 1958. By the time of President Nixon's visit to China in February 1972, the only agreement reached at the talks was on the repatriation of Chinese students from the United States and 40 Americans from China. That deal was hammered out in 1955 within six weeks of the talks' beginning; MacFarquhar (ed.), *Sino-American Relations, 1949–1971*, p. 104. One reason for Ambassador Wang's assessment may have been the successful new tactics which the Kennedy administration adopted in 1961 for keeping the PRC out of the Chinese seat in the UN; ibid., p. 184; SCMP 2648, pp. 36–40.

70 MacFarquhar, *Sino-American Relations*, p. 182; the quotation is from Kennedy's aide, Theodore Sorensen.

71 Ibid., pp. 183–4; Hilsman, *To Move a Nation*, pp. 302–3.

72 Young, *Negotiating with the Chinese Communists*, pp. 116–17, 244–5; Hilsman, *To Move a Nation*, p. 304; Wang, 'Nine Years of Sino-U.S. Talks', p. 46.

73 *Qi Qian Ren Dahui Ziliao*, pp. 1–6. For a brief discussion of this valuable source, see Ch. 7, n. 27.

74 In addition, at one point Liu referred scornfully to the concept of a communist party as a party of the 'whole people', an unmistakable reference to the new party constitution ratified at the CPSU's 22nd Congress; *Qi Qian Ren Dahui Ziliao*, p. 57.

75 '*Diren yi tiantian lanxiaqu, women yi tiantian haoqilai*'; ibid., p. 1.

76 Ibid., pp. 2–3.

77 Ibid., pp. 3–4.

78 Ibid., pp. 4–5.

79 Ibid., pp. 5–6.

80 Translated in Schram (ed.), *Mao Tse-tung Unrehearsed*, p. 181.

81 *Qi Qian Ren Dahui Ziliao*, pp. 87, 100. The precise financial implications are detailed in the next chapter. The North Korean and North Vietnamese delegates to the CPSU's 22nd Congress maintained silence on the Soviet–Albanian quarrel and emulated China in strongly attacking American 'imperialist intervention'; Griffith, *Albania and the Sino-Soviet Rift*, p. 104.

82 Schram, *Mao Tse-tung Unrehearsed*, p. 101.

83 This point was made in Liu's report; *Qi Qian Ren Dahui Ziliao*, p. 28.

PART TWO: FALSE DAWN

CHAPTER 7

[1] Earlier examples exist; e.g. the meeting held by Mao on 30 Apr. 1957 on the eve of the Rectification Campaign; see *Origins* I, p. 210.

[2] *DSNB*, p. 277; Bo Yibo, *Ruogan Zhongda Juece* 2, p. 1014.

[3] Guangdong Teaching Materials, p. 315.

[4] Cong Jin, *Quzhe Fazhande Suiyue*, p. 400.

[5] According to the early Qing scholar, Huang Zongxi (Huang Tsung-hsi): 'Today only if the toil and trouble everywhere and the strain on the people are grievous enough to endanger one's prince, do ministers feel compelled to discuss the proper means for governing and leading the people. As long as these do not affect the dynasty's existence, widespread toil, trouble, and strain are regarded as trifling problems, even by supposedly true ministers.' See de Bary, *Waiting for the Dawn*, p. 95.

[6] Huang Daoxia, Dai Zhou, Yu Zhan, & Zhonggong Zhongyang Xuanchuanbu Xuanchuanju (eds.), *Zhonghua Renmin Gongheguo 40 Nian Dashiji (1949–1989)* (A chronology of 40 years of the PRC, 1949–1989), p. 166.

[7] See Table Intro. 3.

[8] The figures may understate the magnitude of the increase in the prices of consumer goods, according to Nicholas Lardy (personal communication).

[9] Ma Qibin, *et al.* (eds.), *Zhongguo Gongchan Dang Zhizheng Sishinian (1949–1989)* (The CCP's 40 years in power, 1949–1989), p. 211. Chen Yun pushed this proposal after the Seven Thousand Cadres Conference as the best way to supply protein to urban residents; see below Ch. 8. Mao made on-the-spot inquiries into urban living standards in December 1961; see Zhonggong Jiangsu Shengwei Dangshi Gongzuo Weiyuanhui & Jiangsu Sheng Dang'anju (eds.), *Mao Zedong zai Jiangsu*, pp. 80–1.

[10] *Liu Shaoqi Xuanji, xia*, p. 358.

[11] Wu & Wakeman, *Bitter Winds*, pp. 72–3, 83.

[12] Ibid.

[13] Jiang Huaxuan, Zhang Weiping, & Xiao Sheng, *Zhongguo Gongchan Dang Huiyi Gaiyao*, p. 466; Cong Jin, *Quzhe Fazhande Suiyue*, p. 400.

[14] Bo Yibo, *Ruogan Zhongda Juece* 2, pp. 1014–16 is an example of an important source which is silent on who proposed the size of the conference; another is in Lin Zhijian (ed.), *Xin Zhongguo Yaoshi Shuping* (Commentary on important events in new China), p. 270. Cong Jin, *Quzhe Fazhande Suiyue*, p. 400, states it was Mao; so does Zheng Qian & Han Gang, *Wannian Suiyue: 1956 Nianhoude Mao Zedong*, p. 155. The attribution of the idea to Liu, Zhou, and Deng is in Zhang Tianrong, 'Guanyu yijiuliuer nian qiqian ren dahuide jige wenti', on p. 6 of the mimeograph version of 12 May 1981 which was circulated for opinions. This passage was excised when the article, clearly regarded as the definitive, semi-official analysis of the conference, was published shortly thereafter in *DSYJ*, No. 5, 1981, p. 20, and the

excision was maintained when the *DSYJ* article was reprinted in Zhu Chengjia (ed.), *Zhonggong Dang Shi Yanjiu Lunwen Xuan* (A selection of research papers on CCP history), p. 526, and in Guofang Daxue, *Cankao Ziliao* 24, p. 13. (Both Zhang Tianrong and Cong Jin helped compile *Cankao Ziliao*.) Was the passage removed because it was inaccurate, or was it thought better to exercise discretion over this information?

One puzzle is how a clearly well-informed author like Zhang Tianrong could have got this wrong; another puzzle is why Cong Jin attributed the decision to Mao when the conventional account of the conference in the average party history is silent on who had the idea of holding such a large conference. Nor are these issues of idle pedantry. If Liu, Zhou, and Deng did jointly put forward the proposal for an extraordinary conference, it was probably a very rare instance of Mao's colleagues collaborating to twist his arm to do something, and the Chairman would probably have been quite suspicious about their motives. Informant S suggests that the GLF had accustomed people to big meetings and that the Seven Thousand Cadres Conference was not so unusual, but a massive meeting before which Mao would have to accept some responsibility for a national disaster was surely in a different category.

15 For a discussion of these matters, see *Origins* II, *passim*, and below.

16 Bo Yibo, *Ruogan Zhongda Juece* 2, p. 1073.

17 The speech is translated in Schram, *Mao Tse-tung Unrehearsed*, pp. 158–87 from a Chinese version that became available during the Cultural Revolution; this passage is from p. 158. The official Chinese version in *Mao Zedong Zhuzuo Xuandu* (Selected readings from the works of Mao Zedong), *xia*, pp. 814–38, was published with the admission that sections 3 and 5 had been omitted, presumably because they seemed inappropriate when the speech was finally published in the mid-1980s; this passage is on p. 814. A full Chinese version for internal distribution is printed in Guofang Daxue, *Cankao Ziliao* 24, pp. 1–12. In this version, as in the version translated by Schram, section 3 is about which classes the CCP should unite with and section 5 is about the international communist movement.

18 See Deng Xiaoping's description of party leaders at the *xian* level and above in his speech to the conference; *Deng Xiaoping Wenxuan (1938–1965)*, p. 281.

19 Bo Yibo, *Ruogan Zhongda Juece* 2, p. 1019.

20 Hu Sheng & Zhonggong Zhongyang Dangshi Yanjiushi, *Zhongguo Gongchan Dangde Qishi Nian*, p. 378.

21 According to Zhang Tianrong, 'Guanyu yijiuliuer nian qiqian ren dahuide jige wenti', p. 6. This passage, too, was excised from the version in *DSYJ*, No. 5, 1981, p. 20, probably because it exposed the helter-skelter nature of CCP activities at this time. But it should be added that editing for the *DSYJ* version was in some cases clearly done to save space by omitting or paraphrasing passages that simply repeated material from conference reports and discussions presumably available to insiders allowed to read *DSYJ*. Cases of rewriting for the most part seem to reflect nothing more sinister than the universal tendency of authors and editors to tinker with a text right up to press day, but for consistency, the present work will continue to use the mimeographed text.

22 It occupies almost 70 pages in *Liu Shaoqi Xuanji, xia*, pp. 349–417, almost as much as his report to the CCP's 8th Congress in 1956. Lack of time to consider so critical and voluminous a report in detail may have been an

additional reason for Mao to suggest it should be presented to the conference unapproved by the Politburo.

23 *Liu Shaoqi Xuanji, xia*, p. 355; the date of the report's submission is given in Teng Wenzao, 'Guanyu qiqian ren dahuide pingjia wenti' (Problems in evaluating the Seven Thousand Cadres Conference) p. 4.

24 While Liu Shaoqi was talking about GLF slogans during his speech to the Seven Thousand Cadres Conference on 27 Jan., Mao made a brief intervention to say that the secretariat had made a first pass at clearing up these matters, but had not finished the job. His withholding of total approval appears not to have been because the report was in any way critical of his own role, but because the secretariat had failed to criticize the media's responsibility for promoting the fervid atmosphere of 1958, a subject which had irritated Mao at least since the Lushan conference. For Mao's intervention, see *Liu Shaoqi Xuanji, xia*, p. 429; for Mao's earlier criticisms of the media, see *Origins* II, pp. 220–1.

25 See Zhang Tianrong, 'Guanyu yijiuliuer nian qiqian ren dahuide jige wenti', p. 21 (*DSYJ*, No. 5, 1981, p. 26). The passage is not completely clear. Deng apparently asked conferees to express their opinions (i.e. criticisms) on the work of the secretariat and undertook to add them to the report if the secretariat investigation proved to have been incomplete: '... bing yaoqiu daohui tongzhi ti yijian, shuo ruguo jianchade bugou, jiu jia'. (In his speech on 27 Jan., Liu Shaoqi used the same formula—*bugou jiu jia*—when suggesting conferees could propose a more extensive list of errors to be included in his written report if they wished; see *Liu Shaoqi Xuanji, xia*, p. 420.) One might assume that the conferees had the report to pore over to enable them to decide if they had anything to supplement it with. That is not explicitly stated, however, and it would have been highly unusual for a report to the Politburo Standing Committee to be released to county-level officials without a direct order from the Chairman; and if Mao had ordered it distributed at the conference, probably Zhang Tianrong would have said so. Nevertheless, it s clear that the conferees had some some kind of a documentary briefing book in front of them because Zhou Enlai referred to it in his speech; see *Qi Qian Ren Dahui Ziliao*, p. 85. For a discussion of this latter source, see nn. 27 and 96 below.

26 See Appendix 2.

27 The text printed in *Liu Shaoqi Xuanji, xia*, pp. 349–417 (translated in *Selected Works of Liu Shaoqi* 2, pp. 328–96, which appeared after this chapter was drafted and so is referred to much less), is incomplete. Fortunately what appears to be a full text is available in *Qi Qian Ren Dahui Ziliao*, which contains also a fuller text of Deng Xiaoping's speech, a very much fuller text of Lin Biao's, and a text of Zhou Enlai's speech unavailable elsewhere. In the case of Liu's speech, the major excision was any reference to the international situation, presumably because of the considerable changes in China's external relations between 1962 and 1985 when *Liu Shaoqi Xuanji, xia*, was published; but there were also substantial omissions on domestic affairs which will be noted. The date of the written report given in *Liu Shaoqi Xuanji, xia*, p. 349, is 27 Jan., but I have accepted Chinese commentators' indications that it was actually circulated the day before it was formally introduced.

28 Cf. *Origins* II, p. 326.

29 *Liu Shaoqi Xuanji, xia*, pp. 350–2.

30 Ibid., pp. 353–4.

31   Cf. *Qi Qian Ren Dahui Ziliao*, pp. 11–14, with *Liu Shaoqi Xuanji, xia*, p. 354.
32   *Qi Qian Ren Dahui Ziliao*, p. 11. For a discussion of Liu's speech, see *Origins* II, pp. 51–4.
33   *Qi Qian Ren Dahui Ziliao*, p. 11.
34   Ibid., p. 12.
35   Ibid., pp. 12–13.
36   Ibid., p. 28.
37   Ibid., p. 13.
38   Ibid., pp. 13–14.
39   Ibid., p. 14.
40   *Liu Shaoqi Xuanji, xia*, p. 355.
41   Ibid., pp. 354–9.
42   Liu had criticized the press on 28 Apr. 1961 after discovering from his own investigations in Hunan that they had trumpeted bogus triumphs; see above, Ch. 3. Mao, too, had criticized the press during the GLF; see *Origins* II, pp. 220–1.
43   *Qi Qian Ren Dahui Ziliao*, pp. 38–9, 41.
44   *Origins* II, pp. 24–7.
45   *Qi Qian Ren Dahui Ziliao*, p. 40.
46   Ibid., pp. 36–7; *Origins* II. pp. 306–9.
47   *Liu Shaoqi Xuanji, xia*, p. 355.
48   *Qi Qian Ren Dahui Ziliao*, pp. 35–6, 41–2, 58, 61.
49   *Liu Shaoqi Xuanji, xia*, pp. 354–9. Many have been discussed above.
50   An alternative explanation is that the strange juxtaposition existed in both the first and second drafts of the report, but that the editors of Liu's selected works dropped the embarrassing defence of Mao and the centre in deference to the more critical thinking about their roles in the GLF that emerged in the post-Mao era.
51   Ibid., pp. 361–7.
52   Ibid., pp. 368–72.
53   Ibid., pp. 429–30.
54   Ibid., pp. 373–94.
55   These were excised from the text in ibid., perhaps because it was water under the bridge, perhaps because it was decided not to subject the individuals pinpointed to the permanent public humiliation that appearance in this book would mean. The examples are included in *Qi Qian Ren Dahui Ziliao*, pp. 35–7. In one case, Liu's report blamed the Ministry of Agriculture for the activities of a *xian* 1st secretary in Henan who had wreaked havoc by following instructions during the GLF, causing the destruction of over 3 million jujube trees, 6,000 four-wheeled carts, and 32 bridges; ibid., p. 35.
56   *Liu Shaoqi Xuanji, xia*, pp. 395–406.
57   'Zenyang jiejue zhege maodun ne? Weiyide daolu, jiu shi quan dang dou yao fucong zhongyang'; ibid., p. 407.
58   Ibid., pp. 408–13.
59   Ibid., p. 414; Bo Yibo, *Ruogan Zhongda Juece* 2, pp. 934–8. For the hints in the March version and the fully formed set in art. 47 of the June version of the Sixty Articles, see *Nongye Jitihua, xia*, pp. 466 (arts. 44–9), 487–8; for the usage in the Seventy Articles, see *Gongye Qiye Fagui*, p. 72; for the rules in the Forty Articles, see *Guofang Daxue, Cankao Ziliao* 23, p. 489. A Chinese political dictionary gives Liu's written report to the Seven Thousand Cadres Conference as the *locus classicus* for the formulation; see Fan Ping & Ye

Duzhu (eds.), *Dangde Jianshe Cidian* (A dictionary of party building), pp. 110–11. This suggests that the formulation, apparently devised between March and June 1961, gradually gained currency among China's leaders and was seized upon as Liu's written report was being drafted as a handy way of encapsulating how they expected their followers to conduct themselves. However, the political 3/8 formula does not seem to have gained the wide popularity of the PLA formula; it is not normally dealt with in PRC political dictionaries, and was not picked up by the major Taiwan listing of mainland political terms, Warren Kuo's *A Comprehensive Glossary of Chinese Communist Terminology*. The original PLA formulation is in *Selected Works of Mao Tse-tung* 4, pp. 155–6.

60 This formulation was itself revamped at the CC's 10th plenum nine months later; *Liu Shaoqi Xuanji, xia*, p. 503, n. 187.

61 See below, Ch. 15.

62 Footnotes in Chinese articles reveal that records of these discussions exist, but regrettably are apparently available only to trusted PRC scholars. I have drawn upon quotations in their works.

63 Schram, *Mao Tse-tung Unrehearsed*, p. 166.

64 Han Gang, '60 niandai qianqi dangnei guanyu shehuizhuyi wentide xin renshi' (New comprehension of problems of socialism within the party in the early 1960s), in Quanguo Zhonggong Dangshi Yanjiuhui (ed.), *Zhongguo Shehuizhuyi Jianshe he Gaige Zhuanti Jiangzuo*, pp. 1–2.

65 Ibid., p. 2.

66 Ibid. The reference to the 'third left line' is a particularly damning one because it was a period that ended in massive defeat for the CCP. This term is used to describe the period of the Jiangxi Soviet, 1931–4, which ended when the Soviet regime had to be evacuated *en masse* in the face of Chiang Kai-shek's fifth 'bandit-extermination campaign'. The resulting Long March from south to northwest China has since been officially portrayed as an epic saga, but it witnessed the decimation of the communist forces before the remnants arrived in Shaanxi province. The third leftist line is considered to have been terminated by the Zunyi conference in Jan. 1935, at which Mao began his rise to power. For the official Maoist version of this period, see the 1945 'Resolution on Party History', in *Selected Works of Mao Tse-tung* 3, pp. 185–93; for a more recent PRC account, see Lu Ji (ed.), *Zhongguo Gongchan Dang Qishi Nian* (Seventy years of the CCP), pp. 199–220.

67 Han Gang, '60 niandai', p. 2.

68 Ibid.; Informant S.

69 Han Gang, '60 niandai', pp. 3–4.

70 Informant S.

71 See above, Ch. 3, pp. 57–8.

72 *Liu Shaoqi Xuanji, xia*, p. 423.

73 For a discussion of subjectivism, one of the three sins attacked during the rectification campaigns of 1942–4 and 1957, see *Origins* I, pp. 111–14.

74 Both Han Gang and Informant S indicated this.

75 Li Xiangqian, 'Qiqian ren dahui shimo' (The story of the seven thousand man meeting), *Dangshi Wenhui*, No. 12, 1992, p. 28.

76 Teng Wenzao, 'Guanyu qiqian ren dahuide pingjia wenti', p. 2.

77 The size of the redrafting committee and the duration of its discussions were revealed by Mao in his speech to the conference; see Schram, *Mao Tse-tung Unrehearsed*, p. 159.

78 Li Xiangqian, 'Qiqian ren dahui shimo', p. 28. Teng Wenzao, 'Guanyu qiqian ren dahuide pingjia', refers discreetly only to a 'responsible person' from one of the regional bureaux; while Ke's leftism has been increasingly discussed by Chinese authors in recent years, he has never been posthumously condemned.

79 For a discussion of the content, impact, and symbolic importance of the Twelve-Year Agricultural Programme, which Chinese, as in this case, normally referred to as the forty article programme, see *Origins* I, pp. 27–9, 90–1, 123–6, 314–15; II, pp. 16, 42, 122, 305.

80 'Go all out, aim high, and achieve greater, faster, better, and more economical results'; for the evolution of the GLF slogan, see ibid. II, pp. 42, 351 (54).

81 Teng Wenzao, 'Guanyu qiqian ren dahuide pingjia', p. 2.

82 Ibid.; the text refers simply to '4, 5, 8', which I have assumed to be shorthand for the proposal to raise grain yields in north China from the 1955 figure of 150 jin per mou to 400 jin, in central China from 208 jin to 500 jin, and in south China from 400 to 800 jin; see *Origins* II, pp. 351–2 (55). The text of the first version of the programme is in *Communist China, 1955–1959: Policy Documents with Analysis*, pp. 119–226. The targets mentioned here are in art. 6 on p. 121.

83 *Origins* II, p. 323.

84 Teng Wenzao, 'Guanyu qiqian ren dahuide pingjia', pp. 2–3; Li Xiangqian, 'Qiqian ren dahui shimo', p. 28. The latter source has the fullest description of Peng Zhen's remarks, but has some excisions.

85 Bo Yibo, *Ruogan Zhongda Juece* 2, p. 1026.

86 See *Origins* I, pp. 141–6 for a discussion of Peng Zhen and the post of General Secretary.

87 Teng Wenzao, 'Guanyu qiqian ren dahuide pingjia', p. 4; Li Xiangqian, 'Qiqian ren dahui shimo', p. 28; Bo Yibo, *Ruogan Zhongda Juece* 2, pp. 1026–7. The sources mention only 'transition' in three or five years, but in the context of the GLF this clearly refers to the heady talk of the transition to communism in the late summer of 1958; see *Origins* II, p. 130.

88 See for instance, MacFarquhar, Cheek, & Wu, *The Secret Speeches of Chairman Mao*, pp. 431, 433.

89 For Mao's disclaimer on the transition issue, see *Chinese Law and Government* 1, No. 4, pp. 41–2.

90 Teng Wenzao, 'Guanyu qiqian ren dahuide pingjia', p. 4; Li Xiangqian, 'Qiqian ren dahui shimo', p. 28.

91 Ibid. It may be a *déformation professionel* of dictators to want to be thought modest. In Volkogonov's *Stalin: Triumph & Tragedy*, there is a quotation from a letter which the Soviet dictator wrote to the prospective publishers of a book for children called *Tales of Stalin's Childhood* stating his opposition to the venture on the grounds that it promoted the cult of personality! This episode is quoted in the review of Volkogonov's book by David Remnick in *The New York Review of Books*, 5 Nov. 1992, p. 14; I am grateful to Jonathan Mirsky for bringing it to my attention.

92 Teng Wenzao, 'Guanyu qiqian ren dahuide pingjia', p. 5.

93 Teng Wenzao suggests either naïvely or disingenuously that Chen Boda's criticism was gratuitous; ibid. In the background, Mao suggested very mild revisions to Liu's text; *Jianguo Yilai Mao Zedong Wengao* 10, pp. 5–9.

94 Teng Wenzao, 'Guanyu qiqian ren dahuide pingjia', p. 5.

95 Ibid. 'Arbitrary' (*zhuanduan*) is Teng Wenzao's description.

⁹⁶ The version of the speech which is included in *Liu Shaoqi Xuanji, xia*, pp. 418–43, has serious omissions. A much fuller version, Liu 27/1/62 mimeo version, is available in mimeographed form in the library of the Fairbank Center, Harvard University. Even this version omits the opening section on the international situation. The contents of this section are indicated by a similar section at the start of Liu's report, however, which is available in the mimeographed collection, *Qi Qian Ren Dahui Ziliao*, which brings together Liu's *report*, but *not his speech*. For readers' convenience, I will refer to the openly published version of Liu's speech where the two are identical.

The reasons for the omissions will become apparent when they are alluded to, but it should be added that the authorities in charge of editing the speeches and articles of Chinese leaders do not see anything strange in publishing expurgated versions in official collections. Such politically correct versions are meant for study (*xuexi*) by—which means the edification of—the 'broad masses'. The full texts are needed only for research (*yanjiu*) by authorized officials and academics, such as those cited in this chapter, to ensure that they do not get things wrong.

⁹⁷ An indication of the trouble he had in composing it is provided by the five heavily revised handwritten pages from the speech reproduced in miniature in Li Xiangqian, 'Qiqian ren dahui shimo', p. 29. Liu had not envisaged making a speech, but Mao suggested it. Liu prepared only an outline, which Mao and other PSC members perused before Liu spoke; Huang Zheng, *Liu Shaoqi Yi Sheng* (A life of Liu Shaoqi), pp. 377, 379.

⁹⁸ See Teng Wenzao, 'Guanyu qiqian ren dahuide ping ia', p. 3.

⁹⁹ See Li Xiangqian, 'Qiqian ren dahui shimo', p. 28. The official text of Liu's speech omits this intervention by Mao, though it includes others; the Liu 27/1/62 mimeo version does not include interventions.

¹⁰⁰ *Liu Shaoqi Xuanji, xia*, pp. 354, 420.

¹⁰¹ The brief reference to Shandong is omitted from the official text of Liu's speech; cf. ibid., p. 419, with Liu 27/1/62 mimeo version, p. 2. This latter text uses the wrong character for 'Hui' in Huimin district

¹⁰² *Liu Shaoqi Xuanji, xia*, p. 420.

¹⁰³ Ibid.

¹⁰⁴ Ibid., pp. 420–1.

¹⁰⁵ Liu 27/1/62 mimeo version, p. 3. By pointing the finger at Henan, Liu was repaying the province's former 1st secretary, Wu Zhipu, for failing to listen to him during the GLF; see *Origins* II, pp. 303–4.

¹⁰⁶ Again, this intervention is not printed in the official text, but it is quoted in Li Xiangqian, 'Qiqian ren dahui shimo', p. 28.

¹⁰⁷ *Liu Shaoqi Xuanji, xia*, p. 421.

¹⁰⁸ '*Bu li san, liu, jiu*'; Cong Jin, *Quzhe Fazhande Suiyue*, p. 432.

¹⁰⁹ According to one report, Liu Shaoqi summoned a meeting at a resort in Huangshan, a mountain range in southern Anhui, immediately after the 1961 Lushan conference, at which officials presented him with their best estimates of the impact of the GLF; Informant W. For whatever reason—fear of provoking the Chairman, or fear of the consequences to the CCP of a major blow to Mao's reputation, or concern that he himself might be brought down if the revelations resulted in a demand for the return of Peng Dehuai, or simply out of a desire to avoid demoralizing cadres—Liu did not present the data to the Seven Thousand Cadres Conference.

¹¹⁰ *Liu Shaoqi Xuanji, xia*, p. 422.

111 The official text has virtually nothing from this substantial portion of Liu's speech (*Liu Shaoqi Xuanji, xia*, p. 426), and thus Liu 27/1/62 mimeo version will be used.

112 Liu emphasized the importance of a more balanced emphasis in the general line by drawing upon a conversation he had had with the PRC's chargé d'affaires accredited to Britain. The latter had told him that the English greatly feared the speed with which the Chinese were progressing. 'What if we stop moving so fast, would they stop fearing us?' asked Liu. With diplomatic finesse, the chargé promptly replied that they would then fear the Chinese even more because they understood that quality was even more important than quantity! (Liu 27/1/62 mimeo version, pp. 7–8.) Liu did not name the official, but the chargé in London then was Huan Xiang; after the Cultural Revolution, as a vice-president of the Academy of Social Sciences, Huan became a major figure in China's international educational exchanges and a prominent participant in Sino-US policy conferences.

113 Ibid., pp. 8–9.

114 Teng Wenzao, 'Guanyu ciqian ren dahuide pingjia', p. 3.

115 *Qi Qian Ren Dahui Ziliao*, p. 22. The appropriate place for this passage was surely where Liu listed as one of the successes of the GLF that collectivization had reached a higher stage with the entry of 500 m. peasants into the communes. *Liu Shaoqi Xuanji, xia*, p. 352. The half-page of praise of the communes (*Qi Qian Ren Dahui Ziliao*, pp. 21–2), including this passage, was excised by the editors of Liu's selected works, presumably because it was so out of joint with the times. Conscientious readers, knowing that they were supposed to derive edification from the works of leading communists, might have wondered how they were to reconcile these words with the dissolution of the communes in the 1980s. For a comment on the influence of Stalin's training in a seminary on his oratory and writings, see Ulam, *Stalin: The Man and his Era*, p. 24.

116 For a brief discussion of the transformation from primary to higher-level APCs, see *Origins* I, pp. 16–19.

117 At least a few mess-halls persisted into 1962 and even beyond; see William Hinton, *Shenfan*, pp. 230–2, which gives a sympathetic view of the mess-hall system.

118 Liu 27/1/62 mimeo version, pp. 9–10.

119 Ibid., pp. 13–14.

120 For Mao's role in these two programmes, see *Origins* I, pp. 27–9, II, pp. 15–19.

121 *Liu Shaoqi Xuanji, xia*, p. 359.

122 The editors of *Liu Shaoqi Xuanji* evidently thought it would not convince readers who, by the time the book was published in 1985, had heard much about Mao's mistakes and witnessed the rehabilitation of Marshal Peng Dehuai, for they omitted this passage from the version of Liu's speech in the book.

123 Liu 27/1/62 mimeo version, p. 7.

124 See *Origins* II, pp. 212–16.

125 Liu 27/1/62 mimeo version, p. 7.

126 As already noted, the mimeo version of Liu's speech does not include interruptions; this one is quoted in Cong Jin, *Quzhe Fazhande Suiyue*, p. 494. For the fullest and most up-to-date account of the Gao–Rao affair, see Teiwes, *Politics at Mao's Court*; Peng Dehuai's role is discussed on

pp. 104–7. Liu used the same term, *yunie*, at the Lushan conference; see *Origins* II, p. 231.

[127] Liu 27/1/62 mimeo version, pp. 6–7. This remark of Mao's seems first to have been revealed in a Red Guard publication during the Cultural Revolution; see *Origins* II, p. 231. It is not clear when Mao said this. Li Rui wrote that Mao accused Peng at the PSC meeting on 31 July 1959, of being deeply involved in the Gao–Rao affair, but does not quote these words; see Li Rui, *Lushan Huiyi Shilu*, p. 217. For the official attack on Peng over this issue in the CC resolution passed at Lushan, see *The Case of Peng Teh-huai, 1959–1968*, p. 41.

[128] Mao Zedong repeated this allegation in June to a North Korean visitor, who might have shown a particular interest in the former commander of the Chinese People's Volunteers in the Korean War; Cong Jin, *Quzhe Fazhande Suiyue*, pp. 494, 496.

[129] For the allegations against Peng of conspiracy with Khrushchev, see Domes, *Peng Te-huai: The Man and the Image*, pp. 87–8; *Origins* II, pp. 225–8. For Gao Gang, see Teiwes, *Politics at Mao's Court*, pp. 47–51.

[130] Again, an accusation made by Liu at Lushan; *Origins* II, p. 178.

[131] Liu 27/1/62 mimeo version, p. 7.

[132] Ibid.

[133] Interestingly, a post-Mao Chinese analyst felt the need to pinpoint Mao's interventions to show that it was not *just* Liu who held these opinions about Peng, so clearly Liu's personal concerns about a pardon for Peng are taken for granted among knowledgeable PRC historians; Cong Jin, *Quzhe Fazhande Suiyue*, p. 496. For a discussion of Gao as a threat to Liu, see Teiwes, *Politics at Mao's Court*, *passim*, but especially ch. 2. For a longer discussion of the threat to Liu posed by Peng Dehuai, see *Origins* II, pp. 230–3. In the original version of his article on the conference, Zhang Tianrong, 'Guanyu yijiuliuer nian', p. 29, quoted some of Liu's remarks about Peng Dehuai, but this damaging glimpse of Liu's behaviour was excised in the *DSYJ* version.

[134] Liu Shaoqi 27/1/62 mimeo version, pp. 16–18. Nearly all of this passage was omitted from *Liu Shaoqi Xuanji*, presumably because by the time of publication, these practices were commonplace and approved.

[135] Li Xiangqian, 'Qiqian ren dahui shimo', p. 8; Huang Zheng, *Liu Shaoqi Yi Sheng*, p. 382.

[136] There is no totally satisfactory version of Lin Biao's speech. One version which has become widely available to scholars in the West is to be found, among other places, on pp. 129–40 of what appears to be an authentic collection of works by Lin from 1937 through 1968, which I have entitled [*Lin Biao Xuanji*] (Selected works of Lin Biao) because the version available to me has no title page and no publication data. This was clearly a collection prepared and distributed during the Cultural Revolution, but confirmation of the accuracy of its version of this particular speech is provided by the very similar quotations from the same speech in Cong Jin, *Quzhe Fazhande Suiyue*, pp. 410–12, and Teng Wenzao, 'Guanyu qiqian ren dahuide pingjia', pp. 5–6. The differences may be explained by the fact that at the Seven Thousand Cadres Conference, as on other occasions, Lin Biao's preferred operating procedure was to avoid speaking from a prepared text, and only to have an official text formally cleared later if it were needed for wider distribution; thus there could exist an informal version based on a tape-

recording, as well as a final official version. On this occasion, as at the CCP's 9th Congress in 1969, a text was prepared in advance, but he did not use it. See Zhang Yunsheng, *Maojiawan Jishi: Lin Biao Mishu Huiyilu* (The true story of Maojiawan: The memoirs of Lin Biao's secretary), p. 210, and Teng Wenzao, 'Guanyu qiqian ren dahuide pingjia', pp. 5–6.

This version omits, however, the bulk of the second part of the speech, which was devoted to the details of military affairs. This section is to be found in the far more complete version of the speech available in the collection *Qi Qian Ren Dahui Ziliao*, pp. 125–61, which was probably compiled shortly after the conference. Comparison of the first version with the relevant portion of the second version reveals that there are omissions and rewritings in both, some of which can be ascribed to politics, some to editing.

137   For instance, shortly after his re-election at the 8th Congress, Lin was absent from the important Politburo meeting held on 20 Oct. 1956 to discuss the prospect of a Soviet invasion of Poland; Wu Lengxi, *Yi Mao Zhuxi* (Remembering Chairman Mao), p. 11.

138   According to [*Lin Biao Xuanji*], p. 60, he addressed a conference of high-ranking army officers in May 1958. This was presumably the enlarged MAC conference, attended by 1,000 senior officers, which began on 27 May; *Origins* II, pp. 66–7.

139   For Lin Biao's denunciations of Peng Dehuai, see for instance Li Rui, *Lushan Huiyi Shilu*, p. 227; *Origins* II, p. 242.

140   They may have had that interest in common then, but when the Cultural Revolution version of Lin Biao's speech was prepared it was no longer politic to include its second sentence: 'As for party work, Comrade Shaoqi's report discusses it very well and very correctly, and I am in complete agreement'; cf. *Qi Qian Ren Dahui Ziliao*, p. 125 and [*Lin Biao Xuanji*], p. 129. Equally, when editors prepared Liu Shaoqi's speech at this conference for posthumous publication after the Cultural Revolution, they decided to omit from a passage on the very great successes of all aspects of military work a phrase dating them 'from the Lushan conference of 1959'; that was of course when Lin Biao took over as defence minister from the disgraced Peng Dehuai, who had been rehabilitated by the time Liu's works were brought out. Cf. *Qi Qian Ren Dahui Ziliao*, p. 9 and *Liu Shaoqi Xuanji, xia*, p. 352. For the coincidence of interests of Liu and Lin on the Peng Dehuai issue in 1959, see *Origins* II, p. 242.

141   [*Lin Biao Xuanji*], p. 132: this reference is not contained in the corresponding passage in *Qi Qian Ren Dahui Ziliao*, p. 129. One possibility is of course that it was added to the Cultural Revolution version when Peng Dehuai was again a prominent target, but the reference is so relatively innocuous that it is hard to see why; another possibility is that it was omitted from the 1962 version because Lin wished not to further anger Peng's old comrades in the military.

142   [*Lin Biao Xuanji*], p. 132; *Qi Qian Ren Dahui Ziliao*, pp. 129-30. There are what appear to be purely editorial differences between the two versions.

143   [*Lin Biao Xuanji*], p. 129; *Qi Qian Ren Dahui Ziliao*, p. 126. There are differences between the two texts, but it is difficult to read political significance into them. Though Lin's choice of words appeared to suggest that he was referring to 1961, 1962, and 1963, it may have been a slip of the tongue not uncommon even in late January when a person has not yet got used to the fact of the new year, especially if, as in this case, he were speaking

before the Chinese lunar new year. In that case, the years to which Lin would have been referring were 1960–2. Lin spoke as if he already knew 'this year's' figures, which would hardly be the case if he were referring to 1962. Alternatively, he may conceivably have been deliberately lowering expectations as far ahead as 1963, in order to pre-empt pessimism and put it into perspective.

144 *Qi Qian Ren Dahui Ziliao*, pp. 127–8; [*Lin Biao Xuanji*], pp. 130–1. Lin put losses before gains in the 1962 version, but interesting y this was reversed in the Cultural Revolution version. Probably Lin mentioned losses first simply because he was acknowledging that they were what dominated discourse at that time. For Mao's anger with Peng Dehuai at Lushan for putting losses before gains, see *Origins* II, p. 214.

The two texts also differ less importantly on one word: in the 1962 version, Lin says that despite the material losses of the GLF, the CCP had gained greatly in spirit (*zai jingshenshang*); the Cultural Revolution version has him saying that the gain had been in construction (*zai jiansheshang*). This was possibly a transcription error in the first version, corrected in the second; but since Lin emphasized the importance of 'spirit' in a number of other places, it is also possible that the first version was correct, but, on reflection, cultural revolutionary editors thought that he had not made enough of the *material gains* of the GLF and so later replaced 'spirit' with 'construction' in this particular passage.

145 [*Lin Biao Xuanji*], pp. 132–4; *Qi Qian Ren Dahui Ziliao*, pp. 130–4. A call to trust the political leadership despite severe economic problems was a feature of the British Conservative party's successful strategy in the general election of 1992, and even more so of President Bush's unsuccessful re-election campaign later the same year.

The texts again differ here: In the Cultural Revolution version there is an additional positive reference to Mao and a longer anti-revisionist passage; but that version understandably omits a description of America as being 'very much a global model' ('*Zai quan shijie lai shuo, Meiguo hen dianxingde*') because of its progress from backwardness to development, and also omits, for less obvious reasons, the description of Britain as an 'already backward old imperialist' country—conceivably, Lin's editors later felt that this description somewhat diminished the significance of Mao's call for China to overtake Britain in fifteen years made at the outset of the GLF (*Origins* II, pp. 15–19).

146 Teng Wenzao, 'Guanyu qiqian ren dahuide pingjia', p. 6.

147 Long after Stalin died, Marshal Georgy Zhukov described the impossibility of persuading him to put Soviet forces on a war footing in 1941 for what seemed to everyone but Stalin the inevitable German attack. Zhukov admitted that he did not insist on it because the military purges of the late 1930s had made it clear what going against the Soviet leader could mean. But he added: 'And yet that is only one aspect of the truth. I'll tell you another. I didn't regard myself as cleverer or more far-sighted than Stalin, or that I had a better understanding of the situation than he had. Like everyone else, I had enormous faith in him, in his ability to find a way out of the most difficult situations. I sensed the danger of a German attack, the feeling was gnawing at my vitals. But my faith in Stalin, and my belief that in the end everything would come out the way he suggested, was stronger.' Quoted in Shukman (ed.), *Stalin's Generals*, pp. 347–8. For Zhou Enlai's remark in

1958, see Li Rui, *'Da Yuejin' Qin Li Ji* (A record of my own experience of the GLF), pp. 331–2.

148 All Chinese commentators are agreed on this: Teng Wenzao, 'Guanyu qiqian ren dahuide pingjia', p. 6; Cong Jin, *Quzhe Fazhande Suiyue*, p. 413; Li, *The Private Life of Chairman Mao*, pp. 387–8. According to this latter source, Mao also much appreciated the speech of Hua Guofeng, then a Hunan provincial official whom Mao was to dub his successor in 1976. Despite the negative reactions to Lin's speech, when Mao was correcting the centre's decision on Liu's speech, he inserted a phrase indicating that the conference had agreed totally with the speeches of *all* PSC members, and ensured that Lin's was widely distributed; *Jianguo Yilai Mao Zedong Wengao* 10, pp. 59–60, 62–5.

149 Thatcher, *The Downing Street Years*, p. 27. The former British Prime Minister was referring to William Whitelaw, whom she appointed Home Secretary and Deputy Prime Minister in her first government in 1979. For the latter's views of Mrs Thatcher, see Whitelaw, *The Whitelaw Memoirs*.

The reaction of Mao's senior colleagues to Lin Biao's approach may have mirrored that of another of Mrs Thatcher's senior colleagues, Chancellor of the Exchequer Nigel Lawson, to her press secretary Bernard Ingham who 'consistently briefed the press on the basis that everything that went right was Margaret's own personal achievement, while everything that went wrong was the fault of her ministers; and Margaret herself increasingly came to see things in these terms'; Lawson, *The View from No. 11*, p. 850.

150 Cong Jin, *Quzhe Fazhande Suiyue*, p. 413; according to another account, Mao quizzed Luo some months later; Huang Yao, *San Ci Danan Buside Luo Ruiqing Dajiang* (General Luo Ruiqing who survived three disasters), pp. 206–7.

151 Teng Wenzao, 'Guanyu qiqian ren dahuide pingjia', pp. 5–6; Huang Yao, *San Ci Danan Buside Luo Ruiqing Dajiang*, pp. 205–6. Ye Qun, herself holding military rank, was in charge of Lin Biao's private office; see Zhang Yunsheng, *Maojiawan Jishi*, *passim*.

152 Li, *The Private Life of Chairman Mao*, pp. 386–7. Mao attended few of the meetings, spending most of his time with young women in 'his' Room 118 in the Great Hall of the People, reading the criticisms in the transcripts of the proceedings; ibid.

153 One Western leader who, like Mao, was regularly avuncular and even inspiring in front of 'the masses' and scatological in private, was Lyndon Johnson; see Goodwin, *Remembering America*, pp. 256–9, 280–1. Since all Mao's post-1949 speeches were initially made *in camera*, the Chairman felt able to pepper his speeches with crudities, not realizing that during the Cultural Revolution they would be distributed, unexpurgated, by the Red Guards.

154 Schram, *Mao Tse-tung Unrehearsed*, pp. 166–7.

155 Ibid., p. 167.

156 Ibid., p. 187.

157 Li Xiannian, speaking the same day in a small group, adopted a similar approach in his self-criticism; *Li Xiannian Wenxuan*, p. 276.

158 This is the analysis of Mao's doctor; Li, *The Private Life of Chairman Mao*, p. 387.

159 Schram, *Mao Tse-tung Unrehearsed*, pp. 170–6; the quotation is on p. 173. Among the foreigners were the British Field-Marshal Montgomery and the

American journalist Edgar Snow (whose interviews with Mao and description of the communist movement in northwest China in the mid-1930s formed the basis of his classic *Red Star over China*). In *The Other Side of the River* (pp. 613–30), written after a long visit to China in 1960, the year in which the Chinese population had a negative growth rate, Snow poured scorn on stories of mass starvation in China, attributing them to Cold War thinking. For his private doubts on this subject, and his desperate appeal for 'FACTS' from Westerners resident in China, see S. Bernard Thomas, *Season of High Adventure: Edgar Snow in China*, pp. 306–8.

160 *Mao Zedong Zhuzuo Xuandu, xia*, p. 833; Schram *Mao Tse-tung Unrehearsed*, p. 180. Mao did not acknowledge the source. For a discussion of the earlier use of this formulation, which Engels imbibed from Hegel, and which was used by both Mao and Chen Yun in 1959, see *Origins* II, p. 164.

161 Schram, *Mao Tse-tung Unrehearsed*, p. 177.

162 Ibid., p. 168.

163 See for instance its impact on a general whom Mao had once invited to be his 'counsellor' on military education; Fan Hao, *Mao Zedong he Tade Guwen* (Mao Zedong and his counsellor), p. 246.

164 See his note to Tian Jiaying on 24 Feb.; *Mao Zedong he tade Mishu Tian Jiaying*, p. 111; also ibid., p. 62. Mao's speech was gone over by some of the party's chief propagandists before the Chairman allowed it to be released to lower level cadres on 10 April; *Jianguo Yilai Mao Zedong Wengao* 10, pp. 54–8.

165 For a discussion of the two fronts in the Chinese leadership, see *Origins* I, pp. 152–6; II, pp. 172–80.

166 Estimating Mao's private decisions from the behaviour of his colleagues is the reverse of but analogous to calculating the existence of a hidden planet from the movement of the light of a star—which was how the planets circling 51 Pegasus were discovered; *US News & World Report*, 30 Oct. 1995, pp. 69–72. In the present instance, one is calculating the relative brightness of the 'red sun in their hearts' by the behaviour of his satellites; see below Ch. 12.

167 Cong Jin, *Quzhe Fazhande Suiyue*, p. 406.

168 Jin Ye, *Huiyi Tan Zhenlin*, pp. 385, 395.

169 Li Xiangqian, 'Qiqian ren dahui shimo', p. 28. This had also been a problem in Guangdong; see *Origins* II, pp. 155–9.

170 Despite Tao Zhu's concurrent responsibilities as 1st secretary of the Central-South region, Tao did not cede the provincial 1st secretaryship to Zhao Ziyang until 1965. Tao Zhu also self-criticized at this conference: *Biji Tao Zhu*, p. 284.

171 Li Xiangqian, 'Qiqian ren dahui shimo', p. 26. I am assuming that the reference in this source to Li Yunzhong is a printer's error. For Mao's attack on Li, see *Mao Zhuxi dui Peng–Huang–Zhang–Zhou fan-dang jituande pipan* (Chairman Mao's criticism of the Peng [Dehuai]–Huang [Kecheng]–Zhang [Wentian]–Zhou [Xiaozhou] anti-party clique), pp. 12–14.

172 *Origins* II, pp. 163–70.

173 Bachman, *Chen Yun and the Chinese Political System*, p. 75.

174 *Selected Works of Zhu De*, p. 395.

175 See above, Ch. 3, p. 65.

176 *Deng Xiaoping Wenxuan (1938–1965)*, pp. 279–99 (*Selected Works of Deng Xiaoping [1938–1965]*, pp. 269–86) appears to include the whole text; at least there are no indications of cuts as with other texts in this volume.

177 *Deng Xiaoping Wenxuan (1938–1965)*, pp. 280–3. Deng's speech earned Mao's approval; *Jianguo Yilai Mao Zedong Wengao* 10, p. 53.

178 Deng formally expressed the obligatory total agreement with Mao's speech (because he was party chairman) and Liu's report (because it was the centre's); *Deng Xiaoping Wenxuan (1938–1965)*, p. 279.

179 Deng had made a similar argument in his speech to the 8th Congress; see *Origins* I, pp. 116–17.

180 The figure for party membership is in Mao's speech; Schram, *Mao Tse-tung Unrehearsed*, p. 179.

181 *Deng Xiaoping Wenxuan (1938–1965)*, pp. 283–9; the quotation is on p. 289. Mao also quoted himself in his speech; Schram, *Mao Tse-tung Unrehearsed*, p. 163. For the origins and early politics surrounding the Qingdao formulation, see *Origins* I, pp. 285–9, 304.

182 *Deng Xiaoping Wenxuan (1938–1965)*, p. 290; Deng was unperturbed by the interruption, saying that was taken care of in the party constitution, which he had presented to the 8th Congress. Mao in his own speech had indeed talked of a prohibition on 'secret' factions; Schram, *Mao Tse-tung Unrehearsed*, p. 183.

183 *Deng Xiaoping Wenxuan (1938–1965)*, p. 290.

184 Ibid., p. 292. This proposal produced an interesting three-way exchange. Liu Shaoqi interrupted Deng to suggest that each party committee should meet once a month for a criticism and self-criticism session; Deng replied that it need not be every month, one a quarter would be fine. Liu agreed to this, whereupon Mao seemingly decided that he, too, had to contribute something to the dialogue and proposed, somewhat unoriginally, that the meetings should involve an examination of work, summing up experience and exchanging opinions.

185 Ibid., pp. 295–6.

186 *Qi Qian Ren Dahui Ziliao*, p. 79.

187 Ibid., p. 81.

188 Ibid., pp. 81–2.

189 Ibid., p. 83.

190 Ibid., pp. 83–4.

191 Ibid., p. 85.

192 Cong Jin, *Quzhe Fazhande Suiyue*, pp. 407–8.

193 *Qi Qian Ren Dahui Ziliao*, p. 79.

194 For a discussion, see *Origins* II, pp. 59–63.

195 See *Origins* I, pp. 86–91; II, pp. 24–5, 55–9. Chen Yun simply retired from active politics for a time.

196 Li Xiannian made an equally unconvincing self-criticism; *Li Xiannian Wenxuan*, pp. 276–9.

197 Bo Yibo, *Ruogan Zhongda Juece* 2, p. 1070.

198 See for instance *Origins* II, pp. 105, 108–13.

199 For a more extended discussion of the issues in 1959, see ibid., pp. 228–33.

200 Cong Jin, *Quzhe Fazhande Suiyue*, pp. 392–5.

201 *Origins* II, pp. 196–200.

202 *Hengdao Lima Peng Jiangjun* (Gallant General Peng), p. 162; his visit is described on pp. 160–8. Only the month it began is given in *Peng Dehuai Tongzhi Guju Jianjie* (A brief guide to Comrade Peng Dehuai's former home), p. 4. The visit lasted from 3 Nov. to 23 Dec.; Long Zhengcai, 'Peng Dehuai dui shehuizhuyi jingji jianshe wentide jianku tansuo' (Peng

Dehuai's arduous probing of the problems of socialist economic construction), *Zhonggong Dangshi Yanjiu*, No. 6, 1988, p. 49. This latter source has a brief description of Peng's activities in the early 1960s, such as they were. For a description of Peng's place of confinement in the Yuan Ming Park on the northwestern outskirts of Beijing, see *Origins* II, pp. 233–7. The poverty that led the young Peng Dehuai to join the revolution was still in evidence when the present author visited his home in 1986; his family was clearly far worse off than those of his fellow-Hunanese, Mao and Liu Shaoqi.

203 Cong Jin, *Quzhe Fazhande Suiyue*, p. 498.

204 According to ibid., p. 497, it contained five parts: on the Lushan conference, on the Gao–Rao affair, on his contacts with foreigners, a recapitulation of his career in the communist movement, and on the military line. The laudable post-Mao effort to vindicate Peng—*Peng Dehuai Zishu*, translated as *Memoirs of a Chinese Marshal*—has considerable shortcomings as a historical document. Most of the book is based on Peng's confessions during the Cultural Revolution; only chs. 14 (on the Korean War) and 15 (on the Lushan affair) are based on his 1962 apologia. Even on a very generous estimate, these chapters include less than 14,000 characters of the reported 80,000 in the latter document. In ch. 15, Peng's discussion covers only the economic issues and explains his behaviour at Lushan in connection with his decision to write to Mao on 14 July 1959. As we have seen, in his speech to the Seven Thousand Cadres Conference, Liu Shaoqi effectively conceded the validity of Peng's economic points, and justified his continuing disgrace entirely on the grounds of his alleged implication in the Gao Gang affair. Peng's 'autobiography' did not reprint his reply on this issue; presumably it was omitted in order to protect the posthumous reputation of Liu Shaoqi. Interestingly, at the time that Cong Jin published his excellent book, he was a senior colonel (equivalent to a brigadier-general) teaching at the National Defence University; it is not inconceivable that he was permitted to make extensive revelations of Peng Dehuai's rebuttal out of PLA dissatisfaction with the extent of the late marshal's public exculpation in the post-Mao era.

205 Wang Nianyi, ' "Wenge" mantan' (Informal notes on the 'Cultural Revolution'), unpub. MS, part 11. The He Long–Peng Dehuai feud is privately acknowledged among Chinese party historians; it is assumed that this is why Mao invited He Long to participate in the small PSC meeting held in the middle of the Lushan conference to denounce Peng. For a description of the PSC meeting, see Li Rui, *Lushan Huiyi Shilu*, pp. 215–61. One of the incidental casualties of Peng's disgrace was the inability of the PLA to authorize the publication of accounts of political work in the Chinese People's Volunteers, an important topic since many Chinese POWs had elected to be repatriated to Taiwan. Analyses and documentation were being discussed and finalized at a conference in Qingdao in August 1959 when the project was overwhelmed by the backwash from Lushan. The MSS were finally published in 1985; *Li Zhimin Huiyilu* (The memoirs of Li Zhimin), pp. 694–8.

206 Han, *Eldest Son*, p. 277.

APPENDIX 2

1 See, for instance, Lieberthal, 'The Great Leap Forward and the Split in the Yenan Leadership', *CHOC* 14, pp. 327–8; Cheek, *Propaganda and Culture in Mao's China: Deng Tuo and the Intelligensia*, ch. 5

² *Liu Shaoqi Xuanji, xia,* p. 355.
³ 'Deng Xiaoping . . . hai zuzhi ren dui ji nianlaide zhongyang wenjian zuole jiancha, dui shujichu gongzuozhongde quedian cuowu, gei zhengzhiju changwei xiele yige baogao . . .', Zhang Tianrong, 'Guanyu yijiuliuer nian qiqian ren dahui', p. 21.
⁴ Teng Wenzao, 'Guanyu qiqian ren dahuide pingjia', p. 4.
⁵ *Jingxin dongpode 'gongting zhenbian' yinmou* (A soul-stirring plot for a 'palace coup'), pp. 1–13; the prefatory note is on p. 13. *Dangdai Zhongguode Beijing* 1, pp. 155–7.
⁶ Hu Sheng & Zhonggong Zhongyang Dangshi Yanjiushi, *Zhongguo Gongchan Dangde Qishi Nian,* p. 390.
⁷ For other Cultural Revolution accounts of the Changguanlou affair, see Ding Wang (ed.), *Beijing Shi Wenhua Da Geming Yundong* (The Great Cultural Revolution movement in Beijing city), pp. 215–33, which is particularly detailed (Peng's order initiating the Beijing operation is quoted on p. 220) (a translation of the Red Guard newspaper article reprinted here is in SCMP[S] 187, pp. 23–36); *Peng zei 'Huairou diaocha' shi Liu, Deng hei silingbu yinmo fanpi zibenzhuyide yanzhong buji, passim*; another Red Guard newspaper article is translated in SCMP 4014, pp. 1–8 and in JPRS 42,966, pp. 92–101. See also Center for Chinese Research Materials, Red Guard Publications, Supplement 1, vol. IV, pp. 1760–74.
⁸ Regrettably, Peng Zhen has apparently never published any explanation of the affair, and when his deputy, Liu Ren, was asked by his wife about Changguanlou in the early 1970s, he vouchsafed curtly: 'I didn't go there; I'm not clear about it'; *Mianhuai Liu Ren Tongzhi* (Remember Comrade Liu Ren), p. 296.
⁹ I am grateful to Michael Schoenhals for this suggestion.

CHAPTER 8

¹ It is possible that there was an economic summary in the delegates' briefing books, but in that case it seems unlikely that Zhou would have spent so much time laying the figures out again. Elsewhere in his speech he skirted a topic that had already been adequately covered; *Qi Qian Ren Dahui Ziliao*, p. 83.
² The three main categories of loans were for military hardware in the Korean War, plants and equipment for the Chinese development programme, and to cover China's trade deficit; ibid., p. 100.
³ See above, Ch. 2.
⁴ *Jingji Dashiji*, pp. 324–5.
⁵ A picture of the building and the conference room inside is contained in *Gongheguo Zhuxi Liu Shaoqi*, pp. 50–1.
⁶ Cong Jin, *Quzhe Fazhande Suiyue*, p. 414; *Jingji Dashiji*, p. 331. The latter source gives the 5 billion yuan figure for the potential 1962 deficit; the higher 6 billion yuan figure was Li Xiannian's contemporary estimate (see next note).
⁷ See Li Xiannian's speech to the State Council conference on 26 Feb. in which he expressed only total agreement with Liu Shaoqi's criticisms of his officials; in fact, Li blandly claimed that financial work, like that in every other field, had had very great successes, but had produced some deficits! The original estimate that there ought to have been a 3.9 billion yuan surplus

for 1958–61 is in this source. *Dangde Wenxian* (Party documents), No. 2, 1989, p. 25. This speech is not included in *Li Xianniar Wenxuan*. While the discovery of the deficits may have come as a horrible surprise to Liu Shaoqi and even Li Xiannian, it is uncertain whether the ministry officials were unaware of them; Nicholas Lardy suggests that they may have not reported them earlier for fear of the consequences (private communication).

8 Liu & Wu, *China's Socialist Economy*, pp. 269–70; *Dcngde Wenxian*, No. 2, 1989, p. 26; Cong Jin, *Quzhe Fazhande Suiyue*, pp. 413–14.

9 Ibid., p. 414; *Jingji Dashiji*, p. 331.

10 *Chen Yun's Strategy*, pp. 185–201. This translation is based on the text in the internally circulated volume *CYWG*, pp. 157–72, not that which appeared later in the openly published official version *CYWX*. There does not appear to be any significant difference between the two, but quotations used from the translation have been checked against both Chinese texts. The Chinese texts are of Chen Yun's remarks to State Council officials on 26 Feb., but the indication is that this was a repeat of the Xilou speech; Cong Jin, *Quzhe Fazhande Suiyue*, p. 414.

11 *Chen Yun's Strategy*, p. 186.

12 Ibid.

13 Ibid., pp. 185–6. The editors point out that probably because the final figures for 1961 were not yet available to Chen, he underestimated the shortfall, which was actually over 47.5 m. tons.

14 Ibid., pp. 186–7. One reason that so much land was withdrawn from cultivation was the disastrous miscalculation made during the GLF that improved farming techniques would make it possible to get more from less; see *Origins* II, pp. 119–28.

15 *Chen Yun's Strategy*, pp. 188–90.

16 Zhonghua Renmin Gongheguo Caizhengbu *et cl.* (eds.), *Zhongguo Caizheng Wenti* (Problems of China's finances; hereafter, *Zhongguo Caizheng Wenti*), p. 11.

17 *Chen Yun's Strategy*, pp. 190–1. There was a circular problem here: because the peasants, too, were short of grain, they were less keen on growing cash crops thus reducing the amount of raw materials available for processing and resale to themselves (ibid., p. 192). The Chinese situation in 1962 appears to have been a variant of that in the Soviet Union during the notorious 'scissors crisis' forty years earlier, when agriculture was in better shape than industry, but enormously high prices were gouged out of the peasants for industrial goods; Nove, *An Economic History of the U.S.S.R.*, pp. 93–6. Peasants did not stop selling grain to the state, but they did stop buying goods, with disastrous impact upon industry; Davies, *The Industrialisation of Soviet Russia* 1, pp. 28–9. Nove argues (p. 140) that the Soviet government then went overboard in its reduction of industrial prices which did not anyway benefit the peasants, because of middlemen. It is an interesting reflection of the urgency of maintaining peasant incentives in China at this time, and perhaps of his knowledge of Soviet history, that Chen Yun did not advocate raising the price of industrial goods to close the 20–30 yuan gap; as he said twice, indiscriminately increasing prices would just earn the CCP the curses of the people (*Chen Yun's Strategy*, p. 196). One Chinese economist, Liang Wensen, claims that the scissors problem existed before 1949, but was gradually solved under the PRC; see Xu *et al.*, *China's Search for Economic Growth*, p. 71. For Mao's rejection of the suggestion that China faced a scis-

sors crisis similar to that of the Soviet Union, see *Selected Works of Mao Zedong* 5, p. 356. Lardy argues forcefully, however, that in general, the terms of rural–urban exchange did not benefit the peasants; Lardy, *Agriculture in China's Modern Economic Development*, pp. 108–10, 112–19.

18 *Chen Yun's Strategy*, p. 191.

19 Ibid., pp. 192–3. The phrase Chen Yun used for the defeat of the revolution was *geming shi hui shibaide*.

20 Ibid., pp. 194–7.

21 See *Origins* II, pp. 165–70. In Deng Liqun, *Xiang Chen Yun Tongzhi Xuexi Zuo Jingji Gongzuo* (Study Comrade Chen Yun on how to do economic work), pp. 111–12, there is an interesting description of Chen Yun's work methods, in connection with a two-week conference on pig-rearing which he summoned during the GLF.

22 See above, Ch. 7.

23 Since each urban resident needed 36 jin a year, the total amount for 100 m. people comes to 3.6 billion jin.

24 *Chen Yun's Strategy*, p. 197. For the urban population in 1961, see *TJNJ, 1983*, p. 103.

25 What is unclear in the calculations of both Chen and the planners is what increase in output their plans demanded. Output in 1962 went up by only about 600 m. jin; indeed, the 1962 figure was still only 65% of the 1957 one; *TJNJ, 1983*, p. 15.

26 *Chen Yun's Strategy*, p. 198.

27 Ibid., pp. 198–9. Chen realized that this would mean even greater grain imports, but his officials had worked out that it was far more cost-effective to do this than to import cotton. A ton of imported cotton cost $700 as compared with $70 for a ton of grain. This meant that the same amount of foreign exchange could cover either a ton of cotton or 10 tons of grain, but the 10 tons of grain could be used to encourage the production of five extra tons of cotton. For a discussion of how the international terms of trade continued to disadvantage Chinese agriculture, see Xu *et al.*, *China's Search for Economic Growth*, p. 72.

28 *Chen Yun's Strategy*, p. 199. Chen listed the main areas for commercial grain production as the provinces of Jilin and Heilongjiang in the northeast, Inner Mongolia in the north, the central Shaanxi plain in the northwest, the Yangtze delta, the Jianghan plain, and the Dongting Lake area in central China, the Chengdu basin in the southwest, and the Pearl River delta in the south.

29 Ibid., pp. 199–200. For the industry-fixation of Chinese planners, attested to by one of them, see *Origins* II, p. 332.

30 Deng Liqun, *Xiang Chen Yun Tongzhi*, p. 5; Cong Jin, *Quzhe Fazhande Suiyue*, p. 416.

31 Deng Liqun, *Xiang Chen Yun Tongzhi*, pp. 6, 8; Cong Jin, *Quzhe Fazhande Suiyue*, p. 417; Bo Yibo, *Ruogan Zhongda Juece* 2, pp. 1053–4. Mao also agreed that the deputy head of the Small Group should be Li Fuchun, chairman of the State Planning Commission. Later Li Xiannian was made a second deputy head, and Premier Zhou Enlai, Vice-Premier Tan Zhenlin (who ran agriculture during the GLF), Vice-Premier Bo Yibo (chairman of the State Economic Commission), Chief-of-Staff Luo Ruiqing, Cheng Zihua (a vice-chairman of the State Planning Commission), Gu Mu (a vice-chairman of the State Economic Commission), Yao Yilin (the minister of commerce), and Xue Muqiao (a leading economist and another vice-chairman of the

State Planning Commission) were made members; Cong Jin, *Quzhe Fazhande Suiyue*, p. 420. Cong Jin gives a very high appraisal of Chen Yun. For some unexplained reason, the decision on the latter's resumption of leadership of the small group seems not to have come formally into effect for another two months, on 19 April; ibid., and *DSNB*, p. 319.

32 See Li Xiangqian, '1962 niande jingji tiaozheng yu yijian fenqi' (The 1962 economic adjustment and differences of opinion), *Zhonggong Dangshi Yanjiu*, No. 6, 1988, p. 62. The basis for this author's statement is one of Liu Shaoqi's confessions early in the Cultural Revolution, in which he said that he learned later of the Chairman's displeasure. The confession is translated in *Issues & Studies* (Taipei), June 1970, p. 95; I have checked this translation against the version transcribed by correspondents of the Japanese newspaper *Mainichi* from Red Guard posters in Beijing. Chen's speech was formally ordered to be distributed on 18 March, *Jingji Dashiji*, p. 327.

33 Strangely, this picture looks like a photograph of a painting, and Zhu De and Lin Biao, at each end of the group, look as if they were added in the studio or the dark-room. Versions of this group pose, minus Lin Biao, became a staple of CCP photographic mythmaking after the Cultural Revolution to revive a vision of the fraternity of the Chinese leadership under Mao. It is, for instance, on the cover of Hua Lin (ed.), *Mao Zedong he tade Zhanyoumen* (Mao Zedong and his comrades-in-arms). In a photograph obtained by the author from the Xinhua News Agency in Beijing in 1986, Zhu De and Lin Biao are missing, and instead, Peng Zhen (who was not a member of the PSC) is visible where Lin Biao was. No one in the group is smiling; rather the group appears to be engaged in serious discussion, and Peng Zhen's presence as the No. 2 man in the CC secretariat seems very natural. This very much more realistic version—Liu's hand is at his collar, Zhou's eyes are half-closed—was published, minus Peng Zhen, in at least two books of Xinhua photographs: Zhonggong Zhongyang Wenxian Yanjiushi & Xinhua Tongxunshe (eds.), *Deng Xiaoping* (p. 86) in 1988 and *Yongheng zhi Ri* (pp. 102–3) in 1989. But in *Gongheguo Zhuxi Liu Shaoqi* (p. 165), published in 1988, and in *Beijing Review* (1–7 July 1991) on the occasion of the 70th anniversary of the CCP, there appeared a version almost but not quite identical with the *Guangming Ribao* one: Lin Biao was still missing. (This is the version published on the cover of the 2nd edn. of Teiwes, *Politics and Purges in China*.) According to Informant S, the true photograph showed Mao, Liu, Zhou, Zhu, Chen, and Deng. For a discussion of official photographs as an aid to the analysis of Chinese élite politics, see MacFarquhar, 'On Photographs', *CQ*, No. 46, 1971, pp. 289–307.

34 Bo Yibo, *Ruogan Zhongda Juece* 2, p. 1052.

35 *Dangde Wenxian*, No. 2, 1989, pp. 26–8.

36 Hong Chenghua & Guo Xiuzhi, *Zhengzhi Tizhi Yange Dashiji*, p. 239. This was a far broader category than the 240,000 central government cadres whom Mao had wanted halved; see Ch. 2.

37 One problem was that many enterprises did not have financial departments of their own to ensure financial discipline; 90 out of Shanxi province's 160 light industrial firms were in that category, according to Li Xiannian; *Dangde Wenxian*, No. 2, 1989, p. 28.

38 *Jingji Dashiji*, pp. 327–8. Presumably, a sizeable proportion of these would simply be transfers back to their old jobs.

39 *Origins* II, pp. 25–7.

40 Duan Yun, *Caizheng Jinrong Lun Zong* (A summary of finance and monetary theory), p. 95.
41 *Jingji Dashiji*, pp. 329–32, 334–5. The text of the Six Articles on Banking issued on 21 Apr. 1962 is reprinted in Guofang Daxue, *Cankao Ziliao* 24, pp. 49–51.
42 *Dangde Wenxian*, No. 2, 1989, p. 28.
43 Only the month is given in *CYWG*, p. 173, and hence in *Chen Yun's Strategy*, p. 202; the date is supplied in *CYWX*, p. 198. The group meeting lasted two days, 7–8 Mar.; Bo Yibo, *Ruogan Zhongda Juece* 2, p. 1054.
44 *Chen Yun's Strategy*, pp. 202–3. In *Origins* I, pp. 57–8, I suggested that the State Economic Commission was set up in 1956 on the Soviet model to formulate the annual plans and thus provide an alternative, more flexible and more dynamic impetus to the economy than that provided by the State Planning Commission with its FYPs. Chen Yun here indicates that, at least by 1962, the Planning Commission was charged with all planning and the State Economic Commission with implementing its plans on a year-to-year basis.
45 Deng Liqun, *Xiang Chen Yun Tongzhi*, p. 82; 'Chen Yun yu Xin Zhongguo Jingji Jianshe' Bianjizu, *Chen Yun yu Xin Zhongguo Jingji Jianshe* (Chen Yun and new China's economic construction), pp. 514–28.
46 Chen discreetly describes Wang only as a 'leading comrade' of the ministry, but it seems unlikely that anyone less senior would have challenged him; *Chen Yun's Strategy*, p. 206. For the two men's clash over steel targets in 1959, see *Origins* II, pp. 165–70.
47 *Chen Yun's Strategy*, pp. 206–7.
48 Ibid., pp. 208–9.
49 Ibid., p. 204.
50 Ibid., pp. 204–5; the quotation is on p. 205. The translation omits the fact that the half jin of fish was meant to last a month, and in one place it puts the amount as one jin, in another as a half-jin; cf. *CYWG*, p. 175. Again, some of the figures do not add up: half a jin of fish per head per month for 60 m. people makes an annual total of 360 m. jin or 180,000 tons, 20% more than Chen was asking the fishermen to catch.
51 *Chen Yun's Strategy*, p. 210.
52 *CYWG* ends with this speech. Chen's next speech, according to his selected works, was made on 13 Mar. 1977, six months after the death of Mao Zedong; *CYWX*, p. 207. However, with Mao's permission, Liu Shaoqi had Chen Yun's writings made required reading for senior officials over the next few months.
53 Deng Liqun, *Xiang Chen Yun Tongzhi*, p. 7.
54 Guofang Daxue, *Cankao Ziliao* 24, p. 61; *Jianguo Yilai Mao Zedong Wengao* 10, pp. 76–7.
55 Guofang Daxue, *Cankao Ziliao* 24, p. 62; Jiang Huaxuan, Zhang Weiping, & Xiao Sheng, *Zhongguo Gongchan Dang Huiyi Gaiyao*, p. 481.
56 The six other major speakers were Li Fuchun on the rustication of the urban population and cutbacks on the industrial front; Li Xiannian on food and foreign trade; Yao Yilin on market prices; Deng Zihui on consolidating the commune system; Xie Fuzhi, the minister of public security, on consolidating the people's democratic dictatorship; and Lin Feng on education; Guofang Daxue, *Cankao Ziliao* 24, p. 62.
57 Ibid.; Jiang Huaxuan, Zhang Weiping, & Xiao Sheng, *Zhongguo Gongchan Dang Huiyi Gaiyao*, p. 481. The missing members of the PSC (Mao, Chen

Yun, and Lin Biao) were said not to be in Beijing. An odd absentee was one of the key economic officials, Bo Yibo. I have counted Marshal Peng Dehuai and Zhang Wentian, in disgrace since the 1959 Lushan conference but still respectively member and alternate member of the Politburo, as not being in good standing.

58 In the absence of complete documentation from the conference, the fullest account of the substantive discussions is to be found in Guofang Daxue, *Cankao Ziliao* 24, pp. 63–77; this source also includes substantial extracts from the small group's report and the directive issued at the end of the conference. Zhou Enlai's speech in *Selected Works of Zhou Enlai* 2, pp. 416–26 is acknowledged to be an extract; but the purported full texts of Liu Shaoqi's speech (in *Liu Shaoqi Xuanji, xia*, pp. 444–9) and of Deng Xiaoping's speech (in *Deng Xiaoping Wenxuan [1938–1965]*, pp. 300–3) do not contain important passages quoted in the Guofang Daxue account.

59 This appears to have been an underestimate, whether deliberate or not, of the 1961 output, which is put in post-Mao statistical handbooks as 153,710,000 tons; *TJNJ, 1983*, p. 158.

60 Grain production did in fact take five years, 1962–5, to surpass the 1957 level; ibid.

61 Basing himself on Chinese pronouncements, Walker gave Heilongjiang's potential grain surplus in 1957 as 3,369,000 tons and Sichuan's as 938,000 tons, making a total of 4,307,000 tons; the figures he gave for provincial grain sales average out at 1,829,200 tons a year for Heilongjiang and 3,619,600 for Sichuan, making a total of 5,448,800 tons a year; see Walker, *Food Grain Procurement and Consumption in China*, pp. 30, 276.

62 *Sichuan Sheng Qing*, p. 234. The figures for 1958–61 are not given.

63 The report's agricultural section is described in Guofang Daxue, *Cankao Ziliao* 24, pp. 65–7.

64 Ibid., p. 67 quotes a single sentence from this section of the report, presumably conveying the main message; but it is possible that the report deliberately did not waste much space on the less crucial aspects of the economic crisis.

65 Ibid.; again a one sentence epitomization; for the rail crisis during the GLF, see *Origins* II, pp. 89, 129.

66 Guofang Daxue, *Cankao Ziliao* 24, pp. 66–8.

67 For Chen Yun, see the introduction to *Chen Yun's Strategy*, pp. xv–xviii; for Li Fuchun, see *Renmin Shouce, 1957*, pp. 109–10.

68 *TJNJ, 1983*, p. 245.

69 This section of the small group's report is detailed in Guofang Daxue, *Cankao Ziliao* 24, pp. 68–9, 72.

70 Ibid., pp. 72–3; the quotation is on p. 73.

71 Ibid., p. 69. Presumably the participant was uncertain about the uniqueness of this movement of population because when he said it was historically unprecedented, he was referring only to China's history.

72 This is the version in ibid., p. 70. The version in *Selected Works of Zhou Enlai* 2, p. 421, is more discreet: 'Only our people's government, which enjoys popular support, could do such a thing.'

73 Guofang Daxue, *Cankao Ziliao* 24, p. 70. There is no indication of these detailed measures in the relevant portion of the excerpt from Zhou's speech in *Selected Works of Zhou Enlai* 2, pp. 421–2. However, Zhou does outline the decision-making process there. The first thought was to rusticate 7 m. urbanites, including 5 m. office staff and workers, but local governments,

doubtless conscious of the recurring political and logistical headaches they would face, suggested that it would be preferable to have just one larger operation, and the figures were increased to 13 m. and 9 m. After further PSC discussions, it was decided to raise the figures for staff and workers from 9 m. to 10 m., and the total number to be moved to 20 m.

74 'Kaiqiang dasi ren buxingde'. Guofang Daxue, *Cankao Ziliao* 24, pp. 70–1; the quotation is on p. 70. The much shorter version of this passage in *Liu Shaoqi Xuanji, xia*, pp. 446–7, does not contain the references to martial law and shooting people. Ever since the May 4th Movement of 1919, it has been the practice of agitating students in China to 'link up' with their peers in other cities. This had occurred during the 1957 Hundred Flowers movement, and would later occur to a much greater degree in the case of the Red Guards during the Cultural Revolution; hence Liu's advice to isolate troubled cities by cutting their rail and road communications.

75 SCMP 4027, pp. 3–4.

76 Ibid., pp. 4, 7. This Chinese account was one of many denunciations of Tao Zhu after his fall during the Cultural Revolution and has therefore to be treated with care. Nevertheless, it was prepared by presumably knowledgeable 'rebels' at the Canton Public Security Bureau, and its details seem *prima facie* credible in the light of what was learned in Hong Kong at the time. Interestingly, no comprehensive explanation of this episode appears to have figured in the post-Cultural Revolution 'reversal of verdicts' on Tao Zhu.

77 Vogel, *Canton under Communism*, p. 295.

78 SCMP 4027, p. 4.

79 Vogel, *Canton under Communism*, p. 294.

80 Ibid., p. 293.

81 Robertson, 'Refugees and Troop Moves—A Report from Hong Kong', *CQ*, No. 11, 1962, p. 113; SCMP 4027, p. 4.

82 Vogel, *Canton under Communism*, pp. 295–6.

83 SCMP 4027, p. 5.

84 *Zeng Sheng Huiyi Lu*, pp. 674–7; Vogel, *Canton under Communism*, pp. 295–6. The latter account dates the incident as occurring on 1 June, but Mayor Zeng Sheng places it on the later date.

85 Guofang Daxue, *Cankao Ziliao* 24, p. 52.

86 Ibid., p. 75; *Deng Xiaoping Wenxuan (1938–1965)*, p. 300.

87 Guofang Daxue, *Cankao Ziliao* 24, p. 75; *Deng Xiaoping Wenxuan (1938–1965)*, p. 301. The account in the latter source omits the numbers involved.

88 Guofang Daxue, *Cankao Ziliao* 24, p. 63.

89 *Liu Shaoqi Xuanji, xia*, pp. 444–6; the quotation is on p. 445.

90 *Selected Works of Zhou Enlai* 2, pp. 419–20.

91 Guofang Daxue, *Cankao Ziliao* 24, p. 63; this idea is not in the version in *Deng Xiaoping Wenxuan (1938–1965)*.

92 Zhou Enlai ensured that Mao knew what was decided at the May conference, and secured his agreement; *Jianguo Yilai Mao Zedong Wengao* 10, pp. 94–6.

CHAPTER 9

1 Guofang Daxue, *Cankao Ziliao* 24, p. 73.

2 A major source in Chinese is the revealing account in Cong Jin, *Quzhe Fazhande Suiyue*, pp. 483–94, 505–17. He pinpoints the crucial role of

Anhui on p. 483; as does the fate of Fengyang county discussed in the Introduction. This work quotes from a number of documents, many of which are to be found in *Nongye Jitihua, xia,* and in Guofang Daxue, *Cankao Ziliao* (of which Cong Jin was a co-editor). The account and the documents still leave question-marks as we shall see. For an analysis of the ecological problems of northern Anhui and the civil strife which they provoked, see Perry, *Rebels and Revolutionaries in North China.*

3 *Anhui Sheng Qing* 1, p. 168. Zeng was an early product of the Whampoa Military Academy, which had been set up in 1924 by Sun Yat-sen with the help of Soviet advisers. The academy commandant was Chiang Kai-shek, but many of the cadets, like Lin Biao, had later become CCP members under the influence of Zhou Enlai, the senior active political instructor at the academy. Zeng joined the party in 1927 at the age of 23.

4 Klein & Clark, *Biographic Dictionary of Chinese Communism* 2, pp. 860–2.

5 Ibid.; for a comparison of his publication record with that of other provincial leaders, see *Origins* II, p. 388 (202). Zeng also wrote frequently for the journal, *Xu yu Shi* (Principle and practice) founded by the Anhui party committee in the first year of the GLF; see Nos. 1, 1958; 3, 10, 12, 1959; 1, 6, 7, 10, 1960.

6 *Mao Zedong he tade Mishu Tian Jiaying,* p. 64.

7 Zeng's contributions to *Xu yu Shi* just cited certainly bear that out; for instance, in his article in the inaugural issue (no. 1, 1958), 'Pochu mixin, jiefang sixiang' (Dispel superstition, liberate thinking), seven of the twelve long paragraphs which constituted the bulk of the article started with the words 'Comrade Mao Zedong tells us . . .' In Apr. 1958, Zeng played a prominent role at a meeting in Shanghai, at which he boasted to Mao about Anhui's achievements in the field of water conservancy; Wu Lengxi, *Yi Mao Zhuxi,* p. 67. In Sept. 1958, Mao praised the practice introduced in an Anhui commune of being able to eat without paying, which precipitated the movement towards mess-halls; Friedman *et al., Chinese Village, Socialist State,* p. 238. Zeng stoutly defended the GLF at Lushan; Li Rui, *Lushan Huiyi Shilu,* p. 97. See also Cong Jin, *Quzhe Fazhande Suiyue,* p. 483.

8 *Anhui Sheng Qing* 1, p. 123.

9 Song Renqiong, Chen Pixian, & Ye Fei, 'Fendou buxide jianqiang zhanshi—Jinian Zeng Xisheng tongzhi shishi 20 zhounian' (A staunch warrior who struggled ceaselessly—Remembering Comrade Zeng Xisheng on the 20th anniversary of his death), *Xinhua Yuebao,* No 8, 1988, p. 35.

10 *Anhui Sheng Qing* 1, p. 290. There is no hint of these 'deviations' in Zeng Xisheng's article on 'The people's communes in Anhui', *Xu yu Shi,* No. 12, 1959.

11 Bian Yanjun, 'Mao Zedong he 1958 nian "Da yue jin" ' (Mao and the 1958 'GLF'), *Dangde Wenxian,* No. 4, 1994, p. 78. Zhou Enlai received a similar letter in March 1960; Li Ping, *Kaiguo Zongli Zhou Enlai,* p. 390.

12 Jiang Kunchi, '60 niandai Zeng Xisheng zai Anhui tuixing zeren tian shimo' (Zeng Xisheng's management of responsibility fields in Anhui in the 1960s), *Dangdai Zhongguo Shi Yanjiu,* No. 1, 1994, pp. 56–7. For Mao's apparent endorsement made in late 1960, see Wu Ren, *Gongheguo Zhongda Shijian Jishi* 3, p. 67.

13 Jiang Kunchi, '60 niandai Zeng Xisheng zai Anhui , p. 57; Cong Jin, *Quzhe Fazhande Suiyue,* p. 483.

14 *Jiang Kunchi*, '60 niandai Zeng Xisheng zai Anhui', p. 57; *Anhui Sheng Qing* 1, p. 290.

15 Jiang Kunchi, '60 niandai Zeng Xisheng zai Anhui', pp. 57–8; Cong Jin, *Quzhe Fazhande Suiyue*, p. 484; *Nongye Jitihua, xia*, p. 501.

16 Jiang Kunchi, '60 niandai Zeng Xisheng zai Anhui', p. 58; Cong Jin, *Quzhe Fazhande Suiyue*, p. 484; *Nongye Jitihua, xia*, p. 501. Also, see below n. 76.

17 Jiang Kunchi, '60 niandai Zeng Xisheng zai Anhui', p. 58; Bo Yibo, *Ruogan Zhongda Juece* 2, pp. 1079–80.

18 Jiang Kunchi, '60 niandai Zeng Xisheng zai Anhui', p. 58. According to one account, a 'responsible cadre' of the East China region vacationing in Anhui in February had relayed to Zeng the demands of some old peasants to be allowed to plant for themselves, and Zeng had taken this as encouragement; when relating the relaying of Mao's new instruction, this account again refers to a 'responsible cadre', whom we know from the source just cited to have been Ke. If Ke were responsible for the earlier encouragement to Zeng, his role becomes extremely curious. Perhaps he changed his line after sensing that Mao was fundamentally dubious about such experiments; Wu Ren, *Gongheguo Zhongda Shijian Jishi* 3, pp. 68–9.

19 Jiang Kunchi, '60 niandai Zeng Xisheng zai Anhui', pp. 58–9. The other leaders addressed were Liu Shaoqi, Zhou Enlai, Deng Xiaoping, Peng Zhen, and Ke Qingshi, the 1st secretary of the East China region and thus Zeng's immediate superior; *Nongye Jitihua, xia*, p. 498. At the start of his letter, Zeng said that since there had been misunderstandings about the Anhui system, he would explain it again.

20 Crook & Crook, *The First Years of Yangyi Commune*, pp. 126, 128. There is an interesting discussion here (pp. 127–8) of how the peasants resisted the official doctrine of equal pay for equal work where women were concerned. Schran, *The Development of Chinese Agriculture, 1950–1959*, pp. 30–1, indicates that the labour day was widely reckoned at 10 work points.

21 Crook & Crook, *The First Years of Yangyi Commune*, pp. 127–8; He, *Mr. China's Son*, pp. 131–2.

22 Crook & Crook, *The First Years of Yangyi Commune*, pp. 129–32.

23 He, *Mr. China's Son*, p. 118.

24 Ibid., pp. 118–19.

25 *Nongye Jitihua, xia*, pp. 609–10. This analysis was given by Hu Kaiming, 1st secretary of Zhangjiakou prefecture, in a speech to a north China agricultural conference in July 1962; Hu sent a copy of the speech to Mao. Hu's remedies are discussed below.

26 Zeng's letter is in ibid., pp. 498–500.

27 *Mao Zedong he tade Mishu Tian Jiaying*, pp. 64–5.

28 Bo Yibo, *Ruogan Zhongda Juece* 2, p. 1080.

29 It is not impossible that Zeng only listed two of the five unities because he could not recall the others.

30 *Nongye Jitihua, xia*, p. 501; Cong Jin, *Quzhe Fazhande Suiyue*, p. 484, also draws attention to this change of nomenclature.

31 *Nongye Jitihua, xia*, pp. 501–2.

32 Cf. ibid., p. 503 (April and July) and Cong Jin, *Quzhe Fazhande Suiyue*, p. 484 (March); Jiang Kunchi, '60 niandai Zeng Xisheng zai Anhui', p. 59.

33 Ibid., pp. 59–60; Bo Yibo, *Ruogan Zhongda Juece* 2, p. 1080; Song Renqiong, Chen Pixian, & Ye Fei, 'Fendou buxide jianqiang zhanshi', p. 35; *Nongye Jitihua, xia*, p. 503; Cong Jin, *Quzhe Fazhande Suiyue*, p. 485. A text

of Mao and Zeng's conversation is printed in Wu Ren, *Gongheguo Zhongda Shijian Jishi* 3, pp. 70–2.

34   *Nongye Jitihua, xia*, pp. 503–4.
35   Ibid., p. 508.
36   Cong Jin, *Quzhe Fazhande Suiyue*, p. 486. In similarly desperate straits in the Soviet Union during World War II, *kolkhoz* chairmen permitted the emergence of a similar responsibility or 'link' system based on families; Hosking, *A History of the Soviet Union*, p. 288.
37   This is also the view of Bo Yibo; *Ruogan Zhongda Juece* 2, p. 1080. In early October, Mao received another investigation report from Hu Yaobang, the YCL 1st secretary, containing cautious criticism of the Anhui experiments; *Jianguo Yilai Mao Zedong Wengao* 9, pp. 574–6.
38   *Nongye Jitihua, xia*, p. 529.
39   According to Mao's doctor, the Chairman's interviews with Zeng and Ke Qingshi at this time were only brief interruptions in three days of sexual dalliance; Li, *The Private Life of Chairman Mao*, p. 362.
40   Jiang Kunchi, '60 niandai Zeng Xisheng zai Anhui', p. 61.
41   Ibid.; Cong Jin, *Quzhe Fazhande Suiyue*, p. 486.
42   *[Liu Shaoqi] Yanlun Ji* (A collection of [Liu Shaoqi's] speeches), p. 227. Liu made two speeches to the Anhui caucus, one in January on the general thrust of the conference, one in February dealing with Zeng Xisheng.
43   Ibid., pp. 227–9.
44   Ibid., pp. 231–2.
45   *Qi Qian Ren Dahui Ziliao*, pp. 35–6.
46   *[Liu Shaoqi] Yanlun Ji*, p. 232.
47   *Nongye Jitihua, xia*, pp. 558–66, esp. pp. 558, 559, 561–2.
48   *[Liu Shaoqi] Yanlun Ji*, pp. 231–2. Zeng moved to Shanghai where he continued to carry out the duties of 2nd secretary of the East China Bureau; in 1965, he was transferred to the secretariat of the Southwest Bureau in Chengdu; Zhou Yueli, 'Zeng Xisheng tongzhide yisheng' (The life of Comrade Zeng Xisheng), *Xueshu Jie* (The world of learning) (Anhui), No. 2, 1995, p. 86.
49   *Nongye Jitihua, xia*, pp. 599–608. The letter is not dated in this source, but elsewhere it is dated May 1962; Zhongguo Nongcun Fazhan Wenti Yanjiuzu (ed.), *Baochan Daohu Ziliao Xuan* (Selection of materials on contracting output to the household; hereafter, *Baochan Daohu Ziliao Xuan*), pp. 4, 317. It was distributed with a brief covering note from Mao on 2 August; possibly it had only just reached him through the bureaucratic machine. The note identifies Qian and asks for opinions on his letter, but does not specify to whom the letter should be sent; *Nongye Jitihua, xia*, p. 599.
50   Ibid.
51   Ibid., pp. 599–600. While acknowledging that 1960 represented a very low base figure, Qian listed natural disasters and nine other major problems which made 1961 a particularly difficult year to register such achievements.
52   Ibid., p. 601.
53   Ibid., pp. 601–2.
54   Ibid., pp. 603–4.
55   Ibid., p. 605.
56   Ibid., pp. 607–8.
57   Cong Jin quotes at length from Qian's letter, but fails to disclose its impact; nor does he make comparisons to indicate whether or not there were fun-

damental differences between the Tao Zhu–Wang Renzhong formulae for acceptable types of individual agricultural labour (see below) and those espoused by Qian or Zeng Xisheng; *Quzhe Fazhande Suiyue*, pp. 490–2.

58 *Baochan Daohu Ziliao Xuan*, pp. 330–9. The source does not reveal to whom this report was directed; perhaps it was to the CC's Rural Work Department work team (see below).

59 Ibid.

60 Ibid., pp. 344–8; Fuli is mentioned on p. 348. For another investigation presenting *baochan daohu*, this time in Shandong, in a mainly favourable light, see ibid., pp. 359–65.

61 For Hu Kaiming's analysis of peasants' lack of enthusiasm for work, see above, n. 25.

62 *Nongye Jitihua, xia*, p. 611.

63 Ibid., p. 614.

64 Ibid., p. 613.

65 Ibid., p. 615. Shortly after writing to Mao, Hu Kaiming began to be criticized following on the Chairman's negative reaction; see Jia Wenping, *Zhenli yu Mingyun* (Truth and destiny), pp. 191–204, 279.

66 *Nongye Jitihua, xia*, pp. 555–7.

67 Ibid., pp. 591–2.

68 Ibid., p. 593.

69 *Mao Zedong he tade Mishu Tian Jiaying*, p. 65.

70 *Nongye Jitihua, xia*, p. 515.

71 Ibid., pp. 596–7, 598.

72 Henan Sheng Tongjiju (ed.), *Henan Jingji Tongji Nianjian, 1989* (Henan yearbook of economic statistics, 1989), p. 130.

73 *Nongye Jitihua, xia*, p. 598.

74 Wang Renzhong, Jin Ming, Yong Wentao, & Yu Mingtao, 'Songshude fengge changcun' (The pine's characteristic is to live for ever), *Xinhua Yuebao*, No. 11, 1989, p. 50; *Jianguo Yilai Mao Zedong Wengao* 10, pp. 114–16. According to the former account, Mao dropped the idea of transforming the Guangxi experience into a CC decision as a result of 'objections' from some comrades, probably including Ke Qingshi.

75 Anecdotal evidence strongly suggests that Wang Renzhong was among Mao's favourite provincial leaders; strong evidence supporting this proposition would be provided at the outset of the Cultural Revolution when Wang Renzhong was Mao's nominee as a deputy head of the newly formed Cultural Revolution Small Group. (See Quan Yanchi, *Tao Zhu zai 'Wenhua Da Geming' zhong*, p. 202; I am grateful to Michael Schoenhals for bringing this to my attention.) One reason for Mao's soft spot for Wang may have been the latter's alleged sycophancy; Li, *The Private Life of Chairman Mao*, pp. 280–2, 299, 379. Another may have been that the latter apparently shared the Chairman's interest in Chinese history. During the dark days of 1961–2, Wang published his reflections on a famous 11th-century historical classic, Sima Guang's *Zizhi Tongjian* (The comprehensive mirror for aid in government), in a Hubei internal party journal as a means of providing guidance to the cadres under his leadership; see Wang Renzhong, *Dushu Biji* (Reading notes). Knowing of this relationship, Tao Zhu may have decided that it would be politic to associate Wang with what could clearly become a controversial political judgement; otherwise, it is difficult to understand why the Guangxi investigation required the simultaneous

attention of both regional leaders. Among Tao and Wang's additional if
extraneous considerations may have been the fact that Guangxi had been
transformed with fanfare into the Guangxi Zhuang Autonomous Region
(GZAR) in the late 1950s; they could well have been reluctant to come to
conclusions which might perforce have led to the un-eating of the GZAR's
1st secretary, the CCP's most senior ethnic Zhuang Wei Guoqing (whose
name is conspicuous by its absence from the available documentation).

76 The Anhui leaders' citations of acceptable factory analogies for what they
were doing may well have been designed to impress Ke, whose other job was
1st secretary of China's leading industrial city, Shanghai. Cong Jin mentions
the sharp criticism by the East China Bureau of Anhui in late June 1962 and
this probably reflected the bureau's earlier views; Quzhe Fazhande Suiyue,
p. 493. Mao's doctor confirms that Ke led the attack on Zeng; Li, The Private
Life of Chairman Mao, p. 376.

77 Bo Yibo, Ruogan Zhongda Juece 2, p. 1079.

78 See below, Ch. 12.

79 Deng Zihui's report of 24 May on problems in the communes was addressed
to the centre and the Chairman (Nongye Jitihua, xia pp. 567–76); his report
of 11 July on agricultural problems was delivered as a speech to the Central
Party School (ibid., pp. 577–89). Deng's findings were presaged by a report
he sent to Mao in Nov. 1961 which the Chairman described as very good;
Jianguo Yilai Mao Zedong Wengao 9, pp. 605–7.

80 Zhongguo Mao Zedong Sixiang Lilun yu Shixian Yanjiuhui Lishihui (ed.),
Mao Zedong Sixiang Cidian (A dictionary of Mao Zedong Thought), p. 90.

81 Nongye Jitihua, xia, pp. 567, 577.

82 Ibid., pp. 567–9, 577–8, 582. Deng Zihui's faith in the role a law could play
in the PRC is interesting if surprising. In fact, the CCP's promise was not
formally broken, although during the Cultural Revolution leftist leaders
employed various devices to persuade the peasantry to return 'voluntarily'
to brigade accounting; see Zweig, Agrarian Radicalism in China, 1968–
1981, pp. 32–49, 98–121.

83 Nongye Jitihua, xia, pp. 570–1, 578–9, 582.

84 Ibid., pp. 579–81.

85 Ibid., p. 581.

86 Ibid., pp. 586, 588.

87 Ibid., p. 586.

88 Ibid., p. 588.

89 Ibid.

90 Ibid., pp. 572–3, 582–3.

91 Ibid., pp. 574–5, 585.

92 Ibid., p. 575.

93 Ibid., pp. 571–2, 579, 583–4.

94 For a discussion, see Oi, State and Peasant in Contemporary China,
pp. 187–226.

95 Nongye Jitihua, xia, pp. 581, 587.

96 Bo Yibo, Ruogan Zhongda Juece 2, pp. 1084–5.

97 Ma Qibin et al., Zhongguo Gongchan Dang Zhizheng Sishi Nian, p. 220. For
Deng's further use of the black cat/white cat analogy, see below, Ch. 12. For
an indication of disagreement at the secretariat meeting, see Xinghuo Liao
Yuan Bianjibu (ed.), Jiefang Jun Jiangling Zhuan (Biographies of PLA generals; hereafter, Jiefang Jun Jiangling Zhuan) 2, p. 65.

[98] Song Renqiong, Chen Pixian, & Ye Fei, 'Fendou buxide jianqiang zhanshi', p. 35.

[99] Bo Yibo, *Ruogan Zhongda Juece* 2, p. 1078. For a latter-day questioning of the 1955 Maoist triumph over collectivization, see *Zhonggong Dangshi Tongxun*, No. 18, 25 Sept. 1994, p. 3.

CHAPTER 10

[1] My use of the term 'non-party' denotes only non-membership of the CCP; it does not signify simply those who were members of no political party, but can include members of the democratic parties. The common CCP (and KMT) term for all people who are not members is *dangwai* (outside the party).

[2] For a discussion of the democratic parties, whose continued existence was a product of their tilt away from the KMT and towards the CCP prior to the formation of the PRC, and of their importance as a symbol of the CCP's willingness to re-establish a united front with the KMT on Taiwan, see *Origins* I, pp. 48–50; for the Anti-Rightist Campaign, see ibid., part 4.

[3] Cong Jin, *Quzhe Fazhande Suiyue*, p. 431; Li Rui, *Lushan Huiyi Shilu*, pp. 60, 72. The relaxation was roughly Jan.–June, 1959.

[4] See Li Weihan, *Huiyi yu Yanjiu, xia*, pp. 859, 864. It also could affect foreign members of the CCP; see the memoirs of Rittenberg & Bennett, *The Man Who Stayed Behind*, pp. 249–50. Rittenberg was more fortunate than many for Lu Dingyi called the Broadcasting Administration and swiftly terminated the attacks.

[5] Cong Jin, *Quzhe Fazhande Suiyue*, pp. 431–2.

[6] See *Origins* II, pp. 310–15.

[7] *Li Weihan Xuanji*, pp. 433–5.

[8] Li Weihan, *Huiyi yu Yanjiu, xia*, p. 865.

[9] *Selected Works of Zhou Enlai* 2, p. 413.

[10] Wang Bangzuo, *Zhongguo Gongchan Dang Tongyi Zhanxian Shi* (A history of the CCP's united front), pp. 530–1.

[11] Li Weihan, who had been a member of Mao's New People's Study Society in Hunan in 1917, had been in the same worker-student group in France as Deng Xiaoping in the early 1920s, but had risen faster than Deng in the party ranks, being briefly in the Politburo when it was first set up on a temporary basis in 1927. As director of the Organization Department in 1933, Li Weihan presided over a public meeting at which Deng was criticized, the fate of supporters of Mao Zedong at that time. At the meeting, Deng was denounced by his second wife Jin Weiying, who declared she wished to draw a clear line between them, organizationally and ideologically. Afterwards, Jin drew a clear line personally, too, by leaving Deng and marrying Li Weihan. See Gao Xin & He Pin, *Gao Gan Dang'an* (Dossiers on high-ranking cadres), pp. 422–3; Guillermaz, *A History of the Chinese Communist Party, 1921–1949*, pp. 62, 150, 243; Harrison, *The Long March to Power*, pp. 230–1; Wang Jianying (ed.), *Zhongguo Gongchan Dang Zuzhi Shi Ziliao Huibian* (A collection of historical material on the organizational history of the CCP), p. 71; Li Weihan, *Huiyi yu Yanjiu, shang*, pp. 195–6.

[12] Li Weihan, *Huiyi yu Yanjiu, xia*, pp. 865–8.

[13] Cong Jin, *Quzhe Fazhande Suiyue*, p. 433.

[14] See for instance the very sparse reports on the 1962 sessions of the NPC and the CPPCC in *Renmin Shouce, 1962*, pp. 3–13.

[15] This was of course the slogan of the victorious Clinton campaign in the 1992 US presidential election.

[16] From 1950, the CCP's first full year in power, to 1965, the last year before the Cultural Revolution, the paper averaged 275 editorials a year. This average was exceeded during 1954-60, and in that period the two most active years were 1958 (442) and 1960 (459), the first and last years of the GLF. In 1961, the paper printed only 245 editorials, a drop of over 46% from the previous year; in January and February, there were actually more editorials than in the equivalent months of 1960, but hereafter the monthly output dropped precipitously. The annual figure fell another 40% to 147 in 1962, and though it rose by over a third to 205 in 1963, this still left 1962-3 as the least active period for the paper's editorial writers in the period before 1966.

[17] *Origins* II, p. 293.

[18] The comparisons and calculations have been made on the basis of the editorial listings in Oksenberg & Henderson, *Research Guide to* People's Daily *Editorials, 1949-1975*.

[19] The only mandatory attendees were the vice-head of state, the chairman of the NPC, and the premier; see art. 43 of the 1954 *Constitution of the PRC*.

[20] For instance, to make his speech 'On the correct handling of contradictions among the people' on 27 Feb. 1957; see *Origins* I, p. 184.

[21] Cong Jin, *Quzhe Fazhande Suiyue*, pp. 432-6. Zhou Enlai also spoke at the SSC, but neither man's speech is included in their official selected works; fortunately, this source has a lengthy account of Liu's speech.

[22] *Selected Works of Zhou Enlai* 2, pp. 366-82, 401-15. Zhonggong Zhongyang Tongyi Zhanxian Gongzuobu & Zhonggong Zhongyang Yanjiushi (eds.), *Zhou Enlai Tongyi Zhanxian Wenxuan* (Selections from Zhou Enlai on the united front; hereafter, *Zhou Enlai Tongyi Zhanxian Wenxuan*), pp. 425-30.

[23] Cong Jin, *Quzhe Fazhande Suiyue*, p. 436.

[24] *Zhongguo Dangdai Wenxue Shi Chugao, shang*, p. 101. His earlier February speech dealt very specifically with the problems of writers and will be dealt with below.

[25] *Selected Works of Zhou Enlai* 2, p. 366.

[26] Ibid., pp. 367-70.

[27] Ibid., p. 370.

[28] See Schwarcz, *Time for Telling Truth is Running Out: Conversations with Zhang Shenfu*, p. 122; see also Mirsky's review of it, 'The Party's Secrets', *New York Review of Books*, 25 Mar. 1993, where this point is made.

[29] *Selected Works of Zhou Enlai* 2, pp. 371-7.

[30] See for instance Mao's discussion of this issue in MacFarquhar, Cheek, & Wu, *The Secret Speeches of Chairman Mao*, pp. 278-9.

[31] *Selected Works of Zhou Enlai* 2, pp. 377-82.

[32] *Zhou Enlai Tongyi Zhanxian Wenxuan*, pp. 426-8. Despite what happened to the intellectuals—excoriated as 'the stinking ninth category'—in the Cultural Revolution, this source (p. 407) draws attention in a note to the significance of Zhou's description of the intellectuals as belonging to the working people.

[33] For the text of the CC order, see *Dangde Wenxian*, No. 2, 1994, pp. 43-8.

[34] 'Dangdai Zhongguode Minzu Gongzuo' Bianjibu (ed.), *Dangdai Zhongguo Minzu Gongzuo Dashiji, 1949-1988* (Chronology of contemporary

China's nationalities work, 1949–1988), p. 161. A quarter of a century later, the Tacheng authorities acknowledged the disastrous impact of the post-GLF famine; see 'Guanghuide Sanshi Nian' Bianjibu (ed.), *Guanghuide Sanshi Nian, 1955–1985* (A glorious thirty years, 1955–1985), p. 662. According to one Chinese account, as many as 70,000 fled; quoted in Dreyer, 'The PLA and Regionalism in Xinjiang', *The Pacific Review*, No. 1, 1994, pp. 43–4.

35 *Zhou Enlai Tongyi Zhanxian Wenxuan*, pp. 428–30.
36 Guofang Daxue, *Cankao Ziliao* 24, pp. 95–106.
37 MacFarquhar, *The Hundred Flowers Campaign and the Chinese Intellectuals*, pp. 195–202.
38 *Origins* II, pp. 310–15.
39 *Zhou Enlai Tongyi Zhanxian Wenxuan*, p. 428.
40 Zhou Zhenxiang & Shao Jingchun (eds.), *Xin Zhongguo Fazhi Jianshe Sishi Nian Yaolan (1949–1988)* (An overview of the construction of a legal system in new China, 1949–1988), p. 291.
41 For the first meeting of what was then called the 'Political Consultative Conference' in 1946, see Pepper, *Civil War in China*, pp. 137–8; for its formal roles in the founding of the PRC and after the creation of the NPC, see van Slyke, *Enemies and Friends*, pp. 208–10, 236–8.
42 *Selected Works of Zhou Enlai* 2, p. 401.
43 Ibid., pp. 401–3. For a discussion of the evolution of the six criteria, see *Origins* I, pp. 262–9; for the original text of the contradictions speech without the six criteria, see MacFarquhar, Cheek, & Wu, *The Secret Speeches of Chairman Mao*, pp. 131–89.
44 *Selected Works of Zhou Enlai* 2, pp. 404–8; *Origins* I, pp. 49–50, 110–19.
45 For Li's long written report to that conference, see *Li Weihan Xuanji*, pp. 432–51. While Li was naturally concerned to build on the friendly atmosphere Zhou had tried to generate, his report was nevertheless permeated with routine categorizations and appraisals, all of them likely to induce in his readership a feeling that though the CCP might need them more now, its fundamental attitudes towards the *dangwai* had not changed.
46 It is significant that in post-Cultural Revolution PRC studies of CCP policies towards the intellectuals in the early 1960s, the only speeches by senior leaders that are commonly reprinted or cited are by these two men. See for instance, Zhonggong Zhongyang Shujichu Yanjiushi Wenhuazu (ed.), *Dang he Guojia Lingdaoren Lun Wenyi* (Party and state leaders on literature and the arts), and Wuhan Shifan Xueyuan Zhongwenxi Dangdai Wenxue Jiaoyanshi (ed.), *Guanyu Dangdai Wenyi Wentide Neibu Jianghua Xuanbian* (Selection of internal speeches on issues in contemporary literature and the arts). Zhou, in particular, has been continually extolled in a seemingly inexhaustible stream of articles and books for his attitude towards and actions in favour of intellectuals. See for instance, *Zhou Enlai yu Wenyi* published in 1980 in two volumes, and Chen Huangmei (ed.), *Zhou Enlai yu Yishujiamen* (Zhou Enlai and artists), published in 1992.
47 See above, Ch. 5, pp. 114–16. The 1959 speech was made in May during the brief rational interlude in the GLF. The three speeches are reprinted in, for instance, *Zhou Enlai yu Wenyi, shang*, pp. 5–46, which also includes Chen Yi's 1962 speech as an appendix (pp. 47–93), and in Zhou Enlai, *Guanyu Wenyi Gongzuode Sanci Jianghua* (Three speeches on literary and art work). The 1962 speech anthologized in works on culture, it should be

noted, is the one to playwrights in Beijing made on 17 Feb., not the one on intellectuals made in Canton on 2 Mar. But it is the latter, not the former, which appears in Zhou's *Selected Works* 2.

48   This was a meeting to prepare for the national conference in Canton the following month; *Zhongguo Dangdai Wenxue Shi Chugao, shang*, p. 101. See also *Zhou Enlai yu Wenyi, shang*, p. 32.

49   'You xie sheng shi wei jiu buken chuanda'; *Zhou Enlai yu Wenyi, shang*, p. 32.

50   *Selected Works of Zhou Enlai* 2, p. 332.

51   *Zhou Enlai yu Wenyi, shang*, p. 32.

52   *Origins* II, pp. 25, 59–63.

53   If one assumes that Zhou had exhibited his customary caution and sent a text of his speech to Mao, one must conclude that the Chairman chose not to confer his imprimatur. Had the Chairman authorized the speech for distribution, provincial leaders like Ke Qingshi would have had to comply.

54   Comparing the 1959, 1961, and 1962 speeches in Zhou Enlai, *Guanyu Wenyi Gongzuode Sanci Jianghua*, we find that the premier referred to Mao about once every two pages in the 1959 text, just over once a page in the 1961 text, and once every 1.5 pages in the 1962 one. Moreover the 1962 frequency is somewhat diluted by the fact that nearly half of the references are to Mao's thought, the common property of the CCP, rather than to the living, breathing leader himself. From Mao's perspective, one might conclude that in 1959, even though the speech had been a short one, Zhou had been decidedly casual in his acknowledgements to his leader; that a suitably chastened premier had been far more circumspect in 1961; and that in the new atmosphere of 1962, Zhou was again tending to skimp on his genuflections.

55   Zhou's account makes it impossible to detect precisely when his first stage gave way to his second; clearly he recognized the significance of the Anti-Rightist Campaign starting in mid-1957; but at one point he seems to date the second stage from the beginning of 1958, at another at the beginning of the autumn of 1959; see *Zhou Enlai yu Wenyi, shang*, p. 33. Only the contemporary commencement of the third stage is clear.

56   *Zhou Enlai yu Wenyi, shang*, pp. 33–4. Zhou gave Shakespeare's plays as an example of something good though foreign. 'Big nation chauvinism' was a phrase coined by the Chinese in 1956 when criticizing the behaviour of the Soviet Union towards its East European satellites; see *Origins* I, pp. 170–1, 365 (11), (13). For a description of the anti-foreign, principally antimissionary, nature of the Boxers, whose motto was *Fu Qing mie yang* (Support the Qing [dynasty], destroy the foreigner), see Esherick, *The Origins of the Boxer Uprising*, esp. ch. 3.

57   *Zhou Enlai yu Wenyi, shang*, pp. 34–5.

58   Ibid., p. 35. Zhou's normal excursions into Marxist theory went no further than ritual quotes from Mao's works. This was a risky reference, partly because Mao certainly considered himself to be the only leader with the authority to manipulate Marxism for Chinese purposes, and partly because the Chairman had rejected Engels's formulation in 1958 by formulating a new 'law of the affirmation of the negation', thus throwing China's ideologues into total confusion; see Schram, *The Thought of Mao Tse-tung*, pp. 137–41. It is possible that in the press of events, Zhou Enlai had missed Mao's theoretical innovation; what is clear is that Zhou was rather pleased with this formulation, for he repeated it later in his speech.

59 *Zhou Enlai yu Wenyi, shang*, pp. 35–7; cf. Schram, *Mao Tse-tung Unrehearsed*, p. 165.

60 *Zhou Enlai yu Wenyi, shang*, pp. 38–9. For a discussion of the gradual acceptance of Mao's 1957 formulation, which he devised at Qingdao that summer, see *Origins* I, pp. 287, 304, 308.

61 *Zhou Enlai yu Wenyi, shang*, pp. 39–43. Zhou would not have been saved by his codicil that it would be contrary to the thought of Chairman Mao to say that there were heroes without faults.

62 Hu Feng was a distinguished party writer who fell foul of the literary bureaucracy and was denounced in 1955 in a campaign in which Mao played a leading backstairs role; see Goldman, *Literary Dissent in Communist China*, ch. 7; Mao's interventions are in *Jianguo Yilai Mao Zedong Wengao* 5, pp. 108–15, 124–5, 130, 144–5, 148–9, 153–66, 168–78.

63 *Zhou Enlai yu Wenyi, shang*, pp. 43–6; the quotation is on p. 45.

64 The speech takes up fifty pages of *Zhou Enlai yu Wenyi, shang*, and contains over 30,000 characters (*Chen Yi Zhuan*, p. 534). While in Canton, Chen had earlier attended a meeting of the standing committee of the MAC; Li Shufa, *Chen Yi Nianpu* (A chronicle of Chen Yi's life) 2, p. 911.

65 *Zhou Enlai yu Wenyi, shang*, p. 58. Chen Yi's quoted remarks underline formal advocacy of a more sensibly supportive policy towards intellectual life in mid-1961—see e.g. the comments of the centre on the Fourteen Articles quoted in *Zhonggong Dangshi Yanjiu*, No. 4, 1993, p. 72—in this sphere as in others, nothing really happened until after the Seven Thousand Cadres Conference.

66 *Chen Yi Zhuan*, p. 530.

67 *Zhou Enlai yu Wenyi, shang*, p. 50. Unlike Zhou who spoke to a joint session of the science and drama conferences, Chen Yi addressed the scientists on 5 March and the playwrights on 6 March. Chen's frequent references to scientists in his 6 March speech suggest that both addresses had a common framework though there were clearly topics in the later one which were irrelevant for the scientists.

68 *Chen Yi Zhuan*, pp. 525, 534.

69 *Zhou Enlai yu Wenyi, shang*, p. 48.

70 Ibid., pp. 48–55; the quotation is on p. 52. Chen quoted Mao as saying at the Seven Thousand Cadres Conference, 'Comrades, you must acknowledge that in the past three years we have sometimes done some stupid things! We are very stupid!' Chen's quotation is close enough to the official version published years later; cf. *Mao Zedong Zhuzuo Xuandu, xia*, p. 833; Schram's translation of a Red Guard version is in *Mao Tse-tung Unrehearsed*, p. 180.

71 Possibly Chen knew and his audience felt that Liu was basically uninterested in culture and would defer to Mao and Zhou in this field. Certainly I have not come across a book equivalent to *Zhou Enlai yu Wenyi* covering 'Liu Shaoqi and literature and the arts'; and a major study of Liu's work in various fields does not include a section or even a chapter on culture; see Lü Xingdou, *Liu Shaoqi he Tade Shiye*.

72 *Zhou Enlai yu Wenyi, shang*, p. 59.

73 Ibid., pp. 60–1.

74 Ibid., pp. 61–3. Chen Yi was obviously referring to himself when he said 'vice-premier', for he had just criticized two plays whose authors seem to have been in the audience. Chen felt they had depicted opportunist characters incorrectly; they were not traitors. Chen may have been subliminally

defending his fellow marshal, Peng Dehuai, who had of course been condemned for 'right opportunism' at the 1959 Lushan conference.

75 Chen, 'Multiplicity in Uniformity: Poetry and the Great Leap Forward', pp. 1–15, esp. p. 5.

76 *Zhou Enlai yu Wenyi, shang*, pp. 63, 86–8; the quotation is on p. 63.

77 Ibid., pp. 66–8, 75, 86, 90–3. Hai Mo's fate during the anti-rightist movement, and the translation of his title, is in Tung & MacKerras, *Drama in the People's Republic of China*, p. 16.

78 *Zhou Enlai yu Wenyi, shang*, pp. 74–5.

79 Ibid., p. 78. There is no way of knowing if, in this case, there is any validity in the common assumption made during the Cultural Revolution that whenever this particular phrase had been used, it represented an implicit criticism of Mao.

80 Ibid., pp. 78–85.

81 Ibid., pp. 58, 79.

82 Wu & Li, *A Single Tear*, pp. 181–2. Wu, then a 'rightist' college teacher less than a year out of a labour reform camp, recalls that his unit party secretary told him he could now be assigned temporary work because of 'the recent change in the party's policy toward intellectuals' heralded by the Canton conference, but warned him to be careful since the political line regularly shifted from left to right.

83 Hsiao, *Traveller Without a Map*, p. 230.

84 *Chen Yi Zhuan*, p. 534; Zhonghua Renmin Gongheguo Waijiaobu & Waijiao Shi Yanjiushi (eds.), *Huainian Chen Yi* (Remember Chen Yi), p. 128.

85 Hu Sheng, 'Hu Qiaomu he dangshi gongzuo' (Hu Qiaomu and party history work), *Zhonggong Dangshi Yanjiu*, No. 1, 1994, p. 75.

86 *Zhongguo Dangdai Wenxue Shi Chugao, shang*, pp. 102–3; for an analysis, see Goldman, *China's Intellectuals: Advise and Dissent*, pp. 46–50.

CHAPTER 11

1 The chief attack was levelled by Yao Wenyuan, later a member of the notorious Gang of Four. His two main polemics were 'On the new historical play *The Dismissal of Hai Rui*', originally published in the Shanghai *Wenhui Bao*, 10 Nov. 1965, translated in *Chinese Studies in History and Philosophy* 2, No. 1, Fall 1968, pp. 13–43; and 'On "Three-Family Village"—The reactionary nature of *Evening Chats at Yenshan* and *Notes from Three-Family Village*', originally jointly published in the Shanghai papers, *Jiefang Ribao* and *Wenhui Bao*, 10 May 1966, and translated in *The Great Socialist Cultural Revolution in China (1)* (hereafter, Yao Wenyuan, 'On "Three-Family Village" '), pp. 29–69.

2 See for instance Goldman, *China's Intellectuals: Advise and Dissent*, pp. 18–38.

3 For a brief biographical sketch of Liao Mosha, see URI, *Who's Who in Communist China* 1, rev. edn., pp. 420–1; Liao was not well enough known to merit a mention in the first (1966) edition of this work. For a brief autobiographical note, see *Liao Mosha Wenji* (The collected works of Liao Mosha) 1, pp. 1–5. Vol. 2 of this four-volume set contains his contributions to 'Notes from a Three-Family Village', his 'confessions' about these articles made during the Cultural Revolution (pp. 444–88), and his post-

Cultural Revolution versions of events (pp. 198–204, 489–95). Liao died on 27 Dec. 1990, at the age of 84, according to an NCNA report from Beijing on 30 Dec. 1990, and was cremated at the Babaoshan Cemetery of Fallen Revolutionaries on 4 Jan. 1991; see FBIS-CHI-91-003, p. 21, and ibid., 010, p. 27. The NCNA was either slightly inaccurate or going by the traditional Chinese system of reckoning people to be one year old on the day of their birth, for Liao himself said that he was born on 16 Jan. 1907, and was therefore not quite 84 at his death; *Liao Mosha Wenji* 1, p. 1.

⁴ *Liao Mosha Wenji* 2, p. 202.
⁵ Cheek, *Propaganda and Culture in Mao's China: Deng Tuo and the Intelligentsia* (hereafter, Cheek, *Propaganda and Culture in Mao's China*), ch. 2. For reminiscences of Deng Tuo in the 1930s and 1940s, see also *Jin-Cha-Ji Ribao* Shi Yanjiuhui (ed.), *Renmin Xinwenjia Deng Tuo* (A journalist of the people, Deng Tuo), pp. 91–124.
⁶ See Cheek, 'Textually Speaking', in MacFarquhar, Cheek, and Wu, *The Secret Speeches of Chairman Mao*, p. 83.
⁷ See 'Xinwenjie Renwu' Bianji Weiyuanhui (ed.), *Xinwenjie Renwu (5): Deng Tuo* (Personalities of the journalistic world [5]: Deng Tuo; hereafter, *Xinwenjie Renwu (5): Deng Tuo*), p. 51.
⁸ Deng Tuo complained about this to friends; Liu Binyan, *A Higher Kind of Loyalty*, p. 55. I am grateful to Timothy Cheek for this reference.
⁹ Cheek, *Propaganda and Culture in Mao's China*, ch. 4; *Zhonggong Dangshi Renwuzhuan* 50, pp. 283–4; *Origins* I, pp. 282, 312; Goldman, 'Mao's Obsession with the Political Role of Literature and the Intellectuals', in MacFarquhar, Cheek, & Wu, *The Secret Speeches of Chairman Mao*, pp. 50–2. The editors of the *Zhonggong Dangshi Renwuzhuan* series of biographies of leading communists made their own unspoken but pointed comment on Mao's long-running feud with Deng Tuo. In the final four volumes of their first 50-volume series, they published the biographies of the four great figures of the revolution in reverse order of current precedence: Zhu De in vol. 47, Liu Shaoqi in 48, Zhou Enlai in 49, ending grandly with Mao in 50. But in vol. 50, as just indicated, they also included the biography of Deng Tuo, suggesting that they believed that Deng had as much right as Mao to be considered a true revolutionary. One can think of no other reason why they would have waited till 1991 to publish a biography of Deng, when a vast amount of material about him, as well as his collected works, had appeared by the mid-1980s.
¹⁰ Wang Bisheng, *Deng Tuo Pingzhuan* (A critical biography of Deng Tuo), p. 178.
¹¹ Ibid., p. 186, attempts to excuse Deng Tuo by saying he could not escape the influence of the times; *Zhonggong Dangshi Renwuzhuan* 50, pp. 287–8 makes the same point, but adds that Deng was already beginning to expose leftism. See also Cheek, *Propaganda and Culture in Mao's China*, ch. 4, where it is suggested that Deng Tuo was obeying Leninist principles of displaying public unity and obedience, reserving the right to debate within the party.
¹² See Qiu Zhizhuo *et al.* (eds.), *Zhonggong Dang Shi Renming Lu* (A record of names in CCP history), pp. 50–1. The formal announcement of the formation of the new CCP regional bureaux had only been made after the CC's 9th plenum in January 1961. If the dating in this source is accurate, the bureaux were presumably set up in advance of the plenum.
¹³ Cheek, 'Introduction' in 'The Politics of Cultural Reform: Deng Tuo and

the Retooling of Chinese Marxism', *Chinese Law and Government*, Winter 1983–4 (hereafter, Cheek, 'Introduction'), p. 10.

14 See Liao Mosha (ed.), *Yi Deng Tuo* (Remembering Deng Tuo), pp. 111–15; the quotation is on p. 113. The exact location of Malancun in Hebei province can be seen in the map in *Xinwenjie Renwu (5): Deng Tuo*, p. 27. The use of a character for 'nan' instead of 'lan' is a pun; as a Fujianese, Deng Tuo pronounced both words 'lan'; see Cheek, 'Introduction' p. 9.

15 Cheek, *Propaganda and Culture in Mao's China*, ch. 5, where the sum is estimated at roughly $7.50. Apparently, Deng Tuo also received 20,000 yuan ($10,000) for the collection of his columns published in book form in 1963.

16 Liao Mosha, *Yi Deng Tuo*, p. 115.

17 Ma Nancun, *Yanshan Yehua* (Evening chats at Yanshan), pp. 5–7; translated by Cheek in *Chinese Law and Government*, Winter 1983–4, pp. 38–40. The editors of *Beijing Wanbao* later claimed that Deng's first article had an inspirational effect, especially upon young people, at a time when national circumstances made many people aimless and dispirited; Liao, *Yi Deng Tuo*, p. 119.

18 Ibid., p. 116; Ma Nancun, *Yanshan Yehua*, calligraphic frontispiece, translated by Cheek in *Chinese Law and Government*, Winter 1983–4, p. 35.

19 Liao Mosha, *Yi Deng Tuo*, p. 115.

20 H. C. Chuang, quoted in Cheek, 'Deng Tuo: A Chinese Leninist Approach to Journalism', in Hamrin & Cheek (eds.), *China's Establishment Intellectuals*, p. 112.

21 *Zhonggong Dangshi Renwuzhuan* 50, p. 290.

22 SCMP 3912, p. 10.

23 *Zhonggong Dangshi Renwuzhuan* 50, p. 291. For Yao's later attacks, see Yao Wenyuan, 'On "Three-Family Village" . . .', pp. 29–69. The Chinese text is more conveniently available in *Mingbao Yuekan* Bianjihui & Ding Wang (eds.), *Zhonggong Wenhua Da Geming Ziliao Huibian, 2: Deng Tuo Xuanji* (A collection of material on the CCP's Great Cultural Revolution, 2: Selected works on Deng Tuo's case; hereafter, Ding Wang, *Deng Tuo Xuanji*), pp. 408–31.

24 On the eve of his fall at the start of the Cultural Revolution, Peng Zhen is reported to have said to a group of political allies: 'I have never lagged behind others in co-operative enterprises, suppression of reactionaries, and opposition to revisionism, but I have been rather backward on the academic side . . . I am ignorant about many things just because my schooling began late'; SCMP(S) 195, p. 27. Liu Ren's remark is in ibid. 175, p. 37. Anyone thinking cabbage control in the capital a bizarre excuse, should consult Nossal, *Dateline-Peking*, pp. 48–9.

25 This point was made to Timothy Cheek by one of the men who edited p. 3 of the paper on which *Yanshan Yehua* appeared.

26 Mao's concern for Wu Han is indicated by his personal handling of the latter's application for CCP membership mentioned below, n. 29. There is also evidence of the two men privately discussing historical issues in 1954; see Gong Yuzhi, Pang Xianzhi, & Shi Zhongquan, *Mao Zedongde Dushu Shenghuo*, pp.11–12.

27 In addition to Yao's polemic cited above, see also the articles collected and translated in *Chinese Studies in History and Philosophy* 2, Nos. 1 (Fall 1968) and 3 (Spring 1969), and *Chinese Studies in History* (a continuation of the

previous journal) 3, Nos. 1 (Fall 1969), 2 (Winter 1969–70), and 3 (Spring 1970).

[28] See *Deng Tuo Wenji* (The collected works of Deng Tuo) 1, p. 469; *Liao Mosha Wenji* 1, pp. 3, 200.

[29] Su Shuangbi & Wang Hongzhi, *Wu Han Zhuan* (A biography of Wu Han), p. 356. According to this source, Wu Han had applied for membership in December 1948. Mao approved the application, but wrote personally to Wu Han to explain that Zhou Enlai would decide when would be the most advantageous moment for Wu's entry into the CCP to take place; ibid., p. 354. Presumably it was delayed because it was felt that Wu Han's support for communist policies would have greater impact on his fellow intellectuals if delivered from outside the CCP. At the point when Wu Han was finally permitted to join in March 1957, Mao seems to have felt that the intellectuals had been either won over to the communist cause or neutralized—see, for example, his speech in Shanghai on 20 Mar. 1957, in MacFarquhar, Cheek, & Wu, *The Secret Speeches of Chairman Mao*, pp. 354–6—so presumably Wu Han's non-party status was less important to the CCP's wooing of his colleagues. For an analysis of Wu Han's united-front work, see Mary G. Mazur, 'Intellectual Activism in China During the 1940s: Wu Han in the United Front and the Democratic League', *CQ* No. 133, 1993, pp. 27–55. An even more striking case of the CCP insisting on a fellow-traveller remaining outside the party was that of Song Qingling (Mme Sun Yat-sen), who was finally granted membership literally on her deathbed—she became a CCP member on 15 May 1981, and died on 29 May 1981; see Sheng Ping (ed.), *Zhongguo Gongchan Dang Renming Dacidian, 1921–1991* (A dictionary of notables of the CCP, 1921–1991), p. 385.

[30] Su Shuangbi & Wang Hongzhi, *Wu Han Zhuan*, p. 355. This appointment came ten months after Wu Han was denied party membership. Wu apparently did not want to accept the municipal post, preferring 'to retire after meritorious service' (*gong cheng shen tui*), but was persuaded to do so by Zhou Enlai. Is there a hint here that Wu Han resented being palmed off with a largely ceremonial post in lieu of party membership and the substantive power he might hope to win with it?

[31] The 1954 and 1965 versions of Wu Han's life of Zhu Yuanzhang (*Zhu Yuanzhang Zhuan*) comprise vol. 2 of *Wu Han Wenji* (The collected works of Wu Han). The first two versions, full of errors according to the author's preface to the 1965 version, were published in 1944 and 1949; ibid., p. 255.

[32] Mao made this remark to Mei Bai, a middle-rank Hubei provincial official whom Wang Renzhong had seconded to the Chairman; see Jia Sinan (ed.), *1915–1976: Mao Zedong Renji Jiaowang Shilu* (1915–1976: Records of Mao Zedong's inter-personal contacts), p. 166.

[33] According to Mao's doctor, the Chairman had much enjoyed the performance of a Hunanese opera about Hai Rui in Changsha in 1958 put on by the provincial 1st secretary Zhou Xiaozhou. While Mao was participating in the 7th plenum in April 1959 in Shanghai, 1st secretary Ke Qingshi arranged a performance of another opera about Hai Rui; Li, *The Private Life of Chairman Mao*, pp. 285–6, 295–7. Dr Li speculates that Zhou Xiaozhou, who was purged along with Peng Dehuai at the 1959 Lushan conference for criticizing the GLF, was implicitly criticizing the Chairman, but this must be regarded as moot since Ke could hardly be accused of harbouring that intention. With hindsight, one Chinese view is that from Mao's first citing

of Hai Rui, he was attempting to lure critics into the open, a judgement which Li Rui, one of Mao's adjunct secretaries in 1959 preferred to leave to historians; Li Rui, *Lushan Huiyi Shilu*, p. 92.

34 *Origins* II, pp. 208–12. In that discussion, I speculated that the then-unidentified 'leading comrade' who persuaded Wu Han to write about Hai Rui might be either Zhou Enlai or Mao himself. As it turns out, it was one of Mao's senior aides. The role of Hu Qiaomu is revealed in, for instance, Xia Nai and Su Shuangbi, *Wu Hande Xueshu Shengya* (Wu Han's academic career), p. 205.

35 A text of the play is contained in *Wu Han Wenji* 4, pp. 376–427; it appeared originally in *Beijing Wenyi* (Beijing literature and art) in Jan. 1961. For a translation of the play see Wu Han, *The Dismissal of Hai Jui*. Descriptions of how the play came to be written can be found in Xia Nai and Su Shuangbi, *Wu Hande Xueshu Shengya*, pp. 112–14; *Wu Han he 'Hai Rui Ba Guan'* (Wu Han and 'The Dismissal of Hai Rui'), pp. 2–5; Su Shuangbi & Wang Hongzhi, *Wu Han Zhuan*, pp. 310–12, 356–7. Another version of the title issue is contained in Zhong Kan, *Kang Sheng Pingzhuan*, p. 175: According to this account, the play was entitled *Hai Rui Ba Guan* from the fourth draft to distinguish it from other plays on Hai Rui, at the suggestion of the director of the Yunnan Plant Research Institute, presumably Wu Han's friend,

36 *Wu Han he 'Hai Rui Ba Guan'*, p. 5. According to Cong Jin, *Quzhe Fazhande Suiyue*, p. 609, it was performed in January. In Su and Wang, *Wu Han Zhuan*, p. 357, the dating of the performance is given as month 11 of 1961, but this is presumably a misprint for month 1.

37 *Liao Mosha Wenji* 2, pp. 80–2. Liao's article triggered a number of other commentaries on Wu Han's play; ibid., p. 447. Liao's article ' "History" and "Drama" ' appeared in *Beijing Wanbao* on 16 Feb. 1961.

38 Yan Qi (ed.), *Zhongguo Ge Minzhu Dangpai Shi Renwuzhuan* (Biographies from the histories of the various democratic parties), p. 347; Su Shuangbi & Wang Hongzhi, *Wu Han Zhuan*, p. 312. Wu Han was understandably delighted when he was informed of the Chairman's words; ibid. Most Chinese accounts are coy about whether or not this dinner took place after Mao had seen a performance of the play or simply read the published text; the wording in Yan Qi could indicate either, though one Western scholar assumes he saw it (Fisher, 'Wu Han: The "Upright Official" as a Model in the Humanities', in Hamrin & Cheek (eds.), *China's Establishment Intellectuals*, p. 165). One would have thought that if Mao had seen the play—and as noted by Chen Yi, Mao did not like going to plays (ch. 10)—this fact would have been given far greater emphasis after the Cultural Revolution, but perhaps official historians wished to protect the Chairman's reputation. Only one source states categorically that Mao said the play was well acted, thus indicating that he saw it; Lin Qingshan, *Kang Sheng Waizhuan*, p. 257. Logic would suggest that, had Mao merely read the play, he would have been more likely to have called in the author than the actor. On the other hand, he might have called in the actor to hear him read some of his lines, precisely because he had no intention of seeing the play on stage. According to one source, Jiang Qing saw the play and took an instant dislike to it; Lin Qingshan, *Lin Biao Zhuan* (A biography of Lin Biao) 1, pp. 145–6.

39 A photograph of the title page of the Mao volume with Mao's signature and the date 28 September is included as a frontispiece in both Xia Nai and Su Shuangbi, *Wu Hande Xueshu Shengya* and Su Shuangbi & Wang Hongzhi,

Wu Han Zhuan. The caption in the former volume explains that the gift was made in 1961. *Selected Works of Mao Tse-tung* 4 had been published on the occasion of National Day (1 Oct.), 1960—'Quarterly Chronicle and Documentation', *CQ*, No. 4, 1960, p. 140—so clearly Wu Han was not on any list of those who ought to receive an inscribed copy on publication. Nor is there anything in the chronology of Wu Han's life in Su & Wang, *Wu Han Zhuan*, p. 357, to suggest why Mao should have made the presentation on 28 Sept. 1961. Perhaps Mao developed the habit of sending out gift copies for National Day.

40 Yan Qi, *Zhongguo Ge Minzhu Dangpai Shi Renwuzhuan*, pp. 338–9.
41 Yao Wenyuan, 'On "Three-Family Village" . . .', p. 33.
42 For a brief discussion of other columns, see Cheek, *Propaganda and Culture in Mao's China*, ch. 5.
43 Informant L.
44 *Liao Mosha Wenji* 2, pp. 198–204.
45 All were senior officials of the municipal party apparatus. Liao Mosha reports meeting Wu Han often from 1959 onwards; *Liao Mosha Wenji* 2, p. 449.
46 Ibid., p. 201.
47 Ibid., p. 203. Liao Mosha goes on sarcastically to suggest that just because 'Notes' was unorganized, its critics felt the need to help organize it, and to lump with it articles written elsewhere by the three columnists, as if they had been plotting together as far back as the 1930s when they did not even know each other; ibid., pp. 203–4.
48 At the start of the Cultural Revolution, there was an outpouring of criticism against the members of the three-family village. In addition to Yao Wenyuan, 'On "Three-Family Village" . . .', the main ones are Lin Chieh (Lin Jie) *et al.* (compilers), 'Teng To's *Evening Chats at Yenshan* is Anti-Party and Anti-socialist Double-talk', and Chi Pen-yu (Qi Benyu), 'On the Bourgeois Stand of *Frontline* and the *Peking Daily*', both published in *The Great Socialist Cultural Revolution in China (2)*, pp. 12–65.
49 See Fisher, 'The "Upright Official" as a Model in the Humanities', pp. 158–9 on Wu Han and Des Forges, 'Liao Mosha, Three Family Village, and Yao Wenyuan: Ambiguous Relationships with the Party Bureaucracy'.
50 'These slanders and attacks, *with Teng To's articles at their core* . . .'; Yao Wenyuan, 'On "Three-Family Village" . . .', p. 50, emphasis added.
51 The translations are in Yao Wenyuan, 'On "Three-Family Village" . . .', p. 39; they do not distort the original (Ma Nancun, *Yanshan Yehua*, pp. 11–13) and are consistent with Cheek's rendering, *Chinese Law and Government*, Winter 1983–4, pp. 51–3. The latter work (pp. 79–85) also includes translated extracts from the Yao diatribe.
52 Yao Wenyuan, 'On "Three-Family Village" . . .', p. 39.
53 Ibid., p. 40; Ding Wang, *Deng Tuo Xuanji*, p. 414. The original article is in Ma Nancun, *Yanshan Yehua*, pp. 78–9.
54 Yao Wenyuan, 'On "Three-Family Village" . . .', pp. 47–8.
55 Ibid., pp. 41–2; Ma Nancun, *Yanshan Yehua*, pp. 60–2; Cheek, 'The Politics of Cultural Reform', pp. 44–6.
56 Cheek, *Propaganda and Culture in Mao's China*, ch. 5.
57 Fisher, 'The "Upright Official" as a Model in the Humanities', p. 171.
58 Des Forges, 'Liao Mosha, Three Family Village, and Yao Wenyuan'; I am also indebted to Huang Jing for an analysis of Liao Mosha's output. Deng Tuo also wrote satiric *zawen* in the 1930s while still in Fujian; Cheek, *Propaganda and Culture in Mao's China*, ch. 1.

572 NOTES TO PAGES 257–8

60 See App. 2.
61 Cheek, *Propaganda and Culture in Mao's China*, ch. 5.
62 Ibid.; Fisher, 'The "Upright Official" as a Model in the Humanities', p. 171;
Des Forges, 'Liao Mosha, Three Family Village, and Yao Wenyuan'.
63 Cartoons, too, reflected the greater tolerance for criticizing bureaucracy
during 1961–2 as compared with 1964–5; see Hua Junwu, *Chinese Satire and
Humour*, for changes in topics and approach during these years.
64 Over the course of many years, since the end of the Cultural Revolution,
the present author has questioned a range of politically sophisticated Beijing residents on this topic. Quite a few remembered reading the offending
articles at the time, but only one was prepared to claim having read political significance into them then or to have marvelled at the temerity of the
authors. According to the leading Western scholar on Deng Tuo, one of the
two offending newspaper columns 'apparently raised no eyebrows' within
Beijing municipal party circles, and there is no available record of any
comment, critical or otherwise, made by Chinese leaders, including Mao,
on either column at the time; Cheek, *Propaganda and Culture in Mao's
China*, ch. 5.

PART THREE: CLASS STRUGGLE

CHAPTER 12

[1] 'Changing Signals' was how Margaret Thatcher described the rightward swing to 'Thatcherism' which she initiated when she became British prime minister in 1979; Thatcher, *The Downing Street Years*, pp. 38–59.

[2] Cong Jin, *Quzhe Fazhande Suiyue*, pp. 505–6.

[3] For a discussion of Mao's choice of Deng Xiaoping as General Secretary in the 1950s, see *Origins* I, pp. 140–5.

[4] Zhonggong Shanghai Shiwei Dangshi Yanjiushi (ed.), *Mao Zedong zai Shanghai* (Mao Zedong in Shanghai), p. 435; *Mao Zedong he tade Mishu Tian Jiaying*, p. 62.

[5] In the period from 1949 up to the Cultural Revolution, there appear to have been only two other times when Mao absented himself from key meetings, and only one of these was prior to 1962. In 1954, he was possibly too embarrassed to attend the 7th CC's 4th plenum at which his one-time favourite Gao Gang was disciplined; the more innocuous official explanation is reported by Teiwes, *Politics at Mao's Court*, p. 121. In the first half of 1966, Mao allowed Liu Shaoqi to preside over the meetings at which the first senior victims of the Cultural Revolution were purged (as he wanted), and policies were devised to deal with the mounting campus unrest (for which he would later be able to hold Liu and Deng Xiaoping accountable). These two meetings, along with the two 1962 ones cited, are listed as major meetings in *Zhongyao Huiyiji, xia*.

[6] In *Quzhe Fazhande Suiyue*, pp. 512–13, Cong Jin glosses over the issue, by indicating that Liu was in charge because Mao was out of the capital. Underlining Mao's lack of activity in the first half of 1962, there are only 38 items for that period reprinted in *Jianguo Yilai Mao Zedong Wengao* 10, of which 16 are items for the period through the Seven Thousand Cadres Conference or follow-ups to it; for the second half of 1962, there are 66 items. One of Mao's concerns in the period after the conference was to get secretarial staff to assist him with international materials and the English language; ibid., pp. 68–9.

[7] *Mao Zedong he tade Mishu Tian Jiaying*, p. 63.

[8] 'Lun gongchan dang yuande xiuyang', *RMRB*, 1 July 1962. For the print run of the pamphlet version, see Liu Xiaoming, *Zhonggong Dangjian Shi, 1949–1976* (A history of CCP party building, 1949–1976), p. 157.

[9] Informant S. Cf. the 1952 revised edition (based on a 1949 Chinese edition) of *How to be a Good Communist*, issued by the Foreign Languages Press, pp. 31–7, with *Selected Works of Liu Shaoqi* 1, pp. 121–8. The editors of the latter version have an interesting footnote (Nos. 76–8, p. 442): 'When this article was reprinted by the People's Publishing House in March 1980, the following editorial note appeared in the Chinese edition: 'In the 1962 edition, after the word "counter-revolutionaries" was added "and reformists". This addition was not by the author himself, but by the editors with the

approval of the author. We are now publishing it in accordance with the 1949 edition.'

One of the passages referred to in the note reads 'It is by unremitting struggle against counter-revolutionaries [and reform sts] that we Communists change society and the world, and at the same time change ourselves.' The insertion of the word 'reformists' in the 1962 version would seem totally contrary to the spirit with which we are now told Liu wished the pamphlet to be imbued; 'reformists' were precisely those courted under united front policies. That the 1980s editors felt free to discard it suggests that Liu accepted the addition reluctantly. One possibility is that the 1962 editor, Kang Sheng, or Chen Boda, who also helped revise the article, suggested the insertion at Mao's behest, or in the belief that this would more clearly reflect Mao's current mood. For Chen Boda's role, see Ye Yonglie, *Chen Boda Qiren*, p. 203.

10 *Origins* II, p. 176.

11 Mao apparently first made the suggestion in 1952 and then again in 1960; Liu Xiaoming, *Zhonggong Dangjian Shi*, pp. 154–5. According to this source and Informant J, Liu was reluctant to have even his article republished let alone his selected works, partly perhaps because of modesty, partly because he did not want to appear to be rivalling Mao, but once the Chairman had raised the matter again in 1960, Liu had to give way, though he still procrastinated. A similar picture is given by Deng Liqun, who was a member of the small group preparing the selected works; see Guo Simin & Tian Yu (eds.), *Wo Yanzhongde Liu Shaoqi* (Liu Shaoqi as I saw him), pp. 433–43. Deng too dates Mao's suggestion as being made in 1960 and a formal secretariat decision on the matter being taken at the end of that year. He does not mention Kang Sheng's role.

12 *Wang Li Yiyan*, p. 11. In addition to Kang Sheng and Deng Liqun, the editorial team included Xiong Fu, a senior journalist and propagandist specializing in international affairs, and Wang Zongyi. This group reported to Liu on their work in Changsha in May 1961 when he was in the midst of his rural investigation and clearly uninterested then and later in poring over old articles; see Huang Zheng, *Liu Shaoqi Yi Sheng* (A life of Liu Shaoqi), pp. 375–6.

13 *Liu Shaoqi Xuanji, shang*, contains the latest version of 'How to be a Good Communist', (pp. 97–167), which is translated in *Selected Works of Liu Shaoqi* I, pp. 107–68.

14 See *Li Xiannian Lun Caizheng Jinrong Maoyi*, 2 vols., *passim*; the particular references are in *xia*, pp. 21, 31, 35. Li Xiannian's fellow economic minister, Li Fuchun, was more cautious or more loyal; addressing an East China regional party conference on 7 June, he referred to both Mao and Liu (*Li Fuchun Xuanji* [Selected works of Li Fuchun], p. 289).

15 *Mao Zedong he tade Mishu Tian Jiaying*, pp. 62–3; there is a picture of Tian and his team with the Chairman and the Hubei 1st secretary, Wang Renzhong, who attended the meeting, at the front of this book.

16 Ibid., pp. 63–4; Bo Yibo, *Ruogan Zhongda Juece* 2, pp. 1083–4.

17 *Mao Zedong he tade Mishu Tian Jiaying*, pp. 64–6.

18 Ibid., pp. 65–6.

19 Ibid., p. 66. This is a curious episode. It seems to concern private plots rather than *baochan daohu*. Presumably the premier sought Tian's opinion because he was the Chairman's mouthpiece, but this source clearly states

that Tian did not seek Mao's opinion; nor is there any indication that Tian based his response on some conversation with Mao or even with Liu Shaoqi.

20 Significantly, a local source retrospectively credits him with 'strengthening the responsibility system'; Zhonggong Xiangtan Shiwei Dangshi Ziliao Zhengji Bangongshi (ed.), *Mao Zedong yu Xiangtan* (Mao Zedong and Xiangtan), pp. 313–14.

21 Bo Yibo, *Ruogan Zhongda Juece* 2, p. 1081.

22 For Liu on legalization, see ibid., p. 1084.

23 I take this to be the meaning of *xiucai* in this context.

24 Informant B; according to this source, Tian was reported as getting extremely heated and calling for the eradication of the cancer of leftism.

25 *Mao Zedong he tade Mishu Tian Jiaying*, p. 67. This presumably means that Liu, Zhou, Zhu De, Chen Yun, and Deng Xiaoping all approved, and that Lin Biao was waiting to see what Mao did. See also Zheng Qian & Han Gang, *Wannian Suiyue: 1956 Nianhoude Mao Zedong*, pp. 177–9. Peng Zhen was also in favour, according to Jia Wenping, *Zhenli yu Mingyun*, p. 193.

26 In his retrospective account, Bo Yibo, *Ruogan Zhongda Juece* 2, p. 1078, gives an estimate of 20 per cent of the peasantry farming under the *baochan daohu* system.

27 *Mao Zedong he tade Mishu Tian Jiaying*, pp. 67–8.

28 Bo Yibo, *Ruogan Zhongda Juece* 2, p. 1086; the leaders included Henan 1st secretary Liu Jianxun and Shandong 1st secretary Tan Qilong.

29 *Mao Zedong he tade Mishu Tian Jiaying*, pp. 67–8; Bo Yibo, *Ruogan Zhongda Juece* 2, p. 1086. According to one source, at some point, Mao indicated his agreement with Deng Zihui's report on *baochan daohu* forwarded to him by Liu; see Lin Qingshan, *Kang Sheng Waizhuan*, p. 196. If Mao did draw the conventional circle on the document as stated in this source, perhaps the Chairman was indicating only that he had read the document, keeping his powder dry for when the time for counter-attack was ripe. This source also claims that Liu Shaoqi and Deng Zihui had been promoting *baochan daohu* all over the country; ibid., p. 194.

30 In 1955, the lieutenant was of course Deng Zihui. For Chen Boda's role at that time, see *Origins* I, pp. 16–19.

31 *Mao Zedong he tade Mishu Tian Jiaying*, pp. 71–2.

32 See above, Ch. 9.

33 'Chen Yun yu Xin Zhongguo Jingji Jianshe' Bianjizu, *Chen Yun yu Xin Zhongguo Jingji Jianshe*, pp. 168–9; Bo Yibo, *Ruogan Zhongda Juece* 2, pp. 1085–6.

34 Cong Jin, *Quzhe Fazhande Suiyue*, pp. 580–1.

35 In repeating this piece of peasant wisdom, Deng on this occasion said that he had heard it from his comrade-in-arms from the Second Field Army, Marshal Liu Bocheng, who had apparently claimed it as a Sichuanese saying; *Deng Xiaoping Wenxuan, 1938–1965*, p. 305. From this one may conclude: (a) that Deng misremembered on one occasion or the other; (b) that he thought it useful to have the support of a respected military figure on this controversial matter; (c) that mice are widespread in China; (d) all of the above. For a text of Deng's speech, see *Fan-geming xiuzhengzhuyi fenzi Deng Xiaoping fandong yanlun* (Reactionary utterances of the counter-revolutionary, revisionist element Deng Xiaoping), pp. 52–60; the relevant passages are on pp. 53–4.

[36] Informant B.

[37] *Selected Works of Liu Shaoqi* 2, pp. 440–1.

[38] Ibid., p. 443.

[39] Ibid, pp. 440, 441. For the view that Liu's remarks to the cadres represented a complete capitulation to Mao, see Bo Yibo, *Ruogan Zhongda Juece* 2, p. 1086, and Ling Zhijun, *Lishi buzai Paihuai* (History does not waver), pp. 89–91. For the confrontation by the swimming-pool, see Huang Zheng, *Liu Shaoqi Yi Sheng*, p. 389.

[40] Wang Zhen *et al.*, 'Recollections and Inheritance—In Memory of Comrade Wang Jiaxiang', *Gongren Ribao* (Workers' daily), 4 Feb. 1981, translated in *FBIS*-CHI-81-038, p. L 4.

[41] See Yang, *From Revolution to Politics*, ch. 5; *Zhonggong Dangshi Renwuzhuan* 33, pp. 16–19.

[42] Zhonggong Zhongyang Wenxian Yanjiushi (ed.), *Mao Zedong zai Qi Dade Baogao he Jianghua Ji* (A collection of reports and speeches by Mao Zedong at the [CCP's] 7th Congress), pp. 230–2; Wang Jianying, *Zhongguo Gongchan Dang Zuzhi Shi Ziliao Huibian*, p. 481.

[43] Wang's wife, Zhu Zhongli, a doctor, looked after Jiang Qing during her hospitalization in the Soviet Union in 1949; see her Zhu Zhongli, *Nühuang Meng: Jiang Qing Waizhuan* (Empress dream: An unofficial biography of Jiang Qing), pp. 104–21.

[44] *Zhonggong Dangshi Renwuzhuan* 33, p. 44. For Wang's wife's account of their years in the Moscow embassy, see Waijiaobu Waijiaoshi Yanjiushi, *Dangdai Zhongguo Shijie Waijiao Shengya* (The diplomatic life in contemporary China), 1, pp. 1–33.

[45] *Origins* II, pp. 227–8.

[46] Wang had been wounded during the fighting against the KMT during the mid-1930s and later contracted tuberculosis; on both occasions, he was eventually sent to the Soviet Union for medical treatment, but he seems to have suffered from poor health ever afterwards; Klein & Clark, *Biographic Dictionary of Chinese Communism* 2, p. 897; Wang Zhen *et al.*, 'Recollections and Inheritance', *FBIS*-CHI-81-038, p. L 10. Mao later commented acidly on the way in which Wang had risen from his sickbed with a new lease of energy to propagate his revisionist views; Gao Shu *et al.* (eds.), *Lishi Juren Mao Zedong* (A giant of history, Mao Zedong), p. 1421.

[47] *Wang Li Yiyan*, p. 9. This source says that the meeting was in 1960, but since it also mentions that Wang Li was in town helping draft the Sixty Articles and this was in 1961 (see above, Ch. 2), I have assumed this is a misprint.

[48] Wang Li, *Xianchang Lishi* (On-the-spot history), p. 75.

[49] *Wang Li Yiyan*, p. 9.

[50] *Wang Li Yiyan*, p. 9; *Zhonggong Dangshi Renwuzhuan* 33, p. 50. The original letter is not included in Wang Jiaxiang Xuanji Bianjizu (ed.), *Wang Jiaxiang Xuanji* (Selected works of Wang Jiaxiang; hereafter, *Wang Jiaxiang Xuanji*), but comparison of two other items in this source (pp. 444–60) with quotations from the letter in Cong Jin, *Quzhe Fazhande Suiyue* (pp. 500–2), suggest that the former are elaborations of the ideas in the letter.

[51] *Wang Jiaxiang Xuanji*, p. 450; for the 1960 polemics, see *Origins* II, pp. 272–4.

[52] *Wang Jiaxiang Xuanji*, pp. 444–5.

[53] Ibid., p. 445.

[54] *Qi Qian Ren Dahui Ziliao*, p. 100.

[55] Wang Li, *Xianchang Lishi*, p. 73.

[56] Dallin, *Diversity in International Communism*, pp. 8–31. See above, Ch. 6.

[57] Gittings, *Survey of the Sino-Soviet Dispute*, p. 155.

[58] Dallin, *Diversity in International Communism*, pp. 650–1.

[59] Ibid., p. 824.

[60] Ibid., pp. 652–3. For the Xinjiang incidents, see above, Ch. 10.

[61] Hoxha, *Reflections on China* 1, pp. 3–29. Although it would be some years before Hoxha would break with Mao, these early musings suggest that he would have agreed with André Malraux when he told President Nixon: 'But China has never helped anyone! Not Pakistan. Not Vietnam. China's foreign policy is a brilliant lie! The Chinese themselves do not believe in it; they believe only in China. Only China!' See *RN: The Memoirs of Richard Nixon*, p. 557.

[62] *Wang Li Yiyan*, pp. 9–10; Wang Li, *Xianchang Lishi*, pp. 72–3; Dallin, *Diversity in International Communism*, p. 652.

[63] *Zeng Sheng Huiyi Lu*, p. 674; Chang, *Friends and Enemies*, pp. 225–6. Later in the year, Mao warned that saboteurs, arsonists, and those who threw bombs in the vicinity of Canton would be executed; Schram, *Mao Tse-tung Unrehearsed*, p. 195.

[64] Whiting, *The Chinese Calculus of Deterrence*, p. 65.

[65] Ibid., p. 67. For Mao's input into the preparation of a public statement on the need for national alertness, see *Jianguo Yilai Mao Zedong Wengao* 10, pp. 101–3. For the concerns of the Ministry of Public Security over urban counter-revolutionary activities, see ibid., pp. 146–7.

[66] Hilsman, *To Move a Nation*, p. 318; Robertson, 'Refugees and Troop Moves—A Report from Hong Kong', p. 114. Enver Hoxha, on the basis of a communication from the Chinese foreign ministry to the Albanian ambassador, noted that 'a state of war' had been declared in Fujian province; Hoxha, *Reflections on China* 1, p. 21. In the documents of Fujian's Lianjiang county, the situation was described as one of 'preparing for war' (*bei zhan*); Guofangbu Qingbaoju [RoC] (ed.), *Fangong Youjidui Tuji Fujian Lianjiang Luhuo Feifang Wenjian Huibian* (Collection of bandit documents captured by anti-communist guerrillas in a raid on Lianjiang, Fujian), p. 36.

[67] Wang, 'Nine Years of Sino-U.S. Talks in Retrospect', p. 48.

[68] Ibid., pp. 48–50; Whiting, *The Chinese Calculus of Deterrence*, p. 68.

[69] Young, *Negotiating with the Chinese Communists*, pp. 250–1. Kennedy had taken the decision not to back Chiang on 20 June; Chang, *Friends and Enemies*, p. 226.

[70] Hilsman, *To Move a Nation*, p. 319. According to William Bundy, former Assistant Secretary of State for East Asia, an important reason why Washington appointed two admirals as ambassadors to the Nationalist government was because they had the professional credibility to pour cold water on the feasibility of an invasion of the mainland; telephone interview, 24 Aug. 1993.

[71] Ma Qibin *et al.*, *Zhongguo Gongchan Dang Zhizheng Sishi Nian*, pp. 221, 223; Chang, *Friends and Enemies*, p. 226. The shooting down of the U-2 plane generated an enormous amount of media attention in China; see SCMP 2820, pp. 1–7; 2821, pp. 1–11; 2822, pp. 1–11; 2823, pp. 1–2. For a retrospective account of how this feat was achieved and a picture of Mao congratulating the troops involved, see 'Dangdai Zhongguo' Congshu

Bianjibu (ed.), *Dangdai Zhongguo Kong Jun* (Contemporary China's air force; hereafter, *Dangdai Zhongguo Kong Jun*), pp. 374–8.

72 Wang, 'Nine Years of Sino-U.S. Talks in Retrospect , p. 50. According to a report in the *South China Morning Post*, 6 April 1996, entitled ' "Secret meeting" makes headlines after 23 years', Zhou Enlai met Chiang Kai-shek on an island somewhere in the South China Sea in late 1963, and agreement was reached on the principle of 'one China' and peaceful reunification.

73 *Origins* II, pp. 255–64, 287.

74 Whiting, *The Chinese Calculus of Deterrence*, p. 60. The tone of this editorial was particularly surprising since it marked the end of the Sino-Indian agreement on trading in Tibet which the Indians had refused to renew; Maxwell, *India's China War*, p. 249.

75 Quoted in Lall, *How Communist China Negotiates*, p. 179; see also ibid., pp. 171–80.

76 Zhonggong Zhongyang Dangxiao Zhonggong Dangshi Jiaoyanshi (ed.), *Zhonggong Dangshi Zhuan Ti Jiangyi: Kaishi Quanmian Jianshe Shehuizhuyi Shiqi* (Lectures on special topics in CCP history: The period of the start of overall construction of socialism; hereafter *Zhonggong Dangshi Zhuan Ti Jiangyi*), pp. 147–8.

77 Schram, *Mao Tse-tung Unrehearsed*, p. 188.

78 Ma Qibin *et al.*, *Zhongguo Gongchan Dang Zhizheng Sishi Nian*, p. 221.

79 6 Aug. is the date given by most sources for the start of the conference; e.g. Liao Gailong *et al.*, *Xin Zhongguo Biannianshi*, p. 485. At least one source, however, gives the opening date as 25 July; Chen Mingxian, *Xin Zhongguo Sishiwu Nian Yanjiu* (Research into 45 years of new China), p. 212; the account in this source suggests that prior to 6 August the meeting was concerned with preparing final drafts to documents, mainly connected with agriculture (Informant S).

80 The 22—Mao actually said 23, but either miscounted or omitted a name— were: PSC members, Mao, Liu, Zhou, Zhu De, Deng Xiaoping; secretariat members Peng Zhen, Li Fuchun, Li Xiannian, Tan Zhenlin; the regional 1st secretaries, Li Jingquan, Ke Qingshi, Tao Zhu, Song Renqiong, Liu Lantao, Li Xuefeng; and 'responsible comrades from the centre': alternate members of the Politburo Chen Boda (editor of *Red Flag*) and Lu Dingyi (director of the CC's Propaganda Department); Xie Fuzhi (Minister of Public Security); Gu Mu (a planner, possibly standing in for Chen Yun); Luo Ruiqing (Chief-of-Staff, probably standing in for Lin Biao); Chen Yi, and Yang Shangkun. Chen Yun and Lin Biao were presumably absent for health reasons. The proposal was apparently that this core group would divide up into smaller groups; Schram, 'New Texts by Mao Zedong, 1921– 1966', *Communist Affairs* 2, No. 2, Apr. 1983, p. 152; *[Mao Zedong] Ziliao Xuanbian* (Selection of [Mao Zedong] materials), p. 269.

81 Bo Yibo, *Ruogan Zhongda Juece* 2, p. 1076. Tan Zhenlin was clearly keen to emphasize that agricultural recovery was around the corner in order to lessen his own culpability for mishandling that sector during the GLF; *Origins* II, pp. 82–5.

82 Li, Tan, Lu, Tao, and Liu were all victims of the Cultural Revolution; for Lu's position at this time, see below, p. 280 and n. 107; for Tao and Liu's, see Bo Yibo, *Ruogan Zhongda Juece* 2, p. 1087.

83 Schram, 'New Texts', p. 152.

84 Ibid., p. 153; *[Mao Zedong] Ziliao Xuanbian*, pp. 269–70.

85 Bo Yibo, *Ruogan Zhongda Juece* 2, pp. 1087-9; for Mao's critique of Deng Zihui, see *Jianguo Yilai Mao Zedong Wengao* 10, pp. 137-40.

86 '*Chengji hen da, wenti bushao, qiantu guangming*'. Schram, 'New Texts', p. 152; *[Mao Zedong] Ziliao Xuanbian*, p. 269; referred to in Origins II, p. 192.

87 Schram, 'New Texts', p. 152; the translation emphasizes the second '*not*', but this is not in the original.

88 Bo Yibo, *Ruogan Zhongda Juece* 2, p. 1074; *[Mao Zedong] Ziliao Xuanbian*, p. 271. In the quotation, Mao was sarcastically making a play on part of the GLF slogan—'Go all out . . .' (*guzu ganjin*)—which was of course still formally in good standing.

89 Ma Qibin *et al.*, *Zhongguo Gongchan Dang Zhizheng Sishi Nian*, p. 221.

90 Schram, *Mao Tse-tung Unrehearsed*, pp. 152, 153.

91 Cf. this assessment by a senior British minister of how former Prime Minister Margaret Thatcher dominated her cabinet colleagues: 'Margaret . . . when there was an issue on which she had already formed a firm view, would start with an unashamedly tendentious introduction of her own, before inviting the responsible and sometimes cowed Minister to have his say. Thus what began as a method for the most expedient conduct of business ended as a means of getting her own way irrespective of the merits or political costs'; Lawson, *The View from No. 11*, p. 128.

92 *Zhonggong Dangshi Zhuan Ti Jiangyi*, p. 149.

93 *[Mao Zedong] Ziliao Xuanbian*, p. 270.

94 As his behaviour at the 1959 Lushan conference had demonstrated; *Origins* II, pp. 219, 222.

95 *[Mao Zedong] Ziliao Xuanbian*, pp. 270-1. This book was put out at the time of the collectivization drive in 1955-6 (*Origins* I, p. 15), and the preface and commentaries had been written by Mao himself; he was thus obliquely self-criticizing his own failure of perception.

96 *[Mao Zedong] Ziliao Xuanbian*, p. 270.

97 Ibid., pp. 270, 271, 272. Again, there may have been a hint of self-criticism here. In 1947, Mao wrote a directive on land reform in the old liberated areas, revising an earlier one issued by Liu Shaoqi which had resulted in leftist excesses, and this probably set the tone for what happened in the new liberated areas; see Zhang Tianrong *et al.* (eds.), *Dangde Jianshe Qishi Nian* (Seventy years of party building), pp. 222-34. Shue, in *Peasant China in Transition* (p. 83) states that it was precisely those old cadres who had been criticized for violent land reform in the old liberated areas who 'were determined not to be criticised again for the same mistake, and they tried to carry out land reform as peacefully as possible . . .' For examples of rural policies in old liberated areas, see Crook & Crook, *Revolution in a Chinese Village* and *Mass Movement in a Chinese Village*; Friedman *et al.*, *Chinese Village, Socialist State*, chs. 2 and 3; Hartford & Goldstein (eds.), *Single Sparks*; Hinton, *Fanshen*. For examples of what happened in new liberated areas, see Shue, *Peasant China in Transition*; Vogel, *Canton under Communism*, chs. 3 and 4. However soft Mao may have considered land reform in retrospect, it doubtless seemed different to the landlords and other local powerholders. The Chairman himself admitted to almost 800,000 executions of various types of enemy, including 'local bullies' and 'evil gentry', carried out in the early years of the regime; see MacFarquhar, Cheek, & Wu, *The Secret Speeches of Chairman Mao*, p. 142.

98 *[Mao Zedong] Ziliao Xuanbian*, p. 270.

99 The fact that Mao saw Hu Kaiming's letter means that it was shown to him by Tian Jiaying, one of whose jobs was to screen letters to the Chairman and only pass on those he thought worthy of his attention.

100 Ibid., pp. 270–2.

101 Mao had also done this after the initial high tide of the GLF; see *Origins* II, pp. 144–59.

102 Mao made some general remarks about the continuing importance of commodities under socialism at Zhengzhou which Chinese commercial specialists regarded as important for their sphere of activity (*Shangye Dashiji*, pp. 55–6), but did not issue the kind of specific instructions that on this occasion he claimed had been disregarded; see his speeches in Mac-Farquhar, Cheek, & Wu, *The Secret Speeches of Chairman Mao*, pp. 443–79.

103 The text has *zhuyi* (principles or -isms); perhaps it should be *jianyi* (suggestions). Mao also cracked the whip over departments that failed to report to him; see *Jianguo Yilai Mao Zedong Wengao* 10, p. 135.

104 *[Mao Zedong] Ziliao Xuanbian*, p. 273; cf. *Origins* II, pp. 24–7.

105 Ma Qibin *et al.*, *Zhongguo Gongchan Dang Zhizheng Sishi Nian*, p. 221. For Deng Zihui's brief attempt at Beidaihe to defend responsibility systems by citing the judgement on the Guangxi experiment by Tao Zhu and Wang Renzhong which Mao had approved (see above Ch. 9), see 'Deng Zihui Wenji' Bianji Weiyuanhui, *Deng Zihui Wenji* (Collected works of Deng Zihui), pp. 613–15.

106 *[Mao Zedong] Ziliao Xuanbian*, p. 271; Bo Yibo, *Ruogan Zhongda Juece* 2, pp. 1006–7.

107 Informant B. According to Lu Dingyi's daughter, he approved of the Anti-Rightist Campaign; Phathanothai, *The Dragon's Pearl*, p. 137. For a description of Lu's simple life-style by a foreign friend of his daughter, see ibid., pp. 123–5.

108 Bo Yibo, *Ruogan Zhongda Juece* 2, p. 1007.

109 Ibid., pp. 1007–8.

110 Li Weihan, *Huiyi yu Yanjiu, xia*, pp. 875–7.

111 An earlier example of Mao using the provinces against the centre was his collectivization drive in 1955.

112 Ma Qibin *et al.*, *Zhongguo Gongchan Dang Zhizheng Sishi Nian*, p. 221.

113 On 29 Feb. 1964, Mao told Kim Il Sung that in the first half of 1962 some people in the party had wanted to dissolve the socialist collective economy in the countryside, and that ameliorating relations with the Soviet Union and the United States was their external programme; Cong Jin, *Quzhe Fazhande Suiyue*, pp. 577–9.

114 According to Bo Yibo, Mao was worrying about 'peaceful evolution' (*heping yanbian*) from 1959 on; Bo Yibo, *Ruogan Zhongda Juece* 2, pp. 1137–70. By the time Bo's volume was published in 1993, the post-Mao Deng regime was also heavily concerned about peaceful evolution, and doubtless this accounts for Bo's unexpectedly understanding account of Mao's 1960s leftism.

115 Mao used the term *youqing* which may have been shorthand for *youqing jihuizhuyi* (right opportunism), the epithet attached to Peng Dehuai in 1959; *[Mao Zedong] Xuexi Wenxuan*, p. 113.

116 According to the original 1958 figures for the summer harvest, the only year in this period for which such figures are available, it amounted that year to almost 15% of the total grain output. Almost two-thirds of the 1958 summer

harvest consisted of winter wheat, harvested in the early summer and constituting almost 90% of total wheat output, estimated then at almost 39 m. tons. The latter figure works out at 10.3% of the total claimed output for that year; Li Debin, Lin Shunbao *et al.* (eds.), *Xin Zhongguo Nongcun Jingji Jishi, 1949.10–1984.9* (Major events in the rural economy of new China, Oct. 1949–Sept. 1984), pp. 187, 199. While the output figures turned out to be exaggerated, it is the proportions that are important. According to post-Cultural Revolution figures, between 1957 and 1963, annual wheat output as a proportion of total grain output fluctuated between a high of 15.4% (1960) and a low of 9.66% (1961), averaging out at 11.7%, not too far off the 10.3% figure derived from the original 1958 claims; *TJNJ, 1983*, p. 158. In other words, Mao could have assumed that the summer wheat crop and/or overall summer harvest was a legitimate basis for estimating the annual total grain output.

117 Bo Yibo, *Ruogan Zhongda Juece* 2, pp. 1073, 1074. According to Bo, Mao was in Shandong, Shanghai, Hangzhou, and Wuhan; according to Mao himself, he also visited the southwest. Bo also reports (p. 1080) that as early as Dec. 1961, Mao was telling Zeng Xisheng confidently that production had recovered. According to another source, everyone at the Beidaihe conference felt there had been a decided turn for the better; Lin Qingshan, *Kang Sheng Waizhuan*, p. 193. By about June 1962, improved rations convinced prisoners in labour reform camps that the famine was over; Wu & Wakeman, *Bitter Winds*, p. 156.

118 *Selected Works of Zhou Enlai* 2, p. 417.

119 *Mao Zedong sixiang wan sui (1969)*, p. 599; Mao, *Miscellany* 2, p. 430. Mao indicated that a month earlier, prior to the harvest, the Shandong cadres had been less sanguine.

120 Li Debin *et al.*, *Xin Zhongguo Nongcun Jingji Jishi*, p. 187; Cong Jin, *Quzhe Fazhande Suiyue*, p. 152. In Shandong, one of the three major wheat-growing provinces on the north China plain, wheat has ripened by early June and is marked by the Tuan Wu (fifth day of the fifth lunar month) festival; Yang, *A Chinese Village*, p. 18. In 1962, the Tuan Wu festival fell on 6 June; Tun, *Annual Customs and Festivals in Peking*, p. 125. Further south, wheat naturally ripens earlier, in May around Shanghai and in April in Fujian, according to a 19th-century horticulturalist; Fortune, *Three Years' Wanderings in China*, p. 307. Thus there should have been plenty of time for estimates of the summer harvest to have reached Mao. As late as 7 July, Deng Xiaoping was cautiously saying that it was not yet clear whether or not grain production would reach 150 m. tons in 1962 (*Deng Xiaoping Wenxuan [1938–1965]*, pp. 304–5), but he was presumably waiting for the first estimates of the autumn harvest; traditionally, this was available by mid-August (Cong Jin, *Quzhe Fazhande Suiyue*, p. 102, n.1).

121 Schram, 'New Texts', p. 152. The State Statistical Bureau came under severe criticism at the start of the GLF which certainly inhibited its ability to sift and publish facts, but by this time its importance had been recognized again; see Li, *The Statistical System of Communist China*, *passim*, but especially chs. 10 and 11.

122 Whiting, *The Chinese Calculus of Deterrence*, p. 21.

123 *Jingji Dashiji*, p. 344. Autumn harvesting, ploughing, and sowing begins in mid-September (SCMP 2596, p. 13) and tapers off in the second half of October (SCMP 2602, p. 11). Li Xiannian was speaking of 'this year's

increase in production' by 25 Sept.; *Li Xiannian Lun Caizheng Jinrong Maoyi, xia*, p. 38. On 23 Sept., as the autumn harvest was getting going, the CC issued a new grain directive. At Mao's behest, the 1962 grain procurement figure was reduced by almost 2 m. tons to just over 32 m. tons, even less than Deng Zihui had advocated in July. But contrary to Deng's advice to fix the procurement figure for up to five years, but reflecting the anticipated agricultural upturn, the directive envisaged a gradual increase in procurement and diminution in imports over that period; bid.; Ma Qibin *et al.*, *Zhongguo Gongchan Dang Zhizheng Sishi Nian*, pp. 221–2. There was a lack of clarity in the relationship between this decision and that issued at the CC's 10th plenum four days later which stated that procurement should be fixed at an appropriate level and maintained for a period of time as Deng Zihui had wanted; ibid., p. 222; Guofang Daxue, *CanKao Ziliao* 24, p. 133. Li Xiannian appeared to square the circle in his speech to the plenum when he talked of stabilization taking place *after* a rise to an appropriate level; *Li Xiannian Lun Caizheng Jinrong Maoyi, xia*, p. 38.

124 Bo Yibo, *Ruogan Zhongda Juece* 2, pp. 1074–5.

125 Ibid. 1, pp. 371–3.

126 For an indication that Mao was already counting on an agricultural upturn as early as December 1961, see Wu Ren, *Gongheguo Zhongda Shijian Jishi* 3, p. 72; see also, Xu Quanxing, *Mao Zedong Wanniande Lilun yu Shixian, 1956–1976* (Mao Zedong's theory and practice in his later years), p. 301.

127 Schram, *Mao Tse-tung Unrehearsed*, p. 9.

128 Cong Jin, *Quzhe Fazhande Suiyue*, p. 509.

129 Ibid., p. 512.

130 Schram, *Mao Tse-tung Unrehearsed*, pp. 189–90. According to Schram, as far back as the Yan'an period, Mao had made clear that the main message he wished to derive from the communist classics was 'class struggle, class struggle, class struggle'; Schram, *Mao's Road to Power* 1, p. xvii.

131 The list of names of the small group of high-level policy-makers which Mao read out and agreed to at Beidaihe did not include Chen Yun's; see above n. 80. Nor does Chen appear among the PSC members at the top table in the photograph published of the 10th plenum; see MacFarquhar, 'On Photographs', between pp. 306–7.

132 Cong Jin, *Quzhe Fazhande Suiyue*, p. 513.

133 Bo Yibo, *Ruogan Zhongda Juece* 2, pp. 1074–5.

134 Cong Jin, *Quzhe Fazhande Suiyue*, p. 513. Interrupting speeches with brief comments was not in itself a sign of disapprobation, but rather a common practice among the Chinese leadership, a function of the informality of most *in camera* meetings and the fact that speeches on such occasions were not considered to be final texts. Mao himself could be interrupted, too, even when making a long, semi-formal speech on a major occasion; see, for instance, MacFarquhar, Cheek, & Wu, *The Secret Speeches of Chairman Mao*, pp. 162, 169, 186, 217–47. But whereas those who interrupted Mao sought to be helpful to the Chairman, the latter often used this device for harassing the speaker, either to indicate hostility by the use of sarcasm and invective, or to suggest unspoken doubts about the speaker's firmness or authority by reinforcing or explicating his remarks. Mao's interruptions of Liu at the 10th plenum were of the latter variety; for perhaps the most notorious example of the former, see Alitto, *The Last Confucian*, pp. 1–3.

135 The CC's Rural Work Department was simply abolished and its functions were transferred to the State Council Office for Agriculture and Forestry. Deng Zihui was dismissed from the directorship of that office, which was then assumed by Tan Zhenlin. Perhaps because of his earlier closeness with Mao, Deng maintained his status as a senior cadre, but he was later dismissed from his deputy premiership and made a vice-chairman of the CPPCC instead. Interestingly, at first Liu Shaoqi referred to Deng formally as 'Comrade Deng Zihui', but after Mao had called him by the friendlier 'Old Deng' (*Deng Lao*) with its tinge of respect, Liu followed suit. Deng had to visit Mao to self-criticize, but he seems to have behaved with unusual courage under fire from his colleagues; see 'Deng Zihui Zhuan' Bianji Weiyuanhui, *Deng Zihui Zhuan*, pp. 565–70. After the plenum, Deng Zihui made an inspection trip in Guangdong with Chen Yi, He Long, and Nie Rongzhen and wrote a 20,000-character memoir; *Zhonggong Dangshi Renwuzhuan* 7, pp. 376–7; *Jiefang Jun Jiangling Zhuan* 2, p. 65.

136 Cong Jin, *Quzhe Fazhande Suiyue*, pp. 513–14; Bo Yibo, *Ruogan Zhongda Juece* 2, p. 1075.

137 Cong Jin, *Quzhe Fazhande Suiyue*, pp. 515–17.

138 Guo Simin & Tian Yu, *Wo Yanzhongde Liu Shaoqi*, pp. 438–9; Ma Qibin et al., *Zhongguo Gongchan Dang Zhizheng Sishi Nian*, p. 222; Xu Quanxing, *Mao Zedong Wanniande Lilun yu Shixian, 1956–1976*, p. 303.

139 Lü Xingdou (ed.), *Mao Zedong he Tade Shiye* (Mao Zedong and his enterprises) 2, p. 705.

140 Schram, *Mao Tse-tung Unrehearsed*, pp. 194–5. Peng Dehuai was referring to the criticism to which he had been subjected by Mao in Yan'an; see *Origins* II, p. 223.

141 Cong Jin, *Quzhe Fazhande Suiyue*, p. 515. Mao actually referred to grade-17 cadres and above; for the identification of that level as equivalent to section chief, see Barnett, *Cadres, Bureaucracy, and Political Power in Communist China*, pp. 41–3, 190–3. See also Huang Zheng, *Liu Shaoqi Yi Sheng*, pp. 392–3.

142 *Jingji Dashiji*, p. 345; Lieberthal, 'The Great Leap Forward and the Split in the Yenan Leadership', pp. 331–5. Mao's editing of the plenum's public communiqué was focused on class issues rather than economics; *Jianguo Yilai Mao Zedong Wengao* 10, pp. 195–8.

143 Hao Weimin (ed.), *Nei Menggu Zizhiqu Shi* (A history of the Inner Mongolian Autonomous Region), p. 207.

144 The decision to make the team the focus of commune activity had been taken in Feb.; Liu & Wu, *China's Socialist Economy*, p. 296. The number of articles on brigade functions consequently shrank from twelve to two, while those on the team expanded from ten to nineteen; it should be noted, however, that one of the brigade articles had several subheads, so that the figure of two is slightly misleading. In some cases, articles were basically lifted wholesale from the brigade section of the document and transferred to the team section, with appropriate change of nomenclature; since many of the articles on the team in the June 1961 version were preserved (e.g. on grain, cash crops, draught animals, work groups, norms, distribution according to labour, financial management), that section had to expand considerably. See *Nongye Jitihua, xia*, pp. 633–41; I am comparing the texts in ibid., pp. 474–91 and 628–49.

145 *Jingji Dashiji*, p. 349.

146 See above, Ch. 3, Table 3.1.
147 According to Liu & Wu, *China's Socialist Economy*, p. 296, the 30-year decision had been taken in Feb., and it is not clear what Deng's role had been at that time. According to another account, Tian Jiaying presented the Chairman with three alternatives on 8 Feb.: 20 years, 40 years, or 'at least 20 years', and on 11 Feb., Mao opted for 'at least 30 years'; see *Zhonggong Dangshi Zhongda Shijian Shushi*, p. 125.
148 See above, Ch. 9.
149 The brigade lost the right to accumulate and no longer controlled welfare. Cf. arts. 25 and 26 in the June 1961 version with arts. 35 and 36 in the Sept. 1962 one; *Nongye Jitihua*, xia, pp. 481, 639–40. A translation of the 1962 version is available in *Issues & Studies*, Oct. 1979, pp. 93–111, and Dec. 1979, pp. 106–15.
150 Arts. 42 (1961) and 27 (1962); *Nongye Jitihua*, xia, pp. 486, 637.
151 Arts. 34 (1961) and 32 (1962); ibid., pp. 483, 638.
152 Art. 40; ibid., p. 642.
153 Ibid., pp. 659–63.
154 Art. 8 (1961 and 1962); ibid., pp. 475, 629.
155 Arts. 6 (1961) and 8 (1962); ibid., pp. 475, 630.
156 See above, Ch. 7, pp. 151–2.
157 Arts. 47 (1961) and 48 (1962); *Nongye Jitihua*, xia, pp. 488, 645.
158 Arts. 44 (1961) and 46 (1962); ibid., pp. 487, 644.
159 Arts. 57 (1961 and 1962); ibid., pp. 490, 648.
160 Bo Yibo, *Ruogan Zhongda Juece* 2, p. 1094.
161 *[Mao Zedong] Ziliao Xuanbian*, p. 276; Schram, *Mao Tse-tung Unrehearsed*, pp. 194, 196; Cong Jin, *Quzhe Fazhande Suiyue*, p. 512. Peng Dehuai had not attended Politburo meetings since Lushan. In an instruction written on 21 Jan. 1965, Mao left it to Peng Zhen to decide which members of the Politburo should receive an important report on planning, adding only that 'anti-party elements' should be excluded; *Jianguo Yilai Mao Zedong Wengao* 11, p. 316. Zhang Wentian, Peng's purported co-conspirator at Lushan, had been assigned to the Economic Research Institute of the Academy of Sciences at the end of 1960, and had been encouraged by the relaxation earlier in 1962 to send Mao a report of his investigations into rural markets—which doubtless also irritated the Chairman; Zhong Chen, Xia Lu, & Ye Lan (eds.), *Lingxiu Jiaowang Shilu Xilie: Mao Zedong* (A series of records of socialization between leaders: Mao Zedong), p. 57. For Zhang's relationship with Peng and his role at Lushan, see *Origins* II, pp. 204–6, 217–18, 222, 236.
162 Bo Yibo, *Ruogan Zhongda Juece* 2, p. 1093. In Feb. 1965, *Red Flag* published three satirical verses, supposedly the lamentations of one of the '*ni*'s, Khrushchev, about the deaths of the other two, 'West *ni*' (Kennedy) in Nov. 1963 and 'East *ni*' (Nehru) in May 1964, written shortly after his own political demise in October 1964; see 'The Lamentations of a Certain Gentleman', translated in JPRS 30,134, 18 May 1965, pp. 55–7.
163 Informant G.
164 For instance, shortly after he had been humiliated at the 8th Congress by being demoted from full to alternate membership of the Politburo, he failed to attend a key meeting of that body on 20 Oct. 1956, pleading illness. Since the agenda was the threat of an imminent Soviet invasion of Poland, and Kang was a leading Chinese 'Soviet expert', he should have been there; Wu

Lengxi, *Yi Mao Zhuxi*, p. 11; *Origins* I, p. 148. The main Chinese sources on Kang Sheng are Zhong Kan, *Kang Sheng Pingzhuan*; and Lin Qingshan, *Kang Sheng Waizhuan*. For identifications of the authors of these post-Cultural Revolution sources, who are hostile to but informative on Kang, see the biography of him by Byron & Pack, *The Claws of the Dragon*, pp. 489–92, which relies particularly on Zhong Kan. Significant sections on Kang are also contained in Shi Zhe, *Feng yu Gu: Shi Zhe Huiyi Lu* (Peaks and valleys: The memoirs of Shi Zhe), pp. 192–229; Liu Xiao, *Chu Shi Sulian*; and *Wang Li Yiyan*, pp. 5–17. A French work heavily focused on Kang, which seems almost exclusively based on Western-language sources, is Faligot & Kauffer, *Kang Sheng et les services secrets chinois (1927–1987)*, translated into English as *The Chinese Secret Service*.

165 The 'eastern sea' referred to the fact that he was born in the coastal province of Shandong; Li Rui, *Lushan Huiyi Shilu*, p. 23. In addition to treating Kang as a reliable political confidante, Mao periodically consulted with him on cultural matters; see for instance *Jianguo Yilai Mao Zedong Wengao* 10, p. 349; 11, pp. 159, 430–1.

166 Kang Sheng was a name adopted in his mid-thirties, the last of many; he was born Zhang Zongke. See Zhong Kan, *Kang Sheng Pingzhuan*, pp. 332, 343.

167 Ibid., pp. 6–13, The principal of the school was Richard Wilhelm, who translated the *I Ching* into German; Byron & Pack, *The Claws of the Dragon*, pp. 42–4. According to this source, Kang Sheng was sent to the German school at the age of 16 because his father disapproved of the debauched life his son pursued with dubious companions; ibid., pp. 38–40.

168 In Zhong Kan, *Kang Sheng Pingzhuan*, p. 17, there is a somewhat grudging admission that Kang was genuinely fired by the revolutionary events at this time.

169 Ibid., pp. 14–28, 333–6; Lin Qingshan, *Kang Sheng Waizhuan*, p. 9. According to Byron & Pack, *The Claws of the Dragon*, p. 72, Kang Sheng did not bother to divorce his first wife. The social sciences department was at this time headed by Qu Qiubai, who was later briefly leader of the CCP; Zhong Kan, *Kang Sheng Pingzhuan*, p. 23.

170 Ibid., pp. 28–30.

171 Byron & Pack, *The Claws of the Dragon*, pp. 103–11. Zhong Kan, *Kang Sheng Pingzhuan*, p. 38, states coyly only that Kang 'participated in leadership work in a certain CCP CC organ'. Shi Zhe, *Feng yu Gu*, p. 116, points out that 90% of CCP organizations in the 'white' areas disappeared between 1929 and 1931, but this was more a tribute to KMT ruthlessness than to Kang Sheng's ineptitude.

172 Shi Zhe, *Feng yu Gu*, p. 116; Zhong Kan, *Kang Sheng Pingzhuan*, pp. 30–1; Lin Qingshan, *Kang Sheng Waizhuan*, pp. 13–14; Byron & Pack, *The Claws of the Dragon*, pp. 76–85, 90.

173 Zhong Kan, *Kang Sheng Pingzhuan*, pp. 38, 57–63, 338, 344; Shi Zhe, *Feng yu Gu*, p. 211; Lin Qingshan, *Kang Sheng Waizhuan*, pp. 41–9; Byron & Pack, *The Claws of the Dragon*, pp. 112–32. The latter work, p. 89, suggests that Wang Ming returned to Moscow leaving a subordinate in charge of the CCP because he was mortally afraid of being caught by the KMT.

174 Shi Zhe, *Feng yu Gu*, p. 213, suggests that Kang Sheng immediately spotted where the power lay as he got off the plane and saw the welcoming committee aligned with Mao. See also Zhong Kan, *Kang Sheng Pingzhuan*, pp. 74–5; Lin Qingshan, *Kang Sheng Waizhuan*, pp. 78–81; Byron & Pack, *The*

Claws of the Dragon, pp. 135–45; Dai Qing, *Liang Shuming, Wang Shiwei, Chu Anping* (id.), p. 51.

[175] Kang Sheng was able to churn out series of articles even while busy with organizational duties; note, for instance, his activities in 1932 as chronicled in Zhong Kan, *Kang Sheng Pingzhuan*, pp. 338–43.

[176] Zhu Zhongli, *Nühuang Meng*, pp. 36–7. According to Shi Zhe, *Feng yu Gu*, p. 220, it was Kang Sheng's wife, Cao Yiou, who personally arranged for the actress Lan Ping to change her name to Jiang Qing.

[177] Zhong Kan, *Kang Sheng Pingzhuan*, pp. 75–7, 347 Byron & Pack, *The Claws of the Dragon*, pp. 145–50. For speculation that Kang Sheng and Jiang Qing may have had a sexual relationship in Shandorg and/or Yan'an, see the latter work, pp. 48–50; Terrill, *The White-Boned Demon*, pp. 18, 136.

[178] The major documents used in the campaign are collected and introduced in Compton, *Mao's China*.

[179] Zhong Kan, *Kang Sheng Pingzhuan*, pp. 77–95. While this source blames Kang Sheng for the executions, and he may well have been guilty of pursuing the original cases against them, the order that they should be killed seems to have been authorized by the ranking local military commander and future marshal, He Long, as KMT troops approached the CCP base area in 1947; see Dai Qing, *Liang Shuming, Wang Shiwei, Chu Anping*, p. 101, and Dai Qing, *Wang Shiwei and 'Wild Lilies'*, pp. 64–9. The rationale seems to have been He's unwillingness to bother looking after a large group of prisoners as he went into battle. This was indicated by a reference to the execution of Wang Shiwei by Mao in his speech to the Seven Thousand Cadres Conference: 'That incident happened at the time when the army was on the march, and the security organs themselves made the decision to execute him; the decision did not come from the Centre. We have often made criticisms on this very matter; we thought that he shouldn't have been executed. If he was a secret agent and wrote articles to attack us and refused to reform till death, why not leave him there or let him go and do labour?' (Schram, *Mao Tse-tung Unrehearsed*, p. 185.)

For Dai Qing's view of Kang Sheng's role, see *Liang Shuming, Wang Shiwei, Chu Anping*, pp. 48–58, 96–7. For Western appraisals of the criticism campaign against Wang Shiwei, see Goldman, *Literary Dissent in Communist China*, pp. 37–42; Apter & Saich, *Revolutionary Discourse in Mao's Republic*, pp. 288–92.

[180] Zhong Kan, *Kang Sheng Pingzhuan*, p. 353. By this time, Kang Sheng was involved in brutal land reform; ibid., pp. 96–105.

[181] The figures were given by Liu Shaoqi in his address on 30 June 1961, in celebration of the 40th anniversary of the CCP; *Collected Works of Liu Shao-ch'i, 1958–1967*, p. 140.

[182] Zhong Kan, *Kang Sheng Pingzhuan*, pp. 106–11; Lin Qingshan, *Kang Sheng Waizhuan*, pp. 121–34; Byron & Pack, *The Claws of the Dragon*, pp. 198–208.

[183] *Origins* I, pp. 148, 359–60, n. 44.

[184] Other cases included Lin Biao (*Origins* I, pp. 146–7; II, p. 65) and Deng Xiaoping, whom Mao refused to subject to the same total disgrace as Liu Shaoqi during the earlier years of the Cultural Revolution.

[185] Zhong Kan, *Kang Sheng Pingzhuan*, pp. 114–32. During Mao's campaign to sell his rectification policies in early 1957, Kang was often audibly in attendance; MacFarquhar, Cheek, & Wu, *The Secret Speeches of Chairman Mao*,

pp. 196, 200, 210, 218, 219, 223, 238, 245, 246, 256, 261, 264, 265. During the GLF, in addition to ideological support, Kang did some research on the issue of agricultural mechanization; *Origins* II, pp. 43–50. According to other sources, he was also a procurer of women and erotica for Mao; Salisbury, *The New Emperors*, pp. 217–21.

[186] Dai Zhixian, *Shan Yu Yu Lai Feng Man Lou* (The mountain rain is about to come; the wind fills the building), p. 70.

[187] Zhong Kan, *Kang Sheng Pingzhuan*, pp. 144–7; Lin Qingshan, *Kang Sheng Waizhuan*, pp. 180–8; Byron & Pack, *The Claws of the Dragon*, pp. 261–7; Terrill, *The White-Boned Demon*, pp. 207–8. See also below, Ch. 17.

[188] Dai Zhixian, *Shan Yu Yu Lai Feng Man Lou*, p. 72.

[189] The Whampoa class lists are in Guangdong Geming Lishi Bowuguan (ed.), *Huangpu Jun Xiao Shi Liao* (Historical materials on the Whampoa Military Academy), pp. 522–87.

[190] Sheng Ping, *Zhongguo Gongchan Dang Renming Dacidian, 1921–1991*, p. 190. For a recent analysis of Liu Zhidan's fate, see Apter & Saich, *Revolutionary Discourse in Mao's Republic*, pp. 49–54.

[191] See the author's preface when the novel was finally published in 1979; Li Jiantong, *Liu Zhidan*, pp. 1–2. Any biography of a major Chinese communist figure shares the hazards of the *Liu Zhidan* novel. While the CCP produced official overviews of its history in 1945 and 1981, these sketches could not deal with all the myriad individual episodes of intra-party conflict and the roles of the hundreds of leading players. Survivors of those quarrels might have been on opposite sides in the past, but in equally good standing decades later, and extremely reluctant to have their past errors recalled. Fictionalization and the invocation of artistic licence were not always successful as protection, as is evidenced by the quarrel which Li Jiantong had with a senior surviving colleague of Liu Zhidan, even though she could claim that the CCP had approved of him in its 1945 resolution (Li Jiantong, *Liu Zhidan*, p. 3). Another device has been discrete accounts of specific episodes or organizations overseen by committees of survivors and experts. This latter technique has been used in the long set of orange-coloured volumes *Zhongguo Gongchan Dang Lishi Ziliao Congshu* (CCP historical materials' series) produced by the Zhonggong Dang Shi Ziliao Chubanshe (CCP historical materials publishing house). The kind of problems involved in CCP historiography may explain why, although there have been many histories of individual military units, the CCP has never produced an official, comprehensive account of its defining episode, the Long March, preferring to cut through the massive and thorny problems of reconciling dozens, perhaps hundreds, of conflicting or at least different points of view, by allowing a foreigner, Harrison Salisbury, to undertake the job; see his *The Long March*. It may also explain why PRC publishers eagerly translate foreign accounts of their politics which express judgements which no Chinese expert could get away with.

[192] *Who's Who in China*, pp. 768–9.

[193] Klein & Clark, *Biographic Dictionary of Chinese Communism* 1, pp. 312–13.

[194] See Xi Zhongxun's own account in *Renminde Hao Zongli* 3, pp. 24–5.

[195] Wen Yu, *Zhongguo 'Zuo' Huo* (China's 'leftist' scourge), pp. 364–5; Cong Jin, *Quzhe Fazhande Suiyue*, p. 511; Li Jiantong, *Liu Zhidan*, preface, pp. 3–4; Bo Yibo, *Ruogan Zhongda Juece* 2, p. 1096.

¹⁹⁶ Cong Jin, *Quzhe Fazhande Suiyue*, p. 511; Li Jiantong, *Liu Zhidan*, preface, pp. 3–4. Since *Liu Zhidan* was published in 1979 before the CCP had got round to making official assessments of the behaviour of senior cadres during the Cultural Revolution and in events leading up to it, Li was careful not to mention Yan Hongyan's name, only referring to him as a Shaanxi cadre; even Kang Sheng was referred to only by the phrase with which he was identified at that time, 'authority on theory' (*'lilun quanwei'*), in quotation marks to demonstrate irony. Zhong Kan, *Kang Sheng Pingzhuan*, pp. 154–6 followed Li Jiantong's account fairly closely, but did not mention even a 'Shaanxi cadre', thus leaving the reader mystified as to how Kang Sheng got to know about *Liu Zhidan*. Lin Qingshan, *Kang Sheng Waizhuan*, pp. 189–90, reported that a 'loyal follower' of Kang's brought the book up in conversation, but that Kang was not interested until told that it was linked with the Gao Gang issue. The episode is not mentioned in Yan Hongyan's biography in the PLA-sponsored series *Jiefang Jun Jiangling Zhuan* 9, p. 460. Yan died early in the Cultural Revolution, reportedly by his own hand; URI, *Who's Who in Communist China* 2, p. 774.

¹⁹⁷ See Teiwes, *Politics at Mao's Court, passim*; *Origins* I p. 47.

¹⁹⁸ Informant I.

¹⁹⁹ Li Jiantong, *Liu Zhidan*, preface, pp. 3–4; Zhong Kan, *Kang Sheng Pingzhuan*, pp. 155–6; Lin Qingshan, *Kang Sheng Waizhuan*, pp. 200–1; Bo Yibo, *Ruogan Zhongda Juece* 2, pp. 1095–6; Wu Lengxi *Yi Mao Zhuxi*, p. 148.

²⁰⁰ Xi Zhongxun claimed Mao really paid no attention to the substance of the matter, and hints that the consideration with which the Chairman treated him thereafter indicates that he did not believe the charges; *Renminde Hao Zongli* 3, pp. 24–6.

²⁰¹ *Origins* I, p. 222.

²⁰² Cong Jin, *Quzhe Fazhande Suiyue*, pp. 515–17; Wen Yu, *Zhongguo 'Zuo' Huo*, p. 367.

²⁰³ *Renminde Hao Zongli* 3, pp. 23–5.

²⁰⁴ Jia became a three-time loser. He had been attacked for his 'right opportunist' views on the economy after the fall of Peng Dehuai in 1959 and then had been rehabilitated after the Seven Thousand Cadres Conference. After coming under fire from Kang Sheng in the *Liu Zhidan* affair, he was sent to the Central Party School to study, but after three reasonably quiet years there, he suffered again during the Cultural Revolution. See Zhou Weiren, *Jia Tuofu Zhuan* (A biography of Jia Tuofu), pp. 124–214.

²⁰⁵ Dai Zhixian. *Shan Yu Yu Lai Feng Man Lou*, p. 77.

²⁰⁶ By then, Xi was the deputy manager of an industrial plant in Luoyang. When Jia Tuofu died in 1967 as a result of Cultural Revolution persecution, Minister of Labour Ma Wenrui, another Shaanxi ex-guerrilla whom the author of *Liu Zhidan* had consulted, was substituted for him as a co-leader of the 'anti-party group'. It would be seventeen years before the 'reversal of verdicts' on this case in 1979. See *Renminde Hao Zongli* 3, p. 25; Zhong Kan, *Kang Sheng Pingzhuan*, pp. 156–61, 381; Lin Qingshan, *Kang Sheng Waizhuan*, pp. 201–4; Li Jiantong, *Liu Zhidan*, pp. 5–6; *Wenhui Bao*, 20 May 1968.

CHAPTER 13

¹ *Origins* I, pp. 46–8, 169–83.

² Ibid. II, pp. 132–4.

3 See above, Ch. 12.
4 See e.g. *Jianguo Yilai Mao Zedong Wengao* 1, pp. 539–41; Bo Yibo, *Ruogan Zhongda Juece* 1, pp. 43–5; 'Dangdai Zhongguo' Congshu Bianjibu (ed.), *Kang Mei Yuan Chao Zhanzheng* (The resist-America support-Korea war), pp. 17–21.
5 This contemporary Western perception has since been confirmed; cf. *Origins* II, pp. 92–100 and Wu Lengxi, *Yi Mao Zhuxi*, p. 75.
6 *Origins* II, loc. cit. According to one account, Mao ordered preparations for the bombardment to begin as early as 17 July 1958, i.e. almost immediately after the Middle East crisis began; Chen Dunde, 'Beidaihe: Mao Zedong ji zhao Ye Fei shangjun mi tan' (Beidaihe: Mao Zedong urgently summons Gen. Ye Fei for secret talks), *Yan Huang Chun Qiu*, No. 7, 1993, p. 48.
7 One of the problems in analysing the Sino-Indian border war is that even the most detailed post-Cultural Revolution accounts do not provide one with the inside information about the Chinese decision-making process comparable to that long available for the Indian side.
8 *Origins* II, pp. 255–7.
9 Maxwell, *India's China War*, pp. 208–16, 231–8; Gopal, *Jawaharlal Nehru* 3, pp. 206–11; Palit, *War in High Himalaya*, pp. 89, 94, 97–9, 105–10. Dr S. Gopal was the Director of India's Ministry of External Affairs' Historical Division in 1960 and was one of the two Indian signatories to the joint report by Chinese and Indian officials produced as a result of the Nehru–Zhou summit. Brigadier (later Major General) Palit was India's Director of Military Operations in 1961–2. One reason for the Indian army's lack of preparedness on the borders with China was that until Oct. 1959, the area had been the sole responsibility of the Intelligence Bureau, essentially a domestic police operation under the Home Ministry, whose director normally reported directly to Nehru. Even after 1959, the Intelligence Bureau had retained control of all intelligence posts on the border; Palit, *War in High Himalaya*, pp. 99–101.
10 Maxwell, *India's China War*, pp. 492–3. One of Maxwell's sources was Zhou Enlai, but he did not indicate how Zhou was supposed to have found out about confidential communications between Moscow and New Delhi.
11 Palit, *War in High Himalaya*, pp. 85, 109–10, 160–1, 170; Maxwell, *India's China War*, pp. 334–45. According to Palit, as early as autumn 1961, Nehru had formed the view that the combination of all these factors would prevent any serious PLA riposte to proposed Indian moves. Since no serious Nationalist threat was in evidence at that point, Palit is perhaps confusing this with the similar but more justifiable estimates made in New Delhi in mid-1962.
12 Palit, *War in High Himalaya*, pp. 111–54. This is also the impression of Chinese analysts; Shi Bo, *1962: Zhong Yin Dazhan Jishi* (A record of the Sino-Indian war), p. 179.
13 Palit, *War in High Himalaya*, pp. 156–60, 170, 173–4; Government of India, *White Paper No. VI*, pp. i, 37–9; Maxwell, *India's China War*, pp. 250–1; Gopal, *Jawaharlal Nehru* 3, p. 211.
14 Sha Li & Min Li (eds.), *Zhongguo 9 Ci Da Fa Bing* (Nine instances of China sending out troops), p. 101. The major Chinese source on the war is Zhong Yin Bianjing Ziwei Fanji Zuozhan Shi Bianxiezu, *Zhong Yin Bianjing Ziwei Fanji Zuozhan Shi* (A history of the counter-attack in self-defence on the Sino-Indian border; hereafter, *Zhong Yin*), pp. 122–7, 141, 143.

[15] Whiting, *The Chinese Calculus of Deterrence*, pp. 75–7; Hinton, *Communist China in World Politics*, p. 296.

[16] See above, Ch. 12.

[17] SCMP 2755, p. 27.

[18] See above, Ch. 12.

[19] The advance was advised against by the general in charge of India's Western Command; Maxwell, *India's China War*, pp. 252–4. For the Chinese decision to reinforce, see *Zhong Yin*, pp. 132–3.

[20] *Zhong Yin*, pp. 145–8; Gopal, *Jawaharlal Nehru* 3, p 213.

[21] Whiting, *The Chinese Calculus of Deterrence*, pp. 73–4.

[22] Quoted in Palit, *War In High Himalaya*, pp. 79–80.

[23] Quoted in George, *Krishna Menon*, p. 249.

[24] Palit, *War in High Himalaya*, pp. 79–83.

[25] Government of India, *White Paper No. VII*, p. 1.

[26] Ibid., p. 3.

[27] Whiting, *The Chinese Calculus of Deterrence*, p. 80; Maxwell, *India's China War*, p. 267.

[28] Whiting, *The Chinese Calculus of Deterrence*, p. 84; Government of India, *White Paper No. VII*, p. 4.

[29] Brecher, *India and World Politics*, p. 170. Chen Yi's keenness to talk was Menon's reason for their meetings, but it fitted in with the current predilection in Beijing for the *san he yi shao* policy, of which better relations with India was an important component. Menon was later attacked in India for being photographed having a drink with Chen Yi; Maxwell, *India's China War*, p. 267. Chen and Menon met on 22 and 23 July; Liu Shufa, *Chen Yi Nianpu*, p. 926. For confirmation that the meetings were at Chen's request, together with a purported version of the discussion between the two foreign ministers, see Shi Bo, *1962: Zhong Yin Dazhan Jishi* pp. 185–6.

[30] Gopal, *Jawaharlal Nehru* 3, p. 213.

[31] Maxwell, *India's China War*, p. 259; *Origins* II, pp. 255–64.

[32] Government of India, *White Paper No. VII*, p. 18; Maxwell, *India's China War*, pp. 259–61; Whiting, *The Chinese Calculus of Deterrence*, pp. 87–91. Maxwell argued that this had always been the premier's position, that the 26 July note signalled no change, and that the Chinese understood that. Whiting held that Nehru was forced to abandon a more moderate stance.

[33] Ibid., pp. 88–9.

[34] At that time, the deputy foreign minister in overall charge of Africa and Asia was Huang Zhen and colleagues' reminiscences about his activities then give no indication that he was involved in dealings with India prior to the October border war. See Yao Zhongming, Xie Wushen, & Pei Jianzhang (eds.), *Jiangjun, Waijiaojia, Yishujia—Huang Zhen Jinian Wenji* (General, diplomat, artist—a collection of articles in memory of Huang Zhen), pp. 411–23.

[35] Whiting, *The Chinese Calculus of Deterrence*, pp. 91–98.

[36] Ibid., p. 92; see above, Ch. 12.

[37] Whiting, *The Chinese Calculus of Deterrence*, p. 93.

[38] The Chinese leadership did debate entry into the Korean War, but this was a decision involving confronting the world's most powerful military power and involved courting the danger of nuclear retaliation, and anyway, Mao seems to have overruled the majority that was against entry; *Peng Dehuai Zishu*, pp. 257–8; *Memoirs of a Chinese Marshal*, pp 472–4. For additional

confirmation of Mao's supremacy in foreign affairs by a cadre who worked in the CC's International Liaison Department, see *Wang Li Tan Mao Zedong* (Wang Li discusses Mao Zedong), pp. 43–4.

39 Gopal, *Jawaharlal Nehru* 3, p. 212, quotes the writer Han Suyin (*My House has Two Doors*, pp. 267–8) as claiming to have received a message that there would have to be a 'show of force' sometime to make the point that the Chinese had decided on a military solution, but, on examination, the timing, source, and meaning are too vague in Han's account for this intimation to provide any assistance in analysis of Chinese decision-making.

Another hint of possible Chinese military action was received by the Indian Intelligence Bureau in May/June 1962: the Chinese consul in Calcutta secretly warned Indian communist leaders about possible armed action on the border; Palit, *War in High Himalaya*, pp. 176–7. The Chinese Foreign Ministry may well have sensibly anticipated border clashes as a consequence of India's forward policy, and wanted to ensure that Beijing's friends in India were forearmed and able to put a pro-China spin if such events occurred. Another possibility is that the Chinese, well aware that secrets were difficult to keep in India, deliberately fed this 'information' to Indian communists in the confident expectation that it would be picked up by Indian intelligence (whose domestic capabilities were far more impressive than its foreign analyses), and that the Indian army would be deterred from further advances. (Indeed, the hints received by Han Suyin may have had a similar purpose, since Zhou Enlai was well aware that she had an entrée to Nehru.) What is very unlikely is that: (a) as early as May/June, when Wang Jiaxiang's advocacy of a softer line towards India still commanded high-level support, Beijing had decided on a major cross-border assault; (b) even had such a decision been taken, leak-prone citizens of a potentially enemy country would have been forewarned four months in advance. The CCP's propaganda outline on the Sino-Indian conflict for *Chinese* editors was only issued in Nov. 1962; Guofang Daxue, *Cankao Ziliao* 24, pp. 176–82.

40 Waijiaobu Waijiaoshi Bianjishi (ed.), *Xin Zhongguo Waijiao Fengyun* (Major events in new China's foreign affairs) 2, p. 72; *Zhong Yin*, pp. 142–3; 'Dangdai Zhongguo' Congshu Bianjibu (ed.), *Dangdai Zhongguo Junduide Junshi Gongzuo* (Contemporary China's armed forces' military work; hereafter, *Dangdai Zhongguo Junduide Junshi Gongzuo*), p. 617. There is no record of Mao's directives for the 1962 border war in the appropriate (sixth) volume of the most up-to-date and authoritative collection, *Mao Zedong Junshi Wenji* (A collection of Mao Zedong's military writings). Chen Yi is also mentioned in the first source, but not as a key player; the situation was too delicate for even the foreign minister to deal with. During the 1960s, proposals for handling major foreign affairs issues were customarily submitted by Zhou to Mao for approval, and to Liu Shaoqi, Deng Xiaoping, and Peng Zhen for information; Informant D. According to Xue & Pei (eds.), *Diplomacy of Contemporary China*, p. 261: 'Chinese diplomacy, after all, was guided by Chairman Mao and handled under the personal care of Premier Zhou, who did his best to ensure its proper conduct'. Though made in the context of the Cultural Revolution, the comment seemed to have more general significance. The Mao–Zhou relationship in the handling of foreign affairs seems to parallel that of Stalin and Molotov; see Berezhkov, *At Stalin's Side*, pp. 209–10.

41 'Bian fang wu xiao shi bo, shishi lian Beijing'; *Zhong Yin*, p. 144.
42 Whitson, *The Chinese High Command*, Chart D. While the Chinese rank *zhongjiang* is officially translated as Lt.-Gen., it only carries two stars; above it are Marshal (*yuanshuai*), Senior General (*dajiang*; four stars), and General (*shangjiang*; three stars).
43 Maxwell, *India's China War*, pp. 465–6.
44 *Dangdai Zhongguo Junduide Junshi Gongzuo*, pp. €17–18; Li Cheng, Xiao Ji, & Wang Libing (eds.), *Jianguo Yilai Jun Shi Bai Zh ιang Dashi* (A hundred major events in military history since the founding of the nation), p. 186.
45 Gopal, *Jawaharlal Nehru* 3, p. 218; Maxwell, *India's China War*, pp. 271–2.
46 Sha Li & Min Li, *Zhongguo 9 Ci Da Fa Bing*, p. 112; Chen Shiping, *Zhongguo Yuanshuai Liu Bocheng* (Liu Bocheng, Chinese marshal), pp. 525–6; 'Dangdai Zhongguo Renwu Zhuanji' Congshu Bianjibu (ed.), *Liu Bocheng Zhuan* (A biography of Liu Bocheng), pp. 669–74; Xu Yan, *Zhong Yin Bianjiezhi Zhan Lishi Zhenxiang* (The true history of t1e Sino-Indian border war), pp. 111–12. Nicknamed the 'one-eyed dragon' as a result of an early wound, Liu was perhaps the PLA's greatest strategist (with Lin Biao perhaps its greatest tactician). Shortly after the communist conquest of China, Liu was assigned to be the first president of the PLA's staff college, and in 1954 he became director of its General Training Department (Klein & Clark, *Biographic Dictionary of Chinese Communism* 1, pp. 611, 614–15). At the important MAC conference in 1958 (*Origins* II, pp. €3–71), Liu had to self-criticize as a result of an intra-military dispute over 'ɔoctrinairism', and had to be defended by his old comrade-in-arms Deng Xiaoping; Cong Jin, *Quzhe Fazhande Suiyue*, pp. 274–99. Nevertheless, the 69-year-old Liu's role in the Sino-Indian border war indicates that his considerable talents were still valued. Weighing up the Indian dispositions in the eastern sector, he characterized them as 'copper head, tin tail, stiff back, slack belly' (*dong tou, yi wei, bei jin, fu song*); Sha Li & Min Li, *Zhongguo 9 Ci Da Fa Bing*, p. 112.
47 The account in the official PLA chronology is unrevealing; see Junshi Kexue Yuan Junshi Lishi Yanjiubu (ed.), *Zhongguɔ Renmin Jiefang Jun Liushi Nian Dashiji (1927–1987)* (A chronology of 60 years of the Chinese PLA, 1927–1987; hereafter, *Jiefang Jun Liushi Nian Dashiji*), pp. 600–1.
48 Palit, *War in High Himalaya*, pp. 178–81, 183, 187; *Zhong Yin*, pp. 157–60.
49 The Indian military were aware of and concerned about the discrepancy between the McMahon Line and the Indian claim, but were not aware that Beijing had formally rejected the claim.; Palit, *War in High Himalaya*, pp. 188–91.
50 Government of India, *White Paper No. VII*, p. 68.
51 Ibid., pp. 71–3.
52 Ibid., p. 74. The Indian troops found a board near the Dhola post with the Chinese characters for 'This is our river and our mountain'; Maxwell, *India's China War*, p. 320.
53 Government of India, *White Paper No. VII*, pp. 77–8.
54 Maxwell, *India's China War*, pp. 321–31, 343–4. This decision was taken in the absence of the Prime Minister, who had left the previous day for the Commonwealth Prime Ministers' Conference in London. According to one senior Indian officer, 'Menon never actually overrode the professional opinion of his military chiefs, if they were staunch enough to stand firm on their views . . . if a service chief held his ground he would not overrule him'; Palit, *War in High Himalaya*, p. 73.

55 Maxwell, *India's China War*, p. 346; Whiting, *The Chinese Calculus of Deterrence*, pp. 100–2; *Zhong Yin*, pp. 160–1, 510.

56 Maxwell, *India's China War*, pp. 338–42.

57 *Zhong Yin*, p. 161; Whiting, *The Chinese Calculus of Deterrence*, p. 92.

58 Government of India, *White Paper No. VII*, pp. 96–8, 100–2; Whiting, *The Chinese Calculus of Deterrence*, pp. 108–10.

59 *Zhong Yin*, pp. 179–81, 187. This book stresses that India had placed its crack troops along the eastern sector of the border; ibid., pp. 191–2.

60 Whiting, *The Chinese Calculus of Deterrence*, pp. 110–14. For an outsider's assessment of Kaul, see Maxwell, *India's China War*, pp. 193–208, 355–68; for one by a senior officer appointed by Kaul to serve under him, see Palit, *War In High Himalaya*, pp. 71, 76–7, 296; for the latter's account of Kaul's behaviour up to this point in the developing crisis, see ibid., pp. 219–28.

61 Maxwell, *India's China War*, pp. 369–71.

62 Of Nehru's remark, usually only 'free' ('*qingchu diao*' [get rid of]) is translated into Chinese, in statements like 'He openly ordered that [India] must totally "rid" Indian-occupied Chinese territory of Chinese troops'; see *Dangdai Zhongguo Junduide Junshi Gongzuo*, p. 617.

63 Quoted in Whiting, *The Chinese Calculus of Deterrence*, pp. 117–18.

64 Maxwell, *India's China War*, pp. 380–5.

65 Ibid., pp. 391–2.

66 *Zhong Yin*, pp. 189–90; Hu Qingyun, 'Zhong Yin bianjie zhanzheng' (The China–India border war), in Zhongguo Geming Lishi Bowuguan Dangshi Yanjiushi, *Dangshi Yanjiu Ziliao*, No. 11, 1990, p. 614.

67 *Zhong Yin*, pp. 183–4; Wang Xianjin, *Re Xue Bing Shan* (Hot blood, icy mountains), p. 99.

68 *Zhong Yin*, p. 191.

69 For descriptions of the fighting from the Chinese viewpoint see *Zhong Yin*, pp. 195–221; Wang Xianjin, *Re Xue Bing Shan*, pp. 99–102 (western sector), Sha Li & Min Li, *Zhongguo 9 Ci Da Fa Bing*, p. 105. According to Wang, p. 98, dawn in Aksai Chin was 4.30 a.m. by Indian time, 7 a.m. by Beijing time, which prevails even in Tibet, some 2,000 miles to the west. Maxwell, *India's China War*, p. 388, and *Zhong Yin*. p. 198 seem to concur, saying the attack in the east started at 5 a.m. Indian time and 7.30 a.m. Chinese time.

70 Ibid., pp. 222–54; Whiting, *The Chinese Calculus of Deterrence*, pp. 119–21. The Chinese claimed to have responded to massive Indian attacks in both the eastern and western sectors on 20 Oct., but even a source sympathetic to the Chinese case on the border negotiations saw this as a fabrication, turning truth on its head: 'To say that the Indian troops in the western sector "launched a general attack" from their isolated and puny posts was grotesque'; Maxwell, *India's China War*, p. 404.

71 Ibid., pp. 392–4. Gen. Kaul had, however, insisted on going to his home, and tried to continue running his command from there, before giving up on the morning of the Chinese attack; ibid., pp. 385–7, 400. For an insider's account of India's top generals' mishandling of the situation, see Palit, *War in High Himalaya*, pp. 231–75.

72 Gopal, *Jawaharlal Nehru 3*, p. 227, asserts to the contrary that 'even a crisis of this dimension did not endanger Nehru's hold on the people'.

73 Ibid., p. 225; Maxwell, *India's China War*, pp. 405–22. Nehru's pre-condition for talks was the restoration of the *status quo ante* 8 Sept. 1962, when the Dhola post was captured, which would have meant the Chinese having to

relinquish all their recent military gains, but allow the Indians to reoccupy the posts set up under the forward policy. Zhou described Nehru's proposal like one 'forced on a vanquished party', and asked how the Chinese government could possibly agree; quoted in ibid., p. 409. See *Zhong Yin*, pp. 255–67 for a Chinese view of Indian diplomacy.

74 For a description of how Indian political exigencies dictated inappropriate military preparations in the eastern sector, see Maxwell, *India's China War*, pp. 417–28; Maxwell comments in a number of places that Indian units fought bravely and effectively, but were betrayed by incompetent generalship. The quotation from Nehru is on p. 417.

75 Maxwell, *India's China War*, p. 405. For Zhou's wooing of Afro-Asian leaders, see Whiting, *The Chinese Calculus of Deterrence*, pp. 123–4.

76 Ibid., pp. 127–8; Maxwell, *India's China War*, pp. 41C–20; Gopal, *Jawaharlal Nehru* 3, p. 227. Whiting argues convincingly that the article was too long and too detailed to have been prepared after Nehru's rejection of Zhou's talks offer, but it is still possible that the article could have been withheld had Nehru accepted the offer. For the 1959 article, see *Origins* II, p. 259; it had been written by Hu Qiaomu (*Hu Qiaomu Wenj* 1, pp. 618–44). In Hu's absence due to illness from 1961 on, the 1962 article was possibly written by Chen Boda, but when questioned, various officials connected with Chinese propaganda at the time could not recall precisely who the author was. According to the man who supervised its translation, the article went through over two-dozen drafts, with Mao, Liu Shaoqi, and Zhou Enlai contributing amendments, with Mao's becoming the dominant ones. '[T]he blunt, withering, dogmatic style of the original draft had been replaced by something more sophisticated, more subtle, and at the same time more biting, more sarcastic, and much more finely crafted... The final version was a caring little sermon, which angered the Indian leaders even more than a frontal attack would have.' See Rittenberg & Bennett, *The Man Who Stayed Behind*, pp. 263–4.

77 *Origins* II, pp. 8, 255–63, 290.

78 Gopal quotes a Sri Lankan political leader, who had conversations with Mao, Liu Shaoqi, Zhou Enlai, and Chen Yi, in evidence of this hostility; *Jawaharlal Nehru* 3, p. 230.

79 *Zhong Yin*, pp. 270–80; Sha Li & Min Li, *Zhongguo 9 Ci Da Fa Bing*, p. 111; Whitson, *The Chinese High Command*, Chart G; Institute for International Relations (ed.), *Chinese Communist Who's Who* 2, pp. 225–6, 327.

80 A successor had been appointed in consequence of Kaul's illness, but he only lasted a few days in the job because Nehru apparently wanted to help Kaul salvage his reputation; Maxwell, *India's China War*, pp. 423–4. Kaul's replacement and return was only one of a number of changes at senior level in the NEFA units after the first Chinese attack which, whatever the quality of the individual commanders, only produced bureaucratic confusion at a time when all efforts should have been concentrated on military preparedness; ibid., pp. 403–4, 427–8.

81 Ibid., pp. 429–30. Kaul apparently had in mind South Koreans and Nationalist Chinese.

82 Gopal, *Jawaharlal Nehru* 3, p. 228.

83 *Zhong Yin*, pp. 285–342; Sha Li & Min Li, *Zhongguo 9 Ci Da Fa Bing*, pp. 111–12; Hu Qingyun, 'Zhong Yin bianjie zhanzheng', p. 615. The Chinese depiction of their actions was again couched in terms of defence against a

general Indian attack, and Kaul's abortive enterprise on 14 Nov. gave them more justification than they had had on 20 Oct.

[84] A carefully thought-out strategic plan, formulated in 1959, envisaged basing India's main NEFA defences close to its sources of supplies and reinforcements on the plains, forcing an invading Chinese army to accept a dangerously long supply line through the difficult Himalayan terrain. The plan was abandoned because, in the political circumstances of 1962, it would have seemed like ceding Indian territory without a shot; Maxwell, *India's China War*, pp. 425–7. For an opposing view on the Indian decision to hold one particular area, see Palit, *War in High Himalaya*, pp. 256–7.

[85] For a graphic, first-hand description of the paralysis that gripped the Indian high command in the last days of the border war, see ibid., pp. 304–35. For the views of an intimately involved outsider, see Galbraith, *Ambassador's Journal*, pp. 372–456.

[86] Maxwell, *India's China War*, pp. 442–53. Prior to the 1962 war, senior Indian officers and bureaucrats may have assumed there would be Western assistance in the event of such a conflagration; Palit, *War In High Himalaya*, pp. 88, 97. For Menon's reluctance to ask for American weapons, see Galbraith, *Ambassador's Journal*, pp. 378, 386–7.

[87] Cf. Whiting, *The Chinese Calculus of Deterrence*, p. 164. In 1964, the present writer visited Indian military units in Ladakh, of which Aksai Chin is considered a part by India. On that occasion, a junior Indian officer said there was no prospect of India launching a war to take the territory, but that when China's central power waned, as had happened often in its history, then Aksai Chin might be recoverable. The Chinese themselves perhaps drew the wrong conclusions from this successful punitive expedition. In February 1979, Deng Xiaoping decided to teach the Vietnamese a lesson for invading Cambodia and substituting a puppet regime for the Chinese-backed Khmer Rouge government, but while the PLA again managed to penetrate into a certain amount of 'disputed' territory and then withdrew unilaterally, the Chinese troops were badly mauled by battle-hardened Vietnamese troops fighting from good tactical positions. For a Chinese account of Sino-Vietnamese relations, see Guo Ming, *Zhong Yue Guanxi Yanbian Sishi Nian* (Forty years of evolution in Sino-Vietnamese relations).

[88] Another benefit of the Himalayan success according to Mao when hearing a report about it in February 1963 was that it proved that the PLA had grasped politics; [*Mao Zedong*] *Xuexi Ziliao* (Selected materials [of Mao Zedong] for study) 3, p. 49.

[89] This seems to have been Zhou Enlai; Liu Xiao, *Chu Shi Sulian*, pp. 121, 122.

[90] *RMRB*, 2 Nov. 1963, quoted in Gittings, *Survey of the Sino-Soviet Dispute*, p. 178.

[91] Liu Xiao was appropriately to be succeeded by Pan Zili, who had been ambassador to India until the summer.

[92] Liu Xiao, *Chu Shi Sulian*, pp. 119–22.

[93] Floyd, *Mao against Khrushchev*, pp. 158–9.

[94] Liu Xiao, *Chu Shi Sulian*, p. 121; Gittings, *Survey of the Sino-Soviet Dispute*, p. 178.

[95] Liu Xiao, *Chu Shi Sulian*, pp. 122–3.

[96] Waijiaobu Waijiaoshi Bianjishi (ed.), *Xin Zhongguo Waijiao Fengyun* 1, pp. 129–31. When President Nixon went to China eighteen years later, he remembered that snub: 'I knew that Chou had been deeply insulted by Foster

Dulles's refusal to shake hands with him at the Geneva conference in 1954. When I reached the bottom step, therefore, I made a point of extending my hand as I walked toward him. When our hands met, one era ended and another began.' See *RN: The Memoirs of Richard Nixon*, p. 559.

97 Liu Xiao, *Chu Shi Sulian*, p. 122.

98 Whiting, *The Chinese Calculus of Deterrence*, pp. 1–3; Maxwell, *India's China War*, pp. 397–9; Gittings, *Survey of the Sino-Soviet Dispute*, p. 178.

99 *RMRB*, 24, 27 Oct. 1962.

100 When Khrushchev recorded his memoirs after being deposed, the Cuban missile crisis was the first episode he tackled; Sergei Khrushchev, *Khrushchev on Khrushchev*, pp. 234–5.

101 *Khrushchev Remembers*, p. 493.

102 For the problem of when exactly Khrushchev produced his missile plan, see Beschloss, *The Crisis Years*, pp. 382, 386.

103 Ibid., p. 451; see also p. 499.

104 *Khrushchev Remembers*, pp. 492–5; *Khrushchev Remembers: The Last Testament*, p. 583. According to the account in Beschloss, *The Crisis Years*, pp. 382–91, Khrushchev had greater difficulty convincing his closest colleague Anastas Mikoyan than Castro, and Castro agreed without the heated arguments with Khrushchev personally which the latter later wrote about. The difference between Khrushchev and Castro was that the former proclaimed that the main reason for the missiles was to protect Cuba, whereas the latter rejected the need for missiles for that purpose, but accepted them as a means of changing the overall correlation of forces between East and West. According to Zubok & Pleshakov, *Inside the Kremlin's Cold War*, pp. 261–2, the final decision to launch the missile operation was taken by the Defence Council on 24 May 1962, when Khrushchev contrived to share the responsibility for it by insisting that all present sign the directive.

105 Beschloss, *The Crisis Years*, p. 430.

106 For the unfolding of the crisis, see ibid., pp. 431–57; for the economic cost to the Russians and later admission of humiliation, see ibid., pp. 562–3; for Khrushchev's claim of success, see *Khrushchev Remembers*, pp. 498 and 504, where the late Soviet leader states: 'The Caribbean crisis was a triumph of Soviet foreign policy and a personal triumph in my own career as a statesman and as a member of the collective leadership. We achieved, I would say, a spectacular success without having to fire a single shot!' Khrushchev also claimed that Soviet ships ignored the blockade and continued to deliver military equipment to Cuba; ibid., p. 496. For new evidence of Soviet–Cuban interaction from Soviet-era archives, including Khrushchev's concern that Havana might move closer to Beijing, see '1962 Cuban Missile Crisis', *Cold War International History Project Bulletin*, No. 5, Spring 1995, pp. 58 ff.

107 Zhang Dequn, 'Zai Mosike liu nian ban' (Six and a half years in Moscow), *Zhonggong Dangshi Ziliao*, No. 58, June 1996, p. 38; Beschloss, *The Crisis Years*, p. 430.

108 Whiting, *The Chinese Calculus of Deterrence*, p. 15.

109 Of course, the Chinese may have been more realistic about American advance knowledge of the missiles than Khrushchev; ibid.

110 The other major double crisis of the Cold War period occurred in Oct.–Nov. 1956, when there was the conjunction of the Hungarian revolt and its suppression by the Russians and the attack on Egypt by Israeli, British, and French forces. In that case, both crises had been publicly brewing for some

time, but while leaders in Moscow on the one hand and in London, Paris, and Tel Aviv on the other were doubtless grateful that their Cold War antagonists were distracted, they would certainly have pursued their policies anyway. For a brief discussion, see Kyle, *Suez*, pp. 376–7. It is unlikely that anything would have stopped the Soviets from sending their tanks into Hungary, but Prime Minister Imre Nagy must have despaired that the West was distracted and divided by Suez; Nehru, on the other hand, probably benefited because the missile crisis had underlined for a united and responsive West, to whom he like Nagy appealed for help, the need to combat the threat of communism everywhere.

[111] The changing Chinese attitude towards the Soviet Union, obviously influenced heavily by Mao's reassertion of control over foreign affairs, can be seen in Beijing's propaganda output on the alliance: the *People's Daily* commemorated the 1950 Sino-Soviet Treaty for the last time in 1961; in 1962, the treaty was still marked in the Foreign Ministry journal, *Shijie Zhishi*, by a brief article; by 1963, the propagandists had buried the treaty. See Julian Chang, 'Propaganda and Perceptions: The Selling of the Soviet Union in the PRC, 1950–1960', unpub. Ph.D thesis, Harvard University, 1995, ch. 5.

[112] Gittings, *Survey of the Sino-Soviet Dispute*, p. 179.

[113] Dallin, *Diversity in International Communism*, p. 660.

[114] Gittings, *Survey of the Sino-Soviet Dispute*, pp. 181–3. The Russians might have retorted that the bombardment of the offshore islands in 1958 not followed up with an invasion was equally adventurist and capitulationist, even if Mao's humiliation was not as obvious as Khrushchev's.

[115] The North Korean, Burmese, and Malayan parties sided with the CCP at the congress. The Japanese, Indonesian, and Irish parties did not mention the Albanians; Dallin, *Diversity in International Communism*, p. 661.

[116] Wu Xiuquan, *Huiyi yu Huainian*, pp. 344–8.

[117] Griffith, *Albania and the Sino-Soviet Rift*, p. 165.

[118] Wu Xiuquan, *Huiyi yu Huainian*, p. 348.

[119] Ibid., pp. 349–52. Wu explained that in diplomatic parlance, 'regret' (*yihan*) was antagonistic in tone.

[120] Ibid., p. 352. The Poles had good reason to be pleasanter to the Chinese for they considered that Beijing's intervention had been crucial in staving off a Soviet overthrow of the Polish leadership in 1956; see the testimony of Edward Ochab, the then Polish 1st secretary in Toranska, *'Them': Stalin's Polish Puppets*, pp. 67–76.

[121] Wu Xiuquan, *Huiyi yu Huainian*, pp. 358–9; Dallin, *Diversity in International Communism*, p. 662.

[122] The hyper-suspicious Enver Hoxha, ever watchful for evidence of Chinese backsliding, thought that the Chinese speech to the Italian congress was a 'good hard-hitting one' and he characterized the attacks on the CCP at the various East European congresses as being 'launched with hooligan methods', but he remained unconvinced of the value of the overtly reasonable tone of the CCP; Hoxha, *Reflections on China* 1, pp. 30–2.

[123] Floyd, *Mao against Khrushchev*, p. 161. These articles may have been the first products of Kang Sheng's new role as mastermind of anti-Soviet polemics.

[124] Dallin, *Diversity in International Communism*, p. 663.

[125] Wu Xiuquan, *Huiyi yu Huainian*, p. 353.

[126]   Dallin, *Diversity in International Communism*, p. 662.

[127]   Wu Xiuquan, *Huiyi yu Huainian*, pp. 353–6. The statement is contained in Dallin, *Diversity in International Communism*, pp. 664–7. Wu publicly strode up to the rostrum while Novotný was delivering his summing up report and asked the chairman for permission to distribute it after Novotný had seen it. The startled chairman passed it to Novotný, who glanced at it, broke off from his speech, and, with very bad grace, read out the proclamation, to the great delight of the CCP delegation.

[128]   This was illustrated by the five-hour wrangle that took place between the Chinese delegation and their Czech hosts at what should have been a courtesy farewell lunch; Wu Xiuquan, *Huiyi yu Huainian*, pp. 357–8.

[129]   Dallin, *Diversity in International Communism*, pp. 2–3, 745–6; the formal justification for Mongolia's elevation was that it had become a member of the Council for Mutual Economic Assistance, the economic alliance between the Soviet Union and its East European satellites.

[130]   Wu Xiuquan, *Huiyi yu Huainian*, pp. 358–9.

[131]   Ibid., p. 360. Wu may have confused cause and effect. The formal rule laid down by the East Germans said that for a foreign delegate to speak, at least twenty members of the East German party had to back it. The North Koreans and Indonesians protested their inability to take the floor, but to no avail; see Dallin, *Diversity in International Communism*, pp. 746, 762.

[132]   Ibid., p. 750.

[133]   Wu Xiuquan, *Huiyi yu Huainian*, pp. 359–65; Dallin, *Diversity in International Communism*, pp. 761–2. The latter source notes that Wu wore a business suit rather than the customary Chinese tunic, and suggests that he may have been attempting to respond to the implicit charge that China did not understand Western conditions.

CHAPTER 14

[1]   See below, Ch. 19.

[2]   I have not included the plenums of the 7th CC because until about late 1954, when the constitution of the PRC was introduced and the 1st NPC was called, the CCP leaders seem to have seen themselves as occupied still with tasks that were part of the conquest, i.e. gaining control of the political, economic, and social fabric of their country.

[3]   Art. 36 of the 1956 constitution; *Zhongguo Gongchan Dang Di Baci Quanguo Daibiao Dahui Wenjian* (Documents of the 8th National Congress of the CCP), p. 108.

[4]   *Origins* I, pp. 171–2. This plenum was not preceded by a work conference. There may have been two reasons for this: the urgency of the events, and Mao's practice of making foreign as opposed to domestic policy decisions largely on his own, consulting only a few close colleagues.

[5]   Ibid., parts 3 and 4.

[6]   The exception was the three-week gap between the 4th plenum which preceded the second session of the 8th Congress in May 1958 and the 5th which succeeded it. In fact, the second session took the place of a plenum on this occasion, and the two attendant plenums were more for formal purposes. The 5th plenum, for instance, resembled the 1st in that its only significant task was to elect new members to the Politburo in the aftermath of a congress.

[7] *Origins* II, chs. 2 and 3.

[8] Ibid., pp. 128–35.

[9] Ibid., pp. 172–3.

[10] Ibid., part 3.

[11] Deng Zihui, Wang Jiaxiang, Xi Zhongxun, Jia Tuofu, and the other officials who fell at the 10th plenum were of course not as senior as Peng Dehuai or Liu Shaoqi, but their purge still represented a considerable upheaval.

[12] Liao Gailong, Zhao Baoxu, & Du Qinglin, *Dangdai Zhongguo Zhengzhi Dashidian, 1949–1990*, p. 385, states discreetly that the constitution 'united national and international experience'.

[13] *Issues & Studies*, Nov. 1973, p. 96.

[14] Pepper, 'Education for the New Order', *CHOC* 14, pp. 197–203.

[15] See for instance the photographs that accompany the biographies in the series of volumes Xinghuo Liao Yuan Bianjibu (ed.), *Zhongguo Renmin Jiefang Jun: Jiangshuai Minglu* (China's PLA: A record of commanders).

[16] *Origins* II, pp. 36–40, 333–5.

[17] For a description of the buildings, their furnishings, and their uses, see Wu Lengxi, *Yi Mao Zhuxi*, pp. 1–3.

[18] *Jianguo Yilai Mao Zedong Wengao* 9, p. 432. For a medical opinion on Mao's dental problems, see Li, *The Private Life of Chairman Mao*, pp. 99–103.

[19] Informant A.

[20] Li Rui *'Da Yuejin' Qin Li Ji*.

[21] According to one of his secretaries, Lin Ke; *Xinhua Yuebao*, No. 3, 1993, p. 25; and Lin Ke, Xu Tao, & Wu Xujun, *Lishide Zhenshi—Mao Zedong Shenbian Gongzuo Renyuande Zhengyan*, p. 235.

[22] See MacFarquhar, Cheek, & Wu, *The Secret Speeches of Chairman Mao*, p. 12; Wu Lengxi, *Yi Mao Zhuxi*, pp. 145, 151–2.

[23] For a description of this system in operation in the Carter administration, see Brzezinski, *Power and Principle*, pp. 57–74.

[24] If asked, most educated Chinese will assert that in this period, Chinese foreign correspondents were part of their nation's intelligence operations; see also, Faligot & Kauffer, *The Chinese Secret Service*, p. 131. An engaging foreign correspondent of the present author's acquaintance later turned up as a vice-minister of state security.

[25] For an early discussion of one of these publications, see Schwarz, 'The Ts'an-k'ao Hsiao-hsi [*Cankao Xiaoxi*]: How Well Informed are Chinese Officials about the Outside World?', *CQ*, No. 27, 1966, pp. 54–83.

[26] *Bulletin of the Cold War International History Project*, Nos. 6–7, Winter 1995/6, p. 168.

[27] Informant A.

[28] Cf. this comment on Prime Minister Thatcher by one of her erstwhile closest colleagues describing her lack of 'organizational insights': 'Her success in office owed more than she ever acknowledged to the simple bureaucratic skills of people like Sir Robert Armstrong, secretary to the Cabinet.' Howe, *Conflict of Loyalty*, p. 147.

[29] Bartlett, *Monarchs and Ministers*, pp. 28–9.

[30] During the Hundred Flowers in 1957, a professor derided Mao's inspection trips: 'And how can they know the actual situation? At best they can make an inspection tour of the Yellow River and swim in the Yangtze . . . Even if

they talked with the peasants, the peasants would not tell the truth and could only say: "Chairman Mao is great" '; MacFarquhar, *The Hundred Flowers Campaign and the Chinese Intellectuals*, p. 138.

31   *Origins* I, pp. 27–9, 57; II, pp. 20–50, 77–82.

32   For a discussion of the friction between the inner and outer courts, see Bartlett, *Monarchs and Ministers*, ch. 1.

33   This section is based on an analysis of the first six volumes of *Jianguo Yilai Mao Zedong Wengao*.

34   For the imperial system, see Bartlett, *Monarchs and Ministers*, p. 44.

35   One of Mao's most famous early articles was 'Get organized!', *Selected Works* 3, pp. 153–61.

36   See *Origins* II, pp. 59–63.

37   One apparent contra-indication of secretariat power at the 10th plenum was the abolition of the CC's Rural Work Department and the transfer of its functions to the Office of Agriculture and Forestry at the State Council. But since this bureaucratic manoeuvre was accompanied by the replacement of Deng Zihui by Tan Zhenlin, a member of the secretariat, as the director of that office, the secretariat's supervision of this issue area would seem to have been maintained. It is clear that Deng Zihui was being dismissed. It is not clear whether this way of accomplishing it was designed to save his face in some way or was a signal that from now on running agriculture had to do with raising production and not with altering the socialist system in the countryside. For a Zhou report to the secretariat, see *Dangde Wenxian*, No. 3, 1995, p. 37. For a later description of the work of the government, see 'Zhongguo Zhengfu Gongzuo Gaiyao' Bianxiezu (ed.), *Zhongguo Zhengfu Gongzuo Gaiyao* (Outline of the work of the Chinese government).

38   The normal pattern is for detailed accounts of a Chinese leader's involvement in post-1949 politics to emerge only after his death.

39   Almost certainly Huang had not played any role in the secretariat since the dismissal of Marshal Peng Dehuai in 1959 for he had been denounced as a member of Peng's alleged 'military club'; *Origins* II, pp. 239, 242. Tan Zheng, the head of the PLA's General Political Department, who was also officially taken off the secretariat at the 10th plenum, was a late victim of the PLA purge following the Lushan plenum, being accused in October 1960 of still pursuing Peng Dehuai's policies and opposing the new MAC leadership under Lin Biao. He was replaced by a former head of the General Political Department (GPD), Marshal Luo Ronghuan. See *Jiefang Jun Jiangling Zhuan* 7, pp. 507–8.

40   Ibid. 2, p. 287.

41   One gauge of the status of the State Council was its amount of activity. In the three years after its formation in late 1954, it averaged 21 meetings a year, reaching a pre-Cultural Revolution peak of 26 meetings in 1957. In the first year of the GLF, 1958, when central government functions were dispersed to the provinces, whose 1st secretaries were responsible to the secretariat, the number of its meetings dropped to 16, and again to 9 in 1959. A rise to 15 meetings in 1960 may have reflected the preoccupation of the two leaders of the secretariat, Deng and Peng Zhen, with the Sino-Soviet dispute (*Origins* II, p. 293), for in 1961, the number of State Council meetings dropped again to 7. The numbers began to rise with recentralization in 1962, reaching 15 in 1963 (when Deng and Peng were busy with the Socialist Edu-

cation Movement and renewed discussions with the Russians), but then started dropping again, and there were only 8 meetings in 1965, despite the fact that the government was in that year supposedly gearing up for the launch of the nation's 3rd FYP in 1966. See Chang, 'The State Council in Communist China', p. 68.
42 *Origins* II, p. 61.

APPENDIX 3

1 Ulam, *The Bolsheviks*, p. 219.
2 Schapiro, *The Communist Party of the Soviet Union*, pp. 314–15, 447; Tucker, *Stalin in Power*, p. 123; Fainsod, *How Russia is Ruled*, p. 184.
3 See Gong Yuzhi, Pang Xianzhi, & Shi Zhongquan, *Mao Zedongde Dushu Shenghuo, passim.*
4 Li, *The Private Life of Chairman Mao, passim.*
5 In *Hitler and Stalin*, p. 405, Bullock quotes Hitler's architect Albert Speer: 'When, I would ask myself, did Hitler really work?' Speer's own description of Hitler's dinner-table circle is in *Inside the Third Reich*, pp. 176–95.
6 Volkogonov, *Stalin: Triumph and Tragedy*, p. 147.
7 Tucker, *Stalin in Power*, pp. 124–5.
8 Volkogonov, *Lenin*, p. 272; for Hitler, see Stephen Kinzer's report 'Berchtesgaden journal: an unspoiled alpine view, a legacy of demons', *NYT*, 13 Sept. 1995.
9 See Lih, Naumov, & Khlevniuk, *Stalin's Letters to Molotov*, from which it becomes clear that Stalin's subordinates had considerable latitude during his absences.
10 Volkogonov, *Stalin: Triumph and Tragedy*, p. 217.
11 Bracher, *The German Dictatorship*, p. 297; Bullock, *Hitler and Stalin*, p. 404.
12 Toland, *Adolf Hitler*, pp. 374–5. Interestingly, the work habits of each of the four leaders were in sharp contrast to the traditional stereotypes of the 'national character' of the nations they ran: highly disciplined, industrious, and respectful of authority in the cases of China and Germany, highly inefficient, emotional, and idle to the point of anarchy in the case of Russia. Lenin, however, had German blood in his veins, an embarrassing fact for his biographers, for his mother was descended from the Volga Germans; de Madariaga, *Russia in the Age of Catherine the Great*, pp. 361–3 refers to this in a brief description of the origins of this group, deported by Stalin to Central Asia in World War II; see also Volkogonov, *Lenin*, pp. 8–10. For the problems of Lenin's Soviet biographers in this regard, see Fischer, *The Life of Lenin*, pp. 2–3. For China, see Butterfield, *China*, pp. 280–5; for Russia, see Mehnert, *Soviet Man and his World*, p. 30; Smith, *The Russians*, p. 150; Kaiser, *Russia*, ch. 9, 'The Economy: Inefficiency According to Plan'. For the contrasts between Russia and China, see Short, *The Dragon and the Bear*, pp. 28–35. For Russia and Germany, see Smith, *The Russians*, p. 362, and the p. 1 story on the Volga Germans by Steven Erlanger, *NYT*, 9 May 1993; in the latter source, the following passage appears: 'Germans work better than Russians, she [a Volga German] said, echoing a common theme among Russians themselves. It is the reason Germans were invited to Russia in the first place.' The frustrations of what Mao called 'bureaucratism' are of course known in all countries, including these three; for China, see Mathews, *One Billion*, pp. 183–206.

[13] Bullock, *Hitler*, p. 349; Fest, *The Face of the Third Reich*, pp. 77–8; Bracher, *The German Dictatorship*, p. 297.
[14] Quoted in Bullock, *Hitler and Stalin*, p. 150.
[15] *Selected Works of Mao Tse-tung* 1, p. 28.
[16] Cf. Starr, *Continuing the Revolution*, pp. 300–7, and Hitler's statement: 'The conquest of power is a never-ending process . . . the essential thing is not the asssumption of power, but the education of men.' (Quoted in Bullock, *Hitler and Stalin*, p. 431.)
[17] Quoted in Schram, *The Thought of Mao Tse-tung*, p. 167.
[18] Li, *The Private Life of Chairman Mao*, p. 463.
[19] Bullock, *Hitler and Stalin*, p. 374.
[20] Schram, *Mao's Road to Power* 1, pp. xxviii–xxxii, 175–313.
[21] Ibid., pp. 263–4.
[22] Schram, *The Thought of Mao Tse-tung*, p. 17.
[23] The title of one of Mao's most famous speeches, given to the concluding session of the CCP's 7th Congress in 1945; *Selected Works of Mao Tse-tung* 3, pp. 321–3. Of course, the power of the will in human affairs is not confined to dictatorships. Winston Churchill, for instance, overbore inclinations within his cabinet to negotiate peace with Hitler in 1940 by the force of his inner conviction of the inevitability of victory and the power of his personality; unreconciled doubters were silenced by Churchill's ability to appeal over their heads to the people with his stirring oratory. See Charmley, *Churchill: The End of Glory*, pp. 396–419.
[24] Li, *The Private Life of Chairman Mao*, p. 443; Bullock, *Hitler and Stalin*, pp. 383–6.
[25] Ibid., pp. 376, 444.

CHAPTER 15

[1] Cong Jin, *Quzhe Fazhande Suiyue*, p. 519.
[2] *PR*, No. 39, 1962, pp. 5–8; the quotation is on p. 6.
[3] *RMRB*, 11 Jan. 1963; quoted in Baum, *Prelude to Revolution*, pp. 17–18.
[4] These documents were captured by the Nationalists in 1964; Baum, *Prelude to Revolution*, p. 12. The Chinese texts are available in Guofangbu Qingbaoju [RoC] (ed.), *Fangong Youjidui Tuji Fujian Lianjiang Luhuo Feifang Wenjian Huibian*; most of them are translated in Chen (ed.), *Rural People's Communes in Lien-Chiang*, which also has some additional items. Lianjiang was one of three places where the special provincial small group in charge initiated the SEM, the others being Xiamen and Nan'an; 'Dangdai Zhongguo' Congshu Bianjibu (ed.), *Dangdai Zhongguode Fujian* (Contemporary China's Fujian) 1, p. 133.
[5] Chen, *Rural People's Communes in Lien-Chiang*, pp. 109–10.
[6] Zhang Xiangling (ed.), *Heilongjiang Sishi Nian* (Forty years of Heilongjiang), p. 333; *Dangdai Zhongguode Shandong* 1, p. 226; *Dangdai Zhongguode Sichuan* 1, p. 122.
[7] *Mao Zedong sixiang wan sui (1969)*, p. 441. Both men had served under Mao's favourite Wang Renzhong in Hubei, which may have been why the Chairman singled them out for mention rather than the provincial 1st secretaries. Liu Zihou had been in Hubei from 1949, becoming 2nd secretary and provincial governor in the mid-1950s before moving to his native Hebei, where he was currently 2nd secretary. Liu came from Baoding district, the

site of the experiment for which Mao had expressed admiration. Wang Yanchun, also from Hebei, had started his service in Hubei in the mid-1950s, becoming 2nd secretary in 1960 before moving to Hunan in early 1962. See *Zhonggong Renming Lu*, p. 240a; URI, *Who's Who in Communist China* 1, pp. 464–5; 2, p. 703; Sheng Ping, *Zhongguo Gongchan Dang Renming Dacidian, 1921–1991*, pp. 50, 179.

8 Guofang Daxue, *Cankao Ziliao* 24, pp. 168–9.

9 Ibid., pp. 169–71.

10 Later in the year, Anhui province also claimed success in redeeming itself from the capitalist road; ibid., pp. 182–4.

11 According to Mao, the Baoding team had originally intended to handle distribution problems, but had initiated the four cleans in response to popular pressure; *Mao Zedong sixiang wan sui (1969)*, p. 443.

12 'Dangdai Zhongguo' Congshu Bianjibu (ed.), *Dangdai Zhongguode Hebei* (Contemporary China's Hebei) 1, pp. 111–12.

13 *Zhonggong Dangshi Zhuan Ti Jiangyi*, p. 158.

14 *Jianguo Yilai Mao Zedong Wengao* 10, pp. 255–8; CCP CC Party History Research Centre, *History of the Chinese Communist Party*, pp. 302–3; Ma Qibin *et al.*, *Zhongguo Gongchan Dang Zhizheng Sishi Nian*, p. 230. The meeting also discussed the 1963 economic plan, the Forty Articles on Primary Schools, and the Fifty Articles on Middle Schools. For the texts of the latter documents, see *Jiaoyu Nianjian*, pp. 699–705; they were circulated on 23 Mar. 1963 (*Jiaoyu Dashiji*, pp. 328–9).

15 Cong Jin, *Quzhe Fazhande Suiyue*, p. 527.

16 Bo Yibo, *Ruogan Zhongda Juece* 2, p. 1107. Liu's report was made the basis of a CC document on combating revisionism; ibid., p. 1146.

17 Cong Jin, *Quzhe Fazhande Suiyue*, p. 527. This source is usually accurate, but according to one provincial source, the Five-Antis Campaign was initiated in January, and according to others it was 1 March; Hubei Sheng Difang Zhi Bianzuan Weiyuanhui (ed.), *Hubei Sheng Zhi: Dashiji* (Hubei provincial gazeteer: Chronology), p. 678; Zhang Xiangling, *Heilongjiang Sishi Nian*, p. 332; *Zhonggong Dangshi Zhuan Ti Jiangyi*, p. 159. Mao may also have been concerned by a CC Organization Department report in December 1962 that his speech to the Seven Thousand Cadres Conference had sparked desires for more democracy and less centralism, more freedom and less discipline; *Jianguo Yilai Mao Zedong Wengao* 10, p. 241. For the first five-antis campaign in 1951–2, see Lin Yunhui, Fan Shouxin, & Zhang Gong, *1949–1989 Niande Zhongguo, 1: Kaige Xingjinde Shiqi* (China 1949–1989, 1: The period of triumphant advance), pp. 251–61; Barnett, *Communist China: The Early Years, 1949–1955*, pp. 135–71.

18 Ma Yunfei, 'Liu Shaoqi yu liushi niandaide guomin jingji tiaozheng' (Liu Shaoqi and the adjustment of the national economy in the 1960s), *Zhonggong Dangshi Yanjiu*, No. 5, 1988, p. 13. According to another source, this decision was taken at the suggestion of Zhou Enlai, but not until Sept. 1963; Guofang Daxue, *Qishi Nian Jianjie*, p. 513.

19 The Guizhou provincial party, for instance, held meetings after both the 10th plenum and the February work conference, but it was only after the latter that it started talking about socialist education; see *Guizhou Sheng Zhi: Dashiji, 1949–1985 (Zhengqiu yijian gao)* (Guizhou provincial gazeteer: chronology, 1949–1985 [MS circulated for comment]), pp. 103, 105.

[20] Huaibin Xian Zhi Bangongshi (ed.), *Huaibin Xian Zhi, 1951–1983* (Huaibin county gazeteer, 1951–1983), p. 28. In 1962, Henan had responded to the 10th plenum by sending to the centre the materials from three-level cadres conferences in 90 counties. These documents stated that the good situation had earlier prevented people from fully understanding the need for class struggle, but now it was fully exposed; 'Dangdai Zhongguo' Congshu Bianjibu (ed.), *Dangdai Zhongguode Henan* (Contemporary China's Henan; hereafter, *Dangdai Zhongguode Henan*) 1, p. 148.

[21] *Nongye Jitihua, xia*, pp. 674–9.

[22] 'Dangdai Zhongguode Jiangsu' Weiyuanhui & Jiangsu Sheng Dang'anju (eds.), *Jiangsu Sheng Dashiji, 1949–1985* (A chronology of Jiangsu province, 1949–1985; hereafter, *Jiangsu Sheng Dashiji*), pp. 233, 234, 235.

[23] Heilongjiang's slowness may have been due to inefficiency higher up where the campaign was being run. The Tianjin party discussed the five-antis campaign at about the same time, 25 April, at a conference of local industrial and transportation units held on the basis of what had been said on the campaign at a similar meeting at the national level called by the State Economic Commission; *Tianjin Jingji Jianshe Dashiji*, p. 192.

[24] Zhang Xiangling, *Heilongjiang Sishi Nian*, pp. 332–5.

[25] Hao Weimin, *Nei Menggu Zizhiqu Shi*, p. 216.

[26] For an account of how Lei Feng was put up as candidate for model status, see Shu Yun, 'Shi fou xuanchuan Lei Feng, zeng you yi chang zhengyi' (There was a debate about whether or not to propagandize Lei Feng), *Yan Huang Chun Qiu*, 11 May 1993, pp. 4–9.

[27] Li Ming, *Gongheguo Licheng Da Xiezhen* (Major realities in the life of the republic), *shang*, pp. 366–9.

[28] See the article by Lin Ke on the 30th anniversary of the Lei Feng campaign, *RMRB*, 5 Mar. 1993, reproduced in *Xinhua Yuebao*, No. 3, 1993, pp. 25–6. An accompanying *People's Daily* editorial (ibid., pp. 24–5) argued the contemporary relevance of Lei Feng, and the paper also published (ibid., pp. 21–3) a list of all the units and individuals who had been accorded advanced status in the Lei Feng campaign over the previous three decades.

[29] Quoted in Sheridan, 'The Emulation of Heroes', *CQ*, No. 33, 1968, pp. 52–3. For a brief biography of Lei Feng, see Liao Gailong *et al.*, *Xin Zhongguo Biannianshi*, pp. 212–13. For a sardonic account of the Lei Feng campaign by a foreign correspondent resident in Beijing, see Marcuse, *The Peking Papers*, pp. 235–46; for a more sympathetic account by Americans teaching English in Beijing, see Milton & Milton, *The Wind will not Subside*, pp. 63–9.

[30] Liu Binyan, *A Higher Kind of Loyalty*, pp. 197–9.

[31] For instance, in the northeast; *Nongye Jitihua, xia*, p. 672.

[32] Ibid., p. 689; Baum & Teiwes, *Ssu-Ch'ing: The Socialist Education Movement of 1962–1966*, p. 66.

[33] The major figures initially were Peng Zhen, and regional 1st secretaries Ke Qingshi (East China), Li Jingquan (Southwest), and Tao Zhu (Central-South), as well as Jiang Hua (1st secretary, Zhejiang, in whose capital the meeting took place). They were later joined by other regional 1st secretaries: Song Renqiong (Northeast), Li Xuefeng (North China), and Liu Lantao (Northwest), along with Chen Boda and Hu Yaobang (Northwest 3rd secretary). Finally, Zhou Enlai and Deng Xiaoping turned up at the end of the conference. See Zheng Qian & Han Gang, *Wannian Suiyue: 1956 Nianhoude Mao Zedong*, p. 246.

34 Liu was on tour 12 Apr.–16 May; Cong Jin, *Quzhe Fazhande Suiyue*, p. 530. It was during the Indonesia visit that Liu's wife, Wang Guangmei, wore a pearl necklace and the traditional *cheongsam* dress instead of the customary boiler-suit, for which she was arraigned in front of a Red Guard kangaroo court during the Cultural Revolution.

35 Cong Jin, *Quzhe Fazhande Suiyue*, p. 530. This source suggests that this difference was already latent, whereas the argument in this chapter is that the content of the Former Ten Points indicates that Mao had not yet realized that he should be worrying about the top, not the bottom. This source also gives no hint that political considerations lay behind the convening of this meeting in Liu's absence; I am indebted to Huang Jing for this point. For Liu's advocacy of Yan'an-type education which involved students going to the countryside to educate peasants, see *Jianguo Yilai Mao Zedong Wengao* 9, pp. 515–16.

36 Bo Yibo, *Ruogan Zhongda Juece* 2, pp. 1107–8; *Mao Zedong he tade Mishu Tian Jiaying*, p. 73; Informant E. Tian Jiaying was not asked to attend this conference, nor the earlier meeting in Feb. (ibid.), a sign of Mao's mistrust of him.

37 *Mao Zedong sixiang wan sui (1969)*, p. 444.

38 Mao had originally talked in terms of uniting with 90%, but was persuaded by Zhou Enlai to diminish potential enemies from 10% to 5% of the population; Bo Yibo, *Ruogan Zhongda Juece* 2, pp. 1109–10.

39 *Mao Zedong sixiang wan sui (1969)*, p. 445; the translation in Mao, *Miscellany* 2, p. 322, says the opposite.

40 *Mao Zedong sixiang wan sui (1969)*, p. 438.

41 Ibid., p. 443.

42 Baum & Teiwes, *Ssu-Ch'ing*, pp. 58–70. The translations in this volume are of the versions obtained by the Chinese Nationalists in the Lianjiang raid (ibid., pp. 9–10); the official version of the Former Ten Points is available in *Nongye Jitihua, xia*, pp. 680–93. Mao's comments on the Zhejiang documents are in the latter source, pp. 693–4.

43 *Jianguo Yilai Mao Zedong Wengao* 10, pp. 285–9, 292–309; Bo Yibo, *Ruogan Zhongda Juece* 2, pp. 1109–10.

44 *Mao Zedong sixiang wan sui (1969)*, p. 445. For an example of a poor peasant reacting to an excessive tax demand by local party officials by stating publicly that pre-1949 landlords had treated them better under similar circumstances, see Wu & Li, *A Single Tear*, pp. 304–5.

45 Bo Yibo, *Ruogan Zhongda Juece* 2, p. 1106; *Origins* I, pp. 295–7.

46 *Nongye Jitihua, xia*, pp. 671–2.

47 See the report of a French journalist touring China in early 1965 in Karol, *China: The Other Communism*, pp. 165–72.

48 *Nongye Jitihua, xia*, pp. 672–4.

49 Baum & Teiwes, *Ssu-Ch'ing*, p. 70.

50 See the *People's Daily* editorial on the CCP's anniversary on 1 July 1958, 'Nongmin wenti rengran shi genben wenti' (The peasant question still remains the fundamental one).

51 Bo Yibo, *Ruogan Zhongda Juece* 2, pp. 1110–11.

52 Ibid., pp. 1109, 1111–12. For a description of 'trial and error' during the summer of 1963, see Baum, *Prelude to Revolution*, pp. 28–42; *Jiangsu Sheng Dashiji*, pp. 236–7.

53 Informant E.

[54] *Issues & Studies*, June 1970, pp. 95–6.

[55] *Renmin Shouce, 1964*, pp. 343–53.

[56] Bo Yibo, *Ruogan Zhongda Juece* 2, p. 1112. Evidently, all active senior party leaders, bar perhaps Zhou Enlai, had some hand in the drafting of the Latter Ten Points, yet Chinese sources ascribe responsibility differently: One source has stated that Liu Shaoqi and Peng Zhen were in charge of this process; Cong Jin, *Quzhe Fazhande Suiyue*, p. 531; a second said Deng and Tan; *Mao Zedong he tade Mishu Tian Jiaying*, p. 74; a third said Deng and Peng; Informant E. Cultural Revolution sources, like Bo Yibo, reported that the basis of the Latter Ten Points was a report by Peng Zhen to Mao, while Deng supervised the drafting of the document; Baum, *Prelude to Revolution*, p. 43. Bo seems to be the only source to mention Tian's role. For Mao's resentment, see below, Ch. 18. For Mao's participation in the drafting, see *Jianguo Yilai Mao Zedong Wengao* 10, pp. 385–93.

[57] Baum & Teiwes, *Ssu-Ch'ing*, p. 72. Thereafter, the document was peppered with phrases such as 'Comrade Mao Tse-tung has wisely and clearly explained...', 'In accordance with Comrade Mao Tse-tung's instructions...', '... repeatedly study Comrade Mao Tse-tung's instructions...', 'Comrade Mao Tse-tung has repeatedly instructed us...', 'Comrade Mao Tse-tung's instructions... should be directly introduced to the cadres and masses...', '... as advocated by Comrade Mao Tse-tung...', etc.; ibid., pp. 72, 73, 75, 76, 78. See also, Cong Jin, *Quzhe Fazhande Suiyue*, p. 531

[58] A normal tactic in all sorts of political systems. During the long-running dispute between Britain's Chancellor Lawson and Prime Minister Margaret Thatcher over exchange-rate policy in the late 1980s, he and his adviser produced a paper to bridge the differences, which, as Lawson later wrote, 'expressed my views as well as his own. But within that context it bent over backwards to try and accommodate Margaret's.' Lawson, *The View from No. 11*, p. 831.

[59] Baum argued that 'it must be conceded that the pronounced overtones of legalism, liberalism, and political tolerance that permeated the Second Ten Points may have had the effect of tacitly undermining the spirit, if not the letter, of Mao's thesis on class struggle'; *Prelude to Revolution*, p. 59.

[60] *Mao Zedong sixiang wan sui (1969)*, p. 437.

[61] Ibid., p. 441.

[62] The introduction to the Former Ten Points said: 'It has taken us 13 years of practice since the establishment of our government to produce a relatively complete document on the problems in rural work'; the first article of the Latter Ten Points described the SEM as 'even more complicated than the land reform movement'; Baum & Teiwes, *Ssu-Ch'ing*, pp. 58, 75.

[63] For an example of the kind of land reform of which Mao approved, see Hinton, *Fanshen,* which describes the process initiated in an 'old liberated area' before the communist regime was set up.

[64] Baum & Teiwes, *Ssu-Ch'ing*, pp. 63, 70.

[65] Ibid., p. 77.

[66] One reason why Mao turned from Peng Zhen to Chen Boda to draft the Former Ten Points was apparently because he wanted a shorter, sharper document; Bo Yibo, *Ruogan Zhongda Juece* 2, p. 1108.

[67] Baum & Teiwes, *Ssu-Ch'ing*, pp. 73–91.

[68] Ibid., p. 79. Bo Yibo asserts that one of the most important differences between the Former and Latter Ten Points was the considerable elabora-

tion regarding how to unite with 95% of the masses and the cadres; *Ruogan Zhongda Juece* 2, pp. 1113–14.

[69] For a fictional representation based on the author's first-hand observations of the role of envy in the SEM and the permanent disability of a bad class status, see Gu Hua, *A Small Town Called Hibiscus*; for a factual account of how one cadre falsely accused a rival of theft during the SEM, see Chan, Madsen, & Unger, *Chen Village*, pp. 35–40.

[70] For peasant resistance to reclassification of landlords' children, see Li, *The Private Life of Chairman Mao*, pp. 428–9. Doubtless it was convenient to have ready-made targets as each new campaign came along, and if the old target was removed a new one would have to be found, an unsettling prospect.

[71] Baum & Teiwes, *Ssu-Ch'ing*, pp. 82–4, 91–4.

[72] Bo Yibo, *Ruogan Zhongda Juece* 2, pp. 1113, 1114–15.

[73] Baum & Teiwes, *Ssu-Ch'ing*, pp. 75, 83–4.

[74] Ibid., p. 66.

[75] Ibid., p. 64.

[76] Ibid., p. 75.

[77] Harding, *Organizing China*, p. 205.

[78] Baum & Teiwes, *Ssu-Ch'ing*, pp. 74, 90–1.

[79] *Origins* I, pp. 112–16, 189–91.

[80] *Origins* II, pp. 51–5.

[81] Harding, 'The Chinese State in Crisis', *CHOC* 15, pp. 134–8.

[82] Baum, *Prelude to Revolution*, p. 178, n. 3.

CHAPTER 16

[1] Wu Xiuquan, *Huiyi yu Huainian*, p. 366; for a detailed calendar of the polemics, together with quotations from major documents, see Floyd, *Mao against Khrushchev*, pp. 326–95.

[2] Griffith, *The Sino-Soviet Rift*, pp. 105–6, 108.

[3] Hudson, Lowenthal, & MacFarquhar, *The Sino-Soviet Dispute*, pp. 202–3.

[4] Quoted in Griffith, *The Sino-Soviet Rift*, p. 106.

[5] Ibid., pp. 107–8.

[6] For discussions of these, see *Origins* II, pp. 7–11, 255–92.

[7] Griffith, *The Sino-Soviet Rift*, pp. 110–11.

[8] The North Vietnamese, Japanese, Indonesian, Indian, British, and New Zealand communist parties were leaders of the efforts to prevent the CPSU and the CCP from splitting; Gittings, *Survey of the Sino-Soviet Dispute*, pp. 184–5; for an assessment of the positions of such parties—pro-Soviet, pro-Chinese, or neutral—on the issues in dispute, see Griffith, *The Sino-Soviet Rift*, pp. 120–3.

[9] Floyd, *Mao against Khrushchev*, pp. 371–4, 392. Mao actually suggested that Khrushchev might stop over in Beijing in connection with his projected visit to Cambodia. In its reply, the CPSU pointed out that, as already publicly announced, it was Brezhnev not Khrushchev who was planning to visit Cambodia; ibid., p. 395.

[10] Ibid., pp. 390–3.

[11] Ibid., pp. 395–6; Wu Xiuquan, *Huiyi yu Huainian*, p. 367.

[12] Griffith, *The Sino-Soviet Rift*, pp. 114–19.

[13] *The Polemic on the General Line of the International Communist Movement* (hereafter, *The Polemic*), pp. 3–54.

14 Wu Xiuquan, *Huiyi yu Huainian*, p. 368; Ye Yongli, *Chen Boda Qiren*, p. 208.
15 Arbatov, *The System*, p. 95 n.
16 Floyd, *Mao against Khrushchev*, pp. 406-24.
17 Wu Xiuquan, *Huiyi yu Huainian*, p. 367. In addition to being the leading Soviet ideologist, Suslov was the current chair of the China Commission of the CPSU's Presidium (Politburo), a high-level group which had been in existence since 1925; Informant F.
18 Ibid., pp. 368-9.
19 Hoxha, *Reflections on China* I, p. 44.
20 Ibid., pp. 44-5. Chen Yi had taken a similar line within China in 1960; *Origins* II, p. 291.
21 Wu Xiuquan, *Huiyi yu Huainian*, p. 370.
22 Ibid.; Griffith, *The Sino-Soviet Rift*, pp. 149-53; Floyd, *Mao against Khrushchev*, pp. 423-9. Wu gives the impression of blaming Beijing as much as Moscow for these exchanges.
23 Wu Xiuquan, *Huiyi yu Huainian*, p. 371. Wu lifted this phrase approvingly from contemporary Western comment.
24 At the first session, Suslov read out a 70-page paper; Cong Jin, *Quzhe Fazhande Suiyue*, pp. 588-9.
25 Arbatov, *The System*, p. 94.
26 Wu Xiuquan, *Huiyi yu Huainian*, pp. 371-2. The CPSU delegation was under the impression that the CCP delegation would send a Soviet text to Beijing by coded telegram with comments and then await a reply, which would take the form of a final text for delivery at the next session; Arbatov, *The System*, p. 94. Arbatov does not indicate whether this impression was based on a monitoring of Chinese communications by Soviet intelligence.
27 Cong Jin, *Quzhe Fazhande Suiyue*, p. 589. For a brief account of Deng Xiaoping's role at the meetings, see Liu Jintian, *Deng Xiaopingde Licheng* 2, pp. 117-19.
28 Wu Xiuquan, *Huiyi yu Huainian*, p. 371.
29 Arbatov, *The System*, p. 95.
30 *The Polemic*, pp. 4-7.
31 Ibid., pp. 6-12.
32 Ibid., pp. 13-17, 24-5; the quotation is on p. 13.
33 Ibid., pp. 21-4.
34 Ibid., pp. 25-9.
35 Ibid., pp. 29-30.
36 Ibid., pp. 30-3.
37 Ibid., pp. 33-9, 48-50.
38 Ibid., pp. 39-40.
39 Ibid., pp. 42-5.
40 Ibid., pp. 45-8.
41 Ibid., pp. 50-2.
42 Ibid., pp. 526-9.
43 For a brief summary of this Soviet version of recent bloc history, see Griffith, *The Sino-Soviet Rift*, p. 157.
44 *The Polemic*, pp. 529-38.
45 Ibid., p. 539.
46 Ibid.
47 Ibid., p. 563.

48 Ibid., pp. 570–1.
49 *Origins* I, pp. 41–2.
50 *The Polemic*, p. 541.
51 See Michael Schoenhals's translation, 'Mao Zedong: Speeches at the 1957 "Moscow Conference" ', *The Journal of Communist Studies* 2, No. 2, June 1986, pp. 109–26.
52 *The Polemic*, pp. 547–51.
53 Ibid., pp. 551–6.
54 *Origins* II, pp. 10–11, 92–9, 225–6.
55 *The Polemic*, pp. 544–5.
56 Arbatov, *The System*, p. 98.
57 Ibid., p. 97; the two passages are in *The Polemic*, pp. 542, 545.
58 Conquest, *Russia after Khrushchev*, pp. 114–17; Beschloss, *The Crisis Years*, p. 585. Both sources speculate about the possibility of foul play, but indicate that there is no proof that this turn of events was anything more than a piece of good luck for Khrushchev. Kozlov died 21 months later.
59 *Origins* II, p. 278.
60 Beschloss, *The Crisis Years*, p. 586; Arbatov only briefly mentions the test-ban treaty (*The System*, p. 98) and Kozlov's name appears nowhere in his index.
61 The letter was Macmillan's idea; the subsequent Anglo-American discussions on the issue and the text of the letter is in Macmillan, *At the End of the Day*, pp. 455–68.
62 Quoted in Chang, *Friends and Enemies*, p. 236.
63 Ibid., p. 238.
64 Beschloss, *The Crisis Years*, p. 596.
65 Ibid., pp. 598–601.
66 Griffith, *The Sino-Soviet Rift*, p. 158, suggests that this timing was no accident. The Chinese had the same idea; *The Polemic*, p. 98.
67 Wu Xiuquan, *Huiyi yu Huainian*, pp. 372–3.
68 Beschloss, *The Crisis Years*, pp. 622–4.
69 Ibid., pp. 624–6.
70 Wu Xiuquan, *Huiyi yu Huainian*, p. 372; cf. Beschloss, *The Crisis Years*, pp. 622–4.
71 The Sino-Soviet Treaty signed in 1950 was not formally abrogated but was allowed to lapse in 1980 at the end of its 30-year term.
72 Zhou Enlai appears to have been as persuasive as ever on this occasion, for the normally deeply suspicious Enver Hoxha described his talks with the premier as going very well, and the visit overall as a 'great victory' for Albania; Hoxha, *Reflections on China* 1, p. 61.
73 Griffith, *The Sino-Soviet Rift*, pp. 177–89.
74 Ibid., pp. 189–206; Gittings, *Survey of the Sino-Soviet Dispute*, pp. 193–227.
75 The countries were: United Arab Republic (Egypt), Algeria, Morocco, Tunisia, Ghana, Mali, Guinea, Sudan, Ethiopia, Somalia. This paragraph benefits from Adie, 'Chou En-lai on Safari', *CQ*, No. 18, 1964, pp. 174–94.
76 Ibid., p. 175, explains that Zhou was referring to national liberation struggles rather than social revolutions. See also Snow, *The Star Raft*, pp. 75–6; Larkin, *China and Africa, 1949–1970*, p. 70.
77 Qi Li (ed.), *'Zuopai' Lilunjia Fuchen Lu* (A record of the ups and downs of the 'leftist' theoreticians), pp. 210–11. Deputy Foreign Minister Qiao Guanhua and Zhao Yimei, a deputy director of the CC's International Liaison

Department, were nominal members of the group, which also had a seven-person support team. This *fanxiu banzi* (anti-revisionism team) of *xiucai* (scholars), as they were known, should not be confused with the *xuanji banzi* (selected works team) set up earlier to edit the selected works of Mao, Liu Shaoqi, and anyone else the leadership designated for immortalization. This team, led by Kang Sheng, was conveniently located in the same building as the CC secretariat. There was some overlap in the membership of the two teams of *xiucai*. (Communication from Michael Schoenhals.)

78 Except where indicated, most of the material on the writing of the nine polemics came from a participant in the work, Informant I.

79 It subsequently became a secret refuge for foreign revolutionary exiles; Informant I.

80 Many similar complexes existed in other cities all over China; Informant I.

81 Wu Xiuquan, *Huiyi yu Huainian*, p. 374.

82 Ibid., p. 375.

83 Ibid. During the early 1960s, Mao kept a close eye not merely on the writing of the polemics but on all aspects of Sino-Soviet relations and their repercussions; see *Jianguo Yilai Mao Zedong Wengao* 10, pp. 245–54, 262–4, 276–83, 316, 320–4, 330–1, 369–76, 378–9, 394, 414–15, 434–5, 465–6; 11, pp. 12–13, 14–15, 30–2, 36–7, 40–1, 66–7, 68–71, 102, 105–9, 164, 179–81, 204–5, 216–19, 320–1, 339–40, 344–50, 385, 394–5.

84 The first five polemics are excerpted and briefly discussed in Griffith, *The Sino-Soviet Rift*.

85 A striking earlier instance of this phenomenon occurred prior to World War I, when the German Socialist Party voted for increased military spending and later for war credits instead of maintaining its stand against militarism and its solidarity with the socialists of France; Craig, *Germany, 1866–1945*, pp. 296–7.

86 *Origins* I, pp. 39–56. The CCP's first polemic on 'The origin and development of the differences between the leadership of the CPSU and ourselves' confirmed that 'the differences began with the 20th congress of the CPSU'; *The Polemic*, pp. 59–67.

87 For a discussion of Maoists in France, see Fejto, 'A Maoist in France: Jacques Vergès and *Révolution*', *CQ*, No. 19, 1964, pp. 120–7, and a comment on that article by the African-American editor of *Révolution*, Richard Gibson, in ibid., No. 21, 1965, pp. 179–82.

88 According to Informant B, Chen Boda wrote the 9th polemic, but Ye Yonglie, *Chen Boda Qiren*, p. 209, states that Kang Sheng prevented Chen from playing a major role in drafting any of the nine polemics. According to Informant T, the writers were Wu Lengxi and Wang Li.

89 *The Polemic*, pp. 430 ff.

90 Ibid., p. 436.

91 Ibid., pp. 436–9.

92 Ibid., pp. 440–1.

93 Djilas, *The New Class*, *passim*, but esp. pp. 37–69. This book was certainly known in China and could have been read by Mao and other leaders, for it was translated in full in the big-character *Cankao Ziliao* in Aug. 1957 at the suggestion of a cadre who was later designated a rightist, in part for this proposal; Informant I. In Feb. 1963, it was published as a *neibu* (internal) book; information supplied by Michael Schoenhals.

94 *The Polemic*, p. 443.

95 Ibid., pp. 464, 466.
96 Ibid., pp. 471–6.
97 For the development of Mao's thinking on this subject in 1964, see Bo Yibo, *Ruogan Zhongda Juece* 2, pp. 1158–62. Mao had alluded to the importance of revolutionary successors in a speech to a central work conference on 16 June 1964; *Jianguo Yilai Mao Zedong Wengao* 11, p. 87.
98 *The Polemic*, pp. 477–8. For earlier examples of Mao's concern about successors and 'newborn forces' at the grass roots, see *Jianguo Yilai Mao Zedong Wengao* 11, pp. 74–5, 94–5. By the spring of 1965, the CC General Office was publicizing approvingly the news that peasants in 97 Shanxi *xian* had been taught about the five conditions for revolutionary successors; ibid., p. 383.
99 *The Polemic*, p. 479.
100 Despite those attacks, Mao, Liu, and Zhou had signed a conciliatory telegram to Khrushchev on the occasion of his 70th birthday on 17 Apr. 1964; quoted in Medvedev, *Khrushchev*, p. 229.
101 The Russians did the Chinese the courtesy of informing them in advance of the announcement through their ambassador in Beijing; Wu Xiuquan, *Huiyi yu Huainian*, pp. 375–6. The embassy advised exploring the possibility that the Russians might change their policies; Zhang Dequn, 'Zai Mosike liu nian ban', *Zhonggong Dangshi Ziliao*, No. 58, June 1996, p. 40.
102 Hoxha, *Reflections on China* 1, p. 125. The Chinese also moderated their propaganda towards India after the death of Nehru in June 1964 until they had decided that his successor Lal Bahadur Shastri was no different; Sen Gupta, *The Fulcrum of Asia*, pp. 191–3.
103 Hoxha was furious, and wrote in his diary that it would be necessary to expose and fight the revisionist views and actions of the Chinese; Hoxha, *Reflections on China* 1, pp. 125–35.
104 Liu Shaoqi, Deng Xiaoping, and Peng Zhen turned up at the Soviet embassy celebrations of the anniversary, however; Wu Xiuquan, *Huiyi yu Huainian*, pp. 376–8.
105 Khrushchev's successors had criticized him, however, for lacking in circumspection in his off-the-cuff remarks to foreigners about the Chinese, as on the occasion when he referred to Mao as an 'old galosh'; Medvedev, *Khrushchev*, p. 241.
106 Wu Xiuquan, *Huiyi yu Huainian*, pp. 378–81; Griffith, *Sino-Soviet Relations, 1964–1965*, pp. 61–4. In his discussion of the Malinovsky episode, Arbatov (who was not present but was informed of it by Andropov) states that Malinovsky made the remark to Zhou Enlai; *The System*, p. 109. According to another Chinese source, he made it to both men; *Zhonggong Dangshi Zhongda Shijian Shushi*, pp. 207–9.
107 Hoxha, *Reflections on China* 1, p. 177.
108 *The Polemic*, p. 491; Hoxha, *Reflections on China* 1, pp. 181–2.
109 Wu Xiuquan, *Huiyi yu Huainian*, p. 376.
110 Lewis & Xue, *China Builds the Bomb*, pp. 35–72.
111 Nie, *Inside the Red Star*, pp. 701–4.
112 Griffith, *Sino-Soviet Relations, 1964–1965*, pp. 79–88.
113 Erasmus, 'General de Gaulle's Recognition of Peking', *CQ*, No. 18, 1964, pp. 195–200; Lacouture, *De Gaulle: The Ruler, 1945–1970*, pp. 392–3. According to the latter source, for the French leader 'the possession of nuclear weapons was always more than a symbolic gesture: it was the essential attribute of

national independence'; ibid., p. 413. Two months before he died in 1970, de Gaulle, no longer president, was talking about a trip to China which, he said, would be a 'dream fulfilled'; on his death, the Chinese flew the flag over the Forbidden City at half-mast, a mark of the importance they had placed upon French recognition (ibid., pp. 586–7).

114 Agung, *Twenty Years of Indonesian Foreign Policy, 1945–1965*, pp. 431–40; Leifer, *Indonesia's Foreign Policy*, pp. 69–71, 99–105. For Mao's soothing reply to Sukarno's expression of concern about the Sino-Soviet split, see *Jianguo Yilai Mao Zedong Wengao* 10, pp. 421–3.

115 Griffith, *Sino-Soviet Relations, 1964–1965*, pp. 76–9.

116 The first major *secret* decisions were President Kennedy's authorization on 11 May 1961 of the despatch of 400 special forces troops and 100 other military advisers to South Vietnam, and his simultaneous order to the CIA to train South Vietnamese agents for covert action in North Vietnam; *Pentagon Papers*, pp. 79, 82, 90–1.

117 Ibid., pp. 93–111; Gelb & Betts, *The Irony of Vietnam*, pp. 69–80.

118 Ibid., p. 80.

119 'Dangdai Zhongguo' Congshu Bianjibu (ed.), *Dangdai Zhongguo Wai Jiao* (Contemporary China's foreign relations; hereafter, *Dangdai Zhongguo Wai Jiao*), p. 159.

120 *Pentagon Papers*, p. 113.

121 *Dangdai Zhongguo Wai Jiao*, p. 159. The previous year, a Chinese friendship delegation had visited Hanoi, led by Marshal Ye Jianying. The latter enjoyed a special relationship with Ho Chi Minh, having worked closely with him in 1940, training anti-Japanese guerrillas in South China; Fall, *The Two Viet-Nams*, pp. 98, 103.

122 Among the positions which the North Vietnamese shared with the Chinese were antagonism to the partial test-ban treaty and condemnation of Yugoslavia; Griffith, *The Sino-Soviet Rift*, pp. 192–3; id., *Sino-Soviet Relations, 1964–1965*, pp. 66–7. The North Vietnamese Politburo also passed an anti-revisionism resolution in 1963 with only two dissentients: Ho Chi Minh, who abstained, and General Vo Nguyen Giap, who opposed. I am grateful to Hue-Tam Ho Tai for drawing my attention to this. According to one specialist on Vietnam writing in the early 1960s, among the communist leadership, Truong Chinh and Nguyen Duy Trinh favoured China while Le Duan and Vo Nguyen Giap favoured the Soviet Union, with Ho Chi Minh trying to preserve a neutral position in the middle; see Honey, *North Vietnam Today*, pp. 55–8.

123 *Pentagon Papers*, p. 107.

124 Sorensen, *Kennedy*, p. 653. These factors have enabled historians to argue about whether the United States would have sunk into the quagmire had Kennedy lived.

125 Johnson did not pay much attention to Vietnam during his first year in office, other than in the case of the Tonkin Gulf incident; Gelb & Betts, *The Irony of Vietnam*, p. 97.

126 Khong, *Analogies at War*, pp. 97–147, 174–205.

127 *Pentagon Papers*, pp. 254–5.

128 Gelb & Betts, *The Irony of Vietnam*, pp. 100–4. For the then-Secretary of Defence's version of the Tonkin Gulf incidents, see McNamara, *In Retrospect*, ch. 5. After publishing his book, Mr McNamara visited Vietnam and met Gen. Vo Nguyen Giap on 9 Nov. 1995. In response to Mr McNamara's

questioning, the former North Vietnamese Defence Minister asserted that local coastguard ships had attacked an American destroyer on 2 Aug., but that there had been no attack on 4 Aug.; Mr McNamara was quoted as commenting later that he felt '99 and 99–100ths percent sure [the 4 Aug. attack] didn't occur'. See Tim Larimer, 'In Hanoi, ex-foes revisit Vietnam War's turning point', *NYT*, 10 Nov. 1995.

[129] *Pentagon Papers*, pp. 259–70.

[130] Gelb & Betts, *The Irony of Vietnam*, pp. 117–20, 372.

[131] Ibid., pp. 129, 372–3; McNamara, *In Retrospect*, ch. 7.

[132] Guofang Daxue, *Qishi Nian Jianjie*, p. 514. Mao had a tendency to anticipate danger. In Sept. 1960, only a few weeks after the withdrawal of Soviet specialists, he was already speculating on the danger of a Soviet nuclear attack! Wang Dongxing, 'Mao Zhuxi guanhuai women chengzhang' (Chairman Mao paid attention to our maturing), *Yan Huang Chun Qiu*, No. 7, 1993, p. 5.

[133] Yan Fangming, 'San xian jianshe shuping' (A commentary on the construction of the third front), *DSYJ*, No. 4, 1987, p. 71.

[134] The ensuing brief description draws heavily on Yan Fangming, 'San xian jianshe shuping'; and Naughton, 'Industrial Policy During the Cultural Revolution: Military Preparation, Decentralization, and Leaps Forward', in Joseph, Wong, & Zweig (eds.), *New Perspectives on the Cultural Revolution*, pp. 153–81.

[135] Naughton, 'Industrial Policy During the Cultural Revolution', pp. 157–8; there is a map of the third front areas on p. 159. Yan Fangming, 'San xian jianshe shuping', p. 70.

[136] Naughton, 'Industrial Policy During the Cultural Revolution', pp. 157–8.

[137] Yan Fangming, 'San xian jianshe shuping', p. 72.

[138] Lieberthal & Oksenberg, *Policy Making in China*, pp. 186–91. Despite being sidelined, Li Fuchun and Bo Yibo seem to have insisted on their formal responsibility for the third front; see below, n. 146.

[139] Cf. *Origins* I, pp. 63–6 and Yan Fangming, 'San xian jianshe shuping', p. 72.

[140] Cheng Hua, *Zhou Enlai he Tade Mishumen*, p. 12.

[141] Naughton, 'Industrial Policy During the Cultural Revolution', p. 161. For a brief account by a Yunnanese who spent several years in one of the labour battalions set up to help construct the third front, see He, *Mr China's Son*, pp. 135–7.

[142] Naughton argues (p. 163) that by placing initial third front investment in the southwest, China's ability to aid North Vietnam was enhanced, but this rationale would have required the PRC to construct air bases and military staging posts, as indeed it did, not to build key factories vulnerably near the front line. Naughton also suggests that the construction of the third front increased the credibility of Chinese threats to intervene and thus would help to deter the United States; ibid. If so, the device was singularly ineffective; in his analysis of deterrence signalling between Beijing and Washington, Allen Whiting, who was in the State Department working on this subject at the time, gives no indication that American analysts had any idea about the third front, let alone took it into their calculations; see *The Chinese Calculus of Deterrence*, ch. 6.

[143] As in the case of Chiang Kai-shek in 1962, the Americans restrained their eager ally; Gelb & Betts, *The Irony of Vietnam*, p. 99.

[144] Even after the initial commitment of marines in South Vietnam, the Chinese still believed that the Americans would try to avoid using ground

forces in China; see Zhou Enlai's point 4 quoted in Whiting, *The Chinese Calculus of Deterrence*, p. 194.

145 *Dangdai Zhongguo Wai Jiao*, p. 159.

146 For a Chinese view of the problems caused by the third front, see Yan Fangming, 'San xian jianshe shuping', pp. 69, 73. For a brief account of a visit to the third front in the spring of 1965 by two leading economic officials, Li Fuchun and Bo Yibo, see Li Guang'an, Wang Guizhen, & Qin Ming, *Jinian Li Fuchun*, pp. 13–14. For Mao's continuing interest in the third front, see *Jianguo Yilai Mao Zedong Wengao* 11, pp. 182–4, 196–7, 329–30. For the continuing problems caused by the third front in the 1990s, see *NYT*, 11 Dec. 1994, p. 3.

147 *Dangdai Zhongguo Wai Jiao*, p. 160. For a description of the demonstrations by a visiting journalist and resident foreigners, see Karol, *China: The Other Communism*, pp. 200–1, and Milton & Milton, *The Wind will not Subside*, pp. 82–4.

148 Milton & Milton, *The Wind will not Subside*, pp. 4–5.

149 *Dangdai Zhongguo Wai Jiao*, p. 160. This was not clear at the time, for Chinese propaganda dismissed the prospect of 'some tens of thousands of U.S. ground forces' as being unable to 'frighten the Vietnamese people'; quoted in Whiting, *The Chinese Calculus of Deterrence*, p. 183.

150 See André Malraux's interviews with Zhou and Chen in his *Anti-Memoirs*, pp. 383–9, 396–400, and K. S. Karol's interviews with the same men in his *China: The Other Communism*, pp. 448–50, 454–6.

151 In his interview with Edgar Snow on 9 Jan. 1965, which Mao must have known would appear in some form in the American press (a condensed version was published by the *New Republic*, 27 Feb. 1965). See also Snow, *The Long Revolution*, pp. 194, 216, 218.

152 Liao Gailong, Ding Xiaochun, & Li Zhongzhi (eds.) *Zhongguo Gongchan Dang Fazhan Shidian* (A dictionary of the development of the CCP), p. 797. See also *Jianguo Yilai Mao Zedong Wengao* 11, pp. 359–60, 381–2. According to an authoritative Egyptian source, Zhou Enlai told President Nasser in Cairo in June 1965 that Beijing welcomed greater US involvement in Vietnam because it lessened the danger of a nuclear attack upon China; Zhou's rationale appears to have been that the US government would not want to put its own troops in danger of nuclear fall-out; Chanda, *Brother Enemy*, p. 128.

153 Li Jian (ed.), *Xin Zhongguo Liu Ci Fan Qinlue Zhanzheng Shilu* (A record of the six wars by new China against aggression), p. 202; the article on China's role in the Vietnam War in this book by Wang Xian'gen is a shortened version of his earlier book quoted below n. 154. When leaving Changsha, Ho Chi Minh suggested to Mao that they exchange walking sticks, but the Chairman declined saying Ho's was 'too fancy'; Gao Jingzhen, *Pingfan yu Weida*, p. 131.

154 Li Jian, *Xin Zhongguo Liu Ci Fan Qinlue Zhanzheng Shilu*, p. 202; the request for volunteer pilots and (presumably fighting) troops is contained only in Shi Yingfu, *Mimi Chubing Yare Conglin: Yuan Yue Kang Mei Jishi* (Secret jungle warfare: Facts about Aid Vietnam and Resist US), p. 15. All other sources talk only of the request for support troops. Since this book has an approving foreword by Gen. Yang Dezhi one must assume that it is accurate in this important quotation from Le Duan.

Liu Shaoqi presumably headed the Chinese team as the most senior party official under Chairman Mao, in deference to Le Duan's status as senior party leader under Chairman Ho Chi Minh. When Le Duan revisited China in the summer of 1966, Liu was heavily embroiled in the Cultural Revolution and Zhou Enlai received the Vietnamese visitor instead; Wang Xian'gen, *Yuan Yue Kang Mei Shilu* (A record of supporting Vietnam and resisting America), p. 130.

155 For uneasiness in Moscow–Hanoi relations during the 1950s which lent weight to these words, see Thayer, *War by Other Means*, pp. 35–7, 60–3, 159–63.

156 Griffith, *Sino-Soviet Relations, 1964–1965*, pp. 72–4.

157 Ross, *The Indochina Tangle*, pp. 21–3.

158 Shi Yingfu, *Mimi Chubing Yare Conglin*, pp. 3–16.

159 Wang Xian'gen, *Yuan Yue Kang Mei Shilu*, p. 99.

160 Ibid., p. 44. Presumably the formal support of the NPC was sought since the policy contained the seeds of involvement in a major war upon Chinese soil. For documentation on the formal activities of the NPC, see Zhongguo Renda Changweihui Bangongting Yanjiushi (ed.), *Zhonghua Renmin Gongheguo Renmin Daibiao Dahui Wenxian Ziliao Huibian (1949–1990)* (Collection of documentary materials of the PRC's NPC).

161 Wang Xian'gen, *Yuan Yue Kang Mei Shilu*, p. 45; Li Jian, *Xin Zhongguo Liu Ci Fan Qinlue Zhanzheng Shilu*, pp. 202–3.

162 Ibid., pp. 203–5.

163 Li Cheng, Xiao Ji, & Wang Libing, *Jianguo Yilai Jun Shi Bai Zhuang Dashi*, p. 221.

164 Prior to his appointment as a deputy chief-of-staff in April 1963, Li Tianyou had spent over twelve years serving in the Canton Military Region on the Vietnam border, ending up as its commander.

165 Li Jian, *Xin Zhongguo Liu Ci Fan Qinlue Zhanzheng Shilu*, p. 205.

166 At this time, Ho Chi Minh was in Changsha recuperating from heart problems. During a stay of over a month, he was visited by Mao; Xiao Xinli, *Xunshi Dajiang Nanbeide Mao Zedong* (Mao Zedong on inspection tours across the country), pp. 447–50.

167 *Dangdai Zhongguo Wai Jiao*, p. 161; *Jiefang Jun Liushi Nian Dashiji*, pp. 616, 617; Shi Yingfu, *Mimi Chubing Yare Conglin*, pp. 16, 216 (this source also assigns figures to the accomplishments of the various Chinese units; pp. 39, 216); Xie Yixian, *Zhechong yu Gongchu* (Resistance and coexistence), p. 147; Li Jian, *Xin Zhongguo Liu Ci Fan Qinlue Zhanzheng Shilu*, p. 212; Whiting, *The Chinese Calculus of Deterrence*, pp. 186–9; Chanda, *Brother Enemy*, p. 129; *PR*, No. 48, 30 Nov. 1979, p. 14.

According to another source, the withdrawal date was July 1970; Liao Gailong, Ding Xiaochun, & Li Zhongzhi, *Zhongguo Gongchan Dang Fazhan Shidian*, p. 799. According to Informant P, the figures for personnel only include men in uniform and not ordinary Chinese labourers drafted for road-building, etc. If these were to be included, the maximum number of Chinese in Vietnam at any one time was closer to 300,000.

168 *Jiefang Jun Liushi Nian Dashiji*, pp. 616–17; Kong Jun Silingbu Bianyanshi (ed.), *Kong Jun Shi* (A history of the air force), p. 207; *Dangdai Zhongguo Kong Jun*, pp. 396–410; Huang Yuchong, *Yi Dai Tian Jiao–Xin Zhongguo Kong Jun Shi Zhan Lu* (A generation of talented airmen—A record of new China's air force in combat), p. 248. According to another source, the overall figures were: 165 aircraft, 117 warships, 810 tanks and AFV, 15,000 motor vehicles, 30,000 artillery pieces, 1,777,000 rifles and machine guns,

and 1,040 m. rounds of ammunition, and the total cost of the Chinese war effort was 40 billion yuan; Sha Li & Min Li, *Zhongguo 9 Ci Da Fa Bing*, p. 270. For the activities of the PLA Navy, see 'Dangdai Zhongguo' Cong-shu Bianjibu (ed.), *Dangdai Zhongguo Hai Jun* (Contemporary China's navy), pp. 412–31. Again according to Informant P, the official casualty fig-ures are grossly understated, as the deaths only include those who were shipped back to China for treatment and died subsequently. Chinese who were killed and buried in Vietnam were counted as Vietnamese deaths. (The same procedure was apparently followed by the PLA in the Korean War.)

169 Whiting, *The Chinese Calculus of Deterrence*, p. 174
170 Premier Zhou conveyed the policy to President Ayub Khan on 2 April; since he could have done so during the Pakistani leader's visit to Beijing from 2–9 March, had the policy then been agreed, presumably it was not then finalized. Since Zhou paid an official visit to Romania from 23 to 27 March, it was probably formulated before the 23rd, on the assumption that Zhou would have played a major role in drawing it up. An alternative possibility is that the policy had already been adopted by the time of Ayub's March visit, but that the Chinese had not agreed upon how to convey it to the Americans.
171 Zhou had made this point during a visit to Pakistan in 1964; Sen Gupta, *Fulcrum of Asia*, p. 184.
172 Zhou Enlai stopped over in Karachi on 2–3 April 1965 on his way home after brief visits to Romania, Albania, Algeria, and the United Arab Republic; Huai En, *Zhou Zongli Shengping Dashiji*, pp. 450–1; *NYT*, 3 Apr. 1965. Zhou and Ayub met again in Cairo on 28 June Huai En, *Zhou Zongli Shengping Dashiji*, p. 451.
173 *Dangdai Zhongguo Wai Jiao*, pp. 160–1; Xie Yixian, *Zhechong yu Gongchu*, pp. 146–7. These four points were not publicly released through a Pakistani journalist until a year later (Whiting, *The Chinese Calculus of Deterrence*, pp. 193–4) at a point when the Chinese may have been already reasonably satisfied that, at a minimum, the Americans would not attack China.
174 *NYT*, 17 Apr. 1965. A visit by India's Prime Minister Lal Bahadur Shastri, scheduled to take place after Ayub's, was also cancelled in an effort to main-tain even-handedness between the rival South Asian nations. Ayub learned of the postponement while on a visit to the Soviet Union; Gauhar, *Ayub Khan*, p. 302.
175 McMahon, *The Cold War on the Periphery*, pp. 318–24; Barnds, *India, Pakistan, and the Great Powers*, pp. 196–7. For a revealing glimpse of President Johnson's private feelings about the Ayub and Shastri visits and the repercussions of the postponements, see Goodwin, *Remembering America*, pp. 394–6. Ayub eventually met Johnson in Washington in Dec. 1965, but for him the visit to China was well worth the postponement for it greatly strengthened the position of his party in parliamentary elections later in March; see Gauhar, *Ayub Khan*, pp. 289–91. This source does not mention the Zhou–Ayub meeting in Karachi.
176 The then-US ambassador to Pakistan, Walter P. McConaughy, says no such message was passed through him; telephone interview, Aug. 1993. Very senior State Department and CIA officials and National Security Council staff members, to whom I am most indebted for their ready replies to ques-tions by letter or on the telephone, have no recollection of receiving any

such message from Zhou Enlai, via Pakistan or any other source, nor of any reply to such a message. Nevertheless, some kind of communication reached some people in Washington through some intermediary; cf. 'CIA Secret Report on Sino-Vietnamese Reaction to American Tactics in the Vietnam War', *Journal of Contemporary Asia* (Stockholm) 13, No. 2, 1983, p. 269. This document, a very comprehensive analysis of the developing Chinese position, is dated 9 June 1965, and was possibly the CIA's assessment of Chinese intentions in the light of Zhou's message, however delivered. In it, the following references to third-party intermediaries occur: (a) 'Cutting directly across the bold talk of preparation to take "real action" was the not so bold move to disarm a pre-emptive American air strike on bases in south China by privately indicating (to Washington through a third party) that PLA ground forces were not massed on the southern border. (Deleted as secret, 5(B)(2)).' (b) 'The sufficient reason for PLA intervention was asserted privately in the same month by Chou En-lai: an American ground force attack on the North (deleted as secret, 5(B)(2)). (c) Chou also told (deleted as secret, 5(B)(2)) in mid-April that Peiping would send no troops to North Vietnam as long as South Vietnamese or American troops did not invade above the 17th parallel.' In Aug. 1996, the CIA document was released to the present author under the Freedom of Information Act. In this virtually unexpurgated text—though the author's name was erased—no indication was given as to the identity of the 'third party' in (a). However, it was revealed that the recipient of Zhou's confidence in (b) was President Ne Win of Burma, and in (c) Prince Sihanouk of Cambodia. Zhou and Foreign Minister Chen Yi saw Ne Win in Rangoon on 3–4 April after their stopover in Karachi. In mid-April (16–26), Zhou and Chen Yi were in Indonesia for the 10th anniversary of the Bandung Afro-Asian Conference; during that time there was plenty of opportunity for him to talk to Sihanouk, and indeed he called on him on the 17th. (Zhonghua Renmin Gongheguo Waijiaobu & Waijiaoshi Yanjiushi [eds.], *Zhou Enlai Waijiao Huodong Dashiji* [A chronology of Zhou Enlai's activities in foreign affairs], pp. 445–50.) It is also possible that the CIA managed to eavesdrop on Zhou's meeting in Karachi. According to Sidney Rittenberg, Chen Yi told Anna Louise Strong 'in confidence' the three conditions under which China would enter the Vietnam War, believing correctly that they would leak to the US government through her. The date of this manoeuvre is not given; see Rittenberg & Bennett, *The Man Who Stayed Behind*, p. 276. For President Johnson's concern about possible Chinese intervention, see Doris Kearns, *Lyndon Johnson & the American Dream*, pp. 264–5, 270–1.

177   Whiting, *The Chinese Calculus of Deterrence*, p. 179. According to Huang Yuchong, *Yi Dai Tian Jiao*, p. 248, the PLA shot down 25 and damaged 3 US aircraft over Chinese territory between Aug. 1964 and Aug. 1968.

178   Whiting, *The Chinese Calculus of Deterrence*, pp. 175–7.

179   Ibid., pp. 184–5.

180   There is no mention of them in any reports about the agreement or in the information available to American analysts; cf. ibid., pp. 186–7. According to Chen Jian, Chinese sources say that the Chinese and Vietnamese did discuss in detail the modalities for the involvement of Chinese pilots, but Vietnamese sources disagree; see his 'China's Involvement in the Vietnam War, 1964–69', *CQ*, No. 142, 1995, p. 369.

181   Griffith, *Sino-Soviet Relations, 1964–1965*, pp. 74–6.

[182] The desirability of destroying China's nuclear capability with a 'surgical strike' before its development made that too risky an option was apparently considered by Soviet leaders in 1969; Robinson, 'China Confronts the Soviet Union', *CHOC* 15, p. 273; MacFarquhar, 'The Succession to Mao and the End of Maoism', ibid., p. 320. For the dilemma facing a political leader who wishes to purge his party at a time of national danger, cf. Winston Churchill: after he took over as Prime Minister in May 1940, he would have liked to dispense with loyal followers of Neville Chamberlain, but was inhibited by knowing that parliamentary infighting could fatally damage the British government at a time of maximum danger in the war against Nazi Germany; see Roberts, *Eminent Churchillians*, p. 162 For another aspect of Churchill's dilemma, see below Ch. 19, n. 17.

[183] Snow, *The Long Revolution*, p. 17; see below, Ch. 19.

[184] The staff of the Johnson Library in Austin, Texas, failed to locate any such communication from the President to the Chinese in response to a query, though, as one staffer said, a negative result is never final in the case of such a vast archive. Again, senior US government officials, including William Bundy, then Assistant Secretary of State for East Asia, have no recollection of any such message being sent from President to Prime Minister. For an attempt by President Johnson in early 1967 to use a Thai intermediary to initiate high-level talks with the Chinese, see Phathanothai, *The Dragon's Pearl*, pp. 224–41.

[185] Young, *Negotiating with the Chinese Communists*, pp. 268–70.

[186] William Bundy was informed of this in 1993 by Pu Shouchang, one of Zhou Enlai's assistants in 1965; telephone interview with Bundy, 24 Aug. 1993. Firm American statements of policy, as the Taiwan Straits issue in 1962 also demonstrated, seem to have been readily accepted at face value in Beijing.

[187] This issue caused considerable controversy in the mid-1960s among Western analysts who argued over the interpretation of key Chinese articles on global affairs published in 1965–6. See, for instance, Ra'anan, 'Peking's Foreign Policy "Debate", 1965–1966', and Zagoria, 'The Strategic Debate in Peking', both in Tsou, *China in Crisis* 2, pp. 23–71, 237–68; the comment on those articles in Yahuda, 'Kremlinology and the Chinese Strategic Debate, 1965–66', *CQ*, No. 49, 1972, pp. 32–75; the rebuttals by Ra'anan and Zagoria, *CQ*, No. 50, 1972, pp. 343–50; Yahuda's rebuttal of these rebuttals, *CQ*, No. 51, 1972, pp. 547–53; and Harding & Gurtov, *The Purge of Lo Jui-ch'ing: The Politics of Chinese Strategic Planning*. To the best of my knowledge, among the many accusations levelled at the victims of the Cultural Revolution apparently involved in this 'debate', none had to do with Vietnam policy. Though many pre-Cultural Revolution disputes between Mao and his colleagues, including over foreign policy, were thoroughly aired after the Cultural Revolution, I am unaware of any discussion of dissension on this issue. This does not definitively prove there were no debates, on the lines suggested by Western analysts or on others. Some of the participants, notably Deng Xiaoping and Peng Zhen, were still living as of this writing, and this would certainly inhibit Chinese historians. Moreover, after the Sino-Vietnamese war of 1979, Deng in particular would be keen that the Chinese leadership be portrayed as always united on its policy towards the 'ungrateful' Vietnamese communists, and that there should be no suggestion that more could have been done for them in 1965 than was actually done. One major focus of the Western analyses does, however,

require re-examination: the argument that there were profound differences on strategic policy between Luo Ruiqing and Lin Biao, as exhibited particularly in their 1965 20th anniversary articles on the victories over Germany and Japan respectively. According to the most authoritative source on the Lin–Luo struggle and also an establishment biography of Luo Ruiqing, Luo presided over the drafting of Lin Biao's article and both articles were approved by the 'centre', almost certainly Mao in the case of major foreign-policy pronouncements; Huang Yao, *San Ci Danan Buside Luo Ruiqing Dajiang* (General Luo Ruiqing who survived three disasters), ch. 29; *Zhonggong Dangshi Renwuzhuan* 46, p. 60.

PART FOUR: THE END OF THE YAN'AN ROUND TABLE

CHAPTER 17

[1] Bullock, *Hitler and Stalin*, p. 149.

[2] *Origins* I, p. 222, MacFarquhar, Cheek, & Wu, *The Secret Speeches of Chairman Mao*, p. 144; see Ch. 12, p. 296.

[3] While Mao's obsession with the Petöfi syndrome is easily documented, there may have been a deeper cultural reason for his concern with the activities of the intellectuals. Oratory was not traditionally a valued skill; there is no Chinese Demosthenes or Cicero held up as a model for subsequent generations. Unlike the Bolsheviks, who boasted numerous powerful orators, from Lenin down—with the notable exception of Stalin, whose Georgian accent was a disability because it was habitually affected by Russian comedians—no CCP leader ever demonstrated an ability to mount a soap-box and stir citizens to storm a Winter Palace. In closed session, with politically sophisticated audiences, they could have a considerable impact, but more by the matter rather than the manner of their discourse, together with the perceived sincerity with which it was delivered; Mao's contradictions speech on 27 Feb. 1957, and Chen Yi's speech at the Canton conference on 6 Mar. 1962 spring to mind. But leaving aside chats on his tours, Mao, unlike Lenin, or Hitler for that matter, communicated with the 'broad masses' in writing, imperial style, rather than orally. If the hypothesis that CCP leaders did not normally attempt to move the masses with their own tongues is correct, then the compulsion for them to ensure that they controlled those 'engineers of the soul' who were adept at doing so, through media like Peking Opera, was even greater than in the Soviet Union.

[4] Cong Jin, *Quzhe Fazhande Suiyue*, p. 548; Bo Yibo, *Ruogan Zhongda Juece* 2, p. 1226.

[5] Cong Jin emphasizes that Mao did not condemn all old plays and suggests that Ke's actions were based on his (presumably biased) understanding of what the Chairman had said; Cong Jin, *Quzhe Fazhande Suiyue*, p. 548; Bo Yibo, *Ruogan Zhongda Juece* 2, p. 1229, dates Ke's speech as Feb. 1963. For an example of how Ke kept close to Mao during the GLF, see Li Rui, '*Da Yuejin' Qin Li Ji*, p. 326.

[6] Goldman, *China's Intellectuals*, p. 63; Ye Yonglie, *Zhang Chunqiao Fuchen Shi* (The ups and downs of Zhang Chunqiao), pp. 18–19.

[7] Quoted in ibid.

[8] *Zhongguo Dangdai Wenxue Shi Chugao, shang*, p. 107. It is not clear why Zhou chose 108 years, unless he was referring to the period between the Opium War (1839–42) and the CCP victory in 1949; nor have I located the source of the directive.

[9] Cong Jin, *Quzhe Fazhande Suiyue*, p. 549.

[10] Ibid.

11 One of the more important roles which Jiang Qing had played in Shanghai was Nora in *The Doll's House*. In Agnes Smedley's biography of Zhu De, written on the basis of interviews in 1937, the following passage appears: 'As in an aside, he remarked that respectable girls still could not appear on the Chinese stage and that the role of Nora in Ibsen's *The Doll's House* had to be played by young men students who paved the way for modern Chinese womanhood'; *The Great Road*, p. 120. Jiang Qing apparently did not meet and start living with Mao till 1938, but Yan'an was a very small world and she may already have been notorious enough there for Zhu to know of her past and thus to have let slip this otherwise gratuitous remark; Terrill, *The White-Boned Demon*, pp. 138–50.

12 Cong Jin, *Quzhe Fazhande Suiyue*, p. 556; Bo Yibo, *Ruogan Zhongda Juece* 2, p. 1228; Dai Zhixian, *Shan Yu Yu Lai Feng Man Lou*, p. 73; Lin Qingshan, *Jiang Qing Chen Fu Lu* (A record of the ups and downs of Jiang Qing), p. 253. As indicated Jiang Qing was not Mao's first liaison; his affair with an actress called Lily Wu precipitated his divorce from He Zizhen; MacKinnon & MacKinnon, *Agnes Smedley*, pp. 188–92.

13 Braun, *A Comintern Agent in China*, pp. 248–50; Chung & Miller, *Madame Mao*, pp. 45–54; Lin Qingshan, *Jiang Qing Chen Fu Lu*, pp. 238–63; Snow, *Red Star over China*, pp. 522–3; Terrill, *The White-Boned Demon*, pp. 129–61; Witke, *Comrade Chiang Ch'ing*, pp. 148–63; Ye Yonglie, *Lan Ping Wai Zhuan* (An unofficial biography of Lan Ping), p. 90; Zhu Zhongli, *Nüwang Meng*, pp. 30–9. Sources on so controversial a figure as Jiang Qing naturally vary considerably in accuracy; for an assessment of biographies prior to his own (1984), see Terrill, *The White-Boned Demon*, pp. 397–9.

14 Ibid., pp. 182–236; Witke, *Comrade Chiang Ch'ing*, pp. 223–32, 244–75; Zhu Zhongli, *Nüwang Meng*, pp. 104–242.

15 Witke, *Comrade Chiang Ch'ing*, pp. 255–6; this is the only source which says Jiang Qing held this post.

16 Ibid., pp. 233–4, 255; Terrill, *The White-Boned Demon*, p. 190; Zhu Zhongli, *Nüwang Meng*, p. 122.

17 Terrill, *The White-Boned Demon*, pp. 189–97; Witke, *Comrade Chiang Ch'ing*, pp. 232–44; Zhu Zhongli, *Nüwang Meng*, pp. 143–5; *Zhongguo Dangdai Wenxue Shi Chugao, shang*, pp. 41–6; Goldman, *Literary Dissent in Communist China*, pp. 89–93; Goldman, *China's Intellectuals*, pp. 75–6. During the Cultural Revolution, it was alleged that Liu Shaoqi had described *The Inside Story of the Qing Court* as patriotic, a charge which he vigorously rejected at the time in a letter to Mao, and which has been rejected by post-Cultural Revolution authors.

18 *Jianguo Yilai Mao Zedong Wengao* 9, pp. 479, 518, 603–4; 10, pp. 182, 188, 377; 11, pp. 40–1, 61, 81, 89, 130, 193, 204–5, 361–2, 381–4, 468–9, 474.

19 According to Mao's doctor, Jiang Qing was more respectful of Kang Sheng than of any other of Mao's colleagues; Li, *The Private Life of Chairman Mao*, p. 397.

20 Dai Zhixian, *Shan Yu Yu Lai Feng Man Lou*, pp. 80–2; Lin Qingshan, *Kang Sheng Waizhuan*, pp. 184–5.

21 Goldman, *China's Intellectuals*, pp. 43–4.

22 Mao did this on the recommendation of his doctor, Li Zhisui, who had vague but pleasant childhood memories of the original opera upon which Meng Chao's version was based. Mao took offence, however, at the story of

a Song dynasty premier and his concubine because it struck too close to home. Li, *The Private Life of Chairman Mao*, pp. 402–5.

23   Dai Zhixian, *Shan Yu Yu Lai Feng Man Lou*, p. 71; Lin Qingshan, *Kang Sheng Waizhuan*, pp. 186–7; Zhong Kan, *Kang Sheng Pingzhuan*, pp. 143–50; Byron & Pack, *The Claws of the Dragon*, pp. 260–7.

24   Lin Qingshan, *Kang Sheng Waizhuan*, pp. 188–92; Zhong Kan, *Kang Sheng Pingzhuan*, pp. 150–3; Byron & Pack, *The Claws of the Dragon*, pp. 268–9. During the Cultural Revolution, Meng Chao came under the scrutiny of an investigation team headed by Kang himself, and the playwright died in prison.

25   Cong Jin, *Quzhe Fazhande Suiyue*, p. 550.

26   *Zhongguo Dangdai Wenxue Shi Chugao, shang*, p. 107.

27   Goldman, *China's Intellectuals*, p. 43; Cong Jin, *Quzhe Fazhande Suiyue*, p. 550.

28   Ibid., pp. 550–1.

29   Bo Yibo, *Ruogan Zhongda Juece* 2, p. 1226.

30   *Mao Zedong sixiang wan sui!*, p. 26, translated in CB 891, p. 41.

31   Bo Yibo, *Ruogan Zhongda Juece* 2, p. 1226.

32   Ibid., pp. 1220–1.

33   Ibid.; translated in CB 891, p. 41. The official version of the original is now available in *Jianguo Yilai Mao Zedong Wengao* 10, pp. 436–7.

34   In June 1964, Mao stated that in terms of performance, PLA troupes did best, regional troupes were next, and Beijing or central troupes were worst; Mao, *Miscellany* 2, p. 355.

35   Cong Jin, *Quzhe Fazhande Suiyue*, pp. 552–3.

36   *Origins* I, pp. 180–2, 202–7.

37   Cong Jin, *Quzhe Fazhande Suiyue*, p. 553; there is no elaboration of what occurred on this occasion to shock the propaganda establishment.

38   According to ibid., the lead institution was the CC's Propaganda Department; according to Bo Yibo, *Ruogan Zhongda Juece* 2, p. 1221, it was the party group in the Ministry of Culture.

39   Ibid.

40   Cong Jin, *Quzhe Fazhande Suiyue*, p. 553.

41   Ibid.; Bo Yibo, *Ruogan Zhongda Juece* 2, pp. 1221–2.

42   Ibid., p. 1222; *Jianguo Yilai Mao Zedong Wengao* 11, pp. 91–3; *Mao Zedong sixiang wan sui!*, p. 26; translated in CB 891, p. 41. All the Chinese texts contain the mitigating word 'basically' which is not in the CB translation. The emphases, from Mao's original, are in the Bo version. As a reputedly conservative leader publishing his memoirs at a time when the CCP again viewed intellectuals with wary suspicion, Bo was in an awkward position. On the one hand, he agreed with Mao that not enough plays celebrating the revolution and socialism had been staged by that time, but on the other he had to reject Mao's comments as too severe, exaggerated, and restrictive because they were part of the leftism that led to the Cultural Revolution; *Ruogan Zhongda Juece* 2, pp. 1222–3. For his part, Cong Jin quoted approvingly a post-Cultural Revolution (1980) official dictum that both directives were not in accord with actual conditions and produced serious consequences; *Quzhe Fazhande Suiyue*, p. 554.

43   Ibid. Mao kept up his pressure on propaganda officials with comments on philosophy, music, and painting; *Jianguo Yilai Mao Zedong Wengao* 11, pp. 148, 172–3, 339–401.

44   Goldman, *China's Intellectuals*, p. 77.

45 Cong Jin, *Quzhe Fazhande Suiyue*, p. 555.
46 Ibid., p. 556. For Mao's comment, see *Jianguo Yilai Mao Zedong Wengao* 11, p. 113.
47 *Jiang Qing Tongzhi Lun Wenyi* (Comrade Jiang Qing on literature and art), pp. 32–42. Each commentary was given after a viewing of the opera, the last one being on 13 July. An English translation of the May 1970 version of the text is in Snow, *China on Stage*, pp. 256–303.
48 In *Jiang Qing Tongzhi Lun Wenyi*, the July speech is given pride of place (pp. 21–5) to the June one (pp. 26–9), and the July version was the one chosen for translation (Chiang Ching, *On the Revolution of Peking Opera*, pp. 1–7).
49 Cong Jin, *Quzhe Fazhande Suiyue*, pp. 558–9; Bo Yibo, *Ruogan Zhongda Juece* 2, pp. 1228–30.
50 'The Shanghai party and the Beijing party are both grasping [the issue of creating] plays; in Shanghai, old Ke is grasping it personally'; *Jiang Qing Tongzhi Lun Wenyi*, p. 28. For Jiang Qing's relationship with Ke, her exploitation of Shanghai's rivalry with Beijing, and her sarcastic reference to 'Beijing chauvinism', see Terrill, *The White-Boned Demon*, pp. 244–6; Ding Wang, *Beijing Shi Wenhua Da Geming Yundong*, pp. 312–21.
51 Informants H and Q; *Origins* I, p. 203.
52 Chiang, *On the Revolution of Peking Opera*, p. 2. For her figures, see above, Ch. 5. The precise reference to 30 m. people in the 23 June speech (*Jiang Qing Tongzhi Lun Wenyi*, p. 27) became a 'mere handful' of landlords *et al.* in the July one.
53 Chiang, *On the Revolution of Peking Opera*, p. 3. In the earlier speech, Jiang actually said 'I have the right to speak on this point' (*Zhe dian wo you fayan quan*); *Jiang Qing Tongzhi Lun Wenyi*, p. 27.
54 Chiang, *On the Revolution of Peking Opera*, pp. 3–6.
55 *Jianguo Yilai Mao Zedong Wengao* 11, pp. 89–90; Cong Jin, *Quzhe Fazhande Suiyue*, p. 557.
56 Bo Yibo, *Ruogan Zhongda Juece* 2, pp. 1227–8.
57 Cong Jin, *Quzhe Fazhande Suiyue*, pp. 557–8.
58 *Jiang Qing Tongzhi Lun Wenyi*, pp. 63–140.
59 Wu Lengxi, *Yi Mao Zhuxi*, p. 149.
60 Terrill, *The White-Boned Demon*, pp. 245–51.
61 Goldman, *China's Intellectuals*, p. 78; see also Fokkema, 'Creativity and Politics', in *CHOC* 15, pp. 607–11.
62 Birch, 'Literature under Communism', *CHOC* 15, p. 788.
63 See for instance, *Zhongguo Dangdai Wenxue Shi Chugao, shang*, pp. 108, 110, where the prime reason for the severity of the leftist assault was said to be the machinations of Lin Biao, Jiang Qing, Kang Sheng, and acolytes like Yao Wenyuan.
64 Cong Jin comments on how the leftist tide encouraged the emergence of all sorts of critics, whose activities could not be directly attributed to the machinations of Jiang Qing *et al* ; *Quzhe Fazhande Suiyue*, p. 575.
65 Dai Zhixian, *Shan Yu Yu Lai Feng Man Lou*, pp. 117–20; Cong Jin, *Quzhe Fazhande Suiyue*, p. 559.
66 *Zhongguo Dangdai Wenxue Shi Chugao, shang*, pp. 128–9; Goldman, *China's Intellectuals*, pp. 101–7. The first volume of one of the most famous historical sagas written since the founding of the PRC, Yao Xueyin's *Li Zicheng*, appeared in 1963, but the author then stopped publishing till towards the end of the Cultural Revolution when he got Mao's

permission to bring out his second volume; Yao Xueyin's *Li Zicheng* 1, Introduction, pp. 3–5.

67 Cong Jin, *Quzhe Fazhande Suiyue*, p. 561.

68 Mao Dun had long been a prominent Chinese representative on such 'progressive' international bodies as the World Peace Council and the Afro-Asian Solidarity Committee, and had been a delegate to bodies like the Inter-Parliamentary Union; URI, *Who's Who in Communist China* 2, pp. 563–5.

69 Witke, *Comrade Chiang Ch'ing*, pp. 103, 127, 136, 338; Terrill, *The White-Boned Demon*, pp. 103, 163.

70 Cong Jin, *Quzhe Fazhande Suiyue*, p. 561.

71 See for instance, his talk at the 1964 spring festival and his discussions with Mao Yuanxin and Wang Hairong, in *Mao Zedong sixiang wan sui* (*1969*), pp. 455–71, 526–31. For GLF educational policies, see *Origins* II, pp. 108–13.

72 Chen Xiuliang, *Sun Yefang Geming Shengya Liushi Nian* (The sixty-year revolutionary career of Sun Yefang), pp. 70–80 *Sun Yefang Xuanji* (Selected works of Sun Yefang), pp. 294–303, esp. p. 294 n.; Cong Jin, *Quzhe Fazhande Suiyue*, p. 573; Goldman, *China's Intellectuals*, pp. 59–60. For a discussion of Sun Yefang's contribution to the rethinking of industrial management in 1961–3, see Halpern, 'Economic Specialists and the Making of Chinese Economic Policy, 1955–1983', ch. 4. Sun Yefang is admired by his intellectual colleagues for apparently never having admitted error under pressure; Informant I. After the Cultural Revolution, he was lionized; see for instance, Zhongguo Shehui Kexue Yuan Jingji Yanjiusuo Xueshu Ziliaoshi (ed.), *Sun Yefang Jingji Lilun Pinglun* (A discussion of Sun Yefang's economic theories).

73 Cong Jin, *Quzhe Fazhande Suiyue*, p. 574; Goldman, *China's Intellectuals*, pp. 86–7.

74 Ibid., pp. 107–10; Yang Chungui, *Zhongguo Zhexue Sishi Nian, 1949–1989* (Forty years of Chinese philosophy, 1949–1989), pp. 181–4. In mid-Aug. 1964, Kang Sheng took the opportunity of a meeting with Mao to condemn the Institute of Philosophy and Social Science (of the Academy of Sciences) root and branch as an 'institute of antiquities'; Mao, *Miscellany* 2, p. 386.

75 The principal Western sources on Yang Xianzhen are the writings of Carol Lee Hamrin; see her Ph.D thesis 'Alternatives Within Chinese Marxism 1955–1965: Yang Hsien-chen's Theory of Dialectics'; 'Yang Xianzhen: Upholding Orthodox Leninist Theory', in Hamrin & Cheek, *China's Establishment Intellectuals*, pp. 51–91; and 'Yang Xianzhen's Philosophic "Criminal Case" ', *Chinese Law and Government*, Spring–Summer 1991. For a discussion of this episode, see also Byron & Pack, *The Claws of the Dragon*, pp. 275–82. For Chinese sources, see Cong Jin, *Quzhe Fazhande Suiyue*, pp. 561–73; Lin Qingshan, *Kang Sheng Waizhuan*, pp. 205–44; Li Zhenxia, *Dangdai Zhongguo Shi Zhe* (Ten contemporary Chinese philosophers), pp. 50–109; Yang Chungui, *Zhongguo Zhexue Sishi Nian*, pp. 159–71, on the philosophic rather than the political aspects of the affair; Zhong Kan, *Kang Sheng Pingzhuan*, pp. 162–73.

76 *Zhonggong Renming Lu*, app. p. 221. This source, along with Western sources, states that Yang was trained in the Soviet Union and Germany, but there is no confirmation of this in official Chinese sources; Hamrin & Cheek, *China's Establishment Intellectuals*, p. 54, n. 6.

77 For a discussion of Mao's debt to Ai Siqi, see Fogel, *Ai Ssu-ch'i's Contribution to the Development of Chinese Marxism*, ch. 5.
78 Hamrin, 'Yang Xianzhen: Upholding Orthodox Leninist Theory', pp. 59–61.
79 Ibid., pp. 67–9; *Origins* II, p. 236.
80 Hamrin, 'Yang Xianzhen: Upholding Orthodox Leninist Theory', pp. 62–7.
81 Ibid., pp. 67–76.
82 Schram, *The Thought of Mao Tse-tung*, pp. 167–8. For Mao's enthusiastic endorsement of the speech after delivery and his several modifications to the text prior to publication, see *Jianguo Yilai Mao Zedong Wengao* 10, pp. 400–10. For a confirmation of the view that justification of the split with the Soviet Union lay behind Mao's insistence on one dividing into two, see the testimony of a participant in the debate (on Mao's side): Wang Ruoshui, 'The Maid of Chinese Politics: Mao Zedong and his Philosophy of Struggle', *Journal of Contemporary China*, Fall 1995, pp. 73–7.
83 Lin Qingshan, *Kang Sheng Waizhuan*, pp. 205–6. This account has a particular poignancy, since the author was the same Lin Qingshan whose co-authored article had such unfortunate consequences for Yang Xianzhen, whom he greatly admired. See also Cong Jin, *Quzhe Fazhande Suiyue*, pp. 563–4.
84 Hamrin, 'Yang Xianzhen: Upholding Orthodox Leninist Theory', p. 77.
85 Hamrin, 'Yang Xianzhen's Philosophic "Criminal Case" ', p. 111.
86 Ibid., pp. 115–16.
87 Hamrin, however, regards Yang's later defence as 'a bit disingenuous'; Hamrin, 'Yang Xianzhen: Upholding Orthodox Leninist Theory', p. 78.
88 Cong Jin, *Quzhe Fazhande Suiyue*, pp. 564–8; Lin Qingshan, *Kang Sheng Waizhuan*, pp. 207–11; Zhong Kan, *Kang Sheng Pingzhuan*, pp. 162–70, refers to Guan Feng and an 'Anti-revisionist philosophy small group'; according to Michael Schoenhals, no such group actually existed, and Zhong Kan may simply have been loosely referring to the *fanxiu banzi* of which Guan Feng was apparently a member.
89 Cong Jin, *Quzhe Fazhande Suiyue*, p. 565.
90 Schram, *Mao Tse-tung Unrehearsed*, p. 224.
91 See for instance, *Pipan ziliao: Zhongguo Heluxiaofu Liu Shaoqi fan-geming xiuzhengzhuyi yanlunji* (Criticism materials: Collection of the counter-revolutionary revisionist utterances of China's Khrushchev Liu Shaoqi).
92 *Jianguo Yilai Mao Zedong Wengao* 11, pp. 463–4; Cong Jin, *Quzhe Fazhande Suiyue*, pp. 568–70.
93 Byron & Pack, *The Claws of the Dragon*, pp. 280–1. Since the end of the Cultural Revolution, Lin Qingshan has written a number of biographies of leading Cultural Revolution leftists.
94 Goldman, *China's Intellectuals*, p. 102.
95 Witke, *Comrade Chiang Ch'ing*, pp. 103–6, 120–1, 127, 130, 131, 136; Terrill, *The White-Boned Demon*, pp. 52–5, 69, 102–3, 248–51, 263. According to Goldman, Xia Yan, the most important official in the PRC film world and one of the 1930s Shanghai leftists against whom Jiang Qing bore a grudge, was responsible for *Early Spring in February*; see *China's Intellectuals*, pp. 45–6, which includes a description of the plot.
96 Dai Zhixian, *Shan Yu Yu Lai Feng Man Lou*, pp. 95–101; Cong Jin, *Quzhe Fazhande Suiyue*, pp. 568–70. For Mao's comments, see *Jianguo Yilai Mao Zedong Wengao* 11, p. 135.

⁹⁷ Despite his high rank, Tian was not given a seat of honour; Dai Zhixian, *Shan Yu Yu Lai Feng Man Lou*, pp. 87–90.

⁹⁸ Lin Qingshan, *Kang Sheng Waizhuan*, p. 190.

⁹⁹ Goldman, *China's Intellectuals*, p. 82.

¹⁰⁰ For a subtle and exhaustive analysis of Tian Han's *Xie Yaohuan*, see Wagner, *The Contemporary Chinese Historical Drama*, ch. 2; for the suggestion that Tian's link to Zhou protected him for some time, see ibid., pp. 136–7. According to Mao's doctor, Tian Han was also wrongly blamed by Jiang Qing for having written an article praising *Li Huiriang* which led Mao to have it staged in the Zhongnanhai. In fact, Tian Han's article was blamed at the suggestion of Wang Dongxing, with Mao's agreement, in order to prevent Dr Li, the real instigator of the command performance, from becoming the object of Jiang's wrath! Li, *The Private Life of Chairman Mao*, pp. 403–5. According to Jiang Qing's own account, she had earlier asked Tian Han to adapt the play *Red Detachment of Women* as a Peking Opera; he had agreed, but turned in something worse than the original; Witke, *Comrade Chiang Ch'ing*, p. 311.

¹⁰¹ Leaving aside his personal vendettas within the intellectual community, Zhou Yang seems to have been generally in favour of moderate cultural policies until Mao disavowed them, at which point he became a hammer of the right. In contrast to Lu Dingyi, for instance, Zhou had supported Mao's 1957 rectification ideas (*Origins* I, pp. 51–3, 219, 227) but then swung into action during the Anti-Rightist Campaign. Again in contrast to Lu, Zhou Yang supported the policies of Zhou Enlai and Chen Yi in 1961–2, until Mao's antagonism to them was revealed. By early 1965, his position was so leftist that a foreign journalist who interviewed him then was astounded a year later when Zhou was among the first to be purged in the Cultural Revolution; Karol, *China: The Other Communism*, pp. 275–86. One of Zhou's problems was his connection to every major writer criticized since 1949; Wu Zaiping, *Zhurende Qinghuai: Mao Zedong yu Zhongguo Zuojia* (The emotions of a colossus: Mao Zedong and China's writers), p. 64.

CHAPTER 18

¹ Terrill, *The White-Boned Demon*, p. 239. As indicated earlier, during the Cultural Revolution, Wang Guangmei was 'tried' by a Red Guard kangaroo court which demanded she put on the 'decadent' clothes she had worn on Liu's official visit to Indonesia in 1963. It seems likely that Jiang Qing's jealousy of Wang's high-profile role during that trip helped to fuel the Red Guard actions.

² For instance, on 1 Sept. 1963, the cover of *Zhongguo Qingnian*, No. 17, 1963, showed the two, along with Zhou Enlai, in a group shot with the actors in a play on Lei Feng.

³ Cong Jin indicates that the decision was Liu's rather than a suggestion of his wife's to which he agreed; *Quzhe Fazhande Suiyue*, p. 534.

⁴ During the 1992 American presidential campaign, the Clinton camp abandoned the line that his election would buy 'two for the price of one', which had been designed to exploit the undoubted abilities of his lawyer wife, when polling indicated a negative popular reaction because she was not up for election. President Clinton's subsequent assignment of his wife to take charge of his major domestic policy initiative—health care—was at least as

risky a strategy as Mao's and Liu's, with equally momentous, if less lethal, political consequences. The elaborate 1,300-page plan produced under Hillary Rodham Clinton's leadership never made it through the Congress, and a poll taken after the sweeping Republican victory in the 1994 mid-term congressional elections indicated that lack of confidence in the Clinton administration's ability to handle health-care policy was a key ingredient in the disappointment, cynicism, and anger at the Democratic party which led to its defeat; 'Pollsters see a silent storm that swept away Democrats', *NYT*, 16 Nov. 1994, p. A14. Another poll, sponsored by the Democratic Leadership Council which Clinton had headed as Arkansas governor, revealed (according to the DLC's executive director) that it was 'impossible to understimate the amount of damage the health care bill did in shaping the image of President Clinton as a big-government proponent'; 'Moderate Democrats' poll warns Clinton of voter unrest', ibid., 18 Nov. 1994, p. A30. On 9 Jan. 1995, Hillary Clinton, describing herself as having been 'naive and dumb' about national politics, said: 'I regret very much that the efforts on health care were badly misunderstood, taken out of context and used politically against the Administration. I take responsibility for that, and I'm very sorry for that'; 'Hillary Clinton seeking to soften a harsh image', *NYT*, 10 Jan. 1995, p. A1; see also 'The First Lady of paradoxes', *Washington Post Weekly*, 23–9 Jan. 1995, pp. 6–8. Finally in late Feb. 1995, almost four months after the election defeat, the White House revealed to news magazine insider columns that after a 'series of intense discussions', it had been decided that Mrs Clinton's role would henceforth be that of 'adviser' or 'advocate', not manager; *US News & World Report*, 6 Mar. 1995, pp. 29–30; *Newsweek*, 6 Mar. 1995, p. 6. Financial contributors to the Democratic party received a thank-you picture of the President and Mrs Clinton in 1994; in 1995, only the President was in the picture. In the very different political power structure that prevailed in China during the Cultural Revolution, Jiang Qing did not back off, let alone fade from the picture, even when her husband warned her against forming a 'Gang of Four'.

5   Cong Jin, *Quzhe Fazhande Suiyue*, p. 537, uses the terms *zantong* and *zhichi* to express Mao's attitude.

6   For 1960, see *Origins* II, pp. 303–4; for 1961, see above, Ch. 3; for Liu's attitude in 1963, see SCMP 4024, p. 4.

7   Guofang Daxue, *Cankao Ziliao* 24, p. 473.

8   Taoyuan brigade was part of Luwangzhuang commune, which was situated in Funing *xian* in Tangshan special district; ibid., p. 472.

9   Cong Jin, *Quzhe Fazhande Suiyue*, p. 540; SCMP 4024, pp. 4, 12–13. If, as the Cultural Revolution report translated in the latter source also alleged (p. 16), she was protected by five security agents, the local cadres could have hardly failed to realize that she was a VIP.

10 Guofang Daxue, *Cankao Ziliao* 24, pp. 472–3. Long extracts from Wang Guangmei's even longer report, which has still not been made openly available in China, are contained in ibid., pp. 472–84. The full text is in *[Liu Shaoqi] Yanlun Ji* 3, pp. 471–570. The *People's Daily* printed a major attack on Mme Wang's activities in the Hebei countryside on 6. Sept. 1967, translated in SCMP 4024, pp. 1–19. The paper also reproduced a brief *Jiefang Jun Bao* comment on 13 Sept. 1967, translated in SCMP 4025, pp. 16–17. For other negative Cultural Revolution accounts, see Baum, *Prelude to Revolution*, pp. 188–9, n. 1.

11 See above, Ch. 3.
12 Guofang Daxue, *Cankao Ziliao* 24, p. 473. According to the Cultural Revolution account, the party branch had been commended and rewarded on many occasions by the municipal, *xian*, *qu*, and commune party committees; SCMP 4024, p. 4.
13 Cong Jin, *Quzhe Fazhande Suiyue*, p. 540; SCMP 4024, pp. 4, 8, 10, 12.
14 Guofang Daxue, *Cankao Ziliao* 24, pp. 476–7.
15 Ibid., p. 474.
16 Ibid., pp. 477, 481–2.
17 Ibid., pp. 479–80.
18 Ibid., p. 481.
19 Ibid. Wang did not reveal that she and Liu Shaoqi had been greatly impressed by Guan Jingdong's production enthusiasm during the GLF and had entertained him at their home; SCMP 4024, pp. 12–13.
20 Cf. Guofang Daxue, *Cankao Ziliao* 24, pp. 476, 481, and SCMP 4024, pp. 8–9. For other hostile accounts with pictures of Wang Guangmei's activities in Taoyuan, see *Taoyuan diaocha jishi—Jielu Liu Shaoqi Wang Guangmei zai shehuizhuyi jiaoyu yundongzhong fan-dang fan-shehuizhuyi fan-Mao Zedong sixiangde taotian zuixing* (A true record of the Taoyuan investigation—Expose Liu Shaoqi and Wang Guangmei's monstrous anti-party, anti-socialist, anti-Mao Zedong Thought crimes in the Socialist Education Movement); *Wei Dong* (Protect the east), 28 Mar. 1967, p. 4. I am grateful to Michael Schoenhals for the latter reference.
21 SCMP 4024, pp. 7–8.
22 During the Cultural Revolution, allegations were made that in order to boost Taoyuan and Wang Guangmei's achievements there, the brigade was given priority status for the supply of equipment and funds. Anti-Wang exaggeration aside, special help to ensure that 'model' units could maintain standards was the norm; ibid., pp. 18–19.
23 Guofang Daxue, *Cankao Ziliao* 24, p. 475.
24 For the shortage of untapped new leadership talent, see Chan, Madsen, & Unger, *Chen Village*, pp. 52–3. For a novelist's description of the behaviour of a work team in Hunan in early 1964 based on personal experience, see Gu Hua, *A Small Town Called Hibiscus*, pp. 66–128. For a first-hand experience of how a corrupt rural team leader could use his party membership to hold on to power whatever the current political climate, battening on his peasant constituents, threatening them with the Six Articles on Public Security if they balked, shrugging off 'reprimands' from higher authority, getting his debt to the collective forgiven, see Wu & Li, *A Single Tear*, pp 263–306. This account dates from the Cultural Revolution, but the cadre behaviour described replicates that which Wang Guangmei had sought to root out earlier.
25 *Jianguo Yilai Mao Zedong Wengao* 11, pp. 43–6; Bo Yibo, *Ruogan Zhongda Juece* 2, pp. 1115–16.
26 Cong Jin, *Quzhe Fazhande Suiyue*, pp. 534–6.
27 Ibid., p. 533; Bo Yibo, *Ruogan Zhongda Juece* 2, p. 1116.
28 Mao, *Miscellany* 2, p. 387.
29 Bo Yibo, *Ruogan Zhongda Juece* 2, p. 1116.
30 Cong Jin, *Quzhe Fazhande Suiyue*, pp. 536–7; as this source dryly remarks, Liu could not have expected that this concept would be his own undoing. 'Peaceful evolution' of course re-emerged as a prime cause for concern of the post-Mao regime in the 1980s.

[31] Bo Yibo, *Ruogan Zhongda Juece* 2, p. 1116.

[32] Ibid., p. 1118. The directive is in Guofang Daxue, *Cankao Ziliao* 24, pp. 435–6; the association regulations are in ibid., pp. 436–40 and Baum & Teiwes, *Ssu-Ch'ing*, pp. 95–101. See also *Jianguo Yilai Mao Zedong Wengao* 11, pp. 76–7.

[33] In a Cultural Revolution confession; *Issues & Studies*, June 1970, p. 96.

[34] Bo Yibo, *Ruogan Zhongda Juece* 2, pp. 1118–19.

[35] Chen's first and most successful venture of this sort was to latch on to Mao in the late 1930s, some years before his leadership became unquestionable; his last and most disastrous one was cleaving to Lin Biao during the Cultural Revolution.

[36] Informant T. According to this source, Wang Guangmei gave her speech before a very large meeting.

[37] Peng Zhen's replacement may have been necessitated by his recent appointment as head of the five-man group in charge of cultural revolution.

[38] Bo Yibo, *Ruogan Zhongda Juece* 2, p. 1118.

[39] Ibid., pp. 1119–20; *Jianguo Yilai Mao Zedong Wengao* 11, pp. 132–4.

[40] Zheng Qian & Han Gang, *Wannian Suiyue: 1956 Nianhoude Mao Zedong*, p. 260; *Jianguo Yilai Mao Zedong Wengao* 11, pp. 139–41; *Mao Zedong he tade Mishu Tian Jiaying*, p. 75. According to this latter source, Tian was extremely embarrassed with this assignment as he was totally out of sympathy with Liu's leftism.

[41] Liu Zhende, *Wo wei Shaoqi dang Mishu* (I was Shaoqi's secretary), p. 193.

[42] Liao Gailong et al., *Xin Zhongguo Biannianshi*, p. 234. Mao's exact words were: 'This document should be circulated among various comrades at the conference and if everyone agrees it should be distributed nationwide. I agree with the opinions of Chen Boda and Comrade Shaoqi'; *Jianguo Yilai Mao Zedong Wengao* 11, pp. 144–7; Bo Yibo, *Ruogan Zhongda Juece* 2, p. 1123.

[43] The work conference was a high-level one for central leaders and regional 1st secretaries; Jiang Huaxuan, Zhang Weiping, & Xiao Sheng, *Zhongguo Gongchan Dang Huiyi Gaiyao*, p. 508.

[44] See for instance, *Dangdai Zhongguode Henan* 1, p. 148.

[45] Baum & Teiwes, *Ssu-Ch'ing*, p. 104.

[46] Bo Yibo, *Ruogan Zhongda Juece* 2, p. 1121.

[47] Baum, *Prelude to Revolution*, pp. 93–9. The text of the Revised Latter Ten Points is in Baum and Teiwes, *Ssu-Ch'ing*, pp. 102–17. For Liu's tough attitude, see *Jianguo Yilai Mao Zedong Wengao* 11, pp. 194–5.

[48] Former landlords, etc. represented 21%, and cadres with good backgrounds who had gone rotten represented 26%; Bo Yibo, *Ruogan Zhongda Juece* 2, p. 1124. Baum suggests that though such keypoint sites exhibited very high percentages of dismissals, elsewhere the figures may have been considerably lower, so that the overall provincial percentages may have been no higher than 5–10 per cent; *Prelude to Revolution*, pp. 103–4.

[49] Informant I.

[50] Bo Yibo, *Ruogan Zhongda Juece* 2, pp. 1124–5; *Chedi qingsuan Zhao Chuangbi fan-dang fan-shehuizhuyi fan-Mao Zedong sixiangde taotian zuixing* (Thoroughly settle accounts with Zhao Chuangbi's monstrous anti-party, anti-socialist, anti-Mao Zedong Thought crimes), p. 10.

[51] The quotations are from interviews conducted by Helen Siu; see her *Agents and Victims in South China*, pp. 201–2.

52 Bo Yibo, *Ruogan Zhongda Juece* 2, pp. 1124–5. This brief account makes it clear that that at the very least the leader of the brigade had 'shortcomings'; the position of his son suggests nepotism at the very least.

53 Baum, *Prelude to Revolution*, pp. 112–19. For a post-Cultural Revolution account of the ups and downs of the Dazhai model, see Sun Qitai & Xiong Zhiyang, *Dazhai Hongqide Shengqi yu Zhuiluo* (The rise and fall of the Dazhai red flag).

54 Baum, *Prelude to Revolution*, p. 103. For an account of basic-level cadres' experiences in the SEM in late 1964, see ibid., pp. 106–12.

55 It seems highly improbable that the Tianjin party could have commanded such prestigious support by itself; Bo Yibo (see next note) implies that the Tianjin affair was all Chen's doing.

56 Cong Jin, *Quzhe Fazhande Suiyue*, pp. 545–6; Bo Yibo, *Ruogan Zhongda Juece* 2, p. 1124.

57 Zhou Guoquan & Guo Dehong, *Dongluanzhongde Chen Boda* (Chen Boda in the midst of turmoil), p. 9.

58 Bo Yibo, *Ruogan Zhongda Juece* 2, p. 1127. Bo explains that the State Economic Commission, of which he was chairman, was entrusted with writing a directive on behalf of the CC on unleashing the masses in the urban areas; he apparently tried but failed to modify the more extreme measures employed in the rural SEM.

59 According to a foreign member of the CCP resident in Beijing; see Rittenberg & Bennett, *The Man Who Stayed Behind*, p. 284.

60 Bo Yibo, *Ruogan Zhongda Juece* 2, pp. 1117–18; Cong Jin, *Quzhe Fazhande Suiyue*, pp. 543–5. Cong Jin hints mysteriously that the case was linked to Gao Gang, and that the one-time provincial 1st secretary, Zhang Zhongliang (whom he does not refer to as 'comrade') bore much of the blame for this episode. The CC circulated the report of the province and the ministry, with an accompanying note, which is reprinted in Guofang Daxue, *Cankao Ziliao* 24, pp. 434–5. There was also a December report on the plant; for Mao and Bo Yibo's comments, see *Jianguo Yilai Mao Zedong Wengao* 11, pp. 277–9. The verdicts on this case were reversed in 1979; Guofang Daxue, *Qishi Nian Jianjie*, p. 515.

61 Bo Yibo, *Ruogan Zhongda Juece* 2, pp. 1122–3.

62 In the accompanying CC notice and at the start of his long speech, significant portions of which are reprinted in Guofang Daxue, *Cankao Ziliao* 24, pp. 512–20, there are indications that Wang had not been long at the grass roots and was not yet able to talk on the basis of experience (p. 512). For other reports from this gung-ho region, see *Jianguo Yilai Mao Zedong Wengao* 11, pp. 225–6, 259–61.

63 Guofang Daxue, *Cankao Ziliao* 24, pp. 513–14, 516.

64 Wang was in fact pinpointing the basic problem of the CCP in the countryside: the spontaneous tendency of peasants towards capitalism which was a major reason for Mao's collectivization drive in 1955; see *Origins* I, pp. 16–17.

65 This was a foretaste of the post-Mao countryside.

66 Guofang Daxue, *Cankao Ziliao* 24, pp. 514–15; the quotation is on p. 515.

67 Baum & Teiwes, *Ssu-Ch'ing*, p. 63.

68 Guofang Daxue, *Cankao Ziliao* 24, pp. 517–18.

69 *Origins* I, pp. 225–7.

70 Guofang Daxue, *Cankao Ziliao* 24, pp. 518–19.

71 Ibid., pp. 509–10. For confirmation that it was Liu who drafted the approving CC directive, see Bo Yibo, *Ruogan Zhongda Juece* 2, p. 1122. For Mao's prior approval, see *Jianguo Yilai Mao Zedong Wengao* 11, pp. 241–2.

72 Until all the archives are opened, a scholar is of course the prisoner of the data made available; but if significant support were forthcoming from senior officials other than in the Central-South region, doubtless it would have been reprinted or at least referred to.

73 Sichuan mobilized 66,000 cadres into work teams in 1963, and by May 1964, 57% of communes had initiated the SEM; a stepped-up effort took place after the circulation of the Revised Latter Ten Points; *Dangdai Zhongguode Sichuan* 1, pp. 123–4. The conduct of the SEM in another province in Li's region, Guizhou, was so unsatisfactory that the provincial 1st secretary, Zhou Lin, was sacked after a ten-year incumbency, and work teams from the centre and from regional HQ were sent in to run the campaign. A regional secretary, Li Dazhang, took over the provincial party leadership for six months. The despatch of central cadres could indicate an effort by Liu to show that he would not tolerate backsliding in Li Jingquan's region. See 'Dangdai Zhongguo' Congshu Bianjibu (ed.), *Dangdai Zhongguode Guizhou* (Contemporary China's Guizhou) 1, pp. 82–3; He Pin, *Zhongguo Zhangquanzhe* (China's powerholders) 2, p. 1055; Baum, *Prelude to Revolution*, pp. 126, 199, 200.

74 Guofang Daxue, *Cankao Ziliao* 24, pp. 520–1.

75 Cong Jin, *Quzhe Fazhande Suiyue*, p. 540.

76 Guofang Daxue, *Cankao Ziliao* 24, pp. 501–3.

77 Klein & Clark, *Biographic Dictionary of Chinese Communism* 1, pp. 178–9.

78 Guofang Daxue, *Cankao Ziliao* 24, p. 505.

79 Ibid.

80 Ibid., pp. 504, 505. The note of transmittal states that the centre (*zhongyang*) approved the tone of Liu's letter; for Mao's comments, see *Jianguo Yilai Mao Zedong Wengao* 11, pp. 168–71.

81 Guofang Daxue, *Cankao Ziliao* 24, p. 505.

82 This was of course the kind of comment which would arouse Red Guard fury against Liu during the Cultural Revolution.

83 Ibid., pp. 505–6.

84 Ibid., pp. 506–7. For the impact of Liu's humiliation of Jiang Weiqing on Zhang Pinghua, the 1st secretary of Hunan, see *Jianguo Yilai Mao Zedong Wengao* 11, p. 275 n. 1.

85 According to one account (Informant S), at some point in 1961 Deng Xiaoping told Ke Qingshi to promote experiments in *baochan daohu*, and Ke had displayed discipline by passing on this message to Jiang Weiqing. Jiang had refused, pounding the table and insisting that he would only obey the order if it came direct from Mao. Informant S believes that Jiang was so bold because Jiangsu had suffered relatively less than provinces like Anhui, with only a few (!) hundred thousand people dying.

86 Li, *The Private Life of Chairman Mao*, pp. 413–15. One problem with Dr Li's attribution of cause and effect in this instance is that Liu's illness was diagnosed in 'spring' 1964, which in China means the Lunar New Year, which fell in early February that year, whereas Mao's order to abolish the leadership's health bureau was given in August; *Mao Zedong sixiang wan sui (July 1967)*, p. 83. Mao's wishes were anyway evaded. With a few dextrous bureaucratic manoeuvres, the medical establishment ensured that the

leaders' health needs continued to be cared for, and of course Mao did not suffer. In Gao Jingzheng, *Pingfan yu Weida*, p. 30, there is a picture of Mao's medical care card allowing him to use the Beijing Hospital. The caption states: 'Mao rarely visited the hospital, trusting in self-healing with his own will-power and inner strength'!

87   Mao's decision to launch the GLF is one key example; *Origins* II, pp. 15–19. Mao's copying of Khrushchev's somewhat different version of a GLF may reflect a more general phenomenon: leaders of totalitarian states may be motivated to watch closely and, if appropriate, imitate the behaviour of similar leaders. According to one of Stalin's interpreters, after the 1934 Röhm purge, the Soviet leader commented: 'Did you hear what happened in Germany? Hitler, what a great man! This is the way to deal with your political opponents.' The interpreter points out that the German purge occurred in the summer and that the following December the Leningrad party boss, Kirov, was assassinated, giving Stalin the excuse to initiate a widespread purge of Lenin's old guard; Berezhkov, *At Stalin's Side*, pp. 9–10.

88   See for instance, Li, *The Private Life of Chairman Mao*, pp. 229–30, 434–5, 443. Khrushchev was not paranoid enough. A warning of the impending coup against him reached him through his son, but after cursory inquiries he decided that it was bogus; Khrushchev, *Khrushchev on Khrushchev*, pp. 86–122.

89   Conquest, *Russia after Khrushchev*, pp. 77–123; Medvedev, *Khrushchev*, pp. 225–45. 'Hare-brained schemes' was a catch-all phrase used in the CPSU CC indictment to describe Khrushchev's riskier policy initiatives.

90   Khrushchev, *Khrushchev on Khrushchev*, p. 79.

91   According to one analysis, it was Jiang Qing, citing Soviet precedents, who alerted Mao to the danger to his position constituted by Liu Shaoqi's increasingly prominent position and speech-making; *Wang Li Tan Mao Zedong*, p. 79. The very nearly successful attempt to remove Khrushchev in June 1957 may also have influenced Mao's actions; or was it only coincidental that the Chairman reached a compromise with Liu and Peng Zhen on the conduct of the Anti-Rightist Campaign not long after Khrushchev's narrow squeak? See *Origins* I, pp. 293–310.

92   Zhong Chen, Xia Lu, & Ye Lan, *Lingxiu Jiaowang Shilu Xilie: Mao Zedong*, p. 56.

93   Li, *The Private Life of Chairman Mao*, pp. 290–3, 365–9. See below, Ch. 19.

94   Ibid., p. 119.

95   This was what Mao confided to Edgar Snow on 9 Jan. 1965; Snow, *The Long Revolution*, pp. 70, 205.

96   Conquest, *Russia after Khrushchev*, p. 114.

97   Cong Jin, *Quzhe Fazhande Suiyue*, p. 602; Gu Longsheng (ed.), *Mao Zedong Jingji Nianpu* (A chronology of Mao Zedong and economics), p. 615.

98   In *Mao Zedong Jingji Nianpu* the number of pages allocated to each year presumably gives a reliable indicator of the amount of Mao's interest in and activity related to economics: *1958*—35; *1959*—69; *1960*—15; *1961*—33; *1962*—19; *1963*—10; *1964*—30; *1965*—17; *1966*—6. Thereafter, no year merited more than three pages.

99   For Peng Dehuai's comparison of Mao and founding emperors like Qin Shi Huang, see *Origins* II, p. 206.

100 From the *Shi Ji*, quoted in Guisso, Pagani, & Miller, *The First Emperor of China*, p. 22.

101 *Origins* I, pp. 105–7. To judge by the role which Deng Xiaoping continued to play after formally retiring in the late 1980s, it is clear that Mao could never have been sidelined, whatever his nominal status.

102 Why Liu cited Peng Zhen as running the five antis is unclear, since Peng had apparently been replaced by Bo Yibo in that role. Perhaps Peng was the secretariat member charged with overall supervision, as opposed to day-to-day control; or perhaps Liu had forgotten, being more concerned with the rural campaign.

103 Cong Jin, *Quzhe Fazhande Suiyue*, p. 602.

104 *Jianguo Yilai Mao Zedong Wengao* 11, pp. 256–8, 265–74, 286–7; Gu Longsheng, *Mao Zedong Jingji Nianpu*, pp. 615–16.

105 Li, *The Private Life of Chairman Mao*, p. 416; Cong Jin, *Quzhe Fazhande Suiyue*, p. 602; Bo Yibo, *Ruogan Zhongda Juece* 2, p. 1128. Dr Li's misremembers the start of this meeting as being in Jan. 1965; in a lecture at Harvard on 7 Oct. 1994, Dr Li stated that Mao had had a heavy cold.

106 Jiang Huaxuan, Zhang Weiping, & Xiao Sheng, *Zhongguo Gongchan Dang Huiyi Gaiyao*, p. 508. The text of the analysis made by Liu on 15 Dec. is not included in his *Selected Works*. Some sources say the meeting lasted from 15 till 28 Dec.—CCP CC Party History Research Centre, *A History of the Chinese Communist Party*, pp. 314–15; *DSNB*, p. 337; Jiang Huaxuan, Zhang Weiping, & Xiao Sheng, *Zhongguo Gongchan Dang Huiyi Gaiyao*, p. 507; Su Donghai & Fang Kongmu (eds.), *Zhonghua Renmin Gongheguo Fengyun Shilu* (A record of the major events of the PRC) 1, p. 962; others reckon it as concluding on 14 Jan. 1965 when the Twenty-three Articles were issued—Guofang Daxue, *Qishi Nian Jianjie*, pp. 515–16; Huai En, *Zhou Zongli Shengping Dashiji*, p. 448; Huang Zheng, *Liu Shaoqi Yi Sheng* (A life of Liu Shaoqi), p. 398. Certainly meetings continued, perhaps informally, in early January; Bo Yibo, *Ruogan Zhongda Juece* 2, pp. 1130, 1132. The difference in the dating probably reflects the political situation at the time: The work conference under Liu's chairmanship ended on the 28th with agreement on the Seventeen Articles, but Mao continued to hold consultations which led to their transformation into the Twenty-three Articles. Bo says the conference prepared to conclude on the 28th; *Ruogan Zhongda Juece* 2, p. 1128.

107 Su Donghai & Fang Kongmu, *Zhonghua Renmin Gongheguo Fengyun Shilu* 1, p. 962.

108 Mao, *Miscellany* 2, p. 409; *[Mao Zedong] Xuexi Wenxuan* 3, p. 58. Liu's 'late' arrival is curious in a regime whose officials prided themselves on punctuality. Had Mao turned up unexpectedly and deliberately early, thus wrong-footing Liu?

109 The text of the discussion on 20 Dec. which first became available in the West was in *Mao Zedong sixiang wan sui (1969)*, pp. 578–96, translated in Mao, *Miscellany* 2, pp. 408–26. This version has the disadvantage that some of the speakers, notably Liu Shaoqi and Deng Xiaoping, as well as Wang Guangmei's report, are not identified; 'X's were commonly used in texts that emerged during the Cultural Revolution, normally when the person in question had been disgraced. The variant text in *[Mao Zedong] Xuexi Wenxuan* 4, pp. 56–72, omits some passages in the other text, but does give surnames, enabling one to identify Liu and Deng. It also attributes some remarks differently and more convincingly than *Mao Zedong sixiang wan sui (1969)*; e.g. to Deng rather than Mao in one case, and to Mao rather than to an unidentified person in another. In the following discussion, I have relied on both versions.

[110] Bo Yibo, *Ruogan Zhongda Juece* 2, p. 1128.

[111] Jiang Huaxuan, Zhang Weiping, & Xiao Sheng, *Zhongguo Gongchan Dang Huiyi Gaiyao*, p. 509; this analysis is confirmed by the substance of the discussions contained in Mao, *Miscellany* 2, pp. 408–44. See also, Xu Quanxing, *Mao Zedong Wanniande Lilun yu Shixian*, p. 308.

[112] Mao, *Miscellany* 2, pp. 413–14; Bo Yibo, *Ruogan Zhongda Juece* 2, p. 1129.

[113] Mao, *Miscellany* 2, p. 414; *Origins* II, pp. 136–59. In 1959, Tao Zhu was also among the leftists.

[114] Mao, *Miscellany* 2, pp. 415–18. According to Dr Li, Mao's teeth were coated with a green film; *The Private Life of Chairman Mao*, p. 95.

[115] Mao, *Miscellany* 2, p. 418.

[116] *Jianguo Yilai Mao Zedong Wengao* 11, p. 267; Bo Yibo, *Ruogan Zhongda Juece* 2, pp. 1128–9.

[117] Hong Chenghua & Guo Xiuzhi, *Zhengzhi Tizhi Yange Dashiji*, p. 282. According to *Jianguo Yilai Mao Zedong Wengao* 11, p. 268, n. 8, the phrase 'leaders taking the capitalist road' was part of an explanatory comment written in by Bo Yibo; where Mao had written 'these people', Bo had added 'Means those people in the leadership of enterprises resolutely taking the capitalist road'. It is unclear whether Bo appended the explanation, which was included in the version printed for distribution, after consulting Mao or on his own initiative. In the four lines which Bo devotes to this important Mao comment (*Ruogan Zhongda Juece* 2, pp. 1128–9), he does not mention his own role.

[118] Mao, *Miscellany* 2, pp. 411, 412, 414. Zhou Enlai agreed with Mao, seeming to curry favour by pointing out that three senior party members in the government bureaucracy had been sacked.

[119] Ibid., p. 412; Zhao Shenghui, *Zhongguo Gongchan Dang Zuzhi Shi Gangyao* (An outline organizational history of the CCP), pp. 358–9; for the CC's Organization Department's effort to do something about the problem raised by Mao as early as the Ming Tombs Politburo work conference in June 1964; see *id.*, '1965 nian zhongyang zuzhibu guanyu dangde jianshede sange baogaode xingsheng guocheng', *Zhonggong Dangshi Ziliao*, No. 52, pp. 12–21.

[120] According to Bo's own account, however, during the SEM it was impossible to protect factories which had been operating according to the Seventy Articles from being attacked as having come under capitalist control; Bo Yibo, *Ruogan Zhongda Juece* 2, p. 1136.

[121] Mao, *Miscellany* 2, p. 418. Li Xiannian's meaning is somewhat obscure; probably he means that if one does not focus on rectifying the power holders, then one would have to focus on the poorer peasants whom Mao clearly wanted to shield. Mao also emphasized the need to attack first the more dangerous antagonist, party cadres rather than people like former landlords who had already been exposed and squashed, by quoting some lines from the great Tang poet Du Fu:

> If you draw a bow, draw a strong one;
> if you use an arrow, use one that's long,
> If you want to shoot a man, shoot his horse first;
> if you want to seize the enemy, seize their leader first.

Ibid.; Bo Yibo, *Ruogan Zhongda Juece* 2, p. 1129; the translation comes from Watson, *The Columbia Book of Chinese Poetry*, p. 221.

122 Wang Heshou had endeared himself to Mao during the GLF by his fervour for increasing steel output; *Origins* II, pp. 165–70. On this occasion, Mao twice enquired about Wang's fate, evidently unhappy that one of his favourites had been snared as a result of his own policies; Mao, *Miscellany* 2, pp. 419, 422. For a post-Cultural Revolution assignment of the blame in this case, see above, n. 60.

123 Zhao Shenghui, *Zhongguo Gongchan Dang Zuzhi Shi Gangyao*, p. 358.

124 *Mao Zedong sixiang wan sui (1969)*, pp. 591–2; Mao, *Miscellany* 2, pp. 417, 420–1.

125 Ibid., pp. 424, 426.

126 *Jianguo Yilai Mao Zedong Wengao* 11, p. 280; Bo Yibo, *Ruogan Zhongda Juece* 2, p. 1129.

127 Mao sat on Stalin's right; see the picture at the front of Shi Zhe, *Zai Lishi Juren Shenbian* (At the side of a colossus of history).

128 The principal guests were: Wang Jifan, Mao's first cousin, the man responsible for bringing him from Shaoshan to Changsha and thus into the wider world, earning the Chairman's lasting gratitude; Zhang Shizhao, a scholar and educator; Cheng Qian, the KMT commander in Hunan who surrendered the province peacefully to the PLA during the civil war; and Ye Gongzuo, a scholar and calligrapher. The five men chatted in a relaxed manner among themselves while their offspring talked apart. Wang brought his granddaughter Wang Hairong, later a close aide to Mao; Zhang brought his daughter Zhang Hanzhi, later the wife of Foreign Minister Qiao Guanhua; Chen brought his elder daughter; and Ye brought his granddaughter. Mao's daughters Li Min (by He Zizhen) and Li Na (by Jiang Qing) were also there. Jiang Qing came in and out, relaying messages to Mao from officials who called, and joined the party only for dinner. It was held in the Zhongnanhai though not in Mao's residence, according to Informant R; however, among the pictures in Li, *The Private Life of Chairman Mao*, Mao is shown in front of Room 118 (formerly the Beijing Room) in the Great Hall of the People, which was lavishly furnished and reserved for Mao's private use from the beginning of the 1960s (ibid., p. 356). For a brief account of Mao's relationship with Zhang Shizhao, see Lu Haijiang & He Mingzhou (eds.), *Mao Zedong he ta Tongshidaide Ren* (Mao Zedong and his contemporaries), pp. 356–61; for his relationship with Cheng Qian, see ibid., pp. 338–41, and Lü Xingdou, *Mao Zedong he Tade Shiye* 1, pp. 605–8.

129 Gao Jingzheng, *Pingfan yu Weida*, p. 42.

130 Mao is pictured with his personal staff at the Great Hall among the photographs in Li, *The Private Life of Chairman Mao*. Mao's 73rd birthday in 1966 would also be celebrated with a political gesture. With Jiang Qing, he played host to the leading members of the Cultural Revolution small group: Chen Boda, Zhang Chunqiao, Yao Wenyuan, Wang Li, Guan Feng, and Qi Benyu. See Wang Li, *Xianchang Lishi*, p. 100. Wang points out that Lin Biao, Zhou Enlai, Tao Zhu (by then a senior Politburo member), Kang Sheng, and Li Fuchun were not invited.

131 Bo Yibo, *Ruogan Zhongda Juece* 2, p. 1131. According to another account, Peng Zhen, Luo Ruiqing, Yu Qiuli, and Tao Zhu's wife Zeng Zhi also sat at Mao's table; Huang Yao, *San Ci Danan Buside Luo Ruiqing Dajiang*, pp. 235–6.

132 At the December NPC, Zhou Enlai ordered the North China regional bureau and the Shanxi provincial 1st secretaries, Li Xuefeng and Tao Lujia,

to reconfirm Dazhai's achievements in the light of disparaging reports that had reached him; Tao Lujia, *Yige Shengwei Shuji Huiyi Mao Zhuxi* (A provincial party secretary remembers Chairman Mao), pp. 117–20. In the light of Chen Yonggui's later disgrace, Tao underlines the point that the Dazhai leader's leftist mistakes occurred during the Cultural Revolution when he, Tao, was no longer in charge; ibid., pp. 121–7.

133 Sun Qitai & Xiong Zhiyong, *Dazhai Hongqide Shengqing yu Zhuiluo*, pp. 35–69. A picture of Chen Yonggui instructing youth on class issues appeared on the cover of the 1 Dec. 1964 issue (No. 23) of *Zhongguo Qingnian*.

134 Mao, *Miscellany 2*, p. 427; Cong Jin, *Quzhe Fazhande Suiyue*, p. 603.

135 Ibid.; *Jianguo Yilai Mao Zedong Wengao* 11, pp. 280, 283–4. The seventeenth clause merely stated that in principle the previous sixteen clauses applied to the urban areas as well as the rural ones. Cong Jin states that Liu did not confront Mao directly, but Liu's dissent from the Chairman's formulation was disagreement enough to infuriate the latter further as Cong Jin acknowledges (p. 604).

136 Cong Jin, *Quzhe Fazhande Suiyue*, p. 604; Bo Yibo, *Ruogan Zhongda Juece 2*, p. 1131; Li, *The Private Life of Chairman Mao*, pp. 411–12; Mao, *Miscellany 2*, pp. 429–32. According to a hagiographical picture book issued on the occasion of the Mao centenary (with English and Chinese texts), the Chairman was always very meticulous about showing his identity card and registering whenever he attended a meeting; Gao Jingzheng, *Pingfan yu Weida*, p. 29.

137 *Origins* II, p. 222.

138 CB 891, p. 71.

139 Bo Yibo, *Ruogan Zhongda Juece 2*, p. 1128.

140 According to one account, Liu was persuaded by Peng Zhen and Tao Zhu to self-criticize, and he apologized for showing lack of respect by interrupting the Chairman; whereupon Mao angrily said that it was not a matter of respect or not, but a difference of principle between them, the difference between revisionism and anti-revisionism. See Ye Yonglie, *Chen Boda Qiren*, p. 214. According to another account, which may be Ye's source, this came about as a result of behind-the-scenes work by Chen Boda; Wang Li, *Xianchang Lishi*, p. 147; *Wang Li Tan Mao Zedong*, pp. 80–1. In this latter source, Wang Li credits Chen Boda with postponing the Cultural Revolution by a year. Ye's account of the work conference differs from Bo's, in that he says that the sessions in December under Liu's chairmanship were not attended by Mao, and that it was during the January sessions under Deng's chairmanship that Mao made all his *démarches* (*Chen Boda Qiren*, p. 212). Since Bo's account is based on personal recollection refreshed by access to top-level party archives, one must assume his account is more accurate; there would seem to be no obvious reason why he would choose to falsify the sequence of events.

141 Su Donghai & Fang Kongmu, *Zhonghua Renmin Gongheguo Fengyun Shilu* 1, p. 962.

142 Bo Yibo, *Ruogan Zhongda Juece 2*, pp. 1131–2; *Jianguo Yilai Mao Zedong Wengao* 11, pp. 281, 284. (In the latter source, in which the precise wording of Chen Boda's elaboration is given, the new central directive is said to have been No. 815.) Without seeing the complete dossier of central documents, it is impossible to say how unusual a development this was, but Bo

Yibo's reaction suggests that it was virtually unheard of that a central document should be withdrawn after being formally agreed at a meeting at which all major leaders were present. For a discussion of the central document system, see Lieberthal, *Central Documents and Politburo Politics in China*.

[143] See below, Ch. 19.

[144] Lü Yanyu, *Zhonghua Renmin Gongheguo Lishi Jishi: Quzhe Fazhan (1958–1965)* (Historical records of the PRC: Tortuous development, 1958–1965), p. 117. The available text of the discussion of 3 Jan. (Mao, *Miscellany* 2, pp. 437–44) is in striking contrast to that of 20 Dec.; now Mao is doing all the talking with Liu only offering a few defensive comments.

[145] According to Wang Li, this postponed Mao's attack on Liu; see Michael Schoenhals (ed.), 'An Insider's Account of the Cultural Revolution: Wang Li's Memoirs', *Chinese Law and Government*, Nov.–Dec. 1994, p. 16. Interestingly, the American journalist Edgar Snow who was in China from Oct. 1964 to Jan. 1965 saw both Mao and Zhou Enlai; but when he asked to see other leaders, including Liu Shaoqi, he was told by the premier that 'I had no need "to bother" these "busy men" since he could answer any questions I had, and if he couldn't. Mao could'; Thomas, *Season of High Adventure*, p. 312.

[146] This is suggested by the disagreement among recent PRC sources as to the precise dating of the work conference; see above, n. 106.

[147] Mao, *Miscellany* 2, pp. 437–44.

[148] Cong Jin, *Quzhe Fazhande Suiyue*, p. 604.

[149] There is some confusion as to whether Mao forced the State Planning Commission to play host to their supplanters (Lieberthal & Oksenberg, *Policy Making in China*, pp. 189–90) or whether the planners invited them in, trying to foil Mao's initiative by the classic bureaucratic ploy of co-opting and stifling a rival. According to one planner, it was Li Fuchun's suggestion that the new group be inducted into the existing body and gradually take it over (which Mao agreed to); see Bo Yibo, *Ruogan Zhongda Juece* 2, pp. 1205–11. Mao referred to the *xiao jiwei* in a comment on a report from Li Fuchun on 21 Jan. 1965; *Jianguo Yilai Mao Zedong Wengao* 11, pp. 316–17.

[150] For Peng Zhen's role, see Bo Yibo, *Ruogan Zhongda Juece* 2, p. 1132.

[151] Baum & Teiwes, *Ssu-ch'ing*, p. 118. In fact, the small *neibu* pamphlet containing the Twenty-three Articles issued after the conference included only Mao's Former Ten Points.

[152] The legislative history is the account of the deliberations of the US Congress in the process of drawing up and passing bills prepared by congressional aides with the objective of clarifying the intentions of senators and representatives for the benefit of judges who will later be called on to interpret the statutes in the courts. In fact, the legislative history is often ambiguous, offering broad leeway for judicial interpretation. See Melnick, *Regulation and the Courts*, pp. 77, 159, 373–9.

[153] Baum & Teiwes, *Ssu-ch'ing*, pp. 118–26.

[154] On 11 November 1964, the CC's Propaganda Department sent a 250-person work team under a deputy director, Zhang Panshi, into Peking University to conduct the SEM there. The group appears to have been convinced by leftists like Nie Yuanzi, party secretary of the Philosophy Department, who would emerge at the outset of the Cultural Revolution in mid-1966 as a leading campus Maoist, that the whole university was in a

mess and run by 'capitalist roaders'. The work team's report to this effect was supported by Kang Sheng. Peng Zhen and his senior colleagues were considerably worried by this turn of events and sent in municipal party officials to turn the tide. Nie, bolstered by a phone call assuring her of support at the highest levels, persisted. Finally, Peng Zhen reported on the matter to Mao and the Politburo on 1 March 1965. The Chairman apparently accepted Peng's reassurance that Beida president, Lu Ping, was a good comrade, and two days later the secretariat decided to stop the attacks on capitalist roaders at Beida. The Propaganda Department work team was withdrawn, with Lu Dingyi making a report on 5 March, and responsibility for the Beida SEM was transferred to a small Beijing municipal work team headed by a muncipal party secretary, Wan Li. The faculty assembled at the International Hotel for a meeting at which, despite a fierce rearguard action on Nie's part, Lu Ping and his associates were cleared. In July, a second International Hotel conference was held to sort out the problems of the Philosophy and Economics departments, and even Kang Sheng's intervention could not save Nie from criticism. See Wen Jie (ed.), *Ba Zai Qincheng Meng* (Eight years of nightmare in Qincheng), pp. 26–30; *Jiaoyu Dashiji*, p. 370; Hao Ping, 'Reassessing the Starting Point of the Cultural Revolution', *China International Review* (Hawaii), No. 1, Spring 1996, pp. 71–4; Informant U.

[155]   Baum & Teiwes, *Ssu-ch'ing*, p. 120.

[156]   According to *Jianguo Yilai Mao Zedong Wengao* 11, p. 284, seven articles (1, 4, 6, 8, 9, 10, 22) were added and one dropped in the transformation of the seventeen articles into the Twenty-three Articles. The passage about capitalist roaders appeared in art. 2. However, this account also indicates that there was much alteration of the wording, which clearly could have included the existing articles. The 'capitalist roaders' passage does not appear among those quoted in this source (pp. 281–3) as Maoist revisions, and was presumably devised by the trusty Chen Boda. For Zhou's role, see Cong Jin, *Quzhe Fazhande Suiyue*, p. 605.

[157]   The Fujian provincial committee distributed it on 18 Jan.; Baum & Teiwes, *Ssu-ch'ing*, p. 118. Some regional or provincial secretaries, especially those opposed to Liu's stern line, may have passed down advance warning of the new wind blowing in Beijing. For example, on 13 Jan. the Baoding district committee in north China reported their revised SEM practices in line with the spirit of Chairman Mao's directive; Mao commented favourably on the 15th; *Jianguo Yilai Mao Zedong Wengao* 11, pp. 312–13.

[158]   Chan, Madsen, & Unger, *Chen Village*, p. 41. The timing of the arrival of the work team is given as around the end of January in Madsen, *Morality and Power in a Chinese Village*, p. 67.

[159]   Chan, Madsen, & Unger, *Chen Village*, p. 42. For the conduct of the SEM in Chen village, see ibid., pp. 41–73, and Madsen, *Morality and Power*, pp. 67–101.

[160]   Informant R.

[161]   Mao's staff were ordered by the Chairman to participate in the SEM in June 1965; Li, *The Private Life of Chairman Mao*, pp. 422–9; the quotation is on p. 427.

[162]   Of course, they would soon be faced with the even more disruptive repercussions of the Cultural Revolution, by which time Bo would be disgraced and be unable to run interference.

163 Lü Yanyu, *Zhonghua Renmin Gongheguo Lishi Jishi: Quzhe Fazhan*, p. 118.

164 Bo Yibo, *Ruogan Zhongda Juece* 2, pp. 1134–5; *Jueyi Zhushiben Xiuding*, p. 367. An instance of the overlap of the SEM and the early Cultural Revolution is that on 16 May 1966, Tao Zhu gave a report to officials of the Central-South region about the SEM and three days later addressed a mass meeting on the Cultural Revolution; Zheng Xiaofeng & Shu Ling. *Tao Zhu Zhuan*, p. 417.

CHAPTER 19

1 Snow, *The Long Revolution*, p. 17. Snow's interview took place on 10 Dec. 1970. The reference to 'capitalist roaders' actually occurs in art. 2, not art. 1. Coincidentally, Snow had also interviewed Mao on 9 Jan. 1965, just at the time when the Chairman was supposedly making the decision to move against Liu; Thomas, *Season of High Adventure*, pp. 312–15.

2 See for instance Cong Jin, *Quzhe Fazhande Suiyue*, p. 605.

3 *Zhonggong Dangshi Renwuzhuan* 48, p. 120.

4 Quoted in Cong Jin, *Quzhe Fazhande Suiyue*, p. 605.

5 Significantly, while Liu Shaoqi's reputation was rehabilitated after Mao's death, the party line has been that the Revised Latter Ten Points overestimated the seriousness of the situation and was therefore excessively 'leftist'; *Jueyi Zhushiben Xiuding*, pp. 25, 366.

6 See Lü Xingdou, *Liu Shaoqi he Tade Shiye*, pp. 316–17, 401–11, 435–6; Teiwes, *Politics at Mao's Court*, pp. 41–3. See also Schram, *The Thought of Mao Tse-tung*, p. 111; Dittmer, *Liu Shao-ch'i and the Chinese Cultural Revolution*, pp. 244–6. Liu self-criticized for these errors at the outset of the Cultural Revolution; see *Issues & Studies*, June 1970, pp. 93–4.

7 *Origins* I, pp. 177–99.

8 Gao Gang's attempt in 1953 to replace Liu Shaoqi as Mao's number two was inspired in part by the criticisms of Liu and Zhou Enlai which Mao vouchsafed to Gao; Teiwes, *Politics at Mao's Court*, pp. 37–9. Teiwes, whose book is an exhaustive analysis of the Gao Gang affair, concurs with the view of his well-informed oral sources in doubting that Mao wanted Liu removed, but the Chairman's indiscreet and indeed provocative behaviour with so obviously ambitious a lieutenant as Gao allows of alternative explanations. We know enough by now of Mao's deviousness to invoke the time-worn communist party phrase, 'It surely could have been no accident, comrade!' Indeed, the failure of most senior CCP members, including Deng Xiaoping, immediately and forthrightly to reject Gao's lobbying indicates a caution engendered by a belief that Gao could well be acting on Mao's behalf in view of the known closeness between the two men.
  By the time of the Gao Gang affair, Liu had served Mao's purposes in helping dispose of his rival Wang Ming and in building up the Chairman's cult. With the intra-party struggle for leadership long over and civil war against the KMT successfully concluded, Mao may have become less willing to tolerate differences of approach and temperament, or Liu's tendency to go too far right or left when implementing Mao's policy preferences, and have been naggingly conscious that a significant number of senior party bureaucrats had closer ties with Liu than himself. Thus the Gao Gang episode may have been an attempt to demote Liu with Mao remaining

above the battle, awaiting its outcome and preserving his image as a unifying leader. Had Gao succeeded in mobilizing majority support against Liu, Mao could have bowed democratically to the consensus; Liu could have been allowed to survive in a less senior role like Mac's earlier opponents Wang Ming and Li Lisan. As it was, Gao's conspiratorial activities were reported to Mao by Deng Xiaoping and Chen Yun, and the Chairman lost 'deniability'. To have got rid of Liu at this point would have meant throwing the full weight of his own prestige into a factional battle that would have destroyed the Yan'an 'round table' and his own image as its guarantor. Instead, Mao bowed 'democratically' to a different consensus and sacrificed Gao.

From then on, Mao made do with the leadership line-up that he had put together as he was consolidating his power in Yan'an, but as the analyses of this work suggest, and the revelations of Dr Li Zhisui confirm, he was never comfortable with Liu for very long, and grew increasingly concerned about his growing power and his willingness to take a line divergent from his own. It is unnecessary to posit that Mao was continuously seeking to get rid of Liu from the early 1950s on; only to assume that the willingness to engage in unprincipled intrigue which Mao displayed in the run-up to and during the Cultural Revolution was not aberrant.

9 Cf. Margaret Thatcher: 'I've learned one thing in politics. You don't take a decision until you have to'; Clark, *Diaries*, p. 150.

10 See the account by Wang Dongxing, 'Sui Mao Zhuxi chongshang Jinggangshan riji' (Diary of going up to Jinggangshan with Mao again), *Zhonggong Dangshi Ziliao*, No. 40, pp. 124-44.

11 See above, Ch. 16.

12 *Origins* I, pp. 5-7.

13 Mao would have doubtless felt less threatened had he been able to play two potential successors off against each other; cf. how British Prime Minister Harold Wilson felt more at ease when he had two rival heirs-apparent (George Brown and James Callaghan) in the late 1960s, and became increasingly concerned when setbacks to their careers left him for a period with only one (Roy Jenkins); see Pimlott, *Harold Wilson*, pp. 488-91.

14 *Sunday Times* (London), 15 Oct. 1961. This episode is normally referred to by Chinese authors to confirm that Mao had anointed Liu as his successor; see the account of the same conversation in Waijiaobu Waijiaoshi Bianjishi, *Xin Zhongguo Waijiao Fengyun 1*, pp. 48-57. For the record: when briefing Field-Marshal Montgomery prior to his visit to China, the present author suggested that he ask this question and the follow-up question. [It is worthwhile clearing up a discrepancy about the follow-up question between the above two accounts and a recent Chinese version in an otherwise authoritative article. According to the British Field-Marshal, 'I asked who would come next after Liu. He didn't know or care; he himself would be with Karl Marx and they could work it out for themselves in China!' The just cited Chinese version confirms this account in abbreviated fashion, quoting Mao (p. 57) as saying, 'After Liu Shaoqi I don't care ... (*sic*).' In an article written by two Chinese well-acquainted with CCP history, Mao's reply to the succession question was said to have been: 'My successor is, first, Liu Shaoqi and, second, Deng Xiaoping'; Gong Yuzhi & Shi Zhongquan, 'Shidaide zhongtuo, lishide xuanze' (The great trust of the epoch, the choice of history), *Xinhua Wenzhai*, No. 10, 1994, p. 1. This

assertion was, however, made in error; personal communication from Gong Yuzhi.]

Gong and Shi quote Mao as replying to a similar query from Khrushchev in 1957 by saying that after him there were 'Liu Shaoqi, Deng Xiaoping, and Zhou Enlai'. Khrushchev's recollection was different: Mao was critical of Liu, Zhou, and Zhu De. 'The only one of his comrades whom Mao seemed to approve of was Teng Hsiao-p'ing'; *Khrushchev Remembers: The Last Testament*, p. 288. Unlike Kissinger or Montgomery, Khrushchev almost certainly had his own interpreter who could ignore Chinese self-censorship and report what Mao really said; on the other hand, Khrushchev may have misremembered or he may have wanted to spread a little confusion among his old antagonists in Beijing.

15 On the cover of *Zhongguo Qingnian*, No. 3, 1 Feb. 1965, the two men were portrayed side by side at the NPC meeting at which Liu was re-elected state chairman.

16 For the 1961 document, see *Jianguo Yilai Mao Zedong Wengao* 9, pp. 556–9. For the 2nd polemic, see *The Polemic*, p. 123; for Mao's role in the 2nd polemic, see Huang Zheng, *Liu Shaoqi Yi Sheng*, p. 374. For the 9th polemic, see Lin Qingshan, *Lin Biao Zhuan, shang*, p. 201; there is no such tribute to Liu's status in the published version of the 9th polemic.

17 Cong Jin, *Quzhe Fazhande Suiyue*, p. 606. Liu Shaoqi continued to draw up directives for the SEM, for instance in July 1965, though he took care to clear them with Mao before issuing them; *Jianguo Yilai Mao Zedong Wengao* 11, pp. 406–7. Seemingly all-powerful leaders often have to move cautiously for fear of provoking opposition. Winston Churchill took over as Prime Minister from Neville Chamberlain in May 1940 on a wave of popular enthusiasm which he was able to maintain with his leadership and oratory despite subsequent setbacks in the conduct of the war against Nazi Germany. But he found it impossible to win over the Conservative parliamentary party even at the height of the Battle of Britain because of the continuing enmity of its majority of Chamberlain loyalists. Churchill therefore retained and indeed championed Chamberlain in office until the latter had to resign due to ill health. Then Churchill slowly chipped away at the Chamberlainite establishment; but it was not until 14 months after he became premier and eight months after the death of Chamberlain that Churchill felt secure enough to get rid of the late leader's unreconciled followers and radically reconstruct the government in his own image. See Roberts, *Eminent Churchillians*, pp. 137–210.

18 Lin Qingshan, *Lin Biao Zhuan, shang*, p. 201.

19 Deng Xiaoping had been a member of Mao's personal clique back in the early 1930s; *Origins* I, p. 142. For Mao's comment in Dec. 1963 that Deng had been behind him in virtually every vicissitude, see Wang Li, *Xianchang Lishi*, p. 93. For Mao's continuing high appraisal of Deng's abilities even after he had been purged during the Cultural Revolution, see ibid., p. 96. Zhu De, though closely associated with Mao from Jinggangshan days in the late 1920s and always loyal to him when he was leader, had an independent persona; when Mao was in disgrace prior to the Long March, Zhu did not suffer with him, unlike Deng. By 1965, Zhu's political significance was as a Politburo vote upon which Mao could normally rely.

20 Cong Jin, *Quzhe Fazhande Suiyue*, pp. 109–12; *Origins* II, pp. 24–9.

21 Ibid., pp. 59–63.

22 Mao's doctor formed a particularly jaundiced view of Zhou's readiness to trim; e.g. see Li, *The Private Life of Chairman Mao*, pp. 508–11. In an interview printed in the *NYT* on 2 Oct. 1994, Dr Li was even more caustic: 'Zhou was really a slave of Mao. He was absolutely obedient. Whenever I saw him with Mao he acted like a servant with his master. A lot of people think that Zhou protected people, that he was such a good man. But actually everything he did he did under Mao's orders. Mao was on the sedan chair and Zhou was one of his bearers.' In response to a question after a lecture given by him at Harvard University on 7 Oct. 1994, Dr Li was terser still: the relationship between Chairman and Premier could be summed up in three words, 'master and slave'. The pungency of the late Dr Li's comments doubtless reflected in part his distrust of premier Zhou, which permeates his memoir, but no student of PRC politics of the Mao era could doubt that Zhou never deliberately crossed the Chairman.

23 Cheng Hua, *Zhou Enlai he Tade Mishumen*, p. 251.

24 For seven of the ten days, Zhou never went out and did nothing but work on the text, which went through fifteen drafts; Shi Zhongquan, *Zhou Enlaide Zhuoyue Fengxian*, pp. 336–9; Cong Jin, *Quzhe Fazhande Suiyue*, pp. 123–8.

25 Shi Zhongquan, *Zhou Enlaide Zhuoyue Fengxian*, p. 363.

26 Cheng Hua, *Zhou Enlai he Tade Mishumen*, pp. 153, 198, 490. (Cf. the behaviour of Qin Shi Huangdi: 'Once, looking from a mountain top, the emperor was displeased to notice that the carriages and riders of the chancellor (Li Ssu) were very numerous. Someone told this to the chancellor, who diminished his entourage accordingly'; Bodde, 'The State and Empire of Ch'in', *CHOC* 1, p. 71.) There is some disagreement among Zhou's secretaries who contributed to this collection of reminiscences, one stating that the private office was dissolved, another that he cut the number of secretaries from six or seven to two or three. When Zhou had previously been in trouble with Mao in early 1958, he had cut the number from about a dozen to six or seven.

27 As some Chinese put it, Zhou did not have Mao's boldness or vision; see Zhang Suhua, Bian Yanjun, & Wu Xiaomei, *Shuo bujinde Mao Zedong*, pp. 534–5.

28 Like Zhou Enlai, Chen Yun made a full self-criticism at the second session of the 8th Congress; Cong Jin, *Quzhe Fazhande Suiyue*, pp. 128–31.

29 See above, Chs. 7, 8, 12.

30 Cf. Britain's Chancellor of the Exchequer in the late 1980s: '[T]he nature of a modern economy is such that, while there will always be turning points, it is impossible to predict when those turning points will occur. Thus when speaking in a timeless sense about the economy, one should *always* forecast a turning point, while when speaking about the year immediately ahead, one should *never* forecast a turning point—since in a given year the odds are that it will not occur'; Lawson, *The View from No. 11*, p. 807, emphasis in original. Sadly for Chen Yun, who implicitly adopted this stance in 1962, he found himself caught out by the sudden upturn in the Chinese economy.

31 Cong Jin, *Quzhe Fazhande Suiyue*, pp. 580–1. The difference between the behaviour of Zhou Enlai and Chen Yun with regard to Mao is perhaps best captured in this passage on ministership from the early Qing scholar Huang Zongxi (Huang Tsung-hsi): 'The reason for ministership lies in the fact that the world is too big for one man to govern so governance must be shared with colleagues. Therefore, when one goes forth to serve, it is for all-under-

Heaven and not for the prince; it is for all the people and not for one family. When one acts for the sake of all-under-Heaven and its people, then one cannot agree to do anything contrary to the Way even if the prince explicitly constrains one to do so—how much less could one do it without being shown or told! And if it were not in keeping with the true Way, one should not even present oneself to the court—much less sacrifice one's life for the ruler. To act solely for the prince and his dynasty, and attempt to anticipate the prince's unexpressed whims or cravings—this is to have the mind of a eunuch or palace maid. "When the prince brings death and destruction upon himself, if one follows and does the same, this is to serve him as a mistress or some such intimate would". That is the difference between one who is a true minister and one who is not.' De Bary, *Waiting for the Dawn*, pp. 94–5.

³² See above, Ch. 10.
³³ *Origins* II, pp. 55–9. No PRC historian has been willing even to consider the possibility of rivalry between Liu and Zhou.
³⁴ *Origins* II, pp. 63–71. For a far fuller account of the 1958 PLA conference than was available when Origins II was published, see Cong Jin, *Quzhe Fazhande Suiyue*, pp. 274–99, where it is revealed that Peng Dehuai contributed to the military factionalism which played a role in his disgrace.
³⁵ Lin Biao was clearly willing to profit from Peng Dehuai's dismissal. Marshal He Long's presence at the PSC meeting called by Mao to castigate Peng between the conference and the CC's 8th plenum is explicable by the Chairman's knowledge of old animosities between the two men. For a record of the PSC meeting, see Li Rui, *Lushan Huiyi Shilu*, pp. 215–61.
³⁶ *Origins* II, pp. 222–3, 228–33, 237–47.
³⁷ Quoted in Gittings, *The Role of the Chinese Army*, p. 245.
³⁸ *Jiefang Jun Jiangling Zhuan* 2, p. 287; 11, pp. 268–70.
³⁹ Jiang Bo & Li Qing (eds.), *Lin Biao 1959 nian yihou* (Lin Biao after 1959), p. 11. The text of the speech can be found in *Gao Ju Mao Zedong Sixiang Weida Hong Qi* (Raise high the great red banner of Mao Zedong Thought), pp. 145–54 (the quoted passage is on p. 153), or in *[Lin Biao Xuanji]* (Selected works of Lin Biao), pp. 102–19 (where the quotation is on p. 118).
⁴⁰ Jiang Bo & Li Qing (eds.), *Lin Biao 1959 nian yihou*, p. 12.
⁴¹ *Mao Zhuxi Yulu* (Quotations from Chairman Mao). A second edition with a preface by Lin Biao was issued in 1966. For Lin's initial suggestion, see *Jianguo Yilai Mao Zedong Wengao* 9, p. 544.
⁴² Snow, *The Long Revolution*, p. 205.
⁴³ Cf. this appraisal of 'Thatcherism' by the senior British politician who was the first to use the term: 'Thatcherism is, I believe, a useful term, and certainly was at the time. No other modern Prime Minister has given his or her name to a particular constellation of policies and values. However it needs to be used with care. *The wrong definition is "whatever Margaret Thatcher herself at any time did or said"*. The right definition involves a mixture of free markets, financial discipline, firm control over public expenditure, tax cuts, nationalism, "Victorian values" (of the Samuel Smiles self-help variety), privatization and a dash of populism.' (Lawson, *The View from No. 11*, p. 64; emphasis added.) During the Chairman's lifetime, Chinese propagandists struggled in vain against the view that whatever Mao himself at any time did or said was Maoism; only since his death have Chinese party historians been

able to list the elements that constituted the Thought of Mao Zedong and to pinpoint who were their progenitors in addition to Mao. Of course, the fact that Lawson felt obliged to spell out this point suggests considerable frustration that Thatcherism *was* popularly thought, in Britain and abroad, to be whatever Mrs Thatcher did or said. If this equation of leader with a set of political ideals could prevail in a country with a free press and non-Leninist politics, how much more so in Mao's China.

44 Li, *The Private Life of Chairman Mao*, p. 412. On the eve of the Cultural Revolution, in Nov. 1965, Lin Biao proposed and Mao approved that the first two of five principles to guide PLA work in 1956 should be the lively study and use of Mao's works, and the 'four firsts'; *Jianguo Yilai Mao Zedong Wengao* 11, pp. 480–1.

45 When Lin took over, about a third of all companies had no party branches and most platoons had no party cell; eighteen months later, there were party branches in all companies and party cells in 80% of all platoons. See Gittings, *The Role of the Chinese Army*, pp. 246–51. Abolition of ranks was not Lin's suggestion, but resulted from an exchange between Mao and He Long in Aug. 1964; Huang Yao, *San Ci Danan Buside Luo Ruiqing Dajiang*, p. 231. The PLA submitted a formal proposal on 12 Jan. 1965, which Mao approved forthwith; *Jianguo Yilai Mao Zedong Wengao* 11, pp. 308–9. But as early as Dec. 1963, in comments on a military document, the Chairman had called for the text to be amended by substituting 'comrade' for military ranks; ibid. 10, p. 463.

46 Quoted in Gittings, *The Role of the Chinese Army*, pp. 254–5. For an example of Mao calling on his senior colleagues to study Lin Biao's words, see *Jianguo Yilai Mao Zedong Wengao* 11, pp. 237–8.

47 Communications (*jiaotong*) means transportation not the media.

48 *Jianguo Yilai Mao Zedong Wengao* 10, pp. 454–8; Bo Yibo, *Ruogan Zhongda Juece* 2, pp. 1150–1.

49 Bo Yibo, *Ruogan Zhongda Juece* 2, pp. 1151–2; Gittings, *The Role of the Chinese Army*, pp. 256–7. Interestingly, though Mao was keen to involve the PLA in the SEM at least as early as Dec. 1963, that idea does not seem to have borne fruit fast. In Nov. 1964, the prospect was only that high-level experiments would start soon; in Aug. 1965, Mao still had to encourage the PLA to learn from students of an army engineering academy who had participated in the SEM in Heilongjiang; in Oct. 1965, Lin Biao listed participation in the SEM as the PLA's third most important task, after studying Mao's works and grasping strategic and political work, but in November, the SEM did not appear among his five principles to guide PLA work in 1966; see *Jianguo Yilai Mao Zedong Wengao* 10, pp. 432–3, 449–51; 11, pp. 43–6, 223–4, 437–9, 472–3, 480–1.

50 *Origins* I, parts 3 and 4.

51 The analysis of these norms in theory and practice is the focus of Teiwes, *Politics and Purges in China*. Ironically, it was Liu Shaoqi who, in the Yan'an period, had authored the CCP's standard document on the subject: 'Lun dangnei douzheng' (On inner party struggle).

52 It was Deng Xiaoping and Chen Yun who reported Gao Gang's anti-Liu activities to Mao; Teiwes, *Politics at Mao's Court*, pp 108–13.

53 This was presumably why Mao chose not to launch the assault on Wu Han in the pages of *Red Flag*, although it was run by the loyal Chen Boda.

54 Cf. Sherlock Holmes's 'Baker Street Irregulars'.

55 Mao did bring the stalwarts of the central Cultural Revolution group together after their initial successes on the occasion of his 73rd birthday, 26 Dec. 1966; see above, Ch. 18, n. 130.
56 Paranoids are not necessarily fantasists; Mao's suspicions of Tian were not without justification. Though the Chairman presumably did not know it, in 1962 Tian had suppressed the document on which Mao had written that Chen Yun was of 'bourgeois character'; Li, *The Private Life of Chairman Mao*, p. 392.
57 'Both [Hitler and Stalin] owed a great deal of their success as politicians to their ability to disguise, *from allies* as well as opponents, their thoughts and intentions'; Bullock, *Hitler and Stalin*, p. 396 (emphasis added).
58 Li, *The Private Life of Chairman Mao*, p. 405. Michael Schoenhals has pointed out to me that the only recorded occasion on which Jiang Qing said this was to an enlarged MAC meeting on 12 Apr. 1967; see Nankai Daxue Weidong Pipan Wenyi Heixian Liangezhan [yu] "Hong Hai Yan" (ed.), *Wuxian fengguang zai xianfeng* (A limitless vista from the perilous peak), p. 62.
59 Li, *The Private Life of Chairman Mao*, pp. 407–8. Dr Li's book is full of examples of Jiang Qing's obsession with her health and the troubles it caused him; he noted, however, that her maladies all disappeared in 1966 as she emerged in a much heightened political role; ibid., pp. 451–2. Zhang Yufeng was to outlast all her rivals and stay with Mao till his death. According to Informant S, Zhang did not become really important in Mao's household till 1970.
60 Ye Yonglie, *Zhang Chunqiao Fuchen Shi*, p. 122. Most accounts of *The Dismissal of Hai Rui* refer only to the performances in early 1961; if Ye is correct, then either it was restaged or Jiang Qing ordered a special performance. In Cong Jin, *Quzhe Fazhande Suiyue*, p. 609, no mention is made of whether she saw the play. Su Shuangbi & Wang Hongzhi, *Wu Han Zhuan*, p. 317.
61 Guofang Daxue, *Qishi Nian Jianjie*, p. 528; Lin Qingshan, *Kang Sheng Waizhuan*, pp. 249–50.
62 Cong Jin, *Quzhe Fazhande Suiyue*, p. 609.
63 See Goldman, *Literary Dissent in Communist China*, pp. 122–5. Li managed to retain good relations with Jiang Qing despite his refusal; Informant I.
64 *Zheng Fa Hong Qi* (Politics and law red flag), 17 Oct. 1967, p. 5. This revelation from a Red Guard paper is confirmed by Cong Jin's quotation of Mao's remarks to an Albanian military delegation in May 1967; *Quzhe Fazhande Suiyue*, p. 611.
65 Ye Yonglie, *Zhang Chunqiao Fuchen Shi*, pp. 122–3.
66 See ibid., pp. 134–7, for the circumstances of Ke's death while visiting Sichuan.
67 Guofang Daxue, *Qishi Nian Jianjie*, pp. 528–9; *Jueyi Zhushiben Xiuding*, p. 373. According to Informant I, Yao pretended to be ill and secluded himself in the Shanghai Workers' Sanatorium to write the attack on Wu Han. Why was Yao bolder than Li Xifan? He was not constrained by being part of the Beijing party and scene. More importantly, according to Informant I, there was a great deal of ignorance in Beijing and Shanghai of what was going on in ideological circles in the other city. In Peng's Beijing, Jiang Qing was a nuisance, but only a minor player on the ideological scene; in Ke's Shanghai, she had to be seen as a far bigger player, an ideologically congenial emissary from the Chairman. Yao may also have been aware that

an article of his published in May 1964 had been well received by Mao; *Jianguo Yilai Mao Zedong Wengao* 11, p. 99.

68 Mao's and Jiang Qing's accounts are quoted in Cong Jin, *Quzhe Fazhande Suiyue*, pp. 610–11. In Feb. 1967, according to an official version, Mao told a foreigner that at the start the operation had been entirely Jiang Qing's doing (*Jueyi Zhushiben Xiuding*, p. 373). But Michael Schoenhals has suggested to me that this may have been a latter-day attempt to ward off suspicions that Mao had promoted so devious a plot. A Cultural Revolution report of Mao's conversation with Albanians on 3 Feb. (minutes of Mao's meetings with foreigners were circulated) shows that Mao was in on the affair from the start; *[Mao Zedong] Xuexi Ziliao, 1962–1967* (Materials [of Mao Zedong] for study, 1962–1967), pp. 287–8.

69 Cong Jin, *Quzhe Fazhande Suiyue*, p. 616, n. 1; Lin Qingshan, *Kang Sheng Waizhuan*, pp. 249–50; Zhong Kan, *Kang Sheng Pingzhuan*, p. 176. In the latter source (p. 387), however, Kang Sheng's discussion with Mao on this topic is placed in May 1965.

70 Cong Jin, *Quzhe Fazhande Suiyue*, p. 613.

71 Mao had suggested to Jiang Qing that Zhou Enlai and Kang Sheng should be informed, but she had demurred, perhaps wanting this to be exclusively her operation; ibid.; Zhong Kan, *Kang Sheng Pingzhuan*, p. 176. According to the account Mao gave to the Albanians, Jiang Qing took the initiative in saying the draft article should not be shown to Zhou or Kang on the grounds that then Liu Shaoqi and Deng Xiaoping would want to see it; *[Mao Zedong] Xuexi Ziliao, 1962–1967*, p. 288.

72 *Origins* II, pp. 234–6.

73 *Zhonggong Dangshi Zhongda Shijian Shushi*, pp. 320–1. The choice of Peng Zhen to conduct this potentially explosive interview points up his role as the executor of major decisions of the Chairman and the secretariat, but it probably also reflected the knowledge that he was very well able to give as good as he got if Peng Dehuai allowed his resentments to get the better of his discipline and discretion.

74 Ibid., pp. 321–2. Zhou Enlai was receiving Prince Sihanouk of Cambodia.

75 Peng Dehuai, *Memoirs of a Chinese Marshal*, p. 521.

76 Jing Xizhen, *Zai Peng Zong Shenbian* (At the side of chief Peng), p. 114; Wang Chuncai, *Peng Dehuai zai San Xian* (Peng Dehuai in the third front), p. 17. The more official versions of this discussion truncate the passage retailed by Peng to his bodyguard (Jing Xizhen); the impression given is that when Mao referred to Peng possibly being right in connection with Lushan, the Chairman was only referring to Peng's reminder that he (Peng) had given three guarantees at that time of which he (Mao) could only remember two; see e.g. 'Dangdai Zhongguo Renwu Zhuanji' Congshu Bianjibu (ed.), *Peng Dehuai Zhuan* (A biography of Peng Dehuai), p. 697. This latter source (p. 696) states that Peng was summoned to the Zhongnanhai by Mao's secretary, which sounds likely, whereas Jing Xizhen (p. 112) remembers the call as coming from Mao personally. Even if Peng misunderstood Mao on Lushan or Jing misremembered, the key point about this meeting is that the Lushan issue was dismissed as being only of historical interest.

This episode recalls Stalin's hypocritical treatment of Bukharin in the uneasy period after the latter's disgrace and demotion but before his trial and execution. In the spring of 1935, at a banquet for graduating military cadets, Stalin suddenly made the toast: 'Let us drink comrades, to Nikolai

Ivanovich [Bukharin], and let bygones be bygones.' Bukharin's widow, who reported this episode long after Stalin's death, believed that he was testing people's attitudes to her husband; if so, Stalin was presumably taken aback by the 'stormy applause' which greeted the toast and embarrassed Bukharin. See Larina, *This I Cannot Forget*, pp. 65–6.

77 *Zhonggong Dangshi Zhongda Shijian Shushi*, pp. 322–3.

78 Mao made this point during the two-day PSC meeting between the July work conference and the CC's 8th plenum held in August; Li Rui, *Lushan Huiyi Shilu*, p. 238.

79 *Huang Kecheng Zishu*, p. 271. In September, Huang, too, was contacted by central officials, in his case at the lower level of Yang Shangkun, head of the CC's General Office, and An Ziwen, head of its Organization Department. He was told that Mao had decided that he should become a deputy governor of Shanxi province. Huang, delighted at the prospect of doing a job again, asked only to stay on in Beijing till after the 1 Oct. National Day holiday period, but was ordered to leave town immediately. Ironically, the following year he met Yang Shangkun by chance in Taiyuan after the latter, too, had been disgraced and exiled from the capital; ibid., p. 273. This work includes a graphic description of the struggle sessions to which Peng and Huang were subjected at and after Lushan; ibid., pp. 248–70.

80 Another example of Peng's leg-work was informing senior colleagues of central decisions regarding their careers; see *Song Renqiong Huiyilu*, p. 361.

81 *Origins* I, p. 146.

82 Teiwes, *Politics at Mao's Court*, pp. 62–71.

83 Some say that Peng Zhen's failure finally to make it into the post-Mao PSC, after the disgrace and deaths of Gao Gang and Lin Biao long before, was due to Chen Yun's black-ball; Informant P. For the problems between Peng and his colleagues in the northeast, see Teiwes, *Politics at Mao's Court*, pp. 39, 124.

84 As secretary-general of the NPC when Liu was its chairman from 1954 to 1959, Peng seems to have made some efforts to breathe life into the formal superior–inferior relationship between that body and the State Council; *Origins* I, pp. 115–16.

85 The most strongly represented provinces were Hunan, the province of Mao and Liu Shaoqi, and Sichuan, the province of Zhu De and Deng Xiaoping.

86 Informant P.

87 Cf. Wu Lengxi, *Yi Mao Zhuxi*, p. 74, for Mao's insistence that the propaganda organs display military-style discipline at the time of the Taiwan Straits crisis of 1958.

88 An example of Peng Zhen's key role in propaganda work was the 1964 national propaganda work conference; it received directives on culture from Mao, Liu, Deng Xiaoping, and Peng; Zhongyang Xuanchuanbu Bangongting (ed.), *Dangde Xuanchuan Gongzuo Huiyi Gaikuang he Wenxian (1951–1992)* (Summaries and documents of the party's propaganda work conferences, 1951–1992), p. 193.

89 Jiang Huaxuan, Zhang Weiping, & Xiao Sheng, *Zhongguo Gongchan Dang Huiyi Gaiyao*, p. 512.

90 *Origins* I, pp. 180–3, 192–6, 202–7, 270–3, 277–8, 289–92.

91 See above, Ch. 7.

92 This is hardly peculiar to China. A version of the ploy in early modern England came to be popularly known as Morton's Fork: at the suggestion

probably of Archbishop Morton, Henry VII's agents raised money for him from the nobility by asserting that those who spent little must have saved and those who spent much must have means; Chrimes, *Henry VII*, p. 203.

93 Probably processing the article through the chief local party organ, *Jiefang Ribao*, would have required too many senior Shanghai officials getting to know about it in advance with the consequent danger of a leak to Beijing.

94 CCP CC Party History Research Centre, *History of the CCP*, p. 318; Cong Jin, *Quzhe Fazhande Suiyue*, pp. 611–12. In October 1966, Mao quoted himself as having asked about revisionism appearing in 'Beijing' rather than in the CC, but presumably whatever he really said, his audience, including Peng Zhen, took him to mean Beijing as the national capital headed by Mao rather than Beijing as a provincial-level city headed by Peng; see Wang Nianyi, *1949–1989 Niande Zhongguo, 3: Da Dongluande Niandai* (China 1949–1989, 3: A decade of great upheaval), p. 113. I am grateful to Michael Schoenhals for making this point to me.

95 Zhonggong Shanxi Shengwei Dangshi Yanjiushi (ed.), *Peng Zhen Shengping Dashi Nianbiao* (A chronology of the major events in Peng Zhen's life), p. 37.

96 Much of the following account is based on Cong Jin, *Quzhe Fazhande Suiyue*, pp. 612–17. Peng Zhen's whereabouts are unclear: appearance rosters compiled by the US government have no listings for Peng from the period. According to a Red Guard paper, Peng received the Soviet ambassador (in Beijing?) on 9 Nov.; *Dongfang Hong*, 12 Oct. 1967. Knowledge that Peng Zhen would be out of Beijing for some time after 10 Nov. may have dictated the timing of the publication of Yao Wenyuan's article. Wu Han returned home on 11 Nov. to the unpleasant shock of finding Yao's article among the pile of newspapers that awaited him; Su Shuangbi & Wang Hongzhi, *Wu Han Zhuan*, p. 315.

97 Ma Qibin *et al.*, *Zhongguo Gongchan Dang Zhizheng Sishinian*, p. 265; Gu Longsheng, *Mao Zedong Jingji Nianpu*, pp. 633–5.

98 Peng's order to the municipal secretariat may have reflected his own ignorance of and lack of interest in purely intellectual matters; he knew that Deng Tuo's judgement would be better than his own.

99 This was also Wu Han's view; Su Shuangbi & Wang Hongzhi, *Wu Han Zhuan*, pp. 315–16.

100 Cong Jin, *Quzhe Fazhande Suiyue*, p. 618. For an earlier example of the *People's Daily* following the lead of *Beijing Ribao* when Peng Zhen was under pressure, see *Origins* I, p. 206.

101 Officially Yang was transferred to Guangdong as a party secretary there, but he never made it to Canton; Liao Gailong *et al.*, *Xin Zhongguo Biannianshi*, p. 267; Cong Jin, *Quzhe Fazhande Suiyue*, p. 635 n. 1. See also above, n. 79.

102 Li, *The Private Life of Chairman Mao*, pp. 433–4; Ma Qibin *et al.*, *Zhongguo Gongchan Dang Zhizheng Sishi Nian*, p. 264. The meeting at which Mao announced Peng Dehuai's new job and Yang's dismissal was stunned only by the latter; Informant V. Wang Dongxing told Dr Li that he had tried in vain to persuade Mao that he should rather appoint Chen Boda or Hu Qiaomu.

103 Li, *The Private Life of Chairman Mao*, pp. 292–3.

104 Ibid., pp. 365–9.

105 *Origins* II, pp. 242–4. Lin's low profile in the early 1960s is attested to by the paucity and brevity of his utterances; see e.g. *Gao Ju Mao Zedong Sixiang Weida Hong Qi* (Raise high the great red banner of Mao Zedong Thought); *Lin Biao Wenxuan* (Selections from Lin Biao), *xia; [Lin Biao Xuanji]* (Selected works of Lin Biao); *Yi Lin Fu Tongshuai wei Guanghui Bangyang Wuxian Zhongyu Weida Lingxiu Mao Zhuxi* (Take vice-c.-in-c. Lin as a glorious model of boundless loyalty to the great leader Chairman Mao). As late as June 1964, Maj.-Gen. Wu Zili, deputy CO of the Canton military region, had been condemned for seeking to popularize one of Peng Dehuai's earliest revolutionary exploits; Peng's old rival, He Long, was put in charge of the investigation; Ma Qibin *et al.*, *Zhongguo Gongchan Dang Zhizheng Sishi Nian*, p. 248.

106 Huang Yao, *San Ci Danan Buside Luo Ruiqing Dajiang*, pp. 199–200.

107 Ma Qibin *et al.*, *Zhongguo Gongchan Dang Zhizheng Sishi Nian*, p. 248; Li, *The Private Life of Chairman Mao*, pp. 97–8, 157–9, 184–6, 435.

108 Ibid., p. 435.

109 Cong Jin, *Quzhe Fazhande Suiyue*, p. 631.

110 Ma Qibin *et al.*, *Zhongguo Gongchan Dang Zhizheng Sishi Nian*, p. 259.

111 Cong Jin, *Quzhe Fazhande Suiyue*, pp. 631–2; this account has several quotations from Luo's remarks.

112 Ibid., pp. 632–3; Li, *The Private Life of Chairman Mao*, pp. 435–6. Ye Qun spent some 7 hours alone with Mao; Huang Yao, *San Ci Danan Buside Luo Ruiqing Dajiang*, p. 282.

113 Li, *The Private Life of Chairman Mao*, p. 185.

114 See above, Ch. 7, p. 169.

115 When he sought to adulterate Lin Biao's power in 1970–1. For Zhou Enlai's bewilderment at the outset of the Cultural Revolution, see Li Ping, *Kaiguo Zongli Zhou Enlai*, p. 457.

116 Cong Jin, *Quzhe Fazhande Suiyue*, pp. 633–4; Ma Qibin *et al.*, *Zhongguo Gongchan Dang Zhizheng Sishi Nian*, p. 265. Lin Biao had earlier seized the occasion of Yang Shangkun's dismissal to sack his PLA equivalent, Gen. Xiao Xiangrong, head of the MAC's general office; Huang Yao, *San Ci Danan Buside Luo Ruiqing Dajiang*, pp. 274–5. This is the most detailed source on the Lin–Luo struggle; see *passim*. For the final indictment of Luo, see *Gao Ju Mao Zedong Sixiang Weida Hong Qi*, pp. 195–203. For a recent Western attempt to unravel the 'unusually difficult' Luo Ruiqing case, see Teiwes and Sun, *The Tragedy of Lin Biao*, pp. 24–32.

117 See below, p. 460.

118 Liu Shufa, *Chen Yi Nianpu*, 2, p. 1137.

119 Cong Jin, *Quzhe Fazhande Suiyue*, p. 618.

120 Ibid., pp. 618–19.

121 Guofang Daxue, *Cankao Ziliao* 24, p. 604.

122 Cong Jin, *Quzhe Fazhande Suiyue*, p. 621; Ge Hengjun, '1966 nian budui gongzuo zuotanhui ji qi huiyi jiyao shulüe' (An account of the 1966 army forum on literature and art work and its summary), *Zhonggong Dangshi Yanjiu*, No. 3, 1996, pp. 54–8.

123 Guofang Daxue, *Cankao Ziliao* 24, pp. 604–10.

124 Ibid., p. 607. This was a 1930s controversy in which Zhou Yang had been on Mao's side.

125 Ibid., p. 610.

126 Su Shuangbi & Wang Hongzhi, *Wu Han Zhuan*, p. 321.

127 *Chinese Studies in History and Philosophy* 2, No. 1, Fall 1968, pp. 44–8, 56–67.
128 Translated in ibid., pp. 68–107. It had appeared in the *Beijing Ribao* on 27 Dec.; Cong Jin, *Quzhe Fazhande Suiyue*, p. 614. Wu Han's second self-criticism appeared on 12 Jan.
129 Between 1949 and his death, Mao visited Hangzhou 39 times; Xiao Xinli, *Xunshi Dajiang Nanbeide Mao Zedong*, p. 436.
130 Hao Mengbi & Duan Haoran, *Zhongguo Gongchan Dang Liushi Nian*, p. 561. For an account of Tian Jiaying's attempt to excise this passage from the record of Mao's remarks, see Ye Yonglie, *Chen Boda Qiren*, pp. 228–30. Posthumously, Tian succeeded. Of Mao's Hangzhou pronouncements on 21–2 Dec., the only ones quoted in *Jianguo Yilai Mao Zedong Wengao* 11 (pp. 492–3) are on education.
131 *Chinese Studies in History and Philosophy* 2, No. 3, Spring 1969, *passim*. See also Ding Wang, *Wu Han yu 'Hai Rui Ba Guan' Shijian* (The affair of Wu Han and 'Hai Rui dismissed from office'), pp. 547–617.
132 Cong Jin, *Quzhe Fazhande Suiyue*, p. 615. For the background of Guan Feng and other 'radical intellectuals' who rose to prominence in the Cultural Revolution, see Goldman, *China's Intellectuals*, pp. 61–88.
133 See Ding Wang, *Wu Han yu 'Hai Rui Ba Guan' Shijian*, pp. 277–546.
134 Su Shuangbi & Wang Hongzhi, *Wu Han Zhuan*, pp. 322–3.
135 Cong Jin, *Quzhe Fazhande Suiyue*, p. 615.
136 Ibid. p. 616; Zhong Kan, *Kang Sheng Pingzhuan*, pp. 177–8; Lin, *Kang Sheng Waizhuan*, pp. 256–7. The full list of 11 attendees was: Peng Zhen, Lu Dingyi, Kang Sheng, Wu Lengxi, Xu Liqun, Hu Sheng, Yao Zhen, Wang Li, Fan Ruoyu, Liu Ren, Guo Tianfan; *Guofang Daxue*, *Cankao Ziliao* 24, p. 611. Of the five-man group, only Zhou Yang was missing.
137 Cong Jin, *Quzhe Fazhande Suiyue*, pp. 615–16.
138 Ibid., p. 616.
139 Zhonggong Zhongyang Wenxian Yanjiushi (ed.), *Zhu De Nianpu* (A chronicle of Zhu De), p. 543.
140 Cong Jin, *Quzhe Fazhande Suiyue*, p. 618.
141 Liu and Zhou were definitely there; Huai En, *Zhou Zongli Shengping Dashiji*, p. 456.
142 This is confirmed in Wu Lengxi, *Yi Mao Zhuxi*, p. 150
143 Ma Qibin *et al.*, *Zhongguo Gongchan Dang Zhizheng Sishi Nian*, p. 268; Zhong Kan, *Kang Sheng Pingzhuan*, p. 178; Lin Qingshan, *Kang Sheng Waizhuan*, pp. 257–8.
144 Wu Lengxi states that when the PSC endorsed the outline, it told the group to go to Wuhan to get Mao's approval and adds 'we flew to Wuhan'; Wu himself was certainly present; Wu Lengxi, *Yi Mao Zhuxi*, pp. 150–1. Other sources indicating that the whole group went include Zhong Kan, *Kang Sheng Pingzhuan*, p. 178; Lin Qingshan, *Kang Sheng Waizhuan*, p. 258; Mu Xin, *Ban 'Guangming Ribao' Zishu*, p. 278. Huang Ping, 'Lian yu chunqiu—Lu Dingyi zai 1966–1978', *Nanfang Zhoumo*, No. 28, Aug. 1992, says only Peng, Lu and Kang went. Cong Jin confirms that Kang Sheng was there; *Quzhe Fazhande Suiyue*, p. 618, n. 1. But other sources just say that Peng went with the deputy head of the five-man group, Lu Dingyi, and one of the crafters of the outline, Xu Liqun; Ma Qibin *et al.*, *Zhongguo Gongchan Dang Zhizheng Sishi Nian*, p. 268; Cong Jin, *Quzhe Fazhande Suiyue*, p. 616; Su Donghai & Fang Kongmu, *Zhonghua Renmin Gongheguo Fengyun Shilu* 1, p. 1035.

145 Wu Lengxi, *Yi Mao Zhuxi*, p. 150.
146 Cong Jin, *Quzhe Fazhande Suiyue*, p. 616; Ma Qibin *et al.*, *Zhongguo Gongchan Dang Zhizheng Sishi Nian*, p. 268.
147 Cong Jin, *Quzhe Fazhande Suiyue*, p. 616; Lin Qingshan, *Kang Sheng Waizhuan*, p. 258.
148 Cong Jin, *Quzhe Fazhande Suiyue*, p. 616 n. 1; Lin Qingshan, *Kang Sheng Waizhuan*, p. 259; Zhong Kan, *Kang Sheng Pingzhuan*, p. 176.
149 Guofang Daxue, *Cankao Ziliao* 24, pp. 611–13.
150 Ibid., p. 612.
151 Ibid., pp. 612–13.
152 The connection between Liu's absence and Peng's purge is pointed out by Huang Jing in 'Factionalism in Chinese Communist Politics', unpublished Ph.D dissertation, Harvard University, 1995.
153 Li Ping, *Kaiguo Zongli Zhou Enlai* (The PRC's founding premier, Zhou Enlai), p. 436; Snow, *China on Stage*, pp. 21, 122–90. For Peng Zhen's March visit to the third front, see Wang Chuncai, *Peng Dehuai zai San Xian* (Peng Dehuai in the third front), pp. 68–9; regrettably, this source, which tells how Peng Dehuai discreetly avoided being photographed with Peng Zhen in order to avoid embarrassing him further in connection with the Hai Rui issue, gives no precise dating of Peng's expedition. My suggestion that Mao attacked Peng Zhen while he was far from Beijing arises from the virtual certainty that, had Peng been in the capital, he too would have been an inevitable participant in an expanded PSC conference.
154 Cong Jin, *Quzhe Fazhande Suiyue*, pp. 623–5.
155 Wang Nianyi, *1949–1989 Niande Zhongguo, 3: Da Dongluande Niandai*, p. 9.
156 Ye Yonglie, *Chen Boda Qiren*, pp. 222–3; the virtually identical passage appears in an article in Yuan Hao & Jian Min (eds.), *Qian Qiu Gong Zui* (Centuries of meritorious deeds and crimes), pp. 17–18.
157 Wang Nianyi, *Da Dongluande Niandai*, p. 10.
158 Ibid., pp. 10–12. For part of Kang Sheng's speech and a later speech by Chen Boda, see *Lin Biao Wenxuan, xia*, pp. 264–72.
159 For Lin's speech see *Mao Zhuxide Qin Mi Zhanyou Lin Biao Tongzhi Yanlunxuan*, pp. 116–32; Wang Nianyi, *Da Dongluande Niandai*, pp. 16–18.
160 Mao expressed his views in a letter to Jiang Qing; *'Wenhua Da Geming' Yanjiu Ziliao* (Research materials on the 'Great Cultural Revolution'), *shang*, pp. 55–6. Mao's orders on security were later revealed by Zhou to Red Guards; *Zhongyang Shouzhang Jianghua* (Central leaders' speeches) I, p. 249. (Michael Schoenhals drew this to my attention.)
161 According to Liu Zhijian who was at the meeting, Lin Biao's note was longer, making four points: Ye Qun was a virgin on marriage and had been faithful since; she had not been involved with the writer Wang Shiwei in Yan'an; Lin Biao and Ye Qun's children were really theirs; everything that Lu Dingyi's wife had alleged was nonsense. See Wang Nianyi, *Da Dongluande Niandai*, p. 18, n. 1.
162 Ibid., pp. 18–19. For a Cultural Revolution elaboration on the accusation, see the article in *Zhan Bao* (Combat news) 18 Jan. 1967, trans. in SCMP(S) 165, p. 12. During the Cultural Revolution, Lu Dingyi was attacked for advocating the study of the Marxist classics, allegedly as a device to prevent the study of Mao's works, but of course the Chairman heartily approved of more study of such works and encouraged Lu in his endeavours; cf. *Lu*

Dingyi fandui Mao Zedong sixiang tuixing xiuzhengzhuyi jiaoyu luxian yanlun zhaibian (A collection of Lu Dingyi's utterances opposing Mao Zedong Thought and promoting the revisionist educational line), p. 3, no. 5, and *Jianguo Yilai Mao Zedong Wengao* 11, pp. 25–8, 56–7.

163 Michael Schoenhals, 'The CCP Central Case Examination Group (1966–1979)', Center for Pacific Asia Studies, Stockholm University, Working Paper 36, Jan. 1995, pp. 5–6. For the text of Zhou's speech, see *Gao Ju Mao Zedong Sixiang Weida Hong Qi* (Raise the great red banner of Mao Zedong's thought), pp. 19–23.

164 Tao Zhu's promotion was viewed by his wife, Zeng Zhi, with grave foreboding; Zhou Ming, *Lishi zai Zheli Chensi—1966–1976 Nian Jishi* (Ponder history here—A record of the years 1966–1976) 3, p. 1.

165 Wang Nianyi, *Da Dongluande Niandai*, p. 19. For Ye Jianying's links to Zhou Enlai, see Klein & Clark, *Biographic Dictionary of Chinese Communism* 2, p. 106.

166 Quoted in Schoenhals, 'The CCP Central Case Examination Group (1966–1979)', p. 5. This organization, now referred to in post-Cultural Revolution Chinese accounts as the 'Central' Case Examination Group, continued to exist until 1979.

167 Lin Zhijian, *Xin Zhongguo Yaoshi Shuping* (Commentary on important events in new China), p. 307.

168 Schoenhals, 'The CCP Central Case Examination Group (1966–1979)', p. 7. Other senior members of the group were Wang Dongxing, clearly Mao's eyes and ears, Xie Fuzhi, the Minister of Public Security, and General Yang Chengwu, the new acting Chief-of-Staff. Deng Xiaoping was the PSC member formally exercising oversight responsibilities until the 11th plenum, when he was replaced by Kang Sheng; ibid., p. 6. But Zhou Enlai chaired all formal meetings; Schoenhals communication.

CHAPTER 20

1 Wang Nianyi, *Da Dongluande Niandai*, p. 28. Interviews conducted in 1994 with Nie Yuanzi and others involved in this episode have produced contradictory accounts, throwing doubt on the centrality of Cao Yiou's role in provoking the poster; I am grateful to Michael Schoenhals for sharing with me the results of his interviews.

2 Ibid., p. 30.

3 Ibid., p. 34; Ma Qibin *et al.*, *Zhongguo Gongchan Dang Zhizheng Sishi Nian*, pp. 272–3; Zhou Ming, *Lishi zai Zheli Chensi—1966–1976 Nian Jishi* 1, p. 3.

4 The connection between the 'swift' Yangtze current and Mao's ability to swim 15 km. in just over an hour—almost four times as fast as the world record for 10 miles—was not specifically underlined by the Chinese media; consequently the president of the World Professional Marathon Swimming Federation invited the Chairman to enter two 10-mile swimming races in Canada. See 'Quarterly Chronicle and Documentation', *CQ*, No. 28, 1966, pp. 149–52.

5 Ma Qibin *et al.*, *Zhongguo Gongchan Dang Zhizheng Sishi Nian*, p. 275; Lin Zhijian, *Xin Zhongguo Yaoshi Shuping*, p. 314.

6 Li Ping, *Kaiguo Zongli Zhou Enlai*, p. 457.

7 It is unclear whether Peng Dehuai and Zhang Wentian formally retained their posts.

8   For a discussion of Mao's motives, see above Ch. 19, n. 8.
9   Lin Zhijian, *Xin Zhongguo Yaoshi Shuping*, p. 319; Ye Yonglie, *Chen Boda Qiren*, p. 264.
10 Wang Nianyi, *Da Dongluande Niandai*, p. 61; Lin Zhijian, *Xin Zhongguo Yaoshi Shuping*, pp. 325–6.
11 Picking off your opponents one by one is, to be sure, a political tactic not limited to former guerrilla leaders; cf. Lawson, *The View from No. 11*, p. 935, for a description of how Margaret Thatcher demoted her Foreign Secretary first before tackling her Chancellor of the Exchequer.
12 See above Ch. 19, n. 14.
13 There are of course other possibilities. Mao may never have intended Deng to fall, but was unable to insulate him from the attacks on 'capitalist roaders', and the general secretary was swept away like so many others. Since Mao was able to protect Zhou Enlai when need be, this seems unlikely. A more likely alternative possibility is that Mao wanted to teach Deng a lesson, with the aim of rehabilitating him, chastened, for leadership in the future, though this would have been a high-risk strategy since, once Mao had signified a colleague was a legitimate target, the Chairman could not be sure of controlling the struggle tactics of the Red Guards. However, this hypothesis is lent credibility by Deng's return to power in the 1970s, and the fact that, of all the senior victims of the Cultural Revolution, Deng alone never had a formal 'Special Case Group' assigned to assessing his crimes, though information was collected on his past; see Michael Schoenhals, 'The CCP Central Case Examination Group (1966–1979)', *CQ*, No. 145, Mar. 1996, pp. 102–5.
14 This was the title of the *People's Daily* editorial published on 2 June 1966, under Chen Boda's aegis; translated in *The Great Socialist Cultural Revolution in China* 3, pp. 7–10.
15 *Decision of the CC of the CCP concerning the Great Proletarian Cultural Revolution*, pp. 3–5.

CONCLUSIONS

1   Described in part 1 of *Origins* I.
2   MacFarquhar, Cheek, & Wu, *The Secret Speeches of Chairman Mao*, pp. 141–2, 172.
3   Mao's hope that his contradictions speech would generate a national era of good feelings and support for the CCP may have reflected his early admiration for the late Qing reformer, Kang Youwei, whose major treatise on governance was entitled *Da Tong Shu* (The book on great harmony), translated in Thompson, *Ta T'ung Shu: The One-World Philosophy of K'ang Yu-wei*. Mao on occasion employed the term *da tong* to mean communism; see Schram, *Mao Tse-tung*, pp. 25, 27; Schram, *The Thought of Mao Tse-tung*, pp. 18, 91, 102.
4   Cf. this description of the overpowering influence of Prime Minister Margaret Thatcher in her heyday by one of her senior ministers: '. . . her influence was deployed much more opportunistically and instinctively than we should have planned. But throughout Whitehall and Westminster her instinct, her thinking, her authority, was almost always present, making itself felt pervasively, tenaciously and effectively. It came gradually to feel as the months went by, as though the Prime Minister was present, unseen

and unspeaking, at almost every meeting. The questions were always being asked, even if unspoken: how will this play at Number 10? What's the best way of getting the Prime Minister on side for that? And so on.' (Howe, *Conflict of Loyalty*, pp. 249–50.)

As the two paragraphs in the text should indicate, a Mao-centred view of the Chinese polity in this period does not necessitate arguing that Mao could order back the waves, only that he was the overpoweringly dominant political actor. Cf. the following comments on the roles of individual leaders in *Foreign Affairs*, Jan.–Feb. 1994: On Stalin, John Lewis Gaddis wrote: 'There was nothing relaxed, or open, or consensual about Josef Stalin's vision of an acceptable international order; and the more we learn about Soviet history now that the Soviet Union itself has become history, the more difficult it is to separate any aspect of it from the baleful and lingering influence of this remarkable but sinister figure. One need hardly accept a great man theory of history to recognize that in the most authoritarian government the world has ever seen, the authoritarian who ran it did make a difference' (p. 144).

Reviewing Thatcher's memoirs, Robin W. Winks remarked: 'Margaret Thatcher, for good or ill, with or without exclamation points and marginalia, proves the historian's contention that individuals do make a difference' (p. 161).

⁵ Lifton, *Revolutionary Immortality: Mao Tse-tung and the Chinese Cultural Revolution*, p. 19.
⁶ In Debray, *Revolution in the Revolution?*, pp. 120–2, there is a similar discussion of how the ardour of revolutionary organizations is undermined *before* the revolution.
⁷ Cf. this comment on Stalin: 'If Stalin's pursuit and exercise of power had been motivated solely by the enjoyment of power for its own sake, he would never have launched out, immediately after he had eliminated the right as well as the left Opposition, on an undertaking so full of risks as his Second Revolution. If he had been a mere hard-headed realist his success in defeating his rivals for the leadership would have been enough, and he would at least have paused to enjoy his victory. But that view of him fails to understand his need to prove to himself, and to win the recognition of those he had defeated, that he was the successor and equal of Lenin.' (Bullock, *Hitler and Stalin*, p. 382.)
Mao's need was to prove to himself and his colleagues that his concept of the revolution was right.
⁸ Lifton, *Revolutionary Immortality*, p. 31.
⁹ For a discussion of the differences between the Anshan and Magnitogorsk systems, see *Origins* II, pp. 306–9.
¹⁰ *Communist China, 1955–1959*, p. 103.
¹¹ Mao had similarly flinched from over-the-top radicalism in 1959; *Origins* II, pp. 136–59.
¹² Mao never formally embraced the Castroite thesis that there had to be a vanguard but it did not have to be the Marxist-Leninist party, but in practice that seemed to be the case during the Red Guard phase of the Cultural Revolution; cf. Debray, *Revolution in the Revolution?*, pp. 96–7.
¹³ *Origins* I, p. 3.
¹⁴ Cf. Margaret Thatcher: 'So far as she was concerned, she really was going to go on and on and on, as she had told a television interviewer she would.

While she was there, she was not going to give up the levers of power . . .'
(Lawson, *The View from No. 11*, p. 871)

15   *Origins* I, pp. 10, 157–9. The quotation is of course from *2 Henry IV*. See also Li, *The Private Life of Chairman Mao*, *passim*. For paranoia, cf. Stalin who, at the height of his power, felt compelled to keep close watch on the defeated Trotsky and his small band of followers, and was not able to rest easy until his order to assassinate his exiled rival had been successfully carried out; Volkogonov, *Trotsky*, pp. 302–488, *passim*.

16   In his memoirs, *Conflict of Loyalty*, Geoffrey Howe, who served in Margaret Thatcher's governments as Chancellor of the Exchequer and Foreign Secretary, explained how he finally came to resign, thus precipitating a party crisis and her fall: 'Margaret Thatcher was beyond argument a great Prime Minister. Her tragedy is that she may be remembered less for the brilliance of her many achievements than for the recklessness with which she later sought to impose her own increasingly uncompromising views. For Margaret Thatcher in her final years, there was no distinction to be drawn between person, government, party and nation. They merged in her mind as one seamless whole. Her interests were axiomatically those of Britain. Any criticism of her was an unpatriotic act. The insistence on the undivided sovereignty of her own opinion dressed up as the nation's sovereignty was her own undoing.' (p. 691)
     With a few obvious substitutions in that passage, one probably has a close reading of how Mao was regarded by many of his colleagues. Sadly for them and China, Liu did not stand up in a CC plenum and echo the last paragraph of Howe's resignation speech in the House of Commons: 'The conflict of loyalty, of loyalty to my Right Hon. friend the Prime Minister—and, after all, in two decades together that instinct is still very real—and of loyalty to what I perceive to be the true interests of the nation, has become all too great. I no longer believe it is possible to resolve that conflict from within this government. That is why I have resigned. In doing so, I have done what I believe to be right for my party and my country. The time has come for others to consider their own response to the tragic conflict of loyalties with which I have myself wrestled for perhaps too long.' (pp. 702–3)

17   For Bukharin's continuing preference for giving Stalin the benefit of the doubt rather than face reality, even on the eve of his arrest, see the gripping account by his widow; Larina, *This I Cannot Forget*, pp. 246–346. Cf. Molotov's devotion to Stalin and his continuing praise of him after his death despite the latter's imprisonment of his wife; Berezhkov, *At Stalin's Side*, pp. 338–42.

18   Liu Binyan's autobiographical *A Higher Kind of Loyalty* recounts how his long devotion to the CCP was gradually eroded as he realized there were more important values than blind obedience.

19   Berezhkov, *At Stalin's Side*, p. 210.

20   MacFarquhar, 'The Chinese Model and the Underdeveloped World', in Welch, *Political Modernization*, pp. 373–82. For the description of the Yan'an comrades as an 'elect group', see Apter & Saich, *Revolutionary Discourse in Mao's Republic*, p. 265.

21   The phrase was regularly used by Margaret Thatcher to describe those among her colleagues who espoused similar ideological views.

22   One should note, too, that earlier criticisms by Mao of Liu included the latter's leftism on land reform in 1947–8 and rightism on the issue of capitalist

'exploitation' in 1949; Teiwes, *Politics at Mao's Court*, p. 41. For Liu's speeches in Tianjin in 1949, which gave rise to the accusation of rightism, together with commentary, see *Dangde Wenxian* (Party documents), No. 5, 1993, pp. 3–23.

23 Within China, even a party official who had been close to Liu Shaoqi like his former private secretary, ideologue Deng Liqun, accepted the change of heir from Liu to Lin Biao with the reflection that one could not run such a country and party without having a strong grip on military as well as political affairs. Quanguo Dangshi Ziliao Zhengji Gorgzuo Huiyi & Jinian Zhongguo Gongchan Dang Liushi Zhounian Xueshu Taolunhui (eds.), *Dangshi Huiyi Baogao Ji*, p. 153. Of course, this post-Cultural Revolution statement may have been a latter-day rationalization of Deng Liqun's desertion of Liu; at least, it is unclear how officials like Deng could have believed that the almost invisible Lin Biao had a strong grip on political affairs. As for Liu, it is ironic that when military ranks were being formally assigned in 1955 as part of a post-Liberation acknowledgement of contributions to the revolution, he, along with Zhou Enlai and Deng Xiaoping, was mooted as a potential marshal; in Liu's case, the justification was presumably his brief spells as a PLA political commissar in the 1940s. But Mao, whom the appointments committee had assigned the rank of supreme marshal (*da yuanshuai*), refused the title with such withering scorn that his civilian colleagues had no option but to follow suit. See *Song Renqiong Huiyilu*, pp. 323–5.

24 See above, Ch. 19.

25 Liu Binyan (*A Higher Kind of Loyalty*, p. 95) has an additional explanation: 'Mao was much cleverer than Stalin. Why kill off your enemies? Crush them under a label, and if that doesn't work, there's the reformatory, and after that, jail. If Mao had killed off all his political opponents, all the landlords and all the rich, then his rallying cry of four years later—"class struggle must be kept in mind, year in and year out, month in and month out, day in and day out"—would have been pointless. And eight years later, during the Cultural Revolution, the Red Guards would have had no targets on which to focus their revolutionary ardor.'

26 Cf. Georges Sorel, 'the goal is nothing; the movement everything'; quoted in Bullock, *Hitler and Stalin*, p. 438.

27 Mao's attitude towards *luan* is discussed in Solomon, *Mao's Revolution and the Chinese Political Culture*, pp. 474–509.

BIBLIOGRAPHY

'A record of the great events in the struggle between the two lines in the field of higher education', *Jiaoxue Pipan* (Pedagogical critique), 20 August 1967, translated in *Chinese Sociology and Anthropology*, Fall–Winter 1969–70, pp. 17–76.

ADIE, W. A. C. 'Chou En-lai on Safari', *CQ*, No. 18, 1964, pp. 174–94.

AGUNG, IDE ANAK AGUNG GDE. *Twenty Years Indonesian Foreign Policy, 1945–1965*. The Hague: Mouton, 1973.

AHN BYUNG-JOON. *Chinese Politics and the Cultural Revolution: Dynamics of Policy Processes*. Seattle: University of Washington Press, 1976.

ALITTO, GUY S. *The Last Confucian: Liang Shu-ming and the Chinese Dilemma of Modernity*. Berkeley: University of California Press, 1979.

ANDORS, STEPHEN. *China's Industrial Revolution: Politics, Planning, and Management, 1949 to the Present*. London: Martin Robertson, 1977.

Anhui Sheng Renmin Zhengfu Bangongting (ed.). *Anhui Sheng Qing* (Information on Anhui province). Hefei: Anhui renmin chubanshe, vol. 1 (1949–83), 1985; vol. 2 (1949–84), 1986.

Anhui Sheng Tongjiju (ed.). *Anhui Sishi Nian* (40 years of Anhui). Beijing: Zhongguo tongji chubanshe, 1989.

APTER, DAVID E. and TONY SAICH. *Revolutionary Discourse in Mao's Republic*. Cambridge, Mass.: Harvard University Press, 1994.

ARBATOV, GEORGI. *The System: An Insider's Life in Soviet Politics*. New York: Times Books, 1993.

BACHMAN, DAVID M. *Chen Yun and the Chinese Political System*. Berkeley: Institute of East Asian Studies, University of California, 1985.

BANISTER, JUDITH. *China's Changing Population*. Stanford: Stanford University Press, 1987.

BAO RUO-WANG (JEAN PASQUALINI) and RUDOLPH CHELMINSKI. *Prisoner of Mao*. London: Deutsch, 1975.

BARMÉ, GEREMIE and JOHN MINFORD (eds.). *Seeds of Fire: Chinese Voices of Conscience*. New York: Noonday Press, 1989.

BARNDS, WILLIAM J. *India, Pakistan, and the Great Powers*. London: Pall Mall Press for Council on Foreign Relations, 1972.

BARNETT, A. DOAK. *Communist China: The Early Years, 1949–1955*. New York: Praeger, 1964.

—— (with a contribution by EZRA VOGEL). *Cadres, Bureaucracy, and Political Power in Communist China*. New York: Columbia University Press, 1967.

BARRY, ALLAN J. 'The Chinese Food Purchases', *CQ*, No. 8, 1961, pp. 20–33.

BARTLETT, BEATRICE S. *Monarchs and Ministers: The Grand Council in Mid-Ch'ing China, 1723–1820*. Berkeley: University of California Press, 1991.

BAUM, RICHARD. *Prelude to Revolution: Mao, the Party, and the Peasant Question, 1962–66*. New York: Columbia University Press, 1975.

—— and FREDERICK C. TEIWES. *Ssu-Ch'ing: The Socialist Education Movement of 1962–1966*. Berkeley: Center for Chinese Studies, University of California, 1968.

BECKER, JASPER. *Hungry Ghosts: China's Secret Famine*. London: John Murray, 1996.

Beijing Shi Lishi Xuehui (ed.). *Wu Han Jinian Wenji* (A collection of articles in memory of Wu Han). Beijing: Beijing chubanshe, 1984.

BEREZHKOV, VALENTIN M. *At Stalin's Side: His Interpreter's Memoirs from the October Revolution to the Fall of the Dictator's Empire.* New York: Birch Lane Press, 1994.

BESCHLOSS, MICHAEL R. *The Crisis Years: Kennedy and Khrushchev, 1960–1963*. New York: Edward Burlingame Books, 1991.

BIAN YANJUN. 'Mao Zedong he 1958 nian "Da yue jin" ' (Mao and the 1958 'GLF'), *Dangde Wenxian* (Party documents), No. 4, 1994, pp. 75–80.

BIBERAJ, ELEZ. *Albania and China: A Study of an Unequal Alliance.* Boulder, Colo.: Westview, 1986.

BIRCH, CYRIL. 'Literature under Communism', *CHOC* 15, pp. 743–812.

BO YIBO. *Bo Yibo Wenxuan (1937–1992)* (Selections from Bo Yibo, 1937–1992). Beijing: Renmin chubanshe, 1992.

—— *Ruogan Zhongda Juece yu Shijiande Huigu* (A review of certain major decisions and incidents). Beijing: Zhonggong zhongyang dangxiao chubanshe, 1, 1991; 2, 1993.

BODDE, DERK. 'The State and Empire of Ch'in', *CHOC* I pp. 21–102.

BRACHER, KARL DIETRICH. *The German Dictatorship: The Origins, Structure and Consequences of National Socialism.* Harmondsworth: Penguin, 1973.

BRAUN, OTTO A. *A Comintern Agent in China.* London: C. Hurst, 1982.

BRECHER, MICHAEL. *India and World Politics: Krishna Menon's View of the World.* New York: Praeger, 1968.

BRZEZINSKI, ZBIGNIEW. *Power and Principle: Memoirs of the National Security Adviser, 1977–1981.* New York: Farrar Straus Giroux, 1983.

Bujinde Sinian (Inexhaustible memories). Beijing: Zhongyang wenxian chubanshe, 1987.

Bulletin of the Cold War International History Project. Washington, DC: Woodrow Wilson International Center for Scholars, Spring 1992– .

BULLOCK, ALAN. *Hitler: A Study in Tyranny.* London: Ochams, 1952.

—— *Hitler and Stalin: Parallel Lives.* London: Fontana Press, 1993.

BURLATSKY, FEDOR. *Mao Tse-tung: An Ideological and Psychological Portrait.* Moscow: Progress Publishers, 1980.

BUTTERFIELD, FOX. *China: Alive in the Bitter Sea.* New York: Times Books, 1982.

BYRON, JOHN and ROBERT PACK. *The Claws of the Dragon Kang Sheng—the Evil Genius Behind Mao—and His Legacy of Terror in People's China.* New York: Simon & Schuster, 1992.

Caizheng Gongzuo Sanshiwu Nian (Thirty-five years of financial work). Beijing: Zhongguo caizheng jingji chubanshe, 1984.

Cambridge History of China (CHOC). Cambridge and New York: Cambridge University Press, 1, 1986 (Denis Twitchett and Michael Loewe, eds.); 3, Pt 1, 1979 (Denis Twitchett, ed.); 14, 1987, 15, 1991 (Roderick MacFarquhar and John K. Fairbank, eds.).

Case of Peng Teh-huai, 1959–1968, The. Hong Kong: Union Research Institute, 1968.

CCP CC Party History Research Centre (ed.). *History of the Chinese Communist Party—A Chronology of Events (1919–1990)*. Beijing: Foreign Languages Press, 1991.

CHAN, ANITA, RICHARD MADSEN, and JONATHAN UNGER. *Chen Village: The Recent History of a Peasant Community in Mao's China*. Berkeley: University of California Press, 1984.

CHANDA, NAYAN. *Brother Enemy: The War after the War*. San Diego, Cal.: Harcourt Brace Jovanovich, 1986.

CHANG, GORDON H. *Friends and Enemies: The United States, China, and the Soviet Union, 1948–1972*. Stanford: Stanford University Press, 1990.

CHANG, JULIAN. 'Propaganda and Perceptions: The Selling of the Soviet Union in the PRC, 1950–1960', unpub. Ph.D thesis, Harvard University, 1995.

CHANG, PARRIS H. *Power and Policy in China*. University Park, Pa.: Pennsylvania State University Press, 1975.

Chang Duan Lu (A record of the long and the short). Beijing: *Renmin Ribao* chubanshe, 1980.

CHANG WANG-SHAN. 'The State Council in Communist China: A Structural and Functional Analysis, 1954–1965', unpub. MA thesis, Columbia University, New York, n.d.

CHAO KUO-CHÜN. *Agrarian Policy of the Chinese Communist Party, 1921–1959*. London: Asia Publishing House, 1960.

CHARMLEY, JOHN. *Churchill: The End of Glory. A Political Biography*. New York: Harcourt Brace, 1993.

Chedi qingsuan Deng Xiaoping fan-dang fan-shehuizhuyi, fan-Mao Zedong sixiangde taotian zuixing (Thoroughly settle accounts for Deng Xiaoping's monstrous anti-party, anti-socialist, anti-Mao Zedong Thought crimes). 'Hongse lianluozhan' cailiaozu, zhongyang tongzhanbu dongfang hong gongshe, 4 Feb. 1967.

Chedi qingsuan jiu zhong xuanbu yanwangdian shenxiang kexue jishu gongzuozhongde hei xian (Thoroughly settle accounts with the black line of the old CC Propaganda Department, Palace of Hell, towards science and technology work). Shoudu keji jie geming zaofanpai pipan Liu, Deng lianluozhan, July 1967.

Chedi qingsuan Zhao Chuangbi fan-dang fan-shehuizhuyi fan-Mao Zedong sixiangde taotian zuixing (Thoroughly settle accounts with Zhao Chuangbi's monstrous anti-party, anti-socialist, anti-Mao Zedong Thought crimes). Di zong hongweibing Chengdu budui gongyuan shi yi zhandoutuan *et al.*, Sept. 1967.

CHEEK, TIMOTHY. *Propaganda and Culture in Mao's China: Deng Tuo and the Intelligentsia*. Oxford: Oxford University Press, forthcoming.

—— 'Deng Tuo: A Chinese Leninist Approach to Journalism', in Hamrin and Cheek (eds.), *China's Establishment Intellectuals*, pp. 92–123.

—— (ed.). 'The Politics of Cultural Reform: Deng Tuo and the Retooling of Chinese Marxism', *Chinese Law and Government*, Winter 1983–4.

—— 'Studying Deng Tuo: The Academic Politician', *Republican China* 15, No. 2, Apr. 1990.

—— 'Textually Speaking', in MacFarquhar, Cheek, and Wu, *The Secret Speeches of Chairman Mao*, pp. 75–103.

CHEN, C. S. (ed.). *Rural People's Communes in Lien-Chiang*. Stanford: Hoover Institution Press, 1969.

CH'EN, JEROME. 'Writers and Artists Confer', *CQ*, No. 4, 1960, pp. 76–81.

CHEN, S. H. 'Multiplicity in Uniformity: Poetry and the Great Leap Forward', *CQ*, No. 3, 1960, pp. 1–15.

CHEN DIANGUO. 'Qunzhongde tie xin ren' (A close friend of the masses), *RMRB*, 22 May 1980, p. 8.

CHEN DUNDE. 'Beidaihe: Mao Zedong ji zhao Ye Fei shangjiang mi tan' (Beidaihe: Mao Zedong urgently summons Gen. Ye Fei for secret talks), *Yan Huang Chun Qiu*, No. 7, 1993, pp. 48–51.

CHEN HUANGMEI (ed.). *Zhou Enlai yu Yishujiamen* (Zhou Enlai and artists). Beijing: Zhongyang wenxian chubanshe, 1992.

CHEN JIAN. 'China's Involvement in the Vietnam War, 1964–69', *CQ*, No. 142, 1995, pp. 356–87.

CHEN MINGXIAN. *Xin Zhongguo Sishiwu Nian Yanjiu* (Research into 45 years of new China). Beijing: Beijing ligong daxue chubanshe, 1994.

CHEN RULONG (ed.). *Zhonghua Renmin Gongheguo Caizheng Dashiji (1949–1985 nian)* (Financial chronology for the PRC, 1949–1985). Beijing: Zhongguo caizheng jingji chubanshe, 1989.

CHEN SHIPING. *Zhongguo Yuanshuai Liu Bocheng* (Liu Bocheng, Chinese marshal). Beijing: Zhonggong zhongyang dangxiao chubanshe, 1992.

CHEN XIULIANG. *Sun Yefang Geming Shengya Liushi Nian* (The sixty-year revolutionary career of Sun Yefang). Shanghai: Zhishi chubanshe, 1984.

Chen Yi Shici Xuanji (Selected poetry of Chen Yi). Beijing: Renmin wenxue chubanshe, 1977.

Chen Yi Tan Hong yu Zhuan (Chen Yi discusses red and expert). Shanghai: Shanghai renmin chubanshe, 1979.

CHEN YIZI. *Zhongguo: Shinian gaige yu bajiu min yun* (China: The reform decade and the '89 democratic movement). Taipei: Lianjing chuban shiye, 1990.

'Chen Yun Tongzhi Guanyu Pingtande Tanhua He Tongxin' Bianji Xiaozu (ed.). *Chen Yun Tongzhi guanyu Pingtande Tanhua he Tongxin* (Comrade Chen Yun's talks and correspondence on Pingtan). Beijing: Zhongguo quyi chubanshe, 1983.

Chen Yun Tongzhi Wengao Xuanbian (1956–1962) (Selections from Comrade Chen Yun's manuscripts, 1956–1962). Beijing: Renmin chubanshe, 1981.

Chen Yun Wenxuan, 1956–1985 (Selections from Chen Yun, 1956–1985). Beijing: Renmin chubanshe, 1986.

'Chen Yun Yu Xin Zhongguo Jingji Jianshe' Bianjizu. *Chen Yun yu Xin Zhongguo Jingji Jianshe* (Chen Yun and new China's economic construction). Beijing: Zhongyang wenxian chubanshe, 1991.

CHENG, J. CHESTER (ed.). *The Politics of the Chinese Red Army*. Stanford: Hoover Institution Press, 1966.

CHENG CHU-YUAN. *Scientific and Engineering Manpower in Communist China, 1949–1963*. Washington, DC: National Science Foundation, 1965.

CHENG HUA. *Zhou Enlai he tade Mishumen* (Zhou Enlai and his secretaries). Beijing: Zhongguo guangbo dianshi chubanshe, 1992.

Cheng Zihua Huiyilu (Memoirs of Cheng Zihua). Beijing: Jiefang jun chubanshe, 1987.

CHI PEN-YU (QI BENYU). 'On the Bourgeois Stand of *Frontline* and the *Peking Daily*', trans. in *The Great Socialist Cultural Revolution (2)*, q.v.

CHIANG CHING (see also JIANG QING). *On the Revolution of Peking Opera*. Beijing: Foreign Languages Press, 1968.

CHOC, see *Cambridge History of China*.

CHRIMES, S. B. *Henry VII*. London: Eyre Methuen, 1972.

'Chronology of the Two-Road Struggle on the Educational Front in the Past 17 Years', *Jiaoyu Geming*, 6 May 1967, translated in JPRS 41,932 (21 July 1967).

CHUNG CHONG-WOOK. *Maoism and Development: The Politics of Industrial Management in China*. Seoul: Seoul National University Press, 1980.

CHUNG HUA-MIN and ARTHUR MILLER. *Madame Mao*. Hong Kong: Union Research Institute, 1968.

'CIA Secret Report on Sino-Vietnamese Reaction to American Tactics in the Vietnam War', *Journal of Contemporary Asia* (Stockholm) 13, No. 2, 1983, pp. 261–71.

CLARK, ALAN. *Diaries*. London: Phoenix, 1994.

Collected Works of Liu Shao-ch'i, 1958–1967. Hong Kong: Union Research Institute, 1968.

Communist China, 1955–1959: Policy Documents with Analysis. Cambridge, Mass.: Harvard University Press, 1962.

COMPTON, BOYD (ed.). *Mao's China: Party Reform Documents, 1942–44*. Seattle: University of Washington Press, 1952.

CONG JIN. *1949–1989 Niande Zhongguo, 2: Quzhe Fazhande Suiyue* (China 1949–1989, 2: Years of tortuous development). Henan: Henan renmin chubanshe, 1989.

CONQUEST, ROBERT. *Russia after Khrushchev*. New York: Praeger, 1965.

—— *Stalin: Breaker of Nations*. New York: Viking, 1991.

Constitution of the People's Republic of China. Beijing: Foreign Languages Press, rev. trans., 1961.

CRAIG, GORDON A. *Germany, 1866–1945*. New York: Oxford University Press, 1980.

CROOK, DAVID and ISABEL. *Revolution in a Chinese Village: Ten Mile Inn*. London: Routledge & Kegan Paul, 1959.

CROOK, ISABEL and DAVID. *The First Years of Yangyi Commune*. London: Routledge & Kegan Paul, 1966.

—— *Mass Movement in a Chinese Village: Ten Mile Inn*. London: Routledge & Kegan Paul, 1979.

[Cuban Missile Crisis] '1962 Cuban Missile Crisis', *Cold War International History Project Bulletin* (Washington, DC), No. 5, Spring 1995, pp. 58 ff.

Da pipan beijing cailiao (Background material on the great criticism). Beijing: Guojia kewei wenhua geming weiyuanhui bangongshi & Shoudu keji jie geming zaofanpai pipan Liu, Deng lianluozhan, July 1967.

DAI QING. *Liang Shuming, Wang Shiwei, Chu Anping* (id.). Nanjing: Jiangsu wenyi chubanshe, 1989.

—— *Wang Shiwei and 'Wild Lilies': Rectification and Purges in the Chinese Communist Party, 1942–1944*. Armonk, NY: M. E. Sharpe, 1994.

DAI ZHIXIAN. *Shan Yu Yu Lai Feng Man Lou* (The mountain rain is about to come; the wind fills the building). Henan: Henan renmin chubanshe, 1990.

DALLIN, ALEXANDER. *Diversity in International Communism: A Documentary Record, 1961–1963*. New York: Columbia University Press, 1963.

'Dangdai Zhongguo' Congshu Bianjibu (ed.). Beijing: Zhongguo shehui kexue chubanshe, 2 vols., 1989. [Under the supervision of this editorial team, specialized editorial groups prepared the following volumes, published in Beijing by the same publisher.]

    Dangdai Zhongguo Hai Jun (Contemporary China's navy), 1987.

    Dangdai Zhongguo Jingji (Contemporary China's economy), 1987.

    Dangdai Zhongguo Junduide Junshi Gongzuo (Contemporary China's armed forces' military work).

    Dangdai Zhongguo Kong Jun (Contemporary China's air force), 1989.

    Dangdai Zhongguo Shangye (Contemporary China's commerce), 2 vols., 1988.

    Dangdai Zhongguo Wai Jiao (Contemporary China's foreign relations), 1987.

    Dangdai Zhongguode Anhui (Contemporary China's Anhui), 2 vols., 1992.

    Dangdai Zhongguode Beijing (Contemporary China's Beijing), 2 vols., 1989.

    Dangdai Zhongguode Fujian (Contemporary China's Fujian), 2 vols., 1991.

    Dangdai Zhongguode Guizhou (Contemporary China's Guizhou), 2 vols., 1989.

    Dangdai Zhongguode Hebei (Contemporary China's Hebei), 2 vols., 1990.

    Dangdai Zhongguode Henan (Contemporary China's Henan), 2 vols., 1990.

    Dangdai Zhongguode Hunan (Contemporary China's Hunan), 2 vols., 1990.

    Dangdai Zhongguode Jiangsu (Contemporary China's Jiangsu), 2 vols., 1989.

    Dangdai Zhongguode Liangshi Gongzuo (Contemporary China's grain work), 1988.

    Dangdai Zhongguode Shandong (Contemporary China's Shandong), 2 vols., 1989.

    Dangdai Zhongguode Sichuan (Contemporary China's Sichuan), 2 vols., 1990.

    Dangdai Zhongguode Zhejiang (Contemporary China's Zhejiang), 2 vols., 1989.

    Kang Mei Yuan Chao Zhanzheng (The resist-America support-Korea war), 1990.

'Dangdai Zhongguo Renwu Zhuanji' Congshu Bianjibu (ed.). *Chen Yi Zhuan* (A biography of Chen Yi). Beijing: Dangdai Zhongguo chubanshe, 1991.

—— *Liu Bocheng Zhuan* (A biography of Liu Bocheng). Beijing: Dangdai Zhongguo chubanshe, 1992.

—— *Peng Dehuai Zhuan* (A biography of Peng Dehuai). Beijing: Dangdai Zhongguo chubanshe, 1993.

'Dangdai Zhongguo Shangye' Bianjibu (ed.). *Zhonghua Renmin Gongheguo Shangye Dashiji (1958–1978)* (A chronology of commerce in the PRC 1958–1978). N.p.: Shangye chubanshe, 1990.

'Dangdai Zhongguode Jiangsu' Weiyuanhui and Jiangsu Sheng Dang'anju (eds.). *Jiangsu Sheng Dashiji, 1949–1985* (A chronology of Jiangsu province, 1949–1985). Jiangsu: Jiangsu renmin chubanshe, 1988.

'Dangdai Zhongguode Jihua Gongzuo' Bangongshi (ed.). *Zhonghua Renmin*

Gongheguo Guomin Jingji he Shehui Fazhan Jihua Dashi Jiyao, 1949–1985 (A summary chronology of the national economic and social development plans of the PRC, 1949–1985). Beijing: *Hongqi* chubanshe, 1987.

'Dangdai Zhongguode Jingji Guanli' Bianjibu (ed.). *Zhonghua Renmin Gongheguo Jingji Guanli Dashiji* (A chronology of economic management in the PRC). Beijing: Zhongguo jingji chubanshe, 1986.

'Dangdai Zhongguode Minzu Gongzuo' Bianjibu (ed.). *Dangdai Zhongguo Minzu Gongzuo Dashiji, 1949–1988* (Chronology of contemporary China's nationalities work, 1949–1988). Beijing: Minzu chubanshe, 1989.

DAVIES. R. W. *The Industrialisation of Soviet Russia, 1. The Socialist Offensive: The Collectivisation of Soviet Agriculture, 1929–1930.* London: Macmillan, 1980.

DE BARY, WM. THEODORE. *Waiting for the Dawn: A Plan for the Prince; Huang Tsung-hsi's* Ming-i-tai-fang lu. New York: Columbia University Press, 1993.

DE MADARIAGA, ISABEL. *Russia in the Age of Catherine the Great.* New Haven: Yale University Press, 1981.

DEBRAY, RÉGIS. *Revolution in the Revolution?* Harmondsworth: Penguin, 1968.

Decision of the Central Committee of the Chinese Communist Party concerning the Great Proletarian Cultural Revolution. Beijing: Foreign Languages Press, 1966.

DENG LIQUN. *Xiang Chen Yun Tongzhi Xuexi Zuo Jingji Gongzuo* (Study Comrade Chen Yun on how to do economic work). Beijing: Zhonggong zhongyang dangxiao chubanshe, 1981.

—— '1961 nian Guangdong nongcun diaochade yizu cailiao' (Materials from the 1961 investigation into Guangdong villages), *Dangdai Zhongguo Shi Yanjiu* (Research on Contemporary Chinese History), No. 1, 1994.

[DENG] MAOMAO. *Deng Xiaoping: Wode Fuqin* (Deng Xiaoping: My father). Beijing: Zhongyang wenxian chubanshe, shang 1993.

Deng Tuo Wenji (The collected works of Deng Tuo). Beijing: Beijing chubanshe, 4 vols., 1986.

'Deng Xiaoping Da Cidian' Bianji Weiyuanhui. *Deng Xiaoping Da Cidian* (A compendium on Deng Xiaoping). Beijing: *Hongqi* chubanshe, 1994.

Deng Xiaoping fan-dang, fan-shehuizhuyi, fan-Mao Zedong sixiangde yanlun zhaibian (Selection of Deng Xiaoping's anti-party, anti-socialist, anti-Mao Zedong Thought utterances). Beijing: Shoudu hongdaihui Zhongguo renmin daxue sanhong jiu Liu [Shaoqi] Deng [Xiaoping] bingtuan diyi zhidui, Apr. 1967.

Deng Xiaoping Wenxuan (1938–1965) (Selections from Deng Xiaoping, 1938–1965). Beijing: Renmin chubanshe, 1989.

Deng Xiaoping Zibai Shu (Deng Xiaoping's confession). N.p.: N.p., n.d.

'Deng Zihui Wenji' Bianji Weiyuanhui. *Deng Zihui Wenji* (Collected works of Deng Zihui). Beijing: Renmin chubanshe, 1996.

'Deng Zihui Zhuan' Bianji Weiyuanhui. *Deng Zihui Zhuan* (A life of Deng Zihui). Beijing: Renmin chubanshe, 1996.

DES FORGES, ALEXANDER. 'Liao Mosha, Three Family Village, and Yao Wenyuan: Ambiguous Relationships with the Party Bureaucracy', unpub. seminar paper, Harvard University, Jan. 1991.

DING WANG (ed.). *Beijing Shi Wenhua Da Geming Yundong* (The Great Cultural Revolution movement in Beijing city). Hong Kong: *Ming Bao* yuekan she, 1970.

DING WANG (ed.). *Deng Tuo Xuanji* (The selected works of Deng Tuo). Hong Kong: *Ming Bao* yuekan she, 1969.

—— *Wu Han yu 'Hai Rui Ba Guan' Shijian* (The affair of Wu Han and 'Hai Rui dismissed from office'). Hong Kong: *Ming Bao* yuekan she, 1969.

'Dingzhou Juan' Bianji Weiyuanhui (ed.). *Zhongguo Guoqing Congshu—Bai Xianshi Jingji Shehui Diaocha: Dingzhou Juan* (China national conditions series—investigation of the economy and society of 100 *xian* cities: Dingzhou volume). Beijing: Zhongguo dabaike quanshu chubanshe, 1991.

DITTMER, LOWELL. *Liu Shao-ch'i and the Chinese Cultural Revolution: The Politics of Mass Criticism.* Berkeley: University of California Press, 1974.

DJILAS, MILOVAN. *The New Class: An Analysis of the Communist System.* New York: Praeger, 1957.

DOMES, JURGEN. *Peng Te-huai: The Man and the Image.* Stanford: Stanford University Press, 1985.

—— *Socialism in the Chinese Countryside.* London: C. Hurst, 1980.

DOMMEN, ARTHUR J. *Conflict in Laos: The Politics of Neutralization.* London: Pall Mall, 1964.

DONG BAOCUN. *Tan Zhenlin Wai Zhuan* (An unofficial biography of Tan Zhenlin). Beijing: Zuojia chubanshe, 1992.

DONG BIAN, TAN DESHAN, and ZENG ZI (eds.). *Mao Zedong he tade Mishu Tian Jiaying* (Mao Zedong and his secretary Tian Jiaying). Beijing: Zhongyang wenxian chubanshe, 1989.

DONNITHORNE, AUDREY. *China's Economic* System. London: Allen & Unwin, 1967.

Dou Pi Gai Tongxun (Struggle, criticism, transformation newsletter). Beijing.

DREYERS, JUNE. 'The PLA and Regionalism in Xinjiang', *The Pacific Review*, No. 1, 1994, pp. 41–55.

DUAN JUNYI *et al.* 'Shaoqi tongzhi, Henan renmin huainian ni' (Comrade Shaoqi, the people of Henan remember you), *RMRB*, 21 May 1980, p. 2.

DUAN YUN. *Caizheng Jinrong Lun Zong* (A summary of finance and monetary theory). Beijing: Caizheng jingji chubanshe, 1984.

ELEGANT, ROBERT S. *Mao's Great Revolution.* London: Weidenfeld & Nicolson, 1971.

ERASMUS, STEPHEN. 'General de Gaulle's Recognition of Peking', *CQ*, No. 18, 1964, pp. 195–200.

ESHERICK, JOSEPH W. *The Origins of the Boxer Uprising.* Berkeley: University of California Press, 1987.

FAINSOD, MERLE. *How Russia is Ruled.* Cambridge, Mass.: Harvard University Press, rev. edn., 1963.

FALIGOT, ROGER and RÉMI KAUFFER. *The Chinese Secret Service.* London: Headline, 1989. (Originally published in French as *Kang Sheng et les services secrets chinois (1927–1987).* Paris: Éditions Robert Laffont, 1987.)

FALL, BERNARD B. *The Two Viet-Nams.* London: Pall Mall, 1963.

FAN HAO. *Mao Zedong he Tade Guwen* (Mao Zedong and his counsellor). Beijing: Renmin chubanshe, 1993.

FAN PING and YE DUZHU (eds.). *Dangde Jianshe Cidian* (A dictionary of party building). Shanghai: Shanghai renmin chubanshe, 1989.

FAN TIANSHUN, LI YONGFENG, and QI JIANMIN (eds.). *Zhonghua Renmin Gongheguo, 2: 1956–1966* (A comprehensive mirror of the history of the PRC, 2: 1956–1966). Beijing: *Hongqi* chubanshe, 1994 [?].

FANG WEIZHONG (ed.). *Zhonghua Renmin Gongheguo Jingji Dashiji (1949–1980)* (A record of the major economic events of the PRC, 1949–1980). Peking: Zhongguo shehui kexue chubanshe, 1984.

Fan-geming xiuzhengzhuyi fenzi Deng Xiaoping fandong yanlun (Reactionary utterances of the counter-revolutionary, revisionist element Deng Xiaoping). Beijing: Beijing daxue wenhua geming weiyuanhui ziliaozu, Oct. 1967.

FEJTO, FRANÇOIS. 'A Maoist in France: Jacques Vergès and *Révolution*', *CQ*, No. 19, 1964, pp. 120–7.

FENG LANRUI. *Lun Zhongguo Laodongli Shichang* (On China's labour market). Beijing: Zhongguo chengshi chubanshe, 1991.

FEST, JOACHIM C. *The Face of the Third Reich*. London: Maurice Temple Smith, 1982.

FIELD, MICHAEL. *The Prevailing Wind: Witness in Indo-China*. London: Methuen, 1965.

Fifty Years of the Chinese People's Liberation Army. Beijing: Foreign Languages Press, 1978.

FISCHER, LOUIS. *The Life of Lenin*. New York: Harper Colophon, 1965.

FISHER, TOM, 'Wu Han: The "Upright Official" as a Model in the Humanities', in Hamrin and Cheek (eds.), *China's Establishment Intellectuals*, pp. 155–84.

FLOYD, DAVID. *Mao against Khrushchev: A Short History of the Sino-Soviet Conflict*. London: Pall Mall, 1964.

FOGEL, JOSHUA A. *Ai Ssu-ch'i's Contribution to the Development of Chinese Marxism*. Cambridge, Mass.: Council on East Asian Studies, Harvard University, 1987.

FOKKEMA, DOUWE. 'Creativity and Politics', *CHOC* 15, pp. 594–615.

FORTUNE, ROBERT. *Three Years' Wanderings in China*. London: Mildmay Books, repr. 1987.

FRIEDMAN, EDWARD, PAUL G. PICKOWICZ, MARK SELDEN, with KAY ANN JOHNSON. *Chinese Village, Socialist State*. New Haven: Yale University Press, 1991.

GALBRAITH, JOHN KENNETH. *Ambassador's Journal: A Personal Account of the Kennedy Years*. Boston: Houghton Mifflin, 1969.

GAMBLE, SIDNEY D. *Ting Hsien: A North China Rural Community*. Stanford: Stanford University Press, 1968.

GANSU SHENG TONGJIJU (ed.). *Gansu Sishi Nian* (40 years of Gansu). N.p.: Zhongguo tongji chubanshe, 1989.

GAO JINGZHENG (ed.). *Pingfan yu Weida: Mao Zedong Zhongnanhai Yiwu Yishi* (The greatness out of the ordinary: Photographic album of Mao Tse-tung's Zhongnanhai memorabilia). Beijing: Xiyuan chubanshe, 1993.

Gao Ju Mao Zedong Sixiang Weida Hong Qi (Raise high the great red banner of Mao Zedong Thought [Lin Biao selections]). N.p.: N.p., 1966.

GAO KAI and XIONG GUANGJIA (eds.). *Xin Zhongguode Licheng (1 Oct. 1949–1 Oct. 1989)* (The course of new China, 1 Oct. 1949–1 Oct. 1989). Beijing: Zhongguo renmin daxue chubanshe, 1989.

GAO SHU, XING BIN, WANG QIAN, and YANG QING (eds.). *Lishi Juren Mao Zedong* (A giant of history, Mao Zedong). Beijing: Zhongguo renmin daxue chubanshe, 3 vols., 1993.

GAO XIN and HE PIN. *Gao Gan Dang'an: Zhonggong Quangui Guanxi Shi Dian*

(Dossiers on high-ranking cadres: A factual dictionary of the relationships of VIPs in the CCP). Taipei: Xin xinwen wenhua shiye, 1993.

GARVER, JOHN W. *Foreign Relations of the People's Republic of China*. Englewood Cliffs, NJ: Prentice Hall, 1993.

GAUHAR, ALTAF. *Ayub Khan: Pakistan's First Military Ruler*. Lahore: Sang-e-Meel Publications, 1993.

GE HENGJUN. '1966 nian budui gongzuo zuotanhui ji qi huiyi jiyao shulüe' (An account of the 1966 army forum on literature and art work and its summary), *Zhonggong Dangshi Yanjiu* (Research into CCP party history), No. 3, 1966, pp. 54–8.

GELB, LESLIE H., with RICHARD K. BETTS. *The Irony of Vietnam: The System Worked*. Washington, DC: Brookings Institution, 1979.

Geng Biao Huiyilu (The memoirs of Geng Biao). Beijing: Jiefang jun chubanshe, 1991.

GENG SHENG. 'We must definitely seek truth from facts' *Xinwen Yanjiu Ziliao* (Material for research on the press), No. 3, 1980.

GEORGE, T. J. S. *Krishna Menon*. London: Jonathan Cape, 1964.

GIBSON, RICHARD. 'Comment on "A Maoist in France: Jacques Vergès and *Révolution*" ', *CQ*, No. 21, 1965, pp. 179–82.

GITTINGS, JOHN. 'The "Learn from the Army" Campaign', *CQ*, No. 18, 1964, pp. 153–9.

—— *The Role of the Chinese Army*. London: Oxford University Press for the Royal Institute of International Affairs, 1967.

—— *Survey of the Sino-Soviet Dispute: A Commentary and Extracts from the Recent Polemics, 1963–1967*. London: Oxford University Press for the Royal Institute of International Affairs, 1968.

GOLDMAN, MERLE. *China's Intellectuals: Advise and Dissent*. Cambridge, Mass.: Harvard University Press, 1981.

—— *Literary Dissent in Communist China*. Cambridge, Mass.: Harvard University Press, 1967.

GOLDSTEIN, AVERY. *From Bandwagon to Balance-of-Power Politics: Structural Constraints and Politics in China, 1949–1978*. Stanford: Stanford University Press, 1991.

GONG GUZHONG, TANG ZHENNAN, and XIA YUANSHENG. *Mao Zedong Hui Hunan Jishi, 1953–1975* (A record of Mao Zedong's returns to Hunan, 1953–1975). Changsha: Hunan chubanshe, 1993.

GONG YUZHI. *Cong Mao Zedong dao Deng Xiaoping* (From Mao Zedong to Deng Xiaoping). Beijing: Zhonggong dangshi chubanshe, 1994.

—— PANG XIANZHI, and SHI ZHONGQUAN (eds.). *Mao Zedongde Dushu Shenghuo* (Mao Zedong's life of learning). Beijing: Shenghuo, dushu, xinzhi sanlian shudian, 1986.

—— and SHI ZHONGQUAN. *Deng Xiaoping Jianshe You Zhongguo Tese Shehuizhuyi Lilun Xinlun Dagang* (A new outline of Deng Xiaoping's theory of constructing socialism with Chinese characteristics). Shanghai: Shanghai cishu chubanshe, 1994.

—— —— 'Shidaide zhongtuo, lishide xuanze' (The great trust of the epoch, the choice of history), *Xinhua Wenzhai* (New China digest), No. 10, 1994, pp. 1–5.

GOODWIN, RICHARD N. *Remembering America: A Voice from the Sixties*. Boston: Little, Brown, 1988.

GOPAL, SARVEPALLI. *Jawaharlal Nehru: A Biography, 3: 1956–1964.* London: Jonathan Cape, 1984.

Great Socialist Cultural Revolution in China, The. Beijing: Foreign Languages Press, 1, 2, 3, 1966.

GRIFFITH, WILLIAM E. *Albania and the Sino-Soviet Rift.* Cambridge, Mass.: MIT Press, 1963.

—— *Sino-Soviet Relations, 1964–1965.* Cambridge, Mass.: MIT Press, 1967.

—— *The Sino-Soviet Rift.* London: Allen & Unwin, 1964.

GU HUA. *A Small Town Called Hibiscus.* Beijing: Panda Books, 1983.

GU LONGSHENG (ed.). *Mao Zedong Jingji Nianpu* (A chronology of Mao Zedong and economics). Beijing: Zhonggong zhongyang dangxiao chubanshe, 1993.

GU XING and CHENG MEI. *Deng Tuo Zhuan* (A biography of Deng Tuo). Taiyuan: Shanxi jiaoyu chubanshe, 1991.

Guangdong Geming Lishi Bowuguan (ed.). *Huangpu Jun Xiao Shi Liao* (Historical materials on the Whampoa Military Academy). Guangdong: Guangdong renmin chubanshe, 1982.

Guangdong Sheng Gaodeng Yuanxiao 'Zhongguo Gongchan Dang Jian Shi Jiangyi' Bianjizu (ed.). *Zhongguo Gongchan Dang Jian Shi Jiangyi* (Teaching materials for a short history of the CCP). Canton(?): Guangdong renmin chubanshe, 1985.

'Guanghuide Sanshi Nian' Bianjibu (ed.). *Guanghuide Sanshi Nian, 1955–1985* (A glorious thirty years, 1955–1985). Urumqi: Xinjiang renmin chubanshe, 1986.

GUILLERMAZ, JACQUES. *A History of the Chinese Communist Party, 1921–1949.* London: Methuen, 1972.

GUISSO, R. W. L., CATHERINE PAGANI, and DAVID MILLER. *The First Emperor of China.* Toronto: Birch Lane Press, 1989.

Guizhou Sheng Zhi: Dashiji, 1949–1985 (Zhengqiu yijian gao) (Guizhou provincial gazeteer: chronology, 1949–1985 [MS circulated for comment]). N.p.: Guizhou difang zhi bianzuan weiyuanhui, 1989.

GUO JIANRONG (ed.). *Zhongguo Kexue Jishu Jishi (1949–1989)* (The chronicle of China's science and technology, 1949–1989). Beijing: Renmin chubanshe, 1990.

GUO MING. *Zhong Yue Guanxi Yanbian Sishi Nian* (Forty years of evolution in Sino-Vietnamese relations). Nanning: Guangxi renmin chubanshe, 1992.

GUO MORUO. *Five Historical Plays.* Beijing: Foreign Languages Press, 1984.

GUO SIMIN and TIAN YU (eds.). *Wo Yanzhongde Liu Shaoqi* (Liu Shaoqi as I saw him). Shijiazhuang: Hebei renmin chubanshe, 1992.

—— *Wo Yanzhongde Zhu De* (Zhu De as I saw him). Shijiazhuang: Hebei renmin chubanshe, 1992.

Guofang Daxue Dangshi Dangjian Zhengzhi Gongzuo Jiaoyanshi. *Zhongguo Gongchan Dang Qishi Nian Dashi Jianjie* (A summary of the principal events in the 70 years of the CCP). Beijing: Guofang daxue chubanshe, 4th enlarged ed. 1991. [An earlier edition covering the first 60 years of the CCP was issued in 1985.]

Guofangbu Qingbaoju [RoC] (ed.). *Fangong Youjidui Tuji Fujian Lianjiang Luhuo Feifang Wenjian Huibian* (Collection of bandit documents captured by anti-communist guerrillas in a raid on Lianjiang, Fujian). Taipei: Guofangbu qingbaoju, 1964.

Guojia Jingji Weiyuanhui Jingji Faguiju and Beijing Zhengfa Xueyuan Jingjifa Minfa Jiaoyanshi (eds.). *Zhonghua Renmin Gongheguo Gongye Qiye Fagui*

Xuanbian (A selection of the PRC's laws and regulations on industrial enterprises). Beijing: Falü chubanshe, 1981.

Guojia Tongjiju Conghesi (ed.). *Quanguo Gesheng, Zizhiqu, Zhixiashi Lishi Tongji Ziliao Huibian (1949–1989)* (Compendium of historical statistical materials for the nation's provinces, autonomous regions, and cities directly under the central government, 1949–1989). Beijing: Zhongguo tongji chubanshe, 1990.

Guojia Tongjiju Maoyi Wujia Tongjisi (ed.). *Zhongguo Maoyi Wujia Tongji Ziliao (1952–1983)* (Statistical material on China's commercial commodity prices, 1952–1983). Beijing: Zhongguo tongji chubanshe, 1984.

HALLIDAY, JON (ed.). *The Artful Albanian: The Memoirs of Enver Hoxha*. London: Chatto & Windus, 1986.

HALPERN, NINA P. 'Economic Specialists and the Making of Chinese Economic Policy, 1955–1983', unpub. Ph.D thesis, University of Michigan, 1985.

HAMRIN, CAROL LEE. 'Alternatives within Chinese Marxism 1955–1965: Yang Hsien-chen's Theory of Dialectics', unpub. Ph.D thesis, University of Wisconsin, 1975.

—— 'Yang Xianzhen: Upholding Orthodox Leninist Theory', in Hamrin and Cheek (eds.), *China's Establishment Intellectuals*, pp. 51–91.

—— 'Yang Xianzhen's Philosophic "Criminal Case" ', *Chinese Law & Government*, Spring–Summer 1991.

—— and TIMOTHY CHEEK (eds.). *China's Establishment Intellectuals*. Armonk, NY: M. E. Sharpe, 1986.

HAN GANG. '60 niandai qianqi dangnei guanyu shehuizhuyi wentide xin renshi' (New comprehension of problems of socialism within the party in the early 1960s), in Quanguo Zhonggong Dangshi yanjiuhui (ed.), *Zhongguo Shehuizhuyi Jianshe he Gaige Zhuanti Jiangzuo*.

HAN SUYIN. *Eldest Son: Zhou Enlai and the Making of Modern China, 1898–1976*. New York: Kodansha International, 1995.

—— *My House has Two Doors*. London: Jonathan Cape, 1980.

HAO MENGBI and DUAN HAORAN (eds.). *Zhongguo Gongchan Dang Liushi Nian* (Sixty years of the CCP). Beijing: Jiefang jun chubanshe, 2 vols., 1984.

HAO PING. 'Reassessing the Starting Point of the Cultural Revolution', *China International Review* (Hawaii), No. 1, Spring 1966, pp. 66–86.

HAO WEIMIN (ed.). *Nei Menggu Zizhiqu Shi* (A history of the Inner Mongolian Autonomous Region). Huhehot(?): Nei Menggu daxue chubanshe, 1991.

HARDING, HARRY. 'The Chinese State in Crisis', *CHOC* 15, pp. 107–217.

—— *Organizing China: The Problem of Bureaucracy, 1949–1976*. Stanford: Stanford University Press, 1981.

—— and MELVIN GURTOV. *The Purge of Lo Jui-ch'ing: The Politics of Chinese Strategic Planning*. Santa Monica, Cal.: Rand report R-548-PR, 1971.

HARRISON, JAMES PINCKNEY. *The Long March To Power: A History of the Chinese Communist Party, 1921–1972*. London: Macmillan, 1973.

HARTFORD, KATHLEEN and STEVEN M. GOLDSTEIN (eds.). *Single Sparks: China's Rural Revolutions*. Armonk, NY: M. E. Sharpe, 1989.

HE LIYI, with CLAIRE ANNE CHIK. *Mr. China's Son: A Villager's Life*. Boulder, Col.: Westview, 1993.

HE PIN. *Zhongguo Zhangquanzhe: Dalu Juan 1994 Nianban* (China's power-holders: Mainland volume, 1994 edition). Taibei: Yunhao chubanshe, 2 vols., 1994.

HENAN SHENG TONGJIJU (ed.). *Henan Jingji Tongji Nianjian, 1989* (Henan year-book of economic statistics, 1989). Zhengzhou: Zhongguo tongji chubanshe, 1989.

Hengdao Lima Peng Jiangjun (Gallant General Peng). Beijing: Renmin chuban-she, 1979.

HILSMAN, ROGER. *To Move a Nation.* New York: Delta, 1968.

HINTON, HAROLD C. *Communist China in World Politics.* Boston: Houghton Mifflin, 1966.

HINTON, WILLIAM. *Fanshen: A Documentary of Revolution in a Chinese Village.* New York: Monthly Review Press, 1966.

—— *Shenfan: The Continuing Revolution in a Chinese Village.* New York: Vin-tage, 1984.

Home News Library, Xinhua News Agency. *China's Foreign Relations: A Chronology of Events (1949–1989).* Beijing: Foreign Languages Press, 1989.

HONEY, P. J. (ed.). *North Vietnam Today: Profile of a Communist Satellite.* New York: Praeger, 1962.

Hong Chenghua and Guo Xiuzhi (eds.). *Zhonghua Renmin Gongheguo Zhengzhi Tizhi Yange Dashiji (1949–1978)* (A chronology of the major events in the evolution of the political system of the PRC). Beijing: Chunqiu chuban-she, 1987.

Hong Qi Piaopiao (Red flags fluttering). Beijing: Zhongguo qingnian chuban-she, No. 20, 1980.

HOSKING, GEOFFREY. *A History of the Soviet Union, 1917–1991.* London: Fontana, final edn. 1992.

HOWE, GEOFFREY. *Conflict of Loyalty.* London: Macmillan, 1994.

HOXHA, ENVER. *Reflections on China.* Tirana: 8 Nentori, 2 vols., 1979.

HSIAO CH'IEN. *Traveller Without a Map.* Stanford: Stanford University Press, 1993.

HSU KAI-YU (ed.). *Literature of the People's Republic of China.* Bloomington: Indiana University Press, 1980.

HU HUA (ed.). *Zhongguo Shehuizhuyi Geming he Jianshe Shi Jiangyi* (Teaching materials on the history of China's socialist revolution and construction). Bei-jing: Zhongguo renmin daxue chubanshe, 1985.

HU JIAMO. *Peng Dehuai Pingzhuan* (A critical biography of Peng Dehuai). Zhengzhou (?): Henan renmin chubanshe, 1989.

Hu Qiaomu Wenji (Collected writings of Hu Qiaomu). Beijing: Renmin chuban-she, 1, 1992, 2, 1993, 3, 1994

HU QINGYUN. 'Zhong-Yin bianjie zhanzheng' (The China–India border war), *Dangshi Yanjiu Ziliao* (Materials on party history) (Zhongguo Geming Lishi Bowuguan Dangshi Yanjiushi), No. 11, 1990.

HU SHENG. 'Hu Qiaomu he dangshi gongzuo' (Hu Qiaomu and party history work). *Zhonggong Dangshi Yanjiu*, No. 1, 1994, pp. 72–6.

—— and Zhonggong Zhongyang Dangshi Yanjiushi (eds.). *Zhongguo Gongchan Dangde Qishi Nian* (The seventy years of the CCP). Beijing: Zhonggong dangshi chubanshe, 1991.

HUA JUNWU. *Chinese Satire and Humour: Selected Cartoons of Hua Junwu (1955–1982).* Beijing: New World Press, 1984.

HUA LIN (ed.). *Mao Zedong he tade Zhanyoumen* (Mao Zedong and his comrades-in-arms). Beijing: Hualing chubanshe, 1990.

HUAI EN. *Zhou Zongli Shengping Dashiji* (A chronology of Premier Zhou's life). Chengdu: Sichuan renmin chubanshe, 1986.

Huaibin Xian Zhi Bangongshi (ed.). *Huaibin Xian Zhi, 1951–1983* (Huaibin county gazeteer, 1951–1983). N.p.: Henan renmin chubanshe, 1986.

Huainian Liu Shaoqi Tongzhi (Remember Comrade Liu Shaoqi). Changsha: Hunan renmin chubanshe, 1980.

Huainian Mao Zedong Tongzhi (Remember Comrade Mao Zedong). Beijing: Renmin wenxue chubanshe, 1980.

'Huainian Zhou Enlai' Bianji Xiaozu. *Huainian Zhou Enlai* (Remember Zhou Enlai). Beijing: Renmin chubanshe, 1986.

Huang Daoxia, Dai Zhou, Yu Zhan, and Zhonggong Zhongyang Xuanchuanbu Xuanchuanju (eds.). *Zhonghua Renmin Gongheguo 40 Nian Dashiji (1949–1989)* (A chronology of 40 years of the PRC, 1949–1989). Beijing: *Guangming Ribao* chubanshe, 1989.

HUANG JING. 'Factionalism in Chinese Communist Politics', unpub. Ph.D thesis, Harvard University, 1995.

Huang Kecheng Zishu (Huang Kecheng's autobiography). Beijing: Renmin chubanshe, 1994.

HUANG PING. 'Lian yu chunqiu—Lu Dingyi zai 1966–1978', (On spring and autumn—Lu Dingyi in 1966–1978). *Nanfang Zhoumo* (Southern weekend), No. 28, Aug. 1992.

HUANG YAO. *San Ci Danan Buside Luo Ruiqing Dajiang* (General Luo Ruiqing who survived three disasters). Beijing: Zhonggong dangshi chubanshe, 1994.

HUANG YUCHONG. *Yi Dai Tian Jiao—Xin Zhongguo Kong Jun Shi Zhan Lu* (A generation of talented [airmen]—A record of new China's air force in combat). Beijing: Zhonggong zhongyang dangxiao chubanshe, 1992.

HUANG ZHENG. *Liu Shaoqi Yi Sheng* (A life of Liu Shaoqi). Beijing: Zhongyang wenxian chubanshe, 1995.

Hubei Sheng Difang Zhi Bianzuan Weiyuanhui (ed.). *Hubei Sheng Zhi: Dashiji* (Hubei provincial gazeteer: chronology). N.p.: Hubei renmin chubanshe, 1990.

HUCKER, CHARLES O. *China's Imperial Past*. Stanford: Stanford University Press, 1975.

HUDSON, G. F., RICHARD LOWENTHAL, and RODERICK MACFARQUHAR (eds.). *The Sino-Soviet Dispute*. New York: Praeger, 1961.

India, Government of, Ministry of External Affairs. *White Papers: Notes, Memoranda and Letters Exchanged between the Governments of India and China, No. VI, November 1961–July 1962; No. VII, July 1962–October 1962*. Delhi: Government of India Press, 1962.

Institute for International Relations (ed.). *Chinese Communist Who's Who*. Taipei: Institute for International Relations, 2 vols., 1970 and 1971.

International Wheat Council. 'Trade Arrangements Involving Wheat', Secretariat Paper, No. 2, Dec. 1961.

—— 'Trade Arrangements Involving Wheat: 1962/63–1965/66', Secretariat Paper, No. 7, Mar. 1967.

JI XIN'GE, XIONG XIANGHUI, ZHAO WEI, GUO SIMIN, and TIAN YU. *Wo Yanzhongde Zhou Enlai* (The Zhou Enlai I saw). Shijiazhuang: Hebei renmin chubanshe, 1993.

JIA SINAN (ed.). *1915–1976: Mao Zedong Renji Jiaowang Shilu* (1915–1976:

Records of Mao Zedong's interpersonal contacts). Nanjing: Jiangsu wenyi chubanshe, 1989.

JIA WENPING. *Zhenli yu Mingyun: Hu Kaiming Zhuanlüe* (Truth and destiny: A biographical sketch of Hu Kaiming). Beijing: Renmin chubanshe, 1995.

JIANG BO and LI QING (eds.). *Lin Biao 1959 nian yihou* (Lin Biao after 1959). Chengdu: Sichuan renmin chubanshe, 1993.

JIANG BOYING. *Deng Zihui Zhuan* (A biography of Deng Zihui). Shanghai: Shanghai renmin chubanshe, 1986.

JIANG HUAXUAN, ZHANG WEIPING, and XIAO SHENG (eds.). *Zhongguo Gongchan Dang Huiyi Gaiyao* (Essentials of CCP meetings). Shenyang: Shenyang chubanshe, 1991.

JIANG KUNCHI. '60 niandai Zeng Xisheng zai Anhui tuixing zeren tian shimo' (The record of Zeng Xisheng's management of responsibility fields in Anhui in the 1960s), *Dangdai Zhongguo Shi Yanjiu* (Research on the history of contemporary China), No. 1, 1994, pp. 56–61.

JIANG QING (see also CHIANG CHING). *Jiang Qing Tongzhi Lun Wenyi* (Comrade Jiang Qing on literature and art). N.p.: n.p., 1968, Taipei reproduction, 1977.

JIANGBIAN JIACUO. *Banchan Dashi* (Master Panchen). Beijing: Dongfang chubanshe, 1989.

Jianguo Yilai Gongshang Shuishou Dashiji (A chronology of industrial and commercial tax revenues since the founding of the state). Beijing: Zhongguo caizheng jingji chubanshe, 1983.

Jianguo Yilai Mao Zedong Wengao (Manuscripts of Mao Zedong since the founding of the state). Beijing: Zhongyang wenxian chubanshe, 1 (1949–50), 1987; 2 (1951), 1988; 3 (1952), 1989; 4 (1953–4), 1990; 5 (1955), 1991; 6 (1956–7), 7 (1958), 1992; 8 (1959), 1993; 9 (1960–1), 10 (1962–3), 11 (1964–5), 1996.

Jiaoxue Pipan (Pedagogical critique), see 'A record . . .'

Jiaoyu Geming (Educational revolution), see 'Chronology of the two-road struggle . . .'

JIN CHUNMING. *Jianguohou Sanshisan Nian* (The thirty-three years after the founding of the state). Shanghai: Shanghai renmin chubanshe, 1987.

—— ' "Wenge" qiyin: zhong shuo fenyun' (The reasons for the Cultural Revolution: Opinions vary), *Dangshi Wenhui* (Collected writings on party history) (Taiyuan), No. 3, 1995, pp. 2–7.

JIN YE (ed.). *Huiyi Tan Zhenlin* (Remember Tan Zhenlin). Hangzhou: Zhejiang renmin chubanshe, 1992.

JIN ZHENLIN. *Mao Anying* (id.). Beijing: Renmin chubanshe, 1993.

Jin-Cha-Ji Ribao Shi Yanjiuhui (ed.). *Renmin Xinwenjia Deng Tuo* (A journalist of the people, Deng Tuo). Beijing: Renmin chubanshe, 1987.

JING XIZHEN. *Zai Peng Zong Shenbian* (At the side of chief Peng). Chengdu: Sichuan renmin chubanshe, 1982.

Jing'aide Zhou Zongli Women Yongyuan Huainian Ni (Beloved Premier Zhou, we will always remember you). Beijing: Renmin chubanshe, vol. 3, 1977.

Jingxin dongpode 'gongting zhengbian' yinmou (A soul-stirring plot for a 'palace coup'). Beijing: Chedi cuihui jiu Beijing shiwei zhandou bingtuan, July 1967. [Included in Center for Chinese Research Materials, Red Guard Publications, Supplementary Vol. IV, pp. 1760–74.]

Jiti he Geti Shangye Wenjian Xuanbian (Selected documents on collective and individual commerce). Beijing: Zhongguo shangye chubanshe, 1981.

Joint Economic Committee, Congress of the United Sta es. *Chinese Economy Post-Mao*. Washington, DC: US Government Printing Office, 1978.

JOSEPH, WILLIAM A., CHRISTINE P. W. WONG, and DAVID ZWEIG (eds.). *New Perspectives on the Cultural Revolution*. Cambridge, Mass.: Council on East Asian Studies, Harvard University, 1991.

Junshi Kexue Yuan Junshi Lishi Yanjiubu (ed.). *Zhongguo Renmin Jiefang Jun Liushi Nian Dashiji (1927–1987)* (A chronology of 60 years of the Chinese PLAF 1927–1987). Beijing: Junshi kexue chubanshe, 1988.

KAISER, ROBERT G. *Russia: The People and the Power*. New York: Pocket Books, 1976.

KANG SHI'EN. 'Ji Shaoqi tongzhi guancha Daqing youtian' (Remembering Comrade Shaoqi inspecting the Daqing oilfield), *Dangde Wenxian* (Party documents), No. 5, 1993, pp. 24–6.

KARNOW, STANLEY. *Mao and China: From Revolution to Revolution*. London: Macmillan, 1972.

KAROL, K. S. *China: The Other Communism*. London: Heinemann, 1967.

KE AI. *Liu Shaoqi*. Ji'nan: Shandong renmin chubanshe, 1984.

KEARNS, DORIS. *Lyndon Johnson and the American Dream*. New York: Harper & Row, 1976.

Keda Hongweibing: 1, Kexue geming zhuanji (Science and Technology University Red Guard: 1, Special issue on science revolution), No. 2, 1968.

Keji Geming (Science and technology revolution), No. 1, 1967.

Keyan Pipan (Scientific research criticism), No. 2, 1968.

KHONG YUEN FOONG. *Analogies at War: Korea, Munich, Dien Bien Phu, and the Vietnam Decisions of 1965*. Princeton, NJ: Princeton University Press, 1992.

KHRUSHCHEV, N. *Khrushchev Remembers*. London: Andre Deutsch, 1971.

—— *Khrushchev Remembers: The Last Testament*. New York: Bantam Books, 1976.

KHRUSHCHEV, SERGEI. *Khrushchev on Khrushchev: An Inside Account of the Man and his Era*. Boston: Little, Brown, 1990.

KLEIN, DONALD and ANNE B. CLARK. *Biographic Dictionary of Chinese Communism, 1921–1965*. Cambridge, Mass.: Harvard University Press, 2 vols., 1971.

KLOCHKO, MIKHAIL A. *Soviet Scientist in Red China*. Montreal: International Publishers' Representatives, 1964.

Kong Jun Silingbu Bianyanshi (ed.). *Kong Jun Shi* (A history of the air force). Beijing: Jiefang jun chubanshe, 1989.

KORNAI, JANOS. *The Road to a Free Economy. Shifting from a Socialist System: The Example of Hungary*. New York: Norton, 1990.

KUHN, PHILIP A. *Rebellion and its Enemies in Late Imperial China: Militarization and Social Structure, 1796–1864*. Cambridge, Mass.: Council on East Asian Studies, Harvard University, 1980.

KUO, WARREN. *A Comprehensive Glossary of Chinese Communist Terminology*. Taipei: Institute of International Relations, National Chengchi University, 1978.

KYLE, KEITH. *Suez*. New York: St Martin's Press, 1991. London: Weidenfeld and Nicolson, 1991.

LACOUTURE, JEAN. *De Gaulle: The Ruler, 1945–1970*. New York: Norton, 1993.

LALL, ARTHUR. *How Communist China Negotiates*. New York: Columbia University Press, 1968.

LARDY, NICHOLAS R. *Agriculture in China's Modern Economic Development*. Cambridge: Cambridge University Press, 1983.

—— 'The Chinese Economy Under Stress, 1958–1965', *CHOC* 14, pp. 360–97.

—— and KENNETH LIEBERTHAL. *Chen Yun's Strategy for China's Development: A Non-Maoist Alternative*. Armonk, NY: M. E. Sharpe, 1983.

LARINA, ANNA. *This I Cannot Forget: The Memoirs of Nikolai Bukharin's Widow*. New York: W. W. Norton, 1994.

LARKIN, BRUCE D. *China and Africa, 1949–1970: The Foreign Policy of the People's Republic of China*. Berkeley: University of California Press, 1973.

LAWSON, NIGEL. *The View from No. 11: Memoirs of a Tory Radical*. London: Corgi, 1993.

LEIFER, MICHAEL. *Indonesia's Foreign Policy*. London: Allen & Unwin for Royal Institute of International Affairs, 1983.

LEWIS, JOHN WILSON. 'China's Secret Military Papers: "Continuities" and "Revelations" ', *CQ*, No. 18, 1964, pp. 68–78.

—— and XUE LITAI. *China Builds the Bomb*. Stanford: Stanford University Press, 1988.

LI CHEN (ed.). *Quzhe yu Fazhan—Tansuo Daolude Jianxin: 2, shang, 1957–1961; 2, xia, 1962–1965* (Detours and development—hardships along the road of exploration; 2, a, 1957–1961; 2, b, 1962–1965). Changchun: Jilin renmin chubanshe, 1994.

LI CHENG, XIAO JI, and WANG LIBING (eds.). *Jianguo Yilai Jun Shi Baizhuang Dashi* (A hundred major events in military history since the founding of the nation). Beijing: Zhishi chubanshe, 1992.

LI CHOH-MING. *Industrial Development in Communist China*. New York: Praeger, 1964.

—— *The Statistical System of Communist China*. Berkeley: University of California Press, 1962.

LI DEBIN, LIN SHUNBAO, JIN BIHUA, HE FENGQIN, and JIN SHIYING (eds.). *Xin Zhongguo Nongcun Jingji Jishi, 1949.10–1984.9* (Major events in the rural economy of new China, Oct. 1949–Sept. 1984). Beijing: Beijing daxue chubanshe, 1989.

Li Fuchun Xuanji (Selected works of Li Fuchun). Beijing: Zhongguo jihua chubanshe, 1992.

LI GUANG'AN, WANG GUIZHEN, and QIN MING (eds.). *Jinian Li Fuchun* (Remembering Li Fuchun). Beijing: Zhongguo jihua chubanshe, 1990.

LI JIAN (ed.). *Xin Zhongguo Liu Ci Fan Qinlue Zhanzheng Shilu* (A record of the six wars by new China against aggression). Beijing: Zhongguo Guangbo Dianshi chubanshe, 1992.

LI JIANTONG. *Liu Zhidan* (id.). Beijing: Gongren chubanshe, 1979.

LI JUNTING and YANG JINHE (eds.). *Zhongguo Wuzhuang Liliang Tonglan, 1949–1989* (A survey of China's armed forces, 1949–1989). Beijing: Renmin chubanshe, 1990.

LI KE and HAO SHENGZHANG. *'Wenhua Da Geming' zhongde Renmin Jiefang Jun* (The People's Liberation Army in the 'Great Cultural Revolution'). Beijing: Zhonggong dangshi ziliao chubanshe, 1989.

LI MING. *Gongheguo Licheng Da Xiezhen (1949–1993)* (Major realities in the life of the republic, 1949–1993). Beijing: Dang'an chubanshe, 2 vols., 1994.

LI MO (ed.). *Xin Zhongguo Dabolan* (New China review). Guangzhou: Guangdong lüyou chubanshe, 1993.

LI PING. *Kaiguo Zongli Zhou Enlai* (The PRC's founding premier, Zhou Enlai). Beijing: Zhonggong zhongyang dangxiao chubanshe, 1994.

LI RUI. *'Da Yuejin' Qin Li Ji* (A record of my own experience of the GLF). Shanghai: Shanghai yuandong chubanshe, 1996.

—— *Lushan Huiyi Shilu* (A true record of the Lushan Conference). Beijing: Chunqiu chubanshe & Changsha: Hunan jiaoyu chubanshe, 1989. (New edition with additional material published as *Mao Zedong Mishu Shouji: Lushan Huiyi Shilu* (The personal record of Mao Zedong's secretary: A true record of the Lushan Conference). Zhengzhou: Henan renmin chubanshe, 1994.)

LI SHUFA (ed.). *Chen Yi Nianpu* (A chronicle of Chen Yi's life). Beijing: Renmin chubanshe, 2 vols., 1995.

LI WEI. *The Chinese Staff System: A Mechanism for Bureaucratic Control and Integration*. Berkeley: Institute for East Asian Studies, University of California, 1994.

—— 'The Security Service for Chinese Central Leaders'. Unpub. paper.

LI WEIHAN. *Huiyi yu Yanjiu* (Memories and researches). Beijing: Zhonggong dangshi ziliao chubanshe, 2 vols., 1986.

—— *Li Weihan Xuanji* (Selected works of Li Weihan). Beijing: Renmin chubanshe, 1987.

LI XIANGQIAN. 'Qiqian ren dahui shimo' (The story of the seven thousand man meeting), *Dangshi Wenhui* (Collected writings on party history) (Taiyuan), No. 12, 1992.

—— '1962 niande jingji tiaozheng yu yijian fenqi' (The 1962 economic adjustment and differences of opinion), *Zhonggong Dangshi Yanjiu* (Research into CCP history), No. 6, 1988, pp. 59–67.

Li Xiannian Lun Caizheng Jinrong Maoyi (Li Xiannian on finance, banking, and trade). Beijing: Zhongguo caizheng jingji chubanshe, 2 vols., 1992.

Li Xiannian Wenxuan (1935–1988) (Selected works of Li Xiannian, 1935–1988). Beijing: Renmin chubanshe, 1989.

LI YINQIAO. *Zai Mao Zedong Shenbian Shiwu Nian* (Fifteen years at Mao Zedong's side). Shijiazhuang: Hebei renmin chubanshe, 1991.

LI YUMING (ed.). *Zhonghua Renmin Gongheguo Shi Cidian* (A historical dictionary of the PRC). Beijing: Zhongguo guoji guangbo chubanshe, 1989.

LI ZHENXIA (ed.). *Dangdai Zhongguo Shi Zhe* (Ten contemporary Chinese philosophers). Beijing: Huaxia chubanshe, 1991.

Li Zhimin Huiyilu (The memoirs of Li Zhimin). Beijing: Jiefang jun chubanshe, 1993.

LI ZHINING (ed.). *Zhonghua Renmin Gongheguo Jingji Dashidian, 10.1949–1.1987* (Economic dictionary of the PRC, Oct. 1949–Jan. 1987). Jilin: Jilin renmin chubanshe, 1987.

LI ZHISUI, with the editorial assistance of ANNE F. THURSTON. *The Private Life of Chairman Mao*. New York: Random House, 1994.

LIAO GAILONG, DING XIAOCHUN, and LI ZHONGZHI (eds.). *Zhongguo Gongchan Dang Fazhan Shidian* (A dictionary of the development of the CCP). Shenyang: Liaoning jiaoyu chubanshe, 1991.

—— Zhao Baoxu, and Du Qinglin (eds.). *Dangdai Zhongguo Zhengzhi Dashidian, 1949–1990* (A dictionary of contemporary Chinese politics, 1949–1990). Changchun: Jilin wenshi chubanshe, 1991.

—— (chief ed.), Zhuang Puming, Lin Binhui, Cong Jin, Jin Chunming, Tang Zongji, Li Dingguo, Tian Fu (eds.). *Xin Zhongguo Biannianshi (1949–1989)* (The annals of new China, 1949–1989). Beijing: Renmin chubanshe, 1989.

Liao Mosha (ed.). *Ji Deng Tuo* (Remembering Deng Tuo). Fuzhou: Fujian renmin chubanshe, 1980.

Liao Mosha Wenji (The collected works of Liao Mosha). Beijing: Beijing chubanshe, 4 vols., 1986.

Liaoning Wuchanjieji Gemingpai Lianluozhan 'Fa Song Bingtuan'. *Jianjue dadao dongbei diqu dangnei touhao zou zibenzhuyi daolude dangquanpai— Song Renqiong* (Resolutely topple the leading capitalist roader powerholding clique within the party in the Northeast region—Song Renqiong). N.p.: n.p., n.d.

Lieberthal, Kenneth G. 'The Great Leap Forward and the Split in the Yenan Leadership', *CHOC* 14, pp. 293–359.

—— *A Research Guide to Central Party and Government Meetings in China, 1949–1975.* Armonk, NY: M. E. Sharpe, 1976.

—— and Bruce J. Dickson. *A Research Guide to Central Party and Government Meetings in China, 1949–1986.* Armonk, NY: M. E. Sharpe, rev. expanded edn. 1989.

—— and Michel Oksenberg. *Policy Making in China: Leaders, Structures, and Processes.* Princeton, NJ: Princeton University Press, 1988.

—— with James Tong and Sai-Cheung Yeung. *Central Documents and Politburo Politics in China.* Ann Arbor: Center for Chinese Studies, University of Michigan, 1978.

Lifton, Robert Jay. *Revolutionary Immortality: Mao Tse-tung and the Chinese Cultural Revolution.* New York: Vintage Books, 1968.

Lih, Lars T., Oleg V. Naumov, and Oleg V. Khlevniuk (eds.). *Stalin's Letters to Molotov.* New Haven: Yale University Press, 1995.

Lin Biao Wenxuan (Selections from Lin Biao). N.p.: n.p., *xia* n.d.

[*Lin Biao Xuanji* (Selected works of Lin Biao)]. N.p.: n.p., n.d.

Lin Chieh (Lin Jie) *et al.* (comps.). 'Teng To's *Evening Chats at Yenshan* is Anti-Party and Anti-Socialist Double-talk', trans. in *The Great Socialist Cultural Revolution in China (2)*, q.v.

Lin Ke, Xu Tao, and Wu Xujun. *Lishide Zhenshi—Mao Zedong Shenbian Gongzuo Renyuande Zhengyan* (The historical truth—The testimony of personnel who worked at Mao's side). Hong Kong: Liwen chubanshe, 1995.

Lin Qingshan. *Jiang Qing Chen Fu Lu* (A record of the ups and downs of Jiang Qing). Beijing: Zhongguo xinwen chubanshe & Guangzhou: Guangzhou wenhua chubanshe, 2 vols., 1988.

—— *Kang Sheng Waizhuan* (An unofficial biography of Kang Sheng). Beijing: Zhongguo qingnian chubanshe, 1988.

—— *Lin Biao Zhuan* (A biography of Lin Biao). Beijing: Zhishi chubanshe, 2 vols., 1988.

Lin Yunhui, Fan Shouxin, and Zhang Gong. *1949–1989 Niande Zhongguo, 1: Kaige Xingjinde Shiqi* (China 1949–1989, 1: The period of triumphant advance). Henan: Henan renmin chubanshe, 1989.

LIN YUNHUI, LIU YONG, and SHI BAINIAN (eds.). *Renmir Gongheguo Chunqiu Shilu* (The spring and autumn annals of the People's Republic). Beijing: Zhongguo renmin daxue chubanshe, 1992.

LIN ZHIJIAN (ed.). *Xin Zhongguo Yaoshi Shuping* (Commentary on important events in new China). Beijing: Zhonggong dangshi chubanshe, 1994.

LING ZHIJUN. *Lishi buzai Paihuai* (History does not waver). Beijing: Renmin chubanshe, 1996.

LIU AIQIN. *Nuerde Huainian: Huiyi fuqin Liu Shaoqi* (A daughter's memories: Remembering my father Liu Shaoqi). Shijiazhuang: Hebei renmin chubanshe, 1980.

LIU BINYAN. *A Higher Kind of Loyalty: A Memoir by China's Foremost Journalist*. New York: Pantheon, 1990.

LIU FUYUAN, TANG GONGLIE, and LUO LIXING (eds.). *Zhongguo Shehuizhuyi Shangye Jingji* (The economy of socialist commerce in China). Beijing: Zhongguo renmin daxue chubanshe, 1980.

LIU JI (ed.). *Zhongguo Gongchan Dang Qishi Nian* (Seventy years of the CCP). Shanghai: Shanghai renmin chubanshe, 1991.

LIU JINTIAN (ed.). *Deng Xiaopingde Licheng: Yige Wei Ren he Tade Yige Shiji* (Deng Xiaoping's course: A great man and his century). Beijing: Jiefang jun wenyi chubanshe, 2 vols., 1994.

Liu Shaoqi, Collected Works, see *Collected Works of Liu Shao-ch'i*.

LIU SHAOQI (LIU SHAO-CHI). *How to be a Good Communist*. Beijing: Foreign Languages Press, rev. edn. 1952.

Liu Shaoqi, Selected Works, see *Selected Works of Liu Shaoqi*.

Liu Shaoqi fan-dang fan-shehuizhuyi fan-Mao Zedong sixiang yanlun yibai li (One hundred examples of Liu Shaoqi's anti-party, anti-socialist, anti-Mao Zedong Thought utterances). Office for the Study of Chairman Mao's works, Revolutionary Committee of Canton city's Military Control Committee, May 1967.

Liu Shaoqi fan-geming xiuzhengzhuyi yanlun xuanbian (Selection of Liu Shaoqi's counter-revolutionary revisionist utterances). Beijing: Beijing daxue wenhua geming weiyuanhui ziliaozu & Xin Beida gonghe pipan Liu-Deng Lianhezhan, 3 vols., 1967. [See also *Pipan ziliao . . .*]

Liu Shaoqi fan-geming zui'e shi (The history of the counter-revolutionary crimes of Liu Shaoqi). N.p.: Zheng zhao xi zhandoudui, kuiran budong zhandoudui, n.d.

[*Liu Shaoqi Wenxuan* (Selections from Liu Shaoqi)]. N.p.: n.p., n.d.

Liu Shaoqi Xuanji (Selected works of Liu Shaoqi). Beijing: Renmin chubanshe, *shang* 1981, *xia*, 1985.

'Liu Shaoqi Yanjiu Lunwenji' Bianjizu (ed.). *Liu Shaoqi Yanjiu Lunwenji* (A collection of research papers on Liu Shaoqi). Beijing: Zhongyang wenxian chubanshe, 1989.

[*Liu Shaoqi*] *Yanlun Ji* (A collection of [Liu Shaoqi's] speeches). N.p.: n.p., Sept. 1967.

'Liu Shaoqi yu 1962 nian 1 yue 27 ri zai guangdade zhongyang gongzuo huiyishangde jianghua' (Liu Shaoqi's speech of 27 Jan. 1962 to the enlarged [Seven Thousand Cadres] central work conference). N.p.: n.p., n.d. (Mimeographed text available in library of Fairbank Center, Harvard University).

LIU SUINIAN. *China's Socialist Economy: An Outline History (1949–1984)*. Beijing: Beijing Review, 1986.

—— and Wu Qungan (eds.). '*Da Yuejin' he Tiaozheng Shiqide Guomin Jingji (1958–1965)* (The national economy during the 'GLF' and the adjustment period). Harbin: Heilongjiang renmin chubanshe, 1984.

——— ' "Tiaozheng, gonggu, chongshi, tigao" ba zi fangzhende tichu ji zhixing qingkuang' (How the eight character policy 'adjustment, consolidation, filling out, and raising standards' was put forward and implemented), *DSYJ*, No. 6, 1980, pp. 23–35.

Liu Xiao. *Chu Shi Sulian Ba Nian* (Eight years as ambassador to the Soviet Union). Beijing: Zhonggong dangshi ziliao chubanshe, 1986.

Liu Xiaoming. *Zhonggong Dangjian Shi, 1949–1976* (A history of CCP party building, 1949–1976). Beijing: Dangjian duwu chubanshe, 1996.

Liu Xueqi (ed.). *Mao Zedong Feng Fan Cidian* (A dictionary of models of Mao Zedong's style). Beijing: Zhongguo gongren chubanshe, 1991.

—— and Wang Xijing (eds.). *Zhou Enlai Feng Fan Cidian* (A dictionary of models of Zhou Enlai's style). Beijing: Zhongguo gongren chubanshe, 1991.

Liu Zhanming. 'Liu Bobo jiao wo bu pa "gui" ' (Uncle Liu taught me not to fear ghosts), *RMRB*, 15 May 1980, p. 2.

Liu Zhende. *Wo wei Shaoqi dang Mishu* (I was Shaoqi's secretary). Beijing: Zhongyang wenxian chubanshe, 1994.

Long Zhengcai. 'Peng Dehuai dui shehuizhuyi jingji jianshe wentide jianku tansuo' (Peng Dehuai's arduous probing of the problems of socialist economic construction), *Zhonggong Dangshi Yanjiu* (Research into CCP history), No. 6, 1988, pp. 47–53.

Lu Dingyi fandui Mao Zedong sixiang tuixing xiuzhengzhuyi jiaoyu luxian yanlun zhaibian (A collection of Lu Dingyi's utterances opposing Mao Zedong thought and promoting the revisionist educational line). Beijing: Shoudu pipan zichanjieji fandong xueshu 'quanwei' lianluo weiyuanhui, May 1967.

Lu Haijiang and He Mingzhou (eds.). *Mao Zedong he ta Tongshidaide Ren* (Mao Zedong and his contemporaries). Zhengzhou: Henan renmin chubanshe, 1992.

Lü Xingdou (ed.). *Liu Shaoqi he Tade Shiye* (Liu Shaoqi and his enterprises). Beijing: Zhonggong dangshi chubanshe, 1991.

—— *Mao Zedong he Tade Shiye* (Mao Zedong and his enterprises). Beijing: Zhonggong dangshi chubanshe, 2 vols., 1992.

Lü Yanyu. *Zhonghua Renmin Gongheguo Lishi Jishi: Quzhe Fazhan (1958–1965)* (Historical records of the PRC: Tortuous development, 1958–1965). Beijing: Hongqi chubanshe, 1994.

Luo Gengmo. 'Socialism and Inflation', *PR*, No. 44, 1982, pp. 20–2.

Ma Hong and Sun Shangqing (eds.). *Zhongguo Jingji Jiegou Wenti Yanjiu* (Research into problems of China's economic structures). Beijing: Renmin chubanshe, 2 vols., 1981.

Ma Nancun (Deng Tuo). *Yanshan Yehua* (Evening chats at Yanshan). Beijing: Beijing chubanshe, 1979.

Ma Qibin, Chen Wenbin, Lin Yunhui, Cong Jin, Wang Nianyi, Zhang Tianrong, & Bu Weihua (eds.). *Zhongguo Gongchan Dang Zhizheng Sishinian (1949–1989)* (The CCP's 40 years in power, 1949–1989). Beijing: Zhonggong dangshi ziliao chubanshe, 1989; Zhonggong dangshi chubanshe, rev. enlarged edn. 1991.

678 BIBLIOGRAPHY

MA YUNFEI. 'Liu Shaoqi yu liushi niandaide guomin jingji tiaozheng' (Liu Shaoqi and the adjustment of the national economy in the 1960s), *Zhonggong Dangshi Yanjiu* (Research into CCP history), No. 5, 1988, pp. 8–16.

MA YUPING and HUANG YUCHONG (eds.). *Zhongguc Zuotian yu Jintian: 1840–1987 Guoqing Shouce* (China yesterday and today: A handbook of national conditions, 1840–1987). Beijing: Jiefang jun chubanshe, 1989.

McDOUGALL, BONNIE S. *Mao Zedong's 'Talks at the Yan an Conference on Literature and Art': A Translation of the 1943 Text with Commentary*. Ann Arbor: Center for Chinese Studies, University of Michigan, 1980.

MACFARQUHAR, RODERICK. 'The anatomy of collapse', *New York Review of Books*, 26 Sept. 1991.

—— 'The Chinese Model and the Underdeveloped World', in Welch, *Political Modernization*, pp. 373–82.

—— 'The End of the Chinese Revolution', *New York Review of Books*, 20 July 1989.

—— *The Hundred Flowers Campaign and the Chinese Intellectuals*. New York: Praeger, 1960.

—— 'On Photographs', *CQ*, No. 46, 1971, pp. 289–307.

—— *The Origins of the Cultural Revolution, I: Contradictions Among the People, 1956–1957*. London: Oxford University Press; New York: Columbia University Press; both for Royal Institute of International Affairs (RIIA), 1974.

—— *The Origins of the Cultural Revolution, II: The Great Leap Forward, 1958–1960*. London: Oxford University Press; New York: Columbia University Press; both for RIIA, 1983.

—— *The Politics of China, 1949–1989*. New York: Cambridge University Press, 1993.

—— *Sino-American Relations, 1949–1971*. Newton Abbot: David & Charles; New York: Praeger; both for RIIA, 1972.

—— 'The Succession to Mao and the End of Maoism', *CHOC* 15, pp. 305–401.

—— TIMOTHY CHEEK, and EUGENE WU (eds.). *The Secret Speeches of Chairman Mao: From the Hundred Flowers to the Great Leap Forward*. Cambridge, Mass.: Council on East Asian Studies, Harvard University, 1989.

MACKINNON, STEPHEN and JANICE. *Agnes Smedley: The Life and Times of an American Radical*. Berkeley: University of California Press, 1988.

McMAHON, ROBERT J. *The Cold War on the Periphery: The United States, India and Pakistan*. New York: Columbia University Press, 1994.

MACMILLAN, HAROLD. *At the End of the Day, 1961–1963*. New York: Harper & Row, 1973.

McNAMARA, ROBERT S. and BRIAN VANDEMARK. *In Retrospect: The Tragedy and Lessons of Vietnam*. New York: Random House/Times Books, 1995.

MADSEN, RICHARD. *Morality and Power in a Chinese Village*. Berkeley: University of California Press, 1984.

MALRAUX, ANDRÉ. *Anti-Memoirs*. Harmondsworth: Penguin, 1970.

MAOMAO, see [Deng] Maomao.

MAO TSE-TUNG, see *Selected Works of Mao Tse-tung*.

—— *Miscellany of Mao Tse-tung Thought (1949–1968)*. Washington, DC: JPRS 61269-1, -2, 2 vols., 1974.

Mao Zedong Junshi Wenji (A collection of Mao Zedong's military writings). Beijing: Junshi kexue chubanshe & Zhongyang wenxian chubanshe, 6 vols., 1993.

Mao Zedong Nongcun Diaocha Wenji (A collection of Mao Zedong's writings on rural investigation). Beijing: Renmin chubanshe, 1982.

Mao Zedong Shuxin Xuanji (Selected letters of Mao Zedong). Beijing: Renmin chubanshe, 1983.

(For the following, see the classification by Timothy Cheek in MacFarquhar, Cheek, and Wu [eds.]. *The Secret Speeches of Chairman Mao*, pp. 78–81.)

Mao Zedong sixiang wan sui! (Long live Mao Zedong Thought). N.p.: n.p., n.d.

Id., June 1967.

Id., July 1967.

Id., 1967.

Id., 1969.

[Mao Zedong: untitled collection. N.p.: n.p., n.d.]

[Mao Zedong] Xuexi Wenxuan (Selected documents [of Mao Zedong] for study). N.p.: n.p., 4 vols., n.d.

[Mao Zedong] Xuexi Ziliao (Materials [of Mao Zedong] for study). N.p.: n.p., 3 vols., n.d.

Mao Zedong, Zhou Enlai, Liu Shaoqi, Zhu De, Deng Xiaoping, Chen Yun Lun Dangde Qunzhong Gongzuo (Mao Zedong, Zhou Enlai, Liu Shaoqi, Zhu De, Deng Xiaoping, Chen Yun discuss the party's work among the masses). Beijing: Renmin chubanshe, 1990.

Mao Zedong Zhuzuo Xuandu (Selected readings from the works of Mao Zedong). Beijing: Renmin chubanshe, 2 vols., 1986.

Mao Zedong Zhuzuo Xuandu: jia zhongben (Selected readings from the works of Mao Zedong: collection A). Beijing: Renmin chubanshe, 1964.

[Mao Zedong] Ziliao Xuanbian (Selection of [Mao Zedong] materials). N.p.: n.p. [distributed by Center for Chinese Research Materials], 1967.

Mao Zhuxi dui Peng-Huang-Zhang-Zhou fan-dang jituande pipan (Chairman Mao's criticism of the Peng [Dehuai]–Huang [Kecheng]–Zhang [Wentian]–Zhou [Xiaozhou] anti-party clique). N.p.: n.p., n.d.

Mao Zhuxi Yulu (Quotations from Chairman Mao). Guangdong: Zhongguo renmin jiefang jun zong zhengzhi bu, 1966.

Mao Zhuxide geming luxian shengli wan sui—Dangnei liang luxian douzheng dashiji (1921–1969) (Long live the victory of the revolutionary line of Chairman Mao: Major events in the two-line struggle inside the party, 1921–1969). N.p.: n.p., n.d.

Mao Zhuxide Qin Mi Zhanyou Lin Biao Tongzhi Yanlunxuan (Selected utterances of Chairman Mao's dear comrade-in-arms, Comrade Lin Biao). N.p.: Xi'nan zhengfa xueyuan 'Zhengfa bingtuan', Apr. 1967.

MARCUSE, JACQUES. *The Peking Papers: Leaves from the Notebook of a China Correspondent*. London: Arthur Barker, 1967.

MATHEWS, JAY and LINDA. *One Billion: A China Chronicle*. New York: Random House, 1983.

MAXWELL, NEVILLE. *India's China War*. Harmondsworth: Penguin, 1972.

MAZUR, MARY G. 'Intellectual Activism in China During the 1940s: Wu Han in the United Front and the Democratic League', *CQ*, No. 133, 1993, pp. 27–55.

MEDVEDEV, ROY. *Khrushchev*. Oxford: Blackwell, 1982.

MEHNERT, KLAUS. *Soviet Man and his World*. New York: Praeger, 1961.

680 BIBLIOGRAPHY

MELNICK, R. SHEP. *Regulation and the Courts: The Case of the Clean Air Act.* Washington, DC: Brookings, 1983.

Memoirs of a Chinese Marshal: The Autobiographical Notes of Peng Dehuai (1898–1974). Beijing: Foreign Languages Press, 1984.

Mianhuai Liu Ren Tongzhi (Remember Comrade Liu Ren). Beijing: Beijing chubanshe, 1979.

MILTON, DAVID and NANCY DALL MILTON. *The Wind will not Subside: Years in Revolutionary China—1964–1969.* New York: Pantheon, 1976.

Mingbao Yuekan Bianjihui and Ding Wang (eds.). *Zhonggong Wenhua Da Geming Ziliao Huibian, 2: Deng Tuo Xuanji* (A collection of materials on the CCP's Great Cultural Revolution, 2: Selected works on Deng Tuo['s case]. Hong Kong: *Mingbao Yuekan* she, 1969.

MIRSKY, JONATHAN. 'The Party's Secrets', *New York Review of Books*, 25 Mar. 1993, pp. 57–60.

MU XIN. *Ban 'Guangming Ribao' Shi Nian Zishu, 1957–67* (A personal account of running the *Guangming Daily* for ten years, 1957–67). Beijing: Zhonggong dangshi chubanshe, 1994.

Nankai Daxue Weidong, Pipan Wenyi Heixian Liangezhan [Yu] 'Hong Hai Yan' (ed.). *Wuxian Fengguang zai Xianfeng: Jiang Qing Tongzhi Guanyu Wenyi Gemingde Jianghua* (A limitless vista from the perilous peak: Comrade Jiang Qing's speeches on literature and the arts). Tianjin (?): Nankai daxue weidong pipan wenyi heixian liangezhan [yu] 'hong hai yan', 1968.

NAUGHTON, BARRY. 'Industrial Policy During the Cultural Revolution: Military Preparation, Decentralization, and Leaps Forward', in Joseph, Wong, and Zweig (eds.), *New Perspectives on the Cultural Revolution*, pp. 153–81.

NIE RONGZHEN. *Inside the Red Star: The Memoirs of Marshal Nie Rongzhen.* Beijing: New World Press, 1988.

—— *Nie Rongzhen Huiyilu* (Memoirs of Nie Rongzhen). Beijing: Jiefang jun chubanshe, 3 vols., 1983–4.

—— *Nie Rongzhen Junshi Wenxuan* (Selected writings of Nie Rongzhen on military affairs). Beijing: Jiefang jun chubanshe, 1992.

NIXON, RICHARD, *RN: The Memoirs of Richard Nixon.* London: Book Club Associates, 1978.

Nongcun Zhengce Wenjian Xuanbian, 2 (1958–1965) (Selected documents on rural policy, vol. 2, 1958–1965). Beijing: Zhongguo renmin daxue nongye jingjixi ziliaoshi, 1980.

NOSSAL, FREDERICK. *Dateline—Peking.* London: Macdonald, 1962.

NOVE, ALEC. *An Economic History of the U.S.S.R.* Harmondsworth: Penguin, rev. edn. 1982.

OI, JEAN C. *State and Peasant in Contemporary China: The Political Economy of Village Government.* Berkeley: University of California Press, 1989.

OKSENBERG, MICHEL and GAIL HENDERSON. *Research Guide to People's Daily Editorials, 1949–1975.* Ann Arbor: Center for Chinese Studies, University of Michigan, 1982.

PALIT, D. K. *War in High Himalaya: The Indian Army in Crisis, 1962.* New Delhi: Lancer, 1991.

Party History Research Centre of the Central Committee of the Chinese Communist Party. *History of the Chinese Communist Party—A Chronology of Events (1919–1990).* Beijing: Foreign Languages Press, 1991.

Peng Dehuai Tongzhi Guju Jianjie (A brief guide to Comrade Peng Dehuai's former home). Xiangtan *xian*, Hunan: Peng Dehuai tongzhi guju guanlisuo, 1983.

Peng Dehuai Zishu (Peng Dehuai's autobiography). Beijing: Renmin chubanshe, 1981. (Translated as *Memoirs of a Chinese Marshal*, q.v.)

Peng zei 'Huairou diaocha' shi Liu, Deng hei silingbu yinmo fanpi zibenzhuyide yanzhong buji (Traitor Peng's 'Huairou investigation' is a serious step in Liu [Shaoqi] and Deng [Xiaoping's] black headquarters' secret plot to restore capitalism). Beijing: Shoudu hong daihui & Hebei Beijing shiyuan *Hongqi* pi Peng liangezhan, 1 Aug. 1967.

PENG ZHEN. *Lun Xin Zhongguode Zhengfa Gongzuo* (On new China's political and legal work). Beijing: Zhongyang wenxian chubanshe, 1992.

Peng Zhen fan-geming xiuzhengzhuyi yanlun zhaibian (Extracts from Peng Zhen's counter-revolutionary revisionist speeches). Beijing: Zhongguo renmin daxue xin renda gongshe, Mao Zedong sixiang hongweibing, May 1967.

Peng Zhen Wenxuan (1941–1990) (Selected works of Peng Zhen, 1941–1990). Beijing: Renmin chubanshe, 1990.

Pentagon Papers, The. New York: *New York Times*/Bantam, 1971.

PEPPER, SUZANNE. *Civil War in China: The Political Struggle, 1945–1949.* Berkeley: University of California Press, 1978.

—— 'Education for the New Order', *CHOC* 14, pp. 185–217.

—— 'New Directions in Education', *CHOC* 14, pp. 398–431.

PERRY, ELIZABETH J. 'Implications of Household Contracting in China: The Case of Fengyang County', in Rhee (ed.), *China's Reform Politics: Policies and their Implications*, pp. 195–217.

—— *Rebels and Revolutionaries in North China, 1845–1945.* Stanford: Stanford University Press, 1980.

PHATHANOTHAI, SIRIN, with JAMES PECK. *The Dragon's Pearl.* New York: Simon & Schuster, 1994.

PIMLOTT, BEN. *Harold Wilson.* London: Harper Collins, 1992.

Pipan ziliao: Zhongguo Heluxiaofu Liu Shaoqi fan-geming xiuzhengzhuyi yanlunji (Criticism materials: Collection of the counter-revolutionary revisionist utterances of China's Khrushchev Liu Shaoqi). Beijing: Renmin chubanshe ziliaoshi, 3 vols., 1967.

Polemic on the General Line of the International Communist Movement, The. Beijing: Foreign Languages Press, 1965.

PRIOR, JIM. *A Balance of Power.* London: Hamish Hamilton, 1986.

Programme of the Communist Party of the Soviet Union. Moscow: Foreign Languages Publishing House, 1961.

PU NING. *Red in Tooth and Claw: Twenty-Six Years in Communist Chinese Prisons.* New York: Grove Press, 1994.

PYE, LUCIAN. *Mao Tse-tung: The Man in the Leader.* New York: Basic Books, 1976.

—— *The Spirit of Chinese Politics: A Psychocultural Study of the Authority Crisis in Political Development.* Cambridge, Mass.: MIT Press, 1968.

QI BENYU, see CHI PEN-YU.

QI LI (ed.). *'Zuopai' Lilunjia Fuchen Lu* (A record of the ups and downs of the 'leftist' theoreticians). Beijing: Tuanjie chubanshe, 1993.

Qi Qian Ren Dahui Ziliao (Materials from the seven thousand man conference).

N.p.: n.p., mimeo, Dec. 1986. (Available in Fairbank Center Library, Harvard University.)

QING MU. *Zhongguo Yuanshuai Zhu De* (Chinese marshal Zhu De). Beijing: Zhonggong zhongyang dangxiao chubanshe, 1995.

QIU ZHIZHUO et al. (eds.). *Zhonggong Dangshi Renming Lu* (A record of names in CCP history). Chongqing: Chongqing chubanshe, 1986.

QUAN YANCHI. *Lingxiu Lei* (A leader's tears). Beijing: Qiushi chubanshe, 1990.

—— *Mao Zedong: Man not God*. Beijing: Foreign Languages Press, 1992.

—— *Tao Zhu he tade Qinren: Nüer Yanzhongde Fuqin* (Tao Zhu and his family: A father in the eyes of his daughter). Beijing: Beijing chubanshe, 1992.

—— *Tao Zhu zai 'Wenhua Da Geming' zhong* (Tao Zhu in the 'Great Cultural Revolution'). Beijing: Zhonggong zhongyang dangxiao chubanshe, 1991.

Quanguo Dangshi Ziliao Zhengji Gongzuo Huiyi and Jinian Zhongguo Gongchan Dang Liushi Zhounian Xueshu Taolunhui (eds.). *Dangshi Huiyi Baogao Ji* (A collection of reports from the conference on party history). Beijing: Zhonggong zhongyang dangxiao chubanshe, 1982.

Quanguo Zhonggong Dangshi Yanjiuhui (ed.). *Zhongguo Shehuizhuyi Jianshe he Gaige Zhuanti Jiangzuo* (Special lectures on China's socialist construction and reform). N.p.: n.p., 1988.

RA'ANAN, URI. 'Peking's Foreign Policy "Debate", 1965–1966', in Tsou (ed.), *China in Crisis*, pp. 23–71.

Renmin Ribao She Guonei Ziliaozu & Zhongguo Gongye Jingji Xiehui Diaoyanzu (eds.). *Zhongguo Renmin Gongheguo Gongye Deshiji (1949–1990)* (A chronicle of PRC industry, 1949–1990). Changsha: Hunan renmin chubanshe, 1991.

Renmin Shouce (People's handbook). Beijing: *Dagong Bao she*, annual volumes, 1960–5.

Renminde Hao Zongli (The people's good premier). Shanghai: Renmin chubanshe, 1978 (vol. 2), 1979 (vol. 3).

Renminde Zhongcheng Zhanshi: Mianhuai Chen Yi Tongzhi (The people's loyal warrior: Remembering Comrade Chen Yi). Shanghai: Shanghai renmin chubanshe, 1979.

Resolution on CPC History (1949–1981). Beijing: Foreign Languages Press, 1981.

RHEE, SANG-WOO (ed.). *China's Reform Politics: Policies and Their Implications*. Seoul: Sogang University Press, 1986.

RICHMAN, BARRY M. *Industrial Society in Communist China*. New York: Random House, 1969.

RISKIN, CARL. *China's Political Economy: The Quest for Development since 1949*. London: Oxford University Press, 1987.

RITTENBERG, SIDNEY and AMANDA BENNETT. *The Man Who Stayed Behind*. New York: Simon & Schuster, 1993.

ROBERTS, ANDREW. *Eminent Churchillians*. London: Phoenix, 1995.

ROBERTSON, FRANK. 'Refugees and Troop Moves—A Report from Hong Kong', *CQ*, No. 11, 1962, pp. 111–15.

ROBINSON, THOMAS. 'China Confronts the Soviet Union: Warfare and Diplomacy on China's Inner Asian Frontiers', *CHOC* 15, pp. 218–301.

ROSS, ROBERT S. *The Indochina Tangle: China's Vietnam Policy, 1975–1979*. New York: Columbia University Press, 1988.

SALISBURY, HARRISON E. *The Long March: The Untold Story.* New York: Harper & Row, 1985.
—— *The New Emperors: China in the Era of Mao and Deng.* New York: Avon, 1993.
SCHAPIRO, LEONARD. *The Communist Party of the Soviet Union.* London: Eyre & Spottiswoode, 1960.
SCHOENHALS, MICHAEL. 'The CCP Central Case Examination Group (1966–1979)', Center for Pacific Asia Studies, Stockholm University, Working Paper 36, Jan. 1995.
—— 'The Central Case Examination Group (1966–1979)', *CQ*, No. 145, Mar. 1996, pp. 87–111.
—— *Doing Things with Words in Chinese Politics: Five Studies.* Berkeley: Institute of East Asian Studies, University of California, 1992.
—— 'An Insider's Account of the Cultural Revolution: Wang Li's Memoirs', *Chinese Law and Government*, Nov.–Dec. 1994, pp. 5–89.
—— 'Mao Zedong: Speeches at the 1957 "Moscow Conference" ', *The Journal of Communist Studies* 2, No. 2, 1986, pp. 109–26.
SCHRAM, STUART R. ' "Economics in Command?" Ideology and Policy since the Third Plenum, 1978–84', *CQ*, No. 99, Sept. 1994, pp. 417–61.
—— *Mao Tse-tung.* Harmondsworth: Penguin, rev. edn., 1967.
—— *Mao Tse-tung Unrehearsed: Talks and Letters, 1956–71.* Harmondsworth: Penguin, 1974.
—— *Mao's Road to Power: Revolutionary Writings, 1912–1949, 1, The Pre-Marxist Period.* Armonk, NY: M. E. Sharpe, 1992.
—— 'New Texts by Mao Zedong, 1921–1966', *Communist Affairs* 2, No. 2, 1983, pp. 143–65.
—— *The Thought of Mao Tse-tung.* Cambridge: Cambridge University Press, 1989.
SCHRAN, PETER. *The Development of Chinese Agriculture, 1950–1959.* Urbana: University of Illinois Press, 1969.
SCHURMANN, FRANZ. 'China's New Economic Policy—Transition or Beginning', in Li (ed.), *Industrial Development in Communist China*, pp. 65–91.
—— *Ideology and Organization in Communist China.* Berkeley: University of California Press, 1966.
SCHWARCZ, VERA. *Time for Telling Truth is Running Out: Conversations with Zhang Shenfu.* New Haven: Yale University Press, 1992.
SCHWARZ, HENRY G. 'The *Ts'an-k'ao Hsiao-hsi* [*Cankao Xiaoxi*]: How Well Informed are Chinese Officials about the Outside World?', *CQ*, No. 27, 1966, pp. 54–83.
Selected Works of Deng Xiaoping 1938–1965. Beijing: Foreign Languages Press, 1992.
Selected Works of Liu Shaoqi. Beijing: Foreign Languages Press, vol. 1, 1984, vol. 2, 1991.
Selected Works of Mao Tse-tung. Beijing: Foreign Languages Press, vol. 1, vol. 3, 1965, vol. 4, 1961, vol. 5, 1977.
Selected Works of Zhou Enlai. Beijing: Foreign Languages Press, vol. 2, 1989.
Selected Works of Zhu De. Beijing: Foreign Languages Press, 1986.
SEN GUPTA, BHABANI. *The Fulcrum of Asia.* New York: Pegasus, 1970.
SHA LI and MIN LI (eds.). *Zhongguo 9 Ci Da Fa Bing* (Nine instances of China sending out troops). Sichuan: Sichuan wenyi chubanshe, 1992.

SHABAD, THEODORE. *China's Changing* Map. New York: Praeger, rev. edn. 1972.

Shanghai Shehui Kexue Yuan 'Shanghai Jingji' Bianjibu (ed.). *Shanghai Jingji, 1949–1982* (Shanghai's economy, 1949–1982). Shang1ai: Shanghai renmin chubanshe, 1983.

Shanghaishi Tongjiju (ed.). *Shanghai Tongji Nianjian, 1983* (Shanghai statistical yearbook, 1983). Shanghai: Shanghai renmin chubanshe, 1984.

Shangyebu Shangye Jingji Yanjiusuo (ed.). *Xin Zhongguo Shangye Shigao (1949–1982)* (Draft history of commerce in new China 1949–1982). Beijing: Zhongguo caizheng jingji chubanshe, 1984.

Shanxi Sishi Nian Bianji Weiyuanhui (ed.). *Shanxi Sishi Nian, 1949–1989* (Forty years of Shanxi, 1949–1989). Taiyuan: Zhongguo tongji chubanshe, 1989.

SHEN, T. H. *Agricultural Resources of China*. Ithaca, NY: Cornell University Press, 1951.

SHENG PING (ed.). *Zhongguo Gongchan Dang Renming Dacidian, 1921–1991* (A dictionary of notables of the CCP, 1921–1991). Beijing: Zhongguo guoji guangbo chubanshe, 1991.

SHERIDAN, MARY. 'The Emulation of Heroes', *CQ*, No. 33, 1968, pp. 47–72.

SHI BO. *1962: Zhong Yin Dazhan Jishi* (A record of the Sino-Indian war). Beijing: Zhongguo dadi chubanshe, 1993.

SHI DONGBING. *Zuichude Kangzheng: Peng Zhen zai 'Wenhua Da Geming' Qianxi* (The earliest resistance: Peng Zhen on the eve of the 'Great Cultural Revolution'). Beijing: Zhonggong zhongyang dangxiao chubanshe, 1993.

SHI YINGFU. *Mimi Chubing Yare Conglin: Yuan Yue Kang Mei Jishi* (Secret jungle warfare: Facts about aid Vietnam and resist U.S.). Beijing: Jiefang jun wenyi chubanshe, 1990.

SHI ZHE. *Feng yu Gu: Shi Zhe Huiyi Lu* (Peaks and valleys: The memoirs of Shi Zhe). Beijing: *Hongqi* chubanshe, 1992.

—— *Zai Lishi Juren Shenbian: Shi Zhe Huiyi Lu* (At the side of a colossus of history: the memoirs of Shi Zhe). Beijing: Zhongyang wenxian chubanshe, 1991.

SHI ZHONGQUAN. *Mao Zedongde Jianxin Kaituo* (Mao Zedong's arduous exploration). Beijing: Zhonggong dangshi ziliao chubanshe, 1990.

—— *Zhou Enlaide Zhuoyue Fengxian* (Zhou Enlai's ou standing contributions). Beijing: Zhonggong Zhongyang dangxiao chubanshe, 1993.

SHORT, PHILIP. *The Dragon and the Bear: Inside China and Russia Today*. London: Hodder and Stoughton, 1982.

SHU YUN. 'Shi fou xuanchuan Lei Feng, zeng you yi chang zhengyi' (There was a debate about whether or not to propagandize Lei Feng). *Yan Huang Chun Qiu*, 11 May 1993, pp. 4–9.

SHUE, VIVIENNE. *Peasant China in Transition: The Dynamics of Development Toward Socialism, 1949–1956*. Berkeley: University of California Press, 1980.

SHUI JING. 'Zhou Enlaide ling yige shijie' (Another world of Zhou Enlai), *Yan Huang Chun Qiu*, 1 July 1991, pp. 28–36.

SHUKMAN, HAROLD (ed.). *Stalin's Generals*. London: Weidenfeld & Nicolson, 1993.

Sichuan Sheng Tongjiju (ed.). *Sichuan Shehui Tongji Ziliao, 1949–1988* (Statistical material on Sichuan society, 1949–1988). N.p.: Zhongguo tongji chubanshe, 1989.

—— *Sichuan Tongji Nianjian, 1990* (Sichuan statistical yearbook, 1990). N.p.: Zhongguo tongji chubanshe, 1990.

SIU, HELEN F. *Agents and Victims in South China: Accomplices in Rural Revolution*. New Haven: Yale University Press, 1989.

SMEDLEY, AGNES. *The Great Road: The Life and Times of Chu Teh*. New York: Monthly Review Press, 1956.

SMIL, VACLAV. 'China's Energetics: A System Analysis', in Joint Economic Committee, *China's Economy Post-Mao*, pp. 323–69.

SMITH, HEDRICK. *The Russians*. New York: Ballantine Books, rev. edn. 1984.

SNOW, EDGAR. *The Long Revolution*. London: Hutchinson, 1973.

—— *The Other Side of the River: Red China Today*. New York: Random House, 1961; 1970 rev. edn. published by Penguin Books (Harmondsworth) as *Red China Today: The Other Side of the River*.

—— *Red Star over China*. Harmondsworth: Penguin Books, rev. and enlarged edn. 1968.

SNOW, LOIS WHEELER. *China on Stage*. New York: Random House, 1972.

SNOW, PHILIP. *The Star Raft: China's Encounter with Africa*. Ithaca, NY: Cornell University Press, 1989.

SOLINGER, DOROTHY J. *Chinese Business under Socialism: The Politics of Domestic Commerce in Contemporary China, 1949–1980*. Berkeley: University of California Press, 1984.

SOLOMON, RICHARD H. *Mao's Revolution and the Chinese Political Culture*. Berkeley: University of California Press, 1971.

SONG RENQIONG, CHEN PIXIAN, and YE FEI. 'Fendou buxide jianqiang zhanshi—Jinian Zeng Xisheng tongzhi shishi 20 zhounian' (A staunch warrior who struggled ceaselessly—Remembering Comrade Zeng Xisheng on the 20th anniversary of his death), *Xinhua Yuebao* (New China monthly), No. 8, 1988, pp. 34–5.

Song Renqiong Huiyilu (The memoirs of Song Renqiong). Beijing: Jiefang jun chubanshe, 1994.

SORENSEN, THEODORE C. *Kennedy*. London: Hodder & Stoughton, 1965.

SPEER, ALBERT. *Inside the Third Reich*. London: Sphere Books, 1971.

STARR, JOHN BRYAN. *Continuing the Revolution: The Political Thought of Mao*. Princeton, NJ: Princeton University Press, 1979.

State Statistical Bureau. *Ten Great Years*. Beijing: Foreign Languages Press, 1960.

SU DONGHAI and FANG KONGMU (eds.). *Zhonghua Renmin Gongheguo Fengyun Shilu* (A record of the major events of the PRC). Shijiazhuang: Hebei renmin chubanshe, 2 vols., 1994.

SU SHUANGBI (ed.). *Wu Han Zizhuan Shuxin Wenji* (A collection of Wu Han's autobiographical writings and letters). Beijing: Zhongguo renshi chubanshe, 1993.

—— and WANG HONGZHI. *Wu Han Zhuan* (A biography of Wu Han). Beijing: Beijing chubanshe, 1984

SUN QITAI and XIONG ZHIYONG. *Dazhai Hongqide Shengqi yu Zhuiluo* (The rise and fall of the Dazhai red flag). Henan: Henan renmin chubanshe, 1990.

SUN WEIBEN (ed.). *Zhongguo Gongchan Dang Dangwu Gongzuo Dacidian* (Dictionary of CCP party affairs work). Beijing: Zhanwang chubanshe, 1989.

Sun Yefang Xuanji (Selected works of Sun Yefang). Taiyuan: Shanxi renmin chubanshe, 1984.

TANG ZONGJI, ZHENG QIAN, et al. Shi Nian Houde Fngshuo: 'Wenhua Da Geming' Shilunji (An assessment after ten years: A collection of historical articles on the 'Great Cultural Revolution'). Beijing: Zhonggong dangshi ziliao chubanshe, 1987.

TAO LUJIA. Yige Shengwei Shuji Huiyi Mao Zhuxi (A provincial party secretary remembers Chairman Mao). Taiyuan: Shanxi renmin chubanshe, 1993.

'Tao Zhu Wenji' Bianji Weiyuanhui (ed.). Tao Zhu Wenji (Collected works of Tao Zhu). Beijing: Renmin chubanshe, 1987.

'Tao Zhu Wenji' Bianjizu (ed.). Biji Tao Zhu (Written memorials to Tao Zhu). Beijing: Renmin chubanshe, 1990.

Taoyuan diaocha jishi—Jielu Liu Shaoqi Wang Guangmei zai shehuizhuyi jiaoyu yundongzhong fan-dang fan-shehuizhuyi fan-Mao Zedong sixiangde taotian zuixing (A true record of the Taoyuan investigation—Expose Liu Shaoqi and Wang Guangmei's monstrous anti-party, anti-socialist, anti-Mao Zedong Thought crimes in the Socialist Education Movement). Beijing: Zhengfa xueyuan zhengfa gongshe 'Hong weibing' zhan doudui, 1967.

TAYLOR, JAY. China and Southeast Asia: Peking's Relations with Revolutionary Movements. New York: Praeger, 2nd edn. 1976.

TEIWES, FREDERICK C. Leadership, Legitimacy, and Conflict in China. Armonk, NY: M. E. Sharpe, 1984.

—— 'Mao and his Lieutenants', The Australian Journal of Chinese Affairs, Nos. 19–20, 1988, pp. 1–80.

—— Politics and Purges in China: Rectification and the Decline of Party Norms, 1950–1965. Armonk, NY: M. E. Sharpe, 2nd edn., 1993.

—— Politics at Mao's Court: Gao Gang and Party Factionalism in the Early 1950s. Armonk, NY: M. E. Sharpe, 1990.

—— and WARREN SUN. The Tragedy of Lin Biao: Riding the Tiger during the Cultural Revolution, 1966–1971. Hong Kong: Hong Kong University Press, 1996.

TENG WENZAO. 'Guanyu qiqian ren dahuide pingjia wenti' (Problems in evaluating the Seven Thousand Cadres Conference). Mimeographed article available at the Fairbank Center Library, Harvard University.

TERRILL, ROSS. Mao Tse-tung: A Biography. New York: Harper & Row, 1980; updated, Simon & Schuster, 1993.

—— The White-Boned Demon: A Biography of Madame Mao Zedong. New York: William Morrow, 1984.

THATCHER, MARGARET. The Downing Street Years. New York: Harper Collins, 1993.

THAYER, CARLYLE A. War by Other Means: National Liberation and Revolution in Viet-Nam, 1954–1960. Sydney: Allen & Unwin, 1989.

THOMAS, S. BERNARD. Season of High Adventure: Edgar Snow in China. Berkeley: University of California Press, 1996.

THOMPSON, LAURENCE G. Ta T'ung Shu: The One-World Philosophy of K'ang Yu-wei. London: Allen & Unwin, 1958.

THOMPSON, ROGER R. (trans.). Mao Zedong: Report from Xunwu. Stanford: Stanford University Press, 1990.

Tianjin Shehui Kexue Yuan Jingji Yanjiusuo (ed.). Tianjin Jingji Jianshe Dashiji (1949–1987) (A chronology of Tianjin's economic construction, 1949–1987). Tianjin (?): Tianjin shehui kexue yuan (?), 1989 (?).

TOLAND, JOHN. *Adolf Hitler*. New York: Anchor Books, Doubleday, 1976.

TORANSKA, THERESA. *'Them': Stalin's Polish Puppets*. New York: Harper & Row, 1987.

TROTSKY, LEON. *My Life: An Attempt at an Autobiography*. Harmondsworth: Penguin, 1975.

TSOU TANG (ed.). *China in Crisis, 2: China's Policies in Asia and America's Alternatives*. Chicago: University of Chicago Press, 1968.

TUCKER, ROBERT C. *Stalin in Power: The Revolution from Above, 1928–1941*. New York: Norton, 1990.

TUN LI-CH'EN. *Annual Customs and Festivals in Peking* (trans. Derk Bodde). Hong Kong: Hong Kong University Press, 2nd edn. 1965.

TUNG, CONSTANTINE and COLIN MACKERRAS. *Drama in the People's Republic of China*. Albany: State University of New York, 1987.

ULAM, ADAM B. *The Bolsheviks*. New York: Collier Books, 1968.

—— *Stalin: The Man and his Era*. New York: Viking, 1973.

URI (Union Research Institute). *Who's Who in Communist China*. Hong Kong: URI, 2nd edn., 2 vols., 1969.

VAN SLYKE, LYMAN P. *Enemies and Friends: The United Front in Chinese Communist History*. Stanford: Stanford University Press, 1967.

VOGEL, EZRA F. *Canton under Communism: Programs and Politics in a Provincial Capital, 1949–1968*. Cambridge, Mass: Harvard University Press, 1969.

VOLKOGONOV, DMITRI. *Lenin: A New Biography*. New York: Free Press, 1994.

—— *Stalin: Triumph and Tragedy*. Rocklin, Cal.: Prima Publishing, 1992.

—— *Trotsky: The Eternal Revolutionary*. New York: Free Press, 1996.

WAGNER, RUDOLF G. *The Contemporary Chinese Historical Drama: Four Studies*. Berkeley: University of California Press, 1990.

Waijiaobu Waijiaoshi Bianjishi (ed.). *Xin Zhongguo Waijiao Fengyun* (Major events in new China's foreign affairs). Beijing: Shijie zhishi chubanshe, vol. 1, 1990, vol. 2, 1991.

Waijiaobu Waijiaoshi Yanjiushi. *Dangdai Zhongguo Shijie Waijiao Shengya* (The diplomatic life in contemporary China). Beijing: Shijie zhishi chubanshe, vol. 1, 1995.

WALDER, ANDREW G. *Communist Neo-traditionalism: Work and Authority in Chinese Industry*. Berkeley: University of California Press, 1986.

WALKER, KENNETH R. *Food Grain Procurement and Consumption in China*. Cambridge: Cambridge University Press, 1984.

WANG BANGZUO. *Zhongguo Gongchan Dang Tongyi Zhanxian Shi* (A history of the CCP's united front). Shanghai: Shanghai renmin chubanshe, 1991.

WANG BINGNAN. 'Nine Years of Sino–U.S. Talks in Retrospect', *Shijie Zhishi*, Nos. 4–8, 1985, translated in JPRS-CPS-85-079, 7 Aug. 1985.

WANG BISHENG. *Deng Tuo Pingzhuan* (A critical biography of Deng Tuo). Beijing: Qunzhong chubanshe, 1986.

WANG CHUNCAI. *Peng Dehuai zai San Xian* (Peng Dehuai in the third front). Chengdu: Sichuan renmin chubanshe, 1991 [republished with corrections as *Yuanshuaide Zuihou Suiyue: Peng Dehuai zai San Xian* (A marshal's final years: Peng Dehuai in the third front), 1992].

WANG DONGXING. 'Mao Zhuxi guanhuai women chengzhang' (Chairman Mao paid attention to our growth), *Yan Huang Chun Qiu*, No. 7, 1993, pp. 5–6.

—— 'Sui Mao Zhuxi chongshang Jinggangshan riji' (Diary of going up

Jinggangshan again with Chairman Mao), in Zhonggong Dangshi Yanjiushi, *Zhonggong Dangshi Ziliao* (Materials on CCP party history), No. 40, pp. 124–44.

WANG GENGJIN. 'Shehuizhuyi jianshe bixu zunzhong nongye shi jichude guilu' (Socialist construction must respect the law that agriculture is the basis), *Jingji Yanjiu* (Economic Research), No. 12, 1979, pp. 36–8.

WANG GUICHEN and LU XUEYI (eds.). *Nongcun Jingji Dianxing Diaocha— Lingxian Jingji Fazhande Huigu yu Zhanwang* (Investigation of rural economic models—Review of and prospects for Ling *xian*'s economic development). Beijing: Shehui kexue wenxian chubanshe, 1989.

WANG JIANYING (ed.). *Zhongguo Gongchan Dang Zuzhi Shi Ziliao Huibian: Lingdao Jigou Yange he Chengyuan Minglu* (A collection of historical material on the organizational history of the CCP: The evolution of leadership organs and a name-list of their members). Beijing: *Hongqi* chubanshe, 1983.

'Wang Jiaxiang Xuanji' Bianjizu (ed.). *Wang Jiaxiang Xuanji* (Selected works of Wang Jiaxiang). Beijing: Renmin chubanshe, 1989.

WANG JINGJIN, YANG SHUN, WANG ZIPING, LIANG XIAODONG, and YANG GUANSAN (eds.). *Xiangcun Sanshi Nian: Fengyang Nongcun Shehui Jingji Fazhan Shilu (1949–1983 nian)* (30 years of the countryside: A true record of the social and economic development of Fengyang's rural areas, 1949–1983). Beijing: Nongcun duwu chubanshe, 2 vols., 1989.

WANG LI. *Wang Li Tan Mao Zedong* (Wang Li discusses Mao Zedong). N.p.: n.p., 2nd MS. circulated for opinions, 1995.

—— *Wang Li Yiyan* (Wang Li's last words). N.p.: n.p., 1988.

—— *Xianchang Lishi: Wenhua Da Geming Jishi* (On-the-spot history: A record of the Great Cultural Revolution). Hong Kong: Oxford University Press, 1993.

WANG NIANYI. ' "Wenge" mantan' (Informal notes on the 'Cultural Revolution'), unpub. MS.

—— *1949–1989 Niande Zhongguo, 3: Da Dongluande Niandai* (China 1949–1989, 3: A decade of great upheaval). Henan: Henan renmin chubanshe, 1988.

WANG RENZHONG. *Dushu Biji* (Reading notes). Beijing (?): Zhonggong dangshi ziliao chubanshe, 1989.

—— JIN MING, YONG WENTAO, and YU MINGTAO. 'Songshude fengge changcun' (The pine's characteristic is to live forever), *Xinhua Yuebao* (New China monthly), No. 11, 1989, pp. 49–52.

WANG RUOSHUI. 'The Maid of Chinese Politics: Mao Zedong and his Philosophy of Struggle', *Journal of Contemporary China*, Fall 1995, pp. 66–80.

WANG XIAN'GEN. *Yuan Yue Kang Mei Shilu* (A record of supporting Vietnam and resisting America). Chengde: Guoji wenhua chubanshe, 1990.

WANG XIANJIN. *Re Xue Bing Shan* (Hot blood, icy mountains). Beijing: Zhonggong zhongyang dangxiao chubanshe, 1993.

WANG YIFU. *Xin Zhongguo Tongji Shigao* (A draft history of statistics in new China). Beijing: Zhongguo tongji chubanshe, 1986.

WANG ZHEN, LIAO CHENGZHI, XIAO JINGGUANG, WU XIUQUAN, FU ZHONG, FANG QIANG, and ZHONG ZIYUN. 'Recollections and Inheritance—In Memory of Comrade Wang Jiaxiang', *Gongren Ribao* (Workers' Daily), 4 Feb. 1981, translated in *FBIS*-CHI-81-038, pp. L3–12.

WANG ZHIMING and ZHANG BEIGEN. *Zhonghua Renmin Gongheguo Lishi Jishi: Nei Luan Zhou Qi (1965–1969)* (Historical records of the PRC: The sudden onset of internal turmoil, 1965–1969). Beijing: *Hongqi* chubanshe, 1994.

WATSON, BURTON. *The Columbia Book of Chinese Poetry*. New York: Columbia University Press, 1984.

WATT, D. C. (ed.). *Documents on International Affairs, 1961*. London: Oxford University Press for Royal Institute of International Affairs, 1965.

—— *Survey of International Affairs, 1961*. London: Oxford University Press for Royal Institute of International Affairs, 1965.

WEIGELIN-SCHWIEDRZIK, SUSANNE. 'Party Historiography in the People's Republic of China', *Australian Journal of Chinese Affairs*, No. 17, 1987, pp. 77–94.

WELCH, CLAUDE E. Jr (ed.). *Political Modernization: A Reader in Comparative Political Change*. Belmont Cal.: Wadsworth, 1967.

WEN JIE (ed.). *Ba Zai Qincheng Meng* (Eight years of nightmare in Qincheng). Chengdu: Sichuan renmin chubanshe, 1993.

WEN YU. *Zhongguo 'Zuo' Huo* (China's 'leftist' scourge). Beijing: Chaohua chubanshe, 1993.

Wenxian he Yanjiu 1983 (Documents and research, 1983). Beijing: Renmin chubanshe, 1984.

WHITELAW, WILLIAM. *The Whitelaw Memoirs*. London: Aurum Press, 1989.

WHITING, ALLEN S. *The Chinese Calculus of Deterrence: India and Indochina*. Ann Arbor: University of Michigan Press, 1975.

—— 'The Sino-Soviet Split', *CHOC* 14, pp. 478–538.

WHITSON, WILLIAM W., with CHEN-HSIA HUANG. *The Chinese High Command: A History of Communist Military Politics, 1927–71*. London: Macmillan, 1973.

Who's Who in China Editorial Board. *Who's Who in China: Current Leaders*. Beijing: Foreign Languages Press, 1989.

Who's Who in Communist China. Hong Kong: Union Research Institute, rev. edn., 2 vols., 1969.

WILSON, CHARLES F. 'Grain Marketing in Canada', Canadian International Grains Institute, 1979.

WILSON, DICK. *Mao Tse-tung in the Scales of History*. Cambridge: Cambridge University Press, 1977.

WITKE, ROXANE. *Comrade Chiang Ch'ing*. Boston: Little, Brown, 1977.

'Womende Zhou Zongli' Bianjizu (ed.). *Womende Zhou Zongli* (Our Premier Zhou). Beijing: Zhongyang wenxian chubanshe, 1990.

World Bank. *China: Socialist Economic Development*. Washington DC: World Bank, 9 vols., 1981.

WU HAN. *The Dismissal of Hai Rui*. Los Angeles: Bede Press, 1968.

—— *Wu Han he 'Hai Rui Ba Guan'* (Wu Han and *The Dismissal of Hai Rui*). Beijing: Renmin chubanshe, 1979.

WU HAN. *Wu Han Wenji* (The collected works of Wu Han). Beijing: Beijing chubanshe, 4 vols., 1988.

—— *Wu Han Zawen Xuan* (Selected essays of Wu Han). Beijing: Renmin Wenxue chubanshe, 1979.

WU, HARRY and CAROLYN WAKEMAN. *Bitter Winds: A Memoir of My Years in China's Gulag*. New York: John Wiley, 1994.

Wu Lengxi. *Yi Mao Zhuxi: Wo Qinshen Jinglide Ruogar Zhongda Lishi Shijian Pianduan* (Remembering Chairman Mao: Fragments of certain major historical events which I personally experienced). Beijing: Xinhua chubanshe, 1995.

Wu Ningkun and Yikai Li. *A Single Tear*. New York: Atlantic Monthly Press, 1993.

Wu Ren (ed.). *Gongheguo Zhongda Shijian Jishi* (A record of the republic's major incidents). Xi'an: Xibei daxue chubanshe, 3 vols., 1992.

Wu Xiuquan. *Huiyi yu Huainian* (Memoirs and Reminiscences). Beijing: Zhonggong zhongyang dangxiao chubanshe, 1991.

Wu Yuan-Li. *Economic Development and the Use of Energy Resources in Communist China*. New York: Praeger (for the Hoover Institution), 1963.

Wu Zaiping. *Zhurende Qinghuai: Mao Zedong yu Zhongguo Zuojia* (The emotions of a colossus: Mao Zedong and China's writers). Beijing: Zhonggong zhongyang dangxiao chubanshe, 1995.

Wuhan Shifan Xueyuan Zhongwenxi Dangdai Wenxue Jiaoyanshi (ed.). *Guanyu Dangdai Wenyi Wentide Neibu Jianghua Xuanbian* (Selection of internal speeches on issues in contemporary literature and the arts). Wuhan: 1979.

Xia Nai and Su Shuangbi. Wu Hande Xueshu Shengya (Wu Han's academic career). Zhejiang: Zhejiang renmin chubanshe, 1984.

Xiao Xinli (ed.). *Xunshi Dajiang Nanbeide Mao Zedong* (Mao Zedong on inspection tours across the country). Beijing: Zhongguo shehui kexue chubanshe, 1993.

Xie Chuntao. *Da Yuejin Kuanglan* (The raging waves of the GLF). Zhengzhou: Henan renmin chubanshe, 1990.

Xie Minggan and Luo Yuanming (eds.). *Zhongguo Jingji Fazhan Sishinian* (China's forty years of economic development). Beijing [?]: Renmin chubanshe, 1989 [?].

Xie Yixian. *Zhechong yu Gongchu* (Resistance and coexistence). Zhengzhou: Henan renmin chubanshe, 1990.

Xing Zhen. 'Everything Should Start from Reality', *Xinwen Yanjiu Ziliao* (Material for Research on the Press), No. 3, 1980.

Xinhua Tongxunshe Sheyingbu and Jilin Jiaoyu Chubanshe (eds.). *Yongheng zhi Ri* (The unforgettable days). Jilin: Jilin jiaoyu chubanshe, 1989.

Xinghuo Liao Yuan Bianjibu (ed.). *Jiefang Jun Jiangling Zhuan* (Lives of Liberation Army generals). Beijing: Jiefang jun chubanshe, 1– , 1984– .

—— *Zhongguo Renmin Jiefang Jun: Jiangshuai Minglu* (China's PLA: A record of commanders). Beijing: Jiefang jun chubanshe, 1, 1986;2, 3, 1987.

'Xinwenjie Renwu' Bianji Weiyuanhui (ed.). *Xinwenjie Renwu (5): Deng Tuo* (Personalities of the journalistic world [5]: Deng Tuo). Beijing: Xinhua chubanshe, 1985.

Xu Dashen (gen. ed.). *Zhonghua Renmin Gongheguo Shilu* (Records of the PRC). Changchun: Jilin renmin chubanshe, vols. 1–5, 1994.

Xu Dixin. *Wo Guo Shehuizhuyi Jingji Wenti* (Researches into the problem of our nation's socialist economy). Beijing: Beijing chubanshe, 1980.

—— et al. *China's Search for Economic Growth: The Chinese Economy since 1949*. Beijing: New World Press, 1982.

Xu Jizhi. 'Mao Zedong yu Hu Qiaomude shici jiaowang' (Exchanges on poetry between Mao Zedong and Hu Qiaomu), *Dangde Wenxian* (Party documents), No. 6, 1993, pp. 81–6.

XU QUANXING. *Mao Zedong Wanniande Lilun yu Shixian, 1956–1976* (Mao Zedong's theory and practice in his later years). Beijing: Zhongguo dabaike quanshu chubanshe, 1993.

XU XIANG. 'Premier Zhou's Chat with Reporters', *Xinwen Yanjiu Xiliao* (Material for Research on the Press), No. 3, 1980.

XU YAN. *Zhong Yin Bianjiezhi Zhan Lishi Zhenxiang* (The true history of the Sino-Indian border war). Hong Kong: Tiandi tushu, 1993.

Xu yu Shi (Principle and practice) (Anhui).

XUE MOUHONG and PEI JIANZHANG (eds.). *Diplomacy of Contemporary China.* Hong Kong: New Horizon Press, 1990.

XUE MUQIAO. *China's Socialist Economy.* Beijing: Foreign Languages Press, 1981.

—— *Dangqian Woguo Jingji Ruogan Wenti* (Certain problems in our country's economy at present). Beijing: Renmin chubanshe, 1980.

—— *Wo Guo Wujia he Huobi Wenti Yanjiu* (An investigation into the problems of commodity prices and currency in our nation). Beijing: *Hongqi* chubanshe, 1986.

YAHUDA, MICHAEL. 'Kremlinology and the Chinese Strategic Debate, 1965–66', *CQ*, No. 49, 1972, pp. 32–75.

YAN FANGMING. 'San xian jianshe shuping' (A commentary on the construction of the third front), *DSYJ*, No. 4, 1987, pp. 70–3.

YAN QI (ed.). *Zhongguo Ge Minzhu Dangpai Shi Renwuzhuan* (Biographies from the histories of the various democratic parties). Beijing: Huaxia chubanshe, 3 vols., 1991.

YANG, BENJAMIN. *From Revolution to Politics: Chinese Communists on the Long March.* Boulder, Colo.: Westview, 1990.

YANG, MARTIN C. *A Chinese Village: Taitou, Shantung Province.* London: Kegan Paul, Trench, Trubner, 1947.

YANG CHUNGUI (ed.). *Zhongguo Zhexue Sishi Nian, 1949–1989* (Forty years of Chinese philosophy, 1949–1989). Beijing: Zhonggong zhongyang dangxiao chubanshe, 1989.

YANG SHANGKUN. 'Huainian Liu Shaoqi Tongzhi' (In memory of Comrade Liu Shaoqi), *HQ*, No. 8, 1980, trans. in JPRS 75921, 23 June 1980, pp. 13–14.

YAO WENYUAN. 'On "Three-Family Village"—The Reactionary Nature of *Evening Chats at Yenshan* and *Notes from Three-family Village*', trans. in *The Great Socialist Cultural Revolution in China (1)* q.v.

YAO XUEYIN. *Li Zicheng* (id.). Beijing: Qingnian chubanshe, vol. 1, rev. edn. 1977.

YAO ZHONGMING, XIE WUSHEN, and PEI JIANZHANG (eds.). *Jiangjun, Waijiaojia, Yishujia—Huang Zhen Jinian Wenji* (General, diplomat, artist—a collection of articles in memory of Huang Zhen). Beijing: Jiefang jun chubanshe, 1992.

YE YONGLIE. *Chen Boda Qiren* (That man Chen Boda). Changchun: Shidai wenyi chubanshe, 1990.

—— *Hu Qiaomu* (id.). Beijing: Zhonggong zhongyang dangxiao chubanshe, 1994.

—— *Lan Ping Wai Zhuan* (An unofficial biography of Lan Ping). Dalian: Dalian chubanshe, 1988.

—— *Xin Zhongguo Chenzhongde Yi Mu* (A sombre historical episode of new China). Beijing: Zuojia chubanshe, 1993.

YE YONGLIE. *Zhang Chunqiao Fuchen Shi* (The ups and downs of Zhang Chunqiao). Changchun: Shidai wenyi chubanshe, 1988 [Reissued with a third appendix as *Zhang Chunqiao Zhuan* (Biography of Zhang Chunqiao). Beijing: Zuojia chubanshe, 1993.]

Yi Lin Fu Tongshuai wei Guanghui Bangyang Wuxian Zhongyu Weida Lingxiu Mao Zhuxi (Take vice-c.-in-c. Lin as a glorious model of boundless loyalty to the great leader Chairman Mao). Beijing: N.p., *shang*, 1966.

YOUNG, KENNETH T. *Negotiating with the Chinese Communists: The United States Experience, 1953–1967*. New York: McGraw-Hill for the Council on Foreign Relations, 1968.

YU, ANTHONY C. (trans. and ed.). *The Journey to the West*. Chicago: University of Chicago Press, vols. 1–4, 1977–83.

YU JUNDAO and LI JIE (eds.). *Mao Zedong Jiaowang Lu* (A record of Mao Zedong's associations). Beijing: Renmin chubanshe, 1991.

YUAN HAO and JIAN MIN (eds.). *Qian Qiu Gong Zui* (Centuries of meritorious deeds and crimes). Chengdu: Sichuan renmin chubanshe, 1993.

YUAN YONGXI (ed.). *Zhongguo Renkou: Zong Lun* (China's population: General discussion). Beijing: Zhongguo caizheng jingji chubanshe, 1991.

ZAGORIA, DONALD S. *The Sino-Soviet Conflict, 1956–1961*. Princeton, NJ: Princeton University Press, 1962.

—— 'The Strategic Debate in Peking', in Tsou (ed.), *China in Crisis*, pp. 237–68.

ZENG BIJUN and LIN MUXI (eds.). *Xin Zhongguo Jingji Shi, 1949–1989* (An economic history of new China, 1949–1989). Beijing: *Jingji ribao* chubanshe, 1990.

Zeng Sheng Huiyi Lu (The memoirs of Zeng Sheng). Beijing: Jiefang jun chubanshe, 1991.

ZENG XISHENG. 'Pochu mixin, jiefang sixiang' (Dispel superstition, liberate thinking), *Xu yu Shi* (Principle and Practice) (Hefei), No. 1, 1958, pp. 5–11.

Zhanduan Deng, Liu shenxiang keji jiede hei shou (ziliao huibian 5 and 7): Keyan 'Shisi tiao' zhuanji (Cut off the black hand of Liu [Shaoqi, and] Deng [Xiaoping] stretched out towards the scientific and technical circles [5th and 7th collections of material]: Special edition on the 'Fourteen Articles' on science research). Beijing: Shoudu keji jie geming zaofanpai pipan Liu, Deng lianluozhan, June (5th collection), July (7th collection) 1967.

ZHANG DEQUN. 'Zai Mosike liu nian ban' (Six and a half years in Moscow). *Zhonggong Dangshi Ziliao* (Materials on CCP party history), No. 58, June 1996, pp. 31–41.

ZHANG HUA. 'Shilun "Wenhua Da Geming" zhong zhishi qingnian shangshan xiaxiang yundong' (A preliminary examination of the rustication movement for educated youth during the 'Great Cultural Revolution') in Tang Zongji, Zheng Qian, *et al.*, *Shi Nian Houde Pingshuo: 'Wenhua Da Geming' Shilunji*, pp. 141–55.

ZHANG QUANZHEN, HOU GUANGWEN, and WANG YONGSHENG (eds.). *Zhou Enlaide Ganqing Shijie* (The emotional world of Zhou Enlai). Ji'nan: Shandong daxue chubanshe, 1992.

ZHANG RONG. *Fengyun Renwu Jianwen Lu* (A record of interviews with famous persons). Beijing: Zhongguo wenyi chubanshe, 1992.

ZHANG SAI (ed.). *Zhonghua Renmin Gongheguo Tongji Dashiji, 1949–1991* (A chronicle of statistics in the PRC, 1949–1991). Beijing: Zhongguo tongji chubanshe, 1992.

ZHANG SUHUA, BIAN YANJUN, and WU XIAOMEI. *Shuo bujinde Mao Zedong* (An endless story of Mao Zedong). Shenyang: Liaoning renmin chubanshe, 1993.

ZHANG TIANRONG. 'Guanyu yijiuliuer nian qiqian ren dahuide jige wenti' (Some problems relating to the 1962 Seven Thousand Cadres Conference). Beijing: Zhengzhi xueyuan dangshi jiaoyanshi, mimeo., 12 May 1981 (available in library of the Fairbank Center, Harvard University; a version with important excisions was published in *DSYJ*, No. 5, 1981, pp. 19–29).

—— LÜ CHENG, ZHONG BIHUI, and WANG YANSHI (eds.). *Dangde Jianshe Qishi Nian* (Seventy years of party building). Beijing: Zhonggong dangshi chubanshe, 1992.

ZHANG XIANGLING (ed.). *Heilongjiang Sishi Nian* (Forty years of Heilongjiang). Harbin: Heilongjiang renmin chubanshe, 1986.

—— *Grass Soup*. London: Minerva, 1995.

ZHANG XIXIAN. *Chen Bulei yu Chen Boda* (Chen Bulei and Chen Boda). Taiyuan: Shuhai chubanshe, 1993.

ZHANG YUNSHENG. *Maojiawan Jishi: Lin Biao Mishu Huiyilu* (The true story of Maojiawan: The memoirs of Lin Biao's secretary). Beijing: Chunqiu chubanshe, 1988.

ZHANG ZERONG (ed.). *Zhongguo Jingji Tizhi Gaige Jishi* (A chronology of China's economic system reform). Chengdu: Sichuan kexue jishu chubanshe, 1986.

ZHAO DESHENG (ed.). *Zhonghua Renmin Gongheguo Jingji Shi, 1949–1966* (An economic history of the PRC, 1949–1966). Henan: Henan renmin chubanshe, 1989.

—— (ed.). *Zhonghua Renmin Gongheguo Jingji Zhuanti Dashiji, 1949–1966* (PRC chronology on specialized economic topics). Henan: Henan renmin chubanshe, 1989.

ZHAO SHENGHUI. '1965 nian zhongyang zuzhibu guanyu dangde jianshede sange baogaode xingsheng guocheng' (The evolution of the three 1965 reports of the CC's Organization Department on party building), *Zhonggong Dangshi Ziliao* (Materials on CCP history), No. 52, pp. 12–21.

—— *Zhongguo Gongchan Dang Zuzhi Shi Gangyao* (An outline organizational history of the CCP). Anhui: Anhui renmin chubanshe, 1987.

ZHENG QIAN and HAN GANG. *Wannian Suiyue: 1956 Nianhoude Mao Zedong* (The later years: Mao Zedong after the year 1956). Beijing: Zhongguo qingnian chubanshe, 1993.

ZHENG XIAOFENG and SHU LING. *Tao Zhu Zhuan* (A biography of Tao Zhu). Beijing: Zhongguo qingnian chubanshe, 1992.

Zhengzhi Xueyuan Zhonggong Dangshi Jiaoyanshi (ed.). *Zhongguo Gongchan Dang Liushi Nian Dashi Jianjie* (A summary of the principal events in the 60 years of the CCP). Beijing: Guofang daxue chubanshe, 1985.

ZHONG CHEN, XIA LU, and YE LAN (eds.). *Lingxiu Jiaowang Shilu Xilie: Mao Zedong* (A series of records of socialization between leaders: Mao Zedong). Chengdu: Sichuan renmin chubanshe, 1992.

ZHONG KAN. *Kang Sheng Pingzhuan* (A critical biography of Kang Sheng). Beijing: *Hongqi* chubanshe, 1982.

ZHONG PENGRONG. *Zhongguo Zhangjia Fengbo* (China's inflationary storm). Zhengzhou: Henan renmin chubanshe, 1992.

Zhong Yin Bianjing Ziwei Fanji Zuozhan Shi Bianxiezu. *Zhong Yin Bianjing*

Ziwei Fanji Zuozhan Shi (A history of the counter-attack in self-defence on the Sino-Indian border). Beijing: Junshi kexue chubanshe, 1994.

Zhonggong Dangshi Daodu (Guide to CCP history). Beijing: Zhongguo guangbo dianshi chubanshe, 2 vols., 1991.

Zhonggong Dangshi Renwu Yanjiuhui (ed.). *Zhonggong Dangshi Renwuzhuan* (Biographies of personalities in CCP history). Xi'an: Shaanxi renmin chubanshe, 1– , 1980– .

Zhonggong Dangshi Yanjiuhui (ed.). *Xuexi Lishi Jueyi Zhuanji* (A special collection of articles for the study of the *Resolution on [CCP] History*). Beijing: Zhonggong zhongyang dangxiao chubanshe, 1982.

Zhonggong Hebei Shengwei Dangwei Yanjiushi (ed.). *Lingxiu zai Hebei* (Leaders in Hebei). Beijing: Zhonggong dangshi chubanshe, 1993.

Zhonggong Hubei Shengwei Dangshi Ziliao Zhengbian Weiyuanhui (ed.). *Mao Zedong zai Hubei* (Mao Zedong in Hubei). Beijing: Zhonggong dangshi chubanshe, 1993.

Zhonggong Jiangsu Shengwei Dangshi Gongzuo Weiyuanhui and Jiangsu Sheng Dang'anju (eds.). *Mao Zedong zai Jiangsu* (Mao Zedong in Jiangsu). Beijing: Zhonggong dangshi chubanshe, 1993.

Zhonggong Qiyangxian Weiyuanhui (ed.). *Huainian Tao Zhu Tongzhi* (Remember Comrade Tao Zhu). Hunan: Hunan renmin chubanshe, 1979.

'Zhonggong Renming Lu' Bianxiu Weiyuanhui. *Zhonggong Renming Lu* (A record of CCP personnel). Taibei: Guoli zhengzhi daxue guoji guanxi yanjiu zhongxin, 1989.

Zhonggong Shanghai Shiwei Dangshi Yanjiushi (ed.). *Mao Zedong zai Shanghai* (Mao Zedong in Shanghai). Beijing: Zhonggong dangshi chubanshe, 1993.

Zhonggong Shanxi Shengwei Dangshi Yanjiushi (ed.). *Peng Zhen Shengping Dashi Nianbiao* (A chronology of the major events in Peng Zhen's life). Beijing: Zhonggong dangshi chubanshe, 1992.

Zhonggong Sichuan Shengwei Yanjiushi (ed.). *Sichuan Sheng Qing* (Information on Sichuan province). Chengdu: Sichuan renmin chubanshe, 1984.

Zhonggong Xiangtan Shiwei Dangshi Ziliao Zhengji Bangongshi (ed.). *Mao Zedong yu Xiangtan* (Mao Zedong and Xiangtan). Beijing: Zhonggong dangshi chubanshe, 1993.

Zhonggong Zhongyang Bangongting (ed.). *Zhongguo Nongcunde Shehuizhuyi Gaochao* (Socialist high tide in China's countryside). Beijing: Renmin chubanshe, 1956.

Zhonggong Zhongyang Dangshi Yanjiushi (ed.). *Zhonggong Dangshi Dashi Nianbiao* (A chronological table of major events in the history of the CCP). Beijing: Renmin chubanshe, 1987.

—— *Zhonggong Dangshi Ziliao* (Materials on CCP history). Beijing: Zhonggong dangshi chubanshe, 1982– .

—— *Zhongguo Gongchan Dang Lishi Dashiji (1919.5–1987.12)* (A chronology of the history of the CCP). Beijing: Renmin chubanshe, 1989.

Zhonggong Zhongyang Dangshi Yanjiushi Keyanju (ed.). *Mao Zedongde Zuji* (The footprints of Mao Zedong). Beijing: Zhonggong dangshi chubanshe, 1993.

Zhonggong Zhongyang Dangxiao Dangshi Jiaoyanshi. *Zhongguo Gongchan Dang Qishi Niande Licheng he Jingyan* (The 70-year career and experience of the CCP). Beijing: Zhonggong zhongyang dangxiao chubanshe, 1991.

Zhonggong Zhongyang Dangxiao Dangshi Jiaoyanshi Ziliaozu (ed.). *Zhongguo Gongchan Dang Lici Zhongyao Huiyiji, xia* (Collection of various important conferences of the CCP, 2). Shanghai: Shanghai renmin chubanshe, 1983.

Zhonggong Zhongyang Dangxiao Keyan Bangongshi 'Mao Zedong Sixiang Yuanli Jianghua' Bianxiezu (ed.). *Mao Zedong Sixiang Yuanli Jianghua* (Talks on the principles of Mao Zedong Thought). Beijing: Zhongguo qingnian chubanshe, 1983.

Zhonggong Zhongyang Dangxiao Zhonggong Dangshi Jiaoyanshi (ed.). *Sishi Niande Huigu yu Sikao* (Reviews and reflections on forty years). Beijing: Zhonggong zhongyang dangxiao chubanshe, 1991.

—— *Zhonggong Dangshi Zhuanti Jiangyi: Kaishi Quanmian Jianshe Shehuizhuyi Shiqi* (Lectures on special topics in CCP history: The period of the start of overall construction of socialism). Beijing: Zhonggong zhongyang dangxiao chubanshe, 1988.

Zhonggong Zhongyang Shujichu Yanjiushi Wenhuazu (ed.). *Dang he Guojia Lingdaoren Lun Wenyi* (Party and state leaders on literature and the arts). Beijing: Wenhua yishu chubanshe, 1982.

Zhonggong Zhongyang Tongyi Zhanxian Gongzuobu and Zhonggong Zhongyang Wenxian Yanjiushi (eds.). *Zhou Enlai Tongyi Zhanxian Wenxuan* (Selections from Zhou Enlai on the united front). Beijing: Renmin chubanshe, 1984.

Zhonggong Zhongyang Wenjian (CCP CC documents [Twenty-three articles]). N.p.: n.p., 1965.

Zhonggong Zhongyang Wenxian Yanjiushi. *Guanyu Jianguo Yilai Dangde Ruogan Lishi Wentide Jueyi Zhushiben (Xiuding)* (Revised annotated edition of the Resolution on Certain Questions in the History of our Party since the Founding of the State). Beijing: Renmin chubanshe, 1985.

—— *Mao Zedong zai Qi Dade Baogao he Jianghua Ji* (A collection of reports and speeches by Mao Zedong at the [CCP's] 7th Congress). Beijing: Zhongyang wenxian chubanshe, 1995.

—— *Zhou Enlai Jingji Wenxuan* (Selected works of Zhou Enlai on economics). Beijing: Zhongyang wenxian chubanshe, 1993.

—— *Zhu De Nianpu* (A chronicle of Zhu De). Beijing: Renmin chubanshe, 1986.

Zhonggong Zhongyang Wenxian Yanjiushi Mao Zedong Yanjiuzu and Xinhua Chubanshe. *Mao Zedong Huace* (Mao Zedong picture album). Shekou: Xinhua chubanshe, 1993.

Zhonggong Zhongyang Wenxian Yanjiushi and Xinhua Tongxunshe (eds.). *Deng Xiaoping*. Beijing: Zhongyang wenxian chubanshe, 1988.

—— *Gongheguo Zhuxi Liu Shaoqi* (State Chairman Liu Shaoqi). Beijing: Zhongyang wenxian chubanshe, 1988.

Zhonggong Zhongyang Wenxian Yanjiushi and Zhonggong Zhongyang Dangxiao (eds.). *Liu Shaoqi Lun Dangde Jianshe* (Liu Shaoqi on party building). Beijing: Zhongyang wenxian chubanshe, 1991.

Zhonggong Zhongyang Wenxian Yanjiushi and Zhongyang Dang'an Guan, 'Dangde Wenxian' Bianjibu (eds.). *Zhonggong Dangshi Zhongda Shijian Shushi* (An account of major events in CCP history). Beijing: Renmin chubanshe, 1993.

'Zhongguo Baike Nianjian' Bianjibu (ed.). *Zhongguo Baike Nianjian, 1981*

(China encyclopaedic yearbook, 1981). Beijing: Zhongguo Dabaike chubanshe, 1981.

Zhongguo Dangdai Wenxue Shi Chugao (A preliminary draft history of contemporary Chinese literature). Beijing: Renmin wenxue chubanshe, 2 vols., 1981.

Zhongguo Geming Bowuguan (ed.). *Jinian Zhou En'ai* (Remember Zhou Enlai). Beijing: Wenwu chubanshe, 1985.

Zhongguo Geming Bowuguan Dangshi Yanjiushi. *Dangshi Yanjiu Ziliao* (Party history research material). 1981– .

Zhongguo Gongchan Dang Di Baci Quanguo Daibiao Dahui Wenjian (Documents of the 8th National Congress of the CCP). Beijing: Renmin chubanshe, repr. 1980.

'Zhongguo Jiaoyu Nianjian' Bianjibu (ed.). *Zhongguo Jiaoyu Nianjian, 1949–1981* (China education yearbook, 1949–1981). Beijing: Zhongguo dabaike quanshu chubanshe, 1984.

Zhongguo Mao Zedong Sixiang Lilun Yu Shijian Yanjiuhui Lishihui (ed.). *Mao Zedong Sixiang Cidian* (A dictionary of Mao Zedong Thought). Beijing: Zhonggong zhongyang dangxiao chubanshe, 1989.

Zhongguo Nongcun Fazhan Wenti Yanjiuzu (ed.). *Baochan Daohu Ziliao Xuan* (Selection of materials on contracting output to the household). N.p.: n.p., 1981.

Zhongguo Nongye Jingji Xuehui and Zhongguo Shehui Kexue Yuan Nongcun Fazhan Yanjiusuo (eds.). *Deng Zihui Nongye Hezuo Sixiang Xueshu Taolunhui Lunwenji* (A collection of papers from the symposium on Deng Zihui's thinking on agricultural co-operation). Beijing: Nongye chubanshe, 1989.

Zhongguo Nongye Nianjian Bianji Weiyuanhui (ed.). *Zhongguo Nongye Nianjian, 1980* (China agricultural yearbook, 1980). Beijing: Nongye chubanshe, 1981.

Zhongguo Renda Changweihui Bangongting Yanjiushi (ed.). *Zhonghua Renmin Gongheguo Renmin Daibiao Dahui Wenxian Ziliao Huibian (1949–1990)* (Collection of documentary materials of the PRC's NPC). Beijing: Zhongguo minzhu fazhi chubanshe, 1990.

Zhongguo Renkou (China's population): various provincial fascicles (*Fence*). Beijing: Zhongguo caizheng jingji chubanshe, 1987 (*Anhui, Beijing, Hebei, Hunan, Jiangsu, Liaoning, Nei Menggu, Shanghai, Tianjin); 1988 (Gansu, Guangdong, Guangxi, Jilin, Ningxia, Shaanxi, Sichuan, Zhejiang); 1989 (Heilongjiang, Henan, Qinghai, Shanxi); 1990 (Xinjiang)*.

Zhongguo Renmin Geming Junshi Bowuguan (ed.). *Chen Yi Yuanshuai Fengbei Yong Cun* (Marshal Chen Yi's monument will last for ever). Shanghai: Shanghai renmin chubanshe, 1986.

Zhongguo Renmin Jiefang Jun Guofang Daxue Dangshi Dangjian Zhenggong Jiaoyanshi (ed.). *Wenhua Da Geming' Yanjiu Ziliao* (Research materials on the 'Great Cultural Revolution'). Beijing: Guofang daxue, vols. 25–27, 1988.

—— *Zhonggong Dangshi Jiaoxue Cankao Ziliao* (Reference materials for teaching and studying CCP history). Beijing: Guofang daxue, vols. 14–27, 1985–8.

'Zhongguo Shehui Kexue' Jingji Bianjishi (ed.). *Jingjixue Wenji, 1980* (Collection of articles on economics, 1980). Hangzhou: Zhejiang renmin chubanshe, 1982.

Zhongguo Shehui Kexue Yuan Caimao Wuzi Jingji Yanjiusuo and Shangyebu Jiaoyuju (eds.). *Lun Shangpin Liutong: Shangpin Liutong Jingji Lilun Taolunhui Wenji* (On the circulation of commodities: Papers from the symposium on the economic theory of the circulation of commodities). Beijing: Zhongguo shehui kexue chubanshe, 1980.

Zhongguo Shehui Kexue Yuan Gongye Jingji Yanjiusuo Qingbao Ziliaoshi (ed.). *Zhongguo Gongye Jingji Fagui Huibian, 1949–1981* (A collection of laws and regulations on China's industrial economy, 1949–1981). Beijing [?]: Zhongguo shehui kexue yuan chubanshe [?], 1981 [?].

Zhongguo Shehui Kexue Yuan Gongye Jingji Yanjiusuo Qiye Guanli Yanjiushi (ed.). *Zhongguo Gongye Guanli Bufen Tiaoli Huibian* (A collection of some regulations on China's industrial management). Beijing [?]: Dizhi chubanshe, 1980.

Zhongguo Shehui Kexue Yuan Jingji Yanjiusuo Xueshu Ziliaoshi (ed.). *Sun Yefang Jingji Lilun Pinglun* (A discussion of Sun Yefang's economic theories). Beijing: Renmin chubanshe, 1985.

Zhongguo Shehui Kexue Yuan Jingji Yanjiusuo Ziliaoshi, Guojia Jiwei Jingji Yanjiusuo Ziliaoshi, and Jiangsu Sheng Zhexue Shehui Kexue Yanjiusuo Ziliaoshi (eds.). *Shehuizhuyi Jingjizhong Jihua yu Shichangde Guanxi* (The relations between plans and markets in socialist economies). Beijing: Zhongguo shehui kexue chubanshe, 2 vols., 1980.

Zhongguo Shehui Kexue Yuan Wenxue Yanjiusuo and 'Zhongguo Wenxue Yanjiu Nianjian' Bianji Weiyuanhui (eds.). *Zhongguo Wenxue Yanjiu Nianjian, 1981* (Chinese literary research yearbook, 1981). Beijing: Zhongguo shehui kexue chubanshe, 1982.

Zhongguo Shehui Kexue Yuan Wenxue Yanjiusuo Tushu Ziliaoshi (ed.). *Zhou Enlai yu Wenyi* (Zhou Enlai and literature and the arts). Beijing: Zhongguo shehui kexue chubanshe, 2 vols., 1980.

Zhongguo Wenti Yanjiu Zhongxin. *Lin Biao Zhuan Ji* (Lin Biao special collection). Hong Kong: Zilian chubanshe, 1970.

'Zhongguo Zhengfu Gongzuo Gaiyao' Bianxiezu (ed.). *Zhongguo Zhengfu Gongzuo Gaiyao* (Outline of the work of the Chinese government). Beijing: Zhonggong zhongyang dangxiao chubanshe, 1991.

Zhonghua Quanguo Zonggonghui Zhengce Yanjiushi (ed.). *Zhongguo Qiye Lingdao Zhidude Lishi Wenxian* (Historical documents on the leadership system of Chinese enterprises). Beijing: Jingji guanli chubanshe, 1986.

Zhonghua Renmin Gongheguo Caizhengbu, Caizhengliaoxue Yanjiusuo, and Zhongyang Caizheng Jinrong Xueyuan (eds.). *Zhongguo Caizheng Wenti* (Problems of China's finances). Tianjin: Tianjin kexue jishu chubanshe, 1981.

Zhonghua Renmin Gongheguo Guojia Nongye Weiyuanhui Bangongting. *Nongye Jitihua Zhongyao Wenjian Huibian (1958–1981)* (A collection of important documents on agricultural collectivization, 1958–1981). Beijing: Zhonggong zhongyang dangxiao chubanshe, *xia*, 1981.

Zhonghua Renmin Gongheguo Guojia Tongjiju (ed.). *Zhongguo Tongji Nianjian* (China statistical yearbook). Beijing: Zhongguo tongji chubanshe, 1981– .

Zhonghua Renmin Gongheguo Minzhengbu Xingzheng Quhuachu (ed.). *Quanguo Xiangzhen Diming Lu* (A national gazeteer of place-names of townships and villages). Beijing: Cehui chubanshe, 1986.

Zhonghua Renmin Gongheguo Nongyebu Jihuasi (ed.. *Zhongguo Nongcun Jingji Tongji Daquan (1949–1986)* (A compilation of statistics on China's rural economy, 1949–1986). Beijing: Nongye chubanshe, 1989.

Zhonghua Renmin Gongheguo Waijiaobu and Waijiaoshi Yanjiushi (eds.). *Huainian Chen Yi* (Remember Chen Yi). Beijing: Shijie zhishi chubanshe, 1991.

—— *Zhou Enlai Waijiao Huodong Dashiji* (A chronology of Zhou Enlai's activities in foreign affairs). Beijing: Shijie zhishi chubanshe 1993.

Zhonghua Renmin Gongheguo Waijiaobu and Zhonggong Zhongyang Wenxian Yanjiushi (eds.). *Mao Zedong Waijiao Wenxuan* (Mao Zedong's writings on foreign affairs). Beijing: Zhongyang wenxian chubanshe & Shijie zhishi chubanshe, 1994.

Zhongyang Jiaoyu Kexue Yanjiusuo (ed.). *Zhonghua Renmin Gongheguo Jiaoyu Dashiji, 1949*–1982 (A chronology of education in the PRC, 1949–1982). Beijing: Jiaoyu kexue chubanshe, 1983.

Zhongyang Shouzhang Jianghua (Central leaders' speeches). Beijing: Beijing boli zongchang hongweibing lianluozhan, 1967.

Zhongyang Xuanchuanbu Bangongting (ed.). *Dangde Xuanchuan Gongzuo Huiyi Gaikuang he Wenxian (1951–1992)* (Summaries and documents of the party's propaganda work conferences, 1951–1992). Beijing: Zhonggong zhongyang dangxiao chubanshe, 1994.

Zhou Enlai. *Guanyu Wenyi Gongzuode Sanci Jianghua* (Three speeches on literary and art work). Beijing: Renmin chubanshe, 1979.

Zhou Enlai, Selected Works of, see *Selected Works of Zhou Enlai.*

Zhou Enlai Shuxin Xuanji (A selection of Zhou Enlai's letters). Beijing: Zhongyang wenxian chubanshe, 1988.

Zhou Enlai Xuanji (Selected works of Zhou Enlai). Beijing: Renmin chubanshe, *shang,* 1980, *xia,* 1984.

'Zhou Enlai Yanjiu Xueshu Taolunhui Lunwenji' Bianjizu (ed.). *Zhou Enlai Yanjiu Xueshu Taolunhui Lunwenji* (A collection of papers from a research symposium on Zhou Enlai). Beijing: Zhongyang wenxian chubanshe, 1988.

ZHOU GUOQUAN and GUO DEHONG. *Dongluanzhongde Chen Boda* (Chen Boda in the midst of turmoil). Anhui: Anhui renmin chubanshe, 1993.

ZHOU MING (ed.). *Lishi zai Zheli Chensi—1966–1976 Nian Jishi* (Ponder history here—A record of the years 1966–1976). Beijing: Huaxia chubanshe, vols. 1–3, 1986; Taiyuan: Beiyue chubanshe, vols. 4–6, 1989.

ZHOU WEIREN. *Jia Tuofu Zhuan* (A biography of Jia Tuofu). Beijing: Zhonggong dangshi chubanshe, 1993.

Zhou Yang, Xia Yan, Chen Huangmei zai dianying fangmian fan-dang fanshehuizhuyi fan-Mao Zedong sixiang zuixing lu (A record of the anti-party, anti-socialist, anti-Mao Zedong Thought crimes of Zhou Yang, Xia Yan, and Chen Huangmei in the film sector). Beijing: Hongdaihui Beijing dianying xueyuan Jinggangshan wenyi bingtuan *et al.,* vol. 4, n.d.

ZHOU YUELI. 'Zeng Xisheng tongzchide yisheng' (The life of Comrade Zeng Xisheng), *Xueshu Jie* (The world of learning) (Anhui), No. 2, 1995, pp. 82–6.

ZHOU ZHENXIANG and SHAO JINGCHUN (eds.). *Xin Zhongguo Fazhi Jianshe Sishi Nian Yaolan, 1949–1988* (An overview of 40 years of the construction of a legal system in new China, 1949–1988). Beijing: Qunzhong chubanshe, 1990.

ZHU CHENGJIA (ed.). *Zhonggong Dangshi Yanjiu Lunwen Xuan* (A selection of research papers on CCP history). Changsha: Hunan renmin chubanshe, *xia*, 1984.

Zhu De, Selected Works of, see *Selected Works of Zhu De.*

Zhu De fan-dang fan-shehuizhuyi fan-Mao Zedong sixiangde zuixing (Zhu De's anti-party, anti-socialist, anti-Mao Zedong Thought crimes). Beijing: Shoudu chedi pipan Zhu De lianluozhan, 2nd coll., 15 Apr. 1967.

Zhu De Xuanji (Selected works of Zhu De). Beijing: Renmin chubanshe, 1983.

ZHU ZHONGLI. *Nühuang Meng: Jiang Qing Waizhuan* (Empress dream: An unofficial biography of Jiang Qing). Beijing: Dongfang chubanshe, 1988. (Originally published in Hong Kong as Zhu Shan, *Jiang Qing Ye Shi* [An unofficial history of Jiang Qing].

Zhumadian Shi Zhi (Annals of Zhumadian city). Zhengzhou: Henan renmin chubanshe, 1989.

Zhuzuo Da Cidian: Mao Zedong, Zhou Enlai, Liu Shaoqi, Zhu De, Deng Xiaoping, Chen Yun (A dictionary of works: Mao Zedong, etc.). Shenyang: Liaoning renmin chubanshe, vol. 2, 1991.

ZOU AIGUO and XUE JIANHUA. *Zhongguo Da Guang Jiao (1 & 2)* (A panoramic view of China [1 & 2]). Guangdong: Guoji wenhua chuban gongsi, 1989.

ZUBOK, VLADISLAV and CONSTANTINE PLESHAKOV. *Inside the Kremlin's Cold War: From Stalin to Khrushchev.* Cambridge, Mass.: Harvard University Press, 1996.

ZWEIG, DAVID. *Agrarian Radicalism in China, 1968–1981.* Cambridge, Mass.: Harvard University Press, 1989.

INDEX